TENNESSEE WILLIAMS

Tennessee Williams

PLAYS 1957–1980

THE LIBRARY OF AMERICA

Published by arrangement with New Directions Publishing
Corporation, New York, Publisher of the plays of Tennessee
Williams, and The University of the South, copyright proprietor of
the works of Tennessee Williams. For copyrights, see page 990.

CAUTION: Professionals and amateurs are hereby warned that the
plays of Tennessee Williams, being fully protected under the
copyright laws of the United States of America, the British
Commonwealth including the Dominion of Canada, and all other
countries of the Copyright Union, are subject to royalty. All rights,
including professional, amateur, motion picture, recitation, lecturing,
public reading, radio and television broadcasting, and the rights of
translation into foreign languages, are strictly reserved. Particular
emphasis is laid on the question of readings, permission for which
must be secured from the agent for The University of the South,
Casarotto Ramsay & Associates Limited, National House,
60-66 Wardour Street, London WIV 4ND, England.

The paper used in this publication meets the
minimum requirements of the American National Standard for
Information Sciences—Permanence of Paper for Printed
Library Materials, ANSI Z39.48-1984.

Distributed to the trade in the United States
by Penguin Group (USA) Inc.
and in Canada by Penguin Books Canada Ltd.
Library of Congress Catalog Number: 00-030190
For cataloging information, see end of Notes.
ISBN 978-1-883011-87-1
ISBN 1-883011-87-6

Fourth Printing
The Library of America—120

MEL GUSSOW AND KENNETH HOLDITCH
SELECTED THE CONTENTS AND WROTE THE NOTES
FOR THIS VOLUME

Contents

ORPHEUS DESCENDING

For Marion Black Vaccaro

THE PAST, THE PRESENT
AND THE PERHAPS

ONE icy bright winter morning in the last week of 1940, my brave representative, Audrey Wood, and I were crossing the Common in Boston, from an undistinguished hotel on one side to the grandeur of the Ritz-Carlton on the other. We had just read the morning notices of *Battle of Angels*, which had opened at the Wilbur the evening before. As we crossed the Common there was a series of loud reports like gunfire from the street that we were approaching, and one of us said, "My God, they're shooting at us!"

We were still laughing, a bit hysterically, as we entered the Ritz-Carlton suite in which the big brass of the Theatre Guild and director Margaret Webster were waiting for us with that special air of gentle gravity that hangs over the demise of a play so much like the atmosphere that hangs over a home from which a living soul has been snatched by the Reaper.

Not present was little Miriam Hopkins, who was understandably shattered and cloistered after the events of the evening before, in which a simulated on-stage fire had erupted clouds of smoke so realistically over both stage and auditorium that a lot of Theatre Guild first-nighters had fled choking from the Wilbur before the choking star took her bows, which were about the quickest and most distracted that I have seen in a theatre.

It was not that morning that I was informed that the show must close. That morning I was only told that the play must be cut to the bone. I came with a rewrite of the final scene and I remember saying, heroically, "I will crawl on my belly through brimstone if you will substitute this!" The response was gently evasive. It was a few mornings later that I received the *coup de grace*, the announcement that the play would close at the completion of its run in Boston. On that occasion I made an equally dramatic statement, on a note of anguish. "You don't seem to see that I put my heart into this play!"

It was Miss Webster who answered with a remark I have never forgotten and yet never heeded. She said, "You must not wear your heart on your sleeve for daws to peck at!"

Someone else said, "At least you are not out of pocket." I don't think I had any answer for that one, any more than I had anything in my pocket to be out of.

Well, in the end, when the Boston run was finished, I was given a check for $200 and told to get off somewhere and rewrite the play. I squandered half of this subsidy on the first of four operations performed on a cataracted left eye, and the other half took me to Key West for the rewrite. It was a long rewrite. In fact, it is still going on, though the two hundred bucks are long gone.

Why have I stuck so stubbornly to this play? For seventeen years, in fact? Well, nothing is more precious to anybody than the emotional record of his youth, and you will find the trail of my sleeve-worn heart in this completed play that I now call *Orpheus Descending*. On its surface it was and still is the tale of a wild-spirited boy who wanders into a conventional community of the South and creates the commotion of a fox in a chicken coop.

But beneath that now familiar surface it is a play about unanswered questions that haunt the hearts of people and the difference between continuing to ask them, a difference represented by the four major protagonists of the play, and the acceptance of prescribed answers that are not answers at all, but expedient adaptations or surrender to a state of quandary.

Battle was actually my fifth long play, but the first to be given a professional production. Two of the others, *Candles to the Sun* and *Fugitive Kind*, were produced by a brilliant, but semiprofessional group called The Mummers of St. Louis. A third one, called *Spring Storm*, was written for the late Prof. E. C. Mabie's seminar in playwriting at the University of Iowa, and I read it aloud, appropriately in the spring.

When I had finished reading, the good professor's eyes had a glassy look as though he had drifted into a state of trance. There was a long and all but unendurable silence. Everyone seemed more or less embarrassed. At last the professor pushed back his chair, thus dismissing the seminar, and remarked casually and kindly, "Well, we all have to paint our nudes!" And this is the only reference that I can remember anyone making to the play. That is, in the playwriting class, but I do remember that the late Lemuel Ayers, who was a graduate student at

Iowa that year, read it and gave me sufficient praise for its dialogue and atmosphere to reverse my decision to give up the theatre in favor of my other occupation of waiting on tables, or more precisely, handing out trays in the cafeteria of the State Hospital.

Then there was Chicago for a while and a desperate effort to get on the W.P.A. Writers' Project, which didn't succeed, for my work lacked "social content" or "protest" and I couldn't prove that my family was destitute and I still had, in those days, a touch of refinement in my social behavior which made me seem frivolous and decadent to the conscientiously rough-hewn pillars of the Chicago Project.

And so I drifted back to St. Louis, again, and wrote my fourth long play which was the best of the lot. It was called *Not About Nightingales* and it concerned prison life, and I have never written anything since then that could compete with it in violence and horror, for it was based on something that actually occurred along about that time, the literal roasting-alive of a group of intransigent convicts sent for correction to a hot room called "The Klondike."

I submitted it to The Mummers of St. Louis and they were eager to perform it but they had come to the end of their economic tether and had to disband at this point.

Then there was New Orleans and another effort, while waiting on tables in a restaurant where meals cost only two-bits, to get on a Writers' Project or the Theatre Project, again unsuccessful.

And then there was a wild and wonderful trip to California with a young clarinet player. We ran out of gas in El Paso, also out of cash, and it seemed for days that we would never go farther, but my grandmother was an "easy touch" and I got a letter with a $10 bill stitched neatly to one of the pages, and we continued westward.

In the Los Angeles area, in the summer of 1939, I worked for a while at Clark's Bootery in Culver City, within sight of the M-G-M studio and I lived on a pigeon ranch, and I rode between the two, a distance of ten miles, on a secondhand bicycle that I bought for $5.

Then a most wonderful thing happened. While in New Orleans I had heard about a play contest being conducted by the Group Theatre of New York. I submitted all four of the long plays I have mentioned that preceded *Battle of Angels*, plus a group of one-acts called *American Blues*. One fine day I received, when I returned to the ranch on my bike, a telegram saying that I had won a special award of $100 for the one-acts, and it was signed by Harold Clurman, Molly Day Thacher, who is the present Mrs. Elia Kazan, and that fine writer, Irwin Shaw, the judges of the contest.

I retired from Clark's Bootery and from picking squabs at the pigeon ranch. And the clarinet player and I hopped on our bicycles and rode all the way down to Tiajuana and back as far as Laguna Beach, where we obtained, rent free, a small cabin on a small ranch in return for taking care of the poultry.

We lived all that summer on the $100 from the Group Theatre and I think it was the happiest summer of my life. All the days were pure gold, the nights were starry, and I looked so young, or carefree, that they would sometimes refuse to sell me a drink because I did not appear to have reached 21. But toward the end of the summer, maybe only because it was the end of the summer as well as the end of the $100, the clarinet player became very moody and disappeared without warning into the San Bernardino Mountains to commune with his soul in solitude, and there was nothing left in the cabin in the canyon but a bag of dried peas.

I lived on stolen eggs and avocados and dried peas for a week, and also on a faint hope stirred by a letter from a lady in New York whose name was Audrey Wood, who had taken hold of all those plays that I had submitted to the Group Theatre contest, and told me that it might be possible to get me one of the Rockefeller Fellowships, or grants, of $1,000 which were being passed out to gifted young writers at that time. And I began to write *Battle of Angels*, a lyrical play about memories and the loneliness of them. Although my beloved grandmother was living on the pension of a retired minister (I believe it was only $85 a month in those days), and her meager earnings as a piano instructor, she once again stitched some bills to a page of a letter, and I took a bus to St. Louis. *Battle of Angels* was finished late that fall and sent to Miss Wood.

One day the phone rang and, in a terrified tone, my mother

told me that it was long distance, for me. The voice was Audrey Wood's. Mother waited, shakily, in the doorway. When I hung up I said, quietly, "Rockefeller has given me a $1,000 grant and they want me to come to New York." For the first time since I had known her, my mother burst into tears. "I am so happy," she said. It was all she could say.

And so you see it is a very old play that *Orpheus Descending* has come out of, but a play is never an old one until you quit working on it and I have never quit working on this one, not even now. It never went into the trunk, it always stayed on the work bench, and I am not presenting it now because I have run out of ideas or material for completely new work. I am offering it this season because I honestly believe that it is finally finished. About 75 per cent of it is new writing, but what is much more important, I believe that I have now finally managed to say in it what I wanted to say, and I feel that it now has in it a sort of emotional bridge between those early years described in this article and my present state of existence as a playwright.

So much for the past and present. The future is called "perhaps," which is the only possible thing to call the future. And the important thing is not to allow that to scare you.

Tennessee Williams

ACT ONE

SCENE: *The set represents in nonrealistic fashion a general dry-goods store and part of a connecting "confectionery" in a small Southern town. The ceiling is high and the upper walls are dark, as if streaked with moisture and cobwebbed. A great dusty window upstage offers a view of disturbing emptiness that fades into late dusk. The action of the play occurs during a rainy season, late winter and early spring, and sometimes the window turns opaque but glistening silver with sheets of rain. "TORRANCE MERCANTILE STORE" is lettered on the window in gilt of old-fashioned design.*

Merchandise is represented very sparsely and it is not realistic. Bolts of pepperel and percale stand upright on large spools, the black skeleton of a dressmaker's dummy stands meaninglessly against a thin white column, and there is a motionless ceiling fan with strips of flypaper hanging from it.

There are stairs that lead to a landing and disappear above it, and on the landing there is a sinister-looking artificial palm tree in a greenish-brown jardiniere.

But the confectionery, which is seen partly through a wide arched door, is shadowy and poetic as some inner dimension of the play.

Another, much smaller, playing area is a tiny bedroom alcove which is usually masked by an Oriental drapery which is worn dim but bears the formal design of a gold tree with scarlet fruit and fantastic birds.

At the rise of the curtain two youngish middle-aged women, Dolly and Beulah, are laying out a buffet supper on a pair of pink-and-gray-veined marble-topped tables with gracefully curved black-iron legs, brought into the main area from the confectionery. They are wives of small planters and tastelessly overdressed in a somewhat bizarre fashion.

A train whistles in the distance and dogs bark in response from various points and distances. The women pause in their occupations at the tables and rush to the archway, crying out harshly.

DOLLY: Pee Wee!

BEULAH: Dawg!

DOLLY: Cannonball is comin' into th' depot!

BEULAH: You all git down to th' depot an' meet that train!

(*Their husbands slouch through, heavy, red-faced men in clothes that are too tight for them or too loose, and mud-stained boots.*)

PEE WEE: I fed that one-armed bandit a hunnerd nickels an' it coughed up five.

DOG: Must have hed indigestion.

PEE WEE: I'm gonna speak to Jabe about them slots. (*They go out and a motor starts and pauses.*)

DOLLY: I guess Jabe Torrance has got more to worry about than the slot machines and pinball games in that confectionery.

BEULAH: You're not tellin' a lie. I wint to see Dr. Johnny about Dawg's condition. Dawg's got sugar in his urine again, an' as I was leavin' I ast him what was the facks about Jabe Torrance's operation in Mimphis. Well—

DOLLY: What'd he tell you, Beulah?

BEULAH: He said the worse thing a doctor ever can say.

DOLLY: What's that, Beulah?

BEULAH: Nothin' a-tall, not a spoken word did he utter! He just looked at me with those big dark eyes of his and shook his haid like this!

DOLLY (*with doleful satisfaction*): I guess he signed Jabe Torrance's death warrant with just that single silent motion of his haid.

BEULAH: That's exactly what passed through my mind. I understand that they cut him open— (*Pauses to taste something on the table.*)

DOLLY:—An' sewed him right back up!—that's what I heard . . .

BEULAH: I didn't know these olives had seeds in them!

DOLLY: You thought they was stuffed?

BEULAH: Uh-huh. Where's the Temple sisters?

DOLLY: Where d'you think?

BEULAH: Snoopin' aroun' upstairs. If Lady catches 'em at it she'll give those two old maids a touch of her tongue! She's not a Dago for nothin'!

DOLLY: Ha, ha, no! You spoke a true word, honey . . . (*Looks out door as car passes*) Well, I was surprised when I wint up myself!

BEULAH: You wint up you'self?

DOLLY: I did and so did you because I seen you, Beulah.

BEULAH: I never said that I didn't. Curiosity is a human instinct.

DOLLY: They got two separate bedrooms which are not even connectin'. At opposite ends of the hall, and everything is so dingy an' dark up there. Y'know what it seemed like to me? A county jail! I swear to goodness it didn't seem to me like a place for white people to live in!—that's the truth . . .

BEULAH (*darkly*): Well, I wasn't surprised. Jabe Torrance bought that woman.

DOLLY: Bought her?

BEULAH: Yais, he bought her, when she was a girl of eighteen! He bought her and bought her cheap because she'd been thrown over and her heart was broken by that— (*Jerks head toward a passing car, then continues:*) —that Cutrere boy. . . . *Oh*, what a— *Mmmm*, what a—*beautiful* thing he was. . . . And those two met like you struck two stones together and made a fire!—yes—fire . . .

DOLLY: What?

BEULAH: *Fire!*—Ha . . . (*Strikes another match and lights one of the candelabra. Mandolin begins to fade in. The following monologue should be treated frankly as exposition, spoken to audience, almost directly, with a force that commands attention. Dolly does not remain in the playing area, and after the first few sentences, there is no longer any pretense of a duologue.*)

—Well, that was a long time ago, before you and Dog moved into Two River County. Although you must have heard of it. Lady's father was a Wop from the old country and when he first come here with a mandolin and a monkey that wore a little green velvet suit, ha ha.

—He picked up dimes and quarters in the saloons—this was before Prohibition. . . .

—People just called him The Wop, nobody knew his name, just called him 'The Wop,' ha ha ha. . . .

DOLLY (*Off, vaguely*): Anh-hannnh. . . .

(*Beulah switches in the chair and fixes the audience with her eyes, leaning slightly forward to compel their attention. Her voice is rich with nostalgia, and at a sign of restlessness, she rises and comes straight out to the proscenium, like a pitch-man. This monologue should set the nonrealistic key for the whole production.*)

BEULAH: Oh, my law, well, that was Lady's daddy! Then come prohibition an' first thing ennyone knew, The Wop had took to bootleggin' like a duck to water! He picked up a piece of land cheap, it was on the no'th shore of Moon Lake which used to be the old channel of the river and people thought some day the river might swing back that way, and so he got it cheap. . . . (*Moves her chair up closer to proscenium.*) He planted an orchard on it; he covered the whole no'th shore of the lake with grapevines and fruit trees, and then he built little arbors, little white wooden arbors with tables and benches to drink in and carry on in, ha ha! And in the spring and the summer, young couples would come out there, like me and Pee Wee, we used to go out there, an' court up a storm, ha ha, just court up a— storm! Ha ha!—The county was dry in those days, I don't mean dry like now, why, now you just walk a couple of feet off the highway and whistle three times like a jaybird and a nigger pops out of a bush with a bottle of corn!

DOLLY: Ain't that the truth? Ha ha.

BEULAH: But in those days the county was dry for true, I mean bone dry except for The Wop's wine garden. So we'd go out to The Wop's an' drink that Dago red wine an' cut up an' carry on an' raise such cane in those arbors! Why, I remember one Sunday old Doctor Tooker, Methodist minister then, he bust a blood vessel denouncing The Wop in the pulpit!

DOLLY: Lawd have mercy!

BEULAH: Yes, ma'am!—Each of those white wooden arbors had a lamp in it, and one by one, here and there, the lamps would go out as the couples begun to make love . . .

DOLLY: *Oh*—oh . . .

BEULAH: What strange noises you could hear if you listened, calls, cries, whispers, moans—giggles. . . . (*Her voice is soft with recollection*)—And then, one by one, the lamps would be lighted again, and The Wop and his daughter would sing and play Dago songs. . . . (*Bring up mandolin: voice under* 'Dicitencello Vuoi.') But sometimes The Wop would look around for his daughter, and all of a sudden Lady wouldn't be there!

DOLLY: Where would she be?

BEULAH: She'd be with David Cutrere.

DOLLY: Awwwwww—ha ha . . .

BEULAH:—Carol Cutrere's big brother, Lady and him would disappear in the orchard and old Papa Romano, The Wop, would holler, "Lady, Lady!"—no answer whatsoever, no matter how long he called and no matter how loud. . . .

DOLLY: Well, I guess it's hard to shout back, "Here I am, Papa," when where you are is in the arms of your lover!

BEULAH: Well, that spring, no, it was late that summer . . . (*Dolly retires again from the playing area.*)—Papa Romano made a bad mistake. He sold liquor to niggers. The Mystic Crew took action.—They rode out there, one night, with gallons of coal oil—it was a real dry summer—and set that place on fire!—They burned the whole thing up, vines, arbors, fruit trees.—Pee Wee and me, we stood on the dance pavilion across the lake and watched that fire spring up. Inside of tin minutes the whole nawth shore of the lake was a mass of flames, a regular sea of flames, and all the way over the lake we could hear Lady's papa shouting, "Fire, fire, fire!"—as if it was necessary to let people know, and the whole sky lit up with it, as red as Guinea red wine!— Ha ha ha ha. . . . Not a fire engine, not a single engine pulled out of a station that night in Two River County!— The poor old fellow, The Wop, he took a blanket and run up into the orchard to fight the fire singlehanded—*and* burned *alive.* . . . Uh-huh! *burned alive.* . . .

(*Mandolin stops short. Dolly has returned to the table to have her coffee.*)

You know what I sometimes wonder?

DOLLY: No. What do you wonder?

BEULAH: I wonder sometimes if Lady has any suspicion that her husband, Jabe Torrance, was the leader of the Mystic

Crew the night they burned up her father in his wine garden on Moon Lake?

DOLLY: Beulah Binnings, you make my blood run cold with such a thought! How could she live in marriage twenty years with a man if she knew he'd burned her father up in his wine garden?

(*Dog bays in distance.*)

BEULAH: She could live with him in hate. People can live together in hate for a long time, Dolly. Notice their passion for money. I've always noticed when couples don't love each other they develop a passion for money. Haven't you seen that happen? Of course you have. Now there's not many couples that stay devoted forever. Why, some git so they just barely tolerate each other's existence. Isn't that true?

DOLLY: You couldn't of spoken a truer word if you read it out loud from the Bible!

BEULAH: Barely tolerate each other's existence, and some don't even do that. You know, Dolly Hamma, I don't think half as many married min have committed suicide in this county as the Coroner says has done so!

DOLLY (*with voluptuous appreciation of Beulah's wit*): You think it's their wives that give them the deep six, honey?

BEULAH: I don't think so, I know so. Why there's couples that loathe and despise the sight, smell and sound of each other before that round-trip honeymoon ticket is punched at both ends, Dolly.

DOLLY: I hate to admit it but I can't deny it.

BEULAH: But they hang on together.

DOLLY: Yes, they hang on together.

BEULAH: Year after year after year, accumulating property and money, building up wealth and respect and position in the towns they live in and the counties and cities and the churches they go to, belonging to the clubs and so on and so forth and not a soul but them knowin' they have to go wash their hands after touching something the other one just put down! ha ha ha ha ha!—

DOLLY: Beulah, that's an evil laugh of yours, that laugh of yours is evil!

BEULAH (*louder*): Ha ha ha ha ha!—But you know it's the truth.

DOLLY: Yes, she's tellin' the truth! (*Nods to audience.*)

BEULAH: Then one of them—gits—*cincer* or has a—*stroke* or somethin'?—The other one—

DOLLY:—Hauls in the loot?

BEULAH: That's right, hauls in the loot! Oh, my, then you should see how him or her blossoms out. New house, new car, new clothes. Some of 'em even change to a different church!—If it's a widow, she goes with a younger man, and if it's a widower, he starts courtin' some chick, ha ha ha ha ha!

And so I said, I said to Lady this morning before she left for Mamphis to bring Jabe home, I said, "Lady, I don't suppose you're going to reopen the confectionery till Jabe is completely recovered from his operation." She said, "It can't wait for anything that might take that much time." Those are her exact words. It can't wait for anything that might take that much time. Too much is invested in it. It's going to be done over, redecorated, and opened on schedule the Saturday before Easter this spring!—Why?—Because—she knows Jabe is dying and she wants to clean up quick!

DOLLY: An awful thought. But a true one. Most awful thoughts are.

(*They are startled by sudden light laughter from the dim upstage area. The light changes on the stage to mark a division.*)

SCENE ONE

The women turn to see Carol Cutrere in the archway between the store and the confectionery. She is past thirty and, lacking prettiness, she has an odd, fugitive beauty which is stressed, almost to the point of fantasy, by a style of makeup with which a dancer named Valli has lately made such an impression in the bohemian centers of France and Italy, the face and lips powdered white and the eyes outlined and exaggerated with black pencil and the lids tinted blue. Her family name is the oldest and most distinguished in the country.

BEULAH: Somebody don't seem to know that the store is closed.

DOLLY: Beulah?

BEULAH: What?

DOLLY: Can you understand how anybody would deliberately make themselves look fantastic as that?

BEULAH: Some people have to show off, it's a passion with them, anything on earth to get attention.

DOLLY: I sure wouldn't care for that kind of attention. Not me. I wouldn't desire it. . . .

(*During these lines, just loud enough for her to hear them, Carol has crossed to the pay-phone and deposited a coin.*)

CAROL: I want Tulane 0370 in New Orleans. What? Oh. Hold on a minute.

(*Eva Temple is descending the stairs, slowly, as if awed by Carol's appearance. Carol rings open the cashbox and removes some coins; returns to deposit coins in phone.*)

BEULAH: She helped herself to money out of the cashbox.

(*Eva passes Carol like a timid child skirting a lion cage.*)

CAROL: Hello, Sister.

EVA: I'm Eva.

CAROL: Hello, Eva.

EVA: Hello . . . (*Then in a loud whisper to Beulah and Dolly:*) She took money out of the cashbox.

DOLLY: Oh, she can do as she pleases, she's a Cutrere!

BEULAH: Shoot . . .

EVA: What is she doin' barefooted?

BEULAH: The last time she was arrested on the highway, they say that she was naked under her coat.

CAROL (*to operator*): I'm waiting. (*Then to women:*)—I caught the heel of my slipper in that rotten boardwalk out there and it broke right off. (*Raises slippers in hand.*) They say if you break the heel of your slipper in the morning it means you'll meet the love of your life before dark. But it was already dark when I broke the heel of my slipper. Maybe that means I'll meet the love of my life before daybreak. (*The quality of her voice is curiously clear and childlike. Sister Temple appears on stair landing bearing an old waffle iron.*)

SISTER: Wasn't that them?

EVA: No, it was Carol Cutrere!

CAROL (*at phone*): Just keep on ringing, please, he's probably drunk.

(*Sister crosses by her as Eva did.*)

Sometimes it takes quite a while to get through the living-room furniture. . . .

SISTER:—She a *sight?*

EVA: Uh-huh!

CAROL: Bertie?—Carol!—Hi, doll! Did you trip over something? I heard a crash. Well, I'm leaving right now, I'm already on the highway and everything's fixed, I've got my allowance back on condition that I remain forever away from Two River County! I had to blackmail them a little. I came to dinner with my eyes made up and my little black sequin jacket and Betsy Boo, my brother's wife, said, "Carol, you going out to a fancy dress ball?" I said, "Oh, no, I'm just going jooking tonight up and down the Dixie Highway between here and Memphis like I used to when I lived here." Why, honey, she flew so fast you couldn't see her passing and came back in with the ink still wet on the check! And this will be done once a month as long as I stay away from Two River County. . . . (*Laughs gaily.*)— How's Jackie? Bless his heart, give him a sweet kiss for me! Oh, honey, I'm driving straight through, not even stopping for pickups unless you need one! I'll meet you in the Starlite Lounge before it closes, or if I'm irresistibly delayed, I'll certainly join you for coffee at the Morning Call before the all-night places have closed for the day . . . —I— Bertie? Bertie? (*Laughs uncertainly and hangs up.*)—let's see, now. . . . (*Removes a revolver from her trench-coat pocket and crosses to fill it with cartridges back of counter.*)

EVA: What she looking for?

SISTER: Ask her.

EVA (*advancing*): What're you looking for, Carol?

CAROL: Cartridges for my revolver.

DOLLY: She don't have a license to carry a pistol.

BEULAH: She don't have a license to drive a car.

CAROL: When I stop for someone I want to be sure it's someone I want to stop for.

DOLLY: Sheriff Talbott ought to know about this when he gits
back from the depot.

CAROL: Tell him, ladies. I've already given him notice that if
he ever attempts to stop me again on the highway, I'll
shoot it out with him. . . .

BEULAH: When anybody has trouble with the law—

(*Her sentence is interrupted by a panicky scream from Eva,
immediately repeated by Sister. The Temple Sisters scramble
upstairs to the landing. Dolly also cries out and turns, covering her face. A Negro Conjure Man has entered the store. His
tattered garments are fantastically bedizened with many tal-
ismans and good-luck charms of shell and bone and feather.
His blue-black skin is daubed with cryptic signs in white
paint.*)

DOLLY: Git him out, git him out, he's going to mark my
baby!

BEULAH: Oh, shoot, Dolly. . . .

(*Dolly has now fled after the Temple Sisters, to the landing of
the stairs. The Conjure Man advances with a soft, rapid,
toothless mumble of words that sound like wind in dry grass.
He is holding out something in his shaking hand.*)

It's just that old crazy conjure man from Blue Mountain.
He cain't mark your baby.

(*Phrase of primitive music or percussion as Negro moves into
light. Beulah follows Dolly to landing.*)

CAROL (*very high and clear voice*): Come here, Uncle, and let
me see what you've got there. Oh, it's a bone of some kind.
No, I don't want to touch it, it isn't clean yet, there's still
some flesh clinging to it.

(*Women make sounds of revulsion.*)

Yes, I know it's the breastbone of a bird but it's still tainted
with corruption. Leave it a long time on a bare rock in the
rain and the sun till every sign of corruption is burned and

washed away from it, and then it will be a good charm, a white charm, but now it's a black charm, Uncle. So take it away and do what I told you with it. . . .

(*The Negro makes a ducking obeisance and shuffles slowly back to the door.*)

Hey, Uncle Pleasant, give us the Choctaw cry.

(*Negro stops in confectionery.*)

He's part Choctaw, he knows the Choctaw cry.
SISTER TEMPLE: Don't let him holler in *here*!
CAROL: Come on, Uncle Pleasant, *you* know it!

(*She takes off her coat and sits on the R. window sill. She starts the cry herself. The Negro throws back his head and completes it: a series of barking sounds that rise to a high sustained note of wild intensity. The women on the landing retreat further upstairs. Just then, as though the cry had brought him, Val enters the store. He is a young man, about 30, who has a kind of wild beauty about him that the cry would suggest. He does not wear Levi's or a T-shirt, he has on a pair of dark serge pants, glazed from long wear and not excessively tight-fitting. His remarkable garment is a snakeskin jacket, mottled white, black and gray. He carries a guitar which is covered with inscriptions.*)

CAROL (*looking at the young man*): Thanks, Uncle . . .
BEULAH: *Hey, old man, you! Choctaw! Conjure man! Nigguh! Will you go out-a this sto'? So we can come back down stairs?*

(*Carol hands Negro a dollar; he goes out right cackling. Val holds the door open for Vee Talbott, a heavy, vague woman in her forties. She does primitive oil paintings and carries one into the store, saying:*)

VEE: I got m'skirt caught in th' door of the Chevrolet an' I'm afraid I tore it.

(*The women descend into store: laconic greetings, interest focused on Val.*)

Is it dark in here or am I losin' my eyesight? I been painting all day, finished a picture in a ten-hour stretch, just

stopped a few minutes fo' coffee and went back to it again
while I had a clear vision. I think I got it this time. But I'm
so exhausted I could drop in my tracks. There's nothing
more exhausting than that kind of work on earth, it's not
so much that it tires your body out, but it leaves you
drained inside. Y'know what I mean? Inside? Like you was
burned out by something? Well! Still!—You feel you've accomplished something when you're through with it, sometimes you feel—*elevated!* How are you, Dolly?

DOLLY: All right, Mrs. Talbott.

VEE: That's good. How are *you*, Beulah?

BEULAH: Oh, I'm all right, I reckon.

VEE: Still can't make out much. Who is that there? (*Indicates
Carol's figure by the window. A significant silence greets this
question. Vee, suddenly:*)

  Oh! I thought her folks had got her out of the county . . .

(*Carol utters a very light, slightly rueful laugh, her eyes drifting back to Val as she moves back into confectionery.*)

Jabe and Lady back yet?

DOLLY: Pee Wee an' Dawg have gone to the depot to meet
'em.

VEE: Aw. Well, I'm just in time. I brought my new picture
with me, the paint isn't dry on it yet. I thought that Lady
might want to hang it up in Jabe's room while he's conva-
lescin' from the operation, cause after a close shave with
death, people like to be reminded of spiritual things. Huh?
Yes! This is the Holy Ghost ascending. . . .

DOLLY (*looking at canvas*): You didn't put a head on it.

VEE: The head was a blaze of light, that's all I saw in my
vision.

DOLLY: Who's the young man with yuh?

VEE: Aw, excuse me, I'm too worn out to have manners. This
is Mr. Valentine Xavier, Mrs. Hamma and Mrs.— I'm sorry,
Beulah. I never *can* get y' last *name!*

BEULAH: I fo'give you. My name is Beulah Binnings.

VAL: What shall I do with this here?

VEE: Oh, that bowl of sherbet. I thought that Jabe might
need something light an' digestible so I brought a bowl of
sherbet.

DOLLY: What flavor is it?

VEE: Pineapple.

DOLLY: Oh, goody, I love pineapple. Better put it in the ice-box before it starts to melt.

BEULAH (*looking under napkin that covers bowl*): I'm afraid you're lockin' th' stable after the horse is gone.

DOLLY: Aw, is it melted already?

BEULAH: Reduced to juice.

VEE: Aw, shoot. Well, put it on ice anyhow, it might thicken up.

(*Women are still watching Val.*)

Where's the icebox?

BEULAH: In the confectionery.

VEE: I thought that Lady had closed the confectionery.

BEULAH: Yes, but the Frigidaire's still there.

(*Val goes out R. through confectionery.*)

VEE: Mr. Xavier is a stranger in our midst. His car broke down in that storm last night and I let him sleep in the lockup. He's lookin' for work and I thought I'd introduce him to Lady an' Jabe because if Jabe can't work they're going to need somebody to help out in th' store.

BEULAH: That's a good idea.

DOLLY: Uh-huh.

BEULAH: Well, come on in, you all, it don't look like they're comin' straight home from the depot anyhow.

DOLLY: Maybe that wasn't the Cannonball Express.

BEULAH: Or maybe they stopped off fo' Pee Wee to buy some liquor.

DOLLY: Yeah . . . at Ruby Lightfoot's.

(*They move past Carol and out of sight. Carol has risen. Now she crosses into the main store area, watching Val with the candid curiosity of one child observing another. He pays no attention but concentrates on his belt buckle which he is re-pairing with a pocketknife.*)

CAROL: What're you fixing?

VAL: Belt buckle.

CAROL: Boys like you are always fixing something. Could you fix my slipper?

VAL: What's wrong with your slipper?

CAROL: Why are you pretending not to remember me?

VAL: It's hard to remember someone you never met.

CAROL: Then why'd you look so startled when you saw me?

VAL: Did I?

CAROL: I thought for a moment you'd run back out the door.

VAL: The sight of a woman can make me walk in a hurry but I don't think it's ever made me run.—You're standing in my light.

CAROL (*moving aside slightly*): Oh, excuse me. Better?

VAL: Thanks. . . .

CAROL: Are you afraid I'll snitch?

VAL: Do what?

CAROL: Snitch? I wouldn't; I'm not a snitch. But I can prove that I know you if I have to. It was New Year's Eve in New Orleans.

VAL: I need a small pair of pliers. . . .

CAROL: You had on that jacket and a snake ring with a ruby eye.

VAL: I never had a snake ring with a ruby eye.

CAROL: A snake ring with an emerald eye?

VAL: I never had a snake ring with any kind of an eye. . . . (*Begins to whistle softly, his face averted.*)

CAROL (*smiling gently*): Then maybe it was a dragon ring with an emerald eye or a diamond or a ruby eye. You told us that it was a gift from a lady osteopath that you'd met somewhere in your travels and that any time you were broke you'd wire this lady osteopath collect, and no matter how far you were or how long it was since you'd seen her, she'd send you a money order for twenty-five dollars with the same sweet message each time. "I love you. When will you come back?" And to prove the story, not that it was difficult to believe it, you took the latest of these sweet messages from your wallet for us to see. . . . (*She throws back her head with soft laughter. He looks away still further and busies himself with the belt buckle.*)—We followed you through five places before we made contact with you and I was the one that made contact. I went up to the bar where you were standing and touched your jacket and said, "What stuff is this made of?" and when you said it was snakeskin, I said, "I wish you'd told me before I touched it." And you said something not nice. You said, "Maybe that will learn you to hold back your hands." I was drunk by that time which was after midnight. Do you remember what I said to you? I said, "What on earth can you do on this earth but catch at whatever comes near you, with both your hands, until your fingers are broken?" I'd never said that before, or even consciously thought it, but afterwards it seemed like the truest thing that my lips had ever spoken, what on earth can you do but catch at whatever comes near you with both your hands until your fingers are broken. . . . You gave me a quick, sober look. I think you nodded slightly, and then you picked up your guitar and began to sing. After singing you passed the kitty. Whenever paper money was dropped in the kitty you blew a whistle. My cousin Bertie and I dropped in five dollars, you blew the whistle five times and then sat down at our table for a drink, Schenley's with Seven Up. You showed us all those signatures on your guitar. . . . Any correction so far?

VAL: Why are you so anxious to prove I know you?

CAROL: Because I want to know you better and better! I'd like to go out jooking with you tonight.

VAL: What's jooking?

CAROL: Oh, don't you know what that is? That's where you get in a car and drink a little and drive a little and stop and dance a little to a juke box and then you drink a little more and drive a little more and stop and dance a little more to a juke box and then you stop dancing and you just drink and drive and then you stop driving and just drink, and then, finally, you stop drinking. . . .

VAL:—What do you do, then?

CAROL: That depends on the weather and who you're jooking with. If it's a clear night you spread a blanket among the memorial stones on Cypress Hill, which is the local bone orchard, but if it's not a fair night, and this one certainly isn't, why, usually then you go to the Idlewild cabins between here and Sunset on the Dixie Highway. . . .

VAL:—That's about what I figured. But I don't go that route. Heavy drinking and smoking the weed and shacking with strangers is okay for kids in their twenties but this is my thirtieth birthday and I'm all through with that route. (*Looks up with dark eyes.*) I'm not young any more.

CAROL: You're young at thirty—I hope so! I'm twenty-nine!

VAL: Naw, you're not young at thirty if you've been on a Goddam party since you were fifteen!

(*Picks up his guitar and sings and plays "Heavenly Grass." Carol has taken a pint of bourbon from her trench-coat pocket and she passes it to him.*)

CAROL: Thanks. That's lovely. Many happy returns of your birthday, Snakeskin.

(*She is very close to him. Vee enters and says sharply:*)

VEE: Mr. Xavier don't drink.

CAROL: Oh, ex-cuse *me*!

VEE: And if you behaved yourself better your father would not be paralyzed in bed!

(*Sound of car out front. Women come running with various cries. Lady enters, nodding to the women, and holding the door open for her husband and the men following him. She greets the women in almost toneless murmurs, as if too tired to speak. She could be any age between thirty-five and forty-five, in appearance, but her figure is youthful. Her face taut. She is a woman who met with emotional disaster in her girl-hood; verges on hysteria under strain. Her voice is often shrill and her body tense. But when in repose, a girlish softness emerges again and she looks ten years younger.*)

LADY: Come in, Jabe. We've got a reception committee here to meet us. They've set up a buffet supper.

(*Jabe enters. A gaunt, wolfish man, gray and yellow. The women chatter idiotically.*)

BEULAH: Well, look who's here!

DOLLY: Well, *Jabe*!

BEULAH: I don't think he's been sick. I think he's been to Miami. Look at that wonderful color in his face!

DOLLY: I never seen him look better in my life!

BEULAH: Who does he think he's foolin'? Ha ha ha!—not *me*!

JABE: Whew, Jesus—I'm mighty—tired. . . .

(*An uncomfortable silence, everyone staring greedily at the dying man with his tense, wolfish smile and nervous cough.*)

PEE WEE: Well, Jabe, we been feedin' lots of nickels to those one-arm bandits in there.

DOG: An' that pinball machine is hotter'n a pistol.

PEE WEE: Ha ha.

(*Eva Temple appears on stairs and screams for her sister.*)

EVA: Sistuh! Sistuh! Sistuh! Cousin Jabe's here!

(*A loud clatter upstairs and shrieks.*)

JABE: Jesus. . . .

(*Eva rushing at him—stops short and bursts into tears.*)

LADY: Oh, cut that out, Eva Temple!—What were you doin' upstairs?

EVA: I can't help it, it's so good to see him, it's so wonderful to see our cousin again, oh, Jabe, *blessed*!

SISTER: Where's Jabe, where's precious Jabe? Where's our precious cousin?

EVA: Right here, Sister!

SISTER: Well, bless your old sweet life, and lookit the color he's got in his face, will you?

BEULAH: I just told him he looks like he's been to Miami and got a Florida suntan, haha ha!

(*The preceding speeches are very rapid, all overlapping.*)

JABE: I ain't been out in no sun an' if you all will excuse me I'm gonna do my celebratin' upstairs in bed because I'm kind of—worn out. (*Goes creakily to foot of steps while Eva and Sister sob into their handkerchiefs behind him.*)—I see they's been some changes made here. Uh-huh. Uh-huh. How come the shoe department's back here now? (*Instant hostility as if habitual between them.*)

LADY: We always had a problem with light in this store.

JABE: So you put the shoe department further away from the window? That's sensible. A very intelligent solution to the problem, Lady.

LADY: Jabe, you know I told you we got a fluorescent tube coming to put back here.

JABE: Uh-huh. Uh-huh. Well. Tomorrow I'll get me some niggers to help me move the shoe department back front.

LADY: You do whatever you want to, it's your store.

JABE: Uh-huh. Uh-huh. I'm glad you reminded me of it.

(*Lady turns sharply away. He starts up stairs. Pee Wee and Dog follow him up. The women huddle and whisper in the store. Lady sinks wearily into chair at table.*)

BEULAH: That man will never come down those stairs again!

DOLLY: Never in this world, honey.

BEULAH: He has th' death sweat on him! Did you notice that death sweat on him?

DOLLY: An' yellow as butter, just as yellow as—

(*Sister sobs.*)

EVA: Sister, Sister!

BEULAH (*crossing to Lady*): Lady, I don't suppose you feel much like talking about it right now but Dog and me are so worried.

DOLLY: Pee Wee and me are worried sick about it.

LADY:—About what?

BEULAH: Jabe's operation in Memphis. Was it successful?

DOLLY: Wasn't it successful?

(*Lady stares at them blindly. The women, except Carol, close avidly about her, tense with morbid interest.*)

SISTER: Was it too late for surgical interference?

EVA: Wasn't it successful?

(*A loud, measured knock begins on the floor above.*)

BEULAH: Somebody told us it had gone past the knife.

DOLLY: We do hope it ain't hopeless.

EVA: We hope and pray it ain't hopeless.

(*All their faces wear faint, unconscious smiles. Lady looks from face to face; then utters a slight, startled laugh and springs up from the table and crosses to the stairs.*)

LADY (*as if in flight*): Excuse me, I have to go up, Jabe's knocking for me. (*Lady goes upstairs. The women gaze after her.*)

CAROL (*suddenly and clearly, in the silence*): Speaking of knocks, I have a knock in my engine. It goes knock, knock, and I say who's there. I don't know whether I'm in communication with some dead ancestor or the motor's about to drop out and leave me stranded in the dead of night on the Dixie Highway. Do you have any knowledge of mechanics? I'm sure you do. Would you be sweet and take a short drive with me? So you could hear that knock?

VAL: I don't have time.

CAROL: What have you got to do?

VAL: I'm waiting to see about a job in this store.

CAROL: I'm offering you a job.

VAL: I want a job that pays.

CAROL: I expect to pay you.

(*Women whisper loudly in the background.*)

VAL: Maybe sometime tomorrow.

CAROL: I can't stay here overnight; I'm not allowed to stay overnight in this county.

(*Whispers rise. The word "corrupt" is distinguished.*)

(*Without turning, smiling very brightly:*) What are they saying about me? Can you hear what those women are saying about me?

VAL:—Play it cool. . . .

CAROL: I don't like playing it cool! What are they saying about me? That I'm corrupt?

VAL: If you don't want to be talked about, why do you make up like that, why do you—

CAROL: *To show off!*

VAL: What?

CAROL: *I'm an exhibitionist!* I want to be noticed, seen, heard, felt! I want them to know I'm alive! Don't you want them to know you're alive?

VAL: I want to live and I don't care if they know I'm alive or not.

CAROL: Then why do you play a guitar?

VAL: Why do you make a Goddam show of yourself?

CAROL: That's right, for the same reason.

VAL: We don't go the same route. . . . (*He keeps moving away from her; she continually follows him. Her speech is compulsive.*)

CAROL: I used to be what they call a Christ-bitten reformer. You know what that is?—A kind of benign exhibitionist. . . . I delivered stump speeches, wrote letters of protest about the gradual massacre of the colored majority in the county. I thought it was wrong for pellagra and slow starvation to cut them down when the cotton crop failed from army worm or boll weevil or too much rain in summer. I wanted to, tried to, put up free clinics, I squandered the money my mother left me on it. And when that Willie McGee thing came along—he was sent to the chair for having improper relations with a white whore— (*Her voice is like a passionate incantation.*) I made a fuss about it. I put on a potato sack and set out for the capitol on foot. This was in winter. I walked barefoot in this burlap sack to deliver a personal protest to the Governor of the State. Oh, I suppose it was partly exhibitionism on my part, but it wasn't completely exhibitionism; there was something else in it, too. You know how far I got? Six miles out of town—hooted, jeered at, even spit on!—every step of the way—and then arrested! Guess what for? Lewd vagrancy! Uh-huh, that was the charge, "lewd vagrancy," because they said that potato sack I had on was not a respectable garment. . . . Well, all that was a pretty long time ago, and now I'm not a reformer any more. I'm just a "lewd vagrant." And I'm showing the "S.O.B.S." how lewd a "lewd vagrant" can be if she puts her whole heart in it like I do mine! All right. I've told you my story, the story of an exhibitionist. Now I want you to do something for me. Take me out to Cypress Hill in my car. And we'll hear the dead people talk. They do talk there. They chatter together like birds on Cypress Hill, but all they say is one word and that one word is "live," they say "Live, live, live, live, live!" It's all they've learned, it's the only advice they can give.—Just live. . . . (*She opens the door.*) Simple!—a very simple instruction. . . .

(*Goes out. Women's voices rise from the steady, indistinct murmur, like hissing geese.*)

WOMEN'S VOICES:—No, not liquor! Dope!
  —Something not normal all right!
  —Her father and brother were warned by the Vigilantes to keep her out of this county.
  —She's absolutely degraded!
  —Yes, corrupt!
  —Corrupt! (Etc., etc.)

(*As if repelled by their hissing voices, Val suddenly picks up his guitar and goes out of the store as—Vee Talbott appears on the landing and calls down to him.*)

VEE: Mr. Xavier! Where is Mr. Xavier?
BEULAH: Gone, honey.
DOLLY: You might as well face it, Vee. This is one candidate for salvation that you have lost to the opposition.
BEULAH: He's gone off to Cypress Hill with the Cutrere girl.
VEE (*descending*):—If some of you older women in Two River County would set a better example there'd be more decent young people!
BEULAH: What was that remark?
VEE: I mean that people who give drinkin' parties an' get so drunk they don't know which is their husband and which is somebody else's and people who serve on the altar guild and still play cards on Sundays—
BEULAH: Just stop right there! Now I've discovered the source of that dirty gossip!
VEE: I'm only repeating what I've been told by others. I never been to these parties!
BEULAH: No, and you never will! You're a public kill-joy, a professional hypocrite!
VEE: I try to build up characters! You and your drinkin' parties are only concerned with tearin' characters down! I'm goin' upstairs, I'm goin' back upstairs! (*Rushes upstairs.*)
BEULAH: Well, I'm glad I said what I said to that woman. I've got no earthly patience with that sort of hypocriticism. Dolly, let's put this perishable stuff in the Frigidaire and leave here. I've never been so thoroughly disgusted!

DOLLY: Oh, my Lawd. (*Pauses at stairs and shouts:*) PEE WEE! (*Goes off with the dishes.*)

SISTER: Both of those wimmen are as common as dirt.

EVA: Dolly's folks in Blue Mountain are nothin' at all but the poorest kind of white trash. Why, Lollie Tucker told me the old man sits on the porch with his shoes off drinkin' beer out of a bucket!—Let's take these flowers with us to put on the altar.

SISTER: Yes, we can give Jabe credit in the parish notes.

EVA: I'm going to take these olive-nut sandwiches, too. They'll come in handy for the Bishop Adjutant's tea.

(*Dolly and Beulah cross through.*)

DOLLY: We still have time to make the second show.

BEULAH (*shouting*): Dog!

DOLLY: Pee Wee! (*They rush out of store.*)

EVA: Sits on the porch with his shoes off?

SISTER: Drinkin' beer out of a bucket! (*They go out with umbrellas, etc. Men descend stairs.*)

SHERIFF TALBOTT: Well, it looks to me like Jabe will more than likely go under before the cotton comes up.

PEE WEE: He never looked good.

DOG: Naw, but now he looks worse.

(*They cross to door.*)

SHERIFF: Vee!

VEE (*from landing*): Hush that bawling. I had to speak to Lady about that boy and I couldn't speak to her in front of Jabe because he thinks he's gonna be able to go back to work himself.

SHERIFF: Well, move along, quit foolin'.

VEE: I think I ought to wait till that boy gits back.

SHERIFF: I'm sick of you making a goddam fool of yourself over every stray bastard that wanders into this county.

(*Car horn honks loudly. Vee follows her husband out. Sound of cars driving off. Dogs bay in distance as lights dim to indicate short passage of time.*)

SCENE TWO

*A couple of hours later that night. Through the great window
the landscape is faintly luminous under a scudding moonlit sky.
Outside a girl's laughter, Carol's, rings out high and clear and
is followed by the sound of a motor, rapidly going off.*

*Val enters the store before the car sound quite fades out and
while a dog is still barking at it somewhere along the highway.
He says "Christ" under his breath, goes to the buffet table and
scrubs lipstick stain off his mouth and face with a paper napkin,
picks up his guitar which he had left on a counter.*

*Footsteps descending: Lady appears on the landing in a flan-
nel robe, shivering in the cold air; she snaps her fingers impatiently for the old dog, Bella, who comes limping down beside her.
She doesn't see Val, seated on the shadowy counter, and she goes
directly to the phone near the stairs. Her manner is desperate,
her voice harsh and shrill.*

LADY: Ge' me the drugstore, will you? I know the drugstore's closed, this is Mrs. Torrance, my store's closed,
too, but I got a sick man here, just back from the hospital, yeah, yeah, an emergency, wake up Mr. Dubinsky, keep
ringing till he answers, it's an emergency! (*Pause: she mutters under her breath:*) —*Porca la miseria!*—I wish I was
dead, dead, dead. . . .

VAL (*quietly*): No, you don't, Lady.

(*She gasps, turning and seeing him, without leaving the
phone, she rings the cashbox open and snatches out something.*)

LADY: What're you doin' here? You know this store is closed!
VAL: I seen a light was still on and the door was open so I
come back to—
LADY: You see what I got in my hand? (*Raises revolver above
level of counter.*)
VAL: You going to shoot me?
LADY: You better believe it if you don't get out of here,
mister!
VAL: That's all right, Lady, I just come back to pick up my
guitar.
LADY: To pick up your guitar?

(*He lifts it gravely.*)

—Huh. . . .

VAL: Miss Talbott brought me here. I was here when you got back from Memphis, don't you remember?

LADY:—Aw. Aw, yeah. . . . You been here all this time?

VAL: No. I went out and come back.

LADY (*into the phone*): I told you to keep ringing till he answers! Go on, keep ringing, keep ringing! (*Then to Val:*) You went out and come back?

VAL: Yeah.

LADY: What for?

VAL: You know that girl that was here?

LADY: Carol Cutrere?

VAL: She said she had car trouble and could I fix it.

LADY:—Did you fix it?

VAL: She didn't have no car trouble, that wasn't her trouble, oh, she had trouble, all right, but *that* wasn't it. . . .

LADY: What was her trouble?

VAL: She made a mistake about me.

LADY: What mistake?

VAL: She thought I had a sign "Male at Stud" hung on me.

LADY: She thought you—? (*Into phone suddenly:*) Oh, Mr. Dubinsky, I'm sorry to wake you up but I just brought my husband back from the Memphis hospital and I left my box of luminal tablets in the— I got to have some! I ain't slep' for three nights, I'm going to pieces, you hear me, I'm going to pieces, I ain't slept in three nights, I got to have some tonight. Now you look here, if you want to keep my trade, you send me over some tablets. Then bring them yourself, God damn it, excuse my French! Because I'm going to pieces right this minute! (*Hangs up violently.*) —*Mannage la miseria!*—Christ. . . . I'm shivering!—It's cold as a Goddam ice-plant in this store, I don't know why, it never seems to hold heat, the ceiling's too high or something, it don't hold heat at all.—Now what do you want? I got to go upstairs.

VAL: Here. Put this on you.

(*He removes his jacket and hands it to her. She doesn't take it at once, stares at him questioningly and then slowly takes the*

jacket in her hands and examines it, running her fingers cu-
riously over the snakeskin.)

LADY: What is this stuff this thing's made of? It looks like it
was snakeskin.

VAL: Yeah, well, that's what it is.

LADY: What're you doing with a snakeskin jacket?

VAL: It's a sort of a trademark; people call me Snakeskin.

LADY: Who calls you Snakeskin?

VAL: Oh, in the bars, the sort of places I work in—but I've
quit that. I'm through with that stuff now. . . .

LADY: You're a—entertainer?

VAL: I sing and play the guitar.

LADY:—Aw? (*She puts the jacket on as if to explore it.*) It feels
warm all right.

VAL: It's warm from my body, I guess. . . .

LADY: You must be a warm-blooded boy. . . .

VAL: That's right. . . .

LADY: Well, what in God's name are you lookin' for around
here?

VAL:—Work.

LADY: Boys like you don't work.

VAL: What d'you mean by boys like me?

LADY: Ones that play th' guitar and go around talkin' about
how warm they are. . . .

VAL: That happens t' be the truth. My temperature's always a
couple degrees above normal the same as a dog's, it's normal for me the same as it is for a dog, that's the truth. . . .

LADY:—Huh!

VAL: You don't believe me?

LADY: I have no reason to doubt you, but what about it?

VAL:—Why—nothing. . . .

(*Lady laughs softly and suddenly; Val smiles slowly and
warmly.*)

LADY: You're a peculiar somebody all right, you sure are!
How did you get around here?

VAL: I was driving through here last night and an axle broke
on my car, that stopped me here, and I went to the county
jail for a place to sleep out of the rain. Mizz Talbott took

me in and give me a cot in the lockup and said if I hung around till you got back that you might give me a job in the store to help out since your husband was tooken sick.

LADY:—Uh-huh. Well—she was wrong about that. . . . If I took on help here it would have to be local help, I couldn't hire no stranger with a—snakeskin jacket and a guitar . . . and that runs a temperature as high as a dog's! (*Throws back her head in another soft, sudden laugh and starts to take off the jacket.*)

VAL: Keep it on.

LADY: No, I got to go up now and you had better be going . . .

VAL: I got nowhere to go.

LADY: Well, everyone's got a problem and that's yours.

VAL:—What nationality are you?

LADY: Why do you ask me that?

VAL: You seem to be like a foreigner.

LADY: I'm the daughter of a Wop bootlegger burned to death in his orchard!—Take your jacket. . . .

VAL: What was that you said about your father?

LADY: Why?

VAL:—A "Wop bootlegger"?

LADY:—They burned him to death in his orchard! What about it? The story's well known around here.

(*Jabe knocks on ceiling.*)

I got to go up, I'm being called for.

(*She turns out light over counter and at the same moment he begins to sing softly with his guitar: "Heavenly Grass." He suddenly stops short and says abruptly:*)

VAL: I do electric repairs.

(*Lady stares at him softly.*)

I can do all kinds of odd jobs. Lady, I'm thirty today and I'm through with the life that I've been leading. (*Pause. Dog bays in distance.*) I lived in corruption but I'm not corrupted. Here is why. (*Picks up his guitar.*) My life's companion! It washes me clean like water when anything unclean has touched me. . . . (*Plays softly, with a slow smile.*)

LADY: What's all that writing on it?

VAL: Autographs of musicians I run into here and there.

LADY: Can I see it?

VAL: Turn on that light above you.

(*She switches on green-shaded bulb over counter. Val holds the instrument tenderly between them as if it were a child; his voice is soft, intimate, tender.*)

See this name? Leadbelly?

LADY: Leadbelly?

VAL: Greatest man ever lived on the twelve-string guitar! Played it so good he broke the stone heart of a Texas governor with it and won himself a pardon out of jail. . . . And see this name Oliver? King Oliver? That name is immortal, Lady. Greatest man since Gabriel on a horn. . . .

LADY: What's this name?

VAL: Oh. That name? That name is also immortal. The name Bessie Smith is written in the stars!—Jim Crow killed her, John Barleycorn and Jim Crow killed Bessie Smith but that's another story. . . . See this name here? That's another immortal!

LADY: Fats Waller? Is his name written in the stars, too?

VAL: Yes, his name is written in the stars, too. . . .

(*Her voice is also intimate and soft: a spell of softness between them, their bodies almost touching, only divided by the guitar.*)

LADY: You had any sales experience?

VAL: All my life I been selling something to someone.

LADY: So's everybody. You got any character reference on you?

VAL: I have this—letter.

(*Removes a worn, folded letter from a wallet, dropping a lot of snapshots and cards of various kinds on the floor. He passes the letter to her gravely and crouches to collect the dropped articles while she peruses the character reference.*)

LADY (*reading slowly aloud*): "This boy worked for me three months in my auto repair shop and is a real hard worker and is good and honest but is a peculiar talker and that is the reason I got to let him go but would like to—(*Holds letter closer to light.*)—would like to—keep him. Yours truly."

(*Val stares at her gravely, blinking a little.*)

Huh!—Some reference!

VAL:—Is that what it says?

LADY: Didn't you know what it said?

VAL: No.—The man sealed the envelope on it.

LADY: Well, that's not the sort of character reference that will do you much good, boy.

VAL: Naw. I guess it ain't.

LADY:—However. . . .

VAL:—What?

LADY: What people say about you don't mean much. Can you read shoe sizes?

VAL: I guess so.

LADY: What does 75 David mean?

(*Val stares at her, shakes head slowly.*)

75 means seven and one half long and David mean "D" wide. You know how to make change?

VAL: Yeah, I could make change in a store.

LADY: Change for better or worse? Ha ha!—Well— (*Pause.*) Well—you see that other room there, through that arch there? That's the confectionery; it's closed now but it's going to be reopened in a short while and I'm going to compete for the night life in this county, the after-the-movies trade. I'm going to serve setups in there and I'm going to redecorate. I got it all planned. (*She is talking eagerly now, as if to herself.*) Artificial branches of fruit trees in flower on the walls and ceilings!—It's going to be like an orchard in the spring!—My father, he had an orchard on Moon Lake. He made a wine garden of it. We had fifteen little white arbors with tables in them and they were covered with— grapevines and—we sold Dago red wine an' bootleg whiskey and beer.—They burned it up! My father was burned up in it. . . .

(*Jabe knocks above more loudly and a hoarse voice shouts*

"*Lady!*" *Figure appears at the door and calls:* "*Mrs. Torrance?*")

Oh, that's the sandman with my sleeping tablets. (*Crosses to door.*) Thanks, Mr. Dubinsky, sorry I had to disturb you, sorry I—

(*Man mutters something and goes. She closes the door.*)

Well, go to hell, then, old bastard. . . . (*Returns with package.*) —You ever have trouble sleeping?

VAL: I can sleep or not sleep as long or short as I want to.

LADY: Is that right?

VAL: I can sleep on a concrete floor or go without sleeping, without even feeling sleepy, for forty-eight hours. And I can hold my breath three minutes without blacking out; I made ten dollars betting I could do it and I did it! And I can go a whole day without passing water.

LADY (*startled*): Is *that* a *fact?*

VAL (*very simply as if he'd made an ordinary remark*): That's a fact. I served time on a chain gang for vagrancy once and they tied me to a post all day and I stood there all day without passing water to show the sons of bitches that I could do it.

LADY:—I see what that auto repair man was talking about when he said this boy is a peculiar talker! Well—what else can you do? Tell me some more about your self-control!

VAL (*grinning*): Well, they say that a woman can burn a man down. But I can burn down a woman.

LADY: Which woman?

VAL: Any two-footed woman.

LADY (*throws back her head in sudden friendly laughter as he grins at her with the simple candor of a child*):—Well, there's lots of two-footed women round here that might be willin' to test the truth of that statement.

VAL: I'm saying I could. I'm not saying I would.

LADY: Don't worry, boy. I'm one two-footed woman that you don't have to convince of your perfect controls.

VAL: No, I'm done with all that.

LADY: What's the matter? Have they tired you out?

VAL: I'm not tired. I'm disgusted.

LADY: Aw, you're disgusted, huh?

VAL: I'm telling you, Lady, there's people bought and sold in this world like carcasses of hogs in butcher shops!

LADY: You ain't tellin' me nothin' I don't know.

VAL: You might think there's many and many kinds of people in this world but, Lady, there's just two kinds of people, the ones that are bought and the buyers! No!—there's one other kind . . .

LADY: What kind's that?

VAL: The kind that's never been branded.

LADY: You will be, man.

VAL: They got to catch me first.

LADY: Well, then, you better not settle down in this county.

VAL: You know they's a kind of bird that don't have legs so it can't light on nothing but has to stay all its life on its wings in the sky? That's true. I seen one once, it had died and fallen to earth and it was light-blue colored and its body was tiny as your little finger, that's the truth, it had a body as tiny as your little finger and so light on the palm of your hand it didn't weigh more than a feather, but its wings spread out this wide but they was transparent, the color of the sky and you could see through them. That's what they call protection coloring. Camouflage, they call it. You can't tell those birds from the sky and that's why the hawks don't catch them, don't see them up there in the high blue sky near the sun!

LADY: How about in gray weather?

VAL: They fly so high in gray weather the Goddam hawks would get dizzy. But those little birds, they don't have no legs at all and they live their whole lives on the wing, and they sleep on the wind, that's how they sleep at night, they just spread their wings and go to sleep on the wind like other birds fold their wings and go to sleep on a tree. . . . (*Music fades in.*) —They sleep on the wind and . . . (*His eyes grow soft and vague and he lifts his guitar and accompanies the very faint music.*)—never light on this earth but one time when they die!

LADY:—I'd like to be one of those birds.

VAL: So'd I like to be one of those birds; they's lots of people

would like to be one of those birds and never be—corrupted!

LADY: If one of those birds ever dies and falls on the ground
and you happen to find it, I wish you would show it to me
because I think maybe you just imagine there is a bird of
that kind in existence. Because I don't think nothing living
has ever been that free, not even nearly. Show me one of
them birds and I'll say, Yes, God's made one perfect creature!—I sure would give this mercantile store and every bit
of stock in it to be that tiny bird the color of the sky . . .
for one night to sleep on the wind and—float!—around under th'—stars . . .

(*Jabe knocks on floor. Lady's eyes return to Val.*)

—Because I sleep with a son of a bitch who bought me at
a fire sale, and not in fifteen years have I had a single good
dream, not one—oh!—*Shit* . . . I don't know why I'm—
telling a stranger—this. . . . (*She rings the cashbox open.*)
Take this dollar and go eat at the Al-Nite on the highway
and come back here in the morning and I'll put you to
work. I'll break you in clerking here and when the new
confectionery opens, well, maybe I can use you in there.—
That door locks when you close it!—But let's get one thing
straight.

VAL: What thing?

LADY: I'm not interested in your perfect functions, in fact you
don't interest me no more than the air that you stand in. If
that's understood we'll have a good working relation, but
otherwise trouble!—Of course I know you're crazy, but
they's lots of crazier people than you are still running loose
and some of them in high positions, too. Just remember.
No monkey business with me. Now go. Go eat, you're
hungry.

VAL: Mind if I leave this here? My life's companion? (*He
means his guitar.*)

LADY: Leave it here if you want to.

VAL: Thanks, Lady.

LADY: Don't mention it.

(*He crosses toward the door as a dog barks with passionate clarity in the distance. He turns to smile back at her and says:*)

VAL: I don't know nothing about you except you're nice but you are just about the nicest person that I have ever run into! And I'm going to be steady and honest and hard-working to please you and any time you have any more trouble sleeping, I know how to fix that for you. A lady osteopath taught me how to make little adjustments in the neck and spine that give you sound, natural sleep. Well, g'night, now.

(*He goes out. Count five. Then she throws back her head and laughs as lightly and gaily as a young girl. Then she turns and wonderingly picks up and runs her hands tenderly over his guitar as the curtain falls.*)

ACT TWO

SCENE ONE

The store, afternoon, a few weeks later. The table and chair are back in the confectionery. Lady is hanging up the phone. Val is standing just outside the door. He turns and enters. Outside on the highway a mule team is laboring to pull a big truck back on the icy pavement. A Negro's voice shouts: "Hyyyyyyyyy-up."

VAL (*moving to R. window*): One a them big Diamond T trucks an' trailors gone off the highway last night and a six mule team is tryin' t' pull it back on. . . . (*He looks out window.*)

LADY (*coming from behind to R. of counter*): Mister, we just now gotten a big fat complaint about you from a woman that says if she wasn't a widow her husband would come in here and beat the tar out of you.

VAL (*taking a step toward her*): Yeah?—Is this a small pink-headed woman?

LADY: *Pin*-headed woman did you say?

VAL: Naw, I said, "Pink!"—A little pink-haired woman, in a checkered coat with pearl buttons this big on it.

LADY: I talked to her on the phone. She didn't go into such details about her appearance but she did say you got familiar. I said, "How? by his talk or behavior?" And she said, "Both!"—Now I was afraid of this when I warned you last week, "No monkey business here, boy!"

VAL: This little pink-headed woman bought a valentine from me and all I said is my *name* is Valentine to her. Few minutes later a small colored boy come in and delivered the valentine to me with something' wrote on it an' I believe I still got it. . . . (*Finds and shows it to Lady who goes to him. Lady reads it, and tears it fiercely to pieces. He lights a cigarette.*)

LADY: Signed it with a lipstick kiss? You didn't show up for this date?

VAL: No, ma'am. That's why she complained. (*Throws match on floor.*)

LADY: Pick that match up off the floor.

VAL: Are you bucking for sergeant, or something?

(*He throws match out the door with elaborate care. Her eyes follow his back. Val returns lazily toward her.*)

LADY: Did you walk around in front of her that way?

VAL (*at counter*): What way?

LADY: Slew-foot, slew-foot!

(*He regards her closely with good-humored perplexity.*)

Did you stand in front of her like that? That close? In that, that—*position*?

VAL: What position?

LADY: Ev'rything you do is suggestive!

VAL: Suggestive of what?

LADY: Of what you said you was through with—somethin'— *Oh, shoot, you know what I mean.*—Why'd 'ya think I give you a plain, dark business suit to work in?

VAL (*sadly*): Un-hun. . . . (*Sighs and removes his blue jacket.*)

LADY: Now what're you takin' that off for?

VAL: I'm giving the suit back to you. I'll change my pants in the closet. (*Gives her the jacket and crosses into alcove.*)

LADY: Hey! I'm sorry! You hear me? I didn't sleep well last night. Hey! I said I'm sorry! You hear me? (*She enters alcove and returns immediately with Val's guitar and crosses to D.R. He follows.*)

VAL: Le' me have my guitar, Lady. You find too many faults with me and I tried to do good.

LADY: I told you I'm sorry. You want me to get down and lick the dust off your shoes?

VAL: Just give me back my guitar.

LADY: I ain't dissatisfied with you. I'm pleased with you, sincerely!

VAL: You sure don't show it.

LADY: My nerves are all shot to pieces. (*Extends hand to him.*) Shake.

VAL: You mean I ain't fired, so I don't have to quit?

(*They shake hands like two men. She hands him guitar—then silence falls between them.*)

LADY: You see, we don't know each other, we're, we're—just gettin'—acquainted.

VAL: That's right, like a couple of animals sniffin' around each other. . . .

(*The image embarrasses her. He crosses to counter, leans over and puts guitar behind it.*)

LADY: Well, not exactly like that, but—!

VAL: We don't know each other. How do people get to know each other? I used to think they did it by touch.

LADY: By what?

VAL: By touch, by touchin' each other.

LADY (*moving up and sitting on shoe-fitting chair which has been moved to R. window*): Oh, you mean by close—contact!

VAL: But later it seemed like that made them more strangers than ever, uhh, huh, more strangers than ever. . . .

LADY: Then how d'you think they get to know each other?

VAL (*sitting on counter*): Well, in answer to your last question, I would say this: Nobody ever gets to know *no body*! We're all of us sentenced to solitary confinement inside our own skins, for life! You understand me, Lady?—I'm tellin' you it's the truth, we got to face it, we're under a lifelong sentence to solitary confinement inside our own lonely skins for as long as we live on this earth!

LADY (*rising and crossing to him*): Oh, no, I'm not a big optimist but I cannot agree with something as sad as that statement!

(*They are sweetly grave as two children; the store is somewhat dusky. She sits in chair R. of counter.*)

VAL: *Listen!*—When I was a kid on Witches Bayou? After my folks all scattered away like loose chicken's feathers blown around by the wind?—I stayed there alone on the bayou, hunted and trapped out of season and hid from the law!—*Listen!*—All that time, all that lonely time, I felt I was—waiting for something!

LADY: What for?

VAL: What does anyone wait for? For something to happen, for anything to happen, to make things make more sense. . . . It's hard to remember what that feeling was like because I've lost it now, but I was waiting for something like if you ask a question you wait for someone to answer, but you ask the wrong question or you ask the wrong person and the answer don't come.

   Does everything stop because you don't get the answer? No, it goes right on as if the answer was given, day comes after day and night comes after night, and you're still waiting for someone to answer the question and going right on as if the question was answered. And then—well—then. . . .

LADY: Then what?

VAL: You get the make-believe answer.

LADY: What answer is that?

VAL: Don't pretend you don't know because you do!

LADY:—Love?

VAL (*placing hand on her shoulder*): That's the make-believe answer. It's fooled many a fool besides you an' me, that's the God's truth, Lady, and you had better believe it.

(*Lady looks reflectively at Val and he goes on speaking and sits on stool below counter.*)

—I met a girl on the bayou when I was fourteen. I'd had a feeling that day that if I just kept poling the boat down the bayou a little bit further I would come bang into whatever it was I'd been so long expecting!

LADY: Was she the answer, this girl that you met on the bayou?

VAL: She made me think that she was.

LADY: How did she do that?

VAL: By coming out on the dogtrot of a cabin as naked as I was in that flat-bottom boat! She stood there a while with the daylight burning around her as bright as heaven as far as I could see. You seen the inside of a shell, how white that is, pearly white? Her naked skin was like that.—Oh, God, I remember a bird flown out of the moss and its wings made a shadow on her, and then it sung a single, high clear note, and as if she was waiting for that as a kind of a signal to catch me, she turned and smiled, and walked on back in the cabin. . . .

LADY: You followed?

VAL: Yes, I followed, I followed, like a bird's tail follows a bird, I followed!

I thought that she give me the answer to the question, I'd been waiting for, but afterwards I wasn't sure that was it, but from that time the question wasn't much plainer than the answer and—

LADY:—What?

VAL: At fifteen I left Witches Bayou. When the dog died I sold my boat and the gun. . . . I went to New Orleans in this snakeskin jacket. . . . It didn't take long for me to learn the score.

LADY: What did you learn?

VAL: I learned that I had something to sell besides snakeskins and other wild things' skins I caught on the bayou. I was corrupted! That's the answer. . . .

LADY: Naw, that ain't the answer!

VAL: Okay, *you* tell me the answer!

LADY: I don't know the answer, I just know corruption ain't the answer. I know that much. If I thought that was the answer I'd take Jabe's pistol or his morphine tablets and—

(*A woman bursts into store.*)

WOMAN: I got to use your pay-phone!

LADY: Go ahead. Help yourself.

(*Woman crosses to phone, deposits coin. Lady crosses to confectionery. To Val:*)

Get me a coke from the cooler.

(*Val crosses and goes out R. During the intense activity among the choral women, Lady and Val seem bemused as if they were thinking back over their talk before. For the past minute or two a car horn has been heard blowing repeatedly in the near distance.*)

WOMAN (*at phone*): Cutrere place, get me the Cutrere place, will yuh? David Cutrere or his wife, whichever comes to the phone!

(*Beulah rushes in from the street to R.C.*)

BEULAH: Lady, Lady, where's Lady! Carol Cutrere is—!
WOMAN: Quiet, please! I am callin' her brother about her!

(*Lady sits at table in confectionery.*)

(*At phone:*) Who's this I'm talking to? Good! I'm calling about your sister, Carol Cutrere. She is blowing her car horn at the Red Crown station, she is blowing and blowing her car horn at the Red Crown station because my husband give the station attendants instructions not to service her car, and she is blowing and blowing and blowing on her horn, drawing a big crowd there and, Mr. Cutrere, I thought that you and your father had agreed to keep that girl out of Two River County for good, that's what we all understood around here.

(*Car horn.*)

BEULAH (*Listening with excited approval*): Good! Good! Tell him that if—

(*Dolly enters.*)

DOLLY: She's gotten out of the car and—
BEULAH: *Shhh!*

WOMAN: Well, I just wanted to let you know she's back here in town makin' another disturbance and my husband's on the phone now at the Red Crown station—

(*Dolly goes outside and looks off.*)

trying to get the Sheriff, so if she gits picked up again by th' law, you can't say I didn't warn you, Mr. Cutrere.

(*Car horn.*)

DOLLY (*coming back in*): Oh, good! Good!

BEULAH: Where is she, where's she gone now?

WOMAN: You better be quick about it. Yes, I do. I sympathize with you and your father and with Mrs. Cutrere, but Carol cannot demand service at our station, we just refuse to wait on her, she's not— Hello? Hello? (*She jiggles phone violently.*)

BEULAH: What's he doin'? Comin' to pick her up?

DOLLY: Call the Sheriff's office!

(*Beulah goes outside again. Val comes back with a bottle of Coca-Cola—hands it to Lady and leans on juke box.*)

(*Going out to Beulah*) What's goin' on now?

BEULAH (*outside*): Look, look, they're pushing her out of the station driveway.

(*They forget Lady in this new excitement. Ad libs continual. The short woman from the station charges back out of the store.*)

DOLLY: Where is Carol?

BEULAH: Going into the White Star Pharmacy!

(*Dolly rushes back in to the phone.*)

BEULAH (*crossing to Lady*): Lady, I want you to give me your word that if that Cutrere girl comes in here, you won't wait on her! You hear me?

LADY: No.

BEULAH:—What? Will you refuse to wait on her?

LADY: I can't refuse to wait on anyone in this store.

BEULAH: Well, I'd like to know why you can't.

DOLLY: Shhh! I'm on the phone!

BEULAH: Who you phonin' Dolly?

DOLLY: That White Star Pharmacy! I want to make sure that Mr. Dubinsky refuses to wait on that girl! (*Having found and deposited coin*) I want the White Far Starmacy. I mean the—(*Stamps foot*)—White Star Pharmacy!—I'm so upset my tongue's twisted!

(*Lady hands coke to Val. Beulah is at the window.*)

I'm getting a busy signal. Has she come out yet?

BEULAH: No, she's still in the White Star!

DOLLY: Maybe they're not waiting on her.

BEULAH: Dubinsky'd wait on a purple-bottom baboon if it put a dime on th' counter an' pointed at something!

DOLLY: I know she sat at a table in the Blue Bird Café half'n hour last time she was here and the waitresses never came near her!

BEULAH: That's different. They're not foreigners there!

(*Dolly crosses to counter.*)

You can't ostracize a person out of this county unless everybody cooperates. Lady just told me that she was going to wait on her if she comes here.

DOLLY: Lady wouldn't do that.

BEULAH: *Ask* her! She told *me* she would!

LADY (*rising and turning at once to the women and shouting at them*): Oh, for God's sake, no! I'm not going to refuse to wait on her because you all don't like her! Besides I'm delighted that wild girl is givin' her brother so much trouble! (*After this outburst she goes back of the counter.*)

DOLLY (*at phone*): Hush! Mr. Dubinsky! This is Dolly Hamma, Mr. "Dog" Hamma's wife!

(*Carol quietly enters the front door.*)

I want to ask you, is Carol Cutrere in your drugstore?

BEULAH (*warningly*): Dolly!

CAROL: No. She isn't.

DOLLY:—What?

CAROL: She's here.

(*Beulah goes into confectionery. Carol moves toward Val to D.R.C.*)

DOLLY:—Aw!—Never mind, Mr. Dubinsky, I— (*Hangs up furiously and crosses to door.*)

(*A silence in which they all stare at the girl from various positions about the store. She has been on the road all night in an open car: her hair is blown wild, her face flushed and eyes bright with fever. Her manner in the scene is that of a wild animal at bay, desperate but fearless.*)

LADY (*finally and quietly*): Hello, Carol.

CAROL: Hello, Lady.

LADY (*defiantly cordial*): I thought that you were in New Orleans, Carol.

CAROL: Yes, I was. Last night.

LADY: Well, you got back fast.

CAROL: I drove all night.

LADY: In that storm?

CAROL: The wind took the top off my car but I didn't stop.

(*She watches Val steadily; he steadily ignores her; turns away and puts bottles of Coca-Cola on a table.*)

LADY (*with growing impatience*): Is something wrong at home, is someone sick?

CAROL (*absently*): No. No, not that I know of, I wouldn't know if there was, they—may I sit down?

LADY: Why, sure.

CAROL (*crossing to chair at counter and sitting*):—They pay me to stay away so I wouldn't know. . . .

(*Silence. Val walks deliberately past her and goes into alcove.*)

—I think I have a fever, I feel like I'm catching pneumonia, everything's so far away. . . .

(*Silence again except for the faint, hissing whispers of Beulah and Dolly at the back of the store.*)

LADY (*with a touch of exasperation*): Is there something you want?

CAROL: Everything seems miles away. . . .

LADY: Carol, I said is there anything you want here?

CAROL: Excuse me!—yes. . . .

LADY: Yes, what?

CAROL: Don't bother now. I'll wait.

(*Val comes out of alcove with the blue jacket on.*)

LADY: Wait for what, what are you waiting for! You don't have to wait for nothing, just say what you want and if I got it in stock I'll give it to you!

(*Phone rings once.*)

CAROL (*vaguely*):—Thank you—no. . . .

LADY (*to Val*): Get that phone, Val.

(*Dolly crosses and hisses something inaudible to Beulah.*)

BEULAH (*rising*): I just want to wait here to see if she does or she don't.

DOLLY: She just said she would!

BEULAH: Just the same, I'm gonna wait!!

VAL (*at phone*): Yes, sir, she is.—I'll tell her. (*Hangs up and speaks to Lady:*) Her brother's heard she's here and he's coming to pick her up.

LADY: *David Cutrere is not coming in this store!*

DOLLY: Aw-aw!

BEULAH: David Cutrere used to be her lover.

DOLLY: I remember you told me.

LADY (*wheels about suddenly toward the women*): Beulah! Dolly! Why're you back there hissing together like geese? (*Coming from behind counter to R.C.*) Why don't you go to th'—Blue Bird and—have some hot coffee—talk there!

BEULAH: It looks like we're getting what they call the bum's rush.

DOLLY: I never stay where I'm not wanted and when I'm not wanted somewhere I never come back!

(*They cross out and slam door.*)

LADY (*after a pause*): What did you come here for?

CAROL: To deliver a message.

LADY: To me?

CAROL: No.

LADY: Then who?

(*Carol stares at Lady gravely a moment, then turns slowly to look at Val.*)

—Him?—Him?

(*Carol nods slowly and slightly.*)

OK, then, give him the message, deliver the message to him.

CAROL: It's a private message. Could I speak to him alone, please?

(*Lady gets a shawl from a hook.*)

LADY: Oh, for God's sake! Your brother's plantation is ten minutes from here in that sky-blue Cadillac his rich wife give him. Now look, he's on his way here but I won't let him come in, I don't even want his hand to touch the door-handle. I know your message, this boy knows your message, there's nothing private about it. But I tell you, that this boy's not for sale in my store!—Now—I'm going out to watch for the sky-blue Cadillac on the highway. When I see it, I'm going to throw this door open and holler and when I holler, I want you out of this door like a shot from a pistol!—that fast! Understand?

(NOTE: *Above scene is overextended. This can be remedied by a very lively performance. It might also help to indicate a division between the Lady-Val scene and the group scene that follows.*)

(*Lady slams door behind her. The loud noise of the door-slam increases the silence that follows. Val's oblivious attitude is not exactly hostile, but deliberate. There's a kind of purity in it; also a kind of refusal to concern himself with a problem that isn't his own. He holds his guitar with a specially tender concentration, and strikes a soft chord on it. The girl stares at Val; he whistles a note and tightens a guitar string to the pitch of the whistle, not looking at the girl. Since this scene is followed by the emotional scene between Lady and David, it should be keyed somewhat lower than written; it's important that Val should not seem brutal in his attitude toward Carol; there should be an air between them of two lonely children.*)

VAL (*in a soft, preoccupied tone*): You told the lady I work for that you had a message for me. Is that right, Miss? Have you got a message for me?

CAROL (*she rises, moves a few steps toward him, hesitantly. Val whistles, plucks guitar string, changes pitch*): You've spilt some ashes on your new blue suit.

VAL: Is that the message?

CAROL (*moves away a step*): No. No, that was just an excuse to touch you. The message is—

VAL: What?

(*Music fades in—guitar.*)

CAROL:—I'd love to hold something the way you hold your guitar, that's how I'd love to hold something, with such— *tender protection!* I'd love to hold *you* that way, with that same—*tender protection!* (*Her hand has fallen onto his knee, which he has drawn up to rest a foot on the counter stool.*) —*Because you hang the moon for me!*

VAL (*he speaks to her, not roughly but in a tone that holds a long history that began with a romantic acceptance of such declarations as she has just made to him, and that turned gradually to his present distrust. He puts guitar down and goes to her*): Who're you tryin' t' fool beside you'self? You couldn't stand the weight of a man's body on you. (*He casually picks up her wrist and pushes the sleeve back from it.*) What's this here? A human wrist with a bone? It feels like a twig I could snap with two fingers. . . . (*Gently, negligently, pushes collar of her trench coat back from her bare throat and shoulders. Runs a finger along her neck tracing a vein.*) Little girl, you're transparent, I can see the veins in you. A man's weight on you would break you like a bundle of sticks. . . .

(*Music fades out.*)

CAROL (*gazes at him, startled by his perception*): Isn't it funny! You've hit on the truth about me. The act of lovemaking is almost unbearably painful, and yet, of course, I do bear it, because to be not alone, even for a few moments, is worth the pain and the danger. It's dangerous for me because I'm not built for childbearing.

VAL: Well, then, fly away, little bird, fly away before you—get broke. (*He turns back to his guitar.*)

CAROL: Why do you dislike me?

VAL (*turning back*): I never dislike nobody till they interfere with me.

CAROL: How have I interfered with you? Did I snitch when I saw my cousin's watch on you?

VAL (*beginning to remove his watch*):—You won't take my word for a true thing I told you. I'm thirty years old and I'm done with the crowd you run with and the places you run to. The Club Rendezvous, the Starlite Lounge, the Music Bar, and all the night places. Here—(*Offers watch*)—take this Rolex Chronometer that tells the time of the day and the day of the week and the month and all the crazy moon's phases. I never stole nothing before. When I stole that I known it was time for me to get off the party, so take it back, now, to Bertie. . . . (*He takes her hand and tries to force the watch into her fist. There is a little struggle, he can't open her fist. She is crying, but staring fiercely into his eyes. He draws a hissing breath and hurls watch violently across the floor.*)

—That's my message to you and the pack you run with!

CAROL (*flinging coat away*): *I RUN WITH NOBODY!*—I hoped I could run with you. . . . (*Music stops short.*) You're in danger here, Snakeskin. You've taken off the jacket that said: "I'm wild, I'm alone!" and put on the nice blue uniform of a convict! . . . Last night I woke up thinking about you again. I drove all night to bring you this warning of danger. . . . (*Her trembling hand covers her lips.*)—The message I came here to give you was a warning of danger! I hoped you'd hear me and let me take you away before it's—too late.

(*Door bursts open. Lady rushes inside, crying out:*)

LADY: *Your brother's coming, go out! He can't come in!*

(*Carol picks up coat and goes into confectionery, sobbing. Val crosses toward door.*)

Lock that door! Don't let him come in my store!

(*Carol sinks sobbing at table. Lady runs up to the landing of the stairs as David Cutrere enters the store. He is a tall man in hunter's clothes. He is hardly less handsome now than he*

*was in his youth but something has gone: his power is that of a
captive who rules over other captives. His face, his eyes, have
something of the same desperate, unnatural hardness that
Lady meets the world with.*)

DAVID: Carol?

VAL: She's in there. (*He nods toward the dim confectionery into
which the girl has retreated.*)

DAVID (*crossing*): Carol!

(*She rises and advances a few steps into the lighted area of the
stage.*)

You broke the agreement.

(*Carol nods slightly, staring at Val.*)

(*Harshly:*) All right. I'll drive you back. Where's your coat?

(*Carol murmurs something inaudible, staring at Val.*)

Where is her coat, where is my sister's coat?

(*Val crosses below and picks up the coat that Carol has
dropped on the floor and hands it to David. He throws it
roughly about Carol's shoulders and propels her forcefully toward the store entrance. Val moves away to D.R.*)

LADY (*suddenly and sharply*): Wait, please!

(*David looks up at the landing; stands frozen as Lady rushes
down the stairs.*)

DAVID (*softly, hoarsely*): How—are you, Lady?

LADY (*turning to Val*): Val, go out.

DAVID (*to Carol*): Carol, will you wait for me in my car?

(*He opens the door for his sister; she glances back at Val with
desolation in her eyes. Val crosses quickly through the confectionery. Sound of door closing in there. Carol nods slightly as
if in sad response to some painful question and goes out of the
store. Pause.*)

LADY: I told you once to never come in this store.

DAVID: I came for my sister. . . . (*He turns as if to go.*)

LADY: No, wait!

DAVID: I don't dare leave my sister alone on the road.

LADY: I have something to tell you I never told you before. (*She crosses to him. David turns back to her, then moves away to D.R.C.*) —I—carried your child in my body the summer you quit me.

(*Silence.*)

DAVID:—I—didn't know.

LADY: No, no, I didn't write you no letter about it; I was proud then; I had pride. But I had your child in my body the summer you quit me, that summer they burned my father in his wine garden, and you, you washed your hands clean of any connection with a Dago bootlegger's daughter and—(*Her breathless voice momentarily falters and she makes a fierce gesture as she struggles to speak.*)—took that—society girl that—restored your homeplace and give you such—(*Catches breath.*)—wellborn children. . . .

DAVID:—I—didn't know.

LADY: Well, now you do know, you know now. I carried your child in my body the summer you quit me but I had it cut out of my body, and they cut my heart out with it!

DAVID:—I—didn't know.

LADY: I wanted death after that, but death don't come when you *want* it, it comes when you don't want it! I wanted death, then, but I took the next best thing. *You* sold *yourself. I* sold *my* self. *You* was bought. *I* was bought. You made whores of us both!

DAVID:—I—didn't know. . . .

(*Mandolin, barely audible,* "Dicitincello Voie.")

LADY: But that's all a long time ago. Some reason I drove by there a few nights ago; the shore of the lake where my father had his wine garden? You remember? You remember the wine garden of my father?

(*David stares at her. She turns away.*)

No, you don't? You don't remember it even?

DAVID:—Lady, I don't—remember—anything else. . . .

LADY: The mandolin of my father, the songs that I sang with my father in my father's wine garden?

DAVID: Yes, I don't remember anything else. . . .

LADY: *Core Ingrata! Come Le Rose!* And we disappeared and

he would call, *"Lady? Lady?"* (*Turns to him.*) *How could I answer him with two tongues in my mouth!* (*A sharp hissing intake of breath, eyes opened wide, hand clapped over her mouth as if what she said was unendurable to her. He turns instantly, sharply away.*)

(*Music stops short. Jabe begins to knock for her on the floor above. She crosses to stairs, stops, turns.*)

I hold hard feelings!—Don't ever come here again. If your wild sister comes here, send somebody else for her, not you, not you. Because I hope never to feel this knife again in me. (*Her hand is on her chest; she breathes with difficulty.*)

(*He turns away from her; starts toward the door. She takes a step toward him.*)

And don't pity me neither. I haven't gone down so terribly far in the world. I got a going concern in this mercantile store, in there's the confectionery which'll reopen this spring, it's being done over to make it the place that all the young people will come to, it's going to be like—

(*He touches the door, pauses with his back to her.*)

—the wine garden of my father, those wine-drinking nights when you had something better than anything you've had since!

DAVID: Lady— *That's—*

LADY:—*What?*

DAVID:—*True!* (*Opens door.*)

LADY: Go now. I just wanted to tell you my life ain't over.

(*He goes out as Jabe continues knocking. She stands, stunned, motionless till Val quietly re-enters the store. She becomes aware of his return rather slowly; then she murmurs:*)

I made a fool of myself. . . .

VAL: What?

(*She crosses to stairs.*)

LADY: *I made a fool of myself!*

(*She goes up the stairs with effort as the lights change slowly to mark a division of scenes.*)

SCENE TWO

Sunset of that day. Val is alone in the store, as if preparing to go. The sunset is fiery. A large woman opens the door and stands there looking dazed. It is Vee Talbott.

VAL (*turning*): Hello, Mrs. Talbott.

VEE: Something's gone wrong with my eyes. I can't see nothing.

VAL (*going to her*): Here, let me help you. You probably drove up here with that setting sun in your face. (*Leading her to shoe-fitting chair at R. window.*) There now. Set down right here.

VEE: Thank you—so—much. . . .

VAL: I haven't seen you since that night you brought me here to ask for this job.

VEE: Has the minister called on you yet? Reverend Tooker? I made him promise he would. I told him you were new around here and weren't affiliated to any church yet. I want you to go to ours.

VAL:—That's—mighty kind of you.

VEE: The Church of the Resurrection, it's Episcopal.

VAL: Uh, huh.

VEE: Unwrap that picture, please.

VAL: Sure. (*He tears paper off canvas.*)

VEE: It's the Church of the Resurrection. I give it a sort of imaginative treatment. You know, Jabe and Lady have never darkened a church door. I thought it ought to be hung where Jabe could look at it, it might help to bring that poor dying man to Jesus. . . .

(*Val places it against chair R. of counter and crouches before the canvas, studying it long and seriously. Vee coughs nervously, gets up, bends to look at the canvas, sits uncertainly back down. Val smiles at her warmly, then back to the canvas.*)

VAL (*at last*): What's this here in the picture?

VEE: The steeple.

VAL: Aw.—Is the church steeple red?

VEE: Why—no, but—

VAL: Why'd you paint it red, then?

VEE: Oh, well, you see, I—(*Laughs nervously, childlike in her growing excitement.*)—I just, just *felt* it that way! I paint a thing how I feel it instead of always the way it actually is. Appearances are misleading, nothing is what it looks like to the eyes. You got to have—*vision*—*to see!*

VAL:—Yes. Vision. Vision!—to see. . . . (*Rises, nodding gravely, emphatically.*)

VEE: I paint from vision. They call me a visionary.

VAL: Oh.

VEE (*with shy pride*): That's what the New Orleans and Memphis newspaper people admire so much in my work. They call it a primitive style, the work of a visionary. One of my pictures is hung on the exhibition in Audubon Park museum and they have asked for others. I can't turn them out fast enough!—I have to wait for—visions, no, I—I can't paint without—visions . . . I couldn't *live* without visions!

VAL: Have you always had visions?

VEE: No, just since I was born, I— (*Stops short, startled by the absurdity of her answer. Both laugh suddenly, then she rushes on, her great bosom heaving with curious excitement, twisting in her chair, gesturing with clenched hands.*) I was born, I was born with a caul! A sort of thing like a veil, a thin, thin sort of a web was over my eyes. They call that a caul. It's a sign that you're going to have visions, and I did, I had them! (*Pauses for breath; light fades.*) —When I was little my baby sister died. Just one day old, she died. They had to baptize her at midnight to save her soul.

VAL: Uh-huh. (*He sits opposite her, smiling, attentive.*)

VEE: The minister came at midnight, and after the baptism service, he handed the bowl of holy water to me and told me, "Be sure to empty this out on the ground!" —I didn't. I was scared to go out at midnight, with, with—death! in the—house and—I sneaked into the kitchen; I emptied the holy water into the kitchen sink—thunder struck!—the kitchen sink turned black, the kitchen sink turned absolutely black!

(*Sheriff Talbott enters the front door.*)

TALBOTT: Mama! What're you doin'?

VEE: Talkin'.

TALBOTT: I'm gonna see Jabe a minute, you go out and wait in th' car. (*He goes up. She rises slowly, picks up canvas and moves to counter.*)

VEE:—Oh, I—tell you!—since I got into this painting, my whole outlook is different. I can't explain how it is, the difference to me.

VAL: You don't have to explain. I know what you mean. Before you started to paint, it didn't make sense.

VEE:—What—what didn't?

VAL: Existence!

VEE (*slowly and softly*): No—no, it didn't . . . existence didn't make sense. . . . (*She places canvas on guitar on counter and sits in chair.*)

VAL (*rising and crossing to her*): You lived in Two River County, the wife of the county Sheriff. You saw awful things take place.

VEE: Awful! Things!

VAL: Beatings!

VEE: Yes!

VAL: Lynchings!

VEE: Yes!

VAL: Runaway convicts torn to pieces by hounds!

(*This is the first time she could express this horror.*)

VEE: *Chain-gang dogs!*

VAL: Yeah?

VEE: Tear fugitives!

VAL: Yeah?

VEE:—to *pieces*. . . .

(*She had half risen: now sinks back faintly. Val looks beyond her in the dim store, his light eyes have a dark gaze. It may be that his speech is too articulate: counteract this effect by groping, hesitations.*)

VAL (*moving away a step*): But violence ain't quick always. Sometimes it's slow. Some tornadoes are slow. Corruption —rots men's hearts and—rot is slow. . . .

VEE:—How do you—?

VAL: Know? I been a witness, I know!

VEE: *I* been a witness! *I* know!

VAL: We seen these things from seats down front at the show. (*He crouches before her and touches her hands in her lap. Her breath shudders.*) And so you begun to paint your visions. Without no plan, no training, you started to paint as if God touched your fingers. (*He lifts her hands slowly, gently from her soft lap.*) You made some beauty out of this dark country with these two, soft, woman hands. . . .

(*Talbott appears on the stair landing, looks down, silent.*) Yeah, you made some beauty! (*Strangely, gently, he lifts her hands to his mouth. She gasps. Talbott calls out:*)

TALBOTT: *Hey!*

(*Vee springs up, gasping.*)

(*Descending*) *Cut this crap!*

(*Val moves away to R.C.*)

(*To Vee:*) Go out. Wait in the car. (*He stares at Val till Vee lumbers out as if dazed. After a while:*)

Jabe Torrance told me to take a good look at you. (*Crosses to Val.*) Well, now, I've taken that look. (*Nods shortly. Goes out of store. The store is now very dim. As door closes on Talbott, Val picks up painting; he goes behind counter and places it on a shelf, then picks up his guitar and sits on counter. Lights go down to mark a division as he sings and plays "Heavenly Grass."*)

SCENE THREE

As Val finishes the song, Lady descends the stair. He rises and turns on a green-shaded light bulb.

VAL (*to Lady*): You been up there a long time.

LADY:—I gave him morphine. He must be out of his mind. He says such awful things to me. He says I want him to die.

VAL: You sure you don't?

LADY: I don't want no one to die. Death's terrible, Val.

(*Pause. She wanders to the front window R. He takes his guitar and crosses to the door.*) You gotta go now?

VAL: I'm late.

LADY: Late for what? You got a date with somebody?

VAL:—No. . . .

LADY: Then stay a while. Play something. I'm all unstrung. . . .

(*He crosses back and leans against counter; the guitar is barely audible, under the speeches.*)

I made a terrible fool of myself down here today with—

VAL:—That girl's brother?

LADY: Yes, I—threw away——pride. . . .

VAL: His sister said she'd come here to give me a warning. I wonder what of?

LADY (*sitting in shoe-fitting chair*):—I said things to him I should of been too proud to say. . . .

(*Both are pursuing their own reflections; guitar continues softly.*)

VAL: Once or twice lately I've woke up with a fast heart, shouting something, and had to pick up my guitar to calm myself down. . . . Somehow or other I can't get used to this place, I don't feel safe in this place, but I—want to stay. . . . (*Stops short; sound of wild baying.*)

LADY: The chain-gang dogs are chasing some runaway convict. . . .

VAL: *Run boy! Run fast, brother! If they catch you, you never will run again! That's—(He has thrust his guitar under his arm on this line and crossed to the door.)—for sure. . . . (The baying of the dogs changes, becomes almost a single savage note.)* —Uh-huh—the dogs've got him. . . . (*Pause.*) They're tearing him to pieces! (*Pause. Baying continues. A shot is fired. The baying dies out. He stops with his hand on the door; glances back at her; nods; draws the door open. The wind sings loud in the dusk.*)

LADY: *Wait!*

VAL:—Huh?

LADY:—Where do you stay?

VAL:—When?

LADY: Nights.

VAL: I stay at the Wildwood cabins on the highway.

LADY: You like it there?

VAL: Uh-huh.

LADY:—Why?

VAL: I got a comfortable bed, a two-burner stove, a shower and icebox there.

LADY: You want to save money?

VAL: I never could in my life.

LADY: You could if you stayed on the place.

VAL: What place?

LADY: This place.

VAL: Whereabouts on this place?

LADY (*pointing to alcove*): Back of that curtain.

VAL:—Where they try on clothes?

LADY: There's a cot there. A nurse slept on it when Jabe had his first operation, and there's a washroom down here and I'll get a plumber to put in a hot an' cold shower! I'll—fix it up nice for you. . . . (*She rises, crosses to foot of stairs. Pause. He lets the door shut, staring at her.*)

VAL (*moving D.C.*):—I—don't like to be—obligated.

LADY: There wouldn't be no obligation, you'd do me a favor. I'd feel safer at night with somebody on the place. I would; it would cost you nothing! And you could save up that money you spend on the cabin. How much? Ten a week? Why, two or three months from now you'd—save enough money to— (*Makes a wide gesture with a short laugh as if startled.*) Go on! Take a look at it! See if it don't suit you!—All right. . . .

(*But he doesn't move; he appears reflective.*)

LADY (*shivering, hugging herself*): Where does heat go in this building?

VAL (*reflectively*):—Heat rises. . . .

LADY: You with your dog's temperature, don't feel cold, do you? I do! I turn blue with it!

VAL:—Yeah. . . .

(*The wait is unendurable to Lady.*)

LADY: *Well, aren't you going to look at it, the room back there, and see if it suits you or not?!*

VAL:—I'll go and take a look at it. . . .

(*He crosses to the alcove and disappears behind the curtain. A light goes on behind it, making its bizarre pattern translucent: a gold tree with scarlet fruit and white birds in it, formally designed. Truck roars; lights sweep the frosted window. Lady gasps aloud; takes out a pint bottle and a glass from under the counter, setting them down with a crash that makes her utter a startled exclamation: then a startled laugh. She pours a drink and sits in chair R. of counter. The lights turn off behind the alcove curtain and Val comes back out. She sits stiffly without looking at him as he crosses back lazily, goes behind counter, puts guitar down. His manner is gently sad as if he had met with a familiar, expected disappointment. He sits down quietly on edge of counter and takes the pint bottle and pours himself a shot of the liquor with a reflective sigh. Boards creak loudly, contracting with the cold. Lady's voice is harsh and sudden, demanding:*)

LADY: *Well, is it okay or—what!*

VAL: I never been in a position where I could turn down something I got for nothing in my life. I like that picture in there. That's a famous picture, that "September Morn" picture you got on the wall in there. Ha ha! I might have trouble sleeping in a room with that picture. I might keep turning the light on to take another look at it! The way she's cold in that water and sort of crouched over in it, holding her body like that, that—might—ha ha!—sort of keep me awake. . . .

LADY: Aw, you with your dog's temperature and your control of all functions, it would take more than a picture to keep you awake!

VAL: I was just kidding.

LADY: I was just kidding too.

VAL: But you know how a single man is. He don't come home every night with just his shadow.

(*Pause. She takes a drink.*)

LADY: You bring girls home nights to the Wildwood cabins, do you?

VAL: I ain't so far. But I would like to feel free to. That old life is what I'm used to. I always worked nights in cities and if you work nights in cities you live in a different city from those that work days.

LADY: Yes. I know, I—imagine. . . .

VAL: The ones that work days in cities and the ones that work nights in cities, they live in different cities. The cities have the same name but they are different cities. As different as night and day. There's something wild in the country that only the night people know. . . .

LADY: Yeah, I know!

VAL: I'm thirty years old!—but sudden changes don't work, it takes—

LADY:—Time—yes. . . .

(*Slight pause which she finds disconcerting. He slides off counter and moves around below it.*)

VAL: You been good to me, Lady.—Why d'you want me to stay here?

LADY (*defensively*): I told you why.

VAL: For company nights?

LADY: Yeah, to, to!—*guard the store*, nights!

VAL: To be a night watchman?

LADY: Yeah, to be a night *watchman.*

VAL: You feel nervous alone here?

LADY: Naturally now!—Jabe sleeps with a pistol next to him but if somebody broke in the store, he couldn't git up and all I could do is holler!—Who'd *hear* me? They got a telephone girl on the night shift with—sleepin' sickness, I think! Anyhow, why're you so suspicious? You look at me like you thought I was *plottin'.*—Kind people *exist*: Even me! (*She sits up rigid in chair, lips and eyes tight closed, drawing in a loud breath which comes from a tension both personal and vicarious.*)

VAL: I understand, Lady, but. . . . Why're you sitting up so stiff in that chair?

LADY: Ha! (*Sharp laugh; she leans back in chair.*)

VAL: You're still unrelaxed.

LADY: I know.

VAL: Relax. (*Moving around close to her.*) I'm going to show you some tricks I learned from a lady osteopath that took me in, too.

LADY: What tricks?

VAL: How to manipulate joints and bones in a way that makes you feel like a loose piece of string. (*Moves behind her chair. She watches him.*) Do you trust me or don't you?

LADY: Yeah, I trust you completely, but—

VAL: Well then, lean forward a little and raise your arms up and turn sideways in the chair.

(*She follows these instructions.*)

Drop your head. (*He manipulates her head and neck.*) Now the spine, Lady. (*He places his knee against the small of her backbone and she utters a sharp, startled laugh as he draws her backbone hard against his kneecap.*)

LADY: Ha, ha!—That makes a sound like, like, like!—boards contracting with cold in the building, ha, ha!

(*He relaxes.*)

VAL: Better?

LADY: Oh, yes!—much . . . thanks. . . .

VAL (*stroking her neck*): Your skin is like silk. You're light skinned to be Italian.

LADY: Most people in this country think Italian people are dark. Some are but not all are! Some of them are fair . . . very fair. . . . My father's people were dark but my mother's people were fair. Ha ha!

(*The laughter is senseless. He smiles understandingly at her as she chatters to cover confusion. He turns away, then goes above and sits on counter close to her.*)

My mother's mother's sister—come here from Monte Cassino, to die, with relations!—but I think people always die alone . . . with or without relations. I was a little girl then and I remember it took her such a long, long time to die we almost forgot her.—And she was so quiet . . . in a corner. . . . And I remember asking her one time, Zia Teresa, how does it feel to die?—Only a little girl would ask such a question, ha ha! Oh, and I remember her answer. She said—"It's a lonely feeling."

I think she wished she had stayed in Italy and died in a place that she knew. . . . (*Looks at him directly for the first time since mentioning the alcove.*) Well, there is a washroom, and I'll get the plumber to put in a hot and cold shower! Well— (*Rises, retreats awkwardly from the chair. His interest seems to have wandered from her.*) I'll go up and get some clean linen and make up that bed in there.

(*She turns and walks rapidly, almost running, to stairs. He appears lost in some private reflection but as soon as she has disappeared above the landing, he says something under his breath and crosses directly to the cashbox. He coughs loudly to cover the sound of ringing it open; scoops out a fistful of bills and coughs again to cover the sound of slamming drawer shut. Picks up his guitar and goes out the front door of store. Lady returns downstairs, laden with linen. The outer darkness moans through the door left open. She crosses to the door and a little outside it, peering both ways down the dark road. Then she comes in furiously, with an Italian curse, shutting the door with her foot or shoulder, and throws the linen down on counter. She crosses abruptly to cashbox, rings it open and discovers theft. Slams drawer violently shut.*)

Thief! Thief!

(*Turns to phone, lifts receiver. Holds it a moment, then slams it back into place. Wanders desolately back to the door, opens it and stands staring out into the starless night as the scene dims out. Music: blues—guitar.*)

SCENE FOUR

Late that night. Val enters the store, a little unsteadily, with his guitar; goes to the cashbox and rings it open. He counts some bills off a big wad and returns them to the cashbox and the larger wad to the pocket of his snakeskin jacket. Sudden footsteps above; light spills onto stair landing. He quickly moves away from the cashbox as Lady appears on the landing in a white sateen robe; she carries a flashlight.

LADY: Who's that?

(*Music fades out.*)

VAL:—Me.

(*She turns the flashlight on his figure.*)

LADY: Oh, my God, how you scared me!

VAL: You didn't expect me?

LADY: How'd I know it was you I heard come in?

VAL: I thought you give me a room here.

LADY: You left without letting me know if you took it or not. (*She is descending the stairs into store, flashlight still on him.*)

VAL: Catch me turning down something I get for nothing.

LADY: Well, you might have said something so I'd expect you or not.

VAL: I thought you took it for granted.

LADY: I don't take nothing for granted.

(*He starts back to the alcove.*)

Wait!—I'm coming downstairs. . . . (*She descends with the flashlight beam on his face.*)

VAL: You're blinding me with that flashlight.

(*He laughs. She keeps the flashlight on him. He starts back again toward the alcove.*)

LADY: The bed's not made because I didn't expect you.

VAL: That's all right.

LADY: I brought the linen downstairs and you'd cut out.

VAL:—Yeah, well—

(*She picks up linen on counter.*)

Give me that stuff. I can make up my own rack. Tomorrow you'll have to get yourself a new clerk. (*Takes it from her and goes again toward alcove.*) I had a lucky night. (*Exhibits a wad of bills.*)

LADY: *Hey!*

(*He stops near the curtain. She goes and turns on green-shaded bulb over cashbox.*)

—*Did you just open this cashbox?*

VAL:—Why you ask that?

LADY: I thought I heard it ring open a minute ago, that's why I come down here.

VAL:—In your—white satin—kimona?

LADY: *Did you just open the cashbox?!*

VAL:—I wonder who did if I didn't. . . .

LADY: Nobody did if you didn't, but somebody did! (*Opens cashbox and hurriedly counts money. She is trembling violently.*)

VAL: How come you didn't lock the cash up in the safe this evening, Lady?

LADY: Sometimes I forget to.

VAL: That's careless.

LADY:—Why'd you open the cashbox when you come in?

VAL: I opened it twice this evening, once before I went out and again when I come back. I borrowed some money and put it back in the box an' got all this left over! (*Shows her the wad of bills.*) I beat a blackjack dealer five times straight. With this much loot I can retire for the season. . . . (*He returns money to pocket.*)

LADY: *Chicken-feed!*—I'm sorry for you.

VAL: You're sorry for me?

LADY: I'm sorry for you because nobody can help you. I was touched by your—strangeness, your strange talk.— That thing about birds with no feet so they have to sleep on the wind?—I said to myself, "This boy is a bird with no feet so he has to sleep on the wind," and that softened my fool Dago heart and I wanted to help you. . . . Fool, me!—I got what I should of expected. You robbed me while I was upstairs to get sheets to make up your bed!

(*He starts out toward the door.*)

I guess I'm a fool to even feel disappointed.

VAL (*stopping C. and dropping linen on counter*): You're disappointed in me. I was disappointed in you.

LADY (*coming from behind counter*):—How did I disappoint you?

VAL: There wasn't no cot behind that curtain before. You put it back there for a purpose.

LADY: It was back there!—folded behind the mirror.

VAL: It wasn't back of no mirror when you told me three times to go and—

LADY (*cutting in*): I left that money in the cashbox on purpose, to find out if I could trust you.

VAL: You got back th' . . .

LADY: No, no, no, I can't trust you, now I know I can't trust you, I got to trust anybody or I don't want him.

VAL: That's OK, I don't expect no character reference from you.

LADY: I'll give you a character reference. I'd say this boy's a peculiar talker! But I wouldn't say a real hard worker or honest. I'd say a peculiar slew-footer that sweet talks you while he's got his hand in the cashbox.

VAL: I took out less than you owed me.

LADY: Don't mix up the issue. I see through you, mister!

VAL: I see through you, Lady.

LADY: What d'you see through me?

VAL: You sure you want me to tell?

LADY: I'd love for you to.

VAL:—A not so young and not so satisfied woman, that hired a man off the highway to do double duty without paying overtime for it. . . . I mean a store clerk days and a stud nights, and—

LADY: God, no! You—! (*She raises her hand as if to strike at him.*) Oh, God no . . . you cheap little— (*Invectives fail her so she uses her fists, hammering at him with them. He seizes her wrists. She struggles a few moments more, then collapses, in chair, sobbing. He lets go of her gently.*)

VAL: It's natural. You felt—lonely. . . .

(*She sobs brokenly against the counter.*)

LADY: Why did you come back here?

VAL: To put back the money I took so you wouldn't remember me as not honest or grateful— (*He picks up his guitar and starts to the door nodding gravely. She catches her breath; rushes to intercept him, spreading her arms like a crossbar over the door.*)

LADY: NO, NO, DON'T GO . . . I NEED YOU!!!

(*He faces her for five beats. The true passion of her outcry touches him then, and he turns about and crosses to the alcove. . . . As he draws the curtain across it he looks back at her.*)

TO LIVE. . . . TO GO ON LIVING!!!

(*Music fades in—"Lady's Love Song"—guitar. He closes the curtain and turns on the light behind it, making it translucent. Through an opening in the alcove entrance, we see him sitting down with his guitar. Lady picks up the linen and crosses to the alcove like a spellbound child. Just outside it she stops, frozen with uncertainty, a conflict of feelings, but then he begins to whisper the words of a song so tenderly that she is able to draw the curtain open and enter the alcove. He looks up gravely at her from his guitar. She closes the curtain behind her. Its bizarre design, a gold tree with white birds and scarlet fruit in it, is softly translucent with the bulb lighted behind it. The guitar continues softly for a few moments; stops; the stage darkens till only the curtain of the alcove is clearly visible.*)

Curtain

ACT THREE

SCENE ONE

An early morning. The Saturday before Easter. The sleeping alcove is lighted. Val is smoking, half dressed, on the edge of the cot. Lady comes running, panting downstairs, her hair loose, in dressing robe and slippers and calls out in a panicky, shrill whisper.

LADY: Val! Val, he's comin' downstairs!
VAL (*hoarse with sleep*): Who's—what?
LADY: Jabe!
VAL: Jabe?
LADY: I swear he is, he's coming downstairs!
VAL: What of it?
LADY: Jesus, will you get up and put some clothes on? The damned nurse told him that he could come down in the store to check over the stock! You want him to catch you half dressed on that bed there?

VAL: Don't he know I sleep here?

LADY: Nobody knows you sleep here but you and me.

(*Voices above.*)

Oh, God!—they've started.

NURSE: Don't hurry now. Take one step at a time.

(*Footsteps on stairs, slow, shuffling. The professional, nasal cheer of a nurse's voice.*)

LADY (*panicky*): Get your shirt on! Come out!

NURSE: That's right. One step at a time, one step at a time, lean on my shoulder and take one step at a time.

(*Val rises, still dazed from sleep. Lady gasps and sweeps the curtain across the alcove just a moment before the descending figures enter the sight-lines on the landing. Lady breathes like an exhausted runner as she backs away from the alcove and assumes a forced smile. Jabe and the nurse, Miss Porter, appear on the landing of the stairs and at the same moment scudding clouds expose the sun. A narrow window on the landing admits a brilliant shaft of light upon the pair. They have a bizarre and awful appearance, the tall man, his rusty black suit hanging on him like an empty sack, his eyes burning malignantly from his yellow face, leaning on a stumpy little woman with bright pink or orange hair, clad all in starched white, with a voice that purrs with the faintly contemptuous cheer and sweetness of those hired to care for the dying.*)

NURSE: Aw, now, just look at that, that nice bright sun comin' out.

LADY: Miss Porter? It's—it's cold down here!

JABE: What's she say?

NURSE: She says it's cold down here.

LADY: The—the—the air's not warm enough yet, the air's not heated!

NURSE: He's determined to come right down, Mrs. Torrance.

LADY: I know but—

NURSE: Wild horses couldn't hold him a minute longer.

JABE (*exhausted*):—Let's—rest here a minute. . . .

LADY (*eagerly*): Yes! Rest there a minute!

NURSE: Okay. We'll rest here a minute. . . .

(*They sit down side by side on a bench under the artificial palm tree in the shaft of light. Jabe glares into the light like a fierce dying old beast. There are sounds from the alcove. To cover them up, Lady keeps making startled, laughing sounds in her throat, half laughing, half panting, chafing her hands together at the foot of the stairs, and coughing falsely.*)

JABE: Lady, what's wrong? Why are you so excited?

LADY: It seems like a miracle to me.

JABE: What seems like a miracle to you?

LADY: You coming downstairs.

JABE: You never thought I would come downstairs again?

LADY: Not this quick! Not as quick as this, Jabe! Did you think he would pick up as quick as this, Miss Porter?

(*Jabe rises.*)

NURSE: Ready?

JABE: Ready.

NURSE: He's doing fine, knock wood.

LADY: Yes, knock wood, knock wood!

(*Drums counter loudly with her knuckles. Val steps silently from behind the alcove curtain as the Nurse and Jabe resume their slow, shuffling descent of the stairs.*)

(*Moving back to D.R.C.*) You got to be careful not to overdo. You don't want another setback. Ain't that right, Miss Porter?

NURSE: Well, it's my policy to mobilize the patient.

LADY (*to Val in a shrill whisper*): Coffee's boiling, take the Goddamn coffee pot off the burner! (*She gives Val a panicky signal to go in the alcove.*)

JABE: Who're you talking to, Lady?

LADY: To—to—to Val, the clerk! I told him to—get you a—chair!

JABE: Who's that?

LADY: Val, Val, the clerk, you know Val!

JABE: Not yet. I'm anxious to meet him. Where is he?

LADY: Right here, right here, here's Val!

(*Val returns from the alcove.*)

JABE: He's here bright and early.

LADY: The early bird catches the worm!

JABE: That's right. Where is the worm?

LADY (*loudly*): Ha ha!

NURSE: Careful! One step at a time, Mr. Torrance.

LADY: Saturday before Easter's our biggest sales-day of the year, I mean second biggest, but sometimes it's even bigger than Christmas Eve! So I told Val to get here a half hour early.

(*Jabe misses his step and stumbles to foot of stairs. Lady screams. Nurse rushes down to him. Val advances and raises the man to his feet.*)

VAL: Here. Here.

LADY: Oh, my God.

NURSE: Oh, oh!

JABE: I'm all right.

NURSE: Are you sure?

LADY: Are you sure?

JABE: Let me go! (*He staggers to lean against counter, panting, glaring, with a malignant smile.*)

LADY: Oh, my God. Oh, my—God. . . .

JABE: This is the boy that works here?

LADY: Yes, this is the clerk I hired to help us out, Jabe.

JABE: How is he doing?

LADY: Fine, fine.

JABE: He's mighty good-looking. Do women give him much trouble?

LADY: When school lets out the high-school girls are thick as flies in this store!

JABE: How about older women? Don't he attract older women? The older ones are the buyers, they got the money. They sweat it out of their husbands and throw it away! What's your salary, boy, how much do I pay you?

LADY: Twenty-two fifty a week.

JABE: You're getting him cheap.

VAL: I get—commissions.

JABE: Commissions?

VAL: Yes. One percent of all sales.

JABE: Oh? Oh? I didn't know about that.

LADY: I knew he would bring in trade and he brings it in.

JABE: I bet.

LADY: Val, get Jabe a chair, he ought to sit down.

JABE: No, I don't want to sit down. I want to take a look at the new confectionery.

LADY: Oh, yes, yes! Take a look at it! Val, Val, turn on the lights in the confectionery! I want Jabe to see the way I done it over! I'm—real—*proud*!

(*Val crosses and switches on light in confectionery. The bulbs in the arches and the juke box light up.*)

Go in and look at it, Jabe. I am real proud of it!

(*He stares at Lady a moment; then shuffles slowly into the spectral radiance of the confectionery. Lady moves D.C. At the same time a calliope becomes faintly audible and slowly but steadily builds. Miss Porter goes with the patient, holding his elbow.*)

VAL (*returning to Lady*): He looks like death.

LADY (*moving away from him*): *Hush!*

(*Val goes up above counter and stands in the shadows.*)

NURSE: Well, isn't this artistic.

JABE: Yeh. Artistic as hell.

NURSE: I never seen anything like it before.

JABE: Nobody else did either.

NURSE (*coming back to U.R.C.*): Who done these decorations?

LADY (*defiantly*): I did them, all by myself!

NURSE: What do you know. It sure is something artistic.

(*Calliope is now up loud.*)

JABE (*coming back to D.R.*): Is there a circus or carnival in the county?

LADY: What?

JABE: That sounds like a circus calliope on the highway.

LADY: That's no circus calliope. It's advertising the gala opening of the Torrance Confectionery tonight!

JABE: Doing what did you say?

LADY: It's announcing the opening of our confectionery, it's going all over Glorious Hill this morning and all over Sunset and Lyon this afternoon. Hurry on here so you can see it go by the store. (*She rushes excitedly to open the front door as the ragtime music of the calliope approaches.*)

JABE: I married a live one, Miss Porter. How much does that damn thing cost me?

LADY: You'll be surprised how little. (*She is talking with an hysterical vivacity now.*) I hired it for a song!

JABE: How much of a song did you hire it for?

LADY (*closing door*): Next to nothing, seven-fifty an hour! And it covers three towns in Two River County!

(*Calliope fades out.*)

JABE (*with a muted ferocity*): Miss Porter, I married a live one! Didn't I marry a live one? (*Switches off lights in confectionery*) Her daddy "The Wop" was just as much of a live one till he burned up.

(*Lady gasps as if struck.*)

(*With a slow, ugly grin:*) He had a wine garden on the north shore of Moon Lake. The new confectionery sort of reminds me of it. But he made a mistake, he made a bad mistake, one time, selling liquor to niggers. We burned him out. We burned him out, house and orchard and vines and "The Wop" was burned up trying to fight the fire. (*He turns.*) I think I better go up.

LADY:—Did you say "WE"?

JABE:—I have a kind of a cramp. . . .

NURSE (*taking his arm*): Well, let's go up.

JABE:—Yes, I better go up. . . .

(*They cross to stairs. Calliope fades in.*)

LADY (*almost shouting as she moves D.C.*): Jabe, did you say "WE" did it, did you say "WE" did it?

JABE (*at foot of stairs, stops, turns*): Yes, I said *"We"* did it. You heard me, Lady.

NURSE: One step at a time, one step at a time, take it easy.

(*They ascend gradually to the landing and above. The calliope passes directly before the store and a clown is seen, or heard, shouting through megaphone.*)

CLOWN: Don't forget tonight, folks, the gala opening of the Torrance Confectionery, free drinks and free favors, don't forget it, the gala opening of the confectionery.

(*Fade. Jabe and the Nurse disappear above the landing. Calliope gradually fades. A hoarse cry above. The Nurse runs back downstairs, exclaiming:*)

NURSE: He's bleeding, he's having a hemm'rhage! (*Runs to phone.*) Dr. Buchanan's office! (*Turns again to Lady.*) Your husband is having a hemm'rhage!

(*Calliope is loud still. Lady appears not to hear. She speaks to Val:*)

LADY: Did you hear what he said? He said "We" did it, "WE" burned — house — vines — orchard — "The Wop" burned fighting the fire. . . .

(*The scene dims out; calliope fades out.*)

SCENE TWO

Sunset of the same day. At rise Val is alone. He is standing stock-still down center stage, almost beneath the proscenium, in the tense, frozen attitude of a wild animal listening to something that warns it of danger, his head turned as if he were looking off stage left, out over the house, frowning slightly, attentively. After a moment he mutters something sharply, and his body relaxes; he takes out a cigarette and crosses to the store entrance, opens the door and stands looking out. It has been raining steadily and will rain again in a while, but right now it is clearing: the sun breaks through, suddenly, with great brilliance; and almost at the same instant, at some distance, a woman cries out a great hoarse cry of terror and exaltation; the cry is repeated as she comes running nearer.

Vee Talbott appears through the window as if blind and demented, stiff, groping gestures, shielding her eyes with one arm as she feels along the store window for the entrance, gasping for breath. Val steps aside, taking hold of her arm to guide her into the store. For a few moments she leans weakly, blindly panting for breath against the oval glass of the door, then calls out.

VEE: I'm—*struck blind!*

VAL: You can't see?

VEE:—No! Nothing. . . .

VAL (*assisting her to stool below counter*): Set down here, Mrs. Talbott.

VEE:—Where?

VAL (*pushing her gently*): Here.

(*Vee sinks moaning onto stool.*)

What hurt your eyes, Mrs. Talbott, what happened to your eyes?

VEE (*drawing a long, deep breath*): The vision I waited and prayed for all my life long!

VAL: You had a vision?

VEE: I saw the eyes of my Saviour!—They struck me blind. (*Leans forward, clasping her eyes in anguish.*) Ohhhh, they burned out my eyes!

VAL: Lean back.

VEE: Eyeballs burn like fire. . . .

VAL (*going off R.*): I'll get you something cold to put on your eyes.

VEE: I knew a vision was coming, oh, I had many signs!

VAL (*in confectionery*): It must be a terrible shock to have a vision. . . . (*He speaks gravely, gently, scooping chipped ice from the soft-drink cooler and wrapping it in his handkerchief.*)

VEE (*with the naïveté of a child, as Val comes back to her*): I *thought* I would see my Saviour on the day of His passion, which was yesterday, Good Friday, that's when I expected to see Him. But I was mistaken, I was—disappointed. Yesterday passed and nothing, nothing much happened but—today—

(*Val places handkerchief over her eyes.*)

—this afternoon, somehow I pulled myself together and walked outdoors and started to go to pray in the empty church and meditate on the Rising of Christ tomorrow. Along the road as I walked, thinking about the mysteries of Easter, veils!—(*She makes a long shuddering word out of "veils."*)—seemed to drop off my eyes! Light, oh, light! I never have seen such brilliance! It *PRICKED* my eyeballs like *NEEDLES*!

VAL:—Light?

VEE: Yes, yes, light. YOU know, you know we live in light and shadow, that's, that's what we *live* in, a world of—*light* and—*shadow*. . . .

VAL: Yes. In light and shadow. (*He nods with complete understanding and agreement. They are like two children who have found life's meaning, simply and quietly, along a country road.*)

VEE: A world of light and shadow is what we live in, and—it's—confusing. . . .

(*A man is peering in at store window.*)

VAL: Yeah, they—*do* get—*mixed*. . . .

VEE: Well, and then—(*Hesitates to recapture her vision.*)—I heard this clap of thunder! Sky!—Split open!—And there in the split-open sky, I saw, I tell you, I *saw* the TWO HUGE BLAZING EYES OF JESUS CHRIST RISEN!—Not crucified but Risen! I mean Crucified and *then* RISEN!—The blazing eyes of Christ Risen! And then a great— (*Raises both arms and makes a great sweeping motion to describe an apocalyptic disturbance of the atmosphere.*) —His hand!—Invisible!—I didn't *see* his hand!—But it *touched* me—here! (*She seizes Val's hand and presses it to her great heaving bosom.*)

TALBOTT (*appearing R. in confectionery, furiously*): VEE!

(*She starts up, throwing the compress from her eyes. Utters a sharp gasp and staggers backward with terror and blasted ecstacy and dismay and belief, all confused in her look.*)

VEE: You!

TALBOTT: VEE!

VEE: *You!*

TALBOTT (*advancing*): VEE!

VEE (*making two syllables of the word "eyes"*):—The Ey—es! (*She collapses, forward, falls to her knees, her arms thrown about Val. He seizes her to lift her. Two or three men are peering in at the store window.*)

TALBOTT (*pushing Val away*): Let go of her, don't put your hands on my wife! (*He seizes her roughly and hauls her to the door. Val moves up to help Vee.*) Don't move. (*At door, to Val:*) I'm coming back.

VAL: I'm not goin' nowhere.

TALBOTT (*to Dog, as he goes off L. with Vee*): Dog, go in there with that boy.

VOICE (*outside*): Sheriff caught him messin' with his wife.

(*Repeat: Another Voice at a distance. "Dog" Hamma enters and stands silently beside the door while there is a continued murmur of excited voices on the street. The following scene should be underplayed, played almost casually, like the performance of some familiar ritual.*)

VAL: What do you want?

(*Dog says nothing but removes from his pocket and opens a spring-blade knife and moves to D.R. Pee Wee enters. Through the open door—voices.*)

VOICES (*outside*):—Son of a low-down bitch foolin' with—
   —That's right, ought to be—
   —Cut the son of a—

VAL: What do you—?

(*Pee Wee closes the door and silently stands beside it, opening a spring-blade knife. Val looks from one to the other.*)

—It's six o'clock. Store's closed.

(*Men chuckle like dry leaves rattling. Val crosses toward the door; is confronted by Talbott; stops short.*)

TALBOTT: Boy, I said stay here.

VAL: I'm not—goin' nowhere. . . .

TALBOTT: Stand back under that light.

VAL: Which light?

TALBOTT: That light.

(*Points. Val goes behind counter.*)

I want to look at you while I run through some photos of men wanted.

VAL: I'm not wanted.

TALBOTT: A good-looking boy like you is always wanted.

(*Men chuckle. Val stands in hot light under green-shaded bulb. Talbott shuffles through photos he has removed from his pocket.*)

—How tall are you, boy?

VAL: Never measured.

TALBOTT: How much do you weigh?

VAL: Never weighed.

TALBOTT: Got any scars or marks of identification on your face or body?

VAL: No, sir.

TALBOTT: Open your shirt.

VAL: What for? (*He doesn't.*)

TALBOTT: Open his shirt for him, Dog.

(*Dog steps quickly forward and rips shirt open to waist. Val starts forward; men point knives; he draws back.*)

That's right, stay there, boy. What did you do before?

(*Pee Wee sits on stairs.*)

VAL: Before—what?

TALBOTT: Before you come here?

VAL:—Traveled and—played. . . .

TALBOTT: Played?

DOG (*advancing to C.*): What?

PEE WEE: With wimmen?

(*Dog laughs.*)

VAL: No. Played guitar—and sang. . . .

(*Val touches guitar on counter.*)

TALBOTT: Let me see that guitar.

VAL: Look at it. But don't touch it. I don't let nobody but musicians touch it.

(*Men come close.*)

DOG: What're you smiling for, boy?

PEE WEE: He ain't smiling, his mouth's just twitching like a dead chicken's foot.

(*They laugh.*)

TALBOTT: What is all that writing on the guitar?

VAL:—Names. . . .

TALBOTT: What of?

VAL: Autographs of musicians dead and living.

(*Men read aloud the names printed on the guitar: Bessie Smith, Leadbelly, Woody Guthrie, Jelly Roll Morton, etc. They bend close to it, keeping the open knife blades pointed at Val's body; Dog touches neck of the guitar, draws it toward him. Val suddenly springs, with catlike agility, onto the counter. He runs along it, kicking at their hands as they catch at his legs. The Nurse runs down to the landing.*)

MISS PORTER: *What's going on?*

TALBOTT (*at the same time*): *Stop that!*

(*Jabe calls hoarsely above.*)

MISS PORTER (*excitedly, all in one breath, as Jabe calls*): Where's Mrs. Torrance? I got a very sick man up there and his wife's disappeared.

(*Jabe calls out again.*)

I been on a whole lot of cases but never seen one where a wife showed no concern for a—

(*Jabe cries out again. Her voice fades out as she returns above.*)

TALBOTT (*overlapping Nurse's speech*): Dog! Pee Wee! You all stand back from that counter. Dog, why don't you an' Pee Wee go up an' see Jabe. Leave me straighten this boy out, go on, go on up.

PEE WEE: C'mon, Dawg. . . .

(*They go up. Val remains panting on counter.*)

TALBOTT (*sits in shoe chair at R. window. In Talbott's manner there is a curious, half-abashed gentleness, when alone with the boy, as if he recognized the purity in him and was, truly, for the moment, ashamed of the sadism implicit in the occurrence*): Awright, boy. Git on down off th' counter, I ain't gonna touch y'r guitar.

(*Val jumps off counter.*)

But I'm gonna tell you something. They's a certain county I know of which has a big sign at the county line that says, "Nigger, don't let the sun go down on you in this county." That's all it says, it don't threaten nothing, it just says, "Nigger, don't let the sun go down on you in this county!" (*Chuckles hoarsely. Rises and takes a step toward Val.*)

Well, son! You ain't a nigger and this is not that county, but, son, I want you to just imagine that you seen a sign that said to you: "Boy, don't let the sun rise on you in this county." I said "rise," not "go down" because it's too close to sunset for you to git packed an' move on before that. But I think if you value that instrument in your hands as much as you seem to, you'll simplify my job by not allowing the sun tomorrow to rise on you in this county. 'S that understood, now, boy?

(*Val stares at him, expressionless, panting.*)

(*Crossing to door*) I *hope* so. I don't like *violence*. (*He looks back and nods at Val from the door. Then goes outside in the fiery afterglow of the sunset. Dogs bark in the distance. Music fades in: "Dog Howl Blues"—minor—guitar. Pause in which Val remains motionless, cradling guitar in his arms. Then Val's faraway, troubled look is resolved in a slight, abrupt nod of his head. He sweeps back the alcove curtain and enters the alcove and closes the curtain behind him. Lights dim down to indicate a division of scenes.*)

SCENE THREE

Half an hour later. The lighting is less realistic than in the previous scenes of the play. The interior of the store is so dim that only the vertical lines of the pillars and such selected items as the palm tree on the stair landing and the ghostly paper vineyard of the confectionery are plainly visible. The view through the great front window has virtually become the background of the action: A singing wind sweeps clouds before the moon so that the witch-like country brightens and dims and brightens again. The Marshall's hounds are restless: their baying is heard now and then. A lamp outside the door sometimes catches a figure that moves past with mysterious urgency, calling out softly and rais-ing an arm to beckon, like a shade in the under kingdom.

At rise, or when the stage is lighted again, it is empty but foot-steps are descending the stairs as Dolly and Beulah rush into the store and call out, in soft shouts:

DOLLY: Dawg?

BEULAH: Pee Wee?

EVA TEMPLE (*appearing on landing and calling down softly in the superior tone of a privileged attendant in a sick-chamber*): Please don't shout!—Mr. Binnings and Mr. Hamma (*Names of the two husbands*) are upstairs sitting with Jabe. . . . (*She continues her descent. Then Eva Temple appears, sobbing, on landing.*)

—Come down carefully, Sister.

SISTER: Help me, I'm all to pieces. . . .

(*Eva ignores this request and faces the two women.*)

BEULAH: Has the bleedin' quit yit?

EVA: The hemorrhage seems to have stopped. Sister, Sister, pull yourself together, we all have to face these things sometime in life.

DOLLY: Has he sunk into a coma?

EVA: No. Cousin Jabe is conscious. Nurse Porter says his pulse is remarkably strong for a man that lost so much blood. Of course he's had a transfusion.

SISTER: Two of 'em.

EVA (*crossing to Dolly*): Yais, an' they put him on glucose. His strength came back like magic.

BEULAH: She up there?

EVA: *Who?*

BEULAH: Lady!

EVA: No! When last reported she had just stepped into the Glorious Hill Beauty Parlor.

BEULAH: You don't mean it.

EVA: Ask Sister!

SISTER: She's planning to go ahead with—!

EVA:—The gala opening of the confectionery. Switch on the lights in there, Sister.

(*Sister crosses and switches on lights and moves off R. The decorated confectionery is lighted. Dolly and Beulah exclaim in awed voices.*)

—Of course it's not normal behavior; it's downright lunacy, but still that's no excuse for it! And when she called up at five, about one hour ago, it wasn't to ask about Jabe, oh, no, she didn't mention his name. She asked if Ruby Lightfoot had delivered a case of Seagram's. Yais, she just shouted that question and hung up the phone, before I could— (*She crosses and goes off R.*)

BEULAH (*going into confectionery*): *Oh, I understand, now! Now I see what she's up to!* Electric moon, cut-out silver-paper stars and artificial vines? Why, it's her father's wine garden on Moon Lake she's turned this room into!

DOLLY (*suddenly as she sits in shoe chair*): *Here she comes, here she comes!*

(*The Temple Sisters retreat from view in confectionery as Lady enters the store. She wears a hooded rain-cape and carries a large paper shopping bag and paper carton box.*)

LADY: Go on, ladies, don't stop, my ears are burning!

BEULAH (*coming in to U.R.C.*):—Lady, oh, Lady, Lady. . . .

LADY: Why d'you speak my name in that pitiful voice? Hanh? (*Throws back hood of cape, her eyes blazing, and places bag and box on counter.*) Val? Val! Where is that boy that works here?

(*Dolly shakes her head.*)

I guess he's havin' a T-bone steak with French fries and coleslaw fo' ninety-five cents at the Blue Bird. . . .

(*Sounds in confectionery.*)

Who's in the confectionery, is that you, Val?

(*Temple Sisters emerge and stalk past her.*)

Going, girls?

(*They go out of store.*)

Yes, gone! (*She laughs and throws off rain-cape, onto counter, revealing a low-cut gown, triple strand of pearls and a purple satin-ribboned corsage.*)

BEULAH (*sadly*): How long have I known you, Lady?

LADY (*going behind counter, unpacks paper hats and whistles*): A long time, Beulah. I think you remember when my people come here on a banana boat from Palermo, Sicily, by way of Caracas, Venezuela, yes, with a grind-organ and a monkey my papa had bought in Venezuela. I was not much bigger than the monkey, ha ha! You remember the monkey? The man that sold Papa the monkey said it was a very young monkey, but he was a liar, it was a very old monkey, it was on its last legs, ha ha ha! But it was a well-dressed monkey. (*Coming around to R. of counter*) It had a green velvet suit and a little red cap that it tipped and a tambourine that it passed around for money, ha ha ha. . . . The grind-organ played and the monkey danced in the sun, ha ha!—"*O Sole Mio, Da Da Da daaa . . . !*" (*Sits in chair at counter*) —One day, the monkey danced too much in the sun and it was a very old monkey and it dropped dead. . . . My Papa, he turned to the people, he made them a bow and he said, "The show is over, the monkey is dead." Ha ha!

(*Slight pause. Then Dolly pipes up venomously:*)

DOLLY: Ain't it wonderful Lady can be so brave?

BEULAH: Yaiss, wonderful! Hanh. . . .

LADY: For me the show is not over, the monkey is not dead yet! (*Then suddenly:*) Val, is that you, Val?

(*Someone has entered the confectionery door, out of sight, and the draught of air has set the wind-chimes tinkling wildly. Lady rushes forward but stops short as Carol appears. She wears a trench coat and a white sailor's cap with a turned-*)

down brim, inscribed with the name of a vessel and a date, past or future, memory or anticipation.)

DOLLY: Well, here's your first customer, Lady.

LADY (*going behind counter*):—Carol, that room ain't open.

CAROL: There's a big sign outside that says "Open Tonite!"

LADY: It ain't open to you.

CAROL: I have to stay here a while. They stopped my car, you see, I don't have a license; my license has been revoked and I have to find someone to drive me across the river.

LADY: You can call a taxi.

CAROL: I heard that the boy that works for you is leaving tonight and I—

LADY: *Who said he's leaving?*

CAROL (*crossing to counter*): Sheriff Talbott. The County Marshall suggested I get him to drive me over the river since he'd be crossing it too.

LADY: You got some mighty wrong information!

CAROL: Where is he? I don't see him?

LADY: Why d'you keep coming back here bothering that boy? He's not interested in you! Why would he be leaving here tonight?

(*Door opens off as she comes from behind counter.*)

Val, is that you, Val?

(*Conjure Man enters through confectionery, mumbling rapidly, holding out something. Beulah and Dolly take flight out the door with cries of revulsion.*)

No conjure stuff, go away!

(*He starts to withdraw.*)

CAROL (*crossing to U.R.C.*): Uncle! The Choctaw cry! I'll give you a dollar for it.

(*Lady turns away with a gasp, with a gesture of refusal. The Negro nods, then throws back his turkey neck and utters a series of sharp barking sounds that rise to a sustained cry of great intensity and wildness. The cry produces a violent reaction in the building. Beulah and Dolly run out of the store. Lady does not move but she catches her breath. Dog and Pee*)

Wee run down the stairs with ad libs and hustle the Negro out of the store, ignoring Lady, as their wives call: "Pee Wee!" and "Dawg!" outside on the walk. Val sweeps back the alcove curtain and appears as if the cry were his cue. Above, in the sick room, hoarse, outraged shouts that subside with exhaustion. Carol crosses downstage and speaks to the audience and to herself:)

CAROL: Something is still wild in the country! This country used to be wild, the men and women were wild and there was a wild sort of sweetness in their hearts, for each other, but now it's sick with neon, it's broken out sick, with neon, like most other places. . . . I'll wait outside in my car. It's the fastest thing on wheels in Two River County!

(She goes out of the store R. Lady stares at Val with great asking eyes, a hand to her throat.)

LADY *(with false boldness)*: Well, ain't you going with her?

VAL: I'm going with no one I didn't come here with. And I come here with no one.

LADY: Then get into your white jacket. I need your services in that room there tonight.

(Val regards her steadily for several beats.)

(Clapping her hands together twice) Move, move, stop goofing! The Delta Brilliant lets out in half'n hour and they'll be driving up here. You got to shave ice for the setups!

VAL *(as if he thought she'd gone crazy)*: "Shave ice for the setups"? *(He moves up to counter.)*

LADY: Yes, an' call Ruby Lightfoot, tell her I need me a dozen more half-pints of Seagram's. They all call for Seven-and-Sevens. You know how t' sell bottle goods under a counter? It's OK. We're gonna git paid for protection. *(Gasps, touching her diaphragm)* But one thing you gotta watch out for is sellin' to minors. Don't serve liquor to minors. Ask for his driver's license if they's any doubt. Anybody born earlier than—let's see, twenty-one from—oh, I'll figure it later. Hey! Move! Move! Stop goofing!

VAL *(placing guitar on counter)*:—You're the one that's goofing, not me, Lady.

LADY: Move, I said, *move!*

VAL: What kick are you on, are you on a benny kick, Lady? 'Ve you washed down a couple of bennies with a pot of black coffee t' make you come on strong for th' three o'clock show? (*His mockery is gentle, almost tender, but he has already made a departure; he is back in the all-night bars with the B-girls and raffish entertainers. He stands at counter as she rushes about. As she crosses between the two rooms, he reaches out to catch hold of her bare arm and he pulls her to him and grips her arms.*)

LADY: Hey!

VAL: Will you quit thrashin' around like a hooked catfish?

LADY: Go git in y'r white jacket an'—

VAL: Sit down. I want to talk to you.

LADY: I don't have time.

VAL: I got to reason with you.

LADY: It's not possible to.

VAL: You can't open a night-place here this night.

LADY: You bet your sweet life I'm *going* to!

VAL: Not *me*, not *my* sweet life!

LADY: I'm betting *my* life on it! Sweet or *not* sweet, I'm—

VAL: Yours is yours, mine is mine. . . . (*He releases her with a sad shrug.*)

LADY: You don't get the point, huh? There's a man up there that set fire to my father's wine garden and I lost my life in it, yeah, I lost my life in it, *three* lives was lost in it, two *born* lives and *one—not*. . . . I was made to commit a *murder* by him up there! (*Has frozen momentarily*) —I want that man to see the wine garden come open again when he's dying! I want him to hear it coming open again here tonight! While he's dying. It's necessary, no power on earth can stop it. Hell, I don't even want it, it's just necessary, it's just something's got to be done to square things away, to, to, to—be *not defeated! You get me? Just to be not defeated!* Ah, oh, I won't be defeated, not again, in my life! (*Embraces him*) Thank you for staying here with me!—God bless you for it. . . . Now please go and get in your white jacket . . .

(*Val looks at her as if he were trying to decide between a natural sensibility of heart and what his life's taught him since he left Witches' Bayou. Then he sighs again, with the same slight, sad shrug, and crosses into alcove to put on a jacket and remove from under his cot a canvas-wrapped package of his belongings. Lady takes paper hats and carnival stuff from counter, crosses into confectionery and puts them on the tables, then starts back but stops short as she sees Val come out of alcove with his snakeskin jacket and luggage.*)

LADY: That's not your white jacket, that's that snakeskin jacket you had on when you come here.

VAL: I come and I go in this jacket.

LADY: *Go,* did you say?

VAL: Yes, ma'am, I did, I said go. All that stays to be settled is a little matter of wages.

(*The dreaded thing's happened to her. This is what they call "the moment of truth" in the bull ring, when the matador goes in over the horns of the bull to plant the mortal swordthrust.*)

LADY:—So you're—cutting out, are you?

VAL: My gear's all packed. I'm catchin' the southbound bus.

LADY: Uh-huh, in a pig's eye. You're not conning me, mister. She's waiting for you outside in her high-powered car and you're—

(*Sudden footsteps on stairs. They break apart, Val puts suitcase down, drawing back into shadow, as Nurse Porter appears on the stair landing.*)

NURSE PORTER: Miss Torrance, are you down there?

LADY (*crossing to foot of stairs*): Yeah. I'm here. I'm back.

NURSE PORTER: Can I talk to you up here about Mr. Torrance?

LADY (*shouting to Nurse*): I'll be up in a minute. (*Door closes above. Lady turns to Val:*) OK, now, mister. You're scared about something, ain't you?

VAL: I been threatened with violence if I stay here.

LADY: I got paid for protection in this county, plenty paid for it, and it covers you too.

VAL: No, ma'am. My time is up here.

LADY: Y' say that like you'd served a sentence in jail.

VAL: I got in deeper than I meant to, Lady.

LADY: Yeah, and how about me?

VAL (*going to her*): I would of cut out before you got back to the store, but I wanted to tell you something I never told no one before. (*Places hand on her shoulder.*) I feel a true love for you, Lady! (*He kisses her.*) I'll wait for you out of this county, just name the time and the . . .

LADY (*moving back*): Oh, don't talk about love, not to me. It's easy to say "Love, Love!" with fast and free transportation waiting right out the door for you!

VAL: D'you remember some things I told you about me the night we met here?

LADY (*crossing to R.C.*): Yeah, many things. Yeah, temperature of a dog. And some bird, oh, yeah, without legs so it had to sleep on the wind!

VAL (*through her speech*): Naw, not that; not that.

LADY: And how you could burn down a woman? I said "Bull!" I take that back. You can! You can burn down a woman and stamp on her ashes to make sure the fire is put out!

VAL: I mean what I said about gettin' away from . . .

LADY: How long've you held this first steady job in your life?

VAL: Too long, too long!

LADY: Four months and five days, mister. All right! How much pay have you took?

VAL: I told you to keep out all but—

LADY: Y'r living expenses. I can give you the figures to a dime. Eighty-five bucks, no, ninety! Chicken-feed, mister! Y'know how much you got coming? IF you get it? I don't need paper to figure, I got it all in my head. You got five hundred and eighty-six bucks coming to you, not, not chicken-feed, that. But, mister. (*Gasps for breath*) —If you try to walk out on me, now, tonight, without notice!— You're going to get just nothing! A great big zero. . . .

(*Somebody hollers at door off R.: "Hey! You open?" She rushes toward it shouting, "CLOSED! CLOSED! GO AWAY!"— Val crosses to the cashbox. She turns back toward him, gasps:*)

Now you watch your next move and I'll watch mine. You open that cashbox and I swear I'll throw open that door and holler, clerk's robbing the store!

VAL:—Lady?

LADY (*fiercely*): Hanh?

VAL:—Nothing, you've—

LADY:—Hanh?

VAL: Blown your stack. I will go without pay.

LADY (*coming to C.*): Then you ain't understood me! With or without pay, you're staying!

VAL: I've got my gear. (*Picks up suitcase. She rushes to seize his guitar.*)

LADY: Then I'll go up and git mine! And take this with me, just t'make sure you wait till I'm— (*She moves back to R.C. He puts suitcase down.*)

VAL (*advancing toward her*): Lady, what're you—?

LADY (*entreating with guitar raised*): Don't—!

VAL:—Doing with—

LADY:—*Don't!*

VAL:—my guitar!

LADY: *Holding it for security while I*—

VAL: Lady, you been a lunatic since this morning!

LADY: Longer, longer than morning! I'm going to keep hold of your "life companion" while I pack! I am! I am goin' to pack an' go, if you go, where you go!

(*He makes a move toward her. She crosses below and around to counter.*)

You didn't think so, you actually didn't think so? What was I going to do, in your opinion? What, in your opinion, would I be doing? Stay on here in a store full of bottles and boxes while you go far, while you go fast and far, without me having your—forwarding address!—even?

VAL: I'll—give you a forwarding address. . . .

LADY: Thanks, oh, thanks! Would I take your forwarding address back of that curtain? "Oh, dear forwarding address, hold me, kiss me, be faithful!" (*Utters grotesque, stifled cry; presses fist to mouth.*)

(*He advances cautiously, hand stretched toward the guitar. She retreats above to U.R.C., biting lip, eyes flaring. Jabe knocks above.*)

Stay back! You want me to smash it!

VAL (*D.C.*): He's—knocking for you. . . .

LADY: I know! Death's knocking for me! Don't you think I hear him, knock, knock, knock? It sounds like what it is! Bones knocking bones. . . . Ask me how it felt to be coupled with death up there, and I can tell you. My skin crawled when he touched me. But I endured it. I guess my heart knew that somebody must be coming to take me out of this hell! You did. You came. Now look at me! I'm alive once more! (*Convulsive sobbing controlled: continues more calmly and harshly:*)

—*I won't wither in dark!* Got that through your skull? Now. Listen! Everything in this rotten store is yours, not just your pay, but everything Death's scraped together down here!—but Death has got to die before we can go. . . . You got that memorized, now?—Then get into your white jacket!—*Tonight is the gala opening*—(*Rushes through confectionery.*)—*of the confectionery*—

(*Val runs and seizes her arm holding guitar. She breaks violently free.*)

Smash me against a rock and I'll smash your guitar! I will, if you—

(*Rapid footsteps on stairs.*)

Oh, Miss Porter!

(*She motions Val back. He retreats into alcove. Lady puts guitar down beside juke-box. Miss Porter is descending the stairs.*)

NURSE PORTER (*descending watchfully*): You been out a long time.

LADY (*moving U.R.C.*): Yeah, well, I had lots of— (*Her voice expires breathlessly. She stares fiercely, blindly, into the other's hard face.*)

NURSE PORTER:—Of what?

LADY: Things to—things to—take care of. . . . (*Draws a deep, shuddering breath, clenched fist to her bosom.*)

NURSE PORTER: Didn't I hear you shouting to someone just now?

LADY:—Uh-huh. Some drunk tourist made a fuss because I wouldn't sell him no—liquor. . . .

NURSE (*crossing to the door*): Oh. Mr. Torrance is sleeping under medication.

LADY: That's good. (*She sits in shoe-fitting chair.*)

NURSE: I gave him a hypo at five.

LADY:—Don't all that morphine weaken the heart, Miss Porter?

NURSE: Gradually, yes.

LADY: How long does it usually take for them to let go?

NURSE: It varies according to the age of the patient and the condition his heart's in. Why?

LADY: Miss Porter, don't people sort of help them let go?

NURSE: How do you mean, Mrs. Torrance?

LADY: Shorten their suffering for them?

NURSE: Oh, I see what you mean. (*Snaps her purse shut.*) —I see what you mean, Mrs. Torrance. But killing is killing, regardless of circumstances.

LADY: Nobody said killing.

NURSE: You said "shorten their suffering."

LADY: Yes, like merciful people shorten an animal's suffering when he's . . .

NURSE: A human being is not the same as an animal, Mrs. Torrance. And I don't hold with what they call—

LADY (*overlapping*): *Don't give me a sermon*, Miss Porter I just wanted to know if—

NURSE (*overlapping*): I'm not giving a sermon. I just answered your question. If you want to get somebody to shorten your husband's life—

LADY (*jumping up; overlapping*): Why, how dare you say that I—

NURSE: I'll be back at ten-thirty.

LADY: Don't!

NURSE: What?

LADY (*crossing behind counter*): Don't come back at ten-thirty, don't come back.

NURSE: I'm always discharged by the doctors on my cases.

LADY: This time you're being discharged by the patient's wife.

NURSE: That's something we'll have to discuss with Dr. Buchanan.

LADY: I'll call him myself about it. I don't like you. I don't think you belong in the nursing profession, you have cold eyes; I think you like to watch pain!

NURSE: I know why you don't like my eyes. (*Snaps purse shut.*) You don't like my eyes because you know they see clear.

LADY: Why are you staring at *me*?

NURSE: I'm not staring at you, I'm staring at the curtain. There's something burning in there, smoke's coming out! (*Starts toward alcove.*) Oh.

LADY: Oh, no, you don't. (*Seizes her arm.*)

NURSE (*pushes her roughly aside and crosses to the curtain. Val rises from cot, opens the curtain and faces her coolly*): Oh, excuse me! (*She turns to Lady.*) —The moment I looked at you when I was called on this case last Friday morning I knew that you were pregnant.

(*Lady gasps.*)

I also knew the moment I looked at your husband it wasn't by him. (*She stalks to the door. Lady suddenly cries out:*)

LADY: Thank you for telling me what I hoped for is true.

MISS PORTER: You don't seem to have any shame.

LADY (*exalted*): No. I don't have shame. I have—great—joy!

MISS PORTER (*venomously*): Then why don't you get the calliope and the clown to make the announcement?

LADY: You do it for me, save me the money! Make the announcement, all over!

(*Nurse goes out. Val crosses swiftly to the door and locks it. Then he advances toward her, saying:*)

VAL: Is it true what she said?

(*Lady moves as if stunned to the counter; the stunned look gradually turns to a look of wonder. On the counter is a heap of silver and gold paper hats and trumpets for the gala opening of the confectionery.*)

VAL (*in a hoarse whisper*): Is it true or not true, what that woman told you?

LADY: You sound like a scared little boy.

VAL: She's gone out to tell.

(*Pause.*)

LADY: You gotta go now—it's dangerous for you to stay here.
. . . Take your pay out of the cashbox, you can go. Go, go,
take the keys to my car, cross the river into some other
county. You've done what you came here to do. . . .

VAL:—It's true then, it's—?

LADY (*sitting in chair of counter*): True as God's word! I have
life in my body, this dead tree, my body, has burst in
flower! You've given me life, you can go!

(*He crouches down gravely opposite her, gently takes hold of
her knotted fingers and draws them to his lips, breathing on
them as if to warm them. She sits bolt upright, tense, blind as
a clairvoyant.*)

VAL:—Why didn't you tell me before?

LADY:—When a woman's been childless as long as I've been
childless, it's hard to believe that you're still able to bear!—
We used to have a little fig tree between the house and the
orchard. It never bore any fruit, they said it was barren.
Time went by it, spring after useless spring, and it almost
started to—die. . . . Then one day I discovered a small
green fig on the tree they said wouldn't bear! (*She is clasping a gilt paper horn.*) I ran through the orchard. I ran
through the wine garden shouting, "Oh, Father, it's going
to bear, the fig tree is going to bear!"—It seemed such a
wonderful thing, after those ten barren springs, for the
little fig tree to bear, it called for a celebration—I ran to a
closet, I opened a box that we kept Christmas ornaments
in!—I took them out, glass bells, glass birds, tinsel, icicles,
stars. . . . And I hung the little tree with them, I decorated the fig tree with glass bells and glass birds, and silver
icicles and stars, because it won the battle and it would
bear! (*Rises, ecstatic*) Unpack the box! Unpack the box with
the Christmas ornaments in it, put them on me, glass bells
and glass birds and stars and tinsel and snow! (*In a sort of
delirium she thrusts the conical gilt paper hat on her head
and runs to the foot of the stairs with the paper horn. She
blows the horn over and over, grotesquely mounting the stairs,
as Val tries to stop her. She breaks away from him and runs up*

to the landing, blowing the paper horn and crying out:) I've won, I've won, Mr. Death, I'm going to bear! (*Then suddenly she falters, catches her breath in a shocked gasp and awkwardly retreats to the stairs. Then turns screaming and runs back down them, her cries dying out as she arrives at the floor level. She retreats haltingly as a blind person, a hand stretched out to Val, as slow, clumping footsteps and hoarse breathing are heard on the stairs. She moans:*)—Oh, God, oh—God. . . .

(*Jabe appears on the landing, by the artificial palm tree in its dully lustrous green jardiniere, a stained purple robe hangs loosely about his wasted yellowed frame. He is death's self, and malignancy, as he peers, crouching, down into the store's dimness to discover his quarry.*)

JABE: Buzzards! Buzzards! (*Clutching the trunk of the false palm tree, he raises the other hand holding a revolver and fires down into the store. Lady screams and rushes to cover Val's motionless figure with hers. Jabe scrambles down a few steps and fires again and the bullet strikes her, expelling her breath in a great "Hah!" He fires again; the great "Hah!" is repeated. She turns to face him, still covering Val with her body, her face with all the passions and secrets of life and death in it now, her fierce eyes blazing, knowing, defying and accepting. But the revolver is empty; it clicks impotently and Jabe hurls it toward them; he descends and passes them, shouting out hoarsely:*) I'll have you burned! I burned her father and I'll have you burned! (*He opens the door and rushes out onto the road, shouting hoarsely:*) The clerk is robbing the store, he shot my wife, the clerk is robbing the store, he killed my wife!

VAL:—Did it—?
LADY:—Yes!—it did. . . .

(*A curious, almost formal, dignity appears in them both. She turns to him with the sort of smile that people offer in apology for an awkward speech, and he looks back at her gravely, raising one hand as if to stay her. But she shakes her head slightly and points to the ghostly radiance of her make-believe orchard and she begins to move a little unsteadily toward it. Music.*

Lady enters the confectionery and looks about it as people look for the last time at a loved place they are deserting.)

The show is over. The monkey is dead . . .

(*Music rises to cover whatever sound Death makes in the confectionery. It halts abruptly. Figures appear through the great front window of the store, pocket-lamps stare through the glass and someone begins to force the front door open. Val cries out:*)

VAL: Which way!

(*He turns and runs through the dim radiance of the confectionery, out of our sight. Something slams. Something cracks open. Men are in the store and the dark is full of hoarse, shouting voices.*)

VOICES OF MEN (*shouting*):—Keep to the walls! He's armed!
—Upstairs, Dog!
—Jack, the confectionery!

(*Wild cry back of store.*)

Got him. GOT HIM!
—They got him!
—Rope, git rope!
—Git rope from th' hardware section!
—I got something better than rope!
—What've you got?
—What's that, what's he got?
—A BLOWTORCH!
—Christ. . . .

(*A momentary hush.*)

—Come on, what in hell are we waiting for?
—Hold on a minute, I wanta see if it works!
—Wait, Wait!
—LOOK here!

(*A jet of blue flame stabs the dark. It flickers on Carol's figure in the confectionery. The men cry out together in hoarse passion crouching toward the fierce blue jet of fire, their faces lit by it like the faces of demons.*)

—Christ!

—It works!

(*They rush out. Confused shouting behind. Motors start. Fade quickly. There is almost silence, a dog bays in the distance. Then—the Conjure Man appears with a bundle of garments which he examines, dropping them all except the snakeskin jacket, which he holds up with a toothless mumble of excitement.*)

CAROL (*quietly, gently*): What have you got there, Uncle? Come here and let me see.

(*He crosses to her.*)

Oh yes, his snakeskin jacket. I'll give you a gold ring for it.

(*She slowly twists ring off her finger. Somewhere there is a cry of anguish. She listens attentively till it fades out, then nods with understanding.*)

—Wild things leave skins behind them, they leave clean skins and teeth and white bones behind them, and these are tokens passed from one to another, so that the fugitive kind can always follow their kind. . . .

(*The cry is repeated more terribly than before. It expires again. She draws the jacket about her as if she were cold, nods to the old Negro, handing him the ring. Then she crosses toward the door, pausing halfway as Sheriff Talbott enters with his pocket-lamp.*)

SHERIFF: Don't no one move, don't move!

(*She crosses directly past him as if she no longer saw him, and out the door. He shouts furiously:*)

Stay here!

(*Her laughter rings outside. He follows the girl, shouting:*)

Stop! Stop!

(*Silence. The Negro looks up with a secret smile as the curtain falls slowly.*)

SUDDENLY LAST SUMMER

To Anne Meacham

SCENE ONE

The set may be as unrealistic as the decor of a dramatic ballet. It represents part of a mansion of Victorian Gothic style in the Garden District of New Orleans on a late afternoon, between late summer and early fall. The interior is blended with a fantastic garden which is more like a tropical jungle, or forest, in the prehistoric age of giant fern-forests when living creatures had flippers turning to limbs and scales to skin. The colors of this jungle-garden are violent, especially since it is steaming with heat after rain. There are massive tree-flowers that suggest organs of a body, torn out, still glistening with undried blood; there are harsh cries and sibilant hissings and thrashing sounds in the garden as if it were inhabited by beasts, serpents and birds, all of savage nature. . . .

The jungle tumult continues a few moments after the curtain rises; then subsides into relative quiet, which is occasionally broken by a new outburst.

A lady enters with the assistance of a silver-knobbed cane. She has light orange or pink hair and wears a lavender lace dress, and over her withered bosom is pinned a starfish of diamonds.

She is followed by a young blond Doctor, all in white, glacially brilliant, very, very good-looking, and the old lady's manner and eloquence indicate her undeliberate response to his icy charm.

MRS. VENABLE: Yes, this was Sebastian's garden. The Latin names of the plants were printed on tags attached to them but the print's fading out. Those ones there—(*She draws a deep breath*)—are the oldest plants on earth, survivors from the age of the giant fern-forests. Of course in this semi-tropical climate—(*She takes another deep breath*)—some of the rarest plants, such as the Venus flytrap—you know what this is, Doctor? The Venus flytrap?

DOCTOR: An insectivorous plant?

MRS. VENABLE: Yes, it feeds on insects. It has to be kept under glass from early fall to late spring and when it went under glass, my son, Sebastian, had to provide it with fruit flies flown in at great expense from a Florida laboratory that used fruit flies for experiments in genetics. Well, I can't do that, Doctor. (*She takes a deep breath.*) I can't, I just can't do it! It's not the expense but the—

DOCTOR: Effort.

MRS. VENABLE: Yes. So goodbye, Venus flytrap!—like so much else . . . Whew! . . . (*She draws breath.*) —I don't know why, but—! I already feel I can lean on your shoulder, Doctor—Cu?—Cu?

DOCTOR: Cu-kro-wicz. It's a Polish word that means sugar, so let's make it simple and call me Doctor Sugar.

(*He returns her smile.*)

MRS. VENABLE: Well, now, Doctor Sugar, you've seen Sebastian's garden.

(*They are advancing slowly to the patio area.*)

DOCTOR: It's like a well-groomed jungle. . . .

MRS. VENABLE: That's how he meant it to be, nothing was accidental, everything was planned and designed in Sebastian's life and his—(*She dabs her forehead with her handkerchief which she had taken from her reticule*)—work!

DOCTOR: What was your son's work, Mrs. Venable?—besides this garden?

MRS. VENABLE: As many times as I've had to answer that question! D'you know it still shocks me a little?—to realize that Sebastian Venable the poet is still unknown outside of a small coterie of friends, including his mother.

DOCTOR: Oh.

MRS. VENABLE: You see, strictly speaking, his *life* was his occupation.

DOCTOR: I see.

MRS. VENABLE: No, you *don't* see, yet, but before I'm through, you will.—Sebastian was a poet! That's what I meant when I said his life was his work because the work of a poet is the life of a poet and—vice versa, the life of a poet is the work of a poet, I mean you can't separate them, I mean—well, for instance, a salesman's work is one thing and his life is another—or can be. The same thing's true of—doctor, lawyer, merchant, *thief!*—But a poet's life is his work and his work is his life in a special sense because—oh, I've already talked myself breathless and dizzy.

(*The Doctor offers his arm.*)

Thank you.

DOCTOR: Mrs. Venable, did your doctor okay this thing?

MRS. VENABLE (*breathless*): What thing?

DOCTOR: Your meeting this girl that you think is responsible for your son's death?

MRS. VENABLE: I've waited months to face her because I couldn't get to St. Mary's to face her—I've had her brought here to my house. I won't collapse! She'll collapse! I mean her lies will collapse—not my truth—not the truth. . . . *Forward march, Doctor Sugar!*

(*He conducts her slowly to the patio.*)

Ah, we've *made* it, *ha ha!* I didn't know that I was so weak on my pins! Sit down, Doctor. I'm not afraid of using every last ounce and inch of my little, left-over strength in doing just what I'm doing. I'm devoting all that's left of my life, Doctor, to the defense of a dead poet's reputation. Sebastian had no public name as a poet, he didn't want one, he refused to have one. He *dreaded, abhorred!*—false values that come from being publicly known, from fame, from personal—exploitation. . . . Oh, he'd say to me: "Violet? Mother?—You're going to outlive me!!"

DOCTOR: What made him think that?

MRS. VENABLE: Poets are always clairvoyant!—And he had rheumatic fever when he was fifteen and it affected a heart-valve and he wouldn't stay off horses and out of water and so forth. . . . "Violet? Mother? You're going to live longer than me, and then, when I'm gone, it will be yours, in your hands, to do whatever you please with!"—Meaning, of course, his future recognition!—That he *did* want, he wanted it after his death when it couldn't disturb him; then he did want to offer his work to the world. All right. Have I made my point, Doctor? Well, here is my son's work, Doctor, here's his life going *on!*

(*She lifts a thin gilt-edged volume from the patio table as if elevating the Host before the altar. Its gold leaf and lettering catch the afternoon sun. It says* Poem of Summer. *Her face suddenly has a different look, the look of a visionary, an exalted* religieuse. *At the same instant a bird sings clearly and purely in the garden and the old lady seems to be almost young for a moment.*)

DOCTOR (*reading the title*): *Poem of Summer?*

MRS. VENABLE: *Poem of Summer,* and the date of the summer, there are twenty-five of them, he wrote one poem a year which he printed himself on an eighteenth-century hand-press at his—atelier in the—French—Quarter—so no one but he could see it. . . .

(*She seems dizzy for a moment.*)

DOCTOR: He wrote one poem a year?

MRS. VENABLE: One for each summer that we traveled together. The other nine months of the year were really only a preparation.

DOCTOR: Nine months?

MRS. VENABLE: The length of a pregnancy, yes. . . .

DOCTOR: The poem was hard to deliver?

MRS. VENABLE: Yes, even with me! *Without* me, *impossible,* Doctor!—he wrote no poem last summer.

DOCTOR: He died last summer?

MRS. VENABLE: Without me he died last summer, that was his last summer's poem.

(*She staggers; he assists her toward a chair. She catches her breath with difficulty.*)

One long-ago summer—now, why am I thinking of this? —my son, Sebastian, said, "Mother?—Listen to this!"—He read me Herman Melville's description of the Encantadas, the Galapagos Islands. Quote—take five and twenty heaps of cinders dumped here and there in an outside city lot. Imagine some of them magnified into mountains, and the vacant lot, the sea. And you'll have a fit idea of the general aspect of the Encantadas, the Enchanted Isles—extinct volcanos, looking much as the world at large might look— after a last conflagration—end quote. He read me that description and said that we had to go there. And so we did go there that summer on a chartered boat, a four-masted schooner, as close as possible to the sort of a boat that Melville must have sailed on. . . . We saw the Encantadas,

but on the Encantadas we saw something Melville *hadn't*
written about. We saw the great sea-turtles crawl up out of
the sea for their annual egg-laying. . . . Once a year the
female of the sea-turtle crawls up out of the equatorial sea
onto the blazing sand-beach of a volcanic island to dig a
pit in the sand and deposit her eggs there. It's a long
and dreadful thing, the depositing of the eggs in the sand-
pits, and when it's finished the exhausted female turtle
crawls back to the sea half-dead. She never sees her offspring, but we did. Sebastian knew exactly when the sea-
turtle eggs would be hatched out and we returned in time
for it. . . .

DOCTOR: You went back to the—?

MRS. VENABLE: Terrible Encantadas, those heaps of extinct
volcanos, in time to witness the hatching of the sea-turtles
and their desperate flight to the sea!

(*There is a sound of harsh bird-cries in the air. She looks up.*)

—The narrow beach, the color of caviar, was all in motion!
But the sky was in motion, too. . . .

DOCTOR: The sky was in motion, too?

MRS. VENABLE:—Full of flesh-eating birds and the noise of
the birds, the horrible savage cries of the—

DOCTOR: Carnivorous birds?

MRS. VENABLE: Over the narrow black beach of the Encantadas
as the just hatched sea-turtles scrambled out of the sand-
pits and started their race to the sea. . . .

DOCTOR: Race to the sea?

MRS. VENABLE: To escape the flesh-eating birds that made the
sky almost as black as the beach!

(*She gazes up again: we hear the wild, ravenous, harsh cries of
the birds. The sound comes in rhythmic waves like a savage
chant.*)

And the sand all alive, all alive, as the hatched sea-turtles
made their dash for the sea, while the birds hovered and
swooped to attack and hovered and—swooped to attack!
They were diving down on the hatched sea-turtles, turning
them over to expose their soft undersides, tearing the undersides open and rending and eating their flesh. Sebastian

guessed that possibly only a hundredth of one per cent of their number would escape to the sea. . . .

DOCTOR: What was it about this that fascinated your son?

MRS. VENABLE: My son was looking for— (*She stops short with a slight gasp.*) —Let's just say he was interested in sea-turtles!

DOCTOR: That isn't what you started to say.

MRS. VENABLE: I stopped myself just in time.

DOCTOR: Say what you started to say.

MRS. VENABLE: I started to say that my son was looking for God and I stopped myself because I thought you'd think 'Oh, a pretentious young crackpot!'—which Sebastian was *not*!

DOCTOR: Mrs. Venable, doctors look for God, too.

MRS. VENABLE: Oh?

DOCTOR: I think they have to look harder for him than priests since they don't have the help of such well-known guide-books and well-organized expeditions as the priests have with their scriptures and—churches. . . .

MRS. VENABLE: You mean they go on a solitary safari like a poet?

DOCTOR: Yes. Some do. I do.

MRS. VENABLE: I believe, I *believe* you! (*She laughs, startled.*)

DOCTOR: Let me tell you something—the first operation I performed at Lion's View.—You can imagine how anxious and nervous I was about the outcome.

MRS. VENABLE: Yes.

DOCTOR: The patient was a young girl regarded as hopeless and put in the Drum—

MRS. VENABLE: Yes.

DOCTOR: The name for the violent ward at Lion's View because it looks like the inside of a drum with very bright lights burning all day and all night.—So the attendants can see any change of expression or movement among the inmates in time to grab them if they're about to attack. After the operation I stayed with the girl, as if I'd delivered a child that might stop breathing.—When they finally wheeled her out of surgery, I still stayed with her. I walked along by the rolling table holding onto her hand—with my heart in my throat. . . .

(*We hear faint music.*)

—It was a nice afternoon, as fair as this one. And the moment we wheeled her outside, she whispered something, she whispered: "Oh, how blue the sky is!"—And I felt proud, I felt proud and relieved, because up till then her speech, everything that she'd babbled, was a torrent of obscenities!

MRS. VENABLE: Yes, well, now, I can tell you without any hesitation that my son *was* looking for God, I mean for a clear image of him. He spent that whole blazing equatorial day in the crow's-nest of the schooner watching this thing on the beach till it was too dark to see it, and when he came down the rigging he said "Well, now I've seen Him!," and he meant God.—And for several weeks after that he had a fever, he was delirious with it.—

(*The Encantadas music then fades in again, briefly, at a lower level, a whisper.*)

DOCTOR: I can see how he *might* be, I think he *would* be disturbed if he thought he'd seen God's image, an equation of God, in that spectacle you watched in the Encantadas: creatures of the air hovering over and swooping down to devour creatures of the sea that had had the bad luck to be hatched on land and weren't able to scramble back into the sea fast enough to escape that massacre you witnessed, yes, I can see how such a spectacle could be equated with a good deal of—*experience, existence!*—but not with *God*! Can *you*?

MRS. VENABLE: Dr. Sugar, I'm a reasonably loyal member of the Protestant Episcopal Church, but I understood what he meant.

DOCTOR: Did he mean we must rise above God?

MRS. VENABLE: He meant that God shows a savage face to people and shouts some fierce things at them, it's all we see or hear of Him. Isn't it all we ever really see and hear of Him, now?—Nobody seems to know why. . . .

(*Music fades out again.*)

Shall I go on from there?

DOCTOR: Yes, do.

MRS. VENABLE: Well, next?—India—China—

(*Miss Foxhill appears with the medicine. Mrs. Venable sees her.*)

FOXHILL: Mrs. Venable.

MRS. VENABLE: Oh, God—elixir of—. (*She takes the glass.*) Isn't it kind of the drugstore to keep me alive. Where was I, Doctor?

DOCTOR: In the Himalayas.

MRS. VENABLE: Oh yes, that long-ago summer. . . . In the Himalayas he almost entered a Buddhist monastery, had gone so far as to shave his head and eat just rice out of a wood bowl on a grass mat. He'd promised those sly Buddhist monks that he would give up the world and himself and all his worldly possessions to their mendicant order.—Well, I cabled his father, "For God's sake notify bank to freeze Sebastian's accounts!"—I got back this cable from my late husband's lawyer: "Mr. Venable critically ill Stop Wants you Stop Needs you Stop Immediate return advised most strongly. Stop. Cable time of arrival. . . ."

DOCTOR: Did you go back to your husband?

MRS. VENABLE: I made the hardest decision of my life. I stayed with my son. I got him through that crisis too. In less than a month he got up off the filthy grass mat and threw the rice bowl away—and booked us into Shepheard's Hotel in Cairo and the Ritz in Paris—. And from then on, oh, we—still lived in a—world of light and shadow. . . .

(*She turns vaguely with empty glass. He rises and takes it from her.*)

But the shadow was almost as luminous as the light.

DOCTOR: Don't you want to sit down now?

MRS. VENABLE: Yes, indeed I do, before I fall down.

(*He assists her into wheelchair.*)

—Are your hind-legs still on you?

DOCTOR (*still concerned over her agitation*):—My what? Oh— hind legs!—Yes . . .

MRS. VENABLE: Well, then you're not a donkey, you're certainly not a donkey because I've been talking the hind-legs off a donkey—several donkeys. . . . But I had to make it clear to you that the world lost a great deal too when I lost my son last summer. . . . You would have liked my son, he would have been charmed by you. My son, Sebastian, was not a family snob or a money snob but he was a snob, all right. He was a snob about personal charm in people, he insisted upon good looks in people around him, and, oh, he had a perfect little court of young and beautiful people around him always, wherever he was, here in New *Orleans* or New York or on the Riviera or in Paris and Venice, he always had a little entourage of the beautiful and the talented and the young!

DOCTOR: Your son was young, Mrs. Venable?

MRS. VENABLE: Both of us were young, and stayed young, Doctor.

DOCTOR: Could I see a photograph of your son, Mrs. Venable?

MRS. VENABLE: Yes, indeed you could, Doctor. I'm glad that you asked to see one. I'm going to show you not one photograph but two. Here. Here is my son, Sebastian, in a Renaissance pageboy's costume at a masked ball in Cannes. Here is my son, Sebastian, in the same costume at a masked ball in Venice. These two pictures were taken twenty years apart. Now which is the older one, Doctor?

DOCTOR: This photograph looks older.

MRS. VENABLE: The photograph looks older but not the subject. It takes character to refuse to grow old, Doctor—successfully to refuse to. It calls for discipline, abstention. One cocktail before dinner, not two, four, six—a single lean chop and lime juice on a salad in restaurants famed for rich dishes.

(*Foxhill comes from the house.*)

FOXHILL: Mrs. Venable, Miss Holly's mother and brother are—

(*Simultaneously Mrs. Holly and George appear in the window.*)

GEORGE: Hi, Aunt Vi!

MRS. HOLLY: Violet dear, we're here.

FOXHILL: They're here.

MRS. VENABLE: Wait upstairs in my upstairs living room for me.

(*To Miss Foxhill:*)

Get them upstairs. I don't want them at that window during this talk.

(*To the Doctor:*)

Let's get away from the window.

(*He wheels her to stage center.*)

DOCTOR: Mrs. Venable? Did your son have a—well—what kind of a *personal*, well, *private* life did—

MRS. VENABLE: That's a question I wanted you to ask me.

DOCTOR: Why?

MRS. VENABLE: I haven't heard the girl's story except indirectly in a watered-down version, being too ill to go to hear it directly, but I've gathered enough to know that it's a hideous attack on my son's moral character which, being dead, he can't defend himself from. I have to be the defender. Now. Sit down. Listen to me . . .

(*The Doctor sits.*)

. . . before you hear whatever you're going to hear from the girl when she gets here. My son, Sebastian, was chaste. Not c-h-a-s-e-d! Oh, he was chased in that way of spelling it, too, we had to be very fleet-footed I can tell you, with his looks and his charm, to keep ahead of pursuers, every kind of pursuer!—I mean he was c-h-a-s-t-e!— Chaste. . . .

DOCTOR: I understood what you meant, Mrs. Venable.

MRS. VENABLE: And you *believe* me, don't you?

DOCTOR: Yes, but—

MRS. VENABLE: But *what*?

DOCTOR: Chastity at—what age was your son last summer?

MRS. VENABLE: *Forty*, maybe. We really didn't count birthdays. . . .

DOCTOR: He lived a celibate life?

MRS. VENABLE: As strictly as if he'd *vowed* to! This sounds like vanity, Doctor, but really I was actually the only one in his life that satisfied the demands he made of people. Time

after time my son would let people go, dismiss them!—because their, their, their!—*attitude* toward him was—

DOCTOR: Not as pure as—

MRS. VENABLE: My son, Sebastian, demanded! We were a famous couple. People didn't speak of Sebastian and his
mother or Mrs. Venable and her son, they said "Sebastian
and Violet, Violet and Sebastian are staying at the Lido,
they're at the Ritz in Madrid. Sebastian and Violet, Violet
and Sebastian have taken a house at Biarritz for the season," and every appearance, every time we appeared, attention was centered on *us!—everyone else! Eclipsed!* Vanity?
Ohhhh, no, Doctor, you can't call it that—

DOCTOR: I didn't call it that.

MRS. VENABLE:—It wasn't *folie de grandeur*, it was grandeur.

DOCTOR: I see.

MRS. VENABLE: An attitude toward life that's hardly been
known in the world since the great Renaissance princes
were crowded out of their palaces and gardens by successful shopkeepers!

DOCTOR: I see.

MRS. VENABLE: Most people's lives—what are they but trails
of debris, each day more debris, more debris, long, long
trails of debris with nothing to clean it all up but, finally,
death. . . .

(*We hear lyric music.*)

My son, Sebastian, and I constructed our days, each day,
we would—carve out each day of our lives like a piece of
sculpture.—Yes, we left behind us a trail of days like a
gallery of sculpture! But, last summer—

(*Pause: the music continues.*)

I can't forgive him for it, not even now that he's paid for it
with his life!—he let in this—*vandal!* This—

DOCTOR: The girl that—?

MRS. VENABLE: That you're going to meet here this afternoon! Yes. He admitted this vandal and with her tongue
for a hatchet she's gone about smashing our legend, the
memory of—

DOCTOR: Mrs. Venable, what do you think is her reason?

MRS. VENABLE: Lunatics don't have reason!

DOCTOR: I mean what do you think is her—motive?

MRS. VENABLE: What a question!—We put the bread in her mouth and the clothes on her back. People that like you for that or even forgive you for it are, are—*hen's teeth*, Doctor. The role of the benefactor is worse than thankless, it's the role of a victim, Doctor, a sacrificial victim, yes, they want your blood, Doctor, they want your blood on the altar steps of their *outraged, outrageous* egos!

DOCTOR: Oh. You mean she resented the—

MRS. VENABLE: Loathed!—They can't shut her up at St. Mary's.

DOCTOR: I thought she'd been there for months.

MRS. VENABLE: I mean keep her *still* there. She *babbles!* They couldn't shut her up in Cabeza de Lobo or at the clinic in Paris—she babbled, babbled!—smashing my son's reputation.—On the Berengaria bringing her back to the States she broke out of the stateroom and babbled, babbled; even at the airport when she was flown down here, she babbled a bit of her story before they could whisk her into an ambulance to St. Mary's. This is a reticule, Doctor. (*She raises a cloth bag.*) A catch-all, carry-all bag for an elderly lady which I turned into last summer. . . . Will you open it for me, my hands are stiff, and fish out some cigarettes and a cigarette holder.

(*He does.*)

DOCTOR: I don't have matches.

MRS. VENABLE: I think there's a table-lighter on the table.

DOCTOR: Yes, there is.

(*He lights it, it flames up high.*)

My Lord, what a torch!

MRS. VENABLE (*with a sudden, sweet smile*): "So shines a good deed in a naughty world," Doctor—Sugar. . . .

(*Pause. A bird sings sweetly in the garden.*)

DOCTOR: Mrs. Venable?

MRS. VENABLE: Yes?

DOCTOR: In your letter last week you made some reference to a, to a—fund of some kind, an endowment fund of—

MRS. VENABLE: I wrote you that my lawyers and bankers and certified public accountants were setting up the Sebastian Venable Memorial Foundation to subsidize the work of young people like you that are pushing out the frontiers of art and science but have a financial problem. You have a financial problem, don't you, Doctor?

DOCTOR: Yes, we do have that problem. My work is such a *new* and *radical* thing that people in charge of state funds are naturally a little scared of it and keep us on a small budget, so small that—. We need a separate ward for my patients, I need trained assistants, I'd like to marry a girl I can't afford to marry!—But there's also the problem of getting right patients, not just—criminal psychopaths that the State turns over to us for my operation!—because it's—well—risky. . . . I don't want to turn you against my work at Lion's View but I have to be honest with you. There is a good deal of risk in my operation. Whenever you enter the brain with a foreign object . . .

MRS. VENABLE: Yes.

DOCTOR:—Even a needle-thin knife . .

MRS. VENABLE: Yes.

DOCTOR:—In a skilled surgeon's fingers . . .

MRS. VENABLE: Yes.

DOCTOR:—There is a good deal of risk involved in—the operation. . . .

MRS. VENABLE: You said that it pacifies them, it quiets them down, it suddenly makes them peaceful.

DOCTOR: Yes. It does that, that much we already know, but—

MRS. VENABLE: What?

DOCTOR: Well, it will be ten years before we can tell if the immediate benefits of the operation will be lasting or—passing or even if there'd still be—and this is what haunts me about it!—any possibility, afterwards, of—reconstructing a —totally sound person, it may be that the person will always be limited afterwards, relieved of acute disturbances but—*limited,* Mrs. Venable. . . .

MRS. VENABLE: Oh, but what a blessing to them, Doctor, to be just peaceful, to be just suddenly—peaceful. . . .

(*A bird sings sweetly in the garden.*)

After all that horror, after those nightmares: just to be able to lift up their eyes and see—(*She looks up and raises a hand to indicate the sky*)—a sky not as black with savage, devouring birds as the sky that we saw in the Encantadas, Doctor.

DOCTOR:—Mrs. Venable? I can't guarantee that a lobotomy would stop her—*babbling!!*

MRS. VENABLE: That may be, maybe not, but after the operation, who would *believe* her, Doctor?

(*Pause: faint jungle music.*)

DOCTOR (*quietly*): My God. (*Pause.*) —Mrs. Venable, suppose after meeting the girl and observing the girl and hearing this story she babbles—I still shouldn't feel that her condition's—intractable enough! to justify the risks of—suppose I shouldn't feel that non-surgical treatment such as insulin shock and electric shock and—

MRS. VENABLE: SHE'S HAD ALL THAT AT SAINT MARY'S!! Nothing else is left for her.

DOCTOR: But if I disagreed with you? (*Pause.*)

MRS. VENABLE: That's just part of a question: finish the question, Doctor.

DOCTOR: Would you still be interested in my work at Lion's View? I mean would the Sebastian Venable Memorial Foundation still be interested in it?

MRS. VENABLE: Aren't we always more interested in a thing that concerns us personally, Doctor?

DOCTOR: Mrs. Venable!!

(*Catharine Holly appears between the lace window curtains.*)

You're such an innocent person that it doesn't occur to you, it obviously hasn't even occurred to you that anybody less innocent than you are could possibly interpret this offer of a subsidy as—well, as sort of a *bribe*?

MRS. VENABLE (*laughs, throwing her head back*): Name it that —I don't care—. There's just two things to remember. She's a destroyer. My son was a *creator*!—Now if my honesty's shocked you—pick up your little black bag without the subsidy in it, and run away from this garden!—

Nobody's heard our conversation but you and I, Doctor Sugar. . . .

(*Miss Foxhill comes out of the house and calls.*)

MISS FOXHILL: Mrs. Venable?
MRS. VENABLE: What is it, what do you want, Miss Foxhill?
MISS FOXHILL: Mrs. Venable? Miss Holly is here, with—

(*Mrs. Venable sees Catharine at the window.*)

MRS. VENABLE: Oh, my God. There she is, in the window!— I told you I didn't want her to enter my house again, I told you to meet them at the door and lead them around the side of the house to the garden and you didn't listen. I'm not ready to face her. I have to have my five o'clock cock- tail first, to fortify me. Take my chair inside. Doctor? Are you still here? I thought you'd run out of the garden. I'm going back through the garden to the other entrance. Doctor? Sugar? You may stay in the garden if you wish to or run out of the garden if you wish to or go in this way if you wish to or do anything that you wish to but I'm going to have my five o'clock daiquiri, *frozen!*—before I face her. . . .

(*All during this she has been sailing very slowly off through the garden like a stately vessel at sea with a fair wind in her sails, a pirate's frigate or a treasure-laden galleon. The young Doctor stares at Catharine framed by the lace window cur- tains. Sister Felicity appears beside her and draws her away from the window. Music: an ominous fanfare. Sister Felicity holds the door open for Catharine as the Doctor starts quickly forward. He starts to pick up his bag but doesn't. Catharine rushes out, they almost collide with each other.*)

CATHARINE: *Excuse me.*
DOCTOR: *I'm sorry. . . .*

(*She looks after him as he goes into the house.*)

SISTER FELICITY: Sit down and be still till your family come outside.

Dim Out

SCENE TWO

Catharine removes a cigarette from a lacquered box on the table and lights it. The following quick, cadenced lines are accompanied by quick, dancelike movement, almost formal, as the Sister in her sweeping white habit, which should be starched to make a crackling sound, pursues the girl about the white wicker patio table and among the wicker chairs: this can be accompanied by quick music.

SISTER: What did you take out of that box on the table?

CATHARINE: Just a cigarette, Sister.

SISTER: Put it back in the box.

CATHARINE: Too late, it's already lighted.

SISTER: Give it here.

CATHARINE: Oh, please, let me smoke, Sister!

SISTER: Give it here.

CATHARINE: *Please*, Sister Felicity.

SISTER: Catharine, give it here. You know that you're not allowed to smoke at Saint Mary's.

CATHARINE: We're not at Saint Mary's, this is an afternoon out.

SISTER: You're still in my charge. I can't permit you to smoke because the last time you smoked you dropped a lighted cigarette on your dress and started a fire.

CATHARINE: Oh, I did not start a fire. I just burned a hole in my skirt because I was half unconscious under medication. (*She is now back of a white wicker chair.*)

SISTER (*overlapping her*): Catharine, give it here.

CATHARINE: Don't be such a bully!

SISTER: Disobedience has to be paid for later.

CATHARINE: All right, I'll pay for it later.

SISTER (*overlapping*): Give me that cigarette or I'll make a report that'll put you right back on the violent ward, if you don't. (*She claps her hands twice and holds one hand out across the table.*)

CATHARINE (*overlapping*): I'm not being violent, Sister.

SISTER (*overlapping*): Give me that cigarette, I'm holding my hand out for it!

CATHARINE: All right, take it, here, take it!

(*She thrusts the lighted end of the cigarette into the palm of the Sister's hand. The Sister cries out and sucks her burned hand.*)

SISTER: *You burned me with it!*

CATHARINE: I'm sorry, I didn't mean to.

SISTER (*shocked, hurt*): You deliberately burned me!

CATHARINE (*overlapping*): You said give it to you and so I gave it to you.

SISTER (*overlapping*): You stuck the lighted end of that cigarette in my hand!

CATHARINE (*overlapping*): I'm *sick,* I'm *sick!*—of being *bossed* and *bullied!*

SISTER (*commandingly*): *Sit down!*

(*Catharine sits down stiffly in a white wicker chair on forestage, facing the audience. The Sister resumes sucking the burned palm of her hand. Ten beats. Then from inside the house the whirr of a mechanical mixer.*)

CATHARINE: There goes the Waring Mixer, Aunt Violet's about to have her five o'clock frozen daiquiri, you could set a watch by it! (*She almost laughs. Then she draws a deep, shuddering breath and leans back in her chair, but her hands remain clenched on the white wicker arms.*) —We're in Sebastian's garden. *My God, I can still cry!*

SISTER: Did you have any medication before you went out?

CATHARINE: No. I didn't have any. Will you give me some, Sister?

SISTER (*almost gently*): I can't. I wasn't told to. However, I think the doctor will give you something.

CATHARINE: The young blond man I bumped into?

SISTER: Yes. The young doctor's a specialist from another hospital.

CATHARINE: What hospital?

SISTER: A word to the wise is sufficient. . . .

(*The Doctor has appeared in the window.*)

CATHARINE (*rising abruptly*): I knew I was being watched, he's in the window, staring out at me!

SISTER: Sit down and be still. Your family's coming outside.

CATHARINE (*overlapping*): LION'S VIEW, IS IT! DOCTOR?

(*She has advanced toward the bay window. The Doctor draws back, letting the misty white gauze curtains down to obscure him.*)

SISTER (*rising with a restraining gesture which is almost pitying*): Sit down, dear.

CATHARINE: IS IT LION'S VIEW? DOCTOR?!

SISTER: Be still. . . .

CATHARINE: WHEN CAN I STOP RUNNING DOWN THAT STEEP WHITE STREET IN CABEZA DE LOBO?

SISTER: Catharine, dear, sit down.

CATHARINE: I loved him, Sister! Why wouldn't he let me save him? I tried to hold onto his hand but he struck me away and ran, ran, ran in the wrong direction, Sister!

SISTER: Catharine, dear—be still.

(*The Sister sneezes.*)

CATHARINE: Bless you, Sister. (*She says this absently, still watching the window.*)

SISTER: Thank you.

CATHARINE: The Doctor's still at the window but he's too blond to hide behind window curtains, he catches the light, he shines through them. (*She turns from the window.*) —We were *going* to blonds, blonds were next on the menu.

SISTER: Be still now. Quiet, dear.

CATHARINE: Cousin Sebastian said he was famished for blonds, he was fed up with the dark ones and was famished for blonds. All the travel brochures he picked up were advertisements of the blond northern countries. I think he'd already booked us to—Copenhagen or—Stockholm.—Fed up with dark ones, famished for light ones: that's how he talked about people, as if they were—items on a menu.— "That one's delicious-looking, that one is appetizing," or "that one is *not* appetizing"—I think because he was really nearly half-starved from living on pills and salads. . . .

SISTER: *Stop it!*—Catharine, be still.

CATHARINE: He liked me and so I loved him. . . . (*She cries a little again.*) If he'd kept hold of my hand I could have saved him!—Sebastian suddenly said to me last summer: "Let's fly north, little bird—I want to walk under those radiant, cold northern lights—I've never *seen* the aurora borealis!"—Somebody said once or wrote, once: "We're all of us children in a vast kindergarten trying to spell God's name with the wrong alphabet blocks!"

MRS. HOLLY (*offstage*): *Sister?*

(*The Sister rises.*)

CATHARINE (*rising*): I think it's *me* they're calling, they call *me* "Sister," Sister!

SCENE THREE

The Sister resumes her seat impassively as the girl's mother and younger brother appear from the garden. The mother, Mrs. Holly, is a fatuous Southern lady who requires no other description. The brother, George, is typically good-looking, he has the best "looks" of the family, tall and elegant of figure. They enter.

MRS. HOLLY: Catharine, dear! Catharine—

(*They embrace tentatively.*)

Well, well! Doesn't she look fine, George?

GEORGE: Uh huh.

CATHARINE: They send you to the beauty parlor whenever you're going to have a family visit. Other times you look awful, you can't have a compact or lipstick or anything made out of metal because they're afraid you'll swallow it.

MRS. HOLLY (*giving a tinkly little laugh*): I think she looks just splendid, don't you, George?

GEORGE: Can't we talk to her without the nun for a minute?

MRS. HOLLY: Yes, I'm sure it's all right to. Sister?

CATHARINE: Excuse me, Sister Felicity, this is my mother, Mrs. Holly, and my brother, George.

SISTER: How do you do.

GEORGE: How d'ya do.

CATHARINE: This is Sister Felicity. . . .

MRS. HOLLY: We're so happy that Catharine's at Saint Mary's! So very grateful for all you're doing for her.

SISTER (*sadly, mechanically*): We do the best we can for her, Mrs. Holly.

MRS. HOLLY: I'm sure you do. Yes, well—I wonder if you would mind if we had a little private chat with our Cathie?

SISTER: I'm not supposed to let her out of my sight.

MRS. HOLLY: It's just for a minute. You can sit in the hall or the garden and we'll call you right back here the minute the private part of the little talk is over.

(*Sister Felicity withdraws with an uncertain nod and a swish of starched fabric.*)

GEORGE (*to Catharine*): *Jesus! What are you up to? Huh? Sister? Are you trying to RUIN us?!*

MRS. HOLLY: GAWGE! WILL YOU BE QUIET. You're upsetting your sister!

(*He jumps up and stalks off a little, rapping his knee with his zipper-covered tennis racket.*)

CATHARINE: How elegant George looks.

MRS. HOLLY: George inherited Cousin Sebastian's wardrobe but everything else is in probate! Did you know that? That everything else is in probate and Violet can keep it in probate just as long as she wants to?

CATHARINE: Where is Aunt Violet?

MRS. HOLLY: *George, come back here!*

(*He does, sulkily.*)

Violet's on her way down.

GEORGE: Yeah. Aunt Violet has an elevator now.

MRS. HOLLY: Yais, she has, she's had an elevator installed where the back stairs were, and, Sister, it's the cutest little thing you ever did see! It's paneled in Chinese lacquer, black an' gold Chinese lacquer, with lovely bird-pictures on it. But there's only room for two people at a time in it. George and I came down on foot.—I think she's havin' her frozen daiquiri now, she still has a frozen daiquiri promptly at five o'clock ev'ry afternoon in the world . . . in warm weather. . . . Sister, the horrible death of Sebastian just about *killed* her!—She's now slightly better . . . but it's a question of time.—Dear, you know, I'm sure that you understand, why we haven't been out to see you at Saint Mary's. They said you were too disturbed, and a family visit might disturb you more. But I want you to know that nobody, absolutely nobody in the city, knows a thing about what you've been through. Have they, George? Not a thing. Not a soul even knows that you've come back from Europe. When people enquire, when they question us about you, we just say that you've stayed abroad to study something or other. (*She catches her breath.*) Now. Sister?—I want you to please be *very* careful what you say to your Aunt Violet about what happened to Sebastian in Cabeza de Lobo.

CATHARINE: What do you want me to say about what—?

MRS. HOLLY: Just don't repeat that same fantastic story! For my sake and George's sake, the sake of your brother and mother, don't repeat that horrible story again! Not to Violet! Will you?

CATHARINE: Then I am going to have to tell Aunt Violet what happened to her son in Cabeza de Lobo?

MRS. HOLLY: Honey, that's why you're here. She has *INSISTED* on hearing it straight from YOU!

GEORGE: You were the only witness to it, Cathie.

CATHARINE: No, there were others. That *ran.*

MRS. HOLLY: Oh, Sister, you've just had a little sort of a—*nightmare* about it! Now, listen to me, will you, Sister? Sebastian has left, has BEQUEATHED!—to you an' Gawge in his *will*—

GEORGE (*religiously*): *To each of us, fifty grand, each!*—AFTER! TAXES!—GET IT?

CATHARINE: Oh, yes, but if they give me an injection—I won't have any choice but to tell exactly what happened in Cabeza de Lobo last summer. Don't you see? I won't have any choice but to tell the truth. It makes you tell the truth because it shuts something off that might make you able not to and *everything* comes out, decent or *not* decent, you have no control, but always, always the truth!

MRS. HOLLY: Catharine, darling. I don't know the full story, but surely you're not too sick in your *head* to know in your *heart* that the story you've been telling is just—too—

GEORGE (*cutting in*): Cathie, Cathie, you got to forget that story! Can'tcha? For *your* fifty grand?

MRS. HOLLY: Because if Aunt Vi contests the will, and we know she'll contest it, she'll keep it in the courts forever!—We'll be—

GEORGE: It's in PROBATE NOW! And'll never get out of probate until you drop that story—we can't afford to hire lawyers good enough to contest it! So if you don't stop telling that crazy story, we won't have a pot to—cook *greens* in!

(*He turns away with a fierce grimace and a sharp, abrupt wave of his hand, as if slapping down something. Catharine stares at his tall back for a moment and laughs wildly.*)

MRS. HOLLY: Catharine, don't laugh like that, it scares me, Catharine.

(*Jungle birds scream in the garden.*)

GEORGE (*turning his back on his sister*): Cathie, the money is all tied up.

(*He stoops over sofa, hands on flannel knees, speaking directly into Catharine's face as if she were hard of hearing. She raises a hand to touch his cheek affectionately; he seizes the hand and removes it but holds it tight.*)

If Aunt Vi decided to contest Sebastian's will that leaves us all of this cash?!—Am I coming through to you?

CATHARINE: Yes, little brother, you are.

GEORGE: You see, Mama, she's crazy like a coyote!

(*He gives her a quick cold kiss*)

We won't get a single damn penny, honest t' God we won't! So you've just GOT to stop tellin' that story about what you say happened to Cousin Sebastian in Cabeza de Lobo, even if it's what it *couldn't* be, TRUE!—You got to drop it, Sister, you can't tell such a story to civilized people in a civilized up-to-date country!

MRS. HOLLY: Cathie, why, why, why!—did you invent such a tale?

CATHARINE: But, Mother, I DIDN'T invent it. I know it's a hideous story but it's a true story of our time and the world we live in and what did truly happen to Cousin Sebastian in Cabeza de Lobo. . . .

GEORGE: Oh, then you are going to tell it. Mama, she *IS* going to tell it! Right to Aunt Vi, and lose us a hundred thousand!—Cathie? You are a BITCH!

MRS. HOLLY: GAWGE!

GEORGE: I repeat it, a bitch! She isn't crazy, Mama, she's no more crazy than I am, she's just, just—PERVERSE! Was ALWAYS!—perverse. . . .

(*Catharine turns away and breaks into quiet sobbing.*)

MRS. HOLLY: Gawge, Gawge, apologize to Sister, this is no way for you to talk to your sister. You come right back over here and tell your sweet little sister you're sorry you spoke like that to her!

GEORGE (*turning back to Catharine*): I'm sorry, Cathie, but you know we NEED that money! Mama and me, we—Cathie? I got *ambitions*! And, Cathie, I'm YOUNG!—I *want* things, I *need* them, Cathie! So will you please think about ME? Us?

MISS FOXHILL (*offstage*): Mrs. Holly? Mrs. Holly?

MRS. HOLLY: Somebody's callin' fo' me. Catharine, Gawge put it very badly but you know that it's TRUE! WE DO HAVE TO GET WHAT SEBASTIAN HAS LEFT US IN HIS WILL, DEAREST! AND YOU WON'T LET US DOWN? PROMISE? YOU WON'T? LET US DOWN?

GEORGE (*fiercely shouting*): HERE COMES AUNT VI! Mama, Cathie, Aunt Violet's—here is Aunt Vi!

SCENE FOUR

Mrs. Venable enters downstage area. Entrance music.

MRS. HOLLY: *Cathie! Here's Aunt Vi!*

MRS. VENABLE: She sees me and I see her. That's all that's necessary. Miss Foxhill, put my chair in this corner. Crank the back up a little.

(*Miss Foxhill does this business.*)

More. More. Not that much!—Let it back down a little. All right. Now, then. I'll have my frozen daiquiri, now. . . . Do any of you want coffee?

GEORGE: I'd like a chocolate malt.

MRS. HOLLY: Gawge!

MRS. VENABLE: This isn't a drugstore.

MRS. HOLLY: Oh, Gawge is just being Gawge.

MRS. VENABLE: That's what I *thought* he was being!

(*An uncomfortable silence falls. Miss Foxhill creeps out like a burglar. She speaks in a breathless whisper, presenting a cardboard folder toward Mrs. Venable.*)

MISS FOXHILL: Here's the portfolio marked Cabeza de Lobo. It has all your correspondence with the police there and the American consul.

MRS. VENABLE: I asked for the *English transcript*! It's in a separate—

MISS FOXHILL: Separate, yes, here it is!

MRS. VENABLE: Oh . . .

MISS FOXHILL: And here's the report of the private investigators and here's the report of—

MRS. VENABLE: Yes, yes, yes! Where's the doctor?

MISS FOXHILL: On the phone in the library!

MRS. VENABLE: Why does he choose such a moment to make a phone-call?

MISS FOXHILL: He didn't make a phone-call, he received a phone-call from—

MRS. VENABLE: Miss Foxhill, why are you talking to me like a burglar!?

(*Miss Foxhill giggles a little desperately.*)

CATHARINE: Aunt Violet, she's frightened.—Can I move? Can I get up and move around till it starts?

MRS. HOLLY: Cathie, Cathie, dear, did Gawge tell you that he received bids from every good fraternity on the Tulane campus and went Phi Delt because Paul Junior did?

MRS. VENABLE: I see that he had the natural tact and good taste to come here this afternoon outfitted from head to foot in clothes that belonged to my son!

GEORGE: You gave 'em to me, Aunt Vi.

MRS. VENABLE: I didn't know you'd parade them in front of me, George.

MRS. HOLLY (*quickly*): Gawge, tell Aunt Violet how grateful you are for—

GEORGE: I found a little Jew tailor on Britannia Street that makes alterations so good you'd never guess that they weren't cut *out* for me to *begin* with!

MRS. HOLLY: *AND* so reasonable!—Luckily, since it seems that Sebastian's wonderful, wonderful bequest to Gawge an' Cathie is going to be tied up a while!?

GEORGE: Aunt Vi? About the will?

(*Mrs. Holly coughs.*)

I was just wondering if we can't figure out some way to, to—

MRS. HOLLY: Gawge means to EXPEDITE it! To get through the red tape quicker?

MRS. VENABLE: I understand his meaning. Foxhill, get the Doctor.

(*She has risen with her cane and hobbled to the door.*)

MISS FOXHILL (*exits calling*): Doctor!

MRS. HOLLY: Gawge, no more about money.

GEORGE: How do we know we'll ever see her again?

(*Catharine gasps and rises; she moves downstage, followed quickly by Sister Felicity.*)

SISTER (*mechanically*): What's wrong, dear?

CATHARINE: I think I'm just dreaming this, it doesn't seem real!

(*Miss Foxhill comes back out, saying:*)

FOXHILL: He had to answer an urgent call from Lion's View.

(*Slight, tense pause.*)

MRS. HOLLY: Violet! *Not* Lion's View!

(*Sister Felicity had started conducting Catharine back to the patio; she stops her, now.*)

SISTER: Wait, dear.

CATHARINE: What for? I know what's coming.

MRS. VENABLE (*at same time*): Why? are you all prepared to put out a thousand a month plus extra charges for treatments to keep the girl at St. Mary's?

MRS. HOLLY: Cathie? Cathie, dear?

(*Catharine has returned with the Sister.*)

Tell Aunt Violet how grateful you are for her makin' it possible for you to rest an' recuperate at such a sweet, sweet place as St. Mary's!

CATHARINE: No place for lunatics is a sweet, sweet place.

MRS. HOLLY: But the food's good there. Isn't the food good there?

CATHARINE: Just give me written permission not to eat fried grits. I had yard privileges till I refused to eat fried grits.

SISTER: She lost yard privileges because she couldn't be trusted in the yard without constant supervision or even with it because she'd run to the fence and make signs to cars on the highway.

CATHARINE: Yes, I did, I did that because I've been trying for weeks to get a message out of that "sweet, sweet place."

MRS. HOLLY: What message, dear?

CATHARINE: I got panicky, Mother.

MRS. HOLLY: Sister, I don't understand.

GEORGE: What're you scared of, Sister?

CATHARINE: What they might do to me now, after they've done all the rest!—That man in the window's a specialist from Lion's View! We get newspapers. I know what they're . . .

(*The Doctor comes out.*)

MRS. VENABLE: Why, Doctor, I thought you'd left us with just that little black bag to remember you by!

DOCTOR: Oh, no. Don't you remember our talk? I had to answer a call about a patient that—

MRS. VENABLE: This is Dr. Cukrowicz. He says it means "sugar" and we can call him "Sugar"—

(*George laughs.*)

He's a specialist from Lion's View.

CATHARINE (*cutting in*): WHAT DOES HE SPECIALIZE IN?

MRS. VENABLE: Something new. When other treatments have failed.

(*Pause. The jungle clamor comes up and subsides again.*)

CATHARINE: *Do you want to bore a hole in my skull and turn a knife in my brain?* Everything else was done to me!

(*Mrs. Holly sobs. George raps his knee with the tennis racket.*)

You'd have to have my mother's permission for that.

MRS. VENABLE: I'm paying to keep you in a private asylum.

CATHARINE: You're not my legal guardian.

MRS. VENABLE: Your mother's dependent on me. All of you are!—Financially. . . .

CATHARINE: I think the situation is—clear to me, now. . . .

MRS. VENABLE: Good! In that case. . . .

DOCTOR: I think a quiet atmosphere will get us the best results.

MRS. VENABLE: I don't know what you mean by a quiet atmosphere. She shouted, I didn't.

DOCTOR: Mrs. Venable, let's try to keep things on a quiet level, now. Your niece seems to be disturbed.

MRS. VENABLE: She has every reason to be. She took my son from me, and then she—

CATHARINE: Aunt Violet, you're not being fair.

MRS. VENABLE: Oh, aren't I?

CATHARINE (*to the others*): She's not being fair.

(*Then back to Mrs. Venable:*)

Aunt Violet, you know why Sebastian asked me to travel with him.

MRS. VENABLE: Yes, I *do* know why!

CATHARINE: You weren't able to travel. You'd had a— (*She stops short.*)

MRS. VENABLE: Go on! *What* had I had? Are you afraid to say it in front of the Doctor? She meant that I had a stroke.— I DID NOT HAVE A STROKE!—I had a slight aneurism. You know what that is, Doctor? A little vascular convulsion! Not a hemorrhage, just a little convulsion of a blood-vessel.

I had it when I discovered that she was trying to take my son away from me. Then I had it. It gave a little temporary—muscular—contraction.—To one side of my face. . . . (*She crosses back into main acting area.*) These people are not blood-relatives of mine, they're my dead husband's relations. I always detested these people, my dead husband's sister and—her two worthless children. But I did more than my duty to keep their heads above water. To please my son, whose weakness was being excessively softhearted, I went to the expense and humiliation, yes, public humiliation, of giving this girl a debut which was a fiasco. Nobody liked her when I brought her out. Oh, she had some kind of—notoriety! She had a sharp tongue that some people mistook for wit. A habit of laughing in the faces of decent people which would infuriate them, and also reflected adversely on me and Sebastian, too. But, he, Sebastian, was amused by this girl. While I was disgusted, sickened. And halfway through the season, she was dropped off the party lists, yes, dropped off the lists in spite of my position. Why? Because she'd lost her head over a young married man, made a scandalous scene at a Mardi Gras ball, in the middle of the ballroom. Then everybody dropped her like a hot—rock, but— (*She loses her breath.*) My son, Sebastian, still felt sorry for her and took her with him last summer instead of me. . . .

CATHARINE (*springing up with a cry*): I can't change truth, I'm not God! I'm not even sure that He could, I don't think God can change truth! How can I change the story of what happened to her son in Cabeza de Lobo?

MRS. VENABLE (*at the same time*): She was in love with my son!

CATHARINE (*overlapping*): Let me go back to Saint Mary's. Sister Felicity, let's go back to Saint—

MRS. VENABLE (*overlapping*): Oh, no! That's not where you'll go!

CATHARINE (*overlapping*): All right, *Lion's View* but don't ask me to—

MRS. VENABLE (*overlapping*): You *know* that you were!

CATHARINE (*overlapping*): That I was *what*, Aunt Violet?

MRS. VENABLE (*overlapping*): Don't call me "Aunt," you're the niece of my dead husband, not me!

MRS. HOLLY (*overlapping*): Catharine, Catharine, don't upset your— Doctor? Oh, Doctor!

(*But the Doctor is calmly observing the scene, with detachment. The jungle garden is loud with the sounds of its feathered and scaled inhabitants.*)

CATHARINE: I don't want to, I didn't want to come here! I know what she thinks, she thinks I murdered her son, she thinks that I was responsible for his death.

MRS. VENABLE: That's right. I told him when he told me that he was going with you in my place last summer that I'd never see him again and I never did. And only you know why!

CATHARINE: Oh, my God, I—

(*She rushes out toward garden, followed immediately by the Sister.*)

SISTER: Miss Catharine, Miss Catharine—
DOCTOR (*overlapping*): Mrs. Venable?
SISTER (*overlapping*): Miss Catharine?
DOCTOR (*overlapping*): Mrs. Venable?
MRS. VENABLE: What?
DOCTOR: I'd like to be left alone with Miss Catharine for a few minutes.
MRS. HOLLY: George, talk to her, George.

(*George crouches appealingly before the old lady's chair, peering close into her face, a hand on her knee.*)

GEORGE: Aunt Vi? Cathie can't go to Lion's View. Everyone in the Garden District would know you'd put your niece in a state asylum, Aunt Vi.
MRS. VENABLE: Foxhill!
GEORGE: What do you want, Aunt Vi?
MRS. VENABLE: Let go of my chair. Foxhill? Get me away from these people!
GEORGE: Aunt Vi, listen, think of the talk it—
MRS. VENABLE: I can't get up! Push me, push me away!
GEORGE (*rising but holding chair*): I'll push her, Miss Foxhill.
MRS. VENABLE: Let go of my chair or—
MISS FOXHILL: Mr. Holly, I—

GEORGE: I got to talk to her.

(*He pushes her chair downstage.*)

MRS. VENABLE: Foxhill!

MISS FOXHILL: Mr. Holly, she doesn't want you to push her.

GEORGE: I know what I'm doing, leave me alone with Aunt Vi!

MRS. VENABLE: Let go me or I'll *strike* you!

GEORGE: Oh, Aunt Vi!

MRS. VENABLE: Foxhill!

MRS. HOLLY: George—

GEORGE: Aunt Vi?

(*She strikes at him with her cane. He releases the chair and Miss Foxhill pushes her off. He trots after her a few steps, then he returns to Mrs. Holly, who is sobbing into a handkerchief. He sighs, and sits down beside her, taking her hand. The scene fades as light is brought up on Catharine and the Sister in the garden. The Doctor comes up to them. Mrs. Holly stretches her arms out to George, sobbing, and he crouches before her chair and rests his head in her lap. She strokes his head. During this: the Sister has stood beside Catharine, holding onto her arm.*)

CATHARINE: You don't have to hold onto me. I can't run away.

DOCTOR: Miss Catharine?

CATHARINE: What?

DOCTOR: Your aunt is a very sick woman. She had a stroke last spring?

CATHARINE: Yes, she did, but she'll never admit it. . . .

DOCTOR: You have to understand why.

CATHARINE: I do, I understand why. I didn't want to come here.

DOCTOR: Miss Catharine, do you hate her?

CATHARINE: I don't understand what hate is. How can you hate anybody and still be sane? You see, I still think I'm sane!

DOCTOR: You think she did have a stroke?

CATHARINE: She had a slight stroke in April. It just affected one side, the left side, of her face . . . but it was disfiguring, and after that, Sebastian couldn't use her.

DOCTOR: Use her? Did you say use her?

(*The sounds of the jungle garden are not loud but ominous.*)

CATHARINE: Yes, we all use each other and that's what we think of as love, and not being able to use each other is what's—*hate.* . . .

DOCTOR: Do you hate her, Miss Catharine?

CATHARINE: Didn't you ask me that, once? And didn't I say that I didn't understand hate. A ship struck an iceberg at sea—everyone sinking—

DOCTOR: Go on, Miss Catharine!

CATHARINE: But that's no reason for everyone drowning for hating everyone drowning! Is it, Doctor?

DOCTOR: Tell me: what was your feeling for your cousin Sebastian?

CATHARINE: He liked me and so I loved him.

DOCTOR: In what way did you love him?

CATHARINE: The only way he'd accept:—a sort of motherly way. I tried to save him, Doctor.

DOCTOR: From what? Save him from what?

CATHARINE: Completing!—a sort of!—*image!*—he had of himself as a sort of!—*sacrifice* to a!—*terrible* sort of a—

DOCTOR:—God?

CATHARINE: Yes, a—*cruel* one, Doctor!

DOCTOR: How did you feel about that?

CATHARINE: Doctor, my feelings are the sort of feelings that you have in a dream. . . .

DOCTOR: Your life doesn't seem real to you?

CATHARINE: Suddenly last winter I began to write my journal in the third person.

(*He grasps her elbow and leads her out upon forestage. At the same time Miss Foxhill wheels Mrs. Venable off, Mrs. Holly weeps into a handkerchief and George rises and shrugs and turns his back to the audience.*)

DOCTOR: Something happened last winter?

CATHARINE: At a Mardi Gras ball some—some boy that took me to it got too drunk to stand up! (*A short, mirthless note of laughter.*) I wanted to go home. My coat was in the cloakroom, they couldn't find the check for it in his pockets. I said, "Oh, hell, let it go!"—I started out for a taxi. Somebody took my arm and said, "I'll drive you home." He took off his coat as we left the hotel and put it over my shoulders, and then I looked at him and—I don't think I'd ever even seen him before then, really!—He took me home in his car but took me another place first. We stopped near the Duelling Oaks at the end of Esplanade Street. . . . Stopped!—I said, "What for?"—He didn't answer, just struck a match in the car to light a cigarette in the car and I looked at him in the car and I knew "what for"!—I think I got out of the car before he got out of the car, and we walked through the wet grass to the great misty oaks as if somebody was calling us for help there!

(Pause. The subdued, toneless bird-cries in the garden turn to a single bird-song.)

DOCTOR: After that?

CATHARINE: I lost him.—He took me home and said an awful thing to me. "We'd better forget it," he said, "my wife's expecting a child and—." —I just entered the house and sat there thinking a little and then I suddenly called a taxi and went right back to the Roosevelt Hotel ballroom. The ball was still going on. I thought I'd gone back to pick up my borrowed coat but that wasn't what I'd gone back for. I'd gone back to make a scene on the floor of the ballroom, yes, I didn't stop at the cloakroom to pick up Aunt Violet's old mink stole, no, I rushed right into the ballroom and spotted him on the floor and ran up to him and beat him as hard as I could in the face and chest with my fists till— Cousin Sebastian took me away.—After that, the next morning, I started writing my diary in the third person, singular, such as "She's still living this morning," meaning that *I* was. . . . —"WHAT'S NEXT FOR HER? GOD KNOWS!"—I couldn't go out any more.—However one morning my Cousin Sebastian came in my bedroom and said: "Get up!"—Well . . . if you're still alive after dying, well then, you're obedient, Doctor.—I got up. He took me downtown to a place for passport photos. Said: "Mother can't go abroad with me this summer. You're going to go

with me this summer instead of Mother."—If you don't believe me, read my journal of Paris!—"She woke up at daybreak this morning, had her coffee and dressed and took a
brief walk—"

DOCTOR: *Who* did?

CATHARINE: *She* did. *I* did—from the Hotel Plaza Athénée to
the Place de l'Étoile as if pursued by a pack of Siberian
wolves! (*She laughs her tired, helpless laugh.*)—Went right
through all stop signs—couldn't wait for green signals.—
"Where did she think she was going? Back to the Duelling
Oaks?"—Everything chilly and dim but his hot, ravenous
mouth! on—

DOCTOR: Miss Catharine, let me give you something.

(*The others go out, leaving Catharine and the Doctor on-
stage.*)

CATHARINE: Do I have to have the injection again, this time?
What am I going to be stuck with this time, Doctor? I
don't care. I've been stuck so often that if you connected
me with a garden hose I'd make a good sprinkler.

DOCTOR (*preparing needle*): Please take off your jacket.

(*She does. The Doctor gives her an injection.*)

CATHARINE: I didn't feel it.

DOCTOR: That's good. Now sit down.

(*She sits down.*)

CATHARINE: Shall I start counting backwards from a hundred?

DOCTOR: Do you like counting backwards?

CATHARINE: Love it! Just love it! One hundred! Ninety-nine!
Ninety-eight! Ninety-seven. Ninety-six. Ninety—five—. Oh!
—I already feel it! How funny!

DOCTOR: That's right. Close your eyes for a minute.

(*He moves his chair closer to hers. Half a minute passes.*)

Miss Catharine? I want you to give me something.

CATHARINE: Name it and it's yours, Doctor Sugar.

DOCTOR: Give me all your resistance.

CATHARINE: Resistance to what?

DOCTOR: The truth. Which you're going to tell me.

CATHARINE: The truth's the one thing I have never resisted!

DOCTOR: Sometimes people just think they don't resist it, but still do.

CATHARINE: They say it's at the bottom of a bottomless well, you know:

DOCTOR: Relax.

CATHARINE: Truth.

DOCTOR: Don't talk.

CATHARINE: Where was I, now? At ninety?

DOCTOR: You don't have to count backwards.

CATHARINE: At ninety something?

DOCTOR: You can open your eyes.

CATHARINE: Oh, I do feel funny!

(*Silence, pause.*)

You know what I think you're doing? I think you're trying to hypnotize me. Aren't you? You're looking so straight at me and doing something to me with your eyes and your— eyes. . . . Is that what you're doing to me?

DOCTOR: Is that what you *feel* I'm doing?

CATHARINE: Yes! I feel so peculiar. And it's not just the drug.

DOCTOR: Give me all your resistance. See. I'm holding my hand out. I want you to put yours in mine and give me all your resistance. Pass all of your resistance out of your hand to mine.

CATHARINE: Here's my hand. But there's no resistance in it.

DOCTOR: You are totally passive.

CATHARINE: Yes, I am.

DOCTOR: You will do what I ask.

CATHARINE: Yes, I will try.

DOCTOR: You will tell the true story.

CATHARINE: Yes, I will.

DOCTOR: The absolutely true story. No lies, nothing not spoken. Everything told, exactly.

CATHARINE: Everything. Exactly. Because I'll have to. Can I—can I stand up?

DOCTOR: Yes, but be careful. You might feel a little bit dizzy.

(*She struggles to rise, then falls back.*)

CATHARINE: I can't get up! Tell me to. Then I think I could do it.

DOCTOR: Stand up.

(*She rises unsteadily.*)

CATHARINE: How funny! Now I can! Oh, I do feel dizzy! Help me, I'm—

(*He rushes to support her.*)

—about to fall over. . . .

(*He holds her. She looks out vaguely toward the brilliant, steaming garden. Looks back at him. Suddenly sways toward him, against him.*)

DOCTOR: You see, you lost your balance.

CATHARINE: No, I didn't. I did what I wanted to do without you telling me to.

(*She holds him tight against her.*)

Let me! Let! Let! Let me! Let me, let me, oh, let me. . . .

(*She crushes her mouth to his violently. He tries to disengage himself. She presses her lips to his fiercely, clutching his body against her. Her brother George enters.*)

Please hold me! I've been so lonely. It's lonelier than death, if I've gone mad, it's lonelier than death!

GEORGE (*shocked, disgusted*): *Cathie!*—you've got a hell of a nerve.

(*She falls back, panting, covers her face, runs a few paces and grabs the back of a chair. Mrs. Holly enters.*)

MRS. HOLLY: What's the matter, George? Is Catharine ill?

GEORGE: No.

DOCTOR: Miss Catharine had an injection that made her a little unsteady.

MRS. HOLLY: What did he say about Catharine?

(*Catharine has gone out into the dazzling jungle of the garden.*)

SISTER (*returning*): She's gone into the garden.

DOCTOR: That's all right, she'll come back when I call her.

SISTER: It may be all right for you. You're not responsible for her.

(*Mrs. Venable has re-entered.*)

MRS. VENABLE: Call her now!
DOCTOR: Miss Catharine! Come back.

(*To the Sister:*)

Bring her back, please, Sister!

(*Catharine enters quietly, a little unsteady.*)

Now, Miss Catharine, you're going to tell the true story.
CATHARINE: Where do I start the story?
DOCTOR: Wherever you think it started.
CATHARINE: I think it started the day he was born in this house.
MRS. VENABLE: Ha! You see!
GEORGE: Cathie.
DOCTOR: Let's start later than that. (*Pause.*) Shall we begin with last summer?
CATHARINE: Oh. Last summer.
DOCTOR: Yes. Last summer.

(*There is a long pause. The raucous sounds in the garden fade into a bird-song which is clear and sweet. Mrs. Holly coughs. Mrs. Venable stirs impatiently. George crosses downstage to catch Catharine's eye as he lights a cigarette.*)

CATHARINE: Could I—?
MRS. VENABLE: Keep that boy away from her!
GEORGE: She wants to smoke, Aunt Vi.
CATHARINE: Something helps in the—hands. . . .
SISTER: Unh unh!
DOCTOR: It's all right, Sister. (*He lights her cigarette.*) About last summer: how did it begin?
CATHARINE: It began with his kindness and the six days at sea that took me so far away from the—Duelling Oaks that I forgot them, nearly. He was affectionate with me, so sweet and attentive to me, that some people took us for a honeymoon couple until they noticed that we had—separate

staterooms, and—then in Paris, he took me to Patou and Schiaparelli's—*this* is from Schiaparelli's! (*Like a child, she indicates her suit.*) —bought me so many new clothes that I gave away my old ones to make room for my new ones in my new luggage to—travel. . . . I turned into a peacock! Of course, so was *he* one, too. . . .

GEORGE: *Ha Ha!*

MRS. VENABLE: Shh!

CATHARINE: But then I made the mistake of responding too much to his kindness, of taking hold of his hand before he'd take hold of mine, of holding onto his arm and leaning on his shoulder, of appreciating his kindness more than he wanted me to, and, suddenly, last summer, he began to be restless, and—oh!

DOCTOR: Go on.

CATHARINE: The Blue Jay notebook!

DOCTOR: Did you say notebook?

MRS. VENABLE: I know what she means by that, she's talking about the school composition book with a Blue Jay trademark that Sebastian used for making notes and revisions on his "Poem of Summer." It went with him everywhere that he went, in his jacket pocket, even his dinner jacket. I have the one that he had with him last summer. *Foxhill! The Blue Jay notebook!*

(*Miss Foxhill rushes in with a gasp.*)

It came with his personal effects shipped back from Cabeza de Lobo.

DOCTOR: I don't quite get the connection between new clothes and so forth and the Blue Jay notebook.

MRS. VENABLE: I HAVE IT!—Doctor, tell her I've found it.

(*Miss Foxhill hears this as she comes back out of house: gasps with relief, retires.*)

DOCTOR: With all these interruptions it's going to be awfully hard to—

MRS. VENABLE: This is important. I don't know why she mentioned the Blue Jay notebook but I want you to see it. Here it is, here! (*She holds up a notebook and leafs swiftly*

through the pages.) Title? "Poem of Summer," and the date
of the summer—1935. After that: *what? Blank pages, blank
pages,* nothing but *nothing!*—last summer. . . .

DOCTOR: What's that got to do with—?

MRS. VENABLE: His destruction? I'll tell you. A poet's vocation is something that rests on something as thin and
fine as the web of a spider, Doctor. That's all that holds
him *over*!—out of destruction. . . . Few, very few are
able to do it alone! Great help is needed! I *did* give it! She
didn't.

CATHARINE: She's right about that. I failed him. I wasn't able
to keep the web from—breaking. . . . I saw it breaking
but couldn't save or—repair it!

MRS. VENABLE: There now, the truth's coming out. We had
an agreement between us, a sort of contract or covenant
between us which he broke last summer when he broke
away from me and took her with him, not me! When he
was frightened and I knew when and what of, because his
hands would shake and his eyes looked in, not out, I'd
reach across a table and touch his hands and say not a
word, just look, and touch his hands with my hand until his
hands stopped shaking and his eyes looked out, not in, and
in the morning, the poem would be continued. *Continued
until it was finished!*

(*The following ten speeches are said very rapidly, overlapping.*)

CATHARINE: I—couldn't!

MRS. VENABLE: *Naturally* not! He was *mine*! I *knew* how to
help him, I *could*! You didn't, you couldn't!

DOCTOR: These interruptions—

MRS. VENABLE: I would say "You *will*" and he *would*, I—!

CATHARINE: Yes, you see, I failed him! And so, last summer,
we went to Cabeza de Lobo, we flew down there from
where he gave up writing his poem last summer. . . .

MRS. VENABLE: Because he'd broken our—

CATHARINE: Yes! Yes, something had broken, that string of
pearls that old mothers hold their sons by like a—sort of
a—sort of—*umbilical* cord, *long—after* . . .

MRS. VENABLE: She means that I held him back from—

DOCTOR: *Please!*

MRS. VENABLE: *Destruction!*

CATHARINE: All I know is that suddenly, last summer, he wasn't young any more, and we went to Cabeza de Lobo, and he suddenly switched from the evenings to the beach. . . .

DOCTOR: From evenings? To beach?

CATHARINE: I mean from the evenings to the afternoons and from the fa—fash—

(*Silence: Mrs. Holly draws a long, long painful breath. George stirs impatiently.*)

DOCTOR: Fashionable! Is that the word you—?

CATHARINE: Yes. Suddenly, last summer Cousin Sebastian changed to the afternoons and the beach.

DOCTOR: What beach?

CATHARINE: In Cabeza de Lobo there is a beach that's named for Sebastian's name saint, it's known as La Playa San Sebastian, and that's where we started spending all afternoon, every day.

DOCTOR: What kind of beach was it?

CATHARINE: It was a big city beach near the harbor.

DOCTOR: It was a big public beach?

CATHARINE: Yes, public.

MRS. VENABLE: It's little statements like that that give her away.

(*The Doctor rises and crosses to Mrs. Venable without breaking his concentration on Catharine.*)

After all I've told you about his fastidiousness, can you accept such a statement?

DOCTOR: You mustn't interrupt her.

MRS. VENABLE (*overlapping him*): That Sebastian would go every day to some dirty free public beach near a harbor? A man that had to go out a mile in a boat to find water fit to swim in?

DOCTOR: Mrs. Venable, no matter what she says you have to let her say it without any more interruptions or this interview will be useless.

MRS. VENABLE: I won't speak again. I'll keep still, if it kills me.

CATHARINE: I don't want to go on. . . .

DOCTOR: Go on with the story. Every afternoon last summer
your Cousin Sebastian and you went out to this free public
beach?

CATHARINE: No, it wasn't the free one, the free one was
right next to it, there was a fence between the free beach
and the one that we went to that charged a small charge of
admission.

DOCTOR: Yes, and what did you do there?

(*He still stands beside Mrs. Venable and the light gradually
changes as the girl gets deeper into her story: the light concentrates on Catharine, the other figures sink into shadow.*)

Did anything happen there that disturbed you about it?

CATHARINE: Yes!

DOCTOR: What?

CATHARINE: He bought me a swim-suit I didn't want to
wear. I laughed. I said, "I can't wear that, it's a scandal to
the jay-birds!"

DOCTOR: What did you mean by that? That the suit was im-
modest?

CATHARINE: My God, yes! It was a one-piece suit made of
white lisle, the water made it transparent! (*She laughs sadly
at the memory of it.*) —I didn't want to swim in it, but he'd
grab my hand and drag me into the water, all the way in,
and I'd come out looking naked!

DOCTOR: Why did he do that? Did you understand why?

CATHARINE:—Yes! To attract!—Attention.

DOCTOR: He wanted you to attract attention, did he, because
he felt you were moody? Lonely? He wanted to shock you
out of your depression last summer?

CATHARINE: Don't you understand? I was PROCURING
for him!

(*Mrs. Venable's gasp is like the sound that a great hooked fish
might make.*)

She used to do it, *too.*

(*Mrs. Venable cries out.*)

Not consciously! She didn't *know* that she was procuring for
him in the smart, the fashionable places they used to go to

before last summer! Sebastian was shy with people. She wasn't. Neither was I. We both did the same thing for him, made contacts for him, but she did it in nice places and in decent ways and I had to do it the way that I just told you!—Sebastian was lonely, Doctor, and the empty Blue Jay notebook got bigger and bigger, so big it was big and empty as that big empty blue sea and sky. . . . I knew what I was doing. I came out in the French Quarter years before I came out in the Garden District. . . .

MRS. HOLLY: Oh, Cathie! Sister . . .

DOCTOR: Hush!

CATHARINE: And before long, when the weather got warmer and the beach so crowded, he didn't need me any more for that purpose. The ones on the free beach began to climb over the fence or swim around it, bands of homeless young people that lived on the free beach like scavenger dogs, hungry children. . . . So now he let me wear a decent dark suit. I'd go to a faraway empty end of the beach, write postcards and letters and keep up my—third-person journal till it was—five o'clock and time to meet him outside the bathhouses, on the street. . . . He would come out, *followed*.

DOCTOR: Who would follow him out?

CATHARINE: The homeless, hungry young people that had climbed over the fence from the free beach that they lived on. He'd pass out tips among them as if they'd all—shined his shoes or called taxis for him. . . . Each day the crowd was bigger, noisier, greedier!—Sebastian began to be frightened.—At last we stopped going out there. . . .

DOCTOR: And then? After that? After you quit going out to the public beach?

CATHARINE: Then one day, a few days after we stopped going out to the beach—it was one of those white blazing days in Cabeza de Lobo, not a blazing hot *blue* one but a blazing hot *white* one.

DOCTOR: Yes?

CATHARINE: We had a late lunch at one of those open-air restaurants on the sea there.—Sebastian was white as the weather. He had on a spotless white silk Shantung suit and a white silk tie and a white panama and white shoes, white

—white lizard skin—pumps! He—(*She throws back her head in a startled laugh at the recollection*)—kept touching his face and his throat here and there with a white silk handkerchief and popping little white pills in his mouth, and I knew he was having a bad time with his heart and was frightened about it and that was the reason we hadn't gone out to the beach. . . .

(*During the monologue the lights have changed, the surrounding area has dimmed out and a hot white spot is focused on Catharine.*)

"I think we ought to go north," he kept saying, "I think we've done Cabeza de Lobo, I think we've done it, don't you?" *I* thought we'd done it!—but I had learned it was better not to seem to have an opinion because if I did, well, Sebastian, well, you know Sebastian, he always preferred to do what no one else wanted to do, and I always tried to give the impression that I was agreeing reluctantly to his wishes . . . it was a—game. . . .

SISTER: She's dropped her cigarette.

DOCTOR: I've got it, Sister.

(*There are whispers, various movements in the penumbra. The Doctor fills a glass for her from the cocktail shaker.*)

CATHARINE: Where was I? Oh, yes, that five o'clock lunch at one of those fish-places along the harbor of Cabeza de Lobo, it was between the city and the sea, and there were naked children along the beach which was fenced off with barbed wire from the restaurant and we had our table less than a yard from the barbed wire fence that held the beggars at bay. . . . There were naked children along the beach, a band of frightfully thin and dark naked children that looked like a flock of plucked birds, and they would come darting up to the barbed wire fence as if blown there by the wind, the hot white wind from the sea, all crying out, *"Pan, pan, pan!"*

DOCTOR (*quietly*): What's *pan*?

CATHARINE: The word for bread, and they made gobbling noises with their little black mouths, stuffing their little back fists to their mouths and making those gobbling noises, with frightful grins!—Of course we were sorry that we had come to this place but it was too late to go. . . .

DOCTOR (*quietly*): Why was it "too late to go"?

CATHARINE: I told you Cousin Sebastian wasn't well. He was popping those little white pills in his mouth. I think he had popped in so many of them that they had made him feel weak. . . . His, his!—eyes looked—dazed, but he said: "Don't look at those little monsters. Beggars are a social disease in this country. If you look at them, you get sick of the country, it spoils the whole country for you. . . ."

DOCTOR: Go on.

CATHARINE: I'm going on. I have to wait now and then till it gets clearer. Under the drug it has to be a vision, or nothing comes. . . .

DOCTOR: All right?

CATHARINE: Always when I was with him I did what he told me. I didn't look at the band of naked children, not even when the waiters drove them away from the barbed wire fence with sticks!—Rushing out through a wicket gate like an assault party in war!—and beating them screaming away from the barbed wire fence with the sticks. . . . Then! (*Pause.*)

DOCTOR: Go on, Miss Catherine, what comes next in the vision?

CATHARINE: The, the the!—band of children began to—serenade us. . . .

DOCTOR: Do what?

CATHARINE: Play for us! On instruments! Make music!—if you could call it music. . . .

DOCTOR: Oh?

CATHARINE: Their, their—instruments were—instruments of percussion!—Do you know what I mean?

DOCTOR (*making a note*): Yes. Instruments of percussion such as—*drums?*

CATHARINE: I stole glances at them when Cousin Sebastian wasn't looking, and as well as I could make out in the white blaze of the sand-beach, the instruments were tin cans strung together.

DOCTOR (*slowly, writing*): *Tin—cans—strung—together.*

CATHARINE: *And, and, and, and—and!—bits of metal,* other bits of metal that had been flattened out, made into—

DOCTOR: What?

CATHARINE: *Cymbals!* You know? *Cymbals?*

DOCTOR: Yes. Brass plates hit together.

CATHARINE: That's right, Doctor.—Tin cans flattened out and clashed together!—Cymbals. . . .

DOCTOR: Yes. I understand. What's after that, in the vision?

CATHARINE (*rapidly, panting a little*): And others had paper bags, bags made out of—coarse paper!—with something on a string inside the bags which they pulled up and down, back and forth, to make a sort of a—

DOCTOR: Sort of a—?

CATHARINE: Noise like—

DOCTOR: Noise like?

CATHARINE (*rising stiffly from chair*): Ooompa! Oompa! Ooooooompa!

DOCTOR: Ahhh . . . a sound like a *tuba?*

CATHARINE: That's right!—they made a sound like a tuba. . . .

DOCTOR: Oompa, oompa, oompa, like a tuba.

(*He is making a note of the description.*)

CATHARINE: Oompa, oompa, oompa, like a—

(*Short pause.*)

DOCTOR:—Tuba. . . .

CATHARINE: All during lunch they stayed at a—a fairly *close—distance. . . .*

DOCTOR: Go on with the vision, Miss Catharine.

CATHARINE (*striding about the table*): *Oh, I'm going on, nothing could stop it now!!*

DOCTOR: Your Cousin Sebastian was *entertained* by this—concert?

CATHARINE: I think he was *terrified* of it!

DOCTOR: Why was he terrified of it?

CATHARINE: I think he recognized some of the musicians, some of the boys, between childhood and—older. . . .

DOCTOR: What did he do? Did he do anything about it, Miss Catharine?—Did he complain to the manager about it?

CATHARINE: *What* manager? *God?* Oh, *no!*—The manager of the fish-place on the beach? Haha!—No!—You don't understand my cousin!

DOCTOR: What do you mean?

CATHARINE: *He!—accepted!—all!*—as—how!—things!—are! —And thought nobody had any right to complain or interfere in any way whatsoever, and even though he knew that what was awful was awful, that what was wrong was wrong, and my Cousin Sebastian was certainly never sure that anything was wrong!—He thought it unfitting to ever take any action about anything whatsoever!—except to go on doing as something in him directed. . . .

DOCTOR: What did something in him direct him to do?—I mean on this occasion in Cabeza de Lobo.

CATHARINE: After the salad, before they brought the coffee, he suddenly pushed himself away from the table, and said, "They've got to stop that! Waiter, make them stop that. I'm not a well man, I have a heart condition, it's making me sick!"—This was the first time that Cousin Sebastian had ever attempted to correct a human situation!—I think perhaps that *that* was his—fatal error. . . . It was then that the waiters, all eight or ten of them, charged out of the barbed wire wicket gate and beat the little musicians away with clubs and skillets and anything hard that they could snatch from the kitchen!—Cousin Sebastian left the table. He stalked out of the restaurant after throwing a handful of paper money on the table and he fled from the place. I followed. It was all white outside. White hot, a blazing white hot, hot blazing white, at five o'clock in the afternoon in the city of—Cabeza de Lobo. It looked as if—

DOCTOR: It looked as if?

CATHARINE: As if a huge white bone had caught on fire in the sky and blazed so bright it was white and turned the sky and everything under the sky white with it!

DOCTOR:—White . . .

CATHARINE: Yes—white . . .

DOCTOR: You followed your Cousin Sebastian out of the restaurant onto the hot white street?

CATHARINE: Running up and down hill. . . .

DOCTOR: You ran up and down hill?

CATHARINE: No, no! *Didn't!*—move either *way!*—at first, we were—

(*During this recitation there are various sound effects. The percussive sounds described are very softly employed.*)

I rarely made any suggestion but *this* time I *did*. . . .

DOCTOR: What did you suggest?

CATHARINE: Cousin Sebastian seemed to be paralyzed near the entrance of the café, so I said, "Let's go." I remember that it was a very wide and steep white street, and I said, "Cousin Sebastian, down that way is the waterfront and we are more likely to find a taxi near there. . . . Or why don't we go back in?—and have them *call* us a taxi! Oh, let's do! Let's do *that*, that's better!" And he said, "*Mad*, are you *mad*? Go back in that filthy place? Never! That gang of kids shouted vile things about me to the waiters!" "Oh," I said, "then let's go down toward the docks, down there at the bottom of the hill, let's not try to climb the hill in this dreadful heat." And Cousin Sebastian shouted, "Please shut up, let me handle this situation, will you? I want to handle this thing." And he started up the steep street with a hand stuck in his jacket where I knew he was having a pain in his chest from his palpitations. . . . But he walked faster and faster, in panic, but the faster he walked the louder and closer it got!

DOCTOR: What got louder?

CATHARINE: The music.

DOCTOR: The music again.

CATHARINE: The oompa-oompa of the—following band.— They'd somehow gotten through the barbed wire and out on the street, and they were following, following!— up the blazing white street. The band of naked children pursued us up the steep white street in the sun that was like a great white bone of a giant beast that had caught on fire in the sky!—Sebastian started to run and they all screamed at once and seemed to fly in the air, they out-ran him so quickly. I screamed. I heard Sebastian scream, he screamed just once before this flock of black plucked little birds that pursued him and overtook him halfway up the white hill.

DOCTOR: And you, Miss Catharine, what did *you* do, then?

CATHARINE: Ran!

DOCTOR: Ran where?

CATHARINE: Down! Oh, I ran down, the easier direction to run was down, down, down, down!—The hot, white, blazing street, screaming out "Help" all the way, till—

DOCTOR: What?

CATHARINE:—Waiters, police, and others—ran out of buildings and rushed back up the hill with me. When we got back to where my Cousin Sebastian had disappeared in the flock of featherless little black sparrows, he—he was lying naked as they had been naked against a white wall, and this you won't believe, nobody *has* believed it, nobody *could* believe it, nobody, nobody on earth could possibly believe it, and I don't *blame* them!—They had *devoured* parts of him.

(*Mrs. Venable cries out softly.*)

Torn or cut parts of him away with their hands or knives or maybe those jagged tin cans they made music with, they had torn bits of him away and stuffed them into those gobbling fierce little empty black mouths of theirs. There wasn't a sound any more, there was nothing to see but Sebastian, what was left of him, that looked like a big white-paper-wrapped bunch of red roses had been *torn, thrown, crushed!*—against that blazing white wall. . . .

(*Mrs. Venable springs with amazing power from her wheelchair, stumbles erratically but swiftly toward the girl and tries to strike her with her cane. The Doctor snatches it from her and catches her as she is about to fall. She gasps hoarsely several times as he leads her toward the exit.*)

MRS. VENABLE (*offstage*): *Lion's View! State asylum, cut this hideous story out of her brain!*

(*Mrs. Holly sobs and crosses to George, who turns away from her, saying:*)

GEORGE: Mom, I'll quit school, I'll get a job, I'll—

MRS. HOLLY: Hush son! Doctor, can't you say something?

(*Pause. The Doctor comes downstage. Catharine wanders out into the garden followed by the Sister.*)

DOCTOR (*after a while, reflectively, into space*): I think we ought at least to consider the possibility that the girl's story could be true. . . .

The End

SWEET BIRD OF YOUTH

Relentless caper for all those who step
The legend of their youth into the noon

HART CRANE

To Cheryl Crawford

FOREWORD*

When I came to my writing desk on a recent morning, I found lying on my desk top an unmailed letter that I had written. I began reading it and found this sentence: "We are all civilized people, which means that we are all savages at heart but observing a few amenities of civilized behavior." Then I went on to say: "I am afraid that I observe fewer of these amenities than you do. Reason? My back is to the wall and has been to the wall for so long that the pressure of my back on the wall has started to crumble the plaster that covers the bricks and mortar."

Isn't it odd that I said the wall was giving way, not my back? I think so. Pursuing this course of free association, I suddenly remembered a dinner date I once had with a distinguished colleague. During the course of this dinner, rather close to the end of it, he broke a long, mournful silence by lifting to me his sympathetic gaze and saying to me, sweetly, "Tennessee, don't you feel that you are blocked as a writer?"

I didn't stop to think of an answer; it came immediately off my tongue without any pause for planning. I said, "Oh, yes, I've always been blocked as a writer but my desire to write has been so strong that it has always broken down the block and gone past it."

Nothing untrue comes off the tongue that quickly. It is planned speeches that contain lies or dissimulations, not what you blurt out so spontaneously in one instant.

It was literally true. At the age of fourteen I discovered writing as an escape from a world of reality in which I felt acutely uncomfortable. It immediately became my place of retreat, my cave, my refuge. From what? From being called a sissy by the neighborhood kids, and Miss Nancy by my father, because I would rather read books in my grandfather's large and classical library than play marbles and baseball and other normal kid games, a result of a severe childhood illness and of excessive attachment to the female members of my family, who had coaxed me back into life.

*Written prior to the Broadway opening of *Sweet Bird of Youth* and published in the *New York Times* on Sunday, March 8, 1959.

I think no more than a week after I started writing I ran into the first block. It's hard to describe it in a way that will be understandable to anyone who is not a neurotic. I will try. All my life I have been haunted by the obsession that to desire a thing or to love a thing intensely is to place yourself in a vulnerable position, to be a possible, if not a probable, loser of what you most want. Let's leave it like that. That block has always been there and always will be, and my chance of getting, or achieving, anything that I long for will always be gravely reduced by the interminable existence of that block.

I described it once in a poem called "The Marvelous Children."

"He, the demon, set up barricades of gold and purple tinfoil, labeled Fear (and other august titles), which they, the children, would leap lightly over, always tossing backwards their wild laughter."

But having, always, to contend with this adversary of fear, which was sometimes terror, gave me a certain tendency toward an atmosphere of hysteria and violence in my writing, an atmosphere that has existed in it since the beginning.

In my first published work, for which I received the big sum of thirty-five dollars, a story published in the July or August issue of Weird Tales in the year 1928, I drew upon a paragraph in the ancient histories of Herodotus to create a story of how the Egyptian queen, Nitocris, invited all of her enemies to a lavish banquet in a subterranean hall on the shores of the Nile, and how, at the height of this banquet, she excused herself from the table and opened sluice gates admitting the waters of the Nile into the locked banquet hall, drowning her unloved guests like so many rats.

I was sixteen when I wrote this story, but already a confirmed writer, having entered upon this vocation at the age of fourteen, and, if you're well acquainted with my writings since then, I don't have to tell you that it set the keynote for most of the work that has followed.

My first four plays, two of them performed in St. Louis, were correspondingly violent or more so. My first play professionally produced and aimed at Broadway was *Battle of Angels* and it was about as violent as you can get on the stage.

During the nineteen years since then I have only produced five plays that are *not* violent: *The Glass Menagerie, You Touched Me, Summer and Smoke, The Rose Tattoo* and, recently in Florida, a serious comedy called *Period of Adjustment*, which is still being worked on.

What surprises me is the degree to which both critics and audience have accepted this barrage of violence. I think I was surprised, most of all, by the acceptance and praise of *Suddenly Last Summer*. When it was done off Broadway, I thought I would be critically tarred and feathered and ridden on a fence rail out of the New York theatre, with no future haven except in translation for theatres abroad, who might mistakenly construe my work as a castigation of American morals, not understanding that I write about violence in American life only because I am not so well acquainted with the society of other countries.

Last year I thought it might help me as a writer to undertake psychoanalysis and so I did. The analyst, being acquainted with my work and recognizing the psychic wounds expressed in it, asked me, soon after we started, "Why are you so full of hate, anger and envy?"

Hate was the word I contested. After much discussion and argument, we decided that "hate" was just a provisional term and that we would only use it till we had discovered the more precise term. But unfortunately I got restless and started hopping back and forth between the analyst's couch and some Caribbean beaches. I think before we called it quits I had persuaded the doctor that hate was not the right word, that there was some other thing, some other word for it, which we had not yet uncovered, and we left it like that.

Anger, oh yes! And envy, yes! But not hate. I think that hate is a thing, a feeling, that can only exist where there is no understanding. Significantly, good physicians never have it. They never hate their patients, no matter how hateful their patients may seem to be, with their relentless, maniacal concentration on their own tortured egos.

Since I am a member of the human race, when I attack its behavior toward fellow members I am obviously including myself in the attack, unless I regard myself as not human but superior to humanity. I don't. In fact, I can't expose a human weakness on the stage unless I know it through having it my-self. I have exposed a good many human weaknesses and bru-talities and consequently I have them.

I don't even think that I am more conscious of mine than any of you are of yours. Guilt is universal. I mean a strong sense of guilt. If there exists any area in which a man can rise above his moral condition, imposed upon him at birth and long before birth, by the nature of his breed, then I think it is only a willingness to know it, to face its existence in him, and I think that at least below the conscious level, we all face it. Hence guilty feelings, and hence defiant aggressions, and hence the deep dark of despair that haunts our dreams, our creative work, and makes us distrust each other.

Enough of these philosophical abstractions, for now. To get back to writing for the theatre, if there is any truth in the Aristotelian idea that violence is purged by its poetic repre-sentation on a stage, then it may be that my cycle of violent plays have had a moral justification after all. I know that I have felt it. I have always felt a release from the sense of meaninglessness and death when a work of tragic intention has seemed to me to have achieved that intention, even if only approximately, nearly.

I would say that there is something much bigger in life and death than we have become aware of (or adequately recorded) in our living and dying. And, further, to compound this shameless romanticism, I would say that our serious the-atre is a search for that something that is not yet successful but is still going on.

Synopsis of Scenes

ACT ONE

SCENE ONE: A bedroom in the Royal Palms Hotel, somewhere on the Gulf Coast.

SCENE TWO: The same. Later.

ACT TWO

SCENE ONE: The terrace of Boss Finley's house in St.
Cloud.

SCENE TWO: The cocktail lounge and Palm Garden of the
Royal Palms Hotel.

ACT THREE
The bedroom again.

TIME: Modern, an Easter Sunday, from late morning
till late night.

SETTING
AND
"SPECIAL
EFFECTS":

The stage is backed by a cyclorama that should
give a poetic unity of mood to the several specific settings. There are nonrealistic projections
on this "cyc," the most important and constant being a grove of royal palm trees. There
is nearly always a wind among these very tall
palm trees, sometimes loud, sometimes just a
whisper, and sometimes it blends into a the-
matic music which will be identified, when it
occurs, as "The Lament."

During the daytime scenes the cyclorama
projection is a poetic abstraction of semitropi-
cal sea and sky in fair spring weather. At night
it is the palm garden with its branches among
the stars.

The specific settings should be treated as
freely and sparingly as the sets for *Cat on a
Hot Tin Roof* or *Summer and Smoke*. They'll
be described as you come to them in the script.

ACT ONE

SCENE ONE

A bedroom of an old-fashioned but still fashionable hotel some-where along the Gulf Coast in a town called St. Cloud. I think of it as resembling one of those "Grand Hotels" around Sorrento or Monte Carlo, set in a palm garden. The style is vaguely "Moorish." The principal set-piece is a great double bed which should be raked toward the audience. In a sort of Moorish cor-ner backed by shuttered windows, is a wicker tabouret and two wicker stools, over which is suspended a Moorish lamp on a brass chain. The windows are floor length and they open out upon a gallery. There is also a practical door frame, opening onto a cor-ridor: the walls are only suggested.

On the great bed are two figures, a sleeping woman, and a young man awake, sitting up, in the trousers of white silk paja-mas. The sleeping woman's face is partly covered by an eyeless black satin domino to protect her from morning glare. She breathes and tosses on the bed as if in the grip of a nightmare. The young man is lighting his first cigarette of the day.

Outside the windows there is heard the soft, urgent cries of birds, the sound of their wings. Then a colored waiter, Fly, ap-pears at door on the corridor, bearing coffee-service for two. He knocks. Chance rises, pauses a moment at a mirror in the fourth wall to run a comb through his slightly thinning blond hair be-fore he crosses to open the door.

CHANCE: Aw, good, put it in there.

FLY: Yes, suh.

CHANCE: Give me the Bromo first. You better mix it for me, I'm—

FLY: Hands kind of shaky this mawnin'?

CHANCE (*shuddering after the Bromo*): Open the shutters a lit-tle. Hey, I said a little, not much, not that much!

(As the shutters are opened we see him clearly for the first time: he's in his late twenties and his face looks slightly older than that; you might describe it as a "ravaged young face" and yet it is still exceptionally good-looking. His body shows no decline, yet it's the kind of a body that white silk pajamas are,

157

or ought to be, made for. A church bell tolls, and from another church, nearer, a choir starts singing The Alleluia Chorus. It draws him to the window, and as he crosses, he says:)

I didn't know it was—Sunday.

FLY: Yes, suh, it's *Easter* Sunday.

CHANCE (*leans out a moment, hands gripping the shutters*): Uh-huh. . . .

FLY: That's the Episcopal Church they're singin' in. The bell's from the Catholic Church.

CHANCE: I'll put your tip on the check.

FLY: Thank you, Mr. Wayne.

CHANCE (*as Fly starts for the door*): Hey. How did you know my name?

FLY: I waited tables in the Grand Ballroom when you used to come to the dances on Saturday nights, with that real pretty girl you used to dance so good with, Mr. Boss Finley's daughter?

CHANCE: I'm increasing your tip to five dollars in return for a favor which is not to remember that you have recognized me or anything else at all. Your name is Fly—Shoo, Fly. Close the door with no noise.

VOICE OUTSIDE: Just a minute.

CHANCE: Who's that?

VOICE OUTSIDE: George Scudder.

(*Slight pause. Fly exits.*)

CHANCE: How did you know I was here?

(*George Scudder enters: a coolly nice-looking, business-like young man who might be the head of the Junior Chamber of Commerce but is actually a young doctor, about thirty-six or -seven.*)

SCUDDER: The assistant manager that checked you in here last night phoned me this morning that you'd come back to St. Cloud.

CHANCE: So you came right over to welcome me home?

SCUDDER: Your lady friend sounds like she's coming out of ether.

CHANCE: The Princess had a rough night.

SCUDDER: You've latched onto a Princess? (*mockingly*) Gee.

CHANCE: She's traveling incognito.

SCUDDER: Golly, I should think she would, if she's checking in hotels with *you*.

CHANCE: George, you're the only man I know that still says "gee," "golly," and "gosh."

SCUDDER: Well, I'm not the sophisticated type, Chance.

CHANCE: That's for sure. Want some coffee?

SCUDDER: Nope. Just came for a talk. A quick one.

CHANCE: Okay. Start talking, man.

SCUDDER: Why've you come back to St. Cloud?

CHANCE: I've still got a mother and a girl in St. Cloud. How's Heavenly, George?

SCUDDER: We'll get around to that later. (*He glances at his watch.*) I've got to be in surgery at the hospital in twenty-five minutes.

CHANCE: You operate now, do you?

SCUDDER (*opening doctor's bag*): I'm chief-of-staff there now.

CHANCE: Man, you've got it made.

SCUDDER: Why have you come back?

CHANCE: I heard that my mother was sick.

SCUDDER: But you said, "How's Heavenly," not "How's my mother," Chance. (*Chance sips coffee.*) Your mother died a couple of weeks ago. . . .

(*Chance slowly turns his back on the man and crosses to the window. Shadows of birds sweep the blind. He lowers it a little before he turns back to Scudder.*)

CHANCE: Why wasn't I notified?

SCUDDER: You were. A wire was sent you three days before she died at the last address she had for you which was General Delivery, Los Angeles. We got no answer from that and another wire was sent you after she died, the same day of her death and we got no response from that either. Here's the Church Record. The church took up a collection for her hospital and funeral expenses. She was buried nicely in your family plot and the church has also given her a very nice headstone. I'm giving you these details in spite of the fact that I know and everyone here in town knows that you had no interest in her, less than people who knew her only slightly, such as myself.

CHANCE: How did she go?

SCUDDER: She had a long illness, Chance. You know about that.

CHANCE: Yes. She was sick when I left here the last time.

SCUDDER: She was sick at heart as well as sick in her body at that time, Chance. But people were very good to her, especially people who knew her in church, and the Reverend Walker was with her at the end.

(*Chance sits down on the bed. He puts out his unfinished cigarette and immediately lights another. His voice becomes thin and strained.*)

CHANCE: She never had any luck.

SCUDDER: Luck? Well, that's all over with now. If you want to know anything more about that, you can get in touch with Reverend Walker about it, although I'm afraid he won't be likely to show much cordiality to you.

CHANCE: She's gone. Why talk about it?

SCUDDER: I hope you haven't forgotten the letter I wrote you soon after you last left town.

CHANCE: No. I got no letter.

SCUDDER: I wrote you in care of an address your mother gave me about a very important private matter.

CHANCE: I've been moving a lot.

SCUDDER: I didn't even mention names in the letter.

CHANCE: What was the letter about?

SCUDDER: Sit over here so I don't have to talk loud about this. Come over here. I can't talk loud about this. (*Scudder indicates the chair by the tabouret. Chance crosses and rests a foot on the chair.*) In this letter I just told you that a certain girl we know had to go through an awful experience, a tragic ordeal, because of past contact with you. I told you that I was only giving you this information so that you would know better than to come back to St. Cloud, but you didn't know better.

CHANCE: I told you I got no letter. Don't tell me about a letter, I didn't get any letter.

SCUDDER: I'm telling you what I told you in this letter.

CHANCE: All right. Tell me what you told me, don't—don't talk to me like a club, a chamber of something. What did you tell me? What ordeal? What girl? Heavenly? Heavenly? George?

SCUDDER: I see it's not going to be possible to talk about this quietly and so I . . .

CHANCE (*rising to block Scudder's way*): Heavenly? What ordeal?

SCUDDER: We will not mention names. Chance, I rushed over here this morning as soon as I heard you were back in St. Cloud, before the girl's father and brother could hear that you were back in St. Cloud, to stop you from trying to get in touch with the girl and to get out of here. That is absolutely all I have to say to you in this room at this moment. . . . But I hope I have said it in a way to impress you with the vital urgency of it, so you will leave. . . .

CHANCE: Jesus! If something's happened to Heavenly, will you please tell me—what?

SCUDDER: I said no names. We are not alone in this room. Now when I go downstairs now, I'll speak to Dan Hatcher, assistant manager here . . . he told me you'd checked in here . . . and tell him you want to check out, so you'd better get Sleeping Beauty and yourself ready to travel, and I suggest that you keep on traveling till you've crossed the State line. . . .

CHANCE: You're not going to leave this room till you've explained to me what you've been hinting at about my girl in St. Cloud.

SCUDDER: There's a lot more to this which we feel ought not to be talked about to anyone, least of all to you, since you have turned into a criminal degenerate, the only right term for you, but, Chance, I think I ought to remind you that once long ago the father of this girl wrote out a prescription for you, a sort of medical prescription, which is castration. You'd better think about that, that would deprive you of all you've got to get by on. (*He moves toward the steps.*)

CHANCE: I'm used to that threat. I'm not going to leave St. Cloud without my girl.

SCUDDER (*on the steps*): You don't have a girl in St. Cloud. Heavenly and I are going to be married next month. (*He leaves abruptly.*)

(*Chance, shaken by what he has heard, turns and picks up phone, and kneels on the floor.*)

CHANCE: Hello? St. Cloud 525. Hello, Aunt Nonnie? This is Chance, yes Chance. I'm staying at the Royal Palms and I . . . what's the matter, has something happened to Heavenly? Why can't you talk now? George Scudder was here and . . . Aunt Nonnie? Aunt Nonnie?

(*The other end hangs up. The sleeping woman suddenly cries out in her sleep. Chance drops the phone on its cradle and runs to the bed.*)

CHANCE (*bending over her as she struggles out of a nightmare*): Princess! Princess! Hey, *Princess Kos*! (*He removes her eyemask; she sits up gasping and staring wild-eyed about her.*)
PRINCESS: Who are you? Help!
CHANCE (*on the bed*): Hush now. . . .
PRINCESS: Oh . . . I . . . had . . . a *terrible* dream.
CHANCE: It's all right. Chance's with you.
PRINCESS: Who?
CHANCE: Me.
PRINCESS: I don't know who you are!
CHANCE: You'll remember soon, Princess.
PRINCESS: I don't know, I don't know. . . .
CHANCE: It'll come back to you soon. What are you reachin' for, honey?
PRINCESS: Oxygen! Mask!
CHANCE: Why? Do you feel short-winded?
PRINCESS: Yes! I have . . . air . . . shortage!
CHANCE (*looking for the correct piece of luggage*): Which bag is your oxygen in? I can't remember which bag we packed it in. Aw, yeah, the crocodile case, the one with the combination lock. Wasn't the first number zero . . . (*He comes back to the bed and reaches for a bag under its far side.*)
PRINCESS (*as if with her dying breath*): Zero, zero. Two zeros to the right and then back around to . . .
CHANCE: Zero, three zeros, two of them to the right and the last one to the left. . . .
PRINCESS: Hurry! I can't breathe, I'm dying!
CHANCE: I'm getting it, Princess.

PRINCESS: HURRY!

CHANCE: Here we are, I've got it. . . .

(*He has extracted from case a small oxygen cylinder and mask. He fits the inhalator over her nose and mouth. She falls back on the pillow. He places the other pillow under her head. After a moment, her panicky breath subsiding, she growls at him.*)

PRINCESS: Why in hell did you lock it up in that case?

CHANCE (*standing at the head of the bed*): You said to put all your valuables in that case.

PRINCESS: I meant my jewelry, and you know it, you, bastard!

CHANCE: Princess, I didn't think you'd have these attacks any more. I thought that having me with you to protect you would stop these attacks of panic, I . . .

PRINCESS: Give me a pill.

CHANCE: Which pill?

PRINCESS: A pink one, a pinkie, and vodka . . .

(*He puts the tank on the floor, and goes over to the trunk. The phone rings. Chance gives the Princess a pill, picks up the vodka bottle and goes to the phone. He sits down with the bottle between his knees.*)

CHANCE (*pouring a drink, phone held between shoulder and ear*): Hello? Oh, hello, Mr. Hatcher——Oh? But Mr. Hatcher, when we checked in here last night we weren't told that, and Miss Alexandra Del Lago . . .

PRINCESS (*shouting*): *Don't use my name!*

CHANCE: . . . is suffering from exhaustion, she's not at all well, Mr. Hatcher, and certainly not in any condition to travel. . . . I'm sure you don't want to take the responsibility for what might happen to Miss Del Lago . . .

PRINCESS (*shouting again*): *Don't use my name!*

CHANCE: . . . if she attempted to leave here today in the condition she's in . . . do you?

PRINCESS: *Hang up!* (*He does. He comes over with his drink and the bottle to the Princess.*) I want to forget everything, I want to forget who I am. . . .

CHANCE (*handing her the drink*): He said that . . .

PRINCESS (*drinking*): Please shut up, I'm *forgetting*!

CHANCE (*taking the glass from her*): Okay, go on forget. There's nothing better than that, I wish I could do it. . . .

PRINCESS: I can, I will. I'm forgetting . . . I'm forgetting. . . .

(*She lies down. Chance moves to the foot of the bed, where he seems to be struck with an idea. He puts the bottle down on the floor, runs to the chaise and picks up a tape recorder. Taking it back to the bed, he places the recorder on the floor. As he plugs it in, he coughs.*)

What's going on?

CHANCE: Looking for my toothbrush.

PRINCESS (*throwing the oxygen mask on the bed*): Will you please take that away.

CHANCE: Sure you've had enough of it?

PRINCESS (*laughs breathlessly*): Yes, for God's sake, take it away. I must look hideous in it.

CHANCE (*taking the mask*): No, no, you just look exotic, like a Princess from Mars or a big magnified insect.

PRINCESS: Thank you, check the cylinder please.

CHANCE: For what?

PRINCESS: Check the air left in it; there's a gauge on the cylinder that gives the pressure. . . .

CHANCE: You're still breathing like a quarter horse that's been run a full mile. Are you sure you don't want a doctor?

PRINCESS: No, for God's sake . . . no!

CHANCE: Why are you so scared of doctors?

PRINCESS (*hoarsely, quickly*): I don't need them. What happened is nothing at all. It happens frequently to me. Something disturbs me . . . adrenalin's pumped in my blood and I get short-winded, that's all, that's all there is to it . . . I woke up, I didn't know where I was or who I was with, I got panicky . . . adrenalin was released and I got short-winded. . . .

CHANCE: Are you okay now, Princess? Huh? (*He kneels on the bed, and helps straighten up the pillows.*)

PRINCESS: Not quite yet, but I will be. I will be.

CHANCE: You're full of complexes, plump lady.

PRINCESS: What did you call me?

CHANCE: Plump lady.

PRINCESS: Why do you call me that? Have I let go of my figure?

CHANCE: You put on a good deal of weight after that disappointment you had last month.

PRINCESS (*hitting him with a small pillow*): What disappointment? I don't remember any.

CHANCE: Can you control your memory like that?

PRINCESS: Yes. I've had to learn to. What is this place, a hospital? And you, what are you, a male nurse?

CHANCE: I take care of you but I'm not your nurse.

PRINCESS: But you're employed by me, aren't you? For some purpose or other?

CHANCE: I'm not on salary with you.

PRINCESS: What are you on? Just expenses?

CHANCE: Yep. You're footing the bills.

PRINCESS: I see. Yes, I see.

CHANCE: Why're you rubbing your eyes?

PRINCESS: My vision's so cloudy! Don't I wear glasses, don't I have any glasses?

CHANCE: You had a little accident with your glasses.

PRINCESS: What was that?

CHANCE: You fell on your face with them on.

PRINCESS: Were they completely demolished?

CHANCE: One lens cracked.

PRINCESS: Well, please give me the remnants. I don't mind waking up in an intimate situation with someone, but I like to see who it's with, so I can make whatever adjustment seems called for. . . .

CHANCE (*rises and goes to the trunk, where he lights cigarette*): You know what I look like.

PRINCESS: No, I don't.

CHANCE: You did.

PRINCESS: I tell you I don't remember, it's all gone away!

CHANCE: I don't believe in amnesia.

PRINCESS: Neither do I. But you have to believe a thing that happens to you.

CHANCE: Where did I put your glasses?

PRINCESS: Don't ask me. You say I fell on them. If I was in that condition I wouldn't be likely to know where anything is I had with me. What happened last night?

(*He has picked them up but not given them to her.*)

CHANCE: You knocked yourself out.

PRINCESS: Did we sleep here together?

CHANCE: Yes, but I didn't molest you.

PRINCESS: Should I thank you for that, or accuse you of cheating? (*She laughs sadly.*)

CHANCE: I like you, you're a nice monster.

PRINCESS: Your voice sounds young. Are you young?

CHANCE: My age is twenty-nine years.

PRINCESS: That's young for anyone but an Arab. Are you very good-looking?

CHANCE: I used to be the best-looking boy in this town.

PRINCESS: How large is the town?

CHANCE: Fair-sized.

PRINCESS: Well, I like a good mystery novel, I read them to put me to sleep and if they don't put me to sleep, they're good; but this one's a little too good for comfort. I wish you would find me my glasses. . . .

(*He reaches over headboard to hand the glasses to her. She puts them on and looks him over. Then she motions him to come nearer and touches his bare chest with her finger tips.*)

Well, I may have done better, but God knows I've done worse.

CHANCE: What are you doing now, Princess?

PRINCESS: The tactile approach.

CHANCE: You do that like you were feeling a piece of goods to see if it was genuine silk or phony. . . .

PRINCESS: It feels like silk. Genuine! This much I do remember, that I like bodies to be hairless, silky-smooth gold!

CHANCE: Do I meet these requirements?

PRINCESS: You seem to meet those requirements. But I still have a feeling that something is not satisfied in the relation between us.

CHANCE (*moving away from her*): You've had your experiences, I've had mine. You can't expect everything to be settled at once. . . . Two different experiences of two different people. Naturally there's some things that have to be settled between them before there's any absolute agreement.

PRINCESS (*throwing the glasses on the bed*): Take that splintered lens out before it gets in my eye.

CHANCE (*obeying this instruction by knocking the glasses sharply on the bed table*): You like to give orders, don't you?

PRINCESS: It's something I seem to be used to.

CHANCE: How would you like to *take* them? To be a slave?

PRINCESS: What time is it?

CHANCE: My watch is in hock somewhere. Why don't you look at yours?

PRINCESS: Where's mine?

(*He reaches lazily over to the table, and hands it to her.*)

CHANCE: It's stopped, at five past seven.

PRINCESS: Surely it's later than that, or earlier, that's no hour when I'm . . .

CHANCE: Platinum, is it?

PRINCESS: No, it's only white gold. I never travel with anything very expensive.

CHANCE: Why? Do you get robbed much? Huh? Do you get "rolled" often?

PRINCESS: Get what?

CHANCE: "Rolled." Isn't that expression in your vocabulary?

PRINCESS: Give me the phone.

CHANCE: For what?

PRINCESS: I said give me the phone.

CHANCE: I know. And I said for what?

PRINCESS: I want to enquire where I am and who is with me?

CHANCE: Take it easy.

PRINCESS: Will you give me the phone?

CHANCE: Relax. You're getting short-winded again. . . . (*He takes hold of her shoulders.*)

PRINCESS: Please let go of me.

CHANCE: Don't you feel secure with me? Lean back. Lean back against me.

PRINCESS: Lean back?

CHANCE: This way, this way. There . . .

(*He pulls her into his arms: She rests in them, panting a little like a trapped rabbit.*)

PRINCESS: It gives you an awful trapped feeling this, this memory block. . . . I feel as if someone I loved had died lately, and I don't want to remember who it could be.

CHANCE: Do you remember your name?

PRINCESS: Yes, I do.

CHANCE: What's your name?

PRINCESS: I think there's some reason why I prefer not to tell you.

CHANCE: Well, I happen to know it. You registered under a phony name in Palm Beach but I discovered your real one. And you admitted it to me.

PRINCESS: I'm the Princess Kosmonopolis.

CHANCE: Yes, and you used to be known as . . .

PRINCESS (*sits up sharply*): No, stop . . . will you let me do it? Quietly, in my own way? The last place I remember . . .

CHANCE: What's the last place you remember?

PRINCESS: A town with the crazy name of Tallahassee.

CHANCE: Yeah. We drove through there. That's where I reminded you that today would be Sunday and we ought to lay in a supply of liquor to get us through it without us being dehydrated too severely, and so we stopped there but it was a college town and we had some trouble locating a package store, open. . . .

PRINCESS: But we did, did we?

CHANCE (*getting up for the bottle and pouring her a drink*): Oh, sure, we bought three bottles of Vodka. You curled up in the back seat with one of those bottles and when I looked back you were blotto. I intended to stay on the old Spanish Trail straight through to Texas, where you had some oil wells to look at. I didn't stop here . . . I was stopped.

PRINCESS: What by, a cop? Or . . .

CHANCE: No. No cop, but I was arrested by something.

PRINCESS: My car. Where is my car?

CHANCE (*handling her the drink*): In the hotel parking lot, Princess.

PRINCESS: Oh, then, this is a hotel?

CHANCE: It's the elegant old Royal Palms Hotel in the town of St. Cloud.

(*Gulls fly past window, shadows sweeping the blind: they cry out with soft urgency.*)

PRINCESS: Those pigeons out there sound hoarse. They sound like gulls to me. Of course, they could be pigeons with laryngitis.

(*Chance glances at her with his flickering smile and laughs softly.*)

Will you help me please? I'm about to get up.

CHANCE: What do you want? I'll get it.

PRINCESS: I want to go to the window.

CHANCE: What for?

PRINCESS: To look out of it.

CHANCE: I can describe the view to you.

PRINCESS: I'm not sure I'd trust your description. WELL?

CHANCE: Okay, *oopsa-daisy*.

PRINCESS: My God! I said help me up, not . . . toss me onto the carpet! (*Sways dizzily a moment, clutching bed. Then draws a breath and crosses to the window.*)

(*Pauses as she gazes out, squinting into noon's brilliance.*)

CHANCE: Well, what do you see? Give me your description of the view, Princess?

PRINCESS (*faces the audience*): I see a palm garden.

CHANCE: And a four-lane highway just past it.

PRINCESS (*squinting and shielding her eyes*): Yes, I see that and a strip of beach with some bathers and then, an infinite stretch of nothing but water and . . . (*She cries out softly and turns away from the window.*)

CHANCE: What? . . .

PRINCESS: Oh God, I remember the thing I wanted not to. The goddam end of my life! (*She draws a deep shuddering breath.*)

CHANCE (*running to her aid*): What's the matter?

PRINCESS: Help me back to bed. Oh God, no wonder I didn't want to remember, I was no fool!

(*He assists her to the bed. There is an unmistakable sympathy in his manner, however shallow.*)

CHANCE: Oxygen?

PRINCESS (*draws another deep shuddering breath*): No! Where's the stuff? Did you leave it in the car?

CHANCE: Oh, the stuff? Under the mattress. (*Moving to the other side of the bed, he pulls out a small pouch.*)

PRINCESS: A stupid place to put it.

CHANCE (*sits at the foot of the bed*): What's wrong with under the mattress?

PRINCESS (*sits up on the edge of the bed*): There's such a thing as chambermaids in the world, they make up beds, they come across lumps in a mattress.

CHANCE: This isn't pot. What is it?

PRINCESS: Wouldn't that be pretty? A year in jail in one of those model prisons for distinguished addicts. What is it? Don't you know what it is, you beautiful, stupid young man? It's hashish, Moroccan, the finest.

CHANCE: Oh, hash! How'd you get it through customs when you came back for your come-back?

PRINCESS: I didn't get it through customs. The ship's doctor gave me injections while this stuff was winging over the ocean to a shifty young gentleman who thought he could blackmail me for it. (*She puts on her slippers with a vigorous gesture.*)

CHANCE: Couldn't he?

PRINCESS: Of course not. I called his bluff.

CHANCE: You took injections coming over?

PRINCESS: With my neuritis? I had to. Come on give it to me.

CHANCE: Don't you want it packed right?

PRINCESS: You talk too much. You ask too many questions. I need something quick. (*She rises.*)

CHANCE: I'm a new hand at this.

PRINCESS: I'm sure, or you wouldn't discuss it in a hotel room. . . .

(*She turns to the audience, and intermittently changes the focus of her attention.*)

For years they all told me that it was ridiculous of me to feel that I couldn't go back to the screen or the stage as a middle-aged woman. They told me I was an artist, not just a star whose career depended on youth. But I knew in my heart that the legend of Alexandra del Lago couldn't be separated from an appearance of youth. . . .

There's no more valuable knowledge than knowing the right time to go. I knew it. I went at the right time to go. RETIRED! Where to? To what? To that dead planet the moon. . . .

There's nowhere else to retire to when you retire from an art because, believe it or not, I really was once an artist. So I retired to the moon, but the atmosphere of the moon doesn't have any oxygen in it. I began to feel breathless, in that withered, withering country, of time coming after time not meant to come after, and so I discovered . . . Haven't you fixed it yet?

(*Chance rises and goes to her with a cigarette he has been preparing.*)

Discovered this!

And other practices like it, to put to sleep the tiger that raged in my nerves. . . . Why the unsatisfied tiger? In the nerves jungle? Why is anything, anywhere, unsatisfied, and raging? . . .

Ask somebody's good doctor. But don't believe his answer because it isn't . . . the answer . . . if I had just been old but you see, I wasn't old. . . .

I just wasn't young, not young, young. I just wasn't young anymore. . . .

CHANCE: Nobody's young anymore. . . .

PRINCESS: But you see, I couldn't get old with that tiger still in me raging.

CHANCE: Nobody can get old. . . .

PRINCESS: Stars in retirement sometimes give acting lessons. Or take up painting, paint flowers on pots, or landscapes. I could have painted the landscape of the endless, withering country in which I wandered like a lost nomad. If I could paint deserts and nomads, if I could paint . . . hahaha. . . .

CHANCE: SH-Sh-sh-

PRINCESS: Sorry!

CHANCE: Smoke.

PRINCESS: Yes, smoke! And then the young lovers. . . .

CHANCE: Me?

PRINCESS: You? Yes, finally you. But you come after the come-back. Ha . . . Ha . . . The glorious come-back, when I turned fool and came back. . . . The screen's a very clear mirror. There's a thing called a close-up. The camera advances and you stand still and your head, your face, is caught in the frame of the picture with a light blazing on it and all your terrible history screams while you smile. . . .

CHANCE: How do you know? Maybe it wasn't a failure, maybe you were just scared, just chicken, Princess . . . ha-ha-ha. . . .

PRINCESS: Not a failure . . . after that close-up they gasped. . . . People gasped. . . . I heard them whisper, their shocked whispers. Is that her? Is that her? Her? . . . I made the mistake of wearing a very elaborate gown to the *première*, a gown with a train that had to be gathered up as I rose from my seat and began the interminable retreat from the city of flames, up, up, up the unbearably long theatre aisle, gasping for breath and still clutching up the regal white train of my gown, all the way up the forever . . . length of the aisle, and behind me some small unknown man grabbing at me, saying, stay, stay! At last the top of the aisle, I turned and struck him, then let the train fall, forgot it, and tried to run down the marble stairs, tripped of course, fell and, rolled, rolled, like a sailor's drunk whore to the bottom . . . hands, merciful hands without faces, assisted me to get up. After that? Flight, just flight, not interrupted until I woke up this morning. . . . Oh God it's gone out. . . .

CHANCE: Let me fix you another. Huh? Shall I fix you another?

PRINCESS: Let me finish yours. You can't retire with the outcrying heart of an artist still crying out, in your body, in your nerves, in your what? Heart? Oh, no that's gone, that's . . .

CHANCE (*He goes to her, takes the cigarette out of her hand and gives her a fresh one.*) Here, I've fixed you another one . . . Princess, I've fixed you another. . . . (*He sits on the floor, leaning against the foot of the bed.*)

PRINCESS: Well, sooner or later, at some point in your life, the thing that you lived for is lost or abandoned, and then . . . you die, or find something else. This is my something else. . . . (*She approaches the bed.*) And ordinarily I take the most fantastic precautions against . . . detection. . . . (*She sits on the bed, then lies down on her back, her head over the foot, near his.*) I cannot imagine what possessed me to let you know. Knowing so little about you as I seem to know.

CHANCE: I must've inspired a good deal of confidence in you.

PRINCESS: If that's the case, I've gone crazy. Now tell me something. What is that body of water, that sea, out past the palm garden and four-lane highway? I ask you because I remember now that we turned west from the sea when we went onto that highway called the Old Spanish Trail.

CHANCE: We've come back to the sea.

PRINCESS: What sea?

CHANCE: The Gulf.

PRINCESS: The Gulf?

CHANCE: The Gulf of misunderstanding between me and you. . . .

PRINCESS: We don't understand each other? And lie here smoking this stuff?

CHANCE: Princess, don't forget that this stuff is yours, that you provided me with it.

PRINCESS: What are you trying to prove? (*Church bells toll.*) Sundays go on a long time.

CHANCE: You don't deny it was yours.

PRINCESS: What's mine?

CHANCE: You brought it into the country, you smuggled it through customs into the U.S.A. and you had a fair supply of it at that hotel in Palm Beach and were asked to check out before you were ready to do so, because its aroma drifted into the corridor one breezy night.

PRINCESS: What are you trying to prove?

CHANCE: You don't deny that you introduced me to it?

PRINCESS: Boy, I doubt very much that I have any vice that I'd need to introduce to you. . . .

CHANCE: Don't call me "boy."

PRINCESS: Why not?

CHANCE: It sounds condescending. And all my vices were caught from other people.

PRINCESS: What are you trying to prove? My memory's come back now. Excessively clearly. It was this mutual practice that brought us together. When you came in my cabana to give me one of those papaya cream rubs, you sniffed, you grinned and said you'd like a stick too.

CHANCE: That's right. I knew the smell of it.

PRINCESS: What are you trying to prove?

CHANCE: You asked me four or five times what I'm trying to prove, the answer is nothing. I'm just making sure that your memory's cleared up now. You do remember me coming in your cabana to give you those papaya cream rubs?

PRINCESS: Of course I do, Carl!

CHANCE: My name is not Carl. It's Chance.

PRINCESS: You called yourself Carl.

CHANCE: I always carry an extra name in my pocket.

PRINCESS: You're not a criminal, are you?

CHANCE: No ma'am, not me. You're the one that's committed a federal offense.

(*She stares at him a moment, and then goes to the door leading to the hall, looks out and listens.*)

What did you do that for?

PRINCESS (*closing the door*): To see if someone was planted outside the door.

CHANCE: You still don't trust me?

PRINCESS: Someone that gives me a false name?

CHANCE: You registered under a phony one in Palm Beach.

PRINCESS: Yes, to avoid getting any reports or condolences on the disaster I ran from. (*She crosses to the window. There is a pause followed by "The Lament."*) And so we've not arrived at any agreement?

CHANCE: No ma'am, not a complete one.

(*She turns her back to the window and gazes at him from there.*)

PRINCESS: What's the gimmick? The hitch?

CHANCE: The usual one.

PRINCESS: What's that?

CHANCE: Doesn't somebody always hold out for something?

PRINCESS: Are you holding out for something?

CHANCE: Uh-huh. . . .

PRINCESS: What?

CHANCE: You said that you had a large block of stock, more than half ownership in a sort of a second-rate Hollywood Studio, and could put me under contract. I doubted your word about that. You're not like any phony I've met before, but phonies come in all types and sizes. So I held out, even after we locked your cabana door for the papaya cream rubs. . . . You wired for some contract papers we signed. It was notarized and witnessed by three strangers found in a bar.

PRINCESS: Then why did you hold out, still?

CHANCE: I didn't have much faith in it. You know, you can buy those things for six bits in novelty stores. I've been conned and tricked too often to put much faith in anything that could still be phony.

PRINCESS: You're wise. However, I have the impression that there's been a certain amount of intimacy between us.

CHANCE: A certain amount. No more. I wanted to hold your interest.

PRINCESS: Well, you miscalculated. My interest always increases with satisfaction.

CHANCE: Then you're unusual in that respect, too.

PRINCESS: In all respects I'm not common.

CHANCE: But I guess the contract we signed is full of loopholes?

PRINCESS: Truthfully, yes, it is. I can get out of it if I wanted to. And so can the studio. Do you have any talent?

CHANCE: For what?

PRINCESS: Acting, baby, ACTING!

CHANCE: I'm not as positive of it as I once was. I've had more chances than I could count on my fingers, and made the grade almost, but not quite, every time. Something always blocks me. . . .

PRINCESS: What? What? Do you *know*? (*He rises. The lamentation is heard very faintly.*) Fear?

CHANCE: No not fear, but terror . . . otherwise would I be your goddam caretaker, hauling you across the country? Picking you up when you fall? Well would I? Except for that block, by anything less than a star?

PRINCESS: CARL!

CHANCE: Chance. . . . Chance Wayne. You're stoned.

PRINCESS: Chance, come back to your youth. Put off this false, ugly hardness and . . .

CHANCE: And be took in by every con-merchant I meet?

PRINCESS: I'm not a phony, believe me.

CHANCE: Well, then, what is it you want? Come on say it, Princess.

PRINCESS: Chance, come here. (*He smiles but doesn't move.*) Come here and let's comfort each other a little. (*He crouches by the bed; she encircles him with her bare arms.*)

CHANCE: Princess! Do you know something? All this conversation has been recorded on tape?

PRINCESS: What are you talking about?

CHANCE: Listen. I'll play it back to you. (*He uncovers the tape recorder; approaches her with the earpiece.*)

PRINCESS: How did you get that thing?

CHANCE: You bought it for me in Palm Beach. I said that I wanted it to improve my diction. . . .

(*He presses the "play" button on the recorder. The following in the left column can either be on a public address system, or can be cut.*)

(PLAYBACK)

PRINCESS: What is it? Don't you know what it is? You stupid, beautiful young man. It's hashish, Moroccan, the finest.

CHANCE: Oh, hash? How'd you get it through customs when you came back for your "come-back"?

PRINCESS: I didn't get it through customs. The ship's doctor. . . .

PRINCESS: What a smart cookie you are.

CHANCE: How does it feel to be over a great big barrel?

(*He snaps off the recorder and picks up the reels.*)

PRINCESS: This is blackmail is it? Where's my mink stole?

CHANCE: Not stolen.

(*He tosses it to her contemptuously from a chair.*)

PRINCESS: Where is my jewel case?

CHANCE (*picks it up off the floor and throws it on the bed*): Here.

PRINCESS (*opens it up and starts to put on some jewelry*): Every piece is insured and described in detail. Lloyd's in London.

CHANCE: *Who's* a smart cookie, Princess? You want your purse now so you can count your money?

PRINCESS: I don't carry currency with me, just travelers' checks.

CHANCE: I noted that fact already. But I got a fountain pen you can sign them with.

PRINCESS: Ho, Ho!

CHANCE: "Ho, ho!" What an insincere laugh, if that's how you fake a laugh, no wonder you didn't make good in your come-back picture. . . .

PRINCESS: Are you serious about this attempt to blackmail me?

CHANCE: You'd better believe it. Your trade's turned dirt on you, Princess. You understand that language?

PRINCESS: The language of the gutter is understood any-where that anyone ever fell in it.

CHANCE: Aw, then you *do* understand.

PRINCESS: And if I shouldn't comply with this order of yours?

CHANCE: You still got a name, you're still a personage, Princess. You wouldn't want "Confidential" or "Whisper" or "Hush-Hush" or the narcotics department of the F.B.I. to get hold of one of these tape-records, would you? And I'm going to make lots of copies. Huh? Princess?

PRINCESS: You are trembling and sweating . . . you see this part doesn't suit you, you just don't play it well, Chance. . . . (*Chance puts the reels in a suitcase.*) I hate to think of what kind of desperation has made you try to in-timidate me, ME? ALEXANDRA DEL LAGO? with that ridiculous threat. Why it's so silly, it's touching, downright endearing, it makes me feel close to you, Chance.

You were well born, weren't you? Born of good South-ern stock, in a genteel tradition, with just one disadvantage, a laurel wreath on your forehead, given too early, without enough effort to earn it . . . where's your scrapbook,

Chance? (*He crosses to the bed, takes a travelers' checkbook out of her purse, and extends it to her.*) Where's your book full of little theatre notices and stills that show you in the background of . . .

CHANCE: Here! Here! Start signing . . . or . . .

PRINCESS (*pointing to the bathroom*): Or WHAT? Go take a shower under cold water. I don't like hot sweaty bodies in a tropical climate. Oh, you, I do want and will accept, still . . . under certain conditions which I will make very clear to you.

CHANCE: Here. (*Throws the checkbook toward the bed.*)

PRINCESS: Put this away. And your leaky fountain pen. . . . When monster meets monster, one monster has to give way, AND IT WILL NEVER BE ME. I'm an older hand at it . . . with much more natural aptitude at it than you have. . . . Now then, you put the cart a little in front of the horse. Signed checks are payment, delivery comes first. Certainly I can afford it, I could deduct you, as my caretaker, Chance, remember that I was a star before big taxes . . . and had a husband who was a great merchant prince. He taught me to deal with money. . . . Now, Chance, please pay close attention while I tell you the very special conditions under which I will keep you in my employment . . . after this miscalculation. . . .

Forget the legend that I was and the ruin of that legend.

Whether or not I do have a disease of the heart that places an early terminal date on my life, no mention of that, no reference to it ever. No mention of death, never, never a word on that odious subject. I've been accused of having a death wish but I think it's life that I wish for, terribly, shamelessly, on any terms whatsoever.

When I say now, the answer must not be later. I have only one way to forget these things I don't want to remember and that's through the act of love-making. That's the only dependable distraction so when I say now, because I need that distraction, it has to be now, not later.

(*She crosses to the bed: He rises from the opposite side of the bed and goes to the window: She gazes at his back as he looks out the window. Pause: Lamentation.*)

(*Princess, finally, softly.*)

Chance, I need that distraction. It's time for me to find out if you're able to give it to me. You mustn't hang onto your silly little idea that you can increase your value by turning away and looking out a window when somebody wants you. . . . I want you. . . . I say now and I mean now, then and not until then will I call downstairs and tell the hotel cashier that I'm sending a young man down with some travelers' checks to cash for me. . . .

CHANCE (*turning slowly from the window*): Aren't you ashamed, a little?

PRINCESS: Of course I am. Aren't you?

CHANCE: More than a little. . . .

PRINCESS: Close the shutters, draw the curtain across them.

(*He obeys these commands.*)

Now get a little sweet music on the radio and come here to me and make me almost believe that we're a pair of young lovers without any shame.

SCENE TWO

As the curtain rises, the Princess has a fountain pen in hand and is signing checks. Chance, now wearing dark slacks, socks and shoes of the fashionable loafer type, is putting on his shirt and speaks as the curtain opens.

CHANCE: Keep on writing, has the pen gone dry?

PRINCESS: I started at the back of the book where the big ones are.

CHANCE: Yes, but you stopped too soon.

PRINCESS: All right, one more from the front of the book as a token of some satisfaction. I said some, not complete.

CHANCE (*picking up the phone*): Operator— Give me the cashier please.

PRINCESS: What are you doing that for?

CHANCE: You have to tell the cashier you're sending me down with some travelers' checks to cash for you.

PRINCESS: Have to? Did you say have to?

CHANCE: Cashier? Just a moment. The Princess Kosmonopolis. (*He thrusts the phone at her.*)

PRINCESS (*into the phone*): Who is this? But I don't want the
cashier. My watch has stopped and I want to know the
right time . . . five after three? Thank you . . . he says it's
five after three. (*She hangs up and smiles at Chance.*) I'm
not ready to be left alone in this room. Now let's not fight
any more over little points like that, let's save our strength
for the big ones. I'll have the checks cashed for you as soon
as I've put on my face. I just don't want to be left alone in
this place till I've put on the face that I face the world with,
baby. Maybe after we get to know each other, we won't
fight over little points any more, the struggle will stop,
maybe we won't even fight over big points, baby. Will you
open the shutters a little bit please? (*He doesn't seem to hear
her. The lament is heard.*) I won't be able to see my face in
the mirror. . . . Open the shutters, I won't be able to see
my face in the mirror.

CHANCE: Do you want to?

PRINCESS (*pointing*): Unfortunately I have to! Open the
shutters!

(*He does. He remains by the open shutters, looking out as the
lament in the air continues.*)

CHANCE:—I was born in this town. I was born in St. Cloud.

PRINCESS: That's a good way to begin to tell your life story.
Tell me your life story. I'm interested in it, I really would
like to know it. Let's make it your audition, a sort of screen
test for you. I can watch you in the mirror while I put my
face on. And tell me your life story, and if you hold my attention with your life story, I'll know you have talent, I'll
wire my studio on the Coast that I'm still alive and I'm on
my way to the Coast with a young man named Chance
Wayne that I think is cut out to be a great young star.

CHANCE (*moving out on the forestage*): Here is the town I was
born in, and lived in till ten years ago, in St. Cloud. I was
a twelve-pound baby, normal and healthy, but with some
kind of quantity "X" in my blood, a wish or a need to be
different. . . . The kids that I grew up with are mostly still
here and what they call "settled down," gone into business,

married and bringing up children, the little crowd I was in
with, that I used to be the star of, was the snobset, the ones
with the big names and money. I didn't have either . . .
(*The Princess utters a soft laugh in her dimmed-out area.*)
What I had was . . . (*The Princess half turns, brush poised in
a faint, dusty beam of light.*)

PRINCESS: BEAUTY! Say it! Say it! What you had was beauty!
I had it! I say it, with pride, no matter how sad, being
gone, now.

CHANCE: Yes, well . . . the others . . . (*The Princess resumes
brushing hair and the sudden cold beam of light on her goes
out again.*) . . . are all now members of the young social
set here. The girls are young matrons, bridge-players, and
the boys belong to the Junior Chamber of Commerce
and some of them, clubs in New Orleans such as Rex and
Comus and ride on the Mardi Gras floats. Wonderful? No
boring . . . I wanted, expected, intended to get, something better . . . Yes, and I did, I got it. I did things that
fat-headed gang never dreamed of. Hell when they were
still freshmen at Tulane or LSU or Ole Miss, I sang in the
chorus of the biggest show in New York, in "Oklahoma,"
and had pictures in LIFE in a cowboy outfit, tossin' a ten-
gallon hat in the air! YIP . . . EEEEEE! Ha-ha. . . . And
at the same time pursued my other vocation. . . .

  Maybe the only one I was truly meant for, love-making
. . . slept in the social register of New York! Millionaires'
widows and wives and debutante daughters of such famous
names as Vanderbrook and Masters and Halloway and
Connaught, names mentioned daily in columns, whose
credit cards are their faces. . . . And . . .

PRINCESS: What did they pay you?

CHANCE: I gave people more than I took. Middle-aged
people I gave back a feeling of youth. Lonely girls? Understanding, appreciation! An absolutely convincing show of
affection. Sad people, lost people? Something light and up-
lifting! Eccentrics? Tolerance, even odd things they long
for. . . .

  But always just at the point when I might get something
back that would solve my own need, which was great, to
rise to their level, the memory of my girl would pull me

back home to her . . . and when I came home for those
visits, man oh man how that town buzzed with excitement.
I'm telling you, it would blaze with it, and then that thing
in Korea came along. I was about to be sucked into the
Army so I went into the Navy, because a sailor's uniform
suited me better, the uniform was all that suited me,
though. . . .

PRINCESS: Ah-ha!

CHANCE (*mocking her*): Ah-ha. I wasn't able to stand the goddam routine, discipline. . . .

I kept thinking, this stops everything. I was twenty-three,
that was the peak of my youth and I knew my youth
wouldn't last long. By the time I got out, Christ knows, I
might be nearly thirty! Who would remember Chance
Wayne? In a life like mine, you just can't stop, you know,
can't take time out between steps, you've got to keep going right on up from one thing to the other, once you drop
out, it leaves you and goes on without you and you're
washed up.

PRINCESS: I don't think I know what you're talking about.

CHANCE: I'm talking about the parade. THE parade! The
parade! the boys that go places that's the parade I'm talking about, not a parade of swabbies on a wet deck. And so
I ran my comb through my hair one morning and noticed
that eight or ten hairs had come out, a warning signal of a
future baldness. My hair was still thick. But would it be five
years from now, or even three? When the war would be
over, that scared me, that speculation. I started to have bad
dreams. Nightmares and cold sweats at night, and I had
palpitations, and on my leaves I got drunk and woke up
in strange places with faces on the next pillow I had never
seen before. My eyes had a wild look in them in the mirror. . . . I got the idea I wouldn't live through the war,
that I wouldn't come back, that all the excitement and
glory of being Chance Wayne would go up in smoke at the
moment of contact between my brain and a bit of hot steel
that happened to be in the air at the same time and place
that my head was . . . that thought didn't comfort me any.
Imagine a whole lifetime of dreams and ambitions and
hopes dissolving away in one instant, being blacked out like

some arithmetic problem washed off a blackboard by a wet sponge, just by some little accident like a bullet, not even aimed at you but just shot off in space, and so I cracked up, my nerves did. I got a medical discharge out of the service and I came home in civvies, then it was when I noticed how different it was, the town and the people in it. Polite? Yes, but not cordial. No headlines in the papers, just an item that measured one inch at the bottom of page five saying that Chance Wayne, the son of Mrs. Emily Wayne of North Front Street had received an honorable discharge from the Navy as the result of illness and was home to recover . . . that was when Heavenly became more important to me than anything else. . . .

PRINCESS: Is Heavenly a girl's name?

CHANCE: Heavenly is the name of my girl in St. Cloud.

PRINCESS: Is Heavenly why we stopped here?

CHANCE: What other reason for stopping here can you think of?

PRINCESS: So . . . I'm being used. Why not? Even a dead race horse is used to make glue. Is she pretty?

CHANCE (*handing Princess a snapshot*): This is a flashlight photo I took of her, nude, one night on Diamond Key, which is a little sandbar about half a mile off shore which is under water at high tide. This was taken with the tide coming in. The water is just beginning to lap over her body like it desired her like I did and still do and will always, always. (*Chance takes back the snapshot.*) Heavenly was her name. You can see that it fits her. This was her at fifteen.

PRINCESS: Did you have her that early?

CHANCE: I was just two years older, we had each other that early.

PRINCESS: Sheer luck!

CHANCE: Princess, the great difference between people in this world is not between the rich and the poor or the good and the evil, the biggest of all differences in this world is between the ones that had or have pleasure in love and those that haven't and hadn't any pleasure in love, but just watched it with envy, sick envy. The spectators and the performers. I don't mean just ordinary pleasure or the kind you can buy, I mean great pleasure, and nothing that's happened to me or to Heavenly since can cancel out the many long nights without sleep when we gave each other such pleasure in love as very few people can look back on in their lives . . .

PRINCESS: No question, go on with your story.

CHANCE: Each time I came back to St. Cloud I had her love to come back to. . . .

PRINCESS: Something permanent in a world of change?

CHANCE: Yes, after each disappointment, each failure at something, I'd come back to her like going to a hospital. . . .

PRINCESS: She put cool bandages on your wounds? Why didn't you marry this Heavenly little physician?

CHANCE: Didn't I tell you that Heavenly is the daughter of Boss Finley, the biggest political wheel in this part of the country? Well, if I didn't I made a serious omission.

PRINCESS: He disapproved?

CHANCE: He figured his daughter rated someone a hundred, a thousand percent better than me, Chance Wayne. . . . The last time I came back here, she phoned me from the drugstore and told me to swim out to Diamond Key, that she would meet me there. I waited a long time, till almost sunset, and the tide started coming in before I heard the put-put of an outboard motor boat coming out to the sandbar. The sun was behind her, I squinted. She had on a silky wet tank suit and fans of water and mist made rainbows about her . . . she stood up in the boat as if she was water-skiing, shouting things at me an' circling around the sandbar, around and around it!

PRINCESS: She didn't come to the sandbar?

CHANCE: No, just circled around it, shouting things at me. I'd swim toward the boat, I would just about reach it and she'd race it away, throwing up misty rainbows, disappearing in rainbows and then circled back and shouting things at me again. . . .

PRINCESS: What things?

CHANCE: Things like, "Chance go away," "Don't come back to St. Cloud." "Chance, you're a liar." "Chance, I'm sick of your lies!" "My father's right about you!" "Chance, you're no good any more." "Chance, stay away from St. Cloud." The last time around the sandbar she shouted nothing, just waved good-by and turned the boat back to shore.

PRINCESS: Is that the end of the story?

CHANCE: Princess, the end of the story is up to you. You want to help me?

PRINCESS: I want to help you. Believe me, not everybody wants to hurt everybody. I don't want to hurt you, can you believe me?

CHANCE: I can if you prove it to me.

PRINCESS: How can I prove it to you?

CHANCE: I have something in mind.

PRINCESS: Yes, what?

CHANCE: Okay I'll give you a quick outline of this project I have in mind. Soon as I've talked to my girl and shown her my contract, we go on, you and me. Not far, just to New Orleans, Princess. But no more hiding away, we check in at the Hotel Roosevelt there as Alexandra Del Lago and Chance Wayne. Right away the newspapers call you and give a press conference. . . .

PRINCESS: Oh?

CHANCE: Yes! The idea briefly, a local contest of talent to find a pair of young people to star as unknowns in a picture you're planning to make to show your faith in YOUTH, Princess. You stage this contest, you invite other judges, but your decision decides it!

PRINCESS: And you and . . . ?

CHANCE: Yes, Heavenly and I win it. We get her out of St. Cloud, we go to the West Coast together.

PRINCESS: And me?

CHANCE: You?

PRINCESS: Have you forgotten, for instance, that any public attention is what I least want in the world?

CHANCE: What better way can you think of to show the public that you're a person with bigger than personal interest?

PRINCESS: Oh, yes, yes, but not true.

CHANCE: You could pretend it was true.

PRINCESS: If I didn't despise pretending!

CHANCE: I understand. Time does it. Hardens people. Time and the world that you've lived in.

PRINCESS: Which you want for yourself. Isn't that what you want? (*She looks at him then goes to the phone.*) (*in phone*) Cashier?

    Hello Cashier? This is the Princess Kosmonopolis speaking. I'm sending down a young man to cash some travelers' checks for me. (*She hangs up.*)

CHANCE: And I want to borrow your Cadillac for a while. . . .

PRINCESS: What for, Chance?

CHANCE (*posturing*): I'm pretentious. I want to be seen in your car on the streets of St. Cloud. Drive all around town in it, blowing those long silver trumpets and dressed in the fine clothes you bought me. . . . Can I?

PRINCESS: Chance, you're a lost little boy that I really would like to help find himself.

CHANCE: I passed the screen test!

PRINCESS: Come here, kiss me, I love you. (*She faces the audience.*) Did I say that? Did I mean it? (*Then to Chance with arms outstretched.*) What a child you are. . . . Come here. . . . (*He ducks under her arms, and escapes to the chair.*)

CHANCE: I want this big display. Big phony display in your Cadillac around town. And a wad a dough to flash in their faces and the fine clothes you've bought me, on me.

PRINCESS: Did I buy you fine clothes?

CHANCE (*picking up his jacket from the chair*): The finest. When you stopped being lonely because of my company at that Palm Beach Hotel, you bought me the finest. That's the deal for tonight, to toot those silver horns and drive slowly around in the Cadillac convertible so everybody that thought I was washed up will see me. And I have taken my false or true contract to flash in the faces of various people that called me washed up. All right that's the deal. Tomorrow you'll get the car back and what's left of your money. Tonight's all that counts.

PRINCESS: How do you know that as soon as you walk out of this room I won't call the police?

CHANCE: You wouldn't do that, Princess. (*He puts on his jacket.*) You'll find the car in back of the hotel parking lot, and the left-over dough will be in the glove compartment of the car.

PRINCESS: Where will you be?

CHANCE: With my girl, or nowhere.

PRINCESS: Chance Wayne! This was not necessary, all this. I'm not a phony and I wanted to be your friend.

CHANCE: Go back to sleep. As far as I know you're not a bad person, but you just got into bad company on this occasion.

PRINCESS: I am your friend and I'm not a phony. (*Chance turns and goes to the steps.*) When will I see you?

CHANCE (*at the top of the steps*): I don't know—maybe never.

PRINCESS: Never is a long time, Chance, I'll wait.

(*She throws him a kiss.*)

CHANCE: So long.

(*The Princess stands looking after him as the lights dim and the curtain closes.*)

ACT TWO

SCENE ONE

The terrace of Boss Finley's house, which is a frame house of Victorian Gothic design, suggested by a door frame at the right and a single white column. As in the other scenes, there are no walls, the action occurring against the sky and sea cyclorama.

The Gulf is suggested by the brightness and the gulls crying as in Act One. There is only essential porch furniture, Victorian wicker but painted bone white. The men should also be wearing white or off-white suits: the tableau is all blue and white, as strict as a canvas of Georgia O'Keeffe's.

At the rise of the curtain, Boss Finley is standing in the center and George Scudder nearby.

BOSS FINLEY: Chance Wayne had my daughter when she was fifteen.

SCUDDER: That young.

BOSS: When she was fifteen he had her. Know how I know? Some flashlight photos were made of her, naked, on Diamond Key.

SCUDDER: By Chance Wayne?

BOSS: My little girl was fifteen, barely out of her childhood when— (*calling offstage*) Charles—

(*Charles enters.*)

BOSS: Call Miss Heavenly—

CHARLES (*concurrently*): Miss Heavenly. Miss Heavenly. Your daddy wants to see you.

(*Charles leaves.*)

BOSS (*to Scudder*): By Chance Wayne? Who the hell else do you reckon? I seen them. He had them developed by some studio in Pass Christian that made more copies of them than Chance Wayne ordered and these photos were circulated. I seen them. That was when I first warned the son-of-a-bitch to git and out of St. Cloud. But he's back in St. Cloud right now. I tell you—

SCUDDER: Boss, let me make a suggestion. Call off this rally, I mean your appearance at it, and take it easy tonight. Go out on your boat, you and Heavenly take a short cruise on the Starfish. . . .

BOSS: I'm not about to start sparing myself. Oh, I know, I'll have me a coronary and go like that. But not because Chance Wayne had the unbelievable gall to come back to St. Cloud. (*calling offstage*) Tom Junior!

TOM JUNIOR (*offstage*): Yes, sir!

BOSS: Has he checked out yet?

TOM JUNIOR (*entering*): Hatcher says he called their room at the Royal Palms, and Chance Wayne answered the phone, and Hatcher says . . .

BOSS: Hatcher says,—who's Hatcher?

TOM JUNIOR: Dan Hatcher.

BOSS: I hate to expose my ignorance like this but the name Dan Hatcher has no more meaning to me than the name of Hatcher, which is none whatsoever.

SCUDDER (*quietly, deferentially*): Hatcher, Dan Hatcher, is the assistant manager of the Royal Palms Hotel, and the man that informed me this morning that Chance Wayne was back in St. Cloud.

BOSS: Is this Hatcher a talker, or can he keep his mouth shut?

SCUDDER: I think I impressed him how important it is to handle this thing discreetly.

BOSS: Discreetly, like you handled that operation you done on my daughter, so discreetly that a hillbilly heckler is shouting me questions about it wherever I speak?

SCUDDER: I went to fantastic lengths to preserve the secrecy of that operation.

TOM JUNIOR: When Papa's upset he hits out at anyone near him.

BOSS: I just want to know—Has Wayne left?

TOM JUNIOR: Hatcher says that Chance Wayne told him that this old movie star that he's latched on to . . .

SCUDDER: Alexandra Del Lago.

TOM JUNIOR: She's not well enough to travel.

BOSS: Okay, you're a doctor, remove her to a hospital. Call an ambulance and haul her out of the Royal Palms Hotel.

SCUDDER: Without her consent?

BOSS: Say she's got something contagious, typhoid, bubonic plague. Haul her out and slap a quarantine on her hospital door. That way you can separate them. We can remove Chance Wayne from St. Cloud as soon as this Miss Del Lago is removed from Chance Wayne.

SCUDDER: I'm not so sure that's the right way to go about it.

BOSS: Okay, you think of a way. My daughter's no whore, but she had a whore's operation after the last time he had her. I don't want him passin' another night in St. Cloud. Tom Junior.

TOM JUNIOR: Yes, sir.

BOSS: I want him gone by tomorrow—tomorrow commences at midnight.

TOM JUNIOR: I know what to do, Papa. Can I use the boat?

BOSS: Don't ask me, don't tell me nothin'—

TOM JUNIOR: Can I have *The Starfish* tonight?

BOSS: I don't want to know how, just go about it. Where's your sister?

(*Charles appears on the gallery, points out Heavenly lying on the beach to Boss and exits.*)

TOM JUNIOR: She's lyin' out on the beach like a dead body washed up on it.

BOSS (*calling*): Heavenly!

TOM JUNIOR: Gawge, I want you with me on this boat trip tonight, Gawge.

BOSS (*calling*): Heavenly!

SCUDDER: I know what you mean, Tom Junior, but I couldn't be involved in it. I can't even know about it.

BOSS (*calling again*): Heavenly!

TOM JUNIOR: Okay, don't be involved in it. There's a pretty fair doctor that lost his license for helping a girl out of trouble, and he won't be so goddam finicky about doing this absolutely just thing.

SCUDDER: I don't question the moral justification, which is complete without question. . . .

TOM JUNIOR: Yeah, complete without question.

SCUDDER: But I am a reputable doctor, I haven't lost my license. I'm chief of staff at the great hospital put up by your father. . . .

TOM JUNIOR: I said, don't know about it.

SCUDDER: No, sir, I won't know about it . . . (*Boss starts to cough.*) I can't afford to, and neither can your father. . . . (*Scudder goes to gallery writing prescription.*)

BOSS: Heavenly! Come up here, sugar. (*to Scudder*) What's that you're writing?

SCUDDER: Prescription for that cough.

BOSS: Tear it up, throw it away. I've hawked and spit all my life, and I'll be hawking and spitting in the hereafter. You all can count on that.

(*Auto horn is heard.*)

TOM JUNIOR (*leaps up on the gallery and starts to leave*): Papa, he's drivin' back by.

BOSS: Tom Junior.

(*Tom Junior stops.*)

TOM JUNIOR: Is Chance Wayne insane?

SCUDDER: Is a criminal degenerate sane or insane is a question that lots of law courts haven't been able to settle.

BOSS: Take it to the Supreme Court, they'll hand you down a decision on that question. They'll tell you a handsome young criminal degenerate like Chance Wayne is the mental and moral equal of any white man in the country.

TOM JUNIOR: He's stopped at the foot of the drive.

BOSS: Don't move, don't move, Tom Junior.

TOM JUNIOR: I'm not movin', Papa.

CHANCE (*offstage*): Aunt Nonnie! Hey, Aunt Nonnie!

BOSS: What's he shouting?

TOM JUNIOR: He's shouting at Aunt Nonnie.

BOSS: Where is she?

TOM JUNIOR: Runnin' up the drive like a dog-track rabbit.

BOSS: He ain't followin', is he?

TOM JUNIOR: Nope. He's drove away.

(*Aunt Nonnie appears before the veranda, terribly flustered, rooting in her purse for something, apparently blind to the men on the veranda.*)

BOSS: Whatcha lookin' for, Nonnie?

NONNIE (*stopping short*): Oh—I didn't notice you, Tom. I was looking for my *door*-key.

BOSS: Door's open, Nonnie, it's wide open, like a church door.

NONNIE (*laughing*): Oh, ha, ha . . .

BOSS: Why didn't you answer that good-lookin' boy in the Cadillac car that shouted at you, Nonnie?

NONNIE: Oh. I hoped you hadn't seen him. (*Draws a deep breath and comes on to the terrace, closing her white purse.*) That was Chance Wayne. He's back in St. Cloud, he's at the Royal Palms, he's—

BOSS: Why did you snub him like that? After all these years of devotion?

NONNIE: I went to the Royal Palms to warn him not to stay here but—

BOSS: He was out showing off in that big white Cadillac with the trumpet horns on it.

NONNIE: I left a message for him, I—

TOM JUNIOR: What was the message, Aunt Nonnie? Love and kisses?

NONNIE: Just get out of St. Cloud right away, Chance.

TOM JUNIOR: He's gonna git out, but not in that fish-tail Caddy.

NONNIE (*to Tom Junior*): I hope you don't mean violence— (*turning to Boss*) does he, Tom? Violence don't solve problems. It never solves young people's problems. If you will leave it to me, I'll get him out of St. Cloud. I can, I will, I promise. I don't think Heavenly knows he's back in St. Cloud. Tom, you know, Heavenly says it wasn't Chance that— She says it wasn't Chance.

BOSS: You're like your dead sister, Nonnie, gullible as my wife was. You don't know a lie if you bump into it on a street in the daytime. Now go out there and tell Heavenly I want to see her.

NONNIE: Tom, she's not well enough to—

BOSS: Nonnie, you got a whole lot to answer for.

NONNIE: Have I?

BOSS: Yes, you sure have, Nonnie. You favored Chance Wayne, encouraged, aided and abetted him in his corruption of Heavenly over a long, long time. You go get her. You sure do have a lot to answer for. You got a helluva lot to answer for.

NONNIE: I remember when Chance was the finest, nicest, sweetest boy in St. Cloud, and he stayed that way till you, till you—

BOSS: Go get her, go get her! (*She leaves by the far side of the terrace. After a moment her voice is heard calling, "Heavenly? Heavenly?"*) It's a curious thing, a mighty peculiar thing, how often a man that rises to high public office is drug back down by every soul he harbors under his roof. He harbors them under his roof, and they pull the roof down on him. Every last living one of them.

TOM JUNIOR: Does that include me, Papa?

BOSS: If the shoe fits, put it on you.

TOM JUNIOR: How does that shoe fit me?

BOSS: If it pinches your foot, just slit it down the sides a little—it'll feel comfortable on you.

TOM JUNIOR: Papa, you are UNJUST.

BOSS: What do you want credit for?

TOM JUNIOR: I have devoted the past year to organizin' the "Youth for Tom Finley" clubs.

BOSS: I'm carryin' Tom Finley Junior on my ticket.

TOM JUNIOR: You're lucky to have me on it.

BOSS: How do you figure I'm lucky to have you on it?

TOM JUNIOR: I got more newspaper coverage in the last six months than . . .

BOSS: Once for drunk drivin', once for a stag party you thrown in Capitol City that cost me five thousand dollars to hush it up!

TOM JUNIOR: You are so unjust, it . . .

BOSS: And everyone knows you had to be drove through school like a blazeface mule pullin' a plow uphill: flunked out of college with grades that only a moron would have an excuse for.

TOM JUNIOR: I got re-admitted to college.

BOSS: At my insistence. By fake examinations, answers provided beforehand, stuck in your fancy pockets. And your promiscuity. Why, these Youth for Tom Finley clubs are practically nothin' but gangs of juvenile delinquents, wearin' badges with my name and my photograph on them.

TOM JUNIOR: How about your well known promiscuity, Papa? How about your Miss Lucy?

BOSS: Who is Miss Lucy?

TOM JUNIOR (*laughing so hard he staggers*): Who is Miss Lucy? You don't even know who she is, this woman you keep in a fifty-dollar a day hotel suite at the Royal Palms, Papa?

BOSS: What're you talkin' about?

TOM JUNIOR: That rides down the Gulf Stream Highway with a motorcycle escort blowin' their sirens like the Queen of Sheba was going into New Orleans for the day. To use her charge accounts there. And you ask who's Miss Lucy? She don't even talk good of you. She says you're too old for a lover.

BOSS: That is a goddam lie. Who says Miss Lucy says that?

TOM JUNIOR: She wrote it with lipstick on the ladies' room mirror at the Royal Palms.

BOSS: Wrote what?

TOM JUNIOR: I'll quote it to you exactly. "Boss Finley," she wrote, "is too old to cut the mustard."

(*Pause: the two stags, the old and the young one, face each other, panting. Scudder has discreetly withdrawn to a far end of porch.*)

BOSS: I don't believe this story!

TOM JUNIOR: Don't believe it.

BOSS: I will check on it, however.

TOM JUNIOR: I already checked on it. Papa, why don't you get rid of her, huh, Papa?

(*Boss Finley turns away, wounded, baffled: stares out at the audience with his old, bloodshot eyes as if he thought that someone out there had shouted a question at him which he didn't quite hear.*)

BOSS: Mind your own goddam business. A man with a mission, which he holds sacred, and on the strength of which he rises to high public office—crucified in this way, publicly, by his own offspring. (*Heavenly has entered on the gallery.*) Ah, here she is, here's my little girl. (*stopping Heavenly*) You stay here, honey. I think you all had better leave me alone with Heavenly now, huh—yeah. . . . (*Tom Junior and Scudder exit.*) Now, honey, you stay here. I want to have a talk with you.

HEAVENLY: Papa, I can't talk now.

BOSS: It's necessary.

HEAVENLY: I can't, I can't talk now.

BOSS: All right, don't talk, just listen.

(*But she doesn't want to listen, starts away: He would have restrained her forcibly if an old colored manservant, Charles, had not, at that moment, come out on the porch. He carries a stick, a hat, a package, wrapped as a present. Puts them on a table.*)

CHARLES: It's five o'clock, Mister Finley.

BOSS: Huh? Oh—thanks . . .

(*Charles turns on a coach lamp by the door. This marks a formal division in the scene. The light change is not realistic; the light doesn't seem to come from the coach lamp but from a spectral radiance in the sky, flooding the terrace.*)

(*The sea wind sings. Heavenly lifts her face to it. Later that night may be stormy, but now there is just a quickness and freshness coming in from the Gulf. Heavenly is always looking that way, toward the Gulf, so that the light from Point Lookout catches her face with its repeated soft stroke of clarity.*)

(*In her father, a sudden dignity is revived. Looking at his very beautiful daughter, he becomes almost stately. He ap-*)

*proaches her, soon as the colored man returns inside, like an
aged courtier comes deferentially up to a Crown Princess or
Infanta. It's important not to think of his attitude toward
her in the terms of crudely conscious incestuous feeling, but
just in the natural terms of almost any aging father's feeling
for a beautiful young daughter who reminds him of a dead
wife that he desired intensely when she was the age of his
daughter.)*

(*At this point there might be a phrase of stately, Mozartian
music, suggesting a court dance. The flagged terrace may
suggest the parquet floor of a ballroom and the two players'
movements may suggest the stately, formal movements of a
court dance of that time; but if this effect is used, it should be
just a suggestion. The change toward "stylization" ought to be
held in check.*)

BOSS: You're still a beautiful girl.

HEAVENLY: Am I, Papa?

BOSS: Of course you are. Lookin' at you nobody could guess
that—

HEAVENLY (*laughs*): The embalmers must have done a good
job on me, Papa. . . .

BOSS: You got to quit talkin' like that. (*then, seeing Charles*)
Will you get back in the house! (*Phone rings.*)

CHARLES: Yes, sir, I was just—

BOSS: Go on in! If that phone call is for me, I'm in only to
the governor of the state and the president of the Tide-
water Oil Corporation.

CHARLES (*offstage*): It's for Miss Heavenly again.

BOSS: Say she ain't in.

CHARLES: Sorry, she ain't in.

(*Heavenly has moved upstage to the low parapet or sea wall
that separates the courtyard and lawn from the beach. It is
early dusk. The coach lamp has cast a strange light on the setting which is neo-romantic: Heavenly stops by an ornamental
urn containing a tall fern that the salty Gulf wind has
stripped nearly bare. The Boss follows her, baffled.*)

BOSS: Honey, you say and do things in the presence of people as if you had no regard of the fact that people have ears

to hear you and tongues to repeat what they hear. And so you become a issue.

HEAVENLY: Become what, Papa?

BOSS: A issue, a issue, subject of talk, of scandal—which can defeat the mission that—

HEAVENLY: Don't give me your "Voice of God" speech. Papa, there was a time when you could have saved me, by letting me marry a boy that was still young and clean, but instead you drove him away, drove him out of St. Cloud. And when he came back, you took me out of St. Cloud, and tried to force me to marry a fifty-year-old money bag that you wanted something out of—

BOSS: Now, honey—

HEAVENLY:—and then another, another, all of them ones that you wanted something out of. I'd gone, so Chance went away. Tried to compete, make himself big as these big-shots you wanted to use me for a bond with. He went. He tried. The right doors wouldn't open, and so he went in the wrong ones, and— Papa, you married for love, why wouldn't you let me do it, while I was alive, inside, and the boy still clean, still decent?

BOSS: Are you reproaching me for—?

HEAVENLY (*shouting*): Yes, I am, Papa, I am. You married for love, but you wouldn't let me do it, and even though you'd done it, you broke Mama's heart, Miss Lucy had been your mistress—

BOSS: Who is Miss Lucy?

HEAVENLY: Oh, Papa, she was your mistress long before Mama died. And Mama was just a front for you. Can I go in now, Papa? Can I go in now?

BOSS: No, no, not till I'm through with you. What a terrible, terrible thing for my baby to say . . . (*He takes her in his arms.*) Tomorrow, tomorrow morning, when the big after-Easter sales commence in the stores—I'm gonna send you in town with a motorcycle escort, straight to the Maison Blanche. When you arrive at the store, I want you to go directly up to the office of Mr. Harvey C. Petrie and tell him to give you unlimited credit there. Then go down and outfit yourself as if you was—buyin' a trousseau to marry the Prince of Monaco. . . . Purchase a full wardrobe, includin' furs. Keep 'em in storage until winter. Gown? Three, four, five, the most lavish. Slippers? Hell, pairs and pairs of 'em. Not one hat—but a dozen. I made a pile of dough on a deal involvin' the sale of rights to oil under water here lately, and baby, I want you to buy a piece of jewelry. Now about that, you better tell Harvey to call me. Or better still, maybe Miss Lucy had better help you select it. She's wise as a backhouse rat when it comes to a stone,—that's for sure. . . . Now where'd I buy that clip that I give your mama? D'you remember the clip I bought your mama? Last thing I give your mama before she died . . . I knowed she was dyin' when I bought her that clip, and I bought that clip for fifteen thousand dollars mainly to make her think she was going to get well. . . . When I pinned it on her on the nightgown she was wearing, that poor thing started crying. She said, for God's sake, Boss, what does a dying woman want with such a big diamond? I said to her, honey, look at the price tag on it. What does the price tag say? See them five figures, that one and that five and them three aughts on there? Now, honey, make sense, I told her. If you was dying, if there was any chance of it, would I invest fifteen grand in a diamond clip to pin on the neck of a shroud? Ha, haha. That made the old lady laugh. And she sat up as bright as a little bird in that bed with the diamond clip on, receiving callers all day, and laughing and chatting with them, with that diamond clip on inside and she died before midnight, with that diamond clip on her. And not till the very last minute did she believe that the diamonds wasn't a proof that she wasn't dying. (*He moves to terrace, takes off robe and starts to put on tuxedo coat.*)

HEAVENLY: Did you bury her with it?

BOSS: Bury her with it? Hell, no. I took it back to the jewelry store in the morning.

HEAVENLY: Then it didn't cost you fifteen grand after all.

BOSS: Hell, did I care what it cost me? I'm not a small man. I wouldn't have cared one hoot if it cost me a million . . . if at that time I had that kind of loot in my pockets. It would have been worth that money to see that one little smile your mama bird give me at noon of the day she was dying.

HEAVENLY: I guess that shows, demonstrates very clearly, that you have got a pretty big heart after all.

BOSS: Who doubts it then? Who? Who ever? (*He laughs.*)

(*Heavenly starts to laugh and then screams hysterically. She starts going toward the house.*)

(*Boss throws down his cane and grabs her.*)

Just a minute, Missy. Stop it. Stop it. Listen to me, I'm gonna tell you something. Last week in New Bethesda, when I was speaking on the threat of desegregation to white women's chastity in the South, some heckler in the crowd shouted out, "Hey, Boss Finley, how about your daughter? How about that operation you had done on your daughter at the Thomas J. Finley hospital in St. Cloud? Did she put on black in mourning for her appendix?" Same heckler, same question when I spoke in the Coliseum at the state capitol.

HEAVENLY: What was your answer to him?

BOSS: He was removed from the hall at both places and roughed up a little outside it.

HEAVENLY: Papa, you have got an illusion of power.

BOSS: I have power, which is not an illusion.

HEAVENLY: Papa, I'm sorry my operation has brought this embarrassment on you, but can you imagine it, Papa? I felt worse than embarrassed when I found out that Dr. George Scudder's knife had cut the youth out of my body, made me an old childless woman. Dry, cold, empty, like an old woman. I feel as if I ought to rattle like a dead dried-up vine when the Gulf Wind blows, but, Papa—I won't embarrass you any more. I've made up my mind about something. If they'll let me, accept me, I'm going into a convent.

BOSS (*shouting*): You ain't going into no convent. This state is a Protestant region and a daughter in a convent would politically ruin me. Oh, I know, you took your mama's religion because in your heart you always wished to defy me. Now, tonight, I'm addressing the Youth for Tom Finley clubs in the ballroom of the Royal Palms Hotel. My speech is going out over a national TV network, and Missy, you're going to march in the ballroom on my arm. You're going to be wearing the stainless white of a virgin, with a Youth for Tom Finley button on one shoulder and a corsage of lilies on the other. You're going to be on the speaker's platform with me, you on one side of me and Tom Junior on the other, to scotch these rumors about your corruption. And you're gonna wear a proud happy smile on your face, you're gonna stare straight out at the crowd in the ballroom with pride and joy in your eyes. Lookin' at you, all in white like a virgin, nobody would dare to speak or believe the ugly stories about you. I'm relying a great deal on this campaign to bring in young voters for the crusade I'm leading. I'm all that stands between the South and the black days of Reconstruction. And you and Tom Junior are going to stand there beside me in the grand crystal ballroom, as shining examples of white Southern youth—in danger.

HEAVENLY (*defiant*): Papa, I'm not going to do it.

BOSS: I didn't say would you, I said you would, and you will.

HEAVENLY: Suppose I still say I won't.

BOSS: Then you won't, that's all. If you won't, you won't. But there would be consequences you might not like. (*Phone rings.*) Chance Wayne is back in St. Cloud.

CHARLES (*offstage*): Mr. Finley's residence. Miss Heavenly? Sorry, she's not in.

BOSS: I'm going to remove him, he's going to be removed from St. Cloud. How do you want him to leave, in that white Cadillac he's riding around in, or in the scow that totes the garbage out to the dumping place in the Gulf?

HEAVENLY: You wouldn't dare!

BOSS: You want to take a chance on it?

CHARLES (*enters*): That call was for you again, Miss Heavenly.

BOSS: A lot of people approve of taking violent action against corrupters. And on all of them that want to adulterate the pure white blood of the South. Hell, when I was fifteen, I come down barefoot out of the red clay hills as if the Voice of God called me. Which it did, I believe. I firmly believe He called me. And nothing, nobody, nowhere is gonna stop me, never. . . . (*He motions to Charles for gift. Charles hands it to him.*) Thank you, Charles. I'm gonna pay me an early call on Miss Lucy.

(*A sad, uncertain note has come into his voice on this final line. He turns and plods wearily, doggedly off at left.*)

The Curtain Falls

(*House remains dark for short intermission.*)

SCENE TWO

A corner of cocktail lounge and of outside gallery of the Royal Palms Hotel. This corresponds in style to the bedroom set: Victorian with Moorish influence. Royal palms are projected on the cyclorama which is deep violet with dusk. There are Moorish arches between gallery and interior: over the single table, inside, is suspended the same lamp, stained glass and ornately wrought metal, that hung in the bedroom. Perhaps on the gallery there is a low stone balustrade that supports, where steps descend into the garden, an electric light standard with five branches and pear-shaped globes of a dim pearly luster. Somewhere out of the sight-lines an entertainer plays a piano or novachord.

The interior table is occupied by two couples that represent society in St. Cloud. They are contemporaries of Chance's. Behind the bar is Stuff who feels the dignity of his recent advancement from drugstore soda-fountain to the Royal Palms cocktail lounge: he has on a white mess-jacket, a scarlet cummerbund and light blue trousers, flatteringly close-fitted. Chance Wayne was once barman here: Stuff moves with an indolent male grace that he may have unconsciously remembered admiring in Chance.

Boss Finley's mistress, Miss Lucy, enters the cocktail lounge dressed in a ball gown elaborately ruffled and very bouffant like an antebellum Southern belle's. A single blonde curl is arranged to switch girlishly at one side of her sharp little terrier face. She is outraged over something and her glare is concentrated on Stuff who "plays it cool" behind the bar.

STUFF: Ev'nin', Miss Lucy.

MISS LUCY: I wasn't allowed to sit at the banquet table. No. I was put at a little side table, with a couple of state legislators an' wives. (*She sweeps behind the bar in a proprietary fashion.*) Where's your Grant's twelve-year-old? Hey! Do you have a big mouth? I used to remember a kid that jerked sodas at Walgreen's that had a big mouth. . . . Put some ice in this. . . . Is yours big, huh? I want to tell you something.

STUFF: What's the matter with your finger?

(*She catches him by his scarlet cummerbund.*)

MISS LUCY: I'm going to tell you just now. The boss came over to me with a big candy Easter egg for me. The top of the egg unscrewed. He told me to unscrew it. So I unscrewed it. Inside was a little blue velvet jewel box, no not little, a big one, as big as somebody's mouth, too.

STUFF: Whose mouth?

MISS LUCY: The mouth of somebody who's not a hundred miles from here.

STUFF (*going off at the left*): I got to set my chairs. (*Stuff reenters at once carrying two chairs. Sets them at tables while Miss Lucy talks.*)

MISS LUCY: I open the jewel box an' start to remove the great big diamond clip in it. I just got my fingers on it, and start to remove it and the old son of a bitch slams the lid of the box on my fingers. One fingernail is still blue. And the boss says to me, "Now go downstairs to the cocktail lounge and go in the ladies' room and describe this diamond clip with lipstick on the ladies' room mirror down there. Hanh?—" and he put the jewel box in his pocket and slammed the door so hard goin' out of my suite that a picture fell off the wall.

STUFF (*setting the chairs at the table*): Miss Lucy, you are the one that said, "I wish you would see what's written with lipstick on the ladies' room mirror" las' Saturday night.

MISS LUCY: To you! Because I thought I could trust you.

STUFF: Other people were here an' all of them heard it.

MISS LUCY: Nobody but you at the bar belonged to the Youth for Boss Finley Club.

(*Both stop short. They've noticed a tall man who has entered the cocktail lounge. He has the length and leanness and luminous pallor of a face that El Greco gave to his saints. He has a small bandage near the hairline. His clothes are country.*)

Hey, you.

HECKLER: Evenin', ma'am.

MISS LUCY: You with the Hillbilly Ramblers? You with the band?

HECKLER: I'm a hillbilly, but I'm not with no band.

(*He notices Miss Lucy's steady, interested stare. Stuff leaves with a tray of drinks.*)

MISS LUCY: What do you want here?

HECKLER: I come to hear Boss Finley talk. (*His voice is clear but strained. He rubs his large Adam's apple as he speaks.*)

MISS LUCY: You can't get in the ballroom without a jacket and a tie on. . . . I know who you are. You're the heckler, aren't you?

HECKLER: I don't heckle. I just ask questions, one question or two or three questions, depending on how much time it takes them to grab me and throw me out of the hall.

MISS LUCY: Those questions are loaded questions. You gonna repeat them tonight?

HECKLER: Yes, ma'am, if I can get in the ballroom, and make myself heard.

MISS LUCY: What's wrong with your voice?

HECKLER: When I shouted my questions in New Bethesda last week I got hit in the Adam's apple with the butt of a pistol, and that affected my voice. It still ain't good, but it's better. (*Starts to go.*)

MISS LUCY (*goes to back of bar, where she gets jacket, the kind kept in places with dress regulations, and throws it to Heckler*): Wait. Here, put this on. The Boss's talking on a national TV hookup tonight. There's a tie in the pocket. You sit perfectly still at the bar till the Boss starts speaking. Keep your face back of this *Evening Banner.* O.K.?

HECKLER (*opening the paper in front of his face*): I thank you.

MISS LUCY: I thank you, too, and I wish you more luck than you're likely to have.

(*Stuff re-enters and goes to back of the bar.*)

FLY (*entering on the gallery*): Paging Chance Wayne. (*auto horn offstage*) Mr. Chance Wayne, please. Paging Chance Wayne. (*He leaves.*)

MISS LUCY (*to Stuff who has re-entered*): Is Chance Wayne back in St. Cloud?

STUFF: You remember Alexandra Del Lago?

MISS LUCY: I guess I do. I was president of her local fan club. Why?

CHANCE (*offstage*): Hey, Boy, park that car up front and don't wrinkle them fenders.

STUFF: She and Chance Wayne checked in here last night.

MISS LUCY: Well I'll be a dawg's mother. I'm going to look into that. (*Lucy exits.*)

CHANCE (*entering and crossing to the bar*): Hey, Stuff! (*He takes a cocktail off the bar and sips it.*)

STUFF: Put that down. This ain't no cocktail party.

CHANCE: Man, don't you know . . . phew . . . nobody drinks gin martinis with olives. Everybody drinks vodka martinis with lemon twist nowadays, except the squares in St. Cloud. When I had your job, when I was the barman here at the Royal Palms, I created that uniform you've got on. . . . I copied it from an outfit Vic Mature wore in a Foreign Legion picture, and I looked better in it than he did, and almost as good in it as you do, ha, ha. . . .

AUNT NONNIE (*who has entered at the right*): Chance. Chance . . .

CHANCE: Aunt Nonnie! (*to Stuff*) Hey, I want a tablecloth on that table, and a bucket of champagne . . . Mumm's Cordon Rouge. . . .

AUNT NONNIE: You come out here.

CHANCE: But, I just ordered champagne in here. (*Suddenly his effusive manner collapses, as she stares at him gravely.*)

AUNT NONNIE: I can't be seen talking to you. . . .

(*She leads him to one side of the stage. A light change has occurred which has made it a royal palm grove with a bench. They cross to it solemnly. Stuff busies himself at the bar, which is barely lit. After a moment he exits with a few drinks to main body of the cocktail lounge off left. Bar music. Quiereme Mucho.*)

CHANCE (*following her*): Why?

AUNT NONNIE: I've got just one thing to tell you, Chance, get out of St. Cloud.

CHANCE: Why does everybody treat me like a low criminal in the town I was born in?

AUNT NONNIE: Ask yourself that question, ask your conscience that question.

CHANCE: What question?

AUNT NONNIE: You know, and I know you know . . .

CHANCE: Know what?

AUNT NONNIE: I'm not going to talk about it. I just can't talk about it. Your head and your tongue run wild. You can't be trusted. We have to live in St. Cloud. . . . Oh, Chance, why have you changed like you've changed? Why do you live on nothing but wild dreams now, and have no address where anybody can reach you in time to—reach you?

CHANCE: Wild dreams! Yes. Isn't life a wild dream? I never heard a better description of it. . . . (*He takes a pill and a swallow from a flask.*)

AUNT NONNIE: What did you just take, Chance? You took something out of your pocket and washed it down with liquor.

CHANCE: Yes, I took a wild dream and—washed it down with another wild dream, Aunt Nonnie, that's my life now. . . .

AUNT NONNIE: Why, son?

CHANCE: Oh, Aunt Nonnie, for God's sake, have you forgotten what was expected of me?

AUNT NONNIE: People that loved you expected just one thing of you—sweetness and honesty and . . .

(*Stuff leaves with tray.*)

CHANCE (*kneeling at her side*): No, not after the brilliant beginning I made. Why, at seventeen, I put on, directed, and played the leading role in "The Valiant," that one-act play that won the state drama contest. Heavenly played in it with me, and have you forgotten? You went with us as the girls' chaperone to the national contest held in . . .

AUNT NONNIE: Son, of course I remember.

CHANCE: In the parlor car? How we sang together?

AUNT NONNIE: You were in love even then.

CHANCE: God, yes, we were in love! (*He sings softly*)
> "If you like-a me, like I like-a you,
> And we like-a both the same"

TOGETHER:
> "I'd like-a say, this very day,
> I'd like-a change your name."

(*Chance laughs softly, wildly, in the cool light of the palm grove. Aunt Nonnie rises abruptly. Chance catches her hands.*)

AUNT NONNIE: You—*Do*—Take unfair advantage. . . .

CHANCE: Aunt Nonnie, we didn't win that lousy national contest, we just placed second.

AUNT NONNIE: Chance, you didn't place second. You got honorable mention. Fourth place, except it was just called honorable mention.

CHANCE: Just honorable mention. But in a national contest, honorable mention means something. . . . We would have won it, but I blew my lines. Yes, I that put on and produced the damn thing, couldn't even hear the damn lines being hissed at me by that fat girl with the book in the wings. (*He buries his face in his hands.*)

AUNT NONNIE: I loved you for that, son, and so did Heavenly, too.

CHANCE: It was on the way home in the train that she and I—

AUNT NONNIE (*with a flurry of feeling*): I know, I—I—

CHANCE (*rising*): I bribed the Pullman Conductor to let us use for an hour a vacant compartment on that sad, home-going train—

AUNT NONNIE: I know, I—I—

CHANCE: Gave him five dollars, but that wasn't enough, and so I gave him my wrist watch, and my collar pin and tie clip and signet ring and my suit, that I'd bought on credit to go to the contest. First suit I'd ever put on that cost more than thirty dollars.

AUNT NONNIE: Don't go back over that.

CHANCE:—To buy the first hour of love that we had together. When she undressed, I saw that her body was just then, barely, beginning to be a woman's and . . .

AUNT NONNIE: Stop, Chance.

CHANCE: I said, oh, Heavenly, no, but she said yes, and I cried in her arms that night, and didn't know that what I was crying for was—youth, that would go.

AUNT NONNIE: It was from that time on, you've changed.

CHANCE: I swore in my heart that I'd never again come in second in any contest, especially not now that Heavenly was my— Aunt Nonnie, look at this contract. (*He snatches out papers and lights lighter.*)

AUNT NONNIE: I don't want to see false papers.

CHANCE: These are genuine papers. Look at the notary's seal and the signatures of the three witnesses on them. Aunt Nonnie, do you know who I'm with? I'm with Alexandra Del Lago, the Princess Kosmonopolis is my—

AUNT NONNIE: Is your what?

CHANCE: Patroness! Agent! Producer! She hasn't been seen much lately, but still has influence, power, and money— money that can open all doors. That I've knocked at all these years till my knuckles are bloody.

AUNT NONNIE: Chance, even now, if you came back here simply saying, "I couldn't remember the lines, I lost the contest, I—failed," but you've come back here again with—

CHANCE: Will you just listen one minute more? Aunt Nonnie, here is the plan. A local-contest-of-Beauty.

AUNT NONNIE: Oh, Chance.

CHANCE: A local contest of talent that she will win.

AUNT NONNIE: Who?

CHANCE: Heavenly.

AUNT NONNIE: No, Chance. She's not young now, she's faded, she's . . .

CHANCE: Nothing goes that quick, not even youth.

AUNT NONNIE: Yes, it does.

CHANCE: It will come back like magic. Soon as I . . .

AUNT NONNIE: For what? For a fake contest?

CHANCE: For love. The moment I hold her.

AUNT NONNIE: Chance.

CHANCE: It's not going to be a local thing, Aunt Nonnie. It's going to get national coverage. The Princess Kosmonopolis's best friend is that sob sister, Sally Powers. Even you know Sally Powers. Most powerful movie columnist in the world. Whose name is law in the motion . . .

AUNT NONNIE: Chance, lower your voice.

CHANCE: I want people to hear me.

AUNT NONNIE: No, you don't, no you don't. Because if your voice gets to Boss Finley, you'll be in great danger, Chance.

CHANCE: I go back to Heavenly, or I don't. I live or die. There's nothing in between for me.

AUNT NONNIE: What you want to go back to is your clean, unashamed youth. And you can't.

CHANCE: You still don't believe me, Aunt Nonnie?

AUNT NONNIE: No, I don't. Please go. Go away from here, Chance.

CHANCE: Please.

AUNT NONNIE: No, no, go away!

CHANCE: Where to? Where can I go? This is the home of my heart. Don't make me homeless.

AUNT NONNIE: Oh, Chance.

CHANCE: Aunt Nonnie. Please.

AUNT NONNIE (*rises and starts to go*): I'll write to you. Send me an address. I'll write to you.

(*She exits through bar. Stuff enters and moves to bar.*)

CHANCE: Aunt Nonnie . . .

(*She's gone.*)

(*Chance removes a pint bottle of vodka from his pocket and something else which he washes down with the vodka. He stands back as two couples come up the steps and cross the gallery into the bar: they sit at a table. Chance takes a deep breath. Fly enters lighted area inside, singing out "Paging Mr. Chance Wayne, pagin' Mr. Chance Wayne."—Turns about smartly and goes back out through lobby. The name has stirred a commotion at the bar and table visible inside.*)

EDNA: Did you hear *that*? Is *Chance Wayne* back in St. Cloud?

(*Chance draws a deep breath. Then, he stalks back into the main part of the cocktail lounge like a matador entering a bull ring.*)

VIOLET: My God, yes—there he is.

(*Chance reads Fly's message.*)

CHANCE (*to Fly*): Not now, later, later.

(*The entertainer off left begins to play a piano . . . The "evening" in the cocktail lounge is just beginning.*)

(*Fly leaves through the gallery.*)

Well! Same old place, same old gang. Time doesn't pass in St. Cloud. (*To Bud and Scotty*) Hi!

BUD: How are you . . .

CHANCE (*shouting offstage*): (*Fly enters and stands on terrace*) Hey, Jackie . . . (*Piano stops. Chance crosses over to the table that holds the foursome.*) . . . remember my song? Do you —remember my song? . . . You see, he remembers my song. (*The entertainer swings into "It's a Big Wide Wonderful World."*) Now I feel at home. In my home town . . . Come on, everybody—sing!

(*This token of apparent acceptance reassures him. The foursome at the table on stage studiously ignore him. He sings:*)

> "When you're in love you're a master
> Of all you survey, you're a gay Santa Claus.
> There's a great big star-spangled sky up above you,
> When you're in love you're a hero . . .""

Come on! Sing, ev'rybody!

(*In the old days they did; now they don't. He goes on, singing a bit; then his voice dies out on a note of embarrassment. Somebody at the bar whispers something and another laughs. Chance chuckles uneasily and says:*)

What's wrong here? The place is dead.

STUFF: You been away too long, Chance.

CHANCE: Is that the trouble?

STUFF: That's all. . . .

(*Jackie, off, finishes with an arpeggio. The piano lid slams. There is a curious hush in the bar. Chance looks at the table. Violet whispers something to Bud. Both girls rise abruptly and cross out of the bar.*)

BUD (*yelling at Stuff*): Check, Stuff.

CHANCE (*with exaggerated surprise*): Well, *Bud and Scotty*. I didn't see you at all. Wasn't that Violet and Edna at your table? (*He sits at the table between Bud and Scotty*.)

SCOTTY: I guess they didn't recognize you, Chance.

BUD: Violet did.

SCOTTY: Did Violet?

BUD: She said, "My God, Chance Wayne."

SCOTTY: That's recognition and profanity, too.

CHANCE: I don't mind. I've been snubbed by experts, and I've done some snubbing myself. . . . Hey! (*Miss Lucy has entered at left. Chance sees her and goes toward her.*)—Is that Miss Lucy or is that Scarlett O'Hara?

MISS LUCY: Hello there, Chance Wayne. Somebody said that you were back in St. Cloud, but I didn't believe them. I said I'd have to see it with my own eyes before . . . Usually there's an item in the paper, in Gwen Phillips's column saying "St. Cloud youth home on visit is slated to play featured role in important new picture," and me being a movie fan I'm always thrilled by it. . . . (*She ruffles his hair.*)

CHANCE: Never do that to a man with thinning hair. (*Chance's smile is unflinching; it gets harder and brighter.*)

MISS LUCY: Is your hair thinning, baby? Maybe that's the difference I noticed in your appearance. Don't go 'way till I get back with my drink. . . .

(*She goes to back of bar to mix herself a drink. Meanwhile, Chance combs his hair.*)

SCOTTY (*to Chance*): Don't throw away those golden hairs you combed out, Chance. Save 'em and send 'em each in letters to your fan clubs.

BUD: Does Chance Wayne have a fan club?

SCOTTY: The most patient one in the world. They've been waiting years for him to show up on the screen for more than five seconds in a crowd scene.

MISS LUCY (*returning to the table*): Y'know this boy Chance Wayne used to be so attractive I couldn't stand it. But now I can, almost stand it. Every Sunday in summer I used to drive out to the municipal beach and watch him dive off the high tower. I'd take binoculars with me when he put on those free divin' exhibitions. You still dive, Chance? Or have you given that up?

CHANCE (*uneasily*): I did some diving last Sunday.

MISS LUCY: Good, as ever?

CHANCE: I was a little off form, but the crowd didn't notice. I can still get away with a double back somersault and a—

MISS LUCY: Where was this, in Palm Beach, Florida, Chance?

(*Hatcher enters.*)

CHANCE (*stiffening*): Why Palm Beach? Why there?

MISS LUCY: Who was it said they seen you last month in Palm Beach? Oh yes, Hatcher—that you had a job as a beach-boy at some big hotel there?

HATCHER (*stops at steps of the terrace, then leaves across the gallery*): Yeah, that's what I heard.

CHANCE: Had a job—as a beach-boy?

STUFF: Rubbing oil into big fat millionaires.

CHANCE: What joker thought up that one? (*His laugh is a little too loud.*)

SCOTTY: You ought to get their names and sue them for slander.

CHANCE: I long ago gave up tracking down sources of rumors about me. Of course, it's flattering, it's gratifying to know that you're still being talked about in your old home town, even if what they say is completely fantastic. Hahaha.

(*Entertainer returns, sweeps into "Quiereme Mucho."*)

MISS LUCY: Baby, you've changed in some way, but I can't put my finger on it. You all see a change in him, or has he just gotten older? (*She sits down next to Chance.*)

CHANCE (*quickly*): To change is to live, Miss Lucy, to live is to change, and not to change is to die. You know that, don't you? It used to scare me sometimes. I'm not scared of it now. Are you scared of it, Miss Lucy? Does it scare you?

(*Behind Chance's back one of the girls has appeared and signaled the boys to join them outside. Scotty nods and holds up two fingers to mean they'll come in a couple of minutes. The girl goes back out with an angry head-toss.*)

SCOTTY: Chance, did you know Boss Finley was holding a Youth for Tom Finley rally upstairs tonight?

CHANCE: I saw the announcements of it all over town.

BUD: He's going to state his position on that emasculation business that's stirred up such a mess in the state. Had you heard about that?

CHANCE: No.

SCOTTY: He must have been up in some earth satellite if he hasn't heard about that.

CHANCE: No, just out of St. Cloud.

SCOTTY: Well, they picked out a nigger at random and castrated the bastard to show they mean business about white women's protection in this state.

BUD: Some people think they went too far about it. There's been a whole lot of Northern agitation all over the country.

SCOTTY: The Boss is going to state his own position about that thing before the Youth for Boss Finley Rally upstairs in the Crystal Ballroom.

CHANCE: Aw. Tonight?

STUFF: Yeah, t'night.

BUD: They say that Heavenly Finley and Tom Junior are going to be standing on the platform with him.

PAGEBOY (*entering*): Paging Chance Wayne. Paging . . .

(*He is stopped short by Edna.*)

CHANCE: I *doubt* that story, somehow I *doubt* that story.

SCOTTY: You doubt they cut that nigger?

CHANCE: Oh, no, that I don't doubt. You know what that is, don't you? Sex-envy is what that is, and the revenge for sex-envy which is a widespread disease that I have run into personally too often for me to doubt its existence or any manifestation. (*The group push back their chairs, snubbing him. Chance takes the message from the Pageboy, reads it and throws it on the floor.*) Hey, Stuff— What d'ya have to do, stand on your head to get a drink around here?— Later, tell her.—Miss Lucy, can you get that Walgreen's soda jerk to give me a shot of vodka on the rocks? (*She snaps her fingers at Stuff. He shrugs and sloshes some vodka onto ice.*)

MISS LUCY: Chance? You're too loud, baby.

CHANCE: Not loud enough, Miss Lucy. No. What I meant that I doubt is that Heavenly Finley, that only I know in St. Cloud, would stoop to stand on a platform next to her father while he explains and excuses on TV this random emasculation of a young Nigra caught on a street after midnight. (*Chance is speaking with an almost incoherent excitement, one knee resting on the seat of his chair, swaying the chair back and forth. The Heckler lowers his newspaper from his face; a slow fierce smile spreads over his face as he leans forward with tensed throat muscles to catch Chance's burst of oratory.*) No! That's what I do not believe. If I believed it, oh, I'd give you a diving exhibition. I'd dive off municipal pier and swim straight out to Diamond Key and past it, and keep on swimming till sharks and barracuda took me for live bait, brother. (*His chair topples over backward, and he sprawls to the floor. The Heckler springs up to catch him. Miss Lucy springs up too, and sweeps between Chance and the Heckler, pushing the Heckler back with a quick, warning look or gesture. Nobody notices the Heckler. Chance scrambles back to his feet, flushed, laughing. Bud and Scotty outlaugh him. Chance picks up his chair and continues. The laughter stops.*) Because I have come back to St. Cloud to take her out of St. Cloud. Where I'll take her is not to a place anywhere except to her place in my heart. (*He has removed a pink capsule from his pocket, quickly and furtively, and drunk it down with his vodka.*)

BUD: Chance, what did you swallow just now?

CHANCE: Some hundred-proof vodka.

BUD: You washed something down with it that you took out of your pocket.

SCOTTY: It looked like a little pink pill.

CHANCE: Oh, ha ha. Yes, I washed down a goof-ball. You want one? I got a bunch of them. I always carry them with me. When you're not having fun, it makes you have it. When you're having fun, it makes you have more of it. Have one and see.

SCOTTY: Don't that damage the brain?

CHANCE: No, the contrary. It stimulates the brain cells.

SCOTTY: Don't it make your eyes look different, Chance?

MISS LUCY: Maybe that's what I noticed. (*as if wishing to change the subject*) Chance, I wish you'd settle an argument for me.

CHANCE: What argument, Miss Lucy?

MISS LUCY: About who you're traveling with. I heard you checked in here with a famous old movie star.

(*They all stare at him. . . . In a way he now has what he wants. He's the center of attraction: everybody is looking at him, even though with hostility, suspicion and a cruel sense of sport.*)

CHANCE: Miss Lucy I'm traveling with the vice-president and major stockholder of the film studio which just signed me.

MISS LUCY: Wasn't she once in the movies and very well known?

CHANCE: She was and still is and never will cease to be an important, a legendary figure in the picture industry, here and all over the world, and I am now under personal contract to her.

MISS LUCY: What's her name, Chance?

CHANCE: She doesn't want her name known. Like all great figures, world-known, she doesn't want or need and refuses to have the wrong type of attention. Privacy is a luxury to great stars. Don't ask me her name. I respect her too much to speak her name at this table. I'm obligated to her because she has shown faith in me. It took a long hard time to find that sort of faith in my talent that this woman has shown me. And I refuse to betray it at this table. (*His voice rises; he is already "high."*)

MISS LUCY: Baby, why are you sweating and your hands shaking so? You're not sick, are you?

CHANCE: Sick? Who's sick? I'm the least sick one you know.

MISS LUCY: Well, baby, you know you oughtn't to stay in St. Cloud. Y'know that, don't you? I couldn't believe my ears when I heard you were back here. (*to the two boys*) Could you all believe he was back here?

SCOTTY: What did you come back for?

CHANCE: I wish you would give me one reason why I shouldn't come back to visit the grave of my mother and pick out a monument for her, and share my happiness with a girl that I've loved many years. It's her, Heavenly Finley, that I've fought my way up for, and now that I've made it, the glory will be hers, too. And I've just about persuaded the powers to be to let her appear with me in a picture I'm signed for. Because I . . .

BUD: What is the name of this picture?

CHANCE: . . . Name of it? "Youth!"

BUD: Just "Youth?"

CHANCE: Isn't that a great title for a picture introducing young talent? You all look doubtful. If you don't believe me, well, look. Look at this contract. (*Removes it from his pocket.*)

SCOTTY: You carry the contract with you?

CHANCE: I happen to have it in this jacket pocket.

MISS LUCY: Leaving, Scotty? (*Scotty has risen from the table.*)

SCOTTY: It's getting too deep at this table.

BUD: The girls are waiting.

CHANCE (*quickly*): Gee, Bud, that's a clean set of rags you're wearing, but let me give you a tip for your tailor. A guy of medium stature looks better with natural shoulders, the padding cuts down your height, it broadens your figure and gives you a sort of squat look.

BUD: Thanks, Chance.

SCOTTY: You got any helpful hints for my tailor, Chance?

CHANCE: Scotty, there's no tailor on earth that can disguise a sedentary occupation.

MISS LUCY: Chance, baby . . .

CHANCE: You still work down at the bank? You sit on your can all day countin' century notes and once every week they let you slip one in your pockets? That's a fine set-up, Scotty, if you're satisfied with it but it's starting to give you a little pot and a can.

VIOLET (*appears in the door, angry*): Bud! Scotty! Come on.

SCOTTY: I don't get by on my looks, but I drive my own car. It isn't a Caddy, but it's my own car. And if my own mother died, I'd bury her myself; I wouldn't let a church take up a collection to do it.

VIOLET (*impatiently*): Scotty, if you all don't come now I'm going home in a taxi.

(*The two boys follow her into the Palm Garden. There they can be seen giving their wives cab money, and indicating they are staying.*)

CHANCE: The squares have left us, Miss Lucy.

MISS LUCY: Yeah.

CHANCE: Well . . . I didn't come back here to fight with old friends of mine. . . . Well, it's quarter past seven.

MISS LUCY: Is it?

(*There are a number of men, now, sitting around in the darker corners of the bar, looking at him. They are not ominous in their attitudes. They are simply waiting for something, for the meeting to start upstairs, for something. . . . Miss Lucy stares at Chance and the men, then again at Chance, nearsightedly, her head cocked like a puzzled terrier's. Chance is discomfited.*)

CHANCE: Yep . . . How is that Hickory Hollow for steaks? Is it still the best place in town for a steak?

STUFF (*answering the phone at the bar*): Yeah, it's him. He's here. (*Looks at Chance ever so briefly, hangs up.*)

MISS LUCY: Baby, I'll go to the checkroom and pick up my wrap and call for my car and I'll drive you out to the airport. They've got an air-taxi out there, a whirly-bird taxi, a helicopter, you know, that'll hop you to New Orleans in fifteen minutes.

CHANCE: I'm not leaving St. Cloud. What did I say to make you think I was?

MISS LUCY: I thought you had sense enough to know that you'd better.

CHANCE: Miss Lucy, you've been drinking, it's gone to your sweet little head.

MISS LUCY: Think it over while I'm getting my wrap. You still got a friend in St. Cloud.

CHANCE: I still have a girl in St. Cloud, and I'm not leaving without her.

PAGEBOY (*offstage*): Paging Chance Wayne, Mr. Chance Wayne, please.

PRINCESS (*entering with Pageboy*): Louder, young man, louder . . . Oh, never mind, here he is!

(*But Chance has already rushed out onto the gallery. The Princess looks as if she had thrown on her clothes to escape a building on fire. Her blue-sequined gown is unzipped, or partially zipped, her hair is disheveled, her eyes have a dazed, drugged brightness; she is holding up the eyeglasses with the broken lens, shakily, hanging onto her mink stole with the other hand; her movements are unsteady.*)

MISS LUCY: I know who you are. Alexandra Del Lago.

(*Loud whispering. A pause.*)

PRINCESS (*on the step to the gallery*): What? Chance!

MISS LUCY: Honey, let me fix that zipper for you. Hold still just a second. Honey, let me take you upstairs. You mustn't be seen down here in this condition. . . .

(*Chance suddenly rushes in from the gallery: he conducts the Princess outside: she is on the verge of panic. The Princess rushes half down the steps to the palm garden: leans panting on the stone balustrade under the ornamental light standard with its five great pearls of light. The interior is dimmed as Chance comes out behind her.*)

PRINCESS: Chance! Chance! Chance! Chance!

CHANCE (*softly*): If you'd stayed upstairs that wouldn't have happened to you.

PRINCESS: I did, I stayed.

CHANCE: I told you to wait.

PRINCESS: I waited.

CHANCE: Didn't I tell you to wait till I got back?

PRINCESS: I did, I waited forever, I waited forever for you. Then finally I heard those long sad silver trumpets blowing through the palm garden and then—Chance, the most wonderful thing has happened to me. Will you listen to me? Will you let me tell you?

MISS LUCY (*to the group at the bar*): Shhh!

PRINCESS: Chance, when I saw you driving under the window with your head held high, with that terrible stiff-necked pride of the defeated which I know so well; I knew that your come-back had been a failure like mine. And I felt something in my heart for you. That's a miracle, Chance. That's the wonderful thing that happened to me. I felt

something for someone besides myself. That means my
heart's still alive, at least some part of it is, not all of my
heart is dead yet. Part's alive still. . . . Chance, please listen to me. I'm ashamed of this morning. I'll never degrade
you again, I'll never degrade myself, you and me, again by
—I wasn't always this monster. Once I wasn't this monster.
And what I felt in my heart when I saw you returning, defeated, to this palm garden, Chance, gave me hope that I
could stop being a monster. Chance, you've got to help me
stop being the monster that I was this morning, and you
can do it, can help me. I won't be ungrateful for it. I almost died this morning, suffocated in a panic. But even
through my panic, I saw your kindness. I saw a true kindness in you that you have almost destroyed, but that's still
there, a little. . . .

CHANCE: What kind thing did I do?

PRINCESS: You gave my oxygen to me.

CHANCE: Anyone would do that.

PRINCESS: It could have taken you longer to give it to me.

CHANCE: I'm not that kind of monster.

PRINCESS: You're no kind of monster. You're just—

CHANCE: What?

PRINCESS: Lost in the beanstalk country, the ogre's country
at the top of the beanstalk, the country of the flesh-hungry,
blood-thirsty ogre—

(*Suddenly a voice is heard from off.*)

VOICE: Wayne?

(*The call is distinct but not loud. Chance hears it, but doesn't
turn toward it; he freezes momentarily, like a stag scenting
hunters. Among the people gathered inside in the cocktail
lounge we see the speaker, Dan Hatcher. In appearance, dress
and manner he is the apotheosis of the assistant hotel manager,
about Chance's age, thin, blond-haired, trim blond mustache,
suave, boyish, betraying an instinct for murder only by the
ruby-glass studs in his matching cuff links and tie clip.*)

HATCHER: Wayne!

(*He steps forward a little and at the same instant Tom
Junior and Scotty appear behind him, just in view. Scotty*

strikes a match for Tom Junior's cigarette as they wait there. Chance suddenly gives the Princess his complete and tender attention, putting an arm around her and turning her toward the Moorish arch to the bar entrance.)

CHANCE (*loudly*): I'll get you a drink, and then I'll take you upstairs. You're not well enough to stay down here.

HATCHER (*crossing quickly to the foot of the stairs*): Wayne!

(*The call is too loud to ignore: Chance half turns and calls back.*)

CHANCE: Who's that?

HATCHER: Step down here a minute!

CHANCE: Oh, *Hatcher*! I'll be right with you.

PRINCESS: Chance, don't leave me alone.

(*At this moment the arrival of Boss Finley is heralded by the sirens of several squad cars. The forestage is suddenly brightened from off Left, presumably the floodlights of the cars arriving at the entrance to the hotel. This is the signal the men at the bar have been waiting for. Everybody rushes off Left. In the hot light all alone on stage is Chance; behind him, is the Princess. And the Heckler is at the bar. The entertainer plays a feverish tango. Now, off Left, Boss Finley can be heard, his public personality very much "on." Amid the flash of flash bulbs we hear off:*)

BOSS (*off*): Hahaha! Little Bit, smile! Go on, smile for the birdie! Ain't she Heavenly, ain't that the right name for her!

HEAVENLY (*off*): Papa, I want to go in!

(*At this instant she runs in—to face Chance. . . . The Heckler rises. For a long instant, Chance and Heavenly stand there: he on the steps leading to the Palm Garden and gallery; she in the cocktail lounge. They simply look at each other . . . the Heckler between them. Then the Boss comes in and seizes her by the arm. . . . And there he is facing the Heckler and Chance both. . . . For a split second he faces them, half lifts his cane to strike at them, but doesn't strike . . . then pulls Heavenly back off Left stage . . . where the photographing and interviews proceed during what follows. Chance has seen that Heavenly is going to go on the platform with her father. . . . He stands there stunned. . . .)*

PRINCESS: Chance! Chance? (*He turns to her blindly.*) Call the car and let's go. Everything's packed, even the . . . tape recorder with my shameless voice on it. . . .

(*The Heckler has returned to his position at the bar. Now Hatcher and Scotty and a couple of other of the boys have come out. . . . The Princess sees them and is silent. . . . She's never been in anything like this before. . . .*)

HATCHER: Wayne, step down here, will you.

CHANCE: What for, what do you want?

HATCHER: Come down here, I'll tell you.

CHANCE: You come up here and tell me.

TOM JUNIOR: Come on, you chicken-gut bastard.

CHANCE: Why, hello, Tom Junior. Why are you hiding down there?

TOM JUNIOR: You're hiding, not me, chicken-gut.

CHANCE: You're in the dark, not me.

HATCHER: Tom Junior wants to talk to you privately down here.

CHANCE: He can talk to me privately up here.

TOM JUNIOR: Hatcher, tell him I'll talk to him in the washroom on the mezzanine floor.

CHANCE: I don't hold conversations with people in washrooms. . . .

(*Tom Junior infuriated, starts to rush forward. Men restrain him.*)

What is all this anyhow? It's fantastic. You all having a little conference there? I used to leave places when I was told to. Not now. That time's over. Now I leave when I'm ready. Hear that, Tom Junior? Give your father that message. This is my town. I was born in St. Cloud, not him. He was just called here. He was just called down from the hills to preach hate. I was born here to make love. Tell him about that difference between him and me, and ask him which he thinks has more right to stay here. . . . (*He gets no answer from the huddled little group which is restraining Tom Junior from perpetrating murder right there in the cocktail lounge.*

After all, that would be a bad incident to precede the Boss's all-South-wide TV appearance . . . and they all know it. Chance, at the same time, continues to taunt them.) Tom, Tom Junior! What do you want me for? To pay me back for the ball game and picture show money I gave you when you were cutting your father's yard grass for a dollar on Saturday? Thank me for the times I gave you my motor-cycle and got you a girl to ride the buddy seat with you?

Come here! I'll give you the keys to my Caddy. I'll give you the price of any whore in St. Cloud. You still got credit with me because you're Heavenly's brother.

TOM JUNIOR (*almost bursting free*): Don't say the name of my sister!

CHANCE: I said the name of my girl!

TOM JUNIOR (*breaking away from the group*): I'm all right, I'm all right. Leave us alone, will you. I don't want Chance to feel that he's outnumbered. (*He herds them out.*) O.K.? Come on down here.

PRINCESS (*trying to restrain Chance*): No, Chance, don't.

TOM JUNIOR: Excuse yourself from the lady and come on down here. Don't be scared to. I just want to talk to you quietly. Just talk. Quiet talk.

CHANCE: Tom Junior, I know that since the last time I was here something has happened to Heavenly and I—

TOM JUNIOR: Don't—speak the name of my sister. Just leave her name off your tongue—

CHANCE: Just tell me what happened to her.

TOM JUNIOR: Keep your ruttin' voice down.

CHANCE: I know I've done many wrong things in my life, many more than I can name or number, but I swear I never hurt Heavenly in my life.

TOM JUNIOR: You mean to say my sister was had by some-body else—diseased by somebody else the last time you were in St. Cloud? . . . I know, it's possible, it's barely pos-sible that you didn't know what you done to my little sis-ter the last time you come to St. Cloud. You remember that time when you came home broke? My sister had to pick up your tabs in restaurants and bars, and had to cover bad checks you wrote on banks where you had no ac-counts. Until you met this rich bitch, Minnie, the Texas one with the yacht, and started spending week ends on her yacht, and coming back Mondays with money from Minnie to go on with my sister. I mean, you'd sleep with Minnie, that slept with any goddam gigolo bastard she could pick up on Bourbon Street or the docks, and then you would go on sleeping again with my sister. And sometime, during that time, you got something besides your gigolo fee from Minnie and passed it onto my sister, my little sister that had hardly even heard of a thing like that, and didn't know what it was till it had gone on too long and—

CHANCE: I left town before I found out I—

(*The lamentation music is heard.*)

TOM JUNIOR: You found out! Did you tell my little sister?

CHANCE: I thought if something was wrong she'd write me or call me—

TOM JUNIOR: How could she write you or call you, there're no addresses, no phone numbers in gutters. I'm itching to kill you—here, on this spot! . . . My little sister, Heavenly, didn't know about the diseases and operations of whores, till she had to be cleaned and cured—I mean spayed like a dawg by Dr. George Scudder's knife. That's right—by the knife! . . . And tonight—if you stay here tonight, if you're here after this rally, you're gonna get the knife, too. You know? The knife? That's all. Now go on back to the lady, I'm going back to my father. (*Tom Junior exits.*)

PRINCESS (*as Chance returns to her*): Chance, for God's sake, let's go now . . .

(*The Lament is in the air. It blends with the wind-blown sound of the palms.*)

All day I've kept hearing a sort of lament that drifts through the air of this place. It says, "Lost, lost, never to be found again." Palm gardens by the sea and olive groves on Mediterranean islands all have that lament drifting through them. "Lost, lost". . . . The isle of Cyprus, Monte Carlo, San Remo, Torremolenos, Tangiers. They're all places of exile from whatever we loved. Dark glasses, wide-brimmed hats and whispers, "Is that her?" Shocked whispers. . . . Oh, Chance, believe me, after failure comes flight. Nothing ever comes after failure but flight. Face it. Call the car, have them bring down the luggage and let's go on along the Old Spanish Trail. (*She tries to hold him.*)

CHANCE: Keep your grabbing hands off me.

(*Marchers offstage start to sing "Bonnie Blue Flag."*)

PRINCESS: There's no one but me to hold you back from destruction in this place.

CHANCE: I don't want to be held.

PRINCESS: Don't leave me. If you do I'll turn into the monster again. I'll be the first lady of the Beanstalk Country.

CHANCE: Go back to the room.

PRINCESS: I'm going nowhere alone. I can't.

CHANCE (*in desperation*): Wheel chair! (*Marchers enter from the left, Tom Junior and Boss with them.*) Wheel chair! Stuff, get the lady a wheel chair! She's having another attack!

(*Stuff and a Bellboy catch at her . . . but she pushes Chance away and stares at him reproachfully. . . . The Bellboy takes her by the arm. She accepts this anonymous arm and exits. Chance and the Heckler are alone on stage.*)

CHANCE (*as if reassuring, comforting somebody besides himself*): It's all right, I'm alone now, nobody's hanging onto me.

(*He is panting. Loosens his tie and collar. Band in the Crystal Ballroom, muted, strikes up a lively but lyrically distorted variation of some such popular tune as the Liechtensteiner Polka. Chance turns toward the sound. Then, from Left stage, comes a drum majorette, bearing a gold and purple silk banner inscribed, "Youth For Tom Finley," prancing and followed by Boss Finley, Heavenly and Tom Junior, with a tight grip on her arm, as if he were conducting her to a death chamber.*)

TOM JUNIOR: Papa? Papa! Will you tell Sister to march?

BOSS FINLEY: Little Bit, you hold your haid up *high* when we march into that ballroom. (*Music up high . . . They march up the steps and onto the gallery in the rear . . . then start across it. The Boss calling out:*) Now march! (*And they disappear up the stairs.*)

VOICE (*offstage*): Now let us pray. (*There is a prayer mumbled by many voices.*)

MISS LUCY (*who has remained behind*): You still want to try it?

HECKLER: I'm going to take a shot at it. How's my voice?

MISS LUCY: Better.

HECKLER: I better wait here till he starts talkin', huh?

MISS LUCY: Wait till they turn down the chandeliers in the ballroom. . . . Why don't you switch to a question that won't hurt his daughter?

HECKLER: I don't want to hurt his daughter. But he's going to hold her up as the fair white virgin exposed to black lust in the South, and that's his build-up, his lead into his Voice of God speech.

MISS LUCY: He honestly believes it.

HECKLER: I don't believe it. I believe that the silence of God, the absolute speechlessness of Him is a long, long and awful thing that the whole world is lost because of. I think it's yet to be broken to any man, living or any yet lived on earth,—no exceptions, and least of all Boss Finley.

(*Stuff enters, goes to table, starts to wipe it. The chandelier lights go down.*)

MISS LUCY (*with admiration*): It takes a hillbilly to cut down a hillbilly. . . . (*to Stuff*) Turn on the television, baby.

VOICE (*offstage*): I give you the beloved Thomas J. Finley.

(*Stuff makes a gesture as if to turn on the TV, which we play in the fourth wall. A wavering beam of light, flickering, narrow, intense, comes from the balcony rail. Stuff moves his head so that he's in it, looking into it. . . . Chance walks slowly downstage, his head also in the narrow flickering beam of light. As he walks downstage, there suddenly appears on the big TV screen, which is the whole back wall of the stage, the image of Boss Finley. His arm is around Heavenly and he is speaking. . . . When Chance sees the Boss's arm around Heavenly, he makes a noise in his throat like a hard fist hit him low. . . . Now the sound, which always follows the picture by an instant, comes on . . . loud.*)

BOSS (*on TV screen*): Thank you, my friends, neighbors, kinfolk, fellow Americans. . . . I have told you before, but I will tell you again. I got a mission that I hold sacred to perform in the Southland. . . . When I was fifteen I came down barefooted out of the red clay hills. . . . Why? Because the Voice of God called me to execute this mission.

MISS LUCY (*to Stuff*): He's too loud.

HECKLER: Listen!

BOSS: And what is this mission? I have told you before but I will tell you again. To shield from pollution a blood that I think is not only sacred to me, but sacred to Him.

(*Upstage we see the Heckler step up the last steps and make a gesture as if he were throwing doors open. . . . He advances into the hall, out of our sight.*)

MISS LUCY: Turn it down, Stuff.

STUFF (*motioning to her*): Shh!

BOSS: Who is the colored man's best friend in the South? That's right . . .

MISS LUCY: Stuff, turn down the volume.

BOSS: It's me, Tom Finley. So recognized by both races.

STUFF (*shouting*): He's speaking the word. Pour it on!

BOSS: However—I can't and will not accept, tolerate, condone this threat of a blood pollution.

(*Miss Lucy turns down the volume of the TV set.*)

BOSS: As you all know I had no part in a certain operation on a young black gentleman. I call that incident a deplorable thing. That is the one thing about which I am in total agreement with the Northern radical press. It was a deplorable thing. However . . . I understand the emotions that lay behind it. The passion to protect by this violent emotion something that we hold sacred: our purity of our own blood! But I had no part in, and I did

CHANCE: Christ! What lies. What a liar!

MISS LUCY: Wait! . . . Chance, you can still go. I can still help you, baby.

CHANCE (*putting hands on Miss Lucy's shoulders*): Thanks, but no thank you, Miss Lucy. Tonight, God help me, somehow, I don't know how, but somehow I'll take her out of St. Cloud. I'll wake her up in my arms, and I'll give her life back to her. Yes, somehow, God help me, somehow!

not condone the operation performed on the unfortunate colored gentleman caught prowling the midnight streets of our Capitol City. . . .

(*Stuff turns up volume of TV set.*)

HECKLER (*as voice on the TV*): Hey, Boss Finley! (*The TV camera swings to show him at the back of the hall.*) How about your daughter's operation? How about that operation your daughter had done on her at the Thomas J. Finley hospital here in St. Cloud? Did she put on black in mourning for her appendix? . . .

(*We hear a gasp, as if the Heckler had been hit.*)

(*Picture: Heavenly horrified. Sounds of a disturbance. Then the doors at the top of stairs up Left burst open and the Heckler tumbles down. . . . The picture changes to Boss Finley. He is trying to dominate the disturbance in the hall.*)

BOSS: Will you repeat that question. Have that man step forward. I will answer his question. Where is he? Have that man step forward, I will answer his question. . . . Last Friday . . . Last Friday, Good Friday. I said last Friday, Good Friday . . . Quiet, may I have your attention please. . . . Last Friday, Good Friday, I seen a horrible thing on the campus of our great State University, which I built for the State. A hideous straw-stuffed effigy of myself, Tom Finley, was hung and set fire to in the main quadrangle of the college. This outrage was inspired . . . inspired by the Northern radical press. However, that was Good Friday. Today is Easter. I saw that was Good Friday. Today is Easter Sunday and I am in St. Cloud.

(*During this a gruesome, not-lighted, silent struggle has been going on. The Heckler defended himself, but finally has been overwhelmed and rather systematically beaten. . . . The tight intense follow spot beam stayed on Chance. If he had any impulse to go to the Heckler's aid, he'd be discouraged by Stuff and another man who stand behind him, watching him. . . . At the height of the beating, there are*

*bursts of great applause. . . . At a point during it,
Heavenly is suddenly escorted down the stairs, sobbing, and
collapses. . . .)*

Curtain

ACT THREE

*A while later that night: the hotel bedroom. The shutters in the
Moorish Corner are thrown open on the Palm Garden: scattered
sounds of disturbance are still heard: something burns in the
Palm Garden: an effigy, an emblem? Flickering light from it
falls on the Princess. Over the interior scene, the constant serene
projection of royal palms, branched among stars.*

PRINCESS (*pacing with the phone*): Operator! What's happened to my driver?

(*Chance enters on the gallery, sees someone approaching on
other side—quickly pulls back and stands in shadows on the
gallery.*)

You told me you'd get me a driver. . . . Why can't you get
me a driver when you said that you would? Somebody in
this hotel can surely get me somebody to drive me at any
price asked!—out of this infernal . . .

(*She turns suddenly as Dan Hatcher knocks at the corridor
door. Behind him appear Tom Junior, Bud and Scotty, sweaty,
disheveled from the riot in the Palm Garden.*)

Who's that?

SCOTTY: She ain't gonna open, break it in.

PRINCESS (*dropping phone*): What do you want?

HATCHER: Miss Del Lago . . .

BUD: Don't answer till she opens.

PRINCESS: Who's out there! What do you want?

SCOTTY (*to shaky Hatcher*): Tell her you want her out of the
goddam room.

HATCHER (*with forced note of authority*): Shut up. Let me
handle this . . . Miss Del Lago, your check-out time was

three-thirty P.M., and it's now after midnight. . . . I'm
sorry but you can't hold this room any longer.

PRINCESS (*throwing open the door*): What did you say? Will
you repeat what you said! (*Her imperious voice, jewels, furs
and commanding presence abash them for a moment.*)

HATCHER: Miss Del Lago . . .

TOM JUNIOR (*recovering quickest*): This is Mr. Hatcher, assistant manager here. You checked in last night with a character not wanted here, and we been informed he's stayin' in
your room with you. We brought Mr. Hatcher up here to
remind you that the check-out time is long past and—

PRINCESS (*powerfully*): My check-out time at any hotel in the
world is *when I want to check out.* . . .

TOM JUNIOR: This ain't any hotel in the world.

PRINCESS (*making no room for entrance*): Also, I don't talk to
assistant managers of hotels when I have complaints to
make about discourtesies to me, which I do most certainly
have to make about my experiences here. I don't even talk
to managers of hotels, I talk to owners of them. Directly to
hotel owners about discourtesies to me. (*Picks up satin
sheets on bed.*) These sheets are mine, they go with me. And
I have never suffered such dreadful discourtesies to me at
any hotel at any time or place anywhere in the world. Now
I have found out the name of this hotel owner. This is
a chain hotel under the ownership of a personal friend
of mine whose guest I have been in foreign capitals such
as . . . (*Tom Junior has pushed past her into the room.*) What
in hell is he doing in my room?

TOM JUNIOR: Where is Chance Wayne?

PRINCESS: Is that what you've come here for? You can go
away then. He hasn't been in this room since he left this
morning.

TOM JUNIOR: Scotty, check the bathroom. . . . (*He checks a
closet, stoops to peer under the bed. Scotty goes off at right.*)
Like I told you before, we know you're Alexandra Del Lago
traveling with a degenerate that I'm sure you don't know.
That's why you can't stay in St. Cloud, especially after this
ruckus that we— (*Scotty re-enters from the bathroom and indicates to Tom Junior that Chance is not there.*) —Now if
you need any help in getting out of St. Cloud, I'll be—

PRINCESS (*cutting in*): Yes. I want a driver. Someone to drive my car. I want to leave here. I'm desperate to leave here. I'm not able to drive. I have to be driven away!

TOM JUNIOR: Scotty, you and Hatcher wait outside while I explain something to her. . . . (*They go and wait outside the door, on the left end of the gallery.*) I'm gonna git you a driver, Miss Del Lago. I'll git you a state trooper, half a dozen state troopers if I can't get you no driver. O.K.? Some time come back to our town n' see us, hear? We'll lay out a red carpet for you. O.K.? G'night, Miss Del Lago.

(*They disappear down the hall, which is then dimmed out. Chance now turns from where he's been waiting at the other end of the corridor and slowly, cautiously, approaches the entrance to the room. Wind sweeps the Palm Garden; it seems to dissolve the walks; the rest of the play is acted against the night sky. The shuttered doors on the veranda open and Chance enters the room. He has gone a good deal further across the border of reason since we last saw him. The Princess isn't aware of his entrance until he slams the shuttered doors. She turns, startled, to face him.*)

PRINCESS: Chance!

CHANCE: You had some company here.

PRINCESS: Some men were here looking for you. They told me I wasn't welcome in this hotel and this town because I had come here with "a criminal degenerate." I asked them to get me a driver so I can go.

CHANCE: I'm your driver. I'm still your driver, Princess.

PRINCESS: You couldn't drive through the palm garden.

CHANCE: I'll be all right in a minute.

PRINCESS: It takes more than a minute, Chance, will you listen to me? Can you listen to me? I listened to you this morning, with understanding and pity, I did, I listened with pity to your story this morning. I felt something in my heart for you which I thought I couldn't feel. I remembered young men who were what you are or what you're hoping to be. I saw them all clearly, all clearly, eyes, voices, smiles, bodies clearly. But their names wouldn't come back to me. I couldn't get their names back without digging into old programs of plays that I starred in at twenty in which they said, "Madam, the Count's waiting for you," or—Chance? They almost made it. Oh, oh, Franz! Yes, Franz . . . what? Albertzart. Franz Albertzart, oh God, God, Franz Albertzart . . . I had to fire him. He held me too tight in the waltz scene, his anxious fingers left bruises once so violent, they, they dislocated a disc in my spine, and—

CHANCE: I'm waiting for you to shut up.

PRINCESS: I saw him in Monte Carlo not too long ago. He was with a woman of seventy, and his eyes looked older than hers. She held him, she led him by an invisible chain through Grand Hotel . . . lobbies and casinos and bars like a blind, dying lap dog; he wasn't much older than you are now. Not long after that he drove his Alfa-Romeo or Ferrari off the Grand Corniche—accidentally?—Broke his skull like an eggshell. I wonder what they found in it? Old, despaired-of ambitions, little treacheries, possibly even little attempts at blackmail that didn't quite come off, and whatever traces are left of really great charm and sweetness. Chance, Franz Albertzart is Chance Wayne. Will you please try to face it so we can go on together?

CHANCE (*pulls away from her*): Are you through? Have you finished?

PRINCESS: You didn't listen, did you?

CHANCE (*picking up the phone*): I didn't have to. I told you that story this morning—I'm not going to drive off nothing and crack my head like an eggshell.

PRINCESS: No, because you can't drive.

CHANCE: Operator? Long distance.

PRINCESS: You would drive into a palm tree. Franz Albertzart . . .

CHANCE: Where's your address book, your book of telephone numbers?

PRINCESS: I don't know what you think that you are up to, but it's no good. The only hope for you now is to let me lead you by that invisible loving steel chain through Carltons and Ritzes and Grand Hotels and—

CHANCE: Don't you know, I'd die first? I would rather die first . . . (*into phone*) Operator? This is an urgent person-to-person call from Miss Alexandra Del Lago to Miss Sally Powers in Beverly Hills, California. . . .

PRINCESS: Oh, no! . . . Chance!

CHANCE: Miss Sally Powers, the Hollywood columnist, yes, Sally Powers. Yes, well get information. I'll wait, I'll wait. . . .

PRINCESS: Her number is Coldwater five-nine thousand. . . . (*Her hand goes to her mouth—but too late.*)

CHANCE: In Beverly Hills, California, Coldwater five-nine thousand.

(*The Princess moves out onto forestage; surrounding areas dim till nothing is clear behind her but the palm garden.*)

PRINCESS: Why did I give him the number? Well, why not, after all, I'd have to know sooner or later . . . I started to call several times, picked up the phone, put it down again. Well, let him do it for me. Something's happened. I'm breathing freely and deeply as if the panic was over. Maybe it's over. He's doing the dreadful thing for me, asking the answer for me. He doesn't exist for me now except as somebody making this awful call for me, asking the answer for me. The light's on me. He's almost invisible now. What does that mean? Does it mean that I still wasn't ready to be washed up, counted out?

CHANCE: All right, call Chasen's. Try to reach her at Chasen's.

PRINCESS: Well, one thing's sure. It's only this call I care for. I seem to be standing in light with everything else dimmed out. He's in the dimmed out background as if he'd never left the obscurity he was born in. I've taken the light again as a crown on my head to which I am suited by something in the cells of my blood and body from the time of my birth. It's mine, I was born to own it, as he was born to make this phone call for me to Sally Powers, dear faithful custodian of my outlived legend. (*Phone rings in distance.*) The legend that I've outlived. . . . Monsters don't die early; they hang on long. Awfully long. Their vanity's infinite, almost as infinite as their disgust with themselves. . . . (*Phone rings louder: it brings the stage light back up on the hotel bedroom. She turns to Chance and the play returns to a more realistic level.*) The phone's still ringing.

CHANCE: They gave me another number. . . .

PRINCESS: If she isn't there, give my name and ask them where I can reach her.

CHANCE: Princess?

PRINCESS: What?

CHANCE: I have a personal reason for making this phone call.

PRINCESS: I'm quite certain of that.

CHANCE (*into phone*): I'm calling for Alexandra Del Lago. She wants to speak to Miss Sally Powers— Oh, is there any number where the Princess could reach her?

PRINCESS: It will be a good sign if they give you a number.

CHANCE: Oh?—Good, I'll call that number . . . Operator? Try another number for Miss Sally Powers. It's Canyon seven-five thousand . . . Say it's urgent, it's Princess Kosmonopolis . . .

PRINCESS: Alexandra Del Lago.

CHANCE: Alexandra Del Lago is calling Miss Powers.

PRINCESS (*to herself*): Oxygen, please, a little. . . .

CHANCE: Is that you, Miss Powers? This is Chance Wayne talking . . . I'm calling for the Princess Kosmonopolis, she wants to speak to you. She'll come to the phone in a minute. . . .

PRINCESS: I can't. . . . Say I've . . .

CHANCE (*stretching phone cord*): This is as far as I can stretch the cord, Princess, you've got to meet it halfway.

(*Princess hesitates; then advances to the extended phone.*)

PRINCESS (*in a low, strident whisper*): Sally? Sally? Is it really you, Sally? Yes, it's me, Alexandra. It's what's left of me, Sally. Oh, yes, I was there, but I only stayed a few minutes. Soon as they started laughing in the wrong places, I fled up the aisle and into the street screaming Taxi—and never stopped running till now. No, I've talked to nobody, heard nothing, read nothing . . . just wanted—dark . . . What? You're just being kind.

CHANCE (*as if to himself*): Tell her that you've discovered a pair of new stars. Two of them.

PRINCESS: One moment, Sally, I'm—breathless!

CHANCE (*gripping her arm*): And lay it on thick. Tell her to break it tomorrow in her column, in all of her columns, and in her radio talks . . . that you've discovered a pair of young people who are the stars of tomorrow!

PRINCESS (*to Chance*): Go into the bathroom. Stick your head under cold water. . . . Sally . . . Do you really think so? You're not just being nice, Sally, because of old times— Grown, did you say? My talent? In what way, Sally? More depth? More what, did you say? More power!—well, Sally, God bless you, dear Sally.

CHANCE: Cut the chatter. Talk about me and *HEAVENLY*!

PRINCESS: No, of course I didn't read the reviews. I told you I flew, I flew. I flew as fast and fast as I could. Oh. Oh? Oh . . . How very sweet of you, Sally. I don't even care if you're not altogether sincere in that statement, Sally. I think you know what the past fifteen years have been like, because I do have the—"out-crying heart of an—artist." Excuse me, Sally, I'm crying, and I don't have any Kleenex. Excuse me, Sally, I'm crying. . . .

CHANCE (*hissing behind her*): Hey. Talk about me! (*She kicks Chance's leg.*)

PRINCESS: What's that, Sally? Do you really believe so? Who? For what part? Oh, my God! . . . Oxygen, oxygen, quick!

CHANCE (*seizing her by the hair and hissing*): Me! Me!—You bitch!

PRINCESS: Sally? I'm too overwhelmed. Can I call you back later? Sally, I'll call back later. . . . (*She drops phone in a daze of rapture.*) My picture has broken box-office records. In New York and L. A.!

CHANCE: Call her back, get her on the phone.

PRINCESS: Broken box-office records. The greatest comeback in the history of the industry, that's what she calls it. . . .

CHANCE: You didn't mention me to her.

PRINCESS (*to herself*): I can't appear, not yet. I'll need a week in a clinic, then a week or ten days at the Morning Star Ranch at Vegas. I'd better get Ackermann down there for a series of shots before I go on to the Coast. . . .

CHANCE (*at phone*): Come back here, call her again.

PRINCESS: I'll leave the car in New Orleans and go on by plane to, to, to—Tucson. I'd better get Strauss working on publicity for me. I'd better be sure my tracks are covered up well these last few weeks in—hell!—

CHANCE: Here. Here, get her back on this phone.

PRINCESS: Do what?

CHANCE: Talk about me and talk about Heavenly to her.

PRINCESS: Talk about a beach-boy I picked up for pleasure, distraction from panic? Now? When the nightmare is over? Involve my name, which is Alexandra Del Lago with the record of a— You've just been using me. Using me. When I needed you downstairs you shouted, "Get her a wheel chair!" Well, I didn't need a wheel chair, I came up alone, as always. I climbed back alone up the beanstalk to the ogre's country where I live, now, alone. Chance, you've gone past something you couldn't afford to go past; your time, your youth, you've passed it. It's all you had, and you've had it.

CHANCE: Who in hell's talking! Look. (*He turns her forcibly to the mirror.*) Look in that mirror. What do you see in that mirror?

PRINCESS: I see—Alexandra Del Lago, artist and star! Now it's your turn, you look and what do you see?

CHANCE: I see—Chance Wayne. . . .

PRINCESS: The face of a Franz Albertzart, a face that tomorrow's sun will touch without mercy. Of course, you were crowned with laurel in the beginning, your gold hair was wreathed with laurel, but the gold is thinning and the laurel has withered. Face it—pitiful monster. (*She touches the crown of his head.*) . . . Of course, I know I'm one too. But one with a difference. Do you know what that difference is? No, you don't know. I'll tell you. We are two monsters, but with this difference between us. Out of the passion and torment of my existence I have created a thing that I can unveil, a sculpture, almost heroic, that I can unveil, which is true. But you? You've come back to the town you were born in, to a girl that won't see you because you put such rot in her body she had to be gutted and hung on a butcher's hook, like a chicken dressed for Sunday. . . . (*He wheels about to strike at her but his raised fist changes its course and strikes down at his own belly and he bends double with a sick cry. Palm Garden wind: whisper of The Lament.*) Yes, and her brother who was one of my callers, threatens the same thing for you: castration, if you stay here.

CHANCE: That can't be done to me twice. You did that to me this morning, here on this bed, where I had the honor, where I had the great honor . . .

(*Windy sound rises: They move away from each other, he to the bed, she close to her portable dressing table.*)

PRINCESS: Age does the same thing to a woman. . . . (*Scrapes pearls and pillboxes off table top into handbag.*) Well . . .

(*All at once her power is exhausted, her fury gone. Something uncertain appears in her face and voice betraying the fact which she probably suddenly knows, that her future course is not a progression of triumphs. She still maintains a grand air as she snatches up her platinum mink stole and tosses it about her: it slides immediately off her shoulders; she doesn't seem to notice. He picks the stole up for her, puts it about her shoulders. She grunts disdainfully, her back to him; then resolution falters; she turns to face him with great, dark eyes that are fearful, lonely, and tender.*)

PRINCESS: I am going, now, on my way. (*He nods slightly, loosening the Windsor-knot of his knitted black silk tie. Her eyes stay on him.*) Well, are you leaving or staying?

CHANCE: Staying.

PRINCESS: You can't stay here. I'll take you to the next town.

CHANCE: Thanks but no thank you, Princess.

PRINCESS (*seizing his arm*): Come on, you've got to leave with me. My name is connected with you, we checked in here together. Whatever happens to you, my name will be dragged in with it.

CHANCE: Whatever happens to me's already happened.

PRINCESS: What are you trying to prove?

CHANCE: Something's got to mean something, don't it, Princess? I mean like your life means nothing, except that you never could make it, always almost, never quite? Well, something's still got to mean something.

PRINCESS: I'll send a boy up for my luggage. You'd better come down with my luggage.

CHANCE: I'm not part of your luggage.

PRINCESS: What else can you be?

CHANCE: Nothing . . . but not part of your luggage.

(NOTE: *in this area it is very important that Chance's attitude should be self-recognition but* not *self-pity—a sort of deathbed dignity and honesty apparent in it. In both Chance*

*and the Princess, we should return to the huddling-together of
the lost, but not with sentiment, which is false, but with whatever is truthful in the moments when people share doom, face
firing squads together. Because the Princess is really equally
doomed. She can't turn back the clock any more than can
Chance, and the clock is equally relentless to them both. For the
Princess: a little, very temporary, return to, recapture of, the
spurious glory. The report from Sally Powers may be and probably is a factually accurate report: but to indicate she is going
on to further triumph would be to falsify her future. She makes
this instinctive admission to herself when she sits down by
Chance on the bed, facing the audience. Both are faced with
castration, and in her heart she knows it. They sit side by side
on the bed like two passengers on a train sharing a bench.*)

PRINCESS: Chance, we've got to go on.

CHANCE: Go on to where? I couldn't go past my youth, but
I've gone past it.

(*The Lament fades in, continues through the scene to the last
curtain.*)

PRINCESS: You're still young, Chance.

CHANCE: Princess, the age of some people can only be calculated by the level of—level of—rot in them. And by that
measure I'm ancient.

PRINCESS: What am I?—I know, I'm dead, as old Egypt . . .
Isn't it funny? We're still sitting here together, side by side
in this room, like we were occupying the same bench on a
train—going on together . . . Look. That little donkey's
marching around and around to draw water out of a
well. . . . (*She points off at something as if outside a train
window.*) Look, a shepherd boy's leading a flock.—What an
old country, timeless.—Look—

(*The sound of a clock ticking is heard, louder and louder.*)

CHANCE: No, listen. I didn't know there was a clock in this
room.

PRINCESS: I guess there's a clock in every room people live
in. . . .

CHANCE: It goes tick-tick, it's quieter than your heart-beat, but
it's slow dynamite, a gradual explosion, blasting the world we

lived in to burnt-out pieces. . . . Time—who could beat it, who could defeat it ever? Maybe some saints and heroes, but not Chance Wayne. I lived on something, that—time?

PRINCESS: Yes, time.

CHANCE: . . . Gnaws away, like a rat gnaws off its own foot caught in a trap, and then, with its foot gnawed off and the rat set free, couldn't run, couldn't go, bled and died. . . .

(*The clock ticking fades away.*)

TOM JUNIOR (*offstage left*): Miss Del Lago . . .

PRINCESS: I think they're calling our—station. . . .

TOM JUNIOR (*still offstage*): Miss Del Lago, I have got a driver for you.

(*A trooper enters and waits on gallery.*)

(*With a sort of tired grace, she rises from the bed, one hand lingering on her seat-companion's shoulder as she moves a little unsteadily to the door. When she opens it, she is confronted by Tom Junior.*)

PRINCESS: Come on, Chance, we're going to change trains at this station. . . . So, come on, we've got to go on. . . . Chance, please. . . .

(*Chance shakes his head and the Princess gives up. She weaves out of sight with the trooper down the corridor.*)

(*Tom Junior enters from steps, pauses and then gives a low whistle to Scotty, Bud, and third man who enter and stand waiting. Tom Junior comes down bedroom steps and stands on bottom step.*)

CHANCE (*rising and advancing to the forestage*): I don't ask for your pity, but just for your understanding—not even that—no. Just for your recognition of me in you, and the enemy, time, in us all.

(*The curtain closes.*)

The End

PERIOD OF ADJUSTMENT

High Point Over a Cavern

A Serious Comedy

To the director and the cast

The Scene

The action of the play takes place in Ralph Bates'
home, Memphis, Tennessee. The time is Christmas Eve.

ACT ONE

The set is the interior and entrance of a "cute" little Spanish-type suburban bungalow. Two rooms are visible onstage, the living room with its small dining alcove and the bedroom. There are doors to the kitchen and bath. A bit of the stucco exterior surrounds the entrance, downstage right or left. A Christmas wreath is on the door, while above the door is an ornamental porch light, or coach lantern, with amber glass or possibly glass in several colors. The fireplace in the fourth wall of the set is represented by a flickering red light. Of course the living room contains a TV set with its back to the audience, its face to a big sofa that opens into a bed. The dog is a cocker spaniel. There's a rather large Christmas tree, decorated, with a child's toys under it and a woman's fur coat in an open box, but no child and no woman. Ralph Bates, a boyish-looking man in his middle thirties, is approaching the TV set, facing upstage, with a can of beer and opener.

TV COMMERCIAL: Millions of Americans each day are discovering the difference between this new miracle product and the old horse-and-buggy type of cleanser which made washday a torture to Mom and left her too tired at sundown to light up the house with the sunshine of her smile.

RALPH: *No snow!*

(He hoists himself onto a very high bar stool facing the TV.)

TV COMMERCIAL: So don't let unnecessary fatigue cast a shadow over your household, especially not at this—

(He leaps off the stool and crouches to change the channel. He gets snatches of several dramatic and musical offerings, settles for a chorus of "White Christmas," sighs, picks up a poker and stabs at the flickering ruddy light in the fourth wall. It comes up brighter. He crouches to fan the fire with an antique bellows: the fire brightens. He sighs again, hoists himself back onto the brass-studded red-leather-topped stool, which has evidently been removed from the "cute" little bar, which is upstage. For theatrical purpose, this stool is about half a foot higher than any other sitting-surface on the stage. Whenever

Ralph assumes a seat on this stool he is like a judge mounting his judicial bench, except he's not pompous or bewigged about it. He is detached, considering, thinking, and over his face comes that characteristic look of a gentle gravity which is the heart of Ralph. Perhaps his pose should suggest Rodin's "Thinker." Ralph is one of those rare people that have the capacity of heart to truly care, and care deeply, about other people.

(A car horn, urgent, is heard out front, offstage, Ralph slides off the stool and rushes out the front door; he stands under the amber coach lantern. It's snowing, the snowflakes are projected on his figure, tiny, obliquely falling particles of shadow. There's a muffled shout from the car that's stopped below the terrace of the bungalow.)

RALPH (*shouting back*): Hey, there, drive her up under th' carport!

GEORGE (*Texas voice*): Whacha say, boy?

RALPH: PUT 'ER UNDER THE CARPORT!

GEORGE: Wheels won't catch, too steep!

RALPH: Back her all the way out and then shoot 'er up in first!

ISABEL'S VOICE (*high-pitched with strain*): Will you please let me out first, George!

(There is the sound of a car door. Ralph ducks back in, grinning, and seizes a carton of rice.)

RALPH: Yeah, come on in, little lady.

(Isabel appears before the house, small and white-faced with fatigue, eyes dark-circled, manner dazed and uncertain. She wears a cheap navy-blue cloth coat, carries a shiny new patent-leather purse, has on red wool mittens. Ralph pelts her with rice. She ducks the bombardment with a laugh that's more like a sob.)

ISABEL: Oh, no, please! I never want to see rice again in my life, not uncooked anyhow. . . . That fire looks wonderful to me. I'm Isabel Crane, Mr. Bates.

(She removes a red mitten and extends her hand.)

RALPH: I thought you'd married that boy.

(*Both speak in deep Southern voices; hers is distinctly Texan.*)

ISABEL: I mean Mrs. George Haverstick.

(*She says her new name with a hint of grimness.*)

RALPH (*still in the door*): Wait'll I put m'shoes on, I'll come out!

(*This shout is unheard.*)

ISABEL: You have a sweet little house.
RALPH (*with a touch of amiable grimness*): Yeah, we sure do. Wheels cain't git any traction, 'stoo damn steep.

(*He shouts down.*)

LOCK IT UP, LEAVE IT OUT FRONT!—I guess he's gonna do that, yep, that's what he's doin', uh-huh, that's what he's doin. . . .
ISABEL: Does it snow often in Memphis?
RALPH: No, no, rarely, rarely.

(*He gives her a glance. Ralph has a sometimes disconcerting way of seeming either oblivious to a person he's with or regarding the person with a sudden intense concentration, as if he'd just noticed something startling or puzzling about them. But this is a mannerism that the actor should use with restraint.*)

ISABEL: It was snowing all the way down here; it's my first acquaintance with snow except for one little flurry of snow in Saint Louis the day befo' Thanksgivin' day, this is my first real acquaintance with, with—with a real *snow*. . . . What *is* he doing down there?
RALPH: He's unloadin' th' car.
ISABEL: I just want my small zipper bag. Will you please call down to him that's all I want of my things?
RALPH (*shouting*): Leave all that stuff till later. Ha ha. I didn't know you could get all that in a car.
ISABEL: Surely he isn't removing our wedding presents! Is he *insane*, Mr. Bates?

(*She goes to the door.*)

George! Just my small zipper bag, not everything in the car!
Oh, Lord.

(*She retreats into the room.*)

He must think we're going to *live* here for the rest of our
lives! He didn't even warn you all we were coming.

RALPH: He called me up from West Memphis.

ISABEL: Yes, just across the river.

RALPH: What is that car, a Caddy?

ISABEL: It's a fifty-two Cadillac with a mileage close to a hundred and twenty thousand. It ought to be retired with an
old-age pension, Mr. Bates.

RALPH (*at the door*): It looks like one of them funeral limousines.

ISABEL (*wryly*): Mr. Bates, you have hit the nail on the head
with the head of the hammer. That is just what it was. It's
piled up a hundred and twenty thousand miles between
Burkemeyer's Mortuary and various graveyards serving
Greater Saint Louis. JAWGE, CAN YOU HEAR ME, JAWGE?
Excuse me, Mr. Bates.

(*She slips past him onto the terrace again.*)

JAWGE, JUST MY SMALL ZIPPER BAG.

(*Indistinct shout from below. She turns back in.*)

I give up, Mr. Bates.

(*She ducks under his arm to enter the house again and stands
behind Ralph in the doorway.*)

RALPH (*still chuckling at the door*): What's he want with a funeral limousine? On a honeymoon trip?

ISABEL: I asked him that same question and got a very odd
answer. He said there's no better credit card in the world
than driving up at a bank door in a Cadillac limousine.

(*She tries to laugh.*)

Oh, I don't know, I—love Spanish-type architecture,
Spanish mission-type houses, I—don't think you ought to
stand in that door with just that light shirt on you, this is
a—such a—*sweet* house. . . .

(*She seems close to tears. Something in her tone catches his attention and he comes in, closing the door.*)

RALPH: Ha, ha, well, how's it going? Is the marriage in orbit?

ISABEL (*tries to laugh at this, too*): Oh! Will you please do me a favor? Don't encourage him, please don't invite him to spend the night here, Mr. Bates! I'm thinking of your wife, because last night—in Cape Girardeau, Missouri?—he thought it would be very nice to look up an old war buddy he had there, too. He sincerely thought so, and possibly the war buddy thought so, too, but NOT the wife! Oh, no, not *that* lady, no! They'd hardly got through their first beer cans with—remembrances of Korea, when that bright little woman began to direct us to a highway motel which she said was only a hop, skip and jump from their house but turned out to be almost across the state line into— Arkansas? Yaias, Arkansas. I think I can take this off, now!

(*She removes a red woolen muffler. He takes it from her and she murmurs "Thanks."*)

What is holding him up? Why is he—? Mr. Bates, I did tell him that this is one night of the year when you just don't intrude on another young married couple.

RALPH: Aw, come off that, little lady! Why, I been beggin' that boy ever since we got out of the service to come to Memphis. He had to git married to make it. Why, every time I'd git drunk, I'd call that boy on the phone to say "Git to hell down here, you old Texas jack rabbit!" And I'd just about given up hope he'd ever show!

ISABEL: Is he still fooling with luggage?

(*There is a noise outside. Ralph goes to the open door.*)

RALPH: *Hey!*

ISABEL: *What?*

RALPH: Ha ha ha! He put these bags at the door and run back down to the car.

ISABEL: *What* did he—?

RALPH: Gone back down for more luggage. I'll take these in.

ISABEL (*as the bags are brought in*): Those are *my* pieces of luggage! All but the small zipper bag which is all that I wanted!

RALPH (*calling out the open door*): *Hey!*

ISABEL: *What?*

RALPH: *Hey, boy!* He's gotten back in the car an' driven *off*, ha ha!

ISABEL (*rushing to the door*): *Driven? Off?* Did you say? My heavens. You're right, he's *gone!* Mr. Bates, he's *deposited me on your hands and driven away.*

(*She is stunned.*)

Oh, *how funny!* Isn't this *funny!*

(*Laughs wildly, close to sobbing.*)

It's no *surprise* to me, though! All the way down here from Cape Girardeau, where we stopped for our wedding night, Mr. Bates, I had a feeling that the first chance he got to, he would abandon me somewhere!

RALPH: Aw, now, take it easy!

ISABEL: That's what he's done! Put me and my bags in your hands and run away.

RALPH: Aw, now, no! The old boy wouldn't do that, ha ha, for Chrissakes. He just remembered something he had to, had to—go and get at a—drugstore.

ISABEL: If that was the case wouldn't he mention it to me?

RALPH: Aw now, I known that boy a long time and he's always been sort of way out, but never way out that far!

ISABEL: Where is your wife? Where's Mrs. Bates, Mr. Bates?

RALPH: Oh, she's not here, right now.

ISABEL: I'm SUCH A FOOL!

(*She giggles a little hysterically.*)

Oh, I'm such a *fool!* . . . Why didn't I know better, can you answer me that? . . . I hope the news of our approach didn't drive your wife away on Christmas eve, Mr. Bates. . . .

RALPH: No, honey.

ISABEL: He brought up everything but the little blue zipper bag which is all I asked faw! . . . It had my, all my, it had my—*night* things in it. . . .

RALPH: Just let me get you a drink. I'm sorry I don't have any egg nog. But I can make a wonderful hot buttered rum. How about a little hot buttered rum?

ISABEL: Thank you, no, I don't drink. . . .

RALPH: It's never too late to begin to.

ISABEL: No, I don't want liquor.

RALPH: Coffee? Want some hot coffee?

ISABEL: Where is your wife, Mr. Bates?

RALPH: Oh, she's—not here now, I'll tell you about that later.

ISABEL: She will be outraged. This is one night of the year when you don't want outside disturbances—on your hands. . . .

RALPH: I think I know what to give you.

ISABEL: I did expect it but yet I didn't expect it!—I mean it occurred to me, the possibility of it, but I thought I was just being morbid.

RALPH: Aw, now, I know that boy. We been through two wars together, took basic training together and officer's training together. He wouldn't ditch you like that unless he's gone crazy.

ISABEL: George Haverstick is a very sick man, Mr. Bates. He was a patient in neurological at Barnes Hospital in Saint Louis, that's how I met him. I was a student nurse there.

(*She is talking quickly, shrilly. She has a prim, severe manner that disguises her prettiness.*)

RALPH: Yeah? What was wrong with him in the hospital, honey?

ISABEL: If we see him again, if he ever comes back to this house, you will *see* what's wrong. *He shakes!* Sometimes it's just barely noticeable, just a constant, slight tremor, you know, a sort of—vibration, like a—like an electric vibration in his muscles or nerves?

RALPH: Aw. That old tremor has come back on him, huh? He had that thing in Korea.

ISABEL: How bad did he have it in Korea, Mr. Bates?

RALPH: You know—like a heavy drinker—except he didn't drink heavy.

ISABEL: It's like he had Parkinson's disease but he doesn't have it.

(*She speaks like an outraged spinster, which is quite incongruous to her pretty, childlike appearance.*)

RALPH: What in hell is it then?

ISABEL: THAT is a MYSTERY! He shakes, that's all. He just shakes. Sometimes you'd think that he was shaking to pieces. . . . Was that a car out front?

(*She goes to the window.*)

No! I've caught a head cold, darn it.

(*Blows her nose.*)

When I met Mr. George Haverstick— Excuse me, you're watching TV!

RALPH (*turning off set*): Naw, I'm not watchin' TV.

ISABEL: I'm so wound up, sitting in silence all day beside my—silent bridegroom, I can't seem to stop talking now, although I—hardly know you. Yes. I met him at Barnes Hospital, the biggest one in Saint Louis, where I was taking my training as a nurse, he had gone in Barnes instead of the Veterans Hospital because in the Veterans Hospital they couldn't discover any physical cause of this tremor and he thought they just said there wasn't any physical cause in order to avoid having to pay him a physical disability— compensation! I had him as a patient at Barnes Hospital, on the night shift. My, did he keep me running! The little buzzer was never out of his hand. Couldn't sleep under any kind of sedation less than enough to knock an elephant out!—Well, that's where I met George, I was very touched by him, honestly, very, very touched by the boy! I thought he sincerely loved me. . . . Yes, I *have* caught a head cold, or am I crying? I guess it's fatigue—exhaustion.

RALPH: You're just going through a period of adjustment.

ISABEL: Of course at Barnes he got the same diagnosis, or lack of diagnosis, that he'd gotten at the Vets Hospital in Korea and Texas and elsewhere, no physical basis for the tremor, perfect physical health, suggested—psychiatry to him! He blew the roof off! You'd think they'd accused him of beating up his grandmother, at least, if not worse! I swear! Mr. Bates, I still have sympathy for him, but it wasn't fair of him not to let me know he'd quit his job at the airfield till after our marriage. He gave me that information after the wedding, right after the wedding he told me, right on the bridge, Eads Bridge between Saint Louis and East Saint Louis, he said, "Little Bit? Take a good look at Saint Louie because it may be your last one!" I'm quoting him exactly, those were his words. I don't know why I didn't say drive me right back. . . . Isn't it strange that I didn't say turn around on the other side of this bridge and drive me right back? I gave up student nursing at a great hospital to marry a man not honest enough to let me know he'd given up his job till an hour after the wedding!

RALPH: George is a high-strung boy. But they don't make them any better.

ISABEL: A man's opinion of a man! If they don't make them any better than George Haverstick they ought to stop production!

(*Ralph throws back his head, laughing heartily.*)

No, I mean it, if they don't make them better than a man that would abandon his bride in less than—how many hours?—on the doorstep of a war buddy and drive on without her or any apology to her, if that's the best they make them, I say *don't make them!*

(*There is a pause. She has crouched before the fire again, holding her hands out to the flickering glow.*)

Did George tell you on the phone that he's quit his job?

RALPH (*pouring brandy*): What job did he quit, honey?

ISABEL: He was a ground mechanic at Lambert's airfield in Saint Louis. I had lost my job too, I hadn't quit, no, I was politely dismissed. My first day in surgery?—I *fainted!*— when the doctor made the incision and I saw the blood, I keeled over . . .

RALPH: That's understandable, honey.

ISABEL: Not in a nurse, not in a girl that had set her heart on nursing, that—how long has he been gone?

RALPH: Just a few minutes, honey. Xmas Eve traffic is heavy and George being George, he may have stopped at a bar on his way back here. . . . You'd been going steady how long?

ISABEL: Ever since his discharge from Barnes Hopsital. Isn't this suburb called High Point?

RALPH: Yes. High Point over a cavern.

ISABEL: His place was in High Point, too. Another suburb
  called High Point, spelled Hi dash Point—hyphenated.

RALPH: I guess all fair-sized American cities have got a suburb
  called High Point, hyphenated or not, but this is the only
  one I know of that's built on a cavern.

ISABEL (*without really listening to him*): Cavern?

(*She laughs faintly as if it were a weak joke.*)

Well, I said, George, on the bridge, we're not driving down
  to Florida in that case. We're going to find you a job; we're
  going from city to city until you find a new job and I don't
  care if we cross the Rio Grande, we're not going to stop
  until you find one! Did I or didn't I make the right decision? In your opinion, Mr. Bates.

RALPH: Well. How did he react to it?

ISABEL: Stopped talking and started shaking! So violently I
  was scared he would drive that funeral car off the road!
  Ever since then it's been hell! And I am—

(*She springs up from the fireplace chair.*)

—not exactly the spirit of Christmas, am I?

(*She goes to the window to look out; sees nothing but windy
snow. There is a low rumble. A picture falls off the wall.*)

What was that?

RALPH: Oh, nothing. The ground just settled a little. We get
  that all the time here because this suburb, High Point, is
  built over a great big underground cavern and is sinking
  into it gradually, an inch or two inches a year. It would cost
  three thousand dollars to stabilize the foundation of this
  house even temporarily! But it's not publicly known and we
  homeowners and the promoters of the project have got together to keep it a secret till we have sold out, in alphabet-
  ical order, at a loss but not a complete sacrifice. Collusion,
  connivance. Disgusting but necessary.

(*She doesn't hear this, murmurs "What?" as she crosses back to
the window at the sound of a car going by.*)

ISABEL: It's funny, I had a hunch he was going to leave me
  somewhere.

(*She laughs sadly, forlornly, and lets the white window curtains fall together.*)

RALPH: Why don't you take off your coat and sit back down by the fire? That coat keeps the heat off you, honey. That boy's comin' back.

ISABEL: Thank you.

(*She removes her coat.*)

RALPH (*observing with solemn appreciation the perfect neatness of her small body*): I'm *sure* that boy's coming back. I am now *positive* of it! That's a cute little suit you're wearing. Were you married in that?

ISABEL: Yes, I was married in this traveling suit. Appropriately.

RALPH: You couldn't have looked any prettier in white satin.

(*Ralph is at the bar preparing a snifter of brandy for her. Now he puts a match to it and as it flares up blue, she cries out a little.*)

ISABEL: What is, what are you—?

RALPH: Something to warm up your insides, little lady.

ISABEL: Well, isn't that sweet of you? Will it burn if I touch it?

RALPH: Naw, naw, naw, take it, take it.

ISABEL: Beautiful. Let me hold it to warm my hands first, before I—

(*He puts the snifter glass of blue-flaming brandy in her hands and they return to the fireplace.*)

I'm not a drinker, I don't think doctors or nurses have any right to be, but I guess *now*—I'm *out* of the nursing profession! So . . . What a sweet little bar. What a sweet little house. And such a sweet Christmas tree.

RALPH: Yeah. Everything's sweet here. I married a homely girl, honey, but I tried to love her.

(*Isabel doesn't really hear this remark.*)

ISABEL: I hope your wife didn't take your little boy out because we were coming.

RALPH: I sure did make an effort to love that woman. I almost stopped realizing that she was homely.

ISABEL: So he didn't actually tell you he was going to a drugstore, Mr. Bates?

RALPH (*uncomfortably*): He didn't say so. I just figured he was.

ISABEL: I—well, he's abandoned me here.

RALPH: How long've you known George?

ISABEL: I'm afraid I married a stranger.

RALPH: Everybody does that.

ISABEL: Where did you say your wife was?

RALPH: My wife has quit me.

ISABEL: No! You're joking, aren't you?

RALPH: She walked out on me this evening when I let her know I'd quit my job.

ISABEL (*beginning to listen to him*): Surely it's just temporary, Mr. Bates.

RALPH: Nope. Don't think so. I quit my job and so my wife quit me.

ISABEL: I don't think a woman leaves a man as nice as you, Mr. Bates, for such a reason as that.

RALPH: Marriage is an economic arrangement in many ways, let's face it, honey. Also, the situation between us was complicated by the fact that I worked for her father. But that's another story. That's a long other story and you got your mind on George.

ISABEL: I think my pride has been hurt.

RALPH: I told you he's coming back and I'm just as sure of it as I'm sure Dorothea isn't. Or if she does, that she'll find me waiting for her. Ohhhhh, nooooo! I'm cutting out of this High Point over a Cavern on the first military transport I can catch out of Memphis.

ISABEL (*vaguely*): You don't mean that, Mr. Bates, you're talking through your hat, out of hurt feelings, hurt pride.

(*She opens the front door and stands looking out as forlornly as a lost child. She really does have a remarkably cute little figure and Ralph takes slow, continual and rather wistful stock of it with his eyes.*)

RALPH: I got what I had comin' to me, that I admit, for marryin' a girl that didn't attract me.

(*He comes up behind her at the door.*)

ISABEL: Did you say didn't attract you?

RALPH: Naw, she didn't attract me in the beginning. She's one year older'n me and I'm no chicken. But I guess I'm not the only man that would marry the only daughter of an old millionaire with diabetes and gallstones and one kidney. Am I?

ISABEL: It's nice out here.

RALPH: But I'm telling you I'm convinced there is no greater assurance of longevity in this world than one kidney, gallstones an' diabetes! That old man has been cheating the undertaker for yea many years. Seems to thrive on one kidney and . . .

(*He tosses the beer can down the terrace.*)

Oh, they live on anything—nothing!

ISABEL: Do you always throw beer cans on your front lawn, Mr. Bates?

RALPH: Never before in my life. I sure enjoyed it. George is gonna be shocked when he sees me. I sacrificed my youth to—

ISABEL: What?

RALPH: Yep, it's nice out here. I mean, nicer than in there.

ISABEL: You sacrificed your youth?

RALPH: Oh, that. Yeah! I'll tell you more about that unless it bores you.

ISABEL: No.

RALPH: She had fallen into the hands of a psychiatrist when I married this girl. This psychiatrist was charging her father fifty dollars a session to treat her for a condition that he diagnosed as "psychological frigidity." She would shiver violently every time she came within touching distance of a possible boy friend. Well—I think the psychiatrist misunderstood her shivers.

ISABEL: She might have shivered because of—

RALPH: That's what I *mean*! Why, the night I met her, I heard a noise like castanets at a distance. I thought some Spanish dancers were about to come on! Ha ha! Then I noticed her teeth—she had buck teeth at that time which were later extracted!—were chattering together and her whole body was uncontrollably shaking!

ISABEL: We both married into the shakes! But Mr. Bates, I don't think it's very nice of you to ridicule the appearance of your wife.

RALPH: Oh, I'm not!

ISABEL: You WERE!

RALPH: At my suggestion she had the buck teeth extracted. It was like kissing a rock pile before the extractions! I swear!

ISABEL: Now, Mr. Bates.

RALPH: This snow almost feels warm as white ashes out of a— chimney.

ISABEL: Excuse me. I'll get my—sweater.

(*She goes in. He remains on the little paved terrace. When she comes out again in her cardigan, he goes on talking as if there'd been no interruption.*)

RALPH: Yep, her old man was payin' this head-shrinker fifty dollars per session for this condition he diagnosed as "psychological frigidity." I cured her of that completely almost overnight. But at thirty-seven, my age, you ain't middle-aged but you're in the shadow of it and it's a spooky shadow. I mean, when you look at *late* middle-aged couples like the McGillicuddys, my absent wife's parents . . .

ISABEL: Mr. Bates, don't you think I should go downtown and take a hotel room? Even if George comes back, he ought not to find me here like a checked package waiting for him to return with the claim check. Because if you give up your pride, what are you left with, really?

(*She turns and goes back inside. He follows her in. Immediately after they enter, a Negro Girl appears on the terrace.*)

Don't you agree, Mr. Bates?

(*The Girl rings the doorbell.*)

RALPH: *Here he is now. You see?*

(*Isabel, who had sunk onto a hassock before the fireplace, now rises tensely as Ralph calls out:*)

COME ON IN, LOVER BOY! THAT DOOR AIN'T LOCKED!

(*Ralph opens the door.*)

Oh . . . What can I do fo' you, Susie?

(*Susie comes into the room with a sheepish grin.*)

SUSIE: 'Scuse me for comin' to the front door, Mr. Bates, but that snow's wet and I got a hole in muh shoe!

RALPH: You alone?

SUSIE: Yes, suh.

RALPH: They sent you for somethin'?

SUSIE: Yes, suh, they sent me faw th' chile's Santie Claus.

RALPH: Aw, they did, huh? Well, you go right back an' tell the McGillicuddys that "the chile's Santie Claus" is stayin' right here till the chile comes over for it, because I bought it, not them, and I am at least *half* responsible for the "chile's" existence, *also*. Tell them the chile did not come into the world without a father and it's about time for the chile to acknowledge that fact and for them to acknowledge that fact and— How did you git here, Susie?

SUSIE: Charlie brought me.

RALPH: Who's Charlie?

SUSIE: Charlie's they new *showfer*, Mr. Bates.

RALPH: Aw. Well, tell my wife and her folks, the McGillicuddys, that I won't be here tomorrow but "the chile's Santie Claus" will be here under the tree and say that I said Merry Christmas. Can you remember all that?

SUSIE: Yes, suh. (*She turns and shouts through the door:*) Charlie! Don't come up, I'm comin' right down, Charlie!

(*The sound of a Cadillac motor starting is heard below the terrace as Susie leaves. Ralph looks out of the open door till the car is gone, then slams it shut.*)

RALPH: Dig that, will yuh! Sent a colored girl over to collect the kid's Christmas! This is typical of the Stuart McGillicuddys. I'd like to have seen Mr. Stuart McGillicuddy, the look on his face, when that Western Union messenger give him my message of resignation this afternoon and he was at last exposed to my true opinions of him!

ISABEL: You should have let her take the child's Christmas to it.

RALPH: They'll be over. Don't worry. And—I will be waiting for them with both barrels, man—will I blast 'em! Think of the psychiatrist fees that I saved her fat-head father! I even made her think that she was attractive, and over a five-year period got one pay raise when she give birth to my son which she has turned to a sissy.

(*Isabel hasn't listened to his speech.*)

ISABEL: I thought that was George at the door. . . .
RALPH: That's life for you.
ISABEL: What?
RALPH: I said isn't that life for you!
ISABEL: *What* is life for us *all*?

(*She sighs.*)

My philosophy professor at the Baptist college I went to, he said one day, "We are all of us born, live and die in the shadow of a giant question mark that refers to three questions: Where do we *come* from? *Why? And where, oh where, are we going!*"

RALPH: When did you say you got married?
ISABEL: Yesterday. Yesterday morning.
RALPH: That lately? Well, he'll be back before you can say— Joe Blow.

(*He appreciates her neat figure again.*)

ISABEL: What?
RALPH: Nothing.
ISABEL: Well!
RALPH: D'you like Christmas music?
ISABEL: Everything but "White Christmas."

(*As she extends her palms to the imaginary fireplace, Ralph is standing a little behind her, still looking her up and down with solemn appreciation.*)

RALPH: Aw, y' don't like "White Christmas"?
ISABEL: The radio in that car is practically the only thing in it that *works*! We had it on all the time.

(*She gives a little tired laugh.*)

Conversation was impossible, even if there had been a desire to talk! It kept playing "White Christmas" because it was snowing I guess all the way down here, yesterday and—today. . . .

RALPH: A radio in a funeral limousine?

ISABEL: I guess they just played it on the way back from the graveyard. Anyway, once I reached over and turned the volume down. He didn't say anything, he just reached over and turned the volume back up. Isn't it funny how a little thing like that can be so insulting to you? Then I started crying and still haven't stopped! I pretended to be looking out the car window till it got dark.

RALPH: You're just going through a little period of adjustment to each other.

ISABEL: What do you do with a bride left on your doorstep, Mr. Bates?

RALPH: Well, I, *ha ha!*—never *had* that experience!

ISABEL: Before? Well, now you're faced with it, I hope you know how to handle it. You know why I know he's left me? He only took in my bags, he left his own in the car, he brought in all of mine except my little blue zipper overnight bag, *that* he kept for some reason. Perhaps he intends to pick up another female companion who could use its contents.

RALPH: Little lady, you're in a bad state of nerves.

ISABEL: Have you ever been so tired that you don't know what you're doing or saying?

RALPH: Yes. Often.

ISABEL: That's my condition, so make allowances for it. Yes, indeed, that *sure* is a mighty *far* drugstore. . . .

(*She wanders back to the window, and parts the curtain to peer out.*)

RALPH: He seems gone twice as long because you're thinking about it.

ISABEL: I don't know why I should care except for my overnight bag with my toilet articles in it.

RALPH (*obliquely investigating*): Where did you spend last night?

ISABEL (*vaguely*): Where did we spend last night?

RALPH: Yeah. Where did you stop for the night?

ISABEL (*rubbing her forehead and sighing with perplexity*): In a, in a—oh, a tourist camp called the—Old Man River Motel? Yes, the Old Man River Motel.

RALPH: That's a mistake. The first night ought to be spent in a real fine place regardless of what it cost you. It's so important to get off on the right foot.

(*He has freshened his drink and come around to the front of the bar. She has gone back to the window at the sound of a car.*)

If you get off on the wrong foot, it can take a long time to correct it.

(*She nods in slow confirmation of this opinion.*)

Um-hmmm. Walls are built up between people a hell of a damn sight faster than—broken down. . . . Y'want me to give you my word that he's coming back? I will, I'll give you my word. Hey.

(*He snaps his fingers.*)

Had he brought me a Christmas present? If not, *that's* what he's doing. *That* explains where he went to.

(*There is a pause. She sits sadly by the fireplace.*)

What went wrong last night?

ISABEL: Let's not talk about that.

RALPH: I don't mean to pry into such a private, intimate thing, but—

ISABEL: No, let's don't! I'll just put it this way and perhaps you will understand me. In spite of my being a student nurse, till discharged—my experience has been limited, Mr. Bates. Perhaps it's because I grew up in a small town, an only child, too protected. I wasn't allowed to date till my last year at High and then my father insisted on meeting the boys I went out with and laid down pretty strict rules, such as when to bring me home from parties and so forth. If he smelled liquor on the breath of a boy? At the door? That boy would not enter the door! And that little rule ruled out a goodly number.

RALPH: I bet it did. They should've ate peanuts befo' they called for you, honey.

(*He chuckles; reflectively poking at the fire.*)

That's what we done at the Sisters of Mercy Orphans' Home in Mobile.

ISABEL (*touched*): Oh. Were you an *orphan*, Mr. Bates?

RALPH: Yes, I had that advantage.

(*He slides off the high stool again to poke at the fire. She picks up the antique bellows and fans the flames, crouching beside him.*)

ISABEL: So you were an orphan! People that grow up orphans, don't they value love more?

RALPH: Well, let's put it this way. They get it less easy. To get it, they have to give it: so, yeah, they do value it more.

(*He slides back onto the bar stool. She crouches at the fireplace to fan the fire with the bellows; the flickering light brightens their shy, tender faces.*)

ISABEL: But it's also an advantage to have a parent like my daddy.

(*She's again close to tears.*)

Very strict but devoted. Opposed me going into the nursing profession but I had my heart set on it, I thought I had a vocation, I saw myself as a Florence Nightingale nurse. A lamp in her hand? Establishin' clinics in the—upper Amazon country. . . .

(*She laughs a little ruefully.*)

Yais, I had heroic daydreams about myself as a dedicated young nurse working side by side with a—

(*She pauses shyly.*)

RALPH: With a dedicated young doctor?

ISABEL: No, the doctor would be older, well, not too old, but—older. I saw myself passing among the pallets, you know, the straw mats, administering to the plague victims in the jungle, exposing myself to contagion. . . .

(*She exhibits a bit of humor here.*)

RALPH: *Catchin'* it?

ISABEL: Yais, contractin' it eventually *m'self.* . . .

RALPH: What were the symptoms of it?

ISABEL: A slight blemish appearing on the—hands?

(*She gives him a darting smile.*)

RALPH (*joining in the fantasy with her*): Which you'd wear gloves to conceal?

ISABEL: Yais, rubber gloves all the time.

RALPH: A crusty-lookin' blemish or more like a fungus?

(*They laugh together.*)

ISABEL: I don't think I—yais, I did, I imagined it being like *scaa-ales*! Like silver fish scales appearing on my hainds and then progressing gradually to the wrists and *fo'*-arms. . . .

RALPH: And the young doctor discovering you were concealing this condition?

ISABEL: The *youngish middle-aged* doctor, Mr. Bates! Yais, discovering I had contracted the plague myself and then a big scene in which she says, Oh, no, you mustn't touch me but he seizes her passionately in his arms, of course, and—exposes himself to contagion.

(*Ralph chuckles heartily getting off stool to poke at the fire again. She joins him on the floor to fan the flames with the bellows.*)

ISABEL: And love is stronger than death. You get the picture?

RALPH: Yep, I've seen the picture.

ISABEL: We've had a good laugh together. You're a magician, Ralph, to make me laugh tonight in my present situation. George and I never laugh, we never laugh together. Oh, he makes JOKES, YAIS! But we never have a really genuine laugh together and that's a bad sign, I think, because I don't think a married couple can go through life without laughs together any more than they can without tears.

RALPH: Nope.

(*He removes his shoes.*)

Take your slippers off, honey.

ISABEL: I have the funniest sensation in the back of my head, like—

RALPH: Like a tight rope was coming unknotted?

ISABEL: Exactly! Like a tight rope was being unknotted!

(*He removes her slippers and puts them on the hearth, crosses into the bedroom and comes out with a pair of fluffy pink bedroom slippers. He crouches beside her and feels the sole of her stocking.*)

RALPH: Yep, damp. Take those damp stockings off.

ISABEL (*unconsciously following the suggestion*): Does George have a sense of humor? In your opinion? Has he got the ability to laugh at himself and at life and at—human situations? Outside of off-color jokes? In your opinon, Mr. Bates?

RALPH (*taking the damp stockings from her and hanging them over the footlights*): Yes. We had some good laughs together, me an'—"Gawge," ha ha. . . .

ISABEL: We never had any together.

RALPH: That's the solemnity of romantic love, little lady, I mean like Romeo and Juliet was not exactly a joke book, ha ha ha.

ISABEL: "The solemnity of romantic love"!—I wouldn't expect an old war buddy of George's to use an expression like that.

RALPH: Lemme put these on your feet, little lady.

(*She sighs and extends her feet and he slips the soft fleecy pink slippers on them.*)

But you know something? I'm gonna tell you something which isn't out of the joke books either. You got a wonderful boy in your hands, on your hands, they don't make them any better than him and I mean it.

(*He does.*)

ISABEL: I appreciate your loyalty to an old war buddy.

RALPH: Naw, naw, it's not just that.

ISABEL: But if they don't make them any better than George Haverstick, they ought to stop making them, they ought to *cease producing*!

(*She utters a sort of wild, sad laugh which stops as abruptly as it started. Suddenly she observes the bedroom slippers on her feet.*)

What's these, where did they come from?

RALPH: Honey, I just put them on you. Didn't you know?

ISABEL: No!—How strange!—I didn't, I wasn't at all aware of it. . . .

(*They are both a little embarrassed.*)

Where is your wife, Mr. Bates?

RALPH: Honey, I told you she quit me and went home to her folks.

ISABEL: Oh, excuse me, I remember. You told me. . . .

(*Suddenly the blazing logs make a sharp cracking noise; a spark apparently has spit out of the grate onto Isabel's skirt. She gasps and springs up, retreating from the fireplace, and Ralph jumps off the bar stool to brush at her skirt. Under the material of the Angora wool skirt is the equal and warmer softness of her young body. Ralph is abruptly embarrassed, coughs, turns back to the fireplace and picks up copper tongs to shift the position of crackling logs.*
  (*This is a moment between them that must be done just right to avoid misinterpretation. Ralph would never make a play for the bride of a buddy. What should come out of the moment is not a suggestion that he will or might but that Dotty's body never felt that way. He remembers bodies that did. What comes out of Isabel's reaction is a warm understanding of his warm understanding; just that, nothing more, at all.*)

ISABEL: Thank you. This Angora wool is, is—highly inflammable stuff, at least I would—think it—might be. . . .

RALPH: Yeah, and I don't want "Gawge" to come back here and find, a toasted marshmallow bride . . . by my fireplace.

(*They sit down rather self-consciously, Ralph on the high stool, Isabel on the low hassock.*)

ISABEL: Yais . . .

RALPH: Huh?

ISABEL: Daddy opposed me going into nursing so much that he didn't speak to me, wouldn't even look at me for a whole week before I took off for Saint Louie.

RALPH: Aw? Tch!

ISABEL: However, at the last moment, just before the train pulled out of the depot, he came stalking up the platform to the coach window with a gift package and an envelope. The package contained flannel nighties and the envelope had in it a list of moral instructions in the form of prayers such as: "O Heavenly Father, give thy weak daughter strength to—

(*She giggles.*)

"—resist the—"

(*She covers her mouth with a hand to suppress a spasm of laughter.*)

Oh, my Lord. Well, you would have to know Daddy to appreciate the—

RALPH: Honey, I reckon I know your daddy. That's what I meant about the orphan's advantage, honey.

(*They laugh together.*)

ISABEL: We sure do have some good laughs together, Mr. Bates. Now where did I get *these*?

(*She means the bedroom slippers.*)

These aren't mine, where did, how did—? *Oh—yes*, you—

(*They resume their grave contemplation of the fire.*)

"Heavenly Father, give thy weak daughter the strength of will to resist the lusts of men. Amen."

(*Ralph chuckles sadly.*)

And I was never tempted to, *not* to, resist them, till—George. . . .

RALPH: Did George arouse a—?

ISABEL: I don't suppose another man could see George the way I see him: SAW him. So *handsome*? And so *afflicted*? So afflicted and—*handsome*? With that mysterious *tremor*? With those SHAKES?

RALPH: How did "Gawge" come on?

ISABEL: Huh? Oh. No. I don't mean he came on like a—

RALPH: Bull? Exactly?

ISABEL: No, no, no, no. It was very strange, very—strange. . . .

RALPH: What?

ISABEL: He always wanted us to go out on double dates or with a whole bunch of—others. And when we were alone? Together? There was a—funny, oh, a very *odd*—sort of—*timidity!*—between us. . . . And that, of course is what touched me; oh, that—*touched* me. . . .

(*There is a pause in the talk. Ralph descends from his high perch and passes behind her low hassock with a smile behind her back which is a recognition of the truth of her romantic commitment to George. This is also in the slight, tender pat that he gives to the honey-colored crown of her head.*)

And so although I had many strong opportunities to give in to my "weakness" on, on—weekend dates with young interns and doctors at Barnes?—I was never tempted to do so. But with George—

RALPH: You did? Give in?

ISABEL: Mr. Bates, George Haverstick married a virgin, and I can't say for sure that it was my strength of will and not *his* that—deserves the credit. . . .

(*Ralph returns to fireplace with beer.*)

RALPH: Yeah, well. Now I'm going to tell you something about that boy that might surprise you after your experience last night at the Old Man River Motel.

(*He opens a beer can.*)

He always bluffs about his ferocious treatment of women, believe me! To hear him talk you'd think he spared them no pity! However, I happen to know he didn't come on as strong with those dolls in Tokyo and Hong Kong and Korea as he liked to pretend to. Because I heard from those dolls. . . . He'd just sit up there on a pillow and drink that rice wine with them and teach them *English!* Then come downstairs from there, hitching his belt and shouting, *"Oh, man! Oh, brother!"*—like he' laid 'em to waste.

ISABEL: That was not his behavior in the Old Man River Motel. Last night.

RALPH: What went wrong in the Old Man River Motel?

ISABEL: Too many men think that girls in the nursing profession must be—*shock*proof. I'm not, I wasn't—last night. . . .

RALPH: Oh. Was he drunk?

ISABEL: He'd been drinking all day in that heaterless retired funeral hack in a snowstorm to keep himself warm. Since I don't drink, I just had to endure it. Then. We stopped at the Old Man River Motel, as dreary a place as you could find on this earth! The electric heater in our cabin lit up but gave off no heat! Oh, *George* was comfortable there! Threw off his clothes and sat down in front of the heater as if I were not even present.

RALPH: Aw.

ISABEL: Continuing drinking!

RALPH: Aw.

ISABEL: Then began the courtship, and, oh, what a courtship it was, such tenderness, romance! I finally screamed. I locked myself in the bathroom and didn't come out till he had gotten to bed and then I—slept in a chair. . . .

RALPH: You wouldn't—

ISABEL: Mr. Bates, I just couldn't! The atmosphere just wasn't right. And he—

(*She covers her face.*)

—I can't tell you more about it just now except that it was a nightmare, him in the bed, pretending to be asleep, and me in the chair pretending to be asleep too and both of us knowing the other one *wasn't* asleep and, and, and— I can't tell you more about it right now, I just can't tell more than I've told you about it, I—

(*Her sobs become violent and there is a pause.*)

RALPH: Hey! Let me kiss the bride! Huh? Can I kiss the bride?

ISABEL: You're very kind, Mr. Bates. I'm sure you were more understanding with your wife when you were going through this—

RALPH:—period of adjustment? Yeah. That's all it is, it's just a little—period of adjustment.

(*He bestows a kiss on her tear-stained cheek and a pat on her head. She squeezes his hand and sinks down again before the fireplace.*)

ISABEL: It isn't as if I'd given him to believe that I was *experienced*! I made it clear that I *wasn't*. He knows my background and we'd talked at great *length* about my—inhibitions which I know are—*inhibitions*, but—which an understanding husband wouldn't expect his bride to overcome at *once*, in a tourist cabin, after a *long—silent—ride!* —in a *funeral hack* in a *snowstorm* with the *heater not working* in a *shocked! condition!*—having just been told that—we were *both* unemployed, and—

RALPH: Little Bit, Little Bit—you had a sleepless night in that motel—why don't you put in a little sack time now. You need it, honey. Take Dotty's bed in there and think about nothing till morning.

ISABEL: You mean you know, now, that George is not coming back?

RALPH: No. I mean that Dotty's not coming back.

ISABEL: I don't think you ever thought that he would come back for me any more than I did.

RALPH: Take Dotty's bed, get some sleep on that foam-rubber mattress while I sit here and watch the Late Late Show on TV.

ISABEL: But, Mister Bates, if your wife does come back here I wouldn't want her to find a stranger in your bedroom.

RALPH: Honey, finding a stranger in a bedroom is far from being the biggest surprise of a lifetime. So you go on in there and lock the door.

ISABEL: Thank you, Mister Bates.

(*She enters bedroom.*)

I'm only locking the door because of the slight possibility that Mister George Haverstick the fourth might come back drunk and try to repeat the comedy and tragedy of last night. I hope you realize that.

RALPH: Oh, sure. Good night, sleep tight, honey.

(*She locks the bedroom door as Ralph returns to the fireplace.*)

RALPH (*to himself and the audience*): What a bitch of a Christmas.

Curtain

ACT TWO

No time lapse.

Isabel jumps up as a car is heard stopping out front. She looks wildly at Ralph, who gives her a nod and a smile as he crosses to the front door. Snow blows into the living room as he goes out and shouts:

RALPH: HEY!

(*Isabel catches her breath, waiting.*)

Ha ha!

(*Isabel expels her breath and sits down. Ralph, shouting through snow:*)

Your wife thought she was deserted!

GEORGE (*from a distance*): Hey!

(*Isabel springs up and rushes to a mirror to wipe away tears.*
(*A car door is heard slamming in front of the house. Isabel sits down. She immediately rises, rubbing her hands together, and then sits down again. Then she springs up and starts toward the bedroom. Stops short as*
(*George enters.*)

I'm the son of a camel, ha ha! My mother was a camel with two humps, a double hump—dromedary! Ha ha ha!

(*George and Ralph catch each other in a big, rocking hug. Isabel stares, ignored, as the male greetings continue.*)

RALPH: *You ole son of a tail gun!*

GEORGE: *How'sa young squirrel? Ha ha!*

RALPH: *How'sa Texas jack rabbit?*

(*There is a sudden, incongruous stillness. They stare, all three of them, Isabel at George, George and Ralph at each other. George is suddenly embarrassed and says:*)

GEORGE: Well, I see yuh still got yuh dawg.

RALPH: Yeah, m' wife's folks are cat lovers.

GEORGE: You'll get your wife back tomorrow.

RALPH: Hell, I don't want her back.

GEORGE: Y'don't want 'er back?

RALPH: That's right.

GEORGE: Hell, in that case, you won't be able to beat 'er off with a stick, ha ha!

(*His laugh expires as he catches Isabel's outraged look.*)

Won't be able to beat her away from the door with a stick t'morrow. . . .

(*They stare at each other brightly, with little chuckles, a constant series of little chuckles. Isabel feels ignored.*)

ISABEL: I doubt that Mr. Bates means it.

GEORGE: Didn't you all have a kid of some kind? I don't remember if it was a boy or a girl.

ISABEL: The toys under the tree might give you a clue as to that.

RALPH: Yeah, it's a boy, I guess. Drink?

GEORGE: You bet.

(*George goes to the bar and starts mixing drinks.*)

ISABEL: How old is your little boy?

RALPH: Three years old and she's awready made him a sissy.

GEORGE: They'll do it ev'ry time, man.

(*He keeps chuckling, as does Ralph.*)

RALPH: I didn't want this kind of a dawg, either. I wanted a Doberman pinscher, a dawg with some guts, not a whiner! But she wanted a poodle and this flop-eared sad sack of a spaniel was a compromise which turned out to be worse'n a poodle, ha, ha. . . .

GEORGE: I'll bet yuh dollars to doughnuts your wife and kid'll be back here tomorrow.

RALPH (*in his slow drawl*): They won't find me here if they do. I'm all packed to go. I would of been gone when you called but I'm waitin' t' git a call from a boy about t' git married. I want him to come over here an' make a cash offer on all this household stuff since I spent too much on Christmas and won't be around to collect my unemployment.

GEORGE: Come along with us. We got a big car out there an' we're as free as a breeze. Ain't that right, Little Bit?

ISABEL: Don't ask me what's right. I don't know! I *do* know, though, that couples with children don't separate at Christmas, and, George, let your friend work out his problems himself. You don't know the situation and don't have any right to interfere in it. And now will you please go get my little blue zipper bag for me? *Please?*

RALPH (*to George, as if she hadn't spoken*): Naw, I'm just going out to the army airfield a couple miles down the highway and catch the first plane going west.

GEORGE: We'll talk about that.

ISABEL: *George!*

GEORGE: Aw, HERE! I forgot to give you your present! After drivin' almost back into Memphis to find a liquor store open.

(*He extends a gift-wrapped magnum of champagne.*)

RALPH: Lover Jesus, champagne?

GEORGE: Imported and already cold.

RALPH (*glancing briefly at Isabel*): Didn't I tell you that he was buyin' me something? She thought you'd deserted her, boy.

ISABEL: *All right, I'll get it myself! I'll go out and get it out of the car myself!*

(*She rushes out into snow, leaving the door open.*
(*George closes the door without apparently noticing her exit.*)

GEORGE: Boy, you an' me have got a lot to talk over.

RALPH: We sure got lots of territory to cover.

GEORGE: So your goddam marriage has cracked up on yuh, has it?

RALPH: How's yours goin'? So far?

GEORGE: We'll talk about it *later*. Discuss it *thoroughly*! *Later*!

RALPH: Y'got married yestiddy mawnin'?

GEORGE: Yeah.

RALPH: How was last night?

GEORGE: We'll talk about *that* later, too.

(*Isabel rushes into the room in outrage, panting.*)

ISABEL: *I* can't break the lock on that *car*!

GEORGE: Little Bit, I didn't know that you wuh bawn in a barn.

(*He means she left the door open again.*)

ISABEL: I didn't know a lot about you, either!

(*George closes door.*)

Mr. Bates! Mr. Bates!

(*He turns toward her with a vague smile.*)

The gentleman I married refuses to get my zipper bag out of the car or unlock the car so I can get it myself.

(*The phone rings. Ralph picks it up.*)

RALPH (*in a slow, hoarse drawl, at the phone*): Aw, hi, Smokey. I'm glad you got my message. Look. I quit Regal Dairy Products and I'm flyin' out of here late tonight or early to-morrow morning and I thought maybe you might like to look over some of my stuff here, the household equipment, and make me a cash offer for it. I'll take less in cash than a check since I'm not gonna stop at the Coast, I'm flying straight through to Hong Kong so it would be difficult for me to cash yuh check an' of course I expect to make a sac-rifice on the stuff here. Hey! Would you like a beaver-skin coat, sheared beaver-skin coat for Gertrude? Aw. I'd let you have it for a, for a—third off! Aw. Well, anyhow, come over right away, Smokey, and make me an offer in cash on as much of this household stuff as you figure that you could use when you git married. O.K.?

(*He hangs up.*)

GEORGE: Hong Kong?

RALPH: Yeah.

GEORGE: Well, how about that! Back to Miss Lotus Blossom
   in the Pavilion of Joys?

RALPH: I never had it so good. At least not *since.*

ISABEL (*acidly*): Mr. Bates, your character has changed since
   my gypsy husband appeared! He seems to have had an immediate influence on you, and not a good one. May I wash
   up in your bathroom?

(*They both look at her with slight, enigmatic smiles.*)

RALPH: What's that, honey?

ISABEL: Will you let me use your bathroom?

RALPH: Aw, sure, honey. I'm sorry you—

GEORGE: Now what's the matter with her?

(*He turns to Isabel.*)

Now what's the matter with you?

ISABEL: May I talk to you alone? In another room?

RALPH: You all go in the bedroom and straighten things out.

(*Ralph goes out into the snow flurry. George leads Isabel into
next room.*)

GEORGE: Now what's the matter with you?

ISABEL: Is this a sample of how I'm going to be treated?

GEORGE: What do you mean? How have I treated you, huh?

ISABEL: I might as well not be present! For all the attention I
   have been paid since you and your buddy had this tender
   reunion!

GEORGE: Aren't you being a little unreasonable, honey?

ISABEL: I don't think so. George? If you are unhappy, our
   marriage can still be annulled. Y'know that, don't you?

GEORGE: You want to get *out* of it, do you?

(*Ralph comes back in with her traveling case. He sets it down
and goes to the kitchenette.*)

ISABEL: I don't think it's really very unreasonable of me to
   want to be treated as if I LIVED! EXISTED!

GEORGE: Will you quit actin' like a spoiled little bitch? I want
   to tell you something. You're the first woman that ever put
   me down! Sleepin' las' night in a chair? What kind of basis
   is that for a happy marriage?

ISABEL: You had to get drunk on a highway! In a heaterless funeral car, after informing me you had just quit your job! Blasting my eardrums, afterward, with a car radio you wouldn't let me turn down. How was I supposed to react to such kindness? Women are human beings and I am not an exception to that rule, I assure you! I HATED YOU LAST NIGHT AFTER YOU HAD BEEN HATING ME AND TORTURING ME ALL DAY LONG!

(*Ralph comes back into the front room.*)

GEORGE: Torturing you, did you say? WHY DON'T YOU SIMMER DOWN! We ain't ALONE here, y'know!

RALPH (*quietly, from the living room*): You all are just goin' through a perfectly usual little period of adjustment. That's all it is, I told her—

GEORGE: Aw! You all have been talking?

ISABEL: What did you think we'd been doing while you were gone in that instrument of torture you have for a car?

GEORGE: You've got to simmer down to a lower boiling point, baby.

RALPH (*entering the bedroom*): Just goin' through a period of adjustment. . . .

ISABEL: Adjustment to what, Mr. Bates? Humiliation? For the rest of my life? Well, I won't have it! I don't want such an "adjustment." I want to— May I—

(*She sobs.*)

—freshen up a little bit in your bathroom before we drive downtown? To check in at a hotel?

RALPH: Sure you can.

GEORGE: I ain't goin' downtown—or checkin' in no hotel.

(*He goes back into the living room.*)

ISABEL: YOU may do as you *please*! *I'm* checking in a hotel.

RALPH (*offering her a glass*): You never finished your drink.

ISABEL: I don't care to, thanks. Too many people think that liquor solves problems, all problems. I think all it does is *confuse* them!

RALPH: I would say that it—*obfuscates* them a little, but—

ISABEL: Does *what* to them, Mr. Bates?

RALPH: I work crossword puzzles. I—ha ha!—pick up a lot of long words. Obfuscates means obscures. And problems need obfuscation now and then, honey. I don't mean total or permanent obfuscation, I just mean *temporary* obfuscation, that's all.

(*He is touched by the girl and he is standing close to her, still holding the glass out toward her. He has a fine, simple sweetness and gentleness when he's not "bugged" by people.*)

D'ya always say *Mister* to men?

ISABEL: Yes, I do till I know them. I had an old-fashioned upbringing and I can't say I regret it. Yes.

(*She is still peering out the door at her new husband.*)

RALPH: I wish you would say Ralph to me like you *know* me, honey. You got a tension between you, and tensions obfuscate love. Why don't you get that cross look off your face and give him a loving expression? Obfuscate his problems with a sweet smile on your face and—

ISABEL: YOU do that! I'm not in a mood to "obfuscate" his problems. Mr. Bates, I think he'd do better to face them like I'm facing mine, such as the problem of having married a man that seems to dislike me after one day of marriage.

RALPH: Finish this drink and obfuscate that problem because it doesn't exist.

(*He closes the bedroom door. As he comes back to Isabel with the glass, George reopens the door between the two rooms, glares in for a moment and switches the overhead light on, then goes back into the parlor. Ralph smiles tolerantly at this show of distrust which is not justified.*)

ISABEL: You have a sweet little bedroom, Mr. Bates.

RALPH: I married a *sweet, homely* woman. Almost started to *like* her. I can like *anybody,* but—

ISABEL: Mr. Bates? Ralph? This house has a *sweetness* about it!

RALPH: You don't think it's "tacky?"

ISABEL: No. I think it's—sweet!

RALPH: We got it cheap because this section of town is built right over a cavern.

ISABEL (*without listening*): What?

RALPH: This High Point suburb is built over an underground cavern and is gradually sinking down in it. You see those cracks in the walls?

ISABEL: Oh. . . .

(*She hasn't listened to him or looked.*)

Oh! My little blue bag. May I have it?

RALPH (*through the door*): She wants a little blue bag.

GEORGE: *Here, give it to her, goddam it!*

(*He tosses the bag into the bedroom. Isabel screams. Ralph catches the bag.*)

Now whatcha screamin' faw?

ISABEL: Thank heaven Mr. Bates is such a good catch. All my colognes and perfumes are in that bag, including a twenty-five dollar bottle of Vol-de-nuit. Mr. Bates, will it be necessary for me to phone the hotel?

GEORGE: Didn't you hear what I said?

ISABEL: Mr. Bates! Would you mind phoning some clean, inexpensive hotel to hold a room for us tonight?

GEORGE: I said I'm not gonna check in a hotel tonight!

ISABEL: Reserve a *single* room, please!

RALPH: Sure, sure, honey, I'll do that. Now you just rest an' fresh up an'— Come on, George, let her alone here now, so she can rest an' calm down.

(*He leads George back into the parlor.*)

GEORGE: Look at my hands! Willya look at my hands?

RALPH: What about your hands?

GEORGE: Remember that tremor? Which I had in Korea? Those shakes? Which started in Korea?

RALPH: Aw is it come back on yuh?

GEORGE: Are you blind, man?

RALPH: Yeah. How's your drink?

GEORGE: She in the bathroom yet?

RALPH: Naw, she's still in the bedroom.

GEORGE: Wait'll she gits in the bathroom so we can talk.

RALPH: What's your drink, ole son?

GEORGE: Beer's fine. Jesus!

RALPH (*at the bar*): Rough?

GEORGE: Just wait'll she gits in the bathroom so I can tell you about last night.

RALPH: Here.

(*He hands him a beer.*)

GEORGE (*at the bedroom door*): She's still sittin' there bawling on that bed. Step outside a minute.

(*He goes to the front door and out onto the tiny paved porch. The interior dims as Ralph follows him out. For a while they just stand drinking beer with the snow shadows swarming about them.*)

RALPH: Chilly.

GEORGE: I don't feel chilly.

RALPH: *I* do.

(*He pauses.*)

You're not for that little lady in that damn silly little sissy mess of a bedroom!

GEORGE: What's wrong with the bedroom, it looked like a nice little bedroom.

RALPH: A bedroom is just as nice as whoever sleeps in it with you.

GEORGE: I missed that. What was that, now?

(*He rests an arm on Ralph's shoulders.*)

RALPH: How would you like ev'ry time you wint t'bed with your wife, you had to imagine on the bed in the dark that it wasn't her on it with you, in the dark with you, but any one of a list of a thousand or so lovely lays? I done a despicable thing. I married a girl that had no attraction for me excepting I felt sorry for her and her old man's money! I got what I should have gotten: nothing! Just a goddam desk job at Regal Dairy Products, one of her daddy's business operations in Memphis, at eighty-five lousy rutten dollars a week! With my background? In the Air Force?

GEORGE: Man an air record will cut you no ice on the ground. All it leaves you is a—mysterious tremor. Come on back in. I'm freezing to death out here. I'll git her into that bathroom so we can talk.

(*He tosses the beer cans into yard.*)

RALPH: Don't y'know better'n to throw beer cans in a man's front yard?

(*He says this vaguely, glumly, as he follows George back into the cottage and shuts the door behind them. George goes to bedroom.*)

GEORGE (*entering*): Little Bit, you told me you couldn't wait to get under a good hot shower. There's a good shower in that bathroom. Why don't you go and get under that good hot shower?

ISABEL: I have a lot to think over, George.

GEORGE: Think it over under a good shower in that bedroom, will you? I want to take a bath, too.

ISABEL (*suddenly turning to face him from the bed*): George, I feel so lonely!

GEORGE: Yeah, and whose fault is that?

ISABEL: I don't know why I suddenly felt so lonely!

(*She sobs again. He regards her coolly from the door.*)

GEORGE: Little Bit, go in the bathroom and take your shower, so I can go take mine, or do you want us to go in and take one together?

(*She rises with a sigh and goes to bathroom door.*)

Naw, I didn't think so.

(*She enters the bathroom. He waits till the shower starts, then returns to the front room.*)

There now, she's in!

(*He shakes both fists in the air with a grimace of torment.*)

Look! I got to get rid of that girl. I got to get rid of her quick. Jesus, you got to help me. I can't stay with that girl.

RALPH: Man, you're married to her.

GEORGE: You're married to one! Where's yours? You son of a tail gun! Don't tell me I'm married to her when we ain't exchanged five remarks with each other since we drove out of Cape Girardeau where she refused to—has she come out of the bathroom? No!—Even *undress*! But huddled up in a chair all night in a blanket, crying? Because she had the misfortune to be my wife?

RALPH: I wouldn't count on it.

GEORGE: On what?

RALPH: Her thinking it's such a misfortune.

GEORGE: I described to you how we passed the night, last night!

RALPH: Is this girl a virgin?

GEORGE: She is a *cast-iron* virgin! And's going to stay one! Determined!

RALPH: I wouldn't count on that.

GEORGE: I would. I count on it. First thing I do tomorrow is pack her onto a plane back to Saint Louie.

RALPH: You must have done something to shock her.

GEORGE: That's the truth, I tried to sleep with her.

RALPH: Maybe you handled the little lady too rough.

GEORGE: Now don't talk to me like a wise old man of the mountain about how to deal with a woman. Who was it had to make dates for who at Big Springs and who was it even had to make arrangements for you with those Toyko dolls?

RALPH: That's not women, that's gash.

GEORGE: Gash are women.

RALPH: They are used women. You've got a unused woman and got to approach her as one.

GEORGE: She's gonna stay unused as far as I am concerned.

(*He stoops by the Christmas tree.*)

Now what the hell is this thing?

(*He has crouched among the toys under the tree.*)

RALPH: Rocket launcher. Miniature of the rocket-launchin' pad at Cape Canaveral.

GEORGE: No snow! How's it work?

RALPH: Gimme the countdown. I'll show you.

GEORGE: Ten. Nine. Eight. Seven. Six. Five. Four. Three. Two. OWW!

(*The rocket has fired in his face.*)

RALPH: Ain't you got sense enough to stand clear of a rocket launcher? Ha ha! Last week, just last week, I caught the little bugger playin' with a rag doll. Well. I snatched that doll away from him an' pitched it into the fireplace. He tried to pull it out an' burned his hand! Dotty called me a monster! The child screamed "I hate you!" an' kicked my shins black an' blue! But I'll be damned if any son of Ralph Bates will grow up playin' with dolls. Why, I'll bet you he rides this hawss side-saddle! Naw, a sissy tendency in a boy's got to be nipped in the bud, otherwise the bud will blossom.

GEORGE: I would prefer to have a little girl.

(*He says this wistfully, still rubbing his bruised forehead.*)

Little girls prefer Daddy. Female instinct comes out early in them.

RALPH: I wanted a boy but I'm not sure I got one. However, I got him a real red-blooded boy's Christmas, at no small expense for a man in my income bracket!

(*Isabel comes out of the bathroom.*)

I like the kid, I mean I—sure would suffer worse than he would if the neighborhood gang called him "Sissy!" I'm tolerant. By nature. But if I git partial custody of the kid, even one month in summer, I will correct the sissy tendency in him. Because in this world you got to be what your physical sex is or correct it in Denmark. I mean we got a *man's* world coming up, man! Technical! Terrific! And it's gotta be *fearless*! *Terrific!*

ISABEL: Mr. Bates.

GEORGE (*on his way to the door*): Whadaya want?

ISABEL: I called for Mistuh Bates.

GEORGE: Mistuh Bates, Mrs. Haverstick is anxious to talk to you, suh.

ISABEL: I just want to know if you have called the hotel.

RALPH (*entering*): Sure, sure, honey. Don't worry about a thing. Everything's gonna be fine.

ISABEL (*she is in a silk robe*): Thanks, Ralph. You've been awf'ly kind to me. Oh! I helped myself to a little Pepto-Bismol I found in your sweet little bathroom.

RALPH: Aw, that pink stuff? Take it all. I never touch it. It's Dorothea's. She used to get acid stomach.

ISABEL: It's very soothing.

(*George crosses to the bedroom door, head cocked, somewhat suspicious.*)

RALPH: Well, I cured her of that. I doubt that she's hit that Pepto-Bismol bottle once in the last five years.

ISABEL: I rarely suffer from an upset stomach. Rarely as snow in Memphis!

(*She laughs lightly.*)

But the human stomach is an emotional barometer with some people. Some get headaches, others get upset stomachs.

RALPH: Some even git diarrhea.

ISABEL: The combination of nervous strain and— Oh! What's this?

(*She picks up a gorgeously robed statue of the infant Jesus.*)

RALPH: Aw, that.

(*He moves farther into the bedroom. George moves closer to the door.*)

That's the infant of Prague. Prague, Czechoslovakia?

ISABEL: Oh?

RALPH: It was discovered there in the ruins of an old monastery. It has miraculous properties.

ISABEL: Does it?

RALPH: They say that it does. Whoever gives you the Infant of Prague gives you a piece of money to put underneath it for luck. Her father presented this infant to Dorothea so the piece of money was *naturally one penny.* It's s'posed to give you prosperity if you're not prosperous and a child if you're childless. It give us a child but the money is yet to come in, the money's just been goin' out. However, I don't blame the Infant of Prague for that, because—

ISABEL: Mr. Bates? Ralph? You know, very often people can be absolutely blind, stupid, and helpless about their own problems and still have a keen intuition about the problems of others?

RALPH: Yeah?

ISABEL: There is such a tender atmosphere in this sweet little house, especially this little bedroom, you can almost—

touch it, feel it! I mean you can *breathe* the tender atmosphere in it!

RALPH (*in a slow, sad drawl*): The color scheme in this bedroom is battleship gray. And will you notice the cute inscriptions on the twin beds? "His" on this one, "Hers" on that one? The linen's marked his and hers, too. Well. The space between the two beds was no-man's land for a while. Her psychological frigidity was like a, like a—artillery barrage!—between his and hers. I didn't try to break through it the first few nights. Nope. I said to myself, "Let *her* make the first move."

ISABEL: *Did* she?

RALPH: What do *you* think?

ISABEL: I think she *did*.

RALPH: *Right you are!*

(*He gives her a little congratulatory pat on the shoulder.*)

GEORGE: What's this heart-to-heart talk goin' on in here?

RALPH (*chuckling*): Come on out of here, boy. I got something to tell you.

(*He leads George out.*)

GEORGE: What were you up to in there?

RALPH (*whispering loudly*): Go in there, quick, before she gets dressed, you fool!

GEORGE: I'll be damned if I will!

RALPH: I'll turn the TV on loud.

ISABEL (*calling out*): I'll be dressed in a jiffy!

RALPH: Go ON! You just got a jiffy!

GEORGE: Yeah, and I've got some pride, too. She put me down last night, first woman ever to put me down in—

RALPH: I know, you told me, GO IN! Lock the door and—

GEORGE: YOU go in! That's what you WANT to do! I never had a girl yet that you didn't want to take over. This time you're welcome. GO IN! GO BACK IN AND BREATHE THE TENDER ATMOSPHERE OF THAT—

RALPH: Gawge? Hey— You're *shakin'*, man, you're shakin' to pieces! What kind of a son of a bitch d'you take me faw?

GEORGE: The kind which you are, which you always have been!

RALPH: She is right about you. You are not well, son. . . .

GEORGE: Where d'ya git this "son" stuff! Don't call me "son."

RALPH: Then grow up, will yuh! What's your drink? Same?

GEORGE: Same . . .

RALPH: You're shakin' because you want to go in that bedroom. GO IN! Take the bottle in with you! I'll sit here and watch TV till—

(*Isabel has put on her traveling suit. She comes into the living room.*)

—Too late *now*!

ISABEL (*in a sweet Texas drawl*): Mr. Bates? Ralph? It breaks my heart to see all those lovely child's toys under the tree and the little boy not here to have his Christmas.

RALPH: He's with his mother.

ISABEL: I know, but his Christmas is here.

RALPH: He's a Mama's boy. He's better off with his Mama.

ISABEL: How are *you* feeling, now, George?

> (*George grunts and turns to the bar.*
> (*Isabel makes a despairing gesture to Ralph.*
> (*George wheels about abruptly, suspecting some dumb-play.*
> (*Isabel laughs lightly and then sighs deeply.*)

GEORGE: I thought you'd set your heart on a single hotel room tonight.

ISABEL: George, you're shaking worse than I've even seen you.

GEORGE: That's, that's not your problem, that's—*my* problem, not *yours*!

RALPH (*to Isabel*): Honey? Come here a minute.

(*He whispers something to her.*)

ISABEL: Oh, no. No! Mr. Bates, you are confusing the function of a wife with that of a— I feel sorry, I feel very sorry for you not-so-young young men who've depended for love, for tenderness in your lives, on the sort of women available near army camps, in occupied territories! Mr. Bates? Ralph?

RALPH: Just take his hand and lead him into the—

ISABEL: RALPH! NO! BELIEVE ME!
RALPH: All right. . . .

(*There is a pause.*)

ISABEL: Ralph, why did you quit YOUR job? Did you get the
    shakes, too?
GEORGE: Don't get bitchy with him.
ISABEL: I WASN'T BEING BITCHY!
RALPH: She wasn't being bitchy. She asked a logical question.
ISABEL: Just a question!
GEORGE: Can't you mind your own business for a change?
    You got fired too, don't forget! All three of us here is
    jobless!
ISABEL: I am not forgetting.

(*Primly, with dignity.*)

I am not forgetting a thing, and I have a lot to remember.
GEORGE: Good. I hope you remember it. *Memorize* it!

(*He is getting tight.*)

ISABEL (*sniffling a little*): I think I caught cold in that car.
GEORGE: Hell, you were born with a cold—
ISABEL: *Stop that!*   (*Overlapping
GEORGE: In your damn little—   barely
ISABEL: MR. BATES, MAKE HIM STOP!   intelligible*)
RALPH: Let him blow off some steam.
GEORGE: Incurable cold! You didn't catch it from me.
ISABEL: I wish you had shown this side of your nature before,
    just a hint, just a clue, so I'd have known what I was in for.
GEORGE: What hint did you give *me*? What clue did *I* have to
    your nature?
ISABEL: Did I disguise my nature?
GEORGE: You sure in hell did.
ISABEL: In what *way*, tell me, please!
GEORGE: You didn't put the freeze on me at Barnes Hospital!

(*To Ralph.*)

She was nurse at Barnes when I went there for those tests?
To find out the cause of my shakes? She was my night nurse
at Barnes.

ISABEL: Oh, stop! Don't be so crude! How can you be so crude?

GEORGE: She was my night nurse at Barnes and gave me alcohol rubdowns at bedtime.

ISABEL: That was my job. I had to.

GEORGE: Hell, she stroked and petted me with her hands like she had on a pair of silk gloves.

ISABEL: This is insufferable. I am going downtown.

(*She covers her face, sobbing.*)

Just give me carfare downtown.

GEORGE: You remember those dolls with silk gloves on their hands in Tokyo, Ralph? Hell, she could of given them Jap dolls lessons!

ISABEL: I DID NOT TOUCH YOUR BODY EXCEPT AS A NURSE HIRED TO DO IT! YOU KNOW I DIDN'T! I DID NOT TOUCH YOUR BIG OLD LECHEROUS BODY.

GEORGE: How'd you give me a rubdown without touching my body? Huh? How could you give me rubdowns without touching my body? Huh?

ISABEL: Please, please, make him be still. Mr. Bates? You believe me? He's making out I seduced him while I was his nurse.

GEORGE: I didn't say that. Don't say I said that. I didn't say that. I said you had soft little fingers and you knew what you were doing. She'd say, "Turn over." I couldn't turn over. I had to stay on my stomach. I was embarrassed not to.

ISABEL: Ah—I feel nauseated. What filth you have in your mind!

RALPH: Honey? Little lady? Come over and sit here with me. All this will all straighten out. It's going to be all straightened out.

(*George pours himself a drink. The glass slips out of his shaking fingers.*)

GEORGE: *Worse than ever, worse than ever before!* How could I have kept that job? A ground mechanic with hands that can't hold tools?

ISABEL: Go take your tranquillizers. They're in my zipper bag.

GEORGE: Oh, Jesus.

RALPH (*picking up the dropped glass*): See, honey? That boy isn't well. Make some allowances for him. You're both nice kids, both of you, wonderful people. And very good-looking people. I'm afraid you're doomed to be happy for a long time together, soon as this little period of adjustment that you're going through right now passes over.

(*George holds his violently shaking hands in front of him, staring at them fiercely.*
(*He goes to the bedroom.*)

ISABEL: May I call my father, collect?

RALPH: Don't call home, now. Why upset the old people on Christmas Eve?

ISABEL: I'll just say I miss them and want to come home for Christmas.

RALPH: They'll know something's wrong if you go home without your brand-new husband.

ISABEL: Husband! What husband? That man who describes me as a Tokyo whore? Implies that I seduced him in a hospital because I was required to give him alcohol rubdowns at night?

RALPH: All he meant was you excited him, honey.

ISABEL: I assure you that was *not* my intention! I am naturally gentle, I am gentle by nature, and if my touch on his big lecherous body created—*sexual fantasies* in his *mind*!—that's hardly *my* fault, is it?

GEORGE (*returning*): I am sorry that I upset you.

ISABEL: Will you tell him the truth?

GEORGE: Sure I will. What about?

ISABEL: Did I deliberately excite you in Barnes Hospital?

GEORGE: No. I never said that.

ISABEL: Anybody that heard you would get that impression.

GEORGE: You didn't deliberately do it, you just did it because I was horny for you, that's all, that's all, that's—all. . . .

(*He slumps in a chair with a long, despairing sigh.*
(*There is a silent pause.*)

ISABEL: I don't blame you alone, George. I blame myself, too. Not for deliberate sexual provocation, but for not realizing before our marriage yesterday that we were—opposite types.

GEORGE (*sadly*): Yes, opposite types. . . .

ISABEL: *I want to talk to my father!*

GEORGE: Talk to him. Call him. I'll pay Ralph the charges.

ISABEL: May I?

RALPH: Sure, honey, call your folks and wish 'em a Merry Christmas.

ISABEL: Thank you. I will if I can stop crying.

RALPH: George? This little girl needs you. Go on, be nice to her, boy.

GEORGE: I need somebody, too. She hasn't got the incurable shakes, *I* have, *I* got 'em! Was *she* nice to *me*? *Last night*?

ISABEL (*tearfully*): Operator? I want to call long distance, Sweetwater, Texas. Oh-seven-oh-three. No, anybody that answers. It will be Daddy, Mama can't get out of—

(*She sobs.*)

—bed!

(*Ralph makes a sign to George to go over and sit by her. George disregards the suggestion.*)

RALPH: You better hang up and let them call you back. Long distance is very busy on Christmas Eve. Everyone callin' the home folks.

ISABEL: I just hope I stop crying! I don't want Daddy to hear me.

(*She pauses.*)

Poor ole thing. So sweet and faithful to Mama, bedridden with arthritis for seven years, now . . . Hello? What? Oh. You'll call me back when you complete the connection, will you, because it's very important, it's really very urgent. . . .

(*She hangs up. There is silence.*)

RALPH (*finally*): One bad night in a rutten highway motel and you all are acting like born enemies toward each other!

GEORGE: Don't upset her, she's going to talk to her daddy. And tell him she's married to a stinker.

ISABEL: No, I'm not. I'm going to tell him that I am blissfully happy, married to the kindest man in the world, the second kindest, the kindest man next to my daddy!

GEORGE: Thanks.

ISABEL: Waits hand and foot on Mama, bedridden with arthritis.

GEORGE: You told Ralph about that.

ISABEL: And has held down a job in a pharmacy all these years. . . .

GEORGE: Wonderful. I didn't expect to marry a girl in love with her father.

ISABEL: George Haverstick, you are truly a monster!

> (*The phone rings.*
> (*She snatches it up.*)

What?—DAD! OH, PRECIOUS DADDY!

(*She bursts into violent tears.*)

Can't talk, can't talk, can't talk, can't talk, *can't—talk!*

RALPH: Honey, gi' me the phone!

(*She surrenders it to him.*)

Hello? Hi, Pop, merry Christmas. No, this isn't George, this is a buddy of his. Isabel wants to talk to you to tell you how happy she is, but she just broke up with emotion. You know how it is, don't you, Pop? Newlyweds? They're naturally full of emotion. They got to go through a little period of adjustment between them.——Fine, yes, she's fine. She'll talk to you soon as she blows her nose. Hey, honey? Your daddy wants to talk to you.

(*She takes the phone, then bursts into violent sobbing again, covering her mouth and handing the phone back to Ralph.*)

Pop? I'll have to talk for her. She's all shook up.

(*He forces the phone back into Isabel's hand.*)

ISABEL (*choked*): Dad?

(*She bawls again, covering the mouthpiece. Ralph takes the phone back from her.*)

RALPH: Pop? Just talk to her, Pop. She's too shook up to talk back.

(*He forces the phone into her hands again.*)

ISABEL: Dad? How are you, Daddy? Are you? That's wonderful, Daddy. Oh, I'm fine, too. I got married yesterday.
Yesterday . . . How is Mom? Just the same? Daddy? I may
be seeing you soon. Yes. You know I gave up my nursing
job at Barnes when I married and so I have lots of free
time and I might just suddenly pop in on you—*tomorrow!*
——I love you and miss you so much! Good-by, Merry
Christmas, Daddy!

(*She hangs up blindly and goes over to the Christmas tree.*)

I think it's awful your little boy's missing his Christmas.
Such a wonderful Christmas. A choo-choo train with depot
and tunnel, cowboy outfit, chemical set and a set of alphabet blocks. . . .

GEORGE: He knows what he got for his kid, you don't have
to tell him.

(*There is a pause.*)

ISABEL: Well, now, I feel better, after talking to Daddy.

GEORGE: Does it make you feel uplifted, spiritually?

ISABEL: I feel less lonely. That's all.

GEORGE: I wonder if it would have that effect on me if I
called my daddy or mama in Amarillo? That's in Texas, too.
Maybe I'd feel less lonely. Huh, Little Bit?

(*She starts out.*)

Just wait a minute. I want to tell you something. In my
thirty-four years I've been with a fair share of women and
you are the first, you are the first of the lot, that has found
me repulsive.

ISABEL: I don't find you "repulsive," not even your vanity,
George, silly but not repulsive.

RALPH: Hey, now, you all quit this.

GEORGE: Can you stand there and tell me you find me attractive?

ISABEL: I'm afraid I can't, at this moment.

GEORGE: Well, goddam it, what in hell did you marry me
faw?

ISABEL: Mr. Bates, your animal is standing by the door as as
if it wants out. Shall I let it out for you?

RALPH: You two are just goin' through this adjustment period that all young couples go through.

ISABEL: Such a sweet animal! What is this animal's name?

GEORGE: The animal is a dog.

ISABEL: I know it's a dog.

GEORGE: Then why don't you call it a dog!

RALPH: Better put 'er lead on 'er. Her name is Bess.

ISABEL: Shall we take a walk, Bessie? Huh? A nice little run in the snow. See! She does want out. Oh! My coat. . . .

RALPH: Here, put on this one, honey.

(*He takes the beaver coat out of the Christmas box under the tree.*)

ISABEL: Oh, what beautiful sheared beaver! It's your wife's Christmas present?

RALPH: It was but it ain't no more.

ISABEL: How soft! Now I know that you love her. You couldn't feel the softness of this fur and not know it was bought as a present for someone you love.

RALPH: Put it on. It's yours. A wedding present to you.

ISABEL: Oh, no I—

RALPH: WILL YOU PLEASE PUT IT ON YUH?

ISABEL: I guess the snow won't hurt it. Come on, Bessie, that's a good lady, come on. . . .

(*She goes out.*)

GEORGE: I know of *two* animals that want out and one of them ain't no dawg!

ISABEL (*returning*): I heard you say that!

GEORGE: Well, good.

ISABEL: If you want out of our marriage, a divorce isn't necessary. We can just get an annulment! So maybe last night was fortunate after all!

(*She stares at him a moment and then goes back out with the dog. As they leave, the dog is barking at something outside.*
(*George comes up beside Ralph and rests an affectionate arm on his shoulders.*
(*The tempo now becomes very fast.*)

RALPH: You old Texas jack rabbit!

GEORGE: You tail-gunner son of a— How you feel?

RALPH: I feel fine!

(They chuckle shyly together. Then:
(They catch each other in an affectionate bear hug.)

GEORGE: How much money you got?

RALPH: Why?

GEORGE: Remember how we talked about going into something together when we got out of the service? Well, we're out of the service. How much money do you think you can raise?

RALPH: What are *your* assets, Buddy?

GEORGE: I've saved five hundred dollars and can get a thousand for that '52 Caddy.

RALPH: You can't go into no business on as little as that.

GEORGE: You're selling out this house and everything in it, ain't you?

RALPH: I'd have to split it with Dorothea, I reckon.

GEORGE: Look. Let's cut out tomorrow. Let's go to Texas together. We can swing the financing to pick up a piece of ranchland near San Antone and raise us a herd of fine cattle.

RALPH: Why San Antone?

GEORGE: I said near it. It's a beautiful town. A winding river goes through it.

RALPH: Uh-huh. You mentioned "swing the financing." How did you—visualize—that?

GEORGE: Noticed my car out there?

RALPH: That funeral limousine?

GEORGE: We cut out of here tomorrow bright and early and drive straight through to West Texas. In West Texas we git us a colored boy, put a showfer's cap on him an' set him back of the wheel. He drives us up in front of the biggest San Antone bank and there we demand an immediate interview with the president of it. My folks staked out West Texas. The name of the first George Haverstick in West Texas is engraved on the memorial tablet to the Alamo heroes in San Antone! I'm not snowin' you, man! An' they's no better credit card in West Texas than an ancestor's name on that memorial tablet. We will arrive at lunch time an'—invite this bank executive to lunch at the San Antone country club to which I can git us a guest card an' befo' we're in sight of the golf links the financing deal will be swung!

RALPH: Man, a bank president has rode in a awful lot of funeral processions. It's almost one of his main professional duties. He's rode in too many funeral limousines not to know when he's in one. And ain't you afraid that he might, well—notice your shakes?

GEORGE: This little tremor would disappear completely the moment I crossed into Texas!

RALPH: I hope so, man, permanently and completely, but—

GEORGE: Go on. Tear down the project!

RALPH: There's no Ralph Bates, first, second, third, fourth or fifth on that memorial tablet to those—Alamo heroes.

GEORGE: Haven't you blazoned your name in the memory of two wars?

RALPH: Who remembers two wars? Or even one, after some years. There's a great public amnesia about a former war hero.

(*He goes reflectively to the front door.*)

GEORGE: Where you goin'?

RALPH: I'm goin' out to think in this cool night air.

(*He exits onto the paved terrace, switching off the interior lights. George follows gravely. Ralph stoops to light up a string of colored bulbs that cover the arched entrance to carport.*

(*It casts a dim rainbow glow on the terrace. Shadowy flakes of snow drift through it.*)

Why San Antone? Why cattle? Why not electric equipment?

GEORGE: I know San Antone and cattle!

RALPH: And I know electric equipment.

GEORGE: Yes, you can turn on a set of little Christmas tree lights.

RALPH: I don't want to be your ranch hand!

GEORGE: We'd buy in *equal.*

RALPH: How? One minute you say you'll liquidate all your assets that only appear to be an old funeral car, the next you say we'll drive a bank president out in this funeral car, and you want me to put up all that I realize on the sale of this

property here? Your sense of equity is very unequal, and
shit-fire anyhow, even if I sell this property, by remote control, from Hong Kong, and Dotty's folks would sure in
hell block the transaction—well, look at the cracks in this
stucco, y'know how they got there? This Goddam High
Point suburb—*listen!*—happens to be built over a great big
underground cavern into which it is *sinking*!

GEORGE: *Sinking?*

RALPH: I'm not snowing you, man, this whole community
here is gradually sinking, inch by inch by year, into this
subterranean cavern and the property owners and the
real-estate promoters are in collusion to keep this secret
about it: so we can sell out to the next bunch of suckers:
DISGUSTING!

GEORGE: Built over a—

RALPH: *Cavern: yes!—a big subterranean cavern*, but so is
your project, not to mention your *marriage. Cattle!—
Cattle?*

GEORGE: The Texas Longhorn isn't just cattle, it's a—dignified beast.

RALPH: Did you say Texas Longhorn? Son, the Texas
Longhorn is not only dignified, it is *obsolete.*

GEORGE: Historical, yeah, like the Haversticks of West Texas.

RALPH: The Haversticks of West Texas are not yet obsolete,
are they?

GEORGE: I am the last one of 'em an' the prospects of another don't look bright at this moment. But the Texas
Longhorn—

(*He exhales.*)

—compared to modern beef cattle such as your Hereford
or your Black Angus—it has no carcass value.

RALPH: Well, in that case, why don't you *breed* the Black
Angus or the—

GEORGE: I anticipated that question.

RALPH: I hope you're prepared with some answer. . . .

GEORGE (*draws on cigarette and flips it away*): Le' me put it
this way. How would you like to breed a herd of noble cattle, a herd that stood for the frontier days of this country!
—an' ride to the depot one mawnin' in your station wagon,

the name of your ranch stamped on it, to watch these great, dignified beasts being herded onto a string of flatcars, penned in and hauled off to K City packin' houses, Chicago slaughterhouses, the shockin' atrocities which cannot even be thought about without a shudder!—an' wave 'em good-by as if they was off for a mother-lovin' church picnic?

RALPH: It's it's a—heart-breakin' pitcher!

(*He chuckles.*)

But I do love a good steak, ha ha! A prime-cut sirloin, however— What would you want to breed this noble herd for? For *kicks*, for—?

GEORGE: *You* got TV in there, ain't you? Turn on your TV any late afternoon or early evenin' and what do you get—beside the commercials, I mean? A goddam Western, on film. Y'know what I see, outside the camera range? A big painted sign that says: "Haverstick-Bates Ranch"—or "Bates-Haverstick," you can have top billing!—"The Last Stand of the Texas Longhorn, a Dignified Beast! We breed cattle for TV Westerns." We breed us some buffalo, too. The buffalo is also a dignified beast, almost extinct, only thirty thousand head of the buffalo left in this land. We'll increase that number by a sizable fraction. Hell, we could double that number befo' we—

RALPH: Hang up our boots an' saddles under the—dignified sky of West Texas?

GEORGE (*with feeling*): There *is* dignity in that sky! There's dignity in the agrarian, the pastoral—way of—existence! A dignity too long lost out of the—American dream—

(*He is shaking a good deal with emotion.*)

—as it used to be in the West Texas–Haverstick days. . . .

RALPH: But I want to be dignified, too.

GEORGE: Human dignity's what I'm—

RALPH: I don't want to be caught short by a Texas Longhorn while crossing a pasture one mawnin' in West Texas! Ha ha ha. Naw, I don't want to catch me an ass full of Texas Longhorns before I can jump a fence rail out of that West Texas pasture. I—

GEORGE: SHUT UP! WILL YUH? YOU TV WATCHIN', CANNED-BEER DRINKIN', SPANISH-SUBURBAN-STUCCO-TYPE SON OF— Y'KNOW I THINK BEER IS DOPED? DOPED? I THINK THEY DOPE IT TO CREATE A NATIONAL TOLERANCE OF THE TV COMMERCIAL! No— No— I'm sorry I come through Memphis. . . .

(*He moves away, sadly.*)

I cherished a memory of you—

(*Carolers are heard from a distance.*)

—idolized an old picture of which I was suddenly faced with a, with a—*goddam travesty* of it!—When you opened the door and I was confronted with a—DEFEATED! MIDDLE-AGED! NEGATIVE! LOST!—poor bastard . . .

RALPH: What do you think I saw when I opened that door? A ghostly apparition!

GEORGE: ME?

RALPH: A young man I used to know with an old man's af-fliction: the palsy!

GEORGE: Thanks!—I appreciate that.

(*Next door the Carolers sing: "God Rest Ye Merry, Gentle-men, May Nothing Ye Dismay!"*)

Oh, man, oh brother, I sure do appreciate that!

(*He sits down quickly, shaking fiercely, in a metal porch chair, turning it away from Ralph to face the audience. Ralph is immediately and truly contrite.*)

Yeah. In addition to those other changes I mentioned in you, you've now exposed another which is the worst of the bunch. You've turned *vicious*!

RALPH: Aw, now—

GEORGE: Yeah, yeah, bitter and vicious! To ridicule an afflic-tion like *mine*, like *this*, is vicious, *vicious*!

(*He holds up his shaky hand. Ralph reaches his hand out to take it but doesn't. Instead he drops his hand on George's shoulder.*)

Take that mother-grabbin' hand off my shoulder or I'll break it off you!

RALPH: You ridiculed *my* afflictions.

GEORGE: What afflictions?

RALPH: My life has been an affliction.

(*He says this without self-pity, simply as a matter of fact.*)

GEORGE: Now don't make me cry into this can of Budweiser
with that sad, sad story of your childhood in that home for
illegitimate orphans.

RALPH: *Foundlings!* Home. I was not illegitimate.

GEORGE: Foundlings are illegitimate.

RALPH: Not—*necessarily—always* . . .

(*He says this with a humility that might be touching to anyone less absorbed in his own problems than George. Ralph looks
up at the drift of snow from the dark.*)

No, I meant to live a life in a Spanish-type stucco cottage
in a—high point over a cavern, that is an affliction for
someone that wanted and dreamed of—*oh, I wish I could be
the first man in a moon rocket!* No, not the moon, but
Mars, Venus! Hell, I'd like to be transported and trans-
planted to colonize and fertilize, to be the Adam on a—star
in a different *galaxy*, yeah, that far away even!—it's wonderful knowing that such a thing is no longer inconceiv-
able, huh?

GEORGE: You're talking out of character. You're a dedicated
conformist, the most earthbound earth man on earth.

RALPH: If you think that about me, you never known me.

GEORGE (*starts off the terrace*): I'm going walking, alone!

(*He stops abruptly.*)

Naw, if she sees me walking, she'll think I'm out looking
for her.

RALPH: Goddam it, why don't you? Intercept her and don't
say a word, just stick your hand inside that beaver-skin coat
I give her and apply a little soft pressure to her—solar
plexus—putting your other arm around her waist, and
bring her back here, gently. . . .

GEORGE: That's what *you* want to do. Go on, *you* intercept
her! And bring her back here gently!

RALPH: O.K., I *would* like to do it. But do you think I'd *do* it?

GEORGE: Can you honestly say you wouldn't put the make on her if you thought she'd give in?

RALPH: Nope! I wouldn't do it. And if you don't believe me, git back in that funeral hack and drive to West Texas in it, you—*legitimate* bastard.

GEORGE: Nope, I don't think you would. You're too much of a square.

RALPH: *There's her! There she is!*

GEORGE: Where?

RALPH: Corner. Why's she turning around? She must be lost, go get her. Look. She's joining the carolers!

GEORGE: Good, let her stay with them, and sing! Carols!

RALPH: Naw, I better go get her.

GEORGE: Go and get your *own* wife: leave mine alone!

(*Ralph puts his arm around George's shoulder.*)

And I told you to keep your rutten hand off my shoulder.

RALPH: Break it off me.

GEORGE: What I mean is, the point is—you *chose* your afflictions! Married into them. Mine I didn't choose! It just come on me, mysteriously: my shakes. You wouldn't even be interested in the awful implications of an affliction like mine.

(*He holds up his shaking hand.*)

RALPH: Sure, I'm interested in it, but—

GEORGE: S'pose it never lets up? This thing they can't treat or even find the cause of! S'pose I shake all my life like, like — dice in a crap shooter's fist?—Huh?—I mean at all moments of tension, all times of crisis, I shake! . . . Huh? And there's other aspects to it beside the career side. It could affect my love life. Huh? I could start shaking so hard when I started to make out with a girl that I couldn't do it. You know? Couldn't make the scene with her. . . .

(*There is a slight pause.*)

RALPH: Aw. Was that it?

GEORGE: Was what what?

RALPH: Was that the trouble at the Old Man River Motel, last night, you were scared of impotence with her? Was that the problem?

GEORGE: I don't have that problem. I *never* had that problem.

RALPH: No?

GEORGE: *No!*

(*Tense pause.*)

WHY? Do *you* have that problem?

RALPH: Sometimes. I wasn't excited enough by Dotty to satisfy her, sometimes. . . .

GEORGE: The thought of her old man's money couldn't always excite you?

RALPH: Nope, it couldn't always, that's the truth.

(*He switches off the lights, senselessly, and switches them back on again.*)

Poor ole Dotty. She's got so she always wants it and when I can't give it to her I feel guilty, guilty. . . .

(*He turns the Christmas lights off again, turns them back on again.*)

GEORGE: Well, you know *me*. An Eveready battery, built-in in me.

RALPH (*turning to him with a slow, gentle smile*): Yeah, I understand, son.

GEORGE: *Don't be so damned understanding!*

RALPH: Well, there she goes—Mrs. George Haverstick the Fifth. Look. She's going up to the wrong Spanish-type stucco cottage, there's five almost identical ones in this block.

GEORGE: Don't your dawg know where it lives?

RALPH: Aw, it's a dignified beast. A constant Frigidaire pointer. Points at the Westinghouse Frij an' whines for a handout whenever you enter the kitchen. Knows everyone on the block an' pays calls like a new preacher wherever he thinks—

(*Whistles at dog*)

—he might be offered a—

(*Whistles*)

—handout.

(*Voices down the block, hearty, drunken.*)

You better go git your wife. That Spanish-type stucco cottage is occupied by a bachelor decorator and you know how they destroy wimmen. . . . He is running a sort of a unofficial USO at his house. Service men congregate there.

GEORGE: HAH!

(*He is amused by the picture.*)

RALPH: I got to climb back in a back window because you shut this door and I had put the catch on it.

(*He crosses out the door to the carport as George gazes gravely off.*

(*The Carolers are closer. They go into "God Rest Ye Merry, Gentlemen" again.*

(*George is not inclined to be merry. He glares into the starless air.*

(*In the bedroom, a windowpane is smashed and Ralph's arm reaches through, his fingers groping for the window latch. He finds it, gets the window up and clambers through with some muttered invectives against the hostility of the inanimate objects of the world. As soon as he enters the interior, light and sound inside are brought up. Oddly enough, a TV Western is in progress, approaching the climax of an Indian attack or a cattle stampede. It catches Ralph's attention. He turns gravely to the TV set, for the moment forgetting George outside. Gunfire subsides and the dialogue is brought up loud:*)

DIALOGUE

—Save your ammunition, they'll come back.

—HOW LONG HAVE WE GOT?

—Till sundown. They'll hit us again after dark.

—Let's make a run for it now!

—We'll have to abandon the wagons if we make a run for it. The Rio Grande is at least five miles south of here.

—Mount the women, one woman behind each man on the hawses, unhitch the hawses! Then stampede the cattle. That'll give us a cover while we make our break.

—What is our chances, you think?

—You want a *honest* answer or a *comforting* answer?

—Give me the honest answer.

—The comforting answer would have been fifty-fifty: I'll leave you to imagine the honest answer.

—Rosemary? Come here, a minute. Take this pistol. There's five shots in it. Save the fifth shot for yourself. Now git on this hawss behind me.

—Oh, Buck! I'm so scared!

—*Git up!* O.K. sweetheart?

—Yes!

—Hold onto me tight. Dusty, when I count ten, start the cattle stampede.

(*He starts counting, slowly.*)

GEORGE (*to himself as he paces the terrace*): Now I don't even want her. If she asked me for it, I wouldn't give it to her, the way I feel now.

(*Sneezes.*)

Catchin' a cold out here! What's he doing in there, the motherless bastard? BATES! REMEMBER ME?

RALPH (*opening the door*): I thought you'd gone faw your wife.

(*Ralph chuckles and holds the front door open as George withdraws his head from the window and reappears a moment later on the terrace.*
(*Ralph lets him in.*)

GEORGE: Will you look at that? A Western on Christmas eve, even! It's a goddam NATIONAL OBSESSIONAL.

RALPH: Yep, a national homesickness in the American heart for the old wild frontiers with the yelping redskins and the covered wagons on fire and—

GEORGE: Will you look at those miserable shorthorn cattle! Those cows, in this corny Western?

(*They both face the TV. There is a pause.*)

RALPH: Yep—an undignified beast. Man? Buddy? I don't have too much confidence in the project of the Dignified West Texas Longhorn Ranch, even now, but I will go along with you. Don't ask me why. I couldn't tell you why, but I will go along with you. Want to shake on it, Buddy?

GEORGE: That champagne ought to be cold now, let's break out that champagne now.

RALPH: It'll be still colder when you've picked up your wife.

GEORGE: I told you my policy, don't interfere with it, huh?

RALPH: Women are vulnerable creatures.

GEORGE: So's a man.

RALPH (*crosses to the kitchenette door*): I'll open up the champagne while you pick up your wife.

GEORGE: Ralpho? Man?

RALPH: Huh?

GEORGE: Now I know why I come here. You're a *decent! square!*

(*The kitchen door swings closed on them; Carolers are singing out front. After a moment Isabel appears before the house with the dog.*)

(*A Lady Caroler appears on the terrace with a collection plate.*)

ISABEL: Oh—I'm afraid I don't have any money to give you, but—

(*She knocks at the door.*)

Wait!—till they answer the door, I—

(*Raucous voices are heard within.*)

—Some people regard the celebration of the birthday of Jesus as a, as a—sort of a—occasion, excuse for!—just getting drunk and—*disgusting!* I'll probably have to go round the back to get in. . . .

(*Great howls of hilarity have been coming from the back of the cottage, drowning out Isabel's efforts to draw attention to the front door.*)

I'm very sorry, I just don't have any money.

(*The Caroler accepts this in good grace and leaves.*

(Isabel goes around through the carport. A few seconds later George, in a state of Wild West exuberance, comes charging out of the kitchen with the champagne bottle, shouting:)

GEORGE: POWDER RIVER, POWWWWW-der RIV-errrr!—a mile wide and—

RALPH: TWO INCHES DEEP!

(He follows him out as Isabel's head appears through the open window in the dim bedroom: she lifts the dog through and hoists herself over the sill.)

GEORGE: Git me a pitcher with ice and two cans of that Ballantine's ale and I will make us BLACK VELVET!

RALPH: Huh?

GEORGE: Man, you know Black Velvet!

(He is back in the kitchen.)

I made it that time in Hong Kong when we had those girls from the—

(Ralph has gone in behind him. The door swings shut as Isabel picks up the bedside phone in the bedroom.)

ISABEL: Operator? I want a cab right away, it's an *emergency, yaiss!*

(Slight pause.)

Yellow Cab? Checkered! Well, please send a cab right away to— Oh, my goodness, I can't tell you the address, oh, I'll—I'll find out the address and I'll call you right back, right away. . . .

(She hangs up with a little stricken cry, followed by convulsive sobs that she stifles forcibly. On the bed, in the pink-shaded lamplight, she looks like a little girl making a first discovery of life's sorrow. Instinctively she reaches out for the Infant of Prague; at the same time, the Carolers start singing below the terrace: "I Wonder as I Wander." This is a sentimental moment, but not "sticky.")

Little Boy Jesus, so lonesome on your birthday. I know how you feel, *exactly!*—

(*She clasps the infant to her breast, tenderly.*)

—just exactly, because I feel the same way. . . .

Dim Out

INTERMISSION

ACT THREE

No time lapse.
The men return with an open, foaming bottle of champagne,
and pass it back and forth between them before the fireplace, not
noticing that the dog has returned or suspecting Isabel's presence
in the bedroom.

GEORGE: I put them in five categories. Those that worship it,
those that love it, those that just like it, those that don't
like it, those that just tolerate it, those that *don't* tolerate it,
those that can't stand it, and, finally, those that not only
can't stand it but want to cut it off you.

RALPH (*following him with glasses, chuckling*): That's more
than five categories.

GEORGE: How many did I name?

RALPH: I don't know. I lost count.

GEORGE: Well, you know what I mean. And I have married
into that last category. What scares me is that she has had
hospital training and is probably able to do a pretty good
cutting job. You know what I mean?

RALPH: Ha ha, yeah. Wel-l-l. . . .

(*He sets the glasses down and takes the bottle from George. The*
little parlor is flickering with firelight.)

GEORGE: Which class did you marry into? Into the same
category?

RALPH: No. She got to like it. More than I did even.

GEORGE: Now you're braggin'.

RALPH: Love is a very difficult—occupation. You got to work
at it, man. It ain't a thing every Tom, Dick and Harry has

got a true aptitude for. Y'know what I mean? Not every Tom, Dick or Harry understands how to use it. It's not a—offensive weapon. It shouldn't be used like one. Too many guys, they use it like a offensive weapon to beat down a woman with. All right. That rouses resistance. Because a woman has pride, even a woman has pride and resents being raped, and most love-making is rape with these self-regarded—experts! That come downstairs yelling, "Oh, man, Oh, brother," and hitching their belts up like they'd accomplished something.

GEORGE (*getting the allusion and resentful*): You mean me?

RALPH: Naw, naw, will yuh listen a minute? I've got ideas on this subject.

GEORGE: A self-regarded expert!

RALPH: You know Goddam right I'm an expert. I know I never had your good looks but made out better.

GEORGE: One man's opinion!

RALPH: Look! Lissen! You got to use—TENDERNESS!—with it, not roughness like raping, snatch-and-grab roughness but true tenderness with it or—

GEORGE: O.K., build yourself up! If that's what you need to!

RALPH: Naw, now, lissen! You know I know what I'm sayin'!

GEORGE: Sure, self-regarded expert!

(*They are both pretty high now.*)

RALPH: I know what went wrong last night at that Cape Girardeau motel as well as if I had seen it all on TV!

GEORGE: What went wrong is that I found myself hitched up with a woman in the "cut-it-off" category!

(*Isabel is listening to all this in the bedroom. She stands up and sits down, stands up and sits down, barely able to keep from shouting something.*)

RALPH: Aw, naw, aw, naw. I will tell you what happened. Drink your champagne. What happened, man, is this! You didn't appreciate the natural need for using some tenderness with it. Lacking confidence with it, you wanted to hit her, smash her, clobber her with it. You've got violence in you! That's what made you such a good fighter pilot, the best there was! Sexual violence, that's what gives you the shakes, that's what makes you unstable. That's what made you just sit on the straw mats with the Tokyo dolls, drinking sake with them, teaching them English till it was time to come downstairs and holler, "Oh, man, oh, brother" like you had laid them to waste!

(*There is a slight pause. George is sweating, flushed.*)

GEORGE: Who in hell ever told you I—
RALPH: I heard it directly from them. You just sat up there drinkin' sake with 'em an' teachin' 'em English, and then you'd come down shouting, "Oh, man, oh, brother!" like you had laid 'em to waste.
GEORGE: Which of them told you this story?
RALPH: *Which* of them? ALL! EV'RY ONE!

(*They pause. Isabel sits down on the bed again, raises her hands to either side of her face, slowly shaking her head with a gradual comprehension.*)

GEORGE: Man, at this moment I'd like to bust your face in!
RALPH: I'm tryin' to help you. Don't you know that I am tryin' t' help you?

(*A pause. They look away from each other in solemn reverie for some moments. Isabel rises again from the bed but still doesn't move. After some moments she sits back down. She is crying now.*)

RALPH (*continuing gently*): You have got this problem.
GEORGE: In Tokyo I never told you—
RALPH: What?
GEORGE: I was choosy. I had a girl on the side. I mean a nice one. One that I wanted to keep to myself, strictly. I didn't want to expose her to a bunch of—
RALPH: Aw, now, man, you don't have to start fabricating some kind of a *Sayonara* fantasy like this!
GEORGE: How about Big Springs, Texas?
RALPH: What about Big Springs, Texas, besides being boring, I mean, what *else* about it?
GEORGE: Plenty. I fixed you up there. You never got nowhere in Big Springs, Texas, till I opened it up for you.
RALPH: Baby, don't be sore.

GEORGE: Sore, I'm not sore. You've done your damndest to make me feel like a phony, but I'm not sore. *You're* sore. Not *me. I'm* not sore.

RALPH: You sure are shaking.

GEORGE: Yeah, well, I got this tremor. . . . Jesus, my goddam voice is got the shakes too! But you know it's the truth, in Big Springs, Texas, we had the best damn time you ever had in your life, and I broke the ice there, for you.

RALPH: I don't deny that women naturally like you. Everybody likes you! Don't you know that? People never low-rate you! Don't you know that? I like you. That's for sure. But I hate to see you shaking because of—

GEORGE (*cutting in*): Look! We're both free now. Like two birds. You're gonna cut out of this High Point over a Cavern. And we'll buy us a piece of ranchland near San Antone and both of us—

RALPH: Yeah, yeah, let's go back to what we wuh tawkin' about. *Tenderness.* With a *woman.*

GEORGE: I don't want to hear a goddam lecture from you about such a thing as that when here you are, night before Christmas, with just a cocker spaniel and presents under a tree, with no one to *take* them from you!

RALPH (*abruptly*): *Hey!*

GEORGE: *Huh?*

RALPH: Th' *dawg* is back. How *come?*

GEORGE: The dawg come *back,* tha's all. . . .

(*Isabel comes out of the bedroom in coat and hat.*)

ISABEL: Yes, I brought the dog back.

(*A pause, rather long.*)

RALPH: We, uh, we—saw you going up to the wrong— Spanish-type cottage. . . .

ISABEL: I haven't discovered the *right* one, Mr. Bates.

RALPH: I ain't discovered it either.

GEORGE: What kept you so long in the wrong one?

ISABEL: They invited me in and made me sit down to a lovely buffet supper while they looked up the High Point Bates in the phone book.

(*She pauses.*)

I heard your very enlightening conversation from the bedroom. You're a pair of small boys. Boasting, bragging, showing off to each other. . . . I want to call a cab. I'm going downtown, George.

(*He crosses unsteadily to the phone, lifts it and hands it to her with an effort at stateliness.*)

Thank you.

(*To Ralph*)

Do you know the cab number?

GEORGE: Whacha want, yellow, checkered or what? I'll git it for yuh!

RALPH: Put down th' phone.

ISABEL: I'll get one.

(*She dials the operator.*)

GEORGE: Leave her alone. Let her go downtown. She's free to.

(*Ralph takes the phone from her and puts it back in the cradle.*)

ISABEL: Do I have to walk?

(*She goes to the door, opens it and starts out.*)

There's a car in front of your house, Mr. Bates.

RALPH (*rising with sudden energy and rushing to the door*): YEP! IT'S HER OLD MAN'S CAR! Dorothea's papa, my ex-boss!

ISABEL: Perhaps he'll be kind enough to—

RALPH: Go back in, little lady! Stay in the bedroom till I git through this! Then I'll drive you downtown if you're still determined to go.

(*He has drawn her back in the house.*)

SET DOWN, GEORGE! For Chrissakes. Little lady, will you please wait in the bedroom till I get through this hassle with her old man?

ISABEL: It's all so ridiculous. Yes, all right, I will, but please don't forget your promise to take me downtown right afterwards, Mr. Bates!

(*She returns to the bedroom with dignity. Mr. and Mrs. McGillicuddy appear before the house.*
(*They are a pair of old bulls.*)

MRS. MCGILLICUDDY: The first thing to discuss is their joint savings account.

(*Mr. McGillicuddy hammers the knocker on the door.*)

I wish you'd listened to me an' brought your lawyer.

MR. MCGILLICUDDY: I can handle that boy. You keep your mouth out of it. Just collect the silver and china and let me handle the talk.

(*He knocks again, violently, dislodging the Christmas wreath attached to the knocker. Mrs. McGillicuddy picks it up.*)

Now what are you gonna do with that Christmas wreath? You gonna crown him with it?

(*Ralph opens the door.*)

RALPH: Well, Mr. and Mrs. *Mac*!

MR. MCGILLICUDDY (*handing him the wreath*): This come off your knocker.

RALPH: Ha, ha, what a surprise!

MRS. MCGILLICUDDY: We've come to pick up some things of Dorothea's.

RALPH: That's O.K. Take out anything that's hers, but don't touch nothing that belongs to us both.

MRS. MCGILLICUDDY: We've come with a list of things that belong exclusively to Dorothea!

MR. MCGILLICUDDY: Is it true that you called up Emory Sparks at the place you quit your job at and asked him to come over here tonight and make you a cash-on-the-barrel offer for everything in this house?

RALPH: Nope.

MR. MCGILLICUDDY: Then how come Emory's fiancée called up Dorothea to give her that information?

MRS. MCGILLICUDDY (*impatiently*): Come on in here, Susie.

(*Susie is the colored maid. She enters with a large laundry basket.*)

Is that the biggest basket you could find?

SUSIE: Yes, ma'am, it's the laundry basket.

MRS. MCGILLICUDDY: It isn't the large one. You'll have to make several trips up and down those slippery front steps with that little basket.

MR. MCGILLICUDDY: Haven't you got any ice-cream salt?

RALPH: You want to make some ice cream?

MR. MCGILLICUDDY: Susie, before you go down those steps with my daughter's china, you'd better collect some clinkers out of the furnace in the basement.

RALPH: How is she going to get clinkers out of an oil-burning furnace?

MR. MCGILLICUDDY: Oh, that's right. You burn oil. I forgot about that. Well, Susie, you better tote the basket of china down the terrace. Don't try to make the steps with it.

RALPH: She's not takin' no china out of this house.

MR. MCGILLICUDDY: You're not going to sell a goddam thing of my daughter's in this house!

RALPH: All I done was call up Emory Sparks because he's about to get married and invited him over to take a look at this place because I've got to unload it and I can't wait a couple of months to—

MR. MCGILLICUDDY: Now, hold on a minute, war hero!

RALPH: I don't like the way you always call me war hero!

MR. MCGILLICUDDY: *Why?* Ain't that what you *were?*

GEORGE: You're goddam right he was! I flown over seventy bombing missions with this boy in Korea and before that in the—

MR. MCGILLICUDDY: Yes, yes, yes, I know it backwards and forwards, and I know who you are. You are Haverstick, ain't you?

GEORGE: Yeah, you got my name right.

MR. MCGILLICUDDY: Well, Haverstick, the war's over and you two bombers are grounded. Now, Susie, go in the kitchen and get that Mixmaster and that new Rotisserie out in the basket while I collect the silver in that sideboard in there.

RALPH: Susie, don't go in my kitchen. You want to be arrested for trespassing, Susie?

MRS. MCGILLICUDDY: Stuart, you'd better call that policeman in here.

RALPH: No kidding!

MRS. MCGILLICUDDY: We anticipated that you'd make trouble.

RALPH: How does Dorothea feel about you all doing this?

MR. MCGILLICUDDY (*at the door*): OFFICER!—He's coming.

RALPH: How does Dotty feel? What is her attitude toward this kind of—

(*He is trembling. His voice chokes. George rises and puts a hand on Ralph's shoulder as a young Police Officer enters looking embarrassed.*)

MR. MCGILLICUDDY: You know the situation, Lieutenant. We have to remove my daughter's valuables from the house because we've been tipped off this man here, Ralph Bates, is intending to make a quick cash sale of everything in the house and skip out of Memphis tomorrow.

RALPH: THAT'S A GODDAM LIE! WHO TOLD YOU THAT?

MRS. MCGILLICUDDY: Emory Sparks' fiancée is Dorothea's good friend! That's how we got the warning. She called to enquire if Dorothea was serious about this matter. How did Dotty feel, how did she FEEL? I'll tell you! SICK AT HER STOMACH! VIOLENTLY SICK AT HER STOMACH.

RALPH: I should think so, goddam it. I should THINK so! She's got many a fault she got from you two, but, hell, she'd never agree to a piece of cheapness like this any more'n she'd believe that story about me callin'—

MR. MCGILLICUDDY: How could there be any possible doubt about it when Emory Sparks' fiancée—

RALPH: Will you allow me to speak? I did call Emory Sparks and told him my wife had quit me because I had quit my job, and I merely suggested that he come over and kind of look over the stuff here and see if any of all this goddam electric equipment and so forth would be of any use to him since it isn't to me and since I got to have some financial—

(*He becomes suddenly speechless and breathless. George embraces his shoulder.*)

GEORGE: Now, now, son, this is going to work out. Don't blow a gasket over it.

RALPH: I think you folks had better consider some legal angles of what you're up to here.

MR. MCGILLICUDDY (*puffing, red in the face*): Aw, there's no legal angle about it that I don't know, and if there was, I could cope with that, too. I'm prepared to cope with that trouble. You got no goddam position in this town but what I give you!

RALPH: *Oh!* Uh-huh—

(*Mrs. McGillicuddy has gone to the bedroom and discovered Isabel in it.*)

MRS. MCGILLICUDDY: *Stuart, they have a woman in Dotty's bedroom!*

RALPH: George's wife is in there.

MRS. MCGILLICUDDY: How long have you been planning this?

(*She knocks on the bedroom door.*)

Can I come in?

ISABEL: Yes, please.

(*Mrs. McGillicuddy enters the bedroom.*)

MRS. MCGILLICUDDY (*coldly*): I've come to pick up some things that belong to my daughter.

ISABEL: I told my husband we'd dropped in at the wrong time.

MRS. MCGILLICUDDY: May I ask who you are?

ISABEL: I'm Mrs. George Haverstick. You probably saw my husband in the front room.

MRS. MCGILLICUDDY: Your husband's an old friend of Ralph's, one of his wartime buddies?

ISABEL: Yes, he is, Mrs.— I didn't get your name.

MRS. MCGILLICUDDY: All I can say is "Watch out," if he's an old friend of Ralph's!

ISABEL: Why?

MRS. MCGILLICUDDY: Birds of a feather, that's all.

(*Mrs. McGillicuddy opens the closet and starts piling clothes on the bed. In the living room, Mr. McGillicuddy takes a seat in silence.*)

ISABEL: Are you sure you're doing the right thing?

MRS. MCGILLICUDDY (*calling out the door*): Susie!

SUSIE (*entering*): Yes, ma'am?

MRS. MCGILLICUDDY: Take these clothes of Miss Dotty's out to the car.

(*Susie carries out the clothes.*)

ISABEL: I think young people should be given a chance to work things out by themselves.

MRS. MCGILLICUDDY: You have no idea at all of the situation. And I'm sure you have your own problems if you have married a friend of my daughter's husband. Is he living on his war record like Ralph Bates is?

ISABEL: He has a distinguished war record and a nervous disability that was a result of seventy-two flying missions in Korea and, and—more than twice that many in—

MRS. MCGILLICUDDY: *I'm sick of hearing about past glories! Susie!*

(*Susie comes in again.*)

Now pick up all Dotty's shoes on the floor of that closet, put 'em in the bottom of the basket, put some paper over them, and then pile her little undies on top of the paper.— Then! If you still have room in the basket, collect some of the china out of the sideboard and cupboards. Be very careful with that. Don't try to carry too much at one time, Susie. That walk and those steps are a hazard.

(*There has been a prolonged silence in the front room during the scene above, which they have been listening to.*)

MR. MCGILLICUDDY (*at last*): Well, you seem to be living the life of Riley. French champagne. Who was the little girl I saw come out and go back in?

RALPH: Mrs. George Haverstick.

MR. MCGILLICUDDY: That means as much to me as if you said she was a lady from Mars.

RALPH: There's no reason why it should mean anything to you. I just answered your question.

MR. MCGILLICUDDY: Why do you feel so superior to me?

RALPH: Aw. Did you notice that?

MR. MCGILLICUDDY: From the first time I met you. You have always acted very superior to me for some unknown reason.

I'd like to know what it is. You were employed by me till you quit your job today.

RALPH: Does that mean I had to feel inferior to you, Mac?

MR. MCGILLICUDDY: You've started calling me "Mac"?

RALPH: I'm not employed by you, now.

MR. MCGILLICUDDY: If there was a war you could be a war hero again, but in a cold war I don't see how you're going to be such a hero. A cold-war hero, ha ha, is not such a hero, at least not in the newspapers.

(*Gathering confidence*)

Huh? Why don't you answer my question?

RALPH: Which, Mac?

MR. MCGILLICUDDY: Why you feel so rutten superior to me.

RALPH: Can I consider that question? For a minute?

MR. MCGILLICUDDY: Yeah, consider it, will you? I fail to see anything *special* about you, war hero!

(*He lights a cigar with jerky motions. The two younger men stare at his red, puffy face with intolerant smiles.*)

GEORGE: Let me answer for him. He feels superior to you because you're a big male cow, a spiritual male cow.

RALPH: Shut up, George. Well, Mr. Mac? Let me ask you a question. Why did you ask me to marry your daughter?

MR. MCGILLICUDDY: DID WHAT? I NEVER! Done any such thing and—

(*Mrs. McGillicuddy snorts indignantly from the open bedroom door.*)

RALPH: You mean to say you've forgotten that you suggested to me that I marry Dotty?

(*Mrs. McGillicuddy advances from the bedroom door, bearing a French porcelain clock.*)

MR. MCGILLICUDDY: I never forgotten a thing in my adult life, but I never have any such recollections as that. I do remember a conversation I held with you soon after you started to work at Regal Dairy Products an' come to my office to quit because you said you weren't gittin' paid well enough an' th' work was monotonous to you.

RALPH: That's right. Five years ago this winter.

MR. MCGILLICUDDY: I gave you a fatherly talk. I told you monotony was a part of life. And I said I had an eye on you, which I did at that time.

RALPH: How about the rest of the conversation? In which you said that Dotty was your only child, that you had no son, and Dotty was int'rested in me and if Dotty got married her husband would be the heir to your throne as owner of Regal Dairy an' its subsidiaries such as Royal Ice Cream and Monarch Cheese, huh?

MRS. MCGILLICUDDY: HANH!

RALPH: An' you hadn't long for this world because of acute diabetes and so forth and—

MRS. MCGILLICUDDY: HANH!

RALPH: And I would be shot right into your shoes when you departed this world? Well, you sure in hell lingered!

MRS. MCGILLICUDDY: ARE YOU GOING TO STAND THERE LISTENING TO THIS, STUART? I'M NOT!

MR. MCGILLICUDDY: Be still, Mama. I can talk for myself. I did discuss these things with you but how did you arrive at the idea I asked you to marry my daughter?

MRS. MCGILLICUDDY: HANH!

(*George goes to look out the window as if the scene had ceased to amuse him.*)

RALPH: What other way could it be interpreted, Mac?

(*He is no longer angry.*)

MR. MCGILLICUDDY: I offered you a splendid chance in the world which you spit on by your disrespect, your superior—!

RALPH: I respect Dorothea. Always did and still do.

MR. MCGILLICUDDY: I'm talkin' about your attitude to me.

RALPH: I know you are. That's all that you care about, not about Dorothea. You don't love Dotty. She let you down by having psychological problems that you brought on her, that you an' Mrs. Mac gave her by pushing her socially past her social endowments.

MRS. MCGILLICUDDY: WHAT DO YOU MEAN BY THAT?

RALPH: Dotty was never cut out to boost your social position in this city. Which you expected her to. You made her feel inferior all her life.

MRS. MCGILLICUDDY: *Me? Me?*

RALPH: Both of yuh. I respected her, though, and sincerely liked her and I married Dotty. Give me credit for that, and provided her with an—offspring. Maybe not much of an offspring, but an offspring, a male one, at least it started a male one. I can't help it if she's turnin' him into a sissy, I—

MRS. MCGILLICUDDY: MY GOD, STUART, HOW LONG ARE YOU GONNA STAND THERE AND LISTEN TO THIS WITHOUT—

MR. MCGILLICUDDY: *Mama, I told you to keep your mouth outa this!*

RALPH: Yeah, but I MARRIED your baby. Give me credit for that. And provided her with an—offspring!

MRS. MCGILLICUDDY: What does he mean by that? That *he* had the baby, not Dotty?

MR. MCGILLICUDDY: Mama, I told you to keep your mouth out of this.

MRS. MCGILLICUDDY: He talks like he thought he did Dotty a FAVOR!

RALPH:Now, listen. I don't want to be forced into saying unkind things about Dotty. But you all know damn well that Dotty was half a year older than me when I married that girl and if I hadn't you would have been stuck with a lonely, unmarried daughter for the rest of your lives!

MRS. MCGILLICUDDY: *Oh*, my—GOD!

MR. MCGILLICUDDY: Let him talk. I want to hear all, all, all! he has to say about Dotty.

RALPH: You're *going* to hear it, if you stay in my house! I put up a five-year battle between our marriage and your goddam hold on her! You just wouldn't release her!—although I doubt that you wanted her always unmarried.

MRS. MCGILLICUDDY: WHAT MAKES YOU THINK SHE WOULD HAVE STAYED UNMARRIED?

RALPH: The indications, past history, when I met her—

MRS. MCGILLICUDDY: This is too sickening. I can't stand it, Stuart?

MR. MCGILLICUDDY: A bum like you?

RALPH: Don't call *me* a bum!

MR. MCGILLICUDDY: What in hell else *are* you? I give you your
job which you quit today without warning! Carried you in it
despite your indifference to it for—for—for—five—

RALPH: Wait! Like I said. I still respect your daughter, don't
want to say anything not kind about her, but let's face facts.
Who else but a sucker like me, Ralph Bates, would have
married a girl with no looks, a plain, homely girl that
probably no one but me had ever felt anything but just—
SORRY FOR!

MRS. MCGILLICUDDY: OH GOD! STUART, ARE YOU GOING TO
STAND THERE AND LET HIM GO ON WITH THAT TALK?

RALPH: HOW IN HELL DO YOU FIGURE HE'S GOING TO
STOP ME?

MRS. MCGILLICUDDY: OFFICER! CAN'T YOU GET THIS MAN
OUT OF HERE?

OFFICER: No, ma'am. I can't arrest him.

RALPH: ARREST ME FOR WHAT, MRS. MAC?

GEORGE: That's right, arrest him for what?

MRS. MCGILLICUDDY: Stuart? Take out the silver. I don't know
where Susie is. We should have come here with your lawyer
as well as this—*remarkably—incompetent—policeman!*

MR. MCGILLICUDDY: Susie took out the silver.

GEORGE: Naw, she didn't. I got the goddam silver. I'm sitting
on it!

(*He sits on silver, then rises and stuffs it under sofa pillow,
having been discomfited by the forks.*)

MR. MCGILLICUDDY: I guess I'll have to call the Chief of
Police, who's a lodge brother of mine, and get a little more
police co-operation than we have gotten so far.

OFFICER: O.K., you do that, Mister.

MR. MCGILLICUDDY: He'll call you to the phone and give you
exact instructions.

OFFICER: That's all right. If he gives 'em, I'll take 'em.

(*Mrs. McGillicuddy has charged back into the bedroom to collect more things.*)

RALPH: Mr. McGillicuddy, you are the worst thing any person can be: mean-minded, small-hearted, and CHEAP! Out-

standingly and notoriously cheap! It was almost two months before I could *kiss* Dorothea, sincerely, after meeting her father! That's no crap. It wasn't the homeliness that threw me, it was the association she had in my mind with *you*! It wasn't till I found out she despised you as much as I did that I was able to make real love to Dotty.

MR. MCGILLICUDDY: My daughter is *crazy* about me!

RALPH: You're crazy if you *think* so!

(*Mrs. McGillicuddy comes out of the bedroom.*)

MRS. MCGILLICUDDY: All right. All of Dotty's clothes have been taken out. I think we may as well leave now.

MR. MCGILLICUDDY: How about the TV? Which I gave Dotty *last* Christmas?

RALPH: You want the TV? O.K.! Here's the TV!

(*He shoves it to the door and pulls the door open.*)

Take the TV out of here—an' git out with it!

MRS. MCGILLICUDDY: What is that under the tree? It looks like a new fur coat!

RALPH: That's right. A seven-hundred-and-forty-five-dollar sheared-beaver coat that I'd bought for Dotty for Christmas!—but which I have just now presented to Mrs. George Haverstick as her weddin' present.

MR. MCGILLICUDDY: The hell you have! How did you git hold of seven hundred and—

RALPH: From my savings account.

MR. MCGILLICUDDY: That was a *joint* account!

MRS. MCGILLICUDDY: STUART! TAKE THAT COAT! GO ON, PICK UP THAT COAT!

RALPH: By God, if he touches that coat, I'll smash him into next week, and I never hit an old man before in my life.

MRS. MCGILLICUDDY: OFFICER! PICK UP THAT COAT!

RALPH: I'll hit any man that tries to pick up that coat!

OFFICER (*putting down the phone, which he has been talking into quietly*): I talked to my chief. He gave me my instructions. He says not to take any action that might result in publicity, because of Mr. Bates having been a very well-known war hero.

MR. MCGILLICUDDY: Come on, Mama. I'll just have to refer this whole disgusting business to my lawyer tomorrow, put it all in his hands and get the necessary papers to protect our baby.

MRS. MCGILLICUDDY: I just want to say one thing more! Ralph Bates, don't you think for a moment that you are going to escape financial responsibility for the support of your child! Now come on, Stuart!—Isn't it pitiful? All that little boy's Christmas under the tree?

RALPH: Send him over tomorrow to pick it all up. That can go out of the house, the little boy's Christmas can go. . . .

(*They all leave. Isabel enters from bedroom.*)

ISABEL: Mr. Bates! I don't believe that this is what your wife wanted. I'll also bet you that she is outside in that car and if you would just stick your head out the window and call her, she would come running in here.

(*Dorothea comes onto the paved terrace and knocks at the door. Ralph does not move. She knocks again, harder and longer. He starts to rise, sits down again.*)

George, let his wife in the house.

GEORGE: Let's just keep out of this. I reckon he knows what he's doing.

(*A car honks. A Woman's Voice is heard.*)

WOMAN (*off*): Dorothea! Come back! We'll get the police!

DOROTHEA (*calling at the door*): Ralph? Ralph? It's Dotty! I want the child's Christmas things!

RALPH: HE'LL GET THEM HERE OR NOWHERE!

DOROTHEA: *I'm not going to leave here without the child's Christmas things!*—Ralph.

RALPH: *Let him come here alone tomorrow morning.*

DOROTHEA: *You can't do that to a child.*—Ralph!

(*The car honks again, long and loud.*)

RALPH (*shouting back*): Put the kid in a taxi in the morning and I'll let him in to collect his Christmas presents!

MRS. MCGILLICUDDY (*appearing behind Dorothea*): Dorothea! I will not let you humiliate yourself like this! Come away from that door!

DOROTHEA: Mama, stay in the car!

WOMAN: Your father won't wait any longer. He's started the car. He's determined to get the police.

DOROTHEA: RALPH! (*She has removed the door key from her bag.*) I'M COMING IN!

WOMAN: *Dotty, where is your pride!*

(*Dorothea enters and slams the door. The Woman rushes off, crying "Stuart!"*)

(*Dorothea stares at Ralph from the door. He gazes stubbornly at the opposite wall.*)

DOROTHEA: I could tell you'd been drinkin' by your voice. Who are these people you've got staying in the house.

RALPH: Talk about the police! I could get you all arrested for illegal entry!

DOROTHEA: This is your liquor speaking, not you, Ralph.

RALPH: You have abandoned me. You got no right by law to come back into this house and make insulting remarks about my friends.

DOROTHEA: Ralph? Ralph? I know I acted—impetuously this mawnin'. . . .

RALPH: Naw, I think you made the correct decision. You realized that you had tied yourself down to a square peg in a round hole that had now popped out of the hole and consequently would be of no further use to you. You were perfectly satisfied for me to remain at that rutten little desk job, tyrannized over by inferior men, for as long as my— heart kept beating.

DOROTHEA: No, Ralph. I wasn't. MY aim for you was your aim. Independence! A business of your own!

RALPH: Not when you were *faced* with it.

DOROTHEA: You sprung it on me at the wrong moment, Ralph. Our savings account is at a very low ebb.

RALPH: Our savings account is all gone, little woman. It went on Christmas, all of it.

(*He pokes at the fire. There is a pause. The fire crackles and flickers.*)

DOROTHEA: *Mama* says you—bought me a *fur coat* for Christmas.

RALPH: Yeah, she took a look at it. Enquired the price. Wanted to take it off with her.

DOROTHEA: You wouldn't have bought me such a beautiful coat if you didn't still care for me, Ralph. You know that, don't you?

RALPH: I made a decision affecting my whole future life. I know it was a big step, but I had the courage to make it.

DOROTHEA: I've always admired your courage.

RALPH: Hah!—I break the news. You walked right out on me, Dotty, takin' my son that you've turned into a sissy. He won't want these boys' toys under that tree. What he'll want is a doll and a—*tea* set.

DOROTHEA: All of these things are a little too old for Ralph Junior but he'll be delighted with them just the same, Ralph.

(*She takes off her cloth coat.*)

I'm going to try on that wonderful-looking beaver.

RALPH: It's not going out of the house, off you or on you, Dotty.

(*She puts on the beaver-skin coat.*)

DOROTHEA: Oh, how lovely, how lovely! Ralph, it *does* prove you love me!

RALPH: It cleaned out our savings account.

DOROTHEA: Both of us have been guilty of impetuous actions. You must've been awfully lonely, inviting a pair of strangers to occupy our bedroom on Christmas Eve.

RALPH: George Haverstick is not any stranger to me. We both of us died in two wars, repeatedly died in two wars and were buried in suburbs named High Point, but his was hyphenated. H-i-hyphen-Point. Mine was spelled out but was built on a cavern for the daughter and grandchild of Mr. and Mrs. Stuart McGillicuddy. Oh, I told him something which I should have told you five years ago, Dorothea. I married you without love. I married you for—

DOROTHEA: Ralph? Please don't!

RALPH: I married you for your stingy-fisted old papa's promise to—

DOROTHEA: *Ralphie! Don't! I know!*

RALPH:—to make me his Heir Apparent! Assurances, lies! Even broad hints that he would soon kick off!

DOROTHEA: Ralph?

(*She puts her hand over his mouth, beseechingly.*)

Don't you know I know that?

RALPH: Why, you accept it? If you—

DOROTHEA: I was so—

(*She covers her face.*)

RALPH: Cut it out, have some pride!

DOROTHEA: I *do*!

RALPH: In *what*?

DOROTHEA: In *you*!

RALPH: Oh, for the love of— In me? Why, I'm telling you I'm nothin' better'n a goddam—

DOROTHEA: I know, don't tell me again. I always knew it.—I had my nose done over and my front teeth extracted to look better for you, Ralphie!

RALPH: "Ralphie!" *Shoot* . . .

(*Isabel raps discreetly at the bedroom door.*)

Huh? What is it?

ISABEL: I've made some coffee.

DOROTHEA: I *did* improve my appearance, didn't I, Ralph? It was extremely painful.

RALPH: Don't claim you done it for me! Every woman wants to improve on nature any way that she can. Yes! Of course you look better! You think you've won a *argument*?

DOROTHEA: *Me*? *What* argument? *No!* I've come back *crawling*!—not even embarrassed to do so!

(*Isabel comes in from the kitchenette with coffee.*)

Oh, Hello. I didn't know you were—

ISABEL: Mrs. Bates. I'm Isabel Haverstick. I took the liberty of making some coffee in your sweet little kitchen. Mrs. Bates, can I give you some coffee?

DOROTHEA: Thanks, that's awfully sweet of you, Mrs. Haverstick. It's nice of you and your husband to drop in on Ralph, but the situation between Ralph and me has changed. I guess I don't have to explain it. You see I've come home. We only have one bedroom and Ralph and I have an awful lot to talk over.

ISABEL: I understand perfectly. George and I are going to go right downtown.

DOROTHEA (*softening*): You don't have to do that. This sofa lets out to a bed and it's actually more comfortable than the beds in the bedroom. I know, because other times when we've had a falling out, less serious than this time, I have—occupied it.

(*With a little, soft, sad, embarrassed laugh.*)

Of course, I usually called Ralph in before mawnin'. . . .

ISABEL: Oh, but this is no time for strangers to be here with you!

DOROTHEA (*now really warming*): You all stay here! I insist! It's really not easy to get a hotel room downtown with so many folks coming into town for Christmas.

ISABEL: Well, if you're sure, if you're absolutely certain our presence wouldn't be inconvenient at all?—I do love this room. The fire is still burning bright!—and the Christmas tree is so—pretty.

DOROTHEA: I'll tell my mother and father, they're still outside in the car, to drive home and then we'll all have coffee together!

(*She rushes out in her beaver coat.*)

ISABEL: I like her! She's really nice!

RALPH: She came back for the fur coat.

ISABEL: I think she came back for you.

RALPH: She walked out on me this morning because I had liberated myself from a slave's situation!—and she took the kid with her.

ISABEL: You're just going through a—period of adjustment.

RALPH: We've been married six years.

ISABEL: But all that time you've been under terrible strain, hating what you were doing, and maybe taking it out on your wife, Ralph Bates.

(*Dorothea returns.*)

DOROTHEA: All right. I sent them home, much against their objections. I just slammed the car door on them.

RALPH: They comin' back with the police?

DOROTHEA: No. You know they were bluffing.

ISABEL: I think you two should have your coffee alone in your own little bedroom. We'll all get acquainted tomorrow.

DOROTHEA: Ralph?

RALPH (*sadly*): I don't know. We're living over a cavern. . . .

(*He follows Dorothea into the bedroom. It remains dimly lighted.*)

DOROTHEA: But Mama's took all my things! I forgot to ask them back from her. I'll just have to sleep jay-bird since she took even my nighties.

RALPH: Yes, she was fast and thorough, but didn't get out with that seven-hundred-buck beaver coat.

DOROTHEA: I like your friends. But the girl looks terribly nervous. Well-bred, however, and the boy is certainly very good-looking!

RALPH: Thanks.

(*The bedroom dims out as Dorothea enters the bathroom. A silence has fallen between the pair in the living room.*)

ISABEL: Coffee, George?

GEORGE: No, thanks.

ISABEL: Moods change quickly, don't they?

GEORGE: Basic attitudes don't.

ISABEL: Yes, but it takes a long time to form basic attitudes and to know what they are, and meantime you just have to act according to moods.

GEORGE: Is that what you are acting according to, now?

ISABEL: I'm not acting according to anything at all now, I—

(*She sits on a hassock before the fireplace.*)

I don't think she came back just for the coat. Do you?

GEORGE: It's not my business. I don't have any opinion. If that was her reason, Ralph Bates will soon find it out.

ISABEL: Yes . . .

DOROTHEA (*at the door*): Excuse me, may I come in?

ISABEL: Oh, please.

DOROTHEA (*entering*): Mama took all my *things*! Have you got an extra nightie that I could borrow?

ISABEL: Of course I have.

DOROTHEA: I forgot to take anything back. . . .

(*Isabel opens her overnight bag and extends a gossamer night-gown to Dorothea.*)

Oh! How exquisite! No!—that's your honeymoon nightie. Just give me any old plain one!

ISABEL: Really, I have two of them, exactly alike. Please take it!

DOROTHEA: Are you sure?

ISABEL: I'm positive. You take it!

(*She holds up another.*)

See? The same thing exactly, just a different color. I gave you the blue one and kept the pink one for me.

DOROTHEA: Oh. Well, thank you so much.

ISABEL: If you'd prefer the pink one—?

DOROTHEA: I'm delighted with the blue one! Well, g'night, you folks. Sweet dreams.

(*She returns to the dark bedroom. Ralph is prone and motionless on the bed. A tiny light spills from the bathroom door. Dorothea enters the bathroom and closes the door so the bedroom turns pitch-black.*)

GEORGE (*grimly*): D'ya want me to go outside while you undress?

ISABEL: No, I, I—I'm just going to take off my *suit*. I—I, I have a *slip* on, I—

(*She gives him a quick, scared look. The removal of her suit is almost panickily self-conscious and awkward.*)

GEORGE: Well. Ralph and I have decided to—

ISABEL (*fearfully*): *What?*

GEORGE (*finishes his drink, then goes on*): Ralph and I have decided to go in the cattle business, near San Antone.

ISABEL: Who is going to finance it?

(*She has turned out the lamp.*)

GEORGE: We think we can work it out. We have to be smart, and lucky. Just smart and lucky.

(*Isabel drops her skirt to her feet and stands before the flickering fireplace in a slip that the light makes transparent.*)

ISABEL: We all have to be smart and lucky. Or unlucky and silly.

(*Dorothea comes out of the bathroom. Light from the bathroom brightens the bedroom, where Ralph is slowly undressing.*)

RALPH: All right, you're back. But a lot has been discussed and decided on since you cut out of here, Dotty.
DOROTHEA (*picks up something on the dresser*): Good! What?
RALPH: Please don't rub that Vick's Vap-O-Rub on your chest.
DOROTHEA: I'm *not*! This is Hind's honey-almond cream for my *hands!*
RALPH: Aw.

(*She starts taking off her shoes.*
(*In the living room:*)

GEORGE: What're you up to?
ISABEL: Up to?
GEORGE: Standin' in front of that fire with that transparent thing on you. You must know it's transparent.
ISABEL: I honestly didn't even think about that.

(*Isabel crouches by the fire, holding her delicate hands out to its faint, flickering glow.*
(*In the bedroom:*)

RALPH: All right. Here it is. George and me are going to cash in every bit of collateral we possess, including the beaver-skin coat and his fifty-two Caddy to buy a piece of ranch-land near San Antone.
DOROTHEA: Oh. What are you planning to do on this—
RALPH:—ranch? Breed cattle. Texas Longhorns.

(*A pause.*)

DOROTHEA: I like animals, Ralph.
RALPH: Cocker spaniels.

DOROTHEA: No, I like horses, too. I took equitation at Sophie Newcomb's. I even learned how to post.

RALPH: Uh-huh.

DOROTHEA: For a little ole Texas girl she sure does have some mighty French taste in nighties!

RALPH: I don't imagine she suffers from psychological frigidity.

DOROTHEA: Honey, I never suffered from that. Did you believe I really suffered from that?

RALPH: When your father proposed to me—

DOROTHEA: Ralph, don't say things like that! Don't, don't humiliate me!

RALPH: Honey, I—

DOROTHEA: PLEASE don't humiliate me by—

RALPH: HONEY!

(*He goes up to her at the dressing table. Sobbing, she presses her head against him.*)

You KNOW I respect you, honey.

ISABEL (*in the other room*): What an awful, frightening thing it is!

GEORGE: What?

ISABEL: Two people living together, two, two—different worlds!—attempting—existence—together!

(*In the bedroom:*)

RALPH: Honey, will you stop?

DOROTHEA: Respect me, respect me, is that all you can give me when I've loved you so much that sometimes I shake all over at the sight or touch of you? Still? Now? Always?

RALPH: The human heart would never pass the drunk test.

DOROTHEA: Huh?

RALPH: If you took the human heart out of the human body and put a pair of legs on it and told it to walk a straight line, it couldn't do it. It never could pass the drunk test.

DOROTHEA: I love you, baby. And I love animals, too. Hawses, spaniels, longhorns!

RALPH: The Texas longhorn is a—dignified beast.

DOROTHEA: You say that like you thought it was TOO GOOD FOR ME!

RALPH: How do I know that you didn't just come back here for that sheared beaver coat?

(*Living room:*)

ISABEL: I hope they're getting things ironed out between them.

GEORGE: Why?

ISABEL: They need each other. That's why.

GEORGE: Let's mind our own business, huh?

(*Bedroom:*)

DOROTHEA: You'll just have to WONDER! And WONDER!

(*Living room:*)

GEORGE: It's a parallel situation. They're going through a period of adjustment just like us.

(*Bedroom:*)

RALPH: All my life, huh?

DOROTHEA: And I'll have to wonder, too, if you love me, Ralph. There's an awful lot of wondering between people.

RALPH: Come on. Turn out the light. Let's go to bed-ville, baby.

DOROTHEA (*turning out the light*): His or hers?

RALPH: In West Texas we'll get a big one called OURS!

(*In the living room, George has turned on TV and a chorus is singing "White Christmas."*)

GEORGE: Aw. You hate "White Christmas."

(*He turns it down.*)

ISABEL: I don't hate it now, baby.

(*He turns it back up, but softly.*)

DOROTHEA: I'm lookin' *forward* to it. I always wanted a big one, OURS!

RALPH: There's more dignity in it.

DOROTHEA: *Yes!*

(*She giggles breathlessly in the dark.*)

ISABEL (*in the living room*): I think they've talked things over and are working things out.

(*Bedroom:*)

RALPH: Yes. It makes it easy to know if—I mean, you don't have to wonder if—

(*Dorothea giggles in the dark.*)

That long, long, dangerous walk between "His" and "Hers" can be accomplished, or not. . . .

(*Living room:*)

ISABEL: I didn't know until now that the shakes are catching! Why do you keep standing up and sitting back down like a big old jack-in-the-box?

(*A low rumble is heard. It builds. Something falls off a shelf in the kitchenette. Crockery rattles together.*)

WHAT'S THIS!?

GEORGE: Aw, nothin', nothin'.

RALPH (*entering the doorway*): Well, she jus' slipped again!

DOROTHEA (*appearing behind him*): Did you all feel that tremor?

ISABEL: Yes, it felt like an earthquake.

DOROTHEA: We get those little tremors all the time because it seems that this suburb is built over a huge underground cavern and is sinking into it, bit by bit. That's the secret of how we could afford to buy this nice little home of ours at such a knockdown price.

ISABEL: It isn't likely to fall in the cavern *tonight*?

DOROTHEA: No. They say it's going to be gradual, about half an inch every year. Do you all mind if I turn on the light a second to see if there's any new cracks?

ISABEL: No, I'll—put on my robe.

(*She does. The room is lighted.*)

DOROTHEA: Yais! Ralph? A *new* one! This one is a jim-dandy, all the way 'cross the ceiling! See it, honey? All the way 'cross the ceiling. Well—

(*A pause.*)

We will leave you alone now. I still feel badly about you having to sleep on that folding contraption.

RALPH: Anything I can do? Anything I can—

DOROTHEA: Ralph! Leave them alone. Merry Christmas!

(*She shuts the door.*
(*Pause. Isabel stands before fireplace in the fourth wall.*
(*Pause.*)

GEORGE: Isabel? Little Bit? Marriage is a big step for a man to take, especially when he's—nervous. I'm pretty—nervous.

ISABEL: I know.

GEORGE: For a man with the shakes, especially, it's a—big step to take, it's—

ISABEL: I know what you're trying to tell me.

GEORGE (*taking seat on high stool near fire*): Do you, honey?

(*He looks up at her quickly, then down.*)

ISABEL: Of course I do. I expect all men are a little bit nervous about the same thing.

GEORGE: What?

ISABEL: About how they'll be at love-making.

GEORGE: Yeah, well, they don't have the shakes. I mean, not all the others have got a nervous tremor like I've got.

ISABEL: Inside or outside, they've all got a nervous tremor of some kind, sweetheart. The world is a big hospital, and I am a nurse in it, George. The world world's a big hospital, a big neurological ward and I am a student nurse in it. I guess that's still my job!—I love this fire. It feels so good on my skin through this little pink slip. I'm glad she left me the *pink* nightie, tonight.

GEORGE (*huskily*): Yeah, I'm glad she did, too.

(*Isabel retires to slip into her nightgown.*)

I wish I had that—little electric buzzer I—had at— Barnes. . . .

ISABEL: You don't need a buzzer. I'm not way down at the end of a corridor, baby. If you call me, I'll hear you.

(*She returns and hugs her knees, sitting before the fireplace. He rests his head on his cupped hands. She begins to sing softly:*)

> "Now the boat goes round the bend,
>   Good-by, my lover, good-by,
>   It's loaded down with boys and men,
>   Good-by, my lover, good-by!"

RALPH (*in the dark other room*): She's singin'!

(*Pause.*)

DOROTHEA: Papa said you told him that I was—homely! Did you say that, Ralph? That I was homely?

RALPH: Dotty, you used to be homely but you improved in appearance.

DOROTHEA: You never told me you thought I was homely, Ralph.

RALPH: I just meant you had a off-beat kind of face, honey, but—the rest of you is attractive.

DOROTHEA (*giggles*): I always knew *I* was homely but you were good enough lookin' to make *up* for it! Baby—

(*Isabel is singing again, a little forlornly, by the fireplace.*)

ISABEL:
> "Bye low, my baby! Bye low, my baby!
>   Bye low, my baby! Good-by, my lover, good-by!"

(*George whistles softly.*)

Was that for me?

GEORGE: Come here!

ISABEL: No, you come here. It's very nice by the fire.

(*In the other room, as the curtain begins to fall:*)

DOROTHEA: Careful, let me do it!—It isn't mine!

(*She means the borrowed nightgown.*
(*In the front room, George has risen from the bed and is crossing to the fireplace as:*)

The Curtain Falls

THE NIGHT OF THE IGUANA

And so, as kinsmen met a night,
We talked between the rooms,
Until the moss had reached our lips,
And covered up our names.
                    EMILY DICKINSON

The play takes place in the summer of 1940 in a rather rustic and very Bohemian hotel, the Costa Verde, which, as its name implies, sits on a jungle-covered hilltop overlooking the "caleta," or "morning beach" of Puerto Barrio in Mexico. But this is decidedly not the Puerto Barrio of today. At that time—twenty years ago—the west coast of Mexico had not yet become the Las Vegas and Miami Beach of Mexico. The villages were still predominantly primitive Indian villages, and the still-water morning beach of Puerto Barrio and the rain forests above it were among the world's wildest and loveliest populated places.

The setting for the play is the wide verandah of the hotel. This roofed verandah, enclosed by a railing, runs around all four sides of the somewhat dilapidated, tropical-style frame structure, but on the stage we see only the front and one side. Below the verandah, which is slightly raised above the stage level, are shrubs with vivid trumpet-shaped flowers and a few cactus plants, while at the sides we see the foliage of the encroaching jungle. A tall coconut palm slants upward at one side, its trunk notched for a climber to chop down coconuts for rum-cocos. In the back wall of the verandah are the doors of a line of small cubicle bedrooms which are screened with mosquito-net curtains. For the night scenes they are lighted from within, so that each cubicle appears as a little interior stage, the curtains giving a misty effect to their dim inside lighting. A path which goes down through the rain forest to the highway and the beach, its opening masked by foliage, leads off from one side of the verandah. A canvas hammock is strung from posts on the verandah and there are a few old wicker rockers and rattan lounging chairs at one side.

ACT ONE

As the curtain rises, there are sounds of a party of excited female tourists arriving by bus on the road down the hill below the Costa Verde Hotel. Mrs. Maxine Faulk, the proprietor of the hotel, comes around the turn of the verandah. She is a stout, swarthy woman in her middle forties—affable and rapaciously lusty. She is wearing a pair of levis and a blouse that is half unbuttoned. She is followed by Pedro, a Mexican of about twenty—slim and attractive. He is an employee in the hotel and also her casual lover. Pedro is stuffing his shirt under the belt of his pants and sweating as if he had been working hard in the sun. Mrs. Faulk looks down the hill and is pleased by the sight of someone coming up from the tourist bus below.

MAXINE (*calling out*): Shannon! (*A man's voice from below answers:* "Hi!") Hah! (*Maxine always laughs with a single harsh, loud bark, opening her mouth like a seal expecting a fish to be thrown to it.*) My spies told me that you were back under the border! (*to Pedro*) Anda, hombre, anda!

(*Maxine's delight expands and vibrates in her as Shannon labors up the hill to the hotel. He does not appear on the jungle path for a minute or two after the shouting between them starts.*)

MAXINE: Hah! My spies told me you went through Saltillo last week with a busload of women—a whole busload of females, all females, hah! How many you laid so far? Hah!

SHANNON (*from below, panting*): Great Caesar's ghost . . . stop . . . shouting!

MAXINE: No wonder your ass is draggin', hah!

SHANNON: Tell the kid to help me up with this bag.

MAXINE (*shouting directions*): Pedro! Anda—la maléta. Pancho, no seas flojo! Va y trae el equipaje del señor.

(*Pancho, another young Mexican, comes around the verandah and trots down the jungle path. Pedro has climbed up a coconut tree with a machete and is chopping down nuts for rum-cocos.*)

SHANNON (*shouting, below*): Fred? Hey, Fred!

329

MAXINE (*with a momentary gravity*): Fred can't hear you, Shannon. (*She goes over and picks up a coconut, shaking it against her ear to see if it has milk in it.*)

SHANNON (*still below*): Where is Fred—gone fishing?

(*Maxine lops the end off a coconut with the machete, as Pancho trots up to the verandah with Shannon's bag—a beat-up Gladstone covered with travel stickers from all over the world. Then Shannon appears, in a crumpled white linen suit. He is panting, sweating and wild-eyed. About thirty-five, Shannon is "black Irish." His nervous state is terribly apparent; he is a young man who has cracked up before and is going to crack up again—perhaps repeatedly.*)

MAXINE: Well! Lemme look at you!

SHANNON: Don't look at me, get dressed!

MAXINE: Gee, you look like you had it!

SHANNON: You look like you been having it, too. Get dressed!

MAXINE: Hell, I'm dressed. I never dress in September. Don't you know I never dress in September?

SHANNON: Well, just, just—button your shirt up.

MAXINE: How long you been off it, Shannon?

SHANNON: Off what?

MAXINE: The wagon . . .

SHANNON: Hell, I'm dizzy with fever. Hundred and three this morning in Cuernavaca.

MAXINE: Watcha got wrong with you?

SHANNON: Fever . . . fever . . . Where's Fred?

MAXINE: Dead.

SHANNON: Did you say *dead*?

MAXINE: That's what I said. Fred is dead.

SHANNON: How?

MAXINE: Less'n two weeks ago, Fred cut his hand on a fish-hook, it got infected, infection got in his blood stream, and he was dead inside of forty-eight hours. (*to Pancho*) Vete!

SHANNON: Holy smoke. . . .

MAXINE: I can't quite realize it yet. . . .

SHANNON: You don't seem—inconsolable about it.

MAXINE: Fred was an old man, baby. Ten years older'n me. We hadn't had sex together in. . . .

SHANNON: What's that got to do with it?

MAXINE: Lie down and have a rum-coco.

SHANNON: No, no. I want a cold beer. If I start drinking rum-cocos now I won't stop drinking rum-cocos. So Fred is dead? I looked forward to lying in this hammock and talking to Fred.

MAXINE: Well Fred's not talking now, Shannon. A diabetic gets a blood infection, he goes like that without a decent hospital in less'n a week. (*A bus horn is heard blowing from below.*) Why don't your busload of women come on up here? They're blowing the bus horn down there.

SHANNON: Let 'em blow it, blow it. . . . (*He sways a little.*) I got a fever. (*He goes to the top of the path, divides the flowering bushes and shouts down the hill to the bus.*) Hank! Hank! Get them out of the bus and bring 'em up here! Tell 'em the rates are OK. Tell 'em the . . . (*His voice gives out, and he stumbles back to the verandah, where he sinks down onto the low steps, panting.*) Absolutely the worst party I've ever been out with in ten years of conducting tours. For God's sake, help me with 'em because I can't go on. I got to rest here a while. (*She gives him a cold beer.*) Thanks. Look and see if they're getting out of the bus. (*She crosses to the masking foliage and separates it to look down the hill.*) Are they getting out of the bus or are they staying in it, the stingy—daughters of—bitches. . . . Schoolteachers at a Baptist Female College in Blowing Rock, Texas. Eleven, eleven of them.

MAXINE: A football squad of old maids.

SHANNON: Yeah, and I'm the football. Are they out of the bus?

MAXINE: One's gotten out—she's going into the bushes.

SHANNON: Well, I've got the ignition key to the bus in my pocket—this pocket—so they can't continue without me unless they walk.

MAXINE: They're still blowin' that horn.

SHANNON: Fantastic. I can't lose this party. Blake Tours has put me on probation because I had a bad party last month that tried to get me sacked and I am now on probation with Blake Tours. If I lose this party I'll be sacked for sure . . . Ah, my God, are they still all in the bus? (*He heaves himself off the steps and staggers back to the path, dividing the foliage to look down it, then shouts.*) Hank! Get them out of the busssss! Bring them up heeee-re!

HANK'S VOICE (*from below*): They wanta go back in tooooooowwww-n.

SHANNON: They *can't* go back in tooooowwwwn!—Whew— Five years ago this summer I was conducting round-the-world tours for Cook's. Exclusive groups of retired Wall Street financiers. We traveled in fleets of Pierce Arrows and Hispano Suizas.—Are they getting out of the bus?

MAXINE: You're going to pieces, are you?

SHANNON: No! Gone! Gone! (*He rises and shouts down the hill again.*) Hank! come up here! Come on up here a minute! I wanta talk to you about this situation!— Incredible, fantastic . . . (*He drops back on the steps, his head falling into his hands.*)

MAXINE: They're not getting out of the bus.—Shannon . . . you're not in a nervous condition to cope with this party, Shannon, so let them go and you stay.

SHANNON: You know my situation: I lose this job, what's next? There's nothing lower than Blake Tours, Maxine honey.—Are they getting out of the bus? Are they getting out of it now?

MAXINE: Man's comin' up the hill.

SHANNON: Aw. Hank. You gotta help me with him.

MAXINE: I'll give him a rum-coco.

(*Hank comes grinning onto the verandah.*)

HANK: Shannon, them ladies are not gonna come up here, so you better come on back to the bus.

SHANNON: Fantastic.—I'm not going down to the bus and I've got the ignition key to the bus in my pocket. It's going to stay in my pocket for the next three days.

HANK: You can't get away with that, Shannon. Hell, they'll walk back to town if you don't give up the bus key.

SHANNON: They'd drop like flies from sunstrokes on that road. . . . Fantastic, absolutely fantastic . . . (*Panting and sweating, he drops a hand on Hank's shoulder.*) Hank, I want your co-operation. Can I have it? Because when you're out with a difficult party like this, the tour con-

ductor—me—and the guide—you—have got to stick together to control the situations as they come up against us.
It's a test of strength between two men, in this case, and a
busload of old wet *hens*! You know that, don't you?

HANK: Well. . . . (*He chuckles.*) There's this kid that's crying
on the back seat all the time, and that's what's rucked up
the deal. Hell, I don't know if you did or you didn't, but
they all think that you did 'cause the kid keeps crying.

SHANNON: *Hank? Look!* I don't care what they think. A tour
conducted by T. Lawrence Shannon is in his charge, completely—where to go, when to go, every detail of it.
Otherwise I resign. So go on back down there and get
them out of that bus before they suffocate in it. Haul them
out by force if necessary and herd them up here. Hear me?
Don't give me any argument about it. Mrs. Faulk, honey?
Give him a menu, give him one of your sample menus to
show the ladies. She's got a Chinaman cook here, you
won't believe the menu. The cook's from Shanghai, handled the kitchen at an exclusive club there. I got him here
for her, and he's a bug, a fanatic about—whew!—continental cuisine . . . can even make beef Strogonoff and thermi-
dor dishes. Mrs. Faulk, honey? Hand him one of those
—whew!—one of those fantastic sample menus. (*Maxine
chuckles, as if perpetrating a practical joke, as she hands him
a sheet of paper.*) Thanks. Now, here. Go on back down
there and show them this fantastic menu. Describe the view
from the hill, and . . . (*Hank accepts the menu with a
chuckling shake of the head.*) And have a cold Carta Blanca
and. . . .

HANK: You better go down with me.

SHANNON: I can't leave this verandah for at least forty-eight
hours. *What in blazes is this?* A little animated cartoon by
Hieronymus Bosch?

(*The German family which is staying at the hotel, the
Fahrenkopfs, their daughter and son-in-law, suddenly make a
startling, dreamlike entrance upon the scene. They troop
around the verandah, then turn down into the jungle path.
They are all dressed in the minimal concession to decency and
all are pink and gold like baroque cupids in various sizes—*

Rubensesque, splendidly physical. The bride, Hilda, walks astride a big inflated rubber horse which has an ecstatic smile and great winking eyes. She shouts "Horsey, horsey, giddap!" *as she waddles astride it, followed by her Wagnerian-tenor bridegroom, Wolfgang, and her father, Herr Fahrenkopf, a tank manufacturer from Frankfurt. He is carrying a portable shortwave radio, which is tuned in to the crackle and guttural voices of a German broadcast reporting the Battle of Britain. Frau Fahrenkopf, bursting with rich, healthy fat and carrying a basket of food for a picnic at the beach, brings up the rear. They begin to sing a Nazi marching song.*)

SHANNON: Aw—Nazis. How come there's so many of them down here lately?

MAXINE: Mexico's the front door to South America—and the back door to the States, that's why.

SHANNON: Aw, and you're setting yourself up here as a receptionist at both doors, now that Fred's dead? (*Maxine comes over and sits down on him in the hammock.*) Get off my pelvis before you crack it. If you want to crack something, crack some ice for my forehead. (*She removes a chunk of ice from her glass and massages his forehead with it.*)—Ah, God. . . .

MAXINE (*chuckling*): Ha, so you took the young chick and the old hens are squawking about it, Shannon?

SHANNON: The kid asked for it, no kidding, but she's seventeen—less, a month less'n seventeen. So it's serious, it's very serious, because the kid is not just emotionally precocious, she's a musical prodigy, too.

MAXINE: What's that got to do with it?

SHANNON: Here's what it's got to do with it, she's traveling under the wing, the military escort, of this, this—butch vocal teacher who organizes little community sings in the bus. Ah, God! I'm surprised they're not singing now, they must've already suffocated. Or they'd be singing some morale-boosting number like "She's a Jolly Good Fellow" or "Pop Goes the Weasel."—Oh, God. . . . (*Maxine chuckles up and down the scale.*) And each night after supper, after the complaints about the supper and the check-up on the checks by the math instructor, and the vomiting of the supper by several ladies, who have inspected the kitchen—then the kid, the canary, will give a vocal recital. She opens her mouth and out flies Carrie Jacobs Bond or Ethelbert Nevin. I mean after a day of one indescribable torment after another, such as three blowouts, and a leaking radiator in Tierra Caliente. . . . (*He sits up slowly in the hammock as these recollections gather force.*) And an evening climb up sierras, through torrents of rain, around hairpin turns over gorges and chasms measureless to man, and with a thermos-jug under the driver's seat which the Baptist College ladies think is filled with icewater but which I know is filled with iced tequila—I mean after such a day has finally come to a close, the musical prodigy, Miss Charlotte Goodall, right after supper, before there's a chance to escape, will give a heartbreaking and earsplitting rendition of Carrie Jacobs Bond's "End of a Perfect Day"—with absolutely no humor. . . .

MAXINE: Hah!

SHANNON: Yeah, "Hah!" Last night—no, night before last, the bus burned out its brake linings in Chilpancingo. This town has a hotel . . . this hotel has a piano, which hasn't been tuned since they shot Maximilian. This Texas songbird opens her mouth and out flies "I Love You Truly," and it flies straight at *me*, with *gestures*, all right at *me*, till her chaperone, this Diesel-driven vocal instructor of hers, slams the piano lid down and hauls her out of the mess hall. But as she's hauled out Miss Bird-Girl opens her mouth and out flies, "Larry, Larry, I love you, I love you truly!" That night, when I went to my room, I found that I had a roommate.

MAXINE: The musical prodigy had moved in with you?

SHANNON: The *spook* had moved in with me. In that hot room with one bed, the width of an ironing board and about as hard, the spook was up there on it, sweating, stinking, grinning up at me.

MAXINE: Aw, the spook. (*She chuckles.*) So you've got the spook with you again.

SHANNON: That's right, he's the only passenger that got off the bus with me, honey.

MAXINE: Is he here now?

SHANNON: Not far.

MAXINE: On the verandah?

SHANNON: He might be on the other side of the verandah. Oh, he's around somewhere, but he's like the Sioux Indians in the Wild West fiction, he doesn't attack before sundown, he's an after-sundown shadow. . . .

(*Shannon wriggles out of the hammock as the bus horn gives one last, long protesting blast.*)

MAXINE:

>I have a little shadow
>That goes in and out with me,
>And what can be the use of him
>Is more than I can see.
>
>He's very, very like me,
>From his heels up to his head,
>And he always hops before me
>When I hop into my bed.

SHANNON: That's the truth. He sure hops in the bed with me.

MAXINE: When you're sleeping alone, or . . . ?

SHANNON: I haven't slept in three nights.

MAXINE: Aw, you will tonight, baby.

(*The bus horn sounds again. Shannon rises and squints down the hill at the bus.*)

SHANNON: How long's it take to sweat the faculty of a Baptist Female College out of a bus that's parked in the sun when it's a hundred degrees in the shade?

MAXINE: They're staggering out of it now.

SHANNON: Yeah, I've won *this* round, I reckon. What're they doing down there, can you see?

MAXINE: They're crowding around your pal Hank.

SHANNON: Tearing him to pieces?

MAXINE: One of them's slapped him, he's ducked back into the bus, and she is starting up here.

SHANNON: Oh, Great Caesar's ghost, it's the butch vocal teacher.

MISS FELLOWES (*in a strident voice, from below*): Shannon! Shannon!

SHANNON: For God's sake, help me with her.

MAXINE: You know I'll help you, baby, but why don't you lay off the young ones and cultivate an interest in normal grown-up women?

MISS FELLOWES (*her voice coming nearer*): Shannon!

SHANNON (*shouting down the hill*): Come on up, Miss Fellowes, everything's fixed. (*to Maxine*) Oh, God, here she comes chargin' up the hill like a bull elephant on a rampage!

(*Miss Fellowes thrashes through the foliage at the top of the jungle path.*)

SHANNON: Miss Fellowes, never do that! Not at high noon in a tropical country in summer. Never charge up a hill like you were leading a troop of cavalry attacking an almost impregnable. . . .

MISS FELLOWES (*panting and furious*): I don't want advice or instructions, I want the *bus key*!

SHANNON: Mrs. Faulk, this is Miss Judith Fellowes.

MISS FELLOWES: Is this man making a deal with you?

MAXINE: I don't know what you—

MISS FELLOWES: Is this man getting a *kickback* out of you?

MAXINE: Nobody gets any kickback out of me. I turn away more people than—

MISS FELLOWES (*cutting in*): This isn't the Ambos Mundos. It says in the brochure that in Puerto Barrio we stay at the Ambos Mundos in the heart of the city.

SHANNON: Yes, on the plaza—tell her about the plaza.

MAXINE: What about the plaza?

SHANNON: It's hot, noisy, stinking, swarming with flies. Pariah dogs dying in the—

MISS FELLOWES: How is this place better?

SHANNON: The view from this verandah is equal and I think better than the view from Victoria Peak in Hong Kong, the view from the roof-terrace of the Sultan's palace in—

MISS FELLOWES (*cutting in*): I want the view of a clean bed, a bathroom with plumbing that works, and food that is eatable and digestible and not contaminated by filthy—

SHANNON: *Miss Fellowes!*

MISS FELLOWES: Take your hand off my arm.

SHANNON: Look at this sample menu. The cook is a Chinese imported from Shanghai by *me!* Sent here by *me,* year before last, in nineteen thirty-eight. He was the chef at the Royal Colonial Club in—

MISS FELLOWES (*cutting in*): You got a telephone here?

MAXINE: Sure, in the office.

MISS FELLOWES: I want to use it— I'll call collect. Where's the office?

MAXINE (*to Pancho*): Llevala al telefono!

(*With Pancho showing her the way, Miss Fellowes stalks off around the verandah to the office. Shannon falls back, sighing desperately, against the verandah wall.*)

MAXINE: Hah!

SHANNON: Why did you have to . . . ?

MAXINE: Huh?

SHANNON: Come out looking like this! For you it's funny but for me it's. . . .

MAXINE: This is how I *look*. What's wrong with how I *look*?

SHANNON: I told you to button your shirt. Are you so proud of your boobs that you won't button your shirt up?—Go in the office and see if she's calling Blake Tours to get me fired.

MAXINE: She better not unless she pays for the call.

(*She goes around the turn of the verandah.*
(*Miss Hannah Jelkes appears below the verandah steps and stops short as Shannon turns to the wall, pounding his fist against it with a sobbing sound in his throat.*)

HANNAH: Excuse me.

(*Shannon looks down at her, dazed. Hannah is remarkable-looking—ethereal, almost ghostly. She suggests a Gothic cathedral image of a medieval saint, but animated. She could be thirty, she could be forty: she is totally feminine and yet androgynous-looking—almost timeless. She is wearing a cotton print dress and has a bag slung on a strap over her shoulder.*)

HANNAH: Is this the Costa Verde Hotel?

SHANNON (*suddenly pacified by her appearance*): Yes. Yes, it is.

HANNAH: Are you . . . you're not, the hotel manager, are you?

SHANNON: No. She'll be right back.

HANNAH: Thank you. Do you have any idea if they have two vacancies here? One for myself and one for my grandfather who's waiting in a taxi down there on the road. I didn't want to bring him up the hill—till I'd made sure they have rooms for us first.

SHANNON: Well, there's plenty of room here out-of-season—like now.

HANNAH: Good! Wonderful! I'll get him out of the taxi.

SHANNON: Need any help?

HANNAH: No, thank you. We'll make it all right.

(*She gives him a pleasant nod and goes back off down the path through the rain forest. A coconut plops to the ground; a parrot screams at a distance. Shannon drops into the hammock and stretches out. Then Maxine reappears.*)

SHANNON: How about the call? Did she make a phone call?

MAXINE: She called a judge in Texas—Blowing Rock, Texas. Collect.

SHANNON: She's trying to get me fired and she is also trying to pin on me a rape charge, a charge of statutory rape.

MAXINE: What's "statutory rape"? I've never known what that was.

SHANNON: That's when a man is seduced by a girl under twenty. (*She chuckles.*) It's not funny, Maxine honey.

MAXINE: Why do you want the young ones—or think that you do?

SHANNON: I don't want any, any—regardless of age.

MAXINE: Then why do you take them, Shannon? (*He swallows but does not answer.*)—Huh, Shannon.

SHANNON: People need human contact, Maxine honey.

MAXINE: What size shoe do you wear?

SHANNON: I don't get the point of that question.

MAXINE: These shoes are shot and if I remember correctly, you travel with only one pair. Fred's estate included one good pair of shoes and your feet look about his size.

SHANNON: I loved ole Fred but I don't want to fill his shoes, honey.

(*She has removed Shannon's beat-up, English-made oxfords.*)

MAXINE: Your socks are shot. Fred's socks would fit you, too, Shannon. (*She opens his collar.*) Aw-aw, I see you got on your gold cross. That's a bad sign, it means you're thinkin' again about goin' back to the Church.

SHANNON: This is my last tour, Maxine. I wrote my old Bishop this morning a complete confession and a complete capitulation.

(*She takes a letter from his damp shirt pocket.*)

MAXINE: If this is the letter, baby, you've sweated through it, so the old bugger couldn't read it even if you mailed it to him this time.

(*She has started around the verandah, and goes off as Hank reappears up the hill-path, mopping his face. Shannon's relaxed position in the hammock aggravates Hank sorely.*)

HANK: Will you get your ass out of that hammock?

SHANNON: No, I will not.

HANK: Shannon, git out of that hammock! (*He kicks at Shannon's hips in the hammock.*)

SHANNON: Hank, if you can't function under rough circumstances, you are in the wrong racket, man. I gave you instructions, the instructions were simple. I said get them out of the bus and. . . .

(*Maxine comes back with a kettle of water, a towel and other shaving equipment.*)

HANK: Out of the hammock, Shannon! (*He kicks Shannon again, harder.*)

SHANNON (*warningly*): That's enough, Hank. A little familiarity goes a long way, but not as far as you're going. (*Maxine starts lathering his face.*) What's this, what are you . . . ?

MAXINE: Haven't you ever had a shave-and-haircut by a lady barber?

HANK: The kid has gone into hysterics.

MAXINE: Hold still, Shannon.

SHANNON: Hank, hysteria is a natural phenomenon, the common denominator of the female nature. It's the big female weapon, and the test of a man is his ability to cope with

it, and I can't believe you can't. If I believed that you
couldn't, I would not be able—

MAXINE: Hold still!

SHANNON: I'm holding still. (*to Hank*) No, I wouldn't be
able to take you out with me again. So go on back down
there and—

HANK: You want me to go back down there and tell them
you're getting a shave up here in a hammock?

MAXINE: Tell them that Reverend Larry is going back to the
Church so they can go back to the Female College in
Texas.

HANK: I want another beer.

MAXINE: Help yourself, piggly-wiggly, the cooler's in my office right around there. (*She points around the corner of the
verandah.*)

SHANNON (*as Hank goes off*): It's horrible how you got to
bluff and keep bluffing even when hollering "Help!" is all
you're up to, Maxine. *You cut me!*

MAXINE: You didn't hold still.

SHANNON: Just trim the beard a little.

MAXINE: I know. Baby, tonight we'll go night-swimming,
whether it storms or not.

SHANNON: Ah, God. . . .

MAXINE: The Mexican kids are wonderful night-swimmers.
. . . Hah, when I found 'em they were taking the two-
hundred-foot dives off the Quebrada, but the Quebrada
Hotel kicked 'em out for being over-attentive to the lady
guests there. That's how I got hold of them.

SHANNON: Maxine, you're bigger than life and twice as unnatural, honey.

MAXINE: No one's bigger than life-size, Shannon, or even
ever that big, except maybe Fred. (*She shouts* "Fred?" *and
gets a faint answering echo from an adjoining hill.*) Little Sir
Echo is all that answers for him now, Shannon, but. . . .
(*She pats some bay rum on his face.*) Dear old Fred was always a mystery to me. He was so patient and tolerant with
me that it was insulting to me. A man and a woman have
got to challenge each other, y'know what I mean. I mean I
hired those diving-boys from the Quebrada six months before Fred died, and did he care? Did he give a damn when

I started night-swimming with them? No. He'd go night-*fishing*, all night, and when I got up the next day, he'd be preparing to go out fishing again, but he just caught the fish and threw them back in the sea.

(*Hank returns and sits drinking his beer on the steps.*)

SHANNON: The mystery of old Fred was simple. He was just cool and decent, that's all the mystery of him. . . . Get your pair of night-swimmers to grab my ladies' luggage out of the bus before the vocal-teacher gets off the phone and stops them.

MAXINE (*shouting*): Pedro! Pancho! Muchachos! Trae las maletas al anejo! Pronto! (*The Mexican boys start down the path. Maxine sits in the hammock beside Shannon.*) You I'll put in Fred's old room, next to me.

SHANNON: You want me in his socks and his shoes and in his room next to *you*? (*He stares at her with a shocked surmise of her intentions toward him, then flops back down in the hammock with an incredulous laugh.*) Oh no, honey. I've just been hanging on till I could get in this hammock on this verandah over the rain forest and the still-water beach, that's all that can pull me through this last tour in a condition to go back to my . . . original . . . vocation.

MAXINE: Hah, you still have some rational moments when you face the fact that churchgoers don't go to church to hear atheistical sermons.

SHANNON: Goddamit, I never preached an atheistical sermon in a church in my life, and. . . .

(*Miss Fellowes has charged out of the office and rounds the verandah to bear down on Shannon and Maxine, who jumps up out of the hammock.*)

MISS FELLOWES: I've completed my call, which I made collect to Texas.

(*Maxine shrugs, going by her around the verandah. Miss Fellowes runs across the verandah.*)

SHANNON (*sitting up in the hammock*): Excuse me, Miss Fellowes, for not getting out of this hammock, but I . . .

Miss Fellowes? Please sit down a minute, I want to confess something to you.

MISS FELLOWES: *That* ought to be int'restin'! *What?*

SHANNON: Just that—well, like everyone else, at some point or other in life, my life has cracked up on me.

MISS FELLOWES: How does that compensate *us?*

SHANNON: I don't think I know what you mean by *compensate*, Miss Fellowes. (*He props himself up and gazes at her with the gentlest bewilderment, calculated to melt a heart of stone.*) I mean I've just confessed to you that I'm at the end of my rope, and you say, "How does that compensate *us?*" Please, Miss Fellowes. Don't make me feel that any adult human being puts personal compensation before the dreadful, bare fact of a man at the end of his rope who still has to try to go on, to continue, as if he'd never been better or stronger in his whole existence. No, don't do that, it would. . . .

MISS FELLOWES: It would *what?*

SHANNON: Shake if not shatter everything left of my faith in essential . . . human . . . *goodness!*

MAXINE (*returning, with a pair of socks*): Hah!

MISS FELLOWES: Can you sit there, I mean lie there—yeah, I mean *lie* there . . . ! and talk to me about—

MAXINE: Hah!

MISS FELLOWES: "Essential human goodness"? Why, just plain human decency is beyond your imagination, Shannon, so lie there, lie there and *lie* there, we're *going!*

SHANNON (*rising from the hammock*): Miss Fellowes, I thought that I was conducting this party, not you.

MISS FELLOWES: You? You just now *admitted* you're incompetent, as well as. . . .

MAXINE: Hah.

SHANNON: Maxine, will you—

MISS FELLOWES (*cutting in with cold, righteous fury*): Shannon, we girls have worked and slaved all year at Baptist Female College for this Mexican tour, and the tour is a cheat!

SHANNON (*to himself*): Fantastic!

MISS FELLOWES: Yes, *cheat!* You haven't stuck to the schedule and you haven't stuck to the itinerary advertised in the brochure which Blake Tours put out. Now either Blake

Tours is cheating us or you are cheating Blake Tours, and I'm putting wheels in motion—I don't care *what* it costs me—I'm. . . .

SHANNON: Oh, Miss Fellowes, isn't it just as plain to you as it is to me that your hysterical insults, which are not at all easy for any born and bred gentleman to accept, are not . . . *motivated*, *provoked* by . . . anything as *trivial* as the, the . . . the motivations that you're, you're . . . *ascribing* them to? Now can't we talk about the *real, true* cause of. . . .

MISS FELLOWES: Cause of *what*?

(*Charlotte Goodall appears at the top of the hill.*)

SHANNON:—Cause of your *rage* Miss Fellowes, your—
MISS FELLOWES: *Charlotte!* Stay down the hill in the *bus*!
CHARLOTTE: Judy, they're—
MISS FELLOWES: *Obey me! Down!*

(*Charlotte retreats from view like a well-trained dog. Miss Fellowes charges back to Shannon who has gotten out of the hammock. He places a conciliatory hand on her arm.*)

MISS FELLOWES: *Take your hand off my arm!*
MAXINE: Hah!
SHANNON: *Fantastic.* Miss Fellowes, please! No more shouting? Please? Now I really must ask you to let this party of ladies come up here and judge the accommodations for themselves and compare them with what they saw passing through town. Miss Fellowes, there is such a thing as charm and beauty in some places, as much as there's nothing but dull, ugly imitation of highway motels in Texas and—

(*Miss Fellowes charges over to the path to see if Charlotte has obeyed her. Shannon follows, still propitiatory. Maxine says "Hah," but she gives him an affectionate little pat as he goes by her. He pushes her hand away as he continues his appeal to Miss Fellowes.*)

MISS FELLOWES: I've taken a look at those rooms and they'd make a room at the "Y" look like a suite at the Ritz.
SHANNON: Miss Fellowes, I am employed by Blake Tours and so I'm not in a position to tell you quite frankly what mistakes they've made in their advertising brochure. They just

don't know Mexico. I do. I know it as well as I know five
out of all six continents on the—

MISS FELLOWES: *Continent! Mexico?* You never even studied
geography if you—

SHANNON: My degree from Sewanee is *Doctor* of *Divinity*,
but for the past ten years geography's been my *specialty*,
Miss Fellowes, honey! Name any tourist agency I haven't
worked for! You couldn't! I'm only, now, with Blake Tours
because I—

MISS FELLOWES: Because you *what?* Couldn't keep your
hands off innocent, under-age girls in your—

SHANNON: Now, Miss Fellowes. . . . (*He touches her arm
again.*)

MISS FELLOWES: Take your hand off my arm!

SHANNON: For days I've known you were furious and unhappy, but—

MISS FELLOWES: *Oh!* You think it's just *me* that's unhappy!
Hauled in that stifling bus over the byways, off the highways, shook up and bumped up so you could get your rake-
off, is that what you—

SHANNON: What I know is, all I know is, that you are the
leader of the *insurrection!*

MISS FELLOWES: All of the girls in this party have dysentery!

SHANNON: That you can't hold me to blame for.

MISS FELLOWES: I *do* hold you to blame for it.

SHANNON: Before we entered Mexico, at New Laredo, Texas,
I called you ladies together in the depot on the Texas side
of the border and I passed out mimeographed sheets of instructions on what to eat and what *not* to eat, what to
drink, what *not* to drink in the—

MISS FELLOWES: It's not *what* we ate but *where* we ate that
gave us dysentery!

SHANNON (*shaking his head like a metronome*): It is not
dysentery.

MISS FELLOWES: The result of eating in places that would be
condemned by the Board of Health in—

SHANNON: Now wait a minute—

MISS FELLOWES: For disregarding all rules of sanitation.

SHANNON: It is not dysentery, it is not amoebic, it's nothing
at all but—

MAXINE: Montezuma's Revenge! That's what we call it.

SHANNON: I even passed out pills. I passed out bottles of Enteroviaform because I knew that some of you ladies would rather be victims of Montezuma's Revenge than spend cinco centavos on bottled water in stations.

MISS FELLOWES: You sold those pills at a profit of fifty cents per bottle.

MAXINE: Hah-hah! (*She knocks off the end of a coconut with the machete, preparing a rum-coco.*)

SHANNON: Now fun is fun, Miss Fellowes, but an accusation like that—

MISS FELLOWES: I *priced* them in *pharmacies*, because I suspected that—

SHANNON: Miss Fellowes, I am a gentleman, and as a gentleman I can't be insulted like this. I mean I can't accept insults of that kind even from a member of a tour that I am conducting. And, Miss Fellowes, I think you might also remember, you might try to remember, that you're speaking to an ordained minister of the Church.

MISS FELLOWES: *De*-frocked! But still trying to pass himself off as a minister!

MAXINE: How about a rum-coco? We give a complimentary rum-coco to all our guests here. (*Her offer is apparently unheard. She shrugs and drinks the rum-coco herself.*)

SHANNON:—Miss Fellowes? In every party there is always one individual that's discontented, that is not satisfied with all I do to make the tour more . . . unique—to make it different from the ordinary, to give it a personal thing, the Shannon touch.

MISS FELLOWES: The gyp touch, the touch of a defrocked minister.

SHANNON: Miss Fellowes, don't, don't, don't . . . do what . . . you're doing! (*He is on the verge of hysteria, he makes some incoherent sounds, gesticulates with clenched fists, then stumbles wildly across the verandah and leans panting for breath against a post.*) Don't! Break! *Human! Pride!*

VOICE FROM DOWN THE HILL (*a very Texan accent*): Judy? They're taking our luggage!

MISS FELLOWES (*shouting down the hill*): Girls! Girls! Don't let those boys touch your luggage. Don't let them bring your luggage in this dump!

GIRL'S VOICE (*from below*): Judy! We can't stop them!

MAXINE: Those kids don't understand English.

MISS FELLOWES (*wild with rage*): Will you please tell those boys to take that luggage back down to the bus? (*She calls to the party below again.*) Girls! Hold onto your luggage, don't let them take it away! We're going to drive back to A-cap-ul-co! *You hear?*

GIRL'S VOICE: Judy, they want a swim, first!

MISS FELLOWES: I'll be right back. (*She rushes off, shouting at the Mexican boys.*) You! Boys! Muchachos! *You carry that luggage back down!*

(*The voices continue, fading. Shannon moves brokenly across the verandah. Maxine shakes her head.*)

MAXINE: Shannon, give 'em the bus key and let 'em go.

SHANNON: And me do what?

MAXINE: Stay here.

SHANNON: In Fred's old bedroom—yeah, in Fred's old bedroom.

MAXINE: You could do worse.

SHANNON: Could I? Well, then, I'll do worse, I'll . . . do worse.

MAXINE: Aw now, baby.

SHANNON: If I could do worse, I'll do worse. . . . (*He grips the section of railing by the verandah steps and stares with wide, lost eyes. His chest heaves like a spent runner's and he is bathed in sweat.*)

MAXINE: Give me that ignition key. I'll take it down to the driver while you bathe and rest and have a rum-coco, baby.

(*Shannon simply shakes his head slightly. Harsh bird cries sound in the rain forest. Voices are heard on the path.*)

HANNAH: Nonno, you've lost your sun glasses.

NONNO: No. Took them off. No sun.

(*Hannah appears at the top of the path, pushing her grand-father, Nonno, in a wheelchair. He is a very old man but has*) *a powerful voice for his age and always seems to be shouting something of importance. Nonno is a poet and a showman. There is a good kind of pride and he has it, carrying it like a banner wherever he goes. He is immaculately dressed—a linen suit, white as his thick poet's hair; a black string tie; and he is holding a black cane with a gold crook.*)

NONNO: Which way is the sea?

HANNAH: Right down below the hill, Nonno. (*He turns in the wheelchair and raises a hand to shield his eyes.*) We can't see it from here. (*The old man is deaf, and she shouts to make him hear.*)

NONNO: I can feel it and smell it. (*A murmur of wind sweeps through the rain forest.*) It's the cradle of life. (*He is shouting, too.*) Life began in the sea.

MAXINE: These two with your party?

SHANNON: No.

MAXINE: They look like a pair of loonies.

SHANNON: Shut up.

(*Shannon looks at Hannah and Nonno steadily, with a relief of tension almost like that of someone going under hypnosis. The old man still squints down the path, blindly, but Hannah is facing the verandah with a proud person's hope of acceptance when it is desperately needed.*)

HANNAH: How do you do.

MAXINE: Hello.

HANNAH: Have you ever tried pushing a gentleman in a wheelchair uphill through a rain forest?

MAXINE: Nope, and I wouldn't even try it *downhill.*

HANNAH: Well, now that we've made it, I don't regret the effort. What a view for a painter! (*She looks about her, panting, digging into her shoulder-bag for a handkerchief, aware that her face is flushed and sweating.*) They told me in town that this was the ideal place for a painter, and they weren't —*whew*—exaggerating!

SHANNON: You've got a scratch on your forehead.

HANNAH: Oh, is that what I felt.

SHANNON: Better put iodine on it.

HANNAH: Yes, I'll attend to that—*whew*—later, thank you.

MAXINE: Anything I can do for you?

HANNAH: I'm looking for the manager of the hotel.

MAXINE: Me—speaking.

HANNAH: Oh, *you're* the manager, *good*! How do you do, I'm Hannah Jelkes, Mrs. . . .

MAXINE: Faulk, Maxine Faulk. What can I do for you folks? (*Her tone indicates no desire to do anything for them.*)

HANNAH (*turning quickly to her grandfather*): Nonno, the manager is a *lady* from the *States*.

(*Nonno lifts a branch of wild orchids from his lap, ceremonially, with the instinctive gallantry of his kind.*)

NONNO (*shouting*): Give the lady these—botanical curiosities! —you picked on the way up.

HANNAH: I believe they're wild orchids, isn't that what they are?

SHANNON: Laelia tibicina.

HANNAH: Oh!

NONNO: But tell her, Hannah, tell her to keep them in the icebox till after dark, they draw bees in the sun! (*He rubs a sting on his chin with a rueful chuckle.*)

MAXINE: Are you all looking for rooms here?

HANNAH: Yes, we are, but we've come without reservations.

MAXINE: Well, honey, the Costa Verde is closed in September —except for a few special guests, so. . . .

SHANNON: They're special guests, for God's sake.

MAXINE: I thought you said they didn't come with your party.

HANNAH: Please let us be special guests.

MAXINE: *Watch out!*

(*Nonno has started struggling out of the wheelchair. Shannon rushes over to keep him from falling. Hannah has started toward him, too, then seeing that Shannon has caught him, she turns back to Maxine.*)

HANNAH: In twenty-five years of travel this is the first time we've ever arrived at a place without advance reservations.

MAXINE: Honey, that old man ought to be in a hospital.

HANNAH: Oh, no, no, he just sprained his ankle a little in Taxco this morning. He just needs a good night's rest, he'll be on his feet tomorrow. His recuperative powers are absolutely amazing for someone who is ninety-seven years *young*.

SHANNON: Easy, Grampa. Hang on. (*He is supporting the old man up to the verandah.*) Two steps. One! Two! Now you've made it, Grampa.

(*Nonno keeps chuckling breathlessly as Shannon gets him onto the verandah and into a wicker rocker.*)

HANNAH (*breaking in quickly*): I can't tell you how much I appreciate your taking us in here now. It's—providential.

MAXINE: Well, I can't send that old man back down the hill —right now—but like I told you the Costa Verde's practically closed in September. I just take in a few folks as a special accommodation and we operate on a special basis this month.

NONNO (*cutting in abruptly and loudly*): Hannah, tell the lady that my perambulator is temporary. I will soon be ready to crawl and then to toddle and before long I will be leaping around here like an—old—mountain—goat, ha-ha-ha-ha. . . .

HANNAH: Yes, I explained that, Grandfather.

NONNO: I don't like being on wheels.

HANNAH: Yes, my grandfather feels that the decline of the western world began with the invention of the wheel. (*She laughs heartily, but Maxine's look is unresponsive.*)

NONNO: And tell the manager . . . the, uh, lady . . . that I know some hotels don't want to take dogs, cats or monkeys and some don't even solicit the patronage of infants in their late nineties who arrive in perambulators with flowers instead of rattles . . . (*He chuckles with a sort of fearful, slightly mad quality. Hannah perhaps has the impulse to clap a hand over his mouth at this moment but must stand there smiling and smiling and smiling.*) . . . and a brandy flask instead of a teething ring, but tell her that these, uh, concessions to man's seventh age are only temporary, and. . . .

HANNAH: Nonno, I told her the wheelchair's because of a sprained ankle, Nonno!

SHANNON (*to himself*): Fantastic.

NONNO: And after my siesta, I'll wheel it back down the hill, I'll kick it back down the hill, right into the sea, and tell her. . . .

HANNAH: Yes? What, Nonno? (*She has stopped smiling now. Her tone and her look are frankly desperate.*) What shall I tell her now, Nonno?

NONNO: Tell her that if she'll forgive my disgraceful longevity and this . . . temporary decrepitude . . . I will present her with the last signed . . . compitty [*he means* "copy"] of my first volume of verse, published in . . . when, Hannah?

HANNAH (*hopelessly*): The day that President Ulysses S. Grant was inaugurated, Nonno.

NONNO: *Morning Trumpet!* Where is it—you have it, give it to her right now.

HANNAH: Later, a little later! (*Then she turns to Maxine and Shannon.*) My grandfather is the poet Jonathan Coffin. He is ninety-seven years *young* and will be ninety-eight years *young* the fifth of next month, October.

MAXINE: Old folks are remarkable, yep. The office phone's ringing—excuse me, I'll be right back. (*She goes around the verandah.*)

NONNO: Did I talk too much?

HANNAH (*quietly, to Shannon*): I'm afraid that he did. I don't think she's going to take us.

SHANNON: She'll take you. Don't worry about it.

HANNAH: Nobody would take us in town, and if we don't get in here, I would have to wheel him back down through the rain forest, and then *what*, then *where*? There would just be the road, and no direction to move in, except out to sea— and I doubt that we could make it divide before us.

SHANNON: That won't be necessary. I have a little influence with the patrona.

HANNAH: Oh, then, do use it, please. Her eyes said *no* in big blue capital letters.

(*Shannon pours some water from a pitcher on the verandah and hands it to the old man.*)

NONNO: What is this—libation?

SHANNON: Some icewater, Grampa.

HANNAH: Oh, that's kind of you. Thank you. I'd better give him a couple of salt tablets to wash down with it. (*Briskly she removes a bottle from her shoulder-bag.*) Won't you have some? I see you're perspiring, too. You have to be careful not to become dehydrated in the hot seasons under the Tropic of Cancer.

SHANNON (*pouring another glass of water*): Are you a little *financially* dehydrated, too?

HANNAH: That's right. Bone-dry, and I think the patrona suspects it. It's a logical assumption, since I pushed him up here myself, and the patrona has the look of a very logical woman. I am sure she knows that we couldn't afford to hire the taxi driver to help us up here.

MAXINE (*calling from the back*): Pancho?

HANNAH: A woman's practicality when she's managing something is harder than a man's for another woman to cope with, so if you have influence with her, please do use it. Please try to convince her that my grandfather will be on his feet tomorrow, if not tonight, and with any luck whatsoever, the money situation will be solved just as quickly. Oh, here she comes back, do help us!

(*Involuntarily, Hannah seizes hold of Shannon's wrist as Maxine stalks back onto the verandah, still shouting for Pancho. The Mexican boy reappears, sucking a juicy peeled mango—its juice running down his chin onto his throat.*)

MAXINE: Pancho, run down to the beach and tell Herr Fahrenkopf that the German Embassy's waiting on the phone for him. (*Pancho stares at her blankly until she repeats the order in Spanish.*) Dile a Herr Fahrenkopf que la embajada alemana lo llama al telefono. Corre, corre! (*Pancho starts indolently down the path, still sucking noisily on the mango.*) I said *run*! Corre, corre! (*He goes into a leisurely loping pace and disappears through the foliage.*)

HANNAH: What graceful people they are!

MAXINE: Yeah, they're graceful like cats, and just as dependable, too.

HANNAH: Shall we, uh, . . . *register* now?

MAXINE: You all can register later but I'll have to collect six dollars from you first if you want to put your names in the pot for supper. That's how I've got to operate here out of season.

HANNAH: Six? Dollars?

MAXINE: Yeah, three each. In season we operate on the continental plan but out of season like this we change to the modified American plan.

HANNAH: Oh, what is the, uh . . . modification of it? (*She gives Shannon a quick glance of appeal as she stalls for time, but his attention has turned inward as the bus horn blows down the hill.*)

MAXINE: Just two meals are included instead of all three.

HANNAH (*moving closer to Shannon and raising her voice*): Breakfast and dinner?

MAXINE: A continental breakfast and a cold lunch.

SHANNON (*aside*): Yeah, very cold—cracked ice—if you crack it yourself.

HANNAH (*reflectively*): Not dinner.

MAXINE: No! Not dinner.

HANNAH: Oh, I see, uh, but . . . we, uh, operate on a special basis ourselves. I'd better explain it to you.

MAXINE: How do you mean "operate,"—on what "basis"?

HANNAH: Here's our card. I think you may have heard of us. (*She presents the card to Maxine.*) We've had a good many write-ups. My grandfather is the oldest living and practicing poet. *And* he gives recitations. I . . . paint . . . water colors and I'm a "quick sketch artist." We travel together. We pay our way as we go by my grandfather's recitations and the sale of my water colors and quick character sketches in charcoal or pastel.

SHANNON (*to himself*): I have fever.

HANNAH: I usually pass among the tables at lunch and dinner in a hotel. I wear an artist's smock—picturesquely dabbed with paint—wide Byronic collar and flowing silk tie. I don't push myself on people. I just display my work and smile at them sweetly and if they invite me to do so sit down to make a quick character sketch in pastel or charcoal. If not? Smile sweetly and go on.

SHANNON: What does Grandpa do?

HANNAH: We pass among the tables together slowly. I introduce him as the world's oldest living and practicing poet. If invited, he gives a recitation of a poem. Unfortunately all of his poems were written a long time ago. But do you know, he has started a new poem?

For the first time in twenty years he's started another poem!

SHANNON: Hasn't finished it yet?

HANNAH: He still has inspiration, but his power of concentration has weakened a little, of course.

MAXINE: Right now he's not concentrating.

SHANNON: Grandpa's catchin' forty winks. Grampa? Let's hit the sack.

MAXINE: Now wait a minute. I'm going to call a taxi for these folks to take them back to town.

HANNAH: Please don't do that. We tried every hotel in town and they wouldn't take us. I'm afraid I have to place myself at your . . . mercy.

(*With infinite gentleness Shannon has roused the old man and is leading him into one of the cubicles back of the verandah. Distant cries of bathers are heard from the beach. The afternoon light is fading very fast now as the sun has dropped behind an island hilltop out to sea.*)

MAXINE: Looks like you're in for one night. Just one.

HANNAH: Thank you.

MAXINE: The old man's in number 4. You take 3. Where's your luggage—no luggage?

HANNAH: I hid it behind some palmettos at the foot of the path.

SHANNON (*shouting to Pancho*): Bring up her luggage. Tu, flojo . . . las maletas . . . baja las palmas. Vamos! (*The Mexican boys rush down the path.*) Maxine honey, would you cash a postdated check for me?

MAXINE (*shrewdly*): Yeah—mañana, maybe.

SHANNON: Thanks—generosity is the cornerstone of your nature.

(*Maxine utters her one-note bark of a laugh as she marches around the corner of the verandah.*)

HANNAH: I'm dreadfully afraid my grandfather had a slight stroke in those high passes through the sierras. (*She says this with the coolness of someone saying that it may rain before nightfall. An instant later, a long, long sigh of wind sweeps the hillside. The bathers are heard shouting below.*)

SHANNON: Very old people get these little "cerebral accidents," as they call them. They're not regular strokes,
they're just little cerebral . . . incidents. The symptoms
clear up so quickly that sometimes the old people don't
even know they've had them.

(*They exchange this quiet talk without looking at each other.
The Mexican boys crash back through the bushes at the top of
the path, bearing some pieces of ancient luggage fantastically
plastered with hotel and travel stickers indicating a vast range
of wandering. The boys deposit the luggage near the steps.*)

SHANNON: How many times have you been around the
world?

HANNAH: Almost as many times as the world's been around
the sun, and I feel as if I had gone the whole way on foot.

SHANNON (*picking up her luggage*): What's your cell number?

HANNAH (*smiling faintly*): I believe she said it was cell number 3.

SHANNON: She probably gave you the one with the leaky
roof. (*He carries the bags into the cubicle. Maxine is visible to
the audience only as she appears outside the door to her office
on the wing of the verandah.*) But you won't find out till it
rains and then it'll be too late to do much about it but
swim out of it. (*Hannah laughs wanly. Her fatigue is now
very plain. Shannon comes back out with her luggage.*) Yep,
she gave you the one with the leaky roof so you take mine
and. . . .

HANNAH: Oh, no, no, Mr. Shannon, I'll find a dry spot if it
rains.

MAXINE (*from around the corner of the verandah*): Shannon!

(*A bit of pantomime occurs between Hannah and Shannon.
He wants to put her luggage in cubicle number 5. She catches
hold of his arm, indicating by gesture toward the back that it
is necessary to avoid displeasing the proprietor. Maxine shouts
his name louder. Shannon surrenders to Hannah's pleading
and puts her luggage back in the leaky cubicle number 3.*)

HANNAH: Thank you so much, Mr. Shannon. (*She disappears
behind the mosquito netting. Maxine advances to the verandah angle as Shannon starts toward his own cubicle.*)

MAXINE (*mimicking Hannah's voice*): "Thank you so much, Mr. Shannon."

SHANNON: Don't be bitchy. Some people say thank you sincerely. (*He goes past her and down the steps from the end of the verandah.*) I'm going down for a swim now.

MAXINE: The water's blood temperature this time of day.

SHANNON: Yeah, well, I have a fever so it'll seem cooler to me. (*He crosses rapidly to the jungle path leading to the beach.*)

MAXINE (*following him*): Wait for me, I'll. . . .

(*She means she will go down with him, but he ignores her call and disappears into the foliage. Maxine shrugs angrily and goes back onto the verandah. She faces out, gripping the railing tightly and glaring into the blaze of the sunset as if it were a personal enemy. Then the ocean breathes a long cooling breath up the hill, as Nonno's voice is heard from his cubicle.*)

NONNO:

> How calmly does the orange branch
> Observe the sky begin to blanch,
> Without a cry, without a prayer,
> With no expression of despair. . . .

(*And from a beach cantina in the distance a marimba band is heard playing a popular song of that summer of 1940, "Palabras de Mujer"—which means "Words of Women."*)

Slow Dim Out and Slow Curtain

ACT TWO

Several hours later: near sunset.

The scene is bathed in a deep golden, almost coppery light; the heavy tropical foliage gleams with wetness from a recent rain.

Maxine comes around the turn of the verandah. To the formalities of evening she has made the concession of changing from levis to clean white cotton pants, and from a blue work shirt to a pink one. She is about to set up the folding cardtables for the evening meal which is served on the verandah. All the while she is talking, she is setting up tables, etc.

MAXINE: Miss Jelkes?

(*Hannah lifts the mosquito net over the door of cubicle number 3.*)

HANNAH: Yes, Mrs. Faulk?

MAXINE: Can I speak to you while I set up these tables for supper?

HANNAH: Of course, you may. I wanted to speak to you, too. (*She comes out. She is now wearing her artist's smock.*)

MAXINE: Good.

HANNAH: I just wanted to ask you if there's a tub-bath Grandfather could use. A shower is fine for me—I prefer a shower to a tub—but for my grandfather there is some danger of falling down in a shower and at his age, although he says he is made out of India rubber, a broken hipbone would be a very serious matter, so I. . . .

MAXINE: What I wanted to say is I called up the Casa de Huéspedes about you and your Grampa, and I can get you in there.

HANNAH: Oh, but we don't want to *move*!

MAXINE: The Costa Verde isn't the right place for you. Y'see, we cater to folks that like to rough it a little, and—well, frankly, we cater to younger people.

(*Hannah has started unfolding a cardtable.*)

HANNAH: Oh yes . . . uh . . . well . . . the, uh, Casa de Huéspedes, that means a, uh, sort of a rooming house, Mrs. Faulk?

MAXINE: Boarding house. They feed you, they'll even feed you on credit.

HANNAH: Where is it located?

MAXINE: It has a central location. You could get a doctor there quick if the old man took sick on you. You got to think about that.

HANNAH: Yes, I—(*She nods gravely, more to herself than Maxine.*)—I *have* thought about that, but. . . .

MAXINE: What are you doing?

HANNAH: Making myself useful.

MAXINE: Don't do that. I don't accept help from guests here.

(*Hannah hesitates, but goes on setting the tables.*)

HANNAH: Oh, please, let me. Knife and fork on one side, spoon on the . . . ? (*Her voice dies out.*)

MAXINE: Just put the plates on the napkins so they don't blow away.

HANNAH: Yes, it is getting breezy on the verandah. (*She continues setting the table.*)

MAXINE: Hurricane winds are already hitting up coast.

HANNAH: We've been through several typhoons in the Orient. Sometimes *outside* disturbances like that are an almost welcome distraction from *inside* disturbances, aren't they? (*This is said almost to herself. She finishes putting the plates on the paper napkins.*) When do you want us to leave here, Mrs. Faulk?

MAXINE: The boys'll move you in my station wagon tomorrow—no charge for the service.

HANNAH: That is very kind of you. (*Maxine starts away.*) Mrs. Faulk?

MAXINE (*turning back to her with obvious reluctance*): Huh?

HANNAH: Do you know jade?

MAXINE: Jade?

HANNAH: Yes.

MAXINE: Why?

HANNAH: I have a small but interesting collection of jade pieces. I asked if you know jade because in jade it's the craftsmanship, the carving of the jade, that's most important about it. (*She has removed a jade ornament from her blouse.*) This one, for instance—a miracle of carving. Tiny as it is, it has two figures carved on it—the legendary Prince Ahk and Princess Angh, and a heron flying above them. The artist that carved it probably received for this miraculously delicate workmanship, well, I would say perhaps the price of a month's supply of rice for his family, but the merchant who employed him sold it, I would guess, for at least three hundred pounds sterling to an English lady who got tired of it and gave it to me, perhaps because I painted her not as she was at that time but as I could see she must have looked in her youth. Can you see the carving?

MAXINE: Yeah, honey, but I'm not operating a hock shop here, I'm trying to run a hotel.

HANNAH: I know, but couldn't you just accept it as security for a few days' stay here?

MAXINE: You're completely broke, are you?

HANNAH: Yes, we are—completely.

MAXINE: You say that like you're proud of it.

HANNAH: I'm not proud of it or ashamed of it either. It just happens to be what's happened to us, which has never happened before in all our travels.

MAXINE (*grudgingly*): You're telling the truth, I reckon, but I told you the truth, too, when I told you, when you came here, that I had just lost my husband and he'd left me in such a financial hole that if living didn't mean more to me than money, I'd might as well have been dropped in the ocean with him.

HANNAH: Ocean?

MAXINE (*peacefully philosophical about it*): I carried out his burial instructions exactly. Yep, my husband, Fred Faulk, was the greatest game fisherman on the West Coast of Mexico— he'd racked up unbeatable records in sailfish, tarpon, kingfish, barracuda—and on his deathbed, last week, he requested to be dropped in the sea, yeah, right out there in that bay, not even sewed up in canvas, just in his fisherman outfit. So now old Freddie the Fisherman is feeding the fish—fishes' revenge on old Freddie. How about that, I ask you?

HANNAH (*regarding Maxine sharply*): I doubt that he regrets it.

MAXINE: I do. It gives me the shivers.

(*She is distracted by the German party singing a marching song on the path up from the beach. Shannon appears at the top of the path, a wet beachrobe clinging to him. Maxine's whole concentration shifts abruptly to him. She freezes and blazes with it like an exposed power line. For a moment the "hot light" is concentrated on her tense, furious figure. Hannah provides a visual counterpoint. She clenches her eyes shut for a moment, and when they open, it is on a look of stoical despair of the refuge she has unsuccessfully fought for. Then Shannon approaches the verandah and the scene is his.*)

SHANNON: Here they come up, your conquerors of the world, Maxine honey, singing "Horst Wessel." (*He chuckles fiercely, and starts toward the verandah steps.*)

MAXINE: Shannon, wash that sand off you before you come on the verandah.

(*The Germans are heard singing the "Horst Wessel" marching song. Soon they appear, trooping up from the beach like an animated canvas by Rubens. They are all nearly nude, pinked and bronzed by the sun. The women have decked themselves with garlands of pale green seaweed, glistening wet, and the Munich-opera bridegroom is blowing on a great conch shell. His father-in-law, the tank manufacturer, has his portable radio, which is still transmitting a shortwave broadcast about the Battle of Britain, now at its climax.*)

HILDA (*capering, astride her rubber horse*): Horsey, horsey, horsey!

HERR FAHRENKOPF (*ecstatically*): London is burning, the heart of London's on fire! (*Wolfgang turns a handspring onto the verandah and walks on his hands a few paces, then tumbles over with a great whoop. Maxine laughs delightedly with the Germans.*) Beer, beer, beer!

FRAU FAHRENKOPF: Tonight champagne!

(*The euphoric horseplay and shouting continue as they gambol around the turn of the verandah. Shannon has come onto the porch. Maxine's laughter dies out a little sadly, with envy.*)

SHANNON: You're turning this place into the Mexican Berchtesgaden, Maxine honey?

MAXINE: I told you to wash that sand off. (*Shouts for beer from the Germans draw her around the verandah corner.*)

HANNAH: Mr. Shannon, do you happen to know the Casa de Huéspedes, or anything about it, I mean? (*Shannon stares at her somewhat blankly.*) We are, uh, thinking of . . . *moving* there tomorrow. Do you, uh, recommend it?

SHANNON: I recommend it along with the Black Hole of Calcutta and the Siberian salt mines.

HANNAH (*nodding reflectively*): I suspected as much. Mr. Shannon, in your touring party, do you think there might be anyone interested in my water colors? Or in my character sketches?

SHANNON: I doubt it. I doubt that they're corny enough to please my ladies. *Oh-oh! Great Caesar's ghost. . . .*

(*This exclamation is prompted by the shrill, approaching call of his name. Charlotte appears from the rear, coming from the hotel annex, and rushes like a teen-age Medea toward the verandah. Shannon ducks into his cubicle, slamming the door so quickly that a corner of the mosquito netting is caught and sticks out, flirtatiously. Charlotte rushes onto the verandah.*)

CHARLOTTE: *Larry!*

HANNAH: Are you looking for someone, dear?

CHARLOTTE: Yeah, the man conducting our tour, Larry Shannon.

HANNAH: Oh, Mr. Shannon. I think he went down to the beach.

CHARLOTTE: I just now saw him coming up from the beach. (*She is tense and trembling, and her eyes keep darting up and down the verandah.*)

HANNAH: Oh. Well. . . . But. . . .

CHARLOTTE: Larry? Larry! (*Her shouts startle the rain-forest birds into a clamorous moment.*)

HANNAH: Would you like to leave a message for him, dear?

CHARLOTTE: No. I'm staying right here till he comes out of wherever he's hiding.

HANNAH: Why don't you just sit down, dear. I'm an artist, a painter. I was just sorting out my water colors and sketches in this portfolio, and look what I've come across. (*She selects a sketch and holds it up.*)

SHANNON (*from inside his cubicle*): Oh, God!

CHARLOTTE (*darting to the cubicle*): Larry, let me in there!

(*She beats on the door of the cubicle as Herr Fahrenkopf comes around the verandah with his portable radio. He is bug-eyed with excitement over the news broadcast in German.*)

HANNAH: Guten abend.

(*Herr Fahrenkopf jerks his head with a toothy grin, raising a hand for silence. Hannah nods agreeably and approaches him with her portfolio of drawings. He maintains the grin as she displays one picture after another. Hannah is uncertain whether the grin is for the pictures or the news broadcast. He stares at the pictures, jerking his head from time to time. It is rather like the pantomine of showing lantern slides.*)

CHARLOTTE (*suddenly crying out again*): Larry, open this door
and let me in! I know you're in there, Larry!

HERR FAHRENKOPF: Silence, please, for one moment! This
is a recording of Der Führer addressing the Reichstag
just . . . (*He glances at his wristwatch.*) . . . eight hours
ago, today, transmitted by Deutsches Nachrichtenbüro to
Mexico City. Please! Quiet, bitte!

(*A human voice like a mad dog's bark emerges from the
static momentarily. Charlotte goes on pounding on Shannon's
door. Hannah suggests in pantomime that they go to the back
verandah, but Herr Fahrenkopf despairs of hearing the
broadcast. As he rises to leave, the light catches his polished
glasses so that he appears for a moment to have electric light
bulbs in his forehead. Then he ducks his head in a genial little bow and goes out beyond the verandah, where he performs
some muscle-flexing movements of a formalized nature, like
the preliminary stances of Japanese Suma wrestlers.*)

HANNAH: May I show you my work on the other verandah?

(*Hannah had started to follow Herr Fahrenkopf with her
portfolio, but the sketches fall out, and she stops to gather them
from the floor with the sad, preoccupied air of a lonely child
picking flowers.*

(*Shannon's head slowly, furtively, appears through the window of his cubicle. He draws quickly back as Charlotte darts
that way, stepping on Hannah's spilt sketches. Hannah utters
a soft cry of protest, which is drowned by Charlotte's renewed
clamor.*)

CHARLOTTE: Larry, Larry, Judy's looking for me. Let me
come in, Larry, before she finds me here!

SHANNON: You can't come in. Stop shouting and I'll come out.

CHARLOTTE: All right, come out.

SHANNON: Stand back from the door so I *can*.

(*She moves a little aside and he emerges from his cubicle like
a man entering a place of execution. He leans against the
wall, mopping the sweat off his face with a handkerchief.*)

SHANNON: How does Miss Fellowes know what happened
that night? Did you tell her?

CHARLOTTE: I didn't tell her, she guessed.

SHANNON: Guessing isn't knowing. If she is just guessing, that means she doesn't know—I mean if you're not lying, if you didn't tell her.

(*Hannah has finished picking up her drawings and moves quietly over to the far side of the verandah.*)

CHARLOTTE: Don't talk to me like that.

SHANNON: Don't complicate my life now, please, for God's sake, don't complicate my life now.

CHARLOTTE: Why have you changed like this?

SHANNON: I have a fever. Don't complicate my . . . fever.

CHARLOTTE: You act like you hated me now.

SHANNON: You're going to get me kicked out of Blake Tours, Charlotte.

CHARLOTTE: Judy is, not me.

SHANNON: Why did you sing "I Love You Truly" at me?

CHARLOTTE: Because I do love you truly!

SHANNON: Honey girl, don't you know that nothing worse could happen to a girl in your, your . . . unstable condition . . . than to get emotionally mixed up with a man in my unstable condition, huh?

CHARLOTTE: No, no, no, I—

SHANNON (*cutting through*): Two unstable conditions can set a whole world on fire, can blow it up, past repair, and that is just as true between two people as it's true between. . . .

CHARLOTTE: All I know is you've got to marry me, Larry, after what happened between us in Mexico City!

SHANNON: A man in my condition can't marry, it isn't decent or legal. He's lucky if he can even hold onto his job. (*He keeps catching hold of her hands and plucking them off his shoulders.*) I'm almost out of my mind, can't you see that, honey?

CHARLOTTE: I don't believe you don't love me.

SHANNON: Honey, it's almost impossible for anybody to believe they're not loved by someone they believe they love, but, honey, I love *nobody*. I'm like that, it isn't my fault. When I brought you home that night I told you goodnight in the hall, just kissed you on the cheek like the little girl that you are, but the instant I opened my door, you rushed into my room and I couldn't get you out of it, not even when I, oh God, tried to scare you out of it by, oh God, don't you remember?

(*Miss Fellowes' voice is heard from back of the hotel calling,* "Charlotte!")

CHARLOTTE: Yes, I remember that after making love to me, you hit me, Larry, you struck me in the face, and you twisted my arm to make me kneel on the floor and pray with you for forgiveness.

SHANNON: I do that, I do that always when I, when . . . I don't have a dime left in my nervous emotional bank account—I can't write a check on it, now.

CHARLOTTE: Larry, let me help you!

MISS FELLOWES (*approaching*): Charlotte, Charlotte, Charlie!

CHARLOTTE: Help me and let me help you!

SHANNON: The helpless can't help the helpless!

CHARLOTTE: Let me in, Judy's coming!

SHANNON: Let me go. Go away!

(*He thrusts her violently back and rushes into his cubicle, slamming and bolting the door—though the gauze netting is left sticking out. As Miss Fellowes charges onto the verandah, Charlotte runs into the next cubicle, and Hannah moves over from where she has been watching and meets her in the center.*)

MISS FELLOWES: Shannon, Shannon! Where are you?

HANNAH: I think Mr. Shannon has gone down to the beach.

MISS FELLOWES: Was Charlotte Goodall with him? A young blonde girl in our party—was she with him?

HANNAH: No, nobody was with him, he was completely alone.

MISS FELLOWES: I heard a door slam.

HANNAH: That was mine.

MISS FELLOWES (*pointing to the door with the gauze sticking out*): Is this yours?

HANNAH: Yes, mine. I rushed out to catch the sunset.

(*At this moment Miss Fellowes hears Charlotte sobbing in Hannah's cubicle. She throws the door open.*)

MISS FELLOWES: Charlotte! Come out of there, Charlie! (*She has seized Charlotte by the wrist.*) What's your word worth— nothing? You promised you'd stay away from him! (*Charlotte frees her arm, sobbing bitterly. Miss Fellowes seizes her again, tighter, and starts dragging her away.*) I have talked to your father about this man by long distance and he's getting out a warrant for his arrest, if he dare try coming back to the States after this!

CHARLOTTE: I don't care.

MISS FELLOWES: I do! I'm responsible for you.

CHARLOTTE: I don't want to go back to Texas!

MISS FELLOWES: Yes, you do! And you will!

(*She takes Charlotte firmly by the arm and drags her away behind the hotel. Hannah comes out of her cubicle, where she had gone when Miss Fellowes pulled Charlotte out of it.*)

SHANNON (*from his cubicle*): Ah, God. . . .

(*Hannah crosses to his cubicle and knocks by the door.*)

HANNAH: The coast is clear now, Mr. Shannon.

(*Shannon does not answer or appear. She sets down her portfolio to pick up Nonno's white linen suit, which she had pressed and hung on the verandah. She crosses to his cubicle with it, and calls in.*)

HANNAH: Nonno? It's almost time for supper! There's going to be a lovely, stormy sunset in a few minutes.

NONNO (*from within*): Coming!

HANNAH: So is Christmas, Nonno.

NONNO: So is the Fourth of July!

HANNAH: We're past the Fourth of July. Hallowe'en comes next and then Thanksgiving. I hope you'll come forth sooner. (*She lifts the gauze net over his cubicle door.*) Here's your suit, I've pressed it. (*She enters the cubicle.*)

NONNO: It's mighty dark in here, Hannah.

HANNAH: I'll turn the light on for you.

(*Shannon comes out of his cubicle, like the survivor of a plane crash, bringing out with him several pieces of his clerical garb. The black heavy silk bib is loosely fastened about his panting,*) *sweating chest. He hangs over it a heavy gold cross with an amethyst center and attempts to fasten on a starched round collar. Now Hannah comes back out of Nonno's cubicle, adjusting the flowing silk tie which goes with her "artist" costume. For a moment they both face front, adjusting their two outfits. They are like two actors in a play which is about to fold on the road, preparing gravely for a performance which may be the last one.*)

HANNAH (*glancing at Shannon*): Are you planning to conduct church services of some kind here tonight, Mr. Shannon?

SHANNON: Goddamit, please help me with this! (*He means the round collar.*)

HANNAH (*crossing behind him*): If you're not going to conduct a church service, why get into that uncomfortable outfit?

SHANNON: Because I've been accused of being defrocked and of lying about it, that's why. I want to show the ladies that I'm still a clocked—*frocked!*—minister of the. . . .

HANNAH: Isn't that lovely gold cross enough to convince the ladies?

SHANNON: No, they know I redeemed it from a Mexico City pawnshop, and they suspect that that's where I got it in the first place.

HANNAH: Hold still just a minute. (*She is behind him, trying to fasten the collar.*) There now, let's hope it stays on. The button hole is so frayed I'm afraid that it won't hold the button. (*Her fear is instantly confirmed: the button pops out.*)

SHANNON: Where'd it go?

HANNAH: Here, right under. . . .

(*She picks it up. Shannon rips the collar off, crumples it and hurls it off the verandah. Then he falls into the hammock, panting and twisting. Hannah quietly opens her sketch pad and begins to sketch him. He doesn't at first notice what she is doing.*)

HANNAH (*as she sketches*): How long have you been inactive in the, uh, Church, Mr. Shannon?

SHANNON: What's that got to do with the price of rice in China?

HANNAH (*gently*): Nothing.

SHANNON: What's it got to do with the price of coffee beans in Brazil?

HANNAH: I retract the question. With apologies.

SHANNON: To answer your question politely, I have been inactive in the Church for all but one year since I was ordained a minister of the Church.

HANNAH (*sketching rapidly and moving forward a bit to see his face better*): Well, that's quite a sabbatical, Mr. Shannon.

SHANNON: Yeah, that's . . . quite a . . . sabbatical.

(*Nonno's voice is heard from his cubicle repeating a line of poetry several times.*)

SHANNON: Is your grandfather talking to himself in there?

HANNAH: No, he composes out loud. He has to commit his lines to memory because he can't see to write them or read them.

SHANNON: Sounds like he's stuck on one line.

HANNAH: Yes. I'm afraid his memory is failing. Memory failure is his greatest dread. (*She says this almost coolly, as if it didn't matter.*)

SHANNON: Are you drawing me?

HANNAH: Trying to. You're a very difficult subject. When the Mexican painter Siqueiros did his portrait of the American poet Hart Crane he had to paint him with closed eyes because he couldn't paint his eyes open—there was too much suffering in them and he couldn't paint it.

SHANNON: Sorry, but I'm not going to close my eyes for you. I'm hypnotizing myself—at least trying to—by looking at the light on the orange tree . . . leaves.

HANNAH: That's all right. I can paint your eyes open.

SHANNON: I had one parish one year and then I wasn't defrocked but I was . . . locked out of my church.

HANNAH: Oh . . . Why did they lock you out of it?

SHANNON: Fornication and heresy . . . in the same week.

HANNAH (*sketching rapidly*): What were the circumstances of the . . . uh . . . first offense?

SHANNON: Yeah, the fornication came first, preceded the heresy by several days. A very young Sunday-school teacher asked to see me privately in my study. A pretty little thing— no chance in the world—only child, and both of her parents were spinsters, almost identical spinsters wearing clothes of the opposite sexes. Fooling some of the people some of the time but not me—none of the time. . . . (*He is pacing the verandah with gathering agitation, and the all-inclusive mockery that his guilt produces.*) Well, she declared herself to me—wildly.

HANNAH: A declaration of love?

SHANNON: Don't make *fun* of me, honey!

HANNAH: I wasn't.

SHANNON: The natural, or unnatural, attraction of one . . . lunatic for . . . another . . . that's all it was. I was the goddamnedest prig in those days that even you could imagine. I said, let's kneel down together and pray and we did, we knelt down, but all of a sudden the kneeling position turned to a reclining position on the rug of my study and . . . When we got up? I struck her. Yes, I did, I struck her in the face and called her a damned little tramp. So she ran home. I heard the next day she'd cut herself with her father's straightblade razor. Yeah, the paternal spinster shaved.

HANNAH: Fatally?

SHANNON: Just broke the skin surface enough to bleed a little, but it made a scandal.

HANNAH: Yes, I can imagine that it . . . provoked some comment.

SHANNON: That it did, it did that. (*He pauses a moment in his fierce pacing as if the recollection still appalled him.*) So the next Sunday when I climbed into the pulpit and looked down over all of those smug, disapproving, accusing faces uplifted, I had an impulse to shake them—so I shook them. I had a prepared sermon—meek, apologetic —I threw it away, tossed it into the chancel. Look here, I said, I shouted, I'm tired of conducting services in praise and worship of a senile delinquent—yeah, that's what I said, I shouted! All your Western theologies, the whole mythology of them, are based on the concept of God as a *senile delinquent* and, by God, I will not and cannot continue to conduct services in praise and worship of this, this . . . this. . . . .

HANNAH (*quietly*): Senile delinquent?

SHANNON: Yeah, this angry, petulant old man. I mean he's represented like a bad-tempered childish old, old, sick, peevish man—I mean like the sort of old man in a nursing home that's putting together a jigsaw puzzle and can't put it together and gets furious at it and kicks over the table. Yes, I tell you they *do* that, all our theologies do it—accuse God of being a cruel, senile delinquent, blaming the world and brutally punishing all he created for his own faults in construction, and then, ha-ha, yeah—a thunderstorm broke that Sunday. . . .

HANNAH: You mean *outside* the church?

SHANNON: Yep, it was wilder than I was! And out they slithered, they slithered out of their pews to their shiny black cockroach sedans, ha-ha, and I shouted after them, hell, I even followed them halfway out of the church, shouting after them as they. . . . (*He stops with a gasp for breath.*)

HANNAH: Slithered out?

SHANNON: I shouted after them, go on, go home and close your house windows, all your windows and doors, against the truth about God!

HANNAH: Oh, my heavens. Which is just what they did—poor things.

SHANNON: Miss Jelkes honey, Pleasant Valley, Virginia, was an exclusive suburb of a large city and these poor things were not poor—materially speaking.

HANNAH (*smiling a bit*): What was the, uh, upshot of it?

SHANNON: Upshot of it? Well, I wasn't defrocked. I was just locked out of the church in Pleasant Valley, Virginia, and put in a nice little private asylum to recuperate from a complete nervous breakdown as they preferred to regard it, and then, and then I . . . I entered my present line—tours of God's world conducted by a minister of God with a cross and a round collar to prove it. Collecting evidence!

HANNAH: Evidence of what, Mr. Shannon?

SHANNON (*a touch shyly now*): My personal idea of God, not as a senile delinquent, but as a. . . .

HANNAH: Incomplete sentence.

SHANNON: It's going to storm tonight—a terrific electric storm. Then you will see the Reverend T. Lawrence Shannon's conception of God Almighty paying a visit to the world he created. I want to go back to the Church and preach the gospel of God as Lightning and Thunder . . . and also stray dogs vivisected and . . . and . . . and. . . . (*He points out suddenly toward the sea.*) That's him! There he is now! (*He is pointing out at a blaze, a majestic apocalypse of gold light, shafting the sky as the sun drops into the Pacific.*) His oblivious majesty—and *here I am* on this . . . dilapidated verandah of a cheap hotel, out of season, in a country caught and destroyed in its flesh and corrupted in its spirit by its gold-hungry Conquistadors that bore the flag of the Inquisition along with the Cross of Christ. Yes . . . and. . . . (*There is a pause.*)

HANNAH: Mr. Shannon . . . ?

SHANNON: Yes . . . ?

HANNAH (*smiling a little*): I have a strong feeling you will go back to the Church with this evidence you've been collecting, but when you do and it's a black Sunday morning, look out over the congregation, over the smug, complacent faces for a few old, very old faces, looking up at you, as you begin your sermon, with eyes like a piercing cry for something to still look up to, something to still believe in. And then I think you'll not shout what you say you shouted that black Sunday in Pleasant Valley, Virginia. I think you will throw away the violent, furious sermon, you'll toss *it* into the chancel, and talk about . . . no, maybe talk about . . . nothing . . . just. . . .

SHANNON: What?

HANNAH: Lead them beside still waters because you know how badly they need the still waters, Mr. Shannon.

(*There is a moment of silence between them.*)

SHANNON: Lemme see that thing. (*He seizes the sketch pad from her and is visibly impressed by what he sees. There is another moment which is prolonged to Hannah's embarrassment.*)

HANNAH: Where did you say the patrona put your party of ladies?

SHANNON: She had her . . . Mexican concubines put their luggage in the annex.

HANNAH: Where is the annex?

SHANNON: Right down the hill back of here, but all of my ladies except the teen-age Medea and the older Medea have gone out in a glass-bottomed boat to observe the . . . submarine marvels.

HANNAH: Well, when they come back to the annex they're going to observe my water colors with some marvelous submarine prices marked on the mattings.

SHANNON: By God, you're a hustler, aren't you, you're a fantastic cool hustler.

HANNAH: Yes, like *you*, Mr. Shannon. (*She gently removes her sketch pad from his grasp.*) Oh, Mr. Shannon, if Nonno, Grandfather, comes out of his cell number 4 before I get back, will you please look out for him for me? I won't be longer than three shakes of a lively sheep's tail. (*She snatches up her portfolio and goes briskly off the verandah.*)

SHANNON: Fantastic, absolutely fantastic.

(*There is a windy sound in the rain forest and a flicker of gold light like a silent scattering of gold coins on the verandah; then the sound of shouting voices. The Mexican boys appear with a wildly agitated creature—a captive iguana tied up in a shirt. They crouch down by the cactus clumps that are growing below the verandah and hitch the iguana to a post with a piece of rope. Maxine is attracted by the commotion and appears on the verandah above them.*)

PEDRO: Tenemos fiesta!*

PANCHO: Comeremos bien.

PEDRO: Damela, damela! Yo la ataré.

PANCHO: *Yo* la cojí—*yo* la ataré!

PEDRO: Lo que vas a *hacer* es dejarla escapar.

MAXINE: Ammarla fuerte! Ole, ole! No la dejes escapar. Dejala moverse! (*to Shannon*) They caught an iguana.

SHANNON: I've noticed they did that, Maxine.

(*She is holding her drink deliberately close to him. The Germans have heard the commotion and crowd onto the verandah. Frau Fahrenkopf rushes over to Maxine.*)

---

*We're going to have a feast! / We'll eat good. / Give it to me! I'll tie it up. / *I* caught it—*I'll* tie it up! / You'll only let it get away. / Tie it up tight! Ole, ole! Don't let it get away. Give it enough room!

FRAU FAHRENKOPF: What is this? What's going on? A snake? Did they catch a snake?

MAXINE: No. *Lizard.*

FRAU FAHRENKOPF (*with exaggerated revulsion*): *Ouuu . . . lizard!* (*She strikes a grotesque attitude of terror as if she were threatened by Jack the Ripper.*)

SHANNON (*to Maxine*): You like iguana meat, don't you?

FRAU FAHRENKOPF: Eat? *Eat?* A big *lizard?*

MAXINE: Yep, they're mighty good eating—taste like white meat of chicken.

(*Frau Fahrenkopf rushes back to her family. They talk excitedly in German about the iguana.*)

SHANNON: If you mean Mexican chicken, that's no recommendation. Mexican chickens are scavengers and they taste like what they scavenge.

MAXINE: Naw, I mean Texas chicken.

SHANNON (*dreamily*): Texas . . . chicken. . . .

(*He paces restlessly down the verandah. Maxine divides her attention between his tall, lean figure, that seems incapable of stillness, and the wriggling bodies of the Mexican boys lying on their stomachs half under the verandah—as if she were mentally comparing two opposite attractions to her simple, sensual nature. Shannon turns at the end of the verandah and sees her eyes fixed on him.*)

SHANNON: What is the sex of this iguana, Maxine?

MAXINE: Hah, who cares about the sex of an iguana . . . (*He passes close by her.*) . . . except another . . . iguana?

SHANNON: Haven't you heard the limerick about iguanas? (*He removes her drink from her hand and it seems as if he might drink it, but he only sniffs it, with an expression of repugnance. She chuckles.*)

> There was a young gaucho named Bruno
> Who said about love, This I do know:
> Women are fine, and sheep are divine,
> But iguanas are—*Numero Uno!*

(*On "Numero Uno" Shannon empties Maxine's drink over the railing, deliberately onto the humped, wriggling posterior of Pedro, who springs up with angry protests.*)

PEDRO: Me cágo . . . hijo de la . . .
SHANNON: Qué? Qué?
MAXINE: Véte!

(*Shannon laughs viciously. The iguana escapes and both boys rush shouting after it. One of them dives on it and recaptures it at the edge of the jungle.*)

PANCHO: La iguana se escapé.
MAXINE: Cojela, cojela! La cojíste? Si no la cojes, te morderá el culo. La cojíste?
PEDRO: La cojí.*

(*The boys wriggle back under the verandah with the iguana.*)

MAXINE (*returning to Shannon*): I thought you were gonna break down and take a drink, Reverend.
SHANNON: Just the odor of liquor makes me feel nauseated.
MAXINE: You couldn't smell it if you got it *in* you. (*She touches his sweating forehead. He brushes her hand off like an insect.*) Hah! (*She crosses over to the liquor cart, and he looks after her with a sadistic grin.*)
SHANNON: Maxine honey, whoever told you that you look good in tight pants was not a sincere friend of yours.

(*He turns away. At the same instant, a crash and a hoarse, startled outcry are heard from Nonno's cubicle.*)

MAXINE: I knew it, I *knew* it! The old man's took a fall!

(*Shannon rushes into the cubicle, followed by Maxine.*
(*The light has been gradually, steadily dimming during the incident of the iguana's escape. There is, in effect, a division of scenes here, though it is accomplished without a blackout or curtain. As Shannon and Maxine enter Nonno's cubicle, Herr Fahrenkopf appears on the now twilit verandah. He turns on an outsize light fixture that is suspended from overhead, a full pearly-moon of a light globe that gives an unearthly luster to the scene. The great pearly globe is decorated by night insects, large but gossamer moths that have*

---

*The iguana's escaped. / Get it, get it! Have you got it? If you don't, it'll bite your behind. Have you got it? / He's got it.

immolated themselves on its surface: the light through their wings gives them an opalescent color, a touch of fantasy.

(Now Shannon leads the old poet out of his cubicle, onto the facing verandah. The old man is impeccably dressed in snow-white linen with a black string tie. His leonine mane of hair gleams like silver as he passes under the globe.)

NONNO: No bones broke, I'm made out of India rubber!

SHANNON: A traveler-born falls down many times in his travels.

NONNO: Hannah? (*His vision and other senses have so far dete-riorated that he thinks he is being led out by Hannah.*) I'm pretty sure I'm going to finish it here.

SHANNON (*shouting, gently*): I've got the same feeling, Grampa.

(*Maxine follows them out of the cubicle.*)

NONNO: I've never been surer of anything in my life.

SHANNON (*gently and wryly*): I've never been surer of any-thing in mine either.

(*Herr Fahrenkopf has been listening with an expression of en-trancement to his portable radio, held close to his ear, the sound unrealistically low. Now he turns it off and makes an excited speech.*)

HERR FAHRENKOPF: The London fires have spread all the way from the heart of London to the Channel coast! Goering, Field Marshall Goering, calls it "the new phase of conquest!" *Super-firebombs! Each night!*

(*Nonno catches only the excited tone of this announcement and interprets it as a request for a recitation. He strikes the floor with his cane, throws back his silver-maned head and be-gins the delivery in a grand, declamatory style.*)

NONNO:

> Youth must be wanton, youth must be quick,
> Dance to the candle while lasteth the wick,
> Youth must be foolish and. . . .

(*Nonno falters on the line, a look of confusion and fear on his face. The Germans are amused. Wolfgang goes up to Nonno and shouts into his face.*)

WOLFGANG: Sir? What is your age? How old?

(*Hannah, who has just returned to the verandah, rushes up to her grandfather and answers for him.*)

HANNAH: He is ninety-seven years *young*!

HERR FAHRENKOPF: How old?

HANNAH: Ninety-seven—almost a *century young*!

(*Herr Fahrenkopf repeats this information to his beaming wife and Hilda in German.*)

NONNO (*cutting in on the Germans*):
       Youth must be foolish and mirthful and blind,
       Gaze not before and glance not behind,
       Mark not. . . .

(*He falters again.*)

HANNAH (*prompting him, holding tightly onto his arm*):
       Mark not the shadow that darkens the way—

(*They recite the next lines together.*)

       Regret not the glitter of any lost day,
       But laugh with no reason except the red wine,
       For youth must be youthful and foolish and blind!

(*The Germans are loudly amused. Wolfgang applauds directly in the old poet's face. Nonno makes a little unsteady bow, leaning forward precariously on his cane. Shannon takes a firm hold of his arm as Hannah turns to the Germans, opening her portfolio of sketches and addressing Wolfgang.*)

HANNAH: Am I right in thinking you are on your honeymoon? (*There is no response, and she repeats the question in German while Frau Fahrenkopf laughs and nods vehemently.*) Habe ich recht dass Sie auf Ihrer Hochzeitsreise sind? Was für eine hübsche junge Braut! Ich mache Pastell-Skizzen . . . darf ich, würden Sie mir erlauben . . . ? Wurden Sie, bitte . . . bitte. . . .

(*Herr Fahrenkopf bursts into a Nazi marching song and leads his party to the champagne bucket on the table at the left. Shannon has steered Nonno to the other table.*)

NONNO (*exhilarated*): Hannah! What was the *take*?

HANNAH (*embarrassed*): Grandfather, sit down, please stop shouting!

NONNO: Hah? Did they cross your palm with silver or paper, Hannah?

HANNAH (*almost desperately*): Nonno! No more shouting! Sit down at the table. It's time to *eat*!

SHANNON: Chow time, Grampa.

NONNO (*confused but still shouting*): How much did they come across with?

HANNAH: Nonno! *Please!*

NONNO: Did they, did you . . . sell 'em a . . . water color?

HANNAH: No sale, Grandfather!

MAXINE: Hah!

(*Hannah turns to Shannon, her usual composure shattered, or nearly so.*)

HANNAH: He won't sit down or stop shouting.

NONNO (*blinking and beaming with the grotesque suggestion of an old coquette*): Hah? How rich did we strike it, Hannah?

SHANNON: *You* sit down, Miss Jelkes. (*He says it with gentle authority, to which she yields. He takes hold of the old man's forearm and places in his hand a crumpled Mexican bill.*) Sir? Sir? (*He is shouting.*) Five! Dollars! I'm putting it in your pocket.

HANNAH: We can't accept . . . gratuities, Mr. Shannon.

SHANNON: Hell, I gave him five pesos.

NONNO: Mighty good for one poem!

SHANNON: Sir? Sir? The *pecuniary rewards* of a *poem* are *grossly inferior* to its *merits*, always!

(*He is being fiercely, almost mockingly tender with the old man —a thing we are when the pathos of the old, the ancient, the dying is such a wound to our own [savagely beleaguered] nerves and sensibilities that this outside demand on us is beyond our collateral, our emotional reserve. This is as true of Hannah as it is of Shannon, of course. They have both overdrawn their reserves at this point of the encounter between them.*)

NONNO: Hah? Yes. . . . (*He is worn out now, but still shouting.*) We're going to clean up in this place!

SHANNON: You bet you're going to clean up here!

(*Maxine utters her one-note bark of a laugh. Shannon throws a hard roll at her. She wanders amiably back toward the German table.*)

NONNO (*tottering, panting, hanging onto Shannon's arm, thinking it is Hannah's*): Is the, the . . . diningroom . . . crowded? (*He looks blindly about with wild surmise.*)

SHANNON: Yep, it's filled to capacity! There's a big crowd at the door! (*His voice doesn't penetrate the old man's deafness.*)

NONNO: If there's a cocktail lounge, Hannah, we ought to . . . work that . . . first. Strike while the iron is hot, ho, ho, while it's hot. . . . (*This is like a delirium—only as strong a woman as Hannah could remain outwardly impassive.*)

HANNAH: He thinks you're me, Mr. Shannon. Help him into a chair. Please stay with him a minute, I. . . .

(*She moves away from the table and breathes as if she has just been dragged up half-drowned from the sea. Shannon eases the old man into a chair. Almost at once Nonno's feverish vitality collapses and he starts drifting back toward half sleep.*)

SHANNON (*crossing to Hannah*): What're you breathing like that for?

HANNAH: Some people take a drink, some take a pill. I just take a few deep breaths.

SHANNON: You're making too much out of this. It's a natural thing in a man as old as Grampa.

HANNAH: I know, I know. He's had more than one of these little "cerebral accidents" as you call them, and all in the last few months. He was amazing till lately. I had to show his passport to prove that he was the oldest living and practicing poet on earth. We did well, we made expenses and *more*! But . . . when I saw he was failing, I tried to persuade him to go back to Nantucket, but he conducts our tours. He said, "No, *Mexico*!" So here we are on this windy hilltop like a pair of scarecrows. . . . The bus from Mexico City broke down at an altitude of 15,000 feet above sea level. That's when I think the latest cerebral incident happened. It isn't so much the loss of hearing and sight but the . . . dimming out of the mind that I can't bear, because until lately, just lately, his mind was amazingly clear. But yesterday? In Taxco? I spent nearly all we had left on the wheelchair for him and still he insisted that we go on with the trip till we got to the sea, the . . . cradle of life as he calls it. . . . (*She suddenly notices Nonno, sunk in his chair as if lifeless. She draws a sharp breath, and goes quietly to him.*)

SHANNON (*to the Mexican boys*): Servicio! Aqui! (*The force of his order proves effective: they serve the fish course.*)

HANNAH: What a kind man you are. I don't know how to thank you, Mr. Shannon. I'm going to wake him up now. Nonno! (*She claps her hands quietly at his ear. The old man rouses with a confused, breathless chuckle.*) Nonno, linen napkins. (*She removes a napkin from the pocket of her smock.*) I always carry one with me, you see, in case we run into paper napkins as sometimes happens, you see. . . .

NONNO: Wonderful place here. . . . I hope it is à la carte, Hannah, I want a very light supper so I won't get sleepy. I'm going to work after supper. I'm going to finish it here.

HANNAH: Nonno? We've made a friend here. Nonno, this is the Reverend Mr. Shannon.

NONNO (*struggling out of his confusion*): Reverend?

HANNAH (*shouting to him*): Mr. Shannon's an Episcopal clergyman, Nonno.

NONNO: A man of God?

HANNAH: A man of God, on vacation.

NONNO: Hannah, tell him I'm too old to baptize and too young to bury but on the market for marriage to a rich widow, fat, fair and forty.

(*Nonno is delighted by all of his own little jokes. One can see him exchanging these pleasantries with the rocking-chair brigades of summer hotels at the turn of the century—and with professors' wives at little colleges in New England. But now it has become somewhat grotesque in a touching way, this desire to please, this playful manner, these venerable jokes. Shannon goes along with it. The old man touches something in him which is outside of his concern with himself. This part of the scene, which is played in a "scherzo" mood, has an accompanying windy obligato on the hilltop—all through it we hear the wind from the sea gradually rising, sweeping up the hill through the rain forest, and there are fitful glimmers of lightning in the sky.*)

NONNO: But very few ladies ever go past forty if you believe 'em, ho, ho! Ask him to . . . give the blessing. Mexican food needs blessing.

SHANNON: Sir, you give the blessing. I'll be right with you. (*He has broken one of his shoe laces.*)

NONNO: Tell him I will oblige him on one condition.

SHANNON: What condition, sir?

NONNO: That you'll keep my daughter company when I retire after dinner. I go to bed with the chickens and get up with the roosters, ho, ho! So you're a man of God. A benedict or a bachelor?

SHANNON: Bachelor, sir. No sane and civilized woman would have me, Mr. Coffin.

NONNO: What did he say, Hannah?

HANNAH (*embarrassed*): Nonno, give the blessing.

NONNO (*not hearing this*): I call her my daughter, but she's my daughter's daughter. We've been in charge of each other since she lost both her parents in the very first automobile crash on the island of Nantucket.

HANNAH: Nonno, give the blessing.

NONNO: She isn't a modern flapper, she isn't modern and she —doesn't flap, but she was brought up to be a wonderful wife and mother. But . . . I'm a selfish old man so I've kept her all to myself.

HANNAH (*shouting into his ear*): Nonno, Nonno, the blessing!

NONNO (*rising with an effort*): Yes, the blessing. Bless this food to our use, and ourselves to Thy service. Amen. (*He totters back into his chair.*)

SHANNON: Amen.

(*Nonno's mind starts drifting, his head drooping forward. He murmurs to himself.*)

SHANNON: How good is the old man's poetry?

HANNAH: My grandfather was a fairly well-known minor poet before the First World War and for a little while after.

SHANNON: In the minor league, huh?

HANNAH: Yes, a minor league poet with a major league spirit. I'm proud to be his granddaughter. . . . (*She draws a pack*

*of cigarettes from her pocket, then replaces it immediately
without taking a cigarette.*)

NONNO (*very confused*): Hannah, it's too hot for . . . hot
cereals this . . . morning. . . . (*He shakes his head several
times with a rueful chuckle.*)

HANNAH: He's not quite back, you see, he thinks it's morning. (*She says this as if making an embarrassing admission,
with a quick, frightened smile at Shannon.*)

SHANNON: Fantastic—*fantastic.*

HANNAH: That word "fantastic" seems to be your favorite
word, Mr. Shannon.

SHANNON (*looking out gloomily from the verandah*): Yeah,
well, you know we—live on two levels, Miss Jelkes, the realistic level and the fantastic level, and which is the real one,
really. . . .

HANNAH: I would say both, Mr. Shannon.

SHANNON: But when you live on the fantastic level as I have
lately but have got to operate on the realistic level, that's
when you're spooked, that's the spook. . . . (*This is said as
if it were a private reflection.*) I thought I'd shake the spook
here but conditions have changed here. I didn't know the
patrona had turned to a widow, a sort of bright widow spider. (*He chuckles almost like Nonno.*)

(*Maxine has pushed one of those gay little brass-and-glass
liquor carts around the corner of the verandah. It is laden
with an ice bucket, coconuts and a variety of liquors. She
hums gaily to herself as she pushes the cart close to the
table.*)

MAXINE: Cocktails, anybody?

HANNAH: No, thank you, Mrs. Faulk, I don't think we care
for any.

SHANNON: People don't drink cocktails between the fish and
the entrée, Maxine honey.

MAXINE: Grampa needs a toddy to wake him up. Old folks
need a toddy to pick 'em up. (*She shouts into the old man's
ear.*) Grampa! How about a toddy? (*Her hips are thrust out
at Shannon.*)

SHANNON: Maxine, your ass—excuse me, Miss Jelkes—your
hips, Maxine, are too fat for this verandah.

MAXINE: Hah! Mexicans like 'em, if I can judge by the pokes and pinches I get in the busses to town. And so do the Germans. Ev'ry time I go near Herr Fahrenkopf he gives me a pinch or a goose.

SHANNON: Then go near him again for another goose.

MAXINE: Hah! I'm mixing Grampa a Manhattan with two cherries in it so he'll live through dinner.

SHANNON: Go on back to your Nazis, I'll mix the Manhattan for him. (*He goes to the liquor cart.*)

MAXINE (*to Hannah*): How about you, honey, a little soda with lime juice?

HANNAH: Nothing for me, thank you.

SHANNON: Don't make nervous people more nervous, Maxine.

MAXINE: You better let me mix that toddy for Grampa, you're making a mess of it, Shannon.

(*With a snort of fury, he thrusts the liquor cart like a battering ram at her belly. Some of the bottles fall off it; she thrusts it right back at him.*)

HANNAH: Mrs. Faulk, Mr. Shannon, this is childish, please stop it!

(*The Germans are attracted by the disturbance. They cluster around, laughing delightedly. Shannon and Maxine seize opposite ends of the rolling liquor cart and thrust it toward each other, both grinning fiercely as gladiators in mortal combat. The Germans shriek with laughter and chatter in German.*)

HANNAH: Mr. Shannon, stop it! (*She appeals to the Germans.*) Bitte! Nehmen Sie die Spirituosen weg. Bitte, nehmen Sie sie weg.

(*Shannon has wrested the cart from Maxine and pushed it at the Germans. They scream delightedly. The cart crashes into the wall of the verandah. Shannon leaps down the steps and runs into the foliage. Birds scream in the rain forest. Then sudden quiet returns to the verandah as the Germans go back to their own table.*)

MAXINE: Crazy, black Irish protestant son of a . . . protestant!

HANNAH: Mrs. Faulk, he's putting up a struggle not to drink.

MAXINE: Don't interfere. You're an interfering woman.

HANNAH: Mr. Shannon is dangerously . . . disturbed.

MAXINE: I know how to handle him, honey—you just met him today. Here's Grampa's Manhattan cocktail with two cherries in it.

HANNAH: Please don't call him Grampa.

MAXINE: Shannon calls him Grampa.

HANNAH (*taking the drink*): He doesn't make it sound condescending, but you *do*. My grandfather is a gentleman in the true sense of the word, he is a *gentle man*.

MAXINE: What are you?

HANNAH: I am his granddaughter.

MAXINE: Is that all you are?

HANNAH: I think it's enough to be.

MAXINE: Yeah, but you're also a deadbeat, using that dying old man for a front to get in places without the cash to pay even one day in advance. Why, you're dragging him around with you like Mexican beggars carry around a sick baby to put the touch on the tourists.

HANNAH: I told you I had no money.

MAXINE: Yes, and I told you that I was a widow—recent. In such a financial hole they might as well have buried me with my husband.

(*Shannon reappears from the jungle foliage but remains unnoticed by Hannah and Maxine.*)

HANNAH (*with forced calm*): Tomorrow morning, at daybreak, I will go in town. I will set up my easel in the plaza and peddle my water colors and sketch tourists. I am not a weak person, my failure here isn't typical of me.

MAXINE: I'm not a weak person either.

HANNAH: No. By no means, no. Your strength is awe-inspiring.

MAXINE: You're goddam right about that, but how do you think you'll get to Acapulco without the cabfare or even the busfare there?

HANNAH: I will go on shanks' mare, Mrs. Faulk—islanders are good walkers. And if you doubt my word for it, if you really think I came here as a deadbeat, then I will put my grandfather back in his wheelchair and push him back down this hill to the road and all the way back into town.

MAXINE: Ten miles, with a storm coming up?

HANNAH: Yes, I would—I will. (*She is dominating Maxine in this exchange. Both stand beside the table. Nonno's head is drooping back into sleep.*)

MAXINE: I wouldn't let you.

HANNAH: But you've made it clear that you don't want us to stay here for one night even.

MAXINE: The storm would blow that old man out of his wheelchair like a dead leaf.

HANNAH: He would prefer that to staying where he's not welcome, and I would prefer it for him, and for myself, Mrs. Faulk. (*She turns to the Mexican boys.*) Where is his wheelchair? Where is my grandfather's wheelchair?

(*This exchange has roused the old man. He struggles up from his chair, confused, strikes the floor with his cane and starts declaiming a poem.*)

NONNO:

    Love's an old remembered song
    A drunken fiddler plays,
    Stumbling crazily along
    Crooked alleyways.

    When his heart is mad with music
    He will play the—

HANNAH: Nonno, not now, Nonno! He thought someone asked for a poem. (*She gets him back into the chair. Hannah and Maxine are still unaware of Shannon.*)

MAXINE: Calm down, honey.

HANNAH: I'm perfectly calm, Mrs. Faulk.

MAXINE: I'm *not.* That's the trouble.

HANNAH: I understand that, Mrs. Faulk. You lost your husband just lately. I think you probably miss him more than you know.

MAXINE: No, the trouble is Shannon.

HANNAH: You mean his nervous state and his . . . ?

MAXINE: No, I just mean Shannon. I want you to lay off him, honey. You're not for Shannon and Shannon isn't for you.

HANNAH: Mrs. Faulk, I'm a New England spinster who is pushing forty.

MAXINE: I got the vibrations between you—I'm very good at catching vibrations between people—and there sure was a vibration between you and Shannon the moment you got here. That, just that, believe me, nothing but that has made this . . . misunderstanding between us. So if you just don't mess with Shannon, you and your Grampa can stay on here as long as you want to, honey.

HANNAH: Oh, Mrs. Faulk, do I look like a *vamp*?

MAXINE: They come in all types. I've had all types of them here.

(*Shannon comes over to the table.*)

SHANNON: Maxine, I told you don't make nervous people more nervous, but you wouldn't listen.

MAXINE: What you need is a drink.

SHANNON: Let me decide about that.

HANNAH: Won't you sit down with us, Mr. Shannon, and eat something? Please. You'll feel better.

SHANNON: I'm not hungry right now.

HANNAH: Well, just sit down with us, won't you?

(*Shannon sits down with Hannah.*)

MAXINE (*warningly to Hannah*): O.K. O.K. . . .

NONNO (*rousing a bit and mumbling*): Wonderful . . . wonderful place here.

(*Maxine retires from the table and wheels the liquor cart over to the German party.*)

SHANNON: Would you have gone through with it?

HANNAH: Haven't you ever played poker, Mr. Shannon?

SHANNON: You mean you were bluffing?

HANNAH: Let's say I was drawing to an inside straight. (*The wind rises and sweeps up the hill like a great waking sigh from the ocean.*) It *is* going to storm. I hope your ladies aren't still out in that, that . . . glass-bottomed boat, observing the, uh, submarine . . . marvels.

SHANNON: That's because you don't know these ladies. However, they're back from the boat trip. They're down at the cantina, dancing together to the jukebox and hatching new plots to get me kicked out of Blake Tours.

HANNAH: What would you do if you. . . .

SHANNON: Got the sack? Go back to the Church or take the long swim to China. (*Hannah removes a crumpled pack of cigarettes from her pocket. She discovers only two left in the pack and decides to save them for later. She returns the pack to her pocket.*) May I have one of your cigarettes, Miss Jelkes? (*She offers him the pack. He takes it from her and crumples it and throws it off the verandah.*) Never smoke those, they're made out of tobacco from cigarette stubs that beggars pick up off sidewalks and out of gutters in Mexico City. (*He produces a tin of English cigarettes.*) Have these—Benson and Hedges, imported, in an airtight tin, my luxury in my life.

HANNAH: Why—thank you, I will, since you have thrown mine away.

SHANNON: I'm going to tell you something about yourself. You are a lady, a *real* one and a *great* one.

HANNAH: What have I done to merit that compliment from you?

SHANNON: It isn't a compliment, it's just a report on what I've noticed about you at a time when it's hard for me to notice anything outside myself. You took out those Mexican cigarettes, you found you just had two left, you can't afford to buy a new pack of even that cheap brand, so you put them away for later. Right?

HANNAH: Mercilessly accurate, Mr. Shannon.

SHANNON: But when I asked you for one, you offered it to me without a sign of reluctance.

HANNAH: Aren't you making a big point out of a small matter?

SHANNON: Just the opposite, honey, I'm making a small point out of a very large matter. (*Shannon has put a cigarette in his lips but has no matches. Hannah has some and she lights his cigarette for him.*) How'd you learn how to light a match in the wind?

HANNAH: Oh, I've learned lots of useful little things like that. I wish I'd learned some *big* ones.

SHANNON: Such as what?

HANNAH: How to help you, Mr. Shannon. . . .

SHANNON: Now I know why I came here!

HANNAH: To meet someone who can light a match in the wind?

SHANNON (*looking down at the table, his voice choking*): To meet someone who wants to *help me*, Miss Jelkes. . . . (*He makes a quick, embarrassed turn in the chair, as if to avoid her seeing that he has tears in his eyes. She regards him steadily and tenderly, as she would her grandfather.*)

HANNAH: Has it been so long since anyone has wanted to help you, or have you just. . . .

SHANNON: Have I—what?

HANNAH: Just been so much involved with a struggle in yourself that you haven't noticed when people have wanted to help you, the little they can? I know people torture each other many times like devils, but sometimes they do see and know each other, you know, and then, if they're decent, they do want to help each other all that they can. Now will you please help *me*? Take care of Nonno while I remove my water colors from the annex verandah because the storm is coming up by leaps and bounds now.

(*He gives a quick, jerky nod, dropping his face briefly into the cup of his hands. She murmurs* "Thank you" *and springs up, starting along the verandah. Halfway across, as the storm closes in upon the hilltop with a thunderclap and a sound of rain coming, Hannah turns to look back at the table. Shannon has risen and gone around the table to Nonno.*)

SHANNON: Grampa? Nonno? Let's get up before the rain hits us, Grampa.

NONNO: What? What?

(*Shannon gets the old man out of his chair and shepherds him to the back of the verandah as Hannah rushes toward the annex. The Mexican boys hastily clear the table, fold it up and lean it against the wall. Shannon and Nonno turn and face toward the storm, like brave men facing a firing squad. Maxine is excitedly giving orders to the boys.*)

MAXINE: Pronto, pronto, muchachos! Pronto, pronto!* Llevaros todas las cosas! Pronto, pronto! Recoje los platos! Apurate con el mantel!

---

*Hurry, hurry, boys! Pick everything up! Get the plates! Hurry with the table cloth! / We *are* hurrying! / Let the storm wash the plates!

PEDRO: Nos estamos dando prisa!
PANCHO: Que el chubasco lave los platos!

(*The German party look on the storm as a Wagnerian climax. They rise from their table as the boys come to clear it, and start singing exultantly. The storm, with its white convulsions of light, is like a giant white bird attacking the hilltop of the Costa Verde. Hannah reappears with her water colors clutched against her chest.*)

SHANNON: Got them?
HANNAH: Yes, just in time. Here is your God, Mr. Shannon.
SHANNON (*quietly*): Yes, I see him, I hear him, I know him. And if he doesn't know that I know him, let him strike me dead with a bolt of his lightning.

(*He moves away from the wall to the edge of the verandah as a fine silver sheet of rain descends off the sloping roof, catching the light and dimming the figures behind it. Now everything is silver, delicately lustrous. Shannon extends his hands under the rainfall, turning them in it as if to cool them. Then he cups them to catch the water in his palms and bathes his forehead with it. The rainfall increases. The sound of the marimba band at the beach cantina is brought up the hill by the wind. Shannon lowers his hands from his burning forehead and stretches them out through the rain's silver sheet as if he were reaching for something outside and beyond himself. Then nothing is visible but these reaching-out hands. A pure white flash of lightning reveals Hannah and Nonno against the wall, behind Shannon, and the electric globe suspended from the roof goes out, the power extinguished by the storm. A clear shaft of light stays on Shannon's reaching-out hands till the stage curtain has fallen, slowly.*)*

Intermission

---

* *Note:* In staging, the plastic elements should be restrained so that they don't take precedence over the more important human values. It should not seem like an "effect curtain." The faint, windy music of the marimba band from the cantina should continue as the house-lights are brought up for the intermission.

ACT THREE

The verandah, several hours later. Cubicles number 3, 4, and 5 are dimly lighted within. We see Hannah in number 3, and Nonno in number 4. Shannon, who has taken off his shirt, is seated at a table on the verandah, writing a letter to his Bishop. All but this table have been folded and stacked against the wall and Maxine is putting the hammock back up which had been taken down for dinner. The electric power is still off and the cubicles are lighted by oil lamps. The sky has cleared completely, the moon is making for full and it bathes the scene in an almost garish silver which is intensified by the wetness from the recent rainstorm. Everything is drenched—there are pools of silver here and there on the floor of the verandah. At one side a smudge-pot is burning to repel the mosquitoes, which are particularly vicious after a tropical downpour when the wind is exhausted.

Shannon is working feverishly on the letter to the Bishop, now and then slapping at a mosquito on his bare torso. He is shiny with perspiration, still breathing like a spent runner, muttering to himself as he writes and sometimes suddenly drawing a loud deep breath and simultaneously throwing back his head to stare up wildly at the night sky. Hannah is seated on a straight-back chair behind the mosquito netting in her cubicle—very straight herself, holding a small book in her hands but looking steadily over it at Shannon, like a guardian angel. Her hair has been let down. Nonno can be seen in his cubicle rocking back and forth on the edge of the narrow bed as he goes over and over the lines of his first new poem in "twenty-some years"—which he knows is his last one.

Now and then the sound of distant music drifts up from the beach cantina.

MAXINE: Workin' on your sermon for next Sunday, Rev'rend?

SHANNON: I'm writing a very important letter, Maxine. (*He means don't disturb me.*)

MAXINE: Who to, Shannon?

SHANNON: The Dean of the Divinity School at Sewanee. (*Maxine repeats "Sewanee" to herself, tolerantly.*) Yes, and I'd appreciate it very much, Maxine honey, if you'd get Pedro or Pancho to drive into town with it tonight so it will go out first thing in the morning.

MAXINE: The kids took off in the station wagon already—for some cold beers and hot whores at the cantina.

SHANNON: "Fred's dead"—he's lucky. . . .

MAXINE: Don't misunderstand me about Fred, baby. I miss him, but we'd not only stopped sleeping together, we'd stopped talking together except in grunts—no quarrels, no misunderstandings, but if we exchanged two grunts in the course of a day, it was a long conversation we'd had that day between us.

SHANNON: Fred knew when I was spooked—wouldn't have to tell him. He'd just look at me and say, "Well, Shannon, you're spooked."

MAXINE: Yeah, well, Fred and me'd reached the point of just grunting.

SHANNON: Maybe he thought you'd turned into a pig, Maxine.

MAXINE: Hah! You know damn well that Fred respected me, Shannon, like I did Fred. We just, well, you know . . . age difference. . . .

SHANNON: Well, you've got Pedro and Pancho.

MAXINE: Employees. They don't respect me enough. When you let employees get too free with you, personally, they stop respecting you, Shannon. And it's, well, it's . . . humiliating—not to be . . . respected.

SHANNON: Then take more bus trips to town for the Mexican pokes and the pinches, or get Herr Fahrenkopf to "respect" you, honey.

MAXINE: Hah! You kill me. I been thinking lately of selling out here and going back to the States, to Texas, and operating a tourist camp outside some live town like Houston or Dallas, on a highway, and renting out cabins to business executives wanting a comfortable little intimate little place to give a little after-hours dictation to their cute little secretaries that can't type or write shorthand. Complimentary rum-cocos—bathrooms with bidets. I'll introduce the bidet to the States.

SHANNON: Does everything have to wind up on that level with you, Maxine?

MAXINE: Yes and no, baby. I know the difference between loving someone and just sleeping with someone—even I know about that. (*He starts to rise.*) We've both reached a point where we've got to settle for something that works for us in our lives—even if it isn't on the highest kind of level.

SHANNON: I don't want to rot.

MAXINE: You wouldn't. I wouldn't let you! I know your psychological history. I remember one of your conversations on this verandah with Fred. You was explaining to him how your problems first started. You told him that Mama, your Mama, used to send you to bed before you was ready to sleep—so you practiced the little boy's vice, you amused yourself with yourself. And once she caught you at it and whaled your backside with the back side of a hairbrush because she said she had to punish you for it because it made God mad as much as it did Mama, and she had to punish you for it so God wouldn't punish you for it harder than she would.

SHANNON: I was talking to Fred.

MAXINE: Yeah, but I heard it, all of it. You said you loved God and Mama and so you quit it to please them, but it was your secret pleasure and you harbored a secret resentment against Mama and God for making you give it up. And so you got back at God by preaching atheistical sermons and you got back at Mama by starting to lay young girls.

SHANNON: I have never delivered an atheistical sermon, and never would or could when I go back to the Church.

MAXINE: You're not going back to no Church. Did you mention the charge of statutory rape to the Divinity Dean?

SHANNON (*thrusting his chair back so vehemently that it topples over*): Why don't you *let up* on me? You haven't let up on me since I got here this morning! *Let up on me!* Will you please *let up* on me?

MAXINE (*smiling serenely into his rage*): Aw baby. . . .

SHANNON: What do you mean by "aw baby"? What do you want out of me, Maxine honey?

MAXINE: Just to do this. (*She runs her fingers through his hair. He thrusts her hand away.*)

SHANNON: Ah, God. (*Words fail him. He shakes his head with a slight, helpless laugh and goes down the steps from the verandah.*)

MAXINE: The Chinaman in the kitchen says, "No sweat." . . . "No sweat." He says that's all his philosophy. All the Chinese philosophy in three words, "Mei yoo guanchi"— which is Chinese for "No sweat." . . . With your record and a charge of statutory rape hanging over you in Texas, how could you go to a church except to the Holy Rollers with some lively young female rollers and a bushel of hay on the church floor?

SHANNON: I'll drive into town in the bus to post this letter tonight. (*He has started toward the path. There are sounds below. He divides the masking foliage with his hands and looks down the hill.*)

MAXINE (*descending the steps from the verandah*): Watch out for the spook, he's out there.

SHANNON: My ladies are up to something. They're all down there on the road, around the bus.

MAXINE: They're running out on you, Shannon.

(*She comes up beside him. He draws back and she looks down the hill. The light in number 3 cubicle comes on and Hannah rises from the little table that she had cleared for letter-writing. She removes her Kabuki robe from a hook and puts it on as an actor puts on a costume in his dressing room. Nonno's cubicle is also lighted dimly. He sits on the edge of his cot, rocking slightly back and forth, uttering an indistinguishable mumble of lines from his poem.*)

MAXINE: Yeah. There's a little fat man down there that looks like Jake Latta to me. Yep, that's Jake, that's Latta. I reckon Blake Tours has sent him here to take over your party, Shannon. (*Shannon looks out over the jungle and lights a cigarette with jerky fingers.*) Well, let him do it. No sweat! He's coming up here now. Want me to handle it for you?

SHANNON: I'll handle it for myself. You keep out of it, please.

(*He speaks with a desperate composure. Hannah stands just behind the curtain of her cubicle, motionless as a painted figure, during the scene that follows. Jake Latta comes puffing up the verandah steps, beaming genially.*)

LATTA: Hi there, Larry.

SHANNON: Hello, Jake. (*He folds his letter into an envelope.*) Mrs. Faulk honey, this goes air special.

MAXINE: First you'd better address it.

SHANNON: Oh!

(*Shannon laughs and snatches the letter back, fumbling in his pocket for an address book, his fingers shaking uncontrollably. Latta winks at Maxine. She smiles tolerantly.*)

LATTA: How's our boy doin', Maxine?

MAXINE: He'd feel better if I could get him to take a drink.

LATTA: Can't you get a drink down him?

MAXINE: Nope, not even a rum-coco.

LATTA: Let's have a rum-coco, Larry.

SHANNON: You have a rum-coco, Jake. I have a party of ladies to take care of. And I've discovered that situations come up in this business that call for cold, sober judgment. How about you? Haven't you ever made that discovery, Jake? What're you doing here? Are you here with a party?

LATTA: I'm here to pick up your party, Larry boy.

SHANNON: That's interesting! On whose authority, Jake?

LATTA: Blake Tours wired me in Cuernavaca to pick up your party here and put them together with mine cause you'd had this little nervous upset of yours and. . . .

SHANNON: Show me the wire! Huh?

LATTA: The bus driver says you took the ignition key to the bus.

SHANNON: That's right. I have the ignition key to the bus and I have this party and neither the bus or the party will pull out of here till I say so.

LATTA: Larry, you're a sick boy. Don't give me trouble.

SHANNON: What jail did they bail you out of, you fat zero?

LATTA: Let's have the bus key, Larry.

SHANNON: Where did they dig you up? You've got no party in Cuernavaca, you haven't been out with a party since 'thirty-seven.

LATTA: Just give me the bus key, Larry.

SHANNON: In a pig's—snout!—like yours!

LATTA: Where is the reverend's bedroom, Mrs. Faulk?

SHANNON: The bus key is in my pocket. (*He slaps his pants pocket fiercely.*) Here, right here, in my pocket! Want it? Try and get it, Fatso!

LATTA: What language for a reverend to use, Mrs. Faulk. . . .

SHANNON (*holding up the key*): See it? (*He thrusts it back into his pocket.*) Now go back wherever you crawled from. My party of ladies is staying here three more days because several of them are in no condition to travel and neither— neither am I.

LATTA: They're getting in the bus now.

SHANNON: How are you going to start it?

LATTA: Larry, don't make me call the bus driver up here to hold you down while I get that key away from you. You want to see the wire from Blake Tours? Here. (*He produces the wire.*) Read it.

SHANNON: You sent that wire to yourself.

LATTA: From Houston?

SHANNON: You had it sent you from Houston. What's that prove? Why, Blake Tours was nothing, *nothing!*—till they got me. You think they'd let me go?—Ho, ho! Latta, it's caught up with you, Latta, all the whores and tequila have hit your brain now, Latta. (*Latta shouts down the hill for the bus driver.*) Don't you realize what I mean to Blake Tours? Haven't you seen the brochure in which they mention, they brag, that special parties are conducted by the Reverend T. Lawrence Shannon, D.D., noted world traveler, lecturer, son of a minister and grandson of a bishop, and the direct descendant of two colonial governors? (*Miss Fellowes appears at the verandah steps.*) Miss Fellowes has read the brochure, she's memorized the brochure. She knows what it says about me.

MISS FELLOWES (*to Latta*): Have you got the bus key?

LATTA: Bus driver's going to get it away from him, lady. (*He lights a cigar with dirty, shaky fingers.*)

SHANNON: Ha-ha-ha-ha-ha! (*His laughter shakes him back against the verandah wall.*)

LATTA: He's gone. (*He touches his forehead.*)

SHANNON: Why, those ladies . . . have had . . . some of them, most of them if not all of them . . . for the first time in their lives the advantage of contact, social contact, with a gentleman born and bred, whom under no other circumstances they could have possibly met . . . let alone be given the chance to insult and accuse and. . . .

MISS FELLOWES: Shannon! The girls are in the bus and we want to go now, so give up that key. Now!

(*Hank, the bus driver, appears at the top of the path, whistling casually: he is not noticed at first.*)

SHANNON: If I didn't have a decent sense of responsibility to these parties I take out, I would gladly turn over your party —because I don't like your party—to this degenerate here, this Jake Latta of the gutter-rat Lattas. Yes, I would—I would surrender the bus key in my pocket, even to Latta, but I am not that irresponsible, no, I'm not, to the parties that I take out, regardless of the party's treatment of me. I still feel responsible for them till I get them back wherever I picked them up. (*Hank comes onto the verandah.*) Hi, Hank. Are you friend or foe?

HANK: Larry, I got to get that ignition key now so we can get moving down there.

SHANNON: Oh! Then *foe!* I'm disappointed, Hank. I thought you were friend, not foe. (*Hank puts a wrestler's armlock on Shannon and Latta removes the bus key from his pocket. Hannah raises a hand to her eyes.*) O.K., O.K., you've got the bus key. By force. I feel exonerated now of all responsibility. Take the bus and the ladies in it and go. Hey, Jake, did you know they had lesbians in Texas—without the dikes the plains of Texas would be engulfed by the Gulf. (*He nods his head violently toward Miss Fellowes, who springs forward and slaps him.*) Thank you, Miss Fellowes. Latta, hold on a minute. I will not be stranded here. I've had unusual expenses on this trip. Right now I don't have my fare back to Houston or even to Mexico City. Now if there's any truth in your statement that Blake Tours have really authorized you to take over my party, then I am sure they have . . . (*He draws a breath, almost gasping.*) . . . I'm sure they must have given you something in the . . . the nature of . . . *severance* pay? Or at least enough to get me back to the States?

LATTA: I got no money for you.

SHANNON: I hate to question your word, but. . . .

LATTA: We'll drive you back to Mexico City. You can sit up front with the driver.

SHANNON: *You* would do that, Latta. *I'd* find it *humiliating.* Now! Give me my severance pay!

LATTA: Blake Tours is having to refund those ladies half the price of the tour. That's your severance pay. And Miss Fellowes tells me you got plenty of money out of this young girl you seduced in. . . .

SHANNON: Miss Fellowes, did you really make such a . . . ?

MISS FELLOWES: When Charlotte returned that night, she'd cashed two traveler's checks.

SHANNON: After I had spent all my own cash.

MISS FELLOWES: On what? Whores in the filthy places you took her through?

SHANNON: Miss Charlotte cashed two ten-dollar traveler's checks because I had spent all the cash I had on me. And I've never had to, I've certainly never desired to, have relations with whores.

MISS FELLOWES: You took her through ghastly places, such as. . . .

SHANNON: I showed her what she wanted me to show her. Ask her! I showed her San Juan de Letran, I showed her Tenampa and some other places not listed in the Blake Tours brochure. I showed her more than the floating gardens at Xochimilco, Maximilian's Palace, and the mad Empress Carlotta's little homesick chapel, Our Lady of Guadalupe, the monument to Juarez, the relics of the Aztec civilization, the sword of Cortez, the headdress of Montezuma. I showed her what she told me she wanted to see. Where is she? Where is Miss . . . oh, down there with the ladies. (*He leans over the rail and shouts down.*) Charlotte! Charlotte! (*Miss Fellowes seizes his arm and thrusts him away from the verandah rail.*)

MISS FELLOWES: Don't you dare!

SHANNON: Dare what?

MISS FELLOWES: Call her, speak to her, go near her, you, you . . . *filthy!*

(*Maxine reappears at the corner of the verandah, with the ceremonial rapidity of a cuckoo bursting from a clock to announce the hour. She just stands there with an incongruous grin, her big eyes unblinking, as if they were painted on her round beaming face. Hannah holds a gold-lacquered Japanese fan motionless but open in one hand; the other hand touches the netting at the cubicle door as if she were checking an impulse to rush to Shannon's defense. Her attitude has the style of a Kabuki dancer's pose. Shannon's manner becomes courtly again.*)

SHANNON: Oh, all right, I won't. I only wanted her to confirm my story that I took her out that night at her request, not at my . . . suggestion. All that I did was offer my services to her when *she* told *me* she'd like to see things not listed in the brochure, not usually witnessed by ordinary tourists such as. . . .

MISS FELLOWES: Your hotel bedroom? Later? That too? She came back *flea*-bitten!

SHANNON: Oh, now, don't exaggerate, please. Nobody ever got any fleas off Shannon.

MISS FELLOWES: Her clothes had to be fumigated!

SHANNON: I understand your annoyance, but you are going too far when you try to make out that I gave Charlotte fleas. I don't deny that. . . .

MISS FELLOWES: Wait till they get my *report*!

SHANNON: I don't deny that it's possible to get fleabites on a tour of inspection of what lies under the public surface of cities, off the grand boulevards, away from the nightclubs, even away from Diego Rivera's murals, but. . . .

MISS FELLOWES: Oh, preach that in a pulpit, Reverend Shannon *de*-frocked!

SHANNON (*ominously*): You've said that once too often. (*He seizes her arm.*) This time before witnesses. Miss Jelkes? Miss Jelkes!

(*Hannah opens the curtain of her cubicle.*)

HANNAH: Yes, Mr. Shannon, what is it?

SHANNON: You heard what this. . . .

MISS FELLOWES: Shannon! Take your hand off my arm!

SHANNON: Miss Jelkes, just tell me, did you hear what she . . . (*His voice stops oddly with a choked sobbing sound. He runs at the wall and pounds it with his fists.*)

MISS FELLOWES: I spent this entire afternoon and over twenty dollars checking up on this impostor, with long-distance phone calls.

HANNAH: Not impostor—you mustn't say things like that.

MISS FELLOWES: You were locked out of your church!—for atheism and seducing of girls!

SHANNON (*turning about*): In front of God and witnesses, you are lying, lying!

LATTA: Miss Fellowes, I want you to know that Blake Tours was deceived about this character's background and Blake Tours will see that he is blacklisted from now on at every travel agency in the States.

SHANNON: How about Africa, Asia, Australia? The whole world, Latta, God's world, has been the range of my travels. I haven't stuck to the schedules of the brochures and I've always allowed the ones that were willing to see, to *see*!—the underworlds of all places, and if they had hearts to be touched, feelings to feel with, I gave them a priceless chance to feel and be touched. And none will ever forget it, none of them, ever, never! (*The passion of his speech imposes a little stillness.*)

LATTA: Go on, lie back in your hammock, that's all you're good for, Shannon. (*He goes to the top of the path and shouts down the hill.*) O.K., let's get cracking. Get that luggage strapped on top of the bus, we're moving! (*He starts down the hill with Miss Fellowes.*)

NONNO (*incongruously, from his cubicle*):
    How calmly does the orange branch
    Observe the sky begin to blanch. . . .

(*Shannon sucks in his breath with an abrupt, fierce sound. He rushes off the verandah and down the path toward the road. Hannah calls after him, with a restraining gesture. Maxine appears on the verandah. Then a great commotion commences below the hill, with shrieks of outrage and squeals of shocked laughter.*)

MAXINE (*rushing to the path*): Shannon! Shannon! Get back up here, get back up here. Pedro, Pancho, traerme a Shannon. Que está haciendo allí? Oh, my God! Stop him, for God's sake, somebody stop him!

(*Shannon returns, panting and spent. He is followed by Maxine.*)

MAXINE: Shannon, go in your room and stay there until that party's gone.

SHANNON: Don't give me orders.

MAXINE: You do what I tell you to do or I'll have you removed —you know where.

SHANNON: Don't push me, don't pull at me, Maxine.

MAXINE: All right, do as I say.

SHANNON: Shannon obeys only Shannon.

MAXINE: You'll sing a different tune if they put you where they put you in 'thirty-six. Remember 'thirty-six, Shannon?

SHANNON: O.K., Maxine, just . . . let me breathe alone, please. I won't go but I will lie in the . . . hammock.

MAXINE: Go into Fred's room where I can watch you.

SHANNON: Later, Maxine, not yet.

MAXINE: Why do you always come here to crack up, Shannon?

SHANNON: It's the hammock, Maxine, the hammock by the rain forest.

MAXINE: Shannon, go in your room and stay there until I get back. Oh, my God, the money. They haven't paid the mother-grabbin' bill. I got to go back down there and collect their goddam bill before they. . . . Pancho, vijilalo, entiendes? (*She rushes back down the hill, shouting* "Hey! Just a minute down there!")

SHANNON: What did I do? (*He shakes his head, stunned.*) I don't know what I did.

(*Hannah opens the screen of her cubicle but doesn't come out. She is softly lighted so that she looks, again, like a medieval sculpture of a saint. Her pale gold hair catches the soft light. She has let it down and still holds the silver-backed brush with which she was brushing it.*)

SHANNON: God almighty, I . . . what did I do? I don't know what I did. (*He turns to the Mexican boys who have come back up the path.*) Que hice? Que hice?

(*There is breathless, spasmodic laughter from the boys as Pancho informs him that he pissed on the ladies' luggage.*)

PANCHO: Tú measte en las maletas de las señoras!

(*Shannon tries to laugh with the boys, while they bend double with amusement. Shannon's laughter dies out in little choked spasms. Down the hill, Maxine's voice is raised in angry altercation with Jake Latta. Miss Fellowes' voice is lifted and then there is a general rhubarb to which is added the roar of the bus motor.*)

SHANNON: There go my ladies, ha, ha! There go my . . . (*He turns about to meet Hannah's grave, compassionate gaze. He tries to laugh again. She shakes her head with a slight restraining gesture and drops the curtain so that her softly luminous figure is seen as through a mist.*) . . . ladies, the last of my—ha, ha!—ladies. (*He bends far over the verandah rail, then straightens violently and with an animal outcry begins to pull at the chain suspending the gold cross about his neck. Pancho watches indifferently as the chain cuts the back of Shannon's neck. Hannah rushes out to him.*)

HANNAH: Mr. Shannon, stop that! You're cutting yourself doing that. That isn't necessary, so stop it! (*to Pancho:*) Agarrale las manos! (*Pancho makes a halfhearted effort to comply, but Shannon kicks at him and goes on with the furious self-laceration.*) Shannon, let me do it, let me take it off you. Can I take it off you? (*He drops his arms. She struggles with the clasp of the chain but her fingers are too shaky to work it.*)

SHANNON: No, no, it won't come off, I'll have to break it off me.

HANNAH: No, no, wait—I've got it. (*She has now removed it.*)

SHANNON: Thanks. Keep it. Goodbye! (*He starts toward the path down to the beach.*)

HANNAH: Where are you going? What are you going to do?

SHANNON: I'm going swimming. I'm going to swim out to China!

HANNAH: No, no, not tonight, Shannon! Tomorrow . . . tomorrow, Shannon!

(*But he divides the trumpet-flowered bushes and passes through them. Hannah rushes after him, screaming for* "Mrs. Faulk." *Maxine can be heard shouting for the Mexican boys.*)

MAXINE: Muchachos, cojerlo! Atarlo! Está loco. Traerlo aqui. Catch him, he's crazy. Bring him back and tie him up!

(*In a few moments Shannon is hauled back through the bushes and onto the verandah by Maxine and the boys. They rope him into the hammock. His struggle is probably not much of a real struggle—histrionics mostly. But Hannah stands wringing her hands by the steps as Shannon, gasping for breath, is tied up.*)

HANNAH: The ropes are too tight on his chest!

MAXINE: No, they're not. He's acting, acting. He likes it! I know this black Irish bastard like nobody ever knowed him, so you keep out of it, honey. He cracks up like this so regular that you can set a calendar by it. Every eighteen months he does it, and twice he's done it here and I've had to pay for his medical care. Now I'm going to call in town to get a doctor to come out here and give him a knockout injection, and if he's not better tomorrow he's going into the Casa de Locos again like he did the last time he cracked up on me!

(*There is a moment of silence.*)

SHANNON: Miss Jelkes?

HANNAH: Yes.

SHANNON: Where are you?

HANNAH: I'm right here behind you. Can I do anything for you?

SHANNON: Sit here where I can see you. Don't stop talking. I have to fight this panic.

(*There is a pause. She moves a chair beside his hammock. The Germans troop up from the beach. They are delighted by the drama that Shannon has provided. In their scanty swimsuits they parade onto the verandah and gather about Shannon's captive figure as if they were looking at a funny animal in a zoo. Their talk is in German except when they speak directly to Shannon or Hannah. Their heavily handsome figures gleam with oily wetness and they keep chuckling lubriciously.*)

HANNAH: Please! Will you be so kind as to leave him alone?

(*They pretend not to understand her. Frau Fahrenkopf bends over Shannon in his hammock and speaks to him loudly and slowly in English.*)

FRAU FAHRENKOPF: Is this true you make pee-pee all over the suitcases of the ladies from Texas? Hah? Hah? You run down there to the bus and right in front of the ladies you pees all over the luggage of the ladies from Texas?

(*Hannah's indignant protest is drowned in the Rabelaisian laughter of the Germans.*)

HERR FAHRENKOPF: Thees is vunderbar, vunderbar! Hah? Thees is a *epic gesture*! Hah? Thees is the way to demonstrate to ladies that you are a American *gentleman*! Hah?

(*He turns to the others and makes a ribald comment. The two women shriek with amusement, Hilda falling back into the arms of Wolfgang, who catches her with his hands over her almost nude breasts.*)

HANNAH (*calling out*): Mrs. Faulk! Mrs. Faulk! (*She rushes to the verandah angle as Maxine appears there.*) Will you please ask these people to leave him alone. They're tormenting him like an animal in a trap.

(*The Germans are already trooping around the verandah, laughing and capering gaily.*)

SHANNON (*suddenly, in a great shout*): Regression to infantilism, ha, ha, regression to infantilism . . . The infantile protest, ha, ha, ha, the infantile expression of rage at Mama and rage at God and rage at the goddam crib, and rage at the everything, rage at the . . . everything. . . . Regression to infantilism. . . .

(*Now all have left but Hannah and Shannon.*)

SHANNON: Untie me.
HANNAH: Not yet.
SHANNON: I can't stand being tied up.
HANNAH: You'll have to stand it a while.
SHANNON: It makes me panicky.
HANNAH: I know.
SHANNON: A man can die of panic.
HANNAH: Not if he enjoys it as much as you, Mr. Shannon.

(*She goes into her cubicle directly behind his hammock. The cubicle is lighted and we see her removing a small teapot and*) *a tin of tea from her suitcase on the cot, then a little alcohol burner. She comes back out with these articles.*)

SHANNON: What did you mean by that insulting remark?

HANNAH: What remark, Mr. Shannon?

SHANNON: That I enjoy it.

HANNAH: Oh . . . that.

SHANNON: Yes. That.

HANNAH: That wasn't meant as an insult, just an observation. I don't judge people, I draw them. That's all I do, just draw them, but in order to draw them I have to observe them, don't I?

SHANNON: And you've observed, you think you've observed, that I like being tied in this hammock, trussed up in it like a hog being hauled off to the slaughter house, Miss Jelkes.

HANNAH: Who wouldn't like to suffer and atone for the sins of himself and the world if it could be done in a hammock with ropes instead of nails, on a hill that's so much lovelier than Golgotha, the Place of the Skull, Mr. Shannon? There's something almost voluptuous in the way that you twist and groan in that hammock—no nails, no blood, no death. Isn't that a comparatively comfortable, almost voluptuous kind of crucifixion to suffer for the guilt of the world, Mr. Shannon?

(*She strikes a match to light the alcohol burner. A pure blue jet of flame springs up to cast a flickering, rather unearthly glow on their section of the verandah. The glow is delicately refracted by the subtle, faded colors of her robe—a robe given to her by a Kabuki actor who posed for her in Japan.*)

SHANNON: Why have you turned against me all of a sudden, when I need you the most?

HANNAH: I haven't turned against you at all, Mr. Shannon. I'm just attempting to give you a character sketch of yourself, in words instead of pastel crayons or charcoal.

SHANNON: You're certainly suddenly very sure of some New England spinsterish attitudes that I didn't know you had in you. I thought that you were an *emancipated* Puritan, Miss Jelkes.

HANNAH: Who is . . . ever . . . completely?

SHANNON: I thought you were sexless but you've suddenly turned into a woman. Know how I know that? Because you, not me—not me—are taking pleasure in my tied-up condition. All women, whether they face it or not, want to see a man in a tied-up situation. They work at it all their lives, to get a man in a tied-up situation. Their lives are fulfilled, they're satisfied at last, when they get a man, or as many men as they can, in the tied-up situation. (*Hannah leaves the alcohol burner and teapot and moves to the railing where she grips a verandah post and draws a few deep breaths.*) You don't like this observation of you? The shoe's too tight for comfort when it's on your own foot, Miss Jelkes? Some deep breaths again—feeling panic?

HANNAH (*recovering and returning to the burner*): I'd like to untie you right now, but let me wait till you've passed through your present disturbance. You're still indulging yourself in your . . . your Passion Play performance. I can't help observing this self-indulgence in you.

SHANNON: What rotten indulgence?

HANNAH: Well, your busload of ladies from the female college in Texas. I don't like those ladies any more than you do, but after all, they did save up all year to make this Mexican tour, to stay in stuffy hotels and eat the food they're used to. They want to be at home away from home, but you . . . you indulged yourself, Mr. Shannon. You did conduct the tour as if it was just for you, for your own pleasure.

SHANNON: Hell, what pleasure—going through hell all the way?

HANNAH: Yes, but comforted, now and then, weren't you, by the little musical prodigy under the wing of the college vocal instructor?

SHANNON: Funny, ha-ha funny! Nantucket spinsters have their wry humor, don't they?

HANNAH: Yes, they do. They have to.

SHANNON (*becoming progressively quieter under the cool influence of her voice behind him*): I can't see what you're up to, Miss Jelkes honey, but I'd almost swear you're making a pot of tea over there.

HANNAH: That is just what I'm doing.

SHANNON: Does this strike you as the right time for a tea party?

HANNAH: This isn't plain tea, this is poppyseed tea.

SHANNON: Are you a slave to the poppy?

HANNAH: It's a mild, sedative drink that helps you get through nights that are hard for you to get through and I'm making it for my grandfather and myself as well as for you, Mr. Shannon. Because, for all three of us, this won't be an easy night to get through. Can't you hear him in his cell number 4, mumbling over and over and over the lines of his new poem? It's like a blind man climbing a staircase that goes to nowhere, that just falls off into space, and I hate to say what it is. . . . (*She draws a few deep breaths behind him.*)

SHANNON: Put some hemlock in his poppyseed tea tonight so he won't wake up tomorrow for the removal to the Casa de Huéspedes. Do that act of mercy. Put in the hemlock and I will consecrate it, turn it to God's blood. Hell, if you'll get me out of this hammock I'll serve it to him myself, I'll be your accomplice in this act of mercy. I'll say, "Take and drink this, the blood of our—"

HANNAH: Stop it! Stop being childishly cruel! I can't stand for a person that I respect to talk and behave like a small, cruel boy, Mr. Shannon.

SHANNON: What've you found to respect in me, Miss . . . Thin-Standing-Up-Female-Buddha?

HANNAH: I respect a person that has had to fight and howl for his decency and his—

SHANNON: *What* decency?

HANNAH: Yes, for his decency and his bit of goodness, much more than I respect the lucky ones that just had theirs handed out to them at birth and never afterwards snatched away from them by . . . unbearable . . . torments, I. . . .

SHANNON: You *respect* me?

HANNAH: I do.

SHANNON: But you just said that I'm taking pleasure in a . . . voluptuous crucifixion without nails. A . . . what? . . . painless atonement for the—

HANNAH (*cutting in*): Yes, but I think—

SHANNON: Untie me!

HANNAH: Soon, soon. Be patient.

SHANNON: Now!

HANNAH: Not quite yet, Mr. Shannon. Not till I'm reasonably sure that you won't swim out to China, because, you see, I think you think of the . . . "the long swim to China" as another painless atonement. I mean I don't think you think you'd be intercepted by sharks and barracudas before you got past the barrier reef. And I'm afraid you *would be*. It's as simple as that, if that is simple.

SHANNON: What's simple?

HANNAH: Nothing, except for simpletons, Mr. Shannon.

SHANNON: Do you believe in people being tied up?

HANNAH: Only when they might take the long swim to China.

SHANNON: All right, Miss Thin-Standing-Up-Female-Buddha, just light a Benson & Hedges cigarette for me and put it in my mouth and take it out when you hear me choking on it—if that doesn't seem to you like another bit of voluptuous self-crucifixion.

HANNAH (*looking about the verandah*): I will, but . . . where did I put them?

SHANNON: I have a pack of my own in my pocket.

HANNAH: Which pocket?

SHANNON: I don't know which pocket, you'll have to frisk me for it. (*She pats his jacket pocket.*)

HANNAH: They're not in your coat-pocket.

SHANNON: Then look for them in my pants' pockets.

(*She hesitates to put her hand in his pants' pockets, for a moment. Hannah has always had a sort of fastidiousness, a reluctance, toward intimate physical contact. But after the momentary fastidious hesitation, she puts her hands in his pants' pocket and draws out the cigarette pack.*)

SHANNON: Now light it for me and put it in my mouth.

(*She complies with these directions. Almost at once he chokes and the cigarette is expelled.*)

HANNAH: You've dropped it on you—where is it?

SHANNON (*twisting and lunging about in the hammock*): It's under me, under me, burning. Untie me, for God's sake, will you—it's burning me through my pants!

HANNAH: Raise your hips so I can—

SHANNON: I can't, the ropes are too tight. Untie me, un-tieeeee meeeeee!

HANNAH: I've found it, I've got it!

(*But Shannon's shout has brought Maxine out of her office. She rushes onto the verandah and sits on Shannon's legs.*)

MAXINE: Now hear this, you crazy black Irish mick, you! You Protestant black Irish looney, I've called up Lopez, Doc Lopez. Remember him—the man in the dirty white jacket that come here the last time you cracked up here? And hauled you off to the Casa de Locos? Where they threw you into that cell with nothing in it but a bucket and straw and a water pipe? That you crawled up the water pipe? And dropped head-down on the floor and got a concussion? Yeah, and I told him you were back here to crack up again and if you didn't quiet down here tonight you should be hauled out in the morning.

SHANNON (*cutting in, with the honking sound of a panicky goose*): Off, off, off, off, off!

HANNAH: Oh, Mrs. Faulk, Mr. Shannon won't quiet down till he's left alone in the hammock.

MAXINE: Then why don't *you* leave him alone?

HANNAH: I'm not sitting on him and he . . . has to be cared for by someone.

MAXINE: And the someone is *you*?

HANNAH: A long time ago, Mrs. Faulk, I had experience with someone in Mr. Shannon's condition, so I know how necessary it is to let them be quiet for a while.

MAXINE: He wasn't quiet, he was shouting.

HANNAH: He will quiet down again. I'm preparing a sedative tea for him, Mrs. Faulk.

MAXINE: Yeah, I see. Put it out. Nobody cooks here but the Chinaman in the kitchen.

HANNAH: This is just a little alcohol burner, a spirit lamp, Mrs. Faulk.

MAXINE: I know what it is. It goes out! (*She blows out the flame under the burner.*)

SHANNON: Maxine honey? (*He speaks quietly now.*) Stop persecuting this lady. You can't intimidate her. A bitch is no

match for a lady except in a brass bed, honey, and sometimes not even there.

(*The Germans are heard shouting for beer—a case of it to
take down to the beach.*)

WOLFGANG: Eine Kiste Carta Blanca.

FRAU FAHRENKOPF: Wir haben genug gehabt . . . vielleicht
nicht.

HERR FAHRENKOPF: Nein! Niemals genug.

HILDA: Mutter du bist dick . . . aber wir sind es nicht.

SHANNON: Maxine, you're neglecting your duties as a beer-
hall waitress. (*His tone is deceptively gentle.*) They want a
case of Carta Blanca to carry down to the beach, so give it
to 'em . . . and tonight, when the moon's gone down, if
you'll let me out of this hammock, I'll try to imagine you
as a . . . as a nymph in her teens.

MAXINE: A fat lot of good you'd be in your present condition.

SHANNON: Don't be a sexual snob at your age, honey.

MAXINE: Hah! (*But the unflattering offer has pleased her realistically modest soul, so she goes back to the Germans.*)

SHANNON: Now let me try a bit of your poppyseed tea, Miss
Jelkes.

HANNAH: I ran out of sugar, but I had some ginger, some
sugared ginger. (*She pours a cup of tea and sips it.*) Oh, it's
not well brewed yet, but try to drink some now and the—
(*She lights the burner again.*)—the second cup will be better. (*She crouches by the hammock and presses the cup to his
lips. He raises his head to sip it, but he gags and chokes.*)

SHANNON: *Caesar's ghost!*—it could be chased by the witches'
brew from Macbeth.

HANNAH: Yes, I know, it's still bitter.

(*The Germans appear on the wing of the verandah and go
trooping down to the beach, for a beer festival and a moonlight swim. Even in the relative dark they have a luminous
color, an almost phosphorescent pink and gold color of skin.
They carry with them a case of Carta Blanca beer and the
fantastically painted rubber horse. On their faces are smiles of
euphoria as they move like a dream-image, starting to sing a
marching song as they go.*)

SHANNON: Fiends out of hell with the . . . voices of . . . angels.

HANNAH: Yes, they call it "the logic of contradictions," Mr. Shannon.

SHANNON (*lunging suddenly forward and undoing the loosened ropes*): Out! Free! Unassisted!

HANNAH: Yes, I never doubted that you could get loose, Mr. Shannon.

SHANNON: Thanks for your help, anyhow.

HANNAH: Where are you going?

(*He has crossed to the liquor cart.*)

SHANNON: Not far. To the liquor cart to make myself a rum-coco.

HANNAH: Oh. . . .

SHANNON (*at the liquor cart*): Coconut? Check. Machete? Check. Rum? Double check! Ice? The ice-bucket's empty. O.K., it's a night for warm drinks. Miss Jelkes? Would you care to have your complimentary rum-coco?

HANNAH: No thank you, Mr. Shannon.

SHANNON: You don't mind me having mine?

HANNAH: Not at all, Mr. Shannon.

SHANNON: You don't disapprove of this weakness, this self-indulgence?

HANNAH: Liquor isn't your problem, Mr. Shannon.

SHANNON: What is my problem, Mr. Jelkes?

HANNAH: The oldest one in the world—the need to believe in something or in someone—almost anyone—almost anything . . . something.

SHANNON: Your voice sounds hopeless about it.

HANNAH: No, I'm not hopeless about it. In fact, I've discovered something to believe in.

SHANNON: Something like . . . God?

HANNAH: No.

SHANNON: What?

HANNAH: Broken gates between people so they can reach each other, even if it's just for one night only.

SHANNON: One night stands, huh?

HANNAH: One night . . . communication between them on a verandah outside their . . . separate cubicles, Mr. Shannon.

SHANNON: You don't mean physically, do you?

HANNAH: No.

SHANNON: I didn't think so. Then what?

HANNAH: A little understanding exchanged between them, a wanting to help each other through nights like this.

SHANNON: Who was the someone you told the widow you'd helped long ago to get through a crack-up like this one I'm going through?

HANNAH: Oh . . . that. Myself.

SHANNON: You?

HANNAH: Yes. I can help you because I've been through what you are going through now. I had something like your spook—I just had a different name for him. I called him the blue devil, and . . . oh . . . we had quite a battle, quite a contest between us.

SHANNON: Which you obviously won.

HANNAH: I couldn't afford to lose.

SHANNON: How'd you beat your blue devil?

HANNAH: I showed him that I could endure him and I made him respect my endurance.

SHANNON: How?

HANNAH: Just by, just by . . . enduring. Endurance is something that spooks and blue devils respect. And they respect all the tricks that panicky people use to outlast and outwit their panic.

SHANNON: Like poppyseed tea?

HANNAH: Poppyseed tea or rum-cocos or just a few deep breaths. Anything, everything, that we take to give them the slip, and so to keep on going.

SHANNON: To where?

HANNAH: To somewhere like this, perhaps. This verandah over the rain forest and the still-water beach, after long, difficult travels. And I don't mean just travels about the world, the earth's surface. I mean . . . subterranean travels, the . . . the journeys that the spooked and bedevilled people are forced to take through the . . . the *unlighted* sides of their natures.

SHANNON: Don't tell me you have a dark side to your nature.

(*He says this sardonically.*)

HANNAH: I'm sure I don't have to tell a man as experienced and knowledgeable as you, Mr. Shannon, that everything has its shadowy side?

(*She glances up at him and observes that she doesn't have his attention. He is gazing tensely at something off the verandah. It is the kind of abstraction, not vague but fiercely concentrated, that occurs in madness. She turns to look where he's looking. She closes her eyes for a moment and draws a deep breath, then goes on speaking in a voice like a hypnotist's, as if the words didn't matter, since he is not listening to her so much as to the tone and the cadence of her voice.*)

HANNAH: Everything in the whole solar system has a shadowy side to it except the sun itself—the sun is the single exception. You're not listening, are you?

SHANNON (*as if replying to her*): The spook is in the rain forest. (*He suddenly hurls his coconut shell with great violence off the verandah, creating a commotion among the jungle birds.*) Good shot—it caught him right on the kisser and his teeth flew out like popcorn from a popper.

HANNAH: Has he gone off—to the dentist?

SHANNON: He's retreated a little way away for a little while, but when I buzz for my breakfast tomorrow, he'll bring it in to me with a grin that'll curdle the milk in the coffee and he'll stink like a . . . a gringo drunk in a Mexican jail who's slept all night in his vomit.

HANNAH: If you wake up before I'm out, I'll bring your coffee in to you . . . if you call me.

SHANNON (*His attention returns to her*): No, you'll be gone, God help me.

HANNAH: Maybe and maybe not. I might think of something tomorrow to placate the widow.

SHANNON: The widow's implacable, honey.

HANNAH: I think I'll think of something because I have to. I can't let Nonno be moved to the Casa de Huéspedes, Mr. Shannon. Not any more than I could let you take the long swim out to China. You know that. Not if I can prevent it, and when I have to be resourceful, I can be very resourceful.

SHANNON: How'd you get over your crack-up?

HANNAH: I never cracked up, I couldn't afford to. Of course, I nearly did once. I was young once, Mr. Shannon, but I was one of those people who can be young without really having their youth, and not to have your youth when you are young is naturally very disturbing. But I was lucky. My work, this occupational therapy that I gave myself—painting and doing quick character sketches—made me look out of myself, not in, and gradually, at the far end of the tunnel that I was struggling out of I began to see this faint, very faint gray light—the light of the world outside me—and I kept climbing toward it. I had to.

SHANNON: Did it stay a gray light?

HANNAH: No, no, it turned white.

SHANNON: Only white, never gold?

HANNAH: No, it stayed only white, but white is a very good light to see at the end of a long black tunnel you thought would be neverending, that only God or Death could put a stop to, especially when you . . . since I was . . . far from sure about God.

SHANNON: You're still unsure about him?

HANNAH: Not as unsure as I was. You see, in my profession I have to look hard and close at human faces in order to catch something in them before they get restless and call out, "Waiter, the check, we're leaving." Of course sometimes, a few times, I just see blobs of wet dough that pass for human faces, with bits of jelly for eyes. Then I cue in Nonno to give a recitation, because I can't draw such faces. But those aren't the usual faces, I don't think they're even real. Most times I *do* see something, and I can catch it—I *can*, like I caught something in your face when I sketched you this afternoon with your eyes open. Are you still listening to me? (*He crouches beside her chair, looking up at her intently.*) In Shanghai, Shannon, there is a place that's called the House for the Dying—the old and penniless dying, whose younger, penniless living children and grandchildren take them there for them to get through with their dying on pallets, on straw mats. The first time I went there it shocked me, I ran away from it. But I came back later and I saw that their children and grandchildren and the custodians of the place had put little comforts beside their death-pallets, little flowers and opium candies and religious emblems. That made me able to stay to draw their dying faces. Sometimes only their eyes were still alive, but, Mr. Shannon, those eyes of the penniless dying with those last little comforts beside them, I tell you, Mr. Shannon, those eyes looked up with their last dim life left in them as clear as the stars in the Southern Cross, Mr. Shannon. And now . . . now I am going to say something to you that will sound like something that only the spinster granddaughter of a minor romantic poet is likely to say. . . . Nothing I've ever seen has seemed as beautiful to me, not even the view from this verandah between the sky and the still-water beach, and lately . . . lately my grandfather's eyes have looked up at me like that. . . . (*She rises abruptly and crosses to the front of the verandah.*) Tell me, what is that sound I keep hearing down there?

SHANNON: There's a marimba band at the cantina on the beach.

HANNAH: I don't mean that, I mean that scraping, scuffling sound that I keep hearing under the verandah.

SHANNON: Oh, that. The Mexican boys that work here have caught an iguana and tied it up under the verandah, hitched it to a post, and naturally of course it's trying to scramble away. But it's got to the end of its rope, and get any further it cannot. Ha-ha—that's it. (*He quotes from Nonno's poem:* "And still the orange," etc.) Do you have any life of your own—besides your water colors and sketches and your travels with Grampa?

HANNAH: We make a home for each other, my grandfather and I. Do you know what I mean by a home? I don't mean a regular home. I mean I don't mean what other people mean when they speak of a home, because I don't regard a home as a . . . well, as a place, a building . . . a house . . . of wood, bricks, stone. I think of a home as being a thing that two people have between them in which each can . . . well, nest—rest—live in, emotionally speaking. Does that make any sense to you, Mr. Shannon?

SHANNON: Yeah, complete. But. . . .

HANNAH: Another incomplete sentence.

SHANNON: We better leave it that way. I might've said something to hurt you.

HANNAH: I'm not thin skinned, Mr. Shannon.

SHANNON: No, well, then, I'll say it. . . . (*He moves to the liquor cart.*) When a bird builds a nest to rest in and live in, it doesn't build it in a . . . a falling-down tree.

HANNAH: I'm not a bird, Mr. Shannon.

SHANNON: I was making an analogy, Miss Jelkes.

HANNAH: I thought you were making yourself another rum-coco, Mr. Shannon.

SHANNON: Both. When a bird builds a nest, it builds it with an eye for the . . . the relative permanence of the location, and also for the purpose of mating and propagating its species.

HANNAH: I still say that I'm not a bird, Mr. Shannon, I'm a human being and when a member of that fantastic species builds a nest in the heart of another, the question of permanence isn't the first or even the last thing that's considered . . . necessarily? . . . always? Nonno and I have been continually reminded of the impermanence of things lately. We go back to a hotel where we've been many times before and it isn't there any more. It's been demolished and there's one of those glassy, brassy new ones. Or if the old one's still there, the manager or the Maitre D who always welcomed us back so cordially before has been replaced by someone new who looks at us with suspicion.

SHANNON: Yeah, but you still had each other.

HANNAH: Yes. We did.

SHANNON: But when the old gentleman goes?

HANNAH: Yes?

SHANNON: What will you do? Stop?

HANNAH: Stop or go on . . . probably go on.

SHANNON: Alone? Checking into hotels alone, eating alone at tables for one in a corner, the tables waiters call aces.

HANNAH: Thank you for your sympathy, Mr. Shannon, but in my profession I'm obliged to make quick contacts with strangers who turn to friends very quickly.

SHANNON: Customers aren't friends.

HANNAH: They turn to friends, if they're friendly.

SHANNON: Yeah, but how will it seem to be traveling alone after so many years of traveling with. . . .

HANNAH: I will know how it feels when I feel it—and don't say alone as if nobody had ever gone on alone. For instance, you.

SHANNON: I've always traveled with trainloads, planeloads and busloads of tourists.

HANNAH: That doesn't mean you're still not really alone.

SHANNON: I never fail to make an intimate connection with someone in my parties.

HANNAH: Yes, the youngest young lady, and I was on the verandah this afternoon when the latest of these young ladies gave a demonstration of how lonely the intimate connection has always been for you. The episode in the cold, inhuman hotel room, Mr. Shannon, for which you despise the lady almost as much as you despise yourself. Afterwards you are so polite to the lady that I'm sure it must chill her to the bone, the scrupulous little attentions that you pay her in return for your little enjoyment of her. The gentleman-of-Virginia act that you put on for her, your noblesse oblige treatment of her . . . Oh no, Mr. Shannon, don't kid yourself that you ever travel with someone. You have always traveled alone except for your spook, as you call it. He's your traveling companion. Nothing, nobody else has traveled with you.

SHANNON: Thank you for your sympathy, Miss Jelkes.

HANNAH: You're welcome, Mr. Shannon. And now I think I had better warm up the poppyseed tea for Nonno. Only a good night's sleep could make it possible for him to go on from here tomorrow.

SHANNON: Yes, well, if the conversation is over—I think I'll go down for a swim now.

HANNAH: To China?

SHANNON: No, not to China, just to the little island out here with the sleepy bar on it . . . called the Cantina Serena.

HANNAH: Why?

SHANNON: Because I'm not a nice drunk and I was about to ask you a not nice question.

HANNAH: Ask it. There's no set limit on questions here tonight.

SHANNON: And no set limit on answers?

HANNAH: None I can think of between you and me, Mr. Shannon.

SHANNON: That I will take you up on.

HANNAH: Do.

SHANNON: It's a bargain.

HANNAH: Only do lie back down in the hammock and drink a full cup of the poppyseed tea this time. It's warmer now and the sugared ginger will make it easier to get down.

SHANNON: All right. The question is this: have you never had in your life any kind of a lovelife? (*Hannah stiffens for a moment.*) I thought you said there was no limit set on questions.

HANNAH: We'll make a bargain—I will answer your question *after* you've had a full cup of the poppyseed tea so you'll be able to get the good night's sleep you need, too. It's fairly warm now and the sugared ginger's made it much more— (*She sips the cup.*)—palatable.

SHANNON: You think I'm going to drift into dreamland so you can welch on the bargain? (*He accepts the cup from her.*)

HANNAH: I'm not a welcher on bargains. Drink it all. All. *All!*

SHANNON (*with a disgusted grimace as he drains the cup*): *Great* Caesar's *ghost.* (*He tosses the cup off the verandah and falls into the hammock, chuckling.*) The oriental idea of a Mickey Finn, huh? Sit down where I can see you, Miss Jelkes honey. (*She sits down in a straight-back chair, some distance from the hammock.*) Where I can *see* you! I don't have an x-ray eye in the back of my head, Miss Jelkes. (*She moves the chair alongside the hammock.*) Further, further, up further. (*She complies.*) There now. Answer the question now, Miss Jelkes honey.

HANNAH: Would you mind repeating the question.

SHANNON (*slowly, with emphasis*): Have you never had in all of your life and your travels any experience, any encounter, with what Larry-the-crackpot Shannon thinks of as a lovelife?

HANNAH: There are . . . worse things than chastity, Mr. Shannon.

SHANNON: Yeah, lunacy and death are both a little worse, *maybe!* But chastity isn't a thing that a beautiful woman or an attractive man falls into like a booby trap or an overgrown gopher hole, is it? (*There is a pause.*) I still think you are welching on the bargain and I. . . . (*He starts out of the hammock.*)

HANNAH: Mr. Shannon, this night is just as hard for me to get through as it is for you to get through. But it's you that are welching on the bargain, you're not staying in the hammock. Lie back down in the hammock. Now. Yes. Yes, I have had two experiences, well, encounters, with. . . .

SHANNON: *Two*, did you say?

HANNAH: Yes, I said two. And I wasn't exaggerating and don't you say "fantastic" before I've told you both stories. When I was sixteen, your favorite age, Mr. Shannon, each Saturday afternoon my grandfather Nonno would give me thirty cents, my allowance, my pay for my secretarial and housekeeping duties. Twenty-five cents for admission to the Saturday matinee at the Nantucket movie theatre and five cents extra for a bag of popcorn, Mr. Shannon. I'd sit at the almost empty back of the movie theatre so that the popcorn munching wouldn't disturb the other movie patrons. Well . . . one afternoon a young man sat down beside me and pushed his . . . knee against mine and . . . I moved over two seats but he moved over beside me and continued this . . . pressure! I jumped up and screamed, Mr. Shannon. He was arrested for molesting a minor.

SHANNON: Is he still in the Nantucket jail?

HANNAH: No. I got him out. I told the police that it was a Clara Bow picture—it *was* a Clara Bow picture—and I was just overexcited.

SHANNON: Fantastic.

HANNAH: Yes, very! The second experience is much more recent, only two years ago, when Nonno and I were operating at the Raffles Hotel in Singapore, and doing very well there, making expenses and more. One evening in the Palm Court of the Raffles we met this middle-aged, sort of nondescript Australian salesman. You know—plump, bald-spotted, with a bad attempt at speaking with an upper-class accent and terribly overfriendly. He was alone and looked lonely. Grandfather said him a poem and I did a quick character sketch that was shamelessly flattering of him. He paid me more than my usual asking price and gave my grandfather five Malayan dollars, yes, and he even purchased one of my water colors. Then it was Nonno's bedtime. The Aussie salesman asked me out in a sampan with him. Well, he'd been so generous . . . I accepted. I did, I accepted. Grandfather went up to bed and I went out in the sampan with this ladies' underwear salesman. I noticed that he became more and more. . . .

SHANNON: What?

HANNAH: Well . . . *agitated* . . . as the afterglow of the sunset faded out on the water. (*She laughs with a delicate sadness.*) Well, finally, eventually, he leaned toward me . . . we were vis-à-vis in the sampan . . . and he looked intensely, passionately into my eyes. (*She laughs again.*) And he said to me: "Miss Jelkes? Will you do me a favor? Will you do something for me?" "What?" said I. "Well," said he, "if I turn my back, if I look the other way, will you take off some piece of your clothes and let me hold it, just hold it?"

SHANNON: Fantastic!

HANNAH: Then he said, "It will just take a few seconds." "Just a few seconds for what?" I asked him. (*She gives the same laugh again.*) He didn't say for what, but. . . .

SHANNON: His satisfaction?

HANNAH: Yes.

SHANNON: What did you do—in a situation like that?

HANNAH: I . . . gratified his request, I did! And he kept his promise. He did keep his back turned till I said ready and threw him . . . the part of my clothes.

SHANNON: What did he do with it?

HANNAH: He didn't move, except to seize the article he'd requested. I looked the other way while his satisfaction took place.

SHANNON: Watch out for commercial travelers in the Far East. Is that the moral, Miss Jelkes honey?

HANNAH: Oh, no, the moral is oriental. Accept whatever situation you cannot improve.

SHANNON: "When it's inevitable, lean back and enjoy it" is that it?

HANNAH: He'd bought a water color. The incident was embarrassing, not violent. I left and returned unmolested. Oh, and the funniest part of all is that when we got back to the Raffles Hotel, he took the piece of apparel out of his pocket like a bashful boy producing an apple for his schoolteacher and tried to slip it into my hand in the elevator. I wouldn't accept it. I whispered, "Oh, please keep it, Mr. Willoughby!" He'd paid the asking price for my water color and somehow the little experience had been rather touching, I mean it was so *lonely*, out there in the sampan with violet streaks in the sky and this little middle-aged Australian making sounds like he was dying of asthma! And the planet Venus coming serenely out of a fair-weather cloud, over the Straits of Malacca. . . .

SHANNON: And that experience . . . you call that a. . . .

HANNAH: A love experience? Yes. I do call it one.

(*He regards her with incredulity, peering into her face so closely that she is embarrassed and becomes defensive.*)

SHANNON: That, that . . . sad, dirty little episode, you call it a . . . ?

HANNAH (*cutting in sharply*): Sad it certainly was—for the odd little man—but why do you call it "dirty"?

SHANNON: How did you feel when you went into your bedroom?

HANNAH: Confused, I . . . a little confused, I suppose. . . . I'd known about loneliness—but not that degree or . . . depth of it.

SHANNON: You mean it didn't *disgust* you?

HANNAH: Nothing human disgusts me unless it's unkind, violent. And I told you how gentle he was—apologetic, shy, and really very, well, *delicate* about it. However, I do grant you it was on the rather fantastic level.

SHANNON: You're. . . .

HANNAH: I am *what*? "Fantastic"?

(*While they have been talking, Nonno's voice has been heard now and then, mumbling, from his cubicle. Suddenly it becomes loud and clear.*)

NONNO:

>   And finally the broken stem,
>   The plummeting to earth and then. . . .

(*His voice subsides to its mumble. Shannon, standing behind Hannah, places his hand on her throat.*)

HANNAH: What is that for? Are you about to strangle me, Mr. Shannon?

SHANNON: You can't stand to be touched?

HANNAH: Save it for the widow. It isn't for me.

SHANNON: Yes, you're right. (*He removes his hand.*) I could do it with Mrs. Faulk, the inconsolable widow, but I couldn't with you.

HANNAH (*dryly and lightly*): Spinster's loss, widow's gain, Mr. Shannon.

SHANNON: Or widow's loss, spinster's gain. Anyhow it sounds like some old parlor game in a Virginia or Nantucket Island parlor. But . . . I wonder something. . . .

HANNAH: What do you wonder?

SHANNON: If we couldn't . . . *travel* together, I mean just *travel* together?

HANNAH: Could we? In your opinion?

SHANNON: Why not, I don't see why not.

HANNAH: I think the impracticality of the idea will appear much clearer to you in the morning, Mr. Shannon. (*She folds her dimly gold-lacquered fan and rises from her chair.*) Morning can always be counted on to bring us back to a more realistic level. . . . Good night, Mr. Shannon. I have to pack before I'm too tired to.

SHANNON: Don't leave me out here alone yet.

HANNAH: I have to pack now so I can get up at daybreak and try my luck in the plaza.

SHANNON: You won't sell a water color or sketch in that blazing hot plaza tomorrow. Miss Jelkes honey, I don't think you're operating on the realistic level.

HANNAH: Would I be if I thought we could travel together?

SHANNON: I still don't see why we couldn't.

HANNAH: Mr. Shannon, you're not well enough to travel anywhere with anybody right now. Does that sound cruel of me?

SHANNON: You mean that I'm stuck here for good? Winding up with the . . . inconsolable widow?

HANNAH: We all wind up with something or with someone, and if it's someone instead of just something, we're lucky, perhaps . . . unusually lucky. (*She starts to enter her cubicle, then turns to him again in the doorway.*) Oh, and tomorrow. . . . (*She touches her forehead as if a little confused as well as exhausted.*)

SHANNON: What about tomorrow?

HANNAH (*with difficulty*): I think it might be better, tomorrow, if we avoid showing any particular interest in each other, because Mrs. Faulk is a morbidly jealous woman.

SHANNON: *Is* she?

HANNAH: Yes, she seems to have misunderstood our . . . sympathetic interest in each other. So I think we'd better avoid any more long talks on the verandah. I mean till she's thoroughly reassured it might be better if we just say good morning or good night to each other.

SHANNON: We don't even have to say that.

HANNAH: I will, but you don't have to answer.

SHANNON (*savagely*): How about wall-tappings between us by way of communication? You know, like convicts in separate cells communicate with each other by tapping on the walls of the cells? One tap: I'm here. Two taps: are you there? Three taps: yes, I am. Four taps: that's good, we're together. *Christ!* . . . Here, take this. (*He snatches the gold cross from his pocket.*) Take my gold cross and hock it, it's 22-carat gold.

HANNAH: What do you, what are you . . . ?

SHANNON: There's a fine amethyst in it, it'll pay your travel expenses back to the States.

HANNAH: Mr. Shannon, you're making no sense at all now.

SHANNON: Neither are you, Miss Jelkes talking about tomorrow, and. . . .

HANNAH: All I was saying was. . . .

SHANNON: You won't *be* here tomorrow! Had you forgotten you won't be here tomorrow?

HANNAH (*with a slight, shocked laugh*): Yes, I *had*, I'd *forgotten!*

SHANNON: The widow wants you out and out you'll go, even if you sell your water colors like hotcakes to the pariah dogs in the plaza. (*He stares at her, shaking his head hopelessly.*)

HANNAH: I suppose you're right, Mr. Shannon. I must be too tired to think or I've contracted your fever. . . . It had actually slipped my mind for a moment that—

NONNO (*abruptly, from his cubicle*): Hannah!

HANNAH (*rushing to his door*): Yes, what is it, Nonno? (*He doesn't hear her and repeats her name louder.*) Here I am, I'm here.

NONNO: Don't come in yet, but stay where I can call you.

HANNAH: Yes, I'll *hear* you, Nonno. (*She turns toward Shannon, drawing a deep breath.*)

SHANNON: Listen, if you don't take this gold cross that I never want on me again, I'm going to pitch it off the verandah at the spook in the rain forest. (*He raises an arm to throw it, but she catches his arm to restrain him.*)

HANNAH: All right, Mr. Shannon, I'll take it, I'll hold it for you.

SHANNON: Hock it, honey, you've got to.

HANNAH: Well, if I do, I'll mail the pawn ticket to you so you can redeem it, because you'll want it again, when you've gotten over your fever. (*She moves blindly down the verandah and starts to enter the wrong cubicle.*)

SHANNON: That isn't your cell, you went past it. (*His voice is gentle again.*)

HANNAH: I did, I'm sorry. I've never been this tired in all my life. (*She turns to face him again. He stares into her face. She looks blindly out, past him.*) Never! (*There is a slight pause.*) What did you say is making that constant, dry, scuffling sound beneath the verandah?

SHANNON: I told you.

HANNAH: I didn't hear you.

SHANNON: I'll get my flashlight, I'll show you. (*He lurches rapidly into his cubicle and back out with a flashlight.*) It's an iguana. I'll show you. . . . See? The iguana? At the end of its rope? Trying to go on past the end of its goddam rope? Like *you*! Like *me*! Like Grampa with his last poem!

(*In the pause which follows singing is heard from the beach.*)

HANNAH: What is a—what—iguana?

SHANNON: It's a kind of lizard—a big one, a giant one. The Mexican kids caught it and tied it up.

HANNAH: Why did they tie it up?

SHANNON: Because that's what they do. They tie them up and fatten them up and then eat them up, when they're ready for eating. They're a delicacy. Taste like white meat of chicken. At least the Mexicans think so. And also the kids, the Mexican kids, have a lot of fun with them, poking out their eyes with sticks and burning their tails with matches. You know? Fun? Like that?

HANNAH: Mr. Shannon, please go down and cut it loose!

SHANNON: I can't do that.

HANNAH: Why can't you?

SHANNON: Mrs. Faulk wants to eat it. I've got to please Mrs. Faulk, I am at her mercy. I am at her disposal.

HANNAH: I don't understand. I mean I don't understand how anyone could eat a big lizard.

SHANNON: Don't be so critical. If you got hungry enough you'd eat it too. You'd be surprised what people will eat if hungry. There's a lot of hungry people still in the world. Many have died of starvation, but a lot are still living and hungry, believe you me, if you will take my word for it. Why, when I was conducting a party of—*ladies?*—yes, ladies . . . through a country that shall be nameless but in this world, we were passing by rubberneck bus along a tropical coast when we saw a great mound of . . . well, the smell was unpleasant. One of my ladies said, "Oh, Larry, what is that?" My name being Lawrence, the most familiar ladies sometimes call me Larry. I didn't use the four letter word for what the great mound was. I didn't think it was necessary to say it. Then she noticed, and I noticed too, a pair of very old natives of this nameless country, practically naked except for a few filthy rags, creeping and crawling about this mound of . . . and . . . occasionally stopping to pick something out of it, and pop it into their mouths. What? Bits of undigested . . . food particles, Miss Jelkes. (*There is silence for a moment. She makes a gagging sound in her throat and rushes the length of the verandah to the wooden steps and disappears for a while. Shannon continues, to himself and the moon.*) Now why did I tell her that? Because it's true? That's no reason to tell her, because it's true. Yeah. Because it's true was a good reason not to tell her. Except . . . I think I first *faced* it in that nameless country. The gradual, rapid, natural, unnatural—predestined, accidental—cracking up and going to pieces of young Mr. T. Lawrence Shannon, yes, still *young* Mr. T. Lawrence Shannon, by which rapid-slow process . . . his final tour of ladies through tropical countries. . . . Why did I say "tropical"? Hell! Yes! It's always been tropical countries I took ladies through. Does that, does that—huh?—signify something, I wonder? Maybe. Fast decay is a thing of hot climates, steamy, hot, wet climates, and I run back to them like a. . . . Incomplete sentence. . . . Always seducing a lady or two, or three or four or five ladies in the party, but really ravaging her first by pointing out to her the—what?—horrors? Yes, horrors!—of the tropical country being conducted a tour through. My . . . brain's going out now, like a failing —power. . . . So I stay here, I reckon, and live off la patrona for the rest of my life. Well, she's old enough to predecease me. She could check out of here first, and I imagine that after a couple of years of having to satisfy her I might be prepared for the shock of her passing on. . . . Cruelty . . . pity. What is it? . . . Don't know, all I know is. . . .

HANNAH (*from below the verandah*): You're talking to yourself.

SHANNON: No. To you. I knew you could hear me out there, but not being able to see you I could say it easier, you know . . . ?

NONNO:

A chronicle no longer gold,

A bargaining with mist and mould. . . .

HANNAH (*coming back onto the verandah*): I took a closer look at the iguana down there.

SHANNON: You did? How did you like it? Charming? Attractive?

HANNAH: No, it's not an attractive creature. Nevertheless I think it should be cut loose.

SHANNON: Iguanas have been known to bite their tails off when they're tied up by their tails.

HANNAH: This one is tied by its throat. It can't bite its own head off to escape from the end of the rope, Mr. Shannon. Can you look at me and tell me truthfully that you don't know it's able to feel pain and panic?

SHANNON: You mean it's one of God's creatures?

HANNAH: If you want to put it that way, yes, it is. Mr. Shannon, will you please cut it loose, set it free? Because if you don't, I will.

SHANNON: Can you look at *me* and tell *me* truthfully that this reptilian creature, tied up down there, doesn't mostly disturb you because of its parallel situation to your Grampa's dying-out effort to finish one last poem, Miss Jelkes?

HANNAH: Yes, I. . . .

SHANNON: Never mind completing that sentence. We'll play God tonight like kids play house with old broken crates and boxes. All right? Now Shannon is going to go down there with his machete and cut the damn lizard loose so it can run back to its bushes because God won't do it and we are going to play God here.

HANNAH: I knew you'd do that. And I thank you.

(*Shannon goes down the two steps from the verandah with the machete. He crouches beside the cactus that hides the iguana and cuts the rope with a quick, hard stroke of the machete. He turns to look after its flight, as the low, excited mumble in cubicle 3 grows louder. Then Nonno's voice turns to a sudden shout.*)

NONNO: *Hannah! Hannah!* (*She rushes to him, as he wheels himself out of his cubicle onto the verandah.*)

HANNAH: Grandfather! What is it?

NONNO: I! believe! it! is! *finished!* Quick, before I forget it— pencil, paper! Quick! please! Ready?

HANNAH: Yes. All ready, grandfather.

NONNO (*in a loud, exalted voice*):

> How calmly does the orange branch
> Observe the sky begin to blanch
> Without a cry, without a prayer,
> With no betrayal of despair.
>
> Sometime while night obscures the tree
> The zenith of its life will be
> Gone past forever, and from thence
> A second history will commence.
>
> A chronicle no longer gold,
> A bargaining with mist and mould,
> And finally the broken stem
> The plummeting to earth; and then

An intercourse not well designed
For beings of a golden kind
Whose native green must arch above
The earth's obscene, corrupting love.

And still the ripe fruit and the branch
Observe the sky begin to blanch
Without a cry, without a prayer,
With no betrayal of despair.

O Courage, could you not as well
Select a second place to dwell,
Not only in that golden tree
But in the frightened heart of me?

Have you got it?

HANNAH: Yes!

NONNO: All of it?

HANNAH: Every word of it.

NONNO: It is *finished*?

HANNAH: Yes.

NONNO: Oh! God! Finally finished?

HANNAH: Yes, finally finished. (*She is crying. The singing voices flow up from the beach.*)

NONNO: After waiting so long!

HANNAH: Yes, we waited so long.

NONNO: And it's good! It is *good*?

HANNAH: It's—it's. . . .

NONNO: What?

HANNAH: Beautiful, grandfather! (*She springs up, a fist to her mouth.*) Oh, grandfather, I am so happy for you. Thank you for writing such a lovely poem! It was worth the long wait. Can you sleep now, grandfather?

NONNO: You'll have it typewritten tomorrow?

HANNAH: Yes, I'll have it typed up and send it off to *Harper's.*

NONNO: Hah? I didn't hear that, Hannah.

HANNAH (*shouting*): I'll have it typed up tomorrow, and mail it to *Harper's* tomorrow! They've been waiting for it a long time, too! You know!

NONNO: Yes, I'd like to pray now.

HANNAH: Good night. Sleep now, Grandfather. You've finished your loveliest poem.

NONNO (*faintly, drifting off*): Yes, thanks and praise . . .

(*Maxine comes around the front of the verandah, followed by Pedro playing a harmonica softly. She is prepared for a night swim, a vividly striped towel thrown over her shoulders. It is apparent that the night's progress has mellowed her spirit: her face wears a faint smile which is suggestive of those cool, impersonal, all-comprehending smiles on the carved heads of Egyptian or Oriental dieties. Bearing a rum-coco, she approaches the hammock, discovers it empty, the ropes on the floor, and calls softly to Pedro.*)

MAXINE: Shannon ha escapado! (*Pedro goes on playing dreamily. She throws back her head and shouts.*) SHANNON! (*The call is echoed by the hill beyond. Pedro advances a few steps and points under the verandah.*)

PEDRO: Miré. Allé hasta Shannon.

(*Shannon comes into view from below the verandah, the severed rope and machete dangling from his hands.*)

MAXINE: What are you doing down there, Shannon?

SHANNON: I cut loose one of God's creatures at the end of the rope.

(*Hannah, who has stood motionless with closed eyes behind the wicker chair, goes quietly toward the cubicles and out of the moon's glare.*)

MAXINE (*tolerantly*): What'd you do that for, Shannon.

SHANNON: So that one of God's creatures could scramble home safe and free. . . . A little act of grace, Maxine.

MAXINE (*smiling a bit more definitely*): C'mon up here, Shannon. I want to talk to you.

SHANNON (*starting to climb onto the verandah, as Maxine rattles the ice in the coconut shell*): What d'ya want to talk about, Widow Faulk?

MAXINE: Let's go down and swim in that liquid moonlight.

SHANNON: Where did you pick up that poetic expression?

(*Maxine glances back at Pedro and dismisses him with, "Vamos." He leaves with a shrug, the harmonica fading out.*)

MAXINE: Shannon, I want you to stay with me.

SHANNON (*taking the rum-coco from her*): You want a drinking companion?

MAXINE: No, I just want you to stay here, because I'm alone here now and I need somebody to help me manage the place.

(*Hannah strikes a match for a cigarette.*)

SHANNON (*looking toward her*): I want to remember that face. I won't see it again.

MAXINE: Let's go down to the beach.

SHANNON: I can make it down the hill, but not back up.

MAXINE: I'll get you back up the hill. (*They have started off now, toward the path down through the rain forest.*) I've got five more years, maybe ten, to make this place attractive to the male clientele, the middle-aged ones at least. And you can take care of the women that are with them. That's what you can do, you know that, Shannon.

(*He chuckles happily. They are now on the path, Maxine half leading half supporting him. Their voices fade as Hannah goes into Nonno's cubicle and comes back with a shawl, her cigarette left inside. She pauses between the door and the wicker chair and speaks to herself and the sky.*)

HANNAH: Oh, God, can't we stop now? Finally? Please let us. It's so quiet here, now.

(*She starts to put the shawl about Nonno, but at the same moment his head drops to the side. With a soft intake of breath, she extends a hand before his mouth to see if he is still breathing. He isn't. In a panicky moment, she looks right and left for someone to call to. There's no one. Then she bends to press her head to the crown of Nonno's and the curtain starts to descend.*)

The End

NAZI MARCHING SONG

Heute wollen wir ein Liedlein singen,
Trinken wollen wir den kuehlen Wein;
Und die Glaeser sollen dazu klingen,
Denn es muss, es muss geschieden sein.

Gib' mir deine Hand,
Deine weisse Hand,
Leb'wohl, mein Schatz, leb'wohl, mein Schatz
Lebe wohl, lebe wohl,
Denn wir fahren. Boom! Boom!
Denn wir fahren. Boom! Boom!
Denn wir fahren gegen Engelland. Boom! Boom!

Let's sing a little song today,
And drink some cool wine;
The glasses should be ringing
Since we must, we must part.

Give me your hand,
Your white hand,
Farewell, my love, farewell,
Farewell, farewell,
Since we're going—
Since we're going—
Since we're going against England.

THE ECCENTRICITIES
OF A NIGHTINGALE

CHARACTERS

ALMA WINEMILLER
THE REVEREND WINEMILLER, her father
MRS. WINEMILLER, her mother
JOHN BUCHANAN, JR.
MRS. BUCHANAN, his mother
ROGER DOREMUS
VERNON
MRS. BASSETT
ROSEMARY
A TRAVELING SALESMAN

SCENES

The entire action of the play takes place in Glorious Hill, Mississippi. The time is shortly before the First World War.

AUTHOR'S NOTE

Aside from the characters having the same names and the locale remaining the same, I think *The Eccentricities of a Nightingale* is a substantially different play from *Summer and Smoke*, and I prefer it. It is less conventional and melodramatic. I wrote it in Rome one summer and brought it with me to London the fall that *Summer and Smoke* was about to be produced there. But I arrived with it too late. The original version of the play was already in rehearsal.

This radically different version of the play has never been produced on Broadway. I hope that its publication in this volume may lead to its production and that the production may confirm my feeling that it is a better work than the play from which it derived.

ACT ONE

The Feeling of a Singer

SCENE ONE

It is the evening of July 4th of a year shortly before the First World War.

The exterior set is part of a public square in the small Southern town of Glorious Hill, Mississippi. Two stone steps ascend, at the rear, to a public fountain which is in the form of a stone angel (Eternity), in a gracefully crouching position with wings lifted and hands held together in front to form a cup from which water flows. Near the fountain is a small bench. Framing the set above are mossy branches. Behind is a sky with stars beginning to appear.

Before and for a few minutes after the curtain rises, a somewhat-better-than-typical church soprano is heard singing a semi-secular song such as "O That We Two Were Maying."

The Reverend and Mrs. Winemiller, an Episcopal clergyman and his wife, in their early sixties, are on the bench. Sitting on the steps to the fountain is John Buchanan.

The song ends, there is a burst of applause, and while it continues, Miss Alma Winemiller enters from the right. At the same moment a rocket explodes in the sky, casting a momentary white radiance beneath it.

ALMA (*excitedly calling to her parents*): The first sky-rocket! Oh, look at it burst into a million stars!

(*There is a long-drawn "Ahhh" from unseen spectators. After the brief glare the stage seems very dark. Barely visible figures, laughing, chattering, sweep about the fountain like a sudden passage of birds. Alma cries out as if frightened.*)

ALMA: Oh, I'm blinded, I can't see a *thing*! Father, Father, where *are* you?

(*A child imitates her mockingly.*)

REV. WINEMILLER: Here we are, Alma, we're down here on the bench.

ALMA: Oh . . . (*She rushes breathlessly down to them.*)

433

(*The stage lightens again. Alma is dressed in pale yellow and carries a parasol to match.*)

ALMA: The words flew out of my mind. I sang the same verse twice. Was it noticeable? Please open my bag for me, Father. My fingers are frozen stiff. I want my handkerchief. My face and my throat are drenched with perspiration. Was that— Oh, I'm talking too loudly! (*She lowers her voice to a shrill whisper.*) Is that John Buchanan up there by the fountain? I rushed right by him but I think he spoke! Don't look now, he'll know we're talking about him. But I think it is!

REV. WINEMILLER: Suppose it is! What of it? Sit down, Alma.

ALMA: Oh, the Gulf wind is blowing, what a relief! . . . Yes . . . yes, that *is* John Buchanan. . . . (*Her voice quivers over the name. Her father hands her the handkerchief.*) Oh, thank you, Father. Yessssss—that's John Buchanan, he's been home for a week but hasn't called or dropped over . . . I wonder *why*! Don't you think it's *peculiar*?

REV. WINEMILLER: Why "peculiar"?

(*A stout dowager in black lace and pearls approaches John Buchanan and takes his arm.*)

ALMA: His mother stands guard over him like an old dragon! Look at her, keeping time to the music with her lorgnette, one arm hooked through John's, terrified that someone will snatch him from her!

REV. WINEMILLER: Alma, sit still for a minute. Just sit here quietly and listen to the music until you get back a little composure.

ALMA (*in a shrill rapid whisper, staring straight out*): She'll pretend not to see me. I remember the last time John came home from college, no, the time before last, two, two summers ago, while he was still at Johns Hopkins, I was sitting on the front porch one evening. I nodded to him as he went by the house and he lifted his hat and started to come up to me to say hello. Do you know what she did? She immediately stuck her head out of their window and shouted to him, literally shouted to him as if the house had caught fire, "John! John! Come here right this minute! Your father wants you *immediately* in his office!"

REV. WINEMILLER: Do you want them to overhear you?

ALMA: Oh, they're not *there* any more, she's dragged him out of danger!

REV. WINEMILLER: Mrs. Buchanan is always friendly and I don't think it's reasonable of you to blame her for his failure to pay you as much attention as you would like. Now where is your mother gone?

MRS. WINEMILLER (*wistfully, at a distance*): *Where is the ice cream man?*

ALMA: Mother, there *isn't* any ice cream man!

REV. WINEMILLER: I'll have to take her right home. She's on her bad behavior.

ALMA: Has she been talking about the Musée Mécanique?

REV. WINEMILLER: Babbling about it to everybody we meet!

ALMA: Let her go home. She can get home by herself. It's good for her. Oh, I see where she's headed, she's going across the Square to the White Star Pharmacy to treat herself to an ice cream sundae.

REV. WINEMILLER: What a terrible cross to have to bear!

ALMA: The only thing to do with a cross is *bear* it, Father.

REV. WINEMILLER: The failure of a vocation is a terrible thing, and it's all the more terrible when you're not responsible for the failure yourself, when it's the result of a vicious impulse to destroy in some other person.

ALMA: Mother isn't responsible for her condition. You know that.

REV. WINEMILLER: Your mother has *chosen* to be the way she is. She isn't out of her mind. It's all deliberate. One week after our marriage a look came into her eyes, a certain look, a look I can't describe to you, a sort of a cold and secretly spiteful look as if I, who loved her, who was *devoted* to her, had done her some, some—*injury!*—that couldn't be—*mentioned.* . . .

ALMA: I think there are women who feel that way about marriage.

REV. WINEMILLER: They ought not to marry.

ALMA: I know, but they do, they *do*! They are the *ones* that marry! The ones that could bring to marriage the sort of almost—*transcendental! tenderness* that it calls for—what do they do? Teach school! Teach singing! Make a life out of little accomplishments. Father . . . *Look! Mrs. Buchanan is making another entrance!*

(*The dowager approaches her son again.*)

ALMA: She looks so sweet and soft, but under the black lace and pearls is something harder and colder than the stuff that stone angel is made of! And something runs in her veins that's warm and sympathetic as—mineral water! She's come to take her son home. He's too exposed in this place. He might meet a girl without money! A girl who was able to give him nothing but love!

REV. WINEMILLER: Alma, you're talking wildly. I don't like this kind of talk!

ALMA: Oh, yes, oh, yes. She told Miss Preston, who works at the public library, that she was determined that John should make the right kind of marriage for a young doctor to make, a girl with beauty and wealth and social position somewhere in the East!—the Orient where the sun rises! *Ha ha ha!*

(*Mrs. Buchanan calls "John? John? John?" with idiotic persistence, like a bird.*)

REV. WINEMILLER: Alma, I think you had better come home with me, you're not yourself. You're talking almost as wildly as your mother. . . .

ALMA: I'm sorry, Father. Singing in public always leaves me feeling overexcited. You go, you go on home, I'll be all right in a moment or two. I have to wait for Roger. . . .

REV. WINEMILLER: I'm not sure I like you being seen so much and associated in people's minds with that, that— well—that rather *peculiar* young man. . . .

ALMA: You make me think of that story about the Quakers. One Quaker met another Quaker and he said, "Everybody is mad in this world but thee and me, and thou art a little peculiar!" *Ha ha ha!*

REV. WINEMILLER: Why do you laugh like that?

ALMA: Like what, Father?

REV. WINEMILLER: You throw your head back so far it's a wonder you don't break your neck!—Ah, me . . . Hmmm . . . (*He strolls away with a slight parting nod.*)

(*A sky-rocket goes off. There is a long "Ahhh!" from the crowd.*)

(*In dumb play, John's mother tries to lead him from the square, but he protests. Somebody calls her. She reluctantly goes, passing in front of Miss Alma.*)

ALMA (*overbrightly*): Good evening, Mrs. Buchanan.

MRS. BUCHANAN: Why, Miss Alma! I want to congratulate you. I heard you sing and I've never heard anyone sing with quite so much . . . *feeling!* No wonder they call you "the Nightingale of the Delta."

ALMA: It's sweet of you to fib so, I sang so badly.

MRS. BUCHANAN: You're just being modest! (*She simpers, as she goes off.*)

(*Alma had risen from the bench. She now sits down again and closes her eyes, unfolding a fan suspended about her throat.*)

(*John glances down at her, then notices an unexploded fire-cracker. He picks it up, lights it, and tosses it under the bench. It goes off and Alma springs up with a sharp outcry. He laughs and descends the steps and comes over to the bench.*)

JOHN: Hello, Miss Alma.

ALMA: Johnny Buchanan, did you throw that firecracker?

JOHN: Ha ha!

ALMA: It scared me out of my wits! Why, I'm still breathless.

JOHN: Ha ha!

ALMA: Ha ha ha! I think I needed a little shock like that to get me over the shock of my fiasco—on the bandstand!

JOHN: I heard you sing. I liked it.

ALMA: Ha ha ha ha ha! You liked both verses of it? I sang *one twice!* Ha ha ha . . .

JOHN: It was good enough to sing three or four times more.

ALMA: *Chivalry!* Chivalry still survives in the Southern states!

JOHN: Mind if I sit down with you?

ALMA: Oh, please, please *do!* There's room enough for us both. Neither of us is terribly large—in *diameter!* Ha ha ha!

(*He sits down. There is an awkward pause.*)

JOHN: You sang with so much feeling, Miss Alma.

ALMA: The feeling was panic!

JOHN: It sounded O.K. to me.

ALMA: Oh, I can't hear myself sing, I just feel my throat and tongue working and my heart beating fast!—a *hammer* . . .

JOHN: Do you have palpitations when you sing?

ALMA: Sometimes I'm surprised that I don't just drop dead!

JOHN: Then maybe you shouldn't.

ALMA: Oh, afterwards I feel I've done something, and that's a different feeling from what one feels—most times. . . .

JOHN: You seem to be still shaking?

ALMA: That firecracker was a shock to my whole nervous system! Ha ha ha!

JOHN: I'm sorry. I had no idea that you were so nervous.

ALMA: Nobody has a right to be so nervous! You're—you're home for the holidays, are you? I mean home for the rest of the summer?

JOHN: I've finished medical school. But I'm connected with a hospital now, doing laboratory work.

ALMA: Oh, in *what*, how *thrilling*! How thrilling that sounds, in *what*?—Uh?

JOHN: Bacteriology.

ALMA: *That's*—(*She gasps.*)—that's something to do with, with, with a—*microscope*?—Uh?

JOHN: Sometimes you have to look through a microscope.

ALMA: I looked through a telescope once, at Oxford, Mississippi, at the state university when Father delivered the baccalaureate address there one spring. But I've never, never looked through a *microscope*! Tell me, what do you see, I mean, what is it like, through a microscope, if that question makes any sense?—Uh?

JOHN (*slowly*): Well—you see pretty much the same thing that you see through a telescope.

ALMA: Ohhhh?

JOHN: A—a cosmos, a—microcosmos!—part anarchy and—part order. . . .

(*Music is heard again.*)

ALMA: Part anarchy and part order! Oh, the *poetry* of science, the *incredible* poetry of it! Ha ha ha!

JOHN (*vaguely*): Yes . . .

ALMA: Part anarchy and part order—the footprints of God!—Uh?

JOHN: His footprints, maybe, yes . . . but not—God!

ALMA: Isn't it strange? He never really, *really*—exposes Himself! Here and there is a footprint, but even the footprints are not very easy to follow! No, you can't follow. In fact you don't even know which way they're pointing. . . . Ha ha ha!

JOHN: How did we get started on that subject?

ALMA: Heaven knows, but we did!—So you're home for a while! I bet your mother's delighted, she's so crazy about you, constantly singing your praises, tells me you graduated magna cum laude from Johns Hopkins last summer! What are your—future plans?

JOHN: I'm leaving tomorrow.

ALMA: Oh, tomorrow? So soon! As soon as all that?!

JOHN: Just got a wire from an old teacher of mine who's fighting bugs in Cuba.

ALMA: Fighting bugs! In Cuba?

JOHN: Yes. Bugs in Cuba. *Fever* bugs.

ALMA: Ohhhh, fever!—Ha ha ha . . .

JOHN: There's a little epidemic down there with some unusual—aspects, he says. And I've always wanted to visit a Latin country. (*He spreads his knees.*)

ALMA: Oh, those Latins. All they do is dream in the sun, dream, dream in the sun and indulge their senses!

JOHN (*smiling suddenly*): Well, I've heard that cantinas are better than saloons, and they tell me that señoritas are— caviar among females!

ALMA: Be careful you don't get caught. They say that the tropics are a perfect quagmire. People go there and never are *heard* of again!

JOHN: Well, it couldn't be hotter than here, that's one sure thing.

ALMA: Oh, my, isn't it dreadful? Summer isn't the pleasantest time of year to renew your acquaintance with Glorious Hill, Mississippi.—The Gulf wind has failed us this year. It usually cools the nights off, but it has failed us this year.

JOHN: Driving along the river cools you off.

ALMA: How heavenly that sounds, driving along the river to cool off!

JOHN: Does it sound good to you?

ALMA: Almost too good to believe!

JOHN: Why don't we take a drive.

ALMA: What a *divine suggestion*! (*She springs up. But Mrs. Buchanan enters quickly.*)

MRS. BUCHANAN: *John! John, darling!*

JOHN: What is it, Mother?

MRS. BUCHANAN: Your father and I have been searching the whole Square for you!—Excuse us, Miss Alma!

ALMA: Certainly, Mrs. Buchanan. (*She closes her eyes for a moment with a look of infinite desolation.*)

MRS. BUCHANAN (*continuing as she grabs hold of John's arm*): Your father's received a call from Mrs. Arbuckle, but I insist that he must go right to bed; he's about to collapse from exhaustion, and there's absolutely no reason why you can't go and give that woman—please excuse us, Miss Alma!—(*She is dragging him away.*)—the morphine injection, that's all that can be done. . . .

JOHN (*calling back*): Goodbye, Miss Alma.

ALMA: Goodbye! Goodbye! (*She sinks back down on the bench.*)

(*A sky-rocket goes up. The crowd cries "Ahhh!"*)

(*Roger Doremus, a young man with the little excitements of a sparrow, rushes on with his French horn in a case.*)

ROGER: How did it go, my solo on the French horn?

ALMA: I'm!—please get me some water, water, from the fountain, I—I—

ROGER: You're not feeling well?

ALMA: I have to take one of my tablets but my mouth is so dry that I can't swallow the tablet. (*She leans back, touching her throat as Roger crosses anxiously to the fountain.*)

(*The scene dims out.*)

SCENE TWO

The Rectory interior on Christmas Eve of the following winter.
During the interval the soprano sings a traditional Christmas
carol, one not too familiar.

Like all the sets, the Rectory interior is barely suggested, by
window and door frames and a few essential properties.

The Reverend and Mrs. Winemiller are seated on either side
of a small round clawfoot table that supports a cut-glass bowl of
eggnog with cups. Rev. Winemiller faces the fireplace, which is in
the fourth wall and is indicated by a flickering red glow. (Every
interior in the play has a fireplace indicated in this way in the
same position.) Evidently the fire gives little warmth, for the
minister has a lady's lavender woolen shawl wrapped about his
hunched shoulders.

Mrs. Winemiller is never quite silent, although her interior
monologue is never loud enough to be intelligible. She sounds like
a small running brook or a swarm of bees and her face changes
expression as her interior world falls under light and shadow.

Miss Alma is a little outside the lighted area as the scene be-
gins and her responses to Rev. Winemiller's singsong elegiac ru-
minations come out of the shadow where the window frame is
located. In this frame is a small candle.

REV. WINEMILLER (*as if continuing*): Actually we have about
the same number of communicants we've had for the past
ten years, but church attendance has dropped off about,
hmmm, twenty per cent.

ALMA: Just remember what old Doctor Hoctor announced to
his congregation one year, he said to his congregation, "We
haven't had any additions to the congregation this year but
we've had a number of valuable subtractions."

REV. WINEMILLER: In the old days before they had the church
pension fund ministers stayed in the pulpit as long as they
were able to crawl up the chancel.

ALMA: Yes, poor old Doctor Hoctor, he hung on forever!
Much longer than his congregation. They say it finally
dwindled down to just a pair of old ladies, one widow and
one spinster who hated each other so fiercely that one
would sit in the front pew and the other so far in the rear
that old Doctor Hoctor, who had lost his sight but still had

a little hearing, was never quite certain whether she was there or not except when she had the hiccoughs. Ha ha!

REV. WINEMILLER: A man must know when he's outlived his term of usefulness and let go. I'm going to retire next year. . . .

ALMA: But, Father, you won't come into the pension for five more years! What will we live on, what I make teaching singing?

REV. WINEMILLER: The Bishop has hinted to me that if I don't feel able to continue, it might be arranged for me to come into my pension a little bit sooner than I'm due to get it.

ALMA: Ah? (*She suddenly turns out a lamp and rushes back to the window.*) I have never seen anything so ridiculous! Mrs. Buchanan has put on a Santie Claus outfit and is going out their front walk with a sack of presents. I wonder if—John's with her. Yes!—Perhaps they'll . . . Oh, we must get Mother upstairs! They'll come here first, I should think, since we're next door. Yes, they are, they're going to come here first! Mother! Mother! Go upstairs and I'll bring you a piece of fruitcake! Mother? A piece of—! Oh . . . No . . . They're *not* going to come here first. They're crossing the street. (*In a tone of desolation*) They've crossed the street, yes, they've—crossed—the street. . . . You don't suppose they'll—*overlook* us this year?

REV. WINEMILLER: You're constantly at that window spying on the Buchanans.

ALMA: *Spy*ing on the Buchanans? What a notion!

REV. WINEMILLER: You come in the parlor, turn out the lamp, gravitate to that window as if you had to stand by that window to breathe.

ALMA: Why, Father, I've been looking at the snow. I just happened to notice Mrs. Buchanan in her Santie Claus outfit coming out of the . . .

REV. WINEMILLER: The house is surrounded by snow on all four sides and all four sides of the house have windows in them through which you could look at the snow if it is only the snow that holds such a fascination over you.

ALMA: It does, it *does* fascinate me, why, it's the first snow that's fallen on Glorious Hill in more than a hundred years, and when it started falling, they closed all the stores on Front Street and every office in town, even the bank. And all came out, just like overgrown boys, and had snow fights on the street!—Roger Doremus told me . . . No. I don't believe they're going to come here at all. They've gone in the other direction down the block. . . . (*She pours a cup of eggnog, sips it with one hand extended toward the glow of the fireplace.*) The snow reminds me of an old proverb. "Before you love, you must learn how to walk over snow—and leave no footprint. . . ."

(*A carol is heard at some distance.*)

The Methodist carolers have already gone out. I must get . . .

REV. WINEMILLER: Alma. Sit down for a moment. There's something I want to talk to you about.

ALMA (*apprehensively*): I have to get ready to go out with the carolers, Father.

REV. WINEMILLER: They're not going out until half-past eight.

ALMA: That's almost now.

REV. WINEMILLER: Then let them start without you. This is more important.

ALMA: That means it's something unpleasant?

REV. WINEMILLER: Yes, extremely unpleasant and that's why it's important. Alma, I've had one heavy cross to bear. (*He nods toward Mrs. Winemiller.*) One almost insufferable cross. A minister isn't complete without a family, he needs his wife and his family to make a—a social bond—with the parish!

ALMA: Father, I do all I can. More than I have the strength for. I have my vocal pupils. I sing at weddings, I sing at funerals, I swear there's nothing I don't sing at except the conception of infants!

REV. WINEMILLER: Alma, I won't endure that kind—!

ALMA: Excuse me, Father, but you know it's true. And I serve on the Altar Guild and I teach the primary class at Sunday school. I made all their little costumes for the Christmas pageant, their angel wings and dresses, and you know what thanks I got for that! Mrs. Peacock cried out that the costumes were inflammable! Inflammable, she screamed! Exactly as if she thought it was my secret hope, my intention, to burn the children up at the Christmas pageant! No, she said, those costumes are inflammable, if they wear those costumes they can't march in with candles! (*She gasps.*)—And so the candles weren't lighted. They marched in holding little stumps of wax!—holding little dirty stumps of wax! The absurdity of it, as if a wind had blown all the candles out—the whole effect I'd worked so hard to create was destroyed by that woman, and I had to bite my tongue because I couldn't answer, I knew that *you* wouldn't want me to answer back. Oh, I've had to bite my tongue so much it's a wonder I have one left!

REV. WINEMILLER: Please, more calmly, Alma. You're going to swallow your tongue from overexcitement some day, not bite it off from holding back indignation! I asked you to please sit down. Alma— Because of the circumstances, I mean your mother's condition, pitiable, and the never, never outlived notoriety of your Aunt Albertine and the Musée Mécanique . . .

ALMA: Why can't we forget something that happened fifteen years ago?

REV. WINEMILLER: Because other people remember!

ALMA: *I'm* not going to elope with a Mr. Otto Schwarzkopf!

REV. WINEMILLER: We must discuss this quietly.

ALMA: Discuss what quietly? *What!*

REV. WINEMILLER: Alma, someone, Alma—someone, Alma, who is—deeply devoted to you—who has your interests—very much at heart—almost as fond of you as her own daughter!

ALMA: Oh, this is Mrs. Peacock—my bête noire!

REV. WINEMILLER: She was deeply, deeply distressed over something that happened lately. It seems that she overheard someone giving an imitation of you at a young people's party. . . .

ALMA: An imitation? An imitation, Father? Of what? Of what? Of *me!*

REV. WINEMILLER: Yes, of you.

ALMA (*gasping*): What was it they imitated? What did they imitate about me, Father?

REV. WINEMILLER: The point is, Alma—

ALMA: No, please tell me, I want to, I *have* to be told, I must—know . . .

REV. WINEMILLER: What they imitated was your singing, I think, at a wedding.

ALMA: My voice? They imitated my voice?

REV. WINEMILLER: Not your voice but your gestures and facial expressions . . .

ALMA: Ohhh . . . This leaves me quite speechless!

REV. WINEMILLER: You're inclined to—dramatize your songs a—bit too much! You, you get carried away by the, the emotion of it! That's why you choke sometimes and get hoarse when you're singing and Mrs. Peacock says that sometimes you weep!

ALMA: That's not true. It's true that I feel the emotion of a song. Even an ordinary little song like "The Voice That Breathed O'er Eden" or "O Promise Me" or "Because"— why, even commonplace little songs like "I Love You Truly," they have a sincere emotion and a singer must feel it, and when you feel it, you *show* it! A singer's face and hands are part of a singer's *equipment*! Why, even a singer's heart is part of her equipment! That's what they taught me at the Conservatory!

REV. WINEMILLER: I'm sometimes sorry you went to the Conservatory.

ALMA (*in a stricken voice*): All right! I'll give up singing . . . *everything*!

REV. WINEMILLER: The thing for you to give up is your affectations, Alma, your little put-on mannerisms that make you seem—well—slightly *peculiar* to people! It isn't just your singing I'm talking about. In ordinary conversations you get carried away by your emotions or something, I don't know what, and neither does anyone else. You, you, you— *gild the lily*!—You—express yourself in—fantastic highflown —phrases! Your hands fly about you like a pair of wild birds! You, you get out of breath, you—stammer, you— laugh hysterically and clutch at your throat! Now please remember. I wouldn't mention these things if I didn't know that they were just mannerisms, things that you could control, that you can correct! Otherwise I wouldn't mention them to you. Because I can see that you are upset, but you can correct them. All you have to do is *concentrate*. When you're talking, just watch yourself, keep an eye on your hands, and when you're singing, put them in *one* position and *keep* them there. Like *this*!

ALMA: Make a steeple?—No, I'd rather not sing. . . .

REV. WINEMILLER: You're taking altogether the wrong attitude about this.

ALMA: I'll, I'll just give up my—social efforts, Father—all of them!

REV. WINEMILLER: The thing for you to give up is this little band of eccentrics, this collection of misfits that you've gathered about you which you call your club, the ones you say will be meeting *here* next Monday!

ALMA: What a cruel thing to say about a group of sweet and serious people that get together because of—interests in common—cultural interests—who want to create something—vital—in this town!

REV. WINEMILLER: These young people are not the sort of young people that it's an advantage to be identified with! And one thing more—

ALMA: What else, Father?

REV. WINEMILLER: Is it true that you go to the Square with a sack of crumbs?

ALMA: What, what, what?

REV. WINEMILLER: Is it true that you go every day to the Square with a sack of crumbs which you throw to the birds?

ALMA: I scatter breadcrumbs in the Square for the starving birds. *That's* true!

REV. WINEMILLER: Have you thought how it might look to people?

ALMA: I thought it only concerned myself and the birds.

REV. WINEMILLER: Little things like that, an accumulation of them, Alma, little habits, little, little mannerisms, little—peculiarities of behavior—they are what get people known, eventually, as—*eccentrics!* And eccentric people are not happy, they are not happy people, Alma. Eccentrics are—what are you doing?

ALMA (*breathlessly*): I can't open the box, I can't open the box, I can't open the box!

REV. WINEMILLER: Your amytal tablets?

ALMA: I can't open the box!

REV. WINEMILLER: Give it to me.—Hysteria was the beginning of your mother's condition.

ALMA: *I can't breathe!* (*She rushes out.*)

REV. WINEMILLER: Alma! Don't leave the house till you get your mother upstairs! (*She has run out. He turns to his wife and shouts in her ear.*) Grace! This is Christmas Eve and we are going to have callers! You must go up to your bedroom and I will bring you up a piece of fruitcake!

MRS. WINEMILLER (*rousing slightly*): No, oh, no, not till you give me the letter, you've hidden it from me, Albertine's last letter! It's got the new address of the Musée Mécanique!

(*The "Valse Musette" fades in.*)

REV. WINEMILLER (*after a pause*): Grace, listen to me. Albertine has been dead for fifteen years. She and her paramour both died in a fire fifteen years ago, when Mr. Schwarzkopf set fire to the Musée Mécanique.

MRS. WINEMILLER: Oh, I remember the address, Seven Pearl Street!—I must keep that in my mind, that's the new address of the Musée Mécanique, it's Seven Pearl Street—or was it—Seventeen Pearl Street?

(*The doorbell rings.*)

REV. WINEMILLER: *There, there now, visitors!* And look at yourself, how you look! Go upstairs *quickly, quickly!* (*He claps his hands violently together.*)

MRS. WINEMILLER: Yes . . .

(*She makes a confused turn. He leads her out of the lighted area.*)

(*The scene dims out.*)

SCENE THREE

A few minutes later. John and his mother and the Reverend Winemiller are seated in the Rectory parlor. Mrs. Buchanan is ludicrously attired as a female Santa Claus with the incongruous addition of a lorgnon on a silver chain.

She is spotted first before the light comes up on the others.

MRS. BUCHANAN: The children say to me, You're not Santie
Claus, Santie Claus has whiskers, and I say, No, I'm Santie
Claus's *wife*! They're so surprised!

REV. WINEMILLER: I know they must be delighted.

MRS. BUCHANAN: Tickled to death! Having a wife gives him
such a respectability! And how has Grace been lately?

REV. WINEMILLER: A—uh—little disturbed.

MRS. BUCHANAN: All the excitement in the air, don't you
think? Mrs. Santie Claus has something for her, but if she's
a little disturbed, we'll just put it under the tree. Is that
Miss Alma? Oh, it *is*. How *lovely*!

(*Alma's high-pitched laughter is heard. John rises from a hassock before the fireplace.*)

ALMA: *Joyeux Noel!* Ha ha!

MRS. BUCHANAN: How pretty you look, Miss Alma! I was
afraid we'd miss you.

ALMA: I sang one carol and my throat felt scratchy. The com-
bined church choirs are doing Handel's Messiah. (*She
gasps.*) Such dreadful demands on the voice! That's
Thursday. No, no, Friday, Friday evening, in the high
school—goodness, I *am* getting hoarse!—auditorium!

MRS. BUCHANAN: Let John give you a gargle.

ALMA: Nasty gargles. . . . I hate them! The voice is such a
delicate instrument. When was the last time I saw you?
Last—last . . . ?

JOHN: Fourth of July. The band concert in the Square.

ALMA: Oh!—oh, dear, the recollection of that . . . !

JOHN: I heard you sing.

ALMA: Goodness, yes, I still shudder. The same verse twice!

JOHN: Ha ha! And I threw a firecracker at you!

ALMA: Goodness, yes, you *did*! Ha ha! That was so naughty
of you! You always did as a boy, I mean as a little boy, you
always threw—firecrackers! Ha ha!—into the Rectory lawn!
No Fourth of July was complete without— (*She gasps.*)

JOHN: Ha ha! That's right. I had to keep up the tradition.

ALMA (*gasping*): That's right, that's right, you had to keep up
the tradition! Let me give you some—oh, where is it?—
eggnog!

JOHN: We've already been served.

ALMA: Have you? Why, yes, I'm *blind*! I have snow in my eye-lashes. It makes rainbows in the light! What an adventure, just imagine, the first snow that's fallen on Glorious Hill in—how many years? Almost a century. Before it began to snow it rained for two days. Suddenly the temperature fell. The rain froze on the trees, on the lawns, on the bushes and hedges, on the roofs, the steeples, the telephone wires. . . . (*She pauses to gasp for breath.*)

REV. WINEMILLER: Alma, sit down so John can sit down.

ALMA: Yes, forgive me!—Till the whole town was literally sheathed in ice!—And when the sun rose that morning . . . you can't imagine how *dazzling*! It made you suddenly *see* how dull things *usually* are—the trees, oh, the trees, like huge crystal chandeliers!—turned upside down!

MRS. BUCHANAN: It's just like fairyland.

ALMA: Exactly like fairyland.

JOHN: I wish I had five cents for every time someone has said that.

MRS. BUCHANAN: Little John has been north so long it's made him a cynic.

ALMA: Have you lost patience with our romantic clichés?

MRS. BUCHANAN: Little John, Little John, I can see that your shoes are still damp!—We call him Little John and his father we call *Big* John although Little John is almost twice as tall as Big John is!

ALMA: How tall is Little John?

MRS. BUCHANAN: As tall as Jack's beanstalk!

ALMA: I don't think it's fair for a boy to have such curls!

MRS. BUCHANAN: As a boy he was so indifferent to the ladies! But those days are all gone now. Every morning cards and letters this high, to the junior Doctor Buchanan in green pink and lavender ink with all the odors of springtime!

ALMA: What a success he's going to have as a doctor.

MRS. BUCHANAN: His waiting room will be large as a railroad station.

ALMA: At least that large and probably with an annex.

MRS. BUCHANAN: But his love is bugs! He's specializing in something I can't even pronounce.

ALMA: *Bacteriology!* He told me last Fourth of July.

MRS. BUCHANAN (*turning to Rev. Winemiller*): Graduated magna cum laude from Johns Hopkins with the highest marks in the history of the college. Already—think of it— seven fine offers from staffs of various hospitals in the East, and one in California!

ALMA (*gasping*): All the gifts of the gods were showered on him!

MRS. BUCHANAN (*to Rev. Winemiller*): I wanted to have five sons but I only had one. But if I had had fifteen I don't think it would have been reasonable to expect that one of the lot would have turned out *quite* so *fine*!

ALMA: Your mother is proud as a peacock.

MRS. BUCHANAN: Don't you think it's excusable in a mother?

ALMA: Not only excusable but . . . Your cup is empty, John, do let me—fill it!

MRS. BUCHANAN: Don't make him tipsy! John, your shoes *are* damp, I can tell by just looking at them! (*Declining eggnog*) Oh, no, no more for me, I have to climb down some more chimneys!—That sounds like Grace!

(*Mrs. Winemiller is heard descending the stairs, imitating Alma's shrill laugh.*)

REV. WINEMILLER (*anxiously*): Alma, I think your mother is—

ALMA (*gasping*): Oh, excuse me!—I'll see what Mother wants.

(*She rushes out. Mrs. Buchanan touches the minister's arm.*)

MRS. BUCHANAN: Oh, such a tragedy, such a terrible cross for you to bear! Little John, I think we had better go, now, the reindeers must be getting restless.

(*John sneezes. She throws her hands up in terror.*)

I knew it, I knew it, I *knew* it! You *have* caught cold!

JOHN: *Oh, for God's sake!*

MRS. BUCHANAN: *John!*

(*John sneezes again.*)

That settles it, you're going straight home to bed!

(*Mrs. Winemiller rushes into the parlor. Alma follows her.*)

ALMA: Father, Mother *insists* on remaining downstairs. She says that she wasn't ready to go to bed.

MRS. WINEMILLER (*excitedly*): I have found my letter with the address on it. It's Seven Pearl Street in New Orleans. That's where Albertine is with Mr. Schwarzkopf and the Musée Mécanique. Oh, such a lot of news in it!

REV. WINEMILLER: Yes, I am sure. But let's not discuss the news now.

MRS. WINEMILLER (*to Mrs. Buchanan*): Have *you* ever been to the Musée Mécanique?

MRS. BUCHANAN: Long ago, Grace, long ago I—had that pleasure. . . . (*She touches her lips nervously with her lorgnon.*)

MRS. WINEMILLER: Then you know what it is? It's a collection of mechanical marvels, invented and operated by my sister's—husband!—Mr. Otto Schwarzkopf! Mechanical marvels, all of them, but, then, you know, when everything's run by mechanics it takes a mechanical genius to keep them in good condition all of the time and sometimes poor Mr. Schwarzkopf is not in condition to keep them all—in—condition. . . .

MRS. BUCHANAN: Well, this is a mechanical age we live in. . . .

ALMA: Mother, Mrs. Buchanan has brought her son with her and we are so eager to hear about his work and his—studies at—Johns Hopkins!

JOHN: Oh, let's hear about the Museum, Miss Alma.

MRS. WINEMILLER: Yes! That's what I'm telling you about, the Museum!—of mechanical marvels. Do you know what they are? Well, let me tell you. There's the mechanical man that plays the flute. There's the mechanical drummer—oh, such a sweet little boy all made out of tin that shines like a brand new dollar! Boom, boom, boom, beats the drum. Toot, toot, toot, goes the flute. And the mechanical soldier waves his flag, waves it, waves it, and waves it! Ha ha ha!—And oh! *Oh!*—the loveliest thing of all—the mechanical bird-girl! Yes, the mechanical bird-girl is almost the biggest mechanical triumph since the Eiffel Tower, according to people who know. She's made of sterling silver! Every three minutes, right on the dot, a little mechanical bird pops out of her mouth and sings three beautiful notes, as clear as—a bell!

REV. WINEMILLER: Grace, Mrs. Buchanan remembers all of that.

MRS. WINEMILLER: The young man *doesn't*! I don't believe he's seen the Musée Mécanique.

JOHN: No, I've never. It sounds very exciting!

MRS. WINEMILLER: Well, lately, I personally think they have made a mistake. I think it was a mistake to buy the *big snake*!

JOHN: A mechanical snake?

MRS. WINEMILLER: Oh no, a real one, a live one, a boa constrictor. Some meddlesome maddie told them "Big snakes pay good."—So Mr. Schwarzkopf, who is not a practical man, a genius without any business sense whatsoever—mortgaged the whole Museum to pay for this great big snake!— So far, so good!—But! The snake was used to living in a warm climate. It was winter. New Orleans *can* be cold!— The snake seemed chilly, it became *very stupid*, and so they gave it a *blanket*!—Well!—Now in this letter I've just received today—Albertine tells me a *terrible* thing has happened!

JOHN: What did the big snake do?

MRS. WINEMILLER: Nothing!—JUST *swallowed* his *blanket*!

JOHN: I thought you were going to say it swallowed Mr. Schwarzkopf.

MRS. BUCHANAN: Oh, now, Little John, *hush*, you bad boy, you! (*She touches her lips with the lorgnon.*)

MRS. WINEMILLER: Swallowed its blanket!

JOHN: Did the blanket disagree with it?

MRS. WINEMILLER: Disagree with it? I should say it did! What can a stomach, even the stomach of a boa constrictor, do with a heavy blanket?

JOHN: What did they do about the—situation?

MRS. WINEMILLER: Everything they could think of—which wasn't *much* . . . Veterinarians, experts from the—zoo!— Nobody could suggest anything to . . . Finally they sent a telegram to the man who had sold them the snake. "The big snake has swallowed his blanket! What shall we do?"— He'd told them big snakes pay good, but *dead* snakes— what do they pay?—They pay what the little boy shot at! —Well!—Do you know what the man that sold the snake to them wired back?—"All you can do is get on your knees and pray!" That's what he replied.

MRS. BUCHANAN: Oh, now, really! How cruel!

JOHN: Ha ha ha!

ALMA (*desperately*): Mother, I think you—

JOHN: And did they pray for the snake?

MRS. WINEMILLER: They prayed for the big investment!—
They should have stuck to mechanics in the—Museum—
but somebody told them that big snakes pay good. . . .

ALMA: Mother, it's past your bedtime. You go up to bed and
I will bring you a slice of delicious fruitcake. Won't that be
nice?

MRS. WINEMILLER: Yes!—if you really bring it. (*She starts
hurriedly off, then turns and waves to the company.*) Merry
Christmas!

REV. WINEMILLER: She is—well, as you see . . . she's . . .

MRS. BUCHANAN: Yes! A little disturbed right now. All the excitement of the holiday season. Little John, we must be
running along, don't you think? Big John's waiting for us.

JOHN: I've just persuaded Miss Alma to sing us something.

MRS. BUCHANAN: Oh! (*insincerely*) How nice!

(*Alma is at the piano.*)

ALMA: Would you care for something profane or sacred?

JOHN: Oh, something profane, by all means!

REV. WINEMILLER (*weakly*): I think I will try a little of this
eggnog. . . .

(*Miss Alma sings. It is not necessary for the actress to have a
very good voice. If she has no singing voice at all, the song can
be dubbed, the piano placed so her back or her profile will be to
the audience.*)

ALMA (*singing*):

> From the land of the sky-blue water,
> They brought a captive maid,
> Her eyes are lit with lightning,
> Her heart is not afraid!
>
> I stole to her tent at dawning.
> I wooed her with my flute!
> She is sick for the sky-blue water.
> The captive maid is mute. . . .

MRS. BUCHANAN (*interrupting the song*): Oh, how lovely, how lovely, one of my favorite pieces, and such a beautiful voice! —Before I forget it, Mrs. Santie Claus has some gifts to put under your tree. . . .—Where *is* your Christmas tree?

ALMA: Oh, this year we put it up in Father's study!

(*Rev. Winemiller leads Mrs. Buchanan offstage. Alma and John remain by the piano.*)

ALMA: My hands are so stiff from the cold I could hardly touch the right keys. . . .

JOHN: Shall we sit by the fire?

ALMA: Oh, yes, that's a good suggestion . . . an excellent suggestion!

JOHN: You sing very well, Miss Alma.

ALMA: Thank you—thank you . . . (*Pause. She clears her throat.*)

JOHN: Don't they call you "the Nightingale of the Delta"?

ALMA: Sarcastically, perhaps!

(*She has drawn up a hassock to the imagined fireplace. He sits on the floor with his palms extended toward the flickering red glow.*)

I have a lyric soprano. Not strong enough to make a career of singing but just about right for the church and for social occasions and I—teach singing!—But let's—let's talk about you—your—your—life and your—plans! Such a wonderful profession, being a doctor! Most of us lead such empty, useless lives! But a doctor!—Oh!—With his wonderful ability to relieve—human suffering, of which there is always— so—much! (*Her tongue runs away with her.*) I don't think it's just a profession, it's a *vocation*! I think it's something to which some people are just—*appointed by God*! (*She claps her hands together and rolls her eyes.*) Yes, just divinely appointed!—Some of us have no choice but to lead a useless existence—endure for the sake of endurance—but a young doctor, you!—with *surgeon's fingers*!

(*She has sprung up to fill his cup with eggnog. The silver ladle slips from her fingers. She utters a startled cry.*)

Ouuu!—Oh, look what I've done! I've dropped the spoon in the bowl and it is completely submerged! What can I fish it out with, oh, what can I fish it out with?

JOHN: Do you mind if I use my surgeon's fingers?

ALMA: *Ohhhhh—pleeeeeeeease!—do*—ha ha ha! (*She gasps.*)

JOHN: Well—that was not such a delicate operation. . . .

ALMA: Now you must have a napkin to wipe those fingers!

JOHN: My handkerchief will do!

ALMA: No, no, no, no, no, not that beautiful handkerchief with your monogram on it!—probably given you by someone who loves you for—Christmas. . . .

(*She picks up a napkin, grabs his hand, and wipes his fingers with tremulous care.*)

I guess you're totally "booked up," as they say, for the short time you'll be home from your laboratory?

JOHN (*gently*): Just about all.

ALMA: There's a group of young people with interests in common meeting here at the Rectory Monday. Monday evening. I know you'd like them *so* much!—Wouldn't you be able to—drop over? For just a *while*?

JOHN: What sort of interests do they have in common?

ALMA: Oh!—vaguely—*cultural*, I guess. . . . We write things, we read things aloud, we—criticize and—discuss!

JOHN: At what time does it start, this—meeting?

ALMA: Oh, *early*—at eight!

JOHN: I'll—try to make it.

ALMA: Don't say *try* as if it required some Herculean effort. All you have to do is cross the yard.—We serve refreshments, both liquid and solid!

JOHN: Reserve me a seat by the punchbowl.

ALMA (*her voice nearly failing with emotion*): That gives me a splendid idea. I *will* serve punch. Fruit punch with claret in it.—Do you like claret?

JOHN: Oh yes. I'm crazy about it.

ALMA: We *start* so early. We *finish* early, too! You'll have time for something exciting later. Your evenings are long ones, I know that!—I'll tell you *how* I know!—Your *room* is—opposite *mine*. . . .

JOHN: How do you know?

ALMA: Your light—shines in my *window*! ha ha ha!

JOHN: At two or three in the morning?

ALMA: Or *three* or *four*!—in the morning! ha ha!

JOHN: It—wakes you up? (*He smiles warmly. She glances away.*)

ALMA: Ha ha—yes . . .

JOHN: You should have let me know, you should have—complained about it.

ALMA: Complained?—Goodness, no—why *should* I?

JOHN: Well, if it . . .

ALMA: Oh, it . . .

JOHN: It doesn't?

ALMA (*very flustered*): *What?*

JOHN: Wake you up? Disturb your sleep?

ALMA: Oh, no, I'm—awake, already. . . .

JOHN: You must not sleep very well, or maybe you're getting home from late parties, too!

ALMA: The first supposition, I'm afraid, is the right one.

JOHN: I'll give you a prescription for sleeping tablets.

ALMA: Oh no. You misunderstood me. I *finally* sleep, I, I, I—wasn't complaining.

(*He suddenly takes her hand.*)

JOHN: What is the matter?

ALMA: What is the matter? I don't understand that question.

JOHN: Yes, you do. What is the matter, Miss Alma?

(*Mrs. Winemiller has appeared at the edge of the lighted area in her nightgown. She suddenly announces—*)

MRS. WINEMILLER: *Alma has fallen in love with that tall boy!*

ALMA (*springing up*): Mother! What do you want downstairs?

MRS. WINEMILLER: That piece of fruitcake you said you would bring up to me.

ALMA: Go back to your bedroom. I will bring it up.

MRS. WINEMILLER: Now?

ALMA: Yes. Yes, now. Right now!

(*She steals a frightened glance at John, touches her throat as the stage dims out and the returning voices of Mrs. Buchanan and Rev. Winemiller fade in.*)

(*Fade out.*)

ACT TWO

The Tenderness of a Mother

SCENE ONE

The Buchanans'. We see John in pajamas seated on the floor, smoking before the fireplace; nothing else.

His mother, Mrs. Buchanan, enters the lighted area in her lace negligee.

MRS. BUCHANAN: Son?

JOHN: Yes, Mother?

MRS. BUCHANAN: You mustn't misunderstand me about Miss Alma. Naturally I feel sorry for her, too. But, precious, precious! In every Southern town there's a girl or two like that. People feel sorry for them, they're kind to them, but, darling, they keep at a distance, they don't get involved with them. Especially not in a sentimental way.

JOHN: I don't know what you mean about Miss Alma. She's a little bit—quaint, she's very excitable, but—there's nothing *wrong* with her.

MRS. BUCHANAN: Precious, can't you see? Miss Alma is an *eccentric!*

JOHN: You mean she isn't like all the other girls in Glorious Hill?

MRS. BUCHANAN: There's always at least one like her in every Southern town, sometimes, like Miss Alma, rather sweet, sometimes even gifted, and I think that Miss Alma *does* have a rather appealing voice when she doesn't become too carried away by her singing. Sometimes, but not often, pretty. I have seen Miss Alma when she was almost pretty. But never, never *quite.*

JOHN: There are moments when she has beauty.

MRS. BUCHANAN: Those moments haven't occurred when *I* looked at her! Such a wide mouth she has, like the mouth of a clown! And she distorts her face with all those false expressions. However, Miss Alma's looks are beside the point.

JOHN: Her, her eyes are fascinating!

MRS. BUCHANAN: Goodness, yes, disturbing!

JOHN: No, quite lovely, I think. They're never the same for two seconds. The light keeps changing in them like, like— a running stream of clear water. . . .

MRS. BUCHANAN: They have a demented look!

JOHN: She's not demented, Mother.

MRS. BUCHANAN: *Ha!* You should see her in the Square when she feeds the birds.

(*John laughs a little.*)

Talks to them, calls them! "Here, birds, here, birds, here, birdies!" Holding out her hand with some scraps of bread!—huh!—Son, your hair is still damp. It's lucky that Mother peeped in. Now let me rub those curls dry.—My boy's such a handsome boy, and I'm so proud of him! I can see his future so clearly, such a wonderful future! I can see the girl that he will marry! A girl with every advantage, nothing less will do!

JOHN: A girl with money?

MRS. BUCHANAN: Everything, everything! Intelligence, beauty, charm, background—yes! Wealth, wealth, too! It's not to be sneezed at, money, especially in the wife of a young doctor. It takes a while for a doctor to get established, and I want you to take your time and not make any mistakes and go a long, long, long, long way!—further, much further than your dear father, although he hasn't done badly. . . . Yes, Mother can see her future daughter-in-law!—Healthy! Normal! Pretty!

JOHN: A girl like all the others?

MRS. BUCHANAN: Superior to the others!

JOHN: And sort of smug about it?

MRS. BUCHANAN: Oh, people have to be slightly smug sometimes. A little bit snobbish, even. People who have a position have to hold it, and my future daughter-in-law, my coming daughter—she'll have the sort of poise that only comes with the very best of breeding and all the advantages that the best background can give her.

JOHN: She won't be tiresome, will she?

MRS. BUCHANAN: Heavens, no! How could she?

JOHN: I've met some debutantes in Baltimore that found, somehow, a way of being tiresome. . . .

MRS. BUCHANAN: Just wait till you meet the right one! I have already met her, in my dreams! Oh, son, how she will adore you!

JOHN: More than she does herself?

MRS. BUCHANAN: She'll worship the ground you walk on.

JOHN: And her babies, how will they be?

MRS. BUCHANAN: Healthy! Normal!

JOHN: Not little pink and white pigs? With ribbons around their tails?

MRS. BUCHANAN: Ho-ho-ho-ho-ho! Your babies, my son's babies, pigs?! Oh, precious! I see them, I know them, I feel their dear little bodies in my arms! My adorable little grandchildren. Little pink things for the girl. Little blue things for the boy. A nursery full of their funny little toys. Mother Goose illustrations on the wallpaper, and their own wee little table where they sit with their bibs and their silver spoons, just so high, yes, and their own little chairs, their tiny straight back chairs and their wee little rockers, ho, ho, ho!—And on the lawn, on the enormous, grassy, shady lawn of the—Georgian, yes, *Georgian* mansion, not Greek revival, I'm tired of Greek revival!—will be their swing, their shallow pool for goldfish, their miniature train, their pony—oh, no, not a pony, no, no, not a pony!—I knew a little girl, once, that fell off a pony and landed on her head! *Goodness, she grew up to be almost as odd as Miss Alma!*

(*At this point a dim spot of light appears on Miss Alma standing raptly before a window frame at the other side of the stage. A strain of music is heard.*)

JOHN: Miss Alma has asked me over next Monday night!

MRS. BUCHANAN: Oh, I knew it, trying to rope you in!

JOHN: She says there's to be a club meeting at the Rectory. A little group of young people with interests in common.

MRS. BUCHANAN: Oh, yes, I know, I know what they have in common, the freaks of the town! Every Southern town has them and probably every Northern town has them, too. A certain little group that don't fit in with the others, sort of outcast people that have, or imagine they have, little talents for this thing or that thing or the other—over which they make a big fuss among themselves in order to bolster up their poor little, hurt little egos! They band together, they meet at each other's houses once a week, and make believe they're disliked and not wanted at other places because they're special, superior—gifted! . . . Now your curls are all dry! But let me feel your footsies, I want to make sure the footsies are dry, too, I bet anything they're not, I bet they're damp! Let Mother feel them! (*He extends his bare feet.*) Ho, ho, ho, ho! What enormous little footsies!

JOHN (*as she rubs them with towel*): You know, Mama, I never dreamed that you could be such an old tiger. Tigress, I mean.

MRS. BUCHANAN: Every mother's a tiger when her son's future happiness is threatened.

JOHN: I'm not in love with Miss Alma, if that's what you're scared of. I just *respect* her. . . .

MRS. BUCHANAN: For what?

JOHN: I'm not quite sure what it is, but it's something she has, a sort of—*gallantry*, maybe. . . .

MRS. BUCHANAN: Admire her for her good qualities and I am sure she must have some, but *do not get involved*! Don't go to the little club meeting. Make an excuse and don't go. Write a sweet little note explaining that you had forgotten another engagement. Or let Mother do it. Mother can do it sweetly. There won't be any hurt feelings. . . . Now give me that cigarette. I won't leave you to smoke it in bed. That's how fires start. I don't want us all burned up like the Musée Mécanique!

JOHN: Oh, did the Museum burn?

MRS. BUCHANAN: Heavens, yes, that's a story, but it's too long for bedtime. (*She bends to kiss him fondly, with a lingering caress.*) Good night, my precious! Sleep tight!

(*She turns out the light as she leaves. The dim spot remains on Miss Alma a moment longer. . . .*)

ALMA: Oh, my love, my love, your light is out, now—I can sleep!

SCENE TWO

The following Monday evening. The little group is meeting in the Rectory parlor. An animated discussion is in progress.

VERNON: I think it's a question of whether or not we have a serious purpose. I was under the impression that we *had* a serious purpose, but of course, if we *don't* have a serious purpose—

ALMA: Of course we *do* have a serious purpose, but I don't see why that means we have to publish a—manifesto about it!

ROGER: What's wrong with a manifesto?

VERNON: Even if nobody reads the manifesto, it—*crystallizes!* —our purpose, in our own minds.

ALMA: Oh, but to say that we—have such lofty ambitions.

ROGER: But, Miss Alma, *you* are the one who said we were going to make Glorious Hill the *Athens of the Delta!*

ALMA: Yes, but in the manifesto it says the Athens of the whole *South*, and besides an ambition, a hope of that kind, doesn't have to be—published! In a way to publish it—destroys it!—a little. . . .

MRS. BASSETT: The manifesto is beautiful, *perfectly* beautiful, it made me *cry!*

VERNON (*who composed it*): Thank you, Nancy.

ROGER: Boys and girls, the meeting is called to order. Miss Alma will read us the minutes of the last meeting.

MRS. BASSETT: Oh, let's skip the minutes! Who cares what happened last time? Let's concentrate on the present and the future! That's a widow's philosophy!

(*The doorbell rings. Alma drops her papers.*)

Butter-fingers!

ALMA (*breathlessly*): Did I—hear the bell—ring?

(*The bell rings again.*)

Yes!—it did! (*She starts to pick up the papers; they slip again.*)

MRS. BASSETT: Miss Alma, I don't think I've ever seen you quite so nervous!

ALMA: I forgot to mention it!—I . . . invited a . . . guest!— someone just home for the holidays—young Doctor

Buchanan, the old doctor's son, you know!—he—lives next door!—and he . . .

VERNON: I thought we had all agreed not to have outsiders unless we took a vote on them beforehand!

ALMA: It was presumptuous of me, but I'm sure you'll forgive me when you meet him!

(*She flies out. They all exchange excited looks and whispers as she is heard offstage admitting John to the hall.*)

ROSEMARY: I don't care who he is, if a group *is* a group there must be something a *little* exclusive about it!—otherwise it . . .

MRS. BASSETT: *Listen!* Why, she is *hysterical* about him!

(*Miss Alma's excited voice is heard and her breathless laughter offstage racing.*)

ALMA: Well, well, well, our guest of honor has finally made his appearance!

JOHN: Sorry I'm late.

ALMA: Oh, you're not *very* late.

JOHN: Dad's laid up. I have to call on his patients.

ALMA: Oh, is your father *not well*?

JOHN: Just a slight touch of grippe.

ALMA: There's so much going around.

JOHN: These delta houses aren't built for cold weather.

ALMA: Indeed they aren't! The Rectory's made out of paper, I believe.

(*All of this is said offstage, in the hall.*)

ROSEMARY: Her voice has gone up *two octaves*!

MRS. BASSETT: Obviously *infatuated* with him!

ROSEMARY: Oh, my *stars*!

MRS. BASSETT: The last time I was here—the lunatic mother made a sudden entrance!

VERNON: *Shhhh!—girls!*

(*Alma enters with John. He is embarrassed by the curious intensity of her manner and the greedily curious glances of the group.*)

ALMA: Everybody!—this is Doctor John Buchanan, *Junior*!

JOHN: Hello, everybody. I'm sorry if I interrupted the meeting.

MRS. BASSETT: Nothing was interrupted. We'd decided to skip the minutes.

ALMA: Mrs. Bassett says it's a widow's philosophy to skip the minutes. And so we are skipping the minutes—ha, ha, ha! I hope everybody is comfortable?

ROSEMARY: I'm just as cold as Greenland's icy mountains!

ALMA: Rosemary, you always are chilly, even in warm weather. I think you must be thin-blooded!—Here. Take this shawl!

ROSEMARY: No thank you, not a shawl!—at least not a gray woolen shawl, I'm not *that* old yet, that I have to be wrapped in a gray shawl.

ALMA: *Excuse* me, *do forgive* me!—John, I'll put you on this loveseat, next to me.—Well, now we are completely assembled!

MRS. BASSETT: Vernon has his verse play with him tonight!

ALMA (*uneasily*): Is that right, Vernon?

(*He has a huge manuscript in his lap which he solemnly elevates.*)

Oh, I *see* that you have.

ROSEMARY: I thought that I was supposed to read my paper on William Blake at the meeting.

ALMA: Well, obviously we can't have both at once. That would be an embarrassment of riches!—Now why don't we save the verse play, which appears to be rather long, till some more comfortable evening. I think it's too important to hear under any but ideal circumstances, in warmer weather, with—with *music!*—planned to go with it. . . .

ROGER: Yes, let's hear Rosemary's paper on William Blake!

MRS. BASSETT: No, no, no, those dead poets can keep!— Vernon's alive and he's got his verse play with him; he's brought it three times! And each time been disappointed.

VERNON: I am not disappointed not to read my verse play, *that* isn't the point at all, *but*—

ALMA: Shall we take a standing vote on the question?

ROGER: Yes, let's do.

ALMA: Good, good, perfect, let's do! A standing vote. All in favor of postponing the verse play till the next meeting, stand up!

(*Rosemary is late in rising.*)

ROSEMARY: Is this a vote?

(*As she starts to rise Mrs. Bassett jerks her arm.*)

ROGER: Now, Mrs. Bassett, no rough tactics, please!

ALMA: So we'll save the verse play and begin the New Year with it!

(*Rosemary puts on her glasses and rises portentously.*)

ROSEMARY: The poet—William Blake!

MRS. BASSETT: Insane, insane, that man was a mad fanatic!

(*She squints her eyes tight shut and thrusts her thumbs into her ears. The reactions range from indignant to conciliatory.*)

ROGER: Now, Mrs. Bassett!

MRS. BASSETT: This is a free country. I can speak my opinion. And I have *read up* on him. Go on, Rosemary. I wasn't criticizing your paper.

(*But Rosemary sits down, hurt.*)

ALMA: Mrs. Bassett is only joking, Rosemary.

ROSEMARY: No, I don't want to read it if she feels that strongly about it.

MRS. BASSETT: Not a bit, don't be silly! I just don't see why we should encourage the writings of people like that who have already gone into a drunkard's grave!

VARIOUS VOICES (*exclaiming*): Did he? I never heard that about him. Is that true?

ALMA: Mrs. Bassett is mistaken about that. Mrs. Bassett, you have confused Blake with someone else.

MRS. BASSETT (*positively*): Oh, no, don't tell me. I've read up on him and know what I'm talking about. He traveled around with that Frenchman who took a shot at him and landed them both in jail! Brussels, Brussels!

ROGER (*gaily*): Brussels sprouts!

MRS. BASSETT: That's where it happened, fired a gun at him in a drunken stupor, and later one of them died of T.B. in the gutter! All right. I'm finished. I won't say anything more. Go on with your paper, Rosemary. There's nothing like contact with culture!

(*Alma gets up.*)

ALMA: Before Rosemary reads her paper on Blake, I think it would be a good idea, since some of us aren't acquainted with his work, to preface the critical and biographical comments with a reading of one of his loveliest lyric poems.

ROSEMARY: I'm not going to read anything at all! Not I!

ALMA: Then let me read it then. (*She takes a paper from Rosemary.*) . . . This is called "Love's Secret."

(*She clears her throat and waits for a hush to settle. Rosemary looks stonily at the carpet. Mrs. Bassett looks at the ceiling. John coughs.*)

> Never seek to tell thy love,
> Love that never told can be;
> For the gentle wind doth move
> Silently, invisibly.
>
> I told my love, I told my love,
> I told him all my heart.
> Trembling, cold, in ghastly fear
> Did my love depart.
>
> No sooner had he gone from me
> Than a stranger passing by,
> Silently, invisibly,
> Took him with a sigh!

(*There are various effusions and enthusiastic applause.*)

MRS. BASSETT: Honey, you're right. That isn't the man I meant. I was thinking about the one who wrote about the "bought red lips." Who was it that wrote about the "bought red lips"?

ALMA: You're thinking about a poem by Ernest Dowson.

(*The bell rings.*)

MRS. BASSETT: Ohhhhh, the doorbell *again*!

MRS. WINEMILLER (*above*): Alma, Alma!

(*Alma crosses the stage and goes out.*)

ROSEMARY: Aren't you all cold? I'm just freezing to death! I've never been in a house as cold as this!

ALMA (*in the hall*): Why, Mrs. Buchanan! How sweet of you to—drop over. . . .

MRS. BUCHANAN: I can't stay, Alma. I just came to fetch my Little John home.

ALMA: Fetch—John!?

MRS. BUCHANAN: His father's just received an urgent call from old Mrs. Arbuckle's house. The poor woman is in a dreadful pain. John? John, darling? I hate to drag you away but your father can't budge from the house!

ALMA: Mrs. Buchanan, do you know everybody?

MRS. BUCHANAN: Why, yes, I think so.—John? Come, dear! I'm so sorry . . .

(*It is obvious that she is delivering a cool snub to the gathering. There are various embarrassed murmurs as John makes his departure. Miss Alma appears quite stricken.*)

ALMA (*after the departure*): Shall we go on with the reading?

ROSEMARY: "The Poet, William Blake, was born in the year of our Lord, 1757. . . ."

(*Mrs. Winemiller cries out and bursts into the room half in and out of her clothes.*)

MRS. WINEMILLER: Alma, Alma, I've got to go to New Orleans right away, immediately, Alma, by the midnight train. They've closed the Museum, confiscated the marvels! Mr. Schwarzkopf is almost out of his mind. He's going to burn the place up, he's going to set it on fire—before the auction—Monday!

ALMA: *Oh, Mother!* (*She makes a helpless gesture; then bursts into tears and runs out of the room, followed by Mrs. Winemiller.*)

MRS. BASSETT: I think we'd all better go—poor Miss Alma!

ROGER: I move that the meeting adjourn.

VERNON: I second the motion!

MRS. BASSETT: *Poor* Miss Alma! But I knew it was a mistake to have us meet here. (*Sotto voce*) *Nobody* comes to the Rectory any more!—this *always* happens . . . the *mother*!—invariably makes a scene of some kind. . . .

(*They trail off.*)

ROSEMARY (*slowly, wonderingly, as she follows them off*): I don't understand!—What happened?

(*Fade out.*)

SCENE THREE

Later that night.

The interior of the doctor's office is suggested by a chart of anatomy, a black leather divan and an oak desk and chair behind it.

A buzzer sounds in the dark.

VOICES MURMUR ABOVE:
—John?
—Hannh?
—The bell's ringing in the office. You'd better answer it or it will wake up your father.
—All right, Mama.

(*A panicky knocking begins. John enters in pajamas and robe, carrying a book. There are sounds of releasing a lock. Lights go up as Miss Alma enters. She has thrown on a coat over a nightgown, her hair is in disorder, and her appearance very distracted. She is having "an attack."*)

JOHN: Why, it's you, Miss Alma!
ALMA (*panting*): Your father, please.
JOHN: Is something the matter?
ALMA: I have to see your father.
JOHN: Won't I do?
ALMA: No, I think not. Please call your father.
JOHN: Big John's asleep, he's not well.
ALMA: I'm having an attack, I've got to see him!
JOHN: It's after two, Miss Alma.
ALMA: I know the time, I know what time it is! Do you think I'd run over here at two in the morning if I weren't terribly ill?
JOHN: I don't think you would be able to run over here at two in the morning if you *were* terribly ill. Now sit down here. (*He leads her to the divan.*) And stop swallowing air.

ALMA: Swallowing what?

JOHN: Air. You swallow air when you get overexcited. It presses against your heart and starts it pounding. That frightens you more. You swallow more air and get more palpitations and before you know it you're in a state of panic like this. Now you lean back. No, no, lean all the way back and just breathe slowly and deeply. You're not going to suffocate and your heart's going to keep on beating. Look at your fingers, shame on you! You've got them clenched like you're getting ready to hit me. Are you going to hit me? Let those fingers loosen up, now.

ALMA: I can't, I can't, I'm too . . .

JOHN: You couldn't sleep?

ALMA: I couldn't sleep.

JOHN: You felt walled in, the room started getting smaller?

ALMA: I felt—walled in—suffocated!

JOHN: You started hearing your heart as if somebody had stuffed it in the pillow?

ALMA: Yes, like a drum in the pillow.

JOHN: A natural thing. But it scared you. (*He hands her a small glass of brandy.*) Toss this down.

(*He places a hand behind her, raising her shoulders from the divan.*)

ALMA: What is it?

JOHN: Shot of brandy.

ALMA: Oh, that's a stimulant, I need something to calm me.

JOHN: This will calm you.

ALMA: Your father gives me—

JOHN: Let's try this to begin with.

ALMA: He gives me some little white tablets dissolved in—

JOHN: Get this down.

(*She sips and chokes.*)

ALMA: Oh!

JOHN: Went down the wrong way?

ALMA: The muscles of my throat are paralyzed!

JOHN: Undo those fists, undo them, loosen those fingers. (*He presses her hands between his.*)

ALMA: I'm sorry I—woke you up. . . .

JOHN: I was reading in bed. A physicist named Albert
Einstein. I'm going to turn this light out.

ALMA: *Oh, no!*

JOHN: Why not? Are you afraid of the dark?

ALMA: Yes . . .

JOHN: It won't be very dark. I'm going to open these shutters and you can look at the stars while I tell you what I was
reading.

(*He turns off the lamp on the desk. Crossing to the window
frame, he makes a motion of opening shutters. A dim blue radiance floods the stage.*)

I was reading that time is one side of the four-dimensional
continuum that we exist in. I was reading that space is
curved. It turns back on itself instead of going on indefinitely like we used to believe, and it's hanging adrift in
something that's even less than space; it's hanging like a
soap-bubble in something less than space. . . .

ALMA: Where is the . . . ?

JOHN: Brandy? Right here . . . Throat muscles still paralyzed?

ALMA: No, I—think I can—get it down, now. . . .

JOHN: There's nothing wrong with your heart but a little
functional disturbance, but I'll check it for you. Unbutton
your gown.

ALMA: Unbutton? . . .

JOHN: Just the top of your gown.

ALMA: Hadn't I better come back in the morning when your
father is . . . ?

JOHN: Sure. If you'd rather.

ALMA: I—my fingers are . . .

JOHN: Fingers won't work?

ALMA: They are just as if frozen!

JOHN (*kneeling beside her*): Let me. (*He leans over her, unbut-
toning the gown.*) Little pearl buttons . . . (*Stethoscope to her
chest*) Breathe.—Now out . . . Breathe . . . Now out . . .
(*Finally he rises.*) Um-hmmmm.

ALMA: What do you hear in my heart?

JOHN: Just a little voice saying, "Miss Alma is lonesome."

(*She springs up angrily.*)

ALMA: If your idea of helping a patient is to ridicule and insult—

JOHN: My idea of helping you is to tell you the truth.

ALMA (*snatching up her cloak*): Oh, how wise and superior you are! John Buchanan, Junior, graduate of Johns Hopkins, magna cum laude!—Brilliant, yes, as the branches after the ice storm, and just as cold and inhuman! Oh, you put us in our place tonight, my, my little collection of—eccentrics, my club of—fellow misfits! You sat among us like a lord of the earth, the only handsome one there, the one superior one! And oh, how we all devoured you with our eyes, you were like holy bread being broken among us.—But snatched away! Fetched home by your mother with that lame excuse, that invention about Mrs. Arbuckle's turn for the worse. I called the Arbuckles.—Better, much better, they told me, no doctor was called! Oh I suppose you're right to despise us, my little company of the faded and frightened and different and odd and lonely. You don't belong to that club but I hold an office in it! (*She laughs harshly.*)

JOHN: Hush, Miss Alma, you'll wake up the house!

ALMA: Wake up my wealthy neighbors? Oh, no, I mustn't. Everything in this house is *comme il faut.*

(*A clock strikes offstage.*)

Even the clock makes music when it strikes, a dainty little music. Hear it, hear it? It sounds like the voice of your mother, saying, "John? John, darling? We must go home now!" (*She laughs convulsively, then chokes, and seizes the brandy glass.*) And when you marry, you'll marry some Northern beauty. She will have no eccentricities but the eccentricity of beauty and perfect calm. Her hands will have such repose, such perfect repose when she speaks. They won't fly about her like wild birds, oh, no, she'll hold them together, press the little pink tips of her fingers together, making a—steeple—or fold them sweetly and gravely in her lap! She'll only move them when she lifts a tea cup—they won't reach above her when she cries out in the night! Suddenly, desperately—fly up, fly up in the night!—reaching for something—nothing!—clutching at—space. . . .

JOHN: Please! Miss Alma! You are—exhausting yourself. . . .

ALMA: No, the bride will have beauty! (*Her voice is now a shrill whisper; she leans far toward him across the desk.*) The bride will have beauty, beauty! Admirable family background, no lunacy in it, no skeletons in the closet—no Aunt Albertine and Mr. Otto Schwarzkopf, no Musée Mécanique with a shady past!—No, no, nothing morbid, nothing peculiar, nothing eccentric! No—deviations!—But everything perfect and regular as the—tick of that—clock!

MRS. BUCHANAN'S VOICE (*above*): John! John, darling! What on earth is the matter down there?

JOHN (*at the door*): Nothing. Go to sleep, Mother.

MRS. BUCHANAN'S VOICE: Is someone badly hurt?

JOHN: Yes, Mother. Hurt. But not badly. Go back to sleep.

(*He closes the door.*)

Now. You see? You are gasping for breath again. Lie down, lie down. . . .

ALMA: I am not afraid any more and I don't care to lie down.

JOHN: Perhaps, after all, that outburst did you some good.

ALMA: Yes—Yes— (*Then suddenly*) *I'm so ashamed of myself!*

JOHN: You should be proud of yourself. You know, you know, it's surprising how few people there are that dare in this world to say what is in their hearts.

ALMA: I had no right—to talk to you like that. . . .

JOHN: I was—stupid, I—hurt you. . . .

ALMA: No. I hurt myself! I exposed myself. Father is frightened of me and he's right. On the surface I'm still the Episcopal minister's daughter but there's something else that's—

JOHN: Yes, something else! What is it?

ALMA (*slowly shaking her head*): Something—else that's—frantic!

JOHN: A doppelgänger?

ALMA (*nodding slowly*): A—doppelgänger!

JOHN: Fighting for its life in the prison of a little conventional world full of walls and . . .

ALMA: What was it you said about space when you turned the light out?

JOHN: Space, I said, is curved.

ALMA: Then even space is a prison!—not—infinite. . . .

JOHN: A very large prison, even large enough for you to feel free in, Miss Alma. (*He takes her hand and blows his breath on her fingers.*) Are your fingers still frozen?

(*She leans against the desk, turning her face to the audience, closing her eyes.*)

ALMA: Your breath!—is . . . *warm.* . . .

JOHN: Yours, too. Your breath is warm.

ALMA: All human breath is warm—so pitifully! So pitifully warm and soft as children's fingers. . . . (*She turns her face to him and takes his face between the fingers of both her hands.*) The brandy worked very quickly. You know what I feel like now. I feel like a water-lily on a—Chinese lagoon. . . . I will sleep, perhaps. But—I won't see you —again. . . .

JOHN: I'm leaving next Monday.

ALMA: Monday . . .

JOHN: Aren't there any more meetings we could—go to?

ALMA: You don't like meetings.

JOHN: The only meetings I like are between two people.

ALMA: We are two people, we've met—did you like our meeting?

(*John nods, smiling.*)

Then meet me again!

JOHN: I'll take you to see Mary Pickford at the Delta Brilliant tomorrow.

(*Alma throws back her head with a gasping laugh, checks it quickly. She retreats with a slight gasp as Mrs. Buchanan enters in a lace negligee.*)

MRS. BUCHANAN (*with acid sweetness*): Oh, the patient's Miss *Alma*!

ALMA: Yes. Miss Alma's the patient. Forgive me for disturbing you. Good night. (*She turns quickly but with a fleeting glance at John, who grins by the door.*) Au revoir! (*She goes out.*)

MRS. BUCHANAN: And what was the matter with *her*?!

JOHN: Palpitations, Mother. (*He turns out the office light.*) *Haven't* you ever had them?

MRS. BUCHANAN: *Had* them? *Yes!*—But *controlled* them!

(*He laughs gaily on the stairs. She follows with an outraged "Huh!"*)

(*Dim out.*)

SCENE FOUR

The next night, New Year's Eve. Roger and Miss Alma are in the Rectory parlor with a magic lantern.

ROGER: Is it in focus, Miss Alma?
ALMA (*absently*): Yes.

(*The image is completely blurred.*)

ROGER: Are you sure it's in focus?
ALMA (*in a sad whisper*): Yes, perfectly in focus.
ROGER (*rising from behind the lantern*): What is it a picture of?
ALMA (*faintly*): What, Roger?
ROGER: I said, "What is it a picture of?"
ALMA: Why, I can't tell, it seems to be out of focus. . . .
ROGER: You just now said that it was in perfect focus.
ALMA: Excuse me, Roger. My wits are woolgathering.
ROGER: I will turn off the lantern and put the slides away. (*He does so.*) Now let's turn the sofa to face the window so we won't have to twist our necks to gaze at the house next door.—You were expecting him tonight?
ALMA: He'd asked me to go to the movies.
ROGER: Then why did you ask me to bring my magic lantern?
ALMA: Some people called for him at seven. He left the house. I think he'd forgotten he asked me to go to the movies. I just couldn't sit here alone waiting to see if he had, or if he'd remember. I just couldn't bear it!
ROGER: How late is he now?
ALMA: Twenty, no, twenty-five minutes!
ROGER: I think I would go and give him up then.
ALMA: I have, almost. I almost wish I was dead!
ROGER: People who bark up wrong trees . . .
ALMA: Sometimes the only tree you want to bark up is the wrong one. . . . Don't you know that?

ROGER: Miss Alma, we're fond of each other. We get along well together. We have interests in common. Companionship is something.

ALMA: Something, but not enough. I want more than that.— *I see him!*—No . . . No, that isn't him. . . . You and I, we have no desire for each other. They intimated to you at the bank that you'd be advanced more rapidly if you were married. But, Roger, I want more than that. . . . Even if all I get in the end is a button—like Aunt Albertine. . . .

ROGER: A button?

ALMA: You've heard her story?

ROGER: I've heard your mother make some allusions to it, but nothing very—coherent. . . .

ALMA: She grew up, like me, in the shadow of the church. Until one Sunday a strange man came to the service and dropped a ten-dollar bill in the collection plate! —Of course he was immediately invited to dinner at the Rectory. . . . At dinner he sat next to my Aunt Albertine—the next day she bought a plumed hat and the following Wednesday he took her away from the Rectory forever. . . . He'd been married twice already, without a divorce, but bigamy was the least of his delinquencies, and obviously Aunt Albertine found living in sin preferable to life in the Rectory.—Mr. Schwarzkopf was a mechanical genius. They traveled about the South with a sort of show called the Musée Mécanique. I'm sure you've heard Mother speak of it—a collection of mechanical marvels that Mr. Schwarzkopf had created. Among them was a mechanical bird-girl. She was his masterpiece. Every five minutes a tin bird flew out of her mouth and whistled three times, clear as a bell, and flew back in again. She smiled and nodded, lifted her arms as if to embrace a lover. Mr. Schwarzkopf was enchanted by his bird-girl. Everything else was neglected. . . . He'd suddenly get out of bed in the night and go downstairs to wind her up and sit in front of her, drinking, until she seemed alive to him. . . . Then one winter they made a dreadful mistake. They mortgaged the whole Museum to buy a boa constrictor because somebody had told them "Big snakes pay good"—well, this one didn't, it swallowed a blanket and died. . . . You may have heard Mother speak of it. But not of the fire. She refuses to believe in the fire.

ROGER: There was a fire?

ALMA: Oh, yes. Creditors took the Museum and locked Mr. Schwarzkopf out. There was to be an auction of the mechanical marvels but the night before the auction Mr. Schwarzkopf broke into the Museum and set it on fire. Albertine rushed into the burning building and caught Mr. Schwarzkopf by the sleeve of his coat but he broke away from her. When they dragged her out, she was dying, but still holding onto a button she'd torn from his sleeve. "Some people," she said, "don't even die empty-handed!"

ROGER: What did she mean by that?

ALMA: The button, of course . . . all that was left of her darling Mr. Schwarzkopf!

(*The bell rings. She seems paralyzed for a moment, then gasps and rushes out of the lighted area. A moment later her voice is heard.*)

I'd almost given you up!

(*Dim out.*)

ACT THREE
A Cavalier's Plume

SCENE ONE

That night, after the movies, before the angel of the fountain.

ALMA: May we stop here for a moment?

JOHN: You're not cold?

ALMA: No.

(*A silence.*)

JOHN: You've been very quiet, Miss Alma.

ALMA: I always say too much or say too little. The few young men I've gone out with have found me . . . I've only gone out with three at all seriously—and with each one there was a desert between us.

JOHN: What do you mean by a desert?

ALMA: Oh, wide, wide stretches of uninhabitable ground. I'd try to talk, he'd try to talk. Oh, we'd talk quite a lot—but then it would be—exhausted—the talk, the effort. I'd twist the ring on my finger, so hard sometimes it would cut my finger. He'd look at his watch as if he had never seen a watch before. . . . And we would both know that the useless undertaking had come to a close. At the door— (*She turns slowly to the fountain.*) At the door he would say, "I'll call you." "I'll call you" meant goodbye! (*She laughs a little.*)

JOHN (*gently*): Would you care much?

ALMA: Not—not about them. . . .

JOHN: Then about what would you care?

(*Far away nonrealistic baying of a hound. "Valse des Regrets" by Brahms fades in softly.*)

ALMA: They only mattered as shadows of some failure that would come later.

JOHN: What failure?

ALMA: A failure such as—tonight. . . .

JOHN: Tonight is a failure?

ALMA: I think it will be a failure. Look. My ring has cut my finger. No! I shall have to be honest! I can't play any kind of a game! Do you remember what Mother said when she burst into the room? "Alma has fallen in love with that tall boy!" It's true. I had. But longer ago than that. I remember the long afternoons of our childhood when I had to stay indoors and practice my music. I heard your playmates calling you, Johnny, Johnny! Oh, how it used to go through me just to hear your name called. I ran to the window to watch you jump the porch railing, stood at a distance halfway down the block only to keep in sight of your torn red sweater racing about the vacant lot you played in. "Johnny, Johnny!"—It had begun that early, this affliction of love, and it's never let go of me since, but kept on growing and growing. I've lived next door to you all the days of my life, a weak and divided person, lived in your shadow, no, I mean in your brightness which made a shadow I lived in, but lived in adoring awe of your radiance, your strength . . . your singleness. Now Father tells me that I am becoming known as an eccentric. People think me affected, laugh at me, imitate me at parties! I'm marked to be different, it's stamped on me in big letters so people can read from a distance: "This Person Is Strange." . . . Well, I may be eccentric but not so eccentric that I don't have the ordinary human need for love. I have that need, and I must satisfy it, in whatever way my good or bad fortune will make possible for me. . . . One time in the movies I sat next to a strange man. I didn't look at his face, but after a while I felt the pressure of his knee against mine. I thought it might be accidental. I moved aside. But then it began again. I didn't look at him. I sprang from my seat. I rushed out of the theater. I wonder sometimes. If I had dared to look at his face in the queer flickering white light that comes from the screen, and it had been like yours, at *all* like yours, even the *faintest resemblance*— Would I have sprung from my seat, or would I have *stayed*?

JOHN: A dangerous speculation for a minister's daughter!

ALMA: Very dangerous indeed! But not as dangerous as what I did tonight. Didn't you feel it? Didn't you feel the pressure of my—knee?—Tonight?—In the movies?

(*The audience may laugh at this question. Take a count of ten. Perhaps John crosses slowly to drink at the fountain.*)

I have embarrassed you.

JOHN (*gently*): Yes.

ALMA: I told you I had to be honest. Now you take me home. You may take me back to the house between your house and the Episcopal church, you may take me back there, now, unless—unless . . .

JOHN: Unless what, Miss Alma?

ALMA: Unless, unless—by the most unlikely chance in the world you wanted to take me somewhere else!

JOHN: Where is—"somewhere else"?

ALMA: Anywhere that two people could be alone.

JOHN: Oh . . .

ALMA: I told you I had to be honest.

JOHN: We are alone in the Square.

ALMA: I was thinking of—

JOHN: A room?

ALMA: A—little room with—a fireplace . . .

JOHN: One of those rooms that people engage for an hour? A bottle of wine in a bucket of ice—brrr! No!—No ice—No, one of those red wines in straw-covered bottles from Italy. I think they call it—Chianti. . . .

ALMA: Just—four walls and a—fireplace . . .

JOHN: I'm glad you include a fireplace. That might be necessary to take the chill off, Miss Alma.

ALMA: Are there—are there such places?

JOHN: Yes. There have been such places since the beginning of time. Little rooms that seem empty even when you are in them but have sad little tokens of people that occupied them before you, a sprinkle of light pink powder on the dresser, a hairpin on the carpet—a few withered rose petals —in the wastebasket of course an empty pint bottle of some inexpensive whisky. Yes. There is such a place in Glorious Hill—even . . .

ALMA: Do you—know where to find it?

JOHN: I could find it blindfolded.

ALMA: You've been to it often?

JOHN: I grew up in this town. Yes. I remember the place. It wasn't attractive, Miss Alma, you wouldn't like it.

ALMA: I would like it with you.

JOHN: You might think that you would until you got there and then discover you didn't. The first time I went there was with one of those anonymous young ladies who get off the Cannonball Express at midnight and stand aimlessly around the entrance to the waiting room at the depot with one small suitcase like a small dog close to their slippers—that first time I went there because *she* knew of the place. . . . I made an excuse to slip away from the room, and I ran like a rabbit, ha ha, I ran like a rabbit!—I left a white linen jacket over a chair with a wallet containing eight dollars. Later, much later, I believe a year later, yes, the following summer—I went back there again, and the grinning old colored porter handed me the white jacket. "A young lady left it for you, Mistuh Johnny, one time last summer," he told me. The wallet was still in the pocket, and in the wallet was a note from the lady. "Baby, I took five dollars to get me to Memphis."—Ha ha ha—signed "Alice" . . .

ALMA: Alice . . .

JOHN: Yes. Alice. She had a small nose with freckles which is probably still leading her into trouble as straight as a good bird-dog will point at a partridge! Ha ha ha!—No, Miss Alma, you wouldn't care for the place, and besides it's New Year's Eve and it will be crowded, there, and after all, you're not unknown in this town, you're the Nightingale of the Delta! Oh, they wouldn't be people you'd run into at church, but . . . .

ALMA: John, I want to go there. I want to be in a small room with you at midnight when the bells ring!

JOHN: You're quite sure that you want to?

ALMA: Do you see any shadow of doubt in my eyes?

JOHN: No— No, not in your eyes—but of course you know that it might turn out badly.

(*She nods her head slowly and gravely. He grips her gloved hands.*)

It would be an experiment that might fail so miserably that it would have been much better not to have tried it. Because—well—"propinquity," as you call it—just propinquity—sometimes isn't enough. Oh, I wouldn't run out of the room like a rabbit and leave my jacket over the back of the chair! I'm a *big* boy, now! But you know, Miss Alma— or *do* you know?—that regardless of how it was, whether or not the experiment went well or very badly—you must know that I couldn't—couldn't—

ALMA: Go on with it? Yes. I know that.

JOHN: There are many practical reasons.

ALMA: And many impractical reasons. I know all of that!

JOHN: The most important one is the one I'd rather not say, but I guess you know what it is.

ALMA: I know that you don't love me.

JOHN: No. No, I'm not in love with you.

ALMA: I wasn't counting on that tonight or ever.

JOHN: God. Yes, God. You talk as straight as a man and you look right into my eyes and say you're expecting *nothing*?!

ALMA: I'm looking into your eyes but I'm not saying that. I expect a great deal. But for tonight only. Afterwards, nothing, nothing! Nothing at all.

JOHN: Afterwards would come quickly in a room that you rent for an hour.

ALMA: An hour is the lifetime of some creatures.

JOHN: Generations of some creatures can be fitted into an hour, the sort of creatures I see through my microscope. But you're not one of those creatures. You're a complex being. You have that mysterious something, as thin as smoke, that makes the difference between the human and all other beings! An hour isn't a lifetime for you, Miss Alma.

ALMA: Give me the hour, and I'll make a lifetime of it.

JOHN (*smiling a little*): For you, Miss Alma, the name of the stone angel is barely long enough and nothing less than that *could* be!

ALMA: What is the answer, John?

JOHN: Excuse me a minute. I will find a taxi.

ALMA: *Leave something with me to guarantee your return!*

(*Her laughter rings out high and clear, not like a woman's: more like the cry of a bird. He half turns as if startled; then grins wryly, raises an arm, and shouts: "Taxi!"*)

(*The scene dims out.*)

(*A soprano sings: "I Love You" by Grieg, during the change of scene.*)

SCENE TWO

A short while later that night. The skeletal set is a bedroom in a small hotel of the sort that is called, sometimes, a "house of convenience": a place where rooms are let out for periods as brief as an hour. Next door is a night resort. We hear a mechanical piano playing ragtime.

A Negro porter enters and prepares the room for occupants waiting outside. He sets whisky and two glasses on a small round table by the bed. The long shadows of the waiting couple, still outside, are thrown across the lighted area, until the porter withdraws. Then John and Alma enter the lighted area; they stand silent on the edge of it for a moment like timid bathers at the edge of cold water.

JOHN: The room is cold.
ALMA: Will—will—will the fire light?
JOHN: That remains to be seen. . . .
ALMA: Try it, try to light it!

(*He still pauses.*)

What are you waiting for, John?
JOHN: For you to think . . .
ALMA: Think about what?
JOHN: If you really want to go on with this—adventure. . . .
ALMA: My answer is yes! What's yours?

(*Another long pause.*)

JOHN (*finally*): This room reminds me of a hospital room. Even a folding white screen of the sort they put around patients about to expire.
ALMA: Rooms of this kind, are they always like this?
JOHN: You think I've had a vast experience with them?
ALMA: I'm sure you must have had some.
JOHN: Actually, probably not much more than *you've* had.

(*She crosses to the table by the bed.*)

ALMA: Oh, look, I've found a withered rose petal and a sprinkle of powder!
JOHN: That takes the curse off a little.
ALMA: Turn out the light. Let's see how it looks with the light out.

(*He switches off the bare bulb.*)

JOHN: You know what it looks like now? It looks like a cave in Capri that's called the Blue Grotto!
ALMA: Put a match to the fire.

JOHN (*crouching before the fireplace*): The logs are damp.

ALMA: There's paper underneath them.

JOHN: It's damp, too.

ALMA: But try!

JOHN: I shall try, Miss Alma.—But you know I told you this could turn out badly.

ALMA: Yes, I know. You warned me.

(*He strikes a match. A flickering red glow falls upon their figures as he draws the match back from the fire.*)

There, there now, it's *burning!*

JOHN: Temporarily . . .

ALMA: Let's pray it will keep! . . . Put paper on it, put more paper on.

JOHN: I have none!

ALMA: There must be some. Quick, quick, it's expiring! Ring for the boy, ring for the boy! We must have a fire to take the chill off the room!

JOHN: Are you sure that a fire would take the chill off the room?

(*She suddenly seizes her hat and tears off the plume, starts to cast the plume into the fireplace. He seizes her hand.*)

Miss Alma!

ALMA: This plume will burn!

JOHN: *Don't!*

ALMA: This plume will burn! Something has to be sacrificed to a fire.

JOHN (*still gripping her hand that holds the plume*): Miss Alma. Miss Alma. The fire has gone out and nothing will revive it. Take my word for it, nothing!

(*Music is heard very faintly.*)

It never was much of a fire, it never really got started, and now it's out. . . . Sometimes things say things for people. Things that people find too painful or too embarrassing to say, a thing will say it, a thing will say it for them so they don't have to say it. . . . The fire is out, it's gone out, and you feel how the room is now, it's deathly chill. There's no use in staying in it.

(*She turns on the light, walks a few steps from him, twisting her ring. There is a pause.*)

You are twisting your ring. (*He catches hold of her hand again and holds it still.*)

ALMA: How gently a failure can happen! The way that some people die, lightly, unconsciously, losing themselves with their breath. . . .

JOHN: Why—why call it a failure?

ALMA: Why call a spade a spade? I have to be honest. If I had had beauty and desirability and the grace of a woman, it would not have been necessary for me to be honest. My eccentricities—made it necessary. . . .

JOHN: I think your honesty is the plume on your hat. And you ought to wear it proudly.

ALMA: Proudly or not proudly, I shall wear it. Now I must put it back on. Where is my hat?—Oh.—Here—the plume is restored to its place!

(*Downstairs a hoarse whisky contralto starts singing "Hello, my honey, hello, my baby, hello, my ragtime doll!"*)

Who is—what is . . . Oh!—a party—downstairs . . .

JOHN: This is—a honky-tonk.

ALMA: *Yes!* Perhaps I shall get to know it a great deal better!

JOHN: The plume on your hat is lovely, it almost sweeps the ceiling!

ALMA: You *flatterer!* (*She smiles at him with harshness, almost mockery.*)

JOHN: *Don't!*—we have to still like each other!—Don't be *harsh.*

ALMA:

If I wore a tall hat in a sunny room,
I would sweep the ceiling with a cavalier's plume—
If I wore a frock coat on a polished stair,
I would charm a grande dame with my gallant air.
If I wore a . . .

I don't remember the rest of it. Do you?

JOHN:

If I wore a gold sword on a white verandah,
I would shock a simple heart with my heartless candor!

ALMA: Yes, that's how it goes. . . .

(*The music dies out. All over town the church bells begin to ring in various tones, some urgent, some melancholy, some tender, and horns are blown and things exploded or rattled.*)

There. There it is, the New Year! I hope it will be all that you want it to be! (*She says this with a sudden warm sincerity, smiling directly into his face.*) What a strange way we've spent New Year's Eve! Going to a Mary Pickford picture at the Delta Brilliant, having a long conversation in a cold square, and coming to a strange and bare little room like a hospital room where a fire wouldn't burn, in spite of our invocations!—But now—it's another year. . . . Another stretch of time to be discovered and entered and explored, and who knows what we'll find in it? Perhaps the coming true of our most improbable dreams!—I'm not ashamed of tonight! I think that you and I have been honest together, even though we failed!

(*Something changes between them. He reaches above him, turns out the light bulb. Almost invisibly at first a flickering red glow comes from the fireplace. She has lowered the veil attached to her plumed hat. He turns it gently back from her face.*)

ALMA: What are you doing that for?

JOHN: So that I won't get your veil in my mouth when I kiss you. (*He does.*)

(*Alma turns her face to the audience. The stage has darkened but a flickering red glow now falls across their figures. The fire has miraculously revived itself, a phoenix.*)

ALMA: I don't dare to believe it, but look, oh, look, look, John! (*She points at the fireplace from which the glow springs.*) Where did the fire come from?

JOHN: No one has ever been able to answer that question!

(*The red glow brightens.*)

(*The scene dims gradually out.*)

EPILOGUE

The Square, before the stone angel. A Fourth of July night an indefinite time later. Another soprano is singing.

A young traveling salesman approaches the bench on which Alma is seated. Band music is heard.

ALMA: How did you like her voice?

SALESMAN: She sang all right.

ALMA: Her face was blank. She didn't seem to know what to do with her hands. And I didn't think she sang with any emotion. A singer's face and her hands and even her heart are part of her equipment and ought to be used expressively when she sings. That girl is one of my former vocal pupils—I used to teach singing here—and so I feel that I have a right to be critical. I used to sing at public occasions like this. I don't any more.

SALESMAN: Why don't you any more?

ALMA: I'm not asked any more.

SALESMAN: Why's that?

(*Alma shrugs slightly and unfolds her fan. The salesman coughs a little.*)

ALMA: You're a stranger in town?

SALESMAN: I'm a traveling salesman.

ALMA: Ahhhh. A salesman who travels. You're younger than most of them are, and not so fat.

SALESMAN: I'm—uh—just starting out. . . .

ALMA: Oh.—The pyrotechnical display is late in starting.

SALESMAN: What—what did you say?

ALMA: The fireworks, I said. I said they ought to be starting. —I don't suppose you're familiar with this town. This town is Glorious Hill, Mississippi, population five thousand souls and an equal number of bodies.

SALESMAN: Ha ha! An equal number of bodies, that's good, ha ha!

ALMA: Isn't it? My name is Alma. Alma is Spanish for soul. Usted habla Español, señor?

SALESMAN: Un poquito. Usted habla Español, señorita?

ALMA: Tambien! Un poquito.

SALESMAN: Sometimes un poquito is plenty!

ALMA: Yes, indeed, and we have to be grateful for it. Sit down and I'll point out a few of our historical landmarks to you. Directly across the Square is the county courthouse: slaves were sold on the steps before the abolition of slavery in the South; now gray old men with nothing better to do sit on them all day. Over there is the Roman Catholic Church, a small unimpressive building, this being a Protestant town. And there—

(*She points in another direction.*)

—There is the Episcopal church. My father was rector of it before his death. It has an unusual steeple.

(*Her voice is rising in volume and tempo. One or two indistinct figures pause behind the stone bench, whispering, laughing at her. She turns about abruptly, imitating the laughter with a rather frightening boldness: the figures withdraw. She continues.*)

Yes, instead of a cross on top of the steeple, it has an enormous gilded hand with its index finger pointing straight up, accusingly, at—heaven. . . . (*She holds her hand up to demonstrate.*)

(*The young salesman laughs uneasily and glances back of him as other figures appear in silhouette behind them.*)

Are you looking at the angel of the fountain? It's the loveliest thing in Glorious Hill. The angel's name is Eternity. The name is carved in the stone block at the base of the statue, but it's not visible in this light, you'd have to read it with your fingers as if you were blind. . . . Straight ahead but not visible, either, is another part of town: it's concealed by the respectable front of the Square: it's called Tiger Town, it's the part of town that a traveling salesman might be interested in. Are you interested in it?

SALESMAN: What's it got to offer?

ALMA: Saloons, penny arcades, and rooms that can be rented for one hour, which is a short space of time for human beings, but there are living—organisms—only visible through a microscope—that live and die and are succeeded by several generations in an hour, or less than an hour, even. . . .

Oh!—There goes the first sky-rocket! Look at it burst into a million stars!

(*A long-drawn "Ahhh" from the unseen crowd in the Square as a rocket explodes above it and casts a dim gold radiance on Alma's upturned face. She closes her eyes very tightly for a moment, then rises, smiling down at the young salesman.*)

Now would you like to go to Tiger Town? The part of town back of the courthouse?

SALESMAN (*rising, nervously grinning*): Sure, why not, let's go!

ALMA: Good, go ahead, get a taxi, it's better if I follow a little behind you. . . .

SALESMAN: Don't get lost, don't lose me!

(*The salesman starts off jauntily as the band strikes up "The Santiago Waltz."*)

ALMA: Oh, no, I'm not going to lose you before I've lost you!

(*He is out of the lighted area.*)

(*Another rocket explodes, much lower and brighter: The angel, Eternity, is clearly revealed for a moment or two. Alma gives it a little parting salute as she follows after the young salesman, touching the plume on her hat as if to see if it were still there.*)

(*The radiance of the sky-rocket fades out; the scene is dimmed out with it.*)

The End

THE MILK TRAIN DOESN'T STOP HERE ANYMORE

> *"Consume my heart away; sick with desire*
> *And fastened to a dying animal*
> *It knows not what it is; and gather me*
> *Into the artifice of eternity."*
> —FROM *Sailing to Byzantium*
> BY WILLIAM BUTLER YEATS

AUTHOR'S NOTES

Sometimes theatrical effects and devices such as those I have adopted in the third (and I hope final) version of this play are ascribed to affectation or "artiness," so it may be helpful for me to explain a bit of my intention in the use of these effects and devices, and let the play's production justify or condemn them.

I have added to the cast a pair of stage assistants that function in a way that's between the Kabuki Theatre of Japan and the chorus of Greek theatre. My excuse, or reason, is that I think the play will come off better the further it is removed from conventional theatre, since it's been rightly described as an allegory and as a "sophisticated fairy tale."

Stage assistants in Japanese Kabuki are a theatrical expedient. They work on stage during the performance, shifting set pieces, placing and removing properties and furniture. Now and then in this play they have lines to speak, very short ones that serve as cues to the principal performers. . . . They should be regarded, therefore, as members of the cast. They sometimes take a balletic part in the action of the play. They should be dressed in black, very simply, to represent invisibility to the other players. The other players should never appear to see them, even when they speak or take part in the action, except when they appear "in costume."

THE SETTING represents the library and bedroom of the white villa, downstage, and the bedrooms of the pink and blue villinos: most importantly, the terrace of the white villa, I think, should extend the whole width of the proscenium, with a small apron for a white iron bench, a step down from the terrace.

Separations between interior and exterior should not be clearly defined except by lighting. When a single interior is being used, the other interior areas should be masked by light, folding screens, painted to blend with the cyclorama, that is, in sea-and-sky colors: they should be set in place and removed by the stage assistants. The cyclorama and these folding screens represent, preferably in a semi-abstract style, the mountain-sea-sky of Italy's Divina Costiera *in summer.*

Since the villas are, naturally, much farther apart than they can appear on the stage, the director could adopt a convention of having actors, who are to go from one villa to another, make their exits into the wings. They would wait till the stage assistants have removed the screens that mask the next interior to be used, and then come back out and enter that area.

August, 1963.

THE PLAYERS

MRS. GOFORTH
CHRISTOPHER FLANDERS
BLACKIE
THE WITCH OF CAPRI
RUDY, a watchman
GIULIO
SIMONETTA
TWO STAGE ASSISTANTS
   (Sometimes appearing in costume for small parts)
MEMBERS OF THE KITCHEN STAFF

PROLOGUE

At the rise of the curtain, the Stage Assistants are on stage. All the interior areas are masked by their individual screens. The light of the cyclorama suggests early dawn.

ONE: Daybreak: flag-raising ceremony on Mrs. Goforth's mountain.

TWO: Above the oldest sea in the Western world.

ONE: Banner.

(*Two hands it to him. Two places the staff in a socket near the right wings and attaches the flag to it. A fan in the wings whips it out as it is being raised, so that the audience can see the device on it clearly.*)

ONE: The device on the banner is a golden griffin.

TWO: A mythological monster, half lion, and half eagle.

ONE: And completely human.

TWO: Yes, wholly and completely human, that's true.

ONE: We are also a device.

TWO: A theatrical device of ancient and oriental origin.

ONE: With occidental variations, however.

TOGETHER: We are Stage Assistants. We move the screens that mask the interior playing areas of the stage presentation.

ONE: We fetch and carry.

TWO: Furniture and props.

ONE: To make the presentation—the play or masque or pageant—move more gracefully, quickly through the course of the two final days of Mrs. Goforth's existence.

MRS. GOFORTH'S VOICE (*offstage; half sleeping*): Ahhhhhhhh, Meeeeeeeeee . . .

(*There is heard the sound of distant church bells.*)

ONE: The actors will not seem to hear us except when we're in costume.

TWO: They will never see us, except when we're in costume.

ONE: Sometimes we will give them cues for speech and participate in the action.

MRS. GOFORTH'S VOICE (*off stage*): Ahhhhhhh, Ahhhhhh, Ahhhhhh . . .

(*One and Two show no reaction to this human cry.*)

MRS. GOFORTH'S VOICE (*off stage; more wakefully*): Another day, Oh, Christ, Oh, Mother of Christ!

(*There is silence, a pause, as the cyclorama's lighting indicates the progress of the day toward the meridian.*)

ONE *and* TWO (*together*): Our hearts are invisible, too.

(*The fan that whipped out the flag bearing the personal emblem, the griffin, of Mrs. Goforth, dies down and the flag subsides with it, and will not whip out again till the flag-lowering ceremony which will take place during the last three lines of the play.*

(*Now it is noon. Electric buzzers sound from various points on the stage. The Stage Assistants cross rapidly up center and remove a screen, the middle panel of which is topped by Mrs. Goforth's heraldic device, the gold griffin. The library of the white villa is unmasked and the play begins.*)

SCENE ONE

Mrs. Goforth and her secretary, Blackie, are on stage.

MRS. GOFORTH: I made my greatest mistake when I put a fast car in his hands, that red demon sports car, his fighting cock, I called it, which he drove insanely, recklessly, between my estate and the Casino at Monte Carlo, so recklessly that the Police Commissioner of Monaco came personally to ask me. Correction, *beg* me. Correction, *implore* me!—To insist that he go with me in the Rolls with a chauffeur at the wheel, as a protection of his life and of the lives of others.—M. le Commissionaire, I said, for me there are no others.—I know, Madame, he said, but for the others there are others.—Then I confessed to the Commissioner of Police that over this young poet with Romanov blood in his veins, I had no more control than my hands had over the sea-wind or the storms of the sea. At night he had flying dreams, he would thrash his arms like wings, and once his hand, on which he wore a signet

ring with the heavy Romanov crest, struck me in the mouth
and drew blood. After *that, necessarily*—twin beds . . .

BLACKIE: Mrs. Goforth, excuse me, but the last thing I have
typed up is—oh, here it is.—"My first two husbands were
ugly as apes and my third one resembled an ostrich."—
Now if this passage you're dictating to me comes in direct
sequence it will sound as if you had put the fast car in the
hands of the ostrich.

(*There is a long, tempestuous pause.*)

MRS. GOFORTH: Aren't you the sly one, oh, you're sly as ten
flies when you want to give me the needle, aren't you, Miss
Blackie? My first three marriages were into Dun and
Bradstreet's and the Social Register, both!—My first husband, Harlon Goforth, whose name I still carry after three
later marriages—that dignified financier, *tycoon!*—was a
man that Presidents put next to their wives at banquets in
the White House, and you sit there smoking in my face,
when you know I've been told to quit smoking, and you
make a joke of my work with a dead-pan expression on
your Vassar-girl face, in your Vassar-girl voice, and *I will
not tolerate it!*—You know goddamn well I'm talking
about my *fourth* husband, the *last* one, the one I married
for love, who plunged off the Grande Corniche between
Monte Carlo and—died that night in my arms in a clinic at
Nice: and my heart died with him! Forever! (*Her voice
breaks.*)

BLACKIE: I'm sorry, Mrs. Goforth. (*Puts out cigarette.*) I'm
no writer but I do think in writing there has to be some
kind of logical—sequence, continuity—between one bit
and the next bit, and the last thing you dictated to me—

MRS. GOFORTH: Was it something I put on the tape-recorder
in my bedroom after I'd been given one of those injections
that upset my balance at night?

BLACKIE: I took it off your bedroom tape this morning.

MRS. GOFORTH: Always check those night recordings with me
before we begin to work the following morning. We're
working against time, Blackie. Remember, try to remember, I've got two deadlines to meet, my New York publishers and my London publishers, both, have my memoirs on

their Fall List. I said fall. It's already late in August. Now do you see why there's no time for goofing, or must I draw you a picture of autumn leaves falling?

BLACKIE: Mrs. Goforth, I think those publishers' deadlines are unrealistic, not to say cruel, and as for me, I not only have to function as a secretary but as an *editor*, I have to *collate* the material you dictate to me and I'm not being sly or cruel, I'm just being *honest* with you when I tell you—

MRS. GOFORTH (*cutting in*): All cruel people describe themselves as paragons of frankness!

BLACKIE: I think we'd better stop now.

MRS. GOFORTH: *I* think we'd better go *on*, now!

BLACKIE: Mrs. Goforth, the Police Commissioner of Monaco was right when he told you that there were "others." I am one of those "others." I've had no sleep, scarcely any at all and—

MRS. GOFORTH: *You've* had no sleep? What about me, how much sleep do *I* get?

BLACKIE: You sleep till noon or after!

MRS. GOFORTH: Under sedation, with nightmares!

BLACKIE: Your broker is on the phone . . .

(*The Stage Assistants have entered with phone.*)

MRS. GOFORTH (*immediately brightening*): Chuck, baby, how're we doing? Ah-huh, glamour stocks still slipping? Don't hold on to 'em, dump them before they drop under what I bought 'em at, baby. We'll start buying back when they hit the basement level.—Don't give me an argument, Sell! *Sell! Hell!*—It's building into a crash! So, baby, I'm hitting the silk! High, low, jack and the game! Ho ho!

(*She bangs down the phone, exhilarated, and it is removed by one of the Stage Assistants. The other Assistant has rushed to the stage-right wings, and he now appears in a white doctor's jacket. This is one of the costumes that make the Assistants seen and heard by the other actors.*)

ASSISTANT (*as Dr. Lullo*): Buon giorno!

MRS. GOFORTH: What's he wheeling in here that looks like a baby-buggy for a baby from Mars?

(*He is pushing a "mock-up" of a portable X-ray machine.*)

BLACKIE: It's something your doctor in Rome, Dr.—what? Rengucci?—had sent up here to spare you the trouble of interrupting your work to take a new set of pictures to show what progress there is in the healing of the lesion, the lung abscess, that—

MRS. GOFORTH: Oh, so you're having private consultations with that quack in Rome?

BLACKIE: Just routine calls that he told me to make sure to spare you the trouble of—

MRS. GOFORTH: Spare me no trouble, just spare me your goddamn *presumptions!*

DR. LULLO: *Forse più tardi, forse un po' più tardi?*

MRS. GOFORTH: Will you get your sneaky grin out of here? *Va, va. Presto!*

(*He retires quickly from the lighted area. Mrs. Goforth advances both fearfully and threateningly upon the medical apparatus.*)

My outside is public, but my insides are private, and the Rome quack was hired by my bitch daughter that wants to hang black crepe on me. Wants to know if I'm going, and when I'll go. Doesn't know that if and when I do go, she gets one dollar, the rest goes to a—a *cultural foundation!*— named for *me*! Blackie, wheel this thing off the terrace, to the cliff-side of the mountain and shove it over!

BLACKIE: Mrs. Goforth, you mustn't ask me to do ridiculous things.

MRS. GOFORTH: I don't do ridiculous things and don't ask anyone else to do 'em for me. But if you think it's ridiculous of me to show my opinion of Rengucci's presumption and— *Look, watch this! Here we go, perambulator from Mars. Out, down, go!*

(*She thrusts it violently onto the forestage, where it is seized by the Stage Assistants and rushed into the wings. She crosses onto the forestage, leaning forward to watch its fall off the cliff. After a couple of moments, we hear a muted crash that signifies its destruction on the rocky beach under the mountain. Then she straightens, dizzily, with a fierce laugh, and staggers back toward the library area, where Blackie, meanwhile, has closed her notebook and rushed off stage. Heart-beat sounds*) *are heard amplified, as Mrs. Goforth moves distractedly about the library area, calling out breathlessly for Blackie. She presses several buttons on the "intercom" box on the desk: electric buzzers sound from here and there on the stage but no one responds: She washes down a pill with a swig of brandy. The heart-beat sounds subside as her agitation passes. She sinks into the desk chair.)*

Ahhh . . .

(She activates her tape-recorder and speaks into it with a voice that is plaintively childlike.)

Blackie, the boss is sorry she took her nerves out on you. It's those night injections I take for my—neuralgia—neuritis —bursitis. The pick-up pills and the quiet-down pills: nerves shot . . .

(A sea wave booms under the mountain.)

Oh, God, Blackie, I'm *scared!* You know what I'm scared of? Possibly, maybe, the Boss is—dying this summer! On the *Divina Costiera,* under that, that—angry old lion, the sun, and the—insincere sympathy of the— *(Her mood suddenly reverses again.)* No, no, no, I don't want her goddamn sympathy, I'll take that slobbery stuff off the tape and— *Begin! Continue! Dictation! (She rises, paces the forestage with a portable "mike.")*

(A phrase of lyrical music is heard. She stops short, lifting a jeweled hand as if to say "Listen!" Then suddenly the accretion of years is broken through. The stage dims out except for her follow-spot on the forestage.)

"Cloudy symbols of a—high romance . . ." Who said that, where is that from? Check tomorrow, Blackie, in the *Book of Familiar Quotations* . . . Begin, continue dictation.

(A pause, while she paces back and forth.)

The love of true understanding isn't something a man brings up the road to you every day or once in a blue moon, even. But it was brought to me once, almost too late but not quite. . . .

The hard shell of my heart, the calcium deposits grown around it, could still be cracked, broken through, and my last husband broke through it, and I was brought back to life and almost back to—what?—Youth. . . .

The nights, the nights, especially the first one I spent with Alex! The way that a lover undresses, removes his clothes the first night you spend together, is a clue, a definite clue, to your whole future relationship with him, you know. Alex unclothed himself *unconsciously gracefully*, as if before no one in a—room made of windows, and then, unclothed—*correction:* clothed in a god's perfection, his naked body!—he went from window to window, all the way round the bedroom, drawing the curtains together so that daybreak beginning wouldn't wake us early from the sleep after love, which is a heavenly sleep that shouldn't be broken early. Then came to rest in a god's perfection beside me: reached up to turn off the light: I reached up and turned it *back on!*

(*At this point, Mrs. Goforth's watchdogs* (lupos) *set up a great clamor on the inland side of the mountain. A Man shouts. Woman Servants scream in Italian. Somebody calls, "Rudy, Rudy!" Mrs. Goforth is very annoyed by this disruption of her tender recollections: she presses various buttons on the intercom box on her desk.*)

MRS. GOFORTH (*shouting over the dogs*): Che succede! Che fa, Cretini! Stronzi! (*etc.*)

(*The savage barking continues but diminishes a little in volume as a Young Man, who has just been assaulted by dogs, limps and stumbles onto the terrace. He bears a heavy white sack over his shoulder, looking back as if to make sure he's no longer pursued. Blackie appears behind him, panting, looking as if she'd also been roughed up by the dogs.*)

BLACKIE (*to the Young Man*): Places go mad, it's catching, people catch it! (*She draws a breath.*) There's a doctor up here, I'll get him for you.

CHRIS: Can I see Mrs. Goforth?

BLACKIE: Sit down somewhere. I'll see if she can see you, and I'll—

(*The Young Man, Chris, limps out upon the forestage, sinks onto a white iron bench. A wave crashes below the mountain. He looks blankly out at the audience for a moment, then shakes his head and utters a desperate-sounding laugh. Blackie rushes into the library area.*)

Mrs. Goforth, I can't stand this sort of thing!
MRS. GOFORTH: *What?*
BLACKIE: Those dogs of Rudy's, those wolves, attacked a young man just now.
MRS. GOFORTH: What young man, doing what?
BLACKIE: He was climbing the mountain to see you!
MRS. GOFORTH: Who is he, what does he want?
BLACKIE: I didn't stop to ask that. I had to drive the dogs off to keep him from being torn to pieces before I—asked him questions. Look! (*She shows Mrs. Goforth a laceration on her thigh, just over the knee.*) The others just watched and screamed like children at a circus!
MRS. GOFORTH: Sit down, have a brandy. A place like this is always protected by dogs.

(*There is the sound of another wave crashing.*)

CHRIS: *Boom.* (*He discovers that his leather pants, lederhosen, have been split down his thigh.*)
BLACKIE: That gangster's bodyguard, Rudy, just stood there and watched!
MRS. GOFORTH: Blackie, this estate contains things appraised by Lloyd's at over two million pounds sterling, besides my jewels and summer furs, and that's why it has to be guarded against trespassers, uninvited intruders. Have you had your anti-tetanus shot, or—whatever they call it?
BLACKIE: Yes, I'm all right but he isn't. (*She presses a button on the intercom box.*)
MRS. GOFORTH: Who're you calling?
BLACKIE: I'm calling Dr. Lullo.
MRS. GOFORTH: Stop that, leave that to me! Do you think I want to be sued by this trespasser? Get away from my desk. I'm going to buzz Rudy. (*She presses another button.*) Rudy, *dove* Rudy? *Io lo voglio in libreria, subito, presto! Capito?*

(*The Young Man staggers to his feet and calls: "Mrs. Goforth!" Mrs. Goforth picks up a pair of binoculars and gazes out at the terrace. Blackie stares at her with consternation.*)

CHRIS: Mrs. Goforth?

(*Rudy, the watchman, in semi-military costume, appears on the terrace.*)

RUDY: Shut up, stop that shouting. (*He enters the library area.*)

MRS. GOFORTH: Aw. Rudy. What happened, what's the report?

RUDY: I caught this man out there climbing up here from the highway.

BLACKIE: He set the dogs on him.

MRS. GOFORTH: That's what the dogs are here for. Rudy, what's the sign say on the gate on the highway?

RUDY: "Private Property."

MRS. GOFORTH: Just "Private Property," not "Beware of Dogs"?

RUDY: There's nothing about dogs down there.

MRS. GOFORTH: Well, for Chrissake, put up "Beware of Dogs," too. Put it up right away. If this man sues me, I've got to prove *there was a "Beware of Dogs"* sign.

BLACKIE: How can you prove what's not true?

MRS. GOFORTH (*to Rudy*): Go on, hurry it up!

(*Rudy leaves.*)

MRS. GOFORTH (*to Blackie*): Now pull yourself together. What a day! It's too much for me, I'll have to go back to bed. . . .

(*Giulio, the gardener's son, a boy of seventeen, appears on the terrace.*)

GIULIO (*to the Young Man, who is applying an antiseptic to his lacerations*): Come va? Meglio?

CHRIS: *Si, meglio, grazie.* Do you understand English?

GIULIO: Yes, English.

CHRIS: Good. Would you please tell Mrs. Goforth that Mr. Christopher Flanders is here to see her, and— Oh, give her this book, there's a letter in it, and—ask her if I may see

her, don't—don't mention the dogs, just say I—I want
very much to see her, if she's willing to see me. . . .

(*During this exchange on the forestage, Mrs. Goforth has
picked up a pair of binoculars. Giulio knocks at the screen
that represents the door between the terrace and the library.*)

MRS. GOFORTH: Come in, come in, *avanti!*

(*The Boy enters, excitedly.*)

GIULIO: Man bring this up road.

MRS. GOFORTH (*gingerly accepting the book in her hand*):
Young man that dogs bite bring this—(*squints at book*)—
to me?

GIULIO: This, this, brings! Up mountains!

(*She turns the book and squints at a photograph of the author.*)

MRS. GOFORTH: Man resemble this photo?

(*Blackie is still quietly weeping at the desk.*)

GIULIO: *Non capisco.*

MRS. GOFORTH: Man!—*Uomo!*—resemble, look like—this
photo?

GIULIO: Yes, this man. This man that dogs bite on mountain.
(*Points out excitedly toward the Young Man on the bench.*)

MRS. GOFORTH: Well, go back out—*vada fuori e dica*—
Blackie! Tell him to go back out there and say that I am
very upset over the accident with the dogs, but that I
would like to know why he came here without invitation,
and that I am not responsible for anybody that comes here
without invitation!

BLACKIE (*strongly, as she rises*): No, I will not. I will not give
a man nearly killed by dogs such an inhuman message.

MRS. GOFORTH: He hasn't been seriously hurt, he's standing
up now. Listen he's shouting my name.

(*The Young Man has called, "Mrs. Goforth?" in a hoarse,
panting voice. His shirt and one leg of his lederhosen have
been nearly stripped off him. He has the opposite appearance
to that which is ordinarily encountered in poets as they are
popularly imagined. His appearance is rough and weathered;*

his eyes wild, haggard. He has the look of a powerful, battered, but still undefeated, fighter.)

CHRIS: *Mrs. Goforth!*

(*His call is almost imperious. A wave crashes under the mountain: Chris closes his eyes, opens them, crosses to the lounge chair on the terrace and throws himself down in it, dropping a large canvas sack on the terrace tiles. The excited, distant barking of the dogs has now died out. Female voices are still heard exclaiming at a distance, in Italian.*)

MRS. GOFORTH (*looking again through her binoculars*): Pull yourself together. The continent has been overrun by beatniks lately, I've been besieged by them, Blackie. Writers that don't write, painters that don't paint. A bunch of freeloaders, Blackie. They come over here on a Jugoslavian freighter with about a hundred dollars in travelers' checks and the summer addresses of everybody they think they can free-load on. That's why I'm not so sympathetic to them. Look, I made it, I got it because I made it, but they'll never work for a living as long as there is a name on their sucker list, Blackie. Now cut the hysterics now, and go out there and—

BLACKIE: *What?*

MRS. GOFORTH: Interrogate him for me!

BLACKIE: Interrogate? A badly injured young man?

MRS. GOFORTH: Trespasser! Get that straight in case he tries to sue me. (*She continues inspecting him through the binoculars.*) Hmm, he's not bad-looking, in a wild sort of way, but I'm afraid he's a beatnik. He has a beard and looks like he hasn't seen water for bathing purposes in a couple of weeks.

BLACKIE: You would, too, if a pack of wild dogs had attacked you.

MRS. GOFORTH: *Watchdogs, lupos,* defending private property: get that straight. He has on lederhosen. Hmm.—The first time I saw Alex, in the Bavarian Alps, he had on lederhosen and the right legs for 'em, too. And it's odd, it's a coincidence that I was dictating some recollections of Alex, who was a poet, when this young—*trespasser*—got here. Now if the sweat and the filthy appearance just come from the dogs' attack on him, I mean from *meeting* the dogs, you can tell by the smell of him while you're talking to him.

BLACKIE: You want me to go out and smell him? I'm not a dog, Mrs. Goforth.

MRS. GOFORTH: You don't have to be a dog to smell a beatnik. Sometimes they smell to high heaven because not washing is almost a religion with 'em. Why, last summer one of those ones you see in *Life* and *Look*, came up here. I had to talk to him with a handkerchief held to my nose. It was a short conversation and the last one between us.

(*Chris staggers up from the lounge chair and shouts: "Mrs. Goforth."*)

MRS. GOFORTH: What impudence, going on shouting at me like that!

BLACKIE: I think the least you could do is go out there yourself and show some decent concern over the dogs' attack on him.

MRS. GOFORTH: I'm not going to see him till I've checked with my lawyers about my liability, if any. So be a good scout, a nice Brownie den-mother, and go out there and—

BLACKIE: *Interrogate* him?

MRS. GOFORTH: Ask him politely what he wants here, why he came to see me without invitation, and if you get the right answers, put him in the pink villino. And I'll see him later, after my siesta. He might be O.K. for a while, and I could use some male companionship up here since all I've got is you and Generalissimo Rudy for company this summer. I do need male company, Blackie, that's what I need to be me, the old Sissy Goforth, high, low, jack and the game!

BLACKIE: I'll go see if he's seriously hurt.

(*She crosses out, to the terrace, and approaches Chris limping about the forestage.*)

BLACKIE (*to Chris*): How are you, are you all right, now?

CHRIS: Not all right, but better. Could I see Mrs. Goforth?

BLACKIE: Not yet, not right now, but she told me to put you in the little pink guest house, if you can—walk a little. It's a little way down the mountain.

CHRIS: Well, thank God, and— (*He tries to lift his sack and stumbles under its weight.*) Mrs. Goforth, of course . . .
BLACKIE (*calling*): *Giulio! Vieni qui!*

(*Giulio comes on to the terrace.*)

BLACKIE: *Porta questo sacco al villino rosa.*
GIULIO (*lifting sack*): *Pesante!—Dio . . .*
BLACKIE: *Tu sei pesante nella testa!* (*Then to Chris*) You can bathe and rest till Mrs. Goforth feels better and is ready to see you.
CHRIS: Oh.—Thanks . . .

(*He follows her off the terrace. The Stage Assistants fold and remove the screen masking a bed upstage. The bed is small but rococo, and all pink. The Stage Assistants return downstage with the screen and wait near Mrs. Goforth, who is still watching the terrace scene through her binoculars.*)

MRS. GOFORTH (*to herself*): Ah, God . . . (*Raises a hand unconsciously to a pain in her chest.*)

(*The Stage Assistants unfold the screen before her, as the library area is dimmed out.*)

SCENE TWO

The area representing the pink villino is lighted: the light is warm gold afternoon light and striated as if coming through half-open shutters. A cupid is lowered over the bed by a wire: there are smaller cupids on the four posts of the bed. Blackie, Chris, and Giulio enter the narrow lighted area, the young poet limping. Giulio bears the canvas sack with difficulty, muttering "Pesante!"

BLACKIE: Here you are, this is it. Now!
CHRIS: What?
BLACKIE: How are your legs? Mrs. Goforth keeps a doctor on the place, a resident physician, and I think he ought to come here and do a proper job on those dog-bites.
CHRIS: They're not that bad, really.

BLACKIE: Have you had shots?

CHRIS: Shots?

BLACKIE: For tetanus?

CHRIS: Yes, yes, sometime or other. I'm actually just—tired out.

BLACKIE: Giulio, see if the water's running in the bathroom. I'm sure you want to bathe before you rest, Mr. Flanders. Oh, oh, no covers on the bed.

CHRIS: Don't bother about covers on it.

BLACKIE: I think, I have an idea, you're going to sleep a good while, and you might as well sleep comfortably. Giulio. Covers for bed.

GIULIO: *Dove?*

BLACKIE: *Cerca nell' armadio del bagno.*

(*Giulio goes out. Chris sits down on the foot of the narrow bed. His head falls forward.*)

Mr. Flanders! (*He pulls himself up.*) Please try to stay awake till the bed's made up and you've bathed.

CHRIS: Your name is—? (*He rises, unsteadily.*)

BLACKIE: Frances Black, called Blackie.

CHRIS: How do you do. Mine's Flanders, Christopher Flanders.

(*Giulio enters.*)

GIULIO: *Non c'è acqua.*

BLACKIE: Well, tell your papa to turn the water on.

(*Giulio tosses some pink silk sheets on the bed and runs back out.*)

I hope you don't mind camphor, the smell of camphor.

(*He shakes his head slightly, holding onto a bed post.*)

The water ought to be running in a minute.

CHRIS: I hope there's a shower. A tub wouldn't be safe for me. I don't think even drowning would wake me up.

BLACKIE: I'll wait here till you've bathed.

CHRIS: It's wonderful here after—yesterday in—Naples . . .

BLACKIE: Would you please get on the other side of the bed and help me spread these sheets?

(*He staggers around the bed. They make it up.*)

CHRIS: You—

BLACKIE: What?

CHRIS: I wondered if you're related to Mrs. Goforth or if you're—

BLACKIE: Not related. I'm working for Mrs. Goforth: secretarial work. She's writing a sort of—all right, you can sit down, now—she's writing her memoirs and I'm helping her with it, the little, as best I—can. . . .

(*He sinks back onto the bed and drops his head in his hands.*)

Mr. Flanders, the water's turned on, now.

CHRIS (*staggering up*): Oh. Good. Thank you. This way? (*Starts off.*)

BLACKIE: I'll fill the tub for you. Do you want warm or cold water, or—

CHRIS: Cold, please. Let me do it.

BLACKIE: No, just stay on your feet till it's ready for you.

(*She passes him and goes off. There is the sound of running water. He sits exhaustedly on the bed and sways. His forehead strikes the newel-post which is topped by a cupid. The room is full of painted and carved cupids. He looks up at the cupid on the post, shakes his head with a sad, wry grimace, drops his head in his hands, and slumps over again. Blackie returns from the bathroom with a towel-robe. She claps her hands.*)

BLACKIE: I told you to stay on your feet.

CHRIS (*struggling up*): Sorry. What is—I almost said "Where am I?"

BLACKIE: Here's a towel-robe for you. You'd better just duck in and out.

CHRIS (*crossing to door and looking back at her from the threshold*): Is this called the Cupid Room?

BLACKIE: I don't know if it's called that but it should be.

CHRIS (*starting to leave but on threshold*): What a remarkable bathtub, it's almost the size of a deck pool on a steamship.

BLACKIE (*dryly*): Yes, Mrs. Goforth thinks a bathtub should be built for at least two people.

CHRIS (*entering*): She must have been to Japan.

BLACKIE: Yes. She probably owns it.

(*Chris enters the bathroom: There is a splash, a loud gasp.*)

BLACKIE: Oh, I should have warned you, it's mountain spring water.

CHRIS: Does it come from a glacier?

(*Blackie picks up the cords of his rucksack to drag it away from the bedside. She finds it startlingly heavy. She kneels beside it to loosen the drawstrings, draws out a silvery section of some metalwork. She rises guiltily as Chris reappears in the towel-robe.*)

BLACKIE: You're—shivering.

CHRIS: For exercise. Shivering's good exercise.

BLACKIE: I don't think you need any more exercise for a while. How did you get this sack of yours up the mountain?

CHRIS: Carried it—from Genoa.

BLACKIE: I could hardly drag it away from the bed.

CHRIS: Yes, it's heavy with metal. I work in metal, now. I construct mobiles, but it's not the mobiles that are heavy, it's the metalsmith tools.

BLACKIE: You, uh—sell—mobiles, do you?

CHRIS: No, mostly give 'em away. Of course I—

BLACKIE: What?

CHRIS: Some things aren't made to be sold. Oh, you sell them, but they're not made for that, not for selling, they're made for—

BLACKIE: Making them?

CHRIS: Is there something buzzing in the room or is the buzz in my head? Oh, a wasp. It'll fly back out the shutter. Is this a cigarette box? (*Opens box on small bedside table.*) Empty.

BLACKIE: Have a *Nazionale*. (*She offers him the pack.*)

CHRIS: Thank you.

BLACKIE: I'll leave the pack here, I have more in my room.—Your hair's not dry, it's still wet. (*He shakes his head like a spaniel.*) Dry it with the towel and get right into bed. I have to get back to work now. I work here, I do secretarial work and I—

CHRIS: Don't go right away.

BLACKIE: You need to rest, right away.

CHRIS: The ice water woke me up.

BLACKIE: Just temporarily, maybe.

CHRIS: I'll rest much better if I know a bit more, such as— Did Mrs. Goforth remember who I was?

BLACKIE: I don't know about that but she liked your looks, if that's any comfort to you.

CHRIS: I didn't see her. She saw me?

BLACKIE: She inspected you through a pair of military field-glasses before she had me take you to the pink villa with the—king-size bathtub, the pink silk sheets, and the cupids.

CHRIS: Do they, uh—signify something?

BLACKIE: Everything signifies something. I'll—I'll shut the shutters and you get into bed. (*She turns away from him.*)

CHRIS (*sitting on the bed*): What is the program for me when I awake?

BLACKIE (*with her back still toward him*): Don't you make out your own programs?

CHRIS: Not when I'm visiting people. I try to adapt myself as well as I can to their programs, when I'm—visiting people.

BLACKIE: Is that much of the time?

CHRIS: Yes, that's—*most* of the time. . . .

BLACKIE: Well, I think you're in for a while, if you play your cards right. You do want to be in, don't you? After hauling that sack all the way from Genoa and up this mountain to Mrs. Goforth? Or have the pink silk sheets and the cupids scared you, worse than the dogs you ran into?

CHRIS: You have a sharp tongue, Blackie.

BLACKIE: I'm sorry but I was mistaken when I thought I had strong nerves. They're finished for today if not for the season, for—years. . . . (*She starts away.*)

CHRIS: Have a cigarette with me. (*He extends the pack to her.*)

BLACKIE: You want to get some more information from me?

CHRIS: I'd sleep better if I knew a bit more.

BLACKIE: I wouldn't be too sure of *that.*

CHRIS: I've heard, I've been told, that Mrs. Goforth hasn't been well lately.

(*Blackie laughs as if startled.*)

CHRIS: She's lucky to have you with her.

BLACKIE: Why?

CHRIS: I can see you're—sympathetic and understanding about Mrs. Goforth's—condition, but—not sentimental about it. Aren't I right about that?

BLACKIE: I'm not understanding about it, and I'm afraid I've stopped being sympathetic. Mrs. Goforth is a dying monster. (*Rises.*) *Sorry, I'm talking too much!*

CHRIS: No, not enough. Go on.

BLACKIE: Why do you want to hear it?

CHRIS: I've climbed a mountain and fought off a wolf pack to see her.

BLACKIE: *Why?*

CHRIS: No where else to go, now.

BLACKIE: Well, that's an honest admission.

CHRIS: Let's stick to honest admissions.

BLACKIE (*sitting back down by the bed*): All right. I'll give you something to sleep on. You'll probably wish I hadn't but here it is. She eats nothing but pills: around the clock. And at night she has nightmares in spite of morphine injections. I rarely sleep a night through without an electric buzzer by my bed waking me up. I tried ignoring the buzzer, but found out that if I did she'd come stumbling out of her bedroom, onto the terrace, raving into a microphone that's connected to a tape-recorder, stumbling about and raving her—

CHRIS: Raving?

BLACKIE: Yes, her demented memoirs, her memories of her career as a great international beauty which she thinks she still is. I'm here, employed here, to—take down and type up these—

CHRIS: Memories?

BLACKIE: That's enough for you now. Don't you think so?

CHRIS: She doesn't know she's—

BLACKIE: Dying? Oh, no! Won't face it! Apparently never thought that her—legendary—existence—could go on less than forever! Insists she's only suffering from neuralgia, neuritis, allergies, and bursitis! Well? Can you still sleep? After this—bedtime story?

CHRIS: Blackie, I've had a good bit of experience with old dying ladies, scared to death of dying, ladies with lives like Mrs. Goforth's behind them, which they won't think are over, and I've discovered it's possible to give them, at least to offer them, something closer to what they need than what they think they still want. Yes. . . . Would you please throw me the strings of my sack, Blackie?

(*She tosses the strings to the bedside. He hauls the rucksack over, leans out of the bed to open it: removes a mobile.*)

Give her this for me, Blackie. It took me six months to make it. It has a name, a title. It's called "The Earth Is a Wheel in a Great Big Gambling Casino."

(*Music is heard playing softly.*)

BLACKIE:—"The Earth Is—"?

CHRIS: ". . . a Wheel in a Great Big Gambling Casino." I made it on hinges, it has to be unfolded before it's hung up. I think you'd better hang it up before you show it to her, if you don't mind, and in a place where it will turn in the wind, so it will make a—more impressive—impression. . . . And this is for you, this book. (*He hands a book to her.*)

BLACKIE: Poems?

CHRIS: It's a verse-adaptation I made of the writings of a Swami, a great Hindu teacher, my—teacher. Oh. One thing more. I'd like to make a phone call to a friend, an invalid lady, in Sicily—Taormina, a mountain above Taormina.— Would Mrs. Goforth object if I—?

BLACKIE: Not if she doesn't know. What's the number?

(*He gives her the number in Italian and is told that it will not go through for some time.*)

There'll be a delay. Is it very important?

CHRIS: Yes, it is. She's dying. Blackie? You're the kindest person I've met in a long, long time. . . .

BLACKIE (*Drawing a sheet over him*): This sort of thing is just automatic in women.

CHRIS: Only in some of them, Blackie. (*His eyes fall shut.*)

BLACKIE: You're falling asleep.

CHRIS: Yes, automatic—like kindness in some women. . . .

(*He drops his cigarette and she picks it up and crosses to the phone.*)

BLACKIE (*Into the phone*): Mariella? Bring a tray of food up to the pink villa. Better make it cold things. The guest's asleep and won't wake up for hours. (*She hangs up, looks at Chris and exits with book.*)

(*Lights dim on this area and a spot of light immediately picks up Mrs. Goforth on the terrace. The Stage Assistants have set a screen before this area and light is brought up on the forestage which represents the terrace of the white villa. The Stage Assistants remove a wide screen and we see Mrs. Goforth with two servants, Giulio and Simonetta. Mrs. Goforth is preparing to take a sun bath on the terrace. Her appearance is bizarre. She has on a silk robe covered with the signs of the zodiac, and harlequin sunglasses with purple lenses.*)

MRS. GOFORTH (*in her very "pidgin" Italian*): Table here. *Capito? Tabolo.* (*Points.*) *Qui.* On *tabolo*, I want—What are you grinning at?

GIULIO (*very Neapolitan*): *Niente, niente ma scusa!* (*He places table by chaise.*)

SIMONETTA (*giggling*): *Tabolo.*

MRS. GOFORTH: On *tabolo voglio—una bottiglia d'acqua minerale, San Pellegrino, capite, molto ghiacciata: capite?*

(*Simonetta giggles behind her hand at Giulio's antic deference to the Signora. Mrs. Goforth glares suspiciously from one to the other, turning from side to side like a bull wondering which way to charge. Blackie enters the terrace area with the mobile, folded.*)

Che stronzi! Both of 'em.

BLACKIE: You mustn't call them that, it has an insulting meaning.

MRS. GOFORTH: I know what it means and that's what I mean it to mean. Generalissimo Rudy says they sleep together and carry on together some nights right here on my terrace.

BLACKIE: They're from Naples, and—

MRS. GOFORTH: What's that got to do with it?

BLACKIE:—and Generalissimo Rudy wants the girl for himself, so he—

MRS. GOFORTH: *Will you please tell them what I want on the table by this chaise. Here?*

BLACKIE: What do you want on the table?

MRS. GOFORTH: I—want a cold bottle of *acqua minerale*, cigarettes, matches, my Bain-Soleil, my codeine and empirin
tablets, a shot of cognac on the rocks, the Paris *Herald-
Tribune*, the Rome *Daily American*, the Wall Street
Journal, the London *Times* and *Express*, the— Hey, what
did you do with the—

BLACKIE: The visitor?

MRS. GOFORTH: The beatnik trespasser, yes, and what the hell
have you got there that rattles like a string of boxcars crossing a railyard switch?

BLACKIE: The young man's in the pink villa, where you told
me to put him. This is something he gave me for me to
give you. It seems he constructs mobiles.

MRS. GOFORTH: Mobiles? Constructs?

BLACKIE: Yes, those metal decorations. He gives them titles.
This one's called "The Earth Is a Wheel in a Great Big
Gambling Casino."

MRS. GOFORTH: Is it a present—or something he hopes he
can sell me?

BLACKIE: It's a present. He wanted me to suspend it before
you saw it, but since you've already seen it—shall I hang it
up somewhere?

MRS. GOFORTH: No, just put it down somewhere and help me
up. The sun is making me dizzy. I don't know why I came
out here. What am I doing out here?

BLACKIE: I was going to remind you that Dr. Rengucci
warned you not to expose yourself to the sun, till the chest
abscess, the lesion, has healed completely.

MRS. GOFORTH: *I don't have a chest abscess!*—Stop putting
bad mouth on me! Open the door, I'm going in the
library. . . .

(*The Stage Assistants rush out and remove the screen masking
that area as Mrs. Goforth starts toward it, lifting a hand like
a Roman Empress saluting the populace.*)

MRS. GOFORTH (*as she enters the library area*): What did he
have to say?

BLACKIE: The—?

MRS. GOFORTH: *Trespasser*, what did he have to say?

BLACKIE: About what?

MRS. GOFORTH: *Me.*

BLACKIE: He wondered if you remembered him or not.

MRS. GOFORTH: Oh, I might have met him somewhere, sometime or other, when I was still meeting people, interested in it, before they all seemed like the same person over and over and I got tired of the person.

BLACKIE: This young man won't seem like the same person to you.

MRS. GOFORTH: That remains to be— Blackie, y'know what I need to shake off this, this—depression, what would do me more good this summer than all the shots and pills in the pharmaceutical kingdom? I need me a lover.

BLACKIE: What do you mean by "a lover"?

MRS. GOFORTH: I mean a lover! What do *you* mean by a lover, or is that word outside your Vassar vocabulary?

BLACKIE: I've only had one lover, my husband Charles, and I lost Charles last spring.

MRS. GOFORTH: What beats me is how you could have a husband named Charles and not call him Charlie. I mean the fact that you called him Charles and not Charlie describes your whole relationship with him, don't it?

BLACKIE (*flaring*): *Stop about my husband!*

MRS. GOFORTH: The dead are dead and the living are living!

BLACKIE: Not so, I'm not dead but not living!

MRS. GOFORTH: Giulio! (*He has entered the library area with the mineral water.*) *Va al villino rosa e portami qui* the sack—*il sacco!—dell' ospite là.*

BLACKIE: Oh, no, you mustn't do that, that's too undignified of you!

(*Giulio goes out to perform this errand.*)

MRS. GOFORTH: Take care of your own dignity and lemme take care of mine. It's a perfectly natural, legitimate thing to do, to go through the luggage of a trespasser on your place for—possible—weapons, and so forth. . . . (*She sits at the desk.*) Pencil, notebook, dictation.

(*Blackie pays no attention to these demands, but lights a cigarette behind Mrs. Goforth's back as she begins dictating.*)

—Season of '24, costume ball at Cannes. Never mind the style, now. Polish up later. . . .

—Went as Lady Godiva. All of me, gilded, my whole body painted gold, except for—green velvet fig leaf. Breasts? Famous breasts? Nude, nude completely!

—Astride a white horse, led into the ballroom by a young nigger. Correction. A Nubian—slave-boy. Appearance created a riot. Men clutched at my legs, trying to dismount me so they could *mount* me. Maddest party ever, ever imaginable in those days of mad parties. This set the record for madness.—In '29, so much ended, but not for me. I smelt the crash coming, animal instinct—very valuable asset. Put everything into absolutely indestructible utilities such as—Tel. and Tel., *electric power.* . . .

(*Giulio enters with the rucksack.*)

GIULIO: *Ecco, il sacco!* (*Drops it before Mrs. Goforth with a crash that makes her gasp.*)

BLACKIE: May I be excused? I don't want to take part in this.

MRS. GOFORTH: Stay here. You heard that noise, that wasn't just clothes, that was metal.

BLACKIE: Yes, I suppose he's come here to seize the mountain by force of arms.

MRS. GOFORTH (*to Giulio*): Giulio, open, *aprite*!

(*Giulio opens the sack and the inspection begins.*)

BLACKIE: I told you he made mobiles. The sack's full of metal-smith's tools.

MRS. GOFORTH: He hauled this stuff up the mountain?

BLACKIE: It didn't fly up.

MRS. GOFORTH: He must have the back of a dray horse. Tell this idiot to hold the sack upside down and empty it all on the floor, he's taking things out like it was a Christmas stocking.

BLACKIE: I'll do it. He'd break everything. (*She carefully empties the contents of the sack onto the floor.*)

MRS. GOFORTH: See if he's got any travelers' checks and how much they amount to.

BLACKIE (*ignoring this order and picking up a book*): He offered me this book, I forgot to take it.

MRS. GOFORTH (*glaring at the book through her glasses*): *Meanings Known and Unknown.* It sounds like something religious.

BLACKIE: He says it's a verse-adaptation he did of a—

MRS. GOFORTH: Swami Something. See if you can locate the little book they always carry with names and addresses in it. Sometimes it gives you a clue to their backgrounds and—inclinations. Here. This is it. (*Snatches up an address book.*)—Christ, Lady Emerald Fowler, she's been in hell for ten years.—Christabel Smithers, that name rings a long-ago church bell for a dead bitch, too. Mary Cole, *dead!* Laurie Emerson, *dead!* Is he a graveyard sexton? My God, where's his passport?

BLACKIE (*picking it up*): Here.

MRS. GOFORTH: Date of birth: 1928. Hmmm, no chicken, Blackie. How old's that make him?

BLACKIE:—Thirty-five.

(*She lights a cigarette. Mrs. Goforth snatches the cigarette from Blackie's hand. She sets it on the desk and in a moment starts smoking it herself.*)

MRS. GOFORTH: No travelers' checks whatsoever. Did he have some cash on him?

BLACKIE: I don't know, I neglected to frisk him.

MRS. GOFORTH: Did you get him to bathe?

BLACKIE: Yes.

MRS. GOFORTH: How'd he look in the bathtub?

BLACKIE: I'm afraid I can't give you any report on that.

MRS. GOFORTH: Where's his clothes? No clothes, *niente vestiti in sacco?*

GIULIO (*produces one shirt, laundered but not ironed*): *Ecco una camicia, una bella camicia!*

MRS. GOFORTH: One shirt!

BLACKIE: He probably had to check some of his luggage somewhere, in order to get up the—goatpath . . . and the clothes he had on were demolished by Rudy's dogs.

MRS. GOFORTH: Well, put a robe in his room. I know—the Samurai warrior's robe that Alex wore at breakfast. We

always wore robes at breakfast in case we wanted to go back
to bed right after. . . .

(*A Stage Assistant enters with an ancient Japanese robe, with
a belt and sword attached.*)

BLACKIE: Did he keep the sword on him at breakfast?

MRS. GOFORTH: Yes, he did and sometimes he'd draw it out
of the scabbard and poke me with it. Ho ho. Tickle me
with the point of it, ho ho ho ho!

BLACKIE: You weren't afraid he'd—accidentally—?

MRS. GOFORTH: Sure, and it was exciting. I had me a little revolver. I'd draw a bead on him sometimes and I'd say, you
are too beautiful to live, and so you have to die, now,
tonight—tomorrow—

(*The Stage Assistant hands the robe to Blackie, who accepts it
without a glance at him.*)

—put the robe in the pink villino, and then call the Witch
of Capri.

BLACKIE: Which witch?

MRS. GOFORTH: The one that wired me last month: "Are you
still living?" Tell her I am. And get her over for dinner, tell
her it's *urgentissimo*! Everything's *urgentissimo* here this
summer. . . .

(*Phone buzzes on desk. As Blackie starts off, Mrs. Goforth answers the phone.*)

Pronto, pronto, chi parla?—Taormina? Sicilia?—I've placed
no call to that place. (*She slams down the phone.*) —Hmmm,
the summer is coming to life! I'm coming back to life
with it!

(*She presses buttons on her intercom system. Electric buzzers
sound from various points on the stage as the Stage Assistants
cover the library area with the griffin-crested screen.*)

The Scene Dims Out.

SCENE THREE

That evening. The setting is the terrace of the white villa and a small section of Mrs. Goforth's bedroom, upstage left. In this scene, the Stage Assistants may double as Butlers, with or without white jackets. At the curtain's rise, the two screens are lighted, one masking the small dinner table on the forestage, the other Mrs. Goforth; a Stage Assistant stands beside each screen so that they can be removed simultaneously when a chord provides the signal. The middle panel of Mrs. Goforth's screen is topped by a gold-winged griffin to signify that she is "in residence" behind it.

MRS. GOFORTH'S VOICE (*asthmatically*): *Simonetta, la roba.*

(*Simonetta rushes behind the screen with an elaborate Oriental costume.*)

Attenzione, goddamn it, *questa roba molto, molto valore. Va bene. Adesso, parruca!**
SIMONETTA (*emerging from the screen*): *A parruca bionda?*
MRS. GOFORTH: *Nera, nera!*

(*There is heard a reedy chord as on a harmonium. The screens are whisked away. In the stage-left area, we see Mrs. Goforth in the Oriental robe, on the forestage, Rudy in his semi-military outfit pouring himself a drink, and a small section of balustrade on which is a copper brazier, flickering with blue flame. Blackie enters, stage right, with a napkin and silver and sets a third place at the table, Rudy hovers behind her.*)

BLACKIE: Stop breathing down my neck.
MRS. GOFORTH: *Ecco!*

(*She puts on a black Kabuki wig with fantastic ornaments stuck in it. Her appearance is gorgeously bizarre. As she moves, out upon the forestage, there is Oriental music.*)

Well, no comment, Blackie?
BLACKIE: The Witch of Capri has just gotten out of the boat and is getting into the funicular.

*Wig.

MRS. GOFORTH: You kill me, Blackie, you do, you literally kill me. I come out here in this fantastic costume and all you say is the Witch of Capri has landed.

BLACKIE: I told you how fantastic it was when you wore it last week-end, when that Italian screen star didn't show up for dinner, so I didn't think it would be necessary to tell you again, but what I do want to tell you is that I wish you'd explain to Rudy that I find him resistible, and when I say resistible I'm putting it as politely as I know how.

MRS. GOFORTH: What's Rudy doing to you?

BLACKIE: Standing behind me, and—

MRS. GOFORTH: You want him in front of you, Blackie?

BLACKIE: I want him off the terrace while I'm on it.

MRS. GOFORTH: Rudy, you'd better go check my bedroom safe. These rocks I've put on tonight are so hot they're radioactive. (*to Blackie*) Guess what I'm worth on the hoof in this regalia?

BLACKIE: I'm no good at guessing the value of—

MRS. GOFORTH: I can't stand anything false. Even my kidney stones, if I had kidney stones, would be genuine diamonds fit for a Queen's crown, Blackie.

(*Blackie lights a cigarette. Mrs. Goforth takes the cigarette from her.*)

A witch and a bitch always dress up for each other, because otherwise the witch would upstage the bitch, or the bitch would upstage the witch, and the result would be havoc.

BLACKIE: Fine feathers flying in all directions?

MRS. GOFORTH: That's right. The Witch has a fairly large collection of rocks herself, but no important pieces. (*She crosses, smoking, to the table.*) Hey. The table's set for three. Are you having dinner with us?

BLACKIE: Not this evening, thanks, I have to catch up on my typing.

MRS. GOFORTH: Then who's this third place set for?

BLACKIE: The young man in the pink villa, I thought he'd be dining with you.

MRS. GOFORTH: That was presumptuous of you. He's having no meals with me till I know more about him. The Witch of Capri can give me the low-down on him. In fact, the only reason I asked the Witch to dinner was to get the low-down on this mountain climber.

THE WITCH (*at a distance*): Yoo-hoo!

MRS. GOFORTH: Yooo-hooo! She won't be here more than a minute before she makes some disparaging comment on my appearance. Codeine, empirin, brandy, before she gets here. She takes a morbid interest in the health of her friends because her own's on the downgrade.

THE WITCH (*nearer*): Yoo-hoo!

MRS. GOFORTH: Yooo-hooo! Here she comes, here comes the Witch.

(*The Witch of Capri, the Marchesa Constance Ridgeway-Condotti, appears on the terrace. She looks like a creature out of a sophisticated fairy tale, her costume like something that might have been designed for Fata Morgana. Her dress is gray chiffon, paneled, and on her blue-tinted head she wears a cone-shaped hat studded with pearls, the peak of it draped with the material of her dress. Her expressive, claw-like hands are aglitter with gems. At the sight of Mrs. Goforth, she halts dramatically, opening her eyes very wide for a moment, as if confronted by a frightening apparition, then she utters a dramatic little cry and extends her arms in a counterfeit gesture of pity.*)

THE WITCH: *Sissy! Love!*

MRS. GOFORTH: Connie . . .

(*They embrace ritually and coolly, then stand back from each other with sizing-up stares.*)

THE WITCH: Sissy, don't tell me we're having a Chinese dinner.

MRS. GOFORTH: This isn't a Chinese robe, it's a Kabuki dancer's, a Japanese national treasure that Simon Willingham bought me on our reconciliation trip to Japan. It's only some centuries old. I had to sneak it through customs —Japanese customs—by wearing it tucked up under a chinchilla coat. Y'know I studied Kabuki, and got to be very good at it. I was a guest artist once at a thing for typhoon relief, and I can still do it, you see.

(*She opens her lacquered fan and executes some Kabuki dance*

movements, humming weirdly. The effect has a sort of gro-
tesque beauty, but she is suddenly dizzy and staggers against
the table. The Witch utters a shrill cry; Blackie rushes to catch
her and support the table. Mrs. Goforth tries to laugh it off.)

Ha, ha, too much codeine, I took a little codeine for my
neuralgia before you got here.

THE WITCH: Well, I'm suffering, too. We're suffering together. Will you look at my arm. (*She draws up her flowing*
sleeve to expose a bandaged forearm.) The sea is full of
Medusas.

MRS. GOFORTH: Full of what?

THE WITCH: Medusas, you know, those jellyfish that sting.
The Latins call them Medusas, and one of them got me this
morning, a giant one, at the *Piccola Marina*. I want a
martini. . . . I've got to stay slightly drunk to bear the
pain. (*She tosses her parasol to Blackie and advances to the*
liquor cart.) Sissy, your view is a *meraviglia, veramente una*
meraviglia! (*She drains a martini that Blackie pours her,*
then swings full circle and dizzily returns to a chair at the
table.) Do we have to eat?—I'm so full of canapés from
Mona's cocktail do . . .

MRS. GOFORTH: Oh, is that what you're full of? We're having
a very light supper, because the smell of food after codeine
nauseates me, Connie.

BLACKIE: Mrs. Goforth, shouldn't I take something to your
house guest since he's not dining with you?

MRS. GOFORTH: No, meaning no, but you can leave us now,
Blackie. Oh, excuse me, this is my secretary, Miss Black.
Blackie, this is—what's your latest name, Connie?

THE WITCH: I mailed you my wedding invitation the spring
before last spring to some hospital in Boston, the Leahey
Clinic, and never received a word of acknowledgment
from you.

MRS. GOFORTH: Oh, weddings and funerals're things you
show up at or you don't according to where you are and—

(*She rings bell for service: the Stage Assistants appear with*
white towels over their forearms or colored mess-jackets.
Note: Although they sometimes take part in the action of the

play, the characters in the play never appear to notice the Stage Assistants.)

—*other* circumstances: Have a gull's egg, Connie.

THE WITCH: No, thank you, I can't stand gulls.

MRS. GOFORTH: Well, eating their eggs cuts down on their population.

THE WITCH: What is this monster of the deep?

MRS. GOFORTH: *Dentice, dentice freddo.*

THE WITCH: It has a horrid expression on its face.

MRS. GOFORTH: Don't look at it, just eat it.

THE WITCH: Couldn't possibly, thank you.

MRS. GOFORTH: Are you still living on blood transfusions, Connie? That's not good, it turns you into a vampire, a *pipistrella,* ha, ha. . . . Your neck's getting too thin, Connie. Is it true that you had that sheep embryo—plantation in— Switzerland? I heard so. I don't approve of it. It keys you up for a while and then you collapse, completely. The human system can't stand too much stimulation after —sixty. . . .

THE WITCH: What did they find out at the Leahey Clinic, Sissy?

MRS. GOFORTH: Oh, *that*, that was just a little—routine check-up. . . .

THE WITCH: When you called me today I was so relieved I could die: shouted "Hallelujah" silently, to myself. I'd heard such distressing rumors about you lately, Sissy.

MRS. GOFORTH: Rumors? Hell, what rumors?

THE WITCH (*crossing to the bar cart for a refill*): I can't tell you the rumors that have been circulating about you since your house party last month. The ones you brought over from Capri came back to Capri with stories that I love you too much to repeat.

MRS. GOFORTH: Repeat them, Connie, repeat them.

THE WITCH: Are you sure you feel well enough to take them? (*She returns to her chair.*) Well—they said you were, well, that you seemed to be off your rocker. They said you spent the whole night shouting over loudspeakers so nobody could sleep, and that what you shouted was not to be *believed!*

MRS. GOFORTH: Oh, how *nice* of them, Connie. Capri's

turned into a nest of vipers, Connie—and the sea is full of Medusas? Mmm. The Medusas are spawned by the bitches. You want to know the truth behind this gossip? Or would you rather believe a pack of malicious inventions?

THE WITCH: You know I love you, Sissy. What's the truth?

MRS. GOFORTH: Not that.—I'll tell you the truth. (*She rises and indicates the intercom speaker.*) I'm writing my memoirs this summer. I've got the whole place wired for sound, a sort of very elaborate intercom or walkie-talkie system, so I can dictate to my secretary, Blackie. I buzz my secretary any time of the day and night and continue dictating to her. That's the truth, the true story. (*She goes over to The Witch.*)

THE WITCH (*taking her hand*): I'm so glad you told me, Sissy, love!

MRS. GOFORTH: Has it ever struck you, Connie, that life is all memory, except for the one present moment that goes by you so quick you hardly catch it going? It's really all memory, Connie, except for each passing moment. What I just now said to you is a memory now—recollection. Uh-hummm . . . (*She paces the terrace.*) —I'm up now. When I was at the table is a memory, now. (*She arrives at the edge of lighted area downstage right, and turns.*) —when I turned at the other end of the terrace is a memory, now. . . .

(*The Witch gets up and goes toward her.*)

Practically everything is a memory to me, now, so I'm writing my memoirs. . . . (*She points up.*) Shooting star: it's shot:—a memory now. Four husbands, all memory now. All lovers, all memory now.

THE WITCH: So you're writing your memoirs.

MRS. GOFORTH: Devoting all of me to it, and all of my time. . . . At noon today, I was dictating to Blackie on a tape-recorder: the beautiful part of my life, my love with Alex, my final marriage. Alex . . .

THE WITCH (*going to the bar cart*): Oh, the young Russian dancer from the Diaghilev troupe?

MRS. GOFORTH (*returning to her chair*): Oh, God, no, I never married a dancer. Slept with a couple but never married a one. They're too narcissistic for me; they love only mirrors.

Nope, Alex was a young poet with a spirit that was as beautiful as his body, the only one I married that wasn't rich as Croesus. Alex made love without mirrors. He used my eyes for his mirrors. The only husband I've had, of the six I've had, that I could make love to with a bright light burning over the bed. Hundred-watt bulbs overhead! To see, while we loved. . . .

THE WITCH (*going back to the table with the pitcher of martinis*): Are you dictating this. Over a loudspeaker?

MRS. GOFORTH: Ah, God—Alex . . .

THE WITCH: Are you in pain? Do you have a pain in your chest?

MRS. GOFORTH: Why?

THE WITCH: You keep touching your chest.

MRS. GOFORTH: Emotion. I've been very emotional all day. . . . At noon today, a young poet came up the goat-path from the highway just as I was in the emotional— throes—of dictating my memories of young Alex. . . .

THE WITCH (*draining her martini*): Ah-ha.

MRS. GOFORTH: He came up the goatpath from the Amalfi Drive wearing lederhosen like Alex was wearing the first time I set eyes on him.

THE WITCH (*starting to pour another martini*): Ahh-ha!

MRS. GOFORTH (*snatching the pitcher from The Witch and placing it on the floor*): Do you want to hear this story?

THE WITCH: Liquor improves my concentration. Go on. You've met a new poet. What was the name of this poet?

MRS. GOFORTH: His name was on the book.

THE WITCH: Yes, sometimes they do put the author's name on a book.

MRS. GOFORTH (*unamused*): Sanders? No. Manders? No.

THE WITCH: Flanders. Christopher Flanders. (*Makes large eyes.*) Is he still in circulation?

MRS. GOFORTH: I don't know if he's in circulation or not but I do know he came up here to see me and not by the boat and funicular, he—

THE WITCH (*moving toward Mrs. Goforth*): Well, God help you, Sissy.

MRS. GOFORTH: Why, is something wrong with him?

THE WITCH: Not if you're not superstitious. Are you superstitious?

MRS. GOFORTH: What's superstition got to do with—

THE WITCH: I've got to have a wee drop of brandy on this! (*She crosses over to the bar cart.*) This is really uncanny!

MRS. GOFORTH: *Well, come out with it, what?*

THE WITCH (*selecting the brandy bottle*): I think I'd rather not tell you.

MRS. GOFORTH (*commandingly*): *What?*

THE WITCH: Promise me not to be frightened?

MRS. GOFORTH: When've I ever been frightened? Of what? Not even that stiletto you've got for a tongue can scare me! (*She downs her own martini at a gulp.*) So what's the—

THE WITCH: Chris, poor Chris Flanders, he has the bad habit of coming to call on a lady just a step or two ahead of the undertaker. (*She sits down.*) Last summer, at Portofino, he stayed with some Texas oil people, and at supper one night that wicked old Duke of Parma, you know the one that we call the Parma Violet, he emptied a champagne bottle on Christopher's head and he said, "I christen thee, Christopher Flanders, the Angel of Death." The name has stuck to him, Sissy. Why, some people in our age bracket, we're senior citizens, Sissy, would set their dogs on him if he entered their grounds, but since you're not superstitious— Why isn't he dining here with us?

MRS. GOFORTH: I wanted some information about him before I—

THE WITCH: Let him stay here?

MRS. GOFORTH: He's here on probation. (*She rings for Giulio, and then crosses center.*) I put him in the pink villa where he's been sleeping since noon, when he climbed up a goat-path to see me.

THE WITCH (*following Mrs. Goforth*): I hope he's not playing his sleeping trick on you, Sissy.

MRS. GOFORTH: Trick? Sleeping?

THE WITCH: Yes, last summer when he was with that Portofino couple from Texas, they were thrown into panic when they heard his nickname, "Angel of Death," and told him that night to check out in the morning. Well, that night, he swallowed some sleeping pills that night, Sissy, but of course he took the precaution of leaving an early morning call so he could be found and revived before the pills could—

(*Mrs. Goforth abruptly begins to leave.*)

Where're you going, Sissy?

MRS. GOFORTH: Follow me to the pink villa, hurry, hurry, I better make sure he's not playing that trick on me.

(*She rushes off. The Witch laughs wickedly as she follows. The Stage Assistants immediately set a screen before this acting area and the light dims. Then they remove a screen upstage, and we see Chris asleep in the pink villa. A lullaby, perhaps the Brahms one is heard. Mrs. Goforth and The Witch appear just on the edge of the small lighted area.*)

MRS. GOFORTH: Everything's pink in this villa, so it's called the pink villa.

THE WITCH: I see. That's logical, Sissy. Hmmm. There he is, sleeping.

MRS. GOFORTH (*in a shrill whisper as they draw closer to the bed*): Can you tell if he's—?

(*The Witch removes her slippers, creeps to the bedside and touches his wrist.*)

—Well?

THE WITCH: Hush! (*She slips back to Mrs. Goforth.*) You're lucky, Sissy. His pulse seems normal, he's sleeping normally, and he has a good color. (*She slips back to the bed, and bends her face to his.*) Let me see if there's liquor on his breath. No. It's sweet as a baby's.

MRS. GOFORTH: Don't go to bed with him!

THE WITCH: No, that's your privilege, Sissy.

MRS. GOFORTH (*moving downstage from the lighted area in a follow-spot*): Come out here.

THE WITCH (*reluctantly following*): You must have met him before.

MRS. GOFORTH: Oh, somewhere, sometime, when I was still meeting people, before they all seemed like the same person over and over, and I got tired of the—person.

THE WITCH: You know his story, don't you?

(*The Stage Assistants place a section of balustrade, at an angle, beside them, and a copper brazier with the blue flame in it. The flame flickers eerily on The Witch's face as she tells*) *what she knows of Chris. Music plays against her stylized recitation.)*

Sally Ferguson found him at a ski lodge in Nevada where he was working as a ski instructor.

MRS. GOFORTH: A poet, a ski instructor?

THE WITCH: Everything about him was like that, a contradiction. He taught Sally skiing at this Nevada lodge where Sally was trying to prove she was a generation younger than she was, and thought she could get away with it. Well, she should have stuck to the gentle slopes, since her bones had gone dry, but one day she took the ski lift to the top of the mountain, drank a hot buttered rum, and took off like a wild thing, a crazy bird, down the mountain, slammed into a tree, and broke her hip bone. Well, Christopher Flanders carried her back to the ski lodge. We all thought she was done for, but Chris worked a miracle on her that lasted for quite a while. He got her back on her pins after they'd pinned her broken hip together with steel pins. They traveled together, to and from Europe together, but then one time in rough weather, on the promenade deck of one of the *Queen* ships, the *Mary*, he suddenly let go of her, she took a spill and her old hip bone broke again, too badly for steel pins to pin her back together again, and Sally gave up her travels except from one room to another, on a rolling couch pushed by Chris. We all advised her to let Chris go, like Chris had let go of her on the promenade deck of the *Mary*. Would she? Never! She called him "my saint," "my angel," till the day she died. And her children contested her will, so that Chris got nothing, just his poems published, dedicated to Sally. The book won a prize of some kind, and *Vogue* and *Harper's Bazaar* played it up big with lovely photos of Chris looking like what she called him, an angel, a saint. . . .

MRS. GOFORTH: Did he sleep with that old Ferguson bitch? Or was he just her Death Angel?

(*The phone rings on the bedside table: the area has remained softly lighted. Chris starts up, drops back, feigning sleep, as Mrs. Goforth rushes to the phone and snatches it up.*

—*Pronto, dica.*— Taormina, Sicily? No, *sbagliato!*

(*Mrs. Goforth looks with angry suspicion at Chris, who mur-murs as if in sleep. She notices the food tray by the bed, and snatches it up, then returns to The Witch, downstage.*)

He's already making long-distance calls on the phone and look at this! He's had them bring him a food tray, and I am going to remove it, I can't stand guests, especially not in-vited, that act like they're in a hotel, charging calls and call-ing for room service. Come on, I'm turning out the lights.

THE WITCH: My slippers.

(*She slips back to the bed and picks up her slippers, lingering over Chris. Suddenly she bends to kiss him on the mouth. He rolls over quickly, shielding his lower face with an arm and uttering a grunt of distaste.*)

Possum!

(*The lights dim in the area, as The Witch moves downstage. Mrs. Goforth has disappeared.*)

Siss? Sissy! Yoo-hoo!

MRS. GOFORTH (*from a distance*): Yoo-hoo!

THE WITCH (*following*): Yoooooooooo-hoooooooooo . . .

(*The Stage Assistants replace the screen that masked the pink villa bed. Then they fold and remove the screen before Blackie's bed in the blue villa. The area remains dark until a faint dawn light appears on the cyclorama. Then Blackie's bed is lighted, and we see her seated on it, brushing her dark hair with a silver-backed brush.*)

The Scene Dims Out.

SCENE FOUR

It is later that night. The terrace of the white villa. The Watchman, Rudy, sweeps the audience with the beam of his flashlight. We hear a long, anguished "Ahhhh" from behind the screen masking Mrs. Goforth's bed. Rudy, as if he heard the out-cry, turns the flashlight momentarily on the screen behind which it comes. He chuckles, sways drunkenly, then suddenly turns the light beam on Chris who has entered quietly from the wings, stage right.

CHRIS (*shielding his eyes from the flashlight*): Oh. Hello.

RUDY: You still prowling around here?

CHRIS (*agreeably*): No, I'm— Well, yes, I'm— (*His smile fades as Rudy moves in closer.*) I just now woke up hungry. I didn't want to disturb anybody, so I—

RUDY: You just now woke up, huh?

CHRIS: Yes, I—

RUDY: Where'd you just now wake up?

CHRIS: In the, uh, guest house, the—

RUDY: Looking for the dogs again, are you? (*He whistles the dogs awake. They set up a clamor far away.*)

CHRIS: I told you I just now woke up hungry. I came out to see if—

RUDY (*moving still closer and cutting in*): Aw, you woke up *hungry?*

CHRIS: Yes. Famished.

RUDY: How about this, how'd you like to eat this, something like this, huh?

(*He thrusts his stick hard into Chris's stomach. Chris expells his breath in a "hah."*)

'Sthat feel good on your belly? Want some more of that, huh? huh?

(*He drives the stick again into Chris's stomach, so hard that Chris bends over, unable to speak. Blackie rushes onto the terrace in a dressing gown, her hair loose.*)

BLACKIE: *Rudy! What's going on here?*

(*The dogs, roused, are barking, still at a distance.*)

This young man is a guest of Mrs. Goforth. He's staying in the pink villa. Are you all right, Mr. Flanders?

(*Chris can't speak. He leans on a section of balustrade, bent over, making a retching sound.*)

Rudy, get off the terrace!—you drunk gorilla!

RUDY (*grinning*): He's got the dry heaves, Blackie. He woke up hungry and he's got the dry heaves.

CHRIS: *Can't—catch—breath!*

(*From her bed behind the griffin-crested screen, Mrs. Goforth cries out in her sleep, a long, anguished "Ahhhhhh!" The dogs' barking subsides gradually. The "Ahhhhh" is repeated and a faint light appears behind her screen. Blackie turns on Rudy, fiercely.*)

BLACKIE: I said get off the terrace, now get off it.

RUDY: You shoulda told me you—

BLACKIE: Off it, off the terrace!

RUDY (*overlapping Blackie's speech*): You got yourself a boy friend up here, Blackie! You should've let me know that.

BLACKIE: Mr. Flanders, I'll take you back to your place.

CHRIS (*gasping*): Is there—anywhere closer—I could catch my breath?

(*She stands protectively near him as Rudy goes off the terrace, laughing.*

(*The Stage Assistants rush out to remove a screen masking Blackie's bed in the blue villa, indicating "Blackie's bedroom." Chris straightens slowly, still gasping. The Stage Assistants leave. Then Chris and Blackie cross to her villino, represented only by a narrow blue-sheeted bed with a stand beside it that supports an intercom box.*)

BLACKIE: Now tell me just what happened so I can give a report to Mrs. Goforth tomorrow.

CHRIS: The truth is I was looking for something to eat. I've had no food for five days, Blackie, except some oranges that I picked on the road. And you know what the acid, the citric acid in oranges, does to an empty stomach, so I—I woke up feeling as if I had a—a bushel of burning sawdust in my stomach, and I—

BLACKIE: I had food sent to your room. You didn't find it?

CHRIS: No. God, no!

BLACKIE: Then the cook didn't send it, or it was taken out while you were sleeping, and I'm afraid you'll have to wait till morning for something to eat. You see, the only kitchen is in Mrs. Goforth's villa. It's locked up like a bank vault till Mrs. Goforth wakes up and has it opened.

CHRIS: How long is it till morning?

BLACKIE: Oh, my—watch has stopped. I'm a watch-winding person, but I forgot to wind it.

(*The sky has lightened a little and there is the sound of church bells at a distance.*)

CHRIS: The church-bells are waking up on the other mountains.

BLACKIE: Yes, it's, it must be near morning, but morning doesn't begin on Mrs. Goforth's mountain till she sleeps off her drugs and starts pressing buttons for the sun to come up. So—

CHRIS: What?

(*The intercom box comes alive with a shrill electric buzz.*)

BLACKIE: Oh, God, she's awake, buzzing for me!

CHRIS: Oh, then, could you ask her to open the kitchen? A glass of milk, just some milk, is all I—

BLACKIE: Mrs. Goforth isn't buzzing for morning, she's buzzing for me to take dictation and, oh, God, I don't think I can do it. I haven't slept tonight and I just couldn't take it right now, I—

CHRIS: Let me take it for you.

BLACKIE: No. I'll have to answer myself, or she'll come stumbling, raving out, and might fall off the cliff.

(*She presses a button on the intercom box.*)

Mrs. Goforth? Mrs. Goforth?

(*The Stage Assistants remove the screen masking Mrs. Goforth's bed, upstage left. We see her through the gauze curtains enclosing the bed. She pulls a cord, opening the curtains, and speaks hoarsely into a microphone.*)

MRS. GOFORTH: *Blackie? It's night, late night!*

BLACKIE: Yes, it's late, Mrs. Goforth.

MRS. GOFORTH: Don't answer: this is dictation. Don't interrupt me, this is clear as a vision. The death of Harlon Goforth, just now—clearly—remembered, clear as a vision.

It's night, late night, without sleep. He's crushing me under the awful weight of his body. Then suddenly he stops trying to make love to me. He says, "Flora, I have a pain in my head, a terrible pain in my head." And silently, to myself, I say, "Thank God," but out loud I say something else: "Tablets, you want your tablets?" He answers with the groan of—I reach up and turn on the light, and I see—death in his eyes! I see, I know. He has death in his eyes, and something worse in them, terror. I see terror in his eyes. I see it, I feel it, myself, and I get out of the bed, I get out of the bed as if escaping from quicksand! I don't look at him again, I move away from the bed. . . .

(*She rises from the bed, the microphone gripped in her hand.*

I move away from death, terror! I don't look back, I go straight to the door, the door onto the terrace!

(*She moves downstage with the microphone.*)

It's closed, I tear it open, I leave him alone with his death, his—

BLACKIE: She's out of bed, she's going out on the—

(*She rushes into the wings. The light dims on the blue villa bed.*)

MRS. GOFORTH (*dropping the microphone as she moves out on white villa terrace*): I've gone out, now, I'm outside, I'm on the terrace, twenty-five stories over the high, high city of Goforth. I see lights blazing under the high, high terrace but not a light blazing as bright as the blaze of terror that I saw in his eyes!

(*She staggers to the edge of the forestage.*)

Wind, cold wind, clean, clean! Release! Relief! Escape from—

(*She reaches the edges of the orchestra pit. A wave crashes loudly below.*)

I'm lost, blind, dying! I don't know where I—

BLACKIE (*rushing out behind her*): Mrs. Goforth! Don't move! You're at the edge of the cliff!

MRS. GOFORTH (*stopping, her hands over her eyes*): Blackie! (*She sways. Blackie rushes forward to catch her.*) Blackie, don't leave me alone!

(*The stage is blacked out.*)

Intermission.

SCENE FIVE

The scene is the terrace of the white villa the following morning. Mrs. Goforth is standing on the terrace while dictating to Blackie, who sits at a small table. Above the table and about the balustrade are cascades of bougainvillaea. Coins of gold light, reflected from the sea far below, flicker upon the playing area, which is backed by fair sky. There has been a long, reflective pause in the dictation. Mrs. Goforth stands glaring somberly out at the sea.

MRS. GOFORTH: Blackie, I want to begin this chapter on a more serious note.

(*She moves around to the right of the table. Then continues emphatically and loudly.*)

Meaning of life!
BLACKIE: Dictation?
MRS. GOFORTH: Not yet, wait, don't rush me. (*Repeats in a softer tone.*) Meaning of life . . .

(*Chris appears at the far end of the terrace. He wears the Samurai robe. Blackie sees him, but Mrs. Goforth doesn't. Blackie indicates by gesture that he should not approach yet.*)

Yes, I feel this chapter ought to begin with a serious comment on the meaning of life, because y'know, sooner or later, a person's obliged to face it.
BLACKIE: Dictating now, Mrs. Goforth?
MRS. GOFORTH: No, no, thinking—reflecting, I'll raise my hand when I begin the dictation. (*She raises a jeweled hand to demonstrate the signal that she will use.*)

BLACKIE: Begin now?

(*Chris smiles at her tone of voice. Blackie shrugs and closes her notebook, rises quietly, and goes up to Chris, who lights her cigarette.*)

MRS. GOFORTH: One time at Flora's Folly, which was the name of the sixteenth-century coach house, renovated, near Paris where I had my salon, my literary evenings, I brought up the question, "What is the meaning of life?" And do you know they treated it like a joke? Ha ha, very funny, Sissy can't be serious!—but she *was*, she *was*. . . .

CHRIS: I think she's started dictating. Is there something to eat?

BLACKIE: Black coffee and saccharine tablets.

CHRIS: That's *all*?!

BLACKIE: Soon as I get a chance, I'll raid the kitchen for you.

MRS. GOFORTH (*almost plaintively*): Why is it considered ridiculous, bad taste, *mauvais gout*, to seriously consider and discuss the possible meaning of life, and only stylish to assume it's just—what?

(*The Stage Assistants have come out of the wings.*)

ONE: Charade. Game.

TWO (*tossing a spangled ball to his partner*): Pastime.

ONE (*tossing the ball back*): Flora's Folly.

TWO (*tossing the ball back*): Accident of atoms.

ONE (*returning ball*): Resulting from indiscriminate copulation.

(*Blackie throws her cigarette away and returns to her former position. The Stage Assistants withdraw.*)

MRS. GOFORTH: I've often wondered, but I've wondered *more* lately . . . meaning of *life*.

(*The Stage Assistants reappear with a small table and two chairs. They wait in the wings for a moment before placing them. They then retire.*)

Sometimes I think, I suspect, that everything that we do is a way of—*not* thinking about it. Meaning of life, and meaning of death, too. . . . *What in hell are we doing?* (*She raises her jeweled hand.*) Just going from one goddamn frantic distraction to another, till finally one too many goddamn frantic distractions leads to disaster, and blackout? Eclipse of, total of sun?

(*She keeps staring out from the terrace, her head turning slowly right and left, into the swimming gold light below her, murmuring to herself, nodding a little, then shaking her head a little. Her small jeweled hands appear to be groping blindly for something. She coughs from time to time.*)

There's a fog coming in. See it over there, that fog coming in?

BLACKIE: No. It's perfectly clear in all directions this morning.

MRS. GOFORTH: When I woke up this morning, I said to myself—

BLACKIE: Dictation?

MRS. GOFORTH: Shut up! I said to myself, "Oh, God, not morning again, oh, no, no, I can't bear it." But I *did*, I bore it. You really don't see that mist coming in out there?

BLACKIE (*closing her notebook*): Mrs. Goforth, the young man in the pink villa, Mr. Flanders, is waiting out here to see you. He has on the Samurai robe you gave him to wear while his clothes are being repaired, and it's very becoming to him.

MRS. GOFORTH: Call him over.

BLACKIE: Mr. Flanders!

MRS. GOFORTH: Hey, Samurai! *Banzai!*

(*Approaching, Chris ducks under a brilliant cascade of bougainvillaea vine.*)

BLACKIE: You certainly had a long sleep.

CHRIS: Did I ever!

MRS. GOFORTH (*sitting*): Did he ever, ho ho. He slept round the clock, but still has romantic shadows under his eyes! There was a chorus girl in the Follies—I used to be in the Follies, before my first marriage—when she'd show up with circles under her eyes, she'd say, "The blackbirds kissed me last night," meaning she's been too busy to sleep that night, ho ho. . . .

CHRIS: I was busy sleeping, just sleeping. (*He bends over her hand.*)

MRS. GOFORTH: No, no, none of that stuff. Old Georgia swamp-bitches don't go in for hand kissing but—*setzen Sie doon*, and— Are you coming out here for battle with that sword on?

CHRIS (*sitting*): Oh. No, but—I ran into a pack of wild dogs on the mountain, yesterday, when I climbed up here.

MRS. GOFORTH: Yes, I heard about your little misunderstanding with the dogs. You don't seem much the worse for it. You're lucky they didn't get at— (*grins wickedly*) your *face*.

CHRIS: I'm sorry if it disturbed you, but their bite was worse than their bark.

MRS. GOFORTH: The Italians call them *lupos* which means wolves. These watchdogs, they're necessary for the protection of estates like this, but—didn't you notice the "Private Property" sign in English and Italian, and the "Beware of Dogs" sign when you started up that goatpath from the highway?

CHRIS: I don't think I noticed a reference to dogs, no. I don't remember any mention of dogs, in English or Italian.

BLACKIE (*quickly*): Naturally not, the "Beware of Dogs" sign was put up *after* Mr. Flanders' "little misunderstanding with the dogs."

MRS. GOFORTH: Blackie, that is not so.

BLACKIE: Yes, it *is* so, I heard you ordering the sign put up after, just after the—

MRS. GOFORTH (*trembling with fury*): Blackie! You have *work* to do, don't you?

BLACKIE: I've never taken a job that called for collusion in—falsehood!

MRS. GOFORTH (*mocking her*): Oh, what virtue, what high moral character, Blackie.

CHRIS (*cutting in quickly*): Mrs. Goforth, Miss Black, I obviously *did* enter and trespass on private property at my own risk.

MRS. GOFORTH: If that statement's typed up—Blackie, type it up—would you be willing to sign it, Mr. Flanders?

CHRIS: Certainly, yes, of course, but let me write it up in my own handwriting and sign it right now. I'd hate for you to think I'd—

BLACKIE: He was attacked again last night.

MRS. GOFORTH: Again, by dogs?

BLACKIE: Not by dogs, by a dog. Your watchman, Rudy, attacked him because he woke up hungry and came outside to—

MRS. GOFORTH (*rising*): *Blackie, get off the terrace!*

BLACKIE: I want to get off this mountain gone mad with your madness! I try to help you, I try to feel sorry for you because you're—

MRS. GOFORTH: What? What am I?

CHRIS: Please. (*He tears a page out of Blackie's notebook and speaks to her quietly.*) It's all right. Go in.

MRS. GOFORTH: What did you say to that woman?

CHRIS: I said you're very upset, I said you're trembling.

MRS. GOFORTH: *I've been up here surrounded by traitors all summer!* (*She staggers.*) Ahhhhh!

(*Chris helps her into her chair.*)

God! God . . .

CHRIS: Now. (*He scribbles rapidly on the sheet of paper.*) Here. "I, Christopher Flanders, entered a gate marked 'Private' at my own risk and am solely responsible for a—misunderstanding with—dogs." Witnesses? Of the signature?

MRS. GOFORTH: Can you unscrew this bottle? (*She has been trying to open her codeine bottle.*)

CHRIS (*taking it from her and removing the cap*): One?

MRS. GOFORTH: Two.— Thank you.—Brandy on that— (*She indicates liquor cart.*)

CHRIS: Courvoisier?

MRS. GOFORTH: Rémy-Martin.—Thank you.

CHRIS: Welcome. (*He resumes his seat and smiles at her warmly.*) Let me hold that glass for you.

(*She has spilled some of the brandy, her hand is shaking so violently.*)

MRS. GOFORTH: Thank you.—Ahh . . . (*She draws a deep breath, recovering herself.*) You have nice teeth. Are they capped?

(*Chris shakes his head, smiling.*)

Well, you got beautiful teeth. In that respect nature's been favorable to you.

CHRIS: Thank you.

MRS. GOFORTH: Don't thank me, thank your dentist. (*She puts on lipstick, dabbing her nostrils with a bit of disposable tissue.*)

CHRIS: I've never been to a dentist—honestly not.

MRS. GOFORTH: Well, then, thank the Lord for the calcium that you got from your mother's milk. Well, I have a pretty wonderful set of teeth myself. In fact, my teeth are so good people think they are false. But look, look here! (*She takes her large incisors between thumb and forefinger to demonstrate the firmness of their attachment.*) See? Not even a bridge. In my whole mouth I've had exactly three fillings which are still there, put in there ten years ago! See them? (*She opens her mouth wide.*) This tooth here was slightly chipped when my daughter's third baby struck me in the mouth with the butt of a water pistol at Murray Bay. I told my daughter that girl would turn into a problem child, and it sure as hell did.—A little pocket-size bitch, getting bigger! I'm allergic to bitches. Although some people regard me as one myself . . . Sometimes *with* some justification. Want some coffee, Mr. Trojan Horse Guest?

CHRIS: Thanks, yes. Why do you call me that, a Trojan Horse Guest?

MRS. GOFORTH: Because you've arrived here without invitation, like the Trojan Horse got into Troy.

(*She rises shakily to pour him a cup of coffee from a silver urn on the smaller, upstage table. While her back is turned, Chris quietly crumples the sheet from Blackie's notebook and throws it into the orchestra pit.*)

CHRIS: Don't you remember our meeting and conversation at the Ballet Ball, some years ago, quite a few, when you asked me to come here whenever I was in Europe?

MRS. GOFORTH: Passports expire and so do invitations. They've got to be renewed every couple of years.

CHRIS: Has my invitation expired?

MRS. GOFORTH: Coffee. We'll see about that, that remains to be seen. Don't you smoke with your coffee?

CHRIS: Usually, but I—

(*He indicates he has no cigarettes. Mrs. Goforth smiles knowingly and opens a cigarette box on the table.*)

How does it feel, Mrs. Goforth, to be a legend in your own lifetime?

MRS. GOFORTH (*pleased*): If that's a serious question, I'll give it a serious answer. A legend in my own lifetime, yes, I reckon I am. Well, I had certain advantages, endowments to start with: a face people naturally noticed and a figure that was not just sensational, but very durable, too. Some women my age, or younger, 've got breasts that look like a couple of mules hangin' their heads over the top rail of a fence. (*Touches her bosom.*) This is natural, not padded, not supported, and nothing's ever been lifted. Hell, I was born between a swamp and the wrong side of the tracks in One Street, Georgia, but not even that could stop me in my tracks, wrong side or right side, or no side. Hit show-biz at fifteen when a carnival show, I mean the manager of it, saw me and dug me on that *one street* in One Street, Georgia. I was billed at the Dixie Doxy, was just supposed to move my anatomy, but was smart enough to keep my tongue moving, too, and the verbal comments I made on my anatomical motions while in motion were a public delight. So I breezed through show-biz like a tornado, rising from one-week "gigs" in the sticks to star billing in the Follies while still in m'teens, ho ho . . . and I was still in my teens when I married Harlon Goforth, a marriage into the Social Register and Dun and Bradstreet's, both. Was barely out of my teens when I became his widow. Scared to make out a will, he died intestate, so everything went to me.

CHRIS: Marvelous. Amazing.

MRS. GOFORTH: That's right. All my life was and still is, except here, lately I'm a little run down, like a race horse that's been entered in just one race too many, even for me. . . . How do *you* feel about being a legend in your own lifetime? Huh?

CHRIS: Oh, *me*! I don't feel like a—mythological—griffin with gold wings, but this strong fresh wind's reviving me like I'd had a—terrific breakfast!

MRS. GOFORTH: Griffin, what's a griffin?

CHRIS: A force in life that's almost stronger than death. (*He springs up and turns to the booming sea.*) The sea's full of white race horses today. May I—would you mind if I—suggested a program for us? A picnic on the beach, rest on the rocks in the sun till nearly sundown, then we'd come back up here revitalized for whatever the lovely evening had to offer?

MRS. GOFORTH: What do you think it would have to offer?

CHRIS: Dinner on the terrace with the sea still booming? How is that for a program? Say, with music, a couple of tarantella dancers brought up from the village, and—

(*Rudy appears on the terrace.*)

RUDY: Mrs. Goforth, I've taken care of that for you. They're going—on the way out.

MRS. GOFORTH: No trouble?

RUDY: Oh, yeah, sure, they want to see the Signora.

MRS. GOFORTH: No, no, no. I won't see them!

(*But "they" are appearing upstage: the members of her kitchen staff, who have been discharged.*)

Here they come, hold them back!

(*She staggers up, turns her back on them. They cry out to her in Italian. Rudy rushes upstage and herds them violently off. A wave crashes.*)

CHRIS (*quietly*): Boom. What was their—?

MRS. GOFORTH: What?

CHRIS:—transgression?

MRS. GOFORTH: They'd been robbing me blind. He caught them at it. We had—an inventory and discovered that—they'd been robbing me blind like I was—blind. . . .

CHRIS (*his back to her, speaking as if to himself*): When a wave breaks down there, it looks as delicate as a white lace fan, but I bet if it hit you, it would knock you against the rocks and break your bones. . . .

MRS. GOFORTH: What?

CHRIS: I said it's so wonderful here, after yesterday in Naples. . . .

MRS. GOFORTH: What was wrong with yesterday in Naples? Were you picked up for vagrancy in Naples?

CHRIS: I wasn't picked up for anything in Naples.

MRS. GOFORTH: That's worse than being picked up for vagrancy, baby.

(*She chuckles. He grins agreeably.*)

CHRIS: Mrs. Goforth, I'm going to tell you the truth.

MRS. GOFORTH: The truth is all you could tell me that I'd believe—so tell me the truth, Mr. Flanders.

CHRIS: I'll go back a little further than Naples, Mrs. Goforth. I'd drawn out all my savings to come over here this summer on a Jugoslavian freighter that landed at Genoa.

MRS. GOFORTH: You're leading up to financial troubles, aren't you?

CHRIS: Not so much that as—something harder, much harder, for me to deal with, a state of— Well, let me put it this way. Everybody has a sense of *reality* of some kind or other, some kind of sense of things being real or not real in his, his—particular—world. . . .

MRS. GOFORTH: I know what you mean. Go on.

CHRIS: I've lost it lately, this sense of reality in my particular world. We don't all live in the same world, you know, Mrs. Goforth. Oh, we all see the same things—sea, sun, sky, human faces and inhuman faces, but—they're different in *here!* (*Touches his forehead.*) And one person's sense of reality can be another person's sense of—well, of madness!— chaos!—and, and—

MRS. GOFORTH: Go on. I'm still with you.

CHRIS: And when one person's sense of reality, or loss of sense of reality, disturbs another one's sense of reality— I know how mixed up this—

MRS. GOFORTH: Not a bit, clear as a bell, so keep on, y'haven't lost my attention.

CHRIS: Being able to talk: wonderful! When one person's sense of reality seems too—disturbingly different from another person's, uh—

MRS. GOFORTH: Sense of reality. Continue.

CHRIS: Well, he's—avoided! Not welcome! It's—*that sim-ple*. . . . And—yesterday in Naples, I suddenly realized that I was in that situation. (*He turns to the booming sea and says "Boom."*) I found out that I was now a—*leper!*

MRS. GOFORTH: Leopard?

CHRIS: *Leper!*—Boom!

(*She ignores the "boom."*)

Yes, you see, they hang labels, tags of false identification on people that disturb their own sense of reality too much, like the bells that used to be hung on the necks of—lepers!—Boom!

The lady I'd come over to visit, who lives in a castle on the top of Ravello, sent me a wire to Naples. I walked to Naples on foot to pick it up, and picked it up at American Express in Naples, and what it said was: "Not yet, not ready for you, dear—Angel of—Death. . . ."

(*She regards him a bit uncomfortably. He smiles very warmly at her; she relaxes.*)

MRS. GOFORTH: Ridiculous!

CHRIS: Yes, and inconvenient since I'd—

MRS. GOFORTH: Invested all your remaining capital in this standing invitation that had stopped standing, collapsed, ho, ho, ho!

CHRIS:—Yes . . .

MRS. GOFORTH: Who's this bitch at Ravello?

CHRIS: I'd rather forget her name, now.

MRS. GOFORTH: But you see you young people, well, you *reasonably* young people who used to be younger, you get in the habit of being sort of—professional house guests, and as you get a bit older, and who doesn't get a bit older, some more than just a *bit* older, you're still professional house guests, and—

CHRIS: Yes?

MRS. GOFORTH: Oh, you have charm, all of you, you still have your good looks and charm and you all do something creative, such as writing but not writing, and painting but not painting, and that goes fine for a time but—

CHRIS: You've made your point, Mrs. Goforth.

MRS. GOFORTH: No, not yet, quite yet. Your case is special. You've gotten a special nickname, "dear Angel of Death." And it's lucky for you I couldn't be less superstitious, deliberately walk under ladders, think a black cat's as lucky as a white cat, am only against the human cats of this world, of which there's no small number. So! What're you looking around for, Angel of Death, as they call you?

CHRIS: I would love to have some buttered toast with my coffee.

MRS. GOFORTH: Oh, no toast with *my* coffee, buttered, unbuttered—no toast. For breakfast I have only black coffee. Anything solid takes the edge off my energy, and it's the time after breakfast when I do my best work.

CHRIS: What are you working on?

MRS. GOFORTH: My memories, my memoirs, night and day, to meet the publisher's deadlines. The pressure has brought on a sort of nervous breakdown, and I'm enjoying every minute of it because it has taken the form of making me absolutely frank and honest with people. No more pretenses, although I was always frank and honest with people, comparatively. But now much more so. No more pretenses at all . . .

CHRIS: It's wonderful.

MRS. GOFORTH: What?

CHRIS: That you and I have happened to meet at just this time, because I have reached the same point in my life as you say you have come to in yours.

MRS. GOFORTH (*suspiciously*): What? Which? Point?

CHRIS: The point you mentioned, the point of no more pretenses.

MRS. GOFORTH: You say you've reached that point, too?

(*Chris nods, smiling warmly.*)

Hmmmm.

(*The sound is skeptical and so is the look she gives him.*)

CHRIS: It's *true*, I *have*, Mrs. Goforth.

MRS. GOFORTH: I don't mean to call you a liar or even a phantasist, but I don't see how you could afford to arrive at the point of no more pretenses, Chris.

CHRIS: I probably couldn't afford to arrive at that point any more than I could afford to travel this summer.

MRS. GOFORTH: Hmmm. I see. But you traveled?

CHRIS: Yes, mostly on foot, Mrs. Goforth—since—Genoa.

MRS. GOFORTH (*rising and walking near the balustrade*): One of the reasons I took this place here is because it's supposed to be inaccessible except from the sea. Between here and the highway there's just a goatpath, hardly possible to get down, and I thought impossible to get up. Hmm. Yes. Well. But you got yourself up.

CHRIS (*pouring the last of the coffee*): I had to. I had to get up it.

MRS. GOFORTH (*turning back to him and sitting*): Let's play the truth game. Do you know the truth game?

CHRIS: Yes, but I don't like it. I've always made excuses to get out of it when it's played at parties because I think the truth is too delicate and, well, *dangerous* a thing to be played with at parties, Mrs. Goforth. It's nitroglycerin, it has to be handled with the—the carefulest care, or somebody hurts somebody and gets hurt back and the party turns to a—devastating explosion, people crying, people screaming, people even fighting and throwing things at each other. I've seen it happen, and there's no truth in it— that's true.

MRS. GOFORTH: But you say you've reached the same point that I have this summer, the point of no more pretenses, so why can't we play the truth game together, huh, Chris?

CHRIS: Why don't we put it off till—say, after—supper?

MRS. GOFORTH: You play it better on a full stomach, do you?

CHRIS: Yes, you have to be physically fortified for it as well as—morally fortified for it.

MRS. GOFORTH: And you'd like to stay for supper? You don't have any other engagement for supper?

CHRIS: I have no engagements of any kind now, Mrs. Goforth.

MRS. GOFORTH: Well, I don't know about supper. Sometimes I don't want any.

CHRIS: How about after—?

MRS. GOFORTH:—What?

CHRIS: After lunch?

MRS. GOFORTH: Oh, sometimes I don't have lunch, either.

CHRIS: You're not on a healthful regime. You know, the spirit has to live in the body, and so you have to keep the body in a state of repair because it's the home of the—spirit. . . .

MRS. GOFORTH: Hmmm. Are you talking about your spirit and body, or mine?

CHRIS: Yours.

MRS. GOFORTH: One long-ago meeting between us, and you expect me to believe you care more about my spirit and body than your own, Mr. Flanders?

CHRIS: Mrs. Goforth, some people, some people, most of them, get panicky when they're not cared for by somebody, but I get panicky when I have no one to care for.

MRS. GOFORTH: Oh, you seem to be setting yourself up as a—as a saint of some kind. . . .

CHRIS: All I said is I need somebody to care for. I don't say that— (*He has finished his coffee and he crosses to the warmer for more.*) I'm playing the truth game with you. Caring for somebody gives me the sense of being—sheltered, protected. . . .

MRS. GOFORTH: "Sheltered, protected" from what?

CHRIS (*standing above her*): Unreality!—lostness? Have you ever seen how two little animals sleep together, a pair of kittens or puppies? All day they seem so secure in the house of their master, but at night, when they sleep, they don't seem sure of their owner's true care for them. Then they draw close together, they curl up against each other, and now and then, if you watch them, you notice they nudge each other a little with their heads or their paws, exchange little signals between them. The signals mean: we're not in danger . . . sleep: we're close: it's safe here. Their owner's house is never a sure protection, a reliable shelter. Everything going on in it is mysterious to them, and no matter how hard they try to please, how do they know if they please? They hear so many sounds, voices, and see so many things they can't comprehend! Oh, it's ever so much better than the petshop window, but what's become of their mother?—who warmed them and sheltered them and fed them until they were snatched away from her, for no reason they know. We're all of us living in a house we're not used to . . . a house full of—voices, noises, objects, strange shadows, light that's even stranger— We can't understand. We bark and jump around and try to—be—*pleasingly playful* in this big mysterious house but—in our hearts we're all very frightened of it. Don't you think so? Then it gets to be dark. We're left alone with each other. We have to creep close to each other and give those gentle little nudges with our paws and our muzzles before we can slip into—sleep and—rest for the next day's—playtime . . . and the next day's mysteries.

(*He lights a cigarette for her. The Witch enters dramatically on the terrace.*)

THE WITCH: The next day's mysteries! *Ecco, sono qui.*

MRS. GOFORTH (*with unconcealed displeasure*): My Lord, are you still here?

THE WITCH (*as if amazed*): Christopher! Flanders!

CHRIS: How do you do, Mrs.— Oh, I started to say Mrs. Ridgeway but that isn't it, now, is it?

THE WITCH: What a back number you are!

CHRIS (*drawing away from her*): Yes.

MRS. GOFORTH: How'd you miss your return trip to Capri last night? I thought you'd gone back there last night. I had the boatman waiting up for you last night.

THE WITCH: Oh, last *night!* What confusion! (*She puts down her hat and follows Chris.*) When was the last time I saw you?

MRS. GOFORTH: If *you* don't know, why should he?

THE WITCH: Oh, at the wedding banquet those Texas oil people gave me in Portofino, oh, yes, you were staying with them, and so depressed over the loss of—

CHRIS (*cutting in*): Yes. (*He moves toward the balustrade.*)

THE WITCH: You'd taken such beautiful care of that poor old ridiculous woman, but couldn't save her, and, oh, the old Duke of Parma did such a wicked thing to you, poured champagne on your head and—called you—what did he call you?

MRS. GOFORTH: Let him forget it, Connie.

(*The Witch gives her a glance and moves up to Chris.*)

THE WITCH: Something else awful happened and you were involved in some way but I can't remember the details.

CHRIS: Yes, it's better forgotten, Mrs. Goforth is right. Some of the details are much better forgotten if you'll let me—forget them. . . .

(*Mrs. Goforth rises and starts to go inside.*)

THE WITCH: Are you leaving us, Sissy?

MRS. GOFORTH: I'm going to phone the boat house t'make sure there's a boat ready for your trip back to Capri, because I know you want back there as soon as possible, Connie. (*She goes into the library.*)

THE WITCH (*going to the table*): Chris, you're not intending to *stay* here!?

CHRIS: Yes, if I'm invited: I would like to.

THE WITCH: Don't you know, can't you tell? Poor Sissy's going, she's gone. The shock I got last night when I—I had to drink myself blind!—when I saw her condition! (*She comes closer to him.*) You don't want to be stuck with a person in her appalling condition. You're young, have fun. Oh, Chris, you've been foolish too long. The years you devoted to that old Ferguson bitch, and what did you get?

CHRIS (*lighting a cigarette*): Get?

THE WITCH: Yes, get? She *had* you, you were *had!*—*left* you? *Nothing!*—I bet, or why would you be here?

CHRIS: Please don't make me be rude. We don't understand each other, which is natural, but don't make me say things to you that I don't want to say.

THE WITCH: What can you say to me that I haven't heard said?

CHRIS: Have you heard this said to your face about you: that you're the heart of a world that has no heart, the heartless world you live in—has anyone said that to you, Mrs. Ridgeway?

THE WITCH: Condotti, Marchesa Ridgeway-Condotti, Mr. Death Angel Flanders.

CHRIS: Yes, we both have new titles.

THE WITCH (*throwing back her head*): Sally! Laurie! Sissy! It's time for death, old girls, beddy-bye! (*Less shrilly.*) Beddy-bye, old girls, the Death Angel's coming, no dreams . . .

CHRIS: I'm sorry you forced me to say what I feel about you.

THE WITCH: Oh, that. My heart pumps blood that isn't my own blood, it's the blood of anonymous blood donors. And as for the world I live in, you know it as well as I know it. Come to Capri, it's a mountain, too.

CHRIS (*moving away*): You're not afraid of the nickname I've been given?

THE WITCH: No, I think it's a joke that you take seriously, Chris. You've gotten too solemn. (*She follows him.*) Let me take that curse off you. Come to Capri and I'll give you a party, decorated with your mobiles, and—

MRS. GOFORTH (*to Blackie*): See? *She's out there putting the make on—*

(*Blackie leaves as Mrs. Goforth comes from the library toward the terrace.*)

THE WITCH (*to Chris*): You're pale, you look anemic, you look famished, you need someone to put you back in the picture, the social swim. Capri?

(*Mrs. Goforth, on the terrace, advances behind Chris and The Witch.*)

MRS. GOFORTH: What picture? What swim? Capri?

THE WITCH: It's marvelous there this season.

MRS. GOFORTH: The sea is full of Medusas. Didn't you tell me the sea is full of Medusas, and a giant one got you?

THE WITCH (*crossing to her*): Oh, they'll wash out, they'll be washed out by tomorrow.

MRS. GOFORTH: When are *you* going to wash out? I thought you'd washed out last night. I've ordered a boat to take you back to Capri.

THE WITCH: I can't go back to Capri in a dinner gown before sundown. (*She sits at the table and stares at Chris.*)

MRS. GOFORTH: Well, try my hot sulphur baths, or just look the place over, it's worth it. It's worth looking over. Me, I'm about to start work, so I can't talk to you right now. (*She gets The Witch's hat and brings it to her.*) I'm right on the edge of breaking through here today, I'm on a strict discipline, Connie, as I explained last night to you, and— (*She coughs, falls into her chair.*)

THE WITCH: Sissy, I don't like that cough.

MRS. GOFORTH: Hell, do you think I like it? Neuralgia, nerves, overwork, but I'm going to beat it, it isn't going to beat *me*, or it'll be the first thing that ever *did* beat me!

THE WITCH (*rising and going to her*): Be brave, Sissy.

MRS. GOFORTH: Leave me alone, go, Connie, it'll do you in, too. (*She fumbles for a tissue.*)

THE WITCH (*looking wide-eyed at Chris and moving close to him*): Watch out for each other!—Chris, give her the Swami's book you translated. *Ciao!* (*She throws him a kiss and moves off, calling back.*) *Questo è veramente una meraviglia . . . Ciao, arrivederci. . . . Amici!*

(*The Witch goes out of the lighted area and down the goatpath. Chris goes to the table and sits, looking about.*)

MRS. GOFORTH: What are you looking for now?

CHRIS: I was just looking for the cream and sugar.

MRS. GOFORTH: Never touch it. Y'want a saccharine tablet?

CHRIS: Oh, no, thanks, I—don't like the chemical taste.

MRS. GOFORTH (*coming to the table*): Well, it's black coffee or else, I'm afraid, Mr. What?—Chris!

CHRIS: You have *three* villas here?

MRS. GOFORTH: One villa and two villinos. Villino means a small villa. I also have a little grass hut, very Polynesian—(*moving in front of the table*)—down on my private beach too. I have a special use for it, and a funny name for it, too.

CHRIS: Oh?

MRS. GOFORTH: Yes, I call it "the Oubliette." Ever heard of an oubliette?

CHRIS: A place where people are put to be forgotten?

MRS. GOFORTH: That's right, Chris. You've had some education along that line. (*She returns to where he sits.*)

CHRIS: Yes, quite a lot, Mrs. Goforth, especially lately.

MRS. GOFORTH: As for the use of it, well, I've been plagued by imposters lately, the last few summers. The continent has been overrun by imposters of celebrities, writers, actors, and so forth. I mean they arrive and say, like "I am Truman Capote." Well, they look a bit like him so you are taken in by the announcement, "I am Truman Capote," and you receive him cordially only to find out later it isn't the true

Truman Capote, it's the false Truman Capote. Last summer I had the false Truman Capote, and the year before
that I had the false Mary McCarthy. That's before I took to
checking the passports of sudden visitors. Well—(*She moves
to the opposite chair and sits facing him.*) as far as I know
they're still down there in that little grass hut on the beach,
where undesirables are transferred to, when the villas are
overcrowded. The Oubliette. A medieval institution that I
think, personally, was discarded too soon. It was a dun-
geon, where people were put for keeps to be forgotten. You
say you know about it?

(*Chris stares straight at her, not answering by word or gesture.
His look is gentle, troubled.*)

So that's what I call my little grass shack on the beach, I
call it "the Oubliette" from the French verb "*oublier*"
which means to forget, to forget, to put away and—

CHRIS:—forget. . . .

MRS. GOFORTH: And I do really forget 'em. Maybe you think
I'm joking but it's the truth. Can't stand to be made a
Patsy. Understand what I mean?

(*He nods.*)

This is nothing personal. You came with your book—(*picks
up his book of poetry*) with a photograph of you on it, which
still looks like you just, well, ten years younger, but still un-
mistakably you. You're not the false Chris Flanders, I'm
sure about that.

CHRIS: Thank you. I try not to be.

MRS. GOFORTH: However, I don't keep up with the new personalities in the world of art like I used to. Too much a
waste of vital energy, Chris. Of course you're not exactly a
new personality in it: would you say so?

(*Chris smiles and shakes his head slightly.*)

You're almost a veteran in it. I said a veteran, I didn't say a
"has been"— (*She sneezes violently.*) I'm allergic to something around here. I haven't found out just what, but when
I do, oh, brother, watch it go!

CHRIS (*rising and bringing her a clean tissue*): I hope it isn't the bougainvillaea vines.

MRS. GOFORTH: No, it isn't the bougainvillaea, but I'm having an allergy specialist flown down here from Rome to check me with every goddamn plant and animal on the place, and whatever it is has to go.

CHRIS: Have you tried breathing sea water?

MRS. GOFORTH: Oh, you want to drown me?

CHRIS (*returning to his chair and sitting*): Ha ha, no. I meant have you tried snuffing it up in your nostrils to irrigate your nasal passages, Mrs. Goforth, it's sometimes a very effective treatment for—

MRS. GOFORTH: Aside from this allergy and a little neuralgia, sometimes more than a little, I'm a healthy woman. Know how I've kept in shape, my body, the way it still is?

CHRIS: Exercise?

MRS. GOFORTH: Yes! In bed! Plenty of it, still going on! . . . But there's this worship of youth in the States, this Whistler's Mother complex, you know what I mean, this idea that at a certain age a woman ought to resign herself to being a sweet old thing in a rocker. Well, last week-end, a man, a *young* man, came in my bedroom and it wasn't too easy to get him out of it. I had to be very firm about it.

(*Blackie appears on the terrace with a plate of food for Chris. Mrs. Goforth rises.*)

What've you got there, Blackie?

BLACKIE: Mr. Flanders' breakfast. I'm sure he would like some.

MRS. GOFORTH: Aw, now, isn't that thoughtful. Put it down there.

(*As Blackie starts to put it down on the table, Mrs. Goforth indicates the serving table.*

I said down there. And get me my menthol inhaler and Kleenex. I have run out.

(*Blackie sets the plate on the serving table and retires from the lighted area.*

Simonetta!

(*Mrs. Goforth rings and hands the tray to Simonetta as she enters.*)

Take this away. I can't stand the smell of food now.

(*Simonetta goes out.*)

CHRIS (*who has moved toward the serving table and stands stunned*): Mrs. Goforth, I feel that I have, I must have disturbed you, annoyed you—disturbed you because I— (*He crosses back to the table.*)

MRS. GOFORTH: Don't reach for a cigarette till I offer you one.

CHRIS: May I have one, Mrs. Goforth?

MRS. GOFORTH: Take one. Be my Trojan Horse Guest. Wait.

(*She moves beside him.*)

Kiss me for it.

(*Chris doesn't move.*)

Kiss me for it, I told you.

CHRIS (*putting the cigarette away*): Mrs. Goforth, there are moments for kisses and moments not for kisses.

MRS. GOFORTH: This is a "not for kiss" moment?

(*He turns away, and she follows and takes his arm.*)

I've shocked *you* by my ferocity, have I? Sometimes I shock myself by it.

(*They move together toward the balustrade.*)

Look: a coin has two sides. On one side is an eagle, but on the other side is—something else. . . .

CHRIS: Yes, something else, usually some elderly potentate's profile.

(*She laughs appreciatively at his riposte and touches his shoulder. He moves a step away from her.*)

MRS. GOFORTH: Why didn't you grab the plate and run off with it?

CHRIS: Like a dog grabs a bone?

MRS. GOFORTH: Sure! Why not? It might've pleased me to see you show some fight.

CHRIS: I can fight if I have to, but the fighting style of dogs is not my style.

MRS. GOFORTH: *Grab, fight, or go hungry!* Nothing else works.

CHRIS: How is it possible for a woman of your reputation as a patron of arts and artists, to live up here, with all this beauty about you, and yet be—

MRS. GOFORTH: A bitch, a swamp-bitch, a devil? Oh, I see it, the view, but it makes me feel ugly this summer for some reason or other—bitchy, a female devil.

CHRIS: You'd like the view to be ugly to make you feel superior to it?

MRS. GOFORTH (*turning to him*): Why don't we sing that old church hymn:

> "From Greenland's icy mountains to India's coral Isle
> Everything is beautiful . . ."

CHRIS: "Man alone is vile."

MRS. GOFORTH: Hmm. Devils can be driven out of the heart by the touch of a hand on a hand, or a mouth on a mouth. Because, like Alex said once, "Evil isn't a person: evil is a thing that comes sneaky-snaking into the heart of a person, and takes it over: a mean intruder, a *squatter*!"

CHRIS: May I touch your hand, please?

MRS. GOFORTH (*as he does*): Your hand's turned cold. I've shocked the warm blood out of it. Let me rub it back in.

CHRIS: Your hand's cold, too, Mrs. Goforth.

MRS. GOFORTH: Oh, that's just—nervous tension, never mind that. I'll tell you something, Chris, you came here at a time unusually favorable to you. Now we're going to talk turkey. At least *I'm* going to talk turkey. You can talk ducks and geese, but I am going to talk turkey, cold turkey. You've come here at a time when I'm restless, bored, and shocked by the news of deaths of three friends in the States, one, two, three, like firecrackers going off, right together almost, like rat-a-tat-tat blindfolded against the wall.—Well, you see I— (*She moves down to the lower terrace.*) I had a bad scare last winter. I was visiting relatives I'd set up on a grand estate on Long Island when some little psychosomatic symptom gave me a scare. They made a big deal of it, had me removed by a seaplane to the East River where they had an ambulance waiting for me, and whisked me off to a— Know what I said when I was advised to go under the knife the next day? Ha, I'll tell you, ha ha!—Called my law firm and dictated a letter cutting them off with one dollar apiece in my will. . . .

CHRIS (*who has come down to her*): Mrs. Goforth, are you still afraid of— (*He hesitates.*)

MRS. GOFORTH: Death—never even think of it. (*She takes his arm and they move down to a bench, and sit.*)

CHRIS: Death is one moment, and life is so many of them.

MRS. GOFORTH: A million billion of them, if you think in terms of a lifetime as rich as mine's been, Chris.

CHRIS: Yes, life is something, death's nothing. . . .

MRS. GOFORTH: Nothing, nothing, but nothing. I've had to refer to many deaths in my memoirs. Oh, I don't think I'm immortal—I still go to sleep every night wondering if I'll— wake up the next day . . . (*Coughs and gasps for breath.*) —face that angry old lion.

CHRIS: Angry old—?

MRS. GOFORTH:—lion!

CHRIS: The sun? You think it's angry?

MRS. GOFORTH: Naturally, of course—looking down on—? Well, you know what it looks down on. . . .

CHRIS: It seems to accept and understand things today. . . .

MRS. GOFORTH: It's just a big fire-ball that toughens the skin, including the skin of the heart.

CHRIS: How lovely the evenings must be here—when the fishing boats go out on the Gulf of Salerno with their little lamps shining.

MRS. GOFORTH: Well, they call this coast the *Divina Costiera*. That means the divine coast, you know.

CHRIS: Yes, I know. I suppose . . .

MRS. GOFORTH: You suppose what?

CHRIS: I suppose you dine on the terrace about the time the fishing boats go out with their little lamps and the stars come out of the—

MRS. GOFORTH: Firmament. Call it the firmament, not the sky, it's much more classy to call it the firmament, baby. How about spring? You write about spring and live in it, you write about love in the spring, haven't you written

love-poems for susceptible—patrons?—Well! How many
books of poems have you come out with?

CHRIS: Just the one that I brought you.

MRS. GOFORTH: You mean you burnt out as a poet?

CHRIS:—Pardon?

MRS. GOFORTH: You mean you burnt out as a poet?

(*Chris laughs uncomfortably.*)

Why're you laughing? I didn't say anything funny.

CHRIS: I didn't know I was laughing. Excuse me, Mrs.
Goforth. But you are very—direct.

MRS. GOFORTH: Is that shocking?

CHRIS: No. No, not really. In fact I like that about you.

MRS. GOFORTH: But you give that little embarrassed laugh,
like I'd made you uncomfortable.

CHRIS: My nerves are—

MRS. GOFORTH: Gone through like your list of suckers. (*Mrs.
Goforth sneezes and gets up to look for another tissue.*)

CHRIS (*standing*): Mrs. Goforth—if you want me to go—

MRS. GOFORTH: That depends.

CHRIS: What does it depend on?

MRS. GOFORTH: Frankly, I'm very lonely up here this summer.

CHRIS: I can understand that.

MRS. GOFORTH: Now, you're not stupid. You're attractive to
me. You know that you are. You've deliberately set out
to be attractive to me, and you are. So don't be a free-
loader.

(*Chris doesn't speak for a moment.*)

CHRIS (*gently*): Mrs. Goforth, I think you've been exposed to
the wrong kind of people and—

MRS. GOFORTH (*cutting in*): I'm sick of moral blackmail! You
know what that is. People imposing on you by the old, old
trick of making you feel it would be unkind of you not to
permit them to do it. In their hearts they despise you. So
much they can't quite hide it. It pops out in sudden little
remarks and looks they give you. Busting with malice—because you have what they haven't. You know what some
writer called that? "A robust conscience, and the Viking
spirit in life!"

CHRIS (*going back on the terrace*): Oh? Is that what he called it?

MRS. GOFORTH (*following*): He called it that, and I have it! I give away nothing, I sell and I buy in my life, and I've always wound up with a profit, one way or another. You came up that hill from the highway with an old book of poems that you got published ten years ago, by playing on the terrible, desperate loneliness of a rich old broken-hipped woman, who, all she could do, was pretend that someone still loved her. . . .

CHRIS: You're talking about Mrs. Ferguson.

MRS. GOFORTH: Yes, I am.

CHRIS (*moving away from her*): I made her walk again. She published my poems.

MRS. GOFORTH: How long after she published your poems did you let go of her arm so she fell on the deck of a steamship and her hip broke again?

CHRIS: I didn't let her go. She broke away from me—

(*Mrs. Goforth laughs uproariously*)

—if you'll allow me to make a minor correction in the story. We were walking very slowly about the promenade deck of the *Queen Mary*, eight summers ago, more than a year after my poems were published. A young man called to her from a deck chair that we'd just passed, and she wheeled around and broke away from my hand, and slipped and fell, and her hip was broken again. Of course some malicious "friends" blamed me, but—I wouldn't leave her.

MRS. GOFORTH: No? She was still your meal-ticket?

CHRIS: Not at all.

MRS. GOFORTH: Who *was*?

CHRIS (*sitting*): I was fashionable, then.

MRS. GOFORTH: Do you sit down while a lady is standing?

CHRIS (*springing up with a rather ferocious smile*): Sorry, won't you sit down!

(*His tone is so commanding, abruptly, that she does sit down in the chair he jerks out for her.*)

May I tell you something about yourself? It may seem presumptuous of me to tell you this, but I'm going to tell you this: you're suffering more than you need to.

MRS. GOFORTH: I am—

CHRIS (*cutting through her protest*): You're suffering from the worst of all human maladies, of all afflictions, and I don't mean one of the body, I mean the thing people feel when they go from room to room for no reason, and then they go back from room to room for no reason, and then they go *out* for no reason and come back *in* for no reason—

MRS. GOFORTH: You mean I'm alone here, don't you?

(*Chris takes hold of her hand. She snatches it away from him.*)

I'm *working* up here this summer, *working*! *Ever heard of it?*

(*A Stage Assistant appears in the wings as if she had shouted for him. He hands her a letter.*)

This morning's mail brought me this! My London publisher's letter! "Darling Flora: Your book of memoirs, *Facts and a Figure*, will, in my opinion, rank with and possibly—"

(*She squints, unable to decipher the letter further. Chris removes it from her trembling, jeweled hand, and completes the reading.*)

CHRIS: "—rank with and possibly even out-rank the great Marcel Proust's *Remembrance of Things Past* as a social documentation of two continents in three decades. . . ."

MRS. GOFORTH: Well?

CHRIS: A letter like this should fall on a higher mountain.

MRS. GOFORTH: Huh?

CHRIS: A letter like this should be delivered above the snow line of an Alpine peak because it's snow, a snow job.

(*She snatches it back from him.*)

MRS. GOFORTH (*raging*): For you, a blond beatnik, coming from Naples on foot up a goddamn goatpath, wearing at this table a Japanese robe because dogs tore your britches, I think your presumption is not excusable, Mister! It lacks the excuse of much youth, you're not young enough for your moxey. This publisher's not a lover. A lover might snow me, but this man's a business associate, and they don't snow you, not *me*, not *Sissy Goforth*! They don't snow me—*snow me!* They don't get up that early in the morning—

(*Her agitation somehow touches him. His smile turns warm again.*)

—that they could— (*coughs*) snow me. . . .

(*The Stage Assistants lean, whispering together, as they retire from the stage.*)

CHRIS: Of course, without having your publisher's advantage of knowing *Facts and a Figure*—

MRS. GOFORTH: Nothing, not a word of it!

CHRIS: No, not a word, but what I was going to say was that I think you need *companionship*, not just employees about you, up here, but— How often do you see old friends or new friends this summer, Mrs. Goforth? Often or not so often?

MRS. GOFORTH: Hell, all I have to do is pick up a phone to crowd this mountain with—

CHRIS: Crowds? Is it that easy this summer? You're proud. You don't want to ask people up here that might not come, because they're pleasure-seekers, frantic choosers of silly little distractions, and—and—

MRS. GOFORTH: "and—and" *what?*

CHRIS: Your condition, the terrible strain of your work, makes you seem—eccentric, disturbing!— To those sea-level, those lower-than-sea-level, people. . . .

MRS. GOFORTH: *Get to whatever you're leading up to, will you!*

CHRIS: I notice you have trouble reading. I've been told I have a good reading voice.

MRS. GOFORTH: Most human voices are very monotonous to me. Besides, I'm more interested in producing literature this summer than having it read to me.

CHRIS: Mmm—but you do need some agreeable companionship.

MRS. GOFORTH: Right you are about *that*, but how do I know your idea of agreeable companionship is the same as mine? You purr at me like a cat, now, but a cat will purr at you one minute and scratch your eyes out the next.

(He leans back, smiling, working the sword up and down in its scabbard.)

I think you better take off that old sword belt.

CHRIS: There're no buttons on the robe, so without the belt on it—

MRS. GOFORTH: Take it off you!

CHRIS: The *robe*?

MRS. GOFORTH: The *sword* belt. You grin and fiddle with the hilt—the sword—like you had—evil—intentions.

CHRIS: Oh. You suspect I'm a possible assassin?

MRS. GOFORTH: *Take it off, give it here!*

CHRIS: All right. Formal surrender, *unconditional . . . nearly.* *(He takes the sword belt off and hands it to her.)*

MRS. GOFORTH: *O.K., Robert E. Lee! At Appomattox . . .*

(She hurls the sword belt to the terrace tiles behind her. A Stage Assistant darts out of the wings to remove it. The other Assistant laughs off stage.)

CHRIS: Now what can I use for a sash to keep things proper?

MRS. GOFORTH: See if this goes around you, if being proper's so important to you.

(She hands him a brilliant scarf she has been wearing about her throat. He turns upstage to tie the scarf about him. A phone is heard ringing, off stage. Blackie appears from behind the library screen.)

MRS. GOFORTH *(to Blackie)*: Who's calling? My broker again, with the closing quotations?

BLACKIE: The call's for *Mr. Flanders.*

CHRIS: *Me*, for *me*? But who could know I'm up here!

MRS. GOFORTH: Cut the bull. You got a call up here last night. Business is picking up for you.

CHRIS: This is—mystifying!

BLACKIE: The phone's in the library.

CHRIS: Excuse me.

(He goes quickly behind the library screen. Mrs. Goforth crosses toward it but remains, listening, outside it.)

CHRIS (*behind screen*): *Pronto, pronto.* Madelyn!—How are you, how's your dear mother?—Oh, my God!—I meant to come straight down there but—was it, uh, what they call peaceful? (*Pause.*) Oh, I'm so glad, I prayed so hard that it *would* be! And I'm so relieved that it *was.* I did so long to be with you but had to stop on the way. And you? Will you be all right? Yes, I know, *expected*, but still I could be some use in making the necessary arrangements? I'm at Flora Goforth's place, but if you could send a car to pick me up I could— Oh?—Oh?—Well, Madelyn, all I can say is *accept* it.—Bless you, goodbye. *Accept* it.

(*Mrs. Goforth is shaken. She moves to the table as if she had received a personal shock. Chris comes back out. At the same moment, church bells ring in a village below the mountain.*)

CHRIS:—Church bells? In the village?

MRS. GOFORTH: Yes, appropriate, aren't they? Ringing right on a dead cue . . .

CHRIS: I just received news that's—*shocked* me. . . .

MRS. GOFORTH: Another name you have to scratch off the list?

CHRIS: Did you say "list"?

MRS. GOFORTH (*smiling at him cunningly, fiercely*): I went to a spiritualist once. She said to me, "I hear many dead voices calling, 'Flora, Flora.'" I knew she was a fake, then, since all my close friends call me Sissy. I said, "Tell them to mind their own business, play their gold harps and mind their own harp-playing. Sissy Goforth's not ready to go forth yet and won't go forth till she's ready. . . ."

(*Chris extends a hand to her. The bells stop ringing.*)

What are you reaching out for?

CHRIS: Your hand, if I may, Mrs. Goforth. (*He has taken hold of it.*)

MRS. GOFORTH: Hold it but don't squeeze it. The rings cut my fingers.

CHRIS: I'm glad we've talked so frankly, so quickly today. The conversation we had at the ball at the Waldorf in 1950 was a long conversation but not as deep as this one.

MRS. GOFORTH: Who said anything deep? I don't say anything deep in a conversation, not this summer, I save it for my memoirs. Did you say anything deep, in your opinion? If you did, it escaped me, escaped my notice completely. Oh, you've known Swanees. Excuse me, Swamis. You've been exposed to the—intellectual scene, and it's rubbed off on you a little, but only skin-deep, as deep as your little blond beard. . . .

CHRIS: Perhaps I used the wrong word.

(*She places a cigarette in her mouth and waits for him to light it. He turns deliberately away from her, and places a foot on the low balustrade, facing seaward.*)

This "wine-dark sea," it's the oldest sea in the world. . . . Know what I see down there?

MRS. GOFORTH: The sea.

CHRIS: Yes, and a fleet of Roman triremes, those galleys with three banks of oars, rowed by slaves, commanded by commanders headed for conquests. Out for loot. *Boom!* Out for conquering, pillaging, and collecting more slaves. *Boom!* Here's where the whole show started, it's the oldest sea in the Western world, Mrs. Goforth, this sea called the Mediterranean Sea, which means the middle of the earth, was the cradle, of life, not the grave, but the cradle of pagan and Christian—civilizations, this sea, and its connecting river, that old water snake, the Nile.

MRS. GOFORTH: I've been on the Nile. No message. Couple of winters ago I stayed at the Mena House, that hotel under the pyramids. I could see the pyramids, those big-big calcified fools-caps from my breakfast balcony. No message. Rode up to 'em on a camel so I could say I'd done the whole bit.

CHRIS: No message?

MRS. GOFORTH: No message, except you can get seasick on a camel. Yep, you can get mighty seasick on the hump of a camel. Went inside those old king-size tombstones.

CHRIS: No message inside them, either?

MRS. GOFORTH: No message, except the Pharaohs and their families had the idiotic idea they were going to wake up hungry and thirsty and so provided themselves with breakfasts which had gone very stale and dry, and the Pharaohs and families were still sound asleep, ho ho. . . .

(*He still has his back to her. She is obviously annoyed by his loss of attention.*)

And if you look this way, you'll notice I've got a cigarette in my mouth and I'm waiting for you to light it. Didn't that old Sally Ferguson bitch teach you to light a cigarette for a lady?

CHRIS (*facing her*): She wasn't a bitch, unless all old dying ladies are bitches. She was dying, and scared to death of dying, which made her a little—eccentric . . .

(*He has picked up Mrs. Goforth's diamond-studded lighter. He lights her cigarette but doesn't return the lighter to the table. He tosses it in the palm of his hand.*)

MRS. GOFORTH: Thanks. Now put it down.

(*He sits down, smiling, on the low balustrade. There has oc-curred a marked change in his surface attitude toward her: the deferential air has gone completely.*)

I meant my Bulgari lighter, not your—*backside!*

(*He studies the lighter as if to calculate its value. There is a pause.*)

If you don't put that lighter back down on the table, I'm going to call for Rudy! You know Rudy. You've made his acquaintance, I think.

CHRIS: If I don't put it down on the table but in my pocket, and if I were to run down the goatpath with it—how fast can Rudy run?

MRS. GOFORTH: How fast can *you* run? Could you outrun the dogs? Yesterday you didn't outrun the dogs.

CHRIS: That was—uphill, on the other side of your mountain. I think I could get down this side, yes, by the—funicular, I could operate it.

MRS. GOFORTH: Can you outrun a bullet?

CHRIS: Oh, would you have Rudy shoot at me for this lighter?

MRS. GOFORTH: You bet I would. That's a very valuable lighter.

(*Chris laughs and tosses the lighter on the table.*)

CHRIS: Hmmm. On a parapet over the Western world's oldest sea, the lady that owns it had a gangster—

MRS. GOFORTH: The bodyguard of a syndicate gangster!

CHRIS: Yes, the lady that owns it had her bodyguard shoot down a—what?—burnt-out poet who had confiscated a diamond-studded lighter because he was unfed and hungry. He'd been on a five-day fast for—nonsecular reasons, and it had upset his reason.

(*Mrs. Goforth rings the bell on the table. Chris seizes her hand and wrests the bell away from it. She rises from the table and shouts: "Rudy!"*)

CHRIS (*louder than she*): Rudy!

MRS. GOFORTH: You couldn't get away with it!

CHRIS: Oh, yes, I could, if I wanted. (*He tosses the bell back on the table with a mocking grin.*)

MRS. GOFORTH: What a peculiar—puzzlesome young man you are! You came out here like a dandy, kissed my hand, and now you're coming on like a young hood all of a sudden, and I don't like the change, it makes me nervous with you, and now I don't know if I want you around here or not, or if I'm—not superstitious. See? You've made me shaky.

CHRIS: You didn't know I was teasing?

MRS. GOFORTH: No. You're too good at it.

CHRIS (*looking seaward*): I see it, your oubliette on the beach, it looks attractive to me.

MRS. GOFORTH: Help me into my bedroom. (*She tries to rise but falls back into the chair.*) It's time for my siesta.

CHRIS: Could I stay there, a while?

MRS. GOFORTH: Later maybe. Not now. I need to rest.

CHRIS: I meant the grass hut on the beach, not your bedroom.

MRS. GOFORTH: Be still, she's coming back out, my secretary, and I'm not sure I trust her.

CHRIS: Do you trust anybody?

MRS. GOFORTH: Nobody human, just dogs. All except poodles, I never trusted a poodle. . . .

(*Blackie comes onto the terrace.*)

In again, out again, Finnegan! What's it *this* time, Blackie?

BLACKIE: Is it true you've discharged the kitchen staff again, Mrs. Goforth?

MRS. GOFORTH: Yes, it's true. . . . Haven't you heard about the inventory?

BLACKIE: What inventory, inventory of what?

MRS. GOFORTH: I had an intuition that things were disappearing and had Rudy check my list of fabulous china, my Sèvres, Limoges, Lowestoff, against what was still on the mountain. Half of it gone, decimated! And my Medici silver, banquet silver used by the Medicis hundreds of years ago, *gone*!—That's what the inventory disclosed!

BLACKIE: Mrs. Goforth, is it possible you don't remember—

MRS. GOFORTH: *What?*

BLACKIE: You had it removed to a storage house in Naples, in an armored truck.

MRS. GOFORTH: *Me?*

BLACKIE: *You!*

MRS. GOFORTH: *Not true!*

BLACKIE: Mrs. Goforth, when people are very ill and taking drugs for it, they get confused, their memories are confused, they get delusions.

MRS. GOFORTH: *This mountain has been systematically pillaged!*—That's what the inventory—

BLACKIE: An inventory made by the bodyguard of a syndicate gangster?

MRS. GOFORTH: How dare you suggest— *I have a guest at the table!*

BLACKIE: *I will always dare to say what I know to be true!*

MRS. GOFORTH: *Go in, find my checkbook and write out a check for yourself for whatever's coming to you, and bring it out here and I'll sign it for cash, at the Naples branch of my bank! You wanted out, now you got it, so take it! Take it!*

BLACKIE: *Gladly! Gladly!*

MRS. GOFORTH: Mutually *gladly! Go in!*

(*Blackie starts to go. Mrs. Goforth's shouting has brought on a coughing spasm. She covers her mouth with her hands and rushes, in a crouched position, toward the upstage area of the library.*)

CHRIS:—*Boom* . . .

BLACKIE: *Release!*

CHRIS (*pointing at the terrace pavement*): Blackie? Look!— Blood, she's bleeding. . . .

MRS. GOFORTH'S VOICE (*Off stage, hoarsely*): *Dottore, chiama il dottore! Giulio, Simonetta!*

CHRIS: You'd better go in there with her.

BLACKIE: I can't yet. They'll get the doctor for her. (*She moves downstage, gasping.*) You see, she's made me *inhuman!*

(*Simonetta explodes onto the forestage.*)

SIMONETTA: *Signorina, la Signora é molto, molto malata!*

BLACKIE (*going toward her*): *Dov'è la Signora, in camera da letto?*

SIMONETTA: *No, nella biblioteca, con il dottore!* (*She sits on a bench and sobs hysterically.*)

BLACKIE: Well, I'd better go in there.

CHRIS: What shall I do? Anything?

BLACKIE: Yes, stay here, don't go. (*Then, to Simonetta, who is now crying theatrically*) *Ferma questa—commedia.*

(*Simonetta stops crying, and begins straightening up the table.*)

(*To Chris*) Call the hospital in Rome, Salvatore Mundi, and ask for Dr. Rengucci. Tell him what's happening here and a nurse is needed at once. Then come in there, the library, and we'll—

(*Giulio rushes out onto the forestage.*)

GIULIO: *La Signora Goforth vuol' vedere il Signore, presto, molto presto!*

BLACKIE (*to Chris*): She's calling for *you.* I'd better go in first. Make the call and then come to the library.

(*She goes out one way, Chris the other.*)

GIULIO (*to Simonetta*): She's dying?

SIMONETTA: No one's been paid this week. Who will pay us if she dies today?

GIULIO: *Guarda!*

(*He shows her a gold bracelet. Simonetta snatches at it. Giulio
pockets it with a grin, and starts off as she follows.*)

The Scene Dims Out.

SCENE SIX

*Later the same day, toward sundown. The interiors of the white
villa are screened and the terrace is lighted more coolly. Blackie
is seated at the downstage table, jotting in a notebook memo-
randa of things to be done before leaving. The Stage Assistants
stand by the flagstaff ready to lower the banner of Mrs.
Goforth.*

ONE: Cable her daughter that the old bitch is dying.
TWO: The banner of the griffin is about to be lowered.
BLACKIE (*as if translating their speech into a polite para-
    phrase*): Cable Mrs. Goforth's daughter at Point Goforth,
    Long Island, that her mother is not expected to survive the
    night, and I'm waiting for—immediate—instructions.
ONE: Fireworks tonight at Point Goforth, Long Island.
TWO: A champagne fountain.
ONE *and* TWO (*together*): Death: celebration.
BLACKIE: Call police in Amalfi to guard the library safe till
    Rudy has gone.
ONE: Rudy's root-a-toot-tooting through that safe right now.
TWO: He's disappointed to discover that the old bitch still has
    on her most important jewels.
ONE: And she's still conscious—fiercely!
BLACKIE: Contact mortuary. Amalfi.
TWO: That Blackie's a cool one.

(*Chris comes onto the terrace, now wearing his repaired lederhosen and a washed, but unironed, white shirt.*)

CHRIS: Blackie?
BLACKIE (*glancing up*): Oh. I'm making out a list of things
    to do before leaving.
CHRIS: You're not leaving right away, are you?

BLACKIE: Soon as I get instructions from her daughter.

CHRIS: I called the Rome doctor and told him what had happened. He said he's expected it sooner, and there's nothing more to be done that can't be done by the doctor on the place.

BLACKIE: The little doctor, Lullo, has given her a strong shot of adrenalin which was a mistake, I think. She won't go to bed, keeps pressing electric buzzers for Simonetta who's run away, and she's put on all her rings so they won't be stolen. She's more afraid of being robbed of her jewelry than her life. What time would it be in the States?

CHRIS: What time is it here?

BLACKIE: Sundown, nearly.

CHRIS: About seven-thirty here would make it—about two-thirty there.

BLACKIE: Maybe a phone call would get through before a cable.

(*She rises. One of the Stage Assistants brings a phone from the table by the chaise lounge, a little upstage. Blackie takes the phone.*)

Try her daughter's husband at Goforth, Faller and Rush, Incorporated, Plaza 1-9000, while I—

(*She gives Chris the phone, and pours herself a brandy. Rudy comes out with a strongbox from the safe.*)

Who's that? Oh! *You!* What are you taking out?

RUDY: Just what I was told to take out.

BLACKIE: Well, take it out, but don't forget that everything's been listed.

RUDY: I don't forget nothing, Blackie. (*He goes off.*)

STAGE ASSISTANT ONE (*removing the crested screen*): Her bedroom in the white villa.

TWO: The griffin is staring at death, and trying to outstare it.

(*We see Mrs. Goforth seated. She wears a majestic ermine-trimmed robe to which she has pinned her "most important jewels," and rings blaze on her fingers that clench the chair arms.*)

ONE: Her eyes are bright as her diamonds.

TWO: Until she starts bleeding again, she'll give no ground to any real or suspected adversary. . . .

ONE: And *then*?

(*During this exchange between the Assistants, who now back into the wings on their soundless shoes, Blackie has made several other notations. Without looking up at Chris, she asks him:*)

BLACKIE: You're still very hungry, aren't you?

CHRIS: Yes, very.

BLACKIE: The new kitchen staff has arrived. I've put a bottle of milk in your rucksack, and your rucksack is in the library. You'd better just have the milk now. We'll have dinner later together.

CHRIS: Blackie, I've seen her grass hut on the beach, her oubliette, as she calls it. And—I wonder how long I could stay down there before I'd be discovered and—evicted?

BLACKIE: Long as you want to. Indefinitely, I guess. But how would you live down there with the villas all closed?

CHRIS: Oh, on—*frutti di mare*: shellfish. And I'd make a spear for spear-fishing.

BLACKIE: There's no fresh water down there, just the sea water.

CHRIS: I know how to make fresh water out of sea water.

BLACKIE: Why would you want to stay down there?

CHRIS (*as a wave crashes under the mountain*): Boom! I'd like to make a mobile. I'd call it "Boom." The sea and the sky are turning the same color, dissolving into each other. Wine-dark sea and wine-dark sky. In a little while the little fishing boats with their lamps for night fishing will make the sea look like the night sky turned upside down, and you and I will have a sort of valedictory dinner on the terrace.

BLACKIE: Yes, it sounds very peaceful. . . .

(*The bedroom of the white villa is now brightened. Mrs. Goforth staggers from her chair, knocking it over. The Stage Assistants dart out to snatch the small chair and move it farther away, as she leans on a bed post, gasping. Then she draws herself up, advances to the chair's new position a little farther back. She reaches out for it. The Assistants pull it farther. She staggers dizzily after it. The Assistants exchange inquiring*) *looks. They silently agree to allow her the chair and they back out of the area. She sits down with a cry of fury and resumes her fierce contest with death. A reserve of power, triggered by the adrenalin, begins to reanimate her. She rises and drags the chair to a small boudoir table and calls out:)*

MRS. GOFORTH: *Chris? Chris?*

BLACKIE: That's her, she's calling for you. Can you stand to go in there?

CHRIS: Sure I can—it's a professional duty.

(As he turns upstage, the Stage Assistants remove the screen masking the library. He enters that area. One of the Stage Assistants turns the screen perpendicular to the proscenium so that it represents a wall division between bedroom and library. They retire.)

Boom! Mrs. Goforth?

MRS. GOFORTH: Oh, you've finally got here. Stay out there, don't come in here right away. The doctor gave me a shot that's made me a little dizzy, I'll call you in—in a minute. . . . *(She staggers up from the chair, knocking it over.)*

CHRIS: Are you all right, Mrs. Goforth? *(He discovers his sack, removes and opens the milk bottle.)*

MRS. GOFORTH: Just a little unsteady after the shot, the doctor said. The bleeding was from a little blood vessel at the back of my throat. But he thinks I ought to lay off the work for a while, just wind up this volume and save the rest for—sequels. . . .

(Chris opens the milk bottle and sips the milk as if it were sacramental wine.)

Don't you think that's better, since it's such a strain on me?

CHRIS: Yes, I do, I think it's a—*(drinks milk)*—a wise decision. . . . *(He catches some drops of milk that have run down his chin, licks them almost reverently off the palm of his hand.)*

MRS. GOFORTH *(entering the library)*: All that work, the pressure, was burning me up, it was literally burning me up like a house on fire.

CHRIS (*assisting her to the desk chair*): Yes, we—all live in a house on fire, no fire department to call; no way out, just the upstairs window to look out of while the fire burns the house down with us trapped, locked in it.

MRS. GOFORTH: What do you mean by—what windows?

CHRIS (*touching his forehead*): These upstairs windows, not wide enough to crawl out of, just wide enough to lean out of and look out of, and—look and look and look, till we're almost nothing but looking, nothing, almost, but *vision*. . . .

MRS. GOFORTH: Hmmm.—Yes. It isn't as cool out here as it was in my bedroom and this robe I've put on is too heavy. So come on in. We can talk in my bedroom. (*She retires behind the bedroom screen.*)

MRS. GOFORTH'S VOICE (*from behind her screen*): Talking between rooms is a strain on the ears and the vocal cords—so come in, now: I'm ready.

(*He crosses to the screens, stops short.*)

CHRIS: Oh. Sorry. (*He turns away from the screens.*) I'll wait till you've—

MRS. GOFORTH'S VOICE: Modesty? *Modesty?* I wouldn't expect you to suffer from modesty, Chris. I never was bothered with silliness of that kind. If you've got a figure that's pleasing to look at, why be selfish with it?

CHRIS: Yes, it *was* a pleasure, Mrs. Goforth.

MRS. GOFORTH'S VOICE: Then why'd you retreat, back away? In my bedroom, in here, I almost never, if ever, wear a stitch of clothes in summer. I like to feel cool air on my bare skin in summer. Don't you like that? Cool air and cool water on the bare skin in summer's the nicest thing about summer. Huh? Don't you think so, too?

CHRIS: I've found my duffel bag. It wandered in here, for some reason.

MRS. GOFORTH'S VOICE: I had it brought there so I could get your passport for the local police. They want a look at the passport of anyone just arrived.

CHRIS: I see.

MRS. GOFORTH'S VOICE: You'll get it back when you go, you know, there's no hurry, is there?

CHRIS: I'm not sure about that. (*Finds passport.*) Anyway, it's already been returned.

MRS. GOFORTH: We've just been getting acquainted. The preliminaries of a friendship, or any kind of relationship, are the most difficult part, and our talk on the terrace was just a—preliminary.

CHRIS (*wryly, so low that she cannot hear*): Sometimes the preliminaries are rougher than the main bout. (*He is rearranging articles in the rucksack.*)

MRS. GOFORTH: I didn't catch that. What was that?

CHRIS (*to himself*): I didn't mean you to catch it.

MRS. GOFORTH: Stop mumbling and fussing with that metal stuff in the sack. The fussing drowns out the mumbling. D'ya want me to break another blood vessel in my throat talking to you from here?

CHRIS: Are you dressed now, Mrs. Goforth?

MRS. GOFORTH: Hell, I told you I'm never dressed in my bedroom.

CHRIS: You said "rarely if ever"—not "never." (*He sighs and crosses to the door again.*) You have a beautiful body, Mrs. Goforth. It's a privilege to be permitted to admire it. It makes me think of one of those great fountain figures in Scandinavian countries.

MRS. GOFORTH: Yeah, well, baby, a fountain figure is a stone figure and my body isn't a stone figure, although it's been sculpted by several world-famous sculptors, it's still a flesh and blood figure. And don't think it's been easy to keep it the way it still is. I'm going to lie down and rest now on this cool bed. Mmmm, these sheets are so cool—come on in. Why are you standing there paralyzed in that door?

CHRIS: I'm—silent on a peak in—Darien. . . . (*Turns away from the door.*) I came here hoping to be your friend, Mrs. Goforth, but—

MRS. GOFORTH'S VOICE: You said "but" something, but what?

CHRIS: I wouldn't have come here unless I thought I was able to serve some purpose or other, in return for a temporary refuge, a place to rest and work in, where I could get back that sense of reality I've been losing lately, as I tried to explain on the terrace, but— (*He has removed the large mobile under her desk. He climbs on the desk to attach the mobile to the chandelier above it.*) You knew I was hungry but it was "black coffee or else."

MRS. GOFORTH: Is that why you won't come in here?

CHRIS: It would just be embarrassing for us both if I did. (*He jumps off the desk.*)

MRS. GOFORTH: *What's that, what're you doing?*

CHRIS: I hung up a gift I brought you, a mobile called "The Earth Is a Wheel in a Great Big Gambling Casino." And now I think I should leave, I have a long way to go.

MRS. GOFORTH: Just a minute. I'm coming back out there to see this mobile of yours. (*She comes from behind the screen, pulling the regal white robe about her.*) Well, where is it?

CHRIS: Right over your head.

(*She looks up, staggering against the desk.*)

MRS. GOFORTH: It doesn't move, doesn't go.

CHRIS: It will, when it's caught by the wind.

(*The mobile begins to turn, casting faint flickers of light.*)

There now, the winds caught it, it's turning. (*He picks up his canvas sack, preparing to leave.*)

MRS. GOFORTH: (*picking up the phone, suddenly*): *Kitchen, cucina, cucina!—Cucina? Un momento!* (*She thrusts the phone toward Chris.*) Tell the cook what you would like for supper.

CHRIS: Anything, Mrs. Goforth.

MRS. GOFORTH (*into the phone*): O.K.— *Cucina? Senta— Pranzo questa sera.—Pastina in brodo, per cominciare. Capish?—Si!—Poi, una grande pesca, si, si, una grandissima pesca, anche—carne freddo, si, si, carne freddo— Roast Beef, Bif, Beeeeeef!* (*Gasps, catches her breath.*) *Prosciutto, legumi, tutti, tutti legumi. Capito? Poi, un' insalata verde. No, Mista! Insalata mista, Mista!* They don't know their own language. . . . *Poi, dolce, zuppa inglese, frutta, formaggio, tutte formaggio, e vino, vino, bianco e rosso, una bottiglia di Soave e una bottiglia di—* (*gasps for breath again.*) *Valpolicella. Hanh?—Va bene.* . . . (*hangs up.*) This new cook sounds like a—Mau-mau. . . . She'll probably serve us long pig with—shrunk heads on toothpicks stuck in it. . . . (*She tries to laugh, but coughs.*) Now, then, you see, you're not just going to be fed, you're going to be wined and dined in high style tonight on the terrace. But meanwhile, we're going to enjoy a long siesta together in the cool of my bedroom which is full of historical treasures, including myself! (*She crosses to the bedroom doors, beckons him commandingly. He doesn't move.*) Well?!

CHRIS: I'm afraid I came here too late to accept these—invitations.

MRS. GOFORTH: Who else has invited you somewhere?

CHRIS: I've passed the point where I wait for invitations, but I think I'll be welcomed by the elderly spinster lady whose mother died in Taormina today.

MRS. GOFORTH: Not if she's heard your nickname. And Sicily's an island. How'll you get there, can you walk on water?

CHRIS: Your discharged secretary gave me a bottle of milk with some ten thousand lire notes attached to it with a—rubber band. So—goodbye, Mrs. Goforth. (*He bends to hoist his rucksack over his shoulder.*)

MRS. GOFORTH: Mr. Flanders, you have the distinction, the dubious distinction, of being the first man that wouldn't come into my bedroom when invited to enter.

CHRIS: I'm sorry.

MRS. GOFORTH: Man bring this up road, huh? (*She has snatched up his book of poems.*)

CHRIS: No, I—

MRS. GOFORTH: What else? Your book of poems, your calling card? Y'must be running short of 'em. Here take it back! (*She hurls it at his feet.*) I haven't read it but I can imagine the contents. *Facile sentiment!* To be good a poem's got to be tough and to write a good, tough poem you've got to cut your teeth on the marrow bone of this world. I think you're still cutting your milk teeth, Mr. Flanders.

CHRIS: I know you better than you know me. I admire you, admire you so much I almost like you, *almost*. I think if that old Greek explorer, Pytheas, hadn't beat you to it by centuries, you would've sailed up through the Gates of Hercules to map out the Western world, and you would have sailed up farther and mapped it out better than he did. No storm could've driven you back or changed your course. Oh, no, you're nobody's fool, but you're a fool, Mrs. Goforth, if you don't know that finally, sooner or later, you need somebody or something to mean God to you, even if it's a cow on the streets of Bombay, or carved rock on the Easter Islands or—

MRS. GOFORTH: You came here to bring me *God*, did you?

CHRIS: I didn't say God, I said someone or something to—

MRS. GOFORTH: I heard what you said, you said *God*. My eyes are out of focus but not my ears! Well, *bring* Him, I'm ready to lay out a red carpet for Him, but how do you bring Him? Whistle? Ring a bell for Him? (*She snatches a bell off her desk and rings it fiercely.*) Huh? How? What? (*She staggers back against the desk, gasping.*)

CHRIS: I've failed, I've disappointed some people in what they wanted or thought they wanted from me, Mrs. Goforth, but sometimes, once in a while, I've given them what they needed even if they didn't know what it was. I brought it up the road to them, and that's how I got the name that's made me unwelcome this summer.

STAGE ASSISTANT ONE: Tell her about the first time!

STAGE ASSISTANTS (*together*): Tell her, tell her, the first time!

(*They draw back to the wings. Music begins to be heard softly*).

CHRIS:—I was at Mrs. Ferguson's mountain above Palm Springs, the first time. I wasn't used to her world of elegant bitches and dandies. . . . Early one morning I went down the mountain and across the desert on a walking trip to a village in Baja California, where a great Hindu teacher had gathered a group of pupils, disciples, about him. Along the road I passed a rest home that looked like a grand hotel, and just a little farther along, I came to an inlet, an estuary of the ocean, and I stopped for a swim off the beach that was completely deserted. Swam out in the cool water till my head felt cool as the water, then turned and swam back in, but the beach wasn't deserted completely any more. There was a very old gentleman on it. He called "Help!" to me, as if he was in the water drowning, and I was on the shore. I swam in and asked him how I could help him and he said this, he said: "Help me out there! I can't make it alone, I've gone past pain I can bear." I could see it was true. He was elegantly dressed but emaciated, cadaverous. I gave him the help he wanted, I led him out in the water, it wasn't easy. Once he started to panic; I had to hold onto him tight as a lover till he got back his courage and said, "All right." The tide took him as light as a leaf. But just before I did that, and this is the oddest thing, he took out his wallet and thrust all the money in it into my hand. Here take this, he said to me. And I—

MRS. GOFORTH: Took it, did you, you took it?

CHRIS: The sea had no use for his money. The fish in the sea had no use for it, either, so I took it and went on where I was going.

MRS. GOFORTH: How much were you paid for this—service?

CHRIS: It was a very special difficult service. I was well paid for it.

MRS. GOFORTH: Did you tell the old Hindu, the Swami, when you got to his place, that you'd killed an old man on the way and—

CHRIS: I told him that I had helped a dying old man to get through it.

MRS. GOFORTH: What did he say about that?

CHRIS (reflectively): What did he say?—He said, "You've found your vocation," and he smiled. It was a beautiful smile in spite of showing bare gums, and—he held out his hand for the money. The hand was beautiful, too, in spite of being dry skin, pulled tight as a glove, over bones.

MRS. GOFORTH: Did you give him the money?

CHRIS: Yes, they needed the money. I didn't. I gave it to them.

MRS. GOFORTH: I *bet* you did.

CHRIS: I *did*.

MRS. GOFORTH: Did he say thank you for it?

CHRIS: I don't know if he did. You see, they— No, I guess you don't see. They had a belief in believing that too much is said, when feeling, quiet feelings—enough—says more. . . .

And he had a gift for gesture. You couldn't believe how a hand that shriveled and splotched could make such a beautiful gesture of holding out the hand to be helped up from the ground. It made me, so quickly, peaceful. That

was important to me, that sudden feeling of quiet, because
I'd come there, all the way down there, with the—the spec-
tre of lunacy at my heels all the way— He said: "Stay."—
We sat about a fire on the beach that night: Nobody said
anything.

MRS. GOFORTH: No message, he didn't have any message?

CHRIS: Yes, that night it was silence, it was the meaning of
silence.

MRS. GOFORTH: Silence? Meaning?

CHRIS: Acceptance.

MRS. GOFORTH: What of?

CHRIS: Oh, many things, everything, nearly. Such as how to
live and to die in a way that's more dignified than most of
us know how to do it. And of how not to be frightened
of not knowing what isn't meant to be known, acceptance
of not knowing *anything* but the moment of still existing,
until we stop existing—and acceptance of that moment, too.

MRS. GOFORTH: How do you know he wasn't just an old
faker?

CHRIS: How do you know that I'm not just a young one?

MRS. GOFORTH: I don't. You *are* what they call you!

CHRIS (*taking hold of her hand*): As much as *anyone* is what
anyone calls him.

MRS. GOFORTH: A butcher is called a butcher, and that's what
he is. A baker is called a baker, and he's a baker. A—

CHRIS: Whatever they're called, they're men, and being *men*,
they're not known by themselves or anyone else.

MRS. GOFORTH (*presses a button that shrills on the stage*):
Rudy? Rudy!

CHRIS: Your bodyguard's gone, Mrs. Goforth.

(*She goes on pressing the button.*)

He left with the contents of your strongbox, your safe.

MRS. GOFORTH:—I've got on me all my important jewels, and
if Rudy's gone, I want you to go, too. Go on to your next
appointment. You've tired me, you've done me in. This day
has been the most awful day of my life. . . .

CHRIS: I know. That's why you need me here a while longer.

(*He places his arm about her.*)

MRS. GOFORTH: *Don't, don't.* You—*scare* me!

CHRIS: Let me take you into your bedroom, now, and put you to bed, Mrs. Goforth.

MRS. GOFORTH: *No, no,* GO. *Let me* GO!!

(*He releases her and picks up his canvas sack.*)

Hey!

(*He pauses with his back to her.*)

Did somebody tell you I was dying this summer? Yes, isn't that why you came here, because you imagined that I'd be ripe for a soft touch because I'm dying this summer? Come on, for once in your life be honestly frank, be frankly honest with someone! You've been tipped off that old Flora Goforth is about to go forth this summer.

CHRIS: Yes, that's why I came here.

MRS. GOFORTH: Well, I've escorted four husbands to the eternal threshold, and come back alone without them, just with the loot of *three* of them, and, ah, God, it was like I was building a shell of bone round my heart with their goddamn loot, their loot the material for it— It's my turn, now, to go forth, and I've got no choice but to do it. But I'll do it alone. I don't want to be escorted. I want to go forth alone. But you, you counted on touching my heart because you'd heard I was dying, and old dying people are your specialty, your vocation. But you miscalculated with this one. This milk train doesn't stop here anymore. I'll give you some practical advice. Go back to Naples. Walk along Santa Lucia, the bay-front. Yesterday, there, they smelt the smell of no money, and treated you like a used, discarded used person. It'll be different this time. You'll probably run into some Americans at a sidewalk table along there, a party that's in for some shopping from the islands. If you're lucky, they'll ask you to sit down with them and say, "Won't you have something, Chris?"—Well, *have* something, Chris! and if you play your cards right, they might invite you to go back to an island with them. Your best bet is strangers, I guess. Don't work on the young ones or anybody attractive. They're not ripe to be taken. And not the old ones, either, they've been taken too often.

Work on the middle-aged drunks, that's who to work on, Chris, work on them. Sometimes the old milk train still comes to a temporary stop at their crazy station, so concentrate on the middle-aged drunks in Naples.

CHRIS: This isn't the time for such—practical advice. . . .

(*She makes a gasping sound and presses a tissue to her mouth, turning away.*)

MRS. GOFORTH (*facing front*):— A paper rose . . . (*The tissue is dyed red with blood.*) Before you go, help me into my bedroom, I can't make it alone. . . .

(*He conducts her to the screen between the two rooms as the Stage Assistants advance from the wings to remove it.*)

—It's full of historical treasures. The chandelier, if the dealer that sold it to me wasn't a liar, used to hang in Versailles, and the bed, if he wasn't lying, was the bed of Countess Walewska, Napoleon's Polish mistress. It's a famous old bed, for a famous old body. . . .

(*The Stage Assistants remove the screen masking the bed.*)

CHRIS: Yes, it looks like the catafalque of an Empress. (*He lifts her onto the bed, and draws a cover over her.*)

MRS. GOFORTH: *Don't leave me alone till—*

CHRIS: I never leave till the end.

(*She blindly stretches out her jeweled hand. He takes it.*)

MRS. GOFORTH:—*Not so tight, the—*

CHRIS: I know, the rings cut your fingers.

(*He draws a ring off a finger. She gasps. He draws off another. She gasps again.*)

MRS. GOFORTH: Be here, when I wake up.

(*The Stage Assistants place before her bed the screen with the gold-winged griffin on the middle panel. Light dims out on that area, and is brought up on the turning mobile. Music seems to come from the turning mobile that casts very delicate gleams of light on the stage. Blackie appears on the forestage as the Stage Assistants bring out a dinner table and rapidly*)

*set two places. Then they cross to the flagstaff by the right wings
and begin slowly to lower the flag.*)

ONE: Flag-lowering ceremony on the late Mrs. Goforth's
mountain.
TWO: Bugle?

(*A muted bugle is heard from a distance.*)

That's not Taps, that's Reveille.
ONE: It's Reveille always, Taps never, for the gold griffin.
TWO: One more obvious statement is one too many. (*He
snaps his fingers.*) Let's go.

(*They go out with the folded banner. Chris comes from behind
the bedroom screen, onto the terrace where Blackie sits coolly
waiting. She rises and pours wine into a medieval goblet as
she speaks to Chris.*)

BLACKIE:—Is it—is she—?

(*Chris nods as he moves out onto the forestage.*)

Was it what they call "peaceful"?

(*Chris nods again.*)

With all that fierce life in her?
CHRIS: You always wonder afterwards where it's gone, so far,
so quickly. You feel it must be still around somewhere, in
the air. But there's no sign of it.
BLACKIE: Did she say anything to you before she—?
CHRIS: She said to me: "Be here when I wake up." After I'd
taken her hand and stripped the rings off her fingers.
BLACKIE: What did you do with—?
CHRIS (*giving her a quick look that might suggest an understandable shrewdness*): Under her pillow like a Pharaoh's
breakfast waiting for the Pharaoh to wake up hungry. . . .

(*Blackie comes up beside him on the forestage and offers
him the wine goblet. A wave is heard breaking under the
mountain.*)

BLACKIE: The sea is saying the name of your next mobile.
CHRIS: *Boom!*

BLACKIE: What does it mean?

CHRIS: It says "Boom" and that's what it means. No translation, no explanation, just "Boom." (*He drinks from the goblet and passes it back to her.*)

The Curtain Falls Slowly.

THE MUTILATED

PRODUCTION NOTE

The sets are as delicate as Japanese line drawings; they should be so abstract, so spidery, with the exception of Trinket Dugan's bedroom, that the audience will accept the nonrealistic style of the play.

The first set represents The Silver Dollar Hotel on South Rampart Street in New Orleans with the front wall lifted except for a doorframe to the lobby which contains only the desk and switchboard, stage left, a spring-ruptured old sofa, and a Christmas tree which has shed nearly bare of its needles. A few steps curve behind the back wall of the lobby indicating stairway to the floors above. The name of the hotel appears in pale blue neon above the skeleton structure a few moments after the curtain has risen on it.

The verses that appear preceding the play, after various scenes, and at the end of the play will be set to music and sung (probably *a cappella*) as "rounds" by a band of carollers. This band should comprise all the characters in the play and they will be signaled by a pitch pipe. Trinket and Celeste should sing in Trinket's room or as they descend the exterior stairs to the forestage.

SCENE ONE

*The Silver Dollar Hotel on South Rampart Street—the old
French Quarter in New Orleans. At the desk is seated the night
clerk, Bernie, in a swivel chair that leans way back, permitting
him to rest his feet on the low counter. He's reading a comic book.
If the switchboard buzzes, he can make a connection with very
slight change of position. There is a spindling outside staircase of
gray wood to a landing on a level above. For some reason, possibly because it used to be a private frame residence, this stair-
landing only has access to one room. This favored room is
Trinket Dugan's. As the curtain rises, we hear the carollers sing
the first verses of the carol.*

CAROLLERS:

> I think the strange, the crazed, the queer
> Will have their holiday this year
> And for a while, A little while,
> There will be pity for the wild.
> A miracle, A miracle!
> A sanctuary for the wild.
>
> I think the mutilated will
> Be touched by hands that nearly heal,
> At night the agonized will feel
> A comfort that is nearly real.
> A miracle, a miracle!
> A comfort that is nearly real.
>
> The constant star of wanderers
> Will light the forest where they fall
> And they will see and they will hear
> A radiance, A distant call.
> A miracle, a miracle!
> A vision and a distant call.
>
> At last for each someone may come
> And even though he may not stay,
> It may be softer where he was,
> It may be sweeter where he lay.
> A miracle, a miracle!
> Stones may soften where he lay.

(*The carollers finish and disperse. Celeste and her brother, Henry, appear before the hotel. Celeste is a short, plump little woman with a large bosom of which she is excessively proud, wearing low-cut dresses by night and day. She has hennaed hair with bangs and her muskrat jacket was discovered one lucky day in the window of a thrift shop. She has a passion for satins because they fit close and catch light, and pearls cannot be big enough to suit her. She has a very large purse, for shoplifting. Her age is fifty; her spirit, unconquerable.*)

CELESTE: Come on in with me, Henry.

HENRY: No.

CELESTE: Aw, just for a minute. I want you to meet the nice boy on the desk nights. (*She says this with eager cordiality which is rebuffed by her undertaker-brother.*)

HENRY: Look. (*He has produced a notebook and a Waterman pen which he received for Christmas when he was a child of ten.*) I'm gonna write down the address of the Rainbow Bakery for you and the name of the man to talk to when you get down there.

CELESTE: Oh, good, do that, Henry, dear! (*She squeezes his stiff arm against her.*) A girl never had a sweeter brother than you! Y'know that, Henry? How much I appreciate it?

HENRY: I know from experience how much good this'll do. You got no more idea of earning an honest living than flying to the moon.

CELESTE: I'm gonna surprise you, Henry.

HENRY: You got any decent clothes to go to work in?

CELESTE: Blood is thicker than water, ain't it, Henry?

HENRY: I'm not talkin' about blood. I asked if you got a suitable thing to wear to the bakery Monday after New Year's.

CELESTE: I know where I can pick up some real sweet little housedresses, for less than five dollars each and I'll pay you back out of my first week's wages, Henry.

HENRY: You think I'm fool enough to advance you cash for housedresses when right this minute you are staring over my shoulder at the bar on the corner? Now put this address in that suitcase you carry around like a purse. Hell. The size of that old purse would mark you as a shoplifter even if every store in town didn't already know you as one. (*He hands her the bakery address.*)

CELESTE: Don't have my "specs." What's it say?

HENRY: It says 820 Carondelet. That's on a corner, at Carondelet and Dauphine.

CELESTE: Rainbow Bakery, Carondelet and Dauphine, bright and early the first Monday after New Year's. Bless you, Henry, you old sweet thing, you!

HENRY: I'll see if the cook has some old white uniforms for you. You got to wear white in a bakery, I reckon. Well. . . . Oh, what name shall I tell this man when I phone him you're coming?

CELESTE: What name, why my own name of course, Celeste Delacroix Griffin! I'm not ashamed to work in a bakery, Henry, I don't have false pride about it.

HENRY: You don't have pride true or false about anything ever. That's not the point. The point is I don't want you using my name any more. Not there nor anywhere else. I got children growing up here. I don't want you using our name. So give me a madeup name for me to give Mr. Noonan.

CELESTE: —Oh! —Well, give him the name—Agnes Jones. . . .

HENRY: OK. Agnes Jones. (*He starts off abruptly, then stops at the exit and calls back to her.*) —I'll also tell Mr. Noonan that ten a week from your salary gets held back for me till I recover the full amount that it cost me to get you out of the jug.

CELESTE (*calling after him*): See you for Xmas dinner tomorrow, Henry?

HENRY: I never want to see you again in my life, so bum your Xmas dinner off somebody else!

CELESTE: Henry, you don't mean that.

HENRY (*shouting back from a distance*): Yes, I do!

CELESTE: —Yes, he does. Yes, I guess he does. . . . (*A cold wind whines: she raises her hands to her bosom, crossing her arms.*) Well, this time last year, on Xmas eve, Trinket Dugan and I were in her bedroom upstairs. (*On this cue, Trinket Dugan's bedroom is lighted at a low level and we see Trinket in a Japanese kimono, pale rose-colored, seated on the edge of a small, peeling-white, iron bed, holding a schoolchild's notebook on her lap, biting a pencil, about to make an entry in her diary. Her victrola is playing very softly by the bed. A gallon jug of California Tokay is on a tiny table: the wine catches the light with a delicate, jewel-like glow.*)

TRINKET (*aloud*): Dear Diary! Dear Diary! —I have nothing to say. . . . (*She closes the book with a sigh and pours a glass of Tokay.*)

CELESTE: She's up in her room right now, and five will get you fifty, if I had five, that she's got herself a gallon jug of California Tokay. She's a terrible wino: can afford gin, drinks wine. . . . Well. She's rich and selfish. Purse-proud. But mutilated, oh, yes, ha ha, she's a mutilated woman. I know it, I'm the only one who knows it. —That's my ace-in-the-hole. I'm going up there now by these side stairs and offer the peace pipe to her, I'll tell her on the evening of Christ's birthday even a pair of old bitches like Trinket and Celeste should bury the hatchet, forget all past wounds that either's given the other, and drink a toast to the birth of the Babe in the Manger with a sweet golden wine, with Tokay. . . . (*The sound of drunk sailors singing is heard.*) Just a minute! —Business before pleasure. (*Bruno and Slim go by: she opens her mangy old fur to display her bosom but they pass right by, singing, as if she were invisible although she almost straddles the walk.*) Blind drunk! —Otherwise they would have noticed my bosom. Hell, even the sergeant on the desk when I checked out of the pokey took a good look at my bosom, didn't fail to observe it. Well, I'm mighty lucky to still be so firm-breasted when many women past forty or even thirty have boobs like a couple of mules hanging their heads over the top rail of a fence. (*She starts up the outside staircase but is distracted again by a street noise.*)

VOICE: *Bird-Girl, see the Bird-Girl, fifty cents, four bits to see the Bird-Girl!*

CELESTE: Oh-oh, oh-oh, Maxie and the Bird-Girl. (*She chuckles evilly.*) I can make out there if I play my cards right, he's gonna gather a crowd right on this corner, ah-*HAH*!

VOICE (*strident, approaching*): See the Bird-Girl, two bits to see the Bird-Girl!

CELESTE: *OH*-oh! —Dropped the price! (*A fat man, Maxie, appears before the hotel with a cloaked and hooded companion*

who moves with a shuffling, pigeon-toed gait.) Hi, Maxie!
Merry Xmas, Bird-Girl!

MAXIE (*viciously, to Celeste*): Git lost, yuh bum! —See the
Bird-Girl, two bits to see the Bird-Girl uncovered, unmasked, the world's greatest freak attraction! (*A few
drifters pause on the walk. A drunk staggers out of the Silver
Dollar Hotel, digging in his pocket for a quarter.*)

CELESTE (*seeing the drunk is a live one*): Shoot, that's no Bird-
Girl, I know her personally. That's Rampart Street Rose
with chicken feathers glued to her. It's a painful, dangerous
thing, I know from experience, Mister. (*She turns to the
Bird-Girl again.*) Hey, Rose, how much does Maxie pay
you, how much is he payin' you, Rosie? (*Maxie raises a
threatening hand over his head. The Bird-Girl makes angry
bird noises.*) Maxie? Maxie? (*She rushes up close to him.*) I
ain't gonna expose you, just give me five dollars, Maxie.
I just got out of the pokey, gimme five bucks, will yuh? For
a Xmas bottle? Huh, Maxie? To keep my mouth shut,
Maxie?

MAXIE: I'll shut your fat mouth for you, for less'n
five dollars!

CELESTE: Don't raise your hand at me, Maxie!

MAXIE: Go on, go on, get lost!

CELESTE: Why, I was the Bird-Girl myself! Have
you forgotten I was the Bird-Girl myself? Got
two-degree burns when you put that hot glue
on me?

MAXIE: You want trouble? You want trouble, you
want?

BIRD-GIRL: *Awk awk awk!*

CELESTE: No, I want two dollars and twenty cents
to buy a half gallon of California Tokay.

(*A cop enters. The Bird-Girl whistles and croaks
wildly as she flaps off.*)

COP: Break it up.

MAXIE: She's scared th' Bird-Girl away!

BIRD-GIRL (*offstage*): AWK AWK AWK!

MAXIE (*running after her*): Bird-Girl, hey, Bird-
Girl! (*He whistles shrilly. The wind howls.*)

VERY FAST OVERLAPPED

CELESTE (*picking up a loose feather*): Poor Rosie, she lost some feathers, ah, well that's life for you, tch, tch! If she was a bird, the humane society would be interested in her situation but since she's a human being, they couldn't care less. (*She turns to the Cop*): How about that? I mean the irony of it? (*The wind whines coldly.*)

COP: Where you live?

CELESTE: My address? Here, right here! Hotel Silver Dollar.

COP: Get off the street. . . .

CELESTE: Aw, now really!

COP: I know you from night court, go in and stay off the street. (*He moves on. Another sailor appears: Celeste opens her coat, hopefully displaying her bosom.*)

CELESTE: Hello, there, Merry Christmas!

SAILOR (*shoving past her*): Get lost. (*Her vivacious smile fades: she closes her coat like a book with a sad ending.*)

CELESTE: —I am. . . . (*She means lost.*) —When you're lost in this world you're lost and not found, the lost-and-found department is just the lost department, but I'm going in that lobby like I've just come back from the biggest social event of the Goddam season, no shit. . . . (*She starts to the door but freezes just outside it.*) Well, I'll count five and then enter. One. —Two. —Three. —Four. —Four and one-half. —Four and three-quarters. . . . (*Trinket starts a loud lively record on her victrola: four-four tempo—"Santiago Waltz."*) Hmm. Sounds like she's trying to boost her morale up there. I used to boost her morale. I'd say to her every day, forget your mutilation, it's not the end of the world for you or the world. Hell, I'd say, we all have our mutilations, some from birth, some from long before birth, and some from later in life, and some stay with us forever. Well, there's nothing like a week in the pokey to bring out the philosopher in you, but in me it's brought out the chicken in me, too. Scared to enter the lobby of a flea-bag. Four and seven-eighths. —No. Nope. —I need to be morally fortified before I count to five and face that lobby. . . . (*She turns to the outside staircase.*) —What'll I say to her? Well, I'll think of something when I— (*She goes on up to the landing and knocks at the outside door of Trinket's room.*)

TRINKET: Who's knocking at my door?

CELESTE: Me, Celeste, let's bury the hatchet for Christmas.

TRINKET: —We can't bury the hatchet. We hit each other too hard, and now it's too late to forget it.

CELESTE: Think of the wonderful times we had together!

TRINKET: They weren't wonderful times. We bummed around town together, I took you to breakfast, I took you to lunch, I took you to dinner. I took you to the movies. In return for all those favors, I just got envy, resentment, and sly insinuations that if I didn't go on sucking up to you, just for company in my time of despair, you'd give away my secret.

CELESTE: That's not true. No soul knows about your mutilation but me.

TRINKET: You kept reminding me of it. That no soul knew about my mutilation except Celeste. Why would you do that if you didn't mean to threaten me with exposure?

CELESTE: People don't trust each other. I was afraid you'd suddenly get tired of me, bored with me! Trinket? Let me in! I'm scared to pass through the lobby.

TRINKET: —They've checked you out, you've lost your room here, Celeste.

CELESTE: That's what I was afraid of: I suspected! —I see you're drinking Tokay. Let me in for a drink, it will give me the courage to face my situation in the lobby.

TRINKET: Celeste, we're through with each other. You know why. Remember the night you wanted to eat at Commander's Palace in the Garden District? I wanted to eat Chinese. . . . (*She starts addressing the audience instead of Celeste.*) I wanted some Moo Goo Gai Pan at the Chinese place on Dauphine Street. Oh, no, she said, no. If you want to eat boiled rats, go eat Chinese. —I wouldn't dream of it, I told her. Of course I knew two things: she couldn't afford a hamburger at the White Castle, and Moo Goo Gai Pan is made from water chestnuts, snow peas, and breast of chicken, one of the world's most famous and delicate dishes. I turned away from her and walked on without her toward the Chinaman's place. Pretty soon, in fact in less than a minute, I heard the rat-tat-tat of her high heels in pursuit. She caught my elbow. I faced her, her face was *livid* with *hate*. "Who knows except me about your mutilation? Have

I ever exposed you?!" "Let me go, go, go, go," I said, "let me go! Go to Commander's Palace," I said, "or Galatoire's and feast yourself on any dish you crave with imported wine, but go, go, go, let me go, I'm eating Chinese: I want to and I do what I want to!" —Know what she said, then, to me? *"Eat Chinese, you mutilated monster!"* —Well, that didn't improve our friendship. That terminated our friendship. Can you blame me? To taunt an old friend because of a mutilation in order to get a free meal in the place she wanted? (*Celeste resumes pounding at the stair-landing door.*) Go, go, go, go away, it's too late to bury the hatchet!

CELESTE: No, no!

TRINKET: Go, go!

CELESTE: Let me just pass through the room. People are kind at Christmas!

TRINKET: You just want to get in here because you can see this wine and you're a wino!

CELESTE: Me, a wino?

TRINKET: A notorious wino!

CELESTE: You call *me* a wino, sitting in there with your big economy jug of California Tokay, so big you can hardly carry it half a block down Rampart, you being too cheap to have it delivered to you? Ho-ho! (*She rattles the doorknob.*)

TRINKET (*springing up wildly*): Go, go, go, go away, you merciless monster, before I call downstairs to get the police!

CELESTE: You fink, you freak! I'll get even with you, oh, will I ever get even with you, Trinket Dugan! Alias Agnes Jones! (*She rushes back downstairs and into the lobby with an air of bravado. Bernie, the night clerk, has his feet still propped on the desk and the comic book in his lap. Celeste is bold as brass.*) Hi, Bernie, Merry Xmas! Guess what's happened!

BERNIE: Yeah, you got sprung for Christmas.

CELESTE: Got what, Bernie, what, baby?

BERNIE: They let you out of the pokey for Xmas, did they?

CELESTE: Bernie, Bernie, you're lost in the comic-book world, God bless you and let me kiss you, you big sexy thing you, I could jump over this desk and just gobble you up. Oh, baby, let's have a quickie right now, in a vacant room.

BERNIE: —I got a message for you.

CELESTE: Boy, oh, baby, have I got a message for *you*!

BERNIE: Yeah, I bet, but the message I got for you is your stuff's locked up, and is gonna be held in storage till you've paid up your bill here.

CELESTE: —I don't understand this message.

BERNIE: Repeat it to yourself a couple of times and maybe you'll understand it.

CELESTE: You said my stuff—locked up? My personal belongings, no, I don't get this message, it's such a peculiar message that I could repeat it over and over and still be mystified by it.

BERNIE (*making switchboard connections*): Aw, come off it, everyone knows that knows you that you've been in the House of Detention, because you got caught shoplifting at Goodman's department store Monday. You're coming down fast in the world, you used to shoplift at the Canal Street stores and—

CELESTE: What a lie, who said so?

BERNIE: It come out in the papers. *Picayune, Item* and *States.*

CELESTE: Show me the item so I can call my lawyer.

BERNIE: I don't save clippings, press clippings, for kleptos, sister.

CELESTE: It was a false accusation to begin with. My brother, Henry Delacroix Griffin, set them straight and also has got me a job, that's the news, the message, I rushed in here to let you be first to know of it.

BERNIE: It's about time you quit hustling, not because you think so but because the guys you hustle for the price of a bottle or a couple of drinks have eyes to see you with, sister, and what they see is a wino, long in the tooth.

CELESTE: Is this any way to talk to a girl at Xmas?

BERNIE (*with an amiable grin*): Aw, no, face it, you can't make it, Celeste, can't even get away with a little shoplifting at Christmas.

CELESTE (*grandly*): Give me the key to my room, I don't want to stay in this lobby.

BERNIE: You don't have a room here no more. You been checked out and your stuff locked up in the basement by order of Katz.

CELESTE: Katz wouldn't do this to me. When did he do this to me?

BERNIE: When it come out in the papers that a lady identifying herself as Miss Agnes Jones had been arrested shoplifting.

CELESTE: —Agnes Jones is who? Not me!—sounds like a made-up name. My name is Celeste Delacroix Griffin.

BERNIE: Yeah, but we were tipped off that you give a made-up name when the cops picked you up and it's Agnes Jones.

CELESTE: —Who told you such a false story?

BERNIE: Trinket, your old friend, Trinket, saw the newspaper item about your shoplifting rap and said, "Agnes Jones? It's Celeste!"

CELESTE: Me? Agnes Jones? Not me! Agnes Jones is the name she gave at Mercy Hospital when she— I never spoke of it before. She used the name Agnes Jones for her secret operation. (*There is a pause: contemplation.*) I got to go upstairs, I got to go to the little girls' room a minute.

BERNIE: Use the toilet down here.

CELESTE: Get crabs for Christmas? I don't want crabs for Christmas. You use it if you want to be infested with crabs but I'm going to the upstairs john. (*She crosses to the stairs off the lobby and goes up. Bernie answers a switchboard call.*)

BERNIE: Silver Dollar Hotel. —No, gone. —I said GONE. — People *go*! —Checked out of here and left no forwardin' address. Sorry, Merry Christmas. . . . (*The switchboard rings again as Bernie is plugging out. He answers this second ring.*)

TRINKET (*at the phone in her room*): Bernie, is she down there? I mean Celeste.

BERNIE: She's not in the lobby right now.

TRINKET: Good! Then I can come down. I don't want to run into her. (*Bernie plugs out. He unpeels a candy bar and starts munching on it slowly with lazy enjoyment. Celeste returns to the desk with an oddly accomplished smile, more than a mere visit to the "loo" would account for.*)

CELESTE (*excitedly malicious*): —I see there's been a Christmas celebration. Was it organized by Trinket Dugan? Did she put on her Santie Claus suit and ring a cowbell under that sorry tree? I never seen a worse-decorated tree, broken ornaments on it and needles already shedding, it sure looks sad. —Sample bottles of cheap perfume for the ladies and dime-store ties for the gents? Ha ha! Christmas is something you got to do big or don't do it. (*There is a pause.*

Bernie munches his candy bar. Celeste hugs her bosom as if she were still on the chilly street. She watches him munching slowly at his candy bar as he reads a book of cartoons.) Whatcha eatin', Bernie, a candy bar? (*Bernie barely grunts.*) What kind of candy bar is it? O Henry? Baby Ruth? (*Picking up the candy wrapper.*) Aw. A Mr. Goodbar. I never have had one of them. I'm a Hershey milk-chocolate girl. The only thing better than a Hershey milk-chocolate bar is a Hershey almond bar, Bernie. They used to come in the fifty-cent size, when I was in convent school. A girlfriend of mine and me would buy us that fifty-cent bar and eat away on it all afternoon. —Dibs on the last bite, Bernie. Huh? Dibs on the last bite, Bernie? They give me the cold-turkey treatment in the pokey, and that, that—treatment, it—it leaves you with an awful craving for sweets . . . —My mouth is watering, Bernie!

BERNIE: —Yeh, well, swallow or spit. . . . (*He finishes the bar and leans back in his swivel chair, eyes falling shut.*)

CELESTE: —In summer the chocolate sticks to the candy wrapper but in the winter, the wrapper comes off clean . . . (*She licks a tiny bit of chocolate off the candy wrapper.*) —It sure comes off clean in winter. . . .

BERNIE (*sleepily*): Why don't you give up?

CELESTE: Give up, did you say? An easy piece of advice to give but not to follow. (*She moves back to the ruptured sofa under the Christmas tree, removes from the tree a garland of popcorn, and munches it as she speaks.*) Give up? My life? Oh, no. I still have longings, and as long as you have longings, satisfaction is possible. Appetites? —Satisfaction's always possible, Bernie. Cravings? Such as a craving for sweets or liquor or love? Satisfaction is still possible, Bernie, and on a give-and-take basis. Why, just today a man was talking to me. He didn't look in my eyes. He kept his eyes on my breasts. At last I laughed, I said, "Touch 'em, they won't break, they're not soap bubbles and they're not a padded brassiere." — Bernie? —Bernie! —How would you like a quickie in my old room? It wouldn't be the first time, would it, Bernie?

BERNIE: Give up.

CELESTE (*sitting back down*): —Give up is something I never even think of. I'll go on—not to the Rainbow Bakery after

New Year's, that's not for me. —I'm too imaginative to fool with bread. Bread is something that has to be broken in kindness, in friendship or understanding as it was broken among the Apostles at Our Lord's Last Supper. Gee, the cold-turkey treatment sure does leave you hungry and with such a craving for sweets that if I was employed right now at the Rainbow Bakery, the doughnuts and pastry and fruit-cakes, cream puffs and—last year Trinket Dugan had some little fancy cornucopias full of hard candy on the tree, now just stale popcorn. —Katz is a long man to wait for. . . . When do you think he'll— (*Trinket enters the lobby by the interior stairway, she is wild-eyed, shaken. Celeste has snatched up an old copy of the Saturday Evening Post; she has raised it to cover her face but is peeking over the top of the dirty cover.*)

BERNIE (*making a switchboard connection*): Silver Dollar.

TRINKET (*faintly*): Bernie?

CELESTE (*giggling*): —What a funny cartoon! You can't beat the cartoons in the *Saturday Evening Post*!

BERNIE (*into the phone*): No such party here. Nope, no such party. (*He unplugs.*)

TRINKET (*louder*): Bernie! May I speak to you, please?

BERNIE: Sure. What?

TRINKET: Come outside for a moment. This is private, Bernie.

BERNIE: I can't leave the switchboard, Miss Dugan.

TRINKET: I think you'd better. This is a serious matter. I can't speak to you about it in front of that woman.

CELESTE: What a funny cartoon, it's a scream, ho ho ho!

TRINKET: This is something that may call for legal action.

CELESTE (*turning a page*): Here's another funny one, ho ho ho!

TRINKET: On several occasions I found signs that my bed-room had been entered while I was out. Not by the hall door but by the outside entrance, from the stairs outside. The lock wasn't broken. It was entered by someone who held a key to that entrance. Only one person did. Consequently I knew who'd been coming in. Still I re-frained from reporting it to the police: out of pity, Bernie, I made no report, no complaint, although the sneak had been drinking up my wine and picking up money that I deliberately left on the bureau, out of pity. This is a person, Bernie, that I have befriended over a long, long period. You might say supported, even. Bernie, you know that I could afford to stay at a first-class hotel but I've stayed here out of loyalty and friendship. I dressed that Christmas tree. I bought a gift for everyone registered here and put them under the tree. To all employees I passed out a five-dollar gold piece. I pity transients at Christmas. This hotel is full of derelicts, Bernie, lost, lonely, homeless at Christmas. (*Her voice is high and shaky.*) Heaven knows what secret sorrows they carry with them! And very few care!

CELESTE (*throwing down the magazine*): Bernie, get her some music to go with that speech!

TRINKET (*her voice rising*): I've been lucky, financially. I'm not boasting about it. I feel humbly grateful about it. My daddy left me three oil wells in West Texas; one is bone-dry right now, one comes in now and then but the number three well is a gusher, it's a continual gusher. Now, Bernie. I'm not purse-proud. See this? (*She removes a large wad of paper money from her purse.*) —I never walk out of the Silver Dollar Hotel without a wad of money that you could choke a horse with. That's not what I do with it, though. I have a horde of friends in financial trouble. As long as they're loyal to me, I'm devoted to them. I give out gifts called loans, expecting no repayment, except in friendship, Bernie. Bernie, go up to the stair landing and see what some vicious person has scratched on the wall up there. It has to come off right away.

BERNIE: Something's written up there?

TRINKET: No, not written, scratched, I said, scratched, probably with a nail file.

BERNIE: Well, I'll go take a look.

TRINKET (*breathlessly*): Yes, please do, thank you, Bernie. (*He goes up the few steps that curve behind the back wall of the lobby.*)

CELESTE (*in a fierce whisper*): I told you I'd get even. This is just the beginning.

TRINKET: Yes, I knew who did it.

CELESTE: I spent every day for years, for years!

TRINKET: Living off me!

CELESTE: Cheering you up, getting you out of depression, distracting you from your mutilation, you know it! (*Bernie comes back to the lobby.*)

BERNIE: Miss Dugan, I seen it but I don't know how to remove it because it's scratched in the wall.

TRINKET: Cover it with something, with a, with a—with a "no smoking" sign.

BERNIE: The only sign we got's a "no loitering" sign in the downstairs washroom and it wouldn't make sense on the landing.

TRINKET: Cover it up with this calendar. (*She points to a pictorial calendar over the desk.*)

BERNIE: I don't have no thumbtacks here.

TRINKET: Use adhesive tape, then.

BERNIE: Don't have that neither.

TRINKET (*putting money in his hands*): Run to the drugstore next door and get some adhesive tape, fast as you can. Nobody must go up or down those stairs till that vicious lie about me is covered up. Hurry. Otherwise the Silver Dollar Hotel will lose its only good tipper. And for New Year's I'm planning to pass out presents again!

BERNIE: OK, OK.

TRINKET: I'll watch the switchboard for you. (*Bernie goes out. There is a dead silence in lobby. Trinket speaks without looking at Celeste.*) If I were you, I wouldn't sit there much longer.

CELESTE: The calendar won't stay up.

TRINKET: If it doesn't, I'll know who's taken it down and I'll take action.

CELESTE: What action?

TRINKET: *Action!*

CELESTE: How do you know it won't appear other places? There's other places, it might break out like a plague.

TRINKET: Yes, in the House of Detention! Print it on the walls in the House of Detention, cover the prison walls with it!

BERNIE (*returning*): Got it.

TRINKET: Here's the calendar: *hurry!* (*Bernie goes up the short curving flight of steps and disappears behind the back wall of the lobby. The two women are silent.*)

CELESTE (*rising from sofa*): How much a discount do you get on a Xmas tree from last year? I'm covered with needles off it. (*She brushes herself elaborately.*)

TRINKET: I would like for you to return me the key to my outside entrance. I'd be much obliged if you hand it back to me right now so I won't have to put a padlock and a burglar alarm on that door.

CELESTE: I thrown it away long ago.

TRINKET: You know I know that's a lie, and let me warn you that if tonight I discover any evidence that you've been in my room while I'm out, you'll find yourself right back in the House of Detention, yes, right back there tonight.

CELESTE: Tonight I'll be at my brother's for eggnog and fruitcake. Huey P. Long will be there. I love the Kingfish and he seems to find me amusing.

TRINKET: Who *doesn't* find you *absurd*!

CELESTE: Uh-huh, well, I won't be alone with a continual gusher of jealousy in my heart, tonight and all other nights, forever and ever, Amen. (*Bernie returns to the lobby.*)

BERNIE: OK, I got it covered.

CELESTE: So long, Agnes Jones. (*She exits to the street.*)

TRINKET (*to Bernie*): You don't believe it, do you? That vicious lie about me?

BERNIE: Hell, Miss Dugan, I got my own business to mind.

TRINKET: —I—*can't imagine! Impossible to imagine*—malice like *that*! (*The lobby dims out as she goes out to the street and the carollers sing.*)

SCENE TWO

On the forestage is a bench in Jackson Park. Behind it, on the scrim, is a projection of the equestrian statue of Andrew Jackson. Trinket enters and sits on the bench, stiffly.

TRINKET: It's going to take me a little while to recover from that shock. I'm still shivering from it. Yes, I felt close to panic, but now I'll get hold of myself. —Why do I care so much? There's nothing shameful, nothing criminal about an affliction, a—mutilation. . . . (*She shakily lights a cigarette*.) I am *not* Agnes Jones, I am Trinket Dugan, and *I have absolutely no intention of giving up, not a bit in the world, wouldn't dare to or—care to!* —Tonight I'll drive out Agnes Jones, I'll do it right now. How? I'll walk around this bench and when I've walked around it, Agnes Jones will be out of me and never get back in! (*She springs up. The sudden action makes her dizzy: she falls back onto the bench and gasps for breath. Then she rises and starts a slow march about the bench.*) Out, Agnes Jones, out, Agnes Jones, out Agnes Jones. (*She has returned to the front of the bench.*) There, now. It's such a clear, frosty night, I can see my breath in the air and, yes, I'm calming down now. I knew I would and I am. (*She sways a bit and falls back onto the bench. Now she speaks in a different voice: harsh with anger and self-contempt.*) —In the afternoons, old people with nothing else to do come here and stay and stay till the sun is fading away. When they leave here, I come here. I'm the night bench-sitter of Jackson Square. The gates are closed at midnight. It's nearly midnight. My hands are still shaky. It's time for me to go to the Cafe Boheme and have my absinthe frappé at a corner table with an empty chair across from me. Overtipping as if it was necessary to apologize for sitting alone at a table meant for two. *Two!* In life there *has* to be two! —The old winter voice of Agnes Jones is still in me. I said OUT, Agnes Jones, out, out and stay out! Once more around the bench. (*She marches around the bench again.*) —But of course I do have to prepare myself for the possibility that Celeste will be in the Cafe Boheme tonight, and when I come in, is likely to make a vicious remark of some kind. Oh, I'd—sink through the floor, I'd never be able to enter the place again! — OUT, AGNES JONES! (*She arrives in front of the bench.*) —Such a clear, frosty night. Andrew Jackson is all wet, shiny green like he'd rode up out of the sea. Oh, with so much beauty around me, yes, still, even now, why should I have room in me for the ugly, cowardly voice of Agnes Jones. Too much solitude can be corrected, yes, it *must* be corrected. I will correct solitude by—what? —Why not enter the Cafe Boheme tonight like a gladiator, shouting:

"Here I am, the mutilated Trinket Dugan alias—Agnes Jones!" No! Impossible! Couldn't! Not necessary! She can't prove the mutilation unless I expose it to someone. Oh, but not daring to expose the mutilation has made me go without love for three years now, and it's the lack of what I need most that makes me speak to myself with the bitter-old, winter-cold voice of—Agnes Jones: LOVE! —a hand on my *breast*. . . . (*She makes a sound like a hooked fish would make if it could make a sound. She rises, then sits back down: she gives way not to despair but to some inner convulsion which makes her produce these dreadful soft cries. They are accompanied by abrupt, indecisive movements to rise or reach out or— Gradually they subside: she pulls herself together.*) No. No more negative thoughts. Tonight I'll give myself the Christmas gift of a lover, yes, I'll find him tonight and he will be—beautiful! Perfect! —Perhaps he'll be kind, even, so kind I can tell him about my—mutilation. (*She acts out the admission.*) "There's something I feel I should tell you before I—before we—" COULDN'T—get the words out! —Oh, but I'll think of something, if I find him tonight, if that miracle happens tonight at the Cafe Boheme!

VOICE (*offstage*): Gates closing!

TRINKET: Gates closing, must go. . . .

(*She leaves as the bench is dimmed out. The carollers enter.*)

CAROLLERS:

> The lost will find a public place
> Where their names are not unknown
> And there, oh, there an act of grace
> May lift the weight of stone on stone.
> A miracle, a miracle!
> The finding of a love unknown.
>
> Oh, but to love they need to know
> How to walk upon fresh snow
> And leave no footprint where they go,
> Walking on new-fallen snow.
> A miracle, a miracle!
> No footprint on new-fallen snow.

The wounded and the fugitive,
The solitary ones will know
Somewhere a place that's set apart
A place of stillness cool as snow.
A miracle, a miracle!
A place that quiets the outraged heart.

It may be in a public park
That has a bench that's set apart,
And not by daylight, after dark,
With winter mist upon the park.
A miracle, a miracle!
A mist that veils a winter park.

SCENE THREE

The park bench is removed and the scene becomes the interior of the Cafe Boheme. The bar is shaped like a horseshoe; inside is standing Tiger, the proprietor, who was formerly a boxer and a seaman and who is now in his fifties. About the bar are several patrons. The sound of an ambulance is now receding into the distance. Trinket Dugan appears in the lighted area.

TRINKET: Merry Christmas! (*She gets no response. Has Celeste been there, talking against her? She is uncertain whether to stay in the bar, but where else is there to go? Nowhere. She slips quietly, then, to a solitary table, beside the bar. . . . There is a slight pause.*)

WOMAN AT BAR: I can't believe it! Can you? Alive and laughing one second, dead the next!

PIOUS QUEEN (*at the bar*): He told a very sacrilegious story.

TIGER: Hell, don't you think that God has a sense of humor? Ted just laughed a little too loud and bust a blood vessel. Maybe God laughed too.

WOMAN AT BAR: And "bust a blood vessel" too?

TIGER: —It wasn't a bad way to go.

TRINKET (*sitting up straight and stiff and calling out shrilly*): WHO DIED? DID SOMEBODY DIE?

TIGER: Yeah, somebody died, so he died. Somebody always dies, don't he? What yours, Trinket? Name your drinks, everybody, it's all on the house in memory of the deceased. (*They murmur their drinks. Trinket calls out hers as loudly as if she was furious over something: a hand has risen to her mutilated bosom.*)

TRINKET: Absinthe frappé, please, Tiger! (*The old electric piano is started again: it plays another ragtime tune or medley, starting with "Under the Bamboo Tree," as two sailors enter. One is short, named Bruno, one tall, called Slim. Everyone turns to glance at them: it's the tall one they look at, because he shines like a star. Suddenly, Trinket calls shrilly.*) "Tiger, Tiger, burning bright!" —I need my absinthe frappé!

SLIM: Is this the place?

BRUNO: Yeh, yeh, this is the place.

SLIM: Where is he?

BRUNO: What're you shouting about?

SLIM: Why should I whisper, what's there to whisper about?

BRUNO: Don't make you'self conspicuous in this place.

SLIM: Why? Is they somethin' wrong with it?

BRUNO: No. They's nothin' wrong with it except it's special. You notice how quiet people are?

SLIM: Yeah. The place is spooky. Why's a place so quiet on Xmas Eve?

BRUNO: Sit down at the bar.

SLIM: Where's your rich friend, is he here or not here? I want to go if he ain't.

BRUNO: We are ten minutes early.

TIGER: Boys, you can't stay here. This place is off limits to the Navy.

BRUNO: We're just lookin' for someone.

TIGER: Who're you lookin' for, Mac?

BRUNO: —A—a—fellow I met on my last liberty here.

TIGER: What's his name?

BRUNO: His name was Ted.

TIGER: If you mean Ted Dinwiddie, Ted Dinwiddie is dead.

BRUNO: No kidding.

SLIM: Jesus, come on, let's go. I knew somebody had died here.

WOMAN AT BAR: He died here tonight. Screamed and fell off that barstool an hour ago.

PIOUS QUEEN: This one, right next to me.

WOMAN: Th' coroner said he was probably already dead when he hit the floor. . . .

TRINKET (*rising and crossing to the bar*): That is no way to break the news of a death!

SLIM: He died and he's dead, let's go.

BRUNO: Hell, I need a drink first.

TRINKET: The news of a death is shocking to anyone living and it ought to be broken more gently.

BRUNO: Gimme a C.C. and Seven.

TIGER: I told you, you're off limits here.

PIOUS QUEEN (*rising from the barstool*): Boys, boys, I have a room next door and I can provide you both with civilian outfits. In civvies, you know, you can go anywhere in town.

TRINKET: Your clothes wouldn't fit these boys. I have a better suggestion. (*She grips Bruno's elbows.*) Get your buddy outside, I'll wait by the door. (*She goes out of the bar. The electric piano starts up and the voices fade as Trinket departs. She waits tensely on the forestage, then suddenly runs back into the bar, calling out—*) Shore Police are coming!

SLIM: I got no liberty pass.

TIGER: Go out the back way.

BRUNO: I got a liberty pass, I'll go out front. Slim, you go in the "head." (*The light on the bar area dims out as the sailors run in separate directions. Bruno, the short sailor, comes out and stands beside Trinket.*)

TRINKET: Here they come. (*She means the Shore Police: she advances to intercept them as the lights dim out.*) Merry Christmas, boys.

SCENE FOUR

As the scrim closes and lights come up on forestage, the Shore Police ignore Trinket and ask to see Bruno's liberty pass which he produces very slowly.

TRINKET: —He's got his pass: he is my little brother, we are just standing here discussing where to go next.

SHORE POLICE: Yeah, well, don't go in here, this place is off limits.

TRINKET: Oh, we're not going in that bar, we're going to the—the cathedral for the midnight candlelight service. Aren't we, Buddy?

BRUNO: Yes, ma'am. —Sister. (*The Shore Police "case" the bar; they look offstage and then depart.*)

TRINKET: —That's that. Now get your buddy.

BRUNO: I don't wanna insult you, but we're not out looking for whores.

TRINKET: Oh, I'm not insulted, I'm—flattered, but you couldn't be more mistaken. Here, looky here. (*She opens her purse and produces a roll of large bills.*) —See this roll of greenbacks? You could choke a horse with it, if you wanted to choke a horse, but who wants to choke a horse. So money isn't my problem, my problem is not economic, my problem is— (*She raises a trembling hand to her left breast.*)

BRUNO: Is what?

TRINKET: —Human, a human problem. Only one person knows it besides myself. Only one other person in the world knows about it but me.

BRUNO: What's your problem?

TRINKET: This other person who knows it was a person I trusted, but now, just tonight, she betrayed me: in such a horrible way, she— (*She clenches a gloved fist in the air.*)

BRUNO: Are you scared to tell me this problem?

TRINKET: It's a thing, it's a thing, a— (*She can't force herself to confess it.*)

BRUNO (*chuckling*): Everything is a thing.

TRINKET: This is a thing that—

BRUNO: You got a nice little body—have you ever done it outdoors?

TRINKET: What? No!

BRUNO: I've done it outdoors in the Quarter. You just slip between two buildings, out of the light, and it's just as private as it would be in your room.

TRINKET: You're talking about alley cats, and you don't understand: I'm attracted to your friend, I'm waiting out here for him. Get him out of the bar before the wolves snatch him away.

BRUNO: Him? Slim? He's ignorant like a baby. I'm experienced at it.

TRINKET: Slim, his name's Slim?

BRUNO: Forget him.

TRINKET (*calling out*): Slim! Slim! (*Bruno makes another effort to put his hand under her cape. She cries out in panic.*) Stop it! I'm mutilated! (*At this exact moment Celeste's loud, drunken voice is heard.*)

CELESTE: Jingle bells, jingle bells, jingle bells, jingle—bells—jingle—bells. . . . (*It seems to be all she remembers of the song.*)

TRINKET: Oh, God, it's her, it's Celeste, stand in front of me, hide me! (*She clutches Bruno by the lapels of his pea jacket and draws them about her, pressing her face to his chest as Celeste appears and stalks across the forestage, still tonelessly singing.*)

CELESTE: Jingle bells, jingle bells, jingle bells, jingle bells, jingle all the—jingle all the—*wayyyyy!* (*On the word "wayyyyy," she arrives at the lamp post and turns front, opening her coat, her eyes very wide in a farcically lascivious way. She must be trying to attract the attention of someone across the street. Then she resumes the hoarse, toneless chant and stalks off.*)

TRINKET: —Ahhh, God, has she gone? That awful demented creature goes singing at night through the Quarter to catch the attention of near- and far-sighted drunks, and when they hear her in the Cafe Boheme, they all laugh, they all say, "There goes old Madame Goat." Did she see me, she didn't see me, did she? If she'd seen me, she would have shouted a criminal slander about me for which I would have her locked up. Now! Quick! Find your buddy! It's him that I want for Christmas! (*She moves a few steps from Bruno, so that the rest of the speech will seem addressed to herself, rhapsodically.*) Tall, crowned with gold that's so gold it's like his head had caught fire, and I know, I remember the kind of skin that goes with flame-colored hair, it's like snow, it's like sunlight on snow, I remember, I know! (*Slim appears with Celeste, entering from the left. She is stoutly supporting his tall, wobbly frame. Trinket cries out—*) Oh, God, he's been snagged by an old wino, get him away from her, quick! That woman's criminal, a shoplifter, a convicted klepto, evicted, takes old men up alleys for the price of a drink!

CELESTE: *I heard that remark, Agnes Jones!* (*She squares off like a bull about to charge. There should be flashes of bluish-white light on the stage as if an acetylene torch, a soundless one, was drilling the street, throwing fantastically long, tall shadows over the street-fronts. Inside the bar, the electric piano plays a* paso-doble.)

TRINKET: Just out of jail, less than an hour ago, I swear, I swear! Get him away from her quick, quick! She is infested with vermin, lice, LICE!

CELESTE: *I heard that remark!* (*She stamps like a bull pawing the earth before charging.*)

BRUNO: Slim? Hey, Slim! (*But Bruno doesn't approach Celeste who stands guarding Slim.*)

TRINKET (*in a transport, an ecstasy of fury*): Don't just *call* him, go *GET* him!

CELESTE: *Try.* He's felt my *bosom*! He's felt my *breasts, both* of them!

TRINKET (*wildly*): *Shut up, for God's sake, be still!* (*Celeste spits at her from a distance.*) SHE SPITS! —Where's the toad? Wherever a witch spits it produces a *toad*! (*Bruno is amused, now, chuckling drunkenly. Slim rests against the proscenium, with a weak, vague grin.*)

SLIM: Cat-fight.

BRUNO: C'mon, this one here's got money.

SLIM: Aw, frig 'em all.

TRINKET: Oh, I—have a *warning* for you! Celeste? Let me give you this warning! I have engaged the biggest lawyer in town, a criminal lawyer, that never loses a case and I will spare no expense, *no expense*!—to have you committed to the State Hospital for the CRIMINAL INSANE! —Bread and water, not wine! That's what you'll— (*Celeste suddenly charges forward and snatches Trinket's purse from her.*) *Thief, thief, stop thief!* (*With an Indian war whoop, Celeste has dashed offstage. Slim slides slowly down the proscenium edge till he sits against it. There is a change of light and music. The electric piano goes into a number such as "Please Don't Talk About Me When I'm Gone."*) Hah! She snatched an empty purse! I had my money out, look, here, in my hand! (*She holds up her roll of bills.*) —Now, hurry, catch us a taxi be-fore I die on this corner! (*Bruno is getting Slim onto his feet, with soothing, affectionate murmurs as the carollers assemble on the forestage and sing.*)

CAROLLERS:

> For dreamers there will be a night
> That seems more radiant than day,
> And they'll forget, forget they must,
> That light's a thing that will not stay.
> A miracle, a miracle!
> We dream forever and a day.
>
> Now round about and in and out
> We will turn and we will shout.
> Round about and in and out
> Again we turn, again we shout.
> A miracle, a miracle!
> A magic game that children play.

(*The forestage dims out as the carollers disperse.*)

SCENE FIVE

Trinket's bedroom is lighted, as she comes up the outside stairs with Slim, who is leaning heavily on her.

TRINKET: Well, here we are: Did you think we'd ever make it?

SLIM: Yeh, I thought we'd make it.

TRINKET: I wasn't so sure. I mean that we'd make it together. But here we are, together. This is my—little home. . . .

SLIM: Not much to it.

TRINKET: No, there's not much to it, but it's—familiar, it's—home. I lived here before my father's good luck in the oil-fields and I became so attached to this room that I stay on and on. You know, you can love a room you live in like a person you live with, if you live with a person. I don't. I live alone here. I have the advantage of a private, outside entrance, and that's an important advantage, especially if I, when you—have a guest with you at night. I don't, you, uh, don't—always want to have to go through the hotel lobby which I'd have to do at any big hotel with—

SLIM: —With house dicks in it?

TRINKET: With anyone, everyone in it.

SLIM (*suspiciously*): Hmmmm.

TRINKET: You're so tall you make the ceiling seem low. Take off your coat and sit down.

SLIM: Not till I make up my mind if I want to stay here or not.

TRINKET (*nervously*): Oh.

SLIM: "Oh." I can take care of myself in this situation or any Goddam situation that that wop Bruno's ever gotten me into. Las' week-en' he innerduced me to a rich ole freak that had a two-story apartment at the Crescent Hotel. I looked around and I was alone with this freak. I said to the freak, "Something's not natural here," an' the freak said to me: "I'm your slave! I'm your slaaaa-ve!" —I said "OK, slave, show me the color of your money!"

TRINKET (*sadly*): Oh.

SLIM: What do you mean by "oh"?

TRINKET: I just mean oh.

SLIM (*broodingly*): Oh. Then the rich freak says, "Master, I am your slave. My money is green as lettuce and as good as gold." I said, "Slave, forget the description, lemme see it. —Show me the color of your money!"

TRINKET: —Are you speaking to me, or—?

SLIM: I'm telling you something that happened las' week-en' which cost me home leave for Chris'mas. This character, this freak, fell down on her knees an' said: "You hit me, oh, boo, hoo, you hit me." I hadn't touched this freak. But then I got the idea. The freak wanted me to hit her. "OK, slave, get up." The freak got up and I shoved her into a gold frame mirror so hard it cracked the glass. "Now, slave, I don't wanna hear a description of your money, I wanta see it." —What're you messing aroun' with over there?

TRINKET: Me?

SLIM: You.

TRINKET: I'm boiling some water to make you some instant coffee. (*She comes from behind an ornamental screen or hanging.*)

SLIM: Are you having a heart attack?

TRINKET: Oh, no! Why? Why?

SLIM: You keep a hand over your chest. (*He reaches out to pull her hand away. She gasps and retreats.*)

TRINKET: *No, no, no, no, no!* (*In panic, to divert him, she snatches a photograph from the dresser.*) Look at this! Would you recognize me? In this newspaper photo I am standing between the Mayor and the president of the International Trade Mart. Then, at that time, I was in the field of public relations, I was called the Texas Tornado. I planned and organized the funeral of Mr. Depression, yes, I had the idea of burying Mr. Depression, holding an exact imitation of a funeral for him. All civic leaders backed me. There was a parade, I mean a funeral procession—*no, no, no, no!* (*He has stretched his hand out again to remove her hand from her chest.*) —For, for Mr. Depression! (*It should be apparent that this was the climax of her life.*)

SLIM: There's something not natural here.

TRINKET: Oh? No! —Mr. Depression was carried along Canal Street and up Saint Charles with big paper lilies on his twelve-foot coffin and there was a band playing a funeral march and I led the band, I walked in front of it dressed like a widow sobbing in a black veil. (*He reaches again for her hand still clasped in panic to her chest.*) *No, no, no, no, no!* —It went, the procession went, all the way to Audubon Park: and then can you guess what happened? (*Slim, weaving, pays no attention to this.*) —It rained like rain had never fallen before upon the earth! Cats, dogs, crocodiles—ZEBRAS! The procession broke up, band quit, everything dissolved, dispersed in the cloudburst! —Kettle's whistling. . . . (*She rushes back of the screen or hanging.*)

SLIM: Morbid!

TRINKET (*rushing back out*): Here, but let it cool first before you— (*He takes the cup and empties it on the floor.*) —Oh, you spilt it, I'll— (*She rushes back of the screen and back out with a towel, mops up the spilt coffee.*) —Now I'm no longer in public relations at all, it seems like another life in another world to me. It's hard to imagine the energy, confidence, drive I had when I first hit this town. Personalities go through such radical changes when something happens to change the course of their lives. Don't they? Haven't you noticed? (*There is a pause between them. Celeste appears before the hotel. She has two purses: Trinket's and hers. She stands at the foot of the outside stairs to Trinket's room and stamps her foot twice.*)

SLIM: There's somethin' Goddam wrong here, peculiar, not natural, morbid.

TRINKET: —I don't know what it could be except that you won't sit down and you won't take coffee. —Is it something about me? I'm a simple, ordinary person, and you're my guest and I'm your friend, not your slave. I've always maintained that this city is hard on the unformed characters of young people that come here, especially if they, oh, now, please sit down! Do! I'd be so happy!

SLIM: I don't sit down and stay down in any morbid place till I know if I want to stay in it. Be my slave. And show me the lettuce color of your money. —Good as—gold. . . . (*Celeste remains at the foot of the stairs. She stamps her foot twice more.*)

TRINKET (*in a shamed voice.*): It's green as lettuce and it's— good as my father's continual gusher in Texas. . . . (*Celeste stamps her feet twice more and tosses Trinket's purse onto the sidewalk. She stamps on the purse.*)

CELESTE (*in a strange chanting voice, separating each syllable*):
Sa-rah Bern-hardt had one leg.
The oth-er was a wood-en peg.
But good she did, yep, she did good,
Clump-ing on a STUMP OF WOOD!

(*She throws back her head and laughs at the sky.*)

TRINKET: It's a pity so many people choose the night of Our Savior's birth to behave in such a— (*Celeste kicks Trinket's purse into the orchestra pit as a policeman comes on.*)

POLICEMAN: Move along.

CELESTE: That's just what I'm doing. (*She goes off one way, the policeman the other.*)

SLIM: What've you got to drink here?

TRINKET: You don't want more to drink, Slim.

SLIM: Don' argue with me or I'll throw you across a room an'—

TRINKET: Oh, Slim, you don't mean that. You only say that because I'm afraid your friend has led you into the wrong kind of company, Slim. Oh, your hair is red gold, red gold, your skin is like—sunlight on snow. . . .

SLIM: Liquor! Out with it! Quick, before I—

TRINKET: I have nothing but wine here.

SLIM: Produce it, out with it, quick, before I—break you a—mirror!

TRINKET: No one can frighten me, Slim, but— (*She pours a glass of wine from her crystal decanter.*) —here!

SLIM: You take a drink of it, first, I'm takin' no chances.

TRINKET: Why, thank you, I will, I can use it. (*She sips the wine, then offers the glass to him.*)

SLIM: Pour me a clean other glass. I don't wanna drink outa yours an' catch somethin' morbid.

TRINKET: You mustn't talk like that to me, even though you don't mean it. Do you know how long it's been since a man has been in this room? Several years. And it seemed like a lifetime—a *death* time. (*Celeste marches into sight again, stops at the foot of the stairs, and stamps her foot twice as if about to commence the formal parade of a palace guard.*)

SLIM (*falling onto the bed*): I'm paralyzed here in a morbid—situation. . . .

(*Celeste opens her huge purse and removes a key: then she mounts the stairs, saying "Clump!" with each step. Trinket gasps and rushes to bolt the outside door. Celeste tries the door with her key: no luck: then she throws back her head like a dog yowling at the moon and she cries out—*)

CELESTE: Agnes—*JOOOOOO—OOOOOnes!*

TRINKET: Yes, it's the whore that snatched my purse on the street! (*She gasps and turns out the light as if that would protect her from Celeste's maniacal siege.*)

CELESTE: You'll find your empty purse outside in the gutter where I kicked it, you FINK! It's got your rosary in it an' your father's picture standin' next to his GUSHER! You better come out an' get it before the trash-man sweeps it into a sewer!

TRINKET: Celeste, go back to the House of Detention and ask for medical help there. You are out of your mind, howling like a mad dog on my stairs!

CELESTE: You told Bernie and Katz I'd been to jail, you fink.

TRINKET: You scratched a hideous lie on the stairs about me!

CELESTE: I scratched the truth about you! You got two mutilations, not one! The worse mutilation you've got is a crime of the Christian commandments, STINGINESS, CHEAPNESS, PURSE PRIDE! Your rosary's in the gutter with your GUSHER! Goddam, you got me thrown out, out, out! (*She stamps her foot with each "out."*) And everything that I owned locked up in a basement!

TRINKET: You know what you did, I don't have to remind you, and now go back down the stairs before I— I have the phone in my hand! (*She has picked up the telephone.*)

CELESTE: FINK, MUTILATED FINK!

TRINKET (*into the telephone*): BERNIE! (*Celeste runs down the stairs. At the bottom, she stops and looks up sobbing at the sky, weeping like a lost child. There is a pause, a silence. Celeste approaches the orchestra pit, stoops, her hand extended. The purse is handed back to her from below. She returns sobbing to the bottom of the outside staircase; she removes the rosary from Trinket's purse and begins to "tell her beads," sobbing.*) I believe she—

SLIM: —I'd a-been home for Christmas an' not broke Mom's heart if I hadn' gone AWOL las' week-en' but 'stead of home I'm paralyzed here in a morbid situation with a morbid hooker an' Goddam Bruno's gone where?

TRINKET (*at the telephone*): Bernie? Trinket! (*Bernie is lighted dimly at the switchboard in the lobby.*) —Be a doll, Bernie, and fetch me two hamburgers from the White Castle and a big carton of black coffee, and hurry back with it. This is a five-dollar tip night for you, Bernie. (*Celeste stands shivering in a blue spotlight at the foot of the outside stairs.*)

CELESTE: Anyhow, I'm not mutilated. She is. (*Bernie walks past her to the White Castle.*) Bernie? —Sweetheart? (*He ignores her as he goes. Slim falls back onto the bed, Trinket unties his shoes.*)

SLIM (*falling asleep*): Morbid, unnatural—slave. . . .

TRINKET: Oh, please stay awake with me!

SLIM: Ah-gah-wah. . . . (*He rolls away from her and begins to snore.*)

TRINKET: —Well, anyhow, I have somebody here with me. Celeste's alone but I'm not, I'm not alone but she is.

CELESTE (*sinking onto the bottom step of the outside stairs*): No, I'm not mutilated. She is. (*Trinket switches on the radio: it's soundless.*)

TRINKET: —The candlelight service is over. —The Holy Infant has been born in the manger. Now He's under the starry blue robe of His Mother. His blind, sweet hands are fumbling to find her breast. Now He's found it. His sweet, hungry lips are at her rose-petal nipple. —Oh, such *wanting* things lips are, and such *giving* things, breasts! (*The carollers have quietly assembled before the hotel. As the bedroom scene dims out, they begin to sing.*)

CAROLLERS:

> I think for some uncertain reason
> Mercy will be shown this season
> To the wayward and deformed,
> To the lonely and misfit.
> A miracle! a miracle!
> The homeless will be housed and warmed.

SINGLE CAROLLER (*stepping out of the group*):

> I think they will be housed and warmed
> And fed and comforted a while.
> And still not yet, not for a while
> The guileful word, the practiced smile.

CAROLLERS:

> A miracle! a miracle!
> The dark held back a little while.

(*They disperse.*)

SCENE SIX

Daylight comes. Celeste is on the sofa under the Christmas tree, snoring and sighing, her huge purse in her lap. Then Trinket's bedroom is lighted. She is in a kimono, seated on the bed. Slim enters from the hall.

TRINKET: Good morning. I thought you'd gone. (*He grunts disdainfully and turns away from her to comb his hair.*)

SLIM: —You got some free publicity on the bathroom wall down the hall there. It says if you don't mind sex with a mutilated woman, knock at room #307, which is this room number.

TRINKET: Oh. —How horrible of someone. I think I know who it is, the monster that did it.

SLIM: —Where's my wallet?

TRINKET: I *know* I know who did it, the monster last night.

SLIM: You're talking about one thing, I'm talking about another. You being mutilated is your own business except it's a stinking trick to take a fellow to bed without letting him know he's going to bed with someone mutilated. (*She begins to gasp "Ah," first very softly, then building to a scream. He claps his hand over her mouth as Bruno rushes into the room. Slim releases Trinket.*) Hey, Bruno, this Goddam lunatic rolled me! (*Trinket plunges toward the open wall of the room. The sailors drag her back. She writhes grotesquely in their grasp, then collapses to the floor.*) She's got my wallet with eighty-six dollars!

BRUNO: Have you got rocks in your head?

SLIM: I got no rocks in my head, she's got my wallet.

BRUNO: Lady, are you okay? (*Trinket moans, crouching by the bed. Bruno hisses at Slim.*) You lack decent human feelings! —You lack— (*He picks up Trinket and puts her on the bed.*) Are you all right? Are you all right? Huh, Miss?

TRINKET (*faintly*): —Yeah. . . .

BRUNO (*to Trinket*): Are you sure you're all right?

TRINKET: Get him out of here, will you?

BRUNO (*to Slim*): Come out in the hall, rock-head.

SLIM: I got no rocks in my head, she's got my wallet, that mutilated whore has got my wallet, hid somewhere in this fly-trap!

BRUNO: That woman ain't got your wallet, you gave your wallet to me to hold for you, rock-head.

SLIM: I'll count the money left in it. (*They have started to leave.*)

BRUNO: This is the last time I go out on liberty with you, never again, never under any conditions, no time, ever!

(*During this, Trinket has been slowly lifting a trembling hand to her breast.*)

TRINKET: —Ahhhh! (*She opens her diary.*) —Dear Diary, the pain's come back.

(*The singers enter from the wings. The pitch pipe is blown but no one sings. They're waiting for someone. He enters from the upstage door of the hotel lobby, in a black cowboy's suit, with diamond-like brilliants outlining his shirt pockets, belt, holster and the edge of his wide-brimmed hat. The pitch pipe is blown again.*)

CAROLLERS:
        I think—

(*There is a long pause: the pitch pipe is blown.*)

        I think—

(*Long pause: the leader blows long and hard on the pitch pipe.*)

        I think—

(*The leader hurls his pitch pipe to the floor. Then the black-clad cowboy, Jack In Black, steps forward and sings alone with a hand on his holster.*)

JACK IN BLACK:
        I think the ones with measured time
        Before the tolling of the bell
        Will meet a friend and tell their friend
        That nothing's wrong, that all goes well.

CAROLLERS:
        A miracle, a miracle!
        Nothing's wrong and all goes well.

JACK IN BLACK:
        They'll say it once and once again
        Until they say it to themselves,
        And nearly think it may be true,
        No early tolling of the bell.

CAROLLERS:
        A miracle, a miracle!
        Nothing's wrong, all is well!

SCENE SEVEN

*Later that day: it is silver dusk; there is a murmur of rain.
Trinket is dimly lighted in her bedroom: Bernie is back at the
switchboard. Celeste is still on the sofa.*

TRINKET (*at the telephone*): Is she still down there, Bernie?

BERNIE: Her? (*He leans forward in his swivel chair to look.*)
—Yeah. . . .

TRINKET: What's she doing, Bernie?

BERNIE: Nothin'. Sittin'.

TRINKET: She can't sit down there forever, or can she,
Bernie?

BERNIE: No. Katz don't like it. He told me to git her out and
I said then git me a stick of dynamite, will yuh.

TRINKET: —I have been thinking things over this afternoon,
Bernie, and Celeste is not a mentally grown-up person.
She's mentally retarded. You know that, Bernie? Irresponsible. Childish. She doesn't examine her actions, she
can't distinguish between a right and wrong thing, she
acts impulsively, Bernie, like children do. You know how
children act. Impulsively, thoughtlessly, Bernie? Her shoplifting, for instance, is the act of a child. She sees a
thing, she wants it, she picks it up. Like a child picks a
flower. . . .

CELESTE (*rousing slightly*): What's she sayin' about me?

TRINKET: Bernie, you can't hold malice against a child for bad
actions. No matter how much it hurts you, you know the
limitations and you forgive. —Bernie, tell her to come on
up to my room and have a glass of wine with me. I want to
bury the hatchet.

CELESTE (*rising heavily*): What's she saying, huh, Bernie?

BERNIE: Excuse me, Miss Dugan. (*He turns to Celeste.*) You
got a invitation. Miss Dugan wants you to have a glass of
wine upstairs with her.

CELESTE: —Never! —I still have pride!

BERNIE: Yeah, she's comin', Miss Dugan.

CELESTE: Never! I'd sooner die!

BERNIE: G'bye, Miss Dugan. (*He hangs up and leans back
again with his comic book.*)

CELESTE (*She draws her ratty fur coat about her and stalks out-side. There is no hesitation. She goes straight up the outside stairs to Trinket's. Hearing her approaching footsteps, Trinket unlocks the outside door. Celeste enters with an air of dignity.*) I just come up here to tell you my friendship isn't for sale. (*But her eyes gravitate to a cut-glass decanter of Tokay on the table. She stops speaking, her eyes gleam and jaws hang ajar. . . .*)

TRINKET: —It must be raining out there. Your coat looks wet. Let me hang it up by the heater to dry.

CELESTE: Aw, yeah. Thanks. (*Her eyes glitter, fastened on the California Tokay.*)

TRINKET: Sit down, dear. Would you like a glass of Tokay?

CELESTE: Aw, yeah! Thanks!

TRINKET: Help yourself, please. I filled the cut-glass decanter. There's more in the jug.

CELESTE: Where's the jug?

TRINKET: It's right under the table.

CELESTE: Aw, yeah—thanks!

TRINKET: —Well, it seems like old times.

CELESTE: You used to keep those little sweet biscuits, you know, the—

TRINKET: The vanilla cream wafers? Nabiscos?

CELESTE: Yes, yes, Nabiscos!

TRINKET: It's possible I still have some.

CELESTE (*half rising with excitement*): You kept them in a tin box, a round—

TRINKET: Yes, in this round tin box. Let's see if there's any left in it.

TRINKET: Why, yes!

CELESTE: Aw! Good! It's hard to beat a Nabisco vanilla wafer in the way of a sweet cake or cookie.

TRINKET (*with a little shuddering cry of horror*): There's a dead cockroach in the box!

CELESTE: Now, now, now, now, it's just a dead bug in a box, give me the box, I'll get rid of the bug! (*Celeste picks the bug out of the box.*)

TRINKET: Not in the room, out the door!

CELESTE: OK, OK, out the door! (*She tosses the bug out the door and immediately starts munching a wafer.*)

TRINKET (*sadly, imploringly*): Oh, Celeste! You mustn't eat after a cockroach, you can't eat after a cockroach! Don't, please, eat after a cockroach!

CELESTE: Honey, in the best restaurants people eat after cockroaches! Hey! Let's bum around town tomorrow! Huh? Huh? Yeah, we'll bum around town and have lunch together at Arnaud's. Oysters Rockefeller? Yeah, yeah, to begin with! Then a shrimp bisque and—

TRINKET: TODAY I FOUND!

CELESTE: —What? You said you found something today?

TRINKET: Today I found! —A *scorpion* in my bed. . . .

CELESTE: —Is that a insect? Forget it. —Well, then, after Arnaud's—a movie? An afternoon at the movies with a large size Hershey, a big Hershey almond bar, huh? Then home together. Trinket, we got to pick up the thread of our old lives together. It's essential, necessary, we got to! —And go on and on and on and on, like it was! —Because we were happy together before we hurt each other and all that's finished, we won't hurt each other again as long as we live, will we, dear? Uh-uh! —Music? A little radio music?

TRINKET: —I think we ought to go out after while to hear the boys' choir sing at the cathedral. The Christmas afternoon Mass.

CELESTE: M'clothes are too wet to go out again tonight, Trinket. Get the boys' choir on the radio, honey.

TRINKET: The cathedral service is peaceful.

CELESTE: Well, light a candle and let the boys' choir sing on the radio, dear.

TRINKET: No, it's not the same thing. Christ is present, Christ and Our Lady are present in the cathedral, but here. . . . (*A drunken sailor stumbles up the steps. Hearing their voices, he stops, tries the door and knocks.*)

CELESTE: —Somebody's at the door, Trinket . . . (*Her voice is already slurred by the Tokay.*)

TRINKET: —The hotel is full of drunk sailors on leave. Don't let him in, he'll drink the wine up on us.

CELESTE: I'll just peek out.

TRINKET: No, don't *you*, let *me*. I won't admit a drunk sailor after last night. (*She peeks out but the sailor has stumbled back off. She shuts the door.*) —Nobody.

CELESTE: But you opened the door for someone that knocked and how do you know that that someone didn't come in?

TRINKET: Make sense, please. How could he? Where would he be? We'd see anybody that entered.

CELESTE: Not necessarily, Trinket. I've always believed in invisibility. I've always had faith in invisi-*bee*-able *presence!* (*She rises and faces the audience with a mysterious air.*)

TRINKET (*skeptically*): Oh, Celeste, I—

CELESTE: Not so loud.

TRINKET: I remember when you used to see colored aureoles around people's heads, and—

CELESTE: Not aureoles, *auras.*

TRINKET: Yes, auras, different-colored auras and you'd tell their fortunes and characters by the color of the aura. You said mine was purple.

CELESTE: Stop talking. Be still. Act naturally. Give the presence a chance to manifest itself. It will. It's still in the room. Have a little wine, dear. (*She refills their glasses. Jack In Black enters the lobby from the upstage opening. He lounges, smiling, in the downstage entrance. A distant bell starts tolling. Celeste's voice and manner become even more mysterious.*) There was an elderly sister at Sacred Heart Convent School that received invisible presences, and once she told me that if I was ever cut off and forgotten by the blood of my blood and was homeless alone in the world, I would receive the invisible presence of Our Lady in a room I was in. She said that I would smell roses. I smell roses. She said I would smell candles burning. I smell burning candles. She said I would smell incense. I smell incense. I would hear a bell ringing. I hear a bell ringing. (*More singers appear from the wings.*) —I feel it, yes, I feel it, I know it! Our Lady's in the room with us. She entered the room invisible when you opened the door. You opened the door of your heart and Our Lady came in! (*She falls to her knees.*) MARY? MARY? OUR LADY? (*Then, in a loud whisper*): Trinket, kneel beside me! (*Trinket hesitates only a moment, then kneels beside Celeste. There has been a gradual change of light in the room: it now seems to be coming through stained glass windows—a subjective phenomenon of the trance falling over the women. Celeste stretches out a hand as if feeling for the invisible presence. She suddenly cries out and draws back her hand as if it had touched the presence.*)

TRINKET: *What, what?*

CELESTE (*sobbing and rocking on her knees*): I touched Her robe, I touched the robe of Our Lady!

TRINKET: *Where is it, where is the robe of Our Lady?*

CELESTE: *Here!* (*She seizes Trinket's hand and draws it forward.*)

TRINKET (*fallen into the trance*): *Here?*

CELESTE: *Yes, there! Kiss the robe of Our Lady!* (*Both women stretch their hands out and draw them back to their mouths as if kissing the robe.*)

TRINKET (*crying out wildly*): *The pain in my breast is gone!*

CELESTE: *A miracle!*

TRINKET: *Finally!*

CELESTE & TRINKET (*Together*): *Finally, oh, finally!*

JACK IN BLACK (*singing alone*):
>And finally, oh, finally
>The tolling of a ghostly bell
>Cries out farewell, to flesh farewell,
>Farewell to flesh, to flesh farewell!

OTHER SINGERS (*with him*):
>A miracle, a miracle!
>The tolling of a ghostly bell.

(*Celeste and Trinket begin to sing with them*):

SINGERS (*without soloist*):
>The tolling of a ghostly bell
>Will gather us from where we fell,
>And, oh, so lightly will we rise
>With so much wonder in our eyes!
>A miracle, a miracle!
>The light of wonder in our eyes.

(*Jack In Black crosses through them, smiling and lifting his hat.*)

>But that's a dream, for dream we must
>That we're made not of mortal dust.
>There's Jack, there's Jack, there's Jack In Black!

JACK IN BLACK:
>Expect me, but not yet, not yet!

CHORUS:
> A miracle, a miracle!
> He's smiling and it means not yet.

(*The bell stops tolling.*)

JACK IN BLACK (*singing alone*):
> I'm Jack In Black who stacks the deck,
> Who loads the dice and tricks the wheel.
> The bell has stopped because I smile.
> It means forget me for a while.

CHORUS:
> A miracle, a miracle!
> Forget him for a little while.

(*Jack In Black moves his lifted hat from left to right in the style of a matador dedicating his fight to the audience.*)

The Curtain Falls

KINGDOM OF EARTH

(*The Seven Descents of Myrtle*)

SCENE ONE

At rise of the curtain, the stage set, uninhabited, has the mood of a blues song whose subject is loneliness. It is the back of a Mississippi Delta farmhouse, a story and a half high, its walls gray against a sky the same color. On either side of it stand growths of cane, half the height of the house, rattling in a moaning wind. Continually through these sounds is heard the low, insistent murmur of vast waters in flood or near it. This back wall of the house, except for a doorway, is represented by a scrim that will lift when the house is entered. Then the interior will be exposed: a kitchen to the right, a mysterious little "parlor" to the left, a narrow, dark hall between them: a flight of stairs to an upper hall and a low, slant-ceilinged bedroom to the left. The right side of the upper half-story is never used in the play and is always masked. It is a difficult set that requires the inventions of a very gifted designer. A few moments after the curtain rises, a car is heard approaching and stopping close by.

MAN'S VOICE: Hey, Chicken! Chicken!

> (*There is a whine of wind. Then the one being called appears from offstage. He is a young man (30 or 35) in rubber hip boots covered with river slick. He seems a suitable antagonist to a flooding river.*)

WOMAN'S VOICE: We're clearin' out of our place.

CHICKEN: I see.

MAN'S VOICE: We're goin' up to Sunset. That's over the crest of the river.

CHICKEN: That's radio talk. I pay no attention to it.

WOMAN'S VOICE: Sorry we don't have room for you in our car.

CHICKEN: Never mind that. I wouldn't go if I had my own car to go in.

> (*He is staring straight out as if the voices came from the back of the theatre. Dull lightning flickers about the gray place.*)

—So don't worry about it.

WOMAN'S VOICE (*turned openly malicious*): I ain't worried about it, it's your worry, Chicken, but we got word that ole man Sikes might dynamite his south bank levee tonight to

625

save his nawth bank levee, and if he does, this place of yours will be under at least ten foot of water, you know that.

CHICKEN (*raising his voice*): I'd sooner be caught in my house by ten foot of water than caught in the mud on a road between here an' Sunset an' drown like kittens tied in a sack with rocks an' thrown in the river, cause anyhow in this house which is stood out five floods there's something I can climb onto, I can climb on the roof and set on the roof with the chickens till the water goes down. I done that before and can do it again, why, that's how I got my name Chicken, they named me Chicken because I set on the roof with the chickens one time this place was flooded.

WOMAN'S VOICE (*spitefully*): A person could git awful hungry on a roof befo' the water wint down.

CHICKEN: Shit, if I got hungry I'd bite the haid off one of the other chickens and drink its blood.

MAN'S VOICE: I seen a man do that in a freak show once.

WOMAN'S VOICE: Chicken looks like he could do it, an' enjoy it. G'bye, Chicken. Daddy, le's go, we're cold.

(*Motor roars and splutters; the tires spin in the muck.*)

CHICKEN: Seems like you're stuck already. Sorry I don't have room fo' you in the house.

WOMAN'S VOICE: Sorry we don't have room fo' *you* in the car.

(*Tires catch*)

MAN'S VOICE: *Here we go!*

(*The sound of the car and bawling children fade out and we hear the muted warning of the river. The cane stalks make a sad rattling noise in the whining wind. Chicken enters kitchen and strikes a match; lights an oil lamp and warms his hands on its chimney as the glass gets hot. The flame makes grotesque shadows on his dark face. He is a strange-looking young man but also remarkably good-looking with his very light eyes, darker-than-olive skin, and the power and male grace of his body. After his hands are warmed up on the lamp chimney, he crosses with lamp to stove but on the way is distracted by a nude girl's body in a calendar picture, tacked directly over a disordered army cot pushed against kitchen wall. He turns the lamp up higher to see the picture*)

more clearly, one hand at the same time falling involuntar-
ily down his body. But he mutters sharply, "Nah!" and then
goes on to the stove and cupboard. He starts preparing him-
self a pot of coffee, from time to time repeating the Woman's
mocking shout, "Sorry we don't have room for you in the
car." After some moments he abruptly freezes, cocking his
head like an animal at a warning sound. He listens for sev-
eral beats before the audience can hear what he hears—the
sound of an approaching motor. As the sound gets close to the
house, he blows out the lamp and leans over it, as if glaring
out a dim window in the open wall of the set. Then mutters
sharply to himself—)

CHICKEN: *Him!*

(*Motor stops nearby and a Woman's Voice is heard crying out*
something. Chicken grunts, astonished.)

—Him and a *woman*!

(*He sets the lamp down quickly and runs to lock the door be-*
tween the narrow, dark hall and the kitchen. Myrtle and Lot
appear downstage left, by the back door of the house. Neither
is a person that could avoid curious attention. Myrtle is a
rather fleshy young woman, amiably loud-voiced. She is wear-
ing a pink turtle-neck sweater and tight checkered slacks.
Her blond-dyed hair is tied up in a wet silk scarf, magenta-
colored. Her appearance suggests an imitation of a Holly-
wood glamor-girl which doesn't succeed as a good imitation.
Lot comes on behind her, bearing two suitcases with great dif-
ficulty. He is a frail, delicately—you might say exotically—
pretty youth of about twenty. He is ten years younger than
Myrtle, and his frailty makes him look even younger. Myrtle
dominates him in an amiable way.)

MYRTLE: This here ain't the front door of the house.
LOT (*panting*): No. Back.
MYRTLE: Well, then, you just march yourself around to the
    front door, then, cause I'm not about to enter my new
    home for th' first time by th' back door, No, Siree, I'm not!

(*Has already started around house, brushing through the*
canebrake.)

I don't expect you to carry me over the threshold like you ought to but at least you don't have to take me in the back door.

(*Her complaint is affable, gay; she is enormously relieved that the dreadful journey is over safely. Myrtle is a good-natured thing—almost ridiculously so. She has nothing else to meet the world with but good nature. . . . Her vigorous voice fades under the whine of wind. Lot draws a deep, difficult breath and attempts to follow her vigorous lead but can't make it: He staggers coughing against the rain-washed gray wall of the house, dropping his damp, cardboard suitcase. He leans panting against the wet frame wall as Myrtle calls to him from out front, above wind.*)

Hey, Lot, come awn!

(*Inside the dim kitchen, at a safe distance from the dusty windowpane in the imaginary fourth wall, Chicken is leaning stiffly over to look out and listen, like a crouched animal. He is muttering barely audibly to himself. After about ten beats, Myrtle stops waiting out front and comes charging back around the side of the house, imitating the howl of the wind.*)

Woooo! Woooo! That wind is penetratin'! Sharp as a butcher's knife! What's holdin' you up back here?
LOT: No—breath—left . . .

(*She rushes up to him—an avalanche of motherly concern.*)

MYRTLE: Aw, baby, love!
LOT: Shouldn't have tried to carry—luggage . . .

(*He raises his pale, lost eyes to the fading-out sky above Myrtle's look of concern.*)

MYRTLE: Well, I swan!
LOT (*breathlessly, with a touch of disdain*): —What is swan, why swan?
MYRTLE: You'll have to ask my dead Granny, she always said "I swan."
LOT (*lowering his gaze to Myrtle*): To prove she wasn't a goose?

(*He bends, stiffly, to pick up a suitcase but Myrtle snatches it from him.*)

MYRTLE: You come on and stop leaning against those cold, wet boards and let's get into our house! (*She has the suitcase and is trying the back door, saying*—) This door is locked.

LOT: No. Just stuck, always sticks in wet weather.

(*She pulls, the door gives violently and she almost tumbles off the back steps. She recovers, laughing, and hauls the suitcase inside, heading straight up the dark, narrow hall.*)

LOT (*behind her*): Where are you going?

MYRTLE: I'm goin' straight to the parlor. I want the parlor to be my first impression of my new home. Is this the door to the parlor?

LOT: Uh-huh.

MYRTLE: It's stuck, too. (*It gives before her weight.*) *There now!*

LOT: Go in.

MYRTLE: You go in and light the lights in that parlor so I can see it.

LOT (*pressing the switch*): —The lights don't light.

MYRTLE: How come they don't light, baby?

LOT: Sometimes— (*He draws a deep breath.*) —when the river is flooding some places, the electric current that makes the lights light— (*He is talking to her as if she were mentally deficient. He draws another deep breath that wheezes in his throat.*) —is temporarily interrupted, Myrtle.

MYRTLE: How long is temporarily?

LOT: Oh, it comes back on when the— (*deep breath*) —water goes down. These drapes are velvet drapes—neglected lately.

(*He opens them as gently as if they had feeling. Fading gray light enters the parlor.*)

MYRTLE: —Well, this is an elegant parlor, an elegant little parlor.

LOT: My mother did all she could to give some quality to the place but my father— (*deep breath*) —was not just indifferent to the effort she made but opposed it. He was a man that liked to sit in a kitchen and wouldn't let Mother build a dining room onto the house. When he died, howling like a wild beast, Mother was free to transform this place or tear it down to the ground, but life was cruel to Mother. It gave her no time to carry out her plans.

MYRTLE: —She—?

LOT: Outlived my father by shortly less than one year.

MYRTLE: —Sad . . .

LOT: —Yes. —Tragic.

MYRTLE: —Hmmm. A parlor with gold chairs is—like a dream!

LOT: The chandelier is crystal but the pendants are dusty, they've got to be all taken down, one by one, dipped in hot, soapy water. Then rinsed in a bowl of clear water, then dried off with soft tissue paper and hung back up.

(*Chicken grins savagely in the kitchen.*)

Mother and I used to do it, she never allowed the colored girl to touch a thing in this parlor or even come in it. Beautiful things can only be safely cared for by people that know and love them. The day before she died, do you know what she did?

(*Myrtle shakes her head, staring curiously at her exotic young husband.*)

—She climbed a ladder in here and removed each crystal pendant from the little brass hook it hung on, passed it down to me, to be soaped and rinsed and dried, and then replaced on its little brass hook. "Son," she said to me, "help me down off this ladder, I don't know why I'm so tired."

MYRTLE: Baby, you got a mother complex, as they call it, and I'm gonna make you forget it. You hear me?

LOT: You've got a voice that no one in a room with you could help but hear when you speak.

MYRTLE: That's awright. When I speak I want to be heard. Now, baby, this mother complex, I'm gonna get that out of you, Lot, cause I'm not just your wife, I'm also your mother, and I'm not daid, I'm livin'. A-course I don't mean I'm gonna replace her in your heart, but—

(*She draws up one of the little gilded chairs close to the one on which he is seated.*)

LOT: Don't sit on mother's gold chairs. They break too easy.

MYRTLE: You are sittin' on one.

LOT: I'm lighter than you.

MYRTLE: Well! I stand corrected! —Mr. Skin and Bones! — Do I have to stay on my feet in this parlor or can I sit on the sofa?

LOT: Yes, sit on the sofa. (*Slight pause. His head droops forward and his violet-lidded eyes close.*) —The little animal has to make a home of its own. . . .

MYRTLE: I didn't catch that remark.

LOT: —What?

MYRTLE: You said something about an animal.

LOT: I'm too tired to know what I'm saying.

MYRTLE: Are you too tired to hear what *I'm* saying?

LOT: What are you saying?

MYRTLE: I'm saying that all my electric equipment is sitting out there under the leaky roof of your car.

LOT: —Oh. —Yes . . .

MYRTLE: Didn' you tell me you had niggers here working fo' you?

LOT: There's a house girl named Clara and her unmarried husband.

MYRTLE: How do you call this unmarried couple of niggers when you want something done?

LOT: You— (*deep breath*) —have to step outside and ring a bell for 'em.

MYRTLE: Where is this bell you ring for 'em?

LOT: The bell is— (*deep breath*) —in the kitchen.

MYRTLE: Well, kitchen here I come!

(*During the above, Chicken had opened the kitchen door to hear the talk in the parlor. Now he closes and locks the door silently.*)

The unmarried nigra couple're gonna step pretty lively fo' Mrs. Lot Ravenstock.

(*She charges to the kitchen door behind which Chicken is lurking. Lot sways and falls off the chair; staggers to the sofa. Myrtle finds the door locked, rattles the knob and calls out—*)

Who is in there? Who is in this kitchen? —Somebody's in there!

(*She presses her ear to the door. Chicken breathes loudly as if he'd been fighting. Myrtle rattles the knob again and a key*)

*falls to the floor inside the kitchen. Myrtle is startled and sub-
dued: she returns to the parlor as if a little frightened.*)

—If that's a dawg in there, why don't it bark?

LOT: —Dawg?

MYRTLE: That kitchen door was locked or it was stuck mighty
tight. And I swear I heard something breathing right behind it, like a big dawg was in there. Then I rattled the
knob and I heard a key fall to the floor. Will you wake up
an' lissen t'what I tell you?

LOT (*hoarse whisper*): I thought he was hiding in there.

MYRTLE: Who? What?

LOT: —Chicken. . . .

MYRTLE: Chicken? Hiding? A chicken, you say, is hiding in
the kitchen? What are you tawkin about! —No chicken
breathes that loud that I ever met!

LOT: Myrtle, when I say "Chicken" I don't mean the kind of
chicken with feathers, I mean my half brother Chicken who
runs this place for me.

MYRTLE: I'll be switched! This is a piece of news!

LOT: Keep your voice down, please. I got some things to tell
you about the situation on this place.

MYRTLE: —Maybe you should've told me about it before?

LOT: Yes, maybe. But anyhow . . . now . . .

MYRTLE: You are making me nervous. You mean your brother
is hiding in that kitchen while we are sitting in here half
frozen?

LOT: Cain't you talk quiet?

MYRTLE: Not when I am upset. If he is in there, why don't
you call him out?

LOT: He'll come out after while. The sight of a woman talking in this house must have give him a little something to
think about in that kitchen, is what I figure.

MYRTLE: Well, all I can say is— "*Well!*"

LOT: —That's what I figure.

MYRTLE: And that's why you're shaking all over, not cause it's
cold.

LOT: I'm shaking because I am cold with no fire anywhere in
this house except in the kitchen. And it's locked up. With
him in it.

MYRTLE: This makes about as much sense as a Chinese cross-word puzzle to me, but maybe that long, wet ride has injured my brain. Can you explain to me why this half brother of yours would be hiding in the kitchen when we come home, pretending not to be here or—God knows what?!

LOT: Everything can't be explained to you all at once here, Myrtle. Will you try to remember something? Will you just try to get something in your haid?

MYRTLE: What?

LOT: This place is mine. You are my wife. You are now the lady of the house. Is that understood?

MYRTLE: Then why—?

LOT: Sh! Will you? Please? Keep your voice down to something under a shout?

MYRTLE: But—

LOT: Will you? Will you PLEASE?

(*Pause*)

MYRTLE: Awright. (*Sniffs*) Now I got the shivers, too. —If he's in the kitchen, why don't he come out?

LOT: Oh, he'll come out, after he's had three or four drinks in there to work up his nerve.

MYRTLE: You mean he's bashful?

LOT: He's strange by nature, and not accepted around here.

MYRTLE: I think we ought to go call him, it would be more natural to.

LOT: He won't come out till he's ready. Be patient. Do you like sherry wine?

MYRTLE: I don't think I ever had any.

LOT: Some of Miss Lottie's sherry's still left in this ole cut-glass decanter.

MYRTLE (*absently*): Aw. Good. Good. . . .

LOT (*in his thin, breathless voice*): This is Bohemian glass, these here wineglasses are.

MYRTLE: —What dya know. . . .

LOT: Ev'ry afternoon about this time, Miss Lottie would take a glass of this Spanish sherry with a raw egg in it to keep her strength up. It would always revive her, even when she was down to eighty-two pounds, her afternoon sherry and eggs, she called it her sherry flip, would pick her right up and she'd be bright an' lively.

MYRTLE: —Imagine me thinkin' that that was a dawg in there! Yeah, I thought that huffing I heard in there was a big old dawg in the kitchen, locked up in there. I didn't—Ha Ha!—suspect that it was—Ha Ha!—your—*brother*. . . .

(*He begins to cough: the cough shakes him like a dead leaf, and he leans panting against the wall staring at Myrtle with pale, stricken eyes. She gathers him close in her arms. . . .*)

Why, baby! Precious love! —That's an *awful* cough! —I wonder if you could be comin' down with th' flu?

LOT: —Lissen! —He's movin' now!

(*Chicken's frozen attitude by the door was released by the sound of Lot's paroxysm of coughing: He crosses to a cupboard, takes out a jug and takes a long, long drink.*)

—A place with no woman sure does all go to pieces.

MYRTLE: Well, now they's a woman here.

LOT: That's right: we'll make some changes.

MYRTLE: You bet we will. And bright and early tomorrow, the first thing we do after breakfast, we'll, we'll, we'll! —We'll get out that ole stepladder and wash those whatcha-ma-call-ems and make them shine like the chandelier in Loew's State on Main Street in Memphis! And we will—oh, we'll do a whole lot of things as soon as this weather clears up. And soon it's going to be summer. You know that, Sugar? It's going to be summer real soon and—a small animal needs a place of its own.

LOT: Yeah, it'll be summer, the afternoons'll be long, the damp'll dry out of the walls and—

MYRTLE: I'M GONNA MAKE YOU REST! And build you up. You hear me? I'm gonna make you recover your lost strength, baby. —You and me are gonna have us a baby, and if it's a boy, we're going to call it Lot and if it's a girl we're gonna name her Lottie.

LOT (*his eyes falling shut*): If beds could talk what stories they could tell. . . .

MYRTLE: Baby, last night don't count. You was too nervous. I'll tell you something I know that might surprise you. A man is twice as nervous as a woman and you are twice as nervous as a man.

LOT: Do you mean I'm not a man?

MYRTLE: I mean you're a man but superior to a man. (*Hugs him to her and sings—*)

> "Cuddle up a little closer, baby mine.
> Cuddle up and say you'll be my clinging vine!"

Mmmm, Sugar! Last night you touched the deepest chord in my nature which is the maternal chord in me. T'night I'm gonna cradle you in my arms, probably won't sleep, just watch you sleepin' an' hold you all night long, and it'll be better than sleep. Do you know, do you realize what a beautiful thing you are?

LOT: I realize that I resemble my mother.

MYRTLE: To me you resemble just *you*. The first, the most, the *only* refined man in my life. Skin, eyes, hair any girl would be jealous of. A mouth like a flower. Kiss me! (*He submits to a kiss.*) Mmmm. I could kiss you forever!

LOT: I wouldn't be able to breathe.

MYRTLE: You're refined and elegant as this parlor.

LOT: I want you to promise me something. If Chicken asks you, and when he gets drunk he will ask you—

MYRTLE: Chicken will ask me nothing that I won't answer in aces and spades.

LOT: There's something you mustn't answer if he asks you.

MYRTLE: What thing is that, baby?

LOT: If I'm a—

MYRTLE: If you're a what?

LOT: Strong lover. —Tell him I satisfy you.

MYRTLE: Oh, now, baby, there'd be no lie about that. Y'know, they's a lot more to this sex business than two people jumpin' up an' down on each other's eggs. You know that or you *ought* to.

LOT: I'm going to satisfy you when I get my strength back, and meanwhile—make out like I do. Completely. Already. I mean when talking to Chicken.

MYRTLE: Aw, Chicken again, a man that huffs like a dawg an' hides in the kitchen, do you think I'd talk about us to him, about our love with each other? All I want from that man is that he opens the kitchen door so I can go in there and grab hold of that bell and ring the clapper off it for that girl that works here, that Clara. I'll make her step, all right, and step quick, too. The first thing she's gotta do is haul in all that electric equipment settin' in the car, before it gits damp an' rusts on me.

LOT: Myrtle, I told you that when there's danger of flood, the colored help on a place cut out for high ground. —Till the danger's over.

MYRTLE: Then what're we doin' on low ground instid of high ground?

LOT: To protect our property from possible flood damage. This is your house, your home. Aren't you concerned with protecting it for us?

MYRTLE: My house, my home! I never known, I never even suspected, how much havin' property of my own could mean to me till all of a sudden I have some. House, home, land, a little dream of a parlor, elegant as you, refined as you are.

(*During this talk, Chicken has his ear pressed to the kitchen door, fiercely muttering phrases from the talk.*)

LOT: —Chicken calls me a sissy.

MYRTLE: Well, he better not call you no sissy when Myrtle's around. I'll fix his wagon up good, I mean I WILL!

LOT: SHH! —Myrtle, you've got an uncontrollable voice. He's listening to us. —You think you could handle Chicken?

MYRTLE: Want to make a bet on it? I've yet to meet the man that I couldn't handle.

LOT: You ain't met Chicken.

MYRTLE: I'm gonna meet him!—whin he comes outa that kitchen. . . .

LOT: He will, soon, now. It's gettin' dark outside and I heard him set the jug down on the kitchen table.

MYRTLE: Awright, I'm *ready* for him, anytime he comes out, I'm ready to meet him and one thing I want to git straight. Who's going to be running this place, me or this Chicken?

LOT: This place is mine. You're my wife.

MYRTLE: That's what I wanted to know. Then I'm in charge here.

LOT: You're taking the place of Miss Lottie. She ran the house and you'll run it.

MYRTLE: Good. Then that's understood.

LOT: It better be understood. Cause Chicken is not my brother, we're just half brothers and the place went to me. It's mine.

MYRTLE: Did you have diff'rent daddies?

LOT: No, we had diff'rent mothers. *Very* diff'rent mothers!

(*Chicken snorts like a wild horse*)

He's coming out now!

(*Chicken emerges slowly from the kitchen and starts up the dark, narrow hall.*)

MYRTLE: Yes. I hear him coming. Let's go meet him.

LOT: No. Wait here. Sit tight. And remember that you're the lady of the house.

(*Chicken pauses, listening in the dim hall.*)

MYRTLE: It don't seem natural to me.

(*Lot removes an ivory cigarette holder from a coat pocket, puts a cigarette in it and lights it. His hands are shaky.*)

(*nervously*) —A parlor with gold chairs is like a dream!

LOT: —A woman in the house is like a dream.

MYRTLE: —I must be hearing things.

LOT: What did you hear?

MYRTLE: I, I—thought I heard footsteps in the hall.

LOT: Human or animal footsteps?

(*Chicken opens the parlor door.*)

Aw. —Hello, Chicken. Don't come in the parlor till you take off those muddy boots.

(*Chicken disregards this instruction: enters the parlor. Myrtle rises nervously but Lot remains seated, smiling icily through a cloud of cigarette smoke.*)

CHICKEN: They turn you loose from the hospital?

LOT: I wasn't locked in it. A hospital ain't a jail. I was dismissed.

CHICKEN: Couldn't do nothing more for you?

LOT: I was dismissed as cured.

CHICKEN: I see. And who is this woman?

LOT: You mean who is this lady. This lady is my wife. Myrtle, this is Chicken. Chicken, this is Myrtle.

CHICKEN: Why did you all come back here?

LOT: Wanted to is the reason.

CHICKEN: With this flood? In the county?

LOT: That's right. I wanted to see that my mother's things are taken out of the parlor before the downstairs is flooded.

CHICKEN: What good'll that do if the upstairs is flooded, too?

MYRTLE: Oh, my God, the flood won't go *that* high, will it?

CHICKEN: You don't know much about floods.

MYRTLE: All I know is I'm scared to death of deep water.

CHICKEN: Then how come you drove back here through that high water you must've hit south of Sunset?

MYRTLE: I begged Lot to turn back but he was bound an' determined to git us home, I couldn't stop him, he was determined to make it.

CHICKEN: Wanta know something? This time tomorrow, both floors of this house will be full of floodwater.

(*Myrtle draws a long, noisy breath of dismay and terror.*)

The river gauge is thirty-two foot of water at Friar's Point and the crest is still above Memphis. And I just got word from those sons of bitches, Potters, that ole man Sikes is about to blow up the south end of his levee to save the rest of it, he's planning to dynamite it tonight and you—come home just in time for it.

MYRTLE: Lot, baby, I think we ought to turn right around and drive back.

LOT: No. We're home. We're not gonna leave here. Chicken's just tryin' to scare us. Why don't you leave, Chicken, if you're scared of the flood?

CHICKEN: I ain't about to leave here. You know we got this agreement. Have you forgotten about the agreement we signed between us?

LOT: That was before I got married. Now I am.

CHICKEN (*to Myrtle*): Are you his nurse?

MYRTLE: Why, no, I'm Mrs. Lot Ravenstock and have been Mrs. Lot Ravenstock since yesterday mawnin.

CHICKEN: I know of invalid men to marry their nurses, or anyhow live with 'em like they was married.

MYRTLE: We're married, and I wasn't a nurse. Y'know, I don't think I ever seen so little resemblance between two brothers.

CHICKEN: We're half brothers.

LOT: Chicken's much darker complected. Don't you notice?

MYRTLE: There's so little light in the room.

CHICKEN: I work out in the fields and Lot just lays in bed.

LOT: —I'd like some hot coffee, now.

CHICKEN: Coffee's in the kitchen. (*He returns to the kitchen.*)

MYRTLE: Git up, Lot. Come along.

LOT (*remaining on sofa*): How does he impress you?

MYRTLE: I wouldn't call that man a pleasant surprise, and I don't understand why you never mentioned him to me so I'd be a little prepared, but—

LOT: Don't let him scare you.

MYRTLE: I'm not scared of that man, or any man livin'! No, sir!

CHICKEN (*at kitchen door*): Decided y'don't want coffee?

MYRTLE: Be right there.

LOT (*staggering up from the sofa*): If he sees he can bluff an' bully you, that's what he'll do, so remember—we're two against one in this house and the house is ours.

(*They go hand in hand to the kitchen. Chicken sets tin cups on the table.*)

—Myrtle an' I'll have our coffee in china cups.

CHICKEN: The china cups all broke.

LOT: You broke Mother's china cups?

MYRTLE: Lot, baby, china breaks, nobody breaks it on purpose unless there's a fight. This is— I like our kitchen. All but that nakid girl's pitcher on the wall there. I could do without that.

CHICKEN: Jealous of her?

MYRTLE: I think it's pitiful of a strong, grown man like you to pleasure yourself like a kid with that kind of pitcher. I don't have to ask if you're a bachelor now.

CHICKEN: Lot an' me are bachelors, both of us.

MYRTLE: You're a bachelor but my baby ain't.

CHICKEN: Your baby's more of a bachelor than me.

MYRTLE: I'm here to prove he ain't.

CHICKEN: Hmm. I didn't catch your name.

MYRTLE: My maiden name was Myrtle Kane, but now it's legally changed to Mrs. Lot Ravenstock.

CHICKEN: How long've you been Lot's nurse?

MYRTLE: I am nobody's nurse. To repeat that statement.

LOT: We've been married two days, almost.

MYRTLE: My girl-friend, Georgia, said I was robbin' the cradle, you know, cradle snatchin'.

(*No response to her laugh.*)

And I had always boasted that I was too practical-minded for love at first sight but practicality flew out the window whin this boy come in. —I want you to know it turned my bones to water!

LOT: Chicken, we'll have some coffee.

CHICKEN: Pour some out of the coffeepot on the stove.

(*He stares steadily at Myrtle.*)

So you're in the—nursin' profession?

LOT: Myrtle was in show business.

MYRTLE: Why do you keep askin' if I'm a nurse? Oh, I once did a little of what they call practical nursing, took care of a feeble person till he died on me, out of kindness—sympathy. . . .

(*She is pouring coffee into three tin cups.*)

Is everyone's name in the pot? The coffee's still hot.

CHICKEN: Yeah. Show business, huh?

MYRTLE: I've hed all kinds of employment in my life. Respectable employment.

(*She laughs genially and gives Chicken a playful little slap on the shoulder.*)

Oh, in my life I've taken the sweets with the sours, and it's been smooth as silk in my experience and other times rough as a cob. Yais, I've known both in my time. However, I've kept my haid above water, that I can say for myself, and I've rowed my own boat, too. Never had to depend on another soul. No, sir. I've pulled my own weight in this world. Here is my right hand to God, if you don't believe me, and nothing, nobody, never has made me bitter. No sir! What all have I done? I'll tell you all that I've done in my life, and that's a-plenty, yes, siree, a-plenty.

LOT: Myrtle?

MYRTLE: Huh? What, baby?

LOT: I think it's time to bring in that carload of electric equipment.

MYRTLE: Your brother 'n' me'll do that, don't worry about it. Your brother wants to know what all I've done in my life, and I'm gonna tell him. You might find it int'restin', too.

LOT: Yes, I might, if I hadn't already heard it.

(*He sinks into a chair and his eyes fall shut. His eyelids are violet. He sways a little as if he might fall from the chair.*)

MYRTLE: I'll just hit the high spots, baby. Whin I was fifteen I worked as operator of a Photo-matic machine on the beach at Galveston, Texas. I been—you won't believe this but it's true as I'm standin' here before you!—I been the headless woman in a carnival show. All a fake, done with mirrors! Sat in a chair and pretended to have no haid, it was done with mirrors! But completely convincin'!

LOT: Myrtle, skip to show business.

MYRTLE: Baby, that was show business, my first experience in it and it's where my heart still belongs.

CHICKEN: —What is she talkin' about?

LOT (*as if asleep*): Myrtle was in show business.

CHICKEN: Hunh?

LOT (*rousing a bit*): Show him that picture of "The Four Hot Shots from Mobile."

MYRTLE: Oh, that ole snap, that ole publicity still, I wonder if I still got it.

LOT: You showed it to me a minute after we met.

MYRTLE: I'll see if I still got it on me.

LOT: You put it back in your handbag.

MYRTLE: Pandora's box!

CHICKEN: Whose box?

MYRTLE (*a bit nervously*): Cups refilled with coffee. Now let me lead a parade back into that elegant little parlor and I'll show you and tell you about the Four Hot Shots from Mobile. Come along, follow me, boys. . . .

(*She has put the tin cups of coffee on a plate: marches into the parlor and sets the plate down on a table before the couch. Lot and Chicken are still in the kitchen.*)

CHICKEN: Only a lunatic would marry you and you sure have found the right party.

LOT: Is the black bird of jealousy eating at your heart, Chicken?

MYRTLE: Boys, I've found the pitcher of the Four Hot Shots from Mobile and I'm waiting to show it to you.

CHICKEN: She wants you to get up out of the chair and go in Miss Lottie's parlor if you can.

LOT: Sure I can. Without trouble.

(*He gets up and falls to his knees. Chicken laughs and sets him on his feet.*)

CHICKEN: Able to walk or do you have to be carried?

LOT: The long trip made my dizzy.

MYRTLE: *Boys!*

CHICKEN: I bet there's a buzzard circlin' over the house, since you got here.

(*He turns away from Lot and goes to the parlor. Lot leans on the kitchen table a moment. Then gathers a bit of strength and follows into the parlor. Myrtle has had no trouble at all in finding the "publicity still." She gazes at the photograph with a beguilement that it has never failed to give her. Chicken enters the parlor. She turns to him with a warm smile, extending the photo to him. Chicken takes it from her and regards it with considerable interest. Consciously or not, he drops one of his large, dusky hands over his crotch, which is emphasized, pushed out, by his hip boots.*)

MYRTLE: Well, there you are, here we are!

(*Lot sits carefully down on one of the "little gold chairs."*)

Here we are outside the Dew Drop Inn—in the live town of Tallahassee, F-L-A! It's in color, you see.

CHICKEN: Yes, I can see color. Where's these hot shots now, gone back to Mobile?

MYRTLE: —You ast me a sad question, where's them girls. You know somethin'? (*She is sincerely distressed.*)

CHICKEN: I know lots of things but I won't know *that* till you tell me.

MYRTLE (*blows her nose and dabs at her eyes*): From right to left. This tall redhead they called The Statuesque Beauty. (*Chicken grunts—but with interest.*) —her mutilated corpse was found under a trestle three years ago this Spring. (*Chicken grunts again.*) Don't that break your heart?

CHICKEN: No.

MYRTLE: Some one, some pervert I reckon, had cut her up with a knife, writ up in all the papers, you must've heard about it. I'm telling you it just about broke my heart, she was full of vim, vigor and vitality. And *fun*? The Statuesque Beauty was a continual circus.

CHICKEN: Unh. Circus quit now.

MYRTLE: This one next to her, sweet thing, still in her teens, billed as The Gulf Coast Blaze—a victim of a illegal operation.

CHICKEN: Daid?

MYRTLE (*blowing her nose again*): Not livin', brother, bless her old sweet soul. And this one next to her, billed as The Texas Explosion, somehow I feel that her end was saddest of all. Devoured a full bottle of sleeping pills one night in a Wichita, Kansas hotel.

CHICKEN: Suicide, huh?

MYRTLE: Well, brother, you don't devour a full bottle of sleeping pills with much expectation of getting up early to-morrow. Oh, and this one, my God, The Midnight Stawm! —She wint on drugs. Y'see, all of us four girls lived in the same little frame house t' share expenses, y'know, and, well, one night I happened to be passin' down th' hall outside the bedroom of The Midnight Stawm. I smelt a strong smell of incense. I knocked at The Midnight Stawm's door and this strange voice called out "Who's there?" "Me, Myrtle." "Aw, you, come in." So in I wint, and she was sit-tin' there smokin' this thin cigarette with incense burnin' beside her. "What're you smokin'? "I'm smokin' grass," she

answered, "have a stick with me, Myrtle." But instink tole
me not to.

LOT: I'm tired, let's go up now.

MYRTLE (*hugging him to her*): Rest on Myrtle, baby, and
lemme finish the story. At that time, in Mobile, I was totally ignorant thin of things like that, but I had a suspicion
that something had gone wrong with The Midnight Stawm.

CHICKEN: Aw?

MYRTLE: She'd took the first step to what she finally come to.
So we other girls an' me, we talked it over and regretfully
hed to ask The Midnight Stawm to give up her room there
with us. Painful, very. But we didn't want the house raided.
We were clean-livin' girls, as you'd hope to find in show
business. —Here is me, The Petite Personality Kid that had
all the luck in that outfit, and even her luck come mighty
close to petering out once or twice, but character saved me.

CHICKEN: You are The Petite Personality Kid?

MYRTLE: That's how they billed me, brother.

CHICKEN: Built you?

MYRTLE: No, no, billed, not built. It's a term in show business meaning the name by which you're introduced to the
public.

CHICKEN: You been introduced to the public?

MYRTLE: Yes, many times, many places. (*Returns snapshot to
patent-leather purse.*)

CHICKEN: —How did the public like it? (*He gives her a slow,
wolfish grin, his eyes appraising her body.*) —Did they yell
"take it off" or did they yell "keep it on?"

(*Myrtle laughs heartily but with a note of uncertainty.*)

LOT: Myrtle has a personality that the public responds to.

CHICKEN: Aw?

LOT: She received an ovation on TV. I saw it, I heard it. I was
there to audition as— (*draws a long, painful breath*) —MC
for a—"Tonight in Memphis" show. . . .

CHICKEN: Did the public respond to you, too?

LOT: —I—was—interviewed, and— (*He shrugs slightly and
puts a cigarette in an ivory holder.*)

CHICKEN: After this interview, you thought you'd do better
back here? With a stripper to nurse you?

MYRTLE: Now, I don't like that, that's a little uncalled for!

CHICKEN: Did I say something wrong?

LOT: You said something wrong and offensive.

MYRTLE: It's my personality that I sell to the public—mainly.

CHICKEN: Yes, I bet. You kick with the right leg, you kick with the left leg, and between your legs you make your living?

MYRTLE: —Some remarks I deliberately don't hear!

LOT: Chicken, now that I'm home, in *my* home, on *my* land, with *my* wife, filthy talk has got to stop around here, I don't care if it means us getting along without you.

CHICKEN: Aw, you want me to go, now.

MYRTLE: Lot baby didn't mean that!

CHICKEN: What did "Lot baby" mean?

MYRTLE: All he means was we're sittin' here in this elegant little parlor under a crystal glass chandelier and Lot feels and I feel, too, that we should all talk and act like gentlemen an'—ladies!

LOT: I want to go up to bed, while I still have strength to.

CHICKEN: Your nurse'll carry you up.

MYRTLE: Lot, show your brother we're married, let him see the license.

(*Lot produces a paper.*)

CHICKEN: Shit, you can buy those things for two bits in a novelty store to show in a motel where you brought a woman to lay.

MYRTLE: This marriage license is genuine and if you doubt my word for it, call up the TV station in Memphis where we were married.

LOT: Myrtle and I were married on television yesterday morning.

CHICKEN: That statement makes no more sense than if you told me you licked TB and've got the strength of a mule team.

MYRTLE: Want to hear the whole story?

CHICKEN: I like to hear a good joke.

MYRTLE: Brother, this is no joke!

LOT: Let me lie down on this sofa.

MYRTLE: Lie down, baby, and rest your head in my lap while I tell your brother what happened to me in Memphis two days ago.

(*Lot reclines on the sofa with his head in Myrtle's lap. As she tells her story, she strokes his forehead and hair.*)

To start at the beginning, my luck had run out, you know luck does that sometimes, it peters out on you no matter how hard you try and decent and clean you live and close you are to your Saviour. Trials come in a lifetime and you got to face and accept them till the wheel of fortune turns again your way.

CHICKEN: Make this story short.

MYRTLE: Awright, day before yestiddy I happened to be on the street in Memphis for no particular reason and I seen this long line of people, all wimmen, and I said to myself these people are waiting for something, and if that many people are standing in line for something, it must be good.

CHICKEN: Uh-huh. Get on with the story.

MYRTLE: Well, I fell in the line-up with these other ladies and suddenly, all at once, this little Jewish type man come bolting out and hollered, "Ladies, the studio's full, no more admissions today." Everybody went "Awwwww," disappointed, but I said, "Mister, I don't know what this is but I want in on this thing, I been standing here two hours and I want in on this thing, whatever it is!" —I had him by the arm. He give me a funny look, he must've seen something in me, and he said, "Girlie, you just watch where I go and follow me fast as you can without attracting attention." He sort of whispered this to me out of the side of his mouth. So I stepped out of the line. I seen him bustling into a little alleyway back of the TV studio. I followed him around there and in a fire-escape door, and you know where I found myself? On a TV stage! And there I was, right there, right smack in the middle of a TV show, and this nice little plump little man, he had me by the elbow with such a tight grip I don't think a greased alligator could of got loose, and the first I known, d'ya know what I was doin'?

CHICKEN: Hustlin' a fast buck or two?

MYRTLE: I was standin' in front of a mike with cameras and lights on me, telling my story, broadcasting my woes to the world. I started to cry and everyone started to laugh, the studio rocked with 'em laughing. Why, when I was in show business as The Personality Kid, if I'd ever rocked a club like I rocked that TV public, I would, I bet you, hed hed my name in white lights on Broadway, that's the truth, I would of!

CHICKEN: Come to the point of the story if there is one.

MYRTLE: I sobbed and cried and it made me mad that they laughed. Y'know how mad it makes you to pour your heart out at someone an' have him mock you? Well, then I cut loose, I let 'em have it, I hollered out "What's so funny?" And then this little man that had ushered me in the back way, he whispered something to the MC of the show, and to my shock and astonishment a moment later I was led up to and set down on a golden throne and a big gold jewelled crown was set on my haid and the MC shouted to the audience, all applauding, "Hail to the Queen! All hail!" (*She makes a grand gesture.*) "All hail to thee, Queen of the Day!"

LOT: Myrtle, condense the story.

MYRTLE (*oblivious to his suggestion*): WELL! —I'm telling you, brother, I could have dropped through that stage floor to the boiler-room in the basement, whin I realized, that accidentally, just out of the blue, that I hed been chosen, selected as queen for nothing more or less than pouring out my heart to a room full of strangers.

LOT: I was there in that room.

MYRTLE: Yais, that's right, my blessed baby was there. Now then. I was given two choices, to be the "Hollywood-Queen-for-a-Day" or the "Take-Life-Easy Queen."

CHICKEN: This is a bitch of a story.

MYRTLE: Yais, ain't it! Now the "Hollywood-Queen-for-a-Day" is sent to Hollywood, first class on a plane, provided with a sport ensemble for daytime and a formal for night and has her hair styled by the hair stylist for the stars, and she spends eight hours hobnobbing with screen celebrities in famous places. On the other hand, the "Take-Life-Easy Queen" gets a small fortune in electric household equipment. Well, like ev'ry girl in show business, and many out of it, too, Hollywood was my dream, but—

LOT: Tell him why you switched and how we got married on a national hook-up.

MYRTLE: That's what I'm working up to.

CHICKEN: You're working up to it slowly.

MYRTLE: Give me patience, you want to know how this happened!

CHICKEN: Not if it takes till midnight.

MYRTLE: I'm leading up to the climax which is the climax of my life. I hed naturally chosen to be the Hollywood-Queen-for-a-Day and the ceremony was just about finished when somebody touches my arm. I turn around, still in my robe and crown, and there was my precious baby, completely unknown to me then. Gold-haired, soft-voiced, appealing. It was love-at-first-sight, immediate as a surprise, bang, right between my eyes. "Can I have your autograph, please?" is what he said to me. In that instant the love bug hit me, cupid's arrow shot a bull's eye in my heart. We made a date. On this date he said the love bug had bit him too, love-at-first-sight for us both. I phoned the TV studio and told 'em what had happened and I was going to git married and for that reason could I switch to being the Take-It-Easy-Life-Queen with all that electric equipment to start out with. There was no objection but there was a suggestion. "How would you and your husband-to-be like to be married on TV? In a lace bride's gown with a bouquet of lilies?"

LOT: That's the story. Yesterday we were married on TV.

CHICKEN: You acted out a make-believe marriage to fool the public, huh?

MYRTLE: If it wasn't a genuine marriage it sure fooled us.

LOT: It was a genuine marriage performed by a famous revivalist preacher.

MYRTLE: No more disagreeable talk. Back to the kitchen fo' the bell!

(*She rushes back to the kitchen and snatches up a cowbell on the table. Returns to parlor with it.*)

Is this the bell you ring fo' th' unmarried colored couple?

(*Chicken turns to give her a slow, blank look.*)

I am goin' out an' ring this bell and they are gonna bring in my 'lectric equipment before it rusts on me. I got a, I got a—'lectric washer, two of 'em, one fo' clo'se and one for dishes, I got a, I got a—'lectric home permanent set, 'lectric heater an' blanket an' a table model radio-TV set, so many 'lectric appliances we hardly had room enough for 'em in the car. You'll see whin that unmarried couple hauls them in here t' be dried off, an' connected.

CHICKEN: Yeah, I'll see. Go out an' ring the bell. Ring it loud and long, they don't hear good from a distance.

(*Myrtle goes out on the back steps and rings the bell while Chicken and Lot stare silently at each other. She rings the bell loud and long but the only response is moaning wind and a dull flicker of lightning.*)

LOT (*finally speaking*): Well, I guess I surprised you.

CHICKEN: You got a bigger surprise comin' to you.

LOT: What do you mean by that?

CHICKEN: If I said what I mean by it, it wouldn't be as big a surprise to you, would it?

(*Myrtle returns.*)

MYRTLE: I rang an' rang an' got no answer out there.

CHICKEN: Don't let that bother you much. I don't think you all could git it on the roof whin the floodwater fills the house.

LOT: Stop talking about a flood to scare my wife.

MYRTLE: I don't and I can't believe a man would stay in this house if he really thought it was going to be flooded, so I'm not a-tall scared. Now who's going to help me bring in my prizes in the car?

CHICKEN: Your TV husband will do that.

LOT: Chicken will bring it in.

CHICKEN: Oh, no, Chicken won't.

MYRTLE: Thank you both very kindly. I'll bring in what I can carry without your help.

(*She goes out and off.*)

LOT: Help her with it. If you still work on the place.

CHICKEN: I will like shit.

LOT: Let's make an effort to forget what's past and work out a—decent—future.

CHICKEN: There's no future for you. I talked to your doctor before I made out that paper. You remember that agreement between us, witnessed, signed, notarized, giving the place to me when you take the one-way trip to the kingdom of heaven? I never have that paper out of my wallet in here. (*He taps the pocket of his leather jacket.*) —I was curious to know how long I might have to wait. I got your Memphis doctor on the phone to ask about the condition of your lungs. One's gone, he told me, and the other one's going. Limit: six months. Now passed.

(*Myrtle rushes back into the house with a load of portable electric equipment.*)

MYRTLE: I carried in what I can carry and will get some help to bring the heavy stuff in.

(*She enters the parlor: the men ignore her. She sets the electric stuff down, as if she'd forgotten it, observing the tension between the two men. Sad, dull lightning quivers about the house.*)

CHICKEN: Didn't you tell this woman how you bleed?
MYRTLE: Bleed, Lot, baby? Bleed?
CHICKEN: Yeah, Lot baby bleeds. He bleeds like a chicken with its head chopped off. I'm Chicken, he's headless Chicken. Yes, he bleeds, he bleeds. But no, he don't have TB: He just makes a blood donation to Red Cross, only Red Cross is not quick enough to catch it in a—bucket. . . .

(*Lot suddenly springs forward, striking fiercely at Chicken. Chicken pushes him almost gently to the floor. Lot crawls groaning to his feet and staggers into hall and starts to drag himself up the steep, dark, narrow steps.*)

MYRTLE: I don't understand! What is it?
CHICKEN (*mimicking her*): "I don't understand! What is it?"
MYRTLE (*backing up steps*): You scare me!
CHICKEN: "You scare me!"
MYRTLE (*running up a few more steps*): I'm going up with Lot!
CHICKEN: "I'm going up with Lot!"

(*She draws a gasping breath and scrambles up the narrow steps to the bedroom door that Lot has entered. Myrtle comes up behind him and clings to his arm.*)

MYRTLE: I never been so terrified in my life!

LOT (*sadly, reflectively, his eyes searching the dim sky*): Chicken says my doctor said—I'm dying!

MYRTLE: He mocked everything I said, he just stood there and mocked everything I said!

LOT: Can you imagine that? I'm going to die!

MYRTLE: Oh, let's go back, let's drive right back to Memphis!

LOT: —We can't, Myrtle.

MYRTLE: Why can't we? Why can't we drive back?

LOT: I'm going to die, that's why. . . .

(*He glances at her with a soft, surprised, rueful laugh. The scene dims out.*)

Intermission.

SCENE TWO

The upstairs bedroom is lighted by an oil lamp. Late dusk surrounds the house, the "apple green dusk" of an evening clearing after rain which has just stopped. Water is heard running busily along tin gutters, down a spout and into a big mossy barrel beside the back door. Bullfrogs and possibly some crickets are making their forlorn and desultory comments, desultory as the forlorn talk in the bedroom where Myrtle is washing out some things at the rose-bud-printed washbowl and where Lot is in a rocker facing the audience at an angle; the chair is one of those wicker rockers that they have, or used to have, on verandahs of old-fashioned summer hotels in the South. And Lot's fair head, delicately pretty as a girl's, leans against a souvenir pillow from Biloxi. The pillow is made of green satin, the same as the counterpane on the brass bed. The aura of its former feminine occupant, Lot's mother, still persists in this bedroom: a lady who liked violets and lace and mother-of-pearl and decorative fringes on things. . . . Lot is smoking with his long ivory holder; Myrtle is wringing out some nylons as the curtain rises. She glances, from time to time, at her bridegroom as an uneasy scientist might glance at a test tube whose contents had turned an unexpected color. . . . All during this scene between Lot and Myrtle, Chicken is seen in the very dim-lit kitchen, carving something into the kitchen table with a switch-blade knife—on his face a wolfish grin.

MYRTLE: I wish I knew what was going on back of that long ivory cigarette holder and that Mona Lisa smile.

LOT: I got them both from my mother.

MYRTLE: Yes, well, regardless of where you got 'em, they baffle me. We been up here about two hours, I reckon, and all you've said to me is, "I'm dyin', Myrtle." When a couple has been married for twenty or thirty years it's natural for them to fall into long-drawn silences between them because they've talked themselves out, but you and me have been married for less than two days.

LOT: Why didn't you say something to me? I would've answered.

MYRTLE: Thanks. That's a comforting piece of news. —I didn't speak till you lit a cigarette because I thought you'd fallen asleep in that rocker.

LOT: No. I was sitting here thinking.

MYRTLE: I was standin' here thinkin', too, while I washed my nylons and undies.

LOT: Tell me your thoughts, Myrtle.

MYRTLE: I'll tell you one of 'em. Do you think you played fair and square with me when you brought me down here without a word of warning about that man, that animal, down there?

LOT: I thought it was better not to mention Chicken.

MYRTLE: Better for who? For you!

LOT: Yes, for me. You might not've come down here and I couldn't come down here alone.

MYRTLE: Selfishness in your nature isn't a thing to brag of.

LOT: No. I wasn't bragging.

MYRTLE: Every car, truck, wagon, crowds of people on foot headed the opposite way, and you wouldn't turn back! Can you give me a reasonable reason for that?

LOT: —I guess—

MYRTLE: What do you guess?

LOT: I guess I thought in my heart what Chicken told me and wanted to die in this bedroom where I was born. Yes, selfish as hell, but when people are desperate, Myrtle, they only think of themselves.

MYRTLE: Some people. Not all.

LOT: Some people—including me. —Don't hate me for it.

MYRTLE: Whin I love I don't hate.

LOT: You don't have a complex nature. —What time is it, Myrtle?

MYRTLE: My watch don't run. I just wear it now as a bracelet.

LOT: You wound it too tight and broke the springs?

MYRTLE: No, no, baby. Last Fourth of July I wint to a Shriners' picnic on a lake and a couple of drunk Shriners thought it was very funny to throw me in a lake with my watch on, so the works rusted.

LOT: What you should've done to prevent the works from rusting was to take it directly to a jewellers' shop and have the works removed and soaked in oil over-night.

MYRTLE (*sadly*): I should of done many things in my life which I neglected t'do, and not soaking my watch in oil is not the most important I can think of.

LOT: You mean what you regret most is getting married to a—a impotent one-lung sissy who's got one foot in the grave and's about to step in with the other.

MYRTLE: You're putting words in my mouth that I wouldn't speak to anybody I love!

(*She has removed her slacks and is getting into a sheer blouse sprinkled with tiny brilliants and a velveteen skirt.*)

LOT: What're you dressing up for?

MYRTLE: I never keep on slacks after six p.m.

LOT: That outfit you're getting into looks like a costume.

MYRTLE: Baby, all of my dresses are made over from costumes.

LOT (*slowly with little pauses for breath*): This particular one wasn't made over enough to prevent it from still looking like a costume.

MYRTLE: That could be so or not so, but I think it's a sweet little outfit.

LOT: One girl's opinion.

MYRTLE: Yais, an' trusted by her—with your permission.

LOT: I'm not in a position to give or not give permission.

MYRTLE: Lot? Baby? When people are under the weather, it often has the effeck of makin' 'em too critical or sarcastic.

LOT: My mother subscribed to *Vogue* and we both read it. I know the secret of dressing well is to dress in a way that's appropriate to the occasion.

MYRTLE: What occasion is this? Can you tell me?

LOT: It could be the end of the world, but even then—that almost ankle-length imitation velvet skirt might not be appropriate to it.

MYRTLE: This ain't the end of the world, God help me, Jesus, and this skirt is washable velvet.

LOT: There is no such thing as real velvet that's washable, Myrtle.

MYRTLE: Well, I swan, you talk like a dressmaker, Baby.

LOT: My mother, Miss Lottie, had a sense of style that a Paris designer might envy.

MYRTLE: If you talk about her much more, you'll turn me aginst her, Lot.

LOT: —That wouldn't matter. She doesn't exist any more. . . .

MYRTLE: All this style thet she hed, wasn't it wasted down here?

LOT: No, strangely no. In spite of my father who had the taste of a hawg, who ate with his hands and wiped them on his trousers, my mother, Miss Lottie, was socially accepted by sev'ral families with standing in Two River County.

MYRTLE: With so much style, accepted instid of refused, why did she marry this hawg?

LOT: That's a question I can no more answer than if you asked me why God made little green apples.

MYRTLE (*opening closet door in the back wall of the bedroom*): I see, UH-HUH, well, tomorrow, baby, you or me or both of us is gonna clear your mother's clothes outa this closet so I don't have to live out of a suitcase.

LOT: —I'm sorry, but tomorrow—

(*He doesn't complete the sentence. Myrtle's attention is diverted by the loud sound of Chicken pushing his chair back*

*from the kitchen table. He gets up and starts chopping pota-
toes into a hot skillet, dousing them with grease out of a can
on the stove, and tossing into the skillet some strips of bacon.
During the bedroom dialogue, he will pick out the fried bacon
and eat it, all of it, and wipe his fingers on the seat of his
pants. Lot coughs, rackingly. Myrtle feels his forehead.)*

MYRTLE: That's a mean cough you got there, and I don't
need a thermometer to tell me you're runnin' a fever, Baby.
Yes, Sir, burnin' up with it!

LOT (*gasping*): Fever is—the body's protection—reaction—to
the enemy in it—any kind of—infection. . . .

MYRTLE: Sometimes you talk over my head. —I love you, precious baby, I love you and I'm here to protect and care for
you, always! (*She presses her head to his.*)

LOT: Love me but don't smother me with it, Myrtle.

MYRTLE: —What a mean thing to say!

LOT: I didn't mean it that way. I meant I have trouble breathing and when you crouch over me like that, it makes it
harder for me to draw my breath, that's all.

(*He puts another cigarette in the ivory holder. She snatches the
holder away from him.*)

—Give that holder back to me!

MYRTLE: The last thing you need is to smoke!

LOT: It makes no difference now!

MYRTLE: It does to me!

LOT: If you don't return my holder, I'll smoke without it and
nobody's going to stop me—at the end of the world. . . .

MYRTLE: Here! Take it back and drive a nail in your coffin but
don't talk to me about the end of the world, I haven't
come to it yet and don't intend to!

LOT: Thank you, Myrtle.

MYRTLE: Never talk that way to your wife that loves you, my
precious blond-headed baby.

LOT: —I'm no more blond than you are. —My hair is
bleached.

MYRTLE (*shocked*): Did you say your hair is—bleached?

LOT: As bleached as yours. But I do a better job on my hair
than you do on yours because my mother taught me. Ev'ry

morning of the world, and if I'm alive tomorrow I'll do it again, I get up, brush my teeth and obey the calls of nature, and the next thing I do, in the hospital or out, is put a wad of cotton on the tip of an orange stick and dip it into a bottle and rub the roots of my hair so it never shows dark, and I don't use peroxide, I use a special formula which my mother invented and passed on to me. She said with blue eyes and fair skin, I'd look best as a blond, the same as she did. . . .

MYRTLE (*aghast*): Well, I'll be switched. . . .

LOT: Now you're disillusioned with your young husband?

MYRTLE: —I thought at least I had married a natural blond.

LOT: Don't let it throw you and don't imagine you have married a fairy.

MYRTLE: Such an idea would never— (*leaves the statement in air*)

LOT: You've married someone to whom no kind of sex relation was ever as important as fighting sickness and trying with his mother to make, to create, a little elegance in a corner of the earth we lived in that wasn't favorable to it.

MYRTLE: —I—

LOT: —You what?

MYRTLE: —Understand. And I'm going to devote myself to you like a religion, mystery as you are, back of that ivory holder and Mona Lisa smile.

(*Pause. Chicken turns up the lamp in the kitchen and blows on the inscription he has carved into the kitchen table, grins at it. Then carries the lamp to the back wall of the kitchen and peers at the photo-in-color of a nude girl, tacked to the wall. —After a moment, he crosses into the hall and calls out—*)

CHICKEN: Hey, up there, Myrtle, Mrs. Lot Ravenstock. Ain't you all getting hungry for something besides each other?

MYRTLE: Should I answer that man?

LOT: Answer him if you're hungry.

MYRTLE (*calling down from the upper hall*): Lot needs feeding and I could eat something, too.

CHICKEN: Come on down, then.

MYRTLE: All right, thank you, I will.

CHICKEN (*lowering his voice*): Come down in a show costume and put on a show.

(*Myrtle kisses Lot on the forehead as Chicken returns to the kitchen.*)

MYRTLE: Oh, child, you're hot as fire! They say feed a cold and starve a fever, but you got both.

LOT: I'm hungry for nothing.

MYRTLE: You're hungry for love, and you're gonna have supper with it.

LOT: At the same time, with no appetite for either?

MYRTLE: When the sun comes out like a bright new five dollar gold piece, your appetite for both will come out with it.

LOT: All of a sudden the days in this place are long and hot an' yellow and—time gets lost. . . . (*His eyes fall shut.*)

MYRTLE: I oughtn't to go down there after the way he mocked me but I smell fried potatoes which is something I cain't resist.

LOT: If you didn't smell fried potatoes you'd smell chicken. . . .

MYRTLE: What?

LOT: Nothing. Go down in your washable velvet and eat for us both.

MYRTLE: I want to say one thing more before I face that creature in the kitchen. You're precious to me, you're beautiful to me, I love you with all my heart, and if you don't feel good now, you're gonna feel wonderful later and you believe it. Believe it?

LOT (*with closed eyes and an enigmatic smile*): Yes, I do, completely.

MYRTLE: You sure better. Here goes! —To what I don't know. . . .

(*She goes down the hall steps as if approaching a jungle.*)

MYRTLE (*entering the kitchen*): Hi. —Hello. —How are you?

(*He ignores all three salutations.*)

Y'know what I thought I smelt down here?

CHICKEN: Me? Chicken?

MYRTLE: Ha, ha, no. I thought I smelt French fries down here.

CHICKEN: There's potatoes down here but there's nothing French about 'em.

MYRTLE: Bacon with 'em?

CHICKEN: You come down too late for the bacon.

MYRTLE: Oh, did I miss out on it?

CHICKEN: You sure missed out on the bacon but there's some bacon grease in the skillet with the potatoes.

MYRTLE: Bacon grease gives potatoes a wonderful flavor. (*She looks about nervously.*) —Memphis is famous for its French fries.

CHICKEN: 'Sthat what it's famous for?

MYRTLE: Yais. —I worked last winter at a place called the French Fried Heaven.

(*Chicken grunts at this information.*)

—Put on ten pounds. —The way they cooked French fries, they put the potatoes in a wire basket and put the wire basket in deep fat.

CHICKEN: The fried potatoes here come out of a skillet.

MYRTLE: Oh, I didn' expeck you t'have a wire basket here. — In the country. I'll, uh, help myself an' then take a plate up to Lot.

(*As she fills a plate with potatoes, Chicken turns the lamp up.*)

Where do you keep the silver?

CHICKEN: You mean knife an' fork?

MYRTLE: Just a fork. I don't need a knife for potatoes.

(*Chicken grunts.*)

Still hot.

CHICKEN: Who?

MYRTLE: I meant the potatoes.

CHICKEN: Aw. I misunnerstood you.

MYRTLE: —Here's the silver. It needs t'be polished. That colored girl Clara don't make herself very useful, I'll have to talk to her.

CHICKEN (*rising*): Take this chair, this is a good chair for you.

MYRTLE: I don't want to take your chair. You stay where you are.

CHICKEN: No, you take this chair, I've warmed it up for you and I'm going back out for another look at the levee.

MYRTLE: Right away?

(*He is pulling on his hip boots.*)

CHICKEN: I'll stay a while if you want me in here with you.

MYRTLE: This is a perfeck time for us to get better acquainted, don't you think so?

(*She avoids his grinning look and sits gingerly down at the kitchen table.*)

CHICKEN: You don' have enough light.

MYRTLE: Yais, enough, I kin see.

CHICKEN (*pushing oil lamp toward her*): Don't strain your eyesight an' go blind before time to.

MYRTLE (*noticing the knife with which he'd been carving something onto the table*): —Is, uh, this, uh, this switch-blade knife your knife?

CHICKEN: —Is it your or Lot's knife?

MYRTLE: We don't, I don't, he don't—carry a switch-blade knife.

(*Tries to laugh; coughs.*)

CHICKEN: Then I reckon it'd be a safe bet that it's mine.

MYRTLE: Will you please put it away? I never could stand the sight of a big switch-blade knife like that fo' some— reason. . . .

CHICKEN: Why's that?

MYRTLE: —It, it— (*Shakes her head, tremulously.*) —Just, just —makes me uncomf'table always.

CHICKEN: —Reminds you of the end of one of the Mobile Hot Shots?

MYRTLE: —Yais. —No.

CHICKEN: Yais and no are two opposite answers. Maybe you mean maybe. (*He laughs and folds the switch-blade knife and puts it in his pocket.*)

MYRTLE: Maybe I ought to fill another plate fo' Lot an' eat with him upstairs. A sick person is lonesome.

CHICKEN: Eat a little with me befo' you go up. I need some company, too. (*He empties the rest of the potatoes in another plate and starts eating them.*)

MYRTLE (*in a strained voice*): —I think I'll move this lamp a little your way.

(*She shoves it toward his seat at the table. He shoves it back toward hers.*)

A, uh, growin' boy or a—single, unmarried man, specially one in the country, allows his mind to dwell on an' give too much attention to—

CHICKEN: —To what? In your opinion?

MYRTLE: —You know what I'm talkin' about.

CHICKEN: I don't have no idea, not a bit.

MYRTLE: Well, I'll tell you, as if it was necessary. A single man in the country might amuse hisself by cutting a—indecent word and a indecent picture in a kitchen table.

CHICKEN: What brought that up, that subjeck?

MYRTLE: They's no point in me pretendin' I didn't notice these fresh wood-shavings on this table and what's been cut in the wood. I want to say just this. A thing like this's understandable in a, uh, growin' boy in the country but you're past that. You ought to be beyond that. An' you ought to know it's insulting to a clean-livin' woman who is not int'rested or attracted to—indecent things in her life.

CHICKEN: I'm glad you unnerstand that a single man in the country has got to amuse hisself.

MYRTLE: I said a growin' boy in the country, not a—adult— man with a—nawmul—mind.

CHICKEN: Aw. I misunnerstood you. You're not eatin' those good home-fried potatoes. You only like French-fried potatoes?

MYRTLE: —I've said what I hed t'say an' now, if you will excuse me, I'll take this plate up to Lot. (*She rises with plate.*)

CHICKEN: Lemme hold the lamp at the foot of the steps an' watch an' admire your hips as you climb up.

(*She hurries into the hall and he follows with the lamp. She stumbles on the steps and drops the plate.*)

Spilt 'em? On the steps?

MYRTLE: I could of got upstairs with them better without your—watching! Would you be good enough to put a, put some—

CHICKEN: If you mean more potatoes you're outa luck. They's nothin' but grease in th' skillet.

(*They face each other a silent moment. Then Chicken laughs and scrapes the spilt potatoes off the steps back onto the tin plate.*)

Here you are. He'll never know you spilt 'em unless you tell him—

MYRTLE: *I'd* know I spilt 'em an' wouldn't dream of—of not infawmin' my husban' exactly of all that wint on down here. Good night!

CHICKEN: Hurry back down agin, sister! Enjoyed your company down here! Hurry back down.

(*She stumbles rapidly up the steps with the tin plate. As she enters the bedroom, Chicken returns to the kitchen, sets the lamp down by carving and inscription and grins savagely at them. Then he blows out the lamp.*)

SCENE THREE

Immediately afterwards, upstairs. Lot is in the chair, eyes shut.

MYRTLE: Lot? Are you asleep?

LOT: No. No, I'm awake.

MYRTLE: Can you eat a little?

LOT: No. I don't want food.

MYRTLE: I got to tell you something. Something awful. I am still shaking all over. Feel how cold my hand is. Well. I come down in the kitchen. I said I smelled some bacon. He said I come down too slow. The bacon was gone. But I could have some potatoes. So I hed some potatoes. I had to swallow my pride because I was dyin' of hunger not having nothing to eat since that ham sandwich we hed on the road this mawnin. Well. I helped myself to potatoes and then I set down at the table. I started to try to make some polite conversation. Not that I wanted to talk to that son of a bitch but because I knowed that people living together under one roof have got to make some effort to get along.

Well. I notice a pocket knife and some fresh wood shavings in the middle of the table. Well. That was peculiar but I said nothing about it. Then I noticed he kept turning the lamp up. Each time a little bit higher. Then all at once I noticed. I seen the reason. *That man is a lunatic!* You know what he had done? He had cut out a disgusting picture in the table, in the wood of the table, right in front of my plate, a disgusting word and a disgusting pitcher. I!—I started to choke! When I seen it. I sprung up from the table. He says, "What is the matter with you, Myrtle?" Just as innocent-like as you could imagine! Well. I didn't admit that I had seen a damn thing on that table. I just said, "I better take Lot up some food."

LOT (*mysteriously smiling*): What was the picture of? A man or a woman?

MYRTLE: Both!

LOT: Both?

MYRTLE: Yes, both.

LOT: Doing what?

MYRTLE: Can't you imagine what? With his dirty mind?

(*Lot laughs and coughs.*)

You think it's funny?

LOT: I think everything's funny. In this world. I even think it's funny I'm going to die.

MYRTLE: It may surprise you a little but I'm going to tell you what *I* am planning to do. I'm planning to get on the phone and call to THE POlice.

LOT: How are you going to do that?

MYRTLE: He's got into his hip boots. He's going back out on that levee and soon as he goes I'm going to call the police.

LOT: You think they'll come.

MYRTLE: I reckon they will when I tell them he's out of his mind and I am your wife and afraid to stay in the house with him over this night!

LOT: Nobody will come. Nobody will answer the phone.

MYRTLE: Why do you say they won't come?

LOT: Have you forgotten this county is half under water, and the crest of the flood is still coming?

MYRTLE: I keep forgetting that fact because it's like a bad dream I don't believe. And anyhow. Decent people have got to be protected, flood or no flood, yes, come hell or high water.

LOT: —There he goes.

MYRTLE: Who? Chicken?

LOT: Who else is here but you and me and Chicken?

MYRTLE: Well! I'm going down there and try to phone the police.

LOT: See if you can get hold of his wallet.

MYRTLE: What for?

LOT: He's got a paper in it he made me sign. It leaves the place to him if I should die.

MYRTLE: And me? What about me! Left with nothing?

LOT: I don't know if the paper will still be good or not good if I die with a widow.

MYRTLE: —How could I git this paper?

LOT: How well can you hold liquor?

MYRTLE: I guess that question has a point but I don't see it.

LOT: I wondered if you could drink with a man till he passes out but you don't. Chicken's been drinking down there. I've heard him clump the liquor jug on the kitchen table every few minutes or so since we came upstairs, and he was probably drinking a good while before we got here.

MYRTLE: I guess you're drivin' at something but I don't know what.

LOT: Chicken always has on him, in his wallet, that legal paper that leaves this place to him when I go.

MYRTLE: I don't understand what—

LOT: Let me tell you this without interruption, Myrtle, and try to listen to me. Get Chicken drunk but don't get drunk yourself and when he passes out, get this legal paper out of his wallet, tear it to bits and pieces and burn 'em up. Then, as my wife, when I die, this place will be yours, go to you. —Valuable property.

MYRTLE: I don't know how to pretend to not drink but—

LOT: This paper in Lot's wallet—he sleeps on a cot in the kitchen—he keeps this wallet containin' this paper under his pillow like it was sacred to him. Which it is. Sacred. Is my head too vague to explain this?

MYRTLE: You've explained it, but it sounds like a risky suggestion, he's such a bull of a man, and—

LOT: Don't you want this place, all your own, when I go?

MYRTLE: Risky. Suppose he—?

LOT: Anything worth having and doing in this world is risky. So go down and use your charms on him and drink but out of your drink take little sips like a bird while he sloshes down his till he falls on his cot, passed out, and you take out his wallet and out of his wallet take that legal paper and destroy it. Own this place. It would haunt me in my grave and my mother in hers if this place went to Chicken. That paper gone, you'll own a good piece of property and you can run him off it, marry again, and be happy.

MYRTLE: How do I know if—?

LOT: Here's your chance to own something.

MYRTLE: —Is this the reason you married me, baby, an' brought me down here?

LOT: I married and brought you down here to own a place of your own an' be a lady.

MYRTLE: —Well—I'll give it a try. Hmmm. I wasn't called the Petite Personality Kid for nothing.

LOT: Hear him? Coming back in the kitchen?

MYRTLE: Yais, down I go, wish me luck. God knows I'm gonna need it.

LOT: I wish you luck and my mother does, too.

(*Myrtle picks up the oil lamp and starts to the door.*)

Do you have to remove the lamp and leave me gasping in dark?

MYRTLE: Don't I have to light myself down the stairs?

LOT: Go ahead, take it. The moon's out like the bleary eye of a drunkard.

MYRTLE: 'Sthere anything I can do for you 'fore I go down?

LOT: Nothing. Go down. Get the paper.

(*She exits from the bedroom with the lamp. The bedroom is completely dimmed out except for a faint and fitful streak of moonlight on Lot in the rocker.*)

SCENE FOUR

Immediately following, Myrtle descends the stairs with the lamp and the laundry. Hearing her, Chicken returns to the kitchen table and turns up the lamp.

MYRTLE: —I thought you'd gone out of the house.

CHICKEN: —What would I go out for? That wet electric equipment that's gonna git wetter?

MYRTLE: —I'm afraid I let my nerves get the better of me. Let's forget it. I, uh, come down to tell you I'm worried sick about Lot. He has trouble drawing his breath.

CHICKEN: It's hard to draw breath without lungs.

MYRTLE: He won't stop smoking. And says it's the end of the world. I simply couldn't stand it a minute longer without a—drink. Have you got some liquor down here?

CHICKEN: They don't sell me bottle liquor in this county but I can git it by the jug from a—ole colored man that brews a pretty good brew.

MYRTLE: Is, uh, that the jug there?

CHICKEN: Yep, and it ain't drained yet. I'll give you a drink. —I treat you pretty nice, don't I? For a single man in the country?

MYRTLE: We just—haven't yet got used to each other. And this has been a day an' a night that would make any girl nervous with or without nerves in her.

CHICKEN: I guess you want a stiff drink, a pretty stiff one.

MYRTLE: Oh, uh, for me, just average. You have one with me, let's drink together an' git better acquainted. —Oh. This wash. I noticed you have a clothes line in the kitchen. Do you object if I hang up my undies to dry?

CHICKEN: Hang 'em up. (*She daintily hangs up some rayon panties and a brassiere.*) They'll dry out good in the flood.

MYRTLE: Do me a favor and stop reminding me of this—possible flood.

CHICKEN: It's not a possible flood, this flood is certain.

MYRTLE: Let's not—talk about it. I like drinking from a tin cup, I like the metal taste you git from it.

CHICKEN: —Why do you make that whistling noise when you breathe?

MYRTLE: I am choked up with asthma.

CHICKEN: Aw, you got as'ma.

MYRTLE: Oh, no, I haven't got asthma, it's got me. I got that allergy thing. You know about it—I wint to a Memphis doctor who give me the allergy tests and guess what he found out, he found out I was living with a cat and had a allergy to it. Yes, I had a cat I was real, real fond of, cat named Fluffy. Well, they discovered this cat, she had a allergy to me. I had to git rid of Fluffy, it was her or me. First I give her a great big head of a catfish, which was her favorite food. Like the last supper of the condemned. Then chloroformed her. Poor Fluffy. I was so attached to her and her to me. —I wept a bucket full of tears that night! Whew. (*rises*) From the way I suffer from my asthma tonight, I'm willing to bet that there's a cat somewhere on this place.

CHICKEN: I got a cat.

MYRTLE: That explains it.

CHICKEN: I brought her in for company tonight.

(*Lifts a cat in his lap. Myrtle knew the cat was there but pretends to be surprised.*)

MYRTLE: Oh, no wonder I am choking with asthma, git that cat out of here, for heaven's sake, please!

CHICKEN: *Here, Kitty.* (*He lazily seizes cat and pulls up a trap door near the kitchen table and drops cat through it. She drops with a howl and a splash below. He drops the trap door shut.*)

MYRTLE: Why, that cellar is flooded! I heard a splash!

CHICKEN: You said you wanted her out.

MYRTLE: Out the door, not *drowned*!

(*She raises trap door and cries "Kitty!" He nudges her stooping figure with his knee. She screams and rolls on the floor.*)

Oh, my God, you tried to push me in! You tried to drown me!

CHICKEN: Ha ha ha!

MYRTLE: Oh, my God, my God, you tried to drown me!

CHICKEN: Ha ha ha ha ha ha ha!

LOT (*calling weakly above*): *Myrtle, Myrtle!*

CHICKEN: Your lover is calling for you.

MYRTLE (*crawling away on the floor*): Close!—Close that trap door!

CHICKEN: Aw, come on, knock it off! Nobody's going to drown you—Myrtle Turtle!

MYRTLE: You wanted to drown me like you drowned that cat!

CHICKEN: That cat ain't drowned. She swum on top of the wood-pile. —Same as you'd do if I put you down there with her.

MYRTLE: —I—cain't—swim!

CHICKEN: —Can you do anything? —Outside of bed?

MYRTLE: Chicken, please shut that trap door.

(*He kicks it shut.*)

Oh, my heart! How you scared me! (*Gasps and rises weakly.*) Please, I—give me a shot of that—whiskey. . . .

CHICKEN: Go on. Pour you' self one.

MYRTLE (*breathlessly laughing*): I'm afraid to git up! I swear to goodness I am!

CHICKEN: Aw, now, knock it off. I was just fooling a little.

MYRTLE (*cautiously crossing to table*): Where is—where is a cup. My heart is—still beating!

CHICKEN: Shit, if your heart wasn' beatin' you'd be daid!

MYRTLE: Not like this! It's beatin' like a hammer!

CHICKEN: You remember that song?

MYRTLE (*nervously*): Which—which song?

CHICKEN:

"My heart beat like a ham-mer!
Your arms—wound around me tight!
And stars—fell on Alabama—last—night!"

MYRTLE: Yes, I do, I remember.—Do you remember this one? This one's another old-timer!

"Is it true what they say about Dixie?
Is a dream by that stream so sublime?
Do they laugh, do they love
Like they say in ev'ry song!
—If it's true—that's where I—be—long!"

CHICKEN: Ha ha ha ha ha! That one goes back a long way. Yes, siree, Bob, that's a real old-timer!

MYRTLE: And how about this one? Oh, this one is a—

LOT: Myr-*tlllllle*!

MYRTLE: Coming, honey, coming in just a minute!— (*Fearfully as he approaches the table toward her.*)

—Oh, this is fun, this—*singing*—I—love a song-fest, I love a—community—singing! Almost more than anything I can think of.

CHICKEN: Go on and sing! What song?

MYRTLE: —Wait till I—get my drink down! (*She walks in back of table with her whiskey in a tin cup.*)

CHICKEN: Wettin' your whistle, first?

MYRTLE: That's right, wetting my whistle!

CHICKEN: You almost wet something else when I pushed you toward that trap door! Huh, Myrtle? —*Ha ha ha ha ha!*

MYRTLE (*faintly and mirthlessly*): Ha ha ha . . .

CHICKEN: Awright, now, what song was you going to sing for me, next on the program of old-time fav'rites?

MYRTLE: I wish that I had my little ukulele! My—dear ole uke!

CHICKEN: How 'bout a guitar, will that do?

MYRTLE (*with air of delight*): Oh, hev you got a guitar!

CHICKEN: Yeah. Here. (*Removes guitar from back of closet door and hands it to her.*)

MYRTLE: This is a *man*size instrument!

CHICKEN: Don't you like a man-size instrument?

MYRTLE: I'm just wondering if I—

CHICKEN: Oh, I bet you can play it!

MYRTLE: We'll find out if I can.

CHICKEN: Sure you can. What's the number? I'll sing along with you!

MYRTLE: I love the old-time numbers. Don't you love them?

CHICKEN: The old-time tunes are the best.

MYRTLE: Here's one I can pick out with a—few—chords. . . . (*She is almost too breathless to sing.*)

> "They's a long, long trail a-windin'
> Into the land of my dreams!
> Where the nightingale is—"

(*He moves toward the trap door. Her voice dies out in panic.*)

CHICKEN: Whacha stop for?

MYRTLE: You was going to sing with me.

CHICKEN: Sing it through once by you'self so I'll get the words.

MYRTLE: You mean you don't know the words to that old number? I thought everyone does. That song dates back a long ways, it dates back to World War One.

CHICKEN: Then how come you know it? You don't date back that far.

MYRTLE: It's one of those songs that—

CHICKEN: What?

MYRTLE: Never go out of—fashion. —Do me a favor, Chicken. Don't stand there by that trap-door to the cellar. It makes me too nervous to sing. Sit over here by me.

CHICKEN: Aw, you ain't nervous, you just think you're nervous.

MYRTLE: I'm nervous enough to scream.

CHICKEN: Don't scream. Sing! Sing some other old song.

MYRTLE: Like, uh—what?

CHICKEN: How about something religious?

MYRTLE: You really want something religious?

CHICKEN: Yeah, yeah, something from church, something out of the Hymn-book.

MYRTLE: Funny I—know lots of church songs but—can't think of any right now, ha ha! Ain't that funny? Wait a minute! Wait a minute! One's comin' back to me now. Oh, yes. Oh, yes, I got one, ha ha, I got one now! (*Assumes a rapt, grotesquely stiff smile, throws her head back and croons with her eyes half closed.*)

"My feet took a walk in heavenly grass.
All day while the sky shone clear as glass.
My feet took a walk in heavenly grass,
All night while the lonesome stars rolled past.
Then my feet come down to walk on earth,
And my mother cried when she give me birth.
Now my feet walk far and my feet walk fast,
But they still got an itch for heavenly grass.
But they still got an itch for heavenly grass."

CHICKEN: You're gettin' hoarse, Myrtle.

MYRTLE: I thought you was gonna sing with me.

CHICKEN: I don't sing good enough to.

MYRTLE: You got a *good* voice. You know, you always expect a big man is going to sing baritone or bass but they usually sing tenor? You got a sweet tenor voice. Ain't I silly? Gaspin' for breath like this!

CHICKEN: It's that cat allergy thing, you got that allergy thing!

MYRTLE: No, no, it's not cats, it's—!

CHICKEN: It's what? What, Myrtle?

MYRTLE: *Nerves!* A nervous condition!

CHICKEN: You're worried about that cat, that's what's your trouble. I think you're a member of that society, that human humane society, maybe the president of it (*He is pulling on his rubber hip boots.*)

MYRTLE: What's you getting into those rubber boots for?

CHICKEN: I'm going down in the basement to fetch that cat.

MYRTLE: Oh, she's done for, she's gone, now.

CHICKEN: No, she ain't. Come on, let's find that cat. You're worried about her, so let's go down in the basement an' find that cat.

MYRTLE (*backing away from him*): You—*you* do that—if it's possible for you to do.

(*He jerks the trap door open. Myrtle screams and hurls the guitar away as she rushes into the hall and scrambles up the stairs, screaming repeatedly. Chicken howls with laughter; then leaps abruptly into the basement with a splash, calling "pussy, pussy, pussy?" The cat yowls and Chicken laughs. He leaps back up from the trap door, still laughing, with the cat in his hand. He is still laughing and holding the cat as the stage dims out.*)

Intermission.

SCENE FIVE

Immediately following. The bedroom is lighted and, at a much lower level, so are the back steps of the house where Chicken sits with his cat. The parlor is now masked by an opaque transparency. Lot remains in the wicker chair in the bedroom. He is still smoking with his mother's ivory holder and wearing now her white silk wrapper. His "Mona Lisa" smile is more sardonic and the violet shadows about his eyes are deeper. Myrtle stands, panting, in the doorway.

LOT: —From the singing and other commotions I heard down there, I don't need to ask you if you got the paper. —Did you? No, you didn't.

MYRTLE: You listen here! Enough is enough and more than enough is too much!

LOT: You didn't get much liquor down him. —Did you?

MYRTLE: That man, that animal down there, could drink a liquor store dry and walk straight to another!

LOT: I thought you told me there wasn't a man on earth that you weren't able to manage. Well. If that statement was accurate, then either Chicken isn't a man or he isn't on earth. And I think he is both.

MYRTLE: Don't be sarcastic with *me*.

LOT: Don't shout so he can hear you. Can you speak without shouting?

MYRTLE: I said don't be sarcastic with me. I'm not in a mood to take it after what I went through in the kitchen with your so-called brother.

LOT: My opposite type. I hate that man with a passion.

MYRTLE: I'm terrified of him. Is there a key to this door to lock him out?

LOT: No. I hate and despise him with such a passion that if this place or anything on this place became his property—

MYRTLE: S'pose he comes up here and drags me down?

LOT: Neither mother or me could rest in peace in Old Gray Cemetery.

MYRTLE: I'm not in a cemetery. What about me?

LOT: What about you except you—

MYRTLE: There's not just you, there's me. The selfish streak in your nature is wide as the river—flooding!

LOT: Have you ever owned much of anything in your life?

MYRTLE: Yais! My self-respeck an' decency as a woman!

LOT: In addition to that, marvelous as it is, would you like to own and possess entirely as your own a place that's worth much more than it gives appearance of being?

MYRTLE: —Worth what? In cash?

LOT: Over fifty thousand and could increase well-managed. . . . (*Long pause*) —Well? Attractive to you or not?

MYRTLE: I've never owned a stone I could call my own.

LOT: —A pitiful confession, but now's your chance if you want it.

(*A pause as Myrtle reflects.*)

MYRTLE: —Sugar? Baby? Why don't you get in bed instead of sitting at a window in a light silk wrapper?

LOT: I breathe better sitting up in a chair—and can look at the sky.

MYRTLE: The sky's clouded over.

LOT: Once in a while the moon comes out of those fast-moving clouds, and it—says things to me in the soft voice of my mother. . . .

MYRTLE: I wish you would get in bed and let me hold you and love you.

LOT: You don't have to hold me to love me.

MYRTLE: You're shivering. Lemme put something heavier around you like a blanket.

LOT: No, no, don't. I don't want to be smothered.

MYRTLE: Chicken's out of the kitchen, so I am going back in it and fill a hot-water bottle for you an' git you in this bed if you like it or not.

LOT: There's not any hot-water bottle.

MYRTLE: I never travel without one. It's in my traveling case.

LOT: I should've known.

MYRTLE: What?

LOT: —Nothing, and not much of that either.

MYRTLE: That seems to be what you know, but I am going back down there and get hold of that paper, how I don't know, but somehow. And I'm going down there in my show costume as the Personality Kid. (*She changes quickly into the costume.*)

LOT: I think what attracts you back down there is nothing made of rubber and nothing made of paper, whether you face it or not.

MYRTLE: Your fever's gone to your haid, if you think that.

LOT: I don't just think it, I know it. —I won't see daylight again.

MYRTLE: I can pick you up and carry you to the bed and that's what I'm gonna do when I've filled my hot-water bottle.

LOT: Anybody with arms could pick me up—if they wanted to force me against my will.

MYRTLE: Is it against your will to be loved and made well?

LOT: —No. —If you can't make him pass out to get that paper, knock him out with a hammer that's in the drawer of the kitchen table and don't come up here again without that paper. You get that paper and you can pick me up and carry me to the bed with no resistance and I'll—rest in your arms. . . .

MYRTLE: I got to take this lamp to get down the stairs in my—shaky condition.

LOT: Take it. I get enough light from the sky.

(*She goes back into the hall and starts down the steps. She is halfway down them with the lamp when Chicken slams open the back door and enters the lower hall.*)

MYRTLE (*terrified gasp*): HAH! (*She drops the oil lamp on the stairs; it goes out.*)

CHICKEN: Trying to start a fire? Burn your place down? Before it goes under water?

MYRTLE: —I thought—

CHICKEN: Don't strain your brain thinkin'.

MYRTLE: Lot's—Lot's havin' a chill. Terrible. I want to fill up a hot-water bottle for him. Kin I come down?

CHICKEN: Why do you ask to come downstairs in your house?

MYRTLE: I don't possess this house or anything in it except what I brought here with me.

CHICKEN: All that electric equipment to make life easy for you?

(*He laughs and enters the kitchen. Myrtle stops in the downstairs hall and speaks tremulously—*)

MYRTLE: Please do me a favor before I come in the kitchen.

CHICKEN: Such as what? (*He turns up the kitchen lamp.*)

MYRTLE: Of course I know you wuh teasing me with that trap door open, but would you please push the table over it now.

CHICKEN: It ain't open now.

MYRTLE: Open or shut, I couldn't be comf'table in the kitchen unless that table was over that trap-door.

CHICKEN: (*pushing the table with his foot*): You're Mistress of the House, the Lady in it. Whatever you tell me to do I'm obliged t'do it.

(*Myrtle moves nervously to the kitchen threshold.*)

MYRTLE: I'm just a visitor here, but would you push the table over the trap-door a little bit further than that? Please?

CHICKEN: Why, sure, Mrs. Lot Ravenstock. A hired hand on a place always does what pleases the lady and the boss-man. (*He shoves the table further with his foot.*)
   —How's that now, does that suit you?

MYRTLE: (*entering the kitchen*): Yes, thank you, fine, perfeck. I feel much more easy.

CHICKEN: You're a city lady and I'm a country boy with common habits. I hope you'll excuse me for them.

MYRTLE: I've been teased in my life. I had two older brothers, Jack and Jim, that teased me nearly to death. Y'see, my curls were long then. And they would pull them and yell "Ding-dong." Oh, it never hurt much but it always scared me. Holler? Oh, would I holler! Sometimes it wouldn't be necessary for them to pull my curls, they could just say "Ding-Dong" and I'd scream fit to kill and blaze a trail to the house, so you see I'm used to teasing, but so much has happened in the last few hours I feel un-strung. —A little.

CHICKEN: You're walking around like you wuh lookin' fo' something.

MYRTLE: A kettle to boil water in. So I can fill a hot-water bottle in my traveling case.

(*She removes the hot-water bottle from the beat-up case and wanders distractedly about the kitchen.*)

CHICKEN: Why don'tcha put the hot-water bottle down while you look for the kettle so you'll have both your hands free?

MYRTLE: Ha! —What's the matter with me? I sure don't seem to have my head on my—!

(*Chicken rises, setting the cat on the floor.*)

That cat didn't drown in the cellar?

CHICKEN: Shit, no. You can't drown a cat unless you put her in a sack full of rocks. She swum on top of th' woodpile. Didn't you, pussy? (*He hands a kettle to her.*)

MYRTLE: Thanks. (*She sets the kettle on the stove.*)

CHICKEN: —Is that how you do it?

MYRTLE: —Huh?

CHICKEN: —You git the kettle hot first and thin put th' water in it?

MYRTLE: Ha ha! Ain't that *somethin*? Shows how upset I am! I put that empty kettle on the stove without water in it!

CHICKEN: Gimme th' kettle. I'll git you some water in it from the rain barrel out there.

(*Crosses to the door with the kettle and descends to the rain barrel. She follows to the door.*)

MYRTLE: They say rain water's the purest water there is.

CHICKEN: Is that what they say? Well, nothin's too pure for Lot.

MYRTLE: —Not that it matters in a hot-water bottle. . . .

CHICKEN: Yeah, well . . .

(*Hands her the dripping kettle. She returns inside. He watches her back as she moves to the stove and gives a slight wolf whistle. She gets the kettle on the stove with a bang that makes her give a startled laugh.*)

What's the joke? (*She goes on laughing, helplessly.*) Let me in on the joke, it must be a good one.

MYRTLE: I just, just!—*got*—*hysterics!* (*Continues giggling.*)

CHICKEN: They's two ways to stop hysterics in a woman. One way is to give her a slap in the face and the other way is to lay her. Sometimes you got to do both.

MYRTLE: Oh, I'm all right now. I come out of hysterics as quick as I go in them. —How come a handsome young man like you is still single?

CHICKEN: —I'm dark-complected.

MYRTLE: What of it?

CHICKEN: They's not been a woman on this place, not since Miss Lottie died, but the colored girl Clara and she's took to the hills to get away from the flood.

MYRTLE: You mention this flood like it didn't scare you a bit.

CHICKEN: Floods make the land richer.

MYRTLE: What good does that do if you drown?

CHICKEN: I'm not gonna drown. —Are you?

MYRTLE: Lord God Jesus, I pray to my Saviour I won't!

CHICKEN: You'd do better praying to Chicken.

MYRTLE: I'm counting on your protection.

CHICKEN: You better not count on that.

MYRTLE: That's what I'm counting on, Chicken.

CHICKEN: Count on nothing. Set down.

MYRTLE: I prefer to stay on my feet a while if—

CHICKEN: If what?

MYRTLE: —If you don't object.

CHICKEN: Shit, I don't mind if you stand on your head if you want to! But look. I got this old auto cushion I'll put on this here chair and'll make you a nice soft seat. I know a woman don't like a hard seat, does she? Well, here's a real soft cushion for you to sit on while we talk.

MYRTLE: —Thanks! (*She seats herself tensely on the edge of the auto cushion.*)

CHICKEN (*with a slow, wolfish grin*): Now you got *three* cushions?

MYRTLE: —*Three?* —*OH!* —*Ha ha!* —yaissss—three . . .

(*Loud silence in the kitchen.*)

CHICKEN: You feel comf'table?

MYRTLE: Yaiss! Yes, very! Are you?

CHICKEN: I always make myself comfortable as I can.

MYRTLE: Why not? You should! —a man should . . .

CHICKEN: —Should what?

MYRTLE: —Why—uh—make himself as comf'table as he— can . . .

CHICKEN: —How about you? Are you comf'table, too? On those three soft cushions?

MYRTLE: Yes, I told you I was. I'm just a little worried about my husband. I had no idea, I simply had no notion at all that he was in such a bad condition as this. I mean I . . . I just didn't have an idea . . .

CHICKEN: It's like you bought a used car that turned out to be a lemon.

MYRTLE: Oh, that's not how I look at it. That boy has touched the deepest chord in my nature. I mean I . . . (*She suddenly sobs.*)

CHICKEN: Quit that. I want to talk to you.

MYRTLE: Yes, talk!

CHICKEN: I guess you know the setup.

MYRTLE (*struggling for composure*): The what?

CHICKEN: The setup. Do you know it?

MYRTLE (*with a weak attempt at levity*): The only setup I know of is in a dry state they'll serve you a setup for liquor but not the liquor. You got to bring that with you.

CHICKEN: —If I was your lawyer I would advise you not to try to be funny.

MYRTLE: Can't we—joke a little?

CHICKEN: I'd advise you aginst it.

MYRTLE: Awright, I'll take that advice, but, Chicken, do you know that all the electric equipment I won as the Take-Life-Easy Queen is still in that car with a leakin' top bein' rained on?

CHICKEN: Fawgit that stuff. It can't be saved from flood-water. Can you concentrate on the legal setup if I explain it to you, or do you think it's something that don't concern you?

MYRTLE: I'm—anxious to know the—setup. Is the kettle boilin', is that water hot yet?

CHICKEN: Fawgit th' kettle. The fire is low in the stove.

MYRTLE: But I told Lot I'd—

CHICKEN: You don't seem t'want to know about the setup.

MYRTLE: Oh, that's not true, I do!

CHICKEN: I'll explain it to you.

MYRTLE: Yais, wonderful, do that! Whatever concerns this place an' my future life on it is impawtent t' me to understand an' t'know.

CHICKEN: Lot an' me are half brothers. Has that sunk into your haid yet?

MYRTLE: Oh, yes, that I do know. It come out in the, the—conversation we hed when we—first met, this—day.

CHICKEN: That's right. You got that straight. Maybe you know the rest of it.

MYRTLE: Lemme pour you some liquor while you explain the setup.

(*She tries to lift the jug off the table but her hands are too weak and shaky.*)

CHICKEN: Cain't lift the jug, you're so nervous about the setup. Open your mouth and I'll pour some liquor down *you*.

MYRTLE: Thanks, I thank you. I couldn't git through this night without liquor in me. Could you?

CHICKEN: Mouth open.

(*She opens her mouth a little: He presses the mouth of the jug to it. The liquor runs down her chin and neck.*)

MYRTLE: Oh, it's stainin' my dress!

CHICKEN: You wouldn't swallow the liquor, drooled it out.

MYRTLE: I wasn't actually thirsty. You drink some. I like to see a man drink.

CHICKEN: What I am going to do is tell you about the setup, all of it. The rest that you might now know.

MYRTLE: What is the rest of the setup?

CHICKEN: Daddy got Lot in marriage but not me. You're lookin' at what is called a wood's-colt. (*He perches himself on the table and the light is hot on him.*) Whin I was ten years old he married this little blond haided woman that worked in a beauty shop in Clarksdale. Are you list'nin' or still too nervous to lissen?

MYRTLE: I'm list'nin' close. All ears.

CHICKEN: I wouldn't say that about you but I'd advise you to lissen close as you're able to me. This little lady that worked in the beauty parlor in Clarksdale was named Miss Lottie, so when Lot was bawn, he got the name of Lot. Legal; bawn in marriage. Not a wood's-colt. Me—wood's-colt. You know what a wood's-colt is?

MYRTLE: No, I don't know that I know. All I know is you look—

CHICKEN: —Dark-complected?

MYRTLE: Foreign. —Foreign?

CHICKEN: My son of a bitch of a daddy got me offen a dark-complected woman he lived with in Alabama. —What about it?

MYRTLE: Why—nothing!

(*Slight pause.*)

Ain't you drinkin' no more? This awful night?

CHICKEN: Why're you so anxious for me to drink more?

MYRTLE: I don't like drinking alone. It makes me lonesome.

CHICKEN: I can drink you under this kitchen table, tonight.

MYRTLE: I'd rather stay on my feet with the flood you say's coming.

CHICKEN: You'd rather drown standing up?

MYRTLE: Don't talk about drowning. You wouldn't let that happen.

CHICKEN: —Let's get back to the setup. —Lot's mother, Miss Lottie, she thought she was surely going to bury my daddy. Hell, he was sixty when he married Miss Lottie.

MYRTLE: Is that what you mean by the setup?

CHICKEN: Just shut up and listen. —She'd no sooner got married to him that she begun to cheat on him with a good-looking young Greek fellow that had a fruit store in town. Why, ev'ry afternoon, Miss Lottie would say to daddy, "Daddy, I think I will drive in town to buy some fruit to make us a nice fruit salad." And when she got to the store, the store man would let her in and lock the door and she'd stay in for two hours and come out with four or five peaches like it had took her them two hours to pick out that small bag of peaches.

MYRTLE: Why didn't you tell your daddy?

CHICKEN: If I had told him, he'd've told her I told him, and she would of got me thrown outa here in minutes! —Well, she did bury my daddy and the place was hers but she didn't have long to hold it. The Greek sold out his fruit store, quit Miss Lottie, and left. —He just left town but Miss Lottie left the world.

MYRTLE: Daid. Yes. Lot told me. —Tragic.

CHICKEN: Well, she lived long enough to throw me off the place. Called me in her little parlor one day and fired me like a field hand. "Chicken," she said, "I think it's just about time for you to clear off this place and make your own way in the world." I said, "Well, gimme what's comin' to me." —What she give me amounted to just about the

pay that a field hand gets for a week's work. It got me
down the state to Meridian where I worked in a sawmill
till. . . . And then this happened—Miss Lottie couldn't go
on without trips to that fruit store so she quit eating, quit
sleeping—quit breathing. And one month after she died,
Lot started dying. One lung gone and one going, but trying to run this place. Didn't take long for him to find out
he couldn't, so I begun to hear from him. He sent for me
to come back and operate this place for him, sent for me
twice by letter and a third time by wire. First and only wire
I ever got in my life. Chicken, come back, was the message,
I will make a deal with you. —Well, I'm no fool.

MYRTLE: No, no, you're no fool.

CHICKEN: I said, "All right, but I'm going to name the deal,
and here's the deal." I said, "If you want me to run this
place for you, well, here's the deal. Whin you are through
with TB!—it goes to me. . . ."

MYRTLE: TB?

CHICKEN: You ain't paying attention to what I tell you. Not
TB. The place, this *place*!

MYRTLE: —Oh! —So that's the setup.

CHICKEN: Yes, Ma'am, that is the setup.

MYRTLE: Oh. Uh-huh. I see. . . .

CHICKEN: You don't look happy about it!

MYRTLE: Don't I? Well, now, after all, you can't expect me to
be overjoyed about it. I mean, after all, I'm human. And—

CHICKEN: And what?

MYRTLE: —Nothin, nothin but—

CHICKEN: But what?

MYRTLE: —If Lot dies I'm his widow and—

CHICKEN: That's just exactly the point that I'm coming to
later, that's just the little situation we're tryin to git
straightened out right now in this kitchen before the floodwater comes. I got a decision to make.

MYRTLE: What decision?

CHICKEN: A big one. A big one for you and me both. —Have
you ever climbed on a roof?

MYRTLE: Me? Climbed on a roof? No. Not that I can remember. It don't seem—likely. . . . Why? Why do you ask
me if I ever climbed on a roof?

CHICKEN: If you can't climb on a roof Lot won't have a widow when the floodwater comes. Now do you understand why I asked you that question? —Yeah. I can see that you do. So now to go on with what —What's the matt—? Why are you getting up?

(*Myrtle has risen stiffly from the chair with a look of slow and dreadful comprehension. Her breathing is audible and rapid.*)

—Your breath is whistling again. You want the cat out of here?

MYRTLE: *No, no, no, no, no, no, no!*

CHICKEN: I can put her back in the cellar if she is giving you as'ma.

MYRTLE: No, no, no, I'm all right, I'm—*fine*, I'm—all right. . . .

CHICKEN: Then why don't you stay in your seat? Ain't that auto cushion comfortable to sit on?

MYRTLE: Sure, it's—fine!

(*She remains standing, her eyes wide and bright but not focussed. He rises deliberately and picks up the auto cushion, examines it and dusts it and puts it back down again.*)

CHICKEN: You women have got a lot of heat in you. That cushion is warm from your body. Why don't you sit down while I finish explaining the setup?

MYRTLE: Oh, it's all clear now. I understand the setup and I want you to know, here is my right hand to God, that everything you told me is okay as far as I am concerned. I got no designs on nothing. You know it's funny how quickly the human mind changes! Ain't it queer how quick it changes? I had my heart set on a quiet, happy married life. Now what I want most in the world is to return to show business! —that's what I'm going to do, I'm going to cut out all fats and sweets and fried foods and get back my shape and go straight back to show business. It keeps you alive. It keeps you trim. It keeps you alert. It's the business for me. Absolutely no other can compare with it for keeping you healthy and active. —Now I think I can fill that hot-water bottle and take it up to that poor child I married . . . —*God please pity us both!*

(*She starts toward the stove but he seizes her wrist.*)

CHICKEN: I want you to stay sitting here till I've finished talking to you. You going to do that?

MYRTLE: —Why—sure!

CHICKEN: Good. Take a shot of this liquor. It might be good for your as'ma.

MYRTLE: Why, thanks! (*The tin cup shakes: She lifts it with both hands to her lips.*) —thanks. . . .

CHICKEN: So I said to him. I said to my half brother, "Lot, I want this place when you're gone. I been on this place all my life and I want to stay on this place all my life till I die. I was here before you come to it and I want to be here when you go. Is that understood? Is that understood, now, clearly?"

MYRTLE: Yes, yes, clearly, clearly . . .

CHICKEN: Good. So the place goes to Chicken, the place and everything on it goes to Chicken when you die.

MYRTLE: *Me? Die?*

CHICKEN: *Lot!*

MYRTLE: —Oh . . .

CHICKEN: Yes! "OH!"—we got to get things straightened out. . . .

MYRTLE: I told you I—

CHICKEN: Has anyone ever told you you talk too much? If I had married a woman with such a loose mouth, I'd put a stopper in it. "All right," I said. "All right. That's the agreement and I want it on paper, so let's put it on paper. Otherwise I don't stay." He said, "Stay, stay, we'll put it on paper," so we put it on paper. Had it drawn up, legal. Notary seal. Witnesses' names put on it. Signed in their presence! Now! (*Removes wallet and unfolds from about it a thick rubber band.*) I got this paper to prove it. The paper we drawn up between us with a notary seal and names of witnesses on it.

(*She stretches out her hand as he produces the paper from his wallet.*)

Oh, no. Someone's got itchy fingers. —Look but don't touch! —Understand? I never let this paper out of my hands. I sleep with this paper underneath my pillow and when I wake up in the mawning, you know what I find? I find my hand clutching my wallet with this paper in it. Even in my sleep I protect this paper! I guard it with my life and my soul and my body. Because it gives me this place when my half brother is gone! So now you see.

MYRTLE: Oh, yes, now I see.

CHICKEN: You ain't even looking at it. Look at this paper, will you? (*He shakes it in front of her.*) Does it look legal to you? You see this notary seal and names of witnesses on it? You see Lot's signature on it and my signature on it?

MYRTLE: Yes, yes!

CHICKEN: You want more light so you can see it more clearly? (*He turns up the lamp.*) There now, you can see it clearly!

MYRTLE: —It, it—sure looks—legal.

CHICKEN: —Yeah, but—you never can tell. . . .

MYRTLE: —What?

CHICKEN: A smart Jew lawyer might find some loopholes in it or make some if some wasn't there! —'specially if there was a widow surviving. . . . —I guess you think that I'm hard. Well, I got to be hard. A man and his life both got to be equally hard. Made out of the same hard thing. Man, rock. Life, rock. Otherwise one will break and the one that breaks won't be life. The one that breaks is the soft one and that's never life. If one is the soft one, the soft one that breaks will be man, not life, no, no, not life! —that's rock . . . yep—rock! Solid rock. . . . —Now then if you're satisfied that this is a legal paper I'll put it away.

MYRTLE: Of course I can see it is legal.

CHICKEN: But law is tricky. I never figured that Lot was going to git married. I certainly never thought he'd leave a widow. So I am faced with this important decision. Whether or not to haul you up on the roof when the house is flooded. Because if I do, then Lot will have a widow and this thing here might not be worth the paper it's typewritten on. You see what I mean about it? You see why I got to think this whole thing out step by step as careful as possible, do you? —Naw, I never thought he would leave a widow. You see? You see how easy it is to git buggered up? Law is a tricky thing. I never would of dreamed that son of a bitch would marry and leave a widow. And maybe now that changes the situation. Maybe now this agreement will not hold up in a court of law.

MYRTLE: I wouldn't—worry about it.

CHICKEN: Naw, you wouldn't worry about it. Why would you worry about it? You'd git the place, not Chicken!

MYRTLE: I, I, I—don't want this place! What would I do with this place?

CHICKEN: Want it or not you'd git it if bein his widow makes this paper—

MYRTLE (*rising stiffly*): Look, Chicken!

CHICKEN: —makes this paper not good!

MYRTLE: Chicken, Chicken, look here!

CHICKEN: That's what he figured. Son of a bitch thought he'd screw me by leaving a widow. But one thing he didn't count on was the house being flooded and him and his widow both—

MYRTLE: Oh, now, look here, Chicken!

CHICKEN: Him and his widow both!

MYRTLE: Chicken!

CHICKEN: —drowned in it!—unless I haul his widow up on the roof.

MYRTLE: *Chicken, I—can't catch my breath!* I got a bad asthma attack, it's that—

CHICKEN: Huh?

MYRTLE (*gasping*): Allergy thing, that—

CHICKEN: You want the cat out of here?

MYRTLE: Not, not, not in the—cellar but—

CHICKEN: Come on, pussy. You go set in the parlor.

(*He lifts the cat and crosses into the hall with her, shoves her into the parlor and kicks the door shut. Myrtle stands gasping like a fish out of water, leaning for support against table.*)

MYRTLE: Chicken, this, this, this joke is gone on too long. I, I. We, we.

CHICKEN: Take a good breath. Then talk.

MYRTLE: I'm trying to catch one! —Lot an' me, we—ain't—married!

CHICKEN: You an Lot ain't married?

MYRTLE: No, a-course not! Are you kiddin? (*She tries to laugh.*)

You didn't *believe* that, did you? Ha ha! I'm surprised at you for being so, so—gullible! Ha ha!—ha—ha . . . —Why, me and that boy are no more married than the man in the moon!

CHICKEN: He showed me a license.

MYRTLE: Yeah, but you said yourself you can buy those things for two bits at a novelty store to git you a hotel room to lay a woman!

CHICKEN: And the "Just Married" sign and the old shoes tied to the car?

MYRTLE: A joke, can't you take a joke? Ha ha!

CHICKEN: This is no jokin' matter.

MYRTLE: Well, it was just a joke, Chicken, it was all just a joke, Ha ha!

(*Her laugh is hollow: it expires in a gasp.*)

CHICKEN: Yeah. Well. *Maybe.*

MYRTLE: They's no maybe about it. I ought to know I'm not married!

CHICKEN: No?

MYRTLE: No! Look, whin I take that step, a step as serious in my life as marriage would be, I wouldn't take it with a—TB case! You want to know something? You want to know something, Chicken?

CHICKEN: Yeah, I want to know something.

MYRTLE: That poor boy bleaches his hair, not only has TB but bleaches his hair. Look, now, seriously! Do you imagine that I'd give up a career in show business to marry a, a, to marry a, to, to, to marry a—

CHICKEN: —What's wrong now?

MYRTLE (*with a grimace*): Throat's! Stopped!

CHICKEN: Choked on lies!

MYRTLE: No! No!

CHICKEN: That's what you done, you choked you'self on lies!

MYRTLE: Now, Chicken.

CHICKEN: "Now, Chicken."

MYRTLE: Oh, don't mock me, please!

CHICKEN: I think I better take a new look at that paper. Go up and git me that paper.

MYRTLE: Which, which paper?

CHICKEN: This license you say you got from a novelty store.

MYRTLE: Lot's, Lot's got it, he's got it! I, I don't have it, Lot's got it!

CHICKEN: Jesus. I never seen anybody in such a condition as you seem to be in.

MYRTLE: I told you about how scared I am of— (*She turns away, gasping as if drowning.*) —water! (*Gasps twice and clutches chair back.*) —Ever since I was baptized by a preacher that held me under—too *long.* . . .

CHICKEN: I'm not going to hold you under. Shit. It wouldn't be necessary to hold you under. If you can't climb on the roof when the house is flooded, and I don't reckon you can. It wouldn't be necessary to hold you under. Unless you float like a cork. Do you float like a cork?

MYRTLE: Oh, God, Chicken, why don't you take my word? I'm not Lot's widow, I mean I won't be his widow if he dies, cause we ain't married.

CHICKEN: Go up an git that paper.

MYRTLE: —Whin?

CHICKEN: Now.

MYRTLE: Wait till I catch my breath.

CHICKEN: Git the paper now and catch your breath later.

MYRTLE: I can't climb stairs without breath. And Lot's water's boiling, the kettle is boiling, I'll fill his hot-water bottle.

CHICKEN: All right. Fill his hot-water bottle and git that paper and bring it down here so I can give it a careful examination.

MYRTLE: Help me. I can't—do—this!

(*She drops the hot-water bottle. Chicken picks it up and fills it by the stove.*)

CHICKEN: Now go up and give him his hot-water bottle and git that marriage license while you're up there.

(*She starts upstairs.*)

CHICKEN (*to her back*): Hurry.

MYRTLE: I'm goin' fast as I can, unable to breathe!

CHICKEN: You're breathin'.

(*She opens the bedroom door and calls softly.*)

MYRTLE: Lot? Lot, baby? Are you asleep, Lot, baby?

(*Light falls on him: He looks like a Far Eastern idol. He doesn't answer except by rocking his wicker chair in the pool of moonlight.*)

How are you, now, Lot, baby?

LOT: You know how I am: still breathing. Have you got Chicken drunk yet?

MYRTLE: I don't think he's gonna get drunk, liquor don't seem to affect him.

LOT: Then you won't get the paper and he'll get the place.

MYRTLE: —Well . . .

LOT: You sound resigned to it, Myrtle.

MYRTLE: —If this house is flooded, both floors, could *you* get me up on the roof?

LOT: Aw. Chicken has offered to get you up on the roof.

MYRTLE: You brought me here and put me at his mercy, don't forget that.

LOT: I thought you could handle Chicken.

MYRTLE: You gave me no warning.

CHICKEN (*impatiently, below stairs*): Hey! Come on!

LOT: What's he want? Just your company down there?

MYRTLE: I got your hot-water bottle. Here's your hot-water bottle.

LOT: My chill's gone now. I'm burning up with fever. What I need's an ice pack.

MYRTLE: Honey, you know there ain't no ice in this house.

LOT: What were you doing down there with Chicken?

MYRTLE: I was waitin' for the kettle to boil so I could fill up this hot-water bottle which you don't want no more.

LOT: You know something?

MYRTLE: Huh?

LOT: I think you're a whore.

MYRTLE (*sadly, almost gently*): Lot, baby, that is the most cruel thing that anybody has ever said to me in my entire life. Here is my right hand to God! After all that I have suffered to stay on the straight and narrow, to be called a whore by my just married husband.

LOT: I said it looks like I married a prostitute and brought her home for Chicken.

MYRTLE: I know, I know what you said, you don't have to re-peat it. The strange thing about this is, *I*, I haven't blamed *you*! *You* are blaming *me*!

(*Dialogue overlaps.*)

LOT: I married a whore and . . .

MYRTLE: Here I'm standing, here, full of TB germs because you . . .

LOT: . . . brought her back here to Chicken.

MYRTLE: . . . lied! Lied to me! And have bleached hair and—

LOT: Goddam whore an' brought her back here to Chicken for him to lay while I die up here in this rocker, you *common*-trash!

MYRTLE: God! —How mean people are! —I'm going down-stairs after that.

LOT: Sure, and it makes how many times you gone down them!? To Chicken?

MYRTLE: This time is the last time. I'm not going to come back up. Not till you call me up and apologize to me and maybe not even then. No, not even then—maybe. . . .

(*Starts out: Turns back and roots in his coat pocket: coat hangs on hook on wall.*)

LOT: What are you doing? What did you take from my coat?

MYRTLE: Our marriage license! Your half brother wants to look at it to see if it's real.

(*She starts out again: Lot begins to laugh softly as she closes the door. She pushes it open again and says—*)

—What are you laughing at?

LOT: At life! —I think it's funny.

MYRTLE: —I think it's like a bad dream. . . .

LOT: —A bad dream can be funny!

MYRTLE: —I guess it can. At that. . . . (*Closes door rather softly. Chicken waits in the hall. She descends.*)

SCENE SIX

(*Myrtle enters kitchen.*)

MYRTLE: Here it is, this is it. (*Hands him the license.*) You can see it's no good.

CHICKEN: —It's got signatures on it.

MYRTLE: Sure, they put signatures on 'em to make 'em look real, but—

CHICKEN: This looks like a genuine license to me.

MYRTLE: I give you my right hand to God! —That thing is fake!

CHICKEN: Don't give me your right hand to God. I don't want it and He don't want it neither. Nobody wants your right or left hand to nothing. However, I'll keep this thing. I'll put it with my legal agreement with Lot. (*He folds the license into his wallet and studies her somberly.*) Are you able to write?

MYRTLE: Why, uh—yais!

CHICKEN: I don't mean just your name.

MYRTLE: No! Yais, I mean yais! —I been through four grades of school.

CHICKEN: Take a seat at this table. I'm gonna give you a little test in writing. (*He tears a sheet from a writing tablet and sets it before her with a pen and an ink bottle.*) You say you are able to write, and I am able to read. You see this pin an' paper I set befo' you?

MYRTLE: Yais! Perfectly! Plainly!

CHICKEN: Do you write standing up?

MYRTLE: Yais! No, I mean no! (*She scrambles into the chair.*)

CHICKEN: Now take this pin and write out on this paper what I tell you to write.

MYRTLE: What do you—?

CHICKEN: Shut up. I'm gonna dictate to you a letter that you will write an' sign and this letter will be to me.

MYRTLE: Why should I write you a letter when, when—you're right here?

CHICKEN: You'll understand why when you write it and write it out plain enough so anybody can read it.

MYRTLE: —My hand is—

CHICKEN: What?

MYRTLE: Shakin'!

CHICKEN: Control it.

MYRTLE: It's hard to control it with my nerves so unstrung.

CHICKEN: Which hand do you write with, with the left or the right?

MYRTLE: Oh, with the right, I'm right-handed.

CHICKEN: Well, give me that shaky right hand.

MYRTLE: What do you want with my hand?

CHICKEN: Stop it shakin'. (*He takes hold of her hand in both of his.*)

MYRTLE: What big hands you got, Chicken.

CHICKEN: Feel the calluses on 'em? I got those calluses on my hands from a life of hard work on this fuckin' place, worked on it like a nigger and got nothin' for it but bed and board and the bed was a cot in the kitchen and the board was no better than slops in the trough of a sow. However, things do change, they do gradually change, you just got to wait and be patient till the time comes to strike and then strike hard. (*He is rubbing her hand between his.*) Now it's comin', that time. This place is gonna be mine when the house is flooded an' I won't be unhappy sittin' on the roof of it till the flood goes down.

MYRTLE: No. Me neither. I'll be—pleased and—relieved!

CHICKEN: You mean if you are still in the land of the livin'.

MYRTLE: Don't make my hand shake again.

CHICKEN: I guess you think that I'm hard.

MYRTLE: I don't think a man should be soft.

CHICKEN: You know what life is made out of?

MYRTLE: Evil, I think it's evil.

CHICKEN: I think that life just plain don't care for the weak. Or the soft. A man and his life. Like I said, a man and his life both got to be made out of the same stuff or one or the other will break and the one that breaks won't be life. Now then. Your hand ain't shakin.

MYRTLE: No. My hand has stopped shaking because . . .

CHICKEN: —What?

MYRTLE: I know in my heart that you don't hate Myrtle.

CHICKEN: I hate nobody and I love nobody. Now pick up that pin, hold it steady, and write down what I tell you.

(*She picks up the pen, grips it.*)

Dip it in the ink, it don't write dry.

(*She wets the pen.*)

Ready?

MYRTLE: Ready, my hand is steady.

CHICKEN: I got to be careful how I word this thing, it's too important for me to bugger it up.

MYRTLE: Let's make two copies of it, one for, for—practice and the other—final.

CHICKEN: Won't be necessary. I got it now. Now write down what I tell you in big letters or print. "Me, Mrs. Lot Ravenstock, if I had a claim on this place called Raven Roost or anything on this place give up and deny all claims when my husband is dead. Because this place goes to Chicken. I known about this setup before my TV marriage and the paper which Chicken holds with notary seal, two names of witnesses on it, still holds good. I declare this. The place and all on it will be Chicken's, all Chicken's, when Lot Ravenstock dies and also if I die too because of river in flood, a natural act of God."

MYRTLE (*who has been scribbling frantically*): "All Chicken's when Lot dies."

CHICKEN: Now put in the punctuation and dot all the i's an' cross all the t's an' sign your name plain at the bottom.

MYRTLE: Yais, Yais, I did, I already did that, Chicken.

CHICKEN: Give it here. (*He takes the paper from her.*) Huh. I bet they never give you no spelling or handwriting prize when you went to school, but anyhow it's possible to read it if the question comes up in case of you being alive when the flood goes down. There's still one question, though. Where's the witnesses and the notary seal so this would hold up in court?

MYRTLE: Oh, we could get them later, we—!

CHICKEN: You wrote this thing because you're scared of drowning. How do I know you wouldn't back out of it when the flood's over with?

MYRTLE: I swear I wouldn't.

CHICKEN: Well, anyhow it's something, and something's better than nothing. It's worth putting in my wallet with Lot's witnessed letter and the true or false license.

MYRTLE: Chicken, trust my word. I've given you my word and never gone back on my word in all my life.

CHICKEN: I'm not counting on your word, but something else about you.

MYRTLE: What? Else? About me?

CHICKEN: —You're weak.

MYRTLE: I've always been weak compared to men, to a man. I think that's natural, don't you?

(*They have been sitting in chairs on opposite sides of the small, square kitchen table, chairs angled toward the audience. Now Chicken rises and moves close to her.*)

CHICKEN: Look me straight in the eyes and answer a question.

MYRTLE: What? Question?

CHICKEN: Can you kiss and like kissin' a man that's been accused of having some black blood in him?

MYRTLE: No! Yes! It would make no diff'rence to me.

CHICKEN: Let's try it out. Put your arms about me an' give me a kiss on the mouth. Mouth open.

(*She complies nervously, gingerly to this request. During the kiss, he puts a hand on her hips.*)

CHICKEN (*releasing her*): —Well? How did it feel? Disgusting?

MYRTLE: No, not a bit. I was pleased an' relieved that you wanted to kiss me, Chicken.

CHICKEN: That kiss was just a beginning. You know that. Does that please and relieve you?

MYRTLE: I'm a warm-natured woman. You might say passionate, even. A Memphis doctor prescribed me a bottle of pills to keep down the heat of my nature, but those pills are worthless. Have no effect, I'm through with them. —Don't you know I would never back down on that letter you dictated to me? Not if I could, never would!

CHICKEN: No, I reckon you wouldn't.

(*Chicken hoists himself onto the kitchen table, directly in front of her, legs spread wide.*)

MYRTLE: Wouldn't you be more comf'tble in a chair?

CHICKEN: I wouldn' be as close to you. —I'm right in front of you now.

MYRTLE: That's a—high—table. I have to strain my neck to look in your face.

CHICKEN (*with a slow, savage grin*): —You don't have to look in my face, my face ain't all they is to me. . . .

(*She begins suddenly to cry like a child.*)

Why're you cryin' fo' something you want an' can have?

(*He snatches up the lamp and blows it out. The kitchen is blacked out: an opaque scrim falls over its open wall. The light brightens in the bedroom where Lot sits in the wicker rocker; the moonlight on him brightens, fades, and brightens again.*)

LOT: Lamp's gone out in the kitchen and I don't hear a sound. —What I've done is deliver a woman to Chicken, brought home a whore for Chicken that he don't have to pay. —A present from the dying.

The Scene Dims Out.

SCENE SEVEN

The lights come up as Chicken lights the lamp on the table. He is still perched on the table and Myrtle is still on a chair so close to the table that she's between his boots, and she looks as if she had undergone an experience of exceptional nature and magnitude.

CHICKEN: Let there be light. That's what they say that God said on the first day of creation.

(*Slight pause as he fastens the clasp of his belt.*)

MYRTLE: Chicken, I want you to know that—

CHICKEN: What do you want me to know that I don't know?

MYRTLE: That that's the first time I've gone that far with a man, no matter how strongly attracted.

CHICKEN: You mean on the first date?

MYRTLE: I mean practickly never.

CHICKEN: Maybe when instink is powerful enough, then practice is not necessary. But in my opinion, them little white tablets you take to keep your nature down you oughta send back to the Memphis doctor an' demand a refund on whatever they cost you.

MYRTLE: It's possible that the tablets are meant for ordinary attraction but not for terrific attraction.

CHICKEN: Like a levee holds back a river up till a point where the pressure is too strong for it?

MYRTLE: Yes, like that. Exackly.

(*She rises from her chair and makes a weak-kneed effort to climb on the table.*)

CHICKEN: What're you doin'?

MYRTLE: Tryin' to climb up beside you an' lean on your shoulder.

CHICKEN: Naw, naw, stay in your chair a while longer. I don't like to touch or be touched by a woman right after havin' such close relations with her.

MYRTLE (*returning to her chair, humbly*): Are you disgusted with her?

CHICKEN: Just not int'rested in her.

MYRTLE: How long does that feelin' last?

CHICKEN: Sometimes five or tin minutes.

MYRTLE: Minutes kin seem like hours whin the attraction's terrific.

CHICKEN: —I wonder something about you.

MYRTLE (*nervously*): Wh—what do you wonder?

CHICKEN: If the attraction would still be terrific if I was to tell you the talk an' suspicion about me are based on fact.

MYRTLE: —What, uh, talk an' suspicion?

CHICKEN: That I got colored blood in me.

(*Note: Myrtle has the typical southern lower-class dread and awe of Negroes.*)

MYRTLE: Oh, I, why, I—I know they's no truth in that.

CHICKEN (*grinning at her savagely*): How do you know they isn't?

MYRTLE: Lot would of *tole* me.

CHICKEN: I come near to killin' him once fo' sayin' I had colored blood an' Lot hasn't forgotten; he's not so dumb he don't know that if he told you, I'd know.

MYRTLE: Thin why would you tell me thet you—

CHICKEN: I thought you oughta know after havin' such close relations.

(*Shaken and awed by the disclosure, she rises from her chair and pulls it back from the table.*)

CHICKEN: Why'd you do that, Mrs. Lot Ravenstock?

MYRTLE: —Why'd I do what did I do, I—

CHICKEN: You moved your chair back from the table like a monster was on it.

MYRTLE: You wuh swingin' your boots with mud on 'em stainin' my blouse, an'—

CHICKEN: Your blouse was awready stained. Has to be washed in floodwater.

MYRTLE: Chicken, fo' God's sake, don't mention a possible flood to a girl scared as I am of water.

CHICKEN: Move your chair back where it was.

MYRTLE: I don't know where it was.

CHICKEN: Then what do you know? Nothin'?

(*Myrtle moves her chair back to approximately its former position.*)

MYRTLE: Was it here?

CHICKEN: About. Now lissen to me. My mother had colored blood in her. She wasn't black but she wasn't white neither, and that's why I'm dark complected with freckled eyes an' live the life of a dawg that nobody owns and owns nothing. Ask any dawg on a road or a street, any dawg, any road, any street, if that ain't th' fuckin' truth which is made me suspicioned around here. So. Are you cryin' agin?

MYRTLE: —With, with—nervous—sympathy fo' you.

CHICKEN: Keep it, shove it, forget it. I don't want it. When you want sympathy, then is when you're in trouble. Up to your ass, up to your tits, up to your eyebrows in it, ask any dawg in the street, includin' you'self.

MYRTLE: Please don't talk thet way to me. (*She moves her chair back a little, still sniffling.*)

CHICKEN (*broodingly*): One night last winter, for instance, I come up to this girl at the Dixie Star, a night-place on the highway. This girl I come up to politely was known as Desperate Dotty because she put out for men right and left and up the center an' down it.

MYRTLE: —No self-respeck?

CHICKEN: No self-respeck an' no white tablets from the quack in Memphis, but I was so horny that night my balls were achin', so I come up to this girl when the man she was with fell outa their booth to th' floor an' laid there belchin' an' snorin'. I spoke to this girl politely. "Hello, how are you, Miss Bows, terrible weather," and so forth. Then lowered my voice an' leaned on th' table toward her, an' said "Miss Bows, this man you're with here t'night cain't do you no good, any dawg on th' road can tell you that, so why not step over his laigs an' sit in a clean booth with me, I got almost a full pint of Four Roses on me." —What did I git fo' this polite invitation?

MYRTLE (*still sniffling*): I don't, I should, I—

CHICKEN: I'll tell you what I got. She give me a quick, mean look an' said, "Nigger, stay in your place." That's it. That's how it is with me an' wimmen around here. Talk, suspicion, insult. An' when Miss Lottie, Lot's mother, dismissed me off this place, she said to me, "Chicken, I don't want my son to be known as half brother to a nigra." Wonderful, huh? Yeah, great. I'll tell you what her son does to amuse himself here. He gits in his dead mother's clothes—panties, brassiere, slippers, dress, an' a wig he made out of cornsilk. Ask any dawg in the street!

MYRTLE: —Oh, I—wouldn't ask any dawg a, a, a—thing like thet, I—

CHICKEN: Comes downstairs lookin' jus' like her an' sits in her parlor, talkin' to himself in the same voice as hers. OK? —Well, I'm back here, now, alone, suspicioned, despised.

MYRTLE: —I, uh—

CHICKEN: Oh, if I walk in town, I can go to the movies an' sit in th' white section an' watch a female actriss messin' around in a wrapper that you can almost see through. Shit,

I've seen kids play with themselves at The Delta Brilliant an' I don't blame 'em. The movie industry is run by ole men with hot pants, you can ask any dawg in the street if that's not true. Pool hall, I can go to the pool hall, but nobody's anxious to git me in a game with 'em. Can go to the highway night-place, an' sit by myself, left out of the conversation, talked about in whispers. So what I do, practickly everything, I do by myself, you can ask any dawg that.

MYRTLE: You should, I would—pay no attention, rise above talk an' suspicion you know ain't true.

CHICKEN: I just now told you it was. Oh, but naw. You don't wanta believe it after the close relation we had between us, naw, your folks in Mobile wuh so ignorant an' low class they filtered your mind with the idea that you'd be ruined like poisoned by havin' a close relation to someone with colored blood. So? Yais, so. I know.

MYRTLE: I was just, just simply—I was surprised for a—minute, which is over with now.

CHICKEN: You're still holdin' onto th' arms of that chair with your haid leant back like you was about to be electrocuted.

MYRTLE: I been through a good deal t'day, more than some girls go through in their whole lifetimes.

CHICKEN: Like the Four Hot Shots from Mobile?

(*He gets off the table and moves to the back door which is the only solid enclosure of the set—the rest is created by lighting.*)

MYRTLE (*rising fearfully*): Where are you goin'?

CHICKEN: The river's louder. I'm goin' to look at the levee.

MYRTLE: What good does it do to look at it?

CHICKEN: I can tell if the levee will hold the crest or not.

MYRTLE: Don't—

(*He goes off.*)

—leave me alone here. . . .

(*The bedroom upstairs is lighted by the moon. Lot is struggling out of the wicker rocker, knocking it over. He staggers to a closet and with his back to the audience, throws off the silk wrapper. He steps quickly into a gauzy white dress and sets a blond wig on his head. He turns around again, gasps, staggers*)

*to the foot of the brass bed and clings to its bars. Then he slides
down them to a kneeling position.)*

LOT: —Will—make it—Miss Lottie! And order them both off
the place!

*(The moon is obscured again and the bedroom returns to
dark, a scrim descending over its front. During this, Myrtle
has stood at the open kitchen door. Now Chicken returns, hip
boots covered with wet mud as when we first saw him.)*

MYRTLE: I thought you'd never git back here.
CHICKEN: You thought wrong, Missy.

(He sits on the table again.)

MYRTLE: —Those five or tin minutes are over with, now, ain't
they?
CHICKEN: Cain't you see the clock?
MYRTLE: A clock is mechanical but a man is human.
CHICKEN: Sometimes you say a true thing.
MYRTLE: I pride myself on that, and another thing I pride my-
self on is noticin' an' appreciatin' a man's appearance.
More, much more, than most girls I look at a man with ap-
preciation. Physical. I notice such things about him as a
strong figure in fine proportion. Mouth? Full. Teeth?
White. Glist'nin'. Why, you look like a man that could hold
back the flood of a river!
CHICKEN: No man can hold back a flood but some can live
through one.
MYRTLE: —With a—with a woman?
CHICKEN: Uh-huh, even with a woman. —How'd you like to
stay on here after Lot's gone?
MYRTLE: —Lit's not put it like thet.
CHICKEN: What other way would you put it?
MYRTLE: No, I don't know what other way I could put it.
And I know thet ev'ry girl in the world has a dream in her
heart that's sweeter an' more precicious to her than any
other.
CHICKEN: What's that dream in her heart?
MYRTLE: That dream is settl'n' down somewhere, sometime,
with a man to who she's very strongly attracted.

CHICKEN: Think it over an' I'll think it over, too. You're not a match fo' the pitcher tacked on the wall, but—

MYRTLE: No, no, but I—know!

CHICKEN: Yais, I'd say you know, an' if it's necessary to climb on the roof tonight, I'll git you up the ladder in the hall upstairs with a blanket in case we need more'n each other to keep us warm.

MYRTLE: What'd we eat up there if we had to stay up there long?

CHICKEN: The chickens'll fly up there, and if a helly-copter don't come over to pick us up, we'll drink some warm chicken blood to keep us goin'.

MYRTLE: Oh, I couldn't do that!

CHICKEN: What people have to do they always do. —So ev'rything understood now?

MYRTLE: I think we've come to a perfeck understandin'.

CHICKEN: Good. Let's have a drink on it. (*He pours liquor into two tin cups.*) —Have you ever been what they call saved?

MYRTLE: Why, yais, I have, I have been saved by you.

CHICKEN: What I was speakin' of is *religious* salvation.

(*He removes her importunate hand from his shoulder and resumes his seat on the table. The lamp light concentrates on him hotly during the monologue, the expression of his credo, that follows. Myrtle is a shadowy presence.*)

MYRTLE: Oh, *religious* salvation.

CHICKEN: That's right.

MYRTLE: Well, I'm not a steady churchgoer, I wake up so tired on Sundays, y'see, but when I'm perplexed or worried over something, I always appeal to my Saviour and, knock on wood, He has never let me down.

(*The bright light is now fixed on Chicken.*)

CHICKEN: Hmm. Uh-huh. —I reckon you'd never guess from me, the way I am now, that I was what they call saved by this preacher Gypsy Smith when he come through here last Spring. But I sure in hell was, I was what they call saved, but it didn't last much longer than a cold in the head. Hmmm. And talking about salvation, I think there's

a good deal of truth in the statement, the saying, that either
you're saved or you ain't, and the best thing to do is find
out which and stick to it. Because with human beings, and
I'm a human being and you are, too, what counts most is—

(*Myrtle perches herself beside him on the table and leans
against him.*)

With human beings, the ones I known in my life, what
counts most is personal satisfaction, and God knows you'll
never get that by denying yourself what you want most in
the world, by straining and struggling for what they call
salvation when it's something you're just not cut out for.
That preacher, that salvation preacher last spring, he
claimed that we had to put up a terrible struggle against
our lustful body. And I did for a while. Y'know, these
preachers all think we got lustful bodies and that's one
thing I know they're right about. Huh?

MYRTLE: Oh, yes. They're right about that. They're not
mistaken.

CHICKEN: And they also believe that we have spiritual gates,
and they preach about how you should haul down those
spiritual gates on your lustful body. Well. Those are two opposite things and one of 'em's got to be stronger if they're
in the same body. One's got to win and one lose. Well, I
tried to haul down my spiritual gates for a while but I
seemed to be reaching up for something that wasn't in me.
You can't haul down your spiritual gates if you don't have
any in you. I think that's the case in my case. I was just created without them. And either you're saved or you ain't,
you can be or never will be, and I think you're a hell of a
lot better off putting all hope of salvation out of your mind
completely than to put up a long, painful struggle that's
bound to be useless. Sooner or later, you're going to back-
slide, and that's that. Hmm? What do you think?

MYRTLE: In my case, I never had that experience, being saved,
not even for a short while, but I do say prayers, anyhow, to
God and to human beings.

CHICKEN: What do you pray for?

MYRTLE: I pray for protection, and right now I feel like that
prayer is going to be answered. Go on talking in that deep

voice of yours. I don't just hear it. It, it—it gives me a sensation in my ears and goes all through my body, it, it—it *vibrates* in me. I don't even hear the river!

CHICKEN (*with a touch of tolerant contempt*): Mmm, mmm-hmmm. What you're saying is you're anxious to please me in order to git on the roof whin the house is flooded.

MYRTLE (*very nervously*): Oh, no, that, that—that's already been settled.

CHICKEN: Things can be settled one way and then unsettled another.

MYRTLE: You wouldn't back out on it now after givin' your word, you couldn't, you're too good a man! God love you, Chicken!

CHICKEN: This house ain't built out of rock or brick or—cement. This is an old wood house. Oh, I'll git you up on the roof whin the levee collapses. But that's no guarantee that the crest of a flood of a river as big as this might not uproot this house like a weed and wash and toss it down and around till not a board or a shingle stuck together.

MYRTLE: Don't, don't—scare me out of my life!

CHICKEN (*sloshing liquor from the jug into their tin cups*): I'll tell you how I look at life in my life, or in any man's life. There's nothing in the world, in this whole kingdom of earth, that can compare with one thing, and that one thing is what's able to happen between a man and a woman, just that thing, nothing more, is perfect. The rest is crap, all of the rest is almost nothing but crap. Just that one thing's good, and if you never had nothing else but that, no property, no success in the world, but still had *that*, why, then I say this life would still be worth something, and you better believe it. Yes, you could come home to a house like a shack, in blazing heat, and look for water and find not a drop to drink, and look for food and find not a single crumb of it. But if on the bed you seen you a woman waiting, maybe not very young or good-looking even, and she looked up at you and said to you "Daddy, I want it," why, then I say you got a square deal out of life, and whoever don't think so has just not had the right woman. That's how I look at it, that's how I see it now, in this kingdom of earth.

(*Lot appears like an apparition in the pool of cool light at the stair-top. He has put on the gauzy white dress to conjure an image of his mother in summer. As he stands above the stairs he puts on a translucent, wide "picture hat;" the crown is trimmed with faded flowers. The effect is both bizarre and beautiful. There is a phrase of music like a muted trumpet playing a blues song. Then Lot starts his descent of the stairs. With each step his gasping for breath is louder, but his agony is transfigured by the sexless passion of the transvestite. He has a fixed smile which is almost ecstatic. Chicken leaps off the kitchen table and goes to the kitchen door. He seems impressed but not surprised. Myrtle is terrified.*)

MYRTLE: Chicken, Oh, God, stop him!

CHICKEN: What faw?

MYRTLE: Take him back up!

CHICKEN: Naw, naw, let him be in Miss Lottie's parlor.

(*At the foot of the stairs, Lot turns blindly towards the parlor. His gasping breath is now like a death rattle. Even in death he has the ecstasy of a transvestite. As he staggers into the bizarre little parlor, the room is lighted with a delicate rose light. There he stands swaying for a few moments; then sinks into one of the little gold chairs, facing the window. Myrtle is panicky but not Chicken. Lot, in his transfiguration, stares blindly. He is even smiling as if on a social occasion. He holds onto his garden hat, holding it by the crown, as if a wind might blow it away. He is swaying back and forth. Chicken's attitude is impassive.*)

—You're dressed fo' summer t'night.

(*Lot is past hearing any remark. He rises from the chair, sways, seems to bow to an applauding audience, then crumples to the floor. Chicken doesn't enter the parlor until Lot's death agony is finished. Only then does he enter and sits gingerly on one of the gilt chairs for a moment. Then, almost tenderly, he moves the lifeless body to the sofa. Myrtle, in a state of mental shock, has retreated to the kitchen and opened the icebox as if it were a place of refuge.*)

MYRTLE: Aigs. Bacon. Slab of it. New potatoes.

(*She removes these reassuring items from the iceless box. An egg or two splatters on the floor. She makes a few more rapid, irresolute turns.*)

Pan? —Pan! —Knife? —Knife!

(*She heads for the wall where these utensils are hanging and discovers her arms are full. Then she rushes back to deposit the foodstuff on the table. Entirely unnoticed by her, an egg or two more splatters on the floor. Then she rushes back to remove the utensils from their hooks.*)

In no condition to—got to!

(*She then instructs herself as if she were a pupil in a very primary cooking class.*)

Slice bacon in pan with knife. —Stove? —Burnin'!

(*Her words are interspersed with slight, breathless sobs. Chicken has stood over the summer gauze apparition of his half brother without a word or gesture. Now he turns out the chandelier and moves with dark satisfaction down the short hall to the kitchen area. He looks about him appraisingly, a man who has come into possessions fiercely desired. Myrtle's back is to him and when he speaks she catches her breath loudly.*)

CHICKEN: Makin' supper?

MYRTLE: What I'm doin' I don't know what I'm doin', I—

CHICKEN: You're doin' a sensible thing since it might be sev'ral days before we have a hot meal again.

MYRTLE (*turning to face him*): Chicken, as Christian people—

CHICKEN: What about Christian people, something or nothing?

MYRTLE: We got to call in a doctor.

CHICKEN: If there was a doctor that hadn't hauled his ass out of Two River County, there's nothin' he could do here but clean up a mess of aigs you dropt on the floor.

MYRTLE: —Lot is—?

CHICKEN: Isn't.

MYRTLE: —God have mercy on my—

CHICKEN: What?

MYRTLE: —The potatoes will be home-fried.

CHICKEN: That's right. Fried in my home. You couldn't peel 'em?

MYRTLE: Cut my finger!

CHICKEN: A nervous woman has a rough time in this world.

(*He stares at her broodingly for a couple of moments as she sucks her cut finger.*)

I don't reckon that, no, I reckon you couldn't.

MYRTLE: Couldn't? What?

CHICKEN: Produce me a son. Produce a child for me, could you? I've always wanted a child from an all-white woman.

MYRTLE: —I want t' be perfeckly frank with you on that subjeck.

CHICKEN: I could tell if you lied on that subjeck or any other.

(*He holds the lamp toward her still panicky face.*)

MYRTLE: I got five adopted children.

CHICKEN: You adopted five children?

MYRTLE: No, what I mean is, Chicken, I hed five children that hed t' be adopted because I wasn' financially able to give these children the care an' attention—an' care a infant child's got t' have, an' so I hed t' hev 'em adopted, all by families with yearly incomes no less 'n two thousan' dollars. Oh, it broke my heart five times. All five was red-headed like me an' cute as a bug.

CHICKEN: I don't want a child that looks like a bug.

MYRTLE: Oh, that's just a, you know, a—expression.

(*He replaces the lamp on the table.*)

No, sir. The deepest chord in my nature is the— Don't that river sound louder? Or am I just more scared to death of it?

CHICKEN: The flood crest is close to here now. (*He starts outside.*)

MYRTLE (*wildly*): *Don't leave me alone here!*

CHICKEN: I'm goin' out th' door for a minute. Sit down. Peel the home-fried potatoes. —I want to look at my land. (*He goes out and moves forward, his face exultant.*)
—*Sing it out, frogs an' crickets, Chicken is king!*

(Myrtle has come out behind him. There is a great booming sound.)

Up! Quick!

(He says this as the curtain is descending.)

End.

SMALL CRAFT WARNINGS

TO BILL BARNES:
YOU SAID TO GO ON, AND I WENT.

TOO PERSONAL?*

THE greatest danger, professionally, of becoming the subject of so many "write-ups" and personal appearances on TV and lecture platforms is that the materials of your life, which are, in the case of all organic writing, the materials of your work, are sort of telegraphed in to those who see you and to those who read about you. So, when you get to the serious organization of this material into your work, people (meaning audiences and critics—all but the few most tolerant whom you naturally regard as the best) have a sort of *déjà vu* or *déjà entendu* reaction to these materials which you have submitted to the cathartic process of your "sullen craft and art."

You may justifiably wonder why a man of my years in his profession, recognizing this hazard, has yet been willing to expose himself (with a frequency which seems almost symptomatic of clinical exhibitionism) to all of these interviews and the fewer, but equally personal, exposures on platform and "the tube."

I can offer you at least two reasons for this phenomenon. One is probably something with which you will immediately empathize. When one has passed through an extensive period of that excess of privacy which is imposed upon a person drifting almost willfullly out of contact with the world, anticipating that final seclusion of the nonbeing, there comes upon him, when that period wears itself out and he is still alive, an almost insatiable hunger for recognition of the fact that he is, indeed, still alive, both as man and artist. That's reason number one. The other is rather comical, I'm afraid. You get a devastatingly bad write-up, and you feel that you are washed up for good. Then some magazine editor gets through to you on that phone in the studio of your tropical retreat, the phone that you never pick up till it's rung so persistently that you assume that your secretary and house guests have been immobilized by nerve gas or something of that nature, and this editor speaks to you as sympathetically

*This was meant to be submitted to *The New York Times* as a preopening piece, but they chose to interview me instead.—T.W.

as the family doctor to a child stricken with a perforated appendix and tells you that he is as shocked as you were by the tasteless exposé-type of interview which appeared about you in a recent issue of some other mag. And then, of course, you forget about work, and you rage yourself into a slather over the iniquities and duplicities of the "interviewer" referred to. You say, "Why, that creature was so drunk he didn't know what street I lived on, and the guy that set me up for him laced my martini with sodium pentothal, and all I remember about this occasion is that my head came off my shoulders and hit the ceiling and I heard myself babbling away like an hysteric and I hadn't the slightest notion that he had a concealed tape recorder with him, and later he offered to play bridge with me that night, and he came over again with the tape recorder in some orifice of his body, I presume, and you know I do not see well and you know I like to hold forth to apparently amiable listeners, and I just assume that when they say 'I am interested only in your work,' that that's what they mean."

Now the editor has you on the hook.

"That's exactly my reaction to the revolting piece and how about letting us do a piece to correct it?"

You grasp at this offer like a drowning rat climbs on to anything that will float it. So you get another write-up. Then after this write-up, which is usually more colorful and better written than the one before, but equally nonserious, if not downright clownish, you feel that it is a life-or-death matter, professionally, with a new play opening somewhere, to correct the hilarious misquotes and exaggerations which embellished the second write-up, and so you go on to others and others. Now at last you have poured out, compulsively and perhaps fatally, all the recent content of your experience which should have been held in reserve for its proper place, which is in the work you're doing every morning (which, in my case, is the writing I do every morning).

Is it or is it not right or wrong for a playwright to put his persona into his work?

My answer is: "What else can he do?"—I mean the very root-necessity of all creative work is to express those things most involved in his experience. Otherwise, is the work, however well executed, not a manufactured, a synthetic thing? I've said, perhaps repeatedly, that I have two major classifications for writing: that which is organic and that which is not. And this opinion still holds.

Now let me attempt to entertain you once more with an anecdote.

Long ago, in the early forties, I attended a very posh party given by the Theatre Guild. I was comfortably and happily seated at a small table with my dear friend Miss Jo Healy, who was receptionist at the Guild in those days, when a lady with eyes that blazed with some nameless frenzy rushed up to me like a guided missile and seized me by the arm and shrieked to me, "You've got to meet Miss Ferber, she's dying to meet you."

Now in those days I was at least pliable, and so I permitted myself to be hauled over to a large table at which were seated a number of Diamond T trucks disguised as ladies.

"Oh, Miss Ferber," shrieked my unknown pilot, "this is Tennessee Williams."

Miss Ferber gazed slowly up and delivered this annihilating one-liner:

"The best I can manage is a mild 'Yippee.' "

"Madam," I said, "I can't even manage that."

Now everyone knows, who is cognizant of the world of letters, that Miss Edna Ferber was a creature of mammoth productivity and success. She was good at doing her thing; her novel and picture sales are fairly astronomical, I would guess.

I bring her up because she represents to me the classic, the archetypal, example of a writer whose work is impersonal, at least upon any recognizable level. I cannot see her in the oil fields of Texas with Rock Hudson and the late James Dean. Nor can I see her in any of her other impressive epics. I see her only as a lady who chose to put down a writer who was then young and vulnerable with such a gratuitously malicious one-liner. I mean without provocation, since I had literally been dragged to the steps of her throne.

So far I have spoken only in defense of the personal kind of writing. Now I assure you that I know it can be overdone. It is the responsibility of the writer to put his experience as a being into work that refines it and elevates it and that makes of it an essence that a wide audience can somehow manage to feel in themselves: "This is true."

In all human experience, there are parallels which permit common understanding in the telling and hearing, and it is the frightening responsibility of an artist to make what is directly or allusively close to his own being communicable and understandable, however disturbingly, to the hearts and minds of all whom he addresses.

T.W.
MARCH 26, 1972

Act I: A bar along the Southern California Coast

Act II: An hour or two later

ACT I

The curtain rises. The sound of ocean wind is heard. The stage is lighted at a very low level.

The scene is a somewhat nonrealistic evocation of a bar on the beach-front in one of those coastal towns between Los Angeles and San Diego. It attracts a group of regular patrons who are nearly all so well known to each other that it is like a community club, and most of these regulars spend the whole evening there. Ideally, the walls of the bar, on all three sides, should have the effect of fog rolling in from the ocean. A blue neon outside the door says: "Monk's Place." The bar runs diagonally from upstage to down; over it is suspended a large varnished sailfish, whose gaping bill and goggle-eyes give it a constant look of amazement. There are about three tables, with red-checked tablecloths. Stage right there is a juke box, and in the wall at right are doors to the ladies' and gents' lavatories. A flight of stairs ascends to the bar-owner's living quarters. The stairs should be masked above the first few steps.

The bar interior is dimly, evenly lit at rise. At some time in the course of the play, when a character disengages himself from the group to speak as if to himself, the light in the bar should dim, and a special spot should illuminate each actor as he speaks.

Monk is behind the bar serving Doc. Monk, the bar-owner, and Doc, who lost his license for heavy drinking but still practices more or less clandestinely, are middle-aged.

At a downstage table sits Violet, at her feet a battered suitcase fastened with a rope. Her eyes are too large for her face, and they are usually moist: her appearance suggests a derelict kind of existence; still, she has about her a pale, bizarre sort of beauty. As Leona Dawson later puts it, she's like a water plant.

MONK (*to Doc*): Notice? (*He nods his head.*) Over there?

    (*Doc emerges from introspection to glance the way indicated by Monk. They both gaze at Violet.*)

VIOLET (*singing a bit, self-conscious under their scrutiny*):
    The wheel of fortune
    Keeps turning around . . .
    (*She can't remember past this.*)

715

DOC (*voice filtered through booze*): Oh, yes, she's a noticeable thing. She has a sort of not-quite-with-it appearance. Amorphous, that's the word. Something more like a possibility than a completed creature.

MONK: What I mean is the *suitcase. With* her.

DOC: Oh, yes, the suitcase. Does she think she's in the waiting room of a depot?

MONK: I think she thinks she's moved in here.

DOC: Oh. That's a possible problem for you there.

MONK: You're Goddam right. I'm running a tavern that's licensed to dispense spirits, not a pad for vagrants. You see, they see those stairs. They know I live up there.

DOC: Yep, they see those stairs to the living quarters above, and it hits them dimly that you might need the solace of their companionship up there some nights when they find it convenient to offer it to you, and I don't need to tell you that this solace of companionship is not the least expensive item on the shelves of the fucking supermarket a man of my age has to spend what's left of his life in. Oh, that solace, that comfort of companionship is on the shelves of the market even for me, but I tell you, the price is inflated on it. I had me one last summer. Remember that plump little Chicano woman used to come in here with me some nights last summer? A little wet-leg woman, nice boobs on her and a national monument for an ass? Well, she came to me for medical attention.

(*Monk laughs heartily at this.*

(*Bill enters the bar; he comes up to it with an overrelaxed amiability like a loser putting up a bold front: by definition, a "stud"—but what are definitions?*

(*Monk mechanically produces Bill's can of Miller's but doesn't open it for him.*)

She had worms, diet of rotten beef tacos, I reckon, or tamales or something. I diagnosed it correctly. I gave her the little bottle and the wooden spoon and I said to her, "Bring me in a sample of your stool for lab analysis." She didn't know what I meant. Language barrier. I finally said, "Señorita, bring a little piece of your shit in the bottle tomorrow." (*He and Monk laugh heartily.*)

(*Bill is worried over the fact his beer can is not opened and served.*)

VIOLET: Hey, Bill . . .

DOC: Some beginning of some romance. Dewormed the lady and laid her in place of payment. Jesus, what a love story. I had her all summer, but in September she met a good-looking young pimp who made her critical of me. She called me a dirty old man, so I let her go.

BILL: Hey, Monk. About that beer.

MONK (*ignoring Bill*): I don't remember you coming in here with a woman.

DOC: We always sat at a back table arguing over the fair expense of her ass.

BILL: Jesus, Monk, how big a tab has Leona run up here!? For Chrissake! (*He leans across the bar and snatches the can of Miller's from Monk's hand. Monk had ignored him only half deliberately and is annoyed by the grab.*)

MONK: Look, I don't run Leona's tab through a computer, since I know she's good for it. If you want the can opened, give it back here. (*He opens the can.*) Now if it was your tab, not hers, I'd worry, but since it's hers, not yours, I don't. OK? No offense, no complaint, just . . .

VIOLET: Bill?

BILL: I could tell you some things.

MONK: Why don't you tell 'em to Violet, she's called you three times.

BILL (*glancing at her*): Hi, Vi.

VIOLET: I had an awful experience today with Mr. Menzies at the amusement arcade. (*Sobbing sound*) Oh, I don't know what to do. Min broke in. Last night. Menzies said I . . . Come over here so I can tell you. Oh, and bring me a beer and a pepperoni, I'm famished. Lonesome and famished.

BILL: You want me to solve both those situations for you?

VIOLET: Yes, please.

BILL (*to Monk*): Another Miller's and a coupla Slim Jims.

MONK: Yep, I got that message. Have you left Leona?

VIOLET: Bill, where's Leona?

BILL: Crying into a stew in her Goddam trailer.

(*Monk opens another beer, and Bill ambles over to Violet with the pepperonis and beer and the smile he meets the world with. It is a hustler's smile, the smile of a professional stud—now aging a bit but still with considerable memorabilia of his young charm.*)

VIOLET: Thanks, Bill . . .

(*Monk is toying with a radio which is over the bar.*)

RADIO VOICE: Heavy seas from Point Conception south to the Mexican border, fog continuing till tomorrow noon, extreme caution should be observed on all highways along this section of the coastline.

MONK (*ironically, turning off radio*): Small craft warnings, Doc.

DOC: That's right, Monk, and you're running a place of refuge for vulnerable human vessels, and . . .

VIOLET (*closer to Bill*): Have you left Leona? For good?

BILL: Just till she gets her knickers out of that twist. She had this brother, a faggot that played the fiddle in church, and whenever she's drunk, she starts to cry up a storm about this little fag that she admitted was arrested for loitering in the Greyhound bus station men's room, and if I say, "Well, he was asking for it," she throws something at me.

VIOLET (*leaning amorously toward him*): A man like you.

BILL: A man like me?

VIOLET: A bull of a man like you. You got arms on you big as the sides of a ham. (*She strokes his bare arm.*)

BILL: That ain't all I got big.

VIOLET: You mean what I think?

BILL: If you can't see you can feel.

(*She reaches under the table, and it is obvious that she is feeling him.*)

A man likes appreciation. Now I got a letter this week from a female guv'ment employee in Sacramento who's a Reagan supporter.

VIOLET: Huh?

BILL: Shit. She ain't seen me since '65 but remembers me clearly and wants me back on her aquabed with her, and

if you've slept in an aquabed it don't matter who's in it
with you.

(*The door bursts open. Leona enters like a small bull making
his charge into the ring. Leona, a large, ungainly woman, is
wearing white clam-digger slacks and a woolly pink sweater.
On her head of dyed corkscrew curls is a sailor's hat which she
occasionally whips off her head to slap something with—the
bar, a tabletop, somebody's back—to emphasize a point. There
are abrupt changes of position at the downstage table at her
entrance, but she notices only Bill there.*)

LEONA: YOUUUUU . . . MOTHER! I was talkin' to you
from the stove and you weren't there!

(*Bill chuckles and winks.*)

Three hours I spent shopping for and preparing a . . .
memorial dinner while you watched TV.

BILL: Stew and veg.

LEONA (*lyrically, as a pop-poem*): Lamb stew with garden fresh
vegetables from the Farmer's Market, seasoned with bay
leaves, and rosemary and thyme.

BILL: Stew.

LEONA: I'd set up a little banquet table in that trailer
tonight, my grandmother's silver and Irish lace tablecloth,
my crystal candlesticks with the vine leaves filigreed on
'em in silver which I'd polished, all spit-polished for this
memorial dinner, set the candles on either side of my single rose vase containing a single talisman rose just opened,
a table like a photo from *House and Garden*. I talk from
the stove to no one. I open the fridge to get out the jel-
lied bouillon, madrilene, topped with . . . "Okayyyy,
ready." I come in and I'm received by the TV set and the
trailer door hanging open, and in the confusion I knock
over and break my cut-glass decanter of Burgundy, imported.

BILL: I went out for a bottle. You'd kilt a fifth of Imp. She
was crying in the stew to save on salt.

LEONA: Without word or a note on the table. You went!
Why? For what?

VIOLET: Leona, Bill's not happy tonight, so let him be.

LEONA: Two people's not happy and one of 'em with *reason*! Is that your suitcase with you? Are you thrown out, evicted? A lady of the street? Oh, my God, here's a good one I heard at the shop today about a pair of street-ladies in Dublin. One enters a pub, elegant but pissed, and she says to the barman, "Two gins for two ladies." He observes her condition and says, "Where is the other lady?" "The other lady," she says, "is in the gutter, resting." (*Only she is amused by the story.*) Oh, well, I thought it was funny. (*Leona sits at table with Violet and Bill.*) Violet, dear, will you look at your nails?

VIOLET: I know, the enamel's chipping.

LEONA: Yes! Exposing the dirt.

(*Violet drops her hands under the table.*)

Oh, my God, forget it, forget the whole enchilada. Not worth a thought.

(*No response.*)

Excuse me a moment. I'm going to press one button three times on that multiselector, and Violet, here's an orange stick for your nails . . . Don't be depressed. A sure cure for depression is the ax.

VIOLET: I'm not depressed.

LEONA (*laughing*): Then you must not be conscious. (*She crosses to the juke box.*) I hope nobody objects to the number I play. It's going to be played here repeatedly tonight, appreciated or not. (*She bends over the juke box to find the desired number, which she herself contributed to the "Classicals" on the box.*) Rock? No! Popular? No! Classicals—yes! Number? Number? Which?

VIOLET: Tell her I'm not depressed.

(*Violet's hand has dropped under the table. It is apparent that she is reaching for Bill.*)

BILL: *She's* depressed . . . and depressing. (*Leans back luxuriously in chair. A look to Leona. He speaks with emphasis, rather than volume.*) . . . Not bad, huh? A definite . . . personal . . . asset?

(*Monk turns up radio. Gets static.*)

LEONA: Do you have to turn that on when I'm . . .

> (*At this precise moment she is caught by the change in attitudes at the downstage table. Her eyes widen; her hands clench; she takes a couple of paces toward the table and crouches a bit to peer under it. Then quick as a shot:*)

YOUUU . . . CUNT!

> (*She charges.*
> (*Violet screams and springs up, overturning her chair.*)

MONK: Hold her!

> (*Bill's massive frame obstructs Leona, not only her motion but her view of Violet. Bill is holding her by both shoulders, grinning into her face.*
> (*The following lines overlap.*)

LEONA: OFF HANDS!
MONK: Nope, nope, nope, nope, nope!
LEONA: McCorkle, DON' YOU . . . !
MONK: Keep her at that table!

> (*During this Monk has crossed from behind the bar.*
> (*Violet has turned about dizzily, then fled into the ladies'.*
> (*Leona stamps on Bill's foot. He yells, falls back an instant, releasing her. As she rushes forward, he gives her a hard slap on the butt; she turns to give him battle, and is caught from behind by Monk. She kicks at Monk's shin, and gives Bill a wallop in the face with her cap.*)

BILL (*rubbing his eyes*): Goddam, she . . .
MONK: I'm havin' no violence here! Never! None! From no one!

> (*A sudden hush falls: a sudden moment of stillness in a corrida.*)

LEONA (*incredulously, profoundly, hurtly, right into Bill's face*): YOU! Let *her*! In front of ME? . . . in PUBLIC! . . . In a BAR!
BILL: What the fuck of it! You hit me right in the eyes with . . .
LEONA (*makes a big-theater turn and shouts*): Where IS she? Where's she gone? (*Receiving no answer—there is still no*

sound from Violet's place of refuge—she suddenly rushes for the stairs.)

MONK: Nobody's up my stairs! Come down those . . .

(*Violet's lamentation begins.*)

LEONA: Aw! She's gone to the LADIES'! Change the name on that door.

MONK: I'm operating a place for gents and ladies. (*He is panting a bit.*)

LEONA: Gents and . . . what?

MONK: Ladies.

LEONA: Aw, now, Monk. I thought you run a clean place but don't come on with . . . her? Lady? Him? Gent? (*She points toward the ladies' room and then toward Bill.*) There's limits to . . .

MONK: Yes. Stay away from . . .

(*Leona had started toward the ladies'. Monk blocks her. She throws her head back and utters an apocalyptic outcry. It's like the outcry of all human protest.*)

No more disturbance of . . .

LEONA (*drawing herself up heroically as she confronts Monk almost nose-to-nose*): LET ME SET YOU STRAIGHT ABOUT WHAT'S A LADY! A lady's a woman, with respect for herself and for relations of others! HER? IN THERE? WAILING? RESPECT FOR? . . . She's got no respect for herself and that is the single respect in which she's correct to! No one could blame her for that! (*She has resumed her pacing and slapping at things with sailor's cap.*) What could she possibly find to respect in herself? She lives like an animal in a room with no bath that's directly over the amusement arcade at the foot of the pier, yeah, right over the billiards, the pinball games, and the bowling alleys at the amusement arcade, it's bang, bang, bang, loud as a TV western all day and all night, and then bang, bang again at eight A.M. It would drive a sane person crazy but she couldn't care less. She don't have a closet, she didn't have a bureau so she hangs her dresses on a piece of rope that hangs across a corner between two nails, and her other possessions she keeps on the floor in boxes.

BILL: What business is it of yours?

LEONA: None, not a Goddam bit! When she was sick? I went there to bring her a chicken. I asked her, where is your silver? She didn't have any silver, not a fork, spoon, or knife, hell, not even a plate, but she ate the chicken, aw, yeah, she ate the chicken like a dog would eat it, she picked it up in her paws and gnawed at it just like a dog. Who came to see if she was living or dead? ME! ONLY! I got her a bureau, I got her a knife, fork, and spoon, I got her china, I got her a change of bed linen for her broken-down cot, and ev'ry day after work I come by that Goddam rathole with a bottle of hot beef bouillon or a chicken or meatloaf to see what she needed and bring it, and then one time I come by there to see what she needed and bring it. The bitch wasn't there. I thought my God she's died or they put her away. I run downstairs, and I heard her screaming with joy in the amusement arcade. She was having herself a ball with a shipload of drunk sailor boys; she hardly had time to speak to me.

BILL: Maybe she'd gotten sick of you. That's a possible reason.

LEONA: It's a possible reason I was sick of her, too, but I'd thought that the bitch was dying of malnutrition, and I thought she was human, and a human life is worth saving or what the shit *is* worth saving. But is she human? She's just a parasite creature, not even made out of flesh but out of wet biscuit dough, she always looks like the bones are dissolving in her.

BILL (*banging his beer bottle on the table*): DO YOU THINK I BELONG TO YOU? I BELONG TO MYSELF, I JUST BELONG TO MYSELF.

LEONA: Aw, you pitiful piece of . . . worthless . . . conceit! (*She addresses the bar.*) . . . Never done a lick of work in his life . . . He has a name for his thing. He calls it Junior. He says he takes care of Junior and Junior takes care of him. How long is that gonna last? How long does he figure Junior is going to continue to provide for him, huh? HUH! . . . Forever or *less* than forever? . . . Thinks the sun rises and sets between his legs and that's the reason I put him in my trailer, feed him, give him beer-money, pretend I don't notice there's five or ten bucks less in my pocketbook in the morning than my pocketbook had in it when I fell to sleep, night before.

BILL: Go out on the beach and tell that to the sea gulls, they'd be more int'rested in it.

VIOLET (*shrilly, from the ladies' room*): Help me, help me, somebody, somebody call the po-liiiiice!

LEONA: Is she howling out the ladies' room window?

VIOLET: How long do I have to stay in here before you get the police?

LEONA: If that fink is howling out the ladies' room window, I'm going out back and throw a brick in at her.

MONK: Leona, now cool it, Leona.

LEONA: I'll pay the damage, I'll pay the hospital expenses.

MONK: Leona, why don't you play your violin number on the box and settle down at a table and . . .

LEONA: When I been insulted by someone, I don't settle down at a table, or nowhere, NOWHERE!

(*Violet sobs and wails as Steve comes into the bar. Steve is wearing a floral-patterned sports shirt under a tan jacket and the greasy white trousers of a short-order cook.*)

STEVE: Is that Violet in there?

LEONA: Who else do you think would be howling out the ladies' room window but her, and you better keep out of this, this is between her and me.

STEVE: What happened? Did you hit Violet?

LEONA: You're Goddam right I busted that filthy bitch in the kisser, and when she comes out of the ladies', if she ever comes out, I'm gonna bust her in the kisser again, and kiss my ass, I'm just the one that can do it! MONK! DRINK! BOURBON SWEET!

MONK: Leona, you're on a mean drunk, and I don't serve liquor to no one on a mean drunk.

LEONA: Well, you can kiss it, too, you monkey-faced mother. (*She slaps the bar top with her sailor hat.*)

STEVE: Hey, did you hit Violet?

(*Bill laughs at this anticlimactic question.*)

LEONA: Have you gone deaf, have you got wax in your ears, can't you hear her howling in there? Did I hit Violet? The answer is yes, and I'm not through with her yet. (*Leona approaches the door of the ladies' room.*) COME ON OUT OF THERE, VIOLET, OR I'LL BREAK IN THE DOOR! (*She bangs her fist on the door, then slaps it contemptuously with her cap, and resumes her pacing.*)

(*Bill keeps grinning and chuckling.*)

STEVE: Why did she hit Violet?

LEONA: Why don't you ask *me* why?

STEVE: Why did you hit Violet?

LEONA: I hit Violet because she acted indecent with that son of a bitch I been supporting for six months in my trailer.

STEVE: What do you mean "indecent"?

LEONA: Jesus, don't you know her habits? Are you unconscious ev'ry night in this bar and in her rathole over the amusement arcade? I mean she acted indecent with her dirty paws under the table. I came in here tonight and saw her hands on the table. The red enamel had nearly all chipped off the nails and the fingernails, black, I mean *black*, like she'd spend every day for a month without washing her hands after making mud-pies with filthy motherless kids, and I thought to myself, it's awful, the degradation a woman can sink down into without respect for herself, so I said to her, Violet, will you look at your hands, will you look at your fingernails, Violet?

STEVE: Is that why you hit Violet?

LEONA: Goddam it, NO! Will you listen? I told her to look at her nails and she said, oh, the enamel is peeling, I know. I mean the dirtiness of the nails was not a thing she could notice, just the chipped red enamel.

STEVE: Is that why you hit Violet?

LEONA: Shit, will you shut up till I tell you why I hit her? I wouldn't hit her just for being unclean, unsanitary. I wouldn't hit her for nothing that affected just her. And now, if you'll pay attention, I'm going to tell you exactly why I did hit her. I got up from the table to play "Souvenir."

STEVE: What is she talking about? What are you talking about?

LEONA: When I come back to the table her hands had disappeared off it. I thought to myself, I'm sorry, I made her ashamed of her hands and she's hiding them now.

STEVE: Is that why you hit Violet?

LEONA: Why do you come in a bar when you're already drunk? No! Listen! It wasn't embarrassment over her filthy nails that had made her take her hands off the table top, it was her old habit, as filthy as her nails. The reason her pitiful hands had disappeared off the table was because under the table she was acting indecent with her hands in the lap of that ape that moved himself into my trailer and tonight will move himself out as fast as he moved himself in. And now do you know why I hit her? If you had balls, which it doesn't look like you do, you would've hit her yourself instead of making me do it.

STEVE: I wasn't there when it happened, but that's the reason you hit her?

LEONA: Yeah, now the reason has got through the fog in your head, which is thick as the fog on the beach.

(*Violet wails from the ladies' room.*)

STEVE: I'm not married to Violet, I never was or will be. I just wanted to know who hit her and why you hit her.

LEONA (*slapping at him with her cap*): Annhh!

STEVE: Don't slap at me with that cap. What do I have to do with what she done or she does?

LEONA: No responsibility? No affection? No pity? You stand there hearing her wailing in the ladies' and deny there's any connection between you? Well, now I feel sorry for her. I regret that I hit her. She can come back out now and I won't hit her again. I see her life, the awfulness of her hands reaching out under a table, automatically creeping under a table into the lap of anything with a thing that she can catch hold of. Let her out of the ladies', I'll never hit her again. I feel too much pity for her, but I'm going out for a minute to breathe some clean air and to get me a drink where a barman's willing to serve me, and then I'll come back to pay up whatever I owe here and say good-bye

to the sailfish, hooked and shellacked and strung up like a
flag over . . . over . . . lesser, much lesser . . . creatures
that never, ever sailed an inch in their . . . lives . . .

(*The pauses at the end of this speech are due to a shift of her
attention toward a young man and a boy who have entered
the bar. Her eyes have followed them as they walked past her to
a table in the front.*

(*She continues speaking, but now as if to herself.*)

. . . When I leave here tonight, none of you will ever see
me again. I'm going to stop by the shop, let myself in with
my passkey and collect my own equipment, which is
enough to open a shop of my own, write a good-bye note
to Flo, she isn't a bad old bitch, I doubled her trade since
I been there, she's going to miss me, poor Flo, then leave
my passkey and cut back to my trailer and pack like lightning and move on to . . .

BILL: . . . Where?

LEONA: Where I go next. You won't know, but you'll know I
went fast.

(*Now she forgets her stated intention of going out of the bar
and crosses to the table taken by the young man and the boy.*

(*The boy, Bobby, wears faded jeans and a sweatshirt on
the back of which is lettered "Iowa to Mexico." The young
man, Quentin, is dressed effetely in a yachting jacket, ma-
roon linen slacks, and a silk neck-scarf. Despite this costume,
he has a quality of sexlessness, not effeminacy. Some years
ago, he must have been remarkably handsome. Now his face
seems to have been burned thin by a fever that is not of the
flesh.*)

LEONA (*suddenly very amiable*): Hi, boys!

QUENTIN: Oh. Hello. Good Evening.

BOBBY (*with shy friendliness*): Hello.

(*Bill is grinning and chuckling. Violet's weeping in the
ladies' room no longer seems to interest anyone in the bar.*)

LEONA (*to Bobby*): How's the corn growing out there where
the tall corn grows?

BOBBY: Oh, it's still growing tall.

LEONA: Good for the corn. What town or city are you from in Iowa?

BOBBY: Goldenfield. It's close to Dubuque.

LEONA: Dubuque, no shoot? I could recite the telephone book of Dubuque, but excuse me a minute, I want to play a selection on the number selector, and I'll come right back to discuss Dubuque with you. Huh? (*She moves as if totally pacified to the juke box and removes some coins from a pocket. They fall to the floor. She starts to bend over to pick them up, then decides not to bother, gives them a slight kick, gets a dollar bill out of a pocket, calling out:*) Monk, gimme change for a buck. (*Leona crosses to Monk at bar, waving a dollar bill.*)

QUENTIN: Barman? . . . Barman? . . . What's necessary to get the barman's attention here, I wonder.

(*Leona crosses back to juke box, stage right. Bobby hands Leona the change he's picked up off the floor. She looks for a number on the juke box.*)

MONK: I heard you. You've come in the wrong place. You're looking for the Jungle Bar, half a mile up the beach.

QUENTIN: Does that mean you'd rather not serve us?

MONK: Let me see the kid's draft card.

BOBBY: I just want a Coke.

QUENTIN: He wants a plain Coca-Cola, I'd like a vodka and tonic.

(*Leona lights up the juke box with a coin and selects a violin number, "Souvenir." A look of ineffable sweetness appears on her face, at the first note of music.*)

BILL: Y' can't insult 'em, there's no way to bring 'em down except to beat 'em and roll 'em.

(*The bar starts to dim, and a special spot comes up on Bill. The violin music on the juke box plays softly under.*)

I noticed him stop at the door before he come in. He was about to go right back out when he caught sight of me. Then he decided to stay. A piss-elegant one like that is asking for it. After a while, say about fifteen minutes, I'll go in the gents' and he'll follow me in there for a look at Junior.

Then I'll have him hooked. He'll ask me to meet him outside by his car or at the White Castle. It'll be a short wait
and I don't think I'll have t'do more than scare him a little. I don't like beating 'em up. They can't help the way
they are. Who can? Not me. Left home at fifteen, and like
Leona says, I've never done a lick of work in my life and I
never plan to, not as long as Junior keeps batting on the
home team, but my time with Leona's run out. She means
to pull out of here and I mean to stay . . .

(*The bar is relighted. Leona is still at the juke box. She is leaning against the juke box, listening intently to the music.*)

MONK (*rapping at the ladies'*): Violet, you can come out, now,
she's playing that violin number.

(*Bill and Steve laugh. The bar starts to dim, and a special
spot comes up on Steve. The violin number still plays under.*)

STEVE: I guess Violet's a pig, all right, and I ought to be
ashamed to go around with her. But a man unmarried,
forty-seven years old, employed as a short-order cook at a
salary he can barely get by on alone, he can't be choosy.
Nope, he has to be satisfied with the Goddam scraps in this
world, and Violet's one of those scraps. She's a pitiful scrap,
but . . . (*He shrugs sadly and lifts the beer bottle to his
mouth.*) . . . something's better than nothing and I had
nothing before I took up with her. She gave me a clap once
and tried to tell me I got it off a toilet seat. I asked the doctor, is it possible to get a clap off a public toilet seat, and he
said, yes, you can get it that way but you *don't*. (*He grins
sadly and drinks again, wobbling slightly.*) . . . Oh, my life,
my miserable, cheap life! It's like a bone thrown to a dog!
I'm the dog, she's the bone. Hell, I know her habits. She's
always down there in that amusement arcade when I go to
pick her up, she's down there as close as she can get to
some Navy kid, playing a pinball game, and one hand is out
of sight. Hustling? I reckon that's it. I know I don't provide for her, just buy her a few beers here, and a hot dog
on the way home. But, Bill, why's he let her mess around
with him? One night he was braggin' about the size of his
tool, he said all he had to do to make a living was wear

tight pants on the street. Life! . . . Throw it to a dog. I'm not a dog, I don't want it. I think I'll sit at the bar and pay no attention to her when she comes out . . .

(*The light in the bar comes up to normal level as the spot fades out. After a moment, Violet comes out of the ladies' room slowly, with a piteous expression. She is dabbing her nostrils with a bit of toilet tissue. Her lips are pursed in sorrow so that she is like travesty of a female saint under torture. She gasps and draws back a little at the sight of Leona; then, discreetly sobbing, she edges onto a bar stool, and Monk gives her a beer. Steve glares at her. She avoids looking at him. Bill grins and chuckles at his table. Leona ignores the fact that Violet has emerged from her retreat. She goes on pacing the bar, but is enthralled by the music.*)

LEONA: My God, what an instrument, it's like a thing in your heart, it's a thing that's sad but better than being happy, in a . . . crazy drunk way . . .

VIOLET (*piteously*): I don't know if I can drink, I feel sick at my stomach.

LEONA: Aw, shit, Violet. Who do you think you're kidding? You'll drink whatever is put in the reach of your paws. (*She slaps herself on the thigh with the sailor cap and laughs.*)

VIOLET: I do feel sick at my stomach.

LEONA: You're lucky you're sick at your stomach because your stomach can vomit, but when you're sick at your heart, that's when it's awful, because your heart can't vomit the memories of your lifetime. I wish my heart could vomit, I wish my heart could throw up the heartbreaks of my lifetime, my days in a beauty shop and my nights in a trailer. It wouldn't surprise me at all if I drove up to Sausalito alone this night. With no one . . .

(*She glances at Bill, who grins and chuckles. Violet sobs piteously again. Leona gives Violet a fairly hard slap on the shoulders with her sailor's cap. Violet cries out in affected terror.*)

Shuddup, I'm not gonna hit you. Steve, take her off that bar stool and put her at a table, she's on a crying jag and it makes me sick.

STEVE (*to Violet*): Come off it, Violet. Sit over here at a table, before you fall off the bar stool.

LEONA: She hasn't got a mark on her, not a mark, but she acts like I'd nearly kilt her, and turns to a weeping willow. But as for that ape that I put up in my trailer, I took him in because a life in a trailer, going from place to place any way the wind blows you, gets to be lonely, sometimes. But that's a mistake I'll not make again . . . knock wood! (*Knocks table top.*)

STEVE (*wishing to smooth troubled waters*): Know what that means, to knock wood? It means to touch the wood of the true cross, Leona. (*He peers gravely and nearsightedly into Leona's face.*)

LEONA: Yeh, for luck, you need it.

MONK (*to Violet at bar*): That's mine! Here's yours. (*She has reached out for Monk's drink.*)

STEVE: Violet, get off that stool and sit at a table.

LEONA: You got to move her. She's got to be moved.

(*Steve accepts this necessity. He supports Violet's frail, liquid figure to a table upstage, but her long, thin arm snakes out to remove Monk's drink from the bar top as she goes.*)
(*The phone rings, and Monk lifts it.*)

MONK: Monk's Place . . . Doc, it's for you.

DOC (*crossing to the end of the bar*): Thanks, Monk.

MONK: The old Doc's worked up a pretty good practice for a man in retirement.

LEONA: Retirement your ass, he was kicked out of the medical profession for performing operations when he was so loaded he couldn't tell the appendix from the gizzard.

MONK: Leona, go sit at your table.

LEONA: You want responsibility for a human life, do you?

MONK: Bill, I think she's ready to go home now.

LEONA: I'll go home when I'm ready and I'll do it alone.

BILL: I seen a circus with a polar bear in it that rode a three-wheel bicycle. That's what you make me think of tonight.

LEONA: You want to know something, McCorkle? I could beat the shit out of you.

BILL: Set down somewhere and shut up.

LEONA: I got a suggestion for you. Take this cab fare . . . (*She throws a handful of silver on the table.*) . . . And go get your stuff out of my trailer. Clear it all out, because when I go home tonight and find any stuff of yours there, I'll pitch it out of the trailer and bolt the door on you. I'm just in the right mood to do it.

BILL: Don't break my heart.

LEONA: What heart? We been in my trailer together for six months and you contributed nothing.

BILL: Shit, for six months I satisfied you in your trailer!

LEONA: You never satisfied nothing but my mother complex. Never mind, forget it, it's forgotten. Just do this. Take this quarter and punch number K-6 three times on the juke box.

BILL: Nobody wants to hear that violin number again.

LEONA: I do, I'm somebody. My brother, my young brother, played it as good if not better than Heifetz on that box. Y'know, I look at you and I ask myself a question. How does it feel to've never had anything beautiful in your life and not even know you've missed it? (*She crosses toward the juke box.*) Walking home with you some night, I've said, Bill, look at the sky, will you look at that sky? You never looked up, just grunted. In your life you've had no experiation . . . experience! Appreciation! . . . of the beauty of God in the sky, so what is your life but a bottle of, can of, glass of . . . one, two, three! (*She has punched the violin selection three times.*)

MONK: The Doc's still on the phone.

LEONA: "Souvenir" is a soft number.

(*The violin number starts to play again on the juke box.*)

DOC (*returning to the bar*): I've got to deliver a baby. Shot of brandy.

LEONA (*returning to Bill's table*): It wouldn't be sad if you didn't know what you missed by coming into this world and going out of it some day without ever having a sense of, experience of and memory of, a beautiful thing in your life such as I have in mine when I remember the violin of and the face of my young brother . . .

BILL: You told me your brother was a fruit.

LEONA: I told you privately something you're repeating in public with words as cheap as yourself. My brother who played this number had pernicious anemia from the age of thirteen and any fool knows a disease, a condition, like that would make any boy too weak to go with a woman, but he was so full of love he had to give it to someone like his music. And in my work, my profession as a beautician, I never seen skin or hair or eyes that could touch my brother's. His hair was a natural blond as soft as silk and his eyes were two pieces of heaven in a human face, and he played on the violin like he was making love to it. I cry! I cry! . . . No, I don't, I *don't* cry! . . . I'm proud that I've had something beautiful to remember as long as I live in my lifetime . . .

(*Violet sniffles softly.*)

When they passed around the plate for the offering at church, they'd have him play in the choir stall and he played and he looked like an angel, standing under the light through the stained glass window. Um-hummm. (*Her expression is rapt.*) . . . And people, even the tightwads, would drop paper money in the plates when he played. Yes, always before the service, I'd give him a shampoo-rinse so that his silky hair, the silkiest hair I've ever known on a human head in my lifetime as a beautician, would look like an angel's halo, touched with heavenly light. Why, people cried like I'm crying and the preacher was still choked up when he delivered the sermon. "Angels of Light," that was it, the number he played that Easter . . . (*She sings a phrase of the song.*) Emotions of people can be worse than people but sometimes better than people, yes, superior to them, and Haley had that gift of making people's emotions uplifted, superior to them! But he got weaker and weaker and thinner and thinner till one Sunday he collapsed in the choir stall, and after that he failed fast, just faded out of this world. Anemia—pernicious . . .

VIOLET (*sobbing*): Anemia, that's what I've got!

LEONA: Don't compare yourself to him, how dare you compare yourself to him. He was too beautiful to live and so he died. Otherwise we'd be living together in my trailer. I'd train him to be a beautician, to bring out the homeliness in . . . I mean the, I mean the . . . (*She is confused for a moment. She lurches into a bar stool and knocks it over.*) I mean I'd train my young brother to lay his hands on the heads of the homely and lonely and bring some beauty out in them, at least for one night or one day or at least for an hour. We'd have our own shop, maybe two of 'em, and I wouldn't give you . . . (*She directs herself to Bill.*) . . . the time of the day, the time of the night, the time of the morning or afternoon, the sight of you never would have entered my sight to make me feel pity for you, no, noooo! (*She bends over Bill's table, resting her spread palms on it, to talk directly into his face.*) The companionship and the violin of my brother would be all I had any need for in my lifetime till my death-time! Remember this, Bill, if your brain can remember. Everyone needs! One beautiful thing! In the course of a lifetime! To save the heart from colluption!

BILL: What is "colluption," fat lady?

LEONA: *CORRUPTION!* . . . Without one beautiful thing in the course of a lifetime, it's all a death-time. A woman turns to a slob that lives with a slob, and life is disgusting to her and she's disgusting to life, and I'm just the one to . . .

BILL (*cutting in*): If you'd rather live with a fruit . . .

LEONA: *Don't say it! Don't say it!* (*She seizes hold of a chair and raises it mightily over her head. Violet screams. Leona hurls the chair to the floor.*) Shit, he's not worth the price of a broken chair! (*Suddenly she bursts into laughter that is prodigious as her anger or even more, it's like an unleashed element of nature. Several patrons of the bar, involuntarily, laugh with her. Abruptly as it started, the laughter stops short. There is total silence except for the ocean sound outside.*)

VIOLET: Steve, love, get me a hot dog with chili and onion, huh? Or maybe a Whopper.

STEVE: Oh, now you want a Whopper, a king-size burger, now, huh? Always got your hand out for something.

VIOLET: That's a cruel injustice. (*Sobs.*)

STEVE: Stop it!

VIOLET: I'm in paiii-in!

LEONA: Look at her, not a mark on her, but says she's in pain and wants a hot dog with everything on it, and I heard on

TV that the Food Administration found insect and rodent parts in some hot dogs sold lately. (*She has been stalking the bar.*) Let her have him for supper! (*Indicates Bill.*)

DOC (*rising from his bar stool*): Well, I better be going. Somebody's about to be born at Treasure Island.

LEONA: That's my trailer court where I keep my trailer. A baby's about to be born there?

BILL: Naw, not a baby, a full-grown adult's about to be born there, and that's why the Doc had t'brace himself with a coupla shots of brandy.

DOC (*turning about on his bar stool, glass in hand*): You can't make jokes about birth and you can't make jokes about death. They're miracles, holy miracles, both, yes, that's what both of them are, even though, now, they're usually surrounded by . . . expedients that seem to take away the dignity of them. Birth? Rubber gloves, boiled water, forceps, surgical shears. And death? . . . The wheeze of an oxygen tank, the jab of a hypodermic needle to put out the panic light in the dying-out eyes, tubes in the arms and the kidneys, absorbent cotton inserted in the rectum to hold back the bowels discharged when the . . . the *being stops.* (*During this speech the bar dims, and a special spot comes up on Doc.*) . . . It's hard to see back of this cloud of . . . irreverent . . . paraphernalia. But behind them both are the holy mysteries of . . . birth and . . . death . . . They're dark as the face of a black man, yes, that's right, a Negro, yes. I've always figured that God is a black man with no light on his face, He moves in the dark like a black man, a Negro miner in the pit of a lightless coal mine, obscured completely by the . . . irrelevancies and irreverencies of public worship . . . standing to sing, kneeling to pray, sitting to hear the banalities of a preacher . . . Monk, did I give you my . . . ?

(*As light comes up in bar, the spot fades out.*)

MONK: Bag? Yeah, here. (*Monk hands a medical kit across the bar.*)

LEONA: I want to know, is nobody going to stop him from going out, in his condition, to deliver a baby? I want to know quick, or I'll stop him myself!

DOC: Thanks. And I'll have a shot of brandy to wash down a Benzedrine tablet to steady my hands.

LEONA: NOBODY, HUH?

DOC: Tonight, as I drove down Canyon Road, I noticed a clear bright star in the sky, and it was right over that trailer court, Treasure Island, where I'm going to deliver a baby. So now I know: I'm going to deliver a new Messiah tonight.

LEONA: The hell you are, you criminal, murdering quack, leggo of that bag!

(Leona rushes Doc and snatches his bag. She starts toward the door but is blocked by one of the men; starts in another direction and is blocked again. She is then warily approached from three or four sides by Monk, Doc, Bill, and Steve as trainers approaching an angry "big cat.")

(All ad-lib during this, and in the lines that follow, Monk, Leona, and Doc speak almost simultaneously, while Steve keeps up a continual placating repetition of "Violet says" and "Have a beer with us, Leona.")

(The effect should almost suggest a quartet in opera: several voices blended but each pursuing its separate plaint.)

MONK: Don't let her out with . . .

DOC: My bag! The instruments in that bag . . .

MONK: Steve, Bill, hold her, I can't with my . . .

DOC: Are worth and insured for . . . over two thousand! If you damage the contents of that bag . . . I'll sue you for their value and for slander!

(Leona sits on Doc's bag at center table.)

LEONA: I'll surrender this bag to you in a courtroom only!

DOC: Very expensive, very, very expensive.

STEVE: Look, she's sitting on Doc's bag. Violet says she's, Leona, Violet wants to, listen, listen, listen Leona, set down and have a beer with us! Violet says she . . .

VIOLET: Not at this table, no, no, I'm scared of Leona, she . . .

STEVE: Violet, shuddup. Leona? Violet's offered you to a . . . drink! Have a drink with us, Leona.

LEONA: I'll stay sitting on it till some action is taken to stop this man from illegal . . .

(*Bill squirts a mouthful of beer at her, and she immediately leaps up to strike at him fiercely with the sailor's cap. In that instant Monk seizes the bag from the chair and tosses it to Doc, who rushes out the door with it.*)

All of you are responsible! . . . If he murders a baby tonight and the baby's mother! Is life worth nothing in here? I'm going out. I am going to make a phone call.

(*Bill makes a move to stop her.*)

Don't you *dare* to! Try to!

MONK: Who're you going to call?

STEVE: Who's she going to call?

LEONA (*to Monk*): That's my business, strictly. I'm not gonna use your phone. (*She charges out the door, and the door is again left open on the sound of surf.*)

MONK: What's she up to?

STEVE: What's she up to, Bill?

BILL (*grinning and shrugging*): I know what she's up to. She's gonna call the office at Treasure Island and tell 'em the Doc's comin' out there to deliver a baby.

MONK: Well, stop her, go stop her!

STEVE: Yeh, you better stop her.

BILL (*indifferently*): She's disappeared in the fog.

MONK: She can get the Doc into serious trouble, and his condition's no better than mine is . . .

BILL: Shit, they know her too well to pay any attention to her call.

MONK: I hate to eighty-six anyone out of my place; I never have done that in the six years I've run it, but I swear to God, I . . . have to avoid . . . disturbance.

VIOLET (*plaintively*): Last week she gave me a perm and a rinse for nothing, and then tonight she turns on me, threatens to kill me.

BILL: Aw, she blows hot and cold, dependin' on whichever way her liquor hits her.

VIOLET: She's got two natures in her. Sometimes she couldn't be nicer. A minute later she . . .

MONK (*at the telephone*): Shut up a minute. Treasure Island? This is Monk speaking from Monk's Place . . . Yeah. Now. If you get a phone call out there from Leona Dawson, you know her, she's got a trailer out there, don't listen to her; she's on a crazy mean drunk, out to make trouble for a capable doctor who's been called by someone out there, an emergency call. So I thought I'd warn you, thank you. (*Monk hangs up the telephone.*)

(*Violet comes downstage, and the light is focused on her.*)

VIOLET: It's perfectly true that I have a room over the amusement arcade facing the pier. But it wasn't like Leona describes it. It took me a while to get it in shipshape condition because I was not a well girl when I moved in there, but I got it clean and attractive. It wasn't luxurious but it was clean and attractive and had an atmosphere to it. I don't see anything wrong with living upstairs from the amusement arcade, facing the pier. I don't have a bath or a toilet but I keep myself clean with a sponge bath at the washbasin and use the toilet in the amusement arcade. Anyhow it was a temporary arrangement, that's all it was, a temporary arrangement . . .

(*Leona returns to the bar. Bill rises quickly and walks over to the bar.*)

LEONA: One, two, button my shoe, three, four, shut the door, five, six, pick up sticks . . . (*No one speaks.*) . . . Silence, absolute silence. Am I being ostracized? (*She goes to the table of Quentin and Bobby.*) Well, boys, what went wrong?
QUENTIN: I'm afraid I don't know what you mean.
LEONA: Sure you know what I mean. You're not talking to each other, you don't even look at each other. There's some kind of tension between you. What is it? Is it guilt feelings? Embarrassment with guilt feelings?
BOBBY: I still don't know what you mean, but, uh . . .
LEONA: "But, uh" what?
QUENTIN: Don't you think you're being a little presumptuous?
LEONA: Naw, I know the gay scene. I learned it from my kid brother. He came out early, younger than this boy here. I know the gay scene and I know the language of it and I know how full it is of sickness and sadness; it's so full of sadness and sickness, I could almost be glad that my little

brother died before he had time to be infected with all that sadness and sickness in the heart of a gay boy. This kid from Iowa, here, reminds me a little of how my brother was, and you, you remind me of how he might have become if he'd lived.

QUENTIN: Yes, you should be relieved he's dead, then.

(*She flops awkwardly into a chair at the table.*)

QUENTIN (*testily*): Excuse me, won't you sit down?

LEONA: D'ya think I'm still standing up?

QUENTIN: Perhaps we took your table.

LEONA: I don't have any table. I'm moving about tonight like an animal in a zoo because tonight is the night of the death-day of my brother and . . . Look, the barman won't serve me, he thinks I'm on a mean drunk, so do me a favor, order a double bourbon and pretend it's for you. Do that, I'll love you for it, and of course I'll pay you for it.

QUENTIN (*calling out*): Barman? I'd like a double bourbon.

MONK: If it's for the lady, I can't serve you.

(*Bill laughs heartily at the next table.*)

QUENTIN: It isn't for the lady, it's for me.

LEONA: How do you like that shit? (*She shrugs.*) Now what went wrong between you before you come in here, you can tell me and maybe I can advise you. I'm practically what they call a faggot's moll.

QUENTIN: Oh. Are you?

LEONA: Yes, I am. I always locate at least one gay bar in whatever city I'm in. I live in a home on wheels, I live in a trailer, so I been quite a few places. And have a few more to go. Now nobody's listening to us, they're involved in their own situations. What went wrong?

QUENTIN: Nothing, exactly. I just made a mistake, and he did, too.

LEONA: Oh. Mistakes. How did you make these mistakes? Nobody's listening, tell me.

QUENTIN: I passed him riding his bicycle up Canyon Road and I stopped my car and reversed it till I was right by his bike and I . . . spoke to him.

LEONA: What did you say to him?

BOBBY: Do you have to talk about it?

QUENTIN: Why not? I said: "Did you really ride that bike all the way from Iowa to the Pacific Coast," and he grinned and said, yes, he'd done that. And I said: "You must be tired?" and he said he was and I said: "Put your bike in the back seat of my car and come home with me for dinner."

LEONA: What went wrong? At dinner? You didn't *give* him the dinner?

QUENTIN: No, I gave him drinks, first, because I thought that after he'd had dinner, he might say: "Thank you, good night."

BOBBY: Let's shut up about that. I had dinner after.

LEONA: After what?

QUENTIN: After . . .

BOBBY: I guess to you people who live here it's just an old thing you're used to, I mean the ocean out there, the Pacific, it's not an *experience* to you any more like it is to me. You say it's the Pacific, but me, I say THE PACIFIC!

QUENTIN: Well, everything is in "caps" at your age, Bobby.

LEONA (*to Quentin*): Do you work for the movies?

QUENTIN: Naturally, what else?

LEONA: Act in them, you're an actor?

QUENTIN: No. Script writer.

LEONA (*vaguely*): Aw, you write movies, huh?

QUENTIN: Mostly rewrite. Adapt. Oh, I had a bit of a setback when they found me too literate for my first assignment . . . converting an epic into a vehicle for the producer's doxy, a grammar school dropout. But the industry is using me now to make blue movies bluer with . . . you know, touches of special . . . erotica . . . lovely.

(*Leona laughs.*)

LEONA: Name?

QUENTIN: Quentin . . . Miss? (*He rises.*)

LEONA: Leona. Dawson. And he's?

QUENTIN: Bobby.

LEONA: Bobby, come back to the party. I want you back here, love. Resume your seat. (*Resting a hand on the boy's stiff shoulder*) . . . You're a literary gent with the suede shitkickers and a brass-button blazer and a . . . (*Flicks his scarf.*)

BILL (*leering from bar*): Ask him if he's got change for a three-dollar bill.

QUENTIN: Yes, if you have the bill.

LEONA: Ignore the peasants. I don't think that monkey-faced mother will serve us that bourbon . . . I never left his bar without leaving a dollar tip on the table, and this is what thanks I get for it, just because it's the death-day of my brother and I showed a little human emotion about it. Now what's the trouble between you and this kid from Iowa where the tall corn blows, I mean grows?

QUENTIN: I only go for straight trade. But this boy . . . look at him! Would you guess he was gay? . . . I didn't, I thought he was straight. But I had an unpleasant surprise when he responded to my hand on his knee by putting his hand on mine.

BOBBY: I don't dig the word "*gay.*" To me they mean nothing, those words.

LEONA: Aw, you've got plenty of time to learn the meanings of words and cynical attitudes. Why he's got eyes like my brother's! Have you paid him?

QUENTIN: For disappointment?

LEONA: Don't be a mean-minded mother. Give him a five, a ten. If you picked up what you don't want, it's your mistake and pay for it.

BOBBY: I don't want money from him. I thought he was nice, I liked him.

LEONA: Your mistake, too. (*She turns to Quentin.*) Gimme your wallet.

(*Quentin hands her his wallet.*)

BOBBY: He's disappointed. I don't want anything from him.

LEONA: Don't be a fool. Fools aren't respected, you fool. (*She removes a bill from the wallet and stuffs it in the pocket of Bobby's shirt. Bobby starts to return it.*) OK, I'll hold it for you till he cuts out of here to make another pickup and remind me to give it back to you when he goes. He wants to pay you, it's part of his sad routine. It's like doing penance . . . penitence.

BILL (*loudly*): Monk, where's the head?

MONK: None of that here, Bill.

QUENTIN (*with a twist of a smile toward Bill*): Pity.

LEONA (*turning to Quentin*): Do you like being alone except for vicious pickups? The kind you go for? If I understood you correctly? . . . Christ, you have terrible eyes, the expression in them! What are you looking at?

QUENTIN: The fish over the bar . . .

LEONA: You're changing the subject.

QUENTIN: No, I'm not, not a bit . . . Now suppose some night I woke up and I found that fantastic fish . . . what is it?

LEONA: Sailfish. What about it?

QUENTIN: Suppose I woke up some midnight and found that peculiar thing swimming around in my bedroom? Up the Canyon?

LEONA: In a fish bowl? Aquarium?

QUENTIN: No, not in a bowl or aquarium: free, unconfined.

LEONA: Impossible.

QUENTIN: Granted. It's impossible. But suppose it occurred just the same, as so many impossible things *do* occur just the same. Suppose I woke up and discovered it there, swimming round and round in the darkness over my bed, with a faint phosphorescent glow in its big goggle-eyes and its gorgeously iridescent fins and tail making a swishing sound as it circles around and about and around and about right over my head in my bed.

LEONA: Hah!

QUENTIN: Now suppose this admittedly preposterous thing did occur. What do you think I would say?

LEONA: To the fish?

QUENTIN: To myself and the fish.

LEONA: . . . I'll be raped by an ape if I can imagine what a person would say in a situation like that.

QUENTIN: I'll tell you what I would say, I would say: "Oh, well . . ."

LEONA: . . . Just "Oh, well"?

QUENTIN: "Oh, well" is all I would say before I went back to sleep.

LEONA: What I would say is: "Get the hell out of here, you goggle-eyed monstrosity of a mother," that's what I'd say to it.

MONK: Leona, let's lighten it up.

QUENTIN: You don't see the point of my story?

LEONA: Nope.

QUENTIN (*to Bobby*): Do *you* see the point of my story?

(*Bobby shakes his head.*)

Well, maybe I don't either.

LEONA: Then why'd you tell it?

QUENTIN: What is the thing that you mustn't lose in this world before you're ready to leave it? The one thing you mustn't lose ever?

LEONA: . . . Love?

(*Quentin laughs.*)

BOBBY: Interest?

QUENTIN: That's closer, much closer. Yes, that's almost it. The word that I had in mind is surprise, though. The capacity for being surprised. I've lost the capacity for being surprised, so completely lost it, that if I woke up in my bedroom late some night and saw that fantastic fish swimming right over my head, I wouldn't be really surprised.

LEONA: You mean you'd think you were dreaming?

QUENTIN: Oh, no. Wide awake. But not really surprised. (*The special spot concentrates on him. The bar dims, but an eerie glow should remain on the sailfish over the bar.*) There's a coarseness, a deadening coarseness, in the experience of most homosexuals. The experiences are quick, and hard, and brutal, and the pattern of them is practically unchanging. Their act of love is like the jabbing of a hypodermic needle to which they're addicted but which is more and more empty of real interest and surprise. This lack of variation and surprise in their . . . "love life" . . . (*He smiles harshly.*) . . . spreads into other areas of . . . "sensibility?" (*He smiles again.*) . . . Yes, once, quite a long while ago, I was often startled by the sense of being alive, of being *myself, living!* Present on earth, in the flesh, yes, for some completely mysterious reason, a single, separate, intensely conscious being, *myself: living!* . . . Whenever I would feel this . . . *feeling*, this . . . shock of . . . what? . . . self-realization? . . . I would be stunned, I would be thunderstruck by it. And by the existence of everything that exists, I'd be lightning-struck with astonishment . . . it would do more than astound me, it would give me a feeling of panic, the sudden sense of . . . I suppose it was like an epileptic seizure, except that I didn't fall to the ground in convulsions; no, I'd be more apt to try to lose myself in a crowd on a street until the seizure was finished . . . They were dangerous seizures. One time I drove into the mountains and smashed the car into a tree, and I'm not sure if I *meant* to do that, or . . . In a forest you'll sometimes see a giant tree, several hundred years old, that's scarred, that's blazed by lightning, and the wound is almost obscured by the obstinately still living and growing bark. I wonder if such a tree has learned the same lesson that I have, not to feel astonishment any more but just go on, continue for two or three hundred years more? . . . This boy I picked up tonight, the kid from the tall corn country, still has the capacity for being surprised by what he sees, hears and feels in this kingdom of earth. All the way up the canyon to my place, he kept saying, *I can't believe it, I'm here, I've come to the Pacific, the world's greatest ocean!* . . . as if nobody, Magellan or Balboa or even the Indians had ever seen it before him; yes, like he'd discovered this ocean, the largest on earth, and so now, because he'd found it himself, it existed, now, for the first time, never before . . . And this excitement of his reminded me of my having lost the ability to say: "My God!" instead of just: "Oh, well." I've asked all the questions, shouted them at deaf heaven, till I was hoarse in the voice box and blue in the face, and gotten no answer, not the whisper of one, nothing at all, you see, but the sun coming up each morning and going down that night, and the galaxies of the night sky trooping onstage like chorines, robot chorines: one, two, three, kick, one two, three, kick . . . Repeat any question too often and what do you get, what's given? . . . A big carved rock by the desert, a . . . monumental symbol of worn-out passion

and bewilderment in you, a stupid stone paralyzed sphinx
that knows no answers that you don't but comes on like
the oracle of all time, waiting on her belly to give out some
outcries of universal wisdom, and if she woke up some midnight at the edge of the desert and saw that fantastic fish
swimming over her head . . . y'know what she'd say, too?
She'd say: "Oh, well" . . . and go back to sleep for another
five thousand years. (*He turns back; and the bar is relighted.
He returns to the table and adjusts his neck-scarf as he speaks
to Bobby.*) . . . Your bicycle's still in my car. Shall I put it on
the sidewalk?

BOBBY: I'll go get it.

QUENTIN: No. You will find it here, by the door. (*Desires no
further exposure to Bobby.*)

LEONA (*to Bobby*): Stay here awhile . . . Set down. He wants
to escape.

BOBBY: From me? (*Meaning "Why?"*)

LEONA (*visibly enchanted by Bobby, whom she associates with her
lost brother*): Maybe more from himself. Stay here awhile.

BOBBY: . . . It's . . . late for the road. (*But he may resume his
seat here.*)

LEONA: On a bike, yeh, too late, with the dreaded fog people
out. Y'know, I got a suggestion. It's sudden but it's terrific.
(*She leans across the table, urgently.*) Put your bike in my
trailer. It's got two bunks.

BOBBY: Thank you but . . .

LEONA: It wouldn't cost you nothing and we'd be company
for each other. My trailer's not ordinary, it's a Fonda deluxe,
stereo with two speakers, color TV with an eight-inch
screen, touchamatic, and baby, you don't look well fed. I'm
a hell of a cook, could qualify as a pro in that line, too.

BILL (*to Steve*): What a desperate pitch. I was the wrong sex.
She wants a fruit in her stinkin' trailer.

LEONA: Nothing stunk in my trailer but what's out now . . .
He can't understand a person wanting to give protection to
another, it's past his little reception. (*To Bobby*) Why're you
staring out into space with visibility zero?

BOBBY (*slowly, with a growing ardor*): I've got a lot of important things to think over alone, new things. I feel new
vibes, vibrations, I've got to sort out alone.

LEONA: Mexico's a dangerous country for you, and there's lonely stretches of road . . . (*She's thinking of herself, too.*)

BOBBY (*firmly but warmly to her*): Yes . . . I need that, now.

LEONA: Baby, are you scared I'd put the make on you?

(*Bill grunts contemptuously but with the knowledge that he is now truly evicted.*)

I don't, like they say, come on heavy . . . never, not with . . . (*She lightly touches Bobby's hand on the table.*) *This* is my touch! Is it *heavy*?

(*Bobby rises. Quentin is seen dimly, setting the bicycle at the door.*)

BOBBY: That man didn't come on heavy. (*Looking out at Quentin.*) His hand on my knee was just a human touch and it seemed natural to me to return it.

LEONA: Baby, his hand had . . . ambitions . . . And, oh, my God, you've got the skin and hair of my brother and even almost the eyes!

BILL: Can he play the fiddle?

BOBBY: In Goldenfield, Iowa, there was a man like that, ran a flower shop with a back room, decorated Chinese, with incense and naked pictures, which he invited boys into. I heard about it. Well, things like that aren't tolerated for long in towns like Goldenfield. There's suspicion and talk and then public outrage and action, and he had to leave so quick he didn't clear out the shop. (*The bar lights have faded out, and the special spot illuminates Bobby.*) A bunch of us entered one night. The drying-up flowers rattled in the wind and the wind-chimes tinkled and the . . . naked pictures were just . . . pathetic, y'know. Except for a sketch of Michelangelo's David. I don't think anyone noticed me snatch it off the wall and stuff it into my pocket. Dreams . . . images . . . nights . . . On the plains of Nebraska I passed a night with a group of runaway kids my age and it got cold after sunset. A lovely wild young girl invited me under a blanket with just a smile, and then a boy, me between, and both of them kept saying "love," one of 'em in one ear and one in the other, till I didn't know which was which "love" in which ear or which . . .

touch . . . The plain was high and the night air . . . exhilarating and the touches not heavy . . . The man with the hangup has set my bike by the door. (*Extends his hand to Leona. The bar is relighted.*) It's been a pleasure to meet a lady like you. Oh, I've got a lot of new adventures, experiences, to think over alone on my speed iron. I think I'll drive all night, I don't feel tired. (*Bobby smiles as he opens the door and nods good-bye to Monk's Place.*)

LEONA: Hey, Iowa to Mexico, the money . . . here's the money! (*She rushes to the door, but Bobby is gone with his bicycle.*)

BILL: He don't want a lousy five bucks, he wants everything in the wallet. He'll roll the faggot and hop back on his bike looking sweet and innocent as her brother fiddling in church.

(*Leona rushes out, calling.*)

STEVE: The Coast is overrun with 'em, they come running out here like animals out of a brushfire.

MONK (*as he goes to each table, collecting the empty cans and bottles, emptying ash trays on a large serving tray*): I've got no moral objections to them as a part of humanity, but I don't encourage them here. One comes in, others follow. First thing you know you're operating what they call a gay bar and it sounds like a bird cage, they're standing three deep at the bar and lining up at the men's room. Business is terrific for a few months. Then in comes the law. The place is raided, the boys hauled off in the wagon, and your place is padlocked. And then a cop or gangster pays you a social visit, big smile, all buddy-buddy. You had a good thing going, a real swinging place, he tells you, but you needed protection. He offers you protection and you buy it. The place is reopened and business is terrific a few months more. And then? It's raided again, and the next time it's reopened, you pay out of your nose, your ears, and your ass. Who wants it? I don't want it. I want a small steady place that I can handle alone, that brings in a small, steady profit. No buddy-buddy association with gangsters and the police. I want to know the people that come in my place so well I can serve them their brand of liquor or beer before they name it, soon as they come in the door. And all their personal problems, I want to know that, too.

(*Violet begins to hum softly, swaying to and fro like a water plant.*
(*When Monk finishes cleaning off the tables, he returns behind the bar. The bar lights dim, and his special spot comes up.*)

I'm fond of, I've got an affection for, a sincere interest in my regular customers here. They send me post cards from wherever they go and tell me what's new in their lives and I am interested in it. Just last month one of them I hadn't seen in about five years, he died in Mexico City and I was notified of the death and that he'd willed me all he owned in the world, his personal effects and a two-hundred-fifty-dollar savings account in a bank. A thing like that is beautiful as music. These things, these people, take the place of a family in my life. I love to come down those steps from my room to open the place for the evening, and when I've closed for the night, I love climbing back up those steps with my can of Ballantine's ale, and the stories, the jokes, the confidences and confessions I've heard that night, it makes me feel not alone . . . I've had heart attacks, and I'd be a liar to say they didn't scare me and don't still scare me. I'll die some night up those steps, I'll die in the night alone, and I hope it don't wake me up, that I just slip away, quietly.

(*Leona has returned. The light in the bar comes up but remains at a low level.*)

LEONA: . . . Is there a steam engine in here? Did somebody drive in here on a steam engine while I was out?
MONK (*returning from his meditation*): . . . Did what?
LEONA: I hear something going huff-huff like an old locomotive pulling into a station. (*She is referring to a sound like a panting dog. It comes from Bill at the unlighted table where Violet is seated between him and Steve.*) . . . Oh, well, my home is on wheels . . . Bourbon sweet, Monk.
MONK: Leona, you don't need another.

LEONA: Monk, it's after midnight, my brother's death-day is over, I'll be all right, don't worry. (*She goes to the bar.*) . . . It was selfish of me to wish he was still alive.

(*A pin-spot of light picks up Violet's tear-stained and tranced face at the otherwise dark table.*)

. . . She's got some form of religion in her hands . . .

Curtain

ACT II

An hour later. "Group singing" is in progress at the table stage right. Leona is not participating. She is sitting moodily at the bar facing front.

VIOLET: "I don't want to set the world on fii-yuh."
STEVE: "I don't want to set the world on fii-yuh."
VIOLET: I like old numbers best. Here's an oldie that I learned from my mother. (*She rises and assumes a sentimental look.*)
       "Lay me where sweet flowers blos-som,
         Where the dainty lily blows
         Where the pinks and violets min-gle,
         Lay me underneath the rose."
LEONA: Shit. Y'don't need a rose to lay her, you could lay her under a cactus and she wouldn't notice the diff-rence.

(*Bill crosses to the bar for a beer.*)

I guess you don't think I'm serious about it, hitting the highway tonight.

(*Bill shrugs and crosses to a downstage table.*)

Well, I am, I'm serious about it. (*She sits at his table.*) An experienced expert beautician can always get work anywhere.
BILL: Your own appearance is a bad advertisement for your line of work.

LEONA: I don't care how I look as long as I'm clean and decent . . . and *self-supporting*. When I haul into a new town, I just look through the yellow pages of the telephone directory and pick out a beauty shop that's close to my trailer camp. I go to the shop and offer to work a couple of days for nothing, and after that couple of days I'm in like Flynn, and on my own terms, which is fifty per cent of charges for all I do, and my tips, of course, too. They like my work and they like my personality, my approach to customers. I keep them laughing.

BILL: You keep me laughing, too.

LEONA: . . . Of course, there's things about you I'll remember with pleasure, such as waking up sometimes in the night and looking over the edge of the upper bunk to see you asleep in the lower. (*Bill leaves the table. She raises her voice to address the bar-at-large.*) Yeah, he slept in the lower 'cause when he'd passed out or nearly, it would of taken a derrick to haul him into the upper bunk. So I gave him the lower bunk and took the upper myself.

BILL: As if you never pass out. Is that the idea you're selling?

LEONA: When I pass out I wake up in a chair or on the floor, oh, no, the floor was good enough for me in your opinion, and sometimes you stepped on me even, yeah, like I was a rug or a bug, because your nature is selfish. You think because you've lived off one woman after another woman after eight or ten women you're something superior, special. Well, you're special but not superior, baby. I'm going to worry about you after I've gone and I'm sure as hell leaving tonight, fog or no fog on the highway, but I'll worry about you because you refuse to grow up and that's a mistake that you make, because you can only refuse to grow up for a limited period in your lifetime and get by with it . . . I *loved* you! . . . I'm not going to cry. It's only being so tired that makes me cry.

(*Violet starts weeping for her.*)

VIOLET: Bill, get up and tell Leona good-bye. She's a lonely girl without a soul in the world.

LEONA: I've got the world in the world, and McCorkle don't have to make the effort to get himself or any part of him up, it's easier to stay down. And as for being lonely, listen, ducks, that applies to every mother's son and daughter of us alive, we were given warning of that before we were born almost, and yet . . . When I come to a new place, it takes me two or three weeks, that's all it takes me, to find somebody to live with in my home on wheels and to find a night spot to hang out in. Those first two or three weeks are rough, sometimes I wish I'd stayed where I was before, but I know from experience that I'll find somebody and locate a night spot to booze in, and get acquainted with . . . friends . . . (*The light has focused on her. She moves down-stage with her hands in her pockets, her face and voice very grave as if she were less confident that things will be as she says.*) And then, all at once, something wonderful happens. All the past disappointments in people I left behind me, just disappear, evaporate from my mind, and I just remember the good things, such as their sleeping faces, and . . . Life! Life! I never just said, "Oh, well," I've always said "Life!" to life, like a song to God, too, because I've lived in my lifetime and not been afraid of . . . changes . . . (*She goes back to the bar.*) . . . However, y'see, I've got this pride in my nature. When I live with a person I love and care for in my life, I expect his respect, and when I see I've lost it, I GO, GO! . . . So a home on wheels is the only right home for me.

(*Violet starts toward Leona.*)

What is she doing here?

(*Violet has weaved to the bar.*)

Hey! What are *you* doing here?
VIOLET: You're the best friend I ever had, the best friend I . . .
(*She sways and sobs like a* religieuse *in the grip of a vision.*)
LEONA: What's that, what're you saying?

(*Violet sobs.*)

She can't talk. What was she saying?
VIOLET: . . . BEST . . . !
LEONA: WHAT?
VIOLET: . . . *Friend!*

LEONA: I'd go further than that, I'd be willing to bet I'm the *only* friend that you've had, and the next time you come down sick nobody will bring you nothing, no chicken, no hot beef bouillon, no chinaware, no silver, and no interest and concern about your condition, and you'll die in your rattrap with no human voice, just bang, bang, bang from the bowling alley and billiards. And when you die you should feel a relief from the conditions you lived in. Now I'm leaving you two suffering, bleeding hearts together, I'm going to sit at the bar. I had a Italian boy friend that taught me a saying, *"Meglior solo que mal accompanota,"* which means that you're better alone than in the company of a bad companion.

(*She starts to the bar, as Doc enters.*)

Back already, huh? It didn't take you much time to deliver the baby. Or did you bury the baby? Or did you bury the mother? Or did you bury them both, the mother and baby?

DOC (*to Monk*): Can you shut up this woman?

LEONA: Nobody can shut up this woman. Quack, quack, quack, Doctor Duck, quack, quack, quack, quack, quack!

DOC: I'M A LICENSED PHYSICIAN!

LEONA: SHOW *me your license. I'll shut up when I see it!*

DOC: A doctor's license to practice isn't the size of a drunken driver's license, you don't put it in a wallet, you hang it on the wall of your office.

LEONA: Here is your office! Which wall is your license hung on? Beside the sailfish or where? Where is your license to practice hung up, in the gents', with other filthy scribbles?!

MONK: Leona, you said your brother's death-day was over and I thought you meant you were . . .

LEONA: THOUGHT I MEANT I WAS *WHAT*?

MONK: You were ready to cool it. BILL! . . . Take Leona home, now.

LEONA: Christ, do you think I'd let him come near me?! Or near my trailer?! Tonight?! (*She slaps the bar several times with her sailor cap, turning to the right and left as if to ward off assailants, her great bosom heaving, a jungle-look in her eyes.*)

VIOLET: Steve, if we don't go now the King-burger stand will shut on us, and I've had nothing but liquids on my stomach all day. So I need a Whopper tonight.

(*Bill laughs.*)

STEVE: You'll get a hot dog with chili and everything on the way home. Get me . . . get me . . . get me. Grab and grope. You disgrace me! . . . your habits.

VIOLET: You're underdeveloped and you blame me.

LEONA (*looking out*): Yes . . . (*She slaps something with her cap.*) Yes!

VIOLET: What did she mean by that? Another sarcastic crack?

LEONA: When I say "yes" it is not sarcastic . . . It means a decision to act.

MONK: The place is closing so will everybody get themselves together now, please.

VIOLET: I do have to have something solid. Too much liquids and not enough solids in the system upsets the whole system. Ask the Doc if it don't. Doc, don't it upset the system, liquids without solids? All day long?

(*Doc has been sunk in profoundly dark and private reflections. He emerges momentarily to reply to Violet's direct question.*)

DOC: If that's a professional question to a doctor whose office is here . . . (*A certain ferocity is boiling in him and directed mostly at himself.*) My fee is . . . another brandy. (*He turns away with a short, disgusted laugh.*)

MONK: Something wrong, Doc?

(*Violet has crossed to Bill, as a child seeking protection.*)

DOC: Why, no, what could be wrong? But a need to put more liquid in my system . . .

LEONA (*convulsively turning about*): Yes . . . yes! (*This no longer relates to anything but her private decision.*)

BILL (*to himself*): I'm not about to spend the night on the beach . . .

VIOLET (*leaning toward Bill*): I am not neither, so why don't we check in somewhere? Us, two, together?

STEVE: I heard that.

LEONA: Yes . . . *yes!*

MONK: I said the place is closing.

VIOLET: Let's go together, us three, and talk things over at the King-burger stand.

STEVE: Being a cook I know the quality of those giant hamburgers called Whoppers, and they're fit only for dog food.

VIOLET: I think we better leave, now. (*Extends her delicate hands to both men.*) Steve? Bill? (*They all rise unsteadily and prepare to leave.*) Bill, you know I feel so protected now. (*Violet, Steve, and Bill start out.*)

LEONA (*stomping the floor with a powerful foot*): Y' WANT YOUR ASS IN A SLING? BEFORE YOU'RE LAID UNDER THAT ROSE?

VIOLET (*shepherded past Leona by Steve and Bill*): If we don't see you again, good luck wherever you're going.

(*They go out the door.*)

LEONA (*rushing after them*): That's what she wants, she wants her ass in a sling!

(*She rushes out the door. A moment or two later, as Monk looks out, and above the boom of the surf, Violet's histrionically shrill outcries are heard. This is followed by an offstage quarrel between Leona and a night watchman on the beach. Their overlapping, ad-lib dialogue continues in varying intensity as background to the business on stage: "If you don't settle down and come along peaceful-like, I'm going to call the wagon! . . ." "Do that, I just dare you to do it—go on, I just dare you to call the wagon! I want to ride in a wagon—it's got wheels, hasn't it—I'll ride any Goddam thing on wheels! . . ." "Oh, no—listen, lady, what's your name anyhow? . . ." "I'm just the one to do it! . . . I tell you my name? I'm going to tell you my name? What's your name? I want your name! Oh boy, do I want your name! . . ." "Listen, please, come on, now, let's take this thing easy . . ." "I've been drinking in this bar, and it's not the first time you . . ." "Let's go! You raise hell every night! . . ." "Every night! This isn't the first time—I've been meaning to report you! Yes, I'm going to report you! Yes, how's that for a switch? . . ." "I'm just trying to do my duty! . . ." "I live in a home on wheels, and every night you try to molest me when*)

I come home! . . ." "No! You're wrong—you're always in
there drinking and raising hell and . . ." "Yeah, but you let
criminals go free, right? . . ." "No, I don't! . . ." "People
can't walk in the street, murdering, robbing, thieving, and
all I do is have a few Goddam drinks, just because it's my
brother's death-day, so I was showing a little human emotion
—take your hands off me! . . ." "Come on now! . . ." "Don't
you put your hands on a lady like me! . . ." "No, I'm
not! . . ." "I'm a Goddam lady! That's what I am, and you
just lay off! . . ." "I've had enough of this! . . ." "Every
night I come out here, you're looking for free drinks, that's
what's the matter with you! . . ." "I've never had a drink
in my life, lady! . . ." "You never had a drink in your
life! . . ." "No, I haven't, I've . . ." "Show me your identification, that's what I want to see! . . ." "I'm just trying to do
my duty . . ." "Look here, old man . . ." "I don't know why
I have to put up with an old dame like you this way . . ."
"Oh!—Oh!—Why you Goddam son of a! . . ." "Now! . . ."
"Don't you talk to me like that . . ." "I'm not talking to
you, I'm telling you to come over here and let me get you to
the telephone here! . . ." "You've been harassing that man
Monk! . . ." "I'm not harassing anybody! . . ." "You're not
harassing anybody? . . ." "You come over to this Monk's Place
every night and raise hell, the whole damn bunch of you, and
a poor man like me trying to earn a few dollars and make a
living for his old woman and . . ." "Let me see your identification! What precinct are you from? . . ." "Oh, yeah . . ."
"Go on, I want that identification, and I want that uniform
off you, and that badge . . ." "You won't do anything of the
sort! . . ." "Oh, yeah . . ." "Yes, I'm doing my job, what I'm
doing is legal! . . ." "I happen to have more influence up at
that station than you . . . Goddam pig! . . ." "I haven't
done nothing to you, I'm just trying to do my job . . ." "Do
your job? . . ." "Yes, and you're giving me a lot of hard
time! . . ." "There's raping and thieving and criminals and
robbers walking the streets, breaking store fronts, breaking
into every bar . . ." "Well, that's not my—listen, lady! I'm
just the night watchman around this beach here. I'm just on
the beach nights, I don't have anything to do with what's
going on somewhere else in the city, just on this beach! . . ."

"You don't know what's going on on the beach . . ." "I know what's going on on the beach, and it's you and that crowd drinking every night, raising hell! . . ." "We're not raising hell every night! . . ." "If I was your husband, golly, I—I—by God I would take care of you, I wouldn't put up with your likes, you and that crowd drinking every night! . . ." "I like that uniform you've got on you, and I'm gonna have it! . . ." "Why do you have to pick on a little man like me for? . . ." "I've seen you sneaking around, Peeping Tom, that's what you are! . . ." "No, that's not so! . . ." "I've seen you sneaking around looking in ladies' windows . . ." "That's not true! I'm just trying to do my duty! I keep telling you . . ." "Yeah, peeping in windows . . ." "No! . . ." "Watching people undress . . ." "No! You . . ." "I've seen you, you lascivious old man! . . ." "I've seen you taking these young men over to your trailer court and making studs out of them! . . ." "Yeah!—Yeah!—Yeah! Men, that's what I take to my trailer! I wouldn't take a palsied old man like you! . . ." "You know damn well I wasn't trying to get you to . . . ! I was trying to get you to this telephone box, where I was going to! . . ." "You will not be able to, old man! . . ." "Listen, Miss, I asked you to give me your identification! You give me your identification so I can tell who you are! . . ." "I want your identification! I've seen you, I've seen you sneaking around the trailer court, I've seen you looking in windows . . ." "Oh, that's a lie! I never did a thing like that in all my life, I go to church. I'm a good Christian man! . . ." "Oh yeah! Yeah! Yeah! . . ." "I could take you in if I were younger, I wouldn't have to call the highway patrol, but I'm going to do that right now! . . ." "Listen, Holy Willie! I've seen your likes in church before! I wouldn't trust you with a . . ." "A little church wouldn't do you any harm neither! . . ." "Old man . . . Yeah! Yeah! . . ." "I've seen you with those young studs! . . ." "Doesn't that make you excited? . . ." "No, by God, it doesn't! . . ." "Is that your problem? . . ." "No, I don't have none! You're the one with the hang-ups and problems—you are a problem! You hang out here all night in that damn Monk's Place! . . ." "I've got my own man, I don't have to worry about any other man, I got my own man in my trailer! . . ." "Anyone want to spend the night with you, he must be a pig then, he must be *some kind of pig living with you! . . ." "Fat old bag of wind, don't you talk to me! . . ." "Look, I'm tired of talking to you, by God, I've put up with you all I'm going to! I told you I was going to call the highway patrol! . . ." "I've seen the way you look at me when you . . ." "That's a lie!—I never . . ." "Yeah! Yeah! . . ." "I—I . . ." "I've seen you skulking around in the dark, looking in windows! . . ." "I don't need your kind! I've got a good woman at home, and she takes care of me, she takes good care of me! If I can get this job done and you'll just settle down and be quiet, we wouldn't have all this noise! . . ." "Does your wife know about the girls you go out with? . . ." "You're trying to incriminate me! . . ." "Does she know about that? . . ." "I know what you're trying to do . . ." "I've seen you . . ." "Trying to get me in trouble! Trying to get me to lose my job here! . . ." "I know what you holy boys are like! . . ." "Why don't you go back in there and raise some more hell with those young studs? . . ." "I ain't doing that neither . . ." "If you'd be quiet! . . ." "Stop harassing! . . ." "I ain't harassing nothing! . . ." "Every time you want a drink, yes? . . ." "I don't, I don't . . .")*

MONK (*to Doc*): Goddam, she's left her suitcase.

DOC (*musing darkly*): . . . Done what?

MONK: She's left that bag in here, which means she's coming back.

DOC: Aw, yeah, a guarantee of it, she's going to provide you with the solace of her companionship up those stairs to the living quarters. (*He faces out from the bar.*) Y'know, that narrow flight of stairs is like the uterine passage to life, and I'd say that strange, that amorphous-looking creature is expecting to enter the world up the uterine passage to your living quarters above. (*He rises, chuckling darkly.*) Is the toilet repaired in the gents' room?

MONK (*listening to noises outside*): Yeh, plumber fixed it today.

(*Doc sighs and lumbers heavily the way pointed by the chalk-white hand signed "GENTS" off stage right.*

(*Monk crosses to the door to assess the disturbance outside. Bill rushes into the bar.*)

BILL: For Chrissake, get an ambulance with a strait jacket for her.

MONK: You mean you can't hold her, you stupid prick?

BILL: No man can hold that woman when she goes ape. Gimme a dime, I'm gonna call the Star of the Sea psycho ward.

MONK: Don't put a hand on that phone.

(*Violet now rushes in the door. She continues her histrionic outcries.*)

VIOLET: They're callin' the wagon for her, she's like a wild thing out there, lock the door, don't let her at me. Hide me, help me! Please! (*She rushes toward the stairs.*)

MONK: Stay down those stairs, pick up your luggage, I'll . . . I'll . . . call a taxi for you.

VIOLET: Steve done nothin' to . . . nothin' . . . Just run!

(*Altercation rises outside. Violet rushes into the ladies'. Monk closes the door and bolts it. Doc returns from the gents', putting on his jacket. His pant cuffs are wet.*)

DOC: The toilet still overflows.

(*Steve calls at the locked door.*)

STEVE: Vi'let? Monk?

(*Monk admits him. Steve enters with a confused look about, two dripping hot dogs in his hand.*)

STEVE: Vi'let, is Vi'let, did Vi'let get back in here?

MONK: Yeh, she's back in the ladies'. (*Monk closes door.*)

STEVE (*shuffling rapidly to the ladies'*): Vi'let? Vi'let? Hear me?

MONK: No. She don't.

STEVE: Vi'let, the King-burger's closed. So I couldn't get a Whopper . . . I got you two dogs, with chili and sauerkraut. You can come out now, Leona's getting arrested. Violet screamed for help to a cop that hates and hassles me ev'ry time I go home.

MONK: Those dogs you're holding are dripping on the floor.

DOC: Committing a nuisance . . .

STEVE: Vi'let, the dogs'll turn cold, the chili's dripping off 'em. You can't stay all night in a toilet, Vi'let.

VIOLET (*from the ladies'*): I can, I will, go away.

STEVE: She says she's gonna stay all night in a toilet. Wow . . . I mean . . . wow. (*Starts eating one of the hot dogs with a slurping sound.*)

MONK: If she's called the law here I want her to shut up in there.

STEVE: Vi'let, shut up in there. Come out for your dog.

VIOLET: Take your dog away and leave me alone. You give me no protection and no support a'tall.

(*Doc utters a laugh that is dark with an ultimate recognition of human absurdity and his own self-loathing.*)

MONK (*touching his chest*): . . . Doc? . . . Have a nightcap with me.

DOC: Thanks, Monk, I could use one.

MONK (*leaning back in chair and tapping his upper abdomen*): Angina or gastritis, prob'ly both.

DOC: In that location, it's gas.

MONK: What happened at Treasure Island?

DOC (*sipping his "shot"*): Tell you when I . . . get this . . . down.

BILL: Time . . . runs out with one and you go to another. Got a call from a woman guv'ment employee in Sacramento. She's got a co-op in a high-rise condominium, lives so high on the hog with payoffs an' all she can't see ground beneath her.

MONK: Why're you shouting, at who?

BILL: Nobody's ever thrown McCorkle out.

MONK: Unusual and not expected things can happen.

(*Leona is heard from off stage: "Okay, you make your phone call, and I'll make mine."*)

So, Doc, how'd it go at the trailer camp?

(*He and Doc are seated in profile at the downstage table. Steve and Bill are silhouetted at the edge of the lighted area.*)

DOC: The birth of the baby was at least three months premature, so it was born dead, of course, and just beginning to look like a human baby . . . The man living with the woman in the trailer said, "Don't let her see it, get it out of the trailer." I agreed with the man that she shouldn't see it, so I put this fetus in a shoe box . . . (*He speaks with diffi-culty, as if compelled to.*) The trailer was right by the beach, the tide was coming in with heavy surf, so I put the shoe box . . . and contents . . . where the tide would take it.

MONK: . . . Are you sure that was legal?

DOC: Christ, no, it wasn't legal . . . I'd barely set the box down when the man came out shouting for me. The woman had started to hemorrhage. When I went back in the trailer, she was bleeding to death. The man hollered at me, "Do something, can't you do something for her!"

MONK: . . . Could you?

DOC: . . . I could have told the man to call an ambulance for her, but I thought of the probable consequences to me, and while I thought about that, the woman died. She was a small woman, but not small enough to fit in a shoe box, so I . . . I gave the man a fifty-dollar bill that I'd received today for performing an abortion. I gave it to him in return for his promise not to remember my name . . . (*He reaches for the bottle. His hand shakes so that he can't refill his shot-glass. Monk fills it for him.*) . . . You see, I can't make out certificates of death, since I have no legal right any more to practice medicine, Monk.

MONK: . . . In the light of what happened, there's something I'd better tell you, Doc. Soon as you left here to deliver that baby, Leona ran out of the bar to make a phone call to the office at Treasure Island, warning them that you were on your way out there to deliver a baby. So, Doc, you may be in trouble . . . If you stay here . . .

DOC: I'll take a Benzedrine tablet and pack and . . .

MONK: Hit the road before morning.

DOC: I'll hit the road tonight.

MONK: Don't let it hit you. (*Stands to shake.*) G'bye, Doc. Keep in touch.

DOC: G'bye, Monk. Thanks for all and the warning.

MONK: Take care, Doc.

STEVE: Yeh, Doc, you got to take care. Bye, Doc.

BILL: No sweat, Doc, g'bye.

(*Doc exits.*)

MONK: That old son of a bitch's paid his dues . . .

(*Altercation rises outside once more: "I'm gonna slap the cuffs on you! . . ." "That does it, let go of me, you fink, you pig!" Approach of a squad car siren is heard at a distance.*)

Yep, coming the law!

BILL: I don't want in on this.

STEVE: Not me neither.

(*They rush out. Squad car screeches to a stop. Leona appears at the door, shouting and pounding.*)

LEONA: MONK! THE PADDY WAGON IS SINGING MY SONG!

(*Monk lets her in and locks the door.*)

MONK: Go upstairs. Can you make it?

(*She clambers up the steps, slips, nearly falls.*
(*Policeman knocks at the door. Monk admits him.*)

Hi, Tony.

TONY: Hi, Monk. What's this about a fight going on here, Monk?

MONK: Fight? Not here. It's been very peaceful tonight. The bar is closed. I'm sitting here having a nightcap with . . .

TONY: Who's that bawling back there?

MONK (*pouring a drink for Tony*): Some dame disappointed in love, the usual thing. Try this and if it suits you, take the bottle.

TONY (*He drinks.*): . . . O.K. Good.

MONK: Take the bottle. Drop in more often. I miss you.

TONY: Thanks, g'night. (*He goes out.*)

MONK: Coast is clear, Leona. (*As Monk puts another bottle on the table, Leona comes awkwardly back down the stairs.*)

LEONA: Monk? Thanks, Monk. (*She and Monk sit at the table. Violet comes out of the ladies' room.*)

VIOLET: Steve? . . . Bill? (*She sees Leona at the table and starts to retreat.*)

LEONA: Aw, hell, Violet. Come over and sit down with us, we're having a nightcap, all of us, my brother's death-day is over.

VIOLET: Why does everyone hate me? (*She sits at the table: drinks are poured from the bottle. Violet hitches her chair close to Monk's. In a few moments she will deliberately drop a matchbook under the table, bend to retrieve it, and the hand on Monk's side will not return to the table surface.*)

LEONA: Nobody hates you, Violet. It would be a compliment to you if they did.

VIOLET: I'd hate to think that I'd come between you and Bill.

LEONA: Don't torture yourself with an awful thought like that. Two people living together is something you don't understand, and since you don't understand it you don't respect it, but, Violet, this being our last conversation, I want to advise something to you. I think you need medical help in the mental department and I think this because you remind me of a . . . of a . . . of a plant of some kind . . .

VIOLET: Because my name is Violet?

LEONA: No, I wasn't thinking of violets, I was thinking of water plants, yeah, plants that don't grow in the ground but float on water. With you everything is such a . . . such a . . . well, you know what I mean, don't you?

VIOLET: Temporary arrangement?

LEONA: Yes, you could put it that way. Do you know how you got into that place upstairs from the amusement arcade?

VIOLET: . . . How?

LEONA: Yes, *how* or *why* or *when?*

VIOLET: . . . Why, I . . . (*She obviously is uncertain on all three points.*)

LEONA: Take your time. And *think.* How, why, when?

VIOLET: Why, I was . . . in L.A., and . . .

LEONA: Are you sure you were in L.A.? Are you sure about even that? Or is everything foggy to you, is your mind in a cloud?

VIOLET: Yes, I was . . .

LEONA: I said take your time, don't push it. Can you come out of the fog?

MONK: Leona, take it easy, we all know Violet's got problems.

LEONA: Her problems are mental problems and I want her to face them, now, in our last conversation. Violet? Can you come out of the fog and tell us how, when, and why you're living out of a suitcase upstairs from the amusement arcade, can you just . . .

MONK: (*cutting in*): She's left the amusement arcade, she left it tonight, she came here with her suitcase.

LEONA: Yeah, she's a water plant, with roots in water, drifting the way it takes her.

(*Violet weeps.*)

And she cries too easy, the water works are back on. I'll give her some music to cry to before I go back to my home on wheels and get it cracking up the Old Spanish Trail. (*She rises from the table.*)

MONK: Not tonight, Leona. You have to sleep off your liquor before you get on the highway in this fog.

LEONA: That's what you think, not what I think, Monk. My time's run out in this place. (*She has walked to the juke box and started the violin piece.*) . . . How, when, and why, and her only answer is tears. Couldn't say how, couldn't say when, couldn't say why. And I don't think she's sure where she was before she come here, any more sure than she is where she'll go when she leaves here. She don't dare remember and she don't dare look forward, neither. Her mind floats on a cloud and her body floats on water. And her dirty fingernail hands reach out to hold onto something she hopes can hold her together. (*She starts back toward the table, stops; the bar dims and light is focused on her.*) . . . Oh, my God, she's at it again, she got a hand under the table. (*Leona laughs sadly.*) Well, I guess she can't help it. It's sad, though. It's a pitiful thing to have to reach under a table to find some reason to live. You know, she's worshipping her idea of God Almighty in her personal church. Why the hell should I care she done it to a nowhere person that I put up in my trailer for a few months? I wish that kid from I-oh-a with eyes like my lost brother had been willing to travel with me, but I guess I scared him. What I think I'll do is turn back to a faggot's moll when I haul up to Sausalito or San Francisco. You always find one in the gay bars that needs a big sister with him, to camp with and laugh and cry with, and I hope I'll find one soon . . . it scares me to be alone in my home on wheels built for two . . . (*She turns as the bar is lighted and goes back to the table.*) Monk, HEY, MONK! What's my tab here t'night?

MONK: Forget it, don't think about it, go home and sleep, Leona. (*He and Violet appear to be in a state of trance together.*)

LEONA: I'm not going to sleep and I never leave debts behind me. This twenty ought to do it. (*She places a bill on the table.*)

MONK: Uh-huh, sure, keep in touch . . .

LEONA: Tell Bill he'll find his effects in the trailer-court office, and when he's hustled himself a new meal ticket, he'd better try and respect her, at least in public. . . . Well . . . (*She extends her hand slightly. Monk and Violet are sitting with closed eyes.*) . . . I guess I've already gone.

VIOLET: G'bye, Leona.

MONK: G'bye . . .

LEONA: "Meglior solo," huh, ducks? (*Leona lets herself out of the bar.*)

MONK: . . . G'bye, Leona.

VIOLET: . . . Monk?

MONK (*correctly suspecting her intent*): You want your suitcase, it's . . .

VIOLET: I don't mean my suitcase, nothing valuable's in it but my . . . undies and . . .

MONK: Then what've you got in mind?

VIOLET: . . . In *what*?

MONK: Sorry. No offense meant. But there's taverns licensed for rooms, and taverns licensed for liquor and food and liquor, and I am a tavern only licensed for . . .

VIOLET (*overlapping with a tone and gesture of such ultimate supplication that it would break the heart of a stone*): I just meant . . . let's go upstairs. Huh? Monk? (*Monk stares at her reflectively for a while, considering all the potential complications of her taking up semi- or permanent residence up there.*) Why're you looking at me that way? I just want a temporary, a night, a . . .

MONK: . . . Yeah, go on up and make yourself at home. Take a shower up there while I lock up the bar.

VIOLET: God love you, Monk, like me. (*She crosses, with a touch of "labyrinthitis," to the stairs and mounts two steps.*) Monk! . . . I'm scared of these stairs, they're almost steep as a ladder. I better take off my slippers. Take my slippers off for me. (*There is a tone in her voice that implies she has already "moved in" . . . She holds out one leg from the steps, then the other. Monk removes her slippers and she goes on up, calling down to him:*) Bring up some beer, sweetheart.

MONK: Yeh, I'll bring some beer up. Don't forget your shower. (*Alone in the bar, Monk crosses downstage.*) I'm going to stay down here till I hear that shower running, I am not going up there till she's took a shower. (*He sniffs the ratty slipper.*) Dirty, worn-out slipper still being worn, sour-smelling with sweat from being worn too long, but still set by the bed to be worn again the next day, walked on here and there on—pointless—errands till the sole's worn through, and even then not thrown away, just padded with cardboard till the cardboard's worn through and still not thrown away, still put on to walk on till it's . . . past all repair . . . (*He has been, during this, turning out lamps in the bar.*) Hey, Violet, will you for Chrissake take a . . . (*This shouted appeal breaks off with a disgusted laugh. He drops the slipper, then grins sadly.*) She probably thinks she'd dissolve in water. I shouldn't of let her stay here. Well, I won't touch her, I'll have no contact with her, maybe I won't even go up there tonight. (*He crosses to open the door. We hear the boom of the ocean outside.*) I always leave the door open for a few minutes to clear the smoke and liquor smell out of the place, the human odors, and to hear the ocean. Y'know, it sounds different this late than it does with the crowd on the beach-front. It has a private sound to it, a sound that's just for itself and for me. (*Monk switches off the blue neon sign. It goes dark outside. He closes door.*)

(*Sound of water running above. He slowly looks toward the sound.*)

That ain't rain.

(*Tired from the hectic night, maybe feeling a stitch of pain in his heart [but he's used to that], Monk starts to the stairs. In the spill of light beneath them, he glances up with a slow smile, wry, but not bitter. A smile that's old too early, but it grows a bit warmer as he starts up the stairs.*)

Curtain

NOTES AFTER THE SECOND
INVITED AUDIENCE:
(And a Troubled Sleep.)

THE play has drifted out of focus: I was almost inclined to think, "My God, this is a play about groping!"

The production of this play, and I think the play itself, deserves something better than that. The designer, the lighting and sound men, have caught perfectly the mood, the poetry, the ambience of the play.

But unfortunately in performance that lyricism—which is, as always, what I must chiefly rely upon as a playwright—is not being fully explored and utilized. At this moment, I must make a number of exceptions which will be made privately: I would say, however, to all the cast that at last night's performance the only parts that were totally and beautifully realized were those of "Doc," "Steve," "Quentin," and "Bobby."

We have now arrived at a point where we must approach this undertaking with the same seriousness—and I do not mean ponderousness but the opposite of ponderousness—that I had buried somewhere in me, beneath the liquor and the drugs that made my life a death-time in the late sixties; a sort of lyric appeal to my remnant of life to somehow redeem and save me—not from life's end, which can't be revealed through any court of appeals, but from a sinking into shadow and eclipse of so much of everything that had made my life meaningful to me.

I am sorry to return to a self-concerned note. Believe me, my concern is now much broader than self-concern, and in this particular instance, the case of this play and its players and its producers and its artists—which all of you certainly are (I doubt that you can believe how much I care for each of you as a person, and with the truest and purest kind of caring)—I would set down as an axiom that a playwright should never direct his work unassisted by someone who shares his concept but is better able to implement it through discipline.

The word "discipline" is not a pretty word to bring up at this point, and yet it must be. I am too old a hand at the abuse of self-discipline to fail to recognize a failure of self-discipline when I see it so nakedly on a stage before audiences.

The clinical name for this failure to discipline the self to achieve its goal is "the impulse toward self-destruction," which is the opposite and dark side of the will to create and to flower.

Self-transcendence, as well as self-discipline, is now in order. Each of us must put aside as best we can his and her personal stake in this adventure, this play, in order to serve its true creation as a whole. Ensemble and entity must take precedence, now, over that Mae West line to her manager, "How did the lady come on tonight?"—the wonderful bitch did not expect to receive a negative response, and she never got one, but it's a pity he didn't catch her act in the "Breckinridge" comeback. Or speak up about it.

Now to specifics about *Small Craft Warnings*:

I know that our designer, Fred Voelpel, will move that sailfish about a foot and a half out from the wall of the bar and have it suspended over the bar directly, with always just a bit of a light on its astonished expression. This will not upstage but will just provide a muted but persistent key to the tender irony which is the keynote to the still-possible success of this play.

Right now what troubles me most—in the way of specific staging and writing—is that, as physical climaxes to both acts, we have such closely corresponding chase-scenes of Violet by Leona. Of course this could be solved by returning to the opening of *Confessional* and starting the play with Violet wailing in the ladies' room and Leona pacing about in the middle of a tirade. This would eliminate one chase scene. However, it would also eliminate the establishment of place, situation, and identification of characters. And, incidentally, it would finally persuade me that I am no longer able to write a Goddam thing for the American theatre.

The other option—which I hope we can take—is to sharply differentiate the second chase scene from the first. I love the return of Steve and Bill, but I don't like the total absence of a "rhubarb" on the beach until the squad car siren is heard. I think something better than this can somehow be managed for us. I think that Leona has been in furious altercation with a cop or watchman on the beach-front all this time, and the sound of it should "bleed under" like the lights "bleed under" Doc's big monologue. But let us be aware it is going on out there, although—for the uses of a really not literal or naturalistic play—it is faded under the monologue till that has scored for us and is then brought up again a few beats preceding Leona's rush back into the bar, because the beach cop has finally had to call the wagon for her.

For a while, let Leona ad-lib the altercation outside at a level set by the director—and meanwhile, I will write it. Let's say, for the moment, it goes something like this:

LEONA: Okay, do that! I just dare you to do that! Call the wagon! I'm willing to ride in a wagon! It's got wheels, I'll ride in any Goddam thing on wheels, I'm just the one to do it! Okay? Want to call the wagon out here for me? What are you waiting for? Me to go? Oh, no, I'm not going yet. Take your hand off my arm, you fuckin' pig! Don't put your hand on the arm of a lady! (*Sound of a slap: then Bill rushes back in to make his phone call.*)

I think that there can be an interior of bar "hold" for this loud outside altercation between Leona and the beach cop right after Monk calls Doc over to the table: he can do this before Bill and Steve enter. And there can be a dramatic tension in Doc's unreadiness to tell of the disasters at Treasure Island for the time that Leona's off-stage rhubarb with the beach cop is heard. At the end of the Doc's story and just after his exit, Leona's voice can be heard again, continuing her rhubarb with the beach cop: "All right, I'm waiting, I am standing here waiting till that wagon gets here"—then the siren begins:

LEONA: That does it, let go of me, you fink, you pig!" (*Having struggled free of the beach cop's clasp on her arm, she now charges back into the bar, crying out:*) MONK! THE PADDY-WAGON IS SINGING MY SONG!

And let us please have "singing," not "playing."
Other specifics:
I think I've already gotten across to you the necessity of building up those elements in the play not concerned with

the groin and the groping so that the audiences will recognize that this is not a sordid piece of writing. Now I think—with the exception of "Steve"—everybody in the cast—except "Monk" and "Doc"—is giving us a Bowery drunk bit, and that's not where the play's at. We don't want to sit out there looking at "vulnerable human vessels" that can touch us with their individual hearts, each at a time of crisis that compels it to cry out.

Finally, unless there's a sudden upsurge of energies and of selective focus, I think we need a later opening than is now scheduled.* I have always opposed an Easter Sunday opening for very personal but understandable reasons. Now I oppose it for reasons that seem almost desperately practical. The play strikes me as inviting disaster unless it is given time to pull itself together from its present state—and I gravely doubt that four more days are enough. It seems to me that the book has to be studied till there is no longer any groping after lines. Till mugging is not substituted for the delivery of the right ones.

I have always suspected that actors regard playwrights as hostile beings, and this has always made me shy around them. I hope you prove me wrong, since we are all sitting together in this small craft and have been warned by two audiences that the sea is very rough.

However, at this moment I prefer the *Marseillaise* to "extreme unction."

Corággio!

T.W.

*Sunday, April 2, 1972.

OUT CRY

"A garden enclosed is my sister . . ."
Song of Solomon, 4:6

DEDICATED TO THE LADY MARIA ST. JUST

A DISPENSABLE FOREWORD

Having the necessary arrogance to assume that a failed production of a play is not necessarily a failed play, I have prepared this new version for publication and subsequent reappearance on other stages.

Here it is, the play, subject to your appraisal upon the printed page, under the distinguished imprimatur of my most loyal advocate in the world of letters, the publishing house of New Directions.

And as for my depression over the failed production, I think it is temporary, a nervous phenomenon responsive to the treatment of a long ocean voyage with an "outside cabin" —slowly West by way of East, a time to get it together, all of it, the memoirs, the new play, and myself.

Hopefully or *Deo volente*, as my grandfather used to say when setting out on a journey in his nineties, the cry is still *en avant*.

T.W.
1973

SYNOPSIS OF SCENES

Before and after the performance: an evening in an unspecified locality.

During the performance: a nice afternoon in a deep Southern town called New Bethesda. Images may be projected on the stage backdrop: they should have a subjective quality, changing subtly with the mood of the play.

PART ONE

Before the performance.

At curtain rise, Felice stands motionless as a hunted creature at the sound of pursuers. He is on the platform of a raked stage, a notebook hanging open from his downstage hand. There should be, at a low level, a number of mechanical sounds suggesting an inhuman quality to the (half underground) vault of a foreign theater at which he has recently arrived. He is staring from the raked platform (on which a fragmentary set has been assembled) at a huge, dark statue upstage, a work of great power and darkly subjective meaning. Something about it, its monolithic presence and its suggestion of things anguished and perverse (in his own nature?) rivet his attention, which is shocked and fearful.

Almost immediately he starts to move toward it, at first slowly and cautiously. The mechanical sounds might increase slightly in volume and tempo as he approaches the upstage edge of the platform. Then he leaps off to the pediment of the sculpture that towers over him and begins a fierce, demonic effort to push it away. It is too heavy to be moved by a man alone. He shouts for assistance.

FELICE: *Is someone, anyone, back here to help me move this— please? I can't alone!* (*There is an echo of his "alone."*) This place has an echo-only answering voice. (*A door slams off stage*) Is that you Fox? Fox! (*There is an echo of his "Fox."*) Impossible! Where did it begin, where, when? (*He runs his hands through his hair.*) This feeling of confusion began when—I can't think where. My God I've tried to conceal it, this confusion, but it's pretty obvious, now that I've shown some evidence of it . . .

(*He has taken some cushions out of an old wicker box in which "props" are carried. His speech is breathless; sometimes ironic, sometimes savage.*)

FELICE (*exhibiting the articles mentioned*): Scratch pad and pencil! (*He kneels, panting, among the cushions.*) The setting isn't Morocco, the cushions just arrived without the sofa! (*He draws a deep breath to compose himself.*) Act One, Scene

One. At rise of curtain I am discovered on stage alone, yes, necessarily alone since she never enters on cue and never in a condition that I can predict anymore.

CLARE (*in a strangulated cry, at a distance*): Felice?

FELICE: I know what that cry means: she's rising reluctantly to the surface of consciousness, I—understand her—reluctance, but sometimes patience—gets impatient, you know . . . Cockroach! (*He sucks in his breath with disgust.*) —A humanizing touch! I think I read somewhere that cockroaches are immune to radiation and so are destined to be among the last organic survivors of—the great "Amen" . . .

CLARE (*same distance, a little clearer*): Felice?

FELICE (*shouting*): Pla-ces! —Fear . . . (*He has glanced upstage and at the "chained monster."*) Fear! —The fierce little man with the drum inside the rib-cage. —Compared to fear grown to panic that has no limit—short of consciousness blowing out and not reviving again—no other emotion a living, feeling creature is able to have, not even love or hate, is comparable in—what? —Force? —Magnitude? —Too rhetorical, that, work over later . . . —Of course you realize that I'm trying to catch you and hold you with an opening monologue that has to be extended through several—rather arbitrary—transitions, only related in a general way to— (*He gestures toward the statue with eyes shut tight.*)

CLARE (*slightly closer*): Where!

FELICE (*flips a page of the pad without otherwise relating to it*): —There is the love and the—substitutions, the surrogate attachments, doomed to brief duration, no matter how— necessary . . . —You can't, you must never catch hold of and cry out to a person, loved or needed as deeply as if loved— "Take care of me, I'm frightened, don't know the next step!" The one so loved and needed would hold you in contempt of human law and resisting arrest. In the heart of this person—him-her—is a little automatic sound apparatus, and it whispers to this person: "Demand! Blackmail! Despicable! Reject it!" —And so the next morning you have to make your own coffee, your own phone calls, and go alone to the doctor to say: "I'm afraid I'm dying."

CLARE (*in the wings*): Felice!

FELICE: Clare! (*He tosses away the scratch pad and pencil.*)

CLARE (*appearing, lighted dimly*): Nobody called me.

FELICE: I yelled my head off.

CLARE: Oh. —Decapitated? —Sorry! —How much time have we got?

FELICE (*to the audience, rising*): Imagine the curtain is down. (*He comes downstage and peeks through the imaginary curtain.*) They're coming in. It's nearly curtain time.

CLARE: Where is everybody?

FELICE: Everybody is somewhere, Clare. —What I have to do now is keep her from getting too panicky to give a good performance in this state theater of a state unknown, but she's not easy to fool, in spite of her—condition.

(*Clare enters, falteringly, blindly: almost at once she encounters the huge statue and utters a terrified outcry.*)

(*Felice drops an article removed from the prop basket.*)

CLARE: *Whose—monstrous aberration—is this?!*

FELICE: *I honestly don't know but it's there and it can't be moved!*

CLARE: It—dominates, it towers over the stage, what play on earth could be performed under this? Not even *Medea* or —*Oedipus Rex!* And— *"Can't be moved,"* did you say?

FELICE (*helplessly*): It—won't be lighted.

CLARE: *If anything is lighted the light will catch it.*

FELICE: *Will you quit shouting with an audience out there?*

CLARE: *You* are shouting.

FELICE: Will you, please, will you—!

CLARE: Will I what?

FELICE: Your chronic hysteria's cracking my nerves, Clare, I—

CLARE: What about my nerves? —I'm also a vertebrate with a nervous system that's been subjected to shock after shock till— (*She stumbles and cries out again.*)

FELICE: CARE! —ful.

CLARE: Felice, that chained monster's *obscene!*

FELICE: I made the same observation, I tried to move it, I couldn't, I called for assistance, I got none, so now we have to forget it. And by now you surely must have noticed that on these long, long tours we run always into certain— *unalterable circumstances* that we just have to—*ignore!*

CLARE (*abruptly controlling her shock*): Yes, I've—noticed that, too, on these long, long tours—unalterable circumstances, "Pox vobiscum," P-O-X—rhymes with Fox. . . —What I'm going to do in my leisure time from now on—while waiting for custom inspectors to, to confiscate things, and so forth, is—

FELICE: Will you please—? *Migraine!*—no codeine left! (*He is clasping his head.*)

CLARE: Is make out a list, un—unabridged—compendium of these—unexpected and—*unalterable—circumstance*, I'll— see you later. . .

(*She starts a slow, unsteady progress downstage, alongside the acting platform: her eyes have an unnatural, feverish brightness.*)

I forget—*unalterable circumstance*, but— Remember the time that destitute old—painter—invited us to tea on the— Viale—something—somewhere and when we arrived—the concierge said, suspiciously, "Oh, him, huh, five flights up, not worth it!" —Five flights up, not worth it! —No, not exactly worth it, the old, old painter was seated in *rigor mortis* before a totally blank canvas, teakettle boiled dry on the—burner—under a skylight—that sort of light through a dirty winter skylight is—*unalterable—circumstance*—but there is no skylight here, I haven't noticed a window— Is this theater under the ground? Is this the subterranean— pleasure-dome of—Kabla—Kubla—Koon?

(*During this speech, Felice has stood transfixed with dismay at her condition, motionless, an astrological chart in his hand.*)

—Sacred river must be—frozen over— (*She collides with something: a startled cry.*) *Felice!*

FELICE: Clare! —Hush!

CLARE: Will you please help me through this nightmare of debris? Why, it's like the surface of a sea where some great ship's gone under, spewing up wreckage!

FELICE: Parasol?

CLARE: Did you say "parasol"? I thought you said "parasol" —a dreadful thought. . .

FELICE: I'm checking props.

CLARE: Props, parasol—I don't want to think what I'm thinking.

FELICE: Strike a match and watch your step back there.

CLARE: Too late for watching my step, since I was conceived and delivered and fell into this—profession? —I will move not a step more till you remember that you are—the remnant of a gentleman *and* my brother— I will stand here motionless as that monster until you—

FELICE: Gloves!—hat. . .

CLARE: I said—

FELICE: Wait one minute, a moment. —You know, I can't tell your highs from your lows any more, Clare.

CLARE: I can't either, it's all one endless—continuum of—endurance. . .

FELICE (*cutting through*): Bowl of soapwater but only one spool.

CLARE (*moving downstage*): After last season's disasters we should have taken a rest on some quiet Riviera instead of touring these primitive faraway places.

FELICE: Clare, you couldn't stop any more than I could.

CLARE: I couldn't unless you stopped with me. (*She sits on the prop basket, stage left.*)

FELICE: We had to go on together. No alternative ever.

CLARE: I suppose when two people have lived together and worked together for such an—incalculably long time—it's natural to feel panicky as I felt when I recovered consciousness in that—travesty of a dressing room back there. You know what woke me up? A squeaky noise and a flapping about of wings up toward the invisible ceiling. I said to myself: "It's a bat," but I wasn't scared—I wasn't even surprised.

(*They both laugh, sadly and lightly.*)

That dressing room is a sight to behold, it's a filthy refrigerator, but I was so exhausted I fell right asleep in a broken-back chair.

FELICE: I'm glad you got some sleep.

CLARE: I'm still half asleep and my voice is going. Listen! My voice is practically gone!

FELICE (*still arranging props*): Phone on piano top.—You never come on stage just before curtain time, without giving me the comforting bit of news that your voice is gone and you'll have to perform in pantomime tonight.

CLARE: It always seems to be true.

FELICE: But somehow never is.

CLARE: I try my best to understand your nervous anxieties. Why don't you try to understand mine a little?

FELICE: I do, but you have so many of them, you know. Will you come on the set, I have new business to give you.

CLARE: And *I* some to give *you*. I want you to look at me on stage, stop avoiding my eyes, I can't act with you when you won't look in my eyes like you really saw me.

FELICE: Clare, I'd continue to see you if I were stone-blind, Clare.

CLARE (*moving toward the proscenium*): Let me have a peek at *them*.

FELICE (*drawing her back*): No! Don't!

CLARE: Why not?

FELICE: When you look at an audience before a performance, you play self-consciously, you don't get lost in the play.

CLARE: Why are we talking to each other like this, like tonight was the end of the world and we're blaming each other for it?

FELICE: You've been resting, I haven't. I'm dead-beat, I'll probably dry up several times tonight.

CLARE: You nearly always tell me your memory's gone when the curtain's about to go up.

FELICE: It always seems to be true.

CLARE: But somehow never is. (*In a frightened voice*) You have on father's astrology shirt.

FELICE (*impatiently*): Yes, I'm already in costume.

CLARE: For *The Two-Character Play*?

FELICE: The other play is canceled.

CLARE: I have to be informed when a performance is canceled, or else I won't perform. Those stairs, those stairs aren't the stairs for *The Two-Character Play*.

FELICE: So far, only parts of the set have arrived.

CLARE: These stairs go nowhere, they stop in space.

FELICE: I have placed your gloves and parasol up there. Climb some steps and I'll say you've gone upstairs.

CLARE: Are you serious? About playing it that way?

FELICE: Desperately.

CLARE: Where is the sofa?

FELICE: It didn't arrive. We'll have to use cushions, Moroccan style.

CLARE: Are you going to throw new speeches at me tonight?

FELICE: Tonight, I feel there'll be a lot of improvisation, but if we're both lost in the play, the bits of improvisation won't matter at all, in fact they may make the play better.

CLARE: I like to know what I'm playing and especially how a play ends. *The Two-Character Play* never had an ending.

FELICE: When the curtain is up and the lights are on, you'll fly like a bird through the play, and if you dry up—use it.

CLARE: Felice, do you have a fever?

FELICE: No. Do you?

CLARE: I'm on fire with panic.

(*She starts toward the proscenium again, to peek out at the audience. He seizes her arm and drags her back.*)

You looked out. Why can't I?

FELICE: You know how bad it is for you.

CLARE: Well, just let me ask you one question. One little question only.

FELICE: All right, ask me, but don't depend on getting much of an answer.

CLARE: Can you tell me how long were we on the way here? It seemed everlasting to me. All those frontiers, I didn't know the world had so many frontiers. And God help me, Felice, I honestly don't remember where we got on the train. Do you?

FELICE: Certainly. Of course.

CLARE: Then where, tell me where?

FELICE: Oh, Clare, don't! Don't, don't question me now, save all questions till after the performance.

CLARE: Is it all right if I make a comment on your appearance?

FELICE: Yes. What?

CLARE: You have lovely hair but there's much too much of it. Why, it's almost as long as mine.

FELICE: I don't think Felice is a man who could force himself to go to a barber often.

CLARE: The part of Felice is not the only part that you play. *The Two-Character Play* is certainly the most unusual play in the repertory, but it isn't the one and only we perform.

FELICE: From now on, it might be.

CLARE: Wouldn't *that* please the company! What would they be doing?

FELICE: I don't have any idea or a particle of interest.

CLARE: Oh! How regal! (*She pauses.*) Is this tour nearly over?

FELICE: It could end tonight if we don't give a brilliant performance.

CLARE: ALL I remember about this last trip—I must've had a fever—is that it would be light and then it would be dark and then it would be light or half light again and then dark again, and the country changed from prairies to mountains and then back to prairies again and then back to mountains, and my watch froze to death, and I tell you honestly I don't have any idea or any suspicion of where we are now except we seem to be in a huge mausoleum of a theater somewhere that seems like nowhere.

(*There is a guttural mumbling of voices from the "house." Felice pounds the stage floor again.*)

FELICE: After the performance, Clare, I'll answer any question you can think of, but I'm not going to hold up the curtain to answer a single one now.

CLARE: Felice, do you think I am not your equal?

FELICE: You're not my equal. You're my superior, Clare.

CLARE: I'm your superior in only one respect. I'm more realistic than you are, and I insist on knowing why no one is here but us two.

FELICE: Do you hear mumbling and growling?

CLARE: Yes, it sounds like a house full of furious unfed apes, but let's get back to my question. Where's everybody? (*She searches for a cigarette.*) Cigarette shortage.

(*She lights a cigarette with shaky fingers. Felice pounds the stage three times.*)

I said where *is* everybody? And I *insist* on an answer.

FELICE: You *insist* on an answer? You're sure you *do* want an answer?

CLARE: I do want an answer, right now.

FELICE: All right, you win, Clare, but I think you'll wish you'd lost. (*He takes a paper from his pocket.*) Here. Look at this.

CLARE: Telegram? You know I'm blind without my reading glasses. Here, strike a lucifer for me.

FELICE: Shortage of matches. (*He strikes a match and hands the telegram to her.*)

CLARE (*reading aloud, slowly*): "Your sister and you are—*insane!*"

FELICE: Signed—"The Company." Charming?

CLARE: "We have all borrowed money to return to—" (*The match goes out. She turns to the piano and strikes a note.*) Well, as they say—

FELICE: What?

CLARE: That sort of wraps things up.

FELICE: The whole company's left us, there is no staff except for two inscrutable stagehands who came in without a word and put up this piece of the set and helped me hang the lights before they—

CLARE: Deserted us, too?

FELICE: I tried to make them talk but they wouldn't or couldn't. They were silent as executioners, wouldn't look at me, even, just put up the door and the curtains and then weren't there any more.

CLARE: Would you recognize them again if they came back?

FELICE: You're the one that recognizes stagehands. I smile and shake hands with them but never remember their names.

CLARE: You're always so absorbed in your work, Felice, that you hardly recognize me—I understand that, but naturally a new company wouldn't, they'd be offended by it and go into a huddle and come to the conclusion that you were a bit *dérangé*, not just an eccentric artist but *un peu dérangé*. And you'd fallen into a habit of shouting out at rehearsals, "Mad, I'm going mad!" So finally they took your word for it, Felice.

FELICE: When you read the telegram did it say that *I* was insane, me, just *me*?

CLARE: Oh, Felice, no, no, it said: "You and your sister." But Felice, you know that artists put so much into their work, that they've got very little left over for acting like other people, their behavior is bound to seem peculiar . . . even freakish. Doesn't that seem logical to you?

FELICE: The company had been with us, except for a death now and then, or a commitment to an asylum now and then, for—

CLARE: How long?

FELICE: A considerable length of time.

CLARE: A considerable length of time is not a very precise statement of exactly how much time.

FELICE (*pounding the stage floor again*): Then *you* tell me how long!

CLARE: I've always left time up to you. (*She pauses.*) Didn't I get you a new piece of fur for the collar on that coat?

FELICE: Yes, but I preferred my mangy sable.

CLARE: Well, never mind that—what are we going to do? Something or nothing whatsoever at all?

FELICE: Only the dead can do nothing at all and get away with it, Clare.

CLARE: Yes, they do get away with it pretty nicely.

FELICE: But we're alive.

CLARE: Yes, unperished and relatively imperishable?

FELICE: The living have to do something.

CLARE: What is it going to be, in your opinion? Has anything occurred to you, or are you still waiting for a last-moment inspiration?

FELICE: We're going to do *The Two-Character Play* as we've never done it before.

CLARE: Impossible.

FELICE: Necessary.

CLARE: Some necessary things are impossible.

FELICE: And some impossible things are necessary.

CLARE: What an argument!

FELICE: No argument—decision.

CLARE: One-sided. Felice Devoto commanding, but you can't be a commander without someone to command. I won't be commanded since I know what would happen. Chaos of improvisation, new speeches thrown at me like stones, as if I'd been condemned to be stoned to death. Would you like to play with me in absolute panic and in total confusion?

Maybe you would, but you won't. No, thank you, Felice. This isn't the first time I've had to save you from self-destruction which would destroy me, too.

FELICE: We'll toss some new speeches back and forth at each other.

CLARE: Not I, said the fly. Felice, if we attempted to give a performance tonight, it would prove it was true.

FELICE: Prove what was true?

CLARE: What the company called us—insane. I'm going back to my dressing room and put on my coat and go to the hotel and sleep and sleep and—

FELICE: Clare, you have your coat on.

(*There is a pause. Clare strikes a chord on the piano.*)

CLARE: Do you have your brandy flask on you?

FELICE: For after the performance, not before.

CLARE: There can't be a performance.

FELICE: What is there going to be?

CLARE: An announcement by Mr. Fox that the company and the stagehands and the sets have yet to arrive here and so the performance is canceled.

FELICE (*gently and firmly*): No. There'll be a performance of *The Two-Character Play*. (*He takes a silver flask from his pocket and offers it to her.*)

CLARE (*drinking from flask*): Do you think—do you think they really do think we're insane, or were they just being bitchy because the long tour has been such a long disappointment?

FELICE: Since they've quit, I see no reason to think about what they think.

CLARE: You don't find it—disturbing? Well, I do, I find it very disturbing, because I—

FELICE: Let's discuss it after the performance.

CLARE: That witch Florence said to me on the train: "Do you and your brother always go into a trance before a performance?"

FELICE: I'm afraid you're a little confused, since that witch Florence wasn't with us this season. (*Felice goes into the wings.*)

CLARE: Even with the lights on it's cold to the bone, bone cold, and in *The Two-Character Play* we can't keep our coats on, we've got to take off our coats and make the audience and ourselves feel it's a summer day in the South.

(*She coughs. He takes off his coat, holds his hand out to take hers. She gives him her hand with a pleading look.*)

FELICE (*patiently*): I don't want your hand. I want your coat.
CLARE: I'm not going to take off my coat in this big, filthy icebox. If you're able to give a performance, do your pantomime for them.

(*Felice tears off Clare's coat. She cries out. He throws their coats behind the sofa; then thumps the stage again with the stick.*)

Felice, try to understand what that telegram did to me. I can't play tonight, not *The Two-Character Play*—why, I can't remember a line.
FELICE: You will when it starts, and we'll get through it somehow.
CLARE: You think you're being brave, but you're just being desperate and irrational. Felice, believe me, I'm not lying, I can't, I couldn't go through it!
FELICE: Clare, you're going to play Clare.
CLARE: I am going back to my dressing room, and you are going to announce the performance is canceled because of impossible circumstances.
FELICE: I am going out right now and announce the change of program, and when I come back, you will be here, on stage.
CLARE: Don't count on that. Sometimes I make decisions and stick to them.
FELICE: Feel my forehead! Sweating!
CLARE: Because you have fever.
FELICE: I'm sweating because it's a hot summer day in the South.
CLARE: —Somebody, a doctor, once told me that I had unusual courage and so did you. I said: "Oh, no, my brother and I are terrified of our shadows!" And he said: "I know that, and that's exactly why I admire your courage so much." What kind of sense does that make? Felice? I'll make the announcement in English, Spanish, and French.

I'll make a lovely announcement that sometimes things just make it impossible to give a performance and I'll, I'll—I'll crouch before them with my hand held out for pity.

(*She falls to her knees. He clasps her shoulders, tenderly.*)

FELICE: The telegram was shocking, but we're both over that now. Now all we have to do is remember that if we're not artists, we're nothing. And play *The Two-Character Play* the best we've ever played it no matter what our condition of panic may be.

CLARE (*raising her hands to his head*): Your hair's grown so long you look hermaphroditic.

FELICE: Yes? Do I? Good. Thank you. (*He thumps the stage floor with the stick and throws it behind the sofa.*)

CLARE: *Bonne chance!* I'll see you later!

(*Disregarding this threat, Felice advances to the proscenium.*)

FELICE (*to the audience*): Good evening, ladies and gentlemen. I want you to know that my sister and I feel deeply honored to take our own small part in this enormously important idea and program of, of—cultural exchange. Of course there have been some, a number of, unexpected difficulties, but being artists of the theater we have been long prepared for working under unexpected conditions. This evening my sister and I are going to perform alone, since the rest of our company has been delayed by, uh, transportation difficulties due to the eccentricities of the weather bird, perhaps I should say the perversities of the weather bird. (*He laughs hollowly.*) However, it so happens that our favorite play in our repertory is a play for two characters, which is logically entitled *The Two-Character Play*. (*He gives the same hollow laugh, followed by a cough.*) This evening we had expected—

CLARE: Poor Felice, he's dried up. (*She puts on her coat.*)

FELICE: This play, this evening, we will now perform for you, and we hope that you will forgive the technical difficulties and problems due to the delay of our company's arrival— unavoidable— (*He bows and steps back into the setting, then speaks commandingly.*) Clare! Places! I'm going to start the play.

CLARE: You'll find me in my dressing room with the weather bird. Oh, Felice, please! *Don't* humiliate yourself!

FELICE: It's *you* that want to disgrace us! Our performance must continue. No escape!

CLARE: If you start *The Two-Character Play* it will be a one-character play, and I'll know the company's telegram is the truth.

(*Felice disappears into the wings. Clare starts blindly off the stage, then stops by the giant's statue and leans her head against its pedestal. There is the sound of curtains opening. The violet dusk of the stage that surrounds the interior set turns lighter, and strange inhuman mocking laughter is heard. At the sound of the laughter, Clare turns quickly about and defiantly faces the house. Felice returns from the wings.*)

FELICE: Clare! Please!

(*The mocking laughter builds. Clare throws off her coat as if accepting a challenge.*)

CLARE (*to Felice*): Do I enter first or do you?

FELICE: Tonight you go in first.

(*Clare returns to the interior set, goes to the piano and strikes a treble note. Felice enters.*)

Your place is by the phone.

CLARE: Yes, by the phone.

FELICE: The performance commences.

(*Clare goes to the phone.*)

FELICE: Who are you calling, Clare? (*She seems not to hear him.*) Clare! Who are you calling?

CLARE: —Not a soul still existing in the world gone away . . .

FELICE: Then why are you holding the phone?

CLARE: I just picked it up to see if it's still connected.

FELICE: Is it?

CLARE: It hums in my ear. Doesn't that mean it's connected?

FELICE: The telephone company would send us a notice before they turned off the phone.

CLARE (*vaguely and sadly*): Sometimes notices aren't—noticed.

FELICE: The house is—

CLARE: Still occupied but they might have the idea it wasn't, since it's not lighted at night and no one still comes and goes.

FELICE: We would have received a notice if one was sent.

CLARE: We can't count on that.

FELICE: We mustn't start counting things that can't be counted on, Clare.

CLARE: We must trust in things—

FELICE: Continuing as they've—

CLARE: Continued?

FELICE: Yes, as they've continued, for such a long time that they seem—

CLARE: Dependable to us.

FELICE: Permanently dependable, yes, but we were—

CLARE: Shocked when the—

FELICE: Lights refused to turn on, and it was lucky the moon was so nearly full that, with the window shades raised, it lighted the downstairs rooms.

CLARE: But we collided with things in the upstairs hall.

FELICE: Now we could find our way around in it blind.

CLARE: We can, we do. Without even touching the walls.

FELICE: It's a small house and we've lived in it always.

CLARE: You say that I was indulging in a bit of somnambulism last night.

FELICE: Clare, you had a restless night.

CLARE: You did, too.

FELICE: In a small house when—

CLARE: One of the occupants has a restless night—

FELICE: It keeps the other awake.

CLARE (*crying out*): *Why do I have to sleep in that death chamber?*

FELICE (*controlled*): We agreed that their room was just a room now. Everything about them's been removed.

CLARE: Except Father's voice in the walls and his eyes in the ceiling so that I can't shut mine. —That night of the accident night, you ran to the foot of the stairs but not a step further, you blocked the steps, I had to force my way past you to the room where—Mother opened the door as if I'd knocked like a visitor not—expected.

FELICE: Stop repeating, repeating!

CLARE: No sign of recognizing me at the door, no greeting, a look of surprise, very slight, till she opened her mouth on a soundless fountain of blood, and Father behind her saw and received me quietly, too, oh, it was a quiet reception that I received at the door, quiet, polite, just a little surprised till the dreadful torrent and Father said, "Not yet, Clare," just as quietly, gently to me as *that*, before they went separate ways, she to the door of the bathroom where she fell and he to the window where he fired again looking out at—*out* . . .

(*Felice strikes his fist on piano keys.*)

And you tell me it isn't their room any more, that it belongs to me now, inherited without effort not to remember what you never entered so have no memory of?

FELICE: I said: "LET IT REST!"

CLARE: Not in that room at night? Who passed that death sentence on me?

FELICE (*with forced quiet*): You weren't in that room last night, you came to the door of mine.

CLARE (*fearfully*): To ask for—a—cigarette . . .

FELICE: We've had no cigarettes since—

CLARE: Is it improper for me not to stay in one place? All night? Alone?

FELICE: You didn't stay in one place, you wandered about the house, upstairs and down as if you were searching for something.

CLARE: Exploring the premises, yes.

FELICE: With a fine-tooth comb. —Did you find it?

CLARE: No, but I came across something, this old memento, this token of— (*She lifts her hand to show a ring.*)

FELICE: What?

CLARE: This ring with my birthstone, the opal called a fire opal.

FELICE: You haven't worn it for so long that I thought it was lost.

(*Evanescent music fades in.*)

CLARE: Mother told me that opals were unlucky.

FELICE: Frigid women are given to little fears and superstitions, and—

CLARE: Opals do have a sinister reputation. And it was a gift from Father.

FELICE: That was enough to prejudice her against it.

CLARE: Sleepless people love rummaging. I look through pockets that I know are empty. I found this ring in the pocket of an old mildewed corduroy coat which I'd forgotten I'd ever owned and didn't care if the stone was unlucky or not.

FELICE: Nothing could be unlucky that's so lovely, Clare. (*He turns it on her finger, a sort of love-making.*)

(*The music stops.*)

CLARE (*Striking the piano key*): Didn't you say that you went out today?

FELICE: Yes, you saw me come in.

CLARE: I didn't see you go out.

FELICE: When you see somebody come in you know he's been out.

CLARE (*skeptically*): How far outside did you go? Past the sunflowers, or—?

FELICE: I went out to the gate, and do you know what I noticed?

CLARE: Something that scared you back in?

FELICE: No, what I saw didn't scare me, but it, it—startled me, though. It was—

CLARE: What?

FELICE: Clare.

CLARE: What?

FELICE (*stage whisper*): You know *The Two-Character Play*.

CLARE (*in a loud stage whisper*): The telegram is still on the set.

FELICE: Clare, there wasn't, there isn't a telegram in *The Two-Character Play*.

CLARE: Then take it off the sofa where I can see it. When you see a thing, you can't think it doesn't exist.

(*He picks up the telegram, crumples it, throwing it out the window.*)

FELICE: There now, it never existed, it was just a moment of panic.

CLARE: What a convenient way to dispose of a panicky moment!

FELICE: Dismissed completely, like that! And now I'll tell you what I saw in the yard when I went out.

CLARE: Yes, do that! Do, please.

FELICE: I saw a sunflower out there that's grown as tall as the house.

CLARE: Felice, you know that's not so!

FELICE: Go out and see for yourself.

(*She tries to laugh.*)

Or just look outside the window, it's in the front yard, on this side.

CLARE: *Front* yard? (*He nods but averts his face with a slight smile.*) Now I know you're fooling.

FELICE: Oh, no, you don't or you'd go look out the window. It shot up quick as Jack's beanstalk, and it's so gold, so brilliant that it—seems to be shouting sensational things about us. Tourists will be attracted?

CLARE: Why are you—?

FELICE: Botanists, you know botanists, they'll flock to New Bethesda to marvel at this marvel, photograph it for the— *National Geographic*, this marvel of nature. This two-headed sunflower taller than a two-story house which is still inhabited by a—recluse brother and sister who never go out any more . . .

CLARE: It's such a long afternoon . . .

FELICE: It's summer, which is our season, but after the afternoon, we have to remember that there are unexpected collisions in an unlighted house, and not always only with —furniture and—walls . . .

CLARE: Call it the poem of two and dark as—

FELICE: Our blood?

CLARE: Yes, why don't you say it? Abnormality! —Say it! And point at me!

FELICE: At myself, first.

CLARE: Now—let's close the child's eyes and—light candles . . .

FELICE: There's no such line in the script.

CLARE (*smiling brightly*): *Tant pire, che peccato,* meaning "too bad."

(*An abrupt change in style of performance occurs at this point, as if they were startled out of a dream.*)

FELICE: —Clare, somebody is knocking. Why don't you go to the door? Don't you hear them knocking?

CLARE: Who?

FELICE: I can't see through the door.

CLARE: I don't hear any knocking. (*He drums the table with his knuckles.*) Oh, yes, now I do, but— (*He drums the table again.*) They're very insistent, aren't they?

FELICE: Go see who's there.

CLARE: I can't imagine. I'm not properly dressed, I'm not fit to be seen.

FELICE: You're perfectly dressed and look unusually well, but me, I don't have a tie on, and this old shirt of Father's, I've sweated through it.

CLARE: That's excusable on a—hot afternoon. You, you let them in and say you'll call me down if it'd be they want to see *me.*

FELICE: Christ, have you reached the point where you're scared to answer the door?

CLARE: Reached and— (*She starts up the spiral stairs that stop in space.*) —The knocking's stopped. —I think they've gone away. —No! Look! They're slipping a slip of paper under the door!

(*They stare fearfully at the doorsill, the supposed piece of paper.*)

FELICE: —They've left.

CLARE: Yes, pick up the—

(*He crosses to the door and makes the gesture of picking up a card: frowns at it, breath audible.*)

FELICE: "Citizens—Relief."

CLARE: —I've never heard of such a thing in my life. Have you ever heard of Citizens Relief?

FELICE: No, I think it's wise to be cautious about things you've never—

CLARE: Heard of. It might be a trick of some kind, an excuse to—

FELICE: Intrude on our—

CLARE: Privacy, yes. Shall we destroy the card or keep it in case of a desperate situation?

FELICE: That's not a thing we seem to have to wait for, is it?

CLARE: Oh, but all the questions we'd have to—

FELICE: —Answer . . .

CLARE: Yes, there'd be interviews and questionnaires to fill out and—

FELICE: Organizations are such—

CLARE: *Cold!*

FELICE: Yes, impersonal things.

CLARE: I'll put the card under grandmother's wedding picture, just in case a desperate situation—

FELICE: Increases in desperation—

CLARE: *Anyway, here it is,* at least we—know where it is. Now I—suppose we have to prepare for—public action against us, since they know we're—still here.

FELICE: What action, such as what?

CLARE: —Removal by force of—eviction?

FELICE: You do ask for trouble by—having notions like that.

CLARE: I don't know what to do next! (*She turns about distractedly, hands clasped together.*)

FELICE: I do, I know.

CLARE: Sit there and stare at that threadbare rose in the carpet till it withers?

(*He has sunk onto the sofa, chin in hands, staring at the carpet.*)

FELICE: And you? What are you doing but clasping your hands together as if in prayer?

CLARE: Nothing unless it's something to pace about the house in a maze of amazement, upstairs, downstairs, day and night, in and out. *Out!* Oh, Felice, I want to go out, today I want to go out, I want to walk on the street—like a favorite of nature in public view without—shame . . .

FELICE: —Oh? —You want to go out calling?

CLAIRE: Yes, out calling!

FELICE: Go out!

CLAIRE: *Alone?* —Not *alone!*

FELICE: Ladies go calling alone on such nice afternoons.

CLARE: You come out calling with me.

FELICE: I can't, I have to stay here.

CLARE: For what?

FELICE: —To guard the house against—

CLARE: What?

FELICE: *Curious—trespassers!* Somebody has to stay on the premises and it has to be me, but you go out calling, Clare. You must have known when you got up this morning that the day would be different for you, not a stay-at-home day, of which there've been so many, but a day for going out calling, smiling, talking. You've washed your hair, it's yellow as corn silk, you've pinned it up nicely, you have on your dressed-up dress that you washed to go out in today, and you have the face of an angel, Clare, you match the fair weather, so carry out your impulse, go out calling. You know what you could do? Everywhere you went calling you could say, "Oh, do you know how idiotic I am? I went out without cigarettes!" And they'd offer you one at each place, and you could slip them into your purse, save them till you got home, and we could smoke them here, Clare. So! Go! (*He opens the door for her.*)

CLARE: Why have you opened the door?

FELICE: For you to go out calling.

CLARE: Oh, how thoughtful, yes, very gentlemanly of you to open the door for me to go outside without parasol or gloves, but not very imaginative of you to imagine that I'd go out alone.

(*They stand a moment staring at each other near the open door; her hands and lips tremble; the slight smile, mocking and tender, twists his mouth.*)

—Suppose I came home alone, and in front of the house there was a collection of people around an ambulance or police car or both? We've had that happen before. People are attracted by a sudden disturbance in a house that seemed vacant. No. I won't go out alone. (*She slams the door shut.*) My legs wouldn't hold me up, and as for smiling and talking, I think I'd have on my face the grimace of a doll and my hair would stick to the sweat on my forehead. Oh, I'd hardly sit down for this friendly call on—what friends?—before I—staggered back up, that is, if, if—the colored girl had been allowed to admit me.

FELICE: It was your idea. You shouted "Out!" not me.

CLARE: I'd never dream of going out without you in your— disturbed—*condition*.

FELICE: And *you* in *yours*.

CLARE: Me, calling, a fire engine shrieks, a revolver—bang— discharges! Would I sit there continuing with the smile and the talk? (*She is sobbing a little: her trembling hand stretches toward him.*) No, I'd spring up, run, run, and my heart would stop on the street!

FELICE (*his smile fading out*): I never believed you'd go calling.

CLARE: Right you were about that if you thought alone—but calling? Yes, I'll do that! Phone-calling is calling! (*She rushes to the telephone and snatches up the receiver.*)

FELICE: Calling, who are you—? *Careful!*

CLARE (*into phone*): Operator, the Reverend Mr. Wiley! Urgent, very, please hurry!

(*Felice tries to wrest the phone from her grasp: for a moment they struggle for it.*)

FELICE: Clare!

CLARE: Reverend Wiley, this is Clare Devoto, yes, you re- member, the daughter of the— (*Then to Felice*) You have to let me go on or he'll think I'm—

FELICE: What are you! Out of your—!

CLARE (*into phone again*): Excuse me, Reverend Wiley, there was—an interruption. My brother and I still live in our par- ents' home after, after the—terrible accident in the house which was reported so maliciously falsely in *The Press- Scimitar*. Father did *not* kill Mother and himself but— The house was, was—broken into by some—

FELICE: Favorite of nature?

CLARE: Housebreaker who murdered our parents, but I think *we* are suspected! Oh, it's hard to stay on here, but we do, we're still here, but such a terrible thing has been going on and on. My brother Felice and I are surrounded by so much suspicion and malice that we almost never, we hardly ever, dare to go out of the house. In the nighttime people stop and linger on the sidewalk and whisper charges, anomalous letters of obscenities are sent us, and *The Press-Scimitar*—sly allusions to us as the deranged children of a father who was a false mystic and, Reverend Wiley, our father was a man who had true psychic, mystical powers, granted only to an Aries whose element is cardinal fire. (*She is sobbing now.*) Oh, I can't tell you how horrifying it's been, why, the neighbor's child has a slingshot and bombards the house with rocks, we heard his *parents* give the slingshot to him and *tell* him to— Ha! *Another rock struck just now!*

(*She drops the phone in panic. He picks it up.*)

FELICE: Mr. Wiley, my sister has a fever.

CLARE: No.

FELICE: She's not herself today, forget what, excuse and— (*He hangs up, wipes sweat off his forehead with trembling hand.*) Wonderful, that does it! Our one chance is privacy, and you babble away to a man who'll think it is his Christian duty to have us *confined* in—

(*She gasps and stumbles to the piano. She strikes a treble note repeatedly on the piano. He snatches her hand from the keyboard and slams the lid down.*)

Clare!

CLARE: You shouldn't have spoken that word! *"Confined!"* That word is not in the—

FELICE: Oh. A prohibited word. When a word can't be used, when it's prohibited, its silence increases its size. It gets larger and larger till it's so enormous that no house can hold it.

CLARE: Then say the word, over and over, you perverse monster, you—!

(*Felice turns away.*)

Scared to? Afraid of a—?

FELICE: I won't do lunatic things. I have to try to pretend there's some sanity here.

CLARE: Oh, is that what you're trying? I thought you were trying to go as far as possible without going past all limits.

(*He turns to face her, furiously. She smiles and forms the word "confined" with her lips; then she says it with a whisper. He snatches up a sofa pillow.*)

Confined, confined!

(*He thrusts the pillow over her mouth, holding her by the shoulder. She struggles as if suffocating. Suddenly she stops struggling and looks out toward the audience. She then speaks in a quiet and flat tone. Completely real.*)

Felice! There is a gunman out there. A man with a gun pointed at me.

FELICE: Clare! Please. (*Felice stares at her helplessly for a few moments, then turns to the audience and says:*) I am afraid there will have to be an interval of about ten minutes while my sister recovers. You see, she is not at all well tonight.

(*Very quietly and gently he leads her off stage. The house-lights go on.*)

An Interval of Ten Minutes

PART TWO

As the houselights dim Felice and Clare enter hurriedly to the side of the stage outside the set.

We see Felice forcibly drawing Clare back onto the set as the curtain rises: both are panting, and there is evidence of struggle between them during the interval. (He points to a bowl by the window.)

FELICE (*her wrist still firmly in his grip*): What is that?—what is it doing here?

CLARE (*defiantly lifting her face to his*): It's equipment for the amusement of children on hot summer afternoons. Have you forgotten how we blew soap bubbles on the back steps those long—

FELICE: On the back steps, yes, but don't remember that we ever blew soap bubbles here in the parlor.

CLARE: Yesterday you said, "There's nothing to do, there's nothing at all to do," kept saying it, wouldn't quit. All right. Here's soap-bubble equipment. Look! Look! I haven't forgotten how! (*She blows a bubble.*)

FELICE: —Beautiful but—they break.

CLARE: You try, it's your turn now.

(*Felice stares at her for a moment: then breaks into [desperate?] laughter.*)

What has struck you so funny?

FELICE: Madness has a funny side to it, Clare. —And we can't turn back into children in public view.

CLARE: That's my line, not yours.

FELICE (*continues to laugh the same way: then suddenly is quite sober*): —I haven't told you something you'll have to know.

CLARE: You're jumping a page.

(*Felice stares at her blankly.*)

CLARE (*solicitous*): —Have you dried up, Felice? (*She leads him to the cushions as if he were senseless: gently pushes him.*) Lean back, breathe quietly, I'll take it— From where?

(*Slight pause.*)

FELICE: When Father gave up his—

CLARE: —When father gave up his equipment, his psychic readings and astrological predictions, a few days before the *un, inexplicable*—accident!—in the house— Well, he didn't give them up, exactly.

FELICE: No, not exactly by choice.

CLARE: Mother had locked up his equipment.

FELICE: Except for this worn-out shirt of his I have on, which bears the signs of the zodiac on it, and his rising sign, and a chart of the sky as it was on the hour before daybreak of the day of his nativity here in New Bethesda!

CLARE: You know, he seemed to—accept. At least he said nothing. Not even when she spoke of State Haven to him. "Yes, I can see your mind is going again. Check yourself into State Haven for a long rest—voluntarily, or I'll—" He didn't answer these threats. He became very quiet. Except when she ordered him to cut down our sacred flowers in front of the house, and said if he didn't do it she would.

FELICE: Yes, Mother, Regina, made several threats of emasculation to—

CLARE: "You cut them down or I will." (*She continues in a different voice.*) "Do that if you dare."

FELICE: And she didn't. And he—

CLARE: Was restlessly quiet. Sat almost continually where you're sitting and stared at that threadbare rose in the carpet's center and it seemed to smolder, yes, that rose seemed to smolder like his eyes and yours, and when a carpet catches fire in a wooden house, the house will catch fire too. Felice, I swear that this is a house made of wood and that rose is smoldering, now! And cloth and wood are two inflammable things. Your eyes make three!

FELICE: No, four! I'm not a one-eyed Cyclops! And adding your eyes makes six!

(*She strikes a sharp note on the piano. He glares at her furiously, but she strikes the note again, louder.*)

—Line!

CLARE: Didn't you tell me you'd thought of something we have to do today?

FELICE: —Yes, it's something we can't put off any longer.

CLARE: The letter of protest to the—

FELICE: No, no, letters of protest are barely even opened, no, what we *must* do today is go out of the house.

CLARE: To some particular place, or—

FELICE: To Grossman's Market.

CLARE: There?!

FELICE: Yes, *there*!

CLARE: We tried that before and turned back.

FELICE: We didn't have a strong enough reason, and it wasn't such a favorable afternoon.

CLARE: This afternoon is—?

FELICE: Much more favorable. And I simply know that it's necessary for us to go to Grossman's Market today since— I've kept this from you, but sometimes the postman still comes through the barricade of sunflowers and that he did some days ago with a notification that no more—

CLARE: —Deliveries?

FELICE: Will be delivered to the steps of—

CLARE: I knew. Payment for costlies has been long—overdue.

FELICE: So out we do have to go to Grossman's Market, directly to Mr. Grossman, and speak personally to him.

CLARE: What would we speak about to him, if we found him?

FELICE: He has an office.

CLARE: His office! Where's his office? Probably tucked away in some never-discovered corner of that shadowy labyrinth of a—

FELICE: We'll ask a clerk to tell us, to take us, to—

CLARE: If the clerk saw us, he'd pretend that he didn't.

FELICE: Not if we enter with some air of assurance and, and— importance about us, as if some unexpected, some, some— providential thing had occurred in our—

CLARE: An air of importance? To nature? And to Grossman's?

FELICE: We're going to enter Grossman's Market today like a pair of—

CLARE: Prosperous, paying customers?

FELICE: Yes, with excellent credit! We'll speak, first, to a clerk and say to him: "Please show us into the office of Mr. Grossman." We are going to go into his office, we are going to tell him convincingly that in spite of all spite and, and—contrary—accusations—Father's insurance policy will be paid to us on, say, the first of next month, yes, on September the first.

CLARE: But we know that it won't be, on the first or last day of any month of the year!

FELICE: We have to say that it *will* be!

CLARE: I don't think, I'm not so sure that—

FELICE: Don't think, don't be sure. You have a resistance to all positive actions.

CLARE: It's *I* that do the little there's still to be done here.

(*They have crossed downstage to opposite sides of the interior set: face out.*)

CLARE (*at a fast pace*): But we've been informed by the—

FELICE (*at a fast pace*): Acme Insurance Company.

CLARE (*at a fast pace*): Yes, they notified us, that courtesy they did offer, and I'm sure that Grossman knows it—doesn't he know everything?—that the insurance money is —what's the word? Confiscated?

FELICE (*at a fast pace*): Forfeited.

CLARE (*at a fast pace*): Yes, the payment of the insurance policy is forfeited in the—what is the word?

FELICE (*at a fast pace*): Event.

CLARE (*at a fast pace*): Yes, in the event of a man— (*She stops, pressing her fist to her mouth.*)

FELICE (*at a fast pace*): In the event of a man killing his wife, then himself, and—

CLARE: Forgetting his children.

FELICE: —That's what's called a legal technicality . . .

(*They turn to each other.*)

CLARE: What do you know about anything legal, Felice? I'm not impressed by your pose of—

FELICE: I know there are situations in which legal technicalities have to be, to be disregarded in the interests of human, human—

CLARE: I'm afraid you underesteem the, the huge inhumanelessness of a company called *the Acme*. Why, they wrote only three sentences to us in reply to the twelve-page appeal that we wrote and rewrote for a week.

FELICE: It was a mistake to appeal, we should have demanded.

CLARE: And you should have taken the letter to the post office instead of putting it on the mailbox for the ancient postman or for the wind to collect it.

FELICE: I put a rock on the note to the postman on the letter to the—*Will you stop driving me mad?*—*The Acme* wouldn't have answered with even three sentences if they hadn't received the twelve-page appeal—and— When terrible accidents happen, details get confused. Like you got confused the accident night? Ran downstairs and phoned a dead doctor, summoned him from a ten-year stay in Old Gray.

CLARE: Who could tell the dead from the living that night?

FELICE: But couldn't remember our address? Told his widow to send him to the house behind the sunflowers? Yes, details do get confused.

CLARE: Not when publicly published.

FELICE: Forgotten, forgotten! Publicly. Now, will you listen to me?

CLARE: Your voice is coming out of your voice box clearly.

FELICE: We must say that what we saw, there was only us to see, and what we saw was Mother with the revolver, first killing Father and then herself and—

CLARE: A simple lie is one thing, but the absolute opposite of the truth is another.

FELICE (*wildly*): *What's the truth in pieces of metal exploding from the hand of a man driven mad by—!*

CLARE: What you suggest is that we confront Mr. Conrad Grossman, that favorite of nature, in this possible office of his—would there be chairs in it for us to sit down in, or would we have to stand at attention facing the, the—firing squad of his glittering, bifocaled eyes? While we stammered out this fabrication which you propose that we—

FELICE (*mockingly*): We could look an inch over his eyes or an inch under his eyes and talk to him very fast, very, very, very—

CLARE: Together?

FELICE: Each of us would have to confirm the statements of the—

CLARE: Other.

FELICE: And keep smiling and saying "Isn't it *wonderful?*" to him.

CLARE: Isn't what *"wonderful"* to him?

FELICE: That, that *Acme* has at, at—last conceded that—

CLARE: Hmmm. Yes, a plan, a plot, but I think this plot, this plan is something we ought to sleep on and carry out early tomorrow, not late today.

FELICE: Today you have on the dress I call your fair-weather matching.

CLARE: Yes, repaired it and washed it in Ivory. The blouse has worn thin. Oh, I'm afraid it's . . . indecent.

FELICE: It's fetching.

CLARE: What did you call it?

FELICE: Fetching, it's very fetching.

CLARE: Fetching what? Oh, fetching new credit at Grossman's?

FELICE: And when you face Mr. Grossman, it wouldn't hurt to give him a fetching smile. Well? Well? Do we do it or forget it?

CLARE: Sometimes our fear is . . .

FELICE: Our private badge of . . .

CLARE: Courage . . .

FELICE: Right! The door is open. Are we going out?

(*Pause. She backs away from him a step.*)

CLARE: See if there are people on the street.

FELICE: Of course there are, there are always people on streets, that's what streets are made for, for people on them.

CLARE: I meant those boys. You know, those vicious boys that—

FELICE: Oh, yes. You stopped on the walk and shouted "Stop!" to the boys. Covered your ears with your hands and shouted "Stop, stop!" They stopped and they crossed the street. I said: "For God's sake, what did you think they were doing? Why did you shout 'Stop' at them?"

CLARE: You heard them, too. You were right beside me.

FELICE: I was right beside you and I heard nothing but ordinary boys' talk.

(*She rushes downstage to one side of the interior set. He goes out to the opposite side. They face out.*

(*Lightning pace, often overlapping: the effect of a Mass recited in a church containing a time bomb about to explode.*)

CLARE (*overlapping*): They were staring and grinning at me and spelling out a—

FELICE (*overlapping*): You said they were spelling out an obscene word at you.

CLARE (*overlapping*): Yes, an obscene word, the same obscene word that somebody scrawled on our back fence.

FELICE (*overlapping*): Yes, you told me that too. I looked at the back fence and nothing was scrawled on it, Clare.

CLARE (*overlapping*): If you heard nothing the last time we went out, why wouldn't you go on alone to the grocery store? Why did you run back with me to the house?

FELICE (*overlapping*): You were panicky. I was scared what you might do.

CLARE (*overlapping*): What did you think I might do?

FELICE (*overlapping*): What Father and Mother did when—

CLARE (*overlapping*): Stop here, we can't go on!

FELICE (*overlapping*): Go on!

CLARE (*overlapping*): Line!

FELICE (*overlapping*): A few days ago you—

CLARE: No, you, you, not I! I can't sleep at night in a house where a revolver is hidden. Tell me where you hid it. We'll smash it, destroy it together—line!

FELICE: I took the cartridges out when I put it away.

CLARE: What good's that do when you know where the cartridges are?

FELICE: I removed them from the revolver, and put them away, where I've deliberately forgotten and won't remember.

CLARE: "Deliberately forgotten!" Worthless! In a dream you'll remember. Felice, there's death in the house and you know where it's waiting.

FELICE: —Do you prefer locked doors of separate buildings?

CLARE: You've been obsessed with locked doors since your stay at State Haven!

FELICE: Yes, I have the advantage of having experienced, once, the comforts, the security, the humanizing influence of—

CLARE: Locked doors!

FELICE: At State Haven!

CLARE: I'm sorry but you'd allowed yourself to lose contact with anything that seemed real.

FELICE: Seemed and real don't fit.

CLARE: Stopped speaking!

FELICE: Had nothing to speak of.

CLARE: Stared without recognition!

FELICE: With nothing to recognize!

CLARE: In a little house filled with familiar—?

FELICE: Nothing can blind you more than the familiar twisted into—

CLARE: I was here, too, and saw nothing familiar twisted into—

FELICE: Oh, I don't think you knew where you were any more, you—

CLARE: Knew enough to get out of bed in the morning instead of crouching under covers all day.

FELICE (*rushes to stairs and starts up them*): Was that a sign of clearer—

CLARE: It was a sign of ability to go on with—

FELICE (*on stairs*): Customary habits!

CLARE: An appearance of—

FELICE (*beside himself, from top of stairs*): Fuck appearance!

CLARE: Hush! —You've hidden the revolver, give it up. I'll take it down to the cellar and smash it with the wood chopper. And then be able to sleep again in this house.

FELICE (*descending the steps to Clare; exhausted, tender*): —People don't know, sometimes, what keeps them awake . . . (*He starts the tape. The pace slows from exhaustion.*)

CLARE: The need to search for—

FELICE: The contents of empty pockets?

CLARE: Not always empty! Sometimes there's a birthstone in them that isn't lucky!

(*Pause: they stare, panting, at each other.*
(*Very slowly, with lost eyes, he closes the door—nearly.*)

FELICE: —You have the face of an angel—I could no more ever, no matter how much you begged me, fire a revolver at you than any impossible, unimaginable thing. Not even to lead you outside a door that can't be closed completely without its locking itself till the end of—

(*She turns to face him.*)

—I haven't completely closed it, it isn't finally closed . . . Clare, don't you know that you haven't an enemy in the world except yourself?

CLARE: —To be your own enemy is to have against you the worst, the most relentless, enemy of all.

FELICE: That I don't need to be told. Clare, the door's still open.

CLARE (*with a slight, sad smile*): Yes, a little, enough to admit the talk of—

FELICE: Are we going out, now, or giving up all but one possible thing?

CLARE: —We're—going out, now. There never really was any question about it, you know.

FELICE: Good. At last you admit it.

(*Pause*)

CLARE (*assuming a different air*): But you're not properly dressed. For this auspicious occasion I want you to look your best. Close the door a moment.

FELICE: If it were closed, it might never open again.

CLARE: I'm just—just going upstairs to fetch your fair-weather jacket and a tie to go with it. (*She turns upstage.*) Oh, but no stairs going off!

FELICE: The set's incomplete.

CLARE: I know, I knew, you told me. I have gone upstairs and you are alone in the parlor. (*She goes up the spiral stairs.*)

FELICE: Yes, I am alone in the parlor with the front door open. —I hear voices from the street, the calls and laughter of demons. "Loonies, loonie, loonies, looo-nies!" —I— shut the door, remembering what I'd said.

CLARE: You said that it might never be opened again. (*She turns abruptly downstage.*) Oh, there you *are*!

FELICE: Yes. Of course, *waiting* for you.

CLARE: I wasn't long, was I?

FELICE: —No, but I wondered if you would actually come back down.

CLARE: Here I am, and here is your jacket, and here is your tie. (*She holds out empty hands.*)

FELICE: The articles are invisible.

CLARE (*with a mocking smile*): Put on your invisible jacket and your invisible tie.

FELICE: —I go through the motions of—

CLARE: Ah, now, what a difference! Run a comb through your hair!

FELICE: —Where is—?

CLARE: The inside jacket pocket. I put it there.

FELICE: —Oh? —Yes—thanks . . . (*He makes the gesture of removing a comb from his invisible jacket.*)

CLARE: Oh, let *me* do it! (*She arranges his hair with her fingers.*)

FELICE: That's enough. That will do.

CLARE: Hold still just one moment longer.

FELICE: No, no, that's enough, Clare.

CLARE: Yes, well, now you look like a gentleman with excellent credit at every store in the town of New Bethesda!

FELICE: Hmmm . . .

CLARE: The door is shut—why did you shut the door?

FELICE: —The wind was blowing dust in.

CLARE: There is no wind at all.

FELICE: There *was*, so I—

CLARE: Shut the door. Will you be able to open it again?

FELICE: —Yes. Of course. (*He starts the tape recorder again. Then, after a hesitant moment, he draws the door open.*)

CLARE: —What are you waiting for?

FELICE: For you to go out.

CLARE: You go first. I'll follow.

FELICE: —How do I know you would?

CLARE: When a thing has been settled, I don't back out.

FELICE: That may be, but you are going out first.

CLARE: Will you come out right behind me or will you bolt the door on me and—

(*He seizes her hand and draws her forcibly to the door. She gasps.*)

FELICE: Out!

CLARE: See if—!

FELICE: There are no boys on the street! Stop this foolishness. Afternoons aren't everlasting you know.

CLARE: May I set my hat straight, *please?* (*She turns to a little dusty gilt-framed oval mirror to put the old straw hat on her head; it should have a touch of pathos but not be ludicrous.*)

FELICE: I thought you hated that hat.

CLARE: I certainly don't regard it as the most stylish piece of headgear in New Bethesda, but—I don't intend to make a call without a hat on my head. (*She removes the sprig of artificial cornflowers from the silk hatband and tries it in another position.*) Well, it just doesn't—

(*Felice snatches the hat off her head and tosses it on the stairs: then thrusts her through the door. She cries out a little as if dashed in cold water. He shuts the door behind them, takes her hand and leads her a few steps forward.*)

FELICE: Are you going to go on shaking like that?

CLARE: I will if you go on pushing me around.

FELICE: It's a—

CLARE: What?

FELICE: —Nice afternoon.

CLARE (*tensely*): Yes!

FELICE: You couldn't ask for a nicer afternoon, if afternoons could be asked for.

CLARE: I—have no complaints about it.

(*Slight pause*)

FELICE: I don't know what we're waiting here for. Do you? (*She makes a sudden startled turn.*)

CLARE: Slingshot in the—!

FELICE: No, no, no!

CLARE: Something moved in—

FELICE: A kangaroo! Jumped!

(*Clare tries to laugh.*)

We're waiting here like it was a bus stop back of the sun-flowers. And it's only a block and a half from here to Grossman's Market. So let's get a move on, slingshots, kangaroos, or—anything you can dream of. The sooner we get started the sooner we'll return with credit established again and livables and—necessities of persistence—three bags full!—including cigarettes . . .

CLARE: We mustn't—seem too greedy—all at once . . .

FELICE: Once we've assured Mr. Grossman that Acme will pay, there'll be no limit.

CLARE: You couldn't ask for a nicer afternoon, but—I think my suggestion was better.

FELICE: What was your suggestion?

CLARE: That *you* go to Grossman's Market and talk to Mr. Grossman.

FELICE: Alone? Without you?

CLARE: Yes, without me. I don't know why, but I'm shaking, I can't control it. It would make a bad impression on Mr. Grossman.

FELICE: You're not going to back out now. I won't allow you.

CLARE: Felice, while you're gone, I could, could, could—make a phone call to "Citizens Relief," you know, those people we wouldn't let in the house. I could tell them to come right over, and answer all their questions, and we would receive their relief even if Mr. Grossman doesn't believe the story.

FELICE: Clare, quit stalling. Let's go now.

CLARE: —I left something in the house.

FELICE: What?

CLARE: I left my—my—

FELICE: You see, you don't know what you left, so it can't be important.

CLARE: Oh, it is, it's very—it's the—cotton I put in my nose when I have a nosebleed, and I feel like I might have one almost any minute. The *lime dust*!

(*She turns quickly to the door but he blocks her, stretching his arms across the doorway. She utters a soft cry and runs around to the window. He reaches the window before she can climb in.*)

FELICE: You're not going to climb in that window!

CLARE: I am! Let me, I have to! I have a pain in my heart!

FELICE: Don't make me drag you by force to Grossman's Market!

CLARE: The moment I get back in I'll call the people from "Citizens Relief"!

FELICE: *Liar! Liar, and coward!*

CLARE: Oh, Felice, I—

(*She runs back to the door. He remains by the window. She enters the interior set and stares out at him, hands clasped tightly together. He steps over the low window sill, and they face each other silently for a moment.*)

FELICE: If we're not able to walk one block and a half to Grossman's Market, we're not able to live in this house or anywhere else but in two separate closed wards at State Haven. So now listen to me, Clare. Either you come back out and go through the program at Grossman's, or I will leave here and never come back here again, and you'll stay on here alone.

CLARE: You know what I'd do if I was left here alone.

FELICE: Yes, I know what she'd do, so I seize her arm and shout into her face: "Out again, the front door!" I try to drag her to it.

CLARE: I catch hold of something, cling to it! Cling to it for dear life!

FELICE: Cling to it!

CLARE: It's not on the set, the newel post of the stairs. I wrap both arms about it and he can't tear me loose.

FELICE: Stay here, stay here alone! When I go out of this house I'll never come back. I'll go and go! Away, away!

CLARE: I'll wait!

FELICE: For *what?*

CLARE: For *you!*

FELICE: That will be a long wait, a longer wait than you imagine. I'm leaving you now. *Good-bye!* (*He steps out over the low sill of the window.*)

CLARE (*calling out after him*): Don't stay long! Hurry back!

FELICE: Hah. (*He comes forward and speaks pantingly to the audience.*) The audience is supposed to imagine that the front of the house, where I am standing now, is shielded by sunflowers, too, but that was impractical as it would cut off the view. I stand here—move not a step further. Impossible without her. No, I can't leave her alone. I feel so exposed, so cold. And behind me I feel the house. It seems to be breathing a faint, warm breath on my back. I feel it the way you feel a loved person standing close behind you. Yes, I'm already defeated. The house is so old, so faded, so warm that, yes, it seems to be breathing. It seems to be whispering to me: "You can't go away. Give up. Come in and stay." Such a *gentle* command! What do I do? Naturally, I obey. (*He turns and enters by the door.*) I come back into the house, very quietly. I don't look at my sister.

CLARE: We're ashamed to look at each other. We're ashamed of having retreated—surrendered so quickly.

FELICE: There is a pause, a silence, our eyes avoiding each other's.

CLARE: Guiltily.

FELICE: No rock hits the house. No insults and obscenities are shouted.

CLARE: The afternoon light.

FELICE: Yes, the afternoon light is unbelievably golden on—

CLARE: The furniture which is so much older than we are—

FELICE: I realize, now, that the house has turned into a prison.

CLARE: I know it's a prison, too, but it's one that isn't strange to us.

(*For the first time since he re-entered the house, they look directly at each other, slowly, with difficulty.*)

FELICE: I don't lift my arms, not willingly. —They are lifted and they extend as if they weren't a part of me. —I don't know what I feel except a sense of—danger and—longing.

CLARE: I—have no—breath.

(*She takes several faltering steps toward him: then rushes into his extended arms: there is a convulsive embrace—like two lovers meeting after a long separation. Her lips are whispering against his face—inaudible words.*)

FELICE: Not—possible, the—stairs don't go upstairs, the steps—stop in—space!

CLARE: There's nothing, then, but—

(*Very gently, he thrusts her away from him: her eyes turn away from him too.*)

FELICE: "A garden enclosed is my sister . . ."

CLARE: What did I do with the card from Citizens Relief?

FELICE: You put it under—

CLARE: Oh. Grandmother's wedding picture. (*She lifts the picture and looks at it yearningly for a moment.*) A coronet of pearls, a hand lifting the veil from her radiant face.

FELICE: Clare, we've seen that picture all our lives. It's the card under the picture you picked the picture up for.

CLARE: To get the office number.

FELICE: Of Citizens Relief. It might close early you know.

CLARE: I'm going to call them at once.

FELICE: Make it just a simple dignified appeal for—necessary —assistance.

CLARE: Simple, dignified, yes.

(*She has crossed to the phone but her hand stops short of the receiver. He picks it up and thrusts it into her hand. She lifts it to her ear.*)

It makes no sound. I feel like screaming "Help, help!"

FELICE: —Is it—?

CLARE (*hanging up the receiver*): Sometimes a phone will go dead temporarily, just for a little while, and come back to life, you know.

FELICE: Yes, I know. Of course.

CLARE: —So we stay here and wait till it's connected again?

FELICE: We might have to wait till after the Relief Office closes. It might be a better idea to ask the people next door if we can use their phone since something's gone wrong with ours.

CLARE: That's right. Why don't you do that?

FELICE: *You* do that. It's the sort of thing you could do better. Look! (*He points at window.*) The woman next door is taking some clothes off her washline. Call her through the window.

(*Clare catches her breath. Then rushes to the window and calls out in a stifled voice:*)

CLARE: Please, may I, please, may we—!

FELICE: Not loud enough, call louder.

CLARE (*turning from the window*): —Did you really imagine that I could call and beg for "Citizens Relief" in front of those malicious people next door, on their phone, in their presence? Why, they gave their son a slingshot to stone the house! Whenever they catch a glimpse of us through a window, they grin like death.

(*Slight pause.*)

FELICE: You asked me what people did when they had nothing at all left to do.

CLARE: I asked you no such thing. (*After a moment, she dips a spool in the soapy water.*)

FELICE: Instead of calling the woman next door through the parlor window, you blow soap bubbles through it. Did you blow the soap bubbles out the window as an appeal to the world? They are lovely as your birthstone. They rise through the fading afternoon light. But they are a sign of surrender, and we know it. —And now I touch her hand lightly, which is a signal that I am about to speak a new line in *The Two-Character Play*. (*He touches her hand.*) Clare, didn't you tell me that yesterday or last night or today you found, you came across, a box of cartridges for Father's revolver?

CLARE: No! No, I—

FELICE: Clare, you say "yes," not "no." And then I pick up the property of the play which she's always hated and dreaded, so much that she refuses to remember that it exists in the play.

CLARE: I've said it's—*unnecessary.*

(*Felice has picked up a revolver from under the sheet music on the piano top.*)

Has it *always* been there?

FELICE: The revolver and the box of cartridges that you found last night have never been anywhere else, not in any performance of the play. Now I remove the blank cartridges and insert the real ones as calmly as if I were removing dead flowers from a vase and putting in fresh ones. Yes, as calmly as—

(*But his fingers are shaking so that the revolver falls to the floor. Clare gasps, then laughs breathlessly.*)

Stop it!

(*Clare covers her mouth with her hands.*)

Now I— (*He pauses.*)

CLARE: Have you forgotten what you do next? Too bad. I don't remember.

FELICE: I haven't forgotten what I do next. I put the revolver in the center of the little table across which we had discussed the attitude of nature toward its creatures that are regarded as *unnatural* creatures, and then I— (*After placing the revolver on the table, he pauses.*)

CLARE: What do you do next?

FELICE: Yes, I put on the tape and then I—I pick up my spool and dip it in the water and blow a soap bubble out the parlor window without the slightest concern about what neighbors may think. Of course, sometimes the soap bubble bursts before it rises, but this time please imagine you see it rising through gold light, above the gold sunflower heads. Now I turn to my sister who has the face of an angel and say to her: "Look! Do you see?" (*He mimes the action of blowing soap bubbles.*)

CLARE: Yes, I do, it's lovely and you made it . . . and it still hasn't broken.

FELICE: Sometimes we do still see the same things at the same time.

CLARE: Yes, and we would till locked in separate buildings and marched out at different hours, you by bullet-eyed guards and me by bullet-eyed matrons. (*She strikes a note on the piano.*) Oh, what a long, long, way we've traveled together, too long, now, for separation. Yes, all the way back to sunflowers and soap bubbles, and there's no turning back on the road even if the road's backward, and backward.

(*The tape machine misses and plays the music at triple tempo, which rises to a sound like a kind of shriek.*

(*Clare removes her white cotton gloves, glances at her brother's tranced face: he stares past her blindly. She draws a breath: then crosses to the machine and stops its playing.*

(*A couple of beats: silence.*)

—Well, that's that. (*She crosses to pick up her cloak.*) Put on your coat, Felice, I'm putting on mine, and I'll remove this —bewitching bit of millinery from my corn-silk head now. (*She takes off her hat, fiercely snatching the sprig of cornflowers from its band and tossing it to the floor.*)

FELICE (*blankly*): What?

CLARE: Felice, come out of the play! The house is completely empty.

FELICE: Walked? Out? All?

CLARE: Yes, yes, were you unconscious? One stood up down front with a grunt and the others all followed suit and shuffled out—en masse! And I'm glad the torture is over!

FELICE: *It—wasn't—your play!*

(*She brings him his coat.*)

CLARE: No, but you *wrote* it for me. Have I expressed my appreciation enough? (*She throws his coat about him and tries to button it.*)

FELICE: Don't! —Don't put things on me I can put on myself! This is not State Haven!

CLARE: —Only three smokables left. Soooo!—they've broken our rice bowl. —Smoke?

(*She hands him a cigarette. He looks out blindly.*)

Here! —And now call Fox. See if there's cash enough to get us out of this place to somewhere further south of the —Arctic Circle.

(*There is a pause. Felice is afraid to call Fox, who may be gone.*)

Well, for God's sake, call him!

FELICE (*calling into the house*): Fox! —*Fox!*

CLARE: Faithful Fox is silent as the proverbial—

FELICE: *Fox!*

CLARE: *Fox, Fox, Fox!*

TOGETHER: *Fox!*

(*There is an echo from their call.*)

CLARE: I'll tell you an unpleasant thought that's entered my head. Fox has absconded with the box-office receipts.

FELICE: Well, we'll track him down.

CLARE: I don't feel like fox hunting.

FELICE: Then what do you feel like?

CLARE (*lying down on the cushions*): Like falling into bed at the nearest hotel and sleeping the next thousand years.

FELICE: Well, go get your things.

CLARE: Get what things?

FELICE: Your purse, your handbag for instance.

CLARE: I don't have one to get.

FELICE: You've lost it again?

CLARE: I told you days ago that my bag had disappeared and it hasn't returned. What have you got in your wallet?

FELICE: Phone numbers and addresses of people mostly forgotten.

CLARE: Did we start with no money or just arrive here with no money?

FELICE: Things have kept disappearing. Isn't that how it was?

CLARE: Don't ask me how anything was, or is, or will be.

FELICE: When you make remarks of that kind, other people take them literally.

CLARE: This still seems like a performance of *The Two-Character Play*. The worst thing that's disappeared in our lives—I'll tell you what it is. Not the company, not Fox, not brandy in your flask, not successes that give confidence to go on—no, none of that. The worst thing that's disappeared in our lives is being aware of what's going on in our lives. We don't dare talk about, it's like a secret that we're conspiring to keep from each other, even though each of us knows that the other one knows it. (*She strikes a piano key.*) Felice, about the play. *The Two-Character Play.* I wonder sometimes if it isn't a little too personal, too special, for most audiences. Maybe—

FELICE: What do you mean by "too special"?

CLARE: Too personal, that's all, such as using our own names in it, and—

FELICE: At the first reading of it, you made a hypocritical remark. You said: "Why, it's like new wine, it has to be properly aged, so don't let's include it in this season's repertory."

CLARE: I said no such thing but I can tell you who did. It was poor old Gwendolyn Forbes that said that, and that's not all she said. She also said *The Two-Character Play* is a tour de force, it's more like an exercise in performance by two star performers, than like a play, a real play.

FELICE: There was never anyone by that name—what name did you say?—in the company.

CLARE: Felice, there was hardly a soul in the company whose name you could remember. The person I'm talking about is the one that burned to death in that hotel fire in—wherever it was—in some place—

FELICE: Oh. Her. She had a passion for incineration. Burned to death in a hotel fire and then had herself cremated.

CLARE: People burned to death don't have themselves cremated. We're both too tired to make sense. Call a limousine to pick us up and take us to a hotel.

(*Felice sits on the piano stool.*)

Felice, you're as tired as I am. Help me get up. My legs are gone.

(*He rises to help her but topples onto the cushions.*)

Thank you. Will we ever get up. We're sitting here panting for breath like a couple of dogs. Last cigarette, unless you have some.

FELICE: No. (*He lights her cigarette.*)

CLARE: We'll share it. Felice, is it possible that *The Two-Character Play* never had an ending? (*She passes the cigarette to him.*)

FELICE: Even if we were what the company called us in the telegram, we'd never attempt to perform a play that had no end to it, Clare.

CLARE: Then tell me how it ends, because I honestly can't remember a bit of it past the point where we stopped tonight.

FELICE: *The Two-Character Play* doesn't have a conventional ending.

CLARE: I don't mind that, that's fine, but what's the unconventional ending? Or can't you remember any better than I can?

(*He hands her the cigarette.*)

It never seems to end but just to stop, and it always seems to stop just short of something of a disturbing nature when you say: "The performance is over."

FELICE: It's possible for a play to have no ending in the usual sense of an ending, in order to make a point about nothing really ending.

CLARE: I didn't know you believed in the everlasting.

FELICE: That's not what I meant at all.

CLARE: I don't think you know what you meant. Things do end, they do actually have to.

FELICE: Well— (*Rising*) Up! Hotel! Grand entrance! We'll face everything tomorrow.

CLARE: Just before the performance you told me that Fox the foxy hasn't made us hotel reservations here, wherever here is!

FELICE: The one hotel in town is directly across the street from the theater, and we'll enter in such grand style that we'll need no reservations.

(*He crosses hurriedly into the wings and she starts to follow, but her exhaustion stops her at the upstage edge of the platform, facing the statue.*)

CLARE (*to the statue*): —Unalterable—circumstance—unaltered . . .

(*Offstage, frantic sounds begin to be heard, running footsteps, fists pounding and feet kicking at metal: muffled cries faintly echoed. This should continue at a varying pitch during Clare's solitary presence on the stage and should sometimes catch her attention.*

(*She slowly turns about to face downstage in a spot of light.*)

Well, he lost his argument about the impossible being necessary tonight. I think the impossible and the necessary pass each other on streets without recognition, could sit side by side without sign of the slightest acquaintance before or now or—ever . . .

(*Metallic crash, off stage.*)

Felice! —Well, it wasn't always all lost. —There were nights of—triumph, ovations—times of public honor! Memorable —celebrations— Crossing the Tiber in an open carriage, over that bridge of stone angels, when, suddenly, a hailstorm stung our faces and hands with little flowers of ice that made us sing and sing! (*She sings a snatch of "Come le rose" or "Dicitencello Vuoie." Stops, hearing distant shouts.*) *Felice?* —Oh, and that night in the wine garden on the Danube, the lights of a river boat, Russian soldiers singing in chorus! (*She sings a verse of the Russian Gypsy song "Coachman, don't whip the horses, I have no where to hurry to, I have no one to love"—(words in Russian). More pounding and shouting, muted.*) Felice! —"Your sister and you— insane, and so—" "Do you always go into a trance before a performance?" —"Yes, and after one, too." —Long dead now, many—gone . . . Felice, Felice!—when he finds that I am not following him as I've done all my life, he won't be coming back here with glad tidings, or a corsage of violets to pin on my—

(*She touches the lapel of her coat as Felice returns. He seems not to see her at first: he's breathless and stunned.*)

Well? —Have we met with some *new*—unalterable circumstance now?

(*He collapses among the cushions.*)

—Yes, I can see there's been another disaster. Let's put the props back into the old prop basket while we—prepare . . . (*She gathers up all but one cushion on which he has fallen and throws them into the battered wicker basket.*) Aren't you going to speak to me? Ever? Again?

FELICE: Clare, I'm afraid we may have to stay here a while.

CLARE: In this frozen country?

FELICE: I meant here in the theater.

CLARE: Oh!

FELICE: Yes, you see the front and back doors are locked from the outside, and as you know this building is windowless as a casket.

CLARE: Does this mean we have to stay here freezing till they open the building in the morning?

FELICE: Clare, there's no guarantee they'll open up the building in the morning or even in the evening or any morning or even after that.

CLARE: Out! Out! Out! (*Crazed with panic, she whirls about and snatches up the "play" phone. She realizes what it is and drops it as if it had scorched her hand.*)

FELICE: Hysteria won't help, Clare.

CLARE: The, the backstage phone?

FELICE: Disconnected as the phone in the play was.

CLARE: I think that this is some sort of dramatic metaphor that you are trying to catch me in, but I refuse to be caught!

FELICE: Even if it were possible to, would I want to?

CLARE: Obviously you accept this, it was your play and this is the end you want!

FELICE: Clare, I want no end but—

CLARE: —But?

FELICE: There seems to be no choice but—

CLARE: To march between the chaplain and warden conducting us to the execution chamber without resistance?

FELICE: The sentence was passed such a long time ago that the dread of execution is worn out. Fear *does* have a limit.

Contrary to my—opening—monologue, even fear has a limit . . .

CLARE (*tonelessly*): Monologue? —Opening?

FELICE (*with a passion of something—self-derision? despair?— but with a passion*): I'd started a new play. —I would have been too tired to finish it, though.

CLARE (*again abstracted*): —Oh . . .

FELICE (*with the same bitter force*): Just this evening, before you entered, I composed the opening monologue of a play that's—*closed! Unopened* . . . (*He throws his head back in a [silent?] self-mocking laugh—make sure it's not self-pity.*) You could put it *this* way. Fear is limited by the ability of a person to care any more.

CLARE: For anything but—

(*She clasps his head against her. A hollow metallic sound is heard.*)

I hear.

FELICE: This empty vault is full of echoes and echoes and echoes. The heat has been turned off and metal contracts with cold.

CLARE: That's a lovely elegiac note in your voice! Are you paralyzed there? Yes, you, but not me, I am not paralyzed, I am going to find the way out. (*She makes aborted moves in several directions, terrified of the dark that surrounds the dimming area of the stage: at each rush stops short with sharply arrested gestures.*) Human Out Cry!

FELICE: Give it up, Clare, give it up, it's useless. There are punctuation marks in life and it's time to admit that they include periods—one of which is final . . .

CLARE: Who do you think you're addressing? You're talking to your insanely practical sister, not to violet-haired Drama Club Ladies, digesting—*vol-au-vent* and *pêche-Melba*. —Felice, please! It's cold. It's not like the cold anywhere on the planet Earth, it's like the cold at the far, the further, the go-no-more last edge of space . . . So it's a prison, this last theater of yours.

FELICE: Yes, it would seem to be one.

CLARE: I've always suspected that theaters are prisons for players . . .

(The sound of distant explosions)

Listen! Gunfire! Bombardment!

FELICE: Or holiday firecrackers blocks away . . .

(The sound of distant gunfire.)

Clare, you're not frightened, are you?

CLARE: I'm too tired to be frightened, at least not yet. That's strange, you know, because I've always had such a dread of being locked up, caught, confined in a place—it's the greatest dread of my life. No, what I feel right now is bone-tired and bone-cold. Otherwise I'd get up and see for myself if these awful mysteries you've reported to me are exactly as you've reported.

FELICE: Do you think I've just imagined them, dreamed them, Clare?

(He goes out the door of the interior set. Clare becomes panicky.)

CLARE: Felice! Where are you going?

FELICE: To get the telegram from the company. (*He returns with it and smoothes it out on the table. He looks at it as if he had just received it.*)

CLARE: You have a dark thought in your head and I think I know what it is.

FELICE: Sometimes we have the same thoughts at the same time.

CLARE: It's getting colder and colder, moment by moment.

FELICE: During the performance—

CLARE: Yes, such as it was or wasn't—

FELICE: It was cold even with the lights on us, but I was so lost in the play that it seemed warm as summer.

CLARE: You're suggesting that—

FELICE: We must go back into the play.

CLARE: But with the stage so dim—

FELICE: If we can imagine summer, we can imagine more light.

CLARE: When we're lost in the play.

FELICE: Yes, completely lost in *The Two-Character Play*.

CLARE: We could try it, we could give it a try.

FELICE: Other alternatives lacking.

CLARE: Could we keep on our coats?

FELICE: Oh, we could, I suppose, but I think the feeling of summer with sunflowers and soap bubbles would come more easily to us if we took our coats off.

CLARE: All right. Do we stop where we stopped tonight or do we look for the ending?

FELICE: Don't worry about the ending, it'll come to us, Clare. I think you'll find it wherever you hid it.

CLARE: Wherever *you* hid it, not me. (*She catches her breath, suddenly, and raises a hand to her mouth.*)

FELICE: Is something wrong?

CLARE: No!—no—

(*He helps her remove her coat. As he removes his, she hugs her shoulders against the cold. He takes the revolver off the table.*)

FELICE: The properties of the play are the properties of our lives. Where would you like me to hide it?

CLARE: Under a sofa pillow?

FELICE: Yes, I guess that will do.

(*He places the revolver under the pillow. Clare starts the tape.*)

CLARE: And we'll find the end of the play?

FELICE: By the time we come to the end, we'll be so lost in the play that—

CLARE: The end will simply happen.

FELICE: Yes, just happen.

CLARE: Where shall we start, at the top of the play, the phone bit?

FELICE: Yes, take your place by the phone. The performance commences.

CLARE: When a performance works out inevitably, it works out well. (*She lifts the telephone.*)

FELICE: Who are you calling, Clare?

CLARE: Not a soul existing in the world gone away.

FELICE (*very fast*): Then why did you pick up the phone?

CLARE: To see if it's still connected.

FELICE: We would have been notified if—

CLARE: It's a mistake to depend on—notification. Especially when a house looks vacant at night. (*She hangs up the phone.*)

FELICE: Night, what a restless night.

CLARE: Wasn't it, though?

FELICE: I didn't sleep at all well and neither did you. I heard you wandering about the house as if you were looking for something.

CLARE: Yes, I was and I found it. (*She pauses.*) Are you lost in the play?

FELICE: Yes, it's a warm August day.

CLARE (*raising a hand, tenderly, to his head*): I'm sure Acme and Mr. Grossman will believe our story. We can believe it ourselves, and then livables, and necessities of persistence will be delivered through the barricade of—

FELICE: Go straight to the tall sunflowers.

CLARE: Quick as that?

FELICE: That quick!

CLARE: Felice, look out the window. There's a giant sunflower out there that's grown as tall as the house.

(*He draws a long breath, then leans out the window.*)

FELICE: *Oh, yes, I see it. Its color's so brilliant that it seems to be shouting!*

CLARE: Keep your eyes on it a minute, it's a sight to be seen.

(*She crosses to the sofa: lifts the pillow beneath which the revolver is concealed: gasps and drops the pillow back: looks toward Felice.*)

FELICE: Hurry, it won't hold!

(*She crosses to him and touches his hand.*)

CLARE: —Magic is a habit.

(*They look slowly up at the sunflower projections.*)

FELICE: —Magic is the habit of our existence . . .

(*The lights fade, and they accept its fading, as a death, somehow transcended.*)

Curtain

VIEUX CARRÉ

INSCRIBED TO KEITH HACK

TIME: The period between winter 1938 and spring 1939.

PLACE: A rooming house, No. 722 Toulouse Street, in the French Quarter of New Orleans.

THE SETTING OF THE PLAY: The stage seems bare. Various playing areas may be distinguished by sketchy partitions and doorframes. In the barrenness there should be a poetic evocation of all the cheap rooming houses of the world. This one is in the Vieux Carré of New Orleans, where it remains standing, at 722 Toulouse Street, now converted to an art gallery. I will describe the building as it was when I rented an attic room in the late thirties, not as it will be designed, or realized for the stage.

It is a three-story building. There are a pair of alcoves, facing Toulouse Street. These alcove cubicles are separated by plywood, which provides a minimal separation (spatially) between the writer (myself those many years ago) and an older painter, a terribly wasted man, dying of tuberculosis, but fiercely denying this circumstance to himself.

A curved staircase ascends from the rear of a dark narrow passageway from the street entrance to the kitchen area. From there it ascends to the third floor, or gabled attic with its mansard roof.

A narrow hall separates the gabled cubicles from the studio (with skylight) which is occupied by Jane and Tye.

Obviously the elevations of these acting areas can be only suggested by a few shallow steps: a realistic setting is impossible, and the solution lies mainly in very skillful lighting and minimal furnishings.

PART ONE

SCENE ONE

WRITER (*spotlighted downstage*): Once this house was alive, it was occupied once. In my recollection, it still is, but by shadowy occupants like ghosts. Now they enter the lighter areas of my memory.

(*Fade in dimly visible characters of the play, turning about in a stylized manner. The spotlight fades on the writer and is brought up on Mrs. Wire, who assumes her active character in the play.*)

MRS. WIRE: Nursie! Nursie—where's my pillows?

(*Nursie is spotlighted on a slightly higher level, looking up fearfully at something. She screams.*)

Hey, what the hell is going on in there!

NURSIE (*running down in a sort of football crouch*): A bat, a bat's in the kitchen!

MRS. WIRE: Bat? I never seen a bat nowhere on these premises, Nursie.

NURSIE: Why, Mizz Wire, I swear it was a bull bat up there in the kitchen. You tell me no bats, why, they's a pack of bats that hang upside down from that ole banana tree in the courtyard from dark till daybreak, when they all scream at once and fly up like a—explosion of—damned souls out of a graveyard.

MRS. WIRE: If such a thing was true—

NURSIE: As God's word is true!

MRS. WIRE: I repeat, if such a thing was true—which it isn't—an' you go tawkin' about it with you big black mouth, why it could ruin the reputation of this rooming house which is the only respectable rooming house in the Quarter. Now where's my pillows, Nursie?

NURSIE (sotto voce *as she arranges the pallet*): Shit . . .

MRS. WIRE: What you say?

NURSIE: I said shoot . . . faw shit. You'd see they're on the cot if you had a light bulb in this hall. (*She is making up the*

829

cot.) What you got against light? First thing God said on the first day of creation was, "Let there be light."

MRS. WIRE: You hear him say that?

NURSIE: You never read the scriptures.

MRS. WIRE: Why should I bother to read 'em with you quotin' 'em to me like a female preacher. Book say this, say that, makes me sick of the book. Where's my flashlight, Nursie?

NURSIE: 'Sunder the pillows. (*She stumbles on a heavy knapsack.*) Lawd! What that there?

MRS. WIRE: Some crazy young man come here wantin' a room. I told him I had no vacancies for Bourbon Street bums. He dropped that sack on the floor and said he'd pick it up tomorrow, which he won't unless he pays fifty cents for storage . . .

NURSIE: It's got something written on it that shines in the dark.

MRS. WIRE: "Sky"—say that's his name. Carry it on upstairs with you, Nursie.

NURSIE: Mizz Wire, I cain't hardly get myself up them steps no more, you know that.

MRS. WIRE: Shoot.

NURSIE: Mizz Wire, I think I oughta inform you I'm thinkin' of retirin'.

MRS. WIRE: *Retirin'* to what, Nursie? The banana tree in the courtyard with the bats you got in your head?

NURSIE: They's lots of folks my age, black an' white, that's called bag people. They just wander round with paper bags that hold ev'rything they possess or they can collect. Nights they sleep on doorsteps: spend days on boxes on corners of Canal Street with a tin cup. They get along: they live—long as intended to by the Lord.

MRS. WIRE: Yor place is with me, Nursie.

NURSIE: I can't please you no more. You keep callin' Nursie, Nursie, do this, do that, with all these stairs in the house and my failin' eyesight. No Ma'am, it's time for me to retire.

(*She crosses upstage. The kitchen area is dimly lighted. Nursie sits at the table with a cup of chicory coffee, eyes large and ominously dark as the continent of her race.*

(*A spot of light picks up the writer dimly at the entrance to the hall.*)

MRS. WIRE: Who? Who?

WRITER: It's—

MRS. WIRE: *You* . . .

WRITER: Mrs. Wire, you're blinding me with that light. (*He shields his left eye with a hand.*)

MRS. WIRE (*switching off the light*): Git upstairs, boy. We'll talk in the mawnin' about your future plans.

WRITER: I have no plans for the future, Mrs. Wire.

MRS. WIRE: That's a situation you'd better correct right quick.

(*The writer, too, collides with the bizarre, colorfully decorated knapsack.*)

WRITER: What's—?

MRS. WIRE: Carry that sack upstairs with you. Nursie refused to.

(*With an effort the writer shoulders the sack and mounts a step or two to the kitchen level.*)

WRITER: Mrs. Wire told me to carry this sack up here.

NURSIE: Just put it somewhere it won't trip me up.

WRITER: Sky? Sky?

NURSIE: She say that's his name. Whose name? I think her mind is goin' on her again. Lately she calls out, "Timmy, Timmy," or she carries on conversations with her dead husband, Horace . . .

WRITER: A name—Sky? (*To himself:*) Shines like a prediction.

(*He drops the knapsack at the edge of the kitchen light and wanders musingly back to the table. Nursie automatically pours him a cup of chicory.*

(*Again the area serving as the entrance passage is lighted, and the sound of a key scraping at a resistant lock is heard.*)

MRS. WIRE (*starting up from her cot*): Who? Who?

(*Jane enters exhaustedly.*)

JANE: Why, Mrs. Wire, you scared me! (*She has an elegance about her and a vulnerability.*)

MRS. WIRE: Miss Sparks, what're you doin' out so late on the streets of the Quarter?

JANE: Mrs. Wire, according to the luminous dial on my watch, it is only ten after twelve.

MRS. WIRE: When I give you a room here . . .

JANE: Gave me? I thought rented . . .

MRS. WIRE (*cutting through*): I told you a single girl was expected in at midnight.

JANE: I'm afraid I didn't take that too seriously. Not since I lived with my parents in New Rochelle, New York, before I went to college, have I been told to be in at a certain hour, and even then I had my own key and disregarded the order more often than not. However! I *am* going to tell you why and where I've gone tonight. I have gone to the all-night drugstore, Waterbury's, on Canal Street, to buy a spray can of Black Flag, which is an insect repellent. I took a cab there tonight and made this purchase because, Mrs. Wire, when I opened the window without a screen in my room, a cockroach, a *flying* cockroach, flew right into my face and was followed by a squadron of others. *Well!* I do *not* have an Oriental, a Buddhistic tolerance for certain insects, least of all a cockroach and even less a flying one. Oh, I've learned to live reluctantly with the ordinary pedestrian kind of cockroach, but to have one fly directly into my face almost gave me convulsions! Now as for the window without a screen, if a screen has not been put in that window by tomorrow, I will buy one for it myself and deduct the cost from next month's rent. (*She goes past Mrs. Wire toward the steps.*)

MRS. WIRE: Hold on a minute, young lady. When you took your room here, you gave your name as Miss Sparks. Now is that young fellow that's living up there with you Mr. Sparks, and if so why did you register as Miss instead of Mrs.?

JANE: I'm sure you've known for some time that I'm sharing my room with a young man, whose name is not Mr. Sparks, whose name is Tye McCool. And if that offends your moral scruples—well—sometimes it offends mine, too.

MRS. WIRE: If I had not been a young lady myself once! Oh yes, once, yaiss! I'd have evicted, both, so fast you'd think that . . .

JANE: No, I've stopped thinking. Just let things happen to me.

(*Jane is now at the stairs and starts up them weakly. Mrs. Wire grunts despairingly and falls back to her cot. Jane enters the kitchen.*)

NURSIE: Why, hello, Miss Sparks.

JANE: Good evening, Nursie—why is Mrs. Wire sleeping in the entrance hall?

NURSIE: Lawd, that woman, she got the idea that 722 Toulouse Street is the address of a jailhouse. And she's the keeper—have some hot chick'ry with me?

JANE: Do you know I still don't know what chicory is? A beverage of some kind?

NURSIE: Why chicory's South'n style coffee.

JANE: Oh, well, thank you, maybe I could try a bit of it to get me up that flight of stairs . . .

(*She sits at the table. Below, the door has opened a third time. The painter called Nightingale stands in the doorway with a pickup.*)

MRS. WIRE: Who? Ah!

NIGHTINGALE (*voice rising*): Well, cousin, uh, Jake . . .

PICKUP (*uneasily*): Blake.

NIGHTINGALE: Yes, we do have a lot of family news to exchange. Come on in. We'll talk a bit more in my room.

MRS. WIRE: In a pig's snout you will!

NIGHTINGALE: Why, Mrs. Wire! (*He chuckles, coughs.*) Are you sleeping in the hall now?

MRS. WIRE: I'm keeping watch on the comings and goings at night of tenants in my house.

NIGHTINGALE: Oh, yes, I know your aversion to visitors at night, but this is my first cousin. I just bumped into him at Gray Goose bus station. He is here for one day only, so I have taken the license of inviting him in for a little family talk since we'll have no other chance.

MRS. WIRE: If you had half the cousins you claim to have, you'd belong to the biggest family since Adam's.

PICKUP: Thanks, but I got to move on. Been nice seeing you—cousin . . .

NIGHTINGALE: Wait—here—take this five. Go to the America Hotel on Exchange Alley just off Canal Street, and I will drop in at noon tomorrow—cousin . . . (*He starts to cough.*)

PICKUP: Thanks, I'll see ya, cousin.

MRS. WIRE: Hah, cousin.

(*Nightingale coughs and spits near her cot.*)

Don't you spit by my bed!

NIGHTINGALE: Fuck off, you old witch!

MR. WIRE: What did you say to me?

NIGHTINGALE: Nothing not said to and about you before! (*He mounts the steps.*)

MRS. WIRE: Nursie! Nursie! (*Receiving no response she lowers herself with a groan onto the cot.*)

NIGHTINGALE (*starting up the stairs*): Midnight staircase—still in—your (*coughs*) fatal position . . . (*He climbs slowly up.*)

(*The writer, Jane, and Nursie are in the kitchen. The crones enter, wild-eyed and panting with greasy paper bags. The kitchen area is lighted.*)

MARY MAUDE: Nursie? Miss Carrie and I ordered a little more dinner this evening than we could eat, so we had the waiter put the remains of the, the—

MISS CARRIE (*her wild eyes very wild*): The steak "Diane," I had the steak Diane and Mary Maude had the chicken "bonne femme." But our eyes were a little bigger than our stomachs.

MARY MAUDE: The sight of too much on a table can kill your appetite! But this food is too good to waste.

MISS CARRIE: And we don't have ice to preserve it in our room, so would you kindly put it in Mrs. Wire's icebox, Nursie.

NURSIE: The last time I done that Miss Wire raised Cain about it, had me throw it right out. She said it didn' smell good.

JANE: I have an icebox in which I'd be glad to keep it for you ladies.

MARY MAUDE: Oh, that's very kind of you!

WRITER (*rising from the kitchen table*): Let me carry it up.

(*He picks up the greasy bags and starts upstairs. Miss Carrie's asthmatic respiration has steadily increased. She staggers with a breathless laugh.*)

MARY MAUDE: Oh, Miss Carrie, you better get right to bed. She's having another attack of her awful asthma. Our room gets no sun, and the walls are so damp, so—dark . . .

(*They totter out of the light together.*)

NURSIE (*averting her face from the bag with a sniff of repugnance*): They didn't go to no restaurant. They been to the garbage pail on the walk outside, don't bother with it, it's spoiled (*pointing upstage*), just put it over there, I'll throw it out.

JANE: I wonder if they'd be offended if I bought them a sack of groceries at Solari's tomorrow.

NURSIE: Offend 'em did you say?

JANE: I meant their pride.

NURSIE: Honey, they gone as far past pride as they gone past mistaking a buzzard for a bluebird.

(*She chuckles. Tye appears. Jane pretends not to notice.*)

JANE: I'm afraid pride's an easy thing to go past sometimes. I am living—I am sharing my studio with a, an addicted—delinquent, a barker at a—stripshow joint. (*She has pretended to ignore Tye's disheveled, drugged, but vulnerably boyish appearance at the edge of the light.*)

TYE (*in a slurred voice*): You wouldn't be tawkin' about—nobody—present . . .

JANE: Why, hello, Tye. How'd you get back so early? How'd you get back at all, in this—condition?

TYE: Honey! If I didn't have my arms full of—packages.

JANE: The less you say out loud about the hot merchandise you've been accumulating here . . .

TYE: Babe, you're asking for a— (*He doubles his fist.*)

JANE: Which I'd return with a kick in the balls! (*She gasps.*) My Lord, did I say that?

MRS. WIRE: What's that shoutin' about?

(*Jane breaks into tears. She falls back into the chair and buries her head in her arms.*)

TYE: Hey, love, come here, I knocked off work early to be with you—do you think I'd really hit you?

JANE: I don't know . . .

TYE: Come to—bed . . .
JANE: Don't lean on me.

(*They cross out of the light. The writer looks after them wistfully as the light dims out.*)

SCENE TWO

The writer has undressed and is in bed. Nightingale coughs—a fiendish, racking cough. He is hacking and spitting up bloody phlegm. He enters his cubicle.

Then across the makeshift partition in the writer's cubicle, unlighted except by a faint glow in its alcove window, another sound commences—a sound of dry and desperate sobbing which sounds as though nothing in the world could ever appease the wound from which it comes: loneliness, inborn and inbred to the bone.

Slowly, as his coughing fit subsides, Nightingale, the quicksketch artist, turns his head in profile to the sound of the sobbing. Then the writer, across the partition, is dimly lighted, too. He is also sitting up on his cot, staring at the partition between his cell and Nightingale's.

Nightingale clears his throat loudly and sings hoarsely and softly a pop song of the era such as "If I Didn't Care" or "Paper Doll." Slowly the audience of one whom he is serenading succeeds in completely stifling the dry sobbing with a pillow. Nightingale's voice rises a bit as he gets up and lights a cigarette; then he goes toward the upstage limit of the dim stage lighting and makes the gesture of opening a door.

He moves into the other gable room of the attic and stands, silent, for several beats of the song as the writer slowly, reluctantly, turns on his cot to face him.

NIGHTINGALE: . . . I want to ask you something.
WRITER: Huh?
NIGHTINGALE: The word "landlady" as applied to Mrs. Wire and all landladies that I've encountered in my life—isn't it the biggest one-word contradiction in the English language? (*The writer is embarrassed by Nightingale's intrusion and steady scrutiny.*) She owns the land, yes, but is the witch a lady? Mind if I switch on your light?

WRITER: The bulb's burned out.

NIGHTINGALE (*chuckles and coughs*): She hasn't replaced a burnt-out light bulb in this attic since I moved here last spring. I have to provide my own light bulbs by unscrewing them from the gentleman's lavatory at the City of the Two Parrots, where I ply my trade. Temporarily, you know. Doing portraits in pastel of the tourist clientele. (*His voice is curiously soft and intimate, more as if he were speaking of personal matters.*)

Of course I . . . (*He coughs and clears his throat.*) . . . *have no shame about it*, no guilt at all, since what I do there is a travesty of my talent, I mean a prostitution of it, I mean, painting these tourists at the Two Parrots, which are actually two very noisy macaws. Oh, they have a nice patio there, you know, palm trees and azaleas when in season, but the cuisine and the service . . . abominable. The menu sometimes includes cockroaches . . . (There are a lot of great eating places in New Orleans, like Galatoire's, Antoine's, Arnaud's in the Vieux Carré and . . . Commander's Palace and Plantation House in the Garden District . . . lovely old mansions, you know, converted to restaurants with a gracious style . . . haunted by dead residents, of course, but with charm . . .)

(*This monologue is like a soothing incantation, interspersed with hoarseness and coughing.*)

Like many writers, I know you're a writer, you're a young man of very few spoken words, compared to my garrulity.

WRITER: Yes, I . . .

NIGHTINGALE: So far, kid, you're practically . . . monosyllabic.

WRITER: I . . . don't feel well . . . tonight.

NIGHTINGALE: That's why I intruded. You have a candle on that box beside your cot.

WRITER: Yes, but no matches.

NIGHTINGALE: I have matches, I'll light it. Talk is easier . . . (*He strikes the match and advances to the writer's bedside.*) . . . between two people visible to each other, if . . . not too sharply . . . (*He lights the candle.*) Once I put up for a night in a flophouse without doors, and a gentleman entered my cubicle without invitation, came straight to my cot and struck a match, leaned over me peering directly into my face . . . and then said, "No," and walked out . . . as if he assumed that I would have said, "Yes." (*He laughs and coughs.*)

(*Pause*)

You're not a man of few words but a boy of no words. I'll just sit on the cot if you don't object.

WRITER: . . . I, uh . . . do need sleep.

NIGHTINGALE: You need some company first. I know the sound of loneliness: heard it through the partition. (*He has sat on the cot. The writer huddles away to the wall, acutely embarrassed.*) . . . Trying not to, but crying . . . why try not to? Think it's unmanly? Crying is a release for man or woman . . .

WRITER: I was taught not to cry because it's . . . humiliating . . .

NIGHTINGALE: You're a victim of conventional teaching, which you'd better forget. What were you crying about? Some particular sorrow or . . . for the human condition.

WRITER: Some . . . particular sorrow. My closest relative died last month.

NIGHTINGALE: Your mother?

WRITER: The mother of my mother, Grand. She died after a long illness just before I left home, and at night I remember . . .

NIGHTINGALE (*giving a comforting pat*): Well, losses must be accepted and survived. How strange it is that we've occupied these adjoining rooms for about three weeks now and have just barely said hello to each other when passing on the stairs. You have interesting eyes.

WRITER: In what way do you mean?

NIGHTINGALE: Isn't the pupil of the left one a little bit lighter?

WRITER: . . . I'm afraid I'm . . . developing a—cataract in that eye.

NIGHTINGALE: That's not possible for a kid.

WRITER: I am twenty-eight.

NIGHTINGALE: What I meant is, your face is still youthful as your vulnerable nature, they go—together. Of course, I'd see an oculist if you suspect there's a cataract.

WRITER: I plan to when I . . . if I . . . can ever afford to . . . the vision in that eye's getting cloudy.

NIGHTINGALE: Don't wait till you can afford to. Go straight away and don't receive the bill.

WRITER: I couldn't do that.

NIGHTINGALE: Don't be so honest in this dishonest world. (*He pauses and coughs.*) Shit, the witch don't sleep in her bedroom you know.

WRITER: Yes, I noticed she is sleeping on a cot in the hall now.

NIGHTINGALE: When I came in now she sprang up and hollered out, "Who?" And I answer her with a hoot owl imitation, "Hoo, Hooo, Hooooo." Why, the lady is all three furies in one. A single man needs visitors at night. Necessary as bread, as blood in the body. Why, there's a saying, "Better to live with your worst enemy than to live alone."

WRITER: Yes, loneliness is an—affliction.

NIGHTINGALE: Well, now you have a friend here.

WRITER (*dryly*): Thanks.

NIGHTINGALE: Of course we're in a madhouse. I wouldn't tolerate the conditions here if the season wasn't so slow that—my financial condition is difficult right now. I don't like insults and *la vie solitaire*—with bedbugs bleeding me like leeches . . . but now we know each other, the plywood partition between us has been dissolved, no more just hellos. So tonight you were crying in here alone. What of it? Don't we all? Have a cigarette.

WRITER: Thanks.

(*Nightingale holds the candle out.*)

I won't smoke it now, I'll save it till morning. I like a cigarette when I sit down to work.

(*Nightingale's steady scrutiny embarrasses him. They fall silent. After several beats, the writer resumes.*)

There's—a lot of human material—in the Quarter for a writer . . .

NIGHTINGALE: I used to hear you typing. Where's your typewriter?

WRITER: I, uh, hocked it.

NIGHTINGALE: That's what I figured. Wha'd you get for it?

WRITER: Ten dollars. It was a secondhand Underwood portable. I'm worried about just how I'll redeem it. (*He is increasingly embarrassed.*)

NIGHTINGALE: Excuse my cusiosity, I mean concern. It's
sympathetic . . . Smoke a cigarette now and have another
for mawnin'. You're not managing right. Need advice
and . . . company in this sad ole house. I'm happy to give
both if accepted.

WRITER: . . . I appreciate . . . both.

NIGHTINGALE: You don't seem experienced yet . . . kid, are
you . . . excuse my blunt approach . . . but are you . . . ?
(*He completes the question by placing a shaky hand on the
writer's crumpled, sheet-covered body.*)

WRITER (*in a stifled voice*): Oh . . . I'm not sure I know . . .
I . . .

NIGHTINGALE: Ain't come out completely, as we put it?

WRITER: Completely, no, just one—experience.

NIGHTINGALE: Tell me about that one experience.

WRITER: I'm not sure I want to discuss it.

NIGHTINGALE: That's no way to begin a confidential friendship.

WRITER: . . . Well, New Year's Eve, I was entertained by a
married couple I had a letter of introduction to when I
came down here, the . . . man's a painter, does popular
bayou pictures displayed in shop windows in the Quarter,
his name is . . .

NIGHTINGALE: Oh, I know him. He's got a good thing going, commercially speaking, tourists buy them calendar illustrations in dreamy rainbow colors that never existed but
in the head of a hack like him.

WRITER: . . . The, uh, atmosphere is . . . effective.

NIGHTINGALE: Oh, they sell to people that don't know paint
from art. Maybe you've never seen artistic paintings. (*His
voice shakes with feverish pride.*) I could do it, in fact I've
done good painting, serious work. But I got to live, and
you can't live on good painting until you're dead, or nearly.

So, I make it, temporarily, as a quick sketch artist. I flatter old bitches by makin' 'em ten pounds lighter and ten years younger and with some touches of—decent humanity in their eyes that God forgot to put there, or they've decided to dispense with, not always easy. But what is? So—you had an experience with the bayou painter? I didn't know he was, oh, inclined to boys, this is killing?

WRITER (*slowly with embarrassment*): It wasn't with Mr. Block, it was with a . . . paratrooper.

NIGHTINGALE: Aha, a paratrooper dropped out of the sky for you, huh? You have such nice smooth skin . . . Would you like a bit of white port? I keep a half pint by my bed to wash down my sandman special when this touch of flu and the bedbugs keep me awake. Just a mo', I'll fetch it, we'll have a nightcap—now that we're acquainted! (*He goes out rapidly, coughing, then rushes back in with the bottle.*)

The witch has removed the glass, we'll have to drink from the bottle. I'll wash my pill down now, the rest is yours. (*He pops a capsule into his mouth and gulps from the bottle, immediately coughing and gagging. He extends the bottle to the writer.*)

(*Pause. The writer half extends his hand toward the bottle, then draws it back and shakes his head.*)

Oh yes, flu is contagious, how stupid of me, I'm sorry.

WRITER: Never mind, I don't care much for liquor.

NIGHTINGALE: Where you from?

WRITER: . . . St. Louis.

NIGHTINGALE: Christ, do people live there?

WRITER: It has a good art museum and a fine symphony orchestra and . . .

NIGHTINGALE: No decent gay life at all?

WRITER: You mean . . .

NIGHTINGALE: You know what I mean. I mean like the . . . paratrooper.

WRITER: Oh. No. There could be but . . . living at home . . .

NIGHTINGALE: Tell me, how did it go with the paratrooper who descended on you at Block's?

WRITER: Well at midnight we went out on the gallery and he, the paratrooper, was out on the lower gallery with a party of older men, antique dealers, they were all singing "Auld Lang Syne."

NIGHTINGALE: How imaginative and *appropriate* to them.

WRITER: —I noticed him down there and he noticed me.

NIGHTINGALE: Noticing him?

WRITER: . . . Yes. He grinned, and hollered to come down; he took me into the lower apartment. It was vacant, the others still on the gallery, you see I . . . couldn't understand his presence among the . . .

NIGHTINGALE: Screaming old faggots at that antique dealer's. Well, they're rich and they buy boys, but that's a scene that you haven't learned yet. So. What happened downstairs?

WRITER: He took me into a bedroom; he told me I looked pale and wouldn't I like a sunlamp treatment. I thought he meant my face so I—agreed—

NIGHTINGALE: Jesus, you've got to be joking.

WRITER: I was shaking violently like I was a victim of—St. Vitus's Dance, you know, when he said, "Undress"!

NIGHTINGALE: But you did.

WRITER: Yes. He helped me. And I stretched out on the bed under the sunlamp and suddenly he—

NIGHTINGALE: . . . turned it off and did you?

WRITER: Yes, that's what happened. I think that he was shocked by my reaction.

NIGHTINGALE: You did *him* or—?

WRITER: . . . I told him that I . . . loved . . . him. I'd been drinking.

NIGHTINGALE: Love can happen like that. For one night only.

WRITER: He said, he laughed and said, "Forget it. I'm flying out tomorrow for training base."

NIGHTINGALE: He said to you, "Forget it," but you didn't forget it.

WRITER: No . . . I don't even have his address and I've forgotten his name . . .

NIGHTINGALE: Still, I think you loved him.

WRITER: . . . Yes. I . . . I'd like to see some of your serious paintings sometime.

NIGHTINGALE: Yeah. You will. Soon. When I get them canvases shipped down from Baton Rouge next week. But meanwhile . . . (*His hand is sliding down the sheet.*) How about this?

WRITER (*with gathering panic*): . . . I think I'd better get some sleep now. I didn't mean to tell you all that. Goodnight, I'm going to sleep.

NIGHTINGALE (*urgently*): This would help you.

WRITER: I need to sleep nights—to work.

NIGHTINGALE: You are alone in the world, and I am, too. Listen. Rain!

(*They are silent. The sound of rain is heard on the roof.*)

Look. I'll give you two things for sleep. First, this. (*He draws back the sheet. The light dims.*) And then one of these pills I call my sandman special.

WRITER: I don't . . .

NIGHTINGALE: Shh, walls have ears! Lie back and imagine the paratrooper.

(*The dim light goes completely out. A passage of blues piano is heard. It is an hour later. There is a spotlight on the writer as narrator, smoking at the foot of the cot, the sheet drawn about him like a toga.*)

WRITER: When I was alone in the room, the visitor having retreated beyond the plywood partition between his cubicle and mine, which was chalk white that turned ash-gray at night, not just he but everything visible was gone except for the lighter gray of the alcove with its window over Toulouse Street. An apparition came to me with the hypnotic effect of the painter's sandman special. It was in the form of an elderly female saint, of course. She materialized soundlessly. Her eyes fixed on me with a gentle questioning look which I came to remember as having belonged to my grandmother during her sieges of illness, when I used to go to her room and sit by her bed and want, so much, to say something or to put my hand over hers, but could do neither, knowing that if I did, I'd betray my feelings with tears that would trouble her more than her illness . . . Now it was she who stood next to my bed for a while. And as I drifted toward sleep, I wondered if she'd witnessed the encounter between the

painter and me and what her attitude was toward such—
perversions? Of longing?

(*The sound of stifled coughing is heard across the plywood partition.*)

Nothing about her gave me any sign. The weightless hands
clasping each other so loosely, the cool and believing gray
eyes in the faint pearly face were as immobile as statuary. I
felt that she neither blamed nor approved the encounter.
No. Wait. She . . . seemed to lift one hand very, very
slightly before my eyes closed with sleep. An almost invisible gesture of . . . forgiveness? . . . through understanding? . . . Before she dissolved into sleep . . .

SCENE THREE

*Tye is in a seminarcotized state on the bed in Jane's room. Jane
is in the hall burdened with paper sacks of groceries; the writer
appears behind her.*

JANE (*brightly*): Good morning.

WRITER (*shyly*): Oh, good morning.

JANE: Such a difficult operation, opening a purse with one
hand.

WRITER: Let me hold the sacks for you.

JANE: Oh, thanks; now then, come in, put the sacks on one of
those chairs. Over the weekend we run out of everything.
Ice isn't delivered on Sundays: milk spoils. Everything of a
perishable kind has got to be replaced. Oh, don't go out.
Have you had a coffee?

WRITER (*looking at Tye*): I was about to but . . .

JANE: Stay and have some with me. Sorry it's instant, can you
stand instant coffee?

WRITER: I beg your pardon?

JANE: Don't mind him, when his eyes are half open it doesn't
mean he is conscious.

TYE: Bullshit, you picked up a kid on the street?

JANE (*suppressing anger*): This is the young man from across
the hall— I'm Jane Sparks, my friend is Tye McCool, and
you are—

WRITER (*pretending to observe a chess board to cover his embarrassment*): What a beautiful chess board!

JANE: Oh, that, yes!

WRITER: Ivory and ebony? Figures?

JANE: The white squares are mother-of-pearl. Do you play chess?

WRITER: Used to. You play together, you and Mr.— McCool?

TYE: Aw, yeh, we play together but not chess. (*He rubs his crotch. Jane and the writer nervously study the chess board.*)

JANE: I play alone, a solitary game, to keep in practice in case I meet a partner.

WRITER: Look. Black is in check.

JANE: My imaginary opponent. I choose sides you see, although I play for both.

WRITER: I'd be happy to—I mean sometimes when you—

TYE (*touching the saucepan on the burner*): OW!

JANE: I set it to boil before I went to the store.

(*Jane sets a cup and doughnuts on the table.*)

TYE: Hey, kid, why don't you take your cup across the hall to your own room?

JANE: Because I've just now—you heard me—invited him to have it here in this room with me.

TYE: I didn't invite him in, and I want you to git something straight: I live here. And if I live in a place I got equal rights in this place, and it just so happens I don't entertain no stranger to look at me undressed.

WRITER (*gulping down his coffee*): Please. Uh, please, I think I'd rather go in my room because I, I've got some work to do there. I always work immediately after my coffee.

JANE: I will not have this young grifter who has established squatter's rights here telling me that I can't enjoy a little society in a place where—frankly I am frantic with loneliness!

(*The writer does not know what to do. Tye suddenly grins. He pulls out a chair for the writer at the table as if it were for a lady.*)

TYE: Have a seat kid, you like one lump or two? Where's the cat? Can I invite the goddam cat to breakfast?

JANE: Tye, you said you were pleased with the robe I gave you for your birthday, but you never wear it.

TYE: I don't dress for breakfast.

JANE: Putting on a silk robe isn't dressing.

(*She removes the robe from a hook and throws it about Tye's shoulders. Automatically he circles her hips with an arm.*)

TYE: Mmm. Good. Feels good.

JANE (*shyly disengaging herself from his embrace*): It ought to. Shantung silk.

TYE: I didn't mean the robe, babe.

JANE: Tye, behave yourself. (*She turns to the writer.*) I've cherished the hope that by introducing Tye to certain little improvements in wearing apparel and language, I may gradually, despite his resistance—

TYE: Ain't that lovely? That classy langwidge she uses?

JANE: Inspire him to—seek out some higher level of employment. (*Ignoring Tye, she speaks.*) I heard that you are a writer?

WRITER: I, uh—write, but—

JANE: What form of writing? I mean fiction or poetry or . . .

TYE: Faggots, they all do something artistic, all of 'em.

JANE (*quickly*): Do you know, I find myself drinking twice as much coffee here as I did in New York. For me the climate here is debilitating. Perhaps because of the dampness and the, and the—very low altitude, really there's no altitude at all, it's slightly under sea level. Have another cup with me?

(*The writer doesn't answer: Jane prepares two more cups of the instant coffee. Tye is staring steadily, challengingly at the writer, who appears to be hypnotized.*)

Of course, Manhattan hasn't much altitude either. But I grew up in the Adirondacks really. We lived on high ground, good elevation.

TYE: I met one of 'em once by accident on the street. You see. I was out of a job, and he came up to me on a corner in the Quarter an' invited me to his place for supper with him. I seen right off what he was an' what he wanted, but I didn't have the price of a poor boy sandwich so I accepted, I went. The place was all Japanese-like, everything very artistic. He said to me, "Cross over that little bridge that crosses my little lake which I made myself and sit on the bench under my willow tree while I make supper for us and bathe an' change my clo'se. I won't be long." So I crossed over the bridge over the lake, and I stretched out under the weepin' willow tree: fell right asleep. I was woke up by what looked like a female but was him in drag. "Supper ready," he—she—said. Then this freak, put her hand on my—I said, "It's gonna cost you more than supper . . ."

JANE: Tye.

TYE: Huh, baby?

JANE: You will *not* continue that story.

TYE: It's a damn good story. What's your objection to it? I ain't got to the part that's really funny. (*He speaks to the writer, who is crossing out of the light.*) Don't you like the story?

(*The writer exits.*)

JANE: Why did you do that?

TYE: Do what?

JANE: You know what, and the boy knew what you meant by it. Why did you want to hurt him with the implication that he was in a class with a common, a predatory transvestite?

TYE: Look Jane . . . You say you was brought up on high ground, good elevation, but you come in here, you bring in here and expose me to a little queer, and . . .

JANE: Does everyone with civilized behavior, good manners, seem to be a queer to you?

TYE: . . . Was it good manners the way he looked at me, Babe?

JANE (*voice rising*): Was it good manners for you to stand in front of him rubbing your—groin the way you did?

TYE: I wanted you to notice his reaction.

JANE: He was just embarrassed.

TYE: You got a lot to learn about life in the Quarter.

JANE: I think that he's a serious person that I can talk to, and I need some one to talk to!

(*Pause*)

TYE: You can't talk to *me* huh?

JANE: With you working all night at a Bourbon Street strip-joint, and sleeping nearly all day? Involving yourself with all the underworld elements of this corrupt city . . .

TYE: 'Sthat all I do? Just that? I never pleasure you, babe?

(*Fade in piano blues. She draws a breath and moves as if half asleep behind Tye's chair.*)

JANE: Yes, you—pleasure me, Tye.

TYE: I try to do my best to, Babe. Sometimes I wonder why a girl—

JANE: Not a girl, Tye. A woman.

TYE: —How did—why did—you get yourself mixed up with me?

JANE: A sudden change of circumstances removed me from—how shall I put it so you'd understand?

TYE: Just—say.

JANE: What I'd thought was myself. So I quit my former connections, I came down here to— (*She stops short.*) Well, to make an adjustment to— (*Pause*) We met by chance on Royal Street when a deluge of rain backed me into a doorway? Didn't know you were behind me until you put your hand on my hip and I turned to say, "Stop that!" but didn't because you were something I'd never encountered before—faintly innocent—boy's eyes. Smiling. Said to myself, "Why not, with nothing to lose!" Of course you pleasure me, Tye! —I'd been alone so long . . .

(*She touches his throat with trembling fingers. He leans sensually back against her. She runs her hand down his chest.*)

Silk on silk is—lovely . . . regardless of the danger.

(*As the light on this area dims, typing begins offstage. The dim-out is completed.*)

SCENE FOUR

A lighted area represents Mrs. Wire's kitchen, in which she is preparing a big pot of gumbo despite the hour, which is midnight. She could be mistaken for a witch from Macbeth *in vaguely modern but not new costume.*

The writer's footsteps catch her attention. He appears at the edge of the light in all that remains of his wardrobe: riding boots and britches, a faded red flannel shirt.

MRS. WIRE: Who, who? —Aw, you, dressed up like a jockey in a donkey race!

WRITER: —My, uh, clothes are at the cleaners.

MRS. WIRE: Do they clean clothes at the pawnshop, yeah, I reckon they do clean clothes not redeemed. Oh. Don't go upstairs. Your room is forfeited, too.

WRITER: . . . You mean I'm . . . ?

MRS. WIRE: A loser, boy, possibly you could git a cot at the Salvation Army.

WRITER (*averting his eyes*): May I sit down a moment?

MRS. WIRE: Why, for what?

WRITER: Eviction presents . . . a problem.

MRS. WIRE: I thought you was gittin' on the WPA Writers' Project? That's what you tole me when I inquired about your prospects for employment, you said, "Oh, I've applied for work on the WPA for writers."

WRITER: I couldn't prove that my father was destitute, and the fact he contributes nothing to my support seemed— immaterial to them.

MRS. WIRE: Why're you shifty-eyed? I never seen a more shifty-eyed boy.

WRITER: I, uh, have had a little eye trouble, lately.

MRS. WIRE: You're gettin' a cataract on your left eye, boy, face it! —Cataracts don't usually hit at your age.

WRITER: I've noticed a lot of things have hit me—prematurely . . .

MRS. WIRE (*stirring gumbo*): Hungry? I bet. I eat at irregular hours. I suddenly got a notion to cook up a gumbo, and when I do, the smell of it is an attraction, draws company in the kitchen. Oh ho—*footsteps fast. Here comes the ladies.*

WRITER: Mrs. Wire, those old ladies are starving, dying of malnutrition.

(*Miss Carrie and Mary Maude appear at the edge of the lighted area with queer, high-pitched laughter or some bizarre relation to laughter.*)

MRS. WIRE: Set back down there, boy. (*Pause.*) Why, Mizz Wayne an' Miss Carrie, you girls still up at this hour!

MISS CARRIE: We heard you moving about and wondered if we could . . .

MARY MAUDE: Be of some assistance.

MRS. WIRE: Shoot, Mrs. Wayne, do you imagine that rusty ole saucepan of yours is invisible to me? Why, I know when I put this gumbo on the stove and lit the fire, it would smoke you ladies out of your locked room. What do you all do in that locked room so much?

MARY MAUDE: We keep ourselves occupied.

MISS CARRIE: We are compiling a cookbook which we hope to have published. A Creole cookbook, recipes we remember from our childhood.

MRS. WIRE: A recipe is a poor substitute for food.

MARY MAUDE (*with a slight breathless pause*): We ought to go out more regularly for meals but our . . . our light bulbs have burned out, so we can't distinguish night from day anymore. Only shadows come in.

MISS CARRIE: Sshh! (*Pause.*) Y'know, I turned down an invitation to dinner this evening at my cousin Mathilde Devereau Pathet's in the Garden District.

MRS. WIRE: Objected to the menu?

MISS CARRIE: No, but you know, very rich people are so inconsiderate sometimes. With four limousines and drivers at their constant disposal, they wouldn't send one to fetch me.

MRS. WIRE: Four? Limousines? Four drivers?

(*A delicate, evanescent music steals in as the scene acquires a touch of the bizarre. At moments the players seem bewildered as if caught in a dream.*)

MISS CARRIE: Oh, yes, four, four . . . spanking new Cadillacs with uniformed chauffeurs!

MRS. WIRE: Now, that's very impressive.

MISS CARRIE: They call Mr. Pathet the "Southern Planter."

MRS. WIRE: Has a plantation, in the Garden District?

MISS CARRIE (*gasping*): Oh, no, no, no, no. He's a mortician, most prominent mortician, buries all the best families in the parish.

MRS. WIRE: And poor relations, too? I hope.

MARY MAUDE: Miss Carrie goes into a family vault when she goes.

MRS. WIRE: When?

MARY MAUDE: Yes, above ground: has a vault reserved in . . .

MISS CARRIE: Let's not speak of that! . . . now.

MRS. WIRE: Why not speak of that? You got to consider the advantage of this connection. Because of the expenses of "The Inevitable" someday, soon, specially with your asthma? No light? And bad nutrition?

MISS CARRIE: The dampness of the old walls in the Quarter—you know how they hold damp. This city is actually eight feet below sea level. Niggers are buried under the ground, and their caskets fill immediately with water.

MRS. WIRE: But I reckon your family vault is above this nigger water level?

MISS CARRIE: Oh, yes, above water level, in fact, I'll be on top of my great-great-uncle, Jean Pierre Devereau, the third.

(*The writer laughs a bit, involuntarily. The ladies glare at him.*)

Mrs. Wire, who is this . . . transient? Young man?

MARY MAUDE: We did understand that this was a guesthouse, not a . . . refuge for delinquents.

MISS CARRIE (*turning her back on the writer*): They do set an exquisite table at the Pathets, with excellent food, but it's not appetizing, you know, to be conducted on a tour of inspection of the business display room, you know, the latest model of caskets on display, and that's what René Pathet does, invariably escorts me, proud as a peacock, through the coffin display rooms before . . . we sit down to dinner. And all through dinner, he discusses his latest clients and . . . those expected shortly.

MRS. WIRE: Maybe he wants you to pick out your casket cause he's noticed your asthma from damp walls in the Quarter.

MISS CARRIE: I do, of course, understand that business is business with him, a night and day occupation.

MRS. WIRE: You know, I always spit in a pot of gumbo to give it special flavor, like a bootblack spits on a shoe. (*She*

pretends to spit in the pot. The crones try to laugh.) Now help
yourself, fill your saucepan full, and I'll loan you a couple
of spoons, but let it cool a while, don't blister your
gums . . . (*Handing them spoons*) . . . and Mrs. Wayne, I'll
be watching the mailbox for Buster's army paycheck.

MARY MAUDE: That boy has never let me down, he's the most
devoted son a mother could hope for.

MRS. WIRE: Yais, if she had no hope.

MARY MAUDE: I got a postcard from him . . .

MRS. WIRE: A postcard can't be cashed.

MARY MAUDE (*diverting Mrs. Wire's attention, she hopes, as
Miss Carrie ladles out gumbo*): Of course, I wasn't prepared
for the circumstance that struck me when I discovered that
Mr. Wayne had not kept up his insurance payments, *that* I
was not prepared for, that it was *lapsed*.

MRS. WIRE (*amused*): I bet you wasn't prepared for a little
surprise like that.

MARY MAUDE: No, not for that nor for the discovery that secretly for years he'd been providing cash and real estate to
that little redheaded doxy he'd kept in Bay St. Louie.

MISS CARRIE: Owwwww!

(*Mrs. Wire whirls about, and Miss Carrie is forced to swallow
the scalding mouthful.*)

MRS. WIRE: I bet that mouthful scorched your throat, Miss
Carrie. Didn't I tell you to wait?

MARY MAUDE: Carrie, give me that saucepan before you spill
it, your hand's so shaky. Thank you, Mrs. Wire. Carrie,
thank Mrs. Wire for her being so concerned always about
our—circumstances here. Now let's go and see what can be
done for that throat. (*They move toward the stairs but do not
exit.*)

MRS. WIRE: Cut it, if all else fails.

(*Something crashes on the stairs. All turn that way. Tye appears dimly, bearing two heavy cartons; he speaks to the writer,
who is nearest to him.*)

TYE: Hey, you, boy?
WRITER: —Me?

TYE: Yeh, yeh, you, I dropped one of these packages on th' steps, so goddam dark I dropped it. And I'd appreciate it if you'd pick it up fo' me an' help me git it upstairs.

WRITER: I'll be—glad to try to . . .

(*Tye focuses dimly on Miss Carrie. He blinks several times in disbelief.*)

TYE: Am I . . . in the right place?

MRS. WIRE (*shouting*): Not in your present condition. Go on back out. Sleep it off in the gutter.

MISS CARRIE (*to Mrs. Wire*): Tragic for such a nice-looking young man to return to his wife in that condition at night.

MRS. WIRE: Practically every night.

(*Miss Carrie and Mary Maude exit.*
(*Tye has almost miraculously managed to collect his dropped packages, and he staggers to stage right where the lower steps to the attic are dimly seen. The writer follows.*)

TYE (*stumbling back against the writer*): Can you make it? Can you make it, kid?

(*They slowly mount the steps. The lighted kitchen is dimmed out. There is a brief pause. A soft light is cast on the attic hall.*)

TYE: Now, kid, can you locate my room key in my pocket?

WRITER: Which, uh—pocket?

TYE: Pan's pocket.

WRITER: Left pocket or—

TYE: —Head—spinnin'—money in hip pocket, key in— right—lef' side. Shit—key befo' I—fall . . .

(*The writer's hand starts to enter a pocket when Tye collapses, spilling the boxes on the floor and sprawling across them.*)

WRITER: You're right outside my cubbyhole. I suggest you rest in there before you—wake up your wife . . .

TYE: M'ole lady, she chews my ass off if I come home this ways . . . (*He struggles heroically to near standing position as the writer guides him into his cubicle.*) . . . This—bed?

(*There is a soft, ghostly laugh from the adjoining cubicle. A match strikes briefly.*)

WRITER: Swing your legs other way, that way's the pillow—would you, uh, like your wet shoes off?

TYE: Shoes? Yes, but nothin' else. Once I—passed out on—Bourbon Street—late night—in a dark doorway—woke up—this guy, was takin' liberties with me and I don't go for that stuff—

WRITER: I don't take advantages of that kind, I am—going back downstairs, if you're comfortable now . . .

TYE: I said to this guy, "Okay, if you wanto blow me, you can pay me one hunnerd dollars—before, not after."

(*Tye's voice dies out. Nightingale becomes visible, rising stealthily in his cubicle and slipping on a robe, as Tye begins to snore.*

(*The attic lights dim out. The lights on the kitchen come up as the writer re-enters.*)

MRS. WIRE: Got that bum to bed? Set down, son. Ha! Notice I called you, son. Where do you go nights?

WRITER: Oh, I walk, I take long solitary walks. Sometimes I . . . I . . .

MRS. WIRE: Sometimes you what? You can say it's none of my business, but I, well, I have a sort of a, well you could say I have a sort of a—maternal—concern. You see, I do have a son that I never see no more, but I worry about him so I reckon it's natural for me to worry about you a little. And get things straight in my head about you—you've changed since you've been in this house. You know that?

WRITER: Yes, I know that.

MRS. WIRE: This I'll tell you, when you first come to my door, I swear I seen and I recognized a young gentleman in you—shy. Shaky, but . . .

WRITER: Panicky! Yes! Gentleman? My folks say so. I wonder.

(*The light narrows and focuses on the writer alone; the speech becomes an interior reflection.*)

I've noticed I do have some troublesome little scruples in my nature that may cause difficulties in my . . . (*He rises and rests his foot on the chair.*) . . . negotiated—truce with —life. Oh—there's a price for things, that's something I've learned in the Vieux Carré. For everything that you purchase in this marketplace you pay out of *here*! (*He thumps his chest.*) And the cash which is the stuff you use in your work can be overdrawn, depleted, like a reservoir going dry in a long season of drought . . .

(*The scene is resumed on a realistic level with a change in the lighting.*)

MRS. WIRE (*passing a bowl of gumbo to the writer*): Here, son, have some gumbo. Let it cool a while. I just pretended to spit in it, you know.

WRITER: I know.

MRS. WIRE: I make the best gumbo, I do the best Creole cookin' in Louisiana. It's God's truth, and now I'll tell you what I'm plannin' to do while your gumbo's coolin'. I'll tell you because it involves a way you could pay your room and board here.

WRITER: Oh?

MRS. WIRE: Uh huh, I'm plannin' to open a lunchroom.

WRITER: On the premises? Here?

MRS. WIRE: On the premises, in my bedroom, which I'm gonna convert into a small dinin' room. So I'm gonna git printed up some bus'ness cards. At twelve noon ev'ry day except Sundays you can hit the streets with these little bus'ness cards announcin' that lunch is bein' served for twenty-five cents, a cheaper lunch than you could git in a greasy spoon on Chartres . . . and no better cooking in the Garden District or the Vieux Carré.

WRITER: Meals for a quarter in the Quarter.

MRS. WIRE: Hey! That's the slogan! I'll print it on those cards that you'll pass out.

WRITER (*dreamily*): Wonderful gumbo.

MRS. WIRE: Why this "Meals for a quarter in the Quarter" is going to put me back in the black, yeah! Boy! . . . (*She throws him the key to his attic rooms. The lights dim out briefly.*)

TYE'S VOICE: Hey! Whatcha doin'? Git yuh fuckin' hands off me!

(*The writer appears dimly in the attic hall outside his room. He stops.*)

NIGHTINGALE'S VOICE: I thought that I was visiting a friend.

TYE'S VOICE: 'S that how you visit a friend, unzippin' his pants an' pullin' out his dick?

NIGHTINGALE'S VOICE: I assure you it was a mistake of— identity . . .

TYE (*becoming visible on the side of the bed in the writer's cubicle*): This ain't my room. Where is my ole lady? Hey, *hey, Jane!*

WRITER: You collapsed in the hall outside your door so I helped you in here.

TYE: Both of you git this straight. No goddam faggot messes with me, never! For less'n a hundred dollars!

(*Jane becomes visible in the hall before this line.*)

A hunnerd dollars, yes, maybe, but not a dime less.

NIGHTINGALE (*emerging from the cubicle in his robe*): I am afraid that you have priced yourself out of the market.

JANE: Tye, come out of there.

TYE: I been interfered with cause you'd locked me out.

WRITER: Miss, uh, Sparks, I didn't touch your friend except to, to . . . offer him my bed till you let him in.

JANE: *Tye, stand up—if you can stand! Stand. Walk.*

(*Tye stumbles against her, and she cries out as she is pushed against the wall.*)

TYE'S VOICE: Locked out, bolted outa my room, to be— molested.

JANE: I heard you name a price, with you everything has a price. Thanks, good night.

(*During this exchange Nightingale in his purple robe has leaned, smoking with a somewhat sardonic look, against the partition between the two cubicles. The writer reappears.*)

NIGHTINGALE: Back so quick? —*Tant pis . . .*

WRITER: I think if I were you, I'd go in your own room and get to bed.

(*The writer enters his cubicle. Nightingale's face slowly turns to a mask of sorrow past expression. There is music. Nightingale puts out his cigarette and enters his cubicle.*

(*Jane undresses Tye. The writer undresses. Nightingale sits on his cot. Tye and Jane begin to make love. Downstairs, Nursie mops the floor, singing to herself. The writer moves slowly to his bed and places his hand on the warm sheets that Tye has left. The light dims.*

(*There is a passage of time.*)

SCENE FIVE

The attic rooms are dimly lit. Nightingale is adjusting a neck-erchief about his wasted throat. He enters the writer's cubicle without knocking.

NIGHTINGALE: May I intrude once more? It's embarrassing—this incident. Not of any importance, nothing worth a second thought. (*He coughs.*) Oh Christ. You know my mattress is full of bedbugs. Last night I smashed one at least the size of my thumbnail, it left a big blood spot on the pillow. (*He coughs and gasps for breath.*) I showed it to the colored woman that the witch calls Nursie, and Nursie told her about it, and she came charging up here and demanded that I exhibit the bug, which I naturally . . . (*A note of uncertainty and fear enters his voice.*)

WRITER: . . . removed from the pillow.

NIGHTINGALE: Who in hell wouldn't remove the remains of a squashed bedbug from his pillow? Nobody I'd want social or any acquaintance with . . . she even . . . intimated that I coughed up the blood, as if I had . . . (*coughs*) consumption.

WRITER (*stripped to his shorts and about to go to bed*): I think with that persistent cough of yours you should get more rest.

NIGHTINGALE: Restlessness. Insomnia. I can't imagine a worse affliction, and I've suffered from it nearly all my life. I consulted a doctor about it once, and he said, "You don't sleep because it reminds you of death." A ludicrous assumption—the only true regret I'd have over leaving this world is that I'd leave so much of my serious work unfinished.

WRITER (*holding the bedsheet up to his chin*): Do show me your serious work.

NIGHTINGALE: I know why you're taking this tone.

WRITER: I am not taking any tone.

NIGHTINGALE: Oh yes you are, you're very annoyed with me because my restlessness, my loneliness, made me so indiscreet as to—offer my attentions to that stupid but—physically appealing young man you'd put on that cot with the idea of reserving him for yourself. And so I do think your tone is a bit hypocritical, don't you?

WRITER: All right, I do admit I find him attractive, too, but I did *not* make a pass at him.

NIGHTINGALE: I heard him warn you.

WRITER: I simply removed his wet shoes.

NIGHTINGALE: Little man, you are sensual, but I, I—am rapacious.

WRITER: And I am tired.

NIGHTINGALE: Too tired to return my visits? Not very appreciative of you, but lack of appreciation is something I've come to expect and almost to accept as if God—the alleged—had stamped on me a sign at birth—"This man will offer himself and not be accepted, not by anyone ever!"

WRITER: Please don't light that candle.

NIGHTINGALE: I shall, the candle is lit.

WRITER: I do wish that you'd return to your side of the wall —well, now I am taking a tone, but it's . . . justified. Now do please get out, get out, I mean it, when I blow out the candle I want to be alone.

NIGHTINGALE: You know, you're going to grow into a selfish, callous man. Returning no visits, reciprocating no . . . caring.

WRITER: . . . Why do you predict that?

NIGHTINGALE: That little opacity on your left eye pupil could mean a like thing happening to your heart. (*He sits on the cot.*)

WRITER: You have to protect your heart.

NIGHTINGALE: With a shell of calcium? Would that improve your work?

WRITER: You talk like you have a fever, I . . .

NIGHTINGALE: I have a fever you'd be lucky to catch, a fever to hold and be held! (*He throws off his tattered silk robe.*) Hold me! Please, please hold me.

WRITER: I'm afraid I'm tired, I need to sleep and . . . I don't want to catch your cold.

(*Slowly with dignity, Nightingale rises from the cot and puts his silk robe on.*)

NIGHTINGALE: And I don't want to catch yours, which is a cold in the heart, that's a hell of a lot more fatal to a boy with literary pretensions.

(*This releases in the writer a cold rage which he has never felt before. He springs up and glares at Nightingale, who is coughing.*)

WRITER (*in a voice quick and hard as a knife*): I think there has been some deterioration in your condition and you ought to face it! A man has got to face everything sometime and call it by its true name, not to try to escape it by— cowardly!—evasion—go have your lungs x-rayed and don't receive the doctor's bill when it's sent! But go there quick, have the disease stated clearly! Don't, don't call it a cold anymore or a touch of the flu!

NIGHTINGALE (*turning with a gasp*): You've gone mad, you've gone out of your mind here, you little one-eyed bitch! (*He coughs again and staggers out of the light.*)

MRS. WIRE'S VOICE: I heard you from the kitchen, boy! Was he molesting you in here? I heard him. Was he molesting you in here? Speak up! You watch out, I'll get the goods on you yet!

NIGHTINGALE'S VOICE: The persecution continues.

SCENE SIX

Daylight appears in the alcove window—daylight tinged with rain. The room of Jane and Tye is lighted. Tye is sprawled, apparently sleeping, in shorts on the studio bed. Jane has just completed a fashion design. She stares at it with disgust, then crumples it and throws it to the floor with a sob of frustration.

JANE: Yes? Who's there?

WRITER: Uh, me, from across the hall, I brought in a letter for you—it was getting rained on.

JANE: Oh, one moment, please. (*She throws a robe over her panties and bra and opens the door.*) A letter for me?

WRITER: The mail gets wet when it rains since the lid's come off the mailbox.

(*His look irresistibly takes in the figure of Tye. Jane tears the letter open and gasps softly. She looks slowly up, with a stunned expression, at the young writer.*)

JANE: Would you care for some coffee?

WRITER: Thanks, no, I just take it in the morning.

JANE: Then please have a drink with me. I need a drink. Please, please come in. (*Jane is speaking hysterically but abruptly controls it.*) Excuse me—would you pour the drinks—I can't. I . . .

WRITER (*crossing to the cabinet*): Will you have . . .

JANE: Bourbon. Three fingers.

WRITER: With?

JANE: Nothing, nothing.

(*The writer glances again at Tye as he pours the bourbon.*)

Nothing . . . (*The writer crosses to her with the drink.*) Nothing. And you?

WRITER: Nothing, thanks. I have to retype the manuscripts soaked in the rain.

JANE: *Manuscripts*, you said? Oh, yes, you're a writer. I knew, it just slipped my mind. The manuscripts were returned? Does that mean rejection? —Rejection is always so painful.

WRITER (*with shy pride*): This time instead of a printed slip there was this personal signed note . . .

JANE: Encouraging—that. Oh, my glass is weeping—an Italian expression. Would you play barman again? Please? (*She doesn't know where to put the letter, which he keeps glancing at.*)

WRITER: Yes, I am encouraged. He says, "This one doesn't quite make it but try us again." *Story* magazine—they print William Saroyan, you know!

JANE: It takes a good while to get established in a creative field.

WRITER: And meanwhile you've got to survive.

JANE: I was lucky, but the luck didn't hold. (*She is taking little sips of the straight bourbon.*)

WRITER: You're—upset by that—letter? I noticed it came from—isn't Ochsner's a clinic?

JANE: Yes, actually. I am, I was. It concerns a relative rather—critically ill there.

WRITER: Someone close to you?

JANE: Yes. Quite close, although lately I hardly recognize the lady at all anymore . . .

(*Tye stirs on the bed; the writer irresistibly glances at him.*)

Pull the sheet over him. I think he unconsciously displays himself like that as if posing for a painter of sensual inclinations. Wasted on me. I just illustrate fashions for ladies.

TYE (*stirring*): Beret? Beret?

(*The writer starts off, pausing at the edge of the light.*)

WRITER: Jane, what was the letter, wasn't it about you?

JANE: Let's just say it was a sort of a personal, signed rejection slip, too.

(*The writer exits with a backward glance.*)

TYE: Where's Beret, where's the goddam cat?

(*Jane is fiercely tearing the letter to bits. The lights dim out.*)

SCENE SEVEN

A dim light comes up on the writer, stage front, as narrator.

WRITER: The basement of the building had been leased by Mrs. Wire to a fashionable youngish photographer, one T. Hamilton Biggs, a very effete man he was, who had somehow acquired a perfect Oxford accent in Baton Rouge, Louisiana. He made a good living in New Orleans out of artfully lighted photos of debutantes and society matrons in the Garden District, but for his personal amusement—he also photographed, more realistically, some of the many young drifters to be found along the streets of the Vieux Carré.

(*The lights go up on the kitchen. Mrs. Wire is seen at the stove, which bears steaming pots of water.*)

MRS. WIRE (*to the writer*): Aw, it's you sneakin' in at two A.M. like a thief.

WRITER: Yes, uh, good night.

MRS. WIRE: Hold on, don't go up yet. He's at it again down there, he's throwin' one of his orgies, and this'll be the last one he throws down there. By God an' by Jesus, the society folk in this city may tolerate vice but not me. Take one of them pots off the stove.

WRITER: You're, uh . . . cooking at this hour?

MRS. WIRE: Not cooking . . . I'm boiling water! I take this pot and you take the other one, we'll pour this water through the hole in this kitchen floor, which is directly over that studio of his!

WRITER: Mrs. Wire, I can't be involved in . . .

MRS. WIRE: Boy, you're employed by me, you're fed and housed here, and you do like I tell you or you'll go on the street. (*She lifts a great kettle off the stove.*) Take that pot off the stove! (*She empties the steaming water on the floor. Almost instant screams are heard below.*) Hahh, down there, what's the disturbance over?!

WRITER: Mrs. Wire, that man has taken out a peace warrant against you, you know that.

MRS. WIRE: Git out of my way, you shifty-eyed little— (*With demonical energy she seizes the other pot and empties it onto the floor, and the screams continue. She looks and runs to the proscenium as if peering out a window.*) Two of 'em run out naked. Got two of you, I'm not done with you yet! . . . you perverts!

WRITER: Mrs. Wire, he'll call the police.

MRS. WIRE: Let him, just let him, my nephew is a lieutenant on the police force! But these Quarter police, why anybody can buy 'em, and that Biggs, he's got big money. Best we be quiet, sit tight. Act real casual-like. If they git in that door, you seen a, you seen a—

WRITER: What?

MRS. WIRE: A drunk spillin' water in here.

WRITER: . . . that much water?

MRS. WIRE: *Hush up!* One contradictory word out of you and I'll brain you with this saucepan here.

(*Nightingale enters in his robe.*)

NIGHTINGALE: May I inquire what this bedlam is about? (*He pants for breath.*) I had just finally managed to . . . (*He gasps.*) This hellish disturbance . . .

MRS. WIRE: May you inquire, yeah, you may inquire. Look. Here's the story! You're in a doped-up condition. Drunk and doped-up you staggered against the stove and accidentally knocked a kettle of boiling water off it. Now that's the story you'll tell in payment of back rent and your habits! . . . disgracing my house!

NIGHTINGALE (*to writer*): *What* is she talking about?

MRS. WIRE: And *you* . . . *one eye!* (*She turns to the writer.*) You say you witnesses it, you back up the story, you heah?

WRITER (*grinning*): Mrs. Wire, the story wouldn't . . . hold water.

MRS. WIRE: I said accidental. In his condition who'd doubt it?

NIGHTINGALE: Hoo, hoo, hoo!

MRS. WIRE: That night court buzzard on the bench, he'd throw the book at me for no reason but the fight that I've put up against the corruption and evil that this Quarter is built on! All I'm asking is . . .

(*Abruptly Miss Carrie and Mary Maude in outrageous negligees burst into the kitchen. At the sight of them, Mrs. Wire starts to scream wordlessly as a peacock at a pitch that stuns the writer but not Nightingale and the crones. Just as abruptly she falls silent and flops into a chair.*)

MISS CARRIE: Oh, Mrs. Wire!

MARY MAUDE: We thought the house had caught fire!

NIGHTINGALE (*loftily*): . . . What a remarkable . . . *tableau vivant* . . . The paddy wagon's approaching. Means night court, you know.

WRITER: . . . I think I'll . . . go to bed now . . .

MRS. WIRE: Like shoot you will!

(*Jane appears, stage right, in a robe. She speaks to the writer, who is nearest to her.*)

JANE: Can you tell me what is going on down here?

WRITER: Miss Sparks, why don't you stay in your room right now?

JANE: Why?

WRITER: There's been a terrible incident down here, I think the police are coming.

(*Mary Maude screams, wringing her hands.*)

MARY MAUDE: Police!

MISS CARRIE: Oh, Mary Maude, this is not time for hysterics. You're not involved, nor am I! We simply came in to see what the disturbance was about.

JANE (*to the writer*): Was Tye here? Was Tye involved in this . . .

WRITER (*in a low voice to Jane*): Nobody was involved but Mrs. Wire. She poured boiling water through a hole in the floor.

MRS. WIRE (*like a field marshal*): Everybody in here stay here and sit tight till the facts are reported.

(*Nursie enters with black majesty. She is humming a church hymn softly, "He walks with me and he talks with me." She remains at the edge of the action, calm as if unaware.*)

I meant ev'ry goddam one of you except Nursie. Nursie! Don't stand there singin' gospel, barefoot, in that old dirty nightgown!

WRITER (*to Jane*): She wants us to support a totally false story.

MRS. WIRE: I tell you—the Vieux Carré is the new Babylon destroyed by evil in Scriptures!!

JANE: It's like a dream . . .

NIGHTINGALE: The photographer downstairs belongs to the Chateau family, one of the finest and most important families in the Garden District.

MRS. WIRE: Oh, do you write the social register now?

NIGHTINGALE: I know he is New Orleans's most prominent society photographer!

MRS. WIRE: I know he's the city's most notorious *per*vert and is occupying space in my building!

MISS CARRIE: Mary Maude and I can't afford the notoriety of a thing like this.

(*Mary Maud cries out and leans against the table.*)

MARY MAUDE: Mrs. Wire, Miss Carrie and I have—positions to maintain!

JANE: Mrs. Wire, surely there's no need for these ladies to be involved in this.

MRS. WIRE: Deadbeats, all, all! Will stay right here and—

JANE: Do what?

MRS. WIRE: —testify to what happened!

NIGHTINGALE: She wishes you all to corroborate her lie! That I, that I! Oh, yes, I'm appointed to assume responsibility for—

PHOTOGRAPHER (*off stage*): Right up there! Burns like this could disfigure me for life!

(*Mrs. Wire rushes to slam and bolt the door.*)

MISS CARRIE (*to Mary Maude*): Honey? Can you move now?

MRS. WIRE: No, she cain't, she stays—which applies to you all!

PHOTOGRAPHER: The fact that she is insane and allowed to remain at large . . . doesn't excuse it.

(*A patrolman bangs at the door.*)

MRS. WIRE: Shh! Nobody make a sound!

PHOTOGRAPHER: Not only she but her tenants; why, the place is a psycho ward.

(*More banging is heard.*)

MRS. WIRE: What's this banging about?

PATROLMAN: Open this door.

PHOTOGRAPHER: One of my guests was the nephew of the District Attorney!

PATROLMAN: Open or I'll force it.

PHOTOGRAPHER: Break it in! Kick it open!

MRS. WIRE (*galvanized*): You ain't comin' in here, you got no warrant to enter, you filthy—morphodite, you!

WRITER: Mrs. Wire, you said not to make a sound.

MRS. WIRE: Make no sound when they're breakin' in my house, you one-eye Jack? (*The banging continues.*) What's the meaning of this, wakin' me up at two A.M. in the mawnin'?

PHOTOGRAPHER: Scalded! Five guests, including two art models!

MRS. WIRE (*overlapping*): You broken the terms of your lease, and it's now broke. I rented you that downstair space for legitimate business, you turned it into a—continual awgy!

PATROLMAN: Open that door, ma'am, people have been seriously injured.

MRS. WIRE: That's no concern of mine! I open no door till I phone my nephew, a lieutenant on the police force, Jim Flynn, who knows the situation I've put up with here, and then we'll see who calls the law on who!

WRITER: I hear more police sirens comin'.

(*The pounding and shouting continue. A patrolman forces entry, followed by another. All during the bit just preceding, Miss Carie and Mary Maude have clung together, their terrified whispers maintaining a low-pitched threnody to the shouting and banging. Now as the two patrolmen enter, their hysteria erupts in shrill screams. The screams are so intense that the patrolmen's attention is directed upon them.*)

PATROLMAN I: Christ! Is this a fuckin' madhouse?

(*Still clinging together, the emaciated crones sink to their knees as if at the feet of an implacable deity.*)

MRS. WIRE (*inspired*): Officers, remove these demented, old horrors. Why, you know what they done? Poured water on the floor of my kitchen, boiling water!

NIGHTINGALE: She's lying. These unfortunate old ladies just came in, they thought the house was on fire.

PHOTOGRAPHER: This woman is the notorious Mrs. Wire, and it was she who screamed out the window. Why, these old women should be hospitalized, naturally, but it's her, her! (*He points at Mrs. Wire from the door.*) that poured the scalding water into my studio, and screamed with delight when my art models and guests ran naked into the street!

MRS. WIRE: There, now, AWGY CONFESSED!!

PATROLMAN I: All out to the wagon!

(*The scene is dimmed out fast. A spot comes up on the writer in the witness box at night court.*)

OLD JUDGE'S VOICE: Let's not have no more beatin' aroun' the bush in this court, young fellow. The question is plain. You're under oath to give an honest answer. Now for the last time, at risk of being held in contempt of court, "Did you or did you not see the proprietor of the rooming house . . ."

MRS. WIRE'S VOICE (*shrilly*): Restaurant and roomin' house respectfully run!

(*The judge pounds his gavel.*)

OLD JUDGE'S VOICE: Defendant will keep silent during the witness' testimony. To repeat the question: "Did you or did you not see this lady here pour boiling water through the floor of her kitchen down into the studio of Mr. T. Hamilton Biggs?"

WRITER (*swallows, then in a low voice*): I, uh . . . think it's unlikely . . . a lady would do such a thing.

OLD JUDGE'S VOICE: Speak up so I can heah you! What's that you said?

WRITER: . . . I said I thought it very unlikely a lady would do such a thing.

(*Laughter is heard in the night court. The judge gavels, then pronounces the verdict.*)

OLD JUDGE'S VOICE: This court finds the defendant, Mrs. Hortense Wire, guilty as charged and imposes a fine of fifty dollars plus damages and releases her on probation in the custody of her nephew, Police Lieutenant James Flynn of New Orleans Parish, for a period of . . .

(*His voice fades out as does the scene. A spotlight comes up on Mrs. Wire in a flannel robe, drinking at the kitchen table. The writer appears hesitantly at the edge of the kitchen light.*)

MRS. WIRE (*without turning*): I know you're standing there, but I don't wanta see you. It sure does surprise me that you'd dare to enter this house again after double-crossing me in court tonight.

WRITER: —I—just came back to pick up my things.

MRS. WIRE: You ain't gonna remove nothing from this place till you paid off what you owe me.

WRITER: You know I'm—destitute.

MRS. WIRE: You get tips from the customers.

WRITER: Nickels and dimes. (*Pause. The sound of rain is heard.*) —Mrs. Wire? (*She turns slowly to look at him.*) Do you think I really intended to lose you that case? Other witnesses had testified I was in the kitchen when you poured those kettles of water through the floor. And the judge knew I could see with at least one eye. I was on the witness stand under oath, couldn't perjure myself. I did try not to answer directly. I *didn't* answer directly. All I said was—

MRS. WIRE: You said what lost me the case, goddam it! Did you expect that old buzzard on the bench to mistake me for a lady, my hair in curlers, me wearin' the late, long ago Mr. Wire's old ragged bathrobe. Shoot! All of you witnesses betrayed me in night court because you live off me an' can't forgive me for it.

WRITER: —I guess you want me to go . . .

MRS. WIRE: To where would you go? How far could you get on your nickels and dimes? You're shiverin' like a wet dog. Set down. Have a drink with me befo' you go up to bed.

WRITER: You mean I can stay? (*She nods slightly. He sits down at the kitchen table, she pours him a drink.*) I don't think I ever saw you drink before, Mrs. Wire.

MRS. WIRE: I only touch this bottle, which also belonged to the late Mr. Wire, before he descended to hell between two crooked lawyers, I touch it only when forced to by such a shocking experience as I had tonight, the discovery that I was completely alone in the world, a solitary ole woman cared for by no one. You know, I heard some doctor say on the radio that people die of loneliness, specially at my age. They do. Die of it, it kills 'em. Oh, that's not the cause that's put on the death warrant, but that's the *true* cause. I tell you, there's so much loneliness in this house that you can hear it. Set still and you can hear it: a sort of awful—soft—groaning in all the walls.

WRITER: All I hear is rain on the roof.

MRS. WIRE: You're still too young to hear it, but I hear it and I feel it, too, like a—ache in ev'ry bone of my body. It makes me want to scream, but I got to keep still. A landlady ain't permitted to scream. It would disturb the ten-

ants. But some time I will, I'll scream, I'll scream loud
enough to bring the roof down on us all.

WRITER: This house is full of people?

MRS. WIRE: People I let rooms to. Less than strangers to me.

WRITER: There's—me. I'm not.

MRS. WIRE: You—just endure my company 'cause you're employed here, boy.

WRITER: Miss Sparks isn't employed here.

MRS. WIRE: That woman is close to no one but the bum she
keeps here. I'll show you. (*She rises and knocks her chair
over, then bawls out as if to Tye.*) More boxes! Take 'em out
an' stay out with 'em, sleep it off on the streets!

(*Jane rises in her dim spot of light. She crosses to the door.*)

JANE (*offstage*): Tye! Tye! I thought I heard Tye down there.

MRS. WIRE: Miss Sparks—don't you know that bum don't
quit work till daybreak and rarely shows here before noon?

JANE: Sorry. Excuse me.

WRITER (*his speech slurred by drink*): God, but I was ignorant
when I came here! This place has been a— I ought to pay
you—tuition . . .

MRS. WIRE: One drink has made you drunk, boy. Go up to
bed. We're goin' on tomorrow like nothing happened. (*He
rises and crosses unsteadily from the kitchen light.*) Be careful
on the steps.

WRITER (*pausing to look back at her*): Good night, Mrs. Wire.
(*He disappears.*)

MRS. WIRE: —It's true, people die of it . . .

(*On the hall stairs the writer meets Nightingale, who speaks
before the writer enters his own cubicle.*)

NIGHTINGALE (*imitating the writer's testimony in night
court*): "I, uh, think it's unlikely a lady would do such a
thing." (*He coughs.*) —A statement belonging in a glossary
of deathless quotations. (*He coughs again.*) —Completely
convinced me you really do have a future in the—literary—
profession.

(*The light builds on Mrs. Wire, and she rises from the kitchen
table and utters a piercing cry. Nursie appears.*)

NURSIE: Mizz Wire, what on earth is it? A bat?

MRS. WIRE: I just felt like screaming, and so I screamed! That's all . . .

(*The lights dim out.*)

Interval

PART TWO

SCENE EIGHT

A spotlight focuses on the writer working at his dilapidated typewriter in his gabled room in the attic.

WRITER: Instinct, it must have been (*He starts typing.*) directed me here, to the Vieux Carré of New Orleans, down country as a—river flows no plan. I couldn't have consciously, deliberately, selected a better place than here to discover—to encounter—my true nature. *Exposition! Shit!*

(*He springs up and kicks at the worn, wobbly table. A lean, gangling young man, whose charming but irresponsible nature is apparent in his genial grin, appears at the entrance of the writer's cubicle.*)

SKY: Having trouble?

WRITER: Even the typewriter objected to those goddamn lines. The ribbon stuck, won't reverse.

SKY: Let me look at it. (*He enters the cubicle.*) Oh, my name is Schuyler but they call me Sky.

WRITER: The owner of the knapsack with "SKY" printed on it, that was—that was deposited here last winter sometime?

SKY (*working on the typewriter*): Right. Landlady won't surrender it to me for less than twenty-five bucks, which is more than I can pay. Yeah, you see—I'm a fugitive from—from legal wedlock in Tampa, Florida, with the prettiest little bitsy piece of it you ever did see. There, now, the ribbon's reversing, it slipped out of the slots like I slipped out of matrimony in Tampa—couldn't you see that?

WRITER: I don't think there's a room in this building where you could be certain it was night or day, and I've . . .

SKY: Something wrong with that eye.

WRITER: Operation. For a cataract. Just waiting till it heals.— Are you staying here?

SKY: Just for a day or two while I look into spots for a jazz musician in the Quarter.

WRITER: There's several jazz combos just around the corner on Bourbon Street.

SKY: Yeah, I know, but they're black and not anxious to work with a honky. So, I'll probably drive on West.

WRITER: How far West?

SKY: The Coast. Is there a toilet up here? I gotta piss. Downstairs john's occupied.

WRITER: I know a girl across the hall with a bathroom, but she's probably sleeping.

SKY: With the angels wetting the roof, would it matter if I did, too?

WRITER: Go ahead.

(*Sky leaps onto the alcove and pisses upstage out of the window.*)

Why'd you decide not to marry?

SKY: Suddenly realized I wasn't ready to settle. The girl, she had a passion for pink, but she extended it out of bounds in the love nest she'd picked out for us. Pink, pink, pink. So I cut out before daybreak.

WRITER: Without a word to the girl?

SKY: A note, "Not ready. Be back." Wonder if she believed it, or if I did. That was Christmas week. I asked permission to leave my knapsack here with the landlady, overnight. She said, "For fifty cents." Extortionary, but I accepted the deal. However was unavoidably detained like they say. Returned last night for my gear and goddam, this landlady here refuses to surrender it to me except for twenty-five bucks. Crazy witch!

(*Mrs. Wire is at the cubicle entrance.*)

MRS. WIRE: What's he doin' up there?

SKY: Admiring the view.

MRS. WIRE: You was urinating out of the window! Jailbird! You ain't been in a hospital four months, you been in the House of Detention for resistin' arrest and assaultin' an officer of the law. I know. You admire the view in the bathroom. I don't allow no trashy behavior here. (*She turns to the writer.*) Why ain't you on the streets with those business cards?

WRITER: Because I'm at the last paragraph of a story.

MRS. WIRE: Knock it off this minute! Why, the streets are swarming this Sunday with the Azalea Festival trade.

WRITER: The time I give to "Meals for a Quarter in the Quarter" has begun to exceed the time originally agreed on, Mrs. Wire.

MRS. WIRE: It's decent, healthy work that can keep you off bad habits, bad company that I know you been drifting into.

WRITER: How would you know anything outside of this moldy, old—

MRS. WIRE: Don't talk that way about this—*historical* old building. Why, 722 Toulouse Street is one of the oldest buildings in the Vieux Carré, and the courtyard, why, that courtyard out there is on the tourist list of attractions!

WRITER: The tourists don't hear you shoutin' orders and insults to your, your—prisoners here!

MRS. WIRE: Two worthless dependents on me, that pair of scavenger crones that creep about after dark.

(*Nightingale coughs in his cubicle. Mrs. Wire raises her voice.*)

And I got that TB case spitting contagion wherever he goes, leaves a track of blood behind him like a chicken that's had it's head chopped off.

NIGHTINGALE: 'sa goddam libelous lie!

MRS. WIRE (*crossing to the entrance of the adjoining cubicle*): Been discharged from the Two Parrots, they told you to fold up your easel and git out!

NIGHTINGALE (*hoarsely*): I'm making notes on these lies, and my friend, the writer, is witness to them!

MRS. WIRE: You is been discharged from the Two Parrots. It's God's truth, I got it from the cashier!

(*Sky chuckles, fascinated. He sits on the edge of the table or cot, taking a cigarette and offering one to the writer. Their casual friendly talk is contrapuntal to the violent altercation in progress outside.*)

She told me they had to scrub the pavement around your easel with a bucket of lye each night, that customers had left without payin' because you'd hawked an' spit by their tables!

NIGHTINGALE: Bucket of lies, not lye, that's what she told you!

MRS. WIRE: They only kept you there out of human pity!

NIGHTINGALE: Pity!

MRS. WIRE: Yais, pity! But finally pity and patience was exhausted, it run out there and it's run out here! Unlock that door! NURSIE!

NURSIE (*off stage*): Now what?

MRS. WIRE: Bring up my keys! Mr. Nightingale's locked himself in! You're gonna find you'self mighty quicker than you expected in a charity ward on your way to a pauper's grave!

WRITER: Mrs. Wire, be easy on him . . .

MRS. WIRE: You ain't heard what he calls me? Why, things he's said to me I hate to repeat. He's called me a fuckin' ole witch, yes, because I stop him from bringin' pickups in here at midnight that might stick a knife in the heart of anyone in the buildin' after they done it to him.

NIGHTINGALE (*in a wheezing voice as he drops onto the cot in his cubicle*): It's you that'll get a knife stuck in you, between your—dried up old—dugs . . .

WRITER (sotto voce, *near tears*): Be easy on him, he's dying.

MRS. WIRE: Not here. He's defamed this place as infested with bedbugs to try to explain away the blood he coughs on his pillow.

WRITER: That's—his last defense against—

MRS. WIRE: The truth, there's no defense against truth. Ev'rything in that room is contaminated, has got to be removed to the incinerator an' burned. Start with the mattress, Nursie!

(*Nursie has entered the lighted area with a bunch of musty keys.*)

NIGHTINGALE: I warn you, if you attempt to enter my room, I'll strike you down with this easel!

MRS. WIRE: You do that, just try, the effort of the exertion would finish you right here! Oh, shoot, here's the master key, opens all doors!

NIGHTINGALE: At your own risk— I'll brain you, you bitch.

MRS. WIRE: Go on in there, Nursie!

NURSIE: Aw, no, not me! I told you I would never go in that room!

MRS. WIRE: We're coming in!

NIGHTINGALE: WATCH OUT!

(*He is backed into the alcove, the easel held over his head like a crucifix to exorcise a demon. A spasm of coughing wracks him. He bends double, dropping the easel, collapses to his knees, and then falls flat upon the floor.*)

NURSIE (*awed*): Is he daid, Mizz Wire?

MRS. WIRE: Don't touch him. Leave him there until the coroner gets here.

NIGHTINGALE (*gasping*): Coroner, your ass—I'll outlive you.

MRS. WIRE: If I dropped dead this second! Nursie, haul out that filthy mattress of his, pour kerosene on it.

NURSIE: Wouldn't touch that mattress with a pole . . .

MRS. WIRE: And burn it. Git a nigger to help you haul everything in here out, it's all contaminated. Why, this whole place could be quarantined!

NURSIE: Furniture?

MRS. WIRE: All! Then wash off your hands in alcohol to prevent infection, Nursie.

NURSIE: Mizz Wire, the courtyard is full of them Azalea Festival ladies that paid admission to enter! You want me to smoke 'em out?

MRS. WIRE: Collect the stuff you can move.

NURSIE: Move where?

MRS. WIRE: Pile it under the banana tree in the courtyard, cover it with tarpaulin, we can burn it later.

NIGHTINGALE: If anyone lays a hand on my personal effects, I'll (*His voice chokes with sobs.*) —I will be back in the Two Parrots tonight. I wasn't fired. I was given a leave of absence till I recovered from . . . asthma . . .

MRS. WIRE (*with an abrupt compassion*): Mr. Nightingale.

NIGHTINGALE: Rossignol!—of the Baton Rouge Rossignols, as any dog could tell you . . .

MRS. WIRE: I won't consult a dawg on this subject. However, the place for you is not here but in the charity ward at St. Vincent's. Rest there till I've made arrangements to remove you.

SKY: The altercation's subsided.

WRITER (*to Sky, who has begun to play his clarinet*): What kind of horn is that?

(*Mrs. Wire appears at the entrance to the writer's cubicle. Sky plays entrance music—"Ta-ta-taaaa!"*)

SKY: It's not a horn, kid, horns are brass. A clarinet's a wood-wind instrument, not a horn.

MRS. WIRE: Yais, now about you all.

SKY: Never mind about us. We're leaving for the West Coast.

(*Mrs. Wire and the writer are equally stunned in opposite ways.*)

MRS. WIRE: —What's he mean, son? You're leavin' with this jailbird?

WRITER: —I—

MRS. WIRE: You won't if I can prevent it, and I know how. In my register book, when you signed in here, you wrote St. Louis. We got your home address, street and number. I'm gonna inform your folks of the vicious ways and companions you been slipping into. They's a shockin' diff'rence between your looks an' manners since when you arrived here an' now, mockin' me with that grin an' that shifty-eyed indifference, evidence you're setting out on a future life of corruption. Address and phone number, I'll write, I'll phone! —You're not leavin' here with a piece of trash *like* that that pissed out the window! —Son, son, don't do it! (*She covers her face, unraveled with emotion. Exchanging a look with Sky, the writer places an arm gingerly about her shoulder.*) You know I've sort of adopted you like the son took away from me by the late Mr. Wire and a—and a crooked lawyer, they got me declared to be—mentally in-competent.

WRITER: Mrs. Wire, I didn't escape from one mother to look for another.

(*Nursie returns, huffing, to the lighted area.*)

NURSIE: Mizz Wire, those tourists ladies, I can't control them, they're pickin' the azaleas off the bushes, and—

MRS. WIRE: That's what I told you to stay in the courtyard to stop.

NURSIE: Oh, I try, but one of 'em jus' called me a impudent ole nigger, and I won't take it. I come here to tell you I QUIT!

MRS. WIRE: AGAIN! COME BACK OUT THERE WITH ME! (*She turns to the writer.*) We'll continue this later. (*She exits with Nursie.*)

WRITER (*to Sky*): —Were you serious about the West Coast offer?

SKY: You're welcome to come along with me. I don't like to travel a long distance like that by myself.

WRITER: How do you travel?

SKY: I've got a beat-up old '32 Ford across the street with a little oil and about half a tank of gas in it. If you want to go, we could share the expense. Have you got any cash?

WRITER: I guess I've accumulated a capital of about thirty-five dollars.

SKY: We'll siphon gas on the way.

WRITER: Siphon?

SKY: I travel with a little rubber tube, and at night I unscrew the top of somebody's gas tank and suck the gas out through the tube and spit it into a bucket and empty it into my car. Is it a deal?

WRITER (*with suppressed excitement*): How would we live on the road?

SKY (*rolling a cigarette with obvious practice*): We'd have to exercise our wits. And our personal charm. And, well, if that don't suffice, I have a blanket in the car, and there's plenty of wide open spaces between here and the Coast. (*He pauses for a beat.*) Scared? Of the undertaking?

WRITER (*smiling slowly*): No—the Coast—starting when?

SKY: Why not this evening? The landlady won't admit me to the house again, but I'll call you. Just keep your window open. I'll blow my clarinet in the courtyard. Let's say about six.

(*The conversation may continue in undertones as the area is dimmed out.*)

SCENE NINE

The lights come up on Jane's studio area. The shuttered doors to the windows overlooking the courtyard below are ajar. Jane is trying to rouse Tye from an unnaturally deep sleep. It is evident that she has been engaged in packing her effects and his.

JANE: Tye, Tye, oh—Christ . . .

(*He drops a bare arm off the disordered bed and moans slightly. She bends over to examine a needle mark on his arm.*)

TYE: —Wh—?

(*Jane crosses to the sink and wets a towel, then returns to slap Tye's face with it. He begins to wake slowly.*)

Some men would beat a chick up for less'n that, y'know.

JANE: All right, get out of bed and beat me up, but get *up*.

TYE (*stroking a promontory beneath the bed sheet*): —Can't you see I *am* up?

JANE: I don't mean that kind of up, and don't bring strip show lewdness in here this—Sunday afternoon.

TYE: Babe, don't mention the show to me t'day.

JANE: I'd like to remind you that when we first stumbled into this—crazy—co-habitation, you promised me you'd quit the show in a week.

TYE: For what? Tight as work is for a dude with five grades of school and no skill training from the Mississippi sticks?

JANE: You could find something less—publicly embarrassing, like a—filling station attendant.

TYE: Ha!

JANE: But of course your choice of employment is no concern of mine now.

TYE: Why not, Babe?

JANE: I'm not "Babe" and not "Chick"!

TYE: You say you're not my chick?

JANE: I say I'm nobody's chick.

TYE: Any chick who shacks with me's my chick.

JANE: This is my place. You just—moved in and stayed.

TYE: I paid the rent this month.

JANE: Half of it, for the first time, my savings being as close to exhaustion as me.

(*There is the sound of a funky piano and a voice on the Bourbon Street corner: "I've stayed around and played around this old town too long." Jane's mood softens under its influence.*)

Lord, I don't know how I managed to haul you to bed.

TYE: Hey, you put me to bed last night?

JANE: It was much too much exertion for someone in my—condition.

TYE (*focusing on her more closely*): —Honey, are you pregnant?

JANE: No, Lord, now who'd be fool enough to get pregnant by a Bourbon Street strip show barker?

TYE: When a chick talks about her condition, don't it mean she's pregnant?

JANE: All female conditions are not pregnancy, Tye. (*She staggers, then finishes her coffee.*) Mine is that of a desperate young woman living with a young bum employed by gangsters and using her place as a depository for hot merchandise. Well, they're all packed. You're packed too.

TYE: —Come to bed.

JANE: No, thank you. Your face is smeared with lipstick; also other parts of you. I didn't know lip rouge ever covered so much—territory.

TYE: I honestly don't remember a fuckin' thing after midnight.

JANE: That I do believe. Now have some coffee, I've warmed it. It isn't instant, it's percolated.

TYE: Who's birthday is it?

JANE: It's percolated in honor of our day of parting.

TYE: Aw, be sweet, Babe, please come back to bed. I need comfort, not coffee.

JANE: You broke a promise to me.

TYE: Which?

JANE: Among the many? You used a needle last night. I saw the mark of it on you.

TYE: No shit. Where?

JANE (*returning to the bedside*): There, right there on your— (*He circles her with his arm and pulls her onto the bed.*) I've been betrayed by a—sensual streak in my nature. Susceptibility to touch. And you have skin like a child. I'd gladly support you if I believed you'd—if I had the means to and the time to. Time. Means. Luck. Things that expire, run out. And all at once you're stranded.

TYE: Jane you—lie down with me and hold me.

JANE: I'm afraid, Tye, we'll just have to hold each other in our memories from now on.

TYE (*childishly*): Don't talk that way. I never had a rougher night in my life. Do I have to think and remember?

JANE: Tye, we've had a long spell of dreaming, but now we suddenly have to.

TYE: Got any aspirin, Babe?

JANE: You're past aspirin, Tye. I think you've gone past all legal—analgesics.

TYE: You say words to me I've never heard before.

JANE: Tye, I've been forced to make an urgent phone call to someone I never wanted to call.

TYE: Call?

JANE: And then I packed your personal belongings and all that lot you've been holding here. Exertion of packing nearly blacked me out. Trembling, sweating—had to bathe and change.

TYE: Babe?

JANE: You're vacating the premises, "Babe." It's *afternoon.*

TYE: Look, if you're knocked up, have the kid. I'm against abortion.

JANE: On moral principles?

TYE: Have the kid, Babe. I'd pull myself together for a kid.

JANE: You didn't for me.

TYE: A baby would be a livin' thing between us, with both our blood.

JANE: Never mind.

(*Voices in the courtyard are heard.*)

NURSIE: Any donations t'keep the cou'tyard up, just drop it in my apron as you go out, ladies! . . .

JANE: Those tourists down there in the courtyard! If I'd known when I took this room it was over a tourist attraction—

TYE: It's the Festival, Babe. It ain't always Festival . . . Gimme my cigarettes, ought to be some left in a pocket.

JANE (*throwing his pants and a fancy sport shirt on the bed*): Here, your clothes, get in them.

TYE (*putting on his shorts*): Not yet. It's Sunday, Babe . . . Where's Beret? I like Beret to be here when I wake up.

JANE: Not even a cat will wait ten, twelve hours for you to sleep off whatever you shot last night. How did a girl well educated and reasonably well brought up get involved in this . . . Oh, I'm talking to myself.

TYE: I hear you, Babe, and I see you.

JANE: Then . . . get up and dressed.

TYE: It's not dark yet, Babe. Y'know I never get dressed till after dark on Sundays.

JANE: Today has to be an exception. I'm . . . expecting a caller, very important to me.

TYE: Fashion designer?

JANE: No. Buyer . . . to look at my illustrations. They're no good, I'm no good. I just had a flair, not a talent, and the flair flared out, I'm . . . finished. These sketches are evidence of it! (*She starts tearing fashion sketches off the wall.*) Look at me! Bangles, jangles! All taste gone! (*She tears off her costume jewelry.*)

TYE: Babe, you're in no shape to meet a buyer.

JANE (*slowly and bitterly*): He's no buyer of anything but me.

TYE: —Buyer of *you*? Look. You said that you were expecting a buyer to look at your drawin's here.

JANE: I know what I said, I said a buyer to look at my illustrations, but what I said was a lie. Among other things, many other undreamed of before, you've taught me to practice deception.

VOICES OFFSTAGE: Edwina, Edwina, come see this dream of a little courtyard. Oh, my, yaiss, like a dream.

JANE: I know what I said, but let's say, Tye, that I experienced last week a somewhat less than triumphant encounter with the buyer of fashion illustrations at *Vogue Moderne*. In fact, it left me too shattered to carry my portfolio home without a shot of Metaxas brandy at the Blue Lantern, which was on the street level of the building. It was there that I met a gentleman from Brazil. He had observed my entrance, the Brazilian, and apparently took me for a hooker, sprang up with surprising agility for a gentleman of his corpulence, hauled me to his table, and introduced me to his *cama-radas*, "Señorita, this is Señor and Señor and Señor," declared me, *"Bonita muy, muy, bonita"*—tried to press a hundred-dollar bill in my hand. Well, some atavistic bit of propriety surfaced and I, like a fool, rejected it—but did accept his business card, just in case— This morning, Tye, I called him. "Senorita Bonita of the Blue Lantern awaits you, top floor of seven-two-two Toulouse," that was the invitation that I phoned in to the message desk— He must have received it by now at the Hotel Royal Orleans, where the Presidential Suite somehow contains him.

TYE: Who're you talkin' about?

JANE: My expected caller, a responsible businessman from Brazil. Sincerely interested in my bankrupt state . . .

TYE: Forget it, come back to bed and I'll undress you, Babe, you need rest.

JANE: The bed bit is finished between us. You're moving out today.

(*He slowly stumbles up, crosses to the table, and gulps coffee, then grasps her arm and draws her to bed.*)

No, no, no, no, no, no!

TYE: Yes, yes, yes, yes, yes!

(*He throws her onto the bed and starts to strip her; she resists; he prevails. As the lights very gradually dim, a Negro singer-pianist at a nearby bar fades in, "Fly a-way! Sweet Kentucky baby-bay, fly, away . . ."*)

MRS. WIRE (*from a few steps below the writer*): What's paralyzed you there? Son?

WRITER: Miss Sparks is crying.

(*Mrs. Wire appears behind the writer in the lighted spot.*)

MRS. WIRE: That woman's moanin' in there don't mean she's in pain. Son, I got a suspicion you never had close relations with wimmen in your life.

JANE: Ohhh!

WRITER: I never heard sounds like that.

(*Jane utters a wild cry. It impresses even Mrs. Wire.*)

TYE'S VOICE: Babe, I don't wanna force you . . .

JANE'S VOICE: Plee-ase! I'm not a thing, I'm not-a-thing!

MRS. WIRE (*shouting*): You all quit that loud fornication in there!

TYE'S VOICE (*shouting back*): Get the fuck downstairs, goddam ole witch!

MRS. WIRE: Howlin' insults at me in my own house, won't tolerate it! (*She bursts into the room.*) Never seen such a disgustin' exhibition!

(*Tye starts to rise from the bed. Jane clings desperately to him.*)

JANE: As! You see!—Mrs. Wire!—Everything is!—packed, he's—moving—today . . .

TYE: The rent is paid in full! So get the fuck outa here!

JANE: Tye, please.

MRS. WIRE: What's in them boxes?

TYE: None of your—

JANE: Our personal—belongings, Mrs. Wire.

MRS. WIRE: That I doubt! The contents of these boxes will be inspected before removed from this place and in the presence of my nephew on the police force!

(*Tye charges toward Mrs. Wire.*)

Don't you expose yourself naykid in my presence! Nursie!

JANE: Mrs. Wire, for once I do agree with you! Can you get him out, please, please get him out!

MRS. WIRE (*averting her face with an air of shocked propriety*): Dress at once and—

NURSIE: Mizz Wire, I got the hospital on the phone.

MRS. WIRE: They sendin' an ambulance for Nightingale?

NURSIE: Soon's they got a bed for him, but they want you to call 'em back and—

MRS. WIRE: St. Vincent's is run by taxpayers' money, I'll remind 'em of that. (*She crosses off stage. Tye slams the door.*)

(*Jane is sobbing on the bed.*)

TYE: Now, Babe.

JANE: If you approach this bed—

TYE: Just want to comfort you, honey. Can't we just rest together? Can't we? Rest and comfort each other?

(*The area dims as the black pianist sings "Kentucky Baby."*)

MRS. WIRE: Cut out that obscene talking up there, I'm on
the phone. Emergency call is from here at 722 Toulouse.
Christ Almighty, you drive me to profane language. You
mean to admit you don't know the location of the most
historical street in the Vieux Carré? You're not talking to
no . . . no nobody, but a personage. Responsible. Reputable. Known to the authorities on the list of attractions.
God damn it, you twist my tongue up with your . . .
Nursie! Nursie! Will you talk to this incompetent . . .
Nursie! Nursie!

(*Nursie appears.*)

Got some idiot on the phone at the hospital. Will you inform this idiot who I am in the Quarter. Phone. Talk.

(*Nursie takes the phone.*)

NURSIE: Stairs . . . took my breath . . .

MRS. WIRE (*snatching back the phone*): Now I want you to
know, this here Nightingale case . . . I don't lack sympathy
for the dying or the hopelessly inflicted . . . (*She kicks at
Nursie beside here.*) Git! But I've got responsibilities to my
tenants. Valuable paying tenants, distinguished society
ladies, will quit my premises this day, I swear they will, if
this Nightingale remains. Why, the State Board of Health
will clap a suit on me unless . . . at once . . . ambulance.
When? At what time? Don't say approximate to me. Emergency means immediate. Not when you drag your arse
around to it. And just you remember I'm a taxpayer . . .
No, no, you not me. I pay, you collect. Now get the ambulance here immediately, 722 Toulouse, with a stretcher

with straps, the Nightingale is violent with fever. (*She slams down the phone.*) Shit!

NURSIE: My guess is they're going to remove you, too.

(*Mrs. Wire leans on Nursie.*)

SCENE TEN

There is a spotlight on the writer, stage front, as narrator.

WRITER: That Sunday I served my last meal for a quarter in the Quarter, then I returned to the attic. From Nightingale's cage there was silence so complete I thought, "He's dead." Then he cried out softly—

NIGHTINGALE: Christ, how long do I have to go on like this?

WRITER: Then, for the first time, I returned his visits. (*He makes the gesture of knocking at Nightingale's door.*) —Mr. Rossignol . . .

(*There is a sound of staggering and wheezing. Nightingale opens the door; the writer catches him as he nearly falls and assists him back to his cot.*)

—You shouldn't try to dress.

NIGHTINGALE: Got to—escape! She wants to commit me to a charnel house on false charges . . .

WRITER: It's raining out.

NIGHTINGALE: A Rossignol will not be hauled away to a charity hospital.

WRITER: Let me call a private doctor. He wouldn't allow them to move you in your—condition . . .

NIGHTINGALE: My faith's in Christ—not doctors . . .

WRITER: Lie down.

NIGHTINGALE: Can't breathe lying—down . . .

WRITER: I've brought you this pillow. I'll put it back of your head. (*He places the pillow gently in back of Nightingale.*) Two plilows help you breathe.

NIGHTINGALE (*leaning weakly back*): Ah—thanks—better . . . Sit down.

(*A dim light comes up on the studio area as Tye lights a joint, sitting on the table.*)

WRITER: Theren' nowhere to sit.

NIGHTINGALE: You mean nowhere not contaminated? (*The writer sits.*) —*God's got to give me time for serious work!* Even God has moral obligations, don't He? —Well, *don't* He?

WRITER: I think that morals are a human invention that He ignores as successfully as we do.

NIGHTINGALE: Christ, that's evil, that is infidel talk. (*He crosses himself.*) I'm a Cath'lic believer. A priest would say that you have fallen from Grace, boy.

WRITER: What's that you're holding?

NIGHTINGALE: Articles left me by my sainted mother. Her tortoise-shell comb with a mother-of-pearl handle and her silver framed mirror.

(*He sits up with difficulty and starts combing his hair before the mirror as if preparing for a social appearance.*)

Precious heirlooms, been in the Rossignol family three generations. I look pale from confinement with asthma. Bottom of box is—toiletries, cosmetics—please!

WRITER: You're planning to make a public appearance, intending to go on the streets with this—advanced case of asthma?

NIGHTINGALE: Would you kindly hand me my Max Factor, my makeup kit?!

WRITER: I have a friend who wears cosmetics at night—they dissolve in the rain.

NIGHTINGALE: If necessary, I'll go into *Sanctuary*!

(*The writer utters a startled, helpless laugh; he shakes with it and leans against the stippled wall.*)

Joke, is it, is it a joke?! Foxes have holes, but the Son of Man hath nowhere to hide His head!

WRITER: Don't you know you're delirious with fever?

NIGHTINGALE: You used to be kind—gentle. In less than four months you've turned your back on that side of your nature, turned rock-hard as the world.

WRITER: I had to survive in the world. Now where's your pills for sleep, you need to rest.

NIGHTINGALE: On the chair by the bed.

(*Pause.*)

WRITER (*softly*): Maybe this time you ought to take more than one.

NIGHTINGALE: Why, you're suggesting suicide to me which is a cardinal sin, would put me in unhallowed ground in—potter's field. I believe in God the Father, God the Son, and God the Holy Ghost . . . you've turned into a killer?

WRITER (*compulsively, with difficulty*): Stop calling it asthma —the flu, a bad cold. Face the facts, deal with them. (*He opens the pillbox.*) Press tab to open, push down, unscrew the top. Here it is where you can reach it.

NIGHTINGALE: —Boy with soft skin and stone heart . . .

(*Pause. The writer blows the candle out and takes Nightingale's hand.*)

WRITER: Hear the rain, let the rain talk to you, I can't.

NIGHTINGALE: Light the candle.

WRITER: The candle's not necessary. You've got an alcove, too, with a window and bench. Keep your eyes on it, she might come in here before you fall asleep.

(*A strain of music is heard. The angel enters from her dark passage and seats herself, just visible faintly, on Nightingale's alcove bench.*)

Do you see her in the alcove?

NIGHTINGALE: Who?

WRITER: Do you feel a comforting presence?

NIGHTINGALE: None.

WRITER: Remember my mother's mother? Grand?

NIGHTINGALE: I don't receive apparitions. They're only seen by the mad.

(*The writer returns to his cubicle and continues as narrator.*)

WRITER: In my own cubicle, I wasn't sure if Grand had entered with me or not. I couldn't distinguish her from a— diffusion of light through the low running clouds. I thought I saw her, but her image was much fainter than it had ever been before, and I suspected that it would fade more and more as the storm of my father's blood obliterated the tenderness of Grand's. I began to pack my belongings. I was about to make a panicky departure to nowhere I could imagine . . . The West Coast? With Sky?

(*He is throwing things into a cardboard suitcase. Nursie appears at the edge of his light with a coffee tray.*)

NURSIE: Mizz Wire knows you're packin' to leave an' she tole me to bring you up this hot coffee and cold biscuits.

WRITER: Thank her. Thank you both.

NURSIE: She says don't make no mistakes.

WRITER (*harshly*): None, never?

NURSIE: None if you can help, and I agree with her about that. She's phoned your folks about you. They're coming down here tomorrow.

WRITER: If she's not bluffing . . .

NURSIE: She ain't bluffin', I heard her on the phone myself. Mizz Wire is gettin' you confused with her son Timmy. Her mind is slippin' again. Been through that before. Can't do it again.

WRITER: We all have our confusions . . . (*He gulps down the coffee as Nursie crosses out of the light.*)

NURSIE (*singing softly*): "My home is on Jordan."

WRITER: Then I started to write. I worked the longest I'd ever worked in my life, nearly all that Sunday. I wrote about Jane and Tye, I could hear them across the narrow hall. —Writers are shameless spies . . .

SCENE ELEVEN

The studio light builds. Jane is sobbing on the bed. Tye is rolling a joint, seated on the table. The clearing sky has faded toward early blue dusk. Tye regards Jane with a puzzled look. Faintly we hear the black singer-pianist. "Bye, bye, blues. Don't cry blues," etc.

TYE: Want a hit, Babe? (*She ignores the question.*) How long have I been asleep? Christ, what are you crying about. Didn't I just give you one helluva Sunday afternoon ball, and you're cryin' about it like your mother died.

JANE: You forced me, you little—pig, you did, you forced me.

TYE: You wanted it.

JANE: I didn't.

TYE: Sure you did. (*Jane is dressing again.*) Honey, you got shadows under your eyes.

JANE: Blackbirds kissed me last night. Isn't that what they say about shadows under the eyes, that blackbirds kissed her last night. The Brazilian must have been blind drunk when he took a fancy to me in the Blue Lantern, mistook me for a hundred-dollar girl. —Tye, I'm not a whore! I'm the Northern equivalent of a lady, fallen, yes, but a lady, not a whore.

TYE: Whores get paid for it, Babe. I never had to.

JANE: You little—prick—! Now I'm talkin' your jive, how do you like it? Does she talk like that when she's smearing you with lipstick, when you ball her, which I know you do, repeatedly, between shows.

TYE: —Who're you talkin' about?

JANE: That headliner at the strip show, the Champagne Girl.

TYE (*gravely*): She's—not with the show no more.

JANE: The headliner's quit the show?

TYE: Yeah, honey, the Champagne Girl is dead an' so she's not in the show.

JANE: You mean—not such a hot attraction any more?

TYE: Don't be funny about it, it ain't funny.

JANE: You mean she's actually—

TYE: Yes. Ackshally. Dead. Real dead, about as dead as dead, which is totally dead— So now you know why I needed a needle to get me through last night.

JANE: —Well, of course that's—

TYE: You was jealous of her . . . (*Jane looks away.*) I never touched the Champagne Girl. She was strictly the property of the Man. Nobody else dared t' touch her.

JANE: The Man—what man?

TYE: The Man—no other name known by— Well—he wasted her.

JANE: —Killed her?—Why?

TYE: Cause she quit sleeping with him. She was offered a deal on the West Coast, Babe. The Man said, "No." The Champagne Girl said, "Yes." So the Man . . . you don't say no to the Man—so if she's going to the West Coast it'll be packed in ice—

(*Voices are heard from the courtyard.*)

TOURIST 1: My slippers are wet through.

(*Piano music is heard.*)

TOUTIST 2: What's next on the tour, or is it nearly finished?

TYE: When the Man is annoyed by something, he piles his lupos in the back seat of his bulletproof limo and he let's 'em loose on the source of his annoyance.

JANE: —Lupos?

TYE: Lupos are those big black dawgs that're used for attack. The Man has three of 'em, and when he patrols his territory at night, they sit in the back seat of his Lincoln, set up there, mouths wide open on their dagger teeth and their black eyes rollin' like dice in a nigger crapshooter's hands. And night before last, Jesus! he let 'em into the Champagne Girl's apartment, and they—well, they ate her. Gnawed her tits off her ribs, gnawed her sweet little ass off. Of course the story is that the Champagne Girl entertained a pervert who killed her and ate her like that, but it's pretty well known it was them lupos that devoured that girl, under those ceiling mirrors and crystal chandeliers in her all white satin bedroom.—Yep—gone—the headliner— Y'know what you say when the Man wastes somebody? You got to say that he or she has "Gone to Spain." So they tole me last night, when people ask you where's the Champagne Girl, answer 'em that the Champagne Girl's gone to Spain. —Sweet kid from Pascagoula.

JANE: Please don't—continue—the story.

TYE: All champagne colored without face or body makeup on her, light gold like pale champagne and not a line, not a pore to be seen on her body! Was she meant for dawg food? I said, was she meant for dawg food? Those lupos ate that kid like she was their—last—supper . . .

JANE (*who has now managed to get round the table*): Tye, Tye, open the shutters!

TYE: Why? You goin' out naked?

JANE: I'm going to vomit and die—in clean air . . . (*She has moved slowly upstage to the gallery with its closed shutters, moving from one piece of furniture to another for support. Now she opens the shutter doors and staggers out onto the gallery, and the tourist ladies' voices are raised in thrilled shock and dismay.*)

TOURIST 1: Look at that!

TOURIST 2: What at?

TOURIST 1: There's a whore at the gallery window! Practically naked!

(*All gallery speeches should overlap.*)

JANE (*wildly*): Out, out, out, out, out!

NURSIE: Miss, Miss Sparks! These are Festival ladies who've paid admission.

JANE: Can't endure any more! Please, please, I'm sick!

TYE: Fawgit it, Babe, come back in.

JANE: It isn't real, it couldn't be—

(*The writer shakes his head with a sad smile.*)

But it was—it is . . . like a dream . . .

TYE: What did you say, Babe?

JANE: Close the gallery door—please?

TYE: Sure, Babe. (*He shuts the door on the voices below.*)

JANE: And—the hall door—bolt it. Why do you bring home nightmare stories to me?!

TYE (*gently*): Babe, you brought up the subject, you asked me about the Champagne Girl, I wasn't planning to tell you. Chair?

JANE: Bed.

TYE: Grass?

JANE: —Coffee.

TYE: Cold.

JANE: —Cold—coffee.

(*Tye pours her a cup and puts it in her trembling hand. He holds the hand and lifts the cup to her lips, standing behind her. He lets his hand fall to her breasts; she sobs and removes the hand.*
(*The singer-pianist is heard again.*)

JANE: . . . Why do you want to stay on here?

TYE: Here's where you are, Babe.

JANE (*shaking her head*): No more. I . . . have to dress . . .
   (*She dresses awkwardly, frantically. He watches in silence.*)

You have to get dressed, too. I told you I was expecting a very important visitor. Tye, the situation's turned impossible on us, face it.

TYE: You're not walkin' out on me.

JANE: Who have I got to appeal to except God, whose phone's disconnected, or this . . . providential . . . protector.

TYE: From the banana republic, a greaseball. And you'd quit me for that?

JANE: You've got to be mature and understanding. At least for once, now dress. The Brazilian is past due . . . I realized your defects, but you touched me like nobody else in my life had ever before or ever could again. But, Tye, I counted on you to grow up, and you refused to. I took you for someone gentle caught in violence and degradation that he'd escape from . . .

TYE: Whatever you took me for, I took you for honest, for decent, for . . .

JANE: Don't be so . . . "Decent"? You ridiculous little . . . sorry, no. Let's not go into . . . abuse . . . Tye? When we went into this it wasn't with any long-term thing in mind. That's him on the steps. Go in the bathroom quiet!

TYE: You go in the bathroom quiet. I'll explain without words.

(*She thrusts his clothes at him. He throws them savagely about the stage.*)

. . . Well?

(*There is a sound on the stairs.*)

Sounds like the footsteps of a responsible man.

(*Tye opens the door. We see hospital interns with a stretcher. Jane stares out. The interns pass again with Nightingale's dying body on the stretcher. The writer is with them. Jane gasps and covers her face with her arm. The writer turns to her.*)

WRITER: It's just—they're removing the painter.

JANE: —*Just!*

TYE: No Brazilian, no buyer?

JANE: No. No sale . . .

WRITER (*standing in the open doorway*): It was getting dim in the room.

TYE: It's almost getting dark.

WRITER: They didn't talk. He smoked his reefer. He looked at her steady in the room getting dark and said . . .

TYE: I see you clear.

WRITER: She turned her face away. He walked around that way and looked at her from that side. She turned her face the other way. She was crying without a sound, and a black man was playing piano at the Four Deuces round the corner, an oldie, right for the atmosphere . . . something like . . .

(*The piano fades in, "Seem like Old Times." Tye begins to sing softly with the piano.*)

JANE: *Don't.*

(*Tye stops the soft singing but continues to stare at Jane.*)

DON'T.

(*Pause.*)

TYE: Jane. You've gotten sort of—skinny. How much weight you lost?

JANE: I . . . . don't know . . .

TYE: Sometimes you walk a block and can't go no further.

(*Pause.*)

JANE: I guess I'm a yellow-cab girl. With limousine aspirations.

TYE: Cut the smart talk, Babe. Let's level.

(*Pause. She extends her hand.*)

Want a hit? Well?

(*Jane nods and take a hit off his cigarette.*)

Huh?

JANE: Well, after all, why not, if you're interested in it. It hasn't been just lately I've lost weight and energy but for more than a year in New York. Some—blood thing—progressing rather fast at my age . . . . I think I had a remission when I met you.

A definite remission . . . here . . . like the world stopped and turned backward, or like it entered another universe—

months! (*She moves convulsively; Tye grips her shoulders.*) . . .
Then . . . it . . . I . . .

TYE: Us?

JANE: No, no, that unnatural tiredness started in again. I went
to Ochsners. Don't you remember when the doctor's letter
was delivered? No, I guess you don't, being half conscious
all the time. It was from Ochsners. It informed me that
my blood count had changed for the worse. It was close
to . . . collapse . . . (*Pause.*) . . . Those are the clinical
details. Are you satisfied with them? Have you any more
questions to ask?

(*She stares at him; he averts his face. She moves around him to
look at his face; he averts it again. She claps it between her
hands and compels him to look at her. He looks down. A
scratching sound is heard at the shutter doors.*)

JANE: That's Beret, let her in. Isn't it nice how cats go away
and come back and—you don't have to worry about them.
So unlike human beings.

(*Tye opens the door. He opens a can of cat food and sets it on
the floor, then crosses to his clothes, collecting them from the
floor.*)

TYE (*gently*): Jane, it's getting dark and I—I better get
dressed now.

JANE (*with a touch of harshness*): Yes, dress—dress . . . (*But
he is lost in reflection, lighting a joint. She snatches it from
his lips.*)
And leave me alone as always in a room that smells, that
reeks of marijuana!

SCENE TWELVE

WRITER (*as narrator*): She was watching him with an unspoken question in her eyes, a little resentful now.

MRS. WIRE'S VOICE (*from off stage, curiously altered*): Why are
those stairs so dark?

(*The light in the studio area is dimmed to half during the
brief scene that follows. The writer rises and stands apprehen-*

*sively alert as Mrs. Wire becomes visible in a yellowed silk robe
with torn lace, a reliquary garment. Her hair is loose, her
steps unsteady, her eyes hallucinated.*)

WRITER (*crossing from the studio, dismayed*): Is that you, Mrs.
   Wire?

MRS. WIRE: Now, Timmy, Timmy, you mustn't cry every time
   Daddy gets home from the road and naturally wants to be
   in bed just with Mommy. It's Daddy's privilege, Mommy's
   —obligation. You'll understand when you're older—you
   see, Daddy finds Mommy attractive.

WRITER (*backing away from the cubicle entrance*): Mrs. Wire,
   you're dreaming.

MRS. WIRE: Things between grownups in love and marriage
   can't be told to a child. (*She sits on the writer's cot.*) Now lie
   down and Mommy will sing you a little sleepy-time song.
   (*She is staring into space. He moves to the cubicle entrance;
   the candle is turned over and snuffed out.*)

MRS. WIRE: "Rock-a-bye, baby, in a tree top, If the wind
   blows, the cradle will rock . . ."

WRITER: Mrs. Wire, I'm not Timothy, I'm not Tim, I'm not
   Timmy. (*He touches her.*)

MRS. WIRE: Dear child given to me of love . . .

WRITER: Mrs. Wire, I'm not your child. I am nobody's child.
   Was maybe, but not now. I've grown into a man, about to
   take his first step out of this waiting station into the world.

MRS. WIRE: Mummy knows you're scared sleeping alone in
   the dark. But the Lord gave us dark for sleep, and Daddy
   don't like to find you took his rightful place . . .

WRITER: Mrs. Wire, I'm no relation to you, none but a tenant that earned his keep a while . . . Nursie! Nursie!

NURSIE (*approaching*): She gone up there? (*Nursie appears.*)
   She gets these spells, goes back in time. I think it musta
   been all that Azalea Festival excitement done it.

MRS. WIRE: "If the bough breaks, the cradle will fall . . ."

NURSIE (*at the cubicle entrance*): Mizz Wire, it's Nursie. I'll
   take you back downstairs.

MRS. WIRE (*rousing a bit*): It all seemed so real. —I even remember lovemaking . . .

NURSIE: Get up, Mizz Wire, come down with Nursie.

MRS. WIRE (*accepting Nursie's support*): Now I'm—old.

(*They withdraw from the light.*)

MRS. WIRE'S VOICE: Ahhhhhhhh . . . Ahhhhhhhh . . . Ahhhh . . . Ahhhhh . . .

(*This expression of despair is lost in the murmur of the wind. The writer sinks onto his cot; the angel of the alcove appears in the dusk.*)

WRITER: Grand! (*She lifts her hand in a valedictory gesture.*) I guess angels warn you to leave a place by leaving before you.

(*The light dims in the cubicle as the writer begins to pack and builds back up in the studio. The writer returns to the edge of the studio light.*)

JANE: You said you were going to get dressed and go back to your place of employment and resume the pitch for the ladies.

TYE: What did you say, Babe?

(*He has finished dressing and is now at the mirror, absorbed in combing his hair. Jane utters a soft, involuntary laugh.*)

JANE: A hundred dollars, the price, and worth it, certainly worth it. I must be much in your debt, way over my means to pay off!

TYE: Well, I ain't paid to make a bad appearance at work. (*He puts on a sport shirt with girls in grass skirts printed on it.*)

JANE: I hate that shirt.

TYE: I know you think it's tacky. Well, I'm tacky, and it's the only clean one I got.

JANE: It isn't clean, not really. And does it express much grief over the Champagne Girl's violent departure to Spain?

TYE: Do you have to hit me with that? What reason . . . ?

JANE: I've really got no reason to hit a goddamn soul but myself that lacked pride to keep my secrets. You know I shouldn't have told you about my—intentions, I should have just slipped away. The Brazilian was far from attractive but —my circumstances required some drastic—compromises.

TYE (*crouching beside her*): You're talking no sense, Jane. The Brazilian's out of the picture; those steps on the stairs were steps of hospital workers coming to take a—pick a dying fruit outa the place.

JANE: *Do you think I expect you back here again?* You'll say yes, assure me now as if forever—but—reconsider—the moment of impulse . . .

TYE: Cut some slack for me, Babe. We all gotta cut some slack for each other in this fucking world. Lissen. You don't have to sweat it.

JANE: Give me another remission; one that lasts!

TYE: Gotta go now, it's late, after dark and I'm dressed.

JANE: Well, zip your fly up unless you're now in the show. (*She rises and zips up his fly, touches his face and throat with trembling fingers.*)

TYE: Jane, we got love between us! Don't ya know that?

JANE (*not harshly*): Lovely old word, love, it's travelled a long way, Tye.

TYE: And still's a long way to go. Hate to leave you alone, but—

JANE: I'm not alone. I've got Beret. An animal is a comforting presence sometimes. I wonder if they'd admit her to St. Vincent's?

TYE: St. Vincent's?

JANE: That charity hospital where they took the painter called Nightingale.

TYE: You ain't going there, honey.

JANE: It strikes me as being a likely destination.

TYE: Why?

JANE: I watched you dress. I didn't exist for you. Nothing existed for you but your image in the mirror. Understandably so. (*With her last strength she draws herself up.*)

TYE: What's understandable, Jane? —You got a fever? (*He rises, too, and stretches out a hand to touch her forehead. She knocks it away.*)

JANE: What's understandable is that your present convenience is about to become an encumbrance. An invalid, of no use, financial or sexual. Sickness is repellent, Tye, demands more care and gives less and less in return. The person you loved —assuming that you *did* love when she was still useful—is now, is now absorbed in preparing herself for oblivion as you were absorbed in your—your image in the—mirror!

TYE (*frightened by her vehemence*): Hey, Jane!

(*Again she strikes away his extended hand.*)

JANE: Readies herself for it as you do for the street! (*She continues as to herself.*) —Withdraws into another dimension. Is indifferent to you except as—caretaker! Is less aware of you than of— (*Panting, she looks up slowly through the skylight.*) —sky that's visible to her from her bed under the skylight—at night, these—filmy white clouds, they move, they drift over the roofs of the Vieux Carré so close that if you have fever you feel as if you could touch them, and bits would come off on your fingers, soft as—cotton candy—

TYE: Rest, Babe. I'll be back early. I'll get Smokey to take over for me at midnight, and I'll come back with tamales and a bottle of vino! (*He crosses out of the light. She rushes to the door.*)

JANE: *No, no, not before daybreak and with a new needle mark on your arm.* Beret? Beret!

(*She staggers wildly out of the light, calling the cat again and again.*)

WRITER: I lifted her from the floor where she'd fallen . . .

(*Various voices are heard exclaiming around the house.*
(*The writer reappears in the studio area supporting Jane, who appears half conscious.*)

Jane? Jane?

JANE: —My cat, I scared it away . . .

NURSIE (*offstage*): What is goin' on up there?

WRITER: She was frightened by something.

JANE: I lost my cat, that's all. —They don't understand . . . (*The writer places her on the bed.*) Alone. I'm alone.

WRITER: She'll be back. Jane didn't seem to hear me. She was looking up at the skylight.

JANE: It isn't blue any more, it's suddenly turned quite dark.

WRITER: It was dark as the question in her eyes. (*The blues piano fades in.*)

JANE: It's black as the piano man playing around the corner.

WRITER: It must be after six. What's the time now?

JANE: Time? What? Oh. Time. My sight is blurred. (*She shows him her wristwatch.*) Can't make out the luminous dial, can you?

WRITER: It says five of twelve.

JANE: An improbable hour. Must have run down.

WRITER: I'll take it off. To wind it. (*He puts the watch to his ear.*) I'm afraid it's broken.

JANE (*vaguely*): I hadn't noticed. —Lately—I tell time by the sky.

WRITER: His name was Sky.

JANE: Tye . . .

WRITER: No, not Tye. Sky was the name of someone who offered me a ride West.

JANE: —I've had fever all day. Did you ask me a question?

WRITER: I said I'd planned a trip to the West Coast with this young vagrant, a musician.

JANE: Young vagrants are irresponsible. I'm not at all surprised—he let you down? Well. I have travel plans, too.

WRITER: With Tye?

JANE: No, I was going alone, not with Tye. What are you doing there?

WRITER: Setting up the chess board. Want to play?

JANE: Oh, yes, you said you play. I'd have a partner for once. But my concentration's—I warn you—it's likely to be— impaired.

WRITER: Want to play white or black?

JANE: You choose.

(*The piano fades in. Jane looks about in a confused way.*)

WRITER: Black. In honor of the musician around the corner.

JANE: —He's playing something appropriate to the occasion as if I'd phoned in a request. How's it go, so familiar?

WRITER:

"Makes no difference how things break,
    I'll still get by somehow
    I'm not sorry, cause it makes no difference now."

JANE: Each of us abandoned to the other. You know this is almost our first private conversation. (*She nearly falls to the floor. He catches her and supports her to the chair at the upstage side of the table.*) Shall we play, let's do. With no distractions at all. (*She seems unable to move; she has a frozen attitude.*)

(*There is a distant sustained high note from Sky's clarinet. They both hear it. Jane tries to distract the writer's attention from the sound and continues quickly with feverish animation. The sound of the clarinet becomes more urgent.*)

Vagrants, I can tell you about them. From experience. Incorirgibly delinquent. Purposeless. Addictive. Grab at you for support when support's what *you* need—gone? Whistling down the last flight, such a lively popular tune. Well, I have travel plans, but in the company of no charming young vagrant. Love Mediterranean countries but somehow missed Spain. I plan to go. Now! Madrid, to visit the Prado, most celebrated museum of all. Admire the Goyas, El Grecos. Hire a car to cross the—gold plains of Toledo.

WRITER: Jane, you don't have to make up stories, I heard your talk with Tye—all of it.

JANE: Then you must have heard his leaving. How his steps picked up speed on the second flight down—started whistling . . .

WRITER: He always whistles down stairs—it's habitual to him—you mustn't attach a special meaning to it.

(*The clarinet music is closer; the sound penetrates the shut windows.*)

JANE: At night the Quarter's so full of jazz music, so many entertainers. Isn't it now your move?

WRITER (*embarrassed*): It's your move, Jane.

JANE (*relinquishing her game*): No yours—your vagrant musician is late but you're not forgotten.

WRITER: I'll call down, ask him to wait till midnight when Tye said he'll be back.

JANE: With tamales and vino to celebrate— (*She staggers to the window, shatters a pane of glass, and shouts.*) —Your friend's coming right down, just picking up his luggage!

(*She leans against the wall, panting, her bleeding hand behind her.*)

Now go, quick. He might not wait, you'd regret it.

WRITER: Can't I do something for you?

JANE: Pour me three fingers of bourbon.

(*She has returned to the table. He pours the shot.*)

Now hurry, hurry. I know that Tye will be back early tonight.

WRITER: Yes, of course he will . . . (*He crosses from the studio light.*)

JANE (*smiling somewhat bitterly*): Naturally, yes, how could I possibly doubt it. With tamales and vino . . . (*She uncloses her fist; the blood is running from palm to wrist. The writer picks up a cardboard laundry box and the typewriter case.*)

WRITER: As I left, I glanced in Jane's door. She seemed to be or was pretending to be—absorbed in her solitary chess game. I went down the second flight and on the cot in the dark passageway was— (*He calls out.*) Beret?

(*For the first time the cat is visible, white and fluffy as a piece of cloud. Nursie looms dimly behind him, a dark solemn fact, lamplit.*)

NURSIE: It's the cat Miss Sparks come runnin' after.

WRITER: Take it to her, Nursie. She's alone up there.

MRS. WIRE: Now watch out, boy. Be careful of the future. It's a long ways for the young. Some makes it and others git lost.

WRITER: I know . . . (*He turns to the audience.*) I stood by the door uncertainly for a moment or two. I must have been frightened of it . . . .

MRS. WIRE: Can you see the door?

WRITER: Yes—but to open it is a desperate undertaking . . . !

(*He does, hesitantly. Transparencies close from either wing. Dim spots of light touch each character of the play in a characteristic position.*

(*As he first draws the door open, he is forced back a few steps by a cacophony of sound: the waiting storm of his future—mechanical racking cries of pain and pleasure, snatches of song. It fades out. Again there is the urgent call of the clarinet. He crosses to the open door.*)

They're disappearing behind me. Going. People you've known in places do that: they go when you go. The earth seems to swallow them up, the walls absorb them like moisture, remain with you only as ghosts; their voices are echoes, fading but remembered.

(*The clarinet calls again. He turns for a moment at the door.*)

This house is empty now.

The End

A LOVELY SUNDAY FOR CREVE COEUR

SCENE ONE

It is late on a Sunday morning, early June, in St. Louis.

The interior is what was called an efficiency apartment in the period of this play, the middle or late thirties. It is in the West End of St. Louis. Attempts to give the apartment brightness and cheer have gone brilliantly and disastrously wrong, and this wrongness is emphasized by the fiercely yellow glare of light through the oversize windows which look out upon vistas of surrounding apartment buildings, vistas that suggest the paintings of Ben Shahn: the dried-blood horror of lower middle-class American urban neighborhoods. The second thing which assails our senses is a combination of counting and panting from the bedroom, to the left, where a marginally youthful but attractive woman, Dorothea, is taking "setting-up exercises" with fearful effort.

SOUND: Ninety-one, *ha!* —ninety-two, *ha!* —ninety-three, *ha!* —ninety-four, *ha!*

This breathless counting continues till one hundred is achieved with a great gasp of deliverance. At some point during the counting, a rather short, plumpish woman, early middle-aged, has entered from the opposite doorway with a copy of the big Sunday St. Louis Post-Dispatch.

The phone rings just as Bodey, who is hard-of-hearing, sits down on a sofa in the middle of the room. Bodey, absorbed in the paper, ignores the ringing phone, but it has caused Dorothea to gasp with emotion so strong that she is physically frozen except for her voice. She catches hold of something for a moment, as if reeling in a storm, then plunges to the bedroom door and rushes out into the living room with a dramatic door-bang.

DOROTHEA: WHY DIDN'T YOU GET THAT PHONE?

BODEY (*rising and going to the kitchenette at the right*): Where, where, what, what phone?

DOROTHEA: Is there more than one phone here? Are there several other phones I haven't discovered as yet?

BODEY: —Dotty, I think these setting-up exercises get you overexcited, emotional, I mean.

905

DOROTHEA (*continuing*): That phone was ringing and I told you when I woke up that I was expecting a phone call from Ralph Ellis who told me he had something very important to tell me and would phone me today before noon.

BODEY: Sure, he had something to tell you but he didn't.

DOROTHEA: Bodey, you are not hearing, or comprehending, what I'm saying at all. Your face is a dead giveaway. I said Ralph Ellis—you've heard me speak of Ralph?

BODEY: Oh, yes, Ralph, you speak continuously of him, that name Ralph Ellis is one I got fixed in my head so I could never forget it.

DOROTHEA: Oh, you mean I'm not permitted to mention the name Ralph Ellis to you?

BODEY (*preparing fried chicken in the kitchenette*): Dotty, when two girls are sharing a small apartment, naturally each of the girls should feel perfectly free to speak of whatever concerns her. I don't think it's possible for two girls sharing a small apartment *not* to speak of whatever concerns her whenever—whatever—*concerns* her, but, Dotty, I know that I'm not your older sister. However, if I was, I would have a suspicion that you have got a crush on this Ralph Ellis, and as an older sister, I'd feel obliged to advise you to, well, look before you leap in that direction. I mean just don't put all your eggs in one basket till you are one hundred percent convinced that the basket is the right one, that's all I mean. . . . Well, this is a lovely Sunday for a picnic at Creve Coeur. . . . Didn't you notice out at Creve Coeur last Sunday how Buddy's slimmed down round the middle?

DOROTHEA: No, I didn't.

BODEY: Huh?

DOROTHEA: Notice.

BODEY: Well, it was noticeable, Dotty.

DOROTHEA: Bodey, why should I be interested in whatever fractional—fluctuations—occur in your twin brother's waistline—as if it was the Wall Street market and I was a heavy investor?

BODEY: You mean you don't care if Buddy shapes up or not?

DOROTHEA: Shapes up for what?

BODEY: Nacherly for you, Dotty.

DOROTHEA: Does he regard me as an athletic event, the high jump or pole vault? Please, please, Bodey, convince him his shape does not concern me at all.

BODEY: Buddy don't discuss his work with me often, but lately he said his boss at Anheuser-Busch has got an eye on him.

DOROTHEA: How could his boss ignore such a sizeable object? —Bodey, what are you up to in that cute little kitchenette?

BODEY: Honey, I stopped by Piggly-Wiggly's yesterday noon when I got off the streetcar on the way home from the office, and I picked up three beautiful fryers, you know, nice and plump fryers.

DOROTHEA: I'd better remain out here till Ralph calls back, so I can catch it myself. (*She lies on the purple carpet and begins another series of formalized exercises.*)

BODEY: The fryers are sizzling so loud I didn't catch that, Dotty. You know, now that the office lets out at noon Saturday, it's easier to lay in supplies for Sunday. I think that Roosevelt did something for the country when he got us half Saturdays off because it used to be that by the time I got off the streetcar from International Shoe, Piggly-Wiggly's on the corner would be closed, but now it's still wide open. So I went in Piggly-Wiggly's, I went to the meat department and I said to the nice old man, Mr. Butts, the butcher, "Mr. Butts, have you got any real nice fryers?" —"You bet your life!" he said, "I must of been expectin' you to drop in. Feel these nice plump fryers." Mr. Butts always lets me feel his meat. The feel of a piece of meat is the way to test it, but there's very few modern butchers will allow you to feel it. It's the German in me. I got to feel the meat to know it's good. A piece of meat can look good over the counter but to know for sure I always want to feel it. Mr. Butts, being German, he understands that, always says to me, "Feel it, go on, feel it." So I felt the fryers. "Don't they feel good and fresh?" I said, "Yes, Mr. Butts, but will they keep till tomorrow?" "Haven't you got any ice in your icebox?" he asked me. I said to him, "I hope so, but ice goes fast in hot weather. I told the girl that shares my apartment with me to put up the card for a twenty-five pound lump of ice but sometimes she forgets to." Well, thank goodness, this time you didn't forget to. You always got so much on your mind in the morning, civics and— other things at the high school. —What are you laughin' at, Dotty? (*She turns around to glance at Dorothea who is covering her mouth to stifle breathless sounds of laughter.*)

DOROTHEA: Honestly, Bodey, I think you missed your calling. You should be in Congress to deliver a filibuster. I never knew it was possible to talk at such length about ice and a butcher.

BODEY: Well, Dotty, you know we agreed when you moved in here with me that I would take care of the shopping. We've kept good books on expenses. Haven't we kept good books? We've never had any argument over expense or disagreements between us over what I should shop for.—OW!

DOROTHEA: Now what?

BODEY: The skillet spit at me. Some hot grease flew in my face. I'll put bakin' soda on it.

DOROTHEA: So you are really and truly frying chickens in this terrible heat?

BODEY: And boiling eggs, I'm going to make deviled eggs, too. Dotty, what is it? You sound hysterical, Dotty!

DOROTHEA (*half strangled with laughter*): Which came first, fried chicken or deviled eggs? —I swear to goodness, you do the funniest things. Honestly, Bodey, you are a source of continual astonishment and amusement to me. Now, Bodey, please suspend this culinary frenzy until the phone rings again so you can hear it this time before it stops ringing for me.

BODEY: Dotty, I was right here and that phone was not ringin'. I give you my word that phone was not makin' a sound. It was quiet as a mouse.

DOROTHEA: Why, it was ringing its head off!

BODEY: Dotty, about some things everyone is mistaken, and this is something you are mistaken about. I think your exercises give you a ringing noise in your head. I think they're too strenuous for you, 'specially on Sunday, a day of rest, recreation . . .

DOROTHEA: We are both entitled to separate opinions, Bodey, but I assure you I do not suffer from ringing in my head.

That phone was RINGING. And why you did not hear it is simply because you don't have your hearing aid on!

(*The shouting is congruent with the fiercely bright colors of the interior.*)

BODEY: I honestly ain't that deaf. I swear I ain't that deaf, Dotty. The ear specialist says I just got this little calcification, this calcium in my—eardrums. But I do hear a telephone ring, a sharp, loud sound like that, I hear it, I hear it clearly.

DOROTHEA: Well, let's hope Ralph won't imagine I'm out and will call back in a while. But do put your hearing aid in. I don't share your confidence in your hearing a phone ring or a dynamite blast without it, and anyway, Bodey, you must adjust to it, you must get used to it, and after a while, when you're accustomed to it, you won't feel complete without it.

BODEY: —Yes, well— This is the best Sunday yet for a picnic at Creve Coeur . . .

DOROTHEA: That we'll talk about later. Just put your hearing aid in before I continue with my exercises. Put it in right now so I can see you.

BODEY: You still ain't finished with those exercises?

DOROTHEA: I've done one hundred bends and I did my floor exercises. I just have these bust development exercises and my swivels and— BODEY! PUT YOUR HEARING AID IN!

BODEY: I hear you, honey, I will. I'll put it on right now.

(*She comes into the living room from the kitchenette and picks up the hearing aid and several large artificial flowers from a table. She hastily moves the newspaper from the sofa to a chair behind her, then inserts the device in an ear with an agonized look.*)

DOROTHEA: It can't be that difficult to insert it. Why, from your expression, you could be performing major surgery on yourself! . . . without anesthesia . . .

BODEY: I'm just—not used to it yet. (*She covers the defective ear with an artificial chrysanthemum.*)

DOROTHEA (*in the doorway*): You keep reminding yourself of it by covering it up with those enormous artificial flowers.

Now if you feel you have to do that, why don't you pick out a flower that's suitable to the season? Chrysanthemums are for autumn and this is June.

BODEY: Yes. June. How about this poppy?

DOROTHEA: Well, frankly, dear, that big poppy is tacky.

BODEY: —The tiger lily?

DOROTHEA (*despairing*): Yes, the tiger lily! Of course, Bodey, the truth of the matter is that your idea of concealing your hearing aid with a big artificial flower is ever so slightly fantastic.

BODEY: —Everybody is sensitive about something . . .

DOROTHEA: But complexes, obsessions must not be cultivated. Well. Back to my exercises. Be sure not to miss the phone. Ralph is going to call me any minute now. (*She starts to close the bedroom door.*)

BODEY: Dotty?

DOROTHEA: Yes?

BODEY: Dotty, I'm gonna ask Buddy to go to Creve Coeur with us again today for the picnic. That's okay with you, huh?

DOROTHEA (*pausing in the doorway*): Bodey, Buddy is your brother and I fully understand your attachment to him. He's got many fine things about him. A really solid character and all that. But, Bodey, I think it's unfair to Buddy for you to go on attempting to bring us together because— well, everyone has a type she is attracted to and in the case of Buddy, no matter how much—I appreciate his sterling qualities and all, he simply isn't— (*She has gone into the bedroom and started swiveling her hips.*)

BODEY: Isn't what, Dotty?

DOROTHEA: A type that I can respond to. You know what I mean. In a romantic fashion, honey. And to me—romance is—essential.

BODEY: Oh—but—well, there's other things to consider besides—romance . . .

DOROTHEA (*swiveling her hips as she talks*): Bodey, can you honestly feel that Buddy and I are exactly right for each other? Somehow I suspect that Buddy would do better looking about for a steady, German-type girl in South St. Louis—a girl to drink beer with and eat Wiener schnitzel and get fat along with him, not a girl—well, a girl already romantically—pour me a little more coffee? —Thanks. — Why do you keep forgetting the understanding between me and Mr. Ellis? Is that fair to Buddy? To build up his hopes for an inevitable letdown?

(*Dorothea stops her swivels and returns to the living room to get the coffee Bodey has poured for her.*)

BODEY: This Mr. T. Ralph Ellis, well . . .

DOROTHEA: Well, *what*?

BODEY: Nothing except . . .

DOROTHEA: *What*?

BODEY: He might not be as reliable as Buddy—in the long run.

DOROTHEA: What is "the long run," honey?

BODEY: The long run is—*life*.

DOROTHEA: Oh, so that is the long run, the long run is life! With Buddy? Well, then give me the short run, I'm sorry, but I'll take the short run, much less exhausting in the heat of the day and the night!

BODEY: Dotty, I tell you, Dotty, in the long run or the short run I'd place my bet on Buddy, not on a—fly-by-night sort of proposition like this, this—romantic idea you got about a man that mostly you see wrote up in—society pages . . .

DOROTHEA: *That is your misconception!* —Of something about which you are in total ignorance, because I rarely step out of the civics classroom at Blewett without seeing Ralph Ellis a few steps down the corridor, pretending to take a drink at the water cooler on my floor which is two floors up from his office!

BODEY: Not really taking a drink but just pretending? Not a good sign, Dotty—pretending . . .

DOROTHEA: What I mean is—we have to arrange secret little encounters of this sort to avoid gossip at Blewett.

BODEY: —Well—

DOROTHEA: *WHAT*?

BODEY: I never trusted pretending.

DOROTHEA: Then why the paper flowers over the hearing aid, dear?

BODEY: That's—just—a little—sensitivity, there . . .

DOROTHEA: Look, you've got to live with it so take off the concealment, the paper tiger lily, and turn the hearing aid up or I will be obliged to finish my hip swivels out here to catch Ralph's telephone call.

BODEY (*as she is turning up the hearing aid, it makes a shrill sound*): See? See?

DOROTHEA: I think you mean hear, hear! —Turn it down just a bit, find the right level for it!

BODEY: Yes, yes, I— (*She fumbles with the hearing aid, dislodging the paper flower.*)

DOROTHEA: For heaven's sake, let me adjust it for you! (*She rushes over to Bodey and fiddles with the hearing aid.*) Now! —Not shrieking. —But can you hear me? I said can you hear me! At this level!?

BODEY: Yes. Where's my tiger lily?

DOROTHEA: Dropped on the fierce purple carpet. Here. (*She picks it up and hands it to Bodey.*) What's wrong with you?

BODEY: I'm—upset. Over this maybe—dangerous—trust you've got in Ralph Ellis's—intentions . . .

DOROTHEA (*dreamily, eyes going soft*): I don't like discussing an intimate thing like this but—the last time I went out in Ralph Ellis's Reo, that new sedan he's got called the Flying Cloud . . .

BODEY: Cloud? Flying?

DOROTHEA (*raising her voice to a shout*): The Reo is advertised as "The Flying Cloud."

BODEY: Oh. Yes. He'd be attracted to that.

DOROTHEA: It was pouring down rain and Art Hill was deserted, no other cars on it but Ralph and I in his Reo. The windows curtained with rain that glistened in the lamplight.

BODEY: Dotty, I hope you're not leading up to something that shouldn't of happened in this Flying Cloud on Art Hill. It really scares me, Dotty . . .

DOROTHEA: Frankly, I was a little frightened myself because—we've never had this kind of discussion before, it's rather—difficult for me but you must understand. I've always drawn a strict line with a man till this occasion.

BODEY: Dotty, do you mean—?

DOROTHEA: It was so magical to me, the windows curtained with rain, the soft look in his eyes, the warmth of his breath that's always scented with clove, his fingers touching so gently as he—

BODEY: Dotty, I don't think I want to know any more about this—experience on Art Hill because, because—I got a suspicion, Dotty, that you didn't hold the line with him.

DOROTHEA: The line just—didn't exist when he parked the car and turned and looked at me and I turned and looked at him. Our eyes, our eyes—

BODEY: Your eyes?

DOROTHEA: Burned the line out of existence, like it had never existed!

BODEY: —I'm not gonna tell this to Buddy!

DOROTHEA: You know, I wasn't aware until then that the Reo was equipped with adjustable seats.

BODEY: Seats that—?

DOROTHEA: Adjusted to pressure, yes, reclined beneath me when he pushed a lever.

BODEY (*distracted from the phonebook which she had begun to leaf through*): —How far did this seat recline beneath you, Dotty?

DOROTHEA: Horizontally, nearly. So gradually though that I didn't know till later, later. Later, not then—the earth was whirling beneath me and the sky was spinning above.

BODEY: Oh-ho, he got you drunk, did he, with a flask of liquor in that Flying Cloud on—

DOROTHEA: Drunk on a single Pink Lady?

BODEY: Pink?

DOROTHEA: Lady. —The mildest sort of cocktail! Made with sloe gin and grenadine.

BODEY: The gin was slow, maybe, but that man is a fast one, seducing a girl with adjustable seats and a flask of liquor in that Flying Cloud on—

DOROTHEA: Not a flask, a cocktail, and not in the Reo but in a small private club called The Onyx, a club so exclusive he had to present an engraved card at the entrance.

BODEY: Oh yes, I know such places!

DOROTHEA: How would you know such places?

BODEY: I seen one at the movies and so did you, at the West End Lyric, the last time you was all broke up from expectin' a call from this Ellis which never came in, so we seen Roy D'Arcy take poor Janet Gaynor to one of them—private clubs to—!

(*Bodey has not found the Blewett number in the phonebook. She dials the operator.*)

Blewett, Blewett, get me the high school named Blewett.

DOROTHEA: Bodey, what are you doing at the phone which I begged you not to use till Ralph has called?

BODEY: Reporting him to Blewett!

DOROTHEA: Bodey, that takes the cake, reporting on the principal of Blewett to Blewett that's closed on Sundays. What a remarkable—

BODEY (*darting about*): Paper, pen!

DOROTHEA: Now what?

BODEY: A written report to the Board of Education of St. Louis. I tell you, that Board will be interested in all details of how that principal of the school system got you lying down drunk and defenseless in his Flying Cloud in a storm on Art Hill, every advantage taken with Valentino sheik tricks on a innocent teacher of civics just up from Memphis.

DOROTHEA: YOU WILL NOT—

BODEY: DON'T TELL ME NOT!

DOROTHEA: LIBEL THE REPUTATION OF A MAN THAT I LOVE, GAVE MYSELF TO NOT JUST FREELY BUT WITH ABANDON, WITH JOY!

BODEY (*aloud as she writes*): Board of Education of St. Louis, Missouri. I think you should know that your principal at Blewett used his position to take disgusting advantage of a young teacher employed there by him for that purpose. I know, I got the facts, including the date and—

(*Dorothea snatches up and crumples the letter.*)

My letter, you tore up my—!

DOROTHEA: Bodey, if you had written and mailed that letter, do you know what you'd have obliged me to do? I would be morally obliged to go personally down to the Board of Education and tell them an *opposite* story which happens to be the *true* one: that I *desired* Ralph Ellis, possibly even more than he did me!

(*Bodey huffs and puffs wordlessly till she can speak.*)

BODEY: —Well, God help you, Dotty. —But I give you my word I won't repeat this to Buddy.

DOROTHEA: How does it concern Buddy?

BODEY: It concerns Buddy and me because Buddy's got deep feelings and respect for you, Dotty. He would respect you too much to cross the proper line before you had stood up together in the First Lutheran Church on South Grand.

DOROTHEA: *Now* you *admit* it!

BODEY: It's you that's makin' admissions of a terrible kind that might shock Buddy out of his serious intentions.

DOROTHEA: You are admitting that—

(*As she had threatened, Dorothea has begun doing her hip swivels in the living room, but now she stops and stares indignantly at Bodey.*)

—you've been deliberately planning and plotting to marry me off to your twin brother so that my life would be just one long Creve Coeur picnic, interspersed with knockwurst, sauerkraut—hot potato salad dinners. —Would I be asked to prepare them? Even in summer? I know what you Germans regard as the limits, the boundaries of a woman's life—*Kirche, Küche, und Kinder*—while being asphyxiated gradually by cheap cigars. I'm sorry but the life I design for myself is not along those lines or in those limits. My life must include romance. Without romance in my life, I could no more live than I could without breath. I've got to find a partner in life, or my life will have no meaning. But what I must have and finally do have is an affair of the heart, two hearts, a true consummated romance—yes consummated, I'm not ashamed! (*She gasps and sways.*)

BODEY: Dotty, Dotty, set down and catch your breath!

DOROTHEA: In this breathless efficiency apartment? —I've got to have space in my life.

BODEY: —Did I tell you that Buddy has made a down payment on a Buick?

DOROTHEA: No, you didn't and why should you, as it does not concern— Oh, my God, Blessed Savior!

BODEY: Dotty, what Dotty? D'you want your, your whatamacallit tablets?

DOROTHEA: Mebaral? No, I have not collapsed yet, but you've just about driven me to it.

BODEY: Take a breather, take a seventh inning stretch while I—

DOROTHEA: Bodey, this room is GLARING; it's not cheerful but GLARING!

BODEY: Stretch out on the sofa and look up, the ceiling is white!

DOROTHEA: I don't know why I'm so out of breath today.

BODEY: Don't do no more exercises. You drink too much coffee an' Cokes. That's stimulants for a girl high-strung like you. With a nervous heart condition.

DOROTHEA: It's functional—not nervous.

BODEY: Lie down a minute.

DOROTHEA: I will rest a little—but not because you say so. (*Between gasps she sinks into a chair.*) You're very bossy—and very inquisitive, too.

BODEY: I'm older'n you, and I got your interests at heart.

DOROTHEA: Whew!

BODEY: Think how cool it will be on the open-air streetcar to Creve Coeur.

DOROTHEA: You must have had your hearing aid off when I said I had other plans.

BODEY: Buddy, I been telling Buddy to cut down on his beer, and Buddy is listening to me. He's cut down to eight a day —from a dozen and will cut down more . . .

DOROTHEA: Bodey, could you stop talking about Buddy this hot Sunday morning? It's not a suitable subject for hot weather. I know brother-sister relationships are deep, but it's not just the beer, it's the almost total lack of interests in common, no topics of conversations, of—of mutual—interest.

BODEY: They could develop. I know Buddy just feels embarrassed. He hasn't opened up yet. Give him time and he will.

DOROTHEA: Bodey, this discussion is embarrassingly pointless in view of the fact that I'm already committed to Ralph Ellis. I still have to do my hip swivels . . .

(*Sipping coffee as she goes, Dorothea returns to the bedroom and resumes her exercises.*)

BODEY (*rushing to the phone*): Olive 2697, Olive 2697! Buddy? Me! *Grosser Gott!* I can't talk now, but you absolutely got to go to Creve Coeur with us this Sunday. —Dress good! Don't smoke cigars! And laugh at her witty remarks. — Well, they *are*, they're witty! She teaches *civics.*

(*The doorbell rings*).

Now be at the Creve Coeur station at 1:30, huh? —Please!— Somebody's at the door, I can't talk now. (*Leaving the phone off the hook, she rushes to the door and opens it.*) Oh. Hello.

HELENA: Good morning.

BODEY: Are you a friend of Dotty's?

(*A stylishly dressed woman with the eyes of a predatory bird appears.*)

HELENA: Of Dorothea's? —Yes.

BODEY: Well, then come on in. Any friend of Dotty's is a friend of mine.

HELENA: Is that so?

BODEY (*discomfited*): Yes, I—got grease on my hand. I was fryin' up some chickens for a picnic.

HELENA: —Well! This is a surprise! (*She makes several turns in a mechanical, rigid fashion, eyes staring.*)

BODEY: Excuse me, I should of—interduced myself.

HELENA: You are Miss Bodenheifer.

BODEY: Hafer, not heifer. (*She laughs nervously.*) Heifer meaning a cow.

HELENA: No conscious association whatsoever. (*She advances forward a step.*) So this is Schlogger Haven?

BODEY: Oh, Schlogger Haven, that's just a joke of Dotty's. The landlord's name is Schlogger, that's all—that's all . . .

HELENA: Dorothea was joking, was she?

BODEY: Yeh, she jokes a lot, full of humor. We have lots of laughs. (*Bodey extends her hand.*)

HELENA: I can imagine you might, Miss Bodenheifer.

BODEY: You can forget the Miss. —Everyone at the office calls me Bodey.

HELENA: But we are not at the office—we are here in Schlogger Haven. (*She continues enigmatically.*) Hmmm . . . I've never ventured this side of Blewett before.

BODY: Never gone downtown?

HELENA: I do nearly all my shopping in the West End, so naturally it amazed me to discover street after street without a shade tree on it, and the glare, the glare, and the heat refracted by all the brick, concrete, asphalt—was so overpowering that I nearly collapsed. I think I must be afflicted with a combination of photo- and heliophobia, both.

BODY (*unconsciously retreating a step as if fearing contagion*): I never heard of neither—but you got *both*?

HELENA: An exceptional sensitivity to both heat and strong light.

BODY: Aw.

HELENA: Yes. Now would you please let Dorothea know I'm here to see her?

BODY: Does Dotty expect you, Miss, uh—

HELENA: Helena Brookmire, no, she doesn't expect me, but a very urgent business matter has obliged me to drop by this early.

BODY: She won't have no one in there with her. She's exercising.

HELENA: But Dorothea and I are well acquainted.

BODY: Well acquainted or not acquainted at all, makes no difference. I think that modern girls emphasize too much these advertised treatments and keep their weight down too much for their health.

HELENA: The preservation of youth requires some sacrifices.

(*She continues to stare about her, blinking her birdlike eyes as if dazzled.*)

BODY: —I guess you and Dotty teach together at Blewett High?

HELENA: —Separately.

BODY: You mean you're not at Blewett where Dotty teaches civics?

HELENA (*as if addressing a backward child*): I teach there, too. When I said separately, I meant we teach separate classes.

BODY: Oh, naturally, yes. (*She tries to laugh.*) I been to high school.

HELENA: Have you?

BODEY: Yes. I know that two teachers don't teach in the same class at the same time, on two different subjects.

HELENA (*opening her eyes very wide*): Wouldn't *that* be peculiar.

BODEY: Yes. That would be peculiar.

HELENA (*chuckling unpleasantly*): It might create some confusion among the students.

BODEY: Yes, I reckon it would.

HELENA: Especially if the subjects were as different as civics and the history of *art*.

(*Bodey attempts to laugh again; Helena imitates the laugh almost exactly.*)

(*Pause*)

This *is*, it really *is*!

BODEY: Is *what*?

HELENA: The most remarkable room that I've ever stepped into! Especially the combination of colors! Such a *vivid* contrast! May I sit down?

BODEY: Yeh, yeh, excuse me, I'm not myself today. It's the heat and the—

HELENA: Colors? —The vivid contrast of colors? (*She removes a pair of round, white-rimmed dark glasses from her purse and puts them on.*) Did Dorothea assist you, Miss Bodenheifer, in decorating this room?

BODEY: No, when Dotty moved in, it was just like it is now.

HELENA: Then you are solely responsible for this inspired selection of colors?

(*There is a loud sputter of hot fat from the kitchenette.*)

BODEY: Excuse me a moment, I got to turn over the fryers in the skillet.

HELENA: Don't let me interrupt your preparations for a picnic.

BODEY: Didn't catch that. I don't hear good sometimes.

HELENA: Oh?

BODEY: You see, I got this calcium deposit in my ears . . . and they advised me to have an operation, but it's very expensive for me and sometimes it don't work.

PHONE VOICE: Booow-deeee!

(*Helena notices but doesn't comment on the unhooked phone.*)

HELENA: I would advise you against it. I had an elderly acquaintance who had this calcification problem and she had a hole bored in her skull to correct it. The operation is called fenestration—it involves a good deal of danger and whether or not it was successful could not be determined since she never recovered consciousness.

BODEY: Never recovered?

HELENA: Consciousness.

BODEY: Yeh, well, I think maybe I'd better learn to live with it.

PHONE VOICE (*shouting again*): Bodeyyyyy—Bodeyyyy—

BODEY: What's that?

HELENA: I was wondering, too. Very strange barking sounds are coming out of the phone.

BODEY (*laughing*): Oh, God, I left it unhooked. (*She snatches it up.*) Buddy, sorry, somebody just dropped in, forgot you was still on the line. Buddy, call me back in a few minutes, huh, Buddy, it's, uh, very important. (*She hangs up the phone.*) That was my brother. Buddy. He says he drunk two beers and made him a liverwurst sandwich before I got back to the phone. Thank God he is so good-natured. . . . He and me are going out on a picnic at Creve Coeur with Dotty this afternoon. My brother is very interested in Dotty.

HELENA: Interested? Romantically?

BODEY: Oh, yes, Buddy's a very serious person.

HELENA (*rising*): —I am very impressed!

BODEY: By what, what by?

HELENA (*with disguised fury*): The ingenuity with which you've fitted yourself into this limited space. Every inch seems to be utilized by some appliance or—*decoration*? (*She picks up a large painted china frog.*) —A frahg?

BODEY: Yes, frawg.

HELENA: So realistically colored and designed you'd almost expect it to croak. —Oh, and you have a canary . . . stuffed!

BODEY: Little Hilda . . . she lived ten years. That's the limit for a canary.

HELENA: Limit of longevity for the species?

BODEY: She broke it by three months.

HELENA: Establishing a record. It's quite heroic, enduring more than ten years in such confinement. What tenacity to existence some creatures do have!

BODEY: I got so attached to it, I took it to a, a—

HELENA: Taxidermist.

BODEY: Excuse me a moment. (*She rushes to the stove in the alcove.*) OW! —Got burnt again.

HELENA (*following curiously*): You were burnt before?

(*Bodey profusely powders her arms with baking soda. Helena backs away.*)

Miss Bodenheifer, *please!* You've sprinkled my clothes with that powder!

BODEY: Sorry, I didn't mean to.

HELENA: Intentional or not, I'm afraid you have! May I have a clothes brush?

BODEY: Look at that, I spilt it on the carpet. (*She rushes to fetch a broom.*)

HELENA: Miss Bodenheifer, I WOULD LIKE A CLOTHES BRUSH, IF YOU HAVE A *CLOTHES* BRUSH! Not a broom. I am not a carpet.

BODEY: AW. SURE. Dotty's got a clothes brush. Oh. Help yourself to some coffee. (*She drops the broom and enters the bedroom.*)

(*Through the open door, Dorothea can be heard counting as she swivels.*)

DOROTHEA'S VOICE: Sixty, *ha!* Sixty-one, *ha!* (*She continues counting but stops when she notices Bodey.*) —The PHONE? Is it the PHONE?

BODEY: Clothes brush. (*Bodey closes the bedroom door and begins opening and shutting drawers as she looks for the clothes brush.*)

DOROTHEA: DON'T, DON'T, DON'T—slam a drawer shut like that! I feel like screaming!

(*Helena opens a closet in the kitchenette; a box falls out.*)

HELENA: The hazards of this place almost equal the horrors.

DOROTHEA (*in the bedroom*): I asked you if the phone rang.

BODEY: No, no, the doorbell.

HELENA (*who has moved to the icebox*): Ah. Ice, mostly melted, what squalor!

(*This dual scene must be carefully timed.*)

DOROTHEA: I presume it's Miss Gluck from upstairs in boudoir cap and wrapper. Bodey, get her out as quickly as possible. The sight of that woman destroys me for the whole day.

HELENA (*still in the kitchenette*): This remnant of ice will not survive in this steaming glass of coffee.

(*A knock at the door is heard.*)

What's that?

(*Sophie Gluck opens the front door and sticks her head in. At the sight of Helena, she withdraws in alarm.*)

Another tenant. *Demented!*

(*Helena moves to the door and slams and bolts it with such force that Sophie, outside, utters a soft cry of confused panic.*)

BODEY: Don't do no more calisthenics if it affecks you this way.

DOROTHEA: Just, just—knock at the door when Miss Gluck has gone back upstairs, that's my—whew!—only—request . . .

BODEY: —Yes, well . . .

DOROTHEA: No coffee, no crullers or she—will stay—down here—forever—ha!

(*The phone rings; Helena picks it up. Bodey emerges from the bedroom with a whisk broom, closing the door behind her. Helena is at the phone.*)

HELENA: Oh, she seems engaged for the moment . . .

BODEY: Aw, the phone! Is it that principal, Ellis?

HELENA (*aside from the phone*): I'm afraid not. It seems to be Dorothea's other admirer—*quel embarras de richesses* . . .

BODEY (*rushing to the phone*): Must be Buddy. —Buddy? Well? —Yeh, good, what suit you got on? Well, take it off.

It don't look good on you, Buddy. Put on the striped suit, Buddy an' the polka dot tie, and, Buddy, if you smoke a cigar at Creve Coeur, excuse yourself and smoke it in the bushes.

HELENA: This is—

BODY: That's right, 'bye.

HELENA: —absolutely bizarre! You found a clothes brush? That's not a clothes brush. It's a whisk broom. Sorry. It doesn't look clean.

BODY: Sorry. My nerves.

HELENA (*taking it and brushing herself delicately here and there*): What was that counting I heard? Is Dorothea counting something in there?

BODY: She's counting her swivels in there.

HELENA: Swivels of what?

BODY: Hip swivels, that's what. She's counting. Every morning she does one hundred bends and one hundred set-ups and one hundred hip swivels.

HELENA: Regardless of weather?

BODY: That's right, regardless of weather.

HELENA: And regardless of— Hmmm . . .

(*Body senses a touch of malice implicit in this unfinished sentence.*)

BODY: —What else, huh?

HELENA: Dorothea has always impressed me as an emotionally fragile type of person who might collapse, just suddenly collapse, when confronted with the disappointing facts of a situation about which she'd allowed herself to have— romantic illusions.

(*It is now Body's turn to say, "Hmmm . . ."*)

—No matter how—well, I hate to say foolish but even intelligent girls can make mistakes of this nature . . . of course we all felt she was attaching too much importance to—

BODY: "We all" is who?

HELENA: Our little group at Blewett.

BODY: Yeh, there's always a gossipy little group, even down at International Shoe where I work there is a gossipy little group that feels superior to the rest of us. Well, personally,

I don't want in with this gossipy little group because the gossip is malicious. Oh, they call it being concerned, but it's not the right kind of concern, naw, I'd hate for that gossipy little group to feel concerned about me, don't want that and don't need it.

HELENA: Understandably, yaiss. I will return this whisk broom to Dorothea.

BODEY: No, no, just return it to me.

HELENA: I have to speak to her and in order to do that I'll have to enter that room. So if you'll excuse me I'll—

(She starts toward the bedroom. Bodey snatches the whisk broom from her with a force that makes Helena gasp.)

BODEY: Miss Brooksit, you're a visitor here but the visit was not expected. Now you excuse me but I got to say you sort of act like this apartment was yours.

HELENA: —What a dismaying idea! I mean I—

BODEY: And excuse me or don't excuse me but I got a very strong feeling that you got something in mind. All right, your mind is your mind, what's in it is yours but keep it to yourself, huh?

HELENA (*cutting in*): Miss Bodenheifer, you seem to be implying something that's a mystery to me.

BODEY: You know what I mean and I know what I mean so where's the mystery, huh?

DOROTHEA (*calling from the bedroom*): Is somebody out there, Bodey?

BODEY: Just Sophie Gluck.

DOROTHEA: Oh, Lord!

HELENA: What was that you called me?

BODEY: I told Dotty that you was Miss Gluck from upstairs.

HELENA: —Gluck?

BODEY: Yeah, Miss Gluck is a lady upstairs that comes downstairs to visit.

HELENA: She comes down to see Dorothea?

BODEY: No, no, more to see me, and to drink coffee. She lost her mother, an' she's got a depression so bad she can't make coffee, so I save her a cup, keep her a cup in the pot. You know for a single girl to lose a mother is a terrible thing. What else can you do? She oughta be down. Week-days she comes down at seven. Well, this is Sunday.

HELENA: Yes. This is Sunday.

BODEY: Sundays she comes down for coffee and a cruller at ten.

HELENA: Cruller? What is a cruller?

BODEY: Aw. You call it a doughnut, but me, bein' German, was raised to call it a cruller.

HELENA: Oh. A cruller is a doughnut but you call it a cruller. Now if you'll excuse me a moment, I will go in there and relieve Dorothea of the mistaken impression that I am Miss Gluck from upstairs who has come down for her coffee and —cruller.

BODEY: Oh, no, don't interrupt her calisthenics.

(*Helena ignores this admonition and opens the bedroom door.*)

DOROTHEA: Why, Helena Brookmire! —What a surprise. I— I—look a—*mess!*

HELENA: I heard this counting and gasping. Inquired what was going on. Your friend Miss—what?

DOROTHEA: You've met Miss Bodenhafer?

HELENA: Yes, she received me very cordially. We've dispensed with introductions. She says any friend of yours is a friend of hers and wants me to call her Bodey as they do at the of-fice. Excuse me, Miss Bodenheifer, I must have a bit of pri-vate conversation—

(*Helena closes the bedroom door, shutting out Bodey.*)

DOROTHEA: Well, I wasn't expecting a visitor today, obviously not this early. You see, I—never receive a visitor here. . . . Is there something too urgent to hold off till Monday, Helena?

HELENA: Have our negotiations with the realty firm of Orthwein and Muller slipped your flighty mind?

DOROTHEA: Oh, the real estate people, but surely on Sunday—

HELENA: Mr. Orthwein called Cousin Dee-Dee last night and she called me this morning that now the news has leaked out and there's competitive bidding for the apartment on Westmoreland Place and the deal must be settled at once.

DOROTHEA: You mean by—?

HELENA: Immediate payment, yes, to pin it down.

DOROTHEA: *Today? Sunday?*

HELENA: The sanctity of a Sunday must sometimes be profaned by business transactions.

(*Bodey has now entered.*)

DOROTHEA: Helena, if you'll just have some coffee and wait in the living room, I will come out as soon as I've showered and dressed.

BODEY: Yeh, yeh, do that. You're embarrassing Dotty, so come back out and—

(*Bodey almost drags Helena out of the bedroom, kicking the bedroom door shut.*)

HELENA: Gracious!

BODEY: Yes, gracious, here! Set down, I'll get you some coffee.

HELENA (*with a sharp laugh*): She said, "I look a mess," and I couldn't contradict her.

BODEY: Here! Your coffee! Your cruller!

HELENA (*haughtily*): I don't care for the cruller, as you call it. Pastries are not included in my diet. However—I'd like a clean napkin. You've splashed coffee everywhere.

BODEY: Sure, we got plenty of napkins. You name it, we got it. (*She thrusts a paper napkin at Helena like a challenge.*)

HELENA: This paper napkin is stained. Would you please give me—

BODEY: Take 'em all. You stained that napkin yourself. (*She thrusts the entire pile of napkins at Helena.*)

HELENA: You shoved the cup at me so roughly the coffee splashed.

(*Helena fastidiously wipes the tabletop. There is a rap at the door.*)

BODEY: Aw, that's Sophie Gluck.

HELENA: I don't care to meet Miss Gluck.

BODEY: Will you set down so I can let in Sophie Gluck?

HELENA: So if you're going to admit her, I will take refuge again in Dorothea's bedroom. . . . There is another matter I've come here to . . .

BODEY (*seizing Helena's arm as she crosses toward the bedroom*): I know what you're up to! —JUST A MINUTE, *BITTE*, SOPHIE! I can guess the other matter you just can't hold your tongue about, but you're gonna hold it. It's not gonna be mentioned to cloud over the day and spoil the Creve Coeur picnic for Dotty, Buddy, an' me! — COMIN', SOPHIE! (*Then, to Helena, fiercely.*) YOU SET BACK DOWN!

(*During this altercation, Dorothea has been standing in the bedroom paralyzed with embarrassment and dismay. Now she calls sweetly through the door, opened a crack.*)

DOROTHEA: Bodey, Bodey, what *is* going on out there? How could a phone be heard above that shouting? Oh, My Blessed Savior, I was bawn on a Sunday, and I am convinced that I shall die on a Sunday! Could you please tell me what is the cause of the nerve-shattering altercations going on out there?

HELENA: Dorothea, Miss Bodenheifer's about to receive Miss Gluck.

DOROTHEA: Oh, no, oh no, Bodey, entertain her upstairs! I'm not in shape for another visit today, especially not—Bodey!

BODEY: Sophie, Sophie, you had me worried about you.

HELENA: I'm afraid, Dorothea, your request has fallen upon a calcified eardrum.

BODEY: You come downstairs so late.

MISS GLUCK: *Sie hat die Tür in mein Kopf zugeschlagen!*

BODEY (*to Helena*): You done that to Sophie!

HELENA: An unknown creature of demented appearance entering like a sneak thief!

BODEY: My best friend in the building!

HELENA: What a pitiful admission!

BODEY: You come here uninvited, not by Dotty or me, since I never heard of you, but got the nerve to call my best friend in the building . . .

MISS GLUCK: *Diese Frau ist ein Spion.*

BODEY: What did you call her?

HELENA: I called that woman demented. What I would call you is intolerably offensive.

MISS GLUCK: *Verstehen Sie?* Spy. *Vom Irrenhaus.*

BODEY: We live here, you don't. See the difference?

HELENA: Thank God for the difference. *Vive la différence.*

DOROTHEA (*coming just inside the living room*): Helena, Bodey.

HELENA: Be calm Dorothea—don't get overexcited.

MISS GLUCK: *Zwei Jahre.* Two years.

DOROTHEA: Why is she coming at me like this?

MISS GLUCK: State asylum.

BODEY: You come here to scrounge money outta Dotty which she ain't got.

MISS GLUCK: *Sie ist hier—mich noch einmal—im Irrenhaus zu bringen.* To take back to hospital.

HELENA: Aside from the total inaccuracy of your assumption and the insulting manner in which you express it—. As you very well know, Dorothea and I are both employed at Blewett. We are both on salary there! And I have not come here to involve myself in your social group but to rescue my colleague from it.

BODEY: Awright, you put it your way, it adds up to the same thing. You want money from Dotty which she ain't got to give you. Dotty is broke, flat broke, and she's been on a big buying spree, so big that just last night I had to loan her the price of a medium bottle of Golden Glow Shampoo, and not only that, I had to go purchase it for her because she come home exhausted. Dotty was too exhausted to walk to the drugstore. Well, me, I was tired, too, after my work at International Shoe and shopping, but out I hoofed it to Liggett's and forked out the forty-nine cents for the medium size Golden Glow from my own pockets, money I set aside for incidentals at the Creve Coeur picnic. There's always—

HELENA (*cutting in*): Miss Bodenheifer, you certainly have a gift for the felicitous phrase such as "out you hoofed it to Liggett's," sorry, sorry, but it does evoke an image.

BODEY: I know what you mean by "hoof it" since you keep repeating "heifer" for "hafer." I'm not too dumb like which you regard me to know why you're struck so funny by "hoof it."

HELENA: You said you "hoofed it," not me.

BODEY: You keep saying "heifer" for "hafer." Me, I'm a sensitive person with feelings I feel, but sensitive to you I am not. Insults from you bounce off me. I just want you to know that you come here shaking your tin cup at the wrong door.

(*As a soft but vibrant counterpoint to this exchange, Sophie, sobbing and rolling her eyes like a* religieuse *in a state of sorrowful vision, continues her slow shuffle toward Dorothea as she repeats in German an account of her violent ejection by Helena.*)

DOROTHEA (*breathlessly*): Bodey, what is she saying? Translate and explain to her I have no knowledge of German.

HELENA: Babbling, just lunatic babbling!

BODEY: One minute, one minute, Dotty. I got to explain to this woman she's wasting her time here and yours—and had the moxie to slam Sophie out of the door.

HELENA: Miss Bodenheifer, it's useless to attempt to intimidate me. . . . I would like the use of your phone for a moment. Then—

DOROTHEA: No calls on the phone!

BODEY: Dotty don't want this phone used; she's expecting a call to come in, but there is a pay phone at Liggett's three blocks east on West Pine and Pearl.

HELENA: Drugstores are shut on Sundays!

DOROTHEA: Quiet! Listen! All! This thing's getting out of hand!

HELENA: I want only to call a taxi for myself and for Dorothea. She's trapped here and should be removed at once. You may not know that just two weeks after she came to Blewett she collapsed on the staircase, and the staff doctor examined her and discovered that Dorothea's afflicted with neuro-circulatory asthenia.

(*Dorothea has disappeared behind the sofa. Miss Gluck is looking down at her with lamentations.*)

MISS GLUCK: BODEY.

BODEY: Moment, Sophie.

MISS GLUCK: Dotty, Dotty . . .

HELENA: What is she saying? Where's Dorothea?

BODEY: Dotty?

MISS GLUCK: *Hier, auf dem Fussboden. Ist fallen.*

HELENA: This Gluck creature has thrown Dorothea onto the floor.

BODEY: *Gott im—! Wo ist—*Dotty?

HELENA: The Gluck has flung her to the floor behind the sofa!

BODEY: Dotty!

HELENA: Dorothea, I'm calling us a cab. Is she conscious?

DOROTHEA: Mebaral—tablet—quick!

BODEY: Mebarals, where?

(*Sophie wails loudly.*)

DOROTHEA: My pocketbook!

BODEY: Hold on now, slowly, slowly—

DOROTHEA: Mebaral! Tablets!

HELENA: My physician told me those tablets are only prescribed for persons with—extreme nervous tension and asthenia.

BODEY: Will you goddam shut up? —Dotty, you just need to—

HELENA: What she needs is to stop these strenuous exercises and avoid all future confrontations with that lunatic from upstairs!

BODEY: Dotty, let me lift you.

DOROTHEA: Oh, oh, noooo, I—can't, I—I am *paralyzed, Bodey!*

BODEY: HEY, YOU BROOKS-IT, TAKE DOTTY'S OTHER ARM. HELP ME CARRY HER TO HER BED WILL YUH?

(*Sophie is moaning through clenched fists.*)

HELENA: All right, all right, but then I shall call my physician!

(*Dorothea is carried into the bedroom and deposited on the bed. Sophie props pillows behind her.*)

DOROTHEA: Meb—my meb . . .

BODEY: Tablets. Bathroom. In your pocketbook.

(*Bodey rushes into the bathroom, then out with a small bottle. Dorothea raises a hand weakly and Bodey drops tablets in it.*)

Dotty, don't swallow, that's three tablets!

DOROTHEA: My sherry to wash it down with—

BODEY: Dotty, take out the *two extra tablets*, Dotty!

HELENA: Sherry? Did she say sherry? Where is it?

DOROTHEA: There, there.

BODEY: Dotty, open your mouth, I got to take out those extras!

HELENA: No glass, you must drink from the bottle.

BODEY: NO! NOOOO!

HELENA: STOP CLUTCHING AT ME!

(*Miss Gluck utters a terrified wail. Dorothea drinks from the bottle and falls back onto the pillows with a gasp.*)

BODEY (*so angry she speaks half in German*): You *Schwein*, you bitch! *Alte böse Katze.* (*She then goes on in English.*) You washed three tablets down Dotty!

DOROTHEA: Now will you BOTH get out so I can breathe!

HELENA: The door's obstructed by Gluck.

BODEY: Sophie, go out, Sophie, go out of here with me for coffee and crullers!

(*Sobbing, Sophie retreats. Bodey grabs a strong hold of Helena's wrist.*)

HELENA: Let go of my wrist. Oh, my God, you have broken. . . . I heard a bone snap in my—!

BODEY: WALK! OUT! MOVE IT! . . .

HELENA (*turning quickly about and retreating behind the sofa*): Miss Bodenheifer, you are a one-woman demonstration of the aptness of the term "Huns" for Germans. . . . And, incidentally, what you broke was not my wrist but my Cartier wristwatch, a birthday present from my Cousin Dee-Dee; you shattered the crystal, and you've broken the minute hand and bent the two others. I am afraid the repair bill will cost you considerably more than keeping Dorothea in Golden Glow Shampoo.

BODEY: It's all right, Sophie, set down right here and I'll. . . . Coffee's still hot for you. Have a coupla crullers. Blow your nose on this napkin and—

(*Helena laughs tonelessly.*)

What's funny, is something funny? You never been depressed, no sorrows in your life ever, yeh, and you call yourself a human.

HELENA: Really, this is fantastic as the—color scheme of this room or the—view through the windows.

(*In the bedroom, Dorothea has staggered from the bed and stumbled to the floor.*)

DOROTHEA: Bodey.

HELENA: Dorothea.

BODEY (*calling through*): Dotty.

HELENA: You really must let me check on her condition.

DOROTHEA (*in the bedroom*): Don't forget . . . phone call.

BODEY: No, Dotty.

DOROTHEA (*faintly, clinging to something*): Tell Miss Brook-mire I've retired for the day.

HELENA: *What?*

BODEY: She's not coming out. She's not coming out till you leave here—

(*Bodey bolts the bedroom door.*)

HELENA: I beg to differ. She *will* and I'll sit here till she does!

(*Miss Gluck has taken a bite of a cruller, dunked in coffee, and begins to blubber, the coffee-soaked cruller dribbling down her chin.*)

BODEY: Look, you upset Sophie!

MISS GLUCK: *Eine—Woche vor—Sonntag—meine Mutter—*

BODEY (*comfortingly*): *Ich weiss*, Sophie, *ich weiss.*

MISS GLUCK: *Gestorben!*

BODEY: But she went *sudden*, huh, Sophie? (*She crouches beside Miss Gluck, removing the dribblings of cruller and coffee from her mouth and chin.*)

HELENA: I don't understand the language, and the scene appears to be private.

BODEY: Yeh, keep out of it. (*She turns to Miss Gluck.*) —Your mother, she didn't hang on like the doctor thought she would, Sophie. Now, face it, it was better sudden, no big hospital bill, just went and is waiting for you in Heaven.

HELENA: With open arms, I presume, and with coffee and crullers.

BODEY: So, Sophie, just be grateful that she went quick with no pain.

MISS GLUCK (*grotesquely tragic*): *Nein, nein, sie hat geschrien!* I woke up runnin'!

BODEY: To her bed, you reached it and she was dead. Just one scream, it was over—wasn't that a mercy?

(*Helena laughs.*)

Sophie, honey, this woman here's not sympathetic. She laughs at sorrow, so maybe you better take the coffee, the cruller—here's another—upstairs, Sophie, and when we get back from the Creve Coeur picnic, I will bring you beautiful flowers, *schöne Blume.* Then I'll come up and sing to you in German—I will sing you to sleep.

(*Miss Gluck slowly rises with coffee and crullers. Bodey conducts her gently to the door.*)

MISS GLUCK (*crying out*): *Ich bin allein, allein! In der Welt, freundlos!*

BODEY: No, no, Sophie, that is negative thinking.

MISS GLUCK: *Ich habe niemand in der Welt!*

BODEY: Sophie, God is with you, I'm with you. Your mother, all your relations are waiting for you in Heaven!

(*Shepherding Miss Gluck into the hall, Bodey repeats this assurance in German.*)

HELENA: Sometimes despair is just being realistic, the only logical thing for certain persons to *feel.* (*She addresses herself with a certain seriousness, now.*) Loss. Despair. I've faced them and actually they have—fortified and protected, not overcome me at all . . .

BODEY (*in the hall with Miss Gluck*): Okay? *Verstehst du,* Sophie?

HELENA (*still ruminating privately*): The weak. The strong. Only important division between living creatures. (*She nods birdlike affirmation.*)

(*Miss Gluck remains visible in the hall, afraid to return upstairs.*)

MISS GLUCK: *Allein, allein.*

(*There is a change in the light. Helena moves a small chair downstage and delivers the following to herself.*)

HELENA: *Allein, allein* means alone, alone. (*A frightened look appears in her eyes.*) Last week I dined alone, alone three nights in a row. There's nothing lonelier than a woman dining alone, and although I loathe preparing food for myself, I cannot bear the humiliation of occupying a restaurant table for one. Dining *au solitaire*! But I would rather starve than reduce my social standards by accepting dinner invitations from that middle-aged gaggle of preposterously vulgar old maids that wants to suck me into their group despite my total abhorrence of all they stand for. Loneliness in the company of five intellectually destitute spinsters is simply loneliness multiplied by five . . .

(*There is a crash in the hallway.*)

DOROTHEA (*from the bedroom*): Is it the phone?

HELENA: Another visit so soon? Miss Bodenheifer, your bereaved friend from upstairs is favoring you with another visit.

MISS GLUCK (*wildly*): *Mein Zimmer is gespukt, gespukt!*

HELENA: "Spooked, spooked"?

BODEY: Sophie, your apartment isn't haunted.

HELENA: Perhaps if you went up with her, it would despook the apartment.

BODEY: Aw, no, I got to stay down and keep a sharp eye on *you.*

HELENA: Which means that she will remain here?

BODEY: Long as she pleases to. What's it to you? She got nothin' contagious. You can't catch heartbreak if you have got no heart.

HELENA: May I suggest that you put her in the back yard in the sun. I think that woman's complexion could stand a touch of color.

BODEY: I am puttin' her nowhere she don't want to be. How about you settin' in the back yard? Some natural color would do your face good for a change.

(*Sensing the hostile "vibes," Miss Gluck moans, swaying a little.*)

HELENA: Miss Bodenheifer, I will not dignify your insults with response or attention!

(*Miss Gluck moans louder.*)

Aren't you able to see that this Miss Gluck is mental? Distressing to hear and to look at! . . . Be that as it may, I shall wait.

BODEY: Sitting? Tight as a tombstone? Huh?

HELENA: I can assure you that for me to remain in this place is at least as unpleasant to me as to you. (*She cries out to Dorothea who is still in the bedroom.*) Dorothea? Dorothea? Can you hear me?

DOROTHEA (*clinging to something in the bedroom*): See you—Blewett—t'morrow . . .

HELENA: No, no, at once, Dorothea, the situation out here is dreadful beyond endurance.

(*Abruptly, Miss Gluck cries out, clutching her abdomen.*)

BODEY: Sophie, what is it, Sophie?

MISS GLUCK: *Heisser Kaffee gibt mir immer Krampf und Durchfall.*

(*This episode in the play must be handled carefully to avoid excessive scatology but keep the humor.*)

BODEY: You got the runs? *Zum Badezimmer?* Sophie's got to go to the bathroom, Dotty.

DOROTHEA: Hasn't she got one upstairs?

BODEY: After hot coffee, it gives her diarrhea!

DOROTHEA: Must she have it down here?

MISS GLUCK (*in German*): *KANN NICHT WARTEN!*

BODEY: She can't wait, here, bathroom, Sophie! *Badezimmer!*

(*Miss Gluck rushes through the bedroom into the bathroom.*)

DOROTHEA: What a scene for Helena to report at Blewett. Miss Gluck, turn on both water faucets full force.

BODEY: Sophie, *beide Wasser rennen.*

DOROTHEA: Bodey, while I am here don't serve her hot coffee again since it results in these—crises!

BODEY: Dotty, you know that Sophie's got this problem.

DOROTHEA: Then send her coffee upstairs.

BODEY: Dotty, you know she needs companionship, Dotty.

DOROTHEA: That I cannot provide her with just now!

(*Bodey returns to the living room.*)

HELENA: How did Dorothea react to Miss Gluck's sudden indisposition?

BODEY: Dotty's a girl that understands human afflictions.

(*There is a crash in the bathroom.*)

DOROTHEA: Phone, Ralph's call—has he—did he?

BODEY: Phone, Dotty? No, no phone.

HELENA: I wouldn't expect—

BODEY (*to Helena*): Watch it!

HELENA: Watch what, Miss Bodenheifer? What is it you want me to watch?

BODEY: That mouth of yours, the tongue in it, with such a tongue in a mouth you could dig your grave with like a shovel!

HELENA (*her laughter tinkling like ice in a glass*): —The syntax of that sentence was rather confusing. You know, I suspect that English is not your native language but one that you've not quite adequately adopted.

BODEY: I was born on South Grand, a block from Tower Grove Park in this city of St. Louis!

HELENA: Ah, the German section. Your parents were German speaking?

BODEY: I learned plenty English at school, had eight grades of school and a year of business college.

HELENA: I see, I see, forgive me. (*She turns to a window, possibly in the "fourth wall."*) Is a visitor permitted to look out the window?

BODEY: A visitor like you's permitted to jump out it.

HELENA (*laughing indulgently*): With so many restrictions placed on one's speech and actions—

(*Bodey turns up her hearing aid so high that it screeches shrilly.*)

DOROTHEA: Is it the phone?

HELENA: Please. Is it controllable, that electric hearing device?

BODEY: What did you say?

(*The screeching continues.*)

HELENA: Ow . . . ow . . .

(*Bodey finally manages to turn down the hearing aid.*)

DOROTHEA: Oh please bring a mop, Bodey. Water's streaming under—the bathroom door. Miss Gluck's flooded the bathroom.

BODEY: What? Bring?

HELENA: *Mop, mop!*

(*Helena moves toward the bedroom door but Bodey shoves her back.*)

BODEY: Stay! Put! Stay put!

(*Bodey grabs a mop from the closet and then rushes into the bedroom.*)

DOROTHEA: See? Water? Flooding?

BODEY: You told her to turn on both faucets. SOPHIE! *Halte das Wasser ab*, Sophie! (*Bodey opens the bathroom door and thrusts in the mop.*) Here, *das Wust, das Wust*, Sophie!

DOROTHEA (*to herself*): This is incredible to me, I simply do not believe it! (*She then speaks to Bodey who has started back toward the living room.*) May I detain you a moment? The truth has finally struck me. Ralph's calls have been intercepted. He has been repeatedly calling me on that phone, and you have been just as repeatedly lying to me that he hasn't.

BODEY: LYING TO—?

DOROTHEA: YES, LYING! (*She stumbles to the door of the bedroom.*) Helena, will *you* please watch that phone for me now?

HELENA (*crossing to the bedroom door*): I'm afraid, Dorothea, that a watched phone never rings!

(*Bodey emerges from the bedroom. She and Helena return to the living room while Dorothea retreats to the bed, shutting the door behind her.*)

What a view through this window, totally devoid of—why, no, a living creature, a pigeon! Capable of flight but perched for a moment in this absolute desolation . . .

Interval

SCENE TWO

The scene is the same as before. The spotlight focuses on the left-hand, "bedroom" portion of the stage where Dorothea, seated at her vanity table and mellowed by her mebaral and sherry "cocktail," soliloquizes.

DOROTHEA (*taking a large swallow of sherry*): Best years of my youth thrown away, wasted on poor Hathaway James. (*She removes his picture from the vanity table and with closed eyes thrusts it out of sight.*) Shouldn't say wasted but so unwisely devoted. Not even sure it was love. Unconsummated love, is it really love? More likely just a reverence for his talent—precocious achievements . . . musical prodigy. Scholarship to Juilliard, performed a concerto with the Nashville Symphony at fifteen. (*She sips more sherry.*) But those dreadful embarrassing evenings on Aunt Belle's front porch in Memphis! He'd say: "Turn out the light, it's attracting insects." I'd switch it out. He'd grab me so tight it would take my breath away, and invariably I'd feel plunging, plunging against me that—that—frantic part of him . . . then he'd release me at once and collapse on the porch swing, breathing hoarsely. With the corner gas lamp shining through the wisteria vines, it was impossible not to notice the wet stain spreading on his light flannel trousers. . . . Miss Gluck, MOP IN!!

(*Miss Gluck, who has timidly opened the bathroom door and begun to emerge, with the mop, into the bedroom, hastily retreats from sight.*)

Such afflictions—visited on the gifted. . . . Finally worked up the courage to discuss the—Hathaway's—problem with the family doctor, delicately but clearly as I could. "Honey, this Hathaway fellow's afflicted with something clinically known as—chronic case of—premature ejaculation—must have a large laundry bill. . . ." "Is it curable, Doctor?" — "Maybe with great patience, honey, but remember you're only young once, don't gamble on it, relinquish him to his interest in music, let him go."

(*Miss Gluck's mop protrudes from the bathroom again.*)

MISS GLUCK, I SAID MOP IN. REMAIN IN BATH-
ROOM WITH WET MOP TILL MOP UP COM-
PLETED. MERCIFUL HEAVENS.

(*Helena and Bodey are now seen in the living room.*)

HELENA: Is Dorothea attempting a conversation with Miss
Gluck in there?

BODEY: No, no just to herself—you gave her the sherry on
top of mebaral tablets.

HELENA: She talks to herself? That isn't a practice that I
would encourage her in.

BODEY: She don't need no encouragement in it, and as for
you, I got an idea you'd encourage nobody in nothing.

DOROTHEA (*in the bedroom*): After Hathaway James, there
was nothing left for me but—CIVICS.

HELENA (*who has moved to the bedroom door the better to hear
Dorothea's "confessions"*): This is not to B. B.!

BODEY: Stop listening at the door. Go back to your pigeon
watching.

HELENA: How long is this apt to continue?

DOROTHEA: Oh, God, thank you that Ralph Ellis has no such
affliction—is healthily aggressive.

HELENA: I have a luncheon engagement in La Due at two!

BODEY: Well, go keep it! On time!

HELENA: My business with Dorothea must take precedence
over anything else! (*Helena pauses to watch with amused suspicion as Bodey "attacks" the Sunday* Post-Dispatch *which she
has picked up from the chair.*) What is that you're doing,
Miss Bodenheifer?

BODEY: Tearing a certain item out of the paper.

HELENA: A ludicrous thing to do since the news will be all
over Blewett High School tomorrow.

BODEY: Never mind tomorrow. There's ways and ways to
break a piece of news like that to a girl with a heart like
Dotty. You wouldn't know about that, no, you'd do it right
now—malicious! —You got eyes like a bird and I don't
mean a songbird.

HELENA: Oh, is that *so?*

BODY: Yeh, yeh, that's so, I know!

(*Pause. Bodey, who has torn out about half of the top page of one section, puts the rest of the paper on the sofa, and takes the section from which the piece has been torn with her as she crosses to the kitchenette, crumpling and throwing the torn piece into the wastebasket on her way.*)

HELENA: Miss Bodenheifer.

BODY (*from the kitchenette*): Hafer!

HELENA: I have no wish to offend you, but surely you're able to see that for Dorothea to stay in these circumstances must be extremely embarrassing to her at least.

BODY: Aw, you think Dotty's embarrassed here, do you?

(*Bodey has begun to line a shoebox with the section of newspaper she took with her. During the following exchange with Helena, Bodey packs the fried chicken and other picnic fare in the shoebox.*)

HELENA: She has hinted it's almost intolerable to her. The visitations of this Gluck person who has rushed to the bathroom, this nightmare of clashing colors, the purple carpet, orange drapes at the windows looking out at that view of brick and concrete and asphalt, lamp shades with violent yellow daisies on them, and wallpaper with roses exploding like bombshells, why it would give her a breakdown! It's giving me claustrophobia briefly as I have been here. Why, this is not a place for a civilized person to possibly exist in!

BODY: What's so civilized about you, Miss Brooks-it? Stylish, yes, civilized, no, unless a hawk or a buzzard is a civilized creature. Now you see, you got a tongue in your mouth, but I got one in mine, too.

HELENA: You are being hysterical and offensive!

BODY: You ain't heard nothing compared to what you'll hear if you continue to try to offer all this concern you feel about Dotty to Dotty in this apartment.

HELENA: Dorothea Gallaway and I keep nothing from each other and naturally I intend, as soon as she has recovered, to prepare her for what she can hardly avoid facing sooner or later and I—

BODEY (*cutting in*): I don't want heartbreak for Dotty. For Dotty I want a—life.

HELENA: A life of—?

BODEY: A life, a *life*—

HELENA: You mean as opposed to a death?

BODEY: Don't get smart with me. I got your number the moment you come in that door like a well-dressed snake.

HELENA: So far you have compared me to a snake and a bird. Please decide which—since the archaeopteryx, the only known combination of bird and snake, is long extinct!

BODEY: Yes, well, you talk with a kind of a hiss. Awright, you just hiss away but not in this room which you think ain't a civilized room. Okay, it's too cheerful for you but for me and Dotty it's fine. And this afternoon, at the picnic at Creve Coeur Lake, I will tell Dotty, gentle, in my own way, if it's necessary to tell her, that this unprincipled man has just been using her. But Buddy, my brother Buddy, if in some ways he don't suit her like he is now, I will see he quits beer, I will see he cuts out his cigars, I will see he continues to take off five pounds a week. And by Dotty and Buddy there will be children—children! —I will never have none, myself, no! But Dotty and Buddy will have beautiful kiddies. Me? Nieces—nephews. . . . —Now you! I've wrapped up the picnic. It's nice and cool at Creve Coeur Lake and the ride on the open-air streetcar is lickety-split through green country and there's flowers you can pull off the bushes you pass. It's a fine excursion. Dotty will forget not gettin' that phone call. We'll stay out till it's close to dark and the fireflies—fly. I will slip away and Buddy will be alone with her on the lake shore. He will smoke no smelly cigar. He will just respectfully hold her hand and say—"I love you, Dotty. Please be mine," not meanin' a girl in a car parked up on Art Hill but—for the long run of life.

HELENA: —Can Dorothea be really attached to your brother? Is it a mutual attraction?

BODEY: Dotty will settle for Buddy. She's got a few reservations about him so far, but at Creve Coeur she'll suddenly recognize the—wonderful side of his nature.

HELENA: Miss Bodenheifer, Dorothea is not intending to remain in this tasteless apartment. Hasn't she informed you that she is planning to share a lovely apartment with me? The upstairs of a duplex on Westmoreland Place?

BODEY: Stylish? Civilized, huh? And too expensive for you to swing it alone, so you want to rope Dotty in, rope her into a place that far from Blewett? Share expenses? You prob'ly mean pay most.

HELENA: To move from such an unsuitable environment must naturally involve some expense.

(*Miss Gluck falls out of the bathroom onto Dorothea's bed.*)

DOROTHEA: MISS GLUCK! CAREFUL! Bodey, Bodey, Sophie Gluck's collapsed on my bed in a cloud of steam!

HELENA: Has Miss Gluck broken a steam pipe?

(*Bodey rushes from the kitchenette into the bedroom.*)

BODEY (*to Helena*): You stay out.

(*Dorothea emerges from the bedroom. She closes the door and leans against it briefly, closing her eyes as if dizzy or faint.*)

HELENA: At last.

DOROTHEA: I'm so mortified.

HELENA: Are you feeling better?

DOROTHEA: Sundays are always different—

HELENA: This one exceptionally so.

DOROTHEA: I don't know why but—I don't quite understand why I am so—agitated. Something happened last week, just a few evenings ago that—

HELENA: Yes? What?

DOROTHEA: Nothing that I'm—something I can't discuss with you. I was and still am expecting a very important phone call—

HELENA: May I ask you from whom?

DOROTHEA: No, please.

HELENA: Then may I hazard a guess that the expected call not received was from a young gentleman who cuts a quite spectacular figure in the country club set but somehow became involved in the educational system?

DOROTHEA: If you don't mind, Helena, I'd much prefer not to discuss anything of a—private nature right now.

HELENA: Yes, I understand, dear. And since you've located that chair, why don't you seat yourself in it?

DOROTHEA: Oh, yes, excuse me. (*She sits down, weakly, her hand lifted to her throat.*) The happenings here today are still a bit confused in my head. I was doing my exercises before you dropped by.

HELENA: And for quite a while after.

DOROTHEA: I was about to—no, I'd taken my shower. I was about to get dressed.

HELENA: But the Gluck intervened. Such discipline! Well! I've had the privilege of an extended meeting with Miss Bodenheifer— (*She lowers her voice.*) She seemed completely surprised when I mentioned that you were moving to Westmoreland Place.

DOROTHEA: Oh, you told her. —I'm glad. —I'm such a coward, I couldn't.

HELENA: Well, I broke the news to her.

DOROTHEA: I—just hadn't the heart to.

(*Miss Gluck advances from the bedroom with a dripping wet mop and a dazed look.*)

HELENA (*to Dorothea*): Can't you see she's already found a replacement?

DOROTHEA: Oh, no, there's a limit even to Bodey's endurance! Miss Gluck, would you please return that wet mop to the kitchen and wring it out. *Küche*—mop—Sophie.

HELENA: Appears to be catatonic.

DOROTHEA (*as she goes into the bedroom to get Bodey*): Excuse me.

(*Bodey enters from the bedroom and takes Miss Gluck, with mop, into the kitchenette.*)

BODEY (*singing nervously in the kitchenette*): "I'm just breezing along with the breeze, pleasing to live, and living to please!"

(*Dorothea returns to the living room.*)

DOROTHEA: How did Bodey take the news I was moving?

HELENA: "That far from *Blewett!*" she said as if it were transcontinental.

DOROTHEA: Well, it is a bit far, compared to this location.

HELENA: Surely you wouldn't compare it to *this* location.

DOROTHEA: Oh, no, Westmoreland Place is a—fashionable address, incomparable in that respect, but it is quite a distance. Of course, just a block from Delmar Boulevard and the Olive Street car-line, that would let me off at—what point closest to Blewett?

HELENA: Dorothea, forget transportation, that problem. We're going by automobile.

DOROTHEA: By—what automobile do you—?

HELENA: I have a lovely surprise for you, dear.

DOROTHEA: Someone is going to drive us?

HELENA: Yes, I will be the chauffeur and you the passenger, dear. You see, my wealthy cousin Dee-Dee, who lives in La Due, has replaced her foreign-made car, an Hispano-Suiza, no less, practically brand-new, with a Pierce Arrow limousine and has offered to sell us the Hispano for just a song! Immediately, as soon as she made me this offer, I applied for a driver's license.

(*A moment of shocked silence is interrupted by a short squawk from Bodey's hearing aid.*)

BODEY (*advancing quickly from the kitchenette*): Limazine? What limazine? With a show-fer?

HELENA: Miss Bodenheifer, how does this concern you?

BODEY: Who's gonna foot the bill for it, that's how!

HELENA: My cousin Dee-Dee in La Due will accept payment on time.

BODEY: Whose time and how much?

HELENA: *Negligible! A rich cousin!* —Oh, my Lord, I've always heard that Germans—

BODEY: Lay off Germans!

HELENA: Have this excessive concern with money matters.

BODEY: *Whose* money?

HELENA: Practicality can be a stupefying—

MISS GLUCK: Bodey?

HELENA: —virtue, if it *is* one.

MISS GLUCK: *Ich kann nicht*—go up.

HELENA: Go up just one step to the kitchen! Please, Dorothea, can't we—have a private discussion, briefly?

MISS GLUCK: *Das Schlafzimmer is gespukt!*

HELENA: Because you see, Dorothea, as I told you, I do have to make a payment on the Westmoreland Place apartment early tomorrow, and so must collect your half of it today.

DOROTHEA: —My half would amount to—?

HELENA: Seventy.

DOROTHEA: Ohhh! —Would the real estate people accept a—postdated check?

HELENA: Reluctantly—very.

DOROTHEA: You see, I had unusually heavy expenses this week—clothes, lingerie, a suitcase . . .

HELENA: Sounds as if you'd been purchasing a trousseau. — Miss Bodenhafer says that her brother, "Buddy," is seriously interested in you. How selfish of you to keep it such a secret!—even from me!

DOROTHEA: Oh, my heavens, has Miss Bodenhafer—how fantastic!

HELENA: Yes, she is a bit, to put it politely.

DOROTHEA: I meant has she given you the preposterous impression that I am interested in her brother? Oh, my Lord, what a fantastic visit you've had! Believe me, the circumstances aren't always so—chaotic. Well! *Il n'y a rien à faire.* When I tell you that she calls her brother Buddy and that he is her *twin!* (*She throws up her arms.*)

HELENA: Identical?

DOROTHEA: Except for gender, alike as two peas in a pod. You're not so gullible, Helena, that you could really imagine for a moment that I'd—you know me better than that!

HELENA: Sometimes when a girl is on the rebound from a disappointing infatuation, she will leap without looking into the most improbable sort of—liaison—

DOROTHEA: Maybe some girls, but certainly not I. And what makes you think that I'm the victim of a "disappointing infatuation," Helena?

HELENA: Sometimes a thing will seem like the end of the world, and yet the world continues.

DOROTHEA: I personally feel that my world is just beginning. . . . Excuse me for a moment. I'll get my checkbook. . . .

(*Dorothea goes into the bedroom. Miss Gluck wanders back into the living room from the kitchenette, wringing her hands and sobbing.*)

HELENA: MISS BODENHEIFER!

BODEY: Don't bother to tell me good-bye.

HELENA: I am not yet leaving.

BODEY: And it ain't necessary to shake the walls when you call me, I got my hearing aid on.

HELENA: Would you be so kind as to confine Miss Gluck to that charming little kitchen while I'm completing my business with Dorothea?

(*Bodey crosses toward Miss Gluck.*)

BODEY: Sophie, come in here with me. You like a deviled egg don't you? And a nice fried drumstick when your—digestion is better? Just stay in here with me.

(*Bodey leads Miss Gluck back to the kitchenette, then turns to Helena.*)

I can catch every word that you say to Dotty in there, and you better be careful the conversation don't take the wrong turn!

MISS GLUCK (*half in German*): *Ich kann nicht* liven opstairs no more, *nimmer, nimmer—kann nicht*—can't go!

BODEY: You know what, Sophie? You better change apartments. There's a brand-new vacancy. See—right over there, the fifth floor. It's bright and cheerful—I used to go up there sometimes—it's a sublet, furnished, everything in cheerful colors. I'll speak to Mr. Schlogger, no, no, to *Mrs.* Schlogger, she makes better terms. Him, bein' paralyzed, he's got to accept 'em, y'know.

MISS GLUCK: I think— (*She sobs.*) —Missus Schlogger don't like me.

BODEY: That's—*impossible*, Sophie. I think she just had a little misunderstanding with your— (*She stops herself.*)

MISS GLUCK: *Meine Mutter, ja—*

BODEY: Sophie, speak of the Schloggers, she's wheeling that old *Halunke* out on their fire escape.

(*The Schloggers are heard from offstage.*)

MR. SCHLOGGER'S VOICE: I didn't say *out* in the sun.

MRS. SCHLOGGER'S VOICE: You said out, so you're out.

BODEY (*shouting out the window*): Oh, my *Gott*, Missus Schlogger, a stranger that didn't know you would think you meant to push him offa the landin'. Haul him back in, you better. Watch his cane, he's about to hit you with it. Amazin' the strength he's still got in his good arm.

MRS. SCHLOGGER'S VOICE: Now you want back in?

(*Helena rises to watch this episode on the fire escape.*)

MR. SCHLOGGER'S VOICE: Not in the kitchen with you.

HELENA (*to herself but rather loudly*). Schloggers, so those are Schloggers.

BODEY (*to Miss Gluck*): She's got him back in. I'm gonna speak to her right now. —HEY MISSUS SCHLOGGER, YOU KNOW MISS GLUCK? AW, SURE YOU REMEM-BER SOPHIE UPSTAIRS IN 4-F? SHE LOST HER MOTHER LAST SUNDAY. Sophie, come here, stick your head out, Sophie. NOW YOU REMEMBER HER, DON'T YOU?

MRS. SCHLOGGER'S VOICE: *Ja, ja.*

BODEY: *JA, JA*, SURE YOU REMEMBER! MRS. SCHLOGGER, POOR SOPHIE CAN'T LIVE ALONE IN 4-F WHERE SHE LOST HER MOTHER. SHE NEEDS A NEW APARTMENT THAT'S BRIGHT AND CHEERFUL TO GET HER OUT OF DEPRESSION. HOW ABOUT THE VACANCY ON THE FIFTH FLOOR FOR SOPHIE. WE GOT TO LOOK OUT FOR EACH OTHER IN TIMES OF SORROW. *VER-STEHEN SIE?*

MRS. SCHLOGGER'S VOICE: I don't know.

BODEY: GIVE SOPHIE THAT VACANCY UP THERE. THEN TERMS I'LL DISCUSS WITH YOU. (*She draws Miss Gluck back from the window.*) Sophie, I think that done it, and that apartment on five is bright and cheerful like here. And you're not gonna be lonely. We got three chairs at this table, and we can work out an arrangement so you can eat here with us, more economical that way. It's no good cooking for one, cookin' and eatin' alone is—lonely after—

(*Helena resumes her seat as Bodey and Miss Gluck return to the kitchenette.*)

HELENA (*with obscure meaning*): Yes— (*She draws a long breath and calls out.*) Dorothea, can't you locate your checkbook in there?

(*Dorothea returns from the bedroom wearing a girlish summer print dress and looking quite pretty.*)

DOROTHEA: I was just slipping into a dress. Now, then, here it is, my checkbook.

HELENA: Good. Where did you buy that new dress?

DOROTHEA: Why, at Scruggs-Vandervoort.

HELENA: Let me remove the price tag. (*As she removes the tag, she looks at it and assumes an amused and slightly superior air.*) Oh, my dear. I must teach you where to find the best values in clothes. In La Due there is a little French boutique, not expensive but excellent taste. I think a woman looks best when she dresses without the illusion she's still a girl in her teens. Don't you?

DOROTHEA (*stung*): —My half will be—how much did you say?

HELENA: To be exact, $82.50.

DOROTHEA: My goodness, that will take a good bite out of my savings. Helena, I thought you mentioned a lower amount. Didn't you say it would be seventy?

HELENA: Yes, I'd forgotten—utilities, dear. Now, we don't want to move into a place with the phone turned off, the lights off. Utilities must be *on*, wouldn't you say?

DOROTHEA: —Yes. —Of course, I don't think I'll be dependent on my savings much longer, and a duplex on Westmoreland Place— (*She writes out a check.*) —is a—quite a—worthwhile—investment . . .

HELENA: I should think it would strike you as one after confinement with Miss Bodenhafer in this nightmare of colors.

DOROTHEA: Oh. —Yes. —Excuse me . . . (*She extends the check slightly.*)

HELENA: —Are you holding it out for the ink to dry on it?

DOROTHEA: —Sorry. —Here. (*She crosses to Helena and hands the check to her.*)

(*Helena puts on her glasses to examine the check carefully. She then folds it, puts it into her purse, and snaps the purse shut.*)

HELENA: Well, that's that. I hate financial dealings but they do have to be dealt with. Don't they?

DOROTHEA: Yes, they seem to . . .

HELENA: Require it. —Oh, contract.

DOROTHEA: Contract? For the apartment?

HELENA: Oh, no, a book on contract bridge, the bidding system and so forth. You do play bridge a little? I asked you once before and you said you did sometimes.

DOROTHEA: Here?

HELENA: Naturally not here. But on Westmoreland Place I hope you'll join in the twice-weekly games. You remember Joan Goode?

DOROTHEA: Yes, vaguely. Why?

HELENA: We were partners in duplicate bridge, which we usually played, worked out our own set of bidding conventions. But now Joan's gone to Wellesley for her Master's degree in, of all things, the pre-Ptolemaic dynasties of Egypt.

DOROTHEA: Did she do that? I didn't know what she did.

HELENA: You were only very casually—

DOROTHEA: Acquainted.

HELENA: My cousin Dee-Dee from La Due takes part whenever her social calendar permits her to. She often sends over dainty little sandwiches, watercress, tomato, sherbets from Zeller's in the summer. And a nicely uniformed maid to serve. Well, now we're converting from auction to contract, which is more complicated but stimulates the mind. — Dorothea, you have an abstracted look. Are you troubled over something?

DOROTHEA: Are these parties mixed?

HELENA: "Mixed" in what manner?

DOROTHEA: I mean would I invite Ralph?

HELENA: I have a feeling that Mr. T. Ralph Ellis might not be able to spare the time this summer. And anyway, professional women do need social occasions without the—male intrusion . . .

DOROTHEA (*with spirit*): I've never thought of the presence of men as being an intrusion.

HELENA: Dorothea, that's just a lingering symptom of your Southern belle complex.

DOROTHEA: In order to be completely honest with you, Helena, I think I ought to tell you—I probably won't be able to share expenses with you in Westmoreland Place for very long, Helena!

HELENA: Oh, is that so? Is that why you've given me the postdated check which you could cancel tomorrow?

DOROTHEA: You know I wouldn't do that, but—

HELENA: Yes, but—you could and possibly you would. . . . Look before you, there stands the specter that confronts you . . .

DOROTHEA: Miss??

HELENA: Gluck, the perennial, the irremediable, Miss Gluck! You probably think me superficial to value as much as I do, cousin Dee-Dee of La Due, contract bridge, possession of an elegant foreign car. Dorothea, only such things can protect us from a future of descent into the Gluck abyss of surrender to the bottom level of squalor. Look at it and tell me honestly that you can afford not to provide yourself with the Westmoreland Place apartment . . . its elevation, its style, its kind of *éclat*.

(*Miss Gluck, who has come out of the kitchenette and moved downstage during Helena's speech, throws a glass of water in Helena's face.*)

DOROTHEA: Bodey, RESTRAIN HER, RESTRAIN MISS GLUCK, SHE'S TURNED VIOLENT.

BODEY: Sophie, no, no. I didn't say you done wrong. I think you done right. I don't think you did enough.

HELENA: Violence does exist in the vegetable kingdom, you see! It doesn't terrify me since I shall soon be safely out of its range. . . . Just let me draw two good deep breaths and I'll be myself again. (*She does so.*) That did it. . . . I'm back in my skin. Oh, Dorothea, we must, must advance in appearances. You don't seem to know how vastly important it is, the move to Westmoreland Place, particularly now at this time when you must escape from reminders

of, specters of, that alternative there! Surrender without
conditions . . .

DOROTHEA: Sorry. I am a little abstracted. Helena, you sound
as if you haven't even suspected that Ralph and I have been
dating . . .

HELENA: Seriously?

DOROTHEA: Well, now that I've mentioned it to you, yes,
quite. You see, I don't intend to devote the rest of my life
to teaching civics at Blewett. I dream, I've always dreamed,
of a marriage someday, and I think you should know that it
might become a reality this summer.

HELENA: With whom?

DOROTHEA: Why, naturally with the person whom I love. And
obviously loves me.

HELENA: T? RALPH? ELLIS?

(*Bodey, still in the kitchenette, nervously sings "Me and My
Shadow."*)

DOROTHEA: I thought I'd made that clear, thought I'd made
everything clear.

HELENA: Oh, Dorothea, my dear. I hope and pray that you
haven't allowed him to take advantage of your—generous
nature.

DOROTHEA: Miss Bodenhafer has the same apprehension.

HELENA: That is the one and only respect in which your
friend, Miss Bodenhafer, and I have something in common.

DOROTHEA: Poor Miss Bodenhafer is terribly naïve for a girl
approaching forty.

HELENA: Miss Bodenhafer is not approaching forty. She has
encountered forty and continued past it, undaunted.

DOROTHEA: I don't believe she's the sort of girl who would
conceal her age.

HELENA (*laughing like a cawing crow*): Dorothea, no girl
could tell me she's under forty and still be singing a song
of that vintage. Why, she knows every word of it, including—what do they call it? The introductory verse? Why is
she cracking hard-boiled eggs in there?

DOROTHEA: She's making deviled eggs for a picnic lunch.

HELENA: Oh. In Forest Park.

DOROTHEA: No, at Creve Coeur.

HELENA: Oh, at Creve Coeur, that amusement park on a lake, of which Miss Bodenheifer gave such a lyrical account. Would you like a Lucky?

DOROTHEA: No. Thank you. My father smoked Chesterfields. Do you know Creve Coeur?

HELENA: Heard of it. Only. You go out, just the two of you?

DOROTHEA: No, her brother, Buddy, usually goes with us on these excursions. They say they've been going out there since they were children, Bodey and Buddy. They still ride the Ferris wheel, you know, and there's a sort of loop-the-loop that takes you down to the lake shore. Seats much too narrow sometimes. You see, it's become embarrassing to me lately, the brother you know . . .

HELENA: Who doesn't interest you?

DOROTHEA: Heavens, no, it's—pathetic. I don't want to hurt Bodey's feelings, but the infatuation is hardly a mutual thing and it never could be, of course, since I am—well, involved with—

HELENA: The dashing, the irresistible new principal at Blewett.

(*Bodey sings.*)

DOROTHEA: —I'd rather not talk about that—prematurely, you know. Ralph feels it's not quite proper for a principal to be involved with a teacher. He's—a very, very scrupulous young man.

HELENA: Oh? Is that the impression he gives you? I'm rather surprised he's given you that impression.

DOROTHEA: I don't see why. Is it just because he's young and attractive with breeding, background? Frequently mentioned in the social columns? Therefore beyond involvement with a person of my ignominious position.

HELENA: Personally, I'd avoid him like a—snakebite!

(*Bodey, in the kitchenette, sings "I'm Just Breezing along with the Breeze" again.*)

Another one of her oldies! The prospect of this picnic at Creve Coeur seems to make her absolutely euphoric.

DOROTHEA: I'm afraid that they're the high points in her life. Sad . . . Helena, I'm very puzzled by your attitude toward

Ralph Ellis. Why on earth would a girl want to avoid a charming young man like Ralph?

HELENA: Perhaps you'll understand a little later.

(*Dorothea glances at her watch and the silent phone.*)

DOROTHEA (*raising her voice*): Bodey, please not quite so loud in there! Miss Brookmire and I are holding a conversation in here, you know. (*She turns back to Helena and continues the conversation with an abrupt vehemence.*) —Helena, that woman wants to absorb my life like a blotter, and I'm not an ink splash! I'm sorry you had to meet her. I'm awfully— embarrassed, believe me.

HELENA: I don't regret it at all. I found her most amusing. Even the Gluck!

DOROTHEA (*resuming with the same intensity*): Bodey wants me to follow the same, same old routine that she follows day in and day out and I—feel sympathy for the loneliness of the girl, but we have nothing, nothing, but *nothing* at all, in common. (*She interrupts herself.*) Shall we have some coffee?

HELENA: Yes, please. I do love iced coffee, but perhaps the ice is depleted.

BODEY (*from the kitchenette*): She knows darn well she used the last piece.

HELENA: Is it still warm?

(*Dorothea has risen and gone into the kitchenette where she pours two cups of coffee.*)

DOROTHEA: It never cools off in this electric percolator, runs out, but never cools off. Do you take cream?

HELENA: No, thank you.

DOROTHEA (*bringing the coffee into the living room*): Bodey does make very good coffee. I think she was born and raised in a kitchen and will probably die in a kitchen if ever she does break her routine that way.

(*Bodey crosses to the kitchen table with Dorothea's purse and hat which she has collected from the living room while Helena and Dorothea sip their coffee.*)

BODEY: Dotty, remember, Buddy is waiting for us at the Creve Coeur station, we mustn't let him think we've stood him up.

DOROTHEA (*sighing*): Excuse me, Helena, there really has been a terrible problem with communication today. (*She crosses to Bodey and adjusts her hearing aid for her.*) Can you hear me clearly, now at last?

BODEY: You got something to tell me?

DOROTHEA: Something I've told you already, frequently, loudly, and clearly, but which you simply will not admit because of your hostility toward Ralph Ellis. I'm waiting here to receive an important call from him, and I am not going anywhere till it's come through.

BODEY: Dotty. It's past noon and he still hasn't called.

DOROTHEA: On Saturday evenings he's out late at social affairs and consequently sleeps late on Sundays.

BODEY: This late?

HELENA: Miss Bodenhafer doesn't know how the privileged classes live.

BODEY: No, I guess not, we're ignorant of the history of art, but Buddy and me, we've got a life going on, you understand, we got a life . . .

DOROTHEA: Bodey, you know I'm sorry to disappoint your plans for the Creve Coeur picnic, but you must realize by now—after our conversation before Miss Brookmire dropped in—that I can't allow this well-meant design of yours to get me involved with your brother to go any further. So that even if I were *not* expecting this important phone call, I would not go to Creve Coeur with you and your brother this afternoon—or ever! It wouldn't be fair to your brother to, to—lead him on that way . . .

BODEY: Well, I did fry up three chickens and I boiled a dozen eggs, but, well, that's—

HELENA: Life for you, Miss Bodenhafer. We've got to face it.

BODEY: But I really was hoping—expecting—

(*Tears appear in Bodey's large, childlike eyes.*)

HELENA: Dorothea, I believe she's beginning to weep over this. Say something comforting to her.

DOROTHEA: Bodey? Bodey? This afternoon you must break the news to your brother that—much as I appreciate his attentions—I am seriously involved with someone else, and I think you can do this without hurting his feelings. Let him have some beer first and a—cigar. . . . And about this super-abundance of chicken and deviled eggs, Bodey, why don't you call some girl who works in your office and get her to go to Creve Coeur and enjoy the picnic with you this afternoon?

BODEY: Buddy and I, we—don't have fun with—strangers . . .

DOROTHEA: Now, how can you call them strangers when you've been working in the same office with these girls at International Shoe for—how many years? Almost twenty? Strangers? Still?

BODEY: —Not all of 'em have been there long as me . . . (*She blows her nose.*)

DOROTHEA: Oh, some of them must have, surely, unless the death rate in the office is higher than—a cat's back.

(*Dorothea smiles half-apologetically at Helena. Helena stifles a malicious chuckle.*)

BODEY: —You see, Dotty, Buddy and me feel so at home with you now.

DOROTHEA: Bodey, we knew that I was here just for a while because it's so close to Blewett. Please don't make me feel *guilty*. I have no reason to, do I?

BODEY: —No, no, Dotty—but don't worry about it. Buddy and me, we are both—big eaters, and if there's somethin' left over, there's always cute little children around Creve Coeur that we could share with, Dotty, so—

DOROTHEA: Yes, there must be. Do that. Let's not prolong this discussion. I see it's painful to you.

BODEY: —Do you? No. It's—you I'm thinking of, Dotty. — Now if for some reason you should change your mind, here is the schedule of the open-air streetcars to Creve Coeur.

HELENA: Yellowing with antiquity. Is it legible still?

BODEY: We'll still be hoping that you might decide to join us, you know that, Dotty.

DOROTHEA: Yes, of course—I know that. Now why don't you finish packing and start out to the station?

BODEY: —Yes. —But remember how welcome you would be if—shoes. (*She starts into the bedroom to put on her shoes.*) I still have my slippers on.

DOROTHEA (*to Helena after Bodey has gone into the bedroom*): So! You've got the postdated check. I will move to Westmoreland Place with you July first, although I'll have to stretch quite a bit to make ends meet in such an expensive apartment.

HELENA: Think of the advantages. A fashionable address, two bedrooms, a baby grand in the front room and—

DOROTHEA: Yes, I know. It would be a very good place to entertain Ralph.

HELENA: I trust that entertaining Ralph is not your only motive in making this move to Westmoreland Place.

DOROTHEA: Not the only, but the principal one.

HELENA (*leaning forward slowly, eyes widening*): Oh, my dear Dorothea! I have the very odd feeling that I saw the name Ralph Ellis in the newspaper. In the society section.

DOROTHEA: In the society section?

HELENA: I think so, yes. I'm sure so.

(*Rising tensely, Dorothea locates the Sunday paper which Bodey had left on the sofa, in some disarray, after removing the "certain item"—the society page. She hurriedly looks through the various sections trying to find the society news.*)

DOROTHEA: Bodey? —BOOO-DEYY!

BODEY: What, Dotty?

DOROTHEA: Where is the society page of the *Post-Dispatch*?

BODEY: —Oh . . .

DOROTHEA: What does "oh" mean? It's disappeared from the paper and I'd like to know where.

BODEY: Dotty, I—

DOROTHEA: What's wrong with you? Why are you upset? I just want to know if you've seen the society page of the Sunday paper?

BODEY: —Why, I—used it to wrap fried chicken up with, honey.

DOROTHEA (*to Helena*): The only part of the paper in which I have any interest. She takes it and wraps fried chicken in it before I get up in the morning! You see what I mean? Do you understand now? (*She turns back to Bodey.*) Please remove the fried chicken from the society page and *let me have it!*

BODEY: —Honey, the chicken makes the paper so greasy that—

DOROTHEA: *I will unwrap it myself!* (*She charges into the kitchenette, unwraps the chicken, and folds out the section of pages.*) —A section has been torn out of it? Why? What for?

BODEY: Is it? I—

DOROTHEA: Nobody possibly could have done it but you. What did you do with the torn out piece of the paper?

BODEY: —I— (*She shakes her head helplessly.*)

DOROTHEA: Here it is! —Crumpled and tossed in the wastebasket!—What for, I wonder? (*She snatches up the crumpled paper from the wastebasket and straightens it, using both palms to press it hard against the kitchen table so as to flatten it. She holds up the torn-out section of the paper so the audience can see a large photograph of a young woman, good looking in a plain fashion, wearing a hard smile of triumph, then she reads aloud in a hoarse, stricken voice.*) Mr. and Mrs. James Finley announce the engagement of their daughter, Miss Constance Finley, to Mr.—T. Ralph Ellis, principal of—

(*Pause. There is much stage business. Dorothea is stunned for some moments but then comes to violent life and action. She picks up the picnic shoebox, thrusts it fiercely into Bodey's hands, opens the door for her but rushes back to pick up Bodey's small black straw hat trimmed with paper daisies, then opens the door for Bodey again with a violent gesture meaning, "Go quick!" Bodey goes. In the hall we hear various articles falling from Bodey's hold and a small, panting gasp. Then there is silence. Helena gets up with a mechanical air of sympathy.*)

HELENA: That woman is sly all right but not as sly as she's stupid. She might have guessed you'd want the society page and notice Mr. Ellis's engagement had been torn out. Anyhow, the news would have reached you at the school tomorrow. Of course I can't understand how you could be taken in by whatever little attentions you may have received from Ralph Ellis.

DOROTHEA: —"Little—attentions?" I assure you they were not—"little attentions," they were—

HELENA: Little attentions which you magnified in your imagination. Well, now, let us dismiss the matter, which has dismissed itself! Dorothea, about the postdated check, I'm not sure the real estate agents would be satisfied with that.

Now surely, Dorothea, surely you have relatives who could help you with a down payment in cash?

DOROTHEA: —Helena, I'm not interested in Westmoreland Place. —Now.

HELENA: What!

DOROTHEA: I've—abandoned that idea. I've decided not to move.

HELENA (*aghast*): —Do you realize what a shockingly irresponsible thing you are doing? Don't you realize that you are placing me in a very unfair position? You led me to believe I could count on your sharing the expense of the place, and now, at the last moment, when I have no time to get hold of someone else, you suddenly—pull out. It's really irresponsible of you. It's a really very irresponsible thing to do.

DOROTHEA: —I'm afraid we wouldn't have really gotten along together. I'm not uncomfortable here. It's only two blocks from the school and—I won't be needing a place I can't afford to entertain—anyone now.—I think I would like to be alone.

HELENA: All I can say is, the only thing I can say is—

DOROTHEA: Don't say it, just, just—leave me alone, now, Helena.

HELENA: Well, that I shall do. You may be right, we wouldn't have gotten along. Perhaps Miss Bodenheifer and her twin brother are much more on your social and cultural level than I'd hoped. And of course there's always the charm of Miss Gluck from upstairs.

DOROTHEA: The prospect of that is not as dismaying to me, Helena, as the little card parties and teas you'd had in mind for us on Westmoreland Place . . .

HELENA: *Chacun à son goût.*

DOROTHEA: Yes, yes.

HELENA (*at the door*): There is rarely a graceful way to say good-bye. (*She exits.*)

(*Pause. Dorothea shuts her eyes very tight and raises a clenched hand in the air, nodding her head several times as if affirming an unhappy suspicion regarding the way of the world. This gesture suffices to discharge her sense of defeat. Now she springs up determinedly and goes to the phone.*)

(*While waiting for a connection, she notices Miss Gluck seated disconsolately in a corner of the kitchenette.*)

DOROTHEA: Now Miss Gluck, now Sophie, we must pull our-selves together and go on. Go on, we must just go on, that's all that life seems to offer and—demand. (*She turns her attention to the phone.*) Hello, operator, can you get me information, please? —Hello? Information? Can you get me the number of the little station at the end of the Delmar car-line where you catch the, the—open streetcar that goes out to Creve Coeur Lake? —Thank you.

MISS GLUCK (*speaking English with difficulty and a heavy German accent*): Please don't leave me alone. I can't go up!

DOROTHEA (*her attention still occupied with the phone*): Creve Coeur car-line station? Look. On the platform in a few minutes will be a plumpish little woman with a big artificial flower over one ear and a stoutish man with her, probably with a cigar. I have to get an important message to them. Tell them that Dotty called and has decided to go to Creve Coeur with them after all so will they please wait. You'll have to shout to the woman because she's—*deaf* . . .

(*For some reason the word "deaf" chokes her and she begins to sob as she hangs up the phone. Miss Gluck rises, sobbing louder.*)

No, no, Sophie, come here. (*Impulsively she draws Miss Gluck into her arms.*) I know, Sophie, I know, crying is a re-lease, but it—inflames the eyes.

(*She takes Miss Gluck to the armchair and seats her there. Then she goes to the kitchenette, gets a cup of coffee and a cruller, and brings them to Sophie.*)

Make yourself comfortable, Sophie.

(*She goes to the bedroom, gets a pair of gloves, then returns and crosses to the kitchen table to collect her hat and pocket-book. She goes to the door, opens it, and says . . .*)

We'll be back before dark.

The Lights Dim Out

CHRONOLOGY

NOTE ON THE TEXTS

NOTES

Chronology

<table>
<tr>
<td>1911</td>
<td>Born March 26 in Columbus, Mississippi, the second child of Edwina Estelle Dakin Williams and Cornelius Coffin Williams, and christened Thomas Lanier Williams III. (Grandfather Thomas Lanier Williams II was an unsuccessful candidate for governor of Tennessee who later served as state railroad commissioner. Father, born 1879 in Knoxville and known as "C.C.," served in the Spanish-American War, worked for a telephone company as a regional manager, and then became a traveling salesman for a Knoxville men's clothing company. Mother, born 1884 in Marysville, Ohio, moved between Ohio and Tennessee before her family settled in Mississippi in 1901. Parents married in 1907; their first child, Rose, was born in 1909.) Lives with mother, sister, and grandparents in the rectory of St. Paul's Church, where grandfather Walter Dakin, an Episcopal priest, serves as minister; father is usually away from home on business.</td>
</tr>
<tr>
<td>1913</td>
<td>Family moves to Nashville when grandfather becomes rector of the Church of the Advent.</td>
</tr>
<tr>
<td>1914</td>
<td>Father takes new job as traveling salesman for a St. Louis shoe company, and continues to be away from family most of the time.</td>
</tr>
<tr>
<td>1915</td>
<td>Family returns to Mississippi when grandfather becomes rector in Canton and then Clarksdale, town in the Mississippi Delta. Williams is read to by grandparents and mother and listens to animal stories told by "Ozzie," his African-American nurse.</td>
</tr>
<tr>
<td>1916</td>
<td>Develops diphtheria during summer, followed by Bright's disease, which leaves him confined to his house and unable to walk for a year and a half. Mother reads to him from Dickens and Shakespeare.</td>
</tr>
<tr>
<td>1918</td>
<td>Father moves family in July to St. Louis, where he has taken a job as a branch manager with the International</td>
</tr>
</table>

Shoe Company. Williams enters Eugene Field Elementary School in September. Intimidated by his father, who calls him "Miss Nancy" because of his sensitivity and shyness.

1919   Brother Walter Dakin Williams, called Dakin, born February 21. Tension increases between his parents.

1920   Williams is sent to Clarksdale to stay with his grandparents when his mother becomes ill.

1922   Father is promoted to sales manager and moves family into better apartment. Williams enters Stix School, where he becomes friends with Hazel Kramer.

1924   Family moves into another apartment. Williams enters Ben Blewett Junior High School and begins writing on a secondhand typewriter given to him by his mother. Short story "Isolated" is printed in the school newspaper in November.

1925   Poem "Demon Smoke" appears in school yearbook. Family spends August in Elkmont, Tennessee, in the Smoky Mountains, where Williams learns to swim. Father's drinking becomes chronic problem. Rose, growing increasingly disturbed and rebellious, is sent to All Saints College in Vicksburg, Mississippi. Friendship with Hazel Kramer continues.

1926   Mother has hysterectomy. Williams enters Soldan High School in January. Family moves in June to apartment in University City just west of St. Louis. Williams enters University City High School.

1927   Wins $5 as third prize from *Smart Set* for writing an answer to the question "Can a good wife be a good sport?" Wins a prize for reviewing the film *Stella Dallas*.

1928   Short story "The Vengeance of Nitocris" published in *Weird Tales*. Rose begins to show signs of a deepening depression. Williams goes with his grandfather Dakin to New York, where they see *Show Boat* on Broadway, then sails to Europe with grandfather and a church group from Mississippi for a tour of the Continent. Visits France, Italy, Switzerland, Germany, the Netherlands, and England.

1929   Graduates from high school and enters the University of
            Missouri at Columbia, intending to study journalism.
            Pledges Alpha Tau Omega fraternity at his father's insis-
            tence. Becomes good friends with Esmeralda Mayes, who
            is also a poet.

1930   Writes one-act play *Beauty Is the Word*, for a modern
            drama class he is auditing. Submits it to the Dramatic
            Arts Club contest and wins honorable mention, the first
            freshman to be so honored.

1931   Works as typist at International Shoe Company during
            the summer. Enrolls in the University of Missouri School
            of Journalism at Columbia.

1932   Completes third year of college, but because he has failed
            ROTC, father makes him leave school and work as a clerk
            at the shoe company. Votes for Socialist candidate Nor-
            man Thomas for president.

1933   Continues writing and has poems accepted for publica-
            tion in various journals. Short story "Stella for Star"
            awarded first prize in the St. Louis Writers' Guild contest.

1935   Suffers collapse from exhaustion in January and is hospi-
            talized. Father allows him to leave the shoe company and
            spend the summer in Memphis with his Dakin grandpar-
            ents. Writes *Cairo! Shanghai! Bombay!*, which is produced
            by an amateur company in Memphis, Williams' first play
            to be staged. Begins reading the stories of Anton
            Chekhov. Returns to St. Louis in the fall and audits
            courses at Washington University.

1936   Admitted to Washington University and writes plays *The
            Magic Tower* and *Candles to the Sun* for the Mummers, a
            St. Louis drama group. Becomes friendly with a group of
            young poets, including Clark Mills McBurney, who intro-
            duces him to the work of Hart Crane. Publishes poetry in
            the university magazine. Deeply moved by seeing Alla
            Nazimova in a touring company of Ibsen's *Ghosts*.

1937   *Candles to the Sun* is performed by the Mummers in St.
            Louis in March. Rose is committed to a psychiatric ward
            in St. Louis, then moved to a Catholic convalescent

home, where she is diagnosed as having dementia praecox (schizophrenia). In the summer she is transferred to the state hospital at Farmington, Missouri, and given insulin shock treatment. Supported by the Rev. and Mrs. Dakin, Williams studies playwriting at the University of Iowa under well-known professors E. C. Mabie and E. P. Conkle. Works on a "living newspaper" drama. *The Fugitive Kind* is produced by the Mummers. Completes a draft of *Spring Storm* late in the year.

1938   Submits *Spring Storm* in March to his playwriting class at the University of Iowa, but it is not well received. Awarded B.A. degree in English by the University of Iowa. Spends summer and fall in St. Louis and submits *Spring Storm* to the Mummers, but they do not produce it. Begins writing *Not About Nightingales* in September after reading newspaper account of inmates suffocated in a steam room in a Pennsylvania prison. The St. Louis Poets' Workshop, which McBurney and William Jay Smith had established, continues to meet in the Williams home. Uses name "Tennessee Williams" for the first time on entry form for Group Theatre play contest. Goes to New Orleans in late December for the first of many stays there and is shocked by the lifestyle in the French Quarter. Soon makes friends, and becomes accustomed to and embraces the free-wheeling attitude of Quarterites.

1939   Moves January 1 to 722 Toulouse in the French Quarter, where he remains several weeks, supporting himself briefly as a waiter. Meets artists and writers, including Lyle Saxon and Roark Bradford, and attempts to secure a position with the Federal Writers' Project. Submits *Fugitive Kind* to the Project and continues work on *Not About Nightingales*. Leaves for California on February 20 with James Parrott, a musician who becomes a close friend. Wins $100 from the Group Theatre in March for one-act play collection. Engages Audrey Wood as his agent after she contacts him; she places "The Field of Blue Children" with *Story* magazine, his first publication using the name "Tennessee." Visits Frieda Lawrence in New Mexico because of his devotion to D. H. Lawrence's work. Returns to St. Louis in December, where he learns that he has been awarded a $1,000 grant from the Rockefeller Foundation.

1940   Moves to New York and enrolls in John Gassner's mod-
        ern drama course at the New School for Social Research.
        Becomes friends with Donald Windham and Gilbert
        Maxwell. Lives for a while in Provincetown, Massachu-
        setts, where he meets and falls in love with Kip Kiernan, a
        dancer. The Theatre Guild opens *Battle of Angels*, di-
        rected by Margaret Webster, in Boston on December 30.
        Becomes friends with Paul Bigelow, who works for the
        Guild.

1941   *Battle of Angels* closes January 11. Receives draft defer-
        ment because of his poor eyesight. Stays briefly in St.
        Louis, Miami, and Key West, where he meets Marion
        Vaccaro, who will become one of his best friends. Re-
        ceives $500 advance from the Theatre Guild to rewrite
        Battle of Angels. Returns to New York and submits the re-
        vised play, which is rejected by the Guild. Hume Cronyn
        takes an option on one-act plays. Spends part of the sum-
        mer in Provincetown. Returns to New Orleans in Sep-
        tember and in November goes to St. Louis, where his
        grandmother Dakin is ill. Takes a job as a cashier at a
        New Orleans restaurant in December. Completes draft of
        a long play, *Stairs to the Roof*.

1942   Stays with friends in New York in January, working on
        several plays and taking a variety of odd jobs. One-act
        plays anthologized in *American Scenes* and *Best One-Act
        Plays*. Collaborates with Donald Windham on a play, *You
        Touched Me!*, based on a D. H. Lawrence story. Spends
        part of the summer in Macon, Georgia, with Paul
        Bigelow, and in Jacksonville, Florida, where he operates a
        teletype for the U.S. Engineers Office. Returns to New
        York, where he stays with friends and continues work on
        You Touched Me! In Texas, meets Margo Jones, a leader in
        the regional theater movement. Meets James Laughlin,
        publisher of New Directions, in December; he becomes a
        close friend.

1943   Rose, still confined in a mental institution, undergoes a
        bilateral prefrontal lobotomy in January. Williams lives in
        a Brooklyn hotel, then moves to the YMCA. Works
        briefly as elevator operator, movie theater usher, and
        bellhop. Returns to St. Louis, where he works on a dra-
        matic adaptation of his story "Portrait of a Girl in

Glass" called "The Gentleman Caller." In May, at the instigation of his agent Audrey Wood, goes to Hollywood to write for MGM at $250 a week. Works on a variety of scripts, including ones for Lana Turner and Margaret O'Brien, and his own "The Gentleman Caller," but is not successful as a screenwriter. Directed by Guthrie McClintic, *You Touched Me!* opens October 13 in Cleveland, Ohio, and is later staged in Pasadena, California.

1944   Grandmother Rose Dakin dies in January in St. Louis, where he is visiting. Kip Kiernan dies from brain tumor in March. Receives a $1,000 grant from Academy of Arts and Letters and goes to Provincetown, where he rewrites "The Gentleman Caller" as a stage play. In September James Laughlin publishes 26 of his poems in *Five Young American Poets* (from this point on, New Directions will publish most of Williams' books). During rehearsals for *The Glass Menagerie*, the new title of "The Gentleman Caller," returns to St. Louis and there is interviewed by a local drama critic, William Inge, an aspiring dramatist himself. *The Glass Menagerie* opens in Chicago on December 26, with Laurette Taylor as Amanda Wingfield. The play receives excellent reviews from drama critics Claudia Cassidy and Ashton Stevens, who write about it repeatedly and are instrumental in making it a hit in Chicago.

1945   *The Glass Menagerie* opens on Broadway on March 31 to generally favorable reviews. Critics have high praise for Laurette Taylor, but some, including George Jean Nathan, have reservations about the play. Two weeks after its opening, it wins the New York Drama Critics Circle Award. Success of the play relieves Williams from the financial troubles that have burdened him; he assigns half of the royalties to his mother. Following eye surgery, goes to Mexico to work on a play called "The Moth," then renamed "Blanche's Chair in the Moon," and later "The Poker Night." New Directions publishes *27 Wagons Full of Cotton and Other One-Act Plays*. Remains in Mexico until August, when he visits Margo Jones in Dallas, then goes to Boston for rehearsals of *You Touched Me!* It debuts in New York on September 25 to generally poor reviews, and closes after 109 performances.

1946   Settles in the French Quarter in New Orleans with Pancho Rodriguez y Gonzales, whom he had met in New Mexico. Writes *Ten Blocks on the Camino Real*. Travels with Rodriguez in May to Taos, where he suffers a severe attack of diverticulitis that requires surgery. Goes to Nantucket for the summer and writes an appreciative letter to Carson McCullers, who soon joins him on the island and shares a house with him and Rodriguez for the summer, beginning an enduring friendship. Meets dramatist Thornton Wilder on Nantucket. Moves in the fall to St. Peter Street in New Orleans and works on two plays, "The Poker Night" and "Chart of Anatomy." Learns of the death of Laurette Taylor. Grandfather Dakin comes to New Orleans to stay with Williams and Rodriguez.

1947   In January, Hume Cronyn produces three Williams plays, including *Portrait of a Madonna*, starring Jessica Tandy, in Los Angeles. Williams travels with Rodriguez and grandfather Dakin to Key West, where actress Miriam Hopkins has a party for them. Sends finished version of "The Poker Night," soon renamed *A Streetcar Named Desire*, to Audrey Wood in March. Meets Irene Selznick, who will produce the play, in Charleston, South Carolina. Settles with Rodriguez in Provincetown, where he meets Frank Merlo. Rodriguez is enraged and they soon end their often tempestuous relationship. Dallas production of "Chart of Anatomy," retitled *Summer and Smoke*, opens July 8. Goes to Los Angeles for a month and sees Jessica Tandy in *Portrait of a Madonna*; she is cast as Blanche in *Streetcar*. Goes to Dallas to see Margo Jones's production of *Summer and Smoke*. Marlon Brando comes to Provincetown in August to read and is cast as Stanley. *A Streetcar Named Desire*, directed by Elia Kazan and starring Tandy, Brando, and Kim Hunter, opens December 3 in New York. Williams leaves for Europe at the end of the year.

1948   Parents separate. *A Streetcar Named Desire* is awarded the Pulitzer Prize and the Drama Critics Circle Award. Williams stays in London, Paris, and Rome, where he meets Truman Capote and Gore Vidal and becomes involved with a young Italian named Salvatore. In England, visits Helen Hayes, who is in rehearsal for *The Glass Menagerie*; meets John Gielgud, Noël Coward, Laurence

Olivier, and Vivien Leigh. Becomes friends with Maria
Britneva (later Lady Maria St. Just). Returns to Paris,
where he meets Jean Cocteau, who wants to stage a
French production of *Streetcar*. In July, his mother and
brother come to London for the British opening of *The
Glass Menagerie*. Returns to U.S. in September on the
Queen Mary with Truman Capote. *One Arm and Other
Stories* is published by New Directions. *Summer and
Smoke*, directed by Margo Jones, opens in New York. In
October Frank Merlo moves in with him, beginning the
longest intimate relationship of his life. Starts work on a
preliminary draft of *Sweet Bird of Youth*. Arranges for
Rose to receive half the royalties from *Summer and
Smoke*. Visits Paul and Jane Bowles in Tangier in Decem-
ber with Frank Merlo.

1949   Arranges for Rose to be transferred from the state hospital to a private sanitarium in Connecticut. Travels in January with Merlo to Italy, where they take an apartment,
and later to Sicily, where they meet Merlo's family. Begins
work on the novel *The Roman Spring of Mrs. Stone*. Starts
to rely heavily on drugs. In March, travels with Merlo,
Capote, and Jack Dunphy to Ischia. Argues frequently
with Capote and others. Goes to London in April and visits with Laurence Olivier, director of the London production of *Streetcar*, and Vivien Leigh, who will star as
Blanche. Returns with Merlo to New York in September,
then goes to Hollywood to advise on the script of the film
version of *The Glass Menagerie*. Moves with Merlo and
grandfather Dakin to Key West in November. Begins
work on *The Rose Tattoo*. New York production of *Streetcar* closes after two years, the longest run of any of his
plays on Broadway.

1950   Goes to New York for the openings of Inge's *Come Back,
Little Sheba* and Carson McCullers' stage adaptation of
The Member of the Wedding. Returns to Key West and
works on *The Rose Tattoo*, which he dedicates to Merlo.
Attends a limited New York run of *Streetcar* starring Uta
Hagen and Anthony Quinn and at the end of May sails
with Merlo and Jane Smith to Europe. In Paris endeavors
to persuade Anna Magnani to star in the stage production
of *The Rose Tattoo* but she declines, feeling that she does
not speak English well enough. With Merlo, again visits

Sicily, where he hopes to learn local dialect for use in *Tattoo*. They settle for a time in Rome, visit Vienna, then return to the U.S. Buys a house on Duncan Street in Key West that he had previously rented. *The Rose Tattoo* has its off-Broadway premiere in Chicago in December.

1951   *The Rose Tattoo*, starring Maureen Stapleton and Eli Wallach and produced by Cheryl Crawford, opens February 3 on Broadway and later wins Tony Award as best play. Transfers Rose to Stony Lodge, clinic near Ossining, New York, where she will spend most of the rest of her life; visits her often and on occasion takes her to visit Carson McCullers in Nyack or to shop in New York. Begins work on revision of *Battle of Angels* that will become *Orpheus Descending*. Travels with Merlo to England, Italy, Spain, Germany, and to Sweden and Denmark for the premieres of *The Rose Tattoo*. Grows increasingly dependent on alcohol and drugs. Goes to London for premiere of the play, then returns to the U.S. Elia Kazan's film of *A Streetcar Named Desire*, with Marlon Brando as Stanley and Vivien Leigh as Blanche, is released.

1952   Visits New Orleans, then goes to Key West, where he revises *Ten Blocks on the Camino Real* and a screenplay that will ultimately become *Baby Doll*. Goes to New York to see José Quintero's successful revival of *Summer and Smoke* in New York in April at Circle in the Square with Geraldine Page; is moved by the direction and acting. Elected to the National Institute of Arts and Letters. Spends summer in Europe with Merlo, with whom his relations are increasingly strained. Frequently sees Anna Magnani, Carson McCullers, and her husband, Reeves McCullers. Returns to Key West.

1953   *Camino Real* opens in New York March 19 after previews in New Haven and Philadelphia, and is not well received. William, depressed by the reviews and attacks from Walter Winchell and Ed Sullivan, returns to Key West to revise *Camino Real* for publication by New Directions. Works on *Cat on a Hot Tin Roof*. Directs Donald Windham's *The Starless Air* at the Playhouse Theatre in Houston. Argues with Windham about the play and their friendship is strained. Visits his grandfather at the Gayoso Hotel in Memphis, where the Reverend Dakin is living.

Travels extensively in Europe with Merlo and Paul Bowles in the summer. Begins work on a short story, "Man Bring This Up Road," that will ultimately become *The Milk Train Doesn't Stop Here Anymore*. Goes with Paul Bowles to Tangier in the fall. Returns to New York with Merlo in October, then goes to New Orleans, with grandfather Dakin, and spends the rest of the year there.

1954   Spends early months of the year in Key West working on *Cat on a Hot Tin Roof*. Continues work on screenplay, now called "Hide and Seek," that will become *Baby Doll*. Gives poetry reading with Carson McCullers in New York in May. Goes with Merlo a month later to Rome, where they join Maria Britneva and travel to Spain. Drinks heavily and takes increasing amounts of drugs. Returns to U.S. in September with Merlo and Anna Magnani for the filming of *The Rose Tattoo* in Key West. Continues work on revision of *Battle of Angels*. *Hard Candy*, his second collection of short stories, is published. Grandfather Dakin suffers a stroke in St. Louis.

1955   After some difficulty, Williams and agent Audrey Wood choose Elia Kazan to direct *Cat on a Hot Tin Roof*. Disagrees with Kazan on the ending of the play but eventually revises third act following Kazan's recommendation. Goes to New Orleans in mid-January to direct *27 Wagons Full of Cotton* and opera based on *Lord Byron's Love Letter* at Tulane University. Attends rehearsals of *Cat on a Hot Tin Roof* in New York. Grandfather Dakin dies February 14 in St. Louis at age 97. *Cat on a Hot Tin Roof*, starring Burl Ives, Barbara Bel Geddes, and Ben Gazzara, opens on Broadway March 24 with the revised third act and is a critical triumph. Subsequently wins the Drama Critics Circle award and the Pulitzer Prize. Film of *The Rose Tattoo* is released. Returns to Key West in April with Carson McCullers; they work together, then go to Havana briefly. In June goes again to Europe for the summer. Learns in July that Margo Jones has died. Suffering from writer's block, Williams continues to rely on drink and drugs. Attends Stockholm opening of the Swedish *Cat on a Hot Tin Roof* and visits his friend Lilla von Saher. Returns to New York to work on the screenplay of *Baby Doll*, and also works on "The Enemy: Time," which will become *Sweet Bird of Youth*.

1956   Goes with Maria Britneva and Marion Vaccaro to Miami,
            where Tallulah Bankhead is starring in a revival of *Street-
            car*; his dissatisfaction with her performance is publicized
            and Williams apologizes to an angry Bankhead. *Sweet
            Bird of Youth*, directed by George Keathley, opens in Mi-
            ami on April 16. Williams goes to Rome alone as the ten-
            sion between him and Merlo increases. In November, *The
            Glass Menagerie* is revived in New York starring Helen
            Hayes as Amanda. The film *Baby Doll*, directed by Elia
            Kazan and starring Carroll Baker and Eli Wallach, is re-
            leased; it is denounced by Cardinal Spellman, and con-
            demned by the Catholic Legion of Decency and other
            groups. Goes to Key West with his mother. First collec-
            tion of poetry, *In the Winter of Cities*, is published.

1957   Travels to New York for revisions and rehearsals of *Or-
            pheus Descending*. Directed by Harold Clurman, the play
            opens on Broadway on March 21 and closes after two
            months; its negative reviews worsen Williams' depression.
            Father dies March 27, and Williams attends funeral in
            Knoxville with his brother Dakin. In June begins
            psychotherapy with Dr. Lawrence S. Kubie, a Freudian
            analyst, who, according to Williams, urges him to quit
            writing and to live as a heterosexual. Spends the summer
            in New York, visiting friends and often going to Stony
            Lodge to see Rose. Works on *Suddenly Last Summer*.

1958   On January 7 *Garden District*, consisting of *Suddenly
            Last Summer* and *Something Unspoken*, premieres Off
            Broadway in New York to favorable reviews. Returns to
            Key West to work on *Sweet Bird of Youth*. Ends his analy-
            sis with Dr. Kubie in March and leaves again for Europe.
            Cat on a Hot Tin Roof opens in London and in August
            the film version, directed by Richard Brooks and starring
            Elizabeth Taylor, Paul Newman, and Burl Ives, is re-
            leased. Returns to Florida in the fall, and collaborates
            with Meade Roberts on script for film of *Orpheus De-
            scending*, which is retitled *The Fugitive Kind*. Continues
            work on *Sweet Bird of Youth* and *Period of Adjustment*,
            which opens on December 29 for a brief run at the Co-
            conut Grove Playhouse.

1959   Goes to New York in February for rehearsals of *Sweet Bird
            of Youth*. Directed by Elia Kazan and starring Geraldine

Page and Paul Newman, it opens on Broadway March 10. Depressed by critical response to the play, Williams leaves New York for Miami and then goes with Marion Vaccaro to Havana, where he meets Fidel Castro, an admirer of Williams' work. Returns with Vaccaro to Key West for a few weeks and in May flies with her to London for the English premiere of *Orpheus Descending*. Returns to New York in June for rehearsals of *The Fugitive Kind*. In July attends a Chicago production of *Suddenly Last Summer* with Diana Barrymore. After the play closes, returns to Havana with Vaccaro and Barrymore. Leaves in August on three-month around-the-world trip. Film of *Suddenly Last Summer*, directed by Joseph L. Mankiewicz and starring Katharine Hepburn, Elizabeth Taylor, and Montgomery Clift, is released.

1960   Settles with Merlo in Key West to work on *The Night of the Iguana* and *Period of Adjustment*. In June goes with his mother, brother Dakin, and Dakin's wife, Joyce, to Los Angeles, where they meet Elvis Presley and Mae West. Returns to Key West to work. Relations with Merlo, who shows signs of illness, are strained. *The Fugitive Kind*, film version of *Orpheus Descending*, directed by Sidney Lumet and starring Marlon Brando and Anna Magnani, is released. *The Night of the Iguana* is staged at Coconut Grove in August. *Period of Adjustment* opens on Broadway.

1961   Works in Key West on revisions of *The Night of the Iguana*. Goes with Vaccaro in January to Europe. In Rome they meet Donald Windham and Sandy Campbell, then settle in Taormina, Sicily, where he works on the play. Returns to Key West in the autumn, depressed by what he sees as his waning career and more and more dependent on liquor and pills. During previews in Detroit, Williams is hospitalized after his dog bites him. After previews in several other cities, *The Night of the Iguana*, starring Bette Davis, Margaret Leighton, and Patrick O'Neal, opens in New York on December 28.

1962   *The Night of the Iguana* wins Drama Critics Circle Award as best play. Buys a multi-story townhouse in the French Quarter in New Orleans, using income from film versions of his plays. Made lifetime member of the American Academy of Arts and Letters. Lucy Freeman collaborates with Williams' mother on her memoir, *Remember Me to Tom*. The Spoleto Festival of the Two Worlds in Italy premieres a version of *The Milk Train Doesn't Stop Here Anymore*. Poet Frederick Nicklaus, who has moved in with Williams and Merlo in Key West, accompanies him to Italy. Contacted in London by Audrey Wood, who informs him that Merlo is very ill, he flies back to the U.S.

1963   *Milk Train* moves to New York January 16 and runs for only two months. Merlo is diagnosed with lung cancer and goes to Key West, then back to New York to stay with Williams and Nicklaus. Williams begins revisions of *Milk Train* in preparation for a revival. Merlo dies in September. After the funeral, Williams and Nicklaus fly to Mexico where *Night of the Iguana* is being filmed by John Huston, with a cast including Ava Gardner, Deborah Kerr, and Richard Burton. Williams begins a period of depression and heavy dependence on drugs that he will call his "Stoned Age."

1964   Revival of *Milk Train*, starring Tallulah Bankhead, Tab Hunter, Ruth Ford, and Marion Seldes opens January 1 and closes after three days. Goes to Jamaica and then to Key West, where Nicklaus leaves him in March. Back in New York, he begins seeing a new analyst and becomes a patient of Dr. Max Jacobson, who provides him with amphetamines and barbiturates in pill and injection form. Writes *Slapstick Tragedy*, consisting of two short plays, *The Gnädiges Fräulein* and *The Mutilated*. Realizing that he should not be alone, given his reliance on alcohol and drugs, he hires the first of a series of paid companions, William Glavin, to move in with him and travel with him. Film of *The Night of the Iguana* released.

1965   *The Glass Menagerie* revived with Maureen Stapleton as Amanda. *Milk Train* is revived again in San Francisco and is positively received. Goes to St. Louis to visit his mother, who has begun to suffer from delusions. Continues work on *Slapstick Tragedy*, other plays, and short stories. *The Eccentricities of a Nightingale*, a revision of *Summer and Smoke*, is published.

1966   *Slapstick Tragedy*, starring Zoe Caldwell, Margaret Leighton, and Kate Reid opens in New York in January and runs for only four days. Williams issues a public statement condemning America's involvement in Vietnam. Reliance on drugs grows, abetted by Dr. Jacobson, and his mental state becomes progressively unstable. Works on the film script of *Milk Train*, then goes with Glavin and Lester Persky, who will produce it, to London. Film of *This Property Is Condemned*, loosely based on his one-act play, is released.

1967   Goes with Glavin to Virgin Islands where parts of "Goforth!" (soon retitled *Boom!*), based on *Milk Train*, are being filmed. Travels in the summer with Glavin to Europe, visiting Sardinia where *Boom!* is now being filmed by director Joseph Losey with a cast including Elizabeth Taylor, Richard Burton, and Noël Coward. Friends such as Audrey Wood and Elia Kazan are increasingly concerned by his dependence on drugs and his mental state. Carson McCullers dies September 29 following a massive stroke. *The Knightly Quest: A Novella and Four Short Stories* is published by New Directions. Attends the world premiere of *The Two-Character Play* in London in December with Audrey Wood.

1968   Production of *Kingdom of Earth* with Harry Guardino, Estelle Parsons, and Brian Bedford premieres in February in Philadelphia and then opens in New York on March 27 under the direction of José Quintero and retitled *The Seven Descents of Myrtle*. It runs only a month. *Boom!* is released to unfavorable reviews. Friend Lilla van Saher dies. Works on revision of *The Two-Character Play* and on a new play, *In the Bar of a Tokyo Hotel*. At the end of the year, suffering increasingly from paranoid symptoms exacerbated by drug use, goes with Glavin to Key West.

1969   Dakin, at Audrey Wood's suggestion, goes to Key West to check on Williams, who has grown confused and disoriented. Dakin arranges for him to be received into the Roman Catholic church on January 10, although Williams will later deny that the conversion was authentic. In the spring, assumes direction of the New York production of *In the Bar of a Tokyo Hotel*, which opens May 11 in New York and is widely condemned by critics.

Receives National Institute of Arts and Letters gold medal and an honorary doctorate from the University of Missouri at Columbia. In June, flies with actress Anne Meacham to Tokyo where they meet writer Yukio Mishima and see part of the Japanese production of *Streetcar*. Returns to Key West, where Glavin joins him, then goes to San Francisco again and to New Orleans to see Pancho Rodriguez. Becomes progressively more dependent on drugs and increasingly paranoid. In September Dakin convinces him to enter Barnes Hospital in St. Louis, where he is placed in the mental ward. Suffers seizures and two heart attacks related to withdrawal from drugs. Recovers sufficiently to return to Key West in December.

1970　Goes to New York in January for revival of *Camino Real*. Discusses his homosexuality in a television interview with David Frost. Marion Black Vaccaro dies in April. At the end of summer, travels with Oliver Evans to New Orleans and then to Hawaii, Hong Kong, Thailand, and Japan, where he meets with Yukio Mishima shortly before Mishima commits ritual suicide. *Dragon Country: A Book of Plays* is published.

1971　Attends rehearsals in Chicago of production of *Out Cry* (a revised version of *The Two-Character Play*), starring Donald Madden and Eileen Herlie. Resumes use of drugs and, in a fit of anger, dismisses his agent, Audrey Wood, who is replaced by Bill Barnes. Revises and expands *Confessional* into full-length play *Small Craft Warnings*. New Directions begins publication of the multi-volume set, *The Theatre of Tennessee Williams*. Speaks out against American involvement in the Vietnam War at a rally at the Cathedral of St. John the Divine in New York in December.

1972　Moves into an apartment in the New Orleans townhouse he had bought in 1962. *Small Craft Warnings* opens in Philadelphia in February and in New York in April. Awarded honorary degree by Purdue University. Appears in *Small Craft Warnings* as the character Doc in an attempt to boost ticket sales. Spends fall and winter in New York, Key West, and New Orleans. Completes first draft of *Memoirs*, using title "Flee, Flee This Sad Hotel." Attends the Venice Film Festival in August as a juror.

Robert Carroll becomes his companion-secretary and travels with him.

1973   *Out Cry*, with Michael York and Cara Duff-MacCormick, opens in New York March 1 and closes after twelve performances. Visits Los Angeles for a new staging of *Streetcar* and meets with Canadian television producer Harry Rasky, who has made a documentary film about him. Travels with Carroll to the Far East and then to Rome. In May Jane Bowles dies and in June William Inge commits suicide. Travels to Rome and then to Tangier to visit Paul Bowles. Works on *The Red Devil Battery Sign*. Saddened in September by the death of Anna Magnani. Awarded the first Centennial Medal of the Cathedral of St. John the Divine. Williams and Robert Carroll separate for a while.

1974   Travels extensively and visits Rose often. Works on *The Red Devil Battery Sign*. Goes to London in March for a revival of *Streetcar* with Claire Bloom. While in England, stays with Lady Maria St. Just (formerly Maria Britneva). In July *Cat on a Hot Tin Roof* is revived in New York with Elizabeth Ashley and Keir Dullea. Short story collection *Eight Mortal Ladies Possessed* is published.

1975   Receives National Arts Club's gold medal for literature in February and is given the key to the city of New York. Works on *This Is (An Entertainment)*. Second novel, *Moise and the World of Reason*, is published in May. In June, *The Red Devil Battery Sign* with Claire Bloom and Anthony Quinn opens in Boston and closes in 10 days. A successful revival of *Sweet Bird of Youth* opens in Boston and then moves to New York; there are also revivals of *Summer and Smoke* and of *The Glass Menagerie* in New York. *Memoirs* is published.

1976   *This Is (An Entertainment)* premieres in January in San Francisco, where Williams meets Lyle Leverich, whom he later selects as his biographer. Harry Rasky's documentary film *Tennessee Williams's South* appears on television. A series of young men alternate with Robert Carroll as paid companions. Returns in October to San Francisco for Leverich's production of *The Two-Character Play*. *The Eccentricities of a Nightingale* premieres in Buffalo, New

York, then moves to New York City November 23. *The Night of the Iguana* is revived in London. Inducted into the American Academy of Arts and Letters in December.

1977   *Vieux Carré* opens in May on Broadway and closes after only five performances. Goes to London in June for the premiere of *The Red Devil Battery Sign*. Second volume of poetry, *Androgyne, Mon Amour*, is published. Develops cataract on his right eye. Works on adapting the *Baby Doll* screenplay into a play, *Tiger Tail*, and writing the play *Creve Coeur*.

1978   *Tiger Tail* debuts in Atlanta but closes quickly. Returns to New Orleans for a public appearance in which he reads his poetry and fiction. The Spoleto Festival in Charleston, South Carolina, stages *Creve Coeur* (later retitled *A Lovely Sunday for Creve Coeur*). *Vieux Carré* is revived in London in August with Sylvia Miles. Mitch Douglas succeeds Bill Barnes as Williams' agent. Publishes collection of essays, *Where I Live*. Travels extensively before taking an apartment at Manhattan Plaza in New York. Brings Rose to New York for the holidays.

1979   *A Lovely Sunday for Creve Coeur* opens in New York on January 1 for a brief run. After his gardener in Key West is murdered, Williams discovers that the man had stolen manuscripts, other papers, and photographs. Works on revisions of *The Milk Train Doesn't Stop Here Anymore* and *Clothes for a Summer Hotel*. Brings Rose to Key West to live in a cottage near him, under the care of a cousin, but the arrangement proves unsatisfactory. *Kirche, Kuchen, und Kinder* opens in New York in September. In December Williams receives Kennedy Center Honors from President Jimmy Carter.

1980   In January *Will Mr. Merriwether Return from Memphis?* premieres in Key West at the opening of the Tennessee Williams Performing Arts Center. *Clothes for a Summer Hotel*, directed by José Quintero and starring Geraldine Page and Kenneth Haigh, opens in Washington, then Chicago, and in New York on March 26, his birthday, which Mayor Ed Koch declares Tennessee Williams Day; it is to be his last play on Broadway during his lifetime. Mother dies on June 1 at age 95. Travels in Europe in

June and July with artist Henry Faulkner. Works at Goodman Theatre in Chicago on three one-act plays. Appointed Distinguished Writer in Residence at the
University of British Columbia in Vancouver, but does
not remain for the full term. The triad of short plays, col-
lectively called *Tennessee Laughs*, is presented at the
Goodman Theatre. Spends holiday season in Key West,
where he arranges for Rose to be returned to the nursing
home in Ossining, New York.

1981   Works on *A House Not Meant to Stand* at Goodman. The
Goodman has a party to celebrate his seventieth birthday,
after which *A House Not Meant to Stand* opens. In April,
former agent Audrey Wood suffers a stroke that leaves her
in a coma. In the summer, works on his version of
Chekhov's *The Sea Gull*, which will become *The Notebook
of Trigorin*, and on *Something Cloudy, Something Clear*.
The latter opens August 24 for a limited run by the Jean
Cocteau Repertory, the last of his plays to debut in New
York during his lifetime. In the fall, two old friends, poet
Oliver Evans and artist Henry Faulkner, die. Along with
Harold Pinter, he is awarded the Common Wealth Award
of $11,000. Luis Sanjurjo replaces Mitch Douglas as his
agent.

1982   Works in Key West on a revision of *A House Not Meant
to Stand*. Travels to New York in February to receive the
city's medallion of honor. *Something Cloudy, Something
Clear* is revived in February by the Jean Cocteau Repertory. Goes to Chicago to discuss staging of the revised
and expanded *A House Not Meant to Stand*, which opens
in April for a limited run. Receives an honorary doctorate
from Harvard in June. Attends staging of several of his
plays at the Williamstown Theater Festival in Williamstown, Massachusetts. Works in Key West on a screenplay,
then travels with Jane Smith to London and Sicily, where
he works on a new play, *The Lingering Hour*. Makes last
public appearance in November at the 92nd Street Y in
New York. Hospitalized in Key West in December suffering from drug toxicity.

1983   In January, visits Jane Smith in New York, returns to Key
West, then goes to New Orleans to arrange the sale of his
townhouse. Flies to Taormina in February for a final brief

visit before returning to New York. Dies on February 24;
the cause of death may have been the result of an over-
dose of Seconal or from asphyxia caused by choking on a
plastic cap of the type used on bottles of nasal spray or
eyedrops. Funeral services are held at the St. Louis Cathedral on March 5; Williams is buried next to his mother in
the Calvary Cemetery in St. Louis.

Note on the Texts

This volume contains 13 plays by Tennessee Williams that were first produced and published between 1957 and 1980. The texts printed here are taken from the first editions of the plays in book form.

Because Williams habitually revised his works, most of his plays exist in multiple versions. Williams revised many of them after initial book publication for editions published by Dramatists Play Service (intended for use by actors and directors), for subsequent American and English book editions, and for the collected edition *The Theatre of Tennessee Williams*, published by New Directions.

The Dramatists Play Service editions of the plays are meant chiefly to aid in staging and omit prefaces and commentary that are part of the texts of the book editions.

Williams revised the book editions of several of his plays relatively soon after their first publication. For the second printing of the first American edition of *Suddenly Last Summer*, published in 1959, Williams omitted several lines of dialogue included in the first printing; for the English edition of *The Milk Train Doesn't Stop Here Anymore*, published in 1965, Williams inserted a passage that does not appear in American editions of the play and made several other changes. Williams' revisions, however, are not always retained in subsequent editions of the plays, which sometimes revert to the texts of the first editions. In certain instances, Williams' revisions cause inconsistencies within a play, and occasionally he deleted or altered potentially objectionable material.

In 1971, New Directions published the first three volumes of *The Theatre of Tennessee Williams*, a collected edition of Williams' plays. Three additional volumes of this eight-volume series were published during Williams' lifetime and incorporated substantial changes in several plays. For example, the version of *Battle of Angels* printed in *The Theatre of Tennessee Williams* incorporates passages from Williams' play *Orpheus Descending*, and the version of *Kingdom of Earth (The Seven Descents of Myrtle)* is a shortened version of the play as first published.

The texts of the first book editions have been chosen for inclusion in the present volume because they are the versions of the plays Williams published for general readers immediately following the plays' composition.

Orpheus Descending is a rewritten version of Williams' play *Battle of Angels*, first staged in 1940 and published in *Pharos* in 1945. Williams completed his revisions for *Orpheus Descending* shortly before the play opened in New York on March 21, 1957, in a production directed by Harold Clurman. The Prologue was omitted in this production but was included when the play was collected in *Orpheus Descending, with Battle of Angels*, published by New Directions on February 5, 1958. The preface, "The Past, the Present and the Perhaps," first appeared in *The New York Times* on March 17, 1957, as "Tennessee Williams on the Past, the Present and the Perhaps."

For the Dramatists Play Service edition of *Orpheus Descending*, published in 1959, Williams changed the order of some of the material in the play. The version of *Battle of Angels* that was included in Volume 1 (1971) of *The Theatre of Tennessee Williams* combines passages from *Battle of Angels* and *Orpheus Descending*; the text of *Orpheus Descending* in Volume 2 of *The Theatre of Tennessee Williams* follows that of the 1958 New Directions edition. The text printed here is taken from the 1958 New Directions edition of *Orpheus Descending, with Battle of Angels*.

By November 1957, had Williams completed the version of *Suddenly Last Summer* that was staged, along with the one-act play "Something Unspoken," as *Garden District* in a production, directed by Herbert Machiz, that opened in New York on January 7, 1958. New Directions published the book version of *Suddenly Last Summer* on April 23, 1958. The Dramatists Play Service edition published in 1969 does not differ significantly from the first New Directions edition.

Williams revised *Suddenly Last Summer* for the 1959 second printing of the New Directions edition, omitting dialogue from Scene One about the Doctor's operations at Lion's View and Sebastian Venable's vision in the Encantadas. The text of *Suddenly Last Summer* included in *Garden District* (London: Secker & Warburg, 1959), follows that of the first printing of the 1958 New Directions edition, as does the version of the play that appears in Volume 3 (1971) of *The Theatre of Tennessee Williams*. The text printed here is taken from the 1958 New Directions first printing of *Suddenly Last Summer*.

Sweet Bird of Youth is derived from "The Big Time Operators," an unfinished play Williams wrote in 1948, and the story "Two on a Party," written in 1951 and 1952, in which a young man travels with an older woman from New Orleans to West Palm Beach. Williams then incorporated some of this material in "The Enemy: Time," a one-act play published in *The Theatre* in March 1959. Williams had

sent a draft of "The Enemy: Time" in January 1956 to George Keathley, manager of the Studio M Playhouse in Coral Gables, Florida,
who then offered to stage the play in the spring of that year.
Williams revised the play, now titled *Sweet Bird of Youth*, in February
and March for its April 16, 1956, opening, and continued to work on
it after Keathley's production closed. In March 1958, Williams told
Audrey Wood, his agent, that he had finished a new draft to submit
to Cheryl Crawford; by the fall, Crawford had agreed to stage a production in New York, and Elia Kazan was hired as its director. In
November 1958 Williams sent his most recent draft to Kazan, who responded in a letter with comments and suggestions. Williams continued to revise the play during rehearsals in February 1959. After a
trial run in Philadelphia, *Sweet Bird of Youth* opened in New York on
March 10, 1959. A version of the play appeared in *Esquire* the following month.

The New Directions edition of *Sweet Bird of Youth* was published
on November 24, 1959. Its preface had appeared, as "Williams' Wells
of Violence," in *The New York Times* on March 8, 1959. The New Directions version of the play differs significantly from the *Esquire* text;
among other changes, Williams removed a scene from Act II and altered several passages in Act III. The acting edition published by
Dramatists Play Service in 1962 makes further changes and includes
an alternate ending after the end of Act III. Both the English edition, published in 1961 by Secker & Warburg, and the version published in Volume 4 (1972) of *The Theatre of Tennessee Williams* follow
the 1959 New Directions edition of *Sweet Bird of Youth*. The text
printed here is taken from the 1959 New Directions edition.

Williams completed the first draft of *Period of Adjustment* in the
fall of 1958. In December 1958 Williams directed a version of the play,
billed as a work in progress, at the Coconut Grove Theatre in
Florida, and he continued to work on it during 1959 and 1960.
Cheryl Crawford announced a Broadway production and named
George Roy Hill as director in April 1960. *Period of Adjustment*
opened in New York on November 10, 1960, and New Directions
published the book version on November 14, 1960. The working
script that Williams had subsequently revised during rehearsals for
the New York opening was published in *Esquire* in December 1960.

Changes were made in the text of *Period of Adjustment* in the second printing of the first edition because New Directions was concerned that the specificity of the setting might expose the firm to a
libel suit. The setting of the play was changed from "Memphis" to
"a mid-southern city," and several, though not all, references to

"Memphis" were changed to "Dixon." Williams made further revisions for the Dramatists Play Service edition published in 1961. The English edition, published by Secker & Warburg in 1961, does not differ significantly from the first printing of the 1959 New Directions edition. The version that appears in Volume 4 (1972) of *The Theatre of Tennessee Williams* follows the second printing of the first New Directions edition but alters a reference to Memphis that was not changed in earlier editions. The text of *Period of Adjustment* printed here is taken from the 1959 New Directions edition, first printing.

The Night of the Iguana was first performed as a one-act play in Spoleto, Italy, on July 2, 1959, in a production directed by Frank Corsaro. (A short story with the same title, completed in 1948 and collected by Williams in *One Arm and Other Stories* in 1954, is remotely related to the play.) Over the next two years, *The Night of the Iguana* became a full-length play, and it was staged in two different versions by Corsaro in fall 1959 and summer 1960. Williams continued to expand and revise the play for the New York production by the Actors Studio, also directed by Corsaro, that opened on December 28, 1961. The working script that Williams had subsequently revised during rehearsals for the December opening was published in *Esquire* in February 1962. The book version of *The Night of the Iguana* was published by New Directions on February 28, 1962. The acting edition published by Dramatists Play Service the following year is a shortened version of the play. Neither the English edition published by Secker & Warburg in 1963 nor the version included in Volume 4 (1972) of *The Theatre of Tennessee Williams* was revised by Williams; the texts of those editions follow that of the 1962 New Directions first edition. The text printed here is taken from the 1962 New Directions edition of *The Night of the Iguana*.

The Eccentricities of a Nightingale is a rewritten version of Williams' play *Summer and Smoke*, first staged in 1948. Williams revised *Summer and Smoke* heavily in 1952, hoping to have his changes incorporated into a London revival of the play, but these revisions were not finished in time for the London production and were not used in subsequent revivals of *Summer and Smoke*. It appears that many of these revisions were incorporated into *The Eccentricities of a Nightingale*. Williams finished working on the play by 1964, and it was published, in *The Eccentricities of a Nightingale and Summer and Smoke*, by New Directions on February 12, 1965. This version of the play was included in Volume 2 (1971) of *The Theatre of Tennessee Williams*. The first Dramatists Play Service edition was published in

1977 and reflects changes made by Williams for the play's first stage production in 1976. The text printed here is taken from the 1965 New Directions *The Eccentricities of a Nightingale and Summer and Smoke*.

In 1958, Williams began working on a series of dialogues based on his story "Man Bring This Up Road," written in 1953 and collected in Williams' *The Knightly Quest* in 1967. By 1962 these dialogues were incorporated into a short play, *The Milk Train Doesn't Stop Here Anymore*, which was staged in July 1962 at the Festival of Two Worlds in Spoleto, Italy. Rehearsals began later that year for another production, directed by Herbert Machiz, that opened in New York on January 10, 1963, and closed after 69 performances. Williams continued to revise and expand the play for a revival staged in Aberdeen, Virginia, in September 1963 and then wrote new scenes for the second New York production, directed by Tony Richardson, which opened on January 1, 1964.

New Directions published the book version of *The Milk Train Doesn't Stop Here Anymore* on June 9, 1964. While the book was in production, Williams discovered that lines from the second scene had been accidentally transposed to the end of the first scene. The error was corrected in some copies of the first printing and in subsequent printings. For the English edition, published by Secker & Warburg in September 1964, Williams added a short passage in Scene 5 and made other changes, mostly to stage directions. Williams did not revise the play for the Dramatists Play Service edition published in 1964 or for the version that appears in Volume 5 (1976) of *The Theatre of Tennessee Williams*. The texts of these editions follow the corrected version of the first New Directions edition. The corrected first printing of the 1964 New Directions edition of *The Milk Train Doesn't Stop Here Anymore* is the text printed here.

Williams completed a draft of *The Mutilated* by the end of 1964. A production of the play, paired with *The Gnädiges Fräulein* under the title *Slapstick Tragedy*, was scheduled for early 1965, but this production was canceled because of insufficient funding. A new production of *Slapstick Tragedy*, to be directed by Alan Schneider, was announced later that year, and a version of the play was published in *Esquire* in August 1965. Williams revised *The Mutilated* while *Slapstick Tragedy* was in rehearsal in early 1966 in New York; the production opened on February 22, 1966. *The Mutilated* was published by Dramatists Play Service in 1967, then revised for inclusion in *Dragon Country: A Book of Plays*, which was published by New Directions on March 30, 1970. Williams did not revise *The Mutilated* after its publication in *Dragon Country*. The text of *The Mutilated* printed here is taken from the 1970 New Directions edition of *Dragon Country: A Book of Plays*.

Kingdom of Earth originated in the short story "The Kingdom of Earth," first published in 1954 by New Directions in a limited edition of Williams' collection *Hard Candy*. The story was adapted for a one-act play that was published in *Esquire* in February 1967; later that year, David Merrick agreed to stage a full-length version of *Kingdom of Earth*. After a trial run in Philadelphia, the play opened in New York on March 27, 1968, in a production directed by José Quintero; for the New York production, Williams changed the title to *The Seven Descents of Myrtle*. New Directions published the book version, *Kingdom of Earth (The Seven Descents of Myrtle)*, on October 31, 1968. Williams made minor revisions in the play for the acting edition, which was published by Dramatists Play Service the following year. The version that is included in Volume 5 (1976) of *The Theatre of Tennessee Williams* is shorter than the New Directions and the Dramatists Play Service versions, because Williams hoped that a shortened version of the play would be revived. The text printed here is taken from the 1968 New Directions edition of *Kingdom of Earth (The Seven Descents of Myrtle)*.

Small Craft Warnings is an expanded version of *Confessional*, a one-act play published in *Dragon Country: A Book of Plays* in 1970. The favorable reception of William Hunt's 1971 production of *Confessional* prompted Bill Barnes, Williams' agent, to contact three New York producers about staging a full-length version. After a New York production was announced, Williams worked on revising and expanding the play during late 1971 and early 1972. Now titled *Small Craft Warnings*, the play went into rehearsal in early 1972 with Hunt as the director. Hunt quit the production while in rehearsal and was replaced at first by Williams, then by Richard Altman. *Small Craft Warnings* opened in New York on April 2, 1972. New Directions published the book version on November 15, 1972. Williams did not revise *Small Craft Warnings* for the English edition published in 1973 by Secker & Warburg or for its inclusion in Volume 5 (1976) of *The Theatre of Tennessee Williams*. The text printed here is taken from the 1972 New Directions edition.

Out Cry is a rewritten version of *The Two-Character Play*, a play Williams began writing in 1966. *The Two-Character Play* was first staged in 1967 in a production directed by James Rosse-Evans and was published in a limited edition by New Directions in 1969. Williams then wrote a new version of the play, using the title *Out Cry*, which was staged in July 1971 in a production directed by George Keathley and was published by New Directions on October 24, 1973. The text printed here is taken from the 1973 New Directions edition, the only edition of *Out Cry* to be published during Williams' lifetime. (Williams later extensively revised the play, again using the title *The Two-Character Play*; this version, which was staged in March 1973 and published by New Directions in 1975, is a distinct work significantly different from both *Out Cry* and the version of *The Two-Character Play* published in 1969.)

Williams began working on *Vieux Carré* in 1976, although some of the play was drawn from plays and stories that Williams had written earlier. A New York production of the play, directed by Arthur Alan Seidelman, was in rehearsal in early 1977. Although Williams did not attend rehearsals for the first New York production, he did send revisions from his hotel in New York to Seidelman and the cast. *Vieux Carré* opened in New York in March 1977 and was revived the following year in two English productions, both directed by Keith Hack. The book version was published by New Directions on June 25, 1979. This was the only edition of *Vieux Carré* published during Williams' lifetime, and is the source of the text printed here.

Williams wrote a one-act play, "Creve Coeur," in San Francisco in 1976. He read the play in 1977 to Craig Anderson, director of the Hudson Theatre Guild in New York, who agreed to stage a production. Williams expanded and revised "Creve Coeur" for a June 1978 production, directed by Keith Hack, at the Spoleto Festival in Charleston, S.C.; then he continued to work on the play for its New York production, changing its title to *A Lovely Sunday for Creve Coeur*. Final revisions were completed while the New York production was in rehearsal in late 1978. *A Lovely Sunday for Creve Coeur*, directed by Keith Hack, opened on January 1, 1979. The book version was published by New Directions on April 30, 1980. Some of the characters and dialogue of *A Lovely Sunday for Creve Coeur* appear in *All Gaul Is Divided*, a screenplay that was published posthumously in *Stopped Rocking and Other Screenplays* (New York: New Directions, 1984). In a 1979 note to *All Gaul Is Divided*, Williams wrote, "I would guess that the 'teleplay' was written almost twenty years before I wrote the play, *A Lovely Sunday for Creve Coeur* . . . The most remarkable thing about the teleplay is that I had *totally* forgotten its existence when I wrote *Creve Coeur* in San Francisco about three years ago." The 1980 New Directions edition of *A Lovely Sunday for Creve Coeur* is the only version of the play published during Williams' lifetime and is the source of the text printed here.

This volume presents the texts of the original printings chosen for inclusion here, but it does not attempt to reproduce features of their typographic design. The texts are presented without change, except for the correction of typographical errors. Spelling, punctuation, and capitalization are often expressive features and are not altered, even when inconsistent or irregular. The following is a list of typographical errors corrected, cited by page and line number: 10.17, an; 31.24, lady; 158.2, *Allelulia*; 187.26, *O'Keefe's*; 199.29, dare?; 201.26, Hanh?—; 221.35, Torremolenas; 261.9, —resist the—; 261.32, Jawge; 262.14, An; 282.10, [ ] May; 303.14, *He*; 317.6, Why'; 320.26, ot; 332.26, rum-coco; 346.13, susspected; 399.8, *Hanna's*; 404.19, our—; 413.4, built; 426.17, 'hasta; 427.7, *Hannnah*; 448.11, how; 451.15, operate; 516.14, you *you*; 517.5, breats; 529.27, She; 552.34, been—; 556.23, look; 564.32, lighter.; 574.4, embarrasing; 574.30, *legumi*; 579.24, wth; 589.39, *shilly*; 592.2, Galatoires; 647.17, Day!; 648.24, lillies; 668.16, ukelele; 695.15, and'; 696.14, weather, and so forth."; 710.9, penathol; 751.26, *Violets*; 753.18, Doc; 755.27, *precinct*; 812.24, sister...; 813.28, glimpe; 829.32, soto; 856.2, S'; 878.10, *it's*; 880.4, Babe,; 884.20, charnal; 909.18, Jut; 957.22, *daises*.

ACKNOWLEDGMENTS

The plays in this volume are published by arrangement with New Directions Publishing Corporation, New York, Publisher of the plays of Tennessee Williams, and with The University of the South, copyright proprietor of the works of Tennessee Williams.

Orpheus Descending. Copyright 1955, 1958, renewed © 1983, 1986 The University of the South.

Suddenly Last Summer. Copyright 1958, renewed © 1986 The University of the South.

Sweet Bird of Youth. Copyright 1959, renewed © 1987 The University of the South.

Period of Adjustment. Copyright 1960, renewed © 1988 The University of the South.

The Night of the Iguana. Copyright 1961, renewed © 1989 The University of the South.

The Eccentricities of a Nightingale. Copyright 1946, renewed © 1992 The University of the South.

The Milk Train Doesn't Stop Here Anymore. Copyright © 1976 The University of the South. The epigraph from "Sailing to Byzantium" by W. B. Yeats, Copyright 1928 by The Macmillan Company, © Renewed 1956 by Georgie Yeats.

The Mutilated. Copyright 1967, renewed © 1995 The University of the South.

Kingdom of Earth (The Seven Descents of Myrtle). Copyright 1967, 1968, 1969, 1975, renewed © 1995, 1996, 1997 The University of the South. "Cuddle Up a Little Closer," Copyright 1908 M. Witmark & Sons. "There's a Long, Long Trail," Copyright 1914 by M. Witmark & Sons. "Is It True What They Say About Dixie," written by Gerald Marks, Sammy Lerner, and Irving Caesar, Inc. Renewed 1963 Marlong Music Inc., Samuel M. Lerner Publications, and Irving Caesar, Inc. "Stars Fell on Alabama" (Perkins-Parrish), © 1934 by Mills Music, Inc., renewed © 1962. "Heavenly Grass" by Tennessee Williams, set to music by Paul Bowles, Copyright 1946 by G. Schirmer, Inc.

Small Craft Warnings. Copyright 1970, 1972, renewed © 1998, 2000 The University of the South.

Out Cry (The Two-Character Play). Copyright 1969, 1973, 1976, renewed © 1997 The University of the South.

Vieux Carré. Copyright © 1977, 1979 The University of the South.

A Lovely Sunday for Creve Coeur. Copyright © 1978, 1980 The University of the South.

Notes

In the notes below, the reference numbers denote page and line of this volume. No note is made for material included in standard desk-reference books such as Webster's *Collegiate, Biographical,* and *Geographical* dictionaries. Biblical quotations are keyed to the King James Version. Quotations from Shakespeare are keyed to *The Riverside Shakespeare,* ed. G. Blakemore Evans (Boston: Houghton Mifflin, 1974). Cast lists and production information are taken from the first book editions of the plays, except for *The Eccentricities of a Nightingale* and *The Mutilated,* where they are taken from Dramatists Play Service editions, and *The Milk Train Doesn't Stop Here Anymore,* where they are taken from Volume 5 of *The Theatre of Tennessee Williams* (New York: New Directions, 1976). For further biographical information than is contained in the Chronology, see Albert J. Devlin (ed.), *Conversations with Tennessee Williams* (Jackson: University Press of Mississippi, 1986); Ronald Hayman, *Tennessee Williams: Everyone Else Is an Audience* (New Haven: Yale University Press, 1993); Lyle Leverich, *Tom: The Unknown Tennessee Williams* (New York: W.W. Norton & Company, 1995); Harry Rasky, *Tennessee Williams: A Portrait in Laughter and Lamentation* (New York: Dodd, 1986); Donald Spoto, *The Kindness of Strangers: The Life of Tennessee Williams* (Boston: Little, Brown and Company, 1985); Dakin Williams and Shepherd Mead, *Tennessee Williams: An Intimate Biography* (New York: Arbor House, 1983); Edwina Dakin Williams as told to Lucy Freeman, *Remember Me to Tom* (New York: Putnam, 1963); Donald Windham (ed.), *Tennessee Williams' Letters to Donald Windham 1940–1965* (New York: Holt, Rinehart & Winston, 1977).

ORPHEUS DESCENDING

1.1   *Orpheus Descending*] *Orpheus Descending* was presented at the Martin Beck Theatre in New York on March 21, 1957, by the Producers Theatre. It was directed by Harold Clurman; the stage set was designed by Boris Aronson, the costumes by Lucinda Ballard, and the lighting by Feder. The cast was as follows: DOLLY HAMMA: Elizabeth Eustis; BEULAH BINNINGS: Jane Rose; PEE WEE BINNINGS: Warren Kemmerling; DOG HAMMA: David Clarke; CAROL CUTRERE: Lois Smith; EVA TEMPLE: Nell Harrison; SISTER TEMPLE: Mary Farrell; UNCLE PLEASANT: John Marriott; VAL XAVIER: Cliff Robertson; VEE TALBOT: Joanna Roos; LADY TORRANCE: Maureen Stapleton;

JABE TORRANCE: Crahan Denton; SHERIFF TALBOTT: R. G. Armstrong; MR. DUBINSKY: Beau Tilden; WOMAN: Janice Mars; DAVID CUTRERE: Robert Webber; NURSE PORTER: Virgilia Chew; FIRST MAN: Albert Henderson; SECOND MAN: Charles Tyner.

3.37–38   "You must not . . . peck at!"]   Cf. *Othello*, I.i.64.

5.7   W.P.A. Writers' Project]   Federal program under the Works Progress Administration to provide work for authors during the Depression.

13.18–19   Mystic Crew]   Williams' name for the Ku Klux Klan.

15.33   *Valli*]   Movie actress Alida Valli (b. 1921).

17.30   Morning Call]   For more than a hundred years a coffee stand in the French Market of New Orleans.

24.7   *"Heavenly Grass."*]   Williams' poem, collected in *In the Winter of Cities* (1956), was set to music by Paul Bowles.

28.15   Willie McGee]   Willie McGee was convicted in 1949 of raping Willamette Hawkins, a white woman, and sentenced to death. The U.S. Supreme Court refused to review McGee's case and despite international protests he was electrocuted in Laurel, Mississippi, on May 8, 1951.

62.20   "September Morn"]   Painting (1912) by French salon artist Paul Emile Chabas (1869–1937); it was widely reproduced, and was banned in some American cities.

SUDDENLY LAST SUMMER

99.1   *Suddenly Last Summer*]   *Suddenly Last Summer*, with *Something Unspoken*, were presented together under the collective title of *Garden District* at the York Theatre on First Avenue in New York on January 7, 1958, by John C. Wilson and Warner Le Roy. It was directed by Herbert Machiz; the scenery was designed by Robert Soule and the costumes by Stanley Simmons. Lighting was by Lee Watson and the incidental music was by Ned Rorem. *Cast of Characters:* MRS. VENABLE: Hortense Alden; DR. CUKROWICZ: Robert Lansing; MISS FOXHILL: Donna Cameron; MRS. HOLLY: Eleanor Phelps; GEORGE HOLLY: Alan Mixon; CATHERINE HOLLY: Anne Meacham; SISTER FELICITY: Nanom-Kiam.

112.32–33   "So shines . . . world,"]   Shakespeare, *The Merchant of Venice*, V.i.91.

SWEET BIRD OF YOUTH

149.1   *Sweet Bird of Youth*]   *Sweet Bird of Youth* was presented at the Martin Beck Theatre in New York on March 10, 1959, by Cheryl Crawford. It was directed by Elia Kazan; the scenery and lighting were by Jo Mielziner, the costumes by Anna Hill Johnstone, and the music by Paul Bowles;

production stage manager, David Pardoll. The cast was as follows: CHANCE WAYNE: Paul Newman; THE PRINCESS KOSMONOPOLIS: Geraldine Page; FLY: Milton J. Williams; MAID: Patricia Ripley; GEORGE SCUDDER: Logan Ramsey; HATCHER: John Napier; BOSS FINLEY: Sidney Blackmer; TOM JUNIOR: Rip Torn; AUNT NONNIE: Martine Bartlett; HEAVENLY FINLEY: Diana Hyland; CHARLES: Earl Sydnor; STUFF: Bruce Dern; MISS LUCY: Madeleine Sherwood; THE HECKLER: Charles Tyner; VIOLET: Monica May; EDNA: Hilda Brawner; SCOTTY: Charles McDaniel; BUD: Jim Jeter; MEN IN BAR: Duke Farley, Ron Harper, Kenneth Blake; PAGE: Glenn Stensel.

149.2–4   *Relentless caper . . . CRANE*]   "Legend" (1925), lines 22–23.

200.16   *novachord.*]   A six-octave electronic keyboard.

203.22   Vic Mature]   Movie actor Victor Mature (1915–99); his films included *Samson and Delilah* (1949) and *Zarak* (1956).

205.2–6   "If you like-a me . . . change your name."]   From "Under the Bamboo Tree" (1902) by Robert Cole and J. Rosamond Johnson.

222.5   *"Bonnie Blue Flag."*]   "The Bonnie Blue Flag" (1861) by Mrs. Annie Chambers-Ketchum and Harry MacCarthy, a popular song of the Confederacy during the Civil War.

PERIOD OF ADJUSTMENT

237.1   *Period of Adjustment*]   *Period of Adjustment* was presented at the Helen Hayes Theatre in New York on November 10, 1960, by Cheryl Crawford. It was directed by George Roy Hill; the scenery and lighting were by Jo Mielziner and the costumes by Partricia Zipprodt; production stage manager, William Chambers. The cast, in order of appearance, was as follows: RALPH BATES: James Daly; ISABEL HAVERSTICK: Barbara Baxley; GEORGE HAVERSTICK: Robert Webber; SUSIE: Helen Martin; LADY CAROLER: Esther Benson; MRS. MCGILLICUDDY: Nancy R. Pollock; MR. MCGILLICUDDY: Lester Mack; THE POLICE OFFICER: Charles McDaniel; DOROTHY BATES: Rosemary Murphy.

301.31   *Sayonara*]   James A. Michener novel (1954) of American soldiers in occupied Japan; it was filmed in 1955 with Marlon Brando and Red Buttons.

322.2   Sophie Newcomb's.]   Women's college in New Orleans.

326.1–4   "Now the boat . . . good-by!"]   From "Goodbye, My Lover, Goodbye," popular English song of the 19th century.

THE NIGHT OF THE IGUANA

327.1   *The Night of the Iguana*]   *The Night of the Iguana* was presented at the Royale Theatre in New York on December 28, 1961, by Charles Bowden, in association with Violla Rubber. It was directed by Frank Corsaro; the scenery was designed by Oliver Smith; lighting by Jean Rosenthal; costumes by Noel Taylor; audio effects by Edward Beyer. The cast, in order of appearance, was as follows: MAXINE FAULK: Bette Davis; PEDRO: James Farentino; PANCHO: Christopher Jones; REVEREND SHANNON: Patrick O'Neal; HANK: Theseus George; HERR FAHRENKOPF: Heinz Hohenwald; FRAU FAHRENKOPF: Lucy Landau; WOLFGANG: Bruce Glover; HILDA: Laryssa Lauret; JUDITH FEL-LOWES: Patricia Roe; HANNAH JELKES: Margaret Leighton; CHARLOTTE GOODALL: Lane Bradbury; JONATHAN COFFIN (NONNO): Alan Webb; JAKE LATTA: Louis Guss.

327.2–6   *And so . . .* DICKINSON]   "I died for Beauty—but was scarce," stanza 3.

329.30–31   Anda . . . del señor.]   Go—the suitcase. Pancho, don't be lazy! Go and get the gentleman's luggage.

335.3–4   Carrie Jacobs Bond or Ethelbert Nevin.]   Bond (1862–1946), songwriter whose works included "A Perfect Day" and "God Remembers When the World Forgets"; Nevin (1862–1901), songwriter whose works included "Little Boy Blue" and "Mighty Lak' a Rose."

336.10–17   I have . . . my bed.]   Cf. Robert Louis Stevenson, "My Shadow," in *A Child's Garden of Verses* (1885).

338.9   Llevala al telefono!]   Show her to the telephone!

356.17–20   How . . . despair]   Adaptation of a poem, "How Still the Lemon on the Branch," one of several Williams wrote in Mexico in 1940.

359.38   "Horst Wessel."]   Nazi party song that became the second national anthem of the Third Reich.

360.24   Berchtesgaden,]   Adolf Hitler's Bavarian mountain villa.

375.27–31   Habe . . . bitte. . . .]   Am I right in thinking that you are on your honeymoon? What a pretty young bride! I'm making pastel sketches . . . may I, will you permit me . . . ? Would you, please . . . please . . .

381.28–29   *Bitte!* . . . weg.]   Please! Take the liquor away. Please, take it away.

398.23–24   vijilalo, entiendes?]   Keep an eye on things, understand?

399.19   Agarrale las manos!]   Grab his hands!

407.5–9   Eine . . . nicht.]   A case of Carta Blanca. / We've had enough . . . maybe not. / No! Never enough. / You're fat, mother . . . but we're not.

THE ECCENTRICITIES OF A NIGHTINGALE

429.1   *The Eccentricities of a Nightingale*] *The Eccentricities of a Nightingale* was presented by Gloria Hope Sher, in association with Neal Du Brock, at the Morosco Theatre, in New York City, on November 23, 1976. It was directed by Edwin Sherin; the scenery was designed by William Ritman; costumes were designed by Theoni V. Aldredge; lighting was by Marc B. Weiss; and the original music was by Charles Gross. The cast, in order of appearance, was as follows: ALMA WINEMILLER: Betsy Palmer; THE REV. WINE-MILLER: Sheppard Strudwick; MRS. WINEMILLER: Grace Carney; MRS. BUCHANAN: Nan Martin; JOHN BUCHANAN, JR.: David Selby; ROGER DORE-MUS: Peter Blaxill; MRS. BASSETT: Jen Jones; ROSEMARY: Patricia Guinan; VERNON: W. P. Dremak; TRAVELING SALESMAN: Thomas Stechschulte.

464.29–30   that Frenchman . . . Brussels!]   During a drunken quarrel in Brussels in July 1873, Paul Verlaine fired a shot at Arthur Rimbaud, wounding him in the arm.

465.28   "bought red lips."]   Cf. Ernest Dowson, "Non Sum Qualis Eram Bonae Sub Regno Cynarae," line 9: "Surely the kisses of her bought red mouth were sweet."

THE MILK TRAIN DOESN'T STOP HERE ANYMORE

489.1   *The Milk Train Doesn't Stop Here Anymore*] *The Milk Train Doesn't Stop Here Anymore* was presented at the Brooks Atkinson Theatre in New York on January 1, 1964, by David Merrick, with Neil Hartley as associate producer and Kermit Kegley as stage manager. Directed by Tony Richardson, the set design was by Rouben Ter-Artunian, the music by Ned Rorem, the lighting by Martin Aronstein, and the hair styles by Michel Kazan. The cast included the following: MRS. GOFORTH: Tallulah Bankhead; CHRISTOPER FLANDERS: Tab Hunter; BLACKIE: Marian Seldes; RUDY: Ralph Roberts; THE WITCH OF CAPRI: Ruth Ford; STAGE ASSISTANTS: Bobby Dean Hooks, Konrad Matthaei.
    An earlier version of *The Milk Train Doesn't Stop Here Anymore* was staged for the first time anywhere at the Festival of Two Worlds in Spoleto, Italy, on July 11, 1962. It reopened in New York on January 10, 1963, produced by Roger L. Stevens and directed by Herbert Machiz, with scenery and lightning by Jo Mielziner, costumes supervision by Fred Voelpel from sketches by Peter Hall, and music by Paul Bowles. The cast included Hermione Baddeley (Flora Goforth), Ann Williams (Francis Black), Clyde Ventura (Giulio), Paul Roebling (Chris Flanders), Maria Tucci (Angelina), Bruce Gibson (Rudy), and Mildred Dunnock (Vera Ridgeway Condotti).

499.12   *Forse . . . tardi?*]   Maybe later, maybe a little later?

500.28   "Cloudy . . . romance]   Cf. John Keats, "When I have fears that I may cease to be."

507.3–7   *Giulio! . . . testa!*] Giulio! Come here! / Take this bag to the pink villa. / Heavy!—God . . . / Your head is heavy!

508.14   *Cerca . . . bagno.*] Look in the bathroom cupboard.

522.15   *Fata Morgana.*] Morgan Le Fay, in Arthurian legend.

524.13–14   *pipistrella,*] Bat.

548.13   *Ecco, sono qui.*] Here they are.

555.15–16   "From Greenland's . . . vile."] Cf. "Missionary Hymn" (1819) by Reginald Heber.

567.19   *Ferma questa—commedia.*] Finish this—comedy.

573.31   silent . . . Darien. . . .] Cf. John Keats, "On First Looking Into Chapman's Homer."

THE MUTILATED

583.1   *The Mutilated*] *The Mutilated* was first presented, as part of a double bill entitled *Slapstick Tragedy*, by Charles Bowden and Lester Persky in association with Sidney Lanier, at the Longacre Theatre, in New York City, on February 22, 1966. It was directed by Alan Schneider; the scenery was designed by Ming Cho Lee; the costumes designed by Noel Taylor; music was composed and selected by Lee Hoiby; and the lighting was by Martin Aronstein. Production was in association with Frenman Productions, Ltd. The cast, in order of appearance, was as follows: CE-LESTE: Kate Reid; HENRY: Ralph Waite; TRINKET: Margaret Leighton; SLIM: James Olson; BRUNO: Ralph Waite; MAXIE: David Sabin; BIRD GIRL: Renee Orin; COP: Jordan Charney; BERNIE: Tom Aldredge; WOMAN AT BAR: Adelle Rasey; PIOUS QUEEN: Dan Bly; TIGER: Henry Oliver; SHORE POLICE: Hank Brunjes.

603.12–13   "Tiger, Tiger, burning bright!"] Cf. William Blake's "The Tiger," line 1.

607.8   paso-doble.] March-time music of Latin American origin.

KINGDOM OF EARTH

623.1   *Kingdom of Earth (The Seven Descents of Myrtle)*] *Kingdom of Earth (The Seven Descents of Myrtle)* was presented at the Ethel Barrymore Theatre in New York on March 27, 1968, by David Merrick. It was directed by José Quintero; the scenery and lighting by Jo Mielziner; costumes by Jane Greenwood. The cast, in order of appearance, was as follows: CHICKEN: Harry Guardino; MYRTLE: Estelle Parsons; LOT: Brian Bedford.

699.35   Gypsy Smith] Rodney "Gypsy" Smith (1860–1947), British-born evangelist.

SMALL CRAFT WARNINGS

707.1   *Small Craft Warnings*] *Small Craft Warnings* was presented at the Truck and Warehouse Theatre in New York on April 2, 1972, by Ecco Productions, Robert Currie, Mario de Maria, William Orton. It was directed by Richard Altman; the scenery and costumes were by Fred Voelpel, lighting by John Gleason; production stage manager, Robert Currie. The cast was as follows: VIOLET: Cherry Davis; DOC: David Hooks; MONK: Gene Fanning; BILL MCCORKLE: Brad Sullivan; LEONA DAWSON: Helena Carroll; STEVE: William Hickey; QUENTIN: Alan Mixon; BOBBY: David Huffman; TONY, THE COP: John David Kees.

709.10–11   *déjà entendu*] Already heard.

709.12   "sullen craft and art."] Cf. Dylan Thomas, "In My Craft or Sullen Art."

711.30–31   oil fields . . . James Dean.] Reference to the 1955 movie version of Edna Ferber's *Giant*, starring Rock Hudson and James Dean.

719.34   Imp.] Imperial, a brand of whisky.

764.14   "Meglior solo,"] Better alone.

764.37   *"labyrinthitis,"*] An inflammation of the inner ear resulting in vertigo.

767.12–13   "Breckinridge" comeback.] At age 78 Mae West returned to the screen in *Myra Breckinridge* (1970), based on Gore Vidal's novel.

767.26   *Confessional*] An early version of *Small Craft Warnings*, published in *Dragon Country* (1970).

OUT CRY

771.1   *Out Cry*] *Out Cry* opened at the Lyceum Theatre in New York on March 1, 1973, produced by David Merrick Arts Foundation and Kennedy Center Productions, Inc., and directed by Peter Glenville. The lighting and stage design were by Jo Mielziner, the costumes by Sandy Cole, with Alan Hall as stage manager. The cast was as follows: FELICE: Michael York; CLARE: Cara Duff-MacCormick. An earlier version of *Out Cry* was presented in Chicago on July 8, 1971, at the Ivanhoe Theatre. It was produced and directed by George Keathley, with Donald Madden and Eileen Herlie in the principal roles. A still earlier version, under the title of *The Two-Character Play*, was offered at the Hampstead Theatre Club.

778.3   "Pox vobiscum,"] Parody of "pax vobiscum" (peace be unto you).

VIEUX CARRÉ

825.1 *Vieux Carré*] The Nottingham Playhouse Production of *Vieux Carré* was presented at The Playhouse Theatre, Nottingham, on May 16, 1978, and at the Piccadilly Theatre, London, on August 9, 1978. It was directed by Keith Hack; stage design was by Voytek, lighting by Francis Reid, costumes by Maria Björnson, and music by Jeremy Nicholas; company stage manager, James Gill. The cast in order of appearance was as follows: MRS. WIRE: Sylvia Miles; NURSIE: Nadia Cattouse; THE WRITER: Karl Johnson; JANE: Di Trevis; NIGHTINGALE: Richard Kane; MARY MAUDE: Betty Hardy; MISS CARRIE: Judith Fellows; TYE: Jonathan Kent; PHOTOGRAPHER: Robin McDonald; SKY: Jack Elliott.

849.16–17 WPA Writers' Project?] See note 5.7.

856.31 *Tant pis . . .*] So much the worse.

864.20 *"He walks with me and he talks with me."*] "In the Garden," hymn composed in 1913 by C. Austin Miles (1868–1946).

885.29–30 Foxes have holes . . . head!] Cf. Matthew 8:20, Luke 9:58.

A LOVELY SUNDAY FOR CREVE COEUR

903.1 *A Lovely Sunday for Creve Coeur*] The New York premiere of *A Lovely Sunday for Creve Coeur* took place at the Hudson Guild Theatre on January 1, 1979. It was directed by Keith Hack; set design by John Conklin; lighting design by Craig Miller; costume design by Linda Fisher; producing director, Craig Anderson. The cast in order of appearance was as follows: DOROTHEA: Shirley Knight; BODEY: Peg Murray; HELENA: Charlotte Moore; MISS GLUCK: Jane Lowry.

914.1 Roy D'Arcy take poor Janet Gaynor] Roy D'Arcy (1894–1969), character actor who specialized in playing lecherous villains; Janet Gaynor (1906–84), star of *Seventh Heaven* (1927) and *Street Angel* (1928).

915.22 *Kirche, Küche, und Kinder*] Church, kitchen, and children.

927.26 *Sie . . . zugeschlagen!*] She slammed the door in my face!

927.39 *Vom Irrenhaus.*] From the insane asylum.

931.11 *Alte böse Katze.*] Vicious old cat.

932.22–24 *Eine . . . Gestorben!*] A—week ago—Sunday—my mother—/ I know, Sophie, I know./ Died!

933.1 *Nein . . . geschrien!*] No, no, she screamed!

933.14–15 *Ich . . . freundlos!*] I am alone, alone! Without a friend in the world!

933.17 *Ich . . . Welt!*] I have no one in the world!

935.16–17   *Heisser . . . Durchfall.*]   Hot coffee always gives me cramps and diarrhea.

935.25   *KANN NICHT WARTEN!*]   Can't wait!

937.14   *Halte das Wasser ab,*]   Turn the water off.

937.15   *das Wust,*]   The mess.

945.1   *Das Schlafzimmer ist gespukt!*]   The bedroom is haunted!

945.23   *Il n'y a rien à faire.*]   There's nothing to be done.

946.36   *Halunke*]   Rascal.

Library of Congress Cataloging-in-Publication Data

Williams, Tennessee, 1911–1983.
   [Plays. Selections]
   Plays / Tennessee Williams.
       p. cm. —(The Library of America 119–120)
   Selection and notes by Mel Gussow and Kenneth Holditch.
   Contents [v. 1] Plays 1937–1955: Spring storm. Not about
nightingales. Battle of angels. I rise in flame, cried the
phoenix. From 27 wagons full of cotton (1946) . . . . The
glass menagerie. A streetcar named Desire. Summer and
smoke. The rose tattoo. Camino Real. From 27 Wagons full
of cotton (1953) . . . . Cat on a hot tin roof—[v. 2] Plays
1957–1980: Orpheus descending. Suddenly last summer. Sweet
bird of youth. Period of adjustment. The night of the iguana.
The eccentricities of a nightingale. The milk train doesn't
stop here anymore. The mutilated. Kingdom of earth (The
seven descents of Myrtle). Small craft warnings. Out cry.
Vieux Carré. A lovely Sunday for Creve Coeur.
       ISBN 1–883011–86–8 (v. I : alk. paper)—ISBN 1–883011–87–6
       (v. 2 : alk. paper)
   I. Gussow, Mel. II. Holditch, Kenneth. III. Title.
       IV. Series.
PS3545.I5365 A6 2000
812'.54—dc21   00-030190

THE LIBRARY OF AMERICA SERIES

The Library of America fosters appreciation and pride in America's literary heritage by publishing, and keeping permanently in print, authoritative editions of America's best and most significant writing. An independent nonprofit organization, it was founded in 1979 with seed money from the National Endowment for the Humanities and the Ford Foundation.

To subscribe to the series or to order individual copies,
please visit www.loa.org or call (800) 964.5778.

*This book is set in 10 point Linotron Galliard,
a face designed for photocomposition by Matthew Carter
and based on the sixteenth-century face Granjon. The paper
is acid-free lightweight opaque and meets the requirements
for permanence of the American National Standards Institute.
The binding material is Brillianta, a woven rayon cloth made
by Van Heek-Scholco Textielfabrieken, Holland. Composition by The Clarinda Company. Printing by
Malloy Incorporated. Binding by Dekker Book-
binding. Designed by Bruce Campbell.*